Frommer's®
England

Our England

by Darwin Porter & Danforth Prince

WE LOVE ENGLAND. IN SPRINGTIME, YOU'LL FIND US IN THE LAKE DISTRICT, beloved stomping ground of the Romantic poets, wandering its secluded valleys and sheep-grazing meadows looking for William Wordsworth's field of golden daffodils. In autumn, winds blow in from the Atlantic, and we'll wander the bleak landscape of the Dartmoor Moors, a mournful terrain that inspired the Sherlock Holmes murder mystery, *Hounds of the Baskervilles.*

Such memories sustain us when the first cold rains of winter descend over London, turning everything gray. To escape, we go to the theater, where a magic world unfolds much as it did in the days of Shakespeare. Regretfully, these days it is no longer good form to toss rotten tomatoes from Covent Garden market if the actors turn in a bad performance.

Who can't love a land that gave us Queen Bess, Princess Di, Elizabeth Taylor, Henry VIII, Cary Grant, Robin Hood, the Beatles, the Rolling Stones, and Sir Winston Churchill? The landscape, pubs, castles, and experiences that await you in England are as diverse and beguiling as the Brits themselves. And what do Brits think of the constant stream of traveling "invaders"? We asked a British friend, who replied, "You colonials are tolerable, I guess. But I'd like you even more if you bought me another pint." In the following pages, we share some of our favorite English experiences with you.

Preposterously photogenic, the picture-book village of **BIBURY** (left) lies deep in the limestone hills of the Cotswolds. The Industrial Revolution passed by this region, and villages such as Bibury have survived more or less intact since their heyday between the 14th and 16th centuries when merchants grew rich from the wool trade. These asymmetrical two-story Arlington Row cottages were built with timber lintels and doors. Small windows make them very dark inside.

The Romans have long departed but their legacy lives on in the Roman baths of **BATH** (above), built around a now-vanished temple dedicated to their goddess, Sulis Minerva. In this far northern climate, these soldiers from the Mediterranean found relief for their ailments in the curative waters. The Romans turned Bath into the first spa town of Britain. Pillars and terraces, along with statues of famous Romans, surround the waters of the Great Bath, depicted above, where a spring still issues vaporous waters.

From the lowliest "caff" (cafeteria) in the working-class districts of Birmingham to the Queen's posh Buckingham Palace suite, class tradition melts at four o'clock every afternoon as the nation pauses to partake of its most beloved ritual: **AFTERNOON TEA (left)**, pictured here in a Cotswold tearoom with freshly-baked scones and berry-laden jam. Entire books have been written on the proper way to make a "cuppa," be it the strong Indian tea, replete with tannin and preferred by macho men, or the watery-weak China tea ordered by delicate ladies in picture hats.

The dramatic, rugged cliffs of **LAND'S END (below)** mark the western point of mainland Britain. This is literally where England comes to an end—in fact, to ancient Cornish mariners it was known as *Pen an Wlas* or "the end of the earth." Coastal paths wind their way through the wild landscape and lead to this majestic headland—its turf-covered cliffs climb 18.30m (60 ft.) above turbulent Atlantic waters.

STONEHENGE (above), the most celebrated prehistoric monument in Europe, remains the ancient mystery of the Salisbury Plain. What was this pile of rocks—a spot to worship the sun, a place to indulge in ritual sacrifices, or an observatory to ponder astronomy? Beginning about 3000 B.C., these monster monoliths—some weighing 40 tons—were moved to this site from afar. The age-old question remains: who moved them here and how did they transport them?

Three enduring symbols of **LONDON (right)** are the black taxi in the left foreground, the clock tower Big Ben in the center, and a red double-decker bus to the right. The clock tower rises over the mock Gothic Palace of Westminster, containing both of the Houses of Parliament (Lords and Commons). Since 1858, Big Ben's clock chimes have sounded faithfully—even BBC radio broadcasts the deep chimes every day; the sounds are a symbol of London.

The nostalgic English—especially after a few pints—can get downright weepy about their **WHITE CLIFFS OF DOVER (above)**. During England's darkest days of World War II, taverns across the land echoed a prediction of peace with the refrain, "there will be bluebirds over the White Cliffs of Dover." The cliffs survived the savage bombing by the Third Reich, and today they still guard the gateway to Britain. For many soldiers these cliffs were the last homeland landscape they saw before sailing across the English Channel to their deaths.

The old fabled flower, fruit, and vegetable market in **LONDON'S COVENT GARDEN (right)** has long since moved to more modern quarters, but in the city's best recycling venture, these elegant Victorian buildings were rescued from the wrecker's ball and beautifully restored. The market is riddled with bustling restaurants and bars, antiques stalls, and fashion boutiques.

MONNOW BRIDGE (right) is an evocative holdover from the Middle Ages in Wales, lying in the market town of Monmouth at the confluence of the Monnow and Wye Rivers.

At **ASCOT (below)**, outside London, the world's finest thoroughbreds compete at the "Royal Meeting." Ascot is not just about horses strutting their stuff. Human "thoroughbreds," their tower hats crowning their regal heads, are also on parade. Younger women still adopt the style of the late Princess Di at her wide-brimmed best, while older women prefer that of the late Queen Mother's picture hats. Men show up in top hats, tailcoats, and striped pants.

New Yorkers may dispute this, but **LONDON'S WEST END (left)** is home to the best and most varied theatrical presentations in the English-speaking world. The Gielgud Theatre honors one of England's towering thespians, the late Sir John Gielgud, also one of the world's greatest Shakespearean actors. Gielgud once lamented that he'd be forever remembered for "that dumb manservant part," a reference to his role as Dudley Moore's butler in the 1981 comedy *Arthur,* which won him an Oscar.

Rush to order the notorious **ENGLISH BREAKFAST (below)** before this cholesterol-rich "plate of deadly sins" is forever forbidden by your doctor. Originating in the greasy spoons of England, the big breakfast became a mandatory staple in upper-class Victorian homes. Pictured here are the works: Cumberland sausage, grilled tomatoes and mushrooms, streaky back bacon, fried eggs sunny-side-up, a side of toast and jam, and a cup of tea served in fine English China.

SHREWSBURY (above)—Built by wealthy wool merchants in the 16th century, timber-framed and gabled houses known as black-and-white buildings (black timber embedded in white plaster) line Fish Street in Shrewsbury (pronounced *shrose*-bury), one of England's best preserved medieval market towns. With some exceptions, traffic is banned along Fish Street, which used to be inhabited by fishmongers—hence, its name.

The quintessential pastime of both the male and female undergraduate at Cambridge University is **"PUNTING" ON THE RIVER CAM (right)**. Ask a Cambridge graduate what he or she best remembers about college days, and you're likely to prompt memories of a carefree time when students leaned on long poles and lazily guided their flat-bottomed crafts along the riverbanks in "back" of the colleges. Visitors can rent a punt and join in on the fun.

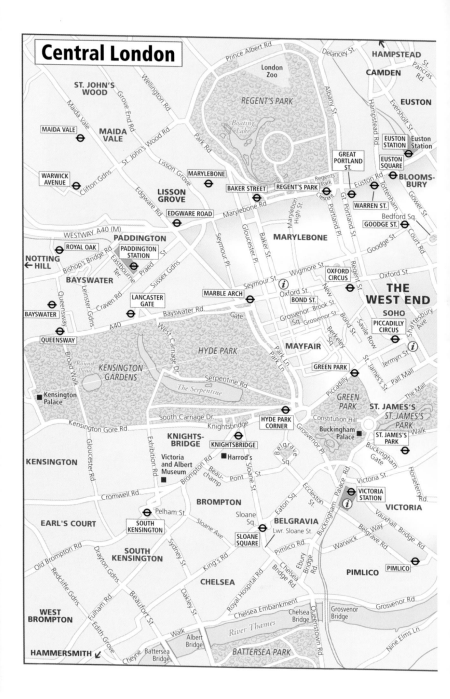

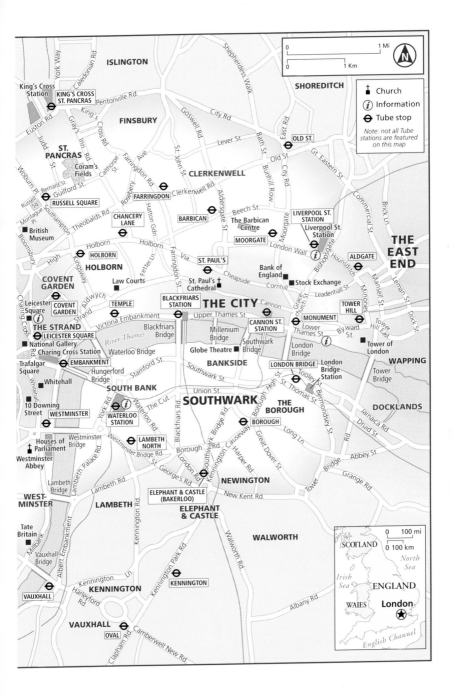

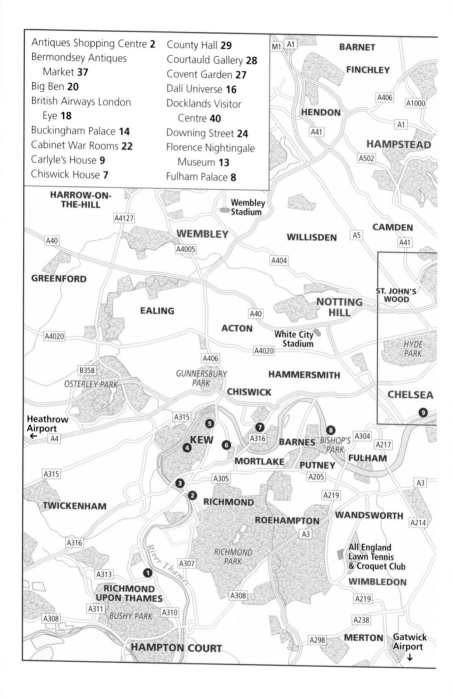

Antiques Shopping Centre **2**
Bermondsey Antiques
   Market **37**
Big Ben **20**
British Airways London
   Eye **18**
Buckingham Palace **14**
Cabinet War Rooms **22**
Carlyle's House **9**
Chiswick House **7**

County Hall **29**
Courtauld Gallery **28**
Covent Garden **27**
Dalí Universe **16**
Docklands Visitor
   Centre **40**
Downing Street **24**
Florence Nightingale
   Museum **13**
Fulham Palace **8**

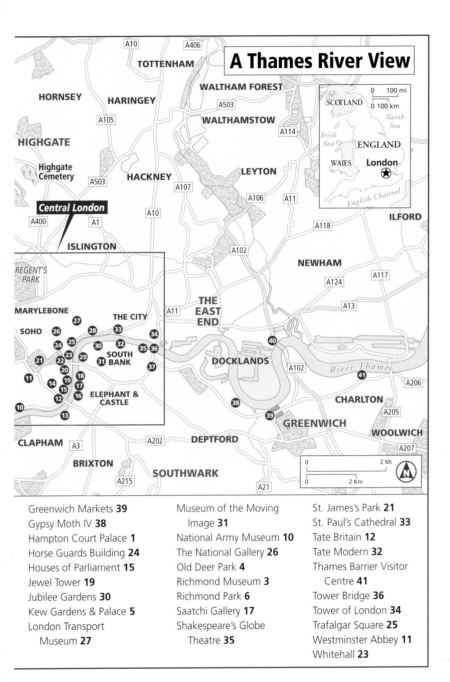

A Thames River View

Greenwich Markets **39**
Gypsy Moth IV **38**
Hampton Court Palace **1**
Horse Guards Building **24**
Houses of Parliament **15**
Jewel Tower **19**
Jubilee Gardens **30**
Kew Gardens & Palace **5**
London Transport
Museum **27**

Museum of the Moving
Image **31**
National Army Museum **10**
The National Gallery **26**
Old Deer Park **4**
Richmond Museum **3**
Richmond Park **6**
Saatchi Gallery **17**
Shakespeare's Globe
Theatre **35**

St. James's Park **21**
St. Paul's Cathedral **33**
Tate Britain **12**
Tate Modern **32**
Thames Barrier Visitor
Centre **41**
Tower Bridge **36**
Tower of London **34**
Trafalgar Square **25**
Westminster Abbey **11**
Whitehall **23**

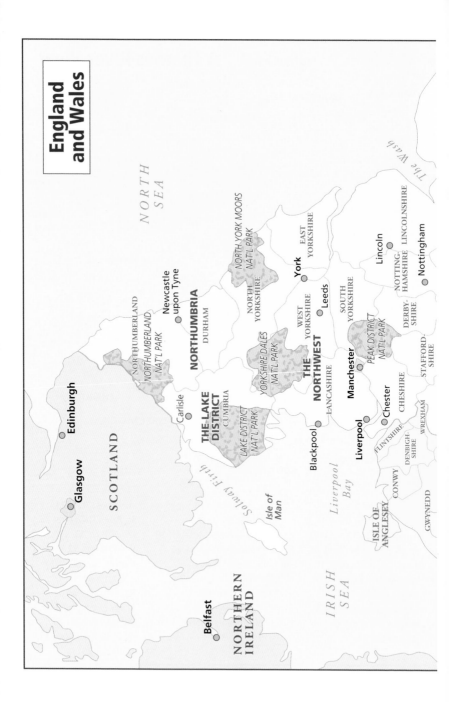

England and Wales

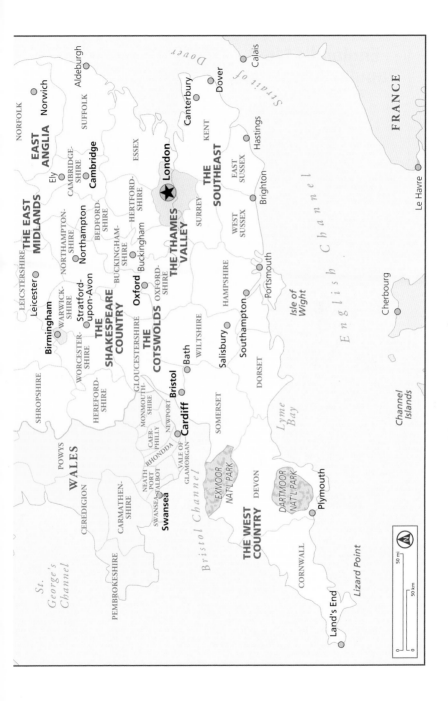

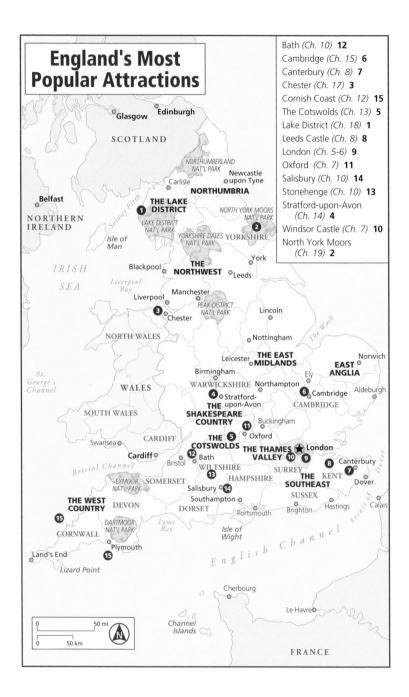

England's Most Popular Attractions

Bath *(Ch. 10)* **12**
Cambridge *(Ch. 15)* **6**
Canterbury *(Ch. 8)* **7**
Chester *(Ch. 17)* **3**
Cornish Coast *(Ch. 12)* **15**
The Cotswolds *(Ch. 13)* **5**
Lake District *(Ch. 18)* **1**
Leeds Castle *(Ch. 8)* **8**
London *(Ch. 5-6)* **9**
Oxford *(Ch. 7)* **11**
Salisbury *(Ch. 10)* **14**
Stonehenge *(Ch. 10)* **13**
Stratford-upon-Avon *(Ch. 14)* **4**
Windsor Castle *(Ch. 7)* **10**
North York Moors *(Ch. 19)* **2**

Frommer's®

England

2009

by Darwin Porter & Danforth Prince

Here's what the critics say about Frommer's:

"Amazingly easy to use. Very portable, very complete."

—Booklist

"Detailed, accurate, and easy-to-read information for all price ranges."
—Glamour Magazine

"Hotel information is close to encyclopedic."

—Des Moines Sunday Register

"Frommer's Guides have a way of giving you a real feel for a place."
—Knight Ridder Newspapers

WILEY

Wiley Publishing, Inc.

Published by:

Wiley Publishing, Inc.

111 River St.
Hoboken, NJ 07030-5774

ISBN 978-0-470-28786-6

Editor: Jennifer Moore, with Naomi Kraus
Production Editor: Heather Wilcox
Cartographer: Guy Ruggiero
Photo Editor: Richard Fox
Production by Wiley Indianapolis Composition Services

Front cover photo: Cumbria Wasdale Head and Illgill Head with a glimpse of Wastwater: close up of a dry stone wall in the foreground
Back cover photo: Oxford, New College: Two students in cloister, staring out at garden beyond

For information on our other products and services or to obtain technical support, please contact our Customer Care Department within the U.S. at 800/762-2974, outside the U.S. at 317/572-3993 or fax 317/572-4002.

Wiley also publishes its books in a variety of electronic formats. Some content that appears in print may not be available in electronic formats.

Manufactured in the United States of America

5   4   3   2   1

Contents

(4) Suggested England Itineraries   91

(5) Settling into London   104

(6) Exploring London   166

(7) The Thames Valley: Royal Windsor & Regal Oxford   228

(8) Kent, Surrey & Sussex: The Garden of England   272

18 The Lake District: Home of the Poets   627

19 Yorkshire & Northumbria: Brontë, Moors & Dales   654

20 Cardiff & South Wales: Dylan Thomas Country   693

21 North Wales: The Peaks of Snowdonia   729

Appendix: Fast Facts, Toll-Free Numbers & Websites   752

Index   761

List of Maps

About the Authors

As a team of veteran travel writers, **Darwin Porter** and **Danforth Prince** have produced numerous titles for Frommer's, including guides to Italy, France, the Caribbean, England, and Germany. A film critic, columnist, and broadcaster, Porter is also a Hollywood biographer. His most recent releases are *Brando Unzipped,* documenting the private life of Marlon Brando, and *Jacko: His Rise and Fall,* the first complete biography ever written on the tumultuous life of Michael Jackson. Prince was formerly employed by the Paris bureau of the *New York Times* and is today the president of Blood Moon Productions and other media-related firms.

An Invitation to the Reader

In researching this book, we discovered many wonderful places—hotels, restaurants, shops, and more. We're sure you'll find others. Please tell us about them, so we can share the information with your fellow travelers in upcoming editions. If you were disappointed with a recommendation, we'd love to know that, too. Please write to:

Frommer's England 2009
Wiley Publishing, Inc. • 111 River St. • Hoboken, NJ 07030-5774

An Additional Note

Please be advised that travel information is subject to change at any time—and this is especially true of prices. We therefore suggest that you write or call ahead for confirmation when making your travel plans. The authors, editors, and publisher cannot be held responsible for the experiences of readers while traveling. Your safety is important to us, however, so we encourage you to stay alert and be aware of your surroundings. Keep a close eye on cameras, purses, and wallets, all favorite targets of thieves and pickpockets.

Other Great Guides for Your Trip:

Frommer's London

MTV England

England For Dummies

Frommer's Scotland

Road Atlas Britain

Frommer's Star Ratings, Icons & Abbreviations

Every hotel, restaurant, and attraction listing in this guide has been ranked for quality, value, service, amenities, and special features using a **star-rating system.** In country, state, and regional guides, we also rate towns and regions to help you narrow down your choices and budget your time accordingly. Hotels and restaurants are rated on a scale of zero (recommended) to three stars (exceptional). Attractions, shopping, nightlife, towns, and regions are rated according to the following scale: zero stars (recommended), one star (highly recommended), two stars (very highly recommended), and three stars (must-see).

In addition to the star-rating system, we also use **seven feature icons** that point you to the great deals, in-the-know advice, and unique experiences that separate travelers from tourists. Throughout the book, look for:

Finds	Special finds—those places only insiders know about
Fun Fact	Fun facts—details that make travelers more informed and their trips more fun
Kids	Best bets for kids and advice for the whole family
Moments	Special moments—those experiences that memories are made of
Overrated	Places or experiences not worth your time or money
Tips	Insider tips—great ways to save time and money
Value	Great values—where to get the best deals

The following **abbreviations** are used for credit cards:

AE	American Express	DISC	Discover	V	Visa
DC	Diners Club	MC	MasterCard		

Frommers.com

Now that you have this guidebook to help you plan a great trip, visit our website at **www.frommers.com** for additional travel information on more than 4,000 destinations. We update features regularly to give you instant access to the most current trip-planning information available. At Frommers.com, you'll find scoops on the best airfares, lodging rates, and car rental bargains. You can even book your travel online through our reliable travel booking partners. Other popular features include:

- Online updates of our most popular guidebooks
- Vacation sweepstakes and contest giveaways
- Newsletters highlighting the hottest travel trends
- Podcasts, interactive maps, and up-to-the-minute events listings
- Opinionated blog entries by Arthur Frommer himself
- Online travel message boards with featured travel discussions

What's New in England & Wales

There will always be an England, as the saying goes, but it won't always be the same. "As time goes by," here are some of the latest developments.

LONDON The big news is the opening of **St. Pancras International,** the new transportation hub for passengers arriving from the Continent on Eurostar. The finest architectural icon from the Age of Steam, with its gargoyles and Gothic Revival towers, has been beautifully restored to receive passengers.

In hotel developments, **Andaz Liverpool Street Hotel,** 40 Liverpool St. (✆ **020/7961-1234**), has opened as part of a new division of Hyatt. Between Shoreditch and Hoxton, this hotel was originally designed by Charles Barry, architect of the Houses of Parliament.

London's burgeoning array of boutique hotels added another charmer to the list, the **Sumner,** 54 Upper Berkeley St., Marble Arch (✆ **020/7723-2244**). Part of an 1820s Georgian terrace, it is one of the finest small hotels in London and is luxuriously appointed.

The biggest development for the luxury market, and generating the most media coverage, is **Haymarket Hotel,** 1 Suffolk Place (✆ **020/7470-4000**), next to the fabled Haymarket Theatre. Of all the hotels of London, this one makes the boldest statement in daring colors—even acid green. Although daringly avant-garde, it still retains many of its original 19th-century John Nash architectural features.

Among restaurants, **Scott's,** 20 Mount St. (✆ **020/7495-7309**), has reopened in a new location in Mayfair. It's been selling "cockles and mussels," along with elegant Dover sole, to Londoners in one place or another since 1851. It is now better than ever. For those who don't like fish, there is always an offering of braised pork cheeks.

It's called **Automat,** 33 Dover St. (✆ **020/7499-3033**), and this Mayfair eatery attracts homesick Yankees and the discerning foodies of London. It's Mayfair's slice of the Big Apple.

Kitschy but chic, **Annex 3,** 16 Little Portland St. (✆ **020/7631-0700**), is one of the best French restaurants in London in spite of its Christmas tree decor. Exceptional products are used in this first-rate cuisine served on the fringe of Soho.

Down in Chelsea, **Tom's Kitchen,** 27 Cale St. (✆ **020/7349-0202**), is a hot new place to dine. This former pub has been stylishly converted into a chic restaurant serving a well-crafted British cuisine in a bustling brasserie atmosphere with an open kitchen.

BATH At the West Country's most elegant hotel architecturally, the famed Royal Crescent, a new restaurant has been installed, called the **Dover House,** 15–16 Royal Crescent (✆ **01225/823333**), serving a finely tuned English cuisine. The setting is romantic, and the dishes often inspired.

BRIGHTON In this seaside resort, **Bill's Produce Store,** the Depot, 100

North St. (℃ **01273/692894**), is all the rage. Bill Collison enjoys a big following among local foodies, buying much of his produce, including fruits and vegetables, from local farmers. You might call him green.

CAMBRIDGE   The innovative restaurant **Cotto,** 183 East Rd. (℃ **01223/ 302010**), above a small deli-bakery, is today one of the leading restaurants of Cambridge, attracting university students when they have money in their pocket. It's known for its no-frills, no-choice, three-course fixed-price dinner, which uses high-quality ingredients.

HENLEY-ON-THAMES   This riverside town, at long last, has a truly elegant place to stay if you head for **Hotel du Vin,** New Street (℃ **01491/848400**), which has been created out of a former brewery, a great example of industrial recycling. It has emerged as the poshest hotel in town and is heavily booked during the famous Royal Regatta held here.

LEEDS   In the northeastern city of Leeds, **Anthony's Restaurant,** 19 Boar Lane (℃ **0113/245-5922**), is the domain of the talented chef, Anthony James Flinn. His take on modern British cuisine has some critics proclaiming him the number-one chef in Yorkshire. He's innovative, even provocative, in his cutting-edge creations, which he calls "molecular gastronomy"—that is, where physics and chemistry principles are applied to the kitchen.

NOTTINGHAM   Once a dreary wasteland for accommodations, this Midlands city has seen the opening of the **Lace Market Hotel,** High Pavement, Lace Market (℃ **0115/8523232**), a boutique

hotel of charm and character. A town house, with its original architecture intact, offers modernized and rather elegant bedrooms for the discerning traveler.

PAINSWICK   In what many English people consider the prettiest village in the Cotswolds, the old Painswick Hotel has been stylishly turned into **Cotswold 88,** Kemps Lane (℃ **01452/813688**), a stylish hotel with terraces of formal gardens. Its interior today looks like a rock star's country manor, very modern and a bit crazy.

SOUTHAMPTON   At this major port along the southern coast, you can find lodgings or good English food at the **White Star Tavern,** 28 Oxford St. (℃ **023/80821990**). It's been turned into a bar-cum-restaurant, a true gastropub serving such classics as wild boar and apple sausage or beer-battered fish.

STRATFORD-UPON-AVON   Foodies flock to **Malbec,** 6 Union St. (℃ **01789/ 269106**), which is now cited as the best place to dine in the Bard's hometown, a former gastronomic wasteland. A market-fresh and unpretentious cuisine served in fashionable surroundings draws diners to this intimate restaurant. The chef and owner, Simon Malin, has been widely acclaimed in British media.

WINDERMERE   David Beckham has already checked out, but the **Samling,** Ambleside Road (℃ **015394/31922**), remains the rage, a hotel fashioned from an 18th-century stone-built manse opening onto panoramic views of the lake. Management bills the Samling as an "uncountry house" hotel, because of its relaxed informality. Yet it offers ultimate comfort in a tranquil setting.

The Best of England & Wales

Planning a trip to England presents a bewildering array of options. We've scoured the country in search of the best places and experiences; in this chapter, we share our very personal and opinionated selections to help you get started.

1 The Best Travel Experiences

- **A Night at the Theater:** The torch passed from Shakespeare still burns brightly. London's theater scene is acknowledged as the finest in the world, with two major subsidized companies: the Royal Shakespeare Company, performing at Stratford-upon-Avon and at the Barbican in London; and the National Theatre on the South Bank in London. Fringe theater offers surprisingly good and often innovative productions staged in venues ranging from church cellars to the upstairs rooms of pubs.

- **Pub-Crawling:** The pursuit of the pint takes on cultural significance in England. Ornate taps fill tankards and mugs in pubs that serve as the social heart of every village and town. Quaint signs for such names as the Red Lion, the White Swan, and the Royal Oak dot the landscape and beckon you in, not only for the pint but also for the conviviality—and perhaps even the entertainment or the food.

- **Motoring through the Cotswolds:** If *driving* involves a determined trip from one place to another, *motoring* is wandering at random. And there's no better place for it than the Cotswolds, less than 161km (100 miles) west of

London, its rolling hills and pasture-lands peppered with ivy-covered inns and honey-colored stone cottages. See chapter 13.

- **Punting on the Cam:** This is Cantabrigian English for gliding along in a flat-bottom boat with a long pole pushed into the River Cam's shallow bed. You bypass the weeping willows along the banks, watch the strolling students along the graveled walkways, and take in the picture-postcard vistas of green lawns along the water's edge. See p. 540.

- **Touring Stately Homes:** England has hundreds of mansions open to visitors, some centuries old, and we tell you about dozens of them. The homes are often surrounded by beautiful gardens; when the owners got fanciful, they added splashing fountains and miniature pagodas or temples.

- **Shopping for Antiques:** Whatever treasure you're looking for, you can find it in England. We're talking Steiff teddy bears, a blunderbuss, an 1890 tin-plate toy train, an egg cup allegedly used by Queen Victoria, a first-edition English print from 1700, or the definitive Henry Harper grandfather clock. No one polishes up their antiques and curios quite as brightly as English dealers. From auction houses to quaint shops, from flea markets to country fairs, England, particularly Victorian England, is for sale.

- **Cruising on Lake Windermere:** Inspired by the lyric poetry of Wordsworth, you can board a boat at Windermere or Bowness and sail England's most famous lake. You'll see the Lake District's scenery, with its tilled valleys lying in the shadow of forbidding peaks, as it was meant to be viewed—from the water. A great jaunt is the round-trip from Bowness to Ambleside, at the head of the lake, and back around to the village of Lakeside, at the southern tip. See chapter 18.

2 The Best of Literary England

- **Samuel Johnson's House** (London; ✆ 020/7353-3745): The backwater at 17 Gough Sq., situated on the north side of Fleet Street, was Johnson's home from 1748 to 1759. Here he worked on his Rambler essays and his dictionary, and here his beloved wife, "Tetty," died in 1752. See p. 194.
- **Keats House** (London; ✆ 020/7435-2062): Most of the poet's brief life was spent in London, where he was born in 1795 in a livery stable run by his father. He moved to Hampstead in 1817 and met his fiancée, Fanny Brawne, there. In this house, he coughed blood into his handkerchief. "That drop of blood is my death warrant," he said. "I must die." He left for Rome in 1820 and died there a year later. See p. 198.
- **Jane Austen Country:** The author of *Pride and Prejudice* and *Sense and Sensibility* wrote of rural delights and a civilized society—set mainly in her beloved Hampshire. In 1809, she moved with her mother to Chawton, 80km (50 miles) south of Bath, where she lived until 1817. Her house is now a museum. Her novels *Persuasion* and *Northanger Abbey* are associated with the city of Bath, where she visited frequently in her youth and lived from 1801 to 1806. In her final year, she moved to 8 College St. in Winchester. She is buried in Winchester Cathedral. See chapter 9.

- **Stratford-upon-Avon** (Warwickshire): The folks who live in touristy Stratford gleefully peddle Shakespeare's literary legacy, including his birthplace, where the son of a glover was born on April 23, 1564. Anne Hathaway's Cottage, in the hamlet of Shottery, is also popular; Shakespeare married Hathaway when he was only 18 years old. See "Stratford-upon-Avon," in chapter 14.
- **Sherwood Forest** (East Midlands): You won't find Errol Flynn in Technicolor-green tights gallivanting through a forest of mighty oaks with his band of merry men. Although most of the forest has been open grassland since the 14th century, it lives on in legend, literature, and lore as the most famous woodland in the world. At the Sherwood Forest Visitor Centre at Edwinstowe, the world of Friar Tuck and Little John lives on. See "Nottinghamshire: Robin Hood Country," in chapter 16.
- **Grasmere** (The Lake District): William Wordsworth lived here with his sister, Dorothy, who commented on the "domestic slip of mountain" behind their home, Dove Cottage. The cottage itself is now part of the Wordsworth Museum, displaying manuscripts and memorabilia. The poet also lived for a time at nearby Rydal Mount, just north of Ambleside (one of his descendants still owns

the property), where you can see gardens landscaped by the poet. Throughout the region, you'll find the landscapes that inspired this giant of English romanticism, including the shores of Ullswater, where Wordsworth saw his famous "host of golden daffodils." See "Grasmere," in chapter 18.

- **Haworth** (West Yorkshire): Second only to Stratford-upon-Avon as a major literary pilgrimage site is the home of the Brontë Parsonage Museum. Here the famous Brontë sisters lived and spun their web of romance. Emily wrote *Wuthering Heights,* Charlotte wrote *Jane Eyre* and *Villette,* and even Anne wrote two novels, *The Tenant of Wildfell Hall* and *Agnes Grey,* though neither measures up to her sisters' works. See "Haworth: Home of the Brontës," in chapter 19.

3 The Best of Legendary England

- **Stonehenge** (near Salisbury, Wiltshire): The most celebrated prehistoric monument in Europe, Stonehenge is some 5,000 years old, but its original purpose remains a mystery. The romantic theory that Stonehenge was "constructed by the Druids" is nonsense; it was completed before the Druids reached Britain in the 3rd century B.C., but the legend persists. See p. 366.

- **Glastonbury Abbey** (Somerset): One of the great abbeys of England and once a center of culture and learning, Glastonbury quickly fell into ruins following the Dissolution of the Monasteries. One story about the abbey says that Jesus came here as a child with Joseph of Arimathea. According to another legend, King Arthur was buried at Glastonbury, the site of the fabled Avalon. See p. 387.

- **Tintagel** (Cornwall): On the windswept Cornish coast, the castle of Tintagel is said to be the birthplace of King Arthur. The castle was actually built much later than the Arthurian legend, around 1150. But who wants to stand in the way of a good story? No one in Cornwall, that's for sure. Tintagel merrily touts the King Arthur legend—in town, you can order an Excaliburger! See "Tintagel Castle: King Arthur's Legendary Lair," in chapter 12.

4 The Best of Ancient & Roman England

- **Roman Painted House** (Dover, Kent): Called Britain's "buried Pompeii," this 1,800-year-old structure has exceptionally well-preserved walls and an under-floor heating system used by the Romans. It's best known for its unique Bacchic murals. See p. 284.

- **Avebury** (west of Marlborough, Wiltshire; east of Bath, Avon): Although not as famous as Stonehenge, this is one of Europe's leading prehistoric monuments. Its circle of more than 100 stones—some of them weighing in at 50 tons—is arrayed on an 11-hectare (28-acre) site. See p. 366.

- **Roman Baths** (Bath, Avon): Dedicated to the goddess Sulis Minerva, the baths were founded in A.D. 75. Among the finest Roman remains in the country, they're still fed by Britain's most famous hot spring. The site of the Temple of Sulis Minerva is excavated and open for viewing. See p. 376.

- **Corinium Museum** (Cirencester, in the Cotswolds): This museum contains one of the best collections of archaeological remains from the Roman occupation of Britain. You'll see Roman mosaics that have remained in Britain, along with provincial sculpture, such as figures of Minerva and Mercury. See p. 454.
- **Hadrian's Wall** (near Hexham, Northumberland): A World Heritage Site, this wall—now in ruins—was ordered built by Hadrian, the Roman emperor, in A.D. 122 to hold back barbarian invasions from the north. Marking the far northern border of the Roman Empire, the wall stretched 118km (73 miles) from Wallsend, or Wall's End, north of Newcastle upon Tyne in the east to Bowness-on-Solway beyond Carlisle in the west. A milecastle (small fort) was added at every mile along the wall. A highlight is Vindolanda, the last of eight successive Roman forts built on a site adjacent to the wall. See "Hexham, Hadrian's Wall & the Pennine Way," in chapter 19.

5 The Best of Norman & Medieval England

- **Battle Abbey** (East Sussex): At this site of the famous Battle of Hastings (fought on Oct 14, 1066), the Normans defeated King Harold's English army. William the Conqueror built a great commemorative abbey here; the high altar of its church was erected over the spot where Harold fell in battle. The abbey was destroyed during the Dissolution of the Monasteries (1538–39). Some ruins and buildings remain, about which Tennyson wrote, "O Garden, blossoming out of English blood." See p. 290.
- **Hastings Castle** (Hastings, East Sussex): Now in ruins, this was the first of the Norman castles erected in England (ca. 1067). The fortress was unfortified in 1216. An audiovisual presentation of the castle's history includes the famous battle of 1066. See p. 291.
- **Rye** (East Sussex): Near the English Channel, this port—one of England's best preserved towns—was a smuggling center for centuries. Louis Jennings once wrote, "Nothing more recent than a Cavalier's Cloak, Hat and Ruffles should be seen on the streets of Rye." See "The Ancient Seaport of Rye," in chapter 8.
- **Dunster Castle** (Somerset): This castle was built on the site of a Norman castle granted to William de Mohun of Normandy by William the Conqueror shortly after his conquest of England. A 13th-century gateway remains from the original fortress. The Luttrell family held possession of the castle and its lands from 1376 until the National Trust took it over in 1976. See p. 391.
- **Warwick Castle** (Warwickshire): This is the finest medieval castle in England, lying on a cliff overlooking the Avon River. Its most powerful commander in the 1400s was the earl of Warwick, who, during the War of the Roses, was called the "Kingmaker." One of the best collections of medieval armor and weapons in Europe is behind its walls. See p. 497.
- **Fountains Abbey & Studley Royal** (southwest of Ripon, in North Yorkshire): These ruins evoke monastic life in medieval England. In 1132, Cistercian monks constructed "a place remote from all the earth." Explore the ruins as well as the Studley Royal, whose lavish 18th-century landscaping is one of the few surviving examples of a Georgian green garden. See p. 674.

- **Conwy Castle** (North Wales): Edward I ordered this masterpiece built after he subdued the last native prince of Wales. Visitors today can tour the royal apartment where Edward brought his queen, Eleanor. The castle's eight towers command the estuary of the River Conwy. See p. 747.

6 The Best of Tudor & Georgian England

- **Hampton Court Palace** (outside London): The most magnificent of the grand residences and royal palaces lining the River Thames west of central London, Hampton Court was built in grand style for Cardinal Wolsey—until Henry VIII snatched it away. Henry added the great hall in 1532, forcing laborers to toil 24 hours a day in shifts. The sheer size of the palace is amazing, and on its grounds is the world's first indoor tennis court. See p. 198.
- **Bath** (Avon): Much magnificent 18th-century architecture remains exactly as Jane Austen saw it, despite repeated World War II bombings. At one time, Bath was the most fashionable spa in Britain. Architect John Wood (1704–54), among others, helped create a city of harmony and beauty, with landscaped terraces, famous crescents such as the Royal Crescent, and Palladian villas. See "Bath: Britain's Most Historic Spa Town," in chapter 10.
- **Kenilworth Castle** (Warwickshire): This castle was the setting for Sir Walter Scott's romantic novel, *Kenilworth,* first published in 1862, which recounts the supposed murder of Amy Robsart, wife of Robert Dudley, earl of Leicester. Elizabeth I had presented Kenilworth Castle to her favorite earl in 1563. The castle was destroyed after the civil war and is now in ruins. See p. 498.

7 The Best of Victorian England

- **Albert Memorial** (Kensington Palace, London): If any statue symbolizes an era, this flamboyant tribute to Victoria's consort, her beloved Albert (1819–61), does; it is the epitome of Victorian excess. The statue depicts Albert holding a catalog of the Great Exhibition. He overlooks the South Kensington Culture Centre, his last legacy. The 4m-high (14-ft.) statue went into place in 1876 and was instantly described as an "outsize reliquary casket." See p. 176.
- **Houses of Parliament** (London): No government building in England symbolizes the Victorian age like the Palace of Westminster, housing Parliament. Replacing a palace destroyed by fire in 1834, it cost £2 million ($4 million) to build, a princely sum at the time. The building was completed in 1860 and turned out to be Gothic fantasy, its facade decorated with monarchs ranging from William the Conqueror to Queen Victoria. See p. 171.
- **Osborne House** (southeast of East Cowes on the Isle of Wight): This was Queen Victoria and Prince Albert's most cherished residence. Constructed at Queen Victoria's own expense, it is imbued with her spirit. The rooms are a perfect period piece of Victoriana, with all their artifacts and stuffy chairs—a cozy clutter best evoked by her sitting room. Grief-stricken at the death of Albert in 1861, the queen requested that the

house be kept as it was upon the death of her husband. See p. 345.

- **Manchester** (Lancashire): A major inland port since 1894, Manchester long had a reputation as a blackened, foggy, and forbidding city, grim and dowdy, the worst of the Midlands. But it has been cleaned up, and today its center is filled with masterpieces of sturdy, solid Victorian architecture, including homes built for the great industrial barons of the 19th century. See "Manchester: Gateway to the North," in chapter 17.

- **National Railway Museum** (York): The first national museum to be built outside of London is devoted to the locomotive that changed the face of Victorian England. Set in an original steam locomotive depot, the museum is filled with railway memorabilia, more than 40 full-size locomotives, plus the century-old Royal Saloon, in which Queen Victoria rode until her death. See p. 659.

8 The Best Museums

- **British Museum** (London): When Sir Hans Sloane died in 1753, he bequeathed to England his vast collection of art and antiquities for only £20,000 ($40,000), forming the nucleus of a collection that would one day embrace everything from the Rosetta Stone to the hotly contested Elgin Marbles (Greece wants them back). It's all here—and much, much more—in one of the world's great museums. See p. 172.

- **National Gallery** (London): One of the world's greatest collections of Western art dazzles the eye. Artists ranging from da Vinci to Rembrandt to Picasso are represented here. The gallery is especially rich in works by Renaissance artists. See p. 175.

- **Tate Britain** (London): Sir Henry Tate, a sugar producer, started the 10,000-piece collection with only 70 paintings. The Tate was considerably enlarged when J. M. W. Turner bequeathed some 300 oils and 19,000 watercolors to England upon his death. The Tate Modern, a repository of avant-garde modern art, is directly across the river. See p. 174.

- **The American Museum** (Claverton, 4km/2½ miles east of Bath, Avon): Housed in a neoclassical country house, this collection presents 2 centuries of American life and styles—including George Washington's mother's recipe for gingerbread. See p. 375.

- **Fitzwilliam Museum** (Cambridge, East Anglia): Although London dominates this list, some outstanding regional museums exist, including this gem near King's College. Exhibits range from paintings by Titian and Renoir to Chinese, Egyptian, and Greek antiquities. See p. 542.

- **Walker Art Gallery** (Liverpool, Lancashire): One of the finest collections of European and British paintings in Britain, this gallery deserves to be better known. A nearly complete study of British paintings is displayed here, from Tudor days to the present. The gallery also owns an outstanding collection of pre-Raphaelites. See p. 615.

- **National Museum Wales** (Cardiff): This museum, Wales's finest, presents the panorama of the history of this little country from prehistoric times until the present. And its collection of 18th-century porcelain is one of the finest in the world. See p. 703.

9 The Best Cathedrals

- **Westminster Abbey** (London): One of the world's greatest Anglo-French Gothic buildings has witnessed a parade of English history—from the crowning of William the Conqueror on Christmas Day 1066 to the funeral of Princess Diana in 1997. With few exceptions, the kings and queens of England have all been crowned here, and many are buried here as well. See p. 170.

- **Canterbury Cathedral** (Canterbury, Kent): The object of countless pilgrimages, as described in Chaucer's *Canterbury Tales,* this cathedral has been rebuilt twice after being destroyed by fires in 1067 and 1174. Thomas à Becket, the archbishop of Canterbury, was murdered here, and his shrine was an important site for pilgrims until the Reformation. See p. 277.

- **Winchester Cathedral** (Winchester, Hampshire): Construction of the cathedral that dominates this ancient city and capital of old Wessex began in 1079. In time, Winchester Cathedral became England's longest medieval cathedral, noted for its 12-bay nave. Many famous people are buried here, including Jane Austen. See p. 327.

- **Salisbury Cathedral** (Salisbury, Wiltshire): The most stylistically unified of England's cathedrals, this edifice was built in the mid–13th century. Its landmark spire—its most striking feature—was completed in 1325. The cathedral epitomizes the Early English style of architecture. See p. 363.

- **Durham Cathedral** (Durham, Yorkshire): Built between 1095 and 1133, this cathedral exemplifies Norman architecture on a broad scale. Its nave, a structure of almost majestic power, is its most notable feature. See p. 687.

- **York Minster** (York, Yorkshire): The largest Gothic cathedral north of the Alps is also among the grandest, with incredible stained-glass windows. Its unusual octagonal Chapter House has a late-15th-century choir screen by William Hyndeley. See p. 660.

- **Llandaff Cathedral** (Llandaff, Wales): Begun under the Normans, this cathedral outside Cardiff makes a dramatic impression. Its west front is one of the best works of medieval art in Wales. That didn't prevent Cromwell's armies from using the edifice as a beer hall. See p. 703.

10 The Best Castles, Palaces & Historic Homes

- **Woburn Abbey** (Woburn, Bedfordshire): A Cistercian abbey for 4 centuries, Woburn Abbey has been visited by everyone from Queen Victoria to Marilyn Monroe. You'll see Queen Victoria's bedroom, and the Canaletto Room, with its 21 perspectives of Venice. The grounds, more popular than the house, include the Wild Animal Kingdom, the best zoological collection in England after the London Zoo. See p. 269.

- **Hatfield House** (Hertfordshire): Hatfield was the childhood home of Elizabeth I, who was under an oak tree there when she learned she had become queen of England. Hatfield remains one of England's largest and finest country houses, with antiques, tapestries, paintings, and even the red silk stockings Elizabeth I wore. See p. 268.

- **Windsor Castle** (Windsor, Berkshire): The largest inhabited stronghold in the world and England's largest castle, Windsor Castle has been a royal abode since William the Conqueror constructed a motte and bailey on the site 4 years after conquering England. Severely damaged by fire in 1992, the castle has been mainly restored. Its major attraction is the great Perpendicular Chapel of St. George's, begun by Edward IV. The chancel is known for its three-tiered stalls, with its misericords (ledges used for support) and ornate carvings. See p. 234.

- **Blenheim Palace** (Woodstock, near Oxford, Oxfordshire): England's answer to Versailles, this extravagant baroque palace was the home of the 11th duke of Marlborough and the birthplace of Sir Winston Churchill. The structure was designed by Sir John Vanbrugh, of Castle Howard fame. Sarah, the duchess of Marlborough, battled the architects and builders from the beginning, wanting "a clean sweet house and garden be it ever so small." That she didn't get—the structure measures 255m (850 ft.) from end to end. Capability Brown designed the gardens. See p. 261.

- **Knole** (near Tunbridge, Kent): Begun in 1456 by the archbishop of Canterbury, Knole is celebrated for its 365 rooms (one for each day of the year), its 52 staircases (for each week of the year), and its seven courts (for each day of the week). Knole, one of England's largest private houses and

set in a 404-hectare (1,000-acre) deer park, is a splendid example of Tudor architecture. See p. 294.

- **Penshurst Place** (near Tunbridge, Kent): One of England's most outstanding country homes, this mansion was the former residence of Elizabethan poet Sir Philip Sidney (1554–86). In its day, the house attracted literati, including Ben Jonson. The original 1346 hall has seen the subsequent addition of Tudor, Jacobean, and neo-Gothic wings. See p. 297.

- **Hever Castle & Gardens** (Edenbridge, Kent): This was the childhood home of Anne Boleyn, second wife of Henry VIII and mother of Queen Elizabeth I. In 1903, William Waldorf Astor, an American multimillionaire and Anglophile, bought the castle, restored it, and landscaped the grounds. From the outside, it still looks as it did in Tudor times, with a moat and drawbridge protecting the castle. See p. 296.

- **Beaulieu Abbey–Palace House** (Beaulieu, in New Forest): Home of the first Lord Montagu, Palace House blends monastic Gothic architecture from the Middle Ages with Victorian trappings. Yet many visitors consider the National Motor Museum, also on the premises and with a collection of more than 250 antique automobiles, more fascinating than the house. See p. 341.

11 The Best Gardens

- **Royal Botanic Gardens, Kew** (near London): A delight in any season, everything blooms in profusion in this 121-hectare (300-acre) garden, from delicate exotics to commonplace flowers and shrubs. An easy trip from London, Kew Gardens, as it's known, possesses the largest herbarium on earth. Famed landscape architect

Capability Brown helped lay out part of the grounds. See p. 200.

- **Sissinghurst Castle Garden** (near Maidstone, Kent): A notorious literary couple, Vita Sackville-West and Harold Nicolson, created this garden. Its flamboyant parentage, unusual landscaping (the grounds were laid between the surviving parts of an

Elizabethan mansion), and location just 34km (21 miles) northeast of Cranbrook make it the most intriguing garden on London's doorstep. Overrun by tourists in summer, it's best in autumn, when the colors peak. See p. 297.

- **Wisley Garden** (Wisley, Kent): Wisley Garden sprawls across 101 hectares

(250 acres), filled with an abundance of flowers and shrubs. Maintained by the Royal Horticultural Society, it ranges from alpinelike meadows to summer carpets of flowers. In early summer, the gardens are brilliant with flowering rhododendrons. The landscaped orchid house alone is worth the trip here. See p. 299.

12 The Best London Experiences

- **Cruising London's Waterways** (Tube: Charing Cross): In addition to the Thames, London is riddled with an antique canal system, complete with towpath walks, bridges, and wharves. Replaced by the railroad, the system was forgotten until rediscovered by a new generation. An urban renewal effort has restored the system, with bridges painted and repaired, and towpaths cleaned up. See "Organized Tours," in chapter 6.

- **Viewing the Turners at the Tate:** Upon his death in 1851, J. M. W. Turner bequeathed his personal collection of 19,000 watercolors and some 300 paintings to the people of Britain. He wanted his finished works, some 100 paintings, displayed under one roof. Today at the Tate, you get not only Turner but also glimpses of the Thames through the museum's windows. How appropriate—the artist lived and died on its banks in Chelsea and painted the river in its many changing moods. See p. 174.

- **Enjoying a Traditional Afternoon Tea:** Nothing is more typically British, and it's a great way to spend an afternoon. We suggest our favorite places for tea (p. 164).

- **Rowing on the Serpentine:** When the weather is right, we like to head to this 17-hectare (41-acre) artificial lake, dating from 1730 and located in Hyde Park. A stream was dammed to

create the artificial lake, whose name derives from its winding, snakelike shape. At the Boathouse, you can rent a boat by the hour. With the right companion, it's one of the most idyllic ways to spend a sunny London afternoon. See p. 179.

- **Wandering through Covent Garden:** George Bernard Shaw got his inspiration for *Pygmalion* here, where the character of Eliza Doolittle sold violets to wealthy operagoers. The old fruit-and-vegetable market, with its Cockney cauliflower peddlers and butchers in blood-soaked aprons, is long gone. But what's left is just as interesting: Today's Covent Garden is London's best example of urban renewal. An antiques market is in the piazza on Monday, a crafts market Tuesday through Saturday. See p. 210.

- **Watching the Sunset at Waterloo Bridge:** Waterloo Bridge is the best place in London to watch the sun set over Westminster. From here, you can also see the last rays of sunlight bounce off the city spires in the East End.

- **Spending an Evening at a West End Theater:** London is the theatrical capital of the world. The live stage offers a unique combination of variety, accessibility, and economy—and a look at next year's Broadway hit. Coverage of the London theater scene begins on p. 211.

- **Crawling the London Pubs:** With some 5,000 pubs within the city limits, enough traditional ones remain, especially in central London. Make a crawl worthwhile by fortifying yourself with a ploughman's lunch or a plate of shepherd's pie. Our favorites include **Grenadier** (p. 224), **Salisbury** (p. 225), and **Red Lion** (p. 226).

13 The Best of Modern Britain

- **Tate Modern** (London): A Bankside Power Station in Southwark was transformed into a vast collection of modern art, even 21st-century avant-garde works. Favorite artists are showcased here, including every painter from Matisse to Andy Warhol, from Salvador Dalí to Picasso and Francis Bacon. In addition to the permanent collection, there are first-rate changing exhibitions. See p. 175.
- **British Airways London Eye** (London): Taking a ride in this "pod," you can see for 40km (25 miles) on a clear day. It's London viewed as a bird might see it. For nearly half an hour, you hover over the city in a slow-motion flight. See p. 195.
- **The Eden Project** (Bodelva, St. Austell): Lying 48km (30 miles) west of Plymouth in breezy Cornwall, this geodesic dome shelters some of the world's most exotic plants, including those rare species that grow in the Amazon. The gardens spread over 51 hectares (125 acres) in a former clay quarry. Locals refer to the attraction as "the Garden of Eden." See p. 427.
- **Castlefield** (Manchester): This historic core has been designated as an urban heritage park, inviting exploration. In a feat of gentrification, city authorities are turning this once-blighted area of warehouses and canals into a thriving community full of restaurants, bars, museums, and art galleries. The first railway station in the world, dating from 1830, has been converted into the Museum of Science and Industry. See "Exploring Castlefield," in chapter 17.
- **National Space Centre** (Leicester): Crowned by a futuristic rocket tower, this is Britain's only attraction dedicated to space science and astronomy. Visitors are taken through eight themed galleries, where they see space rockets, satellites, and capsules. Many attractions are hands-on. See p. 572.

14 The Most Charming Villages

- **Clovelly:** It is said that the little Devon community of Clovelly has been featured on more calendars than any other village in England. Starting at a great height, the village cascades down to the harborfront along narrow, cobblestone High Street. You park your car at the top and make the trip on foot. Supplies are carried down by donkeys. See p. 418.
- **Painswick:** Deep in the heart of the Cotswolds, this old wool town is still remarkably well preserved, its ancient buildings still guarding the narrow streets blanketed by antique cottages of honey-colored stone. Its church is known for the 99 yew trees. According to legend, the Devil won't let the 100th yew tree grow. To the north of the town, its Rococo Garden is visited by people from all over the world. See p. 454.
- **Bibury:** For sheer charm and quaintness, the old Cotswold town Painswick is a rival of Bibury for the title of most picturesque village in

England. Sitting idyllically on the Coln River, Bibury is known for its Arlington Row, a charming cluster of 17th-century weavers' cottages that are remarkably preserved. See p. 461.

- **Chipping Campden:** Elegant, regal Chipping Campden seems frozen in time, fighting other Cotswold villages, Bibury and Painswick, for the title of most beautiful in England. It is a dream of long ago when wealthy wool merchants built honey-stoned cottages in prosperous towns. Look for weather-beaten roofs, original mullioned windows, and a fine

Perpendicular church from the 15th century. See p. 476.

- **Betws-y-Coed:** Deep in the heart of the national park of Snowdonia, this oddly named village lies in a tree-lined valley of the River Conwy. With an antique church, it also comes complete with tumbling rivers and waterfalls set against a backdrop of mountain scenery. The town, which is also known for its eight bridges, makes an ideal center for exploring the attractions of North Wales. See "Betws-y-Coed," in chapter 21.

15 The Best Walks & Hikes

- **New Forest:** Requisitioned by William the Conqueror as a game reserve in 1079, the 375-sq.-km (145-sq.-mile) New Forest isn't very new. Today the New Forest is one of southern England's best rural playgrounds, attracting eight million annual visitors. You can ramble its carefully laid-out trails at leisure, or else take a guided scenic walk offered by the **Forest Commission.** Our favorite is the **Arboretum Sensory Trail,** stretching for .8km (a half-mile). See p. 337.

- **Dartmoor National Park:** Rich in legend and lore, this national park northeast of Plymouth is home to gorges, fields of purple heather, and the Dartmoor pony. The park is criss-crossed with about 805km (500 miles) of walking and hiking trails along with bridle paths. To get the scenic most out of this area, join one of the guided walks offered by the **Dartmoor National Park Authority** (p. 406), ranging from an easy 1½-hour jaunt to 6 long hours of trekking.

- **The Great Cotswold Ramble:** One of the most memorable walks in England is between the two idyllic

villages of Upper and Lower Slaughter. And it's only 1.6km (1 mile). A well-worn footpath, Warden's Way, meanders beside the edge of the swift-flowing River Eye. You pass quaint cottages, antique houses, stately trees, footbridges, and old millponds. You can also extend the walk another 2.5km (1½ miles) to romantic Bourton-on-the-Water. See p. 468.

- **The South Downs Way:** Beginning in the cathedral city of Winchester in the West Country, the South Downs Way, one of the most scenic hikes in the south of England, goes all the way to the town of Eastbourne. The distance across the bucolic terrain is 159km (99 miles). A bridleway forms the trail across these chalk uplands as you traverse miles of woodland. A highlight is the "Cliffs of the Seven Sisters." Bookstores in Winchester sell copies of *A Guide to South Downs Way* by Miles Jebb (Constable Press) and the even more detailed *South Downs Way* by Paul Millmore (Aurum Press).

- **The Cotswolds Way:** One of the great hiking "rambles" of England is the Great Cotswolds Way, a 167km

(104-mile) trail that cuts through some of England's most beautiful scenery in the bucolic Cotswolds. Laid out as late as 1968, the ramble goes from the town of Chipping Campden, arguably the most beautiful in the Cotswolds, in the north, going all the way to the spa city of Bath. The trail is clearly signposted at every intersection en route. The hike takes from 7 to 8 days but, of course, you can stop at any point.

- **Peak District National Park:** A district of moors, dales, green valleys,

waterfalls, and steep hills, the Peak District National Park is the scenic highlight of the East Midlands, covering some 1,404 sq. km (542 sq. miles). The Peak District National Park (p. 574) will supply you with details for hiking through this rugged terrain. The most evocative walk is the Monsal Trail lying between Buxton and Bakewell, two towns that make the best centers for touring the park.

16 The Best Historic Luxury Hotels

- **Brown's Hotel** (London; © 020/ 7493-6020; www.brownshotel.com): All Chippendale and chintz, Brown's was launched by the former manservant to Lord Byron in 1837, and it has been going strong ever since. Today, it occupies 14 historic houses just off Berkeley Square and coddles its well-heeled guests in luxury. See p. 122.

- **Chewton Glen Hotel** (New Milton, Hampshire; © 800/398-4534 in the U.S., or 01425/275341; www.chewton glen.com): This hotel is the best place to stay in southwest England. Service, taste, and quality are its hallmarks. The health club has a stunning design with a centerpiece swimming pool, and the hotel has 28 hectares (70 acres) of manicured grounds. Guest rooms feature period furniture. And the meals served in the Marryat Room Restaurant are prepared with first-rate ingredients. See p. 338.

- **The Lygon Arms** (Broadway, Cotswolds; © 01386/852255; www. thelygonarms.co.uk): Dating from 1532, this fabled inn in the Cotswolds has hosted many famous guests—Charles I used to drop in, and even Oliver Cromwell spent a night here, on the eve of the Battle of

Worcester. Some of the inn's antiques are listed in *The Dictionary of English Furniture*. Request a room in the Tudor Wing with its tilted oak floors and wooden beams. No. 20, with its massive canopied bed, is our favorite. See p. 474.

- **Sharrow Bay Country House Hotel** (Lake Ullswater, the Lake District; © 01768/486301; www.sharrowbay. co.uk): This gem is known as much for its cuisine as for its accommodations. The location alone would justify checking in: a 4.8-hectare (12-acre) site, with several gardens, in a national park on bucolic Lake Ullswater, beneath Barton Fell. The lakeside dining room offers panoramic views of the water, and you can always find something delectable on the menu. See p. 650.

- **Bodysgallen Hall** (Llandudno, North Wales; © 01492/584466; www. bodysgallen.com): One of Wales's greatest country-house hotels, this 17th-century mansion lies on 81 hectares (200 acres) of gardens and parkland. Even though an antique, it oozes with modern comforts while retaining its charms in elegantly furnished suites. See p. 748.

17 The Best Moderately Priced Hotels

- **Sanctuary House Hotel** (London; ℂ 020/7799-4044; www.fullers hotels.com): In a historic building close to Westminster Abbey, a brewery has converted an old building into a traditional English inn with pub downstairs. It's like something you might find in the countryside of England, but instead it's in the historic heart of London. The place is a bit nostalgic, like the food served—all the old favorites such as roast beef, Welsh lamb, and Dover sole. See p. 133.

- **The Fielding Hotel** (London; ℂ 020/7836-8305; www.the-fielding-hotel. co.uk): Named after the novelist Henry Fielding of *Tom Jones* fame, this hotel is one of the most eccentric in London. You'll either love it or hate it. Most guests love its cramped, quirky, quaint aura, and its location at Covent Garden is unbeatable. Everything is old-fashioned and traditional, but if you complain that the bedrooms are too small, Smokey, the African gray parrot, will tell you off! See p. 131.

- **The Hoxton** (London; ℂ 020/7550-1000; www.hoxtonhotels.com): In the increasingly gentrified Shoreditch neighborhood, near London's financial district, this hotel is dedicated to keeping the prices low. As such, it offers one of the best deals in town in comfortable, modern bedrooms. See p. 121.

- **ABode Canterbury** (Canterbury, Kent; ℂ 01227/766266): Since Victoria's day, there has been a hotel standing here, but today it's better than ever and the best in town, although prices remain affordable. See p. 274.

- **The Mermaid Inn** (Rye, Sussex; ℂ 01797/223065; www.mermaid inn.com): England's most famous smugglers' inn, the Mermaid sheltered Elizabeth I on her visit to Rye in 1573. At the time of the queen's visit, the inn had already been operating for 150 years. Still going strong, it leans heavily on English romance— old-world furnishings, some four-poster beds, and even a secret staircase. From its doorstep, the cobblestone streets of ancient Rye await exploration. See p. 286.

- **Powder Mills Hotel** (Battle, Surrey; ℂ 01424/775511; www.powder millshotel.com): Near the famous battlefield at Battle Abbey, this Georgian house stands on 61 hectares (150 acres). This historic property that once catered to luminaries such as the duke of Wellington has been successfully converted to receive paying guests, housing them in style and comfort—all at an affordable price. See p. 290.

- **Apsley House Hotel** (Bath, Avon; ℂ 01225/336966; www.apsley-house. co.uk): Away from the city center, this 1830 house was supposedly constructed for the duke of Wellington. Its owners have restored it and created a period house of character with an ambience of subdued elegance. See p. 371.

- **Chideock House Hotel** (Chideock, Dorset; ℂ 01297/489242; www. chideockhousehotel.com): A former 15th-century thatched house, once used by the Roundheads in 1645, is now a hotel of charm and grace with fireplaces and individually decorated bedrooms. See p. 353.

- **Ravenwood Hall** (Bury St., Edmunds, Suffolk; ℂ 01359/270345; www. ravenwoodhall.co.uk): Deep in the heart of East Anglia, this was once called Tudor Hall. Today, it stands in a 2.7-hectare (7-acre) park and gardens with an outdoor pool and tennis courts. Sleep in a four-poster bed and immerse yourself in old England after having had a good dinner and a toasty "warm-up" at the fireplace. See p. 550.

18 The Best B&Bs

- **New England** (London; ✆ 020/ 7834-1595; www.newenglandhotel. com): If you want a location near Victoria Station, this is one of your best bets in a restored 19th-century town house that's one of the most welcoming in the area. See p. 133.
- **The Jenkins Hotel** (London; ✆ 020/ 7387-2067; www.jenkinshotel.demon. co.uk): Hailed by one London publication as one of the 10 best hotel values in town, the Jenkins was featured on the PBS *Mystery!* series, *Poirot*. Those seeking decent accommodations in Bloomsbury, at an affordable price, have made their way to this address in Cartwright Gardens ever since Maggie Jenkins opened the place in the 1920s. Rooms are small but well furnished, and some of the original Georgian charm remains. See p. 130.
- **Fir Trees** (Windermere; ✆ 01539/ 442272; www.fir-trees.com): This attractive and inviting guesthouse lies near Lake Windermere, so beloved by poets such as Wordsworth. A warm welcome greets you as you're ushered to one of the comfortably furnished bedrooms in this antiques-filled Victorian house that was successfully converted to receive guests. See p. 634.

- **White Vine House** (Rye; ✆ 01797/ 224748; www.whitevinehouse.co.uk): In the romantic old seaport of Rye, this B&B has won many awards for the beauty of its garden and the quality of its restoration in a former 1568 sea captain's house that was but a derelict shell when restored in 1987. The creeper-clad cottage offers inviting bedrooms with both modern comforts and antiques. See p. 287.
- **The Beadles** (Salisbury; ✆ 01980/ 862922; www.guestaccom.co.uk/ 754.htm): This modernized Georgian house with antique furnishings and a view of the cathedral is a standout. It lies 11km (7 miles) from Salisbury in a well-manicured garden with tastefully furnished bedrooms. See p. 361.
- **The Big Sleep Hotel** (Cardiff; ✆ 02920/636363; www.thebig sleephotel.com): In the capital of Wales, this B&B—hailed by *Condé Nast Traveller* as "one of the coolest places to stay"—has been converted from a 1960s office tower. A hotel of affordable prices and chic minimalism, it is owned in part by actor John Malkovich. See p. 699.

19 The Best Restaurants

- **Gordon Ramsay at Claridge's** (London; ✆ 020/7499-0099): Gourmet—and famous Broadway musical producer—Andrew Lloyd Webber has proclaimed this hot chef the finest in London. Maybe that's going a bit far, but Ramsay is dazzling *tout* London with the fare emanating from his pots and pans. Everything he does bears an innovative twist, and though he has learned from the past, he's hardly anchored there. Try anything, but make sure you sample his "cappuccino" of white beans with grated truffles. You'll want to adopt him and take him home. See p. 142.

- **Le Gavroche** (London; ✆ 020/7408-0881): Long known for its top-rate French cuisine, this stellar restaurant has risen to the top again following a bit of a slump in the 1990s. Come here for that grand meal and skip the trip to Paris (we don't really mean that). The menu options are a delight, with such tantalizing dishes as a cassoulet of snails with herb-seasoned frogs' legs. Naturally, the wine cellar is among London's finest. See p. 142.

- **The Square** (London; ✆ 020/7495-7100): One of the great London restaurants to have emerged in the 21st century, this gourmet citadel is the domain of master chef Philip Howard, whose Continental cuisine has dazzled the food critics of London. Howard is justifiably praised for his "magic" in the kitchen and for his use of "stunningly fresh" ingredients, which he deftly concocts into masterpieces. See p. 142.

- **Le Manoir aux Quat' Saisons** (Great Milton, southeast of Oxford, Oxfordshire; ✆ 800/845-4274 in the U.S., or 01844/278881): The country-house hotel and restaurant of self-taught chef Raymond Blanc have brought him a TV series, as well as cookbooks and a school of cuisine. A new lightness, inspired mainly by Japan and the Mediterranean, is more evident in the celebrated chef's creations, and more meatless dishes appear on the seasonal menu. But the intensely French loyalties remain: sweetbread-stuffed pigs' trotters, kidneys, foie gras, even veal tongue. See p. 252.

- **Le Champignon Sauvage** (Cheltenham, the Cotswolds; ✆ 01242/573449): David Everitt-Matthias has awakened the sleepy taste buds of Cheltenham. Thoroughly imbued in the French classics, he also adds more modern and lighter touches to his table d'hôte menus, the finest at this old spa. Some dishes reach into the old English repertoire, including stuffed leg of wild rabbit served with black pudding and turnip sauerkraut. His desserts are acclaimed as the most luscious in England. See p. 459.

- **The Moody Goose** (Bath, Somerset; ✆ 01761/416784): The spa city of Bath offers some of the finest dining in the West Country and, in Bath itself, this English restaurant is the market leader. A most refined cuisine is served here in an elegant Georgian setting. The kitchen is known for its passion for fresh ingredients, and everything is cooked to order and to perfection. See p. 373.

20 The Best Pubs

- **Salisbury** (London; ✆ 020/7836-5863): Glittering cut-glass mirrors, old-fashioned banquettes, and lighting fixtures of veiled bronze girls in flowing togas re-create the Victorian gin-parlor atmosphere in the heart of the West End. Theatergoers drop in for homemade meat pie or a salad buffet before curtain. See p. 225.

- **Grenadier** (London; ✆ 020/7235-3074): Arguably London's most famous pub, and reputedly haunted, the Grenadier was once frequented by the duke of Wellington's officers on leave from fighting Napoleon. It pours the best bloody marys in town, and filet of beef Wellington is always a specialty. See p. 224.

- **The Ship Inn** (Exeter, Devon; ✆ 01392/272040): Frequented by Sir Francis Drake and Sir Walter Raleigh, this pub near Exeter Cathedral is the most celebrated in Devon. It still provides tankards of real ale, the same drink swilled by the likes of Sir John Hawkins. You can also eat here; portions are large, as in Elizabethan times. See p. 399.

- **The Cott Inn** (Dartington, near Totnes, Devon; ✆ **01803/863777**): Constructed in 1320 and believed to be the second-oldest inn in England, the Cott is a low, rambling, two-story building of stone, cob, and plaster under a thatched roof. A gathering place for the locals of Dartington, it's a good place for a drink on a windy night, as log fires keep the lounge and bar snug. See p. 410.

- **The Punch Bowl Inn** (Lanreath, near Looe, Cornwall; ✆ **01503/220778**): Licensed since 1620 as a pub, this was a former rendezvous for smugglers. High-backed settees and old fireplaces evoke the atmosphere of old England. Sample drinks in one of the kitchens—among the few "kitchens" in England licensed as bars. See p. 427.

- **The Turk's Head** (Penzance, Cornwall; ✆ **01736/363093**): Dating from 1233, this durable local favorite is filled with artifacts and timeworn beams. Drinkers take their lagers into a summer garden or retreat inside to the snug chambers when the wind blows cold. See p. 432.

- **The Lamb Inn** (Burford, the Cotswolds; ✆ **01993/823155**): This is our favorite place for a lager in all the Cotswolds. In a mellow old house from 1430 with thick stones and mullioned and leaded windows, it's a good place to spend the night, have a traditional English meal, or quaff a beer. Snacks are served in the timeworn bars and lounges or in a garden in summer. See p. 463.

2

England & Wales in Depth

England was attracting visitors—most of them, especially the Romans and Vikings, unwanted—long before William the Conqueror and his invading Normans crossed the Channel.

That invasion continues today, with millions of foreign visitors winging or boating in to see what all the excitement is about. They are joined by thousands upon thousands of poor immigrants, who have decided that their hope for a good life lies in these great islands whose people once conquered a global empire—two-fifths of the world—on which the sun has long ago set.

The charismatic Princess Di is still a cherished memory. The Beatles are half gone or else paying off crushing divorce settlements. The queen herself is still presiding with grace over a dysfunctional family. In her post-Di humiliation, she's even had her privacy invaded with an intrusive movie and has had to open the doors of Buckingham Palace in August to raise extra funds from those willing to pay her hefty entrance price.

That legendary stiff British upper lip isn't so stiff any more. You get that impression if you visit an English pub, some 5,000 of them in London alone. In some pubs you'll wonder where those famous English manners went, especially if you encounter lager louts ruling the night after too many pints. Some of the clichés remain. The English still consume on a daily basis oceans of fish, served with their soggy chips. However, with the influx of immigrants in the past decades, almost an equal number of curry dishes are devoured as well.

As Victoria and her quaint morals lie sleeping in her grace outside Windsor, London—and England in general—have become cutting edge in music, fashion, culture, art, and even architecture, the latter much too daringly avant-garde for the likes of tradition-minded Prince Charles.

The fading English aristocracy, to pay the tax man, is even opening its castles or manor houses to overnight visitors. So far, the queen isn't running a B&B at Windsor Castle, but many dukes or duchesses are sharing their royal abodes with hordes of tourist invaders. Even theatrical and movie stars, such as Jane Seymour, are renting out, in her case a 14th-century manor near Bath.

As you tour this England with its 60 million people, you'll encounter "Brit ego." The people have a lot to be proud of, along with some shameful scars in their colonization. They did give the world the Magna Carta, and almost everything viewed as "Western," even law. They spearheaded the Industrial Revolution and won nearly all their foreign wars in spite of their Mickey Mouse size.

Before Tony Blair was sent packing from 10 Downing Street, he said, "We Brits are now living in the post–Industrial Age, and we may not quite have reinvented ourselves. But we're doing so every day, and I'm sure our future generations will have many marvelous surprises to spring upon the world."

1 England Today

The England you'll encounter today has moved from the prim and proper Victorianism of the mid–19th century and is an exciting land of change and experiment, being forever altered by the massive arrival of immigrants from around the globe.

It's not a big country, but 2,500 eventful years have left their mark. Traveling in England is like experiencing a living, illustrated history book—the ancient mystery of Stonehenge, Hadrian's Wall left in the north by the Romans, the grand cathedrals, the lofty spires of village churches.

Monuments aside, the highly individualistic people who inhabit England today are an attraction unto themselves. Known for their privacy and reserve, they have endless tolerance for eccentricity.

As a long-term cultural shift, Britain's class system seems to be waning. The average visitor will hardly know that it even exists. Yet the number of titles has grown from some 115 peers (nobles) some 2 centuries ago to almost 2,000 titles today. The explosion in titles derives from the policy of elevating to the peerage anyone who continues in a major way to contribute "to the well-being of Britain"—the late Lord Laurence Olivier, for example.

Britain is the only country in the world that has granted titles to members of labor unions. At the bottom of the rung are knights and ladies (dames) whose titles come from their achievements, perhaps in politics or the arts. Such a title of "Dame Elizabeth" was bestowed on Elizabeth Taylor.

Of course, members of the House of Lords still must come from the peers of the realm; otherwise a politician is "banished" to the House of Commons. As a political issue, there are those who want to abolish the House of Lords. The argument goes that the very nature of Britain's legislative process is deeply rooted in the class system. But to get rid of Britain's aristocracy would necessitate a radical change in Parliament.

One BBC commentator said, "The royals don't rule anymore but they provide us with amusement, which is the only reason we keep them around." Dishing the dirt on the royals lures millions of tabloid readers daily. Times have changed. Contrast today's situation to the

The Bulldog & a Question of Character

The fact that the English have adopted the bulldog as their symbol gives you a clue to their character, at least according to George Orwell, author of *1984* and *Animal Farm*. In 1947 he wrote that millions of Brits "willingly accept as their national emblem the bulldog, an animal noted for its obstinacy, ugliness, and impenetrable stupidity." Orwell, both a socialist and a critic of socialism, had no kindly feelings toward his fellow citizens.

Countless others have attempted to characterize the English, including the writer Arthur Koestler, who described an average Englishman as an "attractive hybrid between an ostrich and a lion: keeping his head in the sand for as long as possible, but when forced to confront reality, capable of heroic deeds."

The Brits have always baffled the Americans, perhaps ever since the latter ceased being Brits and became Americans. Writer Paul Gallico noted: "No one can be as calculatedly rude as the British, which amazes Americans, who do not understand studied insult and can only offer abuse as a substitute."

prolonged press silence about the courtship of King Edward VIII and the American divorcée, Wallis Warfield Simpson, in the 1930s.

The very existence of the monarchy still is a hot political issue to press in a London pub. As Labor's "shadow minister," Jack Straw, longtime critic of the monarchy, said that he would like to see "the type of monarch they have in Norway, or perhaps Sweden. Let the royals shop for groceries like the rest of us. It would signal a classless British society." Even Prince Charles has admitted "that a lot of people need to be taken off the royal payroll and the monarchy scaled back if it is to survive."

Nothing is changing England today more than demographics. The 2001 census listed a population just under 50,000,000, with slightly more females than males. The mean age of England's population is around 39 years, and some 90% of its people were born in the British Isles. Life expectancy for males is 77, for females 81. England's ethnic minorities make up some 15.3% of the population, with Asians forming the largest number of residents.

2 Looking Back at England

FROM MURKY BEGINNINGS TO ROMAN OCCUPATION Britain was probably split off from the continent of Europe some 8 millennia ago by the continental drift and other natural forces. The early inhabitants, the Iberians, were later to be identified with stories of fairies, brownies, and "little people." These are the people whose ingenuity and enterprise are believed to have created Stonehenge (p. 366), but despite that great and mysterious monument, little is known about them.

They were replaced by the iron-wielding Celts, whose massive invasions around 500 B.C. drove the Iberians back to the Scottish Highlands and Welsh mountains, where some of their descendants still live today.

In 54 B.C., Julius Caesar invaded England, but the Romans did not become established there until A.D. 43. They went as far as Caledonia (now Scotland), where they gave up, leaving that land to "the painted ones," or the warring Picts. The wall (p. 689) built by Emperor Hadrian across the north of England marked the northernmost reaches of the Roman Empire. During almost 4 centuries of occupation, the Romans built roads, villas, towns, walls, and fortresses; they farmed the land and introduced first their pagan religions, then Christianity. Agriculture and trade flourished.

FROM ANGLO-SAXON RULE TO THE NORMAN CONQUEST When the Roman legions withdrew, around A.D. 410, they left the country open to waves of invasions by Jutes, Angles, and Saxons, who established themselves in small kingdoms throughout the former Roman colony. From the 8th through the 11th century, the Anglo-Saxons contended with Danish raiders for control of the land.

By the time of the Norman Conquest, the Saxon kingdoms were united under an elected king, Edward the Confessor. His successor was to rule less than a year before the Norman invasion.

The date 1066 is familiar to every English schoolchild. It marked an epic event, the only successful military invasion of Britain in history, and one of England's great turning points: King Harold, the last Anglo-Saxon king, was defeated at the Battle of Hastings, and William of Normandy was crowned William I. To wander those ancient battlefields, visit Hastings (p. 288) and Battle (p. 288).

England's Historical Highlights

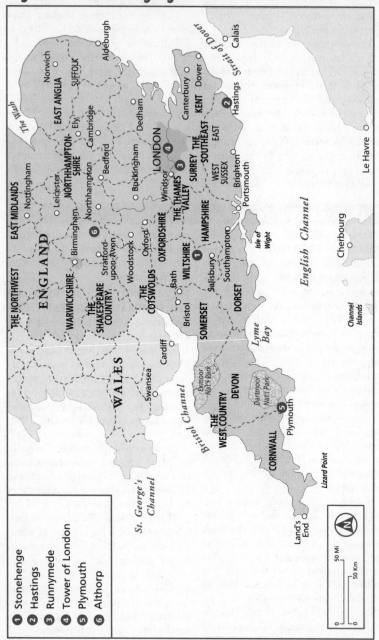

1 Stonehenge
2 Hastings
3 Runnymede
4 Tower of London
5 Plymouth
6 Althorp

King Arthur & the Knights of the Round Table

England's preeminent myth is, of course, the Arthurian legend of Camelot and the Round Table. So compelling was this legend that medieval writers treated it as a tale of chivalry, even though the real Arthur, if he lived, probably did so around the time of the Roman or Saxon invasions. Despite its universal adoption throughout Europe, it was in Wales and southern England that the legend initially developed and blossomed. The story was polished and given a literary form for the first time by Geoffrey of Monmouth around 1135. Combining Celtic myth and Christian and classical symbolism (usually without crediting his sources), Geoffrey forged a fictional history of Britain whose form, shape, and elevated values were centered on the mythical King Arthur. Dozens of other storytellers embellished the written and oral versions of the tale. The resulting stewpot described the birth of Arthur, the exploits of the king and his knights, the establishment of a knightly fellowship of the Round Table, and the search for the Holy Grail, the cup Jesus drank from at the Last Supper. This idyllic and noble kingdom was shattered by the adultery of Arthur's queen, Guinevere, with his favorite knight, Lancelot, and the malice of Mordred, Arthur's illegitimate son.

To visit King Arthur's legendary lair, head to Tintagel Castle (p. 445) in Cornwall.

One of William's first acts was to order a survey of the land he had conquered, assessing all property in the nation for tax purposes. This survey was called the Domesday Book, or "Book of Doom," as some pegged it. The resulting document was completed around 1086 and has been a fertile sourcebook for British historians ever since.

Norman rule had an enormous impact on English society. All high offices were held by Normans, and the Norman barons were given great grants of lands; they built Norman-style castles and strongholds throughout the country. French was the language of the court for centuries—few people realize that heroes such as Richard the Lionheart probably spoke little or no English.

FROM THE RULE OF HENRY II TO THE MAGNA CARTA In 1154, Henry II, the first of the Plantagenets, was crowned (reigned 1154–89). This

---

Dateline

- 54 B.C. Julius Caesar invades England.
- A.D. 43 Romans conquer England.
- 410 Jutes, Angles, and Saxons form small kingdoms in England.
- 500–1066 Anglo-Saxon kingdoms fight off Viking warriors.
- 1066 William, duke of Normandy, invades England, defeats Harold II at the Battle of Hastings.
- 1154 The Plantagenets launch their rule (which lasts until 1399) with the crowning of Henry II.
- 1215 King John signs the Magna Carta at Runnymede.
- 1337 Hundred Years' War between France and England begins.
- 1485 Battle of Boswoth Field ends the War of the Roses between the houses of York and Lancaster; Henry VII launches the Tudor dynasty.
- 1534 Henry VIII brings the Reformation to England and dissolves the monasteries.
- 1558 The accession of Elizabeth I ushers in an era of exploration and a renaissance in science and learning.
- 1588 Spanish Armada defeated.

continues

The Legend of Robin Hood

Another myth that has captured the world's imagination is the legend of Robin Hood, the folk hero of tale and ballad. His slogan, "Take from the rich and give to the poor," fired the imagination of a hardworking, sometimes impoverished English people.

Celebrating their freedom in verdant Sherwood Forest, Robin Hood's eternally youthful band rejoiced in "hearing the twang of the bow of yew and in watching the gray goose shaft as it cleaves the glistening willow wand or brings down the king's proud buck." Life was one long picnic beneath the splendid oaks of a primeval forest, with plenty of ale and flavorful venison poached from the forests of an oppressive king. The clever guerrilla rebel "Robin Hood" waged against authority (represented by the haughty, despotic, and overfed sheriff of Nottingham) was punctuated by heroic exploits and a yearning to win justice for the victims of oppression. Later, such historical figures as the Scottish bandit and soldier of fortune Robert MacGregor, known as Rob Roy (1671–1734), were imbued with the heroism and bravado of Robin Hood, and many English reformers drew upon his heroism as they battled the forces of oppression.

To visit Sherwood Forest, see p. 584.

remarkable character in English history ruled a vast empire—not only most of Britain but Normandy, Anjou, Brittany, and Aquitaine in France.

Henry was a man of powerful physique, both charming and terrifying. He reformed the courts and introduced the system of common law, which still operates in moderated form in England today and also influenced the American legal system. But Henry is best remembered for ordering the infamous murder of Thomas à Becket, archbishop of Canterbury. Henry, at odds with his archbishop, exclaimed, "Who will rid me of this turbulent priest?" His knights, overhearing and taking him at his word, murdered Thomas in front of the high altar in Canterbury Cathedral (p. 277).

Henry's wife, Eleanor of Aquitaine, the most famous woman of her time, was no less of a colorful character. She accompanied her first husband, Louis VII of France, on the Second Crusade, and it was rumored that she had a romantic affair at that time with the Saracen leader,

- 1603 James VI of Scotland becomes James I of England, thus uniting the crowns of England and Scotland.
- 1620 Pilgrims sail from Plymouth on the Mayflower to found a colony in the New World.
- 1629 Charles I dissolves Parliament, ruling alone.
- 1642–49 Civil War between Royalists and Parliamentarians; the Parliamentarians win.

- 1649 Charles I beheaded, and England is a republic.
- 1653 Oliver Cromwell becomes Lord Protector.
- 1660 Charles II restored to the throne with limited power.
- 1665–66 Great Plague and Great Fire decimate London.
- 1688 James II, a Catholic, is deposed, and William and Mary come to the throne, signing a bill of rights.

- 1727 George I, the first of the Hanoverians, assumes the throne.
- 1756–63 In the Seven Years' War, Britain wins Canada from France.
- 1775–83 Britain loses its American colonies.
- 1795–1815 The Napoleonic Wars lead, finally, to the Battle of Waterloo and the defeat of Napoleon.

Saladin. Domestic and political life did not run smoothly, however, and Henry and Eleanor and their sons were often at odds. The pair has been the subject of many plays and films, including *The Lion in Winter, Becket,* and T. S. Eliot's *Murder in the Cathedral.*

Two of their sons were crowned kings of England. Richard the Lionheart actually spent most of his life outside England, on crusades, or in France. John was forced by his nobles to sign the Magna Carta at Runnymede (p. 236), in 1215—another date well known to English schoolchildren.

The Magna Carta guaranteed that the king was subject to the rule of law and gave certain rights to the king's subjects, beginning a process that eventually led to the development of parliamentary democracy as it is known in Britain today. This process would have enormous influence on the American colonies many years later. The Magna Carta became known as the cornerstone of English liberties, though it only granted liberties to the barons. It took the rebellion of Simon de Montfort half a century later to introduce the notion that the common people should also have a voice and representation.

THE BLACK DEATH & THE WARS OF THE ROSES In 1348, half the population died as the Black Death ravaged England. By the end of the century, the population of Britain had fallen from four million to two million.

England also suffered in the Hundred Years' War, which went on intermittently for more than a century. By 1371, England had lost much of its land on French soil. Henry V, immortalized by Shakespeare, revived England's claims to France, and his victory at Agincourt was notable for making obsolete the forms of medieval chivalry and warfare.

After Henry's death in 1422, disputes arose among successors to the crown that resulted in a long period of civil strife, the Wars of the Roses, between the Yorkists, who used a white rose as their symbol, and the Lancastrians with their red rose. The last Yorkist king was Richard III, who got bad press from Shakespeare, but who is defended to this day as a hero by the people of the city of York. Richard was defeated at Bosworth Battlefield (p. 574), and the victory introduced England to the first Tudor, the shrewd and wily Henry VII.

THE TUDORS TAKE THE THRONE The Tudors were unlike the kings who had ruled before them. They introduced into England a strong central monarchy with far-reaching powers. The system worked well under the first three strong and capable Tudor monarchs, but it

---

- **1837** Queen Victoria begins her reign as Britain reaches the zenith of its empire.
- **1901** Victoria dies, and Edward VII becomes king.
- **1914–18** England enters World War I and emerges victorious on the Allied side.
- **1936** Edward VIII abdicates to marry an American divorcée.
- **1939–45** In World War II, Britain stands alone against

Hitler from the fall of France in 1940 until America enters the war in 1941. Dunkirk is evacuated in 1940; bombs rattle London during the Blitz.
- **1945** Germany surrenders. Churchill is defeated; the Labour government introduces the welfare state and begins to dismantle the empire.
- **1952** Queen Elizabeth II ascends the throne.

- **1973** Britain joins the European Union.
- **1979** Margaret Thatcher becomes prime minister.
- **1982** Britain defeats Argentina in the Falklands War.
- **1990** Thatcher is ousted; John Major becomes prime minister.
- **1991** Britain fights with Allies to defeat Iraq.

continues

began to break down later when the Stuarts came to the throne.

Henry VIII is surely the most notorious Tudor. Imperious and flamboyant, a colossus among English royalty, he slammed shut the door on the Middle Ages and introduced the Renaissance to England. He is best known, of course, for his treatment of his six wives and the unfortunate fates that befell five of them.

When his first wife, Catherine of Aragon, failed to produce an heir, and his ambitious mistress, Anne Boleyn, became pregnant, he tried to annul his marriage, but the pope refused, and Catherine contested the action. Defying the power of Rome, Henry had his marriage with Catherine declared invalid and secretly married Anne Boleyn in 1533.

The events that followed had profound consequences and introduced the religious controversy that was to dominate English politics for the next 4 centuries. Henry's break with the Roman Catholic Church and the formation of the Church of England, with himself as supreme head, was a turning point in English history. It led eventually to the Dissolution of the Monasteries, civil unrest, and much social dislocation. The confiscation of the church's land and possessions brought untold wealth into the king's coffers, wealth that was distributed to a new aristocracy that supported the monarch. In one sweeping gesture, Henry destroyed the ecclesiastical culture of the Middle Ages. Among those executed for refusing to cooperate with Henry's changes was Sir Thomas More, humanist, international man of letters, and author of *Utopia*.

Anne Boleyn bore Henry a daughter, the future Elizabeth I, but failed to produce a male heir. She was brought to trial on a trumped-up charge of adultery and beheaded; in 1536, Henry married Jane Seymour, who died giving birth to Edward VI. For his next wife, he looked farther afield and chose Anne of Cleves from a flattering portrait, but she proved disappointing—he called her "The Great Flanders Mare." He divorced her the same year and next picked a pretty young woman from his court, Catherine Howard. She was also beheaded on a charge of adultery but, unlike Anne Boleyn, was probably guilty. Finally, he married an older woman, Catherine Parr, in 1543. She survived him.

Henry's heir, sickly Edward VI (reigned 1547–53), did not live long. He died of consumption—or, as rumor has it, overmedication. He was succeeded by his sister, Mary I (reigned 1553–58), and the trouble Henry had stirred up with the break with Rome came home to roost for the first time. Mary restored the Roman

---

- **1992** Royals are jolted by fire at Windsor Castle and marital troubles of their two sons. Britain joins the European Single Market. Deep recession signals the end of the booming 1980s.
- **1994** England is linked to the Continent by rail via the Channel Tunnel, or Chunnel. Tony Blair elected Labour party leader.

- **1996** The IRA breaks a 17-month cease-fire with a truck bomb at the Docklands that claims two lives. Charles and Di divorce. The government concedes a possible link between mad-cow disease and a fatal brain ailment afflicting humans; British beef imports face banishment globally.

- **1997** London swings again. The Labour party ends 18 years of Conservative rule with a landslide election victory. The tragic death of Diana, Princess of Wales, prompts worldwide outpouring of grief.
- **1998** Prime Minister Tony Blair launches "New Britain"—young, stylish, and informal.

Catholic faith, and her persecution of the adherents of the Church of England earned her the name of "Bloody Mary." Some 300 Protestants were executed, many burned alive at the stake. She made an unpopular and unhappy marriage to Philip of Spain; despite her bloody reputation, her life was a sad one.

Elizabeth I (reigned 1558–1603) came next to the throne, ushering in an era of peace and prosperity, exploration, and a renaissance in science and learning. An entire age was named after her: the Elizabethan age. She was the last great and grand monarch to rule England, and her passion and magnetism were said to match her father's. Through her era marched Drake, Raleigh, Frobisher, Grenville, Shakespeare, Spenser, Byrd, and Hilliard. During her reign, she had to face the appalling precedent of ordering the execution of a fellow sovereign, Mary, Queen of Scots. Her diplomatic skills kept war at bay until 1588, when at the apogee of her reign, the Spanish Armada was defeated. She will be forever remembered as "Good Queen Bess." To see where she lived as a young girl, you can visit Hatfield House (p. 268).

FROM THE RESTORATION TO THE NAPOLEONIC WARS The reign of Charles II was the beginning of a dreadful decade that saw London decimated by the

Great Plague and destroyed by the Great Fire.

His successor, James II, attempted to return the country to Catholicism, an attempt that so frightened the powers that be that Catholics were for a long time deprived of their civil rights. James was deposed in the "Glorious Revolution" of 1688 and succeeded by his daughter Mary (1662–94) and William of Orange (1650–1702). (William of Orange was the grandson of Charles I, the tyrannical king whom Cromwell helped to depose.) This secured a Protestant succession that has continued to this day. These tolerant and levelheaded monarchs signed a bill of rights, establishing the principle that the monarch reigns not by divine right but by the will of Parliament. William outlived his wife, reigning until 1702.

Queen Anne then came to the throne, ruling from 1702 until her own death in 1714. She was the sister of Mary of Orange and was another daughter of James II. The last of the Stuarts, Anne marked her reign with the most significant event, the 1707 Act of Union with Scotland. She outlived all her children, leaving her throne without an heir.

Upon the death of Anne, England looked for a Protestant prince to succeed her and chose George of Hanover who

- **1999** England rushes toward the 21st century with the Millennium Dome at Greenwich.
- **2000** London presides over millennium celebration; gays allowed to serve openly in the military.
- **2002** Queen Elizabeth, the Queen Mother, dies at age 101.
- **2005** Suicide bomb attacks devastate London.
- **2007** Tony Blair steps down; Gordon Brown becomes prime minister.

reigned from 1714 to 1727. Though he spoke only German and spent as little time in England as possible, he was chosen because he was the great-grandson of James I. Beginning with this "distant cousin" to the throne, the reign of George I marked the beginning of the 174-year rule of the Hanoverians who preceded Victoria.

George I left the running of the government to the English politicians and created the office of prime minister. Under the Hanoverians, the powers of Parliament were extended, and the constitutional monarchy developed into what it is today.

The American colonies were lost under the Hanoverian George III, but other British possessions were expanded: Canada was won from the French in the Seven Years' War (1756–63), British control over India was affirmed, and Captain Cook claimed Australia and New Zealand for England. The British became embroiled in the Napoleonic Wars (1795–1815), achieving two of their greatest victories and acquiring two of their greatest heroes: Nelson at Trafalgar and Wellington at Waterloo.

THE INDUSTRIAL REVOLUTION & THE REIGN OF VICTORIA

The mid– to late 18th century saw the beginnings of the Industrial Revolution. This event changed the lives of the laboring class, created a wealthy middle class, and transformed England from a rural, agricultural society into an urban, industrial economy. England was now a world-class financial and military power. Male suffrage was extended, though women were to continue under a series of civil disabilities for the rest of the century. To see the beginnings of the Industrial Revolution, visit Ironbridge (p. 524).

Queen Victoria's reign (1837–1901) coincided with the height of the Industrial Revolution. When she ascended the throne, the monarchy as an institution was in considerable doubt, but her 64-year reign, the longest tenure in English history, was an incomparable success.

The Victorian era was shaped by the growing power of the bourgeoisie, the queen and her consort's personal moral stance, and the perceived moral responsibilities of managing a vast empire. During this time, the first trade unions were formed, a public school system was developed, and railroads were built.

Victoria never recovered from the death of her German husband, Albert. He died from typhoid fever in 1861, and the queen never remarried. Though she had many children, she found them tiresome but was a pillar of family values nonetheless. One historian said her greatest asset was her relative ordinariness.

Middle-class values ruled Victorian England and were embodied by the queen. The racy England of the past went underground. Our present-day view of England is still influenced by the attitudes of the Victorian era, and we tend to forget that English society in earlier centuries was famous for its rowdiness, sexual license, and spicy scandal.

Victoria's son Edward VII (reigned 1901–10) was a playboy who had waited too long in the wings. He is famous for mistresses, especially Lillie Langtry, and his love of elaborate dinners. You can actually spend the night at Langtry Manor Hotel in Bournemouth (p. 347), which the king built for his favorite mistress. During his brief reign, he, too, had an era named after him: the Edwardian age. Under Edward, the country entered the 20th century at the height of its imperial power. At home, the advent of the motorcar and the telephone radically changed social life, and the women's suffrage movement began.

World War I marked the end of an era. It had been assumed that peace, progress, prosperity, empire, and even social improvement would continue indefinitely.

Impressions

"Even a boiled egg tastes of mutton fat in England."
—Norman Douglas, *Old Calabria*, 1915

"For 'tis a low, newspaper, humdrum, law-suit Country."
—Lord Byron, *Don Juan*, 1824

"England is one of the weird mysteries of God's afterthought."
—Henry Adams, letter to John Hay,
December 1900

"England is the paradise of individuality, eccentricity, heresy, anomalies, hobbies and humours."
—George Santayana, "The British Character,"
Soliloquies in England, 1892

World War I and the troubled decades of social unrest, political uncertainty, and the rise of Nazism and fascism put an end to these expectations.

THE WINDS OF WAR   World War II began in 1939, and soon thereafter Britain found a new and inspiring leader, Winston Churchill. Churchill led the nation during its "finest hour." You can visit Churchill's private home, Chartwell in Kent (p. 293) and the underground Cabinet War Rooms (p. 181) in London where he rode out parts of World War II. From the time the Germans took France, Britain stood alone against Hitler. The evacuation of Dunkirk in 1940, the Blitz of London, and the Battle of Britain were dark hours for the British people, and Churchill is remembered for urging them to hold onto their courage. Once the British forces were joined by their American allies, the tide finally turned, culminating in the D-day invasion of German-occupied Normandy. These bloody events are still remembered by many with pride, and with nostalgia for the era when Britain was still a great world power.

The years following World War II brought many changes to England. Britain began to lose its grip on an empire (India became independent in 1947), and the Labour government, which came into power in 1945, established the welfare state and brought profound social change to Britain.

QUEEN ELIZABETH RULES TO THE PRESENT DAY   Upon the death of the "wartime king," George VI, Elizabeth II ascended the throne in 1953. Her reign has seen the erosion of Britain's once-mighty industrial power, and, in recent years, a severe recession.

Political power has seesawed back and forth between the Conservative and Labour parties. Margaret Thatcher, who became prime minister in 1979, seriously eroded the welfare state and was ambivalent toward the European Union. Her popularity soared during the successful Falklands War, when Britain seemed to recover some of its military glory for a brief time.

Though the queen has remained steadfast and punctiliously has performed her ceremonial duties, rumors about the royal family abounded, and in the year 1992, which Queen Elizabeth labeled an *annus horribilis,* a devastating fire swept through Windsor Castle (p. 234), the marriages of several of her children crumbled, and the queen agreed to pay taxes for the first time. Prince Charles and Princess Diana agreed to a separation, and there were ominous rumblings about the future of the House of Windsor. By 1994 and 1995, Britain's economy was improving after several glum years, but Conservative prime minister John Major, heir to Margaret Thatcher's legacy, was coming under increasing criticism.

The IRA, reputedly enraged at the slow pace of peace talks, relaunched its reign of terror across London in February 1996, planting a massive bomb that ripped through a building in London's Docklands, injuring more than 100 people and killing two. Shattered, too, was the 17-month cease-fire by the IRA, which brought hope that peace was at least possible. Another bomb went off in Manchester in June.

Headlines about the IRA bombing gave way to another big bomb: the end of the marriage of Princess Diana and Prince Charles. The Wedding of the Century had become the Divorce of the Century. The lurid tabloids had been right all along about this unhappy pair. But details of the $26-million divorce settlement didn't satisfy the curious: Scrutiny of Prince Charles's relationship with Camilla Parker-Bowles, as well as gossip about Princess Diana's love life, continued in the press.

In 1997, the political limelight now rested on the young Labour Leader Tony Blair. From his rock-star acquaintances to his "New Labour" rhetoric, which is chock-full of pop-culture buzzwords, he was a stark contrast to the more staid Major. His media-savvy personality obviously registered with the British electorate. On May 1, 1997, the Labour Party ended 18 years of Conservative rule with a landslide election victory. At age 44, Blair became Britain's youngest prime minister in 185 years, following in the wake of the largest Labour triumph since Winston Churchill was swept out of office at the end of World War II.

Blair's election—which came just at the moment when London was being touted by the international press for its renaissance in art, music, fashion, and dining—had many British entrepreneurs poised and ready to take advantage of what they perceived as enthusiasm for new ideas and ventures. Comparisons to Harold Macmillan and his reign over the Swinging Sixties were inevitable, and insiders agreed that something was in the air.

However, events took a shocking turn in August 1997 when Princess Diana was killed—along with her companion, Harrods heir Dodi al-Fayed—in a high-speed car crash in Paris. The ancestral home of the late princess at Althorp (p. 568) is open to the public.

"The People's Princess" continued to dominate many headlines in 1998 with bizarre conspiracy theories about her death. But the royal family isn't the real force in Britain today.

Blair led Britain on a program of constitutional reform without parallel in the last century. Critics feared that Blair would one day preside over a "dis-united" Britain, with Scotland breaking away and Northern Ireland forming a self-government.

Of course, the future of the monarchy still remains a hot topic of discussion in Britain. There is little support for doing away with the monarchy in Britain today in spite of wide criticism of the royal family's behavior in the wake of Diana's death. Apparently, if polls are to be believed, some three-quarters of the British populace want the monarchy to continue. Prince Charles is even making a comeback with the British public and has appeared in public—to the delight of the paparazzi—with his longtime mistress, now wife, Camilla Parker-Bowles. At the very least, the monarchy is good for the tourist trade, on which Britain is increasingly dependent. And what would the tabloids do without it?

The big news among royal watchers in Britain early in 2002 was the death of Princess Margaret at age 71, followed 7 weeks later by the death of Queen Mother Elizabeth at the age of 101. The most popular royal, the Queen "Mum" was a symbol of courage and dignity, especially during the tumultuous World

War II years when London was under bombardment from Nazi Germany. The remains of the Queen Mother were laid to rest alongside her husband in the George VI Memorial Chapel at St. George's at Windsor Castle. The ashes of Princess Margaret were also interred with her parents in the same chapel.

At the dawn of the millennium, major social changes occurred in Britain. No sooner had the year 2000 begun than Britain announced a change of its code of conduct for the military, allowing openly gay men and women to serve in the armed forces. The action followed a European court ruling in the fall of 1999 that forbade Britain to discriminate against homosexuals. This change brings Britain in line with almost all other NATO countries, including France, Canada, and Germany. The United States remains at variance with the trend.

After promising beginnings, the 21st century got off to a bad start in Britain. In the wake of mad-cow disease flare-ups, the country was swept by a foot-and-mouth-disease epidemic that disrupted the country's agriculture and threatened one of the major sources of British livelihoods, its burgeoning tourist industry. After billions of pounds in tourism were lost, the panic has now subsided. The government has intervened to take whatever preventive measure it can.

Following the terrorist attack on New York City and Washington on September 11, 2001, Tony Blair and his government joined in a show of support for the United States, condemning the aerial bombardments and loss of life. Not only that, British joined in the war in Afghanistan against the dreaded Taliban. However, by 2003 Blair's backing of George Bush's stance against President Saddam Hussein of Iraq brought his popularity to an all-time low.

Britain's involvement in Iraq remained an unpopular cause. In February 2003, an estimated million protesters, the largest demonstration in the history of London, gathered to oppose military intervention in Iraq.

On an economic front, Britain still shies away from joining the so-called euro umbrella. In June 2003, Tony Blair and Chancellor Gordon Brown declared that abandoning British pound sterling in favor of the euro, prevailing on the Continent, was not right for the country at this time.

England has long endured terrorist attacks from the IRA, but was shaken on the morning of July 7, 2005, when four suicide bombs were detonated on public transportation in London, killing 52 victims. These bombs were the deadliest attacks suffered by the city since the darkest days of World War II.

Following the 2005 election, Blair's population plummeted, and he resigned in May 2007. Succeeding him was Gordon Brown, his chancellor of the exchequer, who became prime minister in June 2007.

3 England's Art & Architecture

No single artist, period, or museum defines England's art and architecture. You can see the country's art in medieval illuminated manuscripts, Thomas Gainsborough portraits, and Damien Hirst's pickled cows. Its architecture ranges from Roman walls and Norman castles to baroque St. Paul's Cathedral and towering postmodern skyscrapers. This section will help you make sense of it all.

CELTIC & MEDIEVAL ART (CA. 9TH C. B.C.–16TH C. A.D.)

Celtic art survived the Roman conquest and medieval Christianity mainly as carved swirls and decorations on the "Celtic Crosses" peppering cemeteries. During the medieval period, colorful Celtic images and illustrations decorated the margins of Bibles and Gospels, giving the books their moniker **"illuminated manuscripts."**

The best example of this art is the **Wilton Diptych** at London's National Gallery, the first truly British painting. It was crafted in the late 1390s for King Richard II by an unknown artist. The **Lindisfarne Gospels** at London's British Library is one of the greatest illuminated manuscripts from the 7th century.

RENAISSANCE & BAROQUE ART (16TH–18TH C.)

The **Renaissance** hit England late, but its museums contain many Old Master paintings from Italy and Germany. A few foreign Renaissance masters did come to work at the English courts and influenced some local artists, but significant Brits didn't emerge until the baroque.

The **baroque,** a more decorative version of the Renaissance approach, mixes compositional complexity and explosions of dynamic fury, movement, color, and figures with an exaggeration of light and dark, called chiaroscuro, and a kind of super-realism based on using peasants as models. The rococo period is baroque art gone awry, frothy and chaotic.

Significant British artists of this period include:

- **Joshua Reynolds (1723–92).** A fussy baroque painter and first president of the Royal Academy of Arts, Reynolds was a firm believer in a painter's duty to celebrate history. Reynolds spent much of his career casting his noble patrons as ancient gods in portrait compositions cribbed from Old Masters. Many of his works are in London's **National Gallery, Tate Britain, Wallace Collection,** and **Dulwich Picture Gallery;** Oxford's **Cathedral Hall;** Liverpool's **Walker Art Gallery;** and Birmingham's **Museum and Art Gallery.**
- **Thomas Gainsborough (1727–88).** Although he was a classical/baroque portraitist like his rival Reynolds, at least Gainsborough could be original. Too bad his tastes ran to rococo pastels, frothy feathered brushwork, and busy compositions. When not immortalizing noble patrons such as Jonathan Buttell (better known as "Blue Boy"), he painted a collection of landscapes just for himself. His works grace the **Victoria Art Gallery** in Bath (where he first came to fame), London's **National Gallery** and **National Portrait Gallery,** Cambridge's **Fitzwilliam Museum,** Oxford's **Cathedral Hall** and **Ashmolean Museum,** Liverpool's **Walker Art Gallery,** and Birmingham's **Museum and Art Gallery.**

PAINTINGS BY THE ROMANTICS (LATE 18TH–19TH C.)

The Romantics felt the Gothic Middle Ages was the place to be. They idealized the romantic tales of chivalry and had a deep respect for nature, human rights, and the nobility of peasantry.

Significant artists of this period include:

- **William Blake (1757–1827).** Romantic archetype Blake snubbed the stuffy Royal Academy of Arts to do his own engraving, prints, illustrations, poetry, and painting. His works were filled with melodrama, muscular figures, and sweeping lines. Judge for yourself at London's **Tate Britain** and Manchester's **Whitworth Art Gallery.**
- **John Constable (1776–1837).** Constable was a great British landscapist whose scenes (especially those of happy, agricultural peasants) got more idealized with each passing year—while his compositions and brushwork became freer. You'll find his best stuff in London's **National Gallery** and **Victoria and Albert Museum,** and in Liverpool's **Walker Art Gallery.**

- **J. M. W. Turner (1775–1851).** "The First Impressionist" was a prolific and multi-talented artist whose mood-laden, freely brushed watercolor landscapes influenced Monet. The River Thames and London, where he lived and died, were frequent subjects. London's **Tate Britain** displays the largest number of Turner's works.
- **Pre-Raphaelites (1848–70s).** This "brotherhood" of painters declared that art had gone all wrong with Italian Renaissance painter Raphael (1483–1520) and set about to emulate the Italian painters who preceded him. The works of Dante Rossetti, William Hunt, and John Millais most evoke this school. Their symbolically imbued, sweetly idealized, hyper-realistic work depicts scenes from Romantic poetry and Shakespeare as much as from the Bible. You can see pre-Raphaelite art at London's **Tate Gallery,** Oxford's **Ashmolean Museum,** Liverpool's **Walker Art Gallery,** and Manchester's **City Art Gallery.**

20TH-CENTURY ART

Art of the last century often followed international schools or styles—no major ones truly originated in Britain—and the major British artists listed here tended to move in and out of styles over their careers:

- **Henry Moore (1898–1986).** A sculptor, Moore saw himself as a sort of reincarnation of Michelangelo. The Henry Moore Institute in Leeds, where he studied, preserves his drawings and sculpture. You'll also find his work at Cambridge's **Fitzwilliam Museum** and **Clare College.**
- **Francis Bacon (1909–92).** A dark and brooding expressionist, Bacon presented man's foibles in formats, such as the triptych (a set of three panels, often hinged and used as an altarpiece), that were usually reserved for religious subjects. Find his works in London, Birmingham, and Manchester's **Whitworth Art Gallery.**
- **David Hockney (b. 1937).** The closest thing to a British Andy Warhol, Hockney employs a less pop-arty style than the famous American—though Hockney does reference modern technologies and culture. His work resides in London and Liverpool.
- **Damien Hirst (b. 1965).** The guy who pickles cows, Hirst is a celebrity/artist whose work sets out to shock. He's a winner of Britain's Turner Prize.

NORMAN ARCHITECTURE (1066–1200)

The oldest surviving architectural style in England dates to when the 1066 Norman Conquest brought the Romanesque era to Britain, where it flourished as the **Norman** style.

Churches in this style were large, with a wide nave and aisles to accommodate the masses who came to hear Mass and worship at the altars of various saints. But to support the weight of all that masonry, the walls had to be thick and solid, giving Norman churches a dark, somber, mysterious, and often oppressive feeling.

White Tower, London

Church Architecture 101

While each architectural era has its distinctive features, there are some elements, floor plans, and terms common to many. This is particularly true of churches, large numbers of which were built in England and Wales from the Middle Ages through the 18th century.

From the Norman period on, most churches consist either of a single, wide **aisle** or a wide central **nave** flanked by two narrower aisles. The aisles are separated from the nave by a row of **columns**, or square stacks of masonry called **piers**, connected by arches.

This main nave/aisle assemblage is usually crossed by a perpendicular corridor called a **transept** near the far, east end of the church so that the floor plan looks like a Latin Cross (shaped like a crucifix). The shorter, east arm of the nave is called the **chancel**; it often houses the **altar** and stalls of the **choir**. If the far end of the chancel is rounded off, it is called an **apse**.

An **ambulatory** is a curving corridor outside the altar and choir area, separating it from the ring of small **chapels** radiating off the chancel and apse.

It's worth pointing out that very few buildings (especially churches) were built in one particular style. Massive, expensive structures often took centuries to complete, during which time tastes would change and plans would be altered.

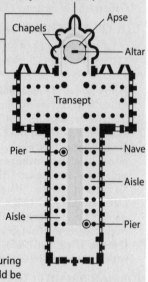

Church Floor Plan

The best examples of Norman architecture include London's **White Tower** (1078), William the Conqueror's first building in Britain at the Tower of London; **Durham Cathedral** (1093–1488), with a Norman floor plan; and **Ely Cathedral** (1083–1189), with a nave and south transept that are perfectly Norman.

GOTHIC ARCHITECTURE (1150–1550)

The French Gothic style invaded England in the late 12th century, trading rounded arches for pointy ones—an engineering discovery that freed church architecture from the heavy, thick walls of Norman structures and allowed ceilings to soar, walls to thin, and windows to proliferate.

The Gothic proper in Britain can be divided into three overlapping periods or styles: **Early English** (1150–1300), **Decorated** (1250–1370), and **Perpendicular** (1350–1550).

The best example of Early English is **Salisbury Cathedral** (1220–65), unique in Europe for the speed with which it was built. The first to use pointy arches was Wells Cathedral (1180–1321), which has 300 statues on its original facade.

The facade, nave, and chapter house of **York Minster** (1220–1480), which preserves the most medieval stained glass in Britain, is **Decorated,** though the chancel is Perpendicular and the transepts are Early English. **Exeter Cathedral** (1112–1206) has an elaborate Decorated facade and fantastic nave vaulting.

The **Perpendicular** King's College Chapel at Cambridge (1446–1515) has England's most magnificent fan vaulting, along with some fine stained glass. **Henry VII's Chapel** (1503–19) in London's Westminster Abbey is textbook Perpendicular.

RENAISSANCE ARCHITECTURE (1550–1650)

It wasn't until the Elizabethan era that the Brits turned to the Renaissance style sweeping the Continent. England's greatest **Renaissance** architect, **Inigo Jones** (1573–1652), brought back from his Italian travels a fevered imagination full of the

Salisbury Cathedral

exactingly classical theories of **Palladianism,** a style derived from the buildings and publications of **Andrea Palladio** (1508–80). However, most English architects at this time tempered the Renaissance style with a heavy dose of Gothic-like elements.

Jones applied his theories of Palladianism to such edifices as **Queen's House** (1616–18 and 1629–35) in Greenwich, and the **Queen's Chapel** (1623–25) in St. James's Palace and the **Banqueting House** (1619–22) in Whitehall, both in London.

BAROQUE ARCHITECTURE (1650–1750)

England's greatest architect was **Christopher Wren** (1632–1723), a scientist and member of Parliament who got the job of rebuilding London after the Great Fire of 1666. He designed 53 replacement churches alone, plus the new St. Paul's Cathedral, which was the crowning achievement of English baroque and of Wren himself. Other proponents of baroque architecture were **John Vanbrugh** (1664–1726) and his mentor and oft-collaborator, **Nicholas Hawksmoor** (1661–1736), who sometimes worked in a more Palladian idiom.

NEOCLASSICAL & GREEK REVIVAL ARCHITECTURE (1714–1837)

Many 18th-century architects cared little for the baroque period, and during the Georgian era (1714–1830) a restrained, simple **neoclassicism** reigned. This **Greek Revival** style was practiced by architects such as **James "Athenian" Stuart** (1713–88), who wrote a book on antiquities after a trip to Greece, and the somewhat less strict **John Soane** (1773–1837).

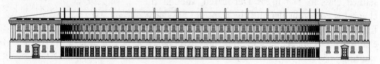

Royal Crescent, Bath

Much of the city of **Bath** was made over in the 18th century, most famously by the father-and-son team of **John Woods, Sr. and Jr.** (1704–54 and 1728–81, respectively). They were responsible, among others, for the **Royal Crescent** (1767–75), where you can visit one house's interior and even lodge in another.

VICTORIAN GOTHIC REVIVAL ARCHITECTURE (1750–1900)

The early Romantic Movement swept up others with rosy visions of the past. This imaginary and fairy-tale version of the Middle Ages led to such creative developments as the pre-Raphaelite painters (see "Paintings by the Romantics," above) and Gothic Revival architects, who really got a head of steam under their movement during the eclectic Victorian era.

Gothic "Revival" is a bit misleading, as its practitioners usually applied their favorite Gothic features at random rather than faithfully re-creating a whole structure.

The best example is the **Palace of Westminster (Houses of Parliament), London** (1835–52). Charles Barry (1795–1860) designed the wonderful British seat of

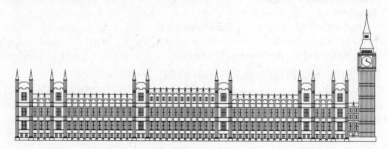

Palace of Westminster, London

government in a Gothic idiom that, more than most, sticks pretty faithfully to the old Perpendicular period's style. His clock tower, usually called Big Ben after its biggest bell, has become an icon of London itself.

20TH-CENTURY ARCHITECTURE

After the World War II Blitz, much of central London had to be rebuilt. Most of the new commercial buildings in the city held to a functional school of architecture aptly named Brutalism. It wasn't until the boom of the late 1970s and 1980s that **postmodern** architecture gave British architects a bold, new direction with a sky-scraper motif.

Stellar examples of modern architecture include **Lloyd's Building** in London (1978–86), the master-piece of Richard Rogers (b. 1933), and **Canary Wharf Tower** (1986), also in London, a complex designed by Cesar Pelli (b. 1926).

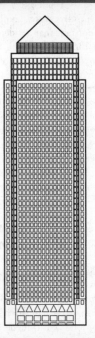

Canary Wharf Tower, London

4 England in Popular Culture: Books, Film, TV & Music

BOOKS

England has produced one of the world's greatest libraries of literature and drama—and not just William Shake-speare. Here is a mere preview of what's out there, at least enough to whet your appetite.

GENERAL & HISTORY Anthony Sampson's *The Changing Anatomy of Britain* (Random House) still gives great insight into the idiosyncrasies of English society; Winston Churchill's *History of the English-Speaking Peoples* (Dodd Mead) is a tour de force in four volumes; while *The Gathering Storm* (Houghton-Mifflin) captures Europe on the brink of World War II.

My Love Affair with England (Ballan-tine), by Susan Allan Toth, tells of Eng-land's "many-layered past" and includes such tidbits as why English marmalade tastes good only when consumed as part of a real (make that greasy) English breakfast.

Britons: Forging the Nation (1707–1837), Yale University Press, by Linda Colley, took more than a decade to finish. Ms. Colley takes the reader from the date of the Act of Union (formally joining Scotland and Wales to England) to the succession of the adolescent Victoria to the British throne. *Children of the Sun* (Basics Books), by Martin Green, por-trays the "decadent" 1920s and the lives of such people as Randolph Churchill, poet Rupert Brooke, the prince of Wales, and Christopher Isherwood.

In *A Writer's Britain* (Knopf), contem-porary English author Margaret Drabble takes readers on a tour of the sacred and haunted literary landscapes of England, places that inspired Hardy, Woolf, Spenser, and Marvell.

Outsiders often paint more penetrating portraits than residents of any culture ever can. In England's case, many have expressed their views of the country at different periods. An early-18th-century portrait is provided by K. P. Moritz in *Journeys of a German in England in 1782* (Holt, Rinehart & Winston), about his travels from London to the Midlands. Nathaniel Hawthorne recorded his impressions in *Our Old Home* (1863), as did Ralph Waldo Emerson in *English Traits* (1856). For an ironic portrait of mid-19th-century Victorian British morals, manners, and society, seek out *Taine's Notes on England* (1872). Henry James's comments on England at the turn of the 20th century in *English Hours* (1905) are worth a read. In *A Passage to England* (St. Martins Press), Nirad Chaudhuri analyzes Britain and the British in a delightful, humorous book—a process continued today by such authors as Salman Rushdie, V. S. Naipaul, and Paul Theroux. Among the interesting portraits written by natives are Cobbet's *Rural Rides* (1830), depicting early-19th-century England; *In Search of England* (Methuen) by H. V. Morton; and *English Journey* (Harper) by J. B. Priestley. For what's really going on behind that serene Suffolk village scene, read Ronald Blythe's *Akenfield: Portrait of an English Village* (Random House).

ART & ARCHITECTURE   For general reference, there's the huge multivolume *Oxford History of English Art* (Oxford University Press) and also the *Encyclopedia of British Art* (Thames Hudson), by David Bindman. *Painting in Britain 1530–1790* (Penguin), by Ellis Waterhouse, covers British art from the Tudor miniaturists to Gainsborough, Reynolds, and Hogarth, while *English Art, 1870–1940* (Oxford University Press), by Dennis Farr, covers the modern period.

On architecture, for sheer amusing, opinionated entertainment, try John Betjeman's *Ghastly Good Taste—the Rise and Fall of English Architecture* (St. Martin's Press). *A History of English Architecture* (Penguin), by Peter Kidson, Peter Murray, and Paul Thompson, covers the subject from Anglo-Saxon to modern times. Nikolaus Pevsner's *The Best Buildings of England: An Anthology* (Viking) and his *Outline of European Architecture* (Penguin) concentrate on the great periods of Tudor, Georgian, and Regency architecture. Mark Girouard has written several books on British architecture including *The Victorian Country House* (Country Life) and *Life in the English Country House* (Yale University Press), a fascinating social/architectural history from the Middle Ages to the 20th century, with handsome illustrations.

ABOUT LONDON   *London Perceived* (Hogarth), by novelist and literary critic V. S. Pritchett, is a witty portrait of the city's history, art, literature, and life. Virginia Woolf's *The London Scene: Five Essays* (Random House) brilliantly depicts the London of the 1930s. *In Search of London* (Methuen), by H. V. Morton, is filled with anecdotal history and well worth reading, though written in the 1950s.

In *London: The Biography of a City* (Penguin), popular historian Christopher Hibbert paints a lively portrait. For some real 17th-century history, you can't beat the *Diary of Samuel Pepys* (written 1660–69); and for the flavor of the 18th century, try Daniel Defoe's *Tour Thro' London About the Year 1725* (Ayer).

Americans in London (William Morrow), by Brian N. Morton, is a street-by-street guide to clubs, homes, and favorite pubs of more than 250 illustrious Americans who made London a temporary home. The *Guide to Literary London* (Batsford), by George Williams, charts literary tours through London from Chelsea to Bloomsbury.

The Architect's Guide to London (Reed International), by Renzo Salvadori, documents 100 landmark buildings with photographs and maps. *Nairn's London* (Penguin), by Ian Nairn, is a stimulating discourse on London's buildings. Donald Olsen's *The City as a Work of Art: London, Paris, and Vienna* (Yale University Press) is a well-illustrated text tracing the evolution of these great cities. *London One: The Cities of London and Westminster* and *London Two: South* (Penguin) are works of love by well-known architectural writers Bridget Cherry and Nikolaus Pevsner. David Piper's *The Artist's London* (Oxford University Press) does what the title suggests—captures the city that artists have portrayed. In *Victorian and Edwardian London* (Batsford), John Betjeman expresses his great love of those eras and their great buildings. *Looking Up in London* (Wiley Academy) by Jane Peyton offers colorful photos of some of London's architectural features.

FICTION & BIOGRAPHY Among English writers are found some of the greatest exponents of mystery and suspense novels, from which a reader can get a good feel for English life both urban and rural. Agatha Christie, P. D. James, and Dorothy Sayers are a few of the familiar names, but the great London character is, of course, Sherlock Holmes, created by Arthur Conan Doyle. Any of these writers will give pleasure and insight into your London experience.

England's literary heritage is so vast, it's hard to select particular titles, but here are a few favorites. Master storyteller Charles Dickens re-creates Victorian London in such books as *Oliver Twist, David Copperfield,* and his earlier satirical *Sketches by Boz.*

Edwardian London and the 1920s and 1930s are captured wonderfully in any of Evelyn Waugh's social satires and comedies; any work from the Bloomsbury group will also prove enlightening, such as Virginia Woolf's *Mrs. Dalloway,* which peers beneath the surface of the London scene. For a portrait of wartime London there's Elizabeth Bowen's *The Heat of the Day;* for an American slant on England and London there's Henry James's *The Awkward Age.*

Among 18th-century figures, there's a great biography of Samuel Johnson by his friend James Boswell, whose *Life of Samuel Johnson* (Modern Library College Editions) was first published in 1791. Antonia Fraser has written several biographies of English monarchs and political figures, including Charles II and Oliver Cromwell. Her most recent is *The Wives of Henry VIII* (Knopf), telling the sad story of the six women foolish enough to marry the Tudor monarch.

Another great Tudor monarch, Elizabeth I, emerges in a fully rounded portrait: *The Virgin Queen, Elizabeth I, Genius of the Golden Age* (Addison-Wesley), by Christopher Hibbert.

Another historian, Anne Somerset, wrote *Elizabeth I* (St. Martin's Press), which was hailed by some critics as the most "readable and reliable" portrait of England's most revered monarch to have emerged since 1934.

No woman—or man, for that matter—had greater influence on London than did Queen Victoria during her long reign (1837–1901). Sarah Ferguson, the duchess of York (Prince Andrew's former wife, "Fergie"), along with Benita Stoney, a professional researcher, captures the era in *Victoria and Albert: A Family Life at Osborne House* (Prentice Hall). One reviewer said that Fergie writes about "England's 19th-century rulers not as historical figures but as a loving couple and caring parents."

Another point of view is projected in *Victoria: The Young Queen* (Blackwell), by Monica Charlot. This book has been praised for its "fresh information"; it traces the life of Victoria until the death of her husband, Prince Albert, in 1861. Queen Elizabeth II granted Charlot access to the Royal Archives.

In *Elizabeth II, Portrait of a Monarch* (St. Martin's Press), Douglas Keay drew on interviews with Prince Philip and Prince Charles.

Richard Ellman's *Oscar Wilde* (Knopf) also reveals such Victorian-era personalities as Lillie Langtry, Gilbert and Sullivan, and Henry James along the way. Quintessential English playwright Noel Coward and the London he inhabited, along with the likes of Nancy Mitford, Cecil Beaton, John Gielgud, Laurence Olivier, Vivien Leigh, Evelyn Waugh, and Rebecca West, are captured in Cole Lesley's *Remembered Laughter* (Knopf). *The Lives of John Lennon* (William Morrow), by Albert Goldman, traces the life of this most famous of all '60s musicians.

Dickens (Harper Perennial), by Peter Ackroyd, is a study of the painful life of the novelist. It's a massive volume, tracing everything from the reception of his first novel, *The Pickwick Papers,* to his scandalous desertion of his wife.

Other good reads include *Wild Spirit: The Story of Percy Bysshe Shelley* (Hodder & Stoughton), by Margaret Morley, a fictionalized biography of the poet. *Gertrude Jekyll* (Viking), by Sally Festing, paints a portrait of the woman called "the greatest artist in horticulture." *Anthony Trollope* (Knopf), by Victoria Glendinning, is a provocative portrait of the English novelist. *Lawrence and the Women: The Intimate Life of D. H. Lawrence* (HarperCollins), by Elaine Feinstein, examines involvements with the female friends and lovers of this passionately sensitive novelist.

CONTEMPORARY LITERATURE

Born to a Jamaican mother and a British father, Zadie Smith is one of the most talented young authors in England. Published in 2000, her bestselling novel, *White Teeth* (Vintage), brought her early acclaim. She followed up with *The Autograph Man* (Vintage, 2002) and *On Beauty* (Penguin, 2005), both of which won prizes for fiction. Her writings are known for their deep penetration of the rainbow-hued races inhabiting Britain today.

The writings of Nick Hornby have earned him the title "European Ambassador of Goodness." An autobiographical work, his first book, *Fever Pitch,* was published in 1992 to both success and acclaim. In subsequent novels, he explores sports, music, "and aimless and obsessive personalities." Several of his works have been adapted for film, including *About a Boy,* starring Hugh Grant.

Influenced by the writing of his father, Sir Kingsley Amis, Martin Amis has written some of the best-known works of English modern literature, especially *Money* in 1986 and *London Fields* in 1989. The *New York Times* called him the undisputed master of "the new unpleasantness." He explores the excesses of the capitalist world, plunging a sword into the heart of grotesque caricatures. His memoir, *Experience,* explored his relationship with his father, and his 2003 novel *Yellow Dog,* although praised by fans, was a disappointment in some quarters.

The English fiction writer Joanne Rowling, writing under the pen name of J. K. Rowling, created the Harry Potter fantasy series, which has sold nearly 400 million copies worldwide and made her an estimated fortune of $1 billion, a first for any author. She was an unemployed single mom when she completed her first novel, *Harry Potter and the Philosopher's Stone* (1997; the American title is *Harry Potter and the Sorcerer's Stone*). In 2007 Rowling released *Harry Potter and the Deathly Hallows,* which she claims will be the last of the series.

Other acclaimed modern writers include Adam Thorpe, a poet, playwright, and novelist. Although born in Paris, he grew up in India. His first novel, *Ulverton* (1992), a panoramic portrait of English rural history, brought him worldwide acclaim. He continues to write today, publishing *Between Each Breath* in 2007.

Another acclaimed and often controversial writer is Irvine Welsh, a brilliant storyteller and—unarguably—one of the funniest and "filthiest" writers in Britain. He shot to fame upon the release of his book, *Trainspotting*, in 1993.

FILM

Some of the greatest stars came from Britain but made their mark in Hollywood, notably Charlie Chaplin, Cary Grant, and violet-eyed Elizabeth Taylor. In spite of its native-born talent, Hollywood even turned to Britain to cast Scarlett O'Hara in the 1939 *Gone With the Wind*.

Great directors, including that master of suspense, Alfred Hitchcock, also moved from London to Hollywood for greater fame. Lord Laurence Olivier frequently was cast in Hollywood films, as were a long line of Shakespeare-trained actors who followed him—Judi Dench, Maggie Smith, Jeremy Irons, Ian McKellen.

Some British films seem to live on forever as in the case of *A Hard Day's Night* (1964), depicting a "typical" day in the life of the Beatles, including many of their famous songs.

Tame by today's standards, *My Beautiful Laundrette* (1985) was a scandal upon its release. It not only brought Daniel Day-Lewis into international renown, but dealt with homosexuality and interracial relationships.

Born in poverty in Northern Ireland, Kenneth Branagh has brought Shakespeare to mainstream audiences, notably with *Much Ado About Nothing* (1993) and a widely acclaimed *Hamlet* (1996).

He's been nominated for four Oscars. Director-writer Mike Leigh's *Secrets & Lies* (1996) was nominated for five Oscars; it depicted a black woman who traces her birth mother to a lower-class white woman.

The happy household of Merchant and Ivory formed a director-producer team that turned out a series of films that achieved international fame, including *Maurice* (1987), *A Room with a View* (1985), and *Howards End* (1992).

Still a great favorite with British students, *Withnail & I* (1987) is set in London in 1969, featuring two unemployed and unemployable actors who go for an idyllic (yeah, right) holiday in the countryside.

Two films depicting unusual stories from the blue-collar ghettos of the north of England were much honored: *Billy Elliot* (2000), where Jamie Bell played a talented young boy who wanted to be a ballet dancer, and *The Full Monty* (1997) in which six unemployed steel worker blokes form a male striptease act.

Four Weddings and a Funeral (1994), a comedy-drama about a group of British friends, starred Hugh Grant giving his most charming performance to date.

24 Hour Party People (2002) was a tale of music, sex, drugs, and larger-than-life characters, plus the birth of one of the most famous dance clubs in the world. The music and dance heritage of Manchester from the late '70s to the early '90s is depicted.

Mr. Madonna himself (Guy Ritchie) is a director-actor-producer-writer who achieved fame with such releases as *Lock, Stock and Two Smoking Barrels* (1998) and *Snatch* (2000), the latter starring Brad Pitt. He's had a bad run of luck in recent years, including when he cast his wife in *Swept Away* (2002). The public was hardly swept away; nor were the critics. But Ritchie is still a young man and might redeem his early promise, although *Revolver* (2005) waited 2 years to find a distributor and then opened and closed overnight.

No films ever equaled the success of the Harry Potter franchise, a series based on the novels of J. K. Rowling. Kicked off in 2001 with *Harry Potter and the Sorcerer's Stone,* the series continues to break box office records. Many Potter fans visit film sites including Alnwick Castle and Christ Church College in Oxford, even Fort William in the Scottish Highlands. The latest, starring Daniel Radcliffe, was *Harry Potter and the Order of the Phoenix* (2007).

The latest film sensation from Britain is the award-winning *Atonement* (2007), in which a 13-year-old charges her older sister's lover of a crime he did not commit. The film stars Keira Knightley and James McAvoy in brilliant performances.

TELEVISION

When in England, tune in to "the Beeb," as the BBC or British Broadcasting Corporation is affectionately known. Whether on radio or TV, nothing is better suited to acquaint you with British life. The stated mission of the BBC is "to inform, educate, and entertain," and it does so magnificently. Check out what's going on at www.bbc.co.uk. Its combined TV and radio services form the largest broadcasting system in the world.

TV shows originating in Britain have often attracted audiences around the world, notably *Monty Python's Flying Circus,* a BBC sketch comedy first aired in 1969, with its surreal plots, innuendo-laden humor, and sight gags. The adjective "pythonesque" had to be invented to define their original comedy. Other British TV hits have included *Mr. Bean* with Rowan Atkinson as the title character, "a child in a grown man's body." The *Da Ali G Show* brought world fame to Sacha Baron Cohen of *Borat* notoriety.

The Office, the title of multiple TV situation comedy shows, found success across the pond.

Current hits include *Big Brother,* which returned for its ninth season in 2008. This is a reality TV show taking its name from George Orwell's 1949 novel, *1984.* Originating in 2001, *Pop Idol* led to an international spinoff, launching such American shows as *American Idol.*

MUSIC

The music performed at Elizabeth I's court, including compositions by Thomas Morley (ca. 1557–1602), have been recorded by the Deller Consort; one of their titles is *Now Is the Month of Maying: Madrigal Masterpieces.*

England's Renaissance church music is best exemplified by English composer William Byrd (1543–1623); listen to his *Cantiones sacrae: 1575,* performed by the Choir of New College, Oxford, and recorded in the New College Chapel for London Records.

Henry Purcell's *Dido and Aeneas* is widely available in several performances. For an example of Purcell's orchestral music, listen to *The Virtuoso Trumpet,* performed by trumpeter Maurice André, who is accompanied by the Academy of St. Martin in the Fields, Sir Neville Mariner conducting.

John Gay's *The Beggar's Opera,* first performed in 1728, is available in a recording by Britain's National Philharmonic Orchestra and the London Opera Chorus for Polygram Records.

The works of the beloved British team of Sir Arthur Sullivan (composer) and Sir W. S. Gilbert (librettist) are widely available. *The Mikado,* performed by the Pro Arte Orchestra and the Glyndebourne Festival Chorus, Sir Malcolm Sargent conducting, is available on CD.

The compositions of Sir Edward Elgar can be heard on the British Philharmonic Orchestra's recording of the *Pomp and*

Circumstance marches, conducted by Andrew Davis.

Two fine recordings of England's modern master, Ralph Vaughan Williams, are his Symphony no. 3 ("Pastoral"), performed by the London Symphony Orchestra; and his *Sea Symphony,* performed by the London Symphony Orchestra and Chorus, with conductor André Previn.

Benjamin Britten's *Ceremony of Carols,* performed by the Choir of St. John's College, Cambridge, and his *Variations for a String Orchestra,* performed by the London Philharmonic Orchestra, with Roger Best on viola, are both fine examples of this preeminent British composer.

A recording of interest to music historians is *All Back Home,* which traces the musical themes of American and Australian folk and blues back to Irish, English, and Scottish roots. The recording includes tracks by Sinead O'Connor, the Everly Brothers, Kate Bush, Bob Dylan, Pete Seeger, the Waterboys, and Thin Lizzy.

Richard Thompson, who performs on *Amnesia,* has been reviewed as one of the most unusual and iconoclastic of modern British folk performers. He uses guitar, mandolin, and hammer dulcimer in his melodies, and his lyrics showcase political and social satire as well as soulfully nostalgic ballads.

Of course, nothing in British musical history has equaled the popular enthusiasm that greeted the British revolution of the 1960s. Aided by improvements in acoustical technology and the changing sociology of Britain, music was suddenly the passionate interest of millions of youthful Brits, setting the scene for a cultural invasion of American shores that hadn't been seen since the 18th century.

It began with the Beatles, of course—John, Paul, George, and Ringo, who won the hearts of every schoolgirl in America when they appeared on the *Ed Sullivan Show* in February 1964. They seemed to be in the vanguard of every cultural and musical movement, and as the 1960s progressed, the Beatles didn't simply capitalize on their success or the musical styles that had originally made them popular. Their music evolved with the times and helped shape the cultural and political texture of their era.

The Beatles were only the first of many British bands who found fertile ground and a receptive audience overseas. They were soon followed by the Rolling Stones, the Who, and David Bowie.

Past Masters is a two-volume retrospective collection of Beatles music. Equally important is their milestone album *Sergeant Pepper,* which was a musical watershed when it was released in 1967.

The Rolling Stones' *Flashpoint* is a textbook study of the spirit of rock 'n' roll, with a guest performance by Eric Clapton on a track entitled "Little Red Rooster." Another Rolling Stone great is *Exile on Main Street.*

These icons were followed by the neo-Brit brats, Oasis, with brothers Liam and Noel Gallagher selling millions of records. Along came Blur, Cast, and Ocean Colour Scene, acknowledging the influence of the Beatles and the Stones. Britain birthed David Bowie, Gary Glitter, the Sex Pistols, the Clash, and Faces. The cities that gave birth to these talents—London, Liverpool, and Manchester—have an ever-changing but always exciting music scene today.

Prince Harry fell hard for the Spice Girls, an English pop group formed in 1994, but David Beckham made off with Posh.

The biggest name today is the Grammy Award–winning Amy Winehouse, mistress of soul, vocal jazz, R&B, and doo-wop. Her personal troubles and beehive hairstyle continue to make tabloid headlines.

Way down the musical scale in pecking order are the London group, the Rakes—"skinny as rakes"—shooting to fame in 2005 with post-punk rock music. From Leeds, the Pigeon Detectives with their indie rock were voted "the band most likely to leap to the main stage in 2007." From Brighton comes the Kooks, both indie and pop rockers who released their second album, "Konk," in the spring of 2008.

Bloc Party, another London group singing indie and rock and post-punk revival, made "Album of the Year" in 2005 with their debut, *Silent Alarm.* Yet another post-punk revival group, Franz Ferdinand, originated in Glasgow as an indie favorite. The band's second album, *You Could Have It So Much Better,* topped the charts in the U.K. An alternative rock group, Coldplay, achieved worldwide fame for their hit single, "Yellow," followed by the success of their debut album, *Parachutes.*

5 Eating & Drinking in England

The late British humorist George Mikes wrote that "the Continentals have good food; the English have good table manners." But the British no longer deserve their reputation for soggy cabbage and tasteless dishes. Contemporary London—and the country as a whole—boasts fine restaurants and sophisticated cuisine.

If you want to see what Britain is eating today, just drop in at Harvey Nichol's Fifth Floor in London's Knightsbridge for its dazzling display of produce from all over the globe.

The buzzword for British cuisine is *magpie,* meaning borrowing ideas from global travels, taking them home, and improving on the original.

A pundit once noted that to dine out in London today requires a knowledge of foreign languages. Increasingly that is true for the rest of England, and, to a lesser degree, Wales as well. Foreign restaurants, especially Indian or Chinese, seem to flourish in almost every village.

All major towns and most definitely all English cities have their immigrant communities, bringing the food of their native lands. In addition to Chinese, Thai and Indonesian restaurants are popping up more and more. Spanish tapas bars (or restaurants) are all the rage, and Japanese cuisine is going over big time with the Brits who flock to sushi places.

For decades now, French and Italian restaurants have been the dining rooms of choice by those who like to dine out. The ranks of British gastronomic restaurants continue to grow, and now even small towns seem to have at least one gastronomic shrine.

Be aware that many of the trendiest, most innovative restaurants are mind-blowingly expensive, especially in London. We've pointed out some innovative but affordable choices in this book, but if you're really trying to save on dining costs, you'll no doubt find yourself falling back on the traditional pub favorites (or better still, turning to an increasingly good selection of ethnic restaurants).

WHAT YOU'LL FIND ON THE MENU IN ENGLAND Of course, many who visit England want to sample the local cuisine. English cooking has been ridiculed for years (those long-boiled Brussels sprouts, for example), but the food is better than ever. The country has wonderful produce, from its Cotswold lamb to its Scottish salmon. You don't always have to dine foreign for a true gastronomic experience. English chefs, many of whom have trained on the Continent, have returned to put more flavor and flair in their native recipes.

On any pub menu, you're likely to encounter such dishes as the **Cornish pasty** (*past-*ee) and **shepherd's pie.** The

Taxes & Tipping

All restaurants and cafes are required to display the prices of their food and drink in a place visible from outside. Charges for service, as well as any minimums or cover charges, must also be made clear. The prices shown must include 17.5% VAT, the so-called "value-added" tax. Most restaurants add a 15% service charge to your bill, but check to make sure. If nothing has been added, leave a 10% to 15% tip. It is by no means considered rude to tip, so feel free to leave something extra if service was good.

first, traditionally made from Sunday-meal leftovers and taken by West Country fishermen for Monday lunch, consists of chopped potatoes, carrots, and onions mixed with seasoning and put into a pastry envelope. The second is a deep dish of chopped cooked beef mixed with onions and seasoning, covered with a layer of mashed potatoes, and served hot. Another version is **cottage pie,** which is minced beef covered with potatoes and also served hot. Of course, these beef dishes are subject to availability. In addition to a pasty, Cornwall also gives us **Stargazy Pie**—a deep-dish fish pie with a crisp crust covering a creamy concoction of freshly caught herring and vegetables.

The most common pub meal, though, is the **ploughman's lunch,** traditional farm-worker's fare, consisting of a good chunk of local cheese, a hunk of home-made crusty white or brown bread, some butter, and a pickled onion or two, washed down with ale. You'll now find such variations as pâté and chutney occasionally replacing the onions and cheese. Or you might find **Lancashire hot pot,** a stew of mutton, potatoes, kidneys, and onions (sometimes carrots). This concoction was originally put into a deep dish and set on the edge of the stove to cook slowly while the workers spent the day at the local mill.

Among the best-known traditional English meals is **roast beef** and **Yorkshire pudding** (the pudding is made with a flour base and cooked under the roast, allowing the fat from the meat to drop onto it). The beef could easily be a large sirloin (rolled loin), which, so the story goes, was named by James I when he was a guest at Houghton Tower, Lancashire. "Arise, Sir Loin," he cried, as he knighted the leg of beef before him with his dagger. Another dish that makes use of a flour base is **toad-in-the-hole,** in which sausages are cooked in batter. Game, especially pheasant and grouse, is also a staple on British tables.

On any menu, you'll find **fresh seafood:** cod, haddock, herring, plaice, and Dover sole, the aristocrat of flatfish. Cod and haddock are used in making British **fish and chips** (chips are fried potatoes or thick french fries), which the true Briton covers with salt and vinegar. If you like **oysters,** try some of the famous Colchester variety. On the west coast, you'll find a not-to-be-missed delicacy: **Morecambe Bay shrimp.** Every region of England has its seafood specialties. In Ely, lying in the marshy fen district of East Anglia, it might be fenland eel pie with a twiggy seaweed as your green vegetable. Amphire also grows here in the salt marshes and along the Norfolk Coast. It's pickled in May and June and appears as a delicacy on many summer menus.

The **East End of London** has quite a few intriguing old dishes, among them tripe and onions. In winter, the Cheshire Cheese tavern on Fleet Street offers a beefsteak, kidney, mushroom, and game pudding in a suet case; in summer, there's a pastry case. East Enders can still be seen on Sunday at the Jellied Eel stall by Petticoat Lane, eating eel, cockles (small clams), mussels, whelks, and winkles—all with a touch of vinegar.

The British call desserts **sweets,** though some people still refer to any dessert as **pudding.** **Trifle** is the most famous English dessert, consisting of sponge cake soaked in brandy or sherry, coated with fruit or jam, and topped with cream custard. A **fool,** such as gooseberry fool, is a light cream dessert whipped up from seasonal fruits. Regional sweets include the **northern flitting dumpling** (dates, walnuts, and syrup mixed with other ingredients and made into a pudding that is easily sliced and carried along when you're "flitting" from place to place). Similarly, **hasty pudding,** a Newcastle dish, is supposed to have been invented by people in a hurry to avoid the bailiff. It consists of stale bread, to which some dried fruit and milk are added before it is put into the oven.

Cheese is traditionally served after dessert as a savory. There are many regional cheeses, the best known being cheddar, a good, solid, mature cheese. Others are the semismooth Caerphilly, from a beautiful part of Wales, and Stilton, a blue-veined crumbly cheese that's often enjoyed with a glass of port.

A TASTE OF WALES   The food served in Wales is often indistinguishable from that in England, but there are a number of specialties you should try that you won't find elsewhere.

The **leek** is one of the national emblems of Wales, and is used in a number of dishes. The selection of the leek for this national honor is lost in the dim past, although associated with St. David, patron saint of Wales. Today the leek is worn on St. Davids Day, March 1, a national holiday.

Among dishes in which the leek is used is **cawl mamgu,** a rich soup or stew. The most commonly used recipe calls for lamb or mutton, turnips (the Welsh call them Swedes), carrots, potatoes, parsnips, onions, and leeks. The **leek pasty,** usually made in the shape of a little leek, is a popular appetizer or side dish.

The potato became a dietary staple of Wales in the 18th century. **Anglesey** eggs feature potatoes and leeks as well as cheese. **Punchnep** is a combination of potatoes and turnips served with heavy cream. **Teisen nionod,** or onion cake, is a tasty, slow-baked potato-and-onion dish.

Most people are familiar with **Welsh rarebit** (or rabbit, if you prefer), but another cheese dish you should try that is not found elsewhere is **Glamorgan sausage,** a meatless concoction of onion, cheese, bread crumbs, and seasonings, shaped like sausages, dipped in bread crumbs, and fried. Another good dish, **skirettes,** is sort of mashed-potato pancake with a difference. The difference is supplied by grated walnuts, prawns, hardboiled eggs, onion, cheddar cheese, and spices. It's all given a bread-crumb coating and baked or deep-fried.

Faggots used to be made of meat fragments left over after pig slaughter, wrapped in membrane that covers the pig's abdominal organs, and shaped like sausages. Today it's all a little more palatable sounding, being made of liver, bacon, onions, bread crumbs, and sage, cooked and served cold.

Rabbit, chicken, turkey, duckling, game, even pheasant appear on the menus, and a rabbit casserole is offered in some restaurants as a Taste of Wales, so popular is the meat. Special dishes include a **poacher's pie** (containing beef, rabbit, chicken, and game) and **Welsh salt duck,** which rivals any offered on Asian menus. Predominant on the list of what to eat while in Wales are freshwater fish and seafood. **Trout and salmon** prevail among the products of rivers and lakes, tumbling practically from the fisherman's creel to your plate, with a little detour through the kitchen. Perhaps you'll get to taste a rare salmon, **gwyniad,** which is found only in Bala Lake. Baked trout with bacon is a favorite.

From the ocean and coastal waters come crabs, lobsters, sewin (sea trout), crayfish, mackerel, herring, Pollack, bass, hake, ling, whiting, and flat fish, as well as cockles, limpets, scallops, and mussels. The Romans were great cockle eaters, as revealed by huge mounds of the shells found in excavating the sites occupied by the long-ago conquerors. You may enjoy the **cockle-and-bacon pie** offered on some menus, or Gower scallops and bacon. Mussel stew and mussel and quee-nie (scallop) cawl, which is like a bouilla-baisse, are popular dishes.

The Welsh word for bread is *bara.* At least once, you should try **laverbread (bara lawr),** which has probably been part of the Welsh diet since prehistoric times. It's made of laver weed, a parch-mentlike seaweed, which is boiled and mixed with oatmeal, shaped into laver-bread cakes, and fried like pancakes. It's full of vitamins and minerals. You'll find it on all Taste of Wales menus, so take a nibble at least. **Bara ceirch,** a flat oatcake, is rolled very thin and cooked on a grid-dle. A rich, currant bread, **bara brith,** is found all over the country, although the ingredients may vary. It's baked in a loaf, and some cooks use raisins and candied citrus peel along with the currants.

Perhaps you'll get a chance to sample **Welsh cakes** made with currants. You may want to buy some at Dylan Thomas's boathouse at Laugharne and munch them with your tea as you look across the wide estuary where the poet had much the same view as his Iron Age predecessors. **Oat biscuits** are another treat, much like the oatmeal cookies you may have had back home. Desserts (*puddings* they're called here, whatever their form) seem to be mainly **fruit crumbles**—blackberry, apple, what have you—topped with custard and/or thick cream.

ENGLISH BREAKFASTS & AFTERNOON TEA

Britain is famous for its enormous breakfast of bacon, eggs, grilled tomato, and fried bread. Some places have replaced this cholesterol festival with a continental breakfast, but you'll still find the traditional morning meal available.

Kipper, or smoked herring, is also a popular breakfast dish. The finest come from the Isle of Man, Whitby, or Loch Fyne, in Scotland. The herrings are split open, placed over oak chips, and slowly cooked to produce a nice pale-brown smoked fish.

Many people still enjoy afternoon tea, which may consist of a simple cup of tea or a formal tea that starts with tiny crust-less sandwiches filled with cucumber or watercress and proceeds through scones, crumpets with jam or clotted cream, fol-lowed by cakes and tarts—all accompanied by a proper pot of tea. The tea at Brown's, in London, is quintessentially English, whereas the Ritz's tea is an elab-orate affair, complete with orchestra and dancing.

In the country, tea shops abound, and in Devon, Cornwall, and the West Coun-try you'll find the best cream teas; they consist of scones spread with jam and thick, clotted Devonshire cream. It's a delicious treat, indeed. People in Britain drink an average of four cups of tea a day, though many younger people prefer cof-fee.

WHAT TO WASH IT ALL DOWN WITH

English pubs serve a variety of cocktails, but their stock in trade is beer: brown beer, or bitter; blond beer, or lager; and very dark beer, or stout. The standard English draft beer is much stronger than American beer and is served "with the chill off" because it doesn't taste good cold. Lager is always chilled, whereas stout can be served either way. Beer is always served straight from the tap, in two sizes: half pint (8 oz.) and pint (16 oz.).

One of the most significant changes in English drinking habits has been the popularity of wine bars, and you will find many to try, including some that turn into discos late at night. Britain isn't known for its wine, though it does produce some medium-sweet fruity whites. Its cider, though, is famous—and mighty potent in contrast to the American variety.

Whisky (spelled without the *e*) refers to Scotch. Canadian and Irish whiskey (spelled with the *e*) are also available, but only the very best stocked bars have American bourbon and rye.

While you're in England, you may want to try the very English drink called **Pimm's,** a mixture developed by James Pimm, owner of a popular London oyster house in the 1840s. Though it can be consumed on the rocks, it's usually served as a Pimm's Cup—a drink that will have any number and variety of ingredients, depending on which part of the world (or empire) you're in. Here, just for fun, is a typical recipe: Take a very tall glass and fill it with ice. Add a thin slice of lemon (or orange), a cucumber spike (or a curl of cucumber rind), and 2 ounces of Pimm's liquor. Then finish with a splash of either lemon or club soda, 7-Up, or Tom Collins mix.

The English tend to drink everything at a warmer temperature than Americans are used to. So if you like ice in your soda, be sure to ask for lots of it, or you're likely to end up with a measly, quickly melting cube or two.

3

Planning Your Trip to England & Wales

Of almost any destination in the world, flying into England, if your documents are in order, is one of the most effortless undertakings in global travel. There are no shots to get, no particular safety precautions, no unusual aspects of planning a trip. With your passport, airline ticket, and enough money, you just go. In general, if you're not bringing any illegal item into the British Isles, Customs officials are courteous and will speed you on your way into your entry in their country.

Of course, before you lift off the ground in your native country, you can do some advance preparation, as will be detailed in this chapter and in the appendix. That could mean checking to see if your passport is up-to-date (or obtaining one if you don't already possess one), or taking care of your health needs before you go, including medication. In the case of London, you might want to make reservations at some highly acclaimed restaurants or even buy tickets in advance to hit plays in London's West End.

In the pages that follow, you'll find everything you need to know about the practicalities of planning your trip in advance: finding the best airfare, deciding when to go, figuring out British currency, and more.

1 Visitor Information

Before you go, you can obtain general information from **Visit Britain** (www.visitbritain.com):

- In the United States: 551 Fifth Ave., 7th Floor, New York, NY 10176-0799 (© **800/462-2748** or 212/986-2266).
- In Canada: Call © **888/VISITUK (847-4885).**
- In Australia: Level 2, 15 Blue St., North Sydney 2060 (© **02/9021-4400**).
- In New Zealand: Fay Richwite Blvd., 17th Floor, 151 Queen St., Auckland (© **0800/700-741**).

For a full information package on London, write to **Visit London,** 2 More London Riverside, 6th Floor, Bermondsey SE1 2RR (© **020/7234-5800;** www.visitlondon.co.uk).

Wales, like England, has a number of regional tourist offices, but the **Visit Wales Centre** is at the Brunel House, 2 Fitzalan Rd., Cardiff CF24 0UY (© **08701/211-255;** www.visitwales.com). Detailed information is also available in London from the Wales Desk at the **Britain Visitors Centre,** 1 Regent St., London SW1Y 4XT (© **0207/808-3838**).

WEBSITES

The most useful site was created by a very knowledgeable source, the British Tourist Authority itself, with U.S. visitors targeted. A wealth of information can be tapped at **www.visitbritain.com**, which lets you order brochures online, provides trip-planning hints, and even allows e-mail questions for prompt answers. All of Great Britain is covered.

Go to **www.baa.com** for a guide and terminal maps for Heathrow, Gatwick, Stansted, and several other airports in the U.K., including flight arrival times, duty-free shops, airport restaurants, and info on getting from the London airports to downtown London. Getting around London can be confusing, so you may want to visit **www.tfl.gov.uk** for up-to-the-minute info on transportation.

You may also wish to check out one of the following websites. **AOL members** can type in the keyword **"Britain"** and find a vibrant guide to the U.K. that gives you the skinny on arts, dining, nightlife, and more. To access the AOL London guide, type in the keyword "London."

At **www.britannia.com**, you'll find much more than a travel guide—it's chock-full of lively features, history, and regional profiles, including sections on Wales and King Arthur.

English Heritage (www.english-heritage.org.uk) has trip planning information, accommodations, and an attractions finder that allows you to search by region. **The National Trust** (www.nationaltrust.org.uk) provides a similar service with a searchable online attractions finder featuring castles, museums, natural wonders, and more. Many hotels and sites that don't have their own Web pages can be found in one of these two directories.

For the latest on London's theater scene, consult **www.officiallondontheatre.co.uk**.

MAPS

Upon arriving in London, you should arm yourself with a detailed street map if you plan to do a lot of walking. London is a maze of narrow streets and "villages" within a vast city, and many addresses are obscure and hard to find.

Plot where you're going before setting out, or otherwise just walk and enjoy discovering London at your whimsy. It's amazing what you'll come across if you have endless time. Otherwise, plot your course so you can cram as much into a precious day as your limited time will allow.

If you plan to motor through England, arm yourself with a road atlas, especially one of the large format ones produced by AA, RAC, Collins, and Ordnance Survey. Virtually every motorway gas (petrol) station in England stocks one or more of the big road atlases.

At **www.multimap.com**, you can access detailed street maps of the whole United Kingdom—just key in the location or even just the postal code, and a map of the area with the location circled will appear. For directions to specific places in London, consult **www.streetmap.co.uk**.

2 Entry Requirements

PASSPORTS

All U.S. citizens, Canadians, Australians, New Zealanders, and South Africans must have a passport with at least 2 months' validity remaining. No visa is required. A passport will allow you to stay in the country for up to 6 months. The immigration officer will also want proof of your intention to return to your point of origin (usually a round-trip ticket) and of visible means of support while you're in Britain. If you're planning to fly from the United States or Canada to the United Kingdom and then on to a country that requires a visa (India, for example), you should secure that visa before you arrive in Britain.

Your valid driver's license and at least 1 year of driving experience are required to drive personal or rented cars.

Cut to the Front of the Airport Security Line as a Registered Traveler

In 2003, the **Transportation Security Administration (TSA;** www.tsa.gov) approved a pilot program to help ease the time spent in line for airport security screenings. In exchange for information and a fee, people can be prescreened as registered travelers, granting them a front-of-the-line position when they fly. The program is run through private firms—the largest and most well known is Steven Brill's **Clear** (www.flyclear.com), and it works like this: Travelers complete an online application providing specific points of personal information including name, addresses for the previous 5 years, birth date, Social Security number, driver's license number, and a valid credit card (you're not charged the **$128 fee** until your application is approved). Print out the completed form and take it, along with proper ID, with you to an "enrollment station" (this can be found in approximately 20 participating airports and in a growing number of American Express offices around the country, for example). It's at this point where it gets seemingly sci-fi. At the enrollment station, a Clear representative will record your biometrics necessary for clearance; in this case, your fingerprints and your irises will be digitally recorded.

Once your application has been screened against no-fly lists, outstanding warrants, and other security measures, you'll be issued a clear plastic card that holds a chip containing your information. Each time you fly through participating airports (and the numbers are steadily growing), go to the Clear Pass station located next to the standard TSA screening line. Here you'll insert your card into a slot and place your finger on a scanner to read your print—when the information matches up, you're cleared to cut to the front of the security line. You'll still have to follow all the procedures of the day like removing your shoes and walking through the x-ray machine, but Clear promises to cut 30 minutes off your wait time at the airport.

On a personal note: Each time I've used my Clear Pass, my travel companions are still waiting to go through security while I'm already sitting down, reading the paper and sipping my overpriced smoothie. Granted, registered traveler programs are not for the infrequent traveler, but for those of us who fly on a regular basis departing from participating airports, it's a perk I'm willing to pay for.

—*David A. Lytle*

For information on how to get a passport, go to "Passports" in the "Fast Facts: England & Wales" section of the appendix (p. 755).

MEDICAL REQUIREMENTS

Unless you're arriving from an area known to be suffering from an epidemic, particularly cholera or yellow fever, inoculations or vaccinations are not required for entry into the U.K.

For more information about health concerns, refer to "Health" (p. 72) later in this chapter.

CUSTOMS
WHAT YOU CAN BRING INTO BRITAIN

Non-E.U. nationals 18 years and over can bring in, duty-free, 200 cigarettes, 100 cigarillos, 50 cigars, or 250 grams of smoking tobacco. This amount is doubled if you live outside Europe. You can also bring in 2 liters of wine and either 1 liter of alcohol more than 22% or 2 liters of wine less than 22%. In addition, you can bring in 60cc (2 oz.) of perfume and a quarter liter (250ml) of eau de toilette. Visitors 15 and older may also bring in other goods totaling £145 ($290); the allowance for those 14 and younger is £73 ($145). (Customs officials tend to be lenient about general merchandise, realizing the limits are unrealistically low.)

You can't bring your pet to Britain. Six months' quarantine is required before it is allowed in. An illegally imported animal may be destroyed.

WHAT YOU CAN TAKE HOME FROM BRITAIN

U.S. Citizens: For specifics on what you can bring back and the corresponding fees, download the invaluable free pamphlet *Know Before You Go* online at **www.cbp.gov**. Or contact the **U.S. Customs & Border Protection (CBP),** 1300 Pennsylvania Ave. NW, Washington, DC 20229 (© **703/526-4200**), and request the pamphlet.

Canadian Citizens: For a clear summary of Canadian rules, write for the booklet *I Declare,* issued by the **Canada Border Services Agency** (© **800/461-9999** in Canada, or 204/983-3500; www.cbsa-asfc.gc.ca).

Australian Citizens: A helpful brochure available from Australian consulates or Customs offices is *Know Before You Go.* For more information, call the **Australian Customs Service** at © **1300/363-263,** or log on to **www.customs.gov.au**.

New Zealand Citizens: Most questions are answered in a free pamphlet available at New Zealand consulates and Customs offices: *New Zealand Customs Guide for Travellers, Notice no. 4.* For more information, contact **New Zealand Customs Service,** The Customhouse, 17–21 Whitmore St., Box 2218, Wellington (© **04/473-6099** or 0800/428-786; www.customs.govt.nz).

3 When to Go

THE WEATHER

Yes, it rains, but you'll rarely get a true downpour—it's heaviest in November (2½ in. on average). British temperatures can range from 30° to 110°F (–1° to 43°C), but they rarely drop below 35°F (2°C) or go above 78°F (26°C). Evenings are cool, even in summer. Note that the British, who consider chilliness to be wholesome, like to keep the thermostats about 10° below the American comfort level. Hotels have central heating systems, which are usually kept just above the goose bump (in Britspeak, "goose pimple") margin.

London's Average Daytime Temperatures & Rainfall

	Jan	Feb	Mar	Apr	May	June	July	Aug	Sept	Oct	Nov	Dec
Temp. (°F)	40	40	44	49	55	61	64	64	59	52	46	42
Temp. (°C)	4	4	7	9	13	16	18	18	15	11	8	6
Rainfall (in.)	2.1	1.6	1.5	1.5	1.8	1.8	2.2	2.3	1.9	2.2	2.5	1.9

Cardiff's Average Daytime Temperatures & Rainfall

	Jan	Feb	Mar	Apr	May	June	July	Aug	Sept	Oct	Nov	Dec
Temp. (°F)	40	40	43	46	52	57	61	61	57	52	44	42
Temp. (°C)	4	4	6	8	11	14	16	16	14	11	7	6
Rainfall (in.)	4.2	3.0	2.9	2.5	2.7	2.6	3.1	4.0	3.8	4.6	4.3	4.6

WHEN YOU'LL FIND BARGAINS

In short, spring offers the countryside at its greenest, autumn brings the bright colors of the northern moorlands, and summer's warmer weather gives rise to the many outdoor music and theater festivals. But winter offers savings across the board and a chance to see Britons going about their everyday lives largely unhindered by tourist invasions.

The cheapest time to travel to Britain is during the off season: from November 1 to December 12 and from December 25 to March 14. In the last few years, the airlines have offered irresistible fares during these periods. And no matter when you travel, keep in mind that weekday flights are cheaper than weekend fares (often by 10% or more).

Rates generally increase between March 14 and June 5, then hit their peak in high travel seasons between June 6 and September 30 and December 13 and 24. July and August are also when most Britons take their holidays, so besides higher prices, you'll have to deal with crowds and limited availability of accommodations.

You can avoid crowds by planning trips for November or January through March. Sure, it may be rainy and cold—but England doesn't shut down when the tourists leave! In fact, the winter season includes some of London's best theater, opera, ballet, and classical music offerings, and gives visitors a more honest view of English life. Additionally, many hotel prices drop by 20%, and cheaper accommodations offer weekly rates (unheard of during peak travel times). By arriving after the winter holidays, you can also take advantage of post-Christmas sales to buy woolens, china, crystal, silver, fashion clothing, handicrafts, and curios.

ENGLAND & WALES CALENDAR OF EVENTS

For an exhaustive list of events beyond those listed here, check **http://events.frommers. com**, where you'll find a searchable, up-to-the-minute roster of what's happening in cities all over the world.

January

London Boat Show, ExCel, Docklands (© **0870/060-0246;** www.london boatshow.com). This is the largest boat show in Europe. Mid-January.

Charles I Commemoration, London. To mark the anniversary of the execution of King Charles I "in the name of freedom and democracy," hundreds of cavaliers march through central London in 17th-century dress, and prayers are said at Whitehall's Banqueting House. Call © **0870/751-5178** for details. Last Sunday in January.

February

Chinese New Year, London. The famous Lion Dancers in Soho perform free on the nearest Sunday to Chinese New Year. Call the London Chinese Community Centre at © **020/7851-6686** (www.chinatownchinese.co.uk). Either in late January or early February (based on the lunar calendar).

Jorvik Festival, York. This 2-week festival celebrates this historic cathedral city's role as a Viking outpost. For more information, call © **01904/543400** or visit www.jorvik-viking-centre.co.uk. Mid-February.

March

St. Davids Day Parade, Cardiff, Wales. The capital of Wales comes to a standstill on Wales's national day, honoring its patron saint with the country's showiest and most fun-filled parade. Contact the Wales Tourist Board, Cardiff Visitor Centre, The Old Library, The Hayes, Cardiff (© **029/ 2087-2087;** www.stdavidsday.org). March 1.

Crufts Dog Show, Birmingham. The English, they say, love their pets more than their offspring. Crufts offers an opportunity to observe the nation's pet lovers doting on 23,000 dogs, representing 209 breeds. It's held at the National Exhibition Centre, Birmingham, West Midlands. Tickets can be purchased at the door. For more information, call © **0870/606-6750** or visit **www.crufts.org.uk**. Early March.

April

John Smith's Grand National Meeting, outside Liverpool. England's premier steeplechase event takes place on a 6.5km (4-mile) course at **Aintree Racecourse,** Aintree (© **0151/522-2929;** www.aintree.co.uk). Early April.

Flora London Marathon. More than 30,000 competitors run from Greenwich Park to Buckingham Palace; call © **020/7902-0200** (www.londonmarathon.co.uk) for information. If you'd like to take the challenge, call during May and June for an application. Mid-April.

Easter Parade, London. A memorable parade of brightly colored floats and marching bands occurs around Battersea Park. Easter Monday.

The Shakespeare Season, Stratford-upon-Avon. The Royal Shakespeare Company begins its annual season, presenting works by the Bard in his hometown, at the **Royal Shakespeare Theatre,** Waterside (© **01789/ 403444;** www.rsc.org.uk). Tickets are available at the box office or through such agents as **Keith Prowse Global Tickets** (© **800/669-8687;** www. keithprowse.com). April to October.

May

Brighton Festival. England's largest arts festival features some 400 different cultural events. For information, call © **01273/709-709;** www.brighton festival.org). Most of May.

Royal Windsor Horse Show. The country's major show-jumping presentation, held at the Home Park in Windsor, Berkshire, is attended by the queen herself. Call © **01753/860-633,** or see **www.royal-windsor-horse-show. co.uk** for more information. Mid-May.

Glyndebourne Festival. One of England's major cultural events, this festival is centered at the 1,200-seat Glyndebourne Opera House in Sussex, some 87km (54 miles) south of London. Tickets, which cost anywhere from £10 to £190 ($20–$380), are available from **Glyndebourne Festival Opera Box Office,** Lewes, East Sussex BN8 5UU (© **01273/812321;** www. glyndebourne.com). Mid-April to late August.

Bath International Music Festival. One of Europe's most prestigious international festivals of music and the arts features as many as 1,000 performers at various venues in Bath. For information, contact the **Bath Festivals,** Abbey Chambers, Kingston Buildings, Bath BA1 1NT (© **01225/463362;** www.bathfestivals.org.uk). Mid-May to early June.

Chelsea Flower Show, London. The best of British gardening, with plants and flowers of the season, is displayed at the Chelsea Royal Hospital. Contact the local British Tourist Authority

Office to find out which overseas reservations agency is handling ticket sales; or contact the **Chelsea Show Ticket Office,** Shows Department, Royal Horticultural Society, 80 Vincent Sq., London SW1P 2PE (✆ **0845/260-5000**; www.rhs.org.uk). Late May.

Chichester Festival Theatre. Some great classic and modern plays are presented at this West Sussex theater. For tickets and information, contact the **Festival Theatre,** Oaklands Park, West Sussex PO19 4AP (✆ **01243/784437**; www.cft.org.uk). The season runs May through October.

June

Royal Academy's Summer Exhibition, London. This institution, founded in 1768, has for some 2 centuries held Summer Exhibitions of living painters at Burlington House, Piccadilly Circus. Call ✆ **0870/848-8484,** or visit **www.royalacademy.org.uk** for more information. Early June to mid-August.

Vodafone Derby Stakes. This famous horse-racing event (the "Darby," as it's called here) is held at Epsom Downs, Epsom, Surrey. Men wear top hats; women, including the queen, put on silly millinery creations. For more details, call ✆ **01372/726311** or check out **www.epsomderby.co.uk.** First week of June.

Trooping the Colour. This is the queen's official birthday parade, a quintessential British event, with exquisite pageantry and pomp as she inspects her regiments and takes their salute, while they parade their colors before her at the Horse Guards Parade, Whitehall. Tickets for the parade and two reviews, held on preceding Saturdays, are allocated by ballot. Applicants must write between January 1 and the end of February, enclosing a self-addressed stamped envelope or International Reply Coupon to the Ticket Office, HQ Household Division, Horse Guards, Whitehall, London SW1X 6AA. Tickets are free. The ballot is held in mid-March, and only successful applicants are informed in April. Call ✆ **020/7414-2479** or visit **www.trooping-the-colour.co.uk** for more details. Held on a day designated in June (not necessarily the queen's actual birthday).

Grosvenor House Art and Antique Fair, London. This very prestigious antiques fair is held at Le Méridien Grosvenor House, Park Lane. For information, contact **Grosvenor House Art and Antiques Fair,** Grosvenor House, 86–90 Park Lane, London W1A 3AA (✆ **020/7399-8100**; www.grosvenor-antiquesfair.co.uk). Mid-June.

City of London Festival. This annual art festival is held in venues throughout the city. Call ✆ **020/7796-4949,** or visit **www.colf.org** for information. Late June to mid-July.

Aldeburgh Festival of Music and the Arts. The composer Benjamin Britten launched this 2-week festival in 1948. For more details on the events and for the year-round program, write to **Aldeburgh Foundation,** High Street, Aldeburgh, Suffolk IP17 1SP (✆ **01728/687110**; www.aldeburgh.co.uk). Mid-to late June.

Royal Ascot Week. Though Ascot Racecourse is open year-round for guided tours, events, exhibitions, and conferences, there are 25 race days throughout the year, with the feature races being the Royal. For information, contact **Ascot Racecourse,** Ascot, Berkshire SL5 7JX (✆ **0870/727-1234**; www.ascot.co.uk). Key race days are the Meeting in June, Diamond Day in late July, and the Festival at Ascot in late September.

The Exeter Summer Festival. The town of Exeter hosts more than 150 events celebrating classical music, ranging from concerts and opera to lectures. Festival dates and offerings vary from year to year; more information is available by contacting the **Exeter Festival Office** at ⓒ **01392/ 277888** (www.exeter.gov.uk). Late June to mid-July.

Lawn Tennis Championships, Wimbledon, London. Ever since players took to the grass courts at Wimbledon in 1877, this tournament has attracted quite a crowd, and there's still an excited hush and a certain thrill at Centre Court. Savor the strawberries and cream that are part of the experience. Early bookings for the world's most famous tennis tournament are strongly advised. Acquiring tickets and overnight lodgings during the annual tennis competitions at Wimbledon can be difficult to arrange independently. Two outfits that book both hotel accommodations and tickets to the event are **Steve Furgal's International Tennis Tours,** 11305 Rancho Bernardo Rd., Ste. 108, San Diego, CA 92127 (ⓒ **800/258-3664** or 858/ 675-3555; www.tours4tennis.com); and **Championship Tennis Tours,** 13951 N. Scottsdale Rd., Ste. 133, Scottsdale, AZ 85254 (ⓒ **800/468- 3664** or 480/429-7700; www.tennis tours.com). Tickets for Centre and Number One courts are obtainable through a lottery. Write in from August to December to **All England Lawn Tennis Club,** P.O. Box 98, Church Road, Wimbledon, London SW19 5AE (ⓒ **020/8944-1066;** www. wimbledon.org). Outside court tickets are available daily, but be prepared to wait in line. Late June to early July.

Shakespeare under the Stars, London. The Bard's works are performed at the **Open Air Theatre,** Inner Circle, Regent's Park, NW1 4NU, in London. Take the Tube to Baker Street. Performances are Monday through Saturday at 8pm; Wednesday, Thursday, and Saturday also at 2:30pm. Call ⓒ **0844/ 826-4242** or visit **www.openair theatre.org.uk** for more information. Previews begin in June and last throughout the summer.

Ludlow Festival. This is one of England's major arts festivals, complete with an open-air Shakespeare performance within the Inner Bailey of Ludlow Castle. Concerts, lectures, readings, exhibitions, and workshops round out the offerings. From March onward, a schedule can be obtained from the box office. Write to **Ludlow Festival Box Office,** Castle Square, Ludlow, Shropshire SY8 1AY; enclose a self-addressed, stamped envelope (ⓒ **01584/872150;** www.ludlowfestival.co.uk). Late June to early July.

Cardiff Festival. In venues across the Welsh capital, this 3-week festival features pop, jazz, theater, street performances, funfairs, opera, comedies, and children's events. Most events are free and take place in public and open-air places. For more information, contact the **Cardiff Festival,** Health Park, Cardiff CF4 4EP (ⓒ **029/2087-2087;** www.cardiff-festival.com). Late June to early August.

July

Henley Royal Regatta. This international rowing competition in Oxfordshire is the premier event on the English social calendar. For more information, call ⓒ **01491/572153** or visit **www.hrr.co.uk.** Early July.

Kenwood Lakeside Concerts, London. These summer concerts on the north side of Hampstead Heath have continued a British tradition of outdoor performances for nearly 50 years.

Fireworks displays and laser shows enliven the premier musical performances. The audience catches the music as it drifts across the lake from the performance shell. For more information, call ✆ 020/7413-1443. Every Saturday from early July to late August.

The Proms, London. A night at "the Proms"—the annual Henry Wood promenade concerts at Royal Albert Hall—attracts music aficionados from around the world. Staged almost daily (except for a few Sun), these traditional concerts were launched in 1895 and are the principal summer engagements for the BBC Symphony Orchestra. Cheering and clapping, Union Jacks on parade, banners, and balloons—it's great summer fun. Call ✆ 020/7589-8212, or check out **www.bbc.co.uk/proms** for more details. Mid-July to mid-September.

Musicfest Aberystwyth. This is a pageant of cultural and sporting events in Aberystwyth, the cultural center of the western section of middle Wales. For more information, contact **Aberystwyth Arts Centre,** Penglais, Aberystwyth SW23 3DE (✆ **01970/623-232;** www.aberystwythartscentre.co.uk). End of July.

August

Skandia Cowes Week, off the Isle of Wight. For details about this yachting festival, call ✆ **01983/295744** or visit **www.skandiacowesweek.co.uk**. Early August.

Pontardawe International Music Festival. The little Welsh village of Pontardawe, lying 13km (8 miles) north of Swansea, attracts some of the world's leading folk and rock musicians for its annual summer concert series. For more information, call ✆ **01792/830200** or see **www.pontardawe festival.org.uk**. Mid-August.

Notting Hill Carnival, Ladbroke Grove, London. Notting Hill is the setting for one of the largest annual street festivals in Europe, attracting more than half a million people. There's live reggae and soul music, plus great Caribbean food. Call ✆ **020/7727-0072,** or see **www.nottinghill carnival.biz** for information. Two days in late August.

International Beatles Week, Liverpool. Tens of thousands of fans gather in Liverpool to celebrate the music of the Fab Four. There's an entire series of concerts by international cover bands, plus tributes, auctions, and tours. **Cavern City Tours,** a local company, offers hotel and festival packages that include accommodations and tickets to tours and events. For information, contact **Cavern City Tours** at ✆ **0151/236-9091** (www.cavernclub.org) or the **Tourist Information Centre** in Liverpool at ✆ **0151/233-2008** (www.visitliverpool.com). Late August.

September

The Landrover Burghley Horse Trials, Lincolnshire. This annual event is staged on the grounds of the largest Elizabethan house in England, Burghley House, Stamford, Lincolnshire (✆ **01780/752131;** www.burghley-horse.co.uk). Early September.

Raising of the Thames Barrier, Unity Way, SE18. Once a year, usually in September, a full test is done on this miracle of modern engineering; all 10 massive steel gates are raised against the low and high tides. Call ✆ **020/8854-8888** for exact date and time.

Horse of the Year Show, NEC Arena. Riders fly from every continent to join in this festive display of horsemanship (much appreciated by the queen). The British press calls it an "equine extravaganza." It's held at **NEC Arena,** in

Birmingham. For more information, call ☎ **01582/711-411** or see **www. hoys.co.uk**. Late September to early October.

The Ascot Festival, Ascot, Berkshire. This is Britain's greatest horse-racing weekend, providing the grand finale to the summer season at Ascot. The 3-day "meeting" combines some of the most valuable racing of the year with other entertainment. A highlight of the festival is the £250,000 ($500,000) Watership Down Stud Sales race, restricted to 2-year-old fillies. Other racing highlights include the Queen Elizabeth II Stakes, with the winning horse crowned champion miler in Europe. To book tickets, call ☎ **0870/727-1234** or visit **www.ascot.co.uk**. Last weekend in September.

October

Quit Rents Ceremony, London. The origins of this ceremony go back so far they have been forgotten. The city solicitor pays the queen's remembrancer (medieval term for collector of the queen's rents) token rents for properties long ago leased—in many cases no longer standing. It's all for fun, show, and tradition. For example, the solicitor will pay the remembrancer two faggots of wood, a billhook, and a hatchet for land in Shropshire; or else 61 nails and six horseshoes for a long-gone forge in the Strand. The ceremony is held at the Royal Courts of Justice. Call ☎ **020/7947-6000** for more information. Early October.

Cheltenham Festival of Literature. This Cotswold event features readings, book exhibitions, and theatrical performances—all in the famed spa town of Gloucestershire. Call ☎ **01242/227979**, or visit **www.cheltenham festivals.co.uk** for more details. Early to mid-October.

Opening of Parliament, London. Ever since the 17th century, when the

English beheaded Charles I, British monarchs have been denied the right to enter the House of Commons. Instead, the monarch opens Parliament in the House of Lords, reading an official speech that is in fact written by the government. Queen Elizabeth II rides from Buckingham Palace to Westminster in a royal coach accompanied by the Yeoman of the Guard and the Household Cavalry. The public galleries are open on a first-come, first-served basis. Call ☎ **020/7219-3107**, or surf the Web to **www.parliament. uk**. Late October to mid-November.

November

London-Brighton Veteran Car Run. This race begins in London's Hyde Park and ends in the seaside resort of Brighton, in East Sussex. Call ☎ **01462/742-818**, or see **www. vccofgb.co.uk** for more details. First Sunday in November.

Guy Fawkes Night, throughout England. This British celebration commemorates the anniversary of the "Gunpowder Plot," an attempt to blow up King James I and Parliament. Huge organized bonfires are lit throughout London, and Guy Fawkes, the plot's most famous conspirator, is burned in effigy. Check *Time Out* for locations. Early November.

Lord Mayor's Procession and Show, the City, London. The queen has to ask permission to enter the square mile in London called the City—and the right of refusal has been jealously guarded by London merchants since the 17th century. Suffice it to say that the lord mayor is a powerful character, and the procession from the Guildhall to the Royal Courts is appropriately impressive. You can watch the procession from the street; the banquet is by invitation only. Call ☎ **020/7222-4345**, or visit **www.lordmayorshow.org** for details. Second Saturday in November.

4 Getting There & Getting Around

GETTING TO ENGLAND & WALES

BY PLANE

The major airport for arrivals from North America is **Heathrow** (LHR) outside London. This is the hub of most airlines, including British Airways and American carriers, and has the best transportation links to London. **Gatwick** (LGW) is the second major airport outside London, but it is much farther from the heart of the city, requiring longer and often more expensive hauls into the city.

Chances are you will not land at London's minor airports, certainly not if you're making a trans-Atlantic crossing; however, you might land at one of these airports if you're winging in from the Continent. They include **Stansted** (STN), **London City** (LCY), **London Luton** (LTN), and **London Southend** (SEN).

If you plan to skip London altogether, you might have a direct flight winging into one of the two leading regional airports of England, including **Manchester** (MAN) and **Birmingham** (BHX).

Chances are you will not use one of the small airports of Wales, since most visitors arrive by rail or car. However, there are airports in the capital of **Cardiff** (CWL) and in the second city of **Swansea** (SWS).

For more contact information than that given below, refer to the list of airlines and their phone numbers and websites in the appendix (p. 756).

British Airways (✆ 800/247-9297; www.britishairways.com) offers flights from 19 U.S. cities to Heathrow and Gatwick airports, as well as many others to Manchester. Nearly every flight is nonstop. With more add-on options than any other airline, British Airways can make a visit to Britain cheaper than you may have expected. Ask about packages that include both airfare and discounted hotel accommodations in Britain.

Known for consistently offering excellent fares, **Virgin Atlantic Airways** (✆ 800/821-5438; www.virgin-atlantic.com) flies daily to either Heathrow or Gatwick from Boston, Newark, New York's JFK, Los Angeles, San Francisco, Washington's Dulles, Miami, Orlando, and Las Vegas.

American Airlines (✆ 800/433-7300; www.aa.com) offers daily flights to Heathrow from half a dozen U.S. gateways—New York's JFK, Chicago, Boston, Miami, Los Angeles, and Dallas.

Depending on the day and season, **Delta Air Lines** (✆ 800/221-1212; www.delta.com) runs either one or two daily nonstop flights between Atlanta and Gatwick. Delta also offers nonstop daily service from Cincinnati.

Northwest Airlines (✆ 800/225-2525 or 800/447-4747; www.nwa.com) flies nonstop from Minneapolis and Detroit to Gatwick.

Continental Airlines (✆ 800/231-0856; www.continental.com) has daily flights to London from Cleveland, Houston, Newark, Orlando, and San Francisco.

United Airlines (✆ 800/864-8331; www.united.com) flies nonstop from New York's JFK and Chicago to Heathrow two or three times daily, depending on the season. United also offers nonstop service from Dulles Airport, near Washington, D.C.; Newark; Los Angeles; and San Francisco.

For travelers departing from Canada, **Air Canada** (✆ 888/247-2262; www.aircanada.com) flies daily to London's Heathrow nonstop from Vancouver, Montreal, and Toronto. There are also frequent direct flights from Calgary, Ottawa, and St. John's. **British Airways** (✆ 800/247-9297) has direct flights from Toronto, Montreal, and Vancouver.

For travelers departing from Australia, **British Airways** (© 1300/767-177) has flights to London from Sydney, Melbourne, Perth, and Brisbane. **Qantas** (© 612/131313; www.qantas.com) offers flights from Australia to London's Heathrow. Direct flights depart from Sydney and Melbourne. Some have the bonus of free stopovers in Bangkok or Singapore.

Departing from New Zealand, **Air New Zealand** (© 800/262-1234 in the U.S., or 0800/737-000 in New Zealand; www.airnz.co.nz) has direct flights to London from Auckland. These flights depart daily.

Short flights from Dublin to London are available through **British Airways** (© 800/247-9297), with four flights daily into London's Gatwick airport, and **Aer Lingus** (© 800/IRISH-AIR [474-7424]; www.aerlingus.com), which flies into Heathrow. Short flights from Dublin to London are also available through **Ryanair** (© 35301/249-7791; www.ryanair.com) and **British Midland** (© 0870/6070555; www.flybmi.com).

LONG-HAUL FLIGHTS: HOW TO STAY COMFORTABLE

- Your choice of airline and airplane will definitely affect your legroom. For England, the research firm Skytrax has posted a list of average seat pitches at **www.airlinequality.com**.
- Emergency exit seats and bulkhead seats typically have the most legroom. Emergency exit seats are usually left unassigned until the day of a flight (to ensure that someone able-bodied fills the seats); it's worth checking in online at home (if the airline offers that option) or getting to the ticket counter early to snag one of these spots for a long flight. Many passengers find that bulkhead seating offers more legroom, but keep in mind that bulkhead seats have no storage space on the floor in front of you.

- To have two seats for yourself in a three-seat row, try for an aisle seat in a center section toward the back of coach. If you're traveling with a companion, book an aisle and a window seat. Middle seats are usually booked last, so chances are good you'll end up with three seats to yourselves. And in the event that a third passenger is assigned the middle seat, he or she will probably be more than happy to trade for a window or an aisle.
- To sleep, avoid the last row of any section or the row in front of an emergency exit, as these seats are the least likely to recline. Avoid seats near highly trafficked toilet areas. Avoid seats in the back of many jets—these can be narrower than those in the rest of coach. Or reserve a window seat so you can rest your head and avoid being bumped in the aisle.
- Get up, walk around, and stretch every 60 to 90 minutes to keep your blood flowing. This helps avoid **deep vein thrombosis,** or "economy-class syndrome."
- Drink water before, during, and after your flight to combat the lack of humidity in airplane cabins. Avoid caffeine and alcohol, which will dehydrate you.

BY CAR FROM CONTINENTAL EUROPE

If you plan to transport a rented car between Britain and France, check in advance with the car-rental company about license and insurance requirements and additional drop-off charges before you begin.

The English Channel is crisscrossed with "drive-on, drive-off" car-ferry services, with many operating from Boulogne and Calais in France. From either of those ports, Sealink ferries will carry you, your luggage, and, if you like, your car. The most popular point of arrival along the English coast is Folkestone.

Taking a car beneath the Channel is more complicated and more expensive. Since the Channel Tunnel's opening (commonly called the "Chunnel"), most passengers have opted to ride the train alone, without being accompanied by their car. The Eurostar trains, discussed below, carry passengers only; **Eurotunnel** trains carry freight cars, trucks, and passenger cars.

The cost of moving a car on Eurotunnel varies according to the season and day of the week. Frankly, it's a lot cheaper to transport your car across by conventional ferryboat, but if you insist, here's what you'll need to know: You'll negotiate both British and French customs as part of one combined process, usually on the English side of the Channel. You can remain within your vehicle even after you drive it onto a flatbed railway car during the 35-minute crossing. (For 19 min. of this crossing, you'll actually be underwater; if you want, you can leave the confines of your car and ride within a brightly lit, air-conditioned passenger car.) When the trip is over, you simply drive off the flatbed railway car and toward your destination. Total travel time between the French and English highway system is about 1 hour. As a means of speeding the flow of perishable goods across the Channel, the car and truck service usually operates 24 hours a day, at intervals that vary from every 15 minutes to once an hour, depending on the time of day. Neither BritRail nor any of the agencies dealing with reservations for passenger trains through the Chunnel will reserve space for your car in advance, and considering the frequency of the traffic on the Chunnel, they're usually not necessary. For information about Eurotunnel car-rail service after you reach England, call © **0870/535-3535,** or go online to **www.eurotunnel.com.**

Duty-free stores, restaurants, and service stations are available to travelers on both sides of the Channel. A bilingual staff is on hand to assist travelers at both the British and French terminals.

BY TRAIN FROM CONTINENTAL EUROPE

Britain's isolation from the rest of Europe led to the development of an independent railway network with different rules and regulations from those observed on the Continent. That's all changing now, but one big difference that may affect you still remains: If you're traveling to Britain from the Continent, *your Eurailpass will not be valid when you get there.*

In 1994, Queen Elizabeth of England and President Francois Mitterrand of France officially opened the Channel Tunnel, or Chunnel, and the Eurostar express passenger train began twice-daily service between London and both Paris and Brussels. In 2003, the completion of a new section of high-speed rail in England, the **Channel Tunnel Rail Link,** shaved 20 minutes off the trip between London and Paris, reducing it to just 2 hours and 35 minutes (or 2 hr., 20 min. to Brussels). This extension allows Eurostar trains to go at the rate of 482kmph (300 mph). One of the great engineering feats of all time, the tunnel is first link between Britain and the Continent since the Ice Age.

So if you're coming to London from say, Rome, your Eurailpass will get you as far as the Chunnel. At that point, you can cross the English Channel aboard the Eurostar, and you'll receive a discount on your ticket. Once in England, you must use a separate BritRail pass or purchase a direct ticket to continue on to your destination.

Rail Europe (© **888/382-7245;** www.raileurope.com) sells direct-service tickets on the Eurostar between Paris or Brussels and London. A one-way fare between Paris and London costs $185 to $214 in second class and $237 to $417 in first class.

In London, make reservations for **Eurostar** by calling © **08705/186-186;** and in the United States, it's © **800/ EUROSTAR** (800/387-6782; www. eurostar.com). Eurostar trains arrive and depart from London's Waterloo Station, Paris's Gare du Nord, and Brussels's Central Station.

BY FERRY/HOVERCRAFT FROM CONTINENTAL EUROPE

P&O Ferries (© **08716/645645;** www. poferries.com) operates car and passenger ferries between Dover and Calais, France (25 sailings a day; 75 min. each way).

BY BUS

Bus connections to Britain from the Continent are generally not comfortable, though some lines are more convenient than others. One line with a relatively good reputation is **Eurolines,** 52 Grosvenor Gardens, SW1W 0AU (© **08705/143-219;** www.eurolines. com). They book passage on buses traveling twice a day between London and Paris (9 hr.); three times a day from Amsterdam (12 hr.); three times a week from Munich (24 hr.); and three times a week from Stockholm (44 hr.). On longer routes, which use alternating drivers, the bus proceeds almost without interruption, taking only occasional breaks for meals.

GETTING AROUND
BY CAR

There's no doubt about it, the best way to explore England, with its little villages and off-the-beaten path attractions, is by car. It's also the most expensive, far more so than the train or bus. For budget-saving suggestions, see below.

Because cars in Britain travel on the left side of the road, steering wheels are positioned on the "wrong" side of the vehicle. Keep in mind that most rental cars are manual, so be prepared to shift with your left hand; you'll pay more for

an automatic—and make sure to request one when you reserve.

Speed limits are in general 50 to 60kmph (30–40 mph) in heavily populated areas, or 110kmph (70 mph) on motorways or "dual carriage ways," as the English call double-lane highways.

In England *you drive on the left* and pass on the right. Road signs are clear and international symbols are used.

Warning: Pedestrian crossings are marked by striped lines (zebra striping) on the road; flashing lights near the curb indicate that drivers must stop and yield the right of way if a pedestrian has stepped out into the zebra zone to cross the street.

It's a good idea to get a copy of the *British Highway Code,* available from almost any petrol or gas station or newsstand in Britain.

Getting the Best Deal on Your Rental Car

The British car-rental market is among the most competitive in Europe. Nevertheless, car rentals are expensive, unless you avail yourself of one of the promotional deals that are frequently offered by British Airways and others. It's always cheaper to arrange a car in advance though one of the big chains such as Hertz or Avis. You might also look into a fly/drive deal.

Car-rental rates vary even more than airline fares. The price you pay depends on the size of the car, where and when you pick it up and drop it off, length of the rental period, where and how far you drive it, whether you purchase insurance, and a host of other factors. It's cheaper to rent a car with a stick shift; if you can't drive a stick shift, you can rent a vehicle with automatic drive but invariably you'll pay more for this convenience.

The best car-rental deals are made in off season, as thousands upon thousands of potential motorists descend on Britain to drive its clogged highways and country lanes in fair weather.

For booking rental cars online, the best deals are usually found at rental-car company websites, although all the major online travel agencies also offer rental-car reservations services. Priceline and Hotwire work well for rental cars, too; the only "mystery" is which major rental company you get, and for most travelers the difference between Hertz, Avis, and Budget is negligible.

Virtually every kind of car imaginable is for rent in England, including an old Rolls-Royce discarded by the queen or a small little budget number from Japan that seats two uncomfortably.

Keep in mind that most companies will only rent to persons 23 years old and above. Many agencies will not rent to people age 70 or older.

Rentals are available through **Avis** (© 800/331-1212; www.avis.com), **Budget** (© 800/800-4000; www.budget.com), and **Hertz** (© 800/654-3001; www.hertz.com). **Kemwel Drive Europe** (© 877/820-0668; www.kemwel.com) is among the cheapest and most reliable of the rental agencies. **AutoEurope** (© 888/223-5555 in the U.S., or 0800/223-5555 in London; www.autoeurope.com) acts as a wholesale company for rental agencies in Europe. For additional listings of the major car-rental agencies in England or Wales, see "Toll-Free Numbers & Websites" in the appendix (p. 756).

When booking your rental car, a few key questions could save you hundreds of dollars:

- Are weekend rates lower than weekday rates? Ask if the rate is the same for pickup Friday morning, for instance, as it is for Thursday night.
- Is a weekly rate cheaper than the daily rate? If you need to keep the car for 4 days, it may be cheaper to keep it for 5, even if you don't need it for that long.
- Does the agency assess a drop-off charge if you do not return the car to the same location where you picked it up? Is it cheaper to pick up the car at the airport compared to a downtown location?
- Are special promotional rates available? If you see an advertised price in your local newspaper, be sure to ask for that specific rate; otherwise you may be charged the standard cost. The terms change constantly, and phone operators may not volunteer information.
- Are discounts available for members of AARP, AAA, frequent-flier programs, or trade unions? If you belong to any of these organizations, you are probably entitled to discounts of up to 30%.
- What is the cost of adding an additional driver's name to the contract?
- How many free miles are included in the price? Free mileage is often negotiable, depending on the length of your rental.
- How much does the rental company charge to refill your gas tank if you return with the tank less than full? Though most rental companies claim these prices are "competitive," fuel is almost always cheaper in town. Try to allow enough time to refuel the car yourself before returning it.

When you reserve a car, make sure you find out the total price, including the 17.5% value-added tax (VAT).

Smart Insurance Tips

Before you drive off in a rental car, be sure you're insured. Hasty assumption about your personal auto insurance or a rental agency's additional coverage could end up costing you tens of thousands of dollars—even if you are involved in an accident that was clearly the fault of another driver.

U.S. drivers who already have their own car insurance are usually covered in the United States for loss of or damage to a rental car and liability in case of injury to any other party involved in an accident. But coverage probably doesn't extend outside the United States. Be sure to find out whether you are covered in England, whether your policy extends to all persons who will be driving the rental car, how much liability is covered in case an outside party is injured in an accident, and whether the type of vehicle you are renting is included under your contract. (Rental trucks, sport utility vehicles, and luxury vehicles such as the Jaguar may not be covered.)

Most **major credit cards** provide some degree of coverage as well—provided they are used to pay for the rental. Terms vary widely, however, so be sure to call your credit card company directly before you rent. But though they will cover damage to or theft of your rental, *credit cards will not cover liability* or the cost of injury to an outside party and/or damage to an outside party's vehicle. If you do not hold an insurance policy or if you are driving outside the United States, you may want to seriously consider purchasing additional liability insurance from your rental company. Be sure to check the terms, however. Some rental agencies only cover liability if the renter is not at fault.

Bear in mind that each credit card company has its own peculiarities. Most American Express Optima cards, for instance, do not provide any insurance. American Express does not cover vehicles valued at over $50,000 when new, such as luxury vehicles or vehicles built on a truck chassis. MasterCard does not provide coverage for loss, theft, or fire damage, and only covers collision if the rental period does not exceed 15 days. Call your own credit card company for details.

Breakdowns

Membership in one of the two major auto clubs can be helpful: the **Automobile Association (AA)** at Norfolk House, Priestly Road, Basingstoke, Hampshire RG24 9NY (© 0870/5444-444), or the **Royal Automobile Club (RAC),** P.O. Box 700, Bristol, Somerset BS99 1RB (© 08000/966-999; www.rac.co.uk). You can join these clubs through your car-rental agent. (Members of AAA in the U.S. can enjoy reciprocity overseas.) There are roadside emergency telephone boxes about every mile along the motorways. If you don't see one, walk down the road for a bit to the blue-and-white marker with an arrow that points to the nearest box. The 24-hour number to call for the AA is © 0800/887-766; for the RAC, it's © 0800/82-82-82. In addition, you can call a police traffic unit that will contact either of the auto clubs on your behalf.

Even if you're not a member, you can call these organizations, though a substantial fee will be involved for nonmembers.

Gasoline

There are plenty of gas ("petrol") stations in England and Wales, especially around cities and big towns and most definitely along the motorways. However, in remote areas they're often few and far between, and many are closed on Sunday. If you're planning a lot of Sunday driving in remote parts, always make sure your tank is full on Saturday.

Note that gasoline costs more in Britain than in North America, and to encourage energy saving the government has imposed a 25% tax on gas.

Parking

In overcrowded cities such as London parking has become a nightmare, and it costs a fortune. Touring English cities by car, especially London, is not recommended. Use public transportation. Even in small villages, parking can be a problem especially in summer. There are just so many spaces.

In general, long- or short-stay car parks are cheaper than using city or town meters, which usually limit you to 2 hours. When you see a yellow line along the edge of a road, that means parking is restricted; refer to the nearest sign to read the conditions. A double yellow line indicates that parking is forbidden at all times.

BY TRAIN

A Eurailpass is not valid in Great Britain, but there are several special passes for train travel outside London. For railroad information, go to Rail Travel centers in the main London railway stations (Waterloo, Kings Cross, Euston, and Paddington).

You can download faxable order forms or order online from BritRail at **www. britainontrack.com**.

BritRail Travel Passes

BritRail passes allow unlimited travel in England, Scotland, and Wales on any British rail scheduled train over the whole of the network during the validity of the pass without restrictions. If you're traveling beyond London anywhere in the United Kingdom and plan to hop on and off the train, consider purchasing a **BritRail Consecutive Pass.** These passes allow you to travel for a consecutive number of days for a flat rate. In first class adults pay $395 for 4 days, $559 for 8 days, $839 for 15 days, $1,065 for 22 days, and $1,259 for 1 month. In second class, fares are $259 for 4 days, $375 for 8 days, $559 for 15 days, $709 for 22 days, and $839 for 1 month. Seniors (60 and older) qualify for discounts in first-class travel and pay $336 for 4 days, $475 for 8 days, $713 for 15 days, $905 for 22 days, and $1,070 for 1 month of first-class travel. Passengers 25 and younger qualify for a **Youth Pass.** In second class rates are $207 for 4 days, $300 for 8 days, $447 for 15 days, $567 for 22 days, and $671 for 1 month. One child (age 14 and younger) can travel free with each adult or senior pass when the **BritRail Family Pass** is requested while buying the adult pass. Additional children pay half the regular adult fare.

A more versatile pass is the **BritRail FlexiPass,** allowing you to travel when you want during a 2-month period of time. In first class, it costs $489 for 4 days, $717 for 8 days, and $1,075 for 15 days of travel. Second class costs $329 for 4 days, $479 for 8 days, and $725 for 15 days of travel.

A **Freedom of Wales Flexi Pass** allows you to discover the small country by bus and rail. The pass also offers 20% discounts on narrow-gauge railways. The pass costs £69 ($138). You're granted 4 days of rail travel and 8 days of bus travel. You can also inquire about passes granting more extended travel time. Check their website at **www.walesflexipass. co.uk**. More information is available from **Arriva Trains Wales,** St. Mary's House, Penarth Road, Cardiff CF10 5DJ (*©* **0845/6061-660**).

For more information on train pass options and on rail vacation packages in England and the U.K., contact **BritRail** (*©* **866/2748-7245;** www.britrail.com).

Travelers who arrive from France by boat and pick up a BritRail train at Dover arrive at **St. Pancras Station,** in the center of London. Those journeying south by rail from Edinburgh arrive at **Kings Cross Station.**

BY BUS

In Britain, a long-distance touring bus is called a "coach," and "buses" are taken for local transportation. An efficient and frequent express motorcoach network—run by National Express and other independent operators—links most of Britain's towns and cities. Destinations off the main route can be easily reached by transferring to a local bus at a stop on the route. Tickets are relatively cheap, often half the price of rail fare, and it's usually cheaper to purchase a round-trip (or "return") ticket than two one-way fares separately.

Victoria Coach Station, on Buckingham Palace Road (*©* **020/7730-3466**), is the departure point for most large coach operators. The coach station is located

Train Routes in England

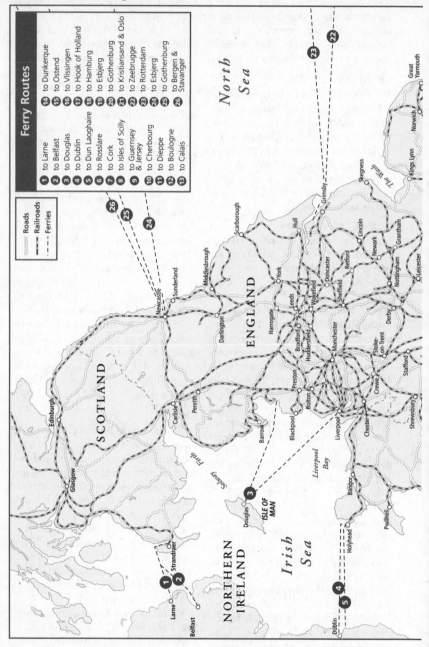

Ferry Routes

❶ to Larne	❽ to Isles of Scilly	⓮ to Dunkerque	㉑ to Kristiansand & Oslo
❷ to Belfast	❾ to Guernsey & Jersey	⓯ to Ostend	㉒ to Zeebrugge
❸ to Douglas	❿ to Cherbourg	⓰ to Vlissingen	㉓ to Rotterdam
❹ to Dublin	⓫ to Dieppe	⓱ to Hook of Holland	㉔ to Esbjerg
❺ to Dun Laoghaire	⓬ to Boulogne	⓲ to Hamburg	㉕ to Gothenburg
❻ to Rosslare	⓭ to Calais	⓳ to Esbjerg	㉖ to Bergen & Stavanger
❼ to Cork		⓴ to Gothenburg	

Roads ══════
Railroads ━━━━
Ferries ┅┅┅┅

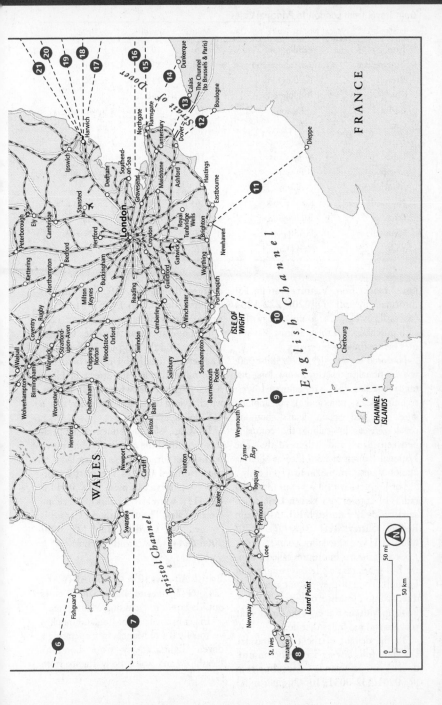

Train Travel from London to Principal Cities

To Station	Typical No. of Trains per Day	Miles	Travel	Time
Bath	Paddington	25	107	1 hr. 11 min.
Birmingham	Euston/Paddington	35	113	1 hr. 37 min.
Bristol	Paddington	46	119	1 hr. 26 min.
Cardiff	Paddington	24	148	2 hr.
Carlisle	Euston	10	299	3 hr. 40 min.
Chester	Euston	16	179	2 hr. 36 min.
Exeter	Paddington	17	174	1 hr. 55 min.
Leeds	Kings Cross	19	185	2 hr. 12 min.
Liverpool	Euston	14	193	2 hr. 34 min.
Manchester	Euston	16	180	2 hr. 27 min.
Newcastle	Kings Cross	26	268	2 hr. 50 min.
Penzance	Paddington	9	305	5 hr.
Plymouth	Paddington	14	226	2 hr. 35 min.
York	Kings Cross	27	188	1 hr. 57 min.

just 2 blocks from Victoria Station. For information, call ✆ **020/7222-1234** (www.tfl.gov.uk), 24 hours a day. For cash purchases, get there at least 30 minutes before the coach departs.

National Express (✆ **0870/580-8080;** www.nationalexpress.com) runs long-distance coaches that are equipped with reclining seats, toilets, and nonsmoking areas. You can obtain details about all coach services by calling the company between 8am and 10pm daily. The National Express ticket office at Victoria Station is open from 6am to 11pm daily.

For journeys within a 56km (35-mile) radius of London, try **Green Line** coach service, 23–27 Endsleigh Rd., Merstham Redhill, Surrey RH1 3LX (✆ **0870/608-7261;** www.greenline.co.uk).

Green Line has bus routes called Country Bus Lines that circle the periphery of London. Though they do not usually go directly into the center of the capital, they hook up with the routes of the Green Line coaches and red buses that do.

To the delight of the frugal traveler, a new no-frills bus service has been introduced in England. **Megabus.com** (✆ **0901/332-0031;** 10p/20¢ per min.)

charges the lowest bus fares in the country—only £1 to £5 ($2–$10) for a single journey on any route. From London, popular stops include Oxford, Brighton, and the old port of Plymouth. The network uses double-decker buses that once rolled through the streets of Hong Kong. Reserve at **www.megabus.com**, which levies a booking charge of less than a U.S. dollar.

In Wales, 65 independent bus operators serve the little country. Public transport guides for local areas are available at tourist offices. One of the most important is **Arriva Cymru** (✆ **08448/004411;** www.arriva.co.uk), servicing North Wales. The area around Cardiff is covered by **Cardiff Bus** (✆ **029/2066-6444;** www.cardiffbus.com).

BY PLANE

British Airways (BA; ✆ **800/AIRWAYS** [247-9297]) flies to more than 20 cities outside London, including Manchester.

To get to the heart of England quickly, visitors fly BA to Manchester, operating a dozen flights a day from London's Heathrow and seven daily flights from Gatwick.

5 Money & Costs

London is becoming one of the most expensive cities on the planet, far more expensive than New York (Brits now view the Big Apple as a bargain basement). London is not as expensive as Tokyo or Oslo, but even an average hotel rate can cost £100 ($200) or more—in many cases, much, much more.

You'll avoid lines at airport ATMs by exchanging at least some money—just enough to cover airport incidentals and transportation to your hotel—before you leave home (though don't expect the exchange rate to be ideal). You can exchange money at your local American Express or Thomas Cook office or at your bank. American Express also dispenses traveler's checks and foreign currency via www.americanexpress.com or *©* **800/ 673-3782,** but they'll charge a $15 order fee and additional shipping costs.

POUNDS & PENCE

Britain's decimal monetary system is based on the pound (£), which is made up of 100 pence (written as "p"). Pounds are also called **quid** by Britons. There are £1 and £2 coins, as well as coins of 50p, 20p, 10p, 5p, 2p, and 1p. Bank notes come in denominations of £5, £10, £20, and £50.

As a general guideline, the price conversions in this book have been computed at the rate of £1 = $2.

ATMs

ATMs, sometimes referred to as "cash machines" or "cashpoints," are widely available in Britain, certainly in all cities and bigger towns, and even at a bank or two in smaller places. But don't always count on it. If you're venturing into rural England, it's always good to have pounds in your pocket.

The **Cirrus** (*©* **800/424-7787;** www.mastercard.com) and **PLUS** (*©* **800/ 843-7587;** www.visa.com) networks span the globe; look at the back of your bank card to see which network you're on, then call or check online for ATM locations at your destination. Be sure you know your personal identification number (PIN) and daily withdrawal limit before you depart.

There are problems involved in the use of ATMs. For example, if you make a mistake and punch your secret code wrong into the machine three times, that machine will swallow your card on the assumption that it is being fraudulently used.

Users with alphabetical rather than numerical PINs may be thrown off by the lack of letters on English cash machines. If your PIN is longer than four digits, check with your bank to see if you can use the first four digits; if not, you will have to get a new number for use in Britain.

To get cash advance by using a credit card at an ATM, ask for a PIN from your credit card company such as Visa before leaving your home country.

Note: Remember that many banks impose a fee every time you use a card at another bank's ATM, and that fee can be higher for international transactions (up to $5 or more) than for domestic ones (where they're rarely more than $2). In addition, the bank from which you withdraw cash may charge its own fee. For international withdrawal fees, ask your bank.

CREDIT CARDS

Credit cards are another safe way to carry money, but their use has become more difficult, especially in England (see below). They also provide a convenient record of all your expenses, and they generally offer relatively good exchange rates. You can usually withdraw cash advances from your credit cards at banks or ATMs, provided you know your PIN. Keep in mind that you'll pay interest from the moment of your withdrawal, even if you pay your monthly bills on time. Also,

The British Pound vs. the U.S. Dollar, the Euro & the Canadian Dollar

Conversion rates between the world's major currencies can and do fluctuate frequently, and their relative differences at the time of your visit could affect the costs of your trip. The chart below should be accepted only for approximate values of relatively small financial transactions. If you're planning on any major expenditures, check for updated ratios at the time of your trip. The chart below was compiled just before this edition's press time with the following ratios: £1 equals approximately US$2, 1.30€, and C$2. For up-to-the-minute currency conversions, check with **www.oanda.com**.

UK£	US$	Euro €	C$	UK£	US$	Euro €	C$
1.00	2.00	1.30	2.00	75.00	150.00	97.50	150.00
2.00	4.00	2.60	4.00	100.00	200.00	130.00	200.00
3.00	6.00	3.90	6.00	125.00	250.00	162.50	250.00
4.00	8.00	5.20	8.00	150.00	300.00	195.00	300.00
5.00	10.00	6.50	10.00	175.00	350.00	227.50	350.00
6.00	12.00	7.80	12.00	200.00	400.00	260.00	400.00
7.00	14.00	9.10	14.00	225.00	450.00	292.50	450.00
8.00	16.00	10.40	16.00	250.00	500.00	325.00	500.00
9.00	18.00	11.70	18.00	275.00	550.00	357.50	550.00
10.00	20.00	13.00	20.00	300.00	600.00	390.00	600.00
15.00	30.00	19.50	30.00	350.00	700.00	455.00	700.00
20.00	40.00	26.00	40.00	400.00	800.00	520.00	800.00
25.00	50.00	32.50	50.00	500.00	1,000.00	650.00	1,000.00
50.00	100.00	65.00	100.00	1,000.00	2,000.00	1,300.00	2,000.00

note that many banks now assess a 1% to 3% "transaction fee" on *all* charges you incur abroad (whether you're using the local currency or your native currency).

There is almost no difference in the acceptance of a debit or a standard credit card.

More and more places in England are moving from the magnetic strip credit card to the new system of "Chip and Pin." With these cards, you must enter a four-digit PIN on a keypad when making a transaction.

In the changeover in technology, some retailers have falsely concluded that they can no longer take swipe cards, or can't take signature cards that don't have PINs. For the time being both the new and old cards are used in shops, hotels, and restaurants regardless of whether they have the old credit and debit cards machines or the new Chip and Pin machines installed. Expect a lot of confusion before you arrive in England or elsewhere.

Warning: Some establishments in Britain might not accept your credit card unless you have a computer chip imbedded in it. The reason? To cut down on credit card fraud.

TRAVELER'S CHECKS

You can buy traveler's checks at most banks, and they are widely accepted in England, although frankly merchants prefer cash. Because of difficulties with credit cards (see above) or ATMs that can reject

What Things Cost in London	UK£	US$	Euro €	C$
Taxi from Heathrow to central London	50.00–70.00	100.00–140.00	65.00–91.00	100.00–140.00
Underground from Heathrow to central London	4.00	8.00	5.20	8.00
Double room at the Dorchester (very expensive)	465.00	930.00	604.50	930.00
Double room at the Hallam Hotel (expensive)	100.00	200.00	130.00	200.00
Double room at the Boston Court (inexpensive)	80.00	160.00	104.00	160.00
Lunch for one at Shepherd's (expensive)	24.00	48.00	31.20	48.00
Lunch for one at Ye Olde Cheshire Cheese (inexpensive)	16.00	32.00	20.80	32.00
Dinner for one, without wine, at Bibendum, the Oyster Bar (expensive)	36.00	72.00	46.80	72.00
Dinner for one, without wine, at Porter's English Restaurant (moderate)	22.00	44.00	28.60	44.00
Dinner for one, without wine, at Cork & Bottle Wine Bar (inexpensive)	18.00	36.00	23.40	36.00
Pint of beer	3.00	6.00	3.90	6.00
Coca-Cola (large)	2.00	4.00	2.60	4.00
Cup of coffee	1.80	3.60	2.35	3.60
Admission to British Museum	Free	Free	Free	Free
Movie Ticket	8.00	16.00	10.40	16.00
Theater ticket	25.00–85.00	50.00–170.00	32.50–110.50	50.00–170.00

your card for no apparent reason, travelers are once again buying traveler's checks for security in case something goes wrong with their plastic. They are offered in denominations of $20, $50, $100, $500, and sometimes $1,000. Generally, you'll pay a service charge ranging from 1% to 4%.

The most popular traveler's checks are offered by **American Express** (© **800/ 528-4800,** or 800/221-7282 for cardholders—this number accepts collect calls, offers service in several foreign languages, and exempts AmEx gold and platinum cardholders from the 1% fee) and **Visa** (© **800/732-1322**). AAA members can obtain Visa checks for a $9.95 fee (for checks up to $1,500) at most AAA offices or by calling © **866/339-3378.** Call © **800/223-9920** for information on **MasterCard** traveler's checks.

American Express, Thomas Cook, Visa, and **MasterCard** offer **foreign**

currency traveler's checks, which are useful if you're traveling to one country, or to the euro zone; they're accepted at locations where dollar checks may not be.

If you carry traveler's checks, keep a record of their serial numbers separate from your checks in the event that they are stolen or lost—you'll get your refund faster.

6 Health

STAYING HEALTHY

Traveling to England doesn't pose any health risk. The tap water is safe to drink, the milk is pasteurized, and health services are good. The crisis regarding mad-cow disease is long over, as is the foot-and-mouth disease epidemic.

England has some of the greatest medical services in the world. And, get this, all the doctors speak English. It is easy to get over-the-counter medicine, and general equivalents of common prescription drugs are available throughout the British Isles.

GENERAL AVAILABILITY OF HEALTHCARE

Contact the **International Association for Medical Assistance to Travelers (IAMAT;** ℭ **716/754-4883,** or 416/652-0137 in Canada; www.iamat.org) for tips on travel and health concerns in the countries you're visiting, and for lists of local, English-speaking doctors. The United States **Centers for Disease Control and Prevention** (ℭ **800/311-3435** or 404/498-1515; www.cdc.gov) provides up-to-date information on health hazards by region or country and offers tips on food safety. The website **www.tripprep.com**, sponsored by a consortium of travel medicine practitioners, may also offer helpful advice on traveling abroad. You can find listings of reliable clinics overseas at the **International Society of Travel Medicine** (www.istm.org).

WHAT TO DO IF YOU GET SICK AWAY FROM HOME

If you need a doctor, your hotel can recommend one, or you can contact your embassy or consulate. Outside London, dial ℭ **100** and ask the operator for the local police, who will give you the name, address, and telephone number of a doctor in your area. *Note:* U.S. visitors who become ill while they're in Britain are eligible only for free *emergency* care. For other treatment, including follow-up care, you'll be asked to pay.

In most cases, your existing health plan will provide the coverage you need. But double-check; you may want to buy **travel medical insurance** instead. (See the section on insurance, under "Fast Facts: England & Wales" in the appendix; p. 752.) Bring your insurance ID card with you when you travel.

If you suffer from a chronic illness, consult your doctor before your departure. For conditions such as epilepsy, diabetes, or heart problems, wear a **MedicAlert Identification Tag** (ℭ **888/ 633-4298** or 209/668-3333; www.medic alert.org), which will immediately alert doctors to your condition and give them access to your records through MedicAlert's 24-hour hot line.

Pack **prescription medications** in your carry-on luggage and carry prescription medications in their original containers, with pharmacy labels—otherwise they won't make it through airport security. Also bring along copies of your prescriptions, in case you lose your pills or run out. Don't forget an extra pair of contact lenses or prescription glasses. Carry the generic name of prescription medicines, in case a local pharmacist is unfamiliar with the brand name.

We list **additional emergency numbers** in the "Fast Facts: England & Wales" section of the appendix, p. 752.

Avoiding "Economy-Class Syndrome"

Deep vein thrombosis, or as it's known in the world of flying, "economy-class syndrome," is a blood clot that develops in a deep vein. It's a potentially deadly condition that can be caused by sitting in cramped conditions—such as an airplane cabin—for too long. During a flight (especially a long-haul flight), get up, walk around, and stretch your legs every 60 to 90 minutes to keep your blood flowing. Other preventative measures include frequent flexing of the legs while sitting, drinking lots of water, and avoiding alcohol and sleeping pills. If you have a history of deep vein thrombosis, heart disease, or another condition that puts you at high risk, some experts recommend wearing compression stockings or taking anticoagulants when you fly; always ask your physician about the best course for you. Symptoms of deep vein thrombosis include leg pain or swelling, or even shortness of breath.

7 Safety

STAYING SAFE

Like all big cities, London has its share of crime, but in general it is one of the safer destinations of Europe. Pickpockets are a major concern, though violent crime is relatively rare, especially in the heart of London, which hasn't seen a Jack the Ripper in a long time. Even so, it is not wise to go walking in parks at night. In London, take all the precautions a prudent traveler would in going anywhere, be it Los Angeles, Paris, or New York. Conceal your wallet or else hold onto your purse, and don't flaunt jewelry or cash. In other words, do as your mother told you.

The same precautions prevail in larger cities such as Birmingham, Leeds, and Manchester. However, in rural Britain you are relatively safe, though if you watch a lot of murder mysteries on TV or read about them in paperbacks, there seem to be a lot of murders going on. Nonetheless, Britain is one of the safer destinations of the world, but the sensible precautions you would heed anywhere prevail, of course. In these uncertain times, it is always prudent to check the U.S. Department of State's travel advisories at **www.travel.state.gov**.

Motorists should know that sleeping in your car is not only potentially dangerous but also illegal in the U.K., and there are always perils linked to hitchhiking, which is not recommended.

Any unrest or protest demonstrations around London's Trafalgar Square should not concern the usual visitor, who is advised to stay out of the area during any demonstrations.

Local law-enforcement officials in Britain have a long history of being fair and impartial to visitors, even those from Third World or Middle Eastern countries. Unlike Germany, England seems to practice great tolerance, more so than parts of America. There is little racial, ethnic, or religious discrimination, including that of sexual preference.

Women traveling alone encounter less aggressive or so-called macho behavior than they will find in such countries as Spain and Italy. Of course, discretion is always advised—that is, don't get in a car, of course, with three lager louts at 2 o'clock in the morning.

8 Specialized Travel Resources

TRAVELERS WITH DISABILITIES

Many London hotels, museums, restaurants, and sightseeing attractions have wheelchair ramps, less so in rural England. Persons with disabilities are often granted special discounts—called "concessions" in Britain—at attractions and, in some cases, nightclubs. Free information and advice is available from **Holiday Care Service,** The Hawkins Suite, Enham Place, Andover SP11 6JS (② **0845/124-9971;** fax 0845/124-9972; www.holidaycare.org.uk).

Many bookstores in London carry *Access in London* (www.accessinlondon. org; £12/$24), a publication listing facilities for persons with disabilities, among other things.

The transport system, cinemas, and theaters are still pretty much off-limits, but **Transport for London** publishes a leaflet called *Access to the Underground,* which gives details of elevators and ramps at individual Underground stations; call ② **020/7222-1234** or visit www.tfl.gov. uk. And **London Black Cab** (② **0845/ 108-3000;** www.londonblackcab.com) vehicles are perfectly suited for those in wheelchairs; the roomy interiors have plenty of room for maneuvering.

London's most visible organization for information about access to theaters, cinemas, galleries, museums, and restaurants is **Artsline,** 54 Chalton St., London NW1 1HS (② **020/7388-2227;** fax 020/7383-2653; www.artsline.org.uk). It offers free information about wheelchair access, theaters with hearing aids, tourist attractions, and cinemas. Artsline mails information to North America, but it's more helpful to contact Artsline once you arrive in London; the line is staffed Monday to Friday 9:30am to 5:30pm.

Many travel agencies offer customized tours and itineraries for travelers with disabilities. **Flying Wheels Travel** (② **507/ 451-5005;** www.flyingwheelstravel.com) offers escorted tours and cruises that emphasize sports and private tours in minivans with lifts. **Access-Able Travel Source** (② **303/232-2979;** www.access-able.com) offers extensive access information and advice for traveling around the world with disabilities. **Accessible Journeys** (② **800/846-4537** or 610/521-0339; www.disabilitytravel.com) caters specifically to slow walkers and wheelchair travelers and their families and friends.

Organizations that offer assistance to travelers with disabilities include **MossRehab** (② **215/663-6000;** www. mossresourcenet.org/travel.htm), which provides a library of accessible-travel resources online; the **American Foundation for the Blind** (AFB; ② **800/ 232-5463** or 212/502-7600; www.afb. org), a referral resource for the blind or visually impaired that includes information on traveling with Seeing Eye dogs; and **SATH** (Society for Accessible Travel & Hospitality; ② **212/447-7284;** www. sath.org), which offers a wealth of travel resources for all types of disabilities and informed recommendations on destinations, access guides, travel agents, tour operators, vehicle rentals, and companion services. **Air Ambulance Card** (② **877/ 424-7633;** www.airambulancecard.com) allows you to preselect top-notch hospitals in case of an emergency.

The "Accessible Travel" link at **Mobility-Advisor.com** (www.mobility-advisor.com) offers a variety of travel resources to persons with disabilities.

Check out the quarterly magazine *Emerging Horizons* (www.emerging horizons.com), published by SATH.

Information for travelers with disabilities going to Wales is available from **Disability Wales,** Bridge House, Caerphilly Business Park, Van Road, Caerphilly CF83 3GW (② **029/2088-7325;** www.disability wales.org). The staff can tell you about facilities suitable in touring, accommodations, restaurants, cafes, pubs, public restrooms, attractions, and other phases of hospitality to make a trip pleasurable.

For more on organizations that offer resources to travelers with disabilities, go to www.frommers.com/planning.

GAY & LESBIAN TRAVELERS

Britain has one of the most active gay and lesbian scenes in the world, centered mainly in London, much less so in Cardiff. Gay bars, restaurants, and centers are also found in all large English cities, notably Bath, Birmingham, Manchester, and especially Brighton.

Lesbian and Gay Switchboard (© 020/7837-7324; www.llgs.org.uk) is open 24 hours a day, providing information about gay-related activities in London or advice in general. London's best gay-oriented bookstore is **Gay's the Word,** 66 Marchmont St., WC1N 1AB (© 020/7278-7654; www.gaystheword.co.uk; Tube: Russell Sq.), the largest such store in Britain. The staff is friendly and helpful and will offer advice about the ever-changing scene in London. It's open Monday through Saturday from 10am to 6:30pm and Sunday from 2 to 6pm. At Gay's the Word and other gay-friendly venues, you can find a number of publications, many free, including the popular *Boyz.* Another free publication is *Pink Paper* (with a good lesbian section), and check out *9X,* filled with data about new clubs and whatever else is hot on the scene.

The International Gay and Lesbian Travel Association (IGLTA; © 954/630-1637; www.iglta.org), the trade association for the gay and lesbian travel industry, offers an online directory of gay- and lesbian-friendly travel businesses.

Many agencies offer tours and travel itineraries specifically for gay and lesbian travelers. **Above and Beyond Tours** (© 800/397-2681; www.abovebeyond tours.com) is a gay and lesbian tour operator. **Now, Voyager** (© 800/255-6951; www.nowvoyager.com) is a well-known San Francisco–based gay-owned and -operated travel service. **Gay.com Travel** (© 415/834-6500; www.gay.com/travel or www.outandabout.com) is an excellent online successor to the popular *Out & About* print magazine. It provides regularly updated information about gay-owned, -oriented, and -friendly lodging, dining, sightseeing, nightlife, and shopping establishments in every important destination worldwide.

The following travel guides are available at many bookstores, or you can order them from any online bookseller: *Spartacus International Gay Guide* (Bruno Gmünder Verlag; www.spartacusworld.com) and *Odysseus: The International Gay Travel Planner* (Odysseus Enterprises, Ltd.); and the *Damron* guides (www.damron.com), with separate, annual books for gay men and lesbians.

For more gay and lesbian travel resources, visit www.frommers.com/planning.

SENIOR TRAVEL

Be advised that in Britain you often have to be a member of an association to get senior discounts. Public-transportation discounts, for example, are available only to holders of British Pension books. However, many attractions do offer discounts for seniors (women 60 or older and men 65 or older). Even if discounts aren't posted, ask if they're available.

If you're older than 60, you're eligible for special 10% discounts on **British Airways** through its Privileged Traveler program. You also qualify for reduced restrictions on APEX cancellations. Discounts are also granted for BA tours and for intra-Britain air tickets booked in North America. **BritRail** offers seniors discounted rates on first-class rail passes around Britain. See "By Train from Continental Europe" in the "Getting There & Getting Around" section, earlier in this chapter.

Don't be shy about asking for discounts, but carry some kind of identification that shows your date of birth. Also, mention you're a senior when you make your reservations. Many hotels offer seniors discounts. In most cities, people older than the age of 60 qualify for reduced admission to theaters, museums, and other attractions, and discounted fares on public transportation.

Members of **AARP,** 601 E St. NW, Washington, DC 20049 (© **888/ 687-2277;** www.aarp.org), get discounts on hotels, airfares, and car rentals. AARP offers members a wide range of benefits, including *AARP The Magazine* and a monthly newsletter. Anyone older than 50 can join.

Many reliable agencies and organizations target the 50-plus market. **Elderhostel** (© **800/454-5768;** www.elderhostel. org) arranges worldwide study programs for those ages 55 and older.

Recommended publications offering travel resources and discounts for seniors include the quarterly magazine *Travel 50 & Beyond* (www.travel50and beyond.com); *Unbelievably Good Deals and Great Adventures That You Absolutely Can't Get Unless You're Over 50* (McGraw-Hill), by Joann Rattner Heilman.

www.frommers.com/planning offers more information and resources on travel for seniors.

FAMILY TRAVEL

If you have enough trouble getting your kids out of the house in the morning, dragging them thousands of miles away may seem like an insurmountable challenge. But family travel can be immensely rewarding, giving you new ways of seeing the world through smaller pairs of eyes.

On airlines, you must request a special menu for children at least 24 hours in advance. If baby food is required, however, bring your own and ask a flight attendant to warm it to the right temperature.

Arrange ahead of time for such necessities as a crib, a bottle warmer, and a car seat (in England, small children aren't allowed to ride in the front seat).

If you're staying with friends in London, you can rent baby equipment from **Chelsea Baby Hire,** 31 Osborne House, 414 Wimbledon Park Rd., SW19 6PW (© 020/8789-9673; www.chelseababy hire.com). **London Black Cab** (© **0845/ 108-3000;** www.londonblackcab.com) is a lifesaver for families; the roomy interior allows a stroller to be lifted right into the cab without unstrapping the baby.

You can find babysitting available at most hotels.

Before you go, help your kids check out London Tourist Board's **Kids Love London** at **www.kidslovelondon.com**, a site created to give kids the lowdown on kid-friendly attractions and events.

To locate those accommodations, restaurants, and attractions that are particularly kid-friendly, refer to the "Kids" icon throughout this guide.

Recommended family-travel Internet sites include **Family Travel Forum** (www. familytravelforum.com), a comprehensive site that offers customized trip planning; **Family Travel Network** (www.familytravel network.com), an award-winning site that offers travel features, deals, and tips; **Traveling Internationally with Your Kids** (www.travelwithyourkids.com), a comprehensive site offering sound advice for long-distance and international travel with children; and **Family Travel Files** (www. thefamilytravelfiles.com), which offers an online magazine and a directory of off-the-beaten-path tours and tour operators for families.

Some Frommer's guides were written specifically for families, including *Frommer's London with Kids, Frommer's Devon & Cornwall with Your family,* and *Frommer's Wales with Your Family.*

For a list of more family-friendly travel resources, turn to the experts at www. frommers.com/planning.

AFRICAN-AMERICAN TRAVELERS

Black Travel Online (www.blacktravel online.com) posts news on upcoming events and includes links to articles and travel-booking sites. **Soul of America** (www.soulofamerica.com) is a comprehensive website, with travel tips, event and family-reunion postings, and sections on historically black beach resorts and active vacations.

Agencies and organizations that provide resources for black travelers include **Rodgers Travel** (✆ 888/823-1775; www.rodgerstravel.com). For more information, check out the following collections and guides: *Go Girl: The Black Woman's Guide to Travel & Adventure* (Eighth Mountain Press), a compilation of travel essays; *The African American Travel Guide* by John Haggins (Hunter Publishing); *Steppin' Out* by Carla Labat (Avalon); *Pathfinders Magazine* (✆ 215/ 438-2140; www.pathfinderstravel.com), which includes articles on everything from Rio de Janeiro to Ghana, as well as information on upcoming ski, dive, golf, and tennis trips.

STUDENT TRAVEL

If you plan to travel outside the U.S., you'd be wise to arm yourself with an **International Student Identity Card (ISIC),** which offers substantial savings on rail passes, plane tickets, and entrance fees. It also provides you with basic health and life insurance and a 24-hour help line. The card is available for $22 from **STA Travel** (✆ 800/781-4040; www.sta.com), the biggest student travel agency in the world. If you're no longer a student but are still 25 or younger, you can get an **International Youth Travel Card (IYTC)** for the same price from the same people, which entitles you to some discounts (but not on museum admissions).

Travel CUTS (✆ 800/592-2887; www.travelcuts.com) offers similar services for both Canadians and U.S. residents.

Irish students should turn to **USIT** (✆ 01/602-1906; www.usitnow.ie).

The International Student House, 229 Great Portland St., W1W 5PN (✆ 020/ 7631-8310; www.ish.org.uk), lies at the foot of Regent's Park in London across from the Tube stop for Great Portland Street. It's a beehive of activity, such as discos and film showings, and rents blandly furnished, institutional rooms. Laundry facilities are available and a key deposit is charged. Reserve way in advance.

University of London Student Union, Malet Street, WC1E 7HY (✆ 020/ 7664-2000; www.ulu.co.uk; Tube: Goodge St. or Russell Sq.), is the best place to go to learn about student activities in the greater London area. The Union has a swimming pool, fitness center, gymnasium, general store, sports shop, ticket agency, banks, bars, inexpensive restaurants, venues for live events, an office of STA Travel, and many other facilities. It's open Monday to Thursday 8:30am to 11pm, Friday 8:30am to 1pm, Saturday 9am to 2pm, and Sunday 9:30am to 10:30pm. Bulletin boards provide a rundown on events; some you may be able to attend, others may be "closed door."

SINGLE TRAVELERS

Many people prefer traveling alone, and for independent travelers, solo journeys offer infinite opportunities to make friends and meet locals. Unfortunately, if you like resorts, tours, or cruises, you're likely to get hit with a "single supplement" to the base price. Single travelers can avoid these supplements, of course, by agreeing to room with other single travelers on the trip. An even better idea is to find a compatible roommate before you go, from one of the many roommate locator agencies.

Travel Buddies Singles Travel Club (✆ 800/998-9099; www.travelbuddies worldwide.com), based in Canada, runs small, intimate, single-friendly group trips and will match you with a roommate free of charge and save you the cost of single supplements. **TravelChums** (© 212/787-2621; www.travelchums.com) is an Internet-only travel-companion matching service with elements of an online personals-type site, hosted by the respected New York–based Shaw Guides travel service.

Many reputable tour companies offer singles-only trips. **Singles Travel International** (© 877/765-6874; www.singlestravelintl.com) offers singles-only trips to London. **Backroads** (© 800/462-2848; www.backroads.com) offers more than 160 active trips to 30 destinations worldwide, including England.

For more information on traveling single, go to www.frommers.com/planning.

9 Sustainable Tourism

Sustainable tourism is conscientious travel. It means being careful with the environments you explore, and respecting the communities you visit. Two overlapping components of sustainable travel are **eco-tourism** and **ethical tourism.** The **International Ecotourism Society (TIES)** defines eco-tourism as responsible travel to natural areas that conserves the environment and improves the well-being of local people. TIES suggests that eco-tourists follow these principles:

- Minimize environmental impact.
- Build environmental and cultural awareness and respect.
- Provide positive experiences for both visitors and hosts.
- Provide direct financial benefits for conservation and for local people.
- Raise sensitivity to host countries' political, environmental, and social climates.
- Support international human rights and labor agreements.

You can find some eco-friendly travel tips and statistics, as well as touring companies and associations—listed by destination under "Travel Choice"—at the TIES website, www.ecotourism.org. Also check out **Ecotravel.com,** which lets you search for sustainable touring companies in several categories (water-based, land-based, spiritually oriented, and so on).

While much of the focus of eco-tourism is about reducing impacts on the natural environment, ethical tourism concentrates on ways to preserve and enhance local economies and communities, regardless of location. You can embrace ethical tourism by staying at a locally owned hotel or shopping at a store that employs local workers and sells locally produced goods.

Responsible Travel (www.responsibletravel.com) is a great source of sustainable travel ideas; the site is run by a spokesperson for ethical tourism in the travel industry. **Sustainable Travel International** (www.sustainabletravelinternational.org) promotes ethical tourism practices, and manages an extensive directory of sustainable properties and tour operators around the world.

In the U.K., **Tourism Concern** (www.tourismconcern.org.uk) works to reduce social and environmental problems connected to tourism. The **Association of Independent Tour Operators (AITO;** www.aito.co.uk) is a group of specialist operators leading the field in making holidays sustainable.

The **Association of British Travel Agents (ABTA;** www.abta.com) acts as a focal point for the U.K. travel industry and is one of the leading groups spearheading responsible tourism.

Volunteer travel has become popular among those who want to venture beyond the standard group-tour experience to learn languages, interact with locals, and make a positive difference

Tips It's Easy Being Green

Here are a few simple ways you can help conserve fuel and energy when you travel:

- Each time you take a flight or drive a car, greenhouse gases release into the atmosphere. You can help neutralize this danger to the planet through "carbon offsetting"—paying someone to invest your money in programs that reduce your greenhouse gas emissions by the same amount you've added. Before buying carbon offset credits, just make sure that you're using a reputable company, one with a proven program that invests in renewable energy. Reliable carbon offset companies include **Carbonfund** (www.carbonfund.org) and **TerraPass** (www.terrapass.org).

    Whenever possible, choose nonstop flights; they generally require less fuel than indirect flights that stop and take off again. Try to fly during the day—some scientists estimate that nighttime flights are twice as harmful to the environment. And pack light—each 15 pounds of luggage on a 5,000-mile flight adds up to 50 pounds of carbon dioxide emitted.

- Where you stay during your travels can have a major environmental impact. To determine the green credentials of a property, ask about trash disposal and recycling, water conservation, and energy use; also question if sustainable materials were used in the construction of the property. The website **www.greenhotels.com** recommends green-rated member hotels around the world that fulfill the company's stringent environmental requirements. Also consult **www.environmentallyfriendlyhotels.com** for more green accommodations ratings.

- At hotels, request that your sheets and towels not be changed daily. (Many hotels already have programs like this in place.) Turn off the lights and air conditioner (or heater) when you leave your room.

- Use public transport where possible—trains, buses, and even taxis are more energy-efficient forms of transport than driving. Even better is to walk or cycle; you'll produce zero emissions and stay fit and healthy on your travels.

- If renting a car is necessary, ask the rental agent for a hybrid, or rent the most fuel-efficient car available. You'll use less gas and save money at the tank.

- Eat at locally owned and operated restaurants that use produce grown in the area. This contributes to the local economy and cuts down on greenhouse gas emissions by supporting restaurants where the food is not flown or trucked in across long distances.

while on vacation. Volunteer travel usually doesn't require special skills—just a willingness to work hard—and programs vary in length from a few days to a number of weeks. Some programs provide free housing and food, but many require volunteers to pay for travel expenses, which can add up quickly.

For general info on volunteer travel, visit **www.volunteerabroad.org** and **www.idealist.org**.

Frommers.com: The Complete Travel Resource

Planning a trip, or just returned? Head to **Frommers.com,** voted Best Travel Site by *PC Magazine.* We think you'll find our site indispensable before, during, and after your travels—with expert advice and tips; independent reviews of hotels, restaurants, attractions, and preferred shopping and nightlife venues; vacation giveaways; and an online booking tool. We publish the complete contents of more than 135 travel guides in our **Destinations** section, covering more than 4,000 places worldwide. Each weekday, we publish original articles that report on **Deals and News** via our free **Frommers.com Newsletters.** What's more, **Arthur Frommer** himself blogs 5 days a week, with cutting opinions about the state of travel in the modern world. We're betting you'll find our **Events** listings an invaluable resource; it's an up-to-the-minute roster of what's happening in cities everywhere—including concerts, festivals, lectures, and more. We've also added weekly **podcasts, interactive maps,** and hundreds of new images across the site. Finally, don't forget to visit our **message boards,** where you can join in conversations with thousands of fellow Frommer's travelers and post your trip report once you return.

Before you commit to a volunteer program, it's important to make sure any money you're giving is truly going back to the local community, and that the work you'll be doing will be a good fit for you. **Volunteer International** (www.volunteerinternational.org) has a helpful list of questions to ask to determine the intentions and the nature of a volunteer program.

10 Packages for the Independent Traveler

Package tours are simply a way to buy the airfare, accommodations, and other elements of your trip (such as car rentals, airport transfers, and sometimes even activities) at the same time and often at discounted prices.

One good source of package deals is the airlines themselves. Most major airlines offer air/land packages, including **American Airlines Vacations** (© 800 /321-2121; www.aavacations.com), **Delta Vacations** (© 800/654-6559; www.deltavacations.com), **Continental Airlines Vacations** (© 800/301-3800; www.covacations.com), and **United Vacations** (© 888/854-3899; www.unitedvacations.com). Several big **online travel agencies**—Expedia, Travelocity,

Orbitz, Site59, and Lastminute.com—also do a brisk business in packages.

Far and away, the most options are with **British Airways Holidays** (© 877/ 428-2228; www.baholidays.com). Its offerings within the British Isles are more comprehensive than those of its competitors and can be tailored to your specific interests and budget. Many tours, such as the 9-day, all-inclusive tour through the great houses and gardens of England, include the ongoing services of a guide and lecturer. But if you prefer to travel independently, without following an organized tour, a sales representative can tailor an itinerary specifically for you, with discounted rates in a wide assortment of big-city hotels. If you opt for this, you can rent a car or choose to take the train. For a free catalog and additional information, call British Airways before you book; some of the company's available options are contingent upon the purchase of a round-trip transatlantic air ticket.

Travel packages are also listed in the travel section of your local Sunday newspaper. Or check ads in the national travel magazines such as *Arthur Frommer's Budget Travel Magazine, Travel + Leisure, National Geographic Traveler,* and *Condé Nast Traveler.*

For more information on Package Tours and for tips on booking your trip, see www.frommers.com/planning.

11 Escorted General-Interest Tours

Escorted tours are structured group tours, with a group leader. The price usually includes everything from airfare to hotels, meals, tours, admission costs, and local transportation.

Abercrombie & Kent (© 800/554-7016; www.abercrombiekent.com) offers extremely upscale escorted tours that are loaded with luxury. They're the best in the business.

Other contenders in the upscale package-tour business include **Maupintour** (© 800/255-4266; www.maupintour.com) and **Tauck World Discovery** (© 800/788-7885; www.tauck.com).

But not all escorted tours are so pricey. Older British folks make up a large portion of the clientele of one of the United Kingdom's largest tour operators, **Wallace Arnold Worldchoice** (© 0845/365-6747; www.waworldchoice.com). Most of the company's tours last between 5 and 10 days, include lodgings (at solid but not particularly extravagant hotels) and most meals, and are reasonably priced.

U.S.-based **Trafalgar Tours** (© 866/544-4434; www.trafalgartours.com) offers more affordable packages with lodgings in unpretentious but comfortable hotels. It's one of Europe's largest tour operators. There may not be a lot of frills, but you can find 7-day itineraries priced from $1,075 per person, double occupancy, without airfare, that include stopovers in Stratford-upon-Avon and Bath; they also offer 8-day packages at first-class hotels in London, starting at $899 per person, double occupancy.

One of Trafalgar's leading competitors, known for roughly equivalent moderately priced tours through Britain, is **Globus & Cosmos Tours** (© 866/755-8581; www.globusandcosmos.com).

Despite the fact that escorted tours require big deposits and predetermine hotels, restaurants, and itineraries, many people derive security and peace of mind from the structure they offer. Escorted tours—whether they're navigated by bus, motorcoach, train, or boat—let travelers sit back and enjoy the trip without having to drive or worry about details. They take you to the maximum number of sights in the minimum amount of time with the least amount of hassle. They're particularly convenient for people with limited mobility and they can be a great way to make new friends.

On the downside, you'll have little opportunity for serendipitous interactions with locals. The tours can be jam-packed with activities, leaving little room for individual sightseeing, whim, or adventure—plus they often focus on the heavily touristed sites, so you miss out on many a lesser known gem.

For more information on escorted general-interest tours, including questions to ask before booking your trip, see www.frommers.com/planning.

12 Special-Interest Trips

BIKE TRIPS

Brits have rediscovered the bicycle: A **National Cycle Network** ⚤⚤ covers about 16,000km (10,000 miles) throughout the country. The network runs from Dover in southeast England to Inverness in the Highlands. Go to **www.sustrans.org.uk** for route maps.

Most routes cross old railway lines, canal towpaths, and riversides. Among the more popular routes are the Sea-to-Sea Cycle Route, a 225km (140-mile) path linking the Irish Sea with the North Sea across the Pennine Hills and into the north Lake District and the Durham Dales. The Essex Cycle Route covers 402km (250 miles) of countryside, going through some of England's most charming villages; the Devon Coast-to-Coast route—our favorite—runs for 145km (90 miles) in southwest England, skirting the edge of Dartmoor; the West Country Way for 399km (248 miles) links the Cornish coast to Bath and Bristol; and the Severn and Thames route for 161km (100 miles) links two of Britain's major rivers.

For a free copy of "Britain for Cyclists," with information on these routes, call the **British Tourist Authority** (© **800/462-2748** in the U.S., and © 888/847-4885 in Canada) or contact the **Cyclists Touring Club,** Parklands, Railton Road, Guildford, Surrey GU2 9JX (© **0870/873-0060;** in Wales call 01544/370666; www.ctc.org.uk), which can suggest routes and provide information. Memberships cost £35 ($70) a year.

A leader in these biking tours since 1974, **Euro-Bike & Walking Tours** ⚤ (© **800/321-6060;** www.eurobike.com in the U.S. and Canada) is currently the best outfitter. For more information, you can also write to Euro-Bike & Walking Tours, P.O. Box 990, DeKalb, IL 60115.

FISHING

Fly-fishing was born here, and it's an art form. Local fishing guides are available to lead you to English waters that are well stocked with trout, perch, grayling, sea bream, Atlantic salmon, and such lesser known species as rudd and roach.

If you prefer to go it alone without a guide, contact the **Salmon & Trout Association,** Fishmonger's Hall, London Bridge, London EC4R 9EL (© **020/7283-5838;** www.salmon-trout.org), for information about British fishing regulations.

An excellent guide to fishing is *Where to Fly Fish in Britain & Ireland,* available on Amazon.com. To learn about fishing holidays, contact **Angling Direct Holidays,** The Homestead, Thurgarton Road, Aldborough Norfolk NR11 2NY (© **01603/407596;** www.anglingdirectholidays.com).

GOLF

Though the sport originated in Scotland, golf has been around in Britain since Edward VII first began stamping over the greens of such courses as Royal Lytham & St. Annes, in England's northwest, or Royal St. Georges, near London.

The unyielding reality is that golf in Britain remains a clubby sport where some of the most prestigious courses are usually reserved exclusively for members. Rules at most British golf courses tend to be stricter in matters of dress code and protocol than their equivalents in the United States.

If, however, your heart is set on enjoying a round or two on the emerald-colored turf of Britain, **Golf International** ⚤, 14 E. 38th St., New York, NY 10016 (© **800/833-1389** or 212/986-9176; www.golfinternational.com), can open doors for you. Golf packages are arranged for anywhere from 7 to 14 days and can include as much or as little golf, on as many different courses, as a participant wants.

Worthy competitors that operate on a less comprehensive scale than Golf International include **Adventures in Golf,** 22 Greeley St., Ste. 7, Merrimack, NH 03054 (© **877/424-7320** or 603/424-7320; www.adventures-in-golf.com); and **Jerry Quinlan's Celtic Golf,** 1129 Rte. 9 South, Cape May Courthouse, NJ 08210 (© **800/535-6148** or 609/465-0600; www.celticgolf.com). Each of their tours is customized and usually includes lodging in anything from simple guesthouses to five-star deluxe manor houses.

HIKING, WALKING & RAMBLING

England and Wales alone have some 161,000km (100,000 miles) of trails and footpaths. The **Ramblers' Association,** Camelford House, 87–90 Albert Embankment, 2nd Floor, London SE1 7TW (© **020/7339-8500,** in Wales 029/2064-4308; www.ramblers.org.uk), has several books and maps on hiking and walking in Great Britain. Prices range from free to £15 ($30).

Wilderness Travel, Inc., 1102 Ninth St., Berkeley, CA 94710 (© **800/368-2794** or 510/558-2488; fax 510/558-2489; www.wildernesstravel.com), also specializes in treks and inn-to-inn hiking tours.

English Lakeland Ramblers ✿, 15404 Beachview Dr., Montclair, VA 22025 (© **800/724-8801** or 703/680-4276; www.ramblers.com), offers 7- or 8-day walking tours for the average active person. On its Lake District tour, you'll stay and have your meals in a charming 17th-century country inn near Ambleside and Windermere. A minibus takes hikers and sightseers daily to trails and sightseeing points. Experts tell you about the area's culture and history and highlight its natural wonders. There are also tours of the Cotswolds, as well as inn-to-inn tours and privately guided tours.

Other contenders include **Country Walkers,** P.O. Box 180, Waterbury, VT 05676 (© **800/464-9255** or 802/244-1387; www.countrywalkers.com). This company's "walking vacations" last 7 days either in the Cotswolds region or the Lake District.

To explore the mountain activities of Wales's Snowdonia National Park, contact Bob Postings at **Pathfinder,** Clynnog Fawr, Tan-yr-allt, Caernarfon, Gwynedd LL54 5NS, in North Wales (© **01286/660202;** www.pathfindersnowdonia.co.uk). Bob and his skilled team specialize in walking the summits, rock climbing, kayaking, and rafting, among other activities.

One of the best outfitters for walks through the West Country and the Cotswolds is **Walking Holidays** ✿ (© **01761/233807;** www.bathwestwalks. com). On these guided tours you take in such attractions as the Wiltshire Downs and the Mendip Hills, as well as the scenery of Exmoor with its coastline.

To read about the vast hiking possibilities of Britain, you can purchase on Amazon.com a copy of *Stilwell's National Trail Companion* (Stilwell Publishing, 2001) by Tim Stilwell, the ultimate where-to-stay guide for walkers, which also documents an extensive national system of 48 hiking trails through Britain.

HORSEBACK RIDING

Horseback riding is one of the reasons many visitors head to England in the first place. It is a country of great horsemen and horsewomen (no pun intended). For details about how to have such a vacation, contact **Cross Country International,** P.O. Box 1170, Millbrook, NY 12545 (© **800/828-8768;** www.equestrianvacations.com). Another choice for equestrian vacations is **Eastern Trekking Associates,** P.O. Box 357, Thomson, GA 30824 (© **888/836-6152** or 706/541-2450; www.horsevacations.com). Small groups of around six riders each are taken on tours of the Exmoor region, arguably the most beautiful district of England. Horseback riding holidays are also arranged in Wales.

A number of American companies offer horseback-riding package tours of Britain. **Equitour** ✪, P.O. Box 807, Dubois, WY 82513 (℗ **800/545-0019** or 307/455-3363; www.ridingtours.com), is one such firm, specializing in package tours for riding enthusiasts who want to experience the horsey traditions of the land of foxes and hounds. Two types of tours can be arranged: stationary tours, with instruction in jumping and dressage during a 7-day period at a stable beside the Bristol Channel or on the fields of Dartmoor, and a "progressive" tour in Wales, with a 7-day trek. Most riders, eager to experience as wide a view of England as possible, opt for the latter, spending nights at different B&Bs or inns and lodging their mount at nearby stables. Accommodations are simple, and prices are kept deliberately low.

UNIVERSITY STUDY PROGRAMS

You can study British literature at renowned universities such as Oxford and Cambridge during the week and then take weekend excursions to the countryside of Shakespeare, Austen, Dickens, and Hardy. While doing your coursework, you can live in dormitories with other students and dine in elaborate halls or the more intimate Fellows' clubs. Study programs in England are not limited to the liberal arts, or to high school or college students. Some programs are designed specifically for teachers and seniors. For more information, contact organizations listed below or in the section "Student Travel," earlier in this chapter.

Affiliated with Richmond College, in London, **American Institute for Foreign Study,** River Plaza, 9 W. Broad St., Stamford, CT 06902 (℗ **866/906-2437** or 203/399-5000; www.aifs.com), offers 4 weeks and up of traveling programs for high school students, and internships and academic programs for college students. There are also programs leading to the British equivalent of an MBA.

Institute of International Education (IIE), U.S. Student Programs Division, 809 United Nations Plaza, New York, NY 10017 (℗ **212/883-8200;** www.iie.org), administers a variety of academic, training, and grant programs for the U.S. Information Agency (USIA), including Fulbright grants. It is especially helpful in arranging enrollments for U.S. students in summer school programs.

Worldwide Classrooms, P.O. Box 1166, Milwaukee, WI 53201 (℗ **414/224-3476;** www.worldwide.edu), produces an extensive listing of schools offering study abroad programs in England.

13 Staying Connected

TELEPHONES

To call England from North America, dial **011** (international code), **44** (Britain's country code), the local area codes (usually three or four digits and found in every phone number we've given in this book), and the local phone number. The local area codes found throughout this book all begin with "0"; you drop the "0" if you're calling from outside Britain, but you need to dial it along with the area code if you're calling from another city or town within Britain. For calls within the same city or town, the local number is all you need.

For **directory assistance** in London, dial ℗ **142;** for the rest of Britain, ℗ **192.**

Within the U.K., despite the growing prevalence of mobile phones, you'll still find at least three kinds of **public pay phones:** Those relatively old-fashioned models that accept only coins; those accepting only prepaid phone cards; and those accepting both phone cards and credit cards. ***Note:*** The "old-fashioned" phone boxes with the royal coat of arms and the bright red coats of paint tend to be maintained by British Telecom and fall into the latter of these three categories. And those telephones that accept credit cards such as Access/MasterCard, Visa, American Express, and Diners Club tend to be most common at airports and large railway stations.

In a "confrontation" with a coin-operated phone, insert your (British) coins before dialing, with the understanding that the minimum charge these days even for calls placed to destinations within the same neighborhood will begin at 30p (60¢)—more, prorated per call, than equivalent calls paid for with a phone card.

Phone cards are issued throughout the U.K. by a wide variety of corporate issuers, and with a wide variety of denominations that begin at £2.50 ($5) to as much as £50 ($100) or higher. Each is reusable until the card's total value has been electronically depleted. Phone cards are sold in post offices, newsstands, and within large retail supermarkets, including branches of Tesco's and Sainsbury's.

To make an **international call** from Britain, dial the international access code **(00),** then the country code, then the area code, and finally the local number. Or call through one of the following long-distance access codes: **AT&T USA Direct** (✆ 1800/CALL-ATT), **Canada Direct** (✆ 0800/890016), **Australia** (✆ 0800/890061), and **New Zealand** (✆ 0800/890064). Common country codes are: U.S. and Canada, **1;** Australia, **61;** New Zealand, **64;** and South Africa, **27.**

For calling **collect** or if you need an international operator, dial ✆ **155.**

Caller beware: Some hotels routinely add outrageous surcharges onto phone calls made from your room. Inquire before you call! It may be a lot cheaper to use your own calling-card number or to find a pay phone.

CELLPHONES

The three letters that define much of the world's wireless capabilities are GSM (Global System for Mobiles), a big, seamless network that makes for easy cross-border cellphone use throughout England and dozens of other countries worldwide. In general, reception is good. But you'll need a Scriber Identity Module Card (SIM). This is a small chip specific for England that gives you a local phone number and plugs you into a regional network. In the U.S., T-Mobile, AT&T Wireless, and Cingular use this quasi-universal system; in Canada, Microcell and some Rogers customers are GSM, and all Europeans and most Australians use GSM. Unfortunately, per-minute charges can be high—usually $1 to $1.50 in western Europe and up to $5 in many other international destinations. Calls to the U.S. average 70p ($1.40) per minute.

For many, **renting** a phone is a good idea. While you can rent a phone from any number of overseas sites, including kiosks at airports and at car-rental agencies, we suggest renting the phone before you leave home. North Americans can rent one before leaving home from **InTouch USA** (✆ **800/872-7626** or 703/222-7161; www.intouchglobal.com) or **RoadPost** (✆ **888/290-1616** or 905/272-5665; www.roadpost.com). InTouch will also, for free, advise you on whether your existing phone will work overseas.

Depending on your business obligations in the U.K., your lifestyle, and your phone habits, **buying a phone** might be economically attractive, since the U.K. is one of the most phone-permeated societies in the world and local competition for your cellphone loyalty is fierce. Once you arrive, stop by a local cellphone shop (T-Mobile, Virgin, Vodafone, and British

Telecom all maintain their respective outlets) and compare their cheapest packages. In some case, buying a no-frills cellphone (at this writing, an example of that was a Nokia 6210) might cost as little as £30 ($60), and in some cases, depending on the promotion of the moment, might carry as much as £10 ($20) of prepaid minutes. From abroad, researching the wide array of options is a daunting task, indeed, but as a means of getting started in your search, click on www.britishtelecom.com.

VOICE-OVER INTERNET PROTOCOL (VoIP)

If you have Web access while traveling, consider a broadband-based telephone service (in technical terms, **Voice over Internet protocol**, or **VoIP**) such as Skype (www.skype.com) or Vonage (www.vonage.com), which allow you to make free international calls from your laptop or in a cybercafe. Neither service requires the people you're calling to also have that service (though there are fees if they do not). Check the websites for details.

INTERNET & E-MAIL
WITH YOUR OWN COMPUTER

More and more hotels, cafes, and retailers in England are signing on as Wi-Fi (wireless fidelity) "hot spots." **T-Mobile Hotspot** (www.t-mobile.com/hotspot or www.t-mobile.co.uk) serves up wireless connections at coffee shops nationwide. **Boingo** (www.boingo.com) and **Wayport** (www.wayport.com) have set up networks in airports and high-class hotel lobbies. iPass providers (see below) also give you access to a few hundred wireless hotel lobby setups. To locate other hot spots that provide **free wireless networks** in cities in England, go to **www.jiwire.com**.

For dial-up access, most business-class hotels offer dataports for laptop modems,

and a few thousand hotels in England now offer free high-speed Internet access. In addition, major Internet service providers (ISPs) have **local access numbers** around the world, allowing you to go online by placing a local call. The **iPass** network also has dial-up numbers around the world. You'll have to sign up with an iPass provider, who will then tell you how to set up your computer for your destination(s). For a list of iPass providers, go to www.ipass.com and click on "Individuals Buy Now." One solid provider is **i2roam** (© 866/811-6209 or 920/233-5863; www.i2roam.com).

Wherever you go, bring a **connection kit** of the right power and phone adapters, a spare phone cord, and a spare Ethernet network cable—or find out whether your hotel supplies them to guests.

WITHOUT YOUR OWN COMPUTER

To find cybercafes check **www.cyber captive.com** and **www.cybercafe.com**. Cybercafes are found in all large U.K. cities, especially London, where they can be found on almost every business street. **easyInternet cafes** (© 020/7241-9000; www.easyeverything.com) has several Great Britain locations.

Aside from formal cybercafes, most **youth hostels** and **public libraries** have Internet access. Avoid **hotel business centers** unless you're willing to pay exorbitant rates.

Internet kiosks appear within the public areas of every large and medium-size airport of the U.K. These usually provide basic Web access for a per-minute fee. More conveniently, if you have access to the business-class lounges of most airlines, including British Airways, Delta, American, Continental, and most of their competitors, free Internet stations are standard features within any of them.

14 Tips on Accommodations

Reserve your accommodations as far in advance as possible, even in the so-called slow months from November to April. Travel to London peaks from May to October, and during that period, it's hard to come by a moderate or inexpensive hotel room. Sometimes you can get better rates by calling the hotel directly. Ask for the type of room you want. If you're sensitive to noise, for example, request a room that's quieter, perhaps in the rear so you won't hear traffic noise out front. Remember that in the older hotels and inns, guest rooms tend to be small and each room is different, often with different plumbing. If you need a bathtub, ask for one or else you might end up with a small shower cubicle.

For tips on surfing for hotel deals online, visit www.frommers.com/planning.

CLASSIFICATIONS

Unlike some countries, England has no rigid hotel classification system. The tourist board grades hotels by stars. Hotels are judged on standards, quality, and hospitality, and are rated "approved," "commended," "highly commended," and "deluxe." Five stars (deluxe) is the highest rating. A classification of "listed" refers to accommodations that are, for the most part, very modest.

All establishments from two stars upward are required to have 100% en suite (private bathroom) facilities. In a one-star hotel, buildings are required to have hot and cold running water in all rooms, but in "listed" hotels, hot and cold running water in rooms is not mandatory. Star ratings are posted outside the buildings. However, the system is voluntary, and many hotels do not participate.

Many hotels, especially older ones, still lack private bathrooms for all rooms. However, most have hot and cold running water, and many have modern wings

with all the amenities (and older sections that are less up-to-date). When making reservations, always ask what section of the hotel you'll be staying in.

All hotels once included in the room price a full English breakfast of bacon and eggs, but today that is true of only some hotels. A continental breakfast is commonly included, usually just tea or coffee and toast.

BED & BREAKFASTS

In towns, cities, and villages throughout Britain, homeowners take in paying guests. Watch for the familiar bed-and-breakfast (B&B) signs. Generally, these are modest family homes, but sometimes they may be built like small hotels, with as many as 15 rooms. If they're that big, they are more properly classified as guesthouses. B&Bs are the cheapest places you can stay in England and still be comfortable.

Reservations for bed-and-breakfast accommodations in London can also be made by writing (not calling) the **British Visitor Centre,** 1 Regent St., London W1. Once in London, you can also visit their office (Tube: Piccadilly Circus).

In addition, Susan Opperman and Rosemary Lumb run **Bed and Breakfast Nationwide,** P.O. Box 2100, Clacton-on-Sea, Essex CO16 9BW, an agency specializing in privately owned bed-and-breakfasts all over Great Britain. Host homes range from small cottages to large manor houses, as well as working farms, and the prices vary accordingly. One thing you can be sure of is that owners have been specially selected for their wish to entertain visitors from overseas. Remember that these are private homes, so hotel-type services are not available. You will, however, be assured of a warm welcome, a comfortable bed, a hearty breakfast, and a glimpse of British life. Write for a free brochure. For bookings in accommodations outside London, call © **01255/ 831235** or fax 01255/831437 daily between 9am and 6pm. Or check out their website at **www.bedandbreakfast nationwide.com**.

FARMHOUSES

In many parts of the country, farmhouses have one, two, even four rooms set aside for paying guests, who usually arrive in the summer months. Farmhouses don't have the facilities of most guesthouses, but they have a rustic appeal and charm, especially for motorists, as they tend to lie off the beaten path. Prices are generally lower than those at bed-and-breakfasts or guesthouses, and sometimes you're offered some good country home cooking (at an extra charge) if you make arrangements in advance.

Farm Stay UK (© **024/7669-6909;** www.farmstayuk.co.uk) publishes an annual directory in early December that includes 1,000 farms and bed-and-breakfasts throughout the United Kingdom. The listings include quality ratings, the number of bedrooms, nearby attractions and activities, prices, and line drawings of each property. Also listed are any special details, such as rooms with four-poster beds or activities on the grounds (fishing, for example). Many farms are geared toward children, who can participate in light chores—gathering eggs or just tagging along—for an authentic farm experience. The approximate prices range from £30 to £60 ($60–$120) a night and include an English breakfast and usually private facilities. (The higher prices are for stays at mansions and manor houses.)

Another option is self-catering accommodations, which are usually cottages or converted barns that cost from £200 ($400) per week and include dishwashers and central heating. Each property is inspected annually not only by the Farm Holiday Bureau but also by the English Tourist Board. The majority of the properties, with the exception of those located in the mountains, are open year-round.

For a copy of the directory called *Farm Stay UK,* contact **Farm Stay UK,** National Agricultural Centre, Stoneleigh Park, Warwickshire CV8 2LG (© **024/ 7669-6909;** www.farmstayuk.co.uk). It costs £4.50 ($9) for postage and may be purchased by credit card.

For apartment, farmhouse, or cottage stays of 2 weeks or more, **Untours** (© **888/868-6871;** www.untours.com) provides exceptional lodgings for reasonable prices—which includes air/ground transportation, cooking facilities, and on-call support from a local resident. Best of all, Untours donates most profits to provide low-interest loans to underprivileged entrepreneurs around the world (see website for details).

NATIONAL TRUST PROPERTIES

The **National Trust Holiday Cottages,** Holiday Booking Office, P.O. Box 536, Melksham, Wiltshire SN12 8SX (© **0844/800-2070;** www.nationaltrust cottages.co.uk), is Britain's leading conservation organization. In addition to the many castles, forests, and gardens it maintains, the National Trust owns almost 350 houses and cottages in some of the most beautiful parts of England, Wales, and Northern Ireland. Some of these properties are in remote and rural locations, some have incomparable views of the coastline, and others stand in the hearts of villages and ancient cities. Most of these comfortable self-catering holiday accommodations are available for rental throughout the year. Many can be booked for midweek or weekend breaks on short notice, particularly in autumn and winter. National Trust properties can sleep from 2 to 12 guests.

Though anyone can book rentals in National Trust properties, it's worth mentioning the trust's U.S. affiliate, the **Royal**

Oak Foundation, 26 Broadway, Ste. 950, New York, NY 10004 (© **800/ 913-6565** or 212/480-2889; www.royal-oak.org), which publishes a full-color 400-page booklet that describes all National Trust holiday rental properties, their facilities, and prices. Copies cost $12 for nonmembers. Individual annual memberships are $55, and family memberships are $90. Benefits include free admission to all National Trust sites and properties open to the public, plus discounts on reservations at cottages and houses owned by them, and discounted air and train travel.

HOLIDAY COTTAGES & VILLAGES

Throughout Britain, fully furnished studios, houses, cottages, "flats" (apartments), and even trailers suitable for families or groups can be rented by the month. From October to March, rents are sometimes reduced by 50%.

The British Tourist Authority and most tourist offices have lists available. The BTA's free *Apartments in London and Holiday Homes* lists rental agencies such as **At Home Abroad, Inc.,** 163 Third Ave., Box 319, New York, NY 10003 (© **212/421-9165;** fax 212/228-4860; www.athomeabroadinc.com). Interested parties should write or fax a description of their needs; At Home Abroad will send listings at no charge.

Cottages 4 You (© **0870/078-2100;** www.cottages4you.co.uk) represents about 9,000 rental properties in the United Kingdom. They have everything from thatch-roofed cottages to castles.

Barclay International Group (BIG), 6800 Jericho Turnpike 212W, Syosset, NY 11791 (© **800/845-6636** or 516/364-0064; www.barclayweb.com), specializes in short-term apartment (flat) rentals in London and cottages in the English countryside. These rentals can be appropriate for families, groups of friends, or businesspeople traveling together and are sometimes less expensive than equivalent stays in hotels. Apartments, available for stays as short as 1 night (though the company prefers that guests stay a minimum of 3 nights and charges a premium if your stay is shorter), are usually more luxurious than you'd imagine. Furnished with kitchens, they offer a low-cost alternative to restaurant meals. For extended stays in the English countryside, BIG has country cottages in such areas as the Cotswolds, the Lake District, and Oxford, as well as farther afield in Scotland and Wales. The company can also arrange tickets for sightseeing attractions, BritRail passes, and various other "extras."

At the cheaper end of the spectrum, there's **Hoseasons Holidays,** Lowestoft, NR32 2LW (© **01502/502588;** www.hoseasons.co.uk), a reservations agent based in Suffolk (East Anglia). They arrange stopovers in at least 400 vacation villages throughout Britain. Though many are isolated in bucolic regions far from any of the sites covered within this guide, others lie within an hour's drive of Stratford-upon-Avon. Don't expect luxury or convenience: Vacation villages in England usually consist of a motley assortment of trailers, noninsulated bungalows, and/or mobile homes perched on cement blocks. They're intended as frugal escapes for claustrophobic urbanites with children. Such a place may not meet your expectations for a vacation in the English countryside (and a minimum stay of 3 nights is usually required), but it's hard to beat the rate.

CHAIN HOTELS

Many American chains, such as Best Western, Hilton, Sheraton, and Travelodge are found throughout Britain. In addition, Britain has a number of leading chains with which North American travelers are generally not familiar. **Thistle**

Britain Bans Public Smoking

Some 4 centuries ago King James I denounced tobacco, calling it "loathsome to the eye, hateful to the nose, harmful to the brain, and dangerous to the lungs."

Britain has now heard his words, banning smoking in most public places, including **hotels, restaurants,** and **pubs** that serve food. Anti-smoking activists welcomed the proposal but criticized the government for letting smokers continue lighting up in some pubs and bars. Still, it's a big step for a country that has long had a love-hate affair with tobacco. Britain's smoky pubs are at the heart of the nation's social life. Since the law was enacted, many hotels have opted to become 100% nonsmoking, even in the bedrooms, while others—at their discretion—have opted to set aside a few of their rooms for smokers. Always ask before booking if you want a room in which you can smoke.

Hotels (© 0871/376-9000; www.thistlehotels.com) is a well-regarded chain of upscale to moderate full-service hotels that caters to both business and leisure travelers. An exclusive chain of government-rated three-crown hotels is called **Malmaison** (© 0845/365-4247; www.malmaison.com). There's not a bad hotel in their post. **Premier Travel Inn** (© 0870/242-8000; www.premiertravel inn.com) is a chain of modern, moderately priced accommodations across the U.K., each one featuring a licensed restaurant.

HOUSE SWAPPING

The market leader in home exchanges is **HomeLink International,** 2937 NW9 Terrace, Fort Lauderdale, FL 33311 (© 800/638-3841 or 954/566-2687; www.homelink.org), which costs $80 to join. This is the oldest, largest, and best home-exchange holiday organization in the world.

A competitor is **Intervac U.S. & International,** 30 Corte San Fernando, Tiburon, CA 94920 (© 800/756-HOME; www.intervacus.com). To hook up with this outfitter, you pay $65 annually. Intervac is adept at securing a list of home exchanges throughout Great Britain.

YOUTH HOSTELS

Youth Hostels Association (England and Wales) operates a network of 230 youth hostels in major cities, in the countryside, and along the coast. You can contact them at Customer Services Department, YHA, Trevelyan House, Dimple Road, Matlock, Derbyshire DE4 3YH (© 0870/770-8868; www.yha.org.uk), for a free map with locations of each youth hostel and full details, including prices.

4

Suggested England Itineraries

Vacations are getting shorter, and a "lean-and-mean" schedule is called for if you want to experience the best of any country in a relatively short span of time. If you're a time-pressed traveler, as most of us are, with only 1 or 2 weeks for England, you may find the first two itineraries helpful. But before planning your schedule, take a moment to review each of England's unique regions.

1 The Regions in Brief

England is a part of the United Kingdom, which is made up of England, Wales, Scotland, and Northern Ireland. Only 130,347 sq. km (50,327 sq. miles)—about the same size as New York State—England has an amazing amount of rural land and natural wilderness and an astonishing regional, physical, and cultural diversity. See the "England and Wales" map in the insert at the beginning of this book for the regions outlined below.

ENGLAND

LONDON   Some seven million Londoners live in this mammoth metropolis, a parcel of land that's more than 1,577 sq. km (609 sq. miles) in size. The City of London proper is merely 2.5 sq. km (1 sq. mile), but the rest of the city is made up of separate villages, boroughs, and corporations. London's neighborhoods and outlying areas are described in chapter 5.

THE THAMES VALLEY   England's most famous river runs westward from Kew to its source in the Cotswolds. A land of meadows, woodlands, attractive villages, small market towns, and rolling hillsides, this is one of England's most scenic areas. Highlights include **Windsor Castle** (Elizabeth II's favorite residence) and nearby **Eton College,** founded by a young Henry VI in 1440. **Henley,** site of the Royal Regatta, remains our favorite Thames-side town; and at the university city of **Oxford,** you can tour the colleges.

THE SOUTHEAST (KENT, SURREY & SUSSEX)   This is the land of Charles Lamb, Virginia Woolf, Sir Winston Churchill, and Henry James. In this region are some of the nation's biggest attractions: **Brighton, Canterbury, Dover,** and dozens of country homes and castles—not only **Hever** and **Leeds castles,** but also **Chartwell,** the more modest abode where Churchill lived. In small villages, such as Rye and Winchelsea in Sussex, you discover the charm of the southeast. Almost all of the Sussex shoreline is built up, and seaside towns, such as Eastbourne and Hastings, are often tacky. In fact, though the area's major attraction is **Canterbury Cathedral,** the **Royal Pavilion at Brighton** rates as an outstanding, extravagant folly. Tea shops, antiques shops, pubs, and small inns abound in the area. Surrey is essentially a commuter suburb of London and is easily reached for day trips.

HAMPSHIRE & WILTSHIRE   Southwest of London, these counties possess two of England's greatest **cathedrals,** Winchester and Salisbury, and one of Europe's most significant prehistoric monuments, **Stonehenge.** Hampshire is bordered on its western side by the woodlands and heaths of **New Forest. Portsmouth** and **Southampton** loom large in naval heritage. You may also want to take a ferry over to the **Isle of Wight,** once Queen Victoria's preferred vacation retreat. In Wiltshire, you encounter the beginning of the **West Country,** with its scenic beauty and monuments. Here you'll find Wilton House, the 17th-century home of the earls of Pembroke, and Old Sarum, the remains of what is believed to have been an Iron Age fortification.

THE SOUTHWEST (DORSET, SOMERSET, DEVON & CORNWALL)   These four counties are the great vacation centers and retirement havens of England. Dorset, associated with Thomas Hardy, is a land of rolling downs, rocky headlands, well-kept villages, and rich farmlands. Somerset—the Somerset of King Arthur and Camelot— offers such magical towns as **Glastonbury.** Devon has both **Exmoor** and **Dartmoor,** and its northern and southern coastlines are peppered with famous resorts such as Lyme Regis and villages such as Clovelly. In Cornwall, you're never more than 32km (20 miles) from the rugged coastline, which ends at **Land's End.** Among the cities worth visiting in these counties are **Bath,** with its impressive Roman baths and Georgian architecture; **Plymouth,** the departure point of the Mayflower; and **Wells,** the site of a great cathedral.

THE COTSWOLDS   A wonderful region to tour, this is a pastoral land of honey-colored limestone villages where rural England unfolds before you like a storybook. In the Middle Ages, wool made the Cotswolders prosperous, but now they put out the welcome mat for visitors, with famously lovely inns and pubs. Start at Burford, the traditional gateway to the region, continue on to Bourton-on-the-Water, Lower and Upper Slaughter, Stow-on-the-Wold, Moreton-in-Marsh, and Chipping Campden, and finish at Broadway. **Cirencester** is the uncrowned capital of the south Cotswolds, and **Cheltenham** is still an elegant Regency spa. Our two favorite villages are **Painswick,** with its minute cottages, and **Bibury,** with Arlington Row, its cluster of former weavers' cottages.

STRATFORD & WARWICK   This region encompasses both Shakespeare country and the Midlands. The Midlands was the birthplace of the Industrial Revolution, which made Britain the first industrialized country in the world. Its foremost tourist town is **Stratford-upon-Avon,** but also drawing visitors are **Warwick Castle,** one of England's great castles, and the ruins of **Kenilworth Castle. Coventry,** heavily bombed in World War II, is visited mainly for its outstanding modern cathedral.

BIRMINGHAM & THE WEST MIDLANDS   The area known as the West Midlands embraces the so-called "Black Country." **Birmingham,** nicknamed "Brum," is Britain's largest city after London. This sprawling metropolis is still characterized by its overpass jungles and tacky suburbs, as well as its great piles of Victorian architecture. Urban renewal is underway. The English marshes cut through the old counties of **Shropshire** and **Herefordshire. Ironbridge Gorge** was at the heart of the Industrial Revolution, and the famous **Potteries** are in Staffordshire.

EAST ANGLIA (ESSEX, CAMBRIDGESHIRE, NORFOLK & SUFFOLK) East Anglia, a semicircular geographic bulge northeast of London, is the name applied to these four very flat counties. The land of John Constable is still filled with the landscapes he painted. The **Fens**—that broad expanse of fertile, black soil lying north of

Cambridge—remains our favorite district. Go there to see **Ely Cathedral. Cambridge,** with its colleges and river, is the chief attraction. The most important museum is the **Fitzwilliam** in Cambridge, but visitors also flock to East Anglia for the scenery and its solitary beauty—fens, salt marshes, and villages of thatched cottages.

THE EAST MIDLANDS (DERBYSHIRE, LEICESTERSHIRE, LINCOLNSHIRE, NORTHAMPTONSHIRE & NOTTINGHAMSHIRE) This area encompasses some of the worst of industrial England, yet there is still great natural beauty to be found, as well as stately homes. These include **Chatsworth** in Derbyshire, the seat of the dukes of Devonshire; **Sulgrave Manor** in Northamptonshire, the ancestral home of George Washington; and **Althorp House,** also in Northamptonshire, the childhood home of Diana, Princess of Wales. **Lincoln** has one of England's great cathedrals, rebuilt in the 13th and 14th centuries. Bostonians like to visit their namesake, the old seaport town of **Boston. Nottingham** recalls Robin Hood, though the deforested Sherwood Forest is obviously not what it was in the outlaw's heyday.

THE NORTHWEST Stretching from Liverpool to the Scottish border, northwest England can be a rustic delight if you steer clear of its industrial pockets. Most people come here to follow in the footsteps of such romantic poets as Wordsworth, who wrote of the beauty of the Lake District (see below). But **Chester, Manchester,** and **Liverpool** merit stopovers along the way. The resort of **Blackpool** is big, brash, and a bit tawdry, drawing the working class of the Midlands for Coney Island–style fun by the sea. In contrast, the Roman city of Chester is a well-preserved medieval town, known for its encircling wall. And Liverpool is culturally alive and always intriguing, if only to see where the Beatles came from, but it also has a branch of London's Tate Gallery.

THE LAKE DISTRICT The literary Lakeland evokes memories of the Wordsworths, Samuel Taylor Coleridge, John Ruskin, and Beatrix Potter, among others. **Windermere** is the best location for touring the area, but there are many other charming towns as well, including **Grasmere** and **Ambleside.** The Lake District contains some of England's most dramatic scenery.

YORKSHIRE & NORTHUMBRIA Yorkshire will be familiar to fans of the Brontës and James Herriot. **York,** with its immense cathedral and medieval streets, is the city to visit, though more and more visitors are calling on the cities of **Leeds** and **Bradford.** Northumbria comprises **Northumberland, Cleveland, Durham,** and **Tyne and Wear** (the area around **Newcastle**). The whole area echoes the ancient border battles between the Scots and English. **Hadrian's Wall,** built by the Romans, is a highlight. The **great cathedral** at Durham is one of Britain's finest examples of Norman church architecture, and **Fountains Abbey** is among the country's greatest ecclesiastical ruins. Country homes abound; here you find **Harewood House** and **Castle Howard.**

WALES

CARDIFF & SOUTH WALES The capital of Wales, **Cardiff** is a large seaport on the tidal estuary of the River Taff. As the center of the small landmass that is Wales, Cardiff admittedly can't be compared very well with London or Edinburgh, but it's a charmer in its own right. Newly restored, the capital invites with such attractions as that treasure-trove, the **National Museum of Wales,** and **Cardiff Castle,** with all its rich architectural detail. If time remains, dip into **South Wales,** which isn't all remnants of the Industrial Revolution but is filled with beauty spots, such as the **Brecon**

Beacons National Park. West of Cardiff is the city of **Swansea,** opening onto Swansea Bay. This is Dylan Thomas country.

NORTH WALES   Even more rewarding in scenery than South Wales, North Wales is a land of mountain peaks, spectacular estuaries, and rugged cliffs brooding over secluded coves, little rivers, valleys, and lakes. Its great towns and villages include **Betws-y-Coed, Llandudno,** and **Conwy,** along with such historic castles as **Harlech, Caernarfon,** and especially **Conwy Castle,** ordered built by Edward I and a masterpiece of medieval architecture. In this region, **Snowdonia National Park** covers 2,176 sq. km (840 sq. miles) of North Wales coastal areas and rugged hills.

2 England in 1 Week

Use the following itinerary to make the most out of a week in England, but feel free to drop a place or two to save a day to relax. One week provides enough time, although barely. Allow a day or two to introduce yourself to some of the attractions of London, such as the **Tower of London** or the **British Museum.** On Day 3 you can head for **Windsor Castle,** and on Days 4 and 5 you can call on the Bard at **Stratford-upon-Avon** with a side trip to **Warwick Castle.** Finally, you can make a quick day trip to Oxford on Day 6, climaxing your final day in England with a trip down the Thames to **Hampton Court Palace.**

Days ❶ & ❷: Arrival in London 🌟🌟🌟
Take a flight that arrives in London as early as possible on **Day 1.** Check into your hotel and enjoy an old-fashioned English breakfast. You might even find yourself skipping lunch.

Take the Tube to **Westminster Abbey** (p. 170), the shrine of the nation where most of England's queens and kings have been crowned and where they are also buried. Check out the fan-vaulted Henry VII's Chapel (one of the loveliest in all of Europe), the shrine to Edward the Confessor, and, for a final look, Poets' Corner, where the literati are buried. After your visit (allow 1½ hr.), stroll by the **Houses of Parliament** and that landmark clock of London, "**Big Ben**" (p. 171).

Continue walking north along **Whitehall,** bypassing **10 Downing Street,** the official residence of the prime minister, and ending at **Trafalgar Square,** the hub of London and its most famous square. See p. 178.

On the north side of the square stands the **National Gallery** (p. 175), where you will be able to see some of the highlights in 1½ hours. Directly north of the square, you enter the precincts of **Covent Garden** (p. 109), with dozens of places for lunch.

Then take the Tube to Charing Cross Station. Armed with a good map, walk along the **Mall** all the way to **Buckingham Palace** (p. 173). If it's late summer, you might even be able to visit the palace when the queen is away.

After a look, head east for the one big attraction of the afternoon, the **Tower of London** (p. 166). The much-photographed Beefeaters conduct hour-long guided tours.

On **Day 2,** take the Tube to Russell Square for your descent on the **British Museum** (p. 172). This is the mammoth home of one of the world's greatest treasure-troves—much of it plundered from other parts of the globe when Britannia ruled the waves. The most exciting of these treasures are the Elgin Marbles, stolen from Greece, and the Rosetta Stone, stolen from Egypt. You'll need at least 2 hours for the most cursory of visits. After the British Museum, head to the

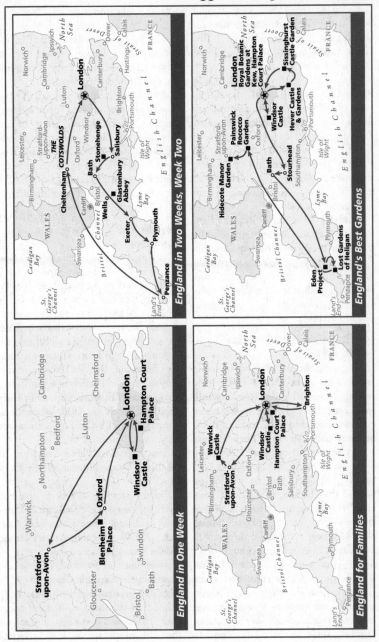

England in Two Weeks, Week Two

England's Best Gardens

England in One Week

England for Families

City, the financial district of London lying in the East End. An evocative and atmospheric luncheon stopover is **Bow Wine Vaults** at 10 Bow Churchyard, EC4; see p. 224.

Fortified for the afternoon, head for **St. Paul's Cathedral** (p. 177), the masterpiece of architect Sir Christopher Wren. At the top you'll be rewarded with one of the most panoramic of all London views.

On the south side of the Thames, pay a visit to **Tate Modern** (p. 175), housing the greatest collection of 20th-century art in Britain. Allow at least 1½ hours for the most cursory of visits.

Head for Westminster Bridge (Tube: Westminster), the embarkation point for a ride on the **British Airways London Eye** (p. 195), the world's largest observation wheel. On a clear day at least, it provides you with a panoramic sweep of 40km (25 miles). It's the most popular ride in London.

Day ❸: A Side Trip to Windsor Castle ⟨★★★⟩

Having sampled the charms of London in just 2 days, make **Day 3** different by heading north of London to visit **Windsor Castle** (p. 234), which the queen prefers as a royal residence even to Buckingham Palace itself. In just half an hour, a fast train from London will deliver you to the royal town of Windsor, site of England's most legendary castle. If you skipped the Changing of the Guard ceremony at Buckingham Palace, you can see an even more exciting pageant taking place here from April to July Monday to Saturday at 11am (off-season hours differ slightly—see p. 234 for more details). Wander through such attractions as **St. George's Chapel,** where some British monarchs are entombed; and visit the **Jubilee Gardens** spread over .8 hectares (2 acres). You'll need at least 2 hours to explore the castle.

Head back to London, arriving at Waterloo or Paddington Station where

you can take the Tube to Hyde Park (Marble Arch). Strolling through this "green lung of London," take in the miniature lake, Serpentine, and listen to protesters at Speakers Corner demanding the overthrow of the government.

After a visit, head for the heart of Mayfair, **Grosvenor Square,** before window-shopping along **Oxford Street** or else **New and Old Bond streets.** End up at the **Burlington Arcade** (p. 205) and have tea at the world's most famous grocery store, **Fortnum & Mason** (p. 164). After tea, walk east into **Piccadilly Circus** (p. 107), the hub of London.

Days ❹ & ❺: Stratford-upon-Avon ⟨★★⟩

From London's Paddington Station, you can be in Stratford-upon-Avon in just 2 hours. After checking into a hotel here for 2 nights, you can begin your tour of the Shakespeare properties, after stopping in at the **Shakespeare Birthplace Trust** (p. 490) and purchasing a global ticket.

After lunch in Stratford, try to visit at least three of the Shakespeare-related properties in the afternoon, including **Shakespeare's Birthplace** (p. 493); **Holy Trinity Church** (p. 492), where he is buried; and **Hall's Croft** (p. 490), where his daughter, Susanna, lived.

That night have dinner and a pint at the **Black Swan,** nicknamed "the Dirty Duck" (p. 489).

On the morning of **Day 5,** continue your exploration of the Shakespeare properties by visiting **Anne Hathaway's Cottage** (p. 490) and **Mary Arden's House (Glebe Farm)/Palmer's Farm** (p. 492).

After lunch in Stratford, head in the afternoon to **Warwick Castle** (p. 497), England's greatest medieval castle lying only 13km (8 miles) northeast of Stratford. Trains run frequently throughout the day between Stratford and the city of Warwick. You can go on a 2-hour tour before the castle closes at 6pm in summer. Return to Stratford for the night.

Instead of going to the Royal Shakespeare Theatre this time, visit the auxiliary theater, the **Swan,** since it presents somewhat more unconventional productions but with actors just as skilled as those who perform in the main theater.

Day ❻: Oxford & Its University ✪✪

Return to London and then transfer on to another fast train leaving from Paddington Station, reaching Oxford in 1½ hours. Five trains run to Oxford every hour.

For atmosphere and affordable food, have lunch at the **Turf Tavern** (p. 260), following in the footsteps of everybody from Elizabeth Taylor to Bill Clinton. We'd then recommend a **2-hour walking tour** that departs at 2pm daily from the **Oxford Tourist Information Centre** (p. 255). This is the best orientation for the highlights of this university city. To crown the afternoon, climb **Carfax Tower** (p. 256) for a panoramic view of the "city of dreaming spires." If there's still time in the afternoon, engage in that popular local pastime: **"Punting the River Cherwell"** (p. 257).

Day ❼: Blenheim Palace ✪✪✪ & Hampton Court Palace ✪✪✪

If you move fast enough, you can see two of England's greatest palaces—each one different—before the day's end. From Oxford, trains depart every 12 minutes to Woodstock, home of **Blenheim Palace** (p. 262), called England's answer to Versailles. The ancestral seat of the dukes of Marlborough, it was also the birthplace of Sir Winston Churchill. After a tour of the palace, lasting 1½ hours, return to Oxford and take a fast train back to London, where you can check into a hotel.

There will still be time in the afternoon to visit **Hampton Court Palace** (p. 198), the 16th-century palace once lived in by the lusty Henry VIII ("the marrying kind"). You can take frequent trains from London for the 21km (13-mile) journey. Allow yourself a minimum of 3 hours to explore this magnificent palace and its great gardens.

3 England in 2 Weeks

Two parts of England are always special treats for us to visit: **West Country** (Wiltshire, Devon, and Cornwall) and the scenic villages of the **Cotswolds.** The highlights of both of these destinations can be reached by public transportation, but schedules and connections can be difficult, consuming precious vacation time. So for your second week in England, we recommend that you rent a car. Since England is such a small island nation, distances from one major attraction to another are relatively short. Of course, if you've already spent 1 week in England, you will have already "conquered" the touristy highlights—**London, Oxford, Stratford-upon-Avon,** and the country's three great palaces: **Windsor Castle, Blenheim Palace,** and **Hampton Court Palace.**

Days ❶–❼

Follow the "England in 1 Week" itinerary as outlined above.

Day ❽: Salisbury ✪✪ & Stonehenge ✪✪✪

The drive from London to the cathedral city of **Salisbury** (coverage begins on p. 358) is only 145km (90 miles) to the southwest. You can easily arrive in time to check into a hotel for the night and visit **Salisbury Cathedral** (p. 363), whose architectural framework may already be familiar to you because of the John Constable paintings. Allow 1½ hours to visit its interior and wander about the cathedral complex.

If you're ready for a busy afternoon, you can head first for **Wilton House** (p. 364), ancestral home of the earls of

Pembroke, where General Eisenhower lived as he plotted the D-day landings on the beaches of Normandy in 1944. Allow 1½ hours for a visit, including strolling through its rose and water gardens and taking a riverside walk.

You'll still have time to descend on ancient **Stonehenge** (p. 366), a visit taking 1½ hours. Lying 14km (9 miles) north of Salisbury, this colossal circle of stones is, of course, one of the world's greatest prehistoric monuments, though still a mystery to archaeologists. It dates from 3000 B.C.

Day ❾: The Spa Town of Bath 🐦🐦🐦

In a trail blazed before you by the likes of Queen Anne and Jane Austen, Bath is the grandest and most elegant city of the West Country, lying 185km (115 miles) west of London. Northwest of Salisbury, a distance of 67km (41 miles), Bath can be easily reached in a morning's drive.

After checking into a hotel and having lunch in Bath, you can view some of its grand squares such as the **Circus** (p. 374), dating from 1754, and take in **Bath Abbey** (p. 375) and the **Pump Room and Roman Baths** (p. 376), all in an afternoon. That evening, try to catch a performance at **Theatre Royal Bath** (p. 376).

Day ❿: Wells 🐦🐦, Glastonbury Abbey 🐦🐦 & Exeter 🐦🐦

A busy day indeed. Leave Bath in the morning and drive 34km (21 miles) southwest to the city of **Wells,** where you can visit its famous **cathedral** (p. 386), dating from the 12th century. The structure is noted for its vast and intricate inverted arches added in 1338. After a visit lasting less than an hour, continue 9.5km (6 miles) to the southwest to visit historic **Glastonbury Abbey** (p. 387), the famous abbey ruins and legendary retreat of King Arthur and Queen Guinevere. Allow 45 minutes for a visit.

Arrive in **Exeter,** the capital of Devon, and check into a hotel. Exeter lies 151km (94 miles) southwest of Bath. If time remains, visit its **cathedral** (p. 390) dating from 1112.

Day ⓫: Plymouth & the Mayflower 🐦🐦

In the morning, drive to **Powderham Castle** (p. 400), the seats of the earls of Devon and a site used in Merchant Ivory's *The Remains of the Day,* starring Anthony Hopkins and Emma Thompson. The location is 13km (8 miles) to the south.

After a visit, continue southwest following the southern coastline of Devon, heading for a luncheon stopover in the port of **Dartmouth,** 56km (35 miles) southeast of Exeter. This is the ancient seaport home of the Royal Naval College.

Continue for the night to the historic seaport of **Plymouth,** a distance of 390km (242 miles) southwest of London. If you arrive in time, you can visit the spot where the *Mayflower* sailed to the New World and walk along the **Barbican** (p. 418), with its maze of narrow streets and old houses. Either in the late afternoon or early in the morning of the next day, visit the **National Marine Aquarium** (p. 415), the best in Britain.

Day ⓬: Penzance 🐦 on the Cornish Coast

A good part of the day will be consumed driving along the southern Devon and Cornish coasts, one of the most historic of England, until you arrive in the city of **Penzance** (p. 430), a distance of 451km (280 miles) southwest of London. Check into a hotel for the night in Penzance.

Spend 2 hours visiting the **Castle on St. Michael's Mount** (p. 432), and try to catch a performance that evening at the **Minack Theatre** (p. 433).

Day ⓭: Cheltenham 🐦

In the morning, cut inland and take the A30 northeast toward the Cotswolds, until you reach the scenic village of **Painswick** (p. 454), where you can break for lunch. After a visit to the **Rococo Garden** (p. 456), continue northeast into Cheltenham, where you can book into a hotel for the night. Try to catch a performance that evening at the **Everyman Theatre** (p. 460). But before dinner and the theater, walk through the historic core of Cheltenham, especially along its **Promenade,** one of the most beautiful thoroughfares in England.

Day ⑭: Driving Through the Cotswolds ✮✮✮

For your final day in England, arm yourself with a good map and set out to explore the most beautiful villages in the Cotswolds. Coverage of these towns and villages is found in chapter 13.

From Cheltenham, and by doing some crisscrossing here and there, you can take in the best of the Cotswolds. Scenic highlights of your day will include **Upper and Lower Slaughter, Bourton-on-the-Water, Bibury, Burford, Stow-on-the-Wold,** and **Moreton-in-Marsh.** Finally, in the north Cotswolds, you arrive in the most scenic town of **Broadway,** with what is arguably the most beautiful High Street in England. However, it's overrun with visitors in summer and charges very high prices. Make your way northeast to the even more charming village of **Chipping Campden,** which you can walk around and explore in 2 hours, spending the night before heading back to London and your final destination in the morning.

4 England for Families

England offers many attractions that kids enjoy. Perhaps your main concern with having children along is pacing yourself with museum time. Our suggestion is to explore **London** for 2 days with family in tow, then spend a good part of the third day wandering around **Windsor Castle** and the little Thames town, followed by a fourth day in **Brighton** with some fun on the beach. On Days 5 and 6, head for **Stratford-upon-Avon** and **Warwick Castle,** concluding with a final day in London and a side trip to **Hampton Court Palace.**

Days ① & ②: Arrival in London ✮✮✮

Your kid has probably been held captive on a long jet plane ride and will be eager for exercise. After a fortifying English breakfast, head for a stroll of an hour or two in **Hyde Park** (p. 196), which is a great way to "find your legs" in a new city. You can walk around Serpentine Lake, created in the 1730s, and even take a boat out if you wish.

Follow this by booking a tour of 1½ hours on the **Original London Sightseeing Tour** (p. 203), which is a traditional double-decker bus with commentary, offering reduced prices for children (free for 4 and younger). This will give you a thorough grounding in the overview of London. Some tours feature the **Changing of the Guard** at Buckingham Palace,

great English pomp and circumstance that thrills all ages.

After the tour, head for the **British Airways London Eye** (p. 195), the world's largest observation wheel, which will take you for a grand sweep in the skies of London in a "pod." Kids love this, and so do adults.

In the afternoon, stroll by the **Houses of Parliament** and **Big Ben** (more for yourself than for the kids), and call at **Westminster Abbey** (p. 170). This is such an awesome sight that even if your kid isn't that interested in churches, there is much to behold here. Later, take a ferry ride down the Thames to the **Tower of London** (p. 166), a sure kid-pleaser, hooking up with one of the red-coated Beefeater tours.

On **Day 2,** descend on the **British Museum** (p. 172) in Bloomsbury when it opens. Even if your kid is not a museum buff, there is wonder here and at times utter fascination, especially in the Egyptian rooms with all those scary mummies.

After lunch in Bloomsbury, head for **Madame Tussauds** (p. 189), where you'll encounter wax effigies of everybody from Mel Gibson to Saddam Hussein. Very young children may be disturbed by some of the "blood-and-gore" exhibitions. To finish off the afternoon, head for the **London Zoo** (p. 196). A total of 8,000 animals, some of the rarest species on earth, wander about the 15-hectare (36-acre) site of fascination.

End your day with a fun-filled stroll through **Battersea Park** (p. 197), where there is, among other attractions, a little zoo just for children.

Day ❸: A Side Trip to Windsor Castle ✫✫✫

Having sampled the charms of London in just 2 days, you can launch **Day 3** by heading out of town to nearby **Windsor Castle** (p. 234). In just half an hour, a train from London will deliver you to Windsor Castle. If you missed the Changing of the Guard ceremony in London, you can see an even more exciting pageant taking place here April to July Monday to Saturday at 11am (winter hours differ—see p. 234 for more details).

The highlight of Windsor Castle for younger children is a perfect miniature **Queen Mary's Dolls' House,** accurate to the most minute detail, even royal toilets that flush in all five bathrooms.

After lunch, stroll through **Eton College** (p. 235), the most famous public school in England (it'd be called private in the United States), wandering the same grounds as Prince William.

For a final attraction, head for **LEGOLAND** (p. 236), outside Windsor, a 61-hectare (150-acre) theme park, with everything from puppet theaters to

"knight-and-dragon" castles. Return to London on a fast train for the night.

Day ❹: A Side Trip to Brighton ✫✫

On **Day 4,** while still based in London, take one of the fast trains from Victoria Station, which will put you in "London by the Sea," as Brighton is called, in 55 minutes.

Even children adore the **Royal Pavilion at Brighton** (p. 311). This faux Indian mogul's palace is like something Disney might have created. Allow 2 hours for a visit.

After a tour and time out for lunch, enjoy the seaside amusements on the boardwalk and even the pebbly beaches if the weather is fair. The **Palace Pier** is filled with video arcades, games, and souvenir stands. Before leaving Brighton, stroll its maze of narrow alleyways, called the **Lanes** (p. 313) and found in the Old Town. Return to London for the night.

Days ❺ & ❻: Stratford-upon-Avon ✫✫ & Warwick Castle ✫✫✫

Check out of your London hotel and take a train from Paddington Station, reaching the town of Stratford-upon-Avon in 2 hours. Check into one of the family-friendly B&Bs for 2 nights.

Few children will want to see plays by the Bard, but many of the sights associated with Shakespeare have appeal for all ages. Of most interest to children—all of which can be seen in 1 day—are **Anne Hathaway's Cottage** (p. 490), **Mary Arden's House and the Shakespeare Countryside Museum** (p. 492), and **Shakespeare's Birthplace** (p. 493).

On **Day 6,** head north for 13km (8 miles) to **Warwick Castle** (p. 497), the finest medieval castle in England. Surrounded by gardens, this 17th-century castle has fairy-tale aspects for most children—and interests grown-ups, too. Kids, along with their families, see fascinating exhibits such as the dungeon and torture chamber (a little frightening for particularly young kids), and a Victorian rose garden and water garden. Family tickets are sold. Have lunch in Warwick and return to Stratford in the afternoon.

If you get back to Stratford in time, you might check out another two attractions of particular interest to children and a diversion from Shakespeareana. The **Teddy Bear Museum,** 19 Greenhill St. (© **01789/293160**), contains dozens upon dozens of teddy bears in various shapes and sizes. Some of these were owned by famous personages such as the Baroness Margaret Thatcher. Hours are daily 9:30am to 5:30pm, and admission is £2.50 ($5).

Children also delight in the **Stratford Butterfly Farm,** Swan's Nest Lane (© **01789/299288**), containing Europe's largest display of butterflies with a mock rainforest as well. It is open June to August daily 10am to dusk, charging £4.50 ($9) for admission. After another overnight in Stratford, return to London in the morning for your final day in England.

Day ❼: A Side Trip to Hampton Court Palace ✶✶✶

On **Day 7,** leave your London hotel and take a train from Waterloo Station to **Hampton Court Palace** (p. 198) on the north side of the Thames, lying 21km (13 miles) west of London. You'll reach it in about half an hour. Allow at least 3 hours for an unhurried visit, nearly 1 hour of which you can spend wandering through the beautiful gardens. You can enjoy lunch at the complex.

From April to September you can take a boat back into London, a 4-hour journey that will bring you to Westminster Pier.

If time remains, use your final time in London to take the kids to the **Natural History Museum** (p. 190). For children, the highlight of this exhibit is the display of 14 complete dinosaur skeletons, with such re-creations as a full-size robotic dinosaur lunching on a freshly killed Tenontosaurus.

5 1 Week in England's Best Gardens

Reaching all of these gardens by public transportation is possible in most cases, but rather awkward. The only way to see all of these gardens in a week is with a rented car. However, you'll need to rent a car for only the last 4 days of the tour. The other gardens in and around London can be reached by public transportation. This tour should be considered only from May to August, when English gardens are at their best.

Day ❶: Arrival in London ✶✶✶

Pay a morning visit to **Kensington Gardens** (p. 176). Adjacent to Hyde Park, these gardens are very different. Once the gardens were reserved for royal owners such as George III. In 1841 young Queen Victoria opened them to "respectably dressed people—but no soldiers, sailors, or servants."

The 111-hectare (274-acre) park is filled with hawthorns, weeping willows, maples, ash, swamp white oaks, and red oaks.

The ideal place for lunch is the **Orangery** in the Kensington Palace Gardens (p. 164). This is also an idyllic place for afternoon tea.

Spend the rest of the afternoon on a romp through **Regent's Park** (p. 196). With its gardens, lake, and zoo, this is like the estate of an English country gentleman covering 191 hectares (472 acres). The park was once a hunting ground for Henry VIII.

Day ❷: Royal Botanic Gardens ✶✶✶ at Kew

On **Day 2,** the world-famous **Royal Botanic Gardens** at Kew (p. 200), set on 121 hectares (300 acres), include pavilions, lakes, greenhouses, and flower-bordered walks. Reached by Tube or boat, these former royal pleasure gardens can easily occupy the good part of your day. Originally planted in 1759 by the mother of King George III, Kew once employed Capability Brown, England's most famous landscaper, to shape and enlarge the gardens. Captain Cook sent men off around the world to collect rare specimens. The Palm House, for example, contains every known variety of palm, including the African cycad.

Day ❸: Windsor Castle ✿✿✿ & Hampton Court Palace ✿✿✿

Get an early start by taking a 30-minute train ride from London's Waterloo or Paddington Station, which will put you in Windsor, site of **Windsor Castle** (p. 234). Visit **St. George's Chapel,** the highlight of the tour, before wandering the **Jubilee Gardens** around the castle (p. 233). In a romantic setting with white rambling roses, among other species, you can wander for at least 30 minutes, taking in the beauty.

Only if you have a car, consider driving to **Windsor Great Park** (p. 236), lying 8km (5 miles) from Windsor along A30. This 14-hectare (35-acre) garden is one of the most spectacular in Europe. Allow at least an hour, maybe more, to visit this park.

Return to London and take the train from Waterloo Station to **Hampton Court Palace** (p. 198), 21km (31 miles) west of London. The ideal time to visit is the first week of July at the time of the **Hampton Court Flower Show** held on the palace grounds. Call ✆ **020/ 8781-9500** for more information. Wend your way through the famous maze—and get lost—before heading back to London.

Day ❹: Hever Castle & Gardens ✿✿ & Sissinghurst Castle Garden ✿✿

On **Day 4,** leave London in a rented car, heading for **Hever Castle and Gardens** (p. 296), where Henry VIII wooed Anne Boleyn. The most celebrated and beautiful is the much-photographed Italian Garden filled with statuary and sculpture dating from Roman days to the Renaissance. Other garden highlights include a rose garden and a Tudor herb garden. Allow at least 1½ hours for a visit to the gardens.

After lunch, spend the afternoon visiting **Sissinghurst Castle Garden** (p. 297). This is the far point of the day's tour, taking you 85km (53 miles) southeast of London.

They are among the most romantic gardens in England and can be overrun with visitors. Highlights include the **White Garden** with its white or silver foliage, the **Spring Garden** that bursts into bloom with enough daffodils to please Wordsworth, and the alluring **Wild Garden** in the orchard. Return to London for the night.

Day ❺: West to Stourhead ✿✿✿

In the county of Wiltshire in the West Country, the gardens of **Stourhead** (p. 390) are the most celebrated example of English landscape gardening in the country. Although a "garden for all seasons," Stourhead is best visited in May and June when its masses of rhododendrons are at their fullest bloom. Built around a 1721 Palladian villa and set on 40 hectares (100 acres), Stourhead is a wonder to behold. It comes complete with rare trees, miles of flowering shrubs, a beautiful lake, classical temples, and grottoes.

Consider an overnight in **Bath** (p. 367).

Day ❻: Eden Project ✿✿ & the Lost Gardens of Heligan ✿✿

From your overnight stopover in Bath, you can drive to the southwest into Cornwall for a look at two of England's most bizarre and mysterious gardens: the Eden Project and Heligan. Visit the **Eden Project** (p. 427) first, lying at Bodelva, St. Austell, a 48km (30-mile) journey west of the city of Plymouth in Devon. This geodesic dome exhibits the world's major plant systems in microcosm, a former china clay pit boasting more than 70,000 plants.

After lunch in the area, continue the short distance south for a visit to the **Lost Gardens of Heligan** (p. 429). This site spreads across 32 hectares (80 acres) near the fishing village of Mevagissey. Once part of a 404-hectare (1,000-acre) Victorian estate, the gardens slumbered for 70 years as they were gradually buried by wild, unchecked overgrowth in Cornwall's subtropical climate.

After a day of fascination, head to St. Mawes (p. 428) or to one of the fishing villages such as Looe (p. 424) or Polperro (p. 424) for the night. These villages lie west of Plymouth.

Day ❼: Painswick Rococo Garden ✶ & Hidcote Manor Garden ✶✶

Get an early start in the morning and drive northeast to the towns of the Cotswolds (chapter 13).

The enchanting village of **Painswick** is arguably the most beautiful in England.

A rare English garden in that it's a throwback to the 1720 style of flamboyant gardens that flourished then, **Painswick Rococo Garden** (p. 456) lies .8km (a half-mile) north of Painswick. Today it has been restored to its original glory. After visiting the gardens, lunch in Painswick before continuing northeast to one of the Cotswold's most beautiful towns, **Chipping Campden** (p. 476).

Lying 6.5km (4 miles) northeast of Chipping Campden, **Hidcote Manor Garden** (p. 478) was created in 1907 by Major Lawrence Johnstone, an American horticulturist. Gardeners throughout the world have found inspiration in this remarkable masterpiece of landscaping with various "parlor rooms" different in texture, scent, shape, and color.

Overnight in Chipping Campden before returning to London.

5

Settling into London

Europe's largest city is like a great wheel, with **Piccadilly Circus** at the hub and dozens of communities branching out from it. In Britspeak, Circus means a circular area at an intersection of streets, not a Barnum & Bailey spectacular under the tent. London is such a conglomeration of neighborhoods, each with its own personality, first-time visitors may be confused until you get the hang of it. You'll probably spend most of your time in the **West End**, where many attractions are located, and in the historic part of London known as the **City**, which includes the Tower of London. This chapter will help you get your bearings.

1 Orientation

ARRIVING
BY PLANE

LONDON HEATHROW AIRPORT West of London in Hounslow (© **0870/ 000-0123;** www.baa.co.uk), Heathrow is one of the world's busiest airports. It has four terminals, each relatively self-contained. Terminal 4, the most modern, handles the long-haul and transatlantic operations of British Airways. Most transatlantic flights on U.S.-based airlines arrive at Terminal 3. Terminals 1 and 2 receive the intra-European flights of several European airlines.

Getting to Central London from Heathrow It takes 45 to 50 minutes by the Underground (Tube) and costs £4 ($8) to make the 24km (15-mile) trip from Heathrow to the center of London. A taxi is likely to cost from £50 to £70 ($100–$140). For more information about Tube or bus connections, call © **020/7222-1234** or go to **www.tfl.gov.uk.**

The British Airport Authority now operates **Heathrow Express** (© **0845/600-1515;** www.heathrowexpress.com), a 161kmph (100-mph) train service running every 15 minutes daily from 5:10am until 11:40pm between Heathrow and Paddington Station in the center of London. Trips cost £15 ($30) each way in economy class, rising to £46 ($92) in first class. Children 14 and younger pay £7.20 ($14) in economy, £23 ($46) in first class. You can save £1 ($2) by booking online or by phone. The trip takes 15 minutes each way between Paddington and terminals 1, 2, and 3, and 23 minutes from Terminal 4. The trains have special areas for wheelchairs. From Paddington, passengers can connect to other trains and the Underground, or you can hail a taxi. You can buy tickets on the train with a £2 ($4) surcharge, or at self-service machines at Heathrow Airport. Tickets are also available from travel agents.

GATWICK AIRPORT While Heathrow still dominates, more and more scheduled flights land at relatively remote **Gatwick** (© **0870/574-7777;** www.baa.co.uk), located some 40km (25 miles) south of London in West Sussex but only a 30-minute train ride away.

Getting to Central London from Gatwick From Gatwick, the fastest way to get to London is via the **Gatwick Express trains** (© 0845/850-1530; www.gatwick express.co.uk), which depart approximately every 15 minutes, daily between 4:35am and 1:35am. The round-trip fare between Gatwick and Victoria Rail Station is £27 ($54) for adults and £13 ($26) for children age 10 and younger. (One-way fares cost £16/$32 for adults and £7.95/$16 for children.) The travel time each way is 30 minutes Monday to Saturday, and 35 minutes on Sunday.

A **taxi** from Gatwick Airport to central London costs from £95 ($190). Fares vary according to a printed price list that defines the fare from Gatwick to whichever neighborhood of London you're traveling to. Meters in this case don't apply because Gatwick lies outside the Metropolitan Police District. For further transportation information, call © 020/7222-1234.

LONDON CITY AIRPORT Some business travelers prefer **London City Airport** (© 020/7646-0088; www.londoncityairport.com) because of its convenient location 5km (3 miles) east of the business centers of Canary Wharf, the Docklands, and the ExCel convention center. If you have business within these districts, the London City Airport is a better arrival point than equivalent flights into Heathrow, Gatwick, or Stansted. Accepting flights from 23 cities throughout western Europe and Scandinavia, it services airlines that include British Airways, Cirrus Airlines, Luxair, KLM, CityJet, OLT, Lufthansa, Scot Airways, Air France, Eastern Airways (not to be confused with the now-defunct, U.S.-based Eastern Airlines), SAS, Darwin Airlines, Swiss International Airlines, and VLM.

Trains on the Docklands Light Railway make runs at 10-minute intervals from City Airport to the Underground station known as "Bank" (short for Bank of England) in the heart of London's financial district, which is known locally as "the City." One-way passage costs £4 ($8) for adults and £1 ($2) for children 15 and younger.

As a final means of getting from the airport to central London, consider boarding London Transport's bus no. 473 or 474, which make frequent runs between the airport and various points in East London, including the Plaistow Tube (Underground) station. From here, you can make connections to virtually any other point in London.

LONDON STANSTED AIRPORT Located some 80km (50 miles) northeast of London's West End, **Stansted**, in Essex (© 0870/000-0303; www.baa.co.uk), handles mostly flights to and from the European continent.

Getting to Central London from Stansted From Stansted, your best bet to central London is the **Stansted Express train** (© 08457/484950; www.stanstedexpress.co.uk) to Liverpool Street Station, which runs every 15 minutes from 6am to 11:45pm and every 30 minutes in the early mornings on weekends. It costs £15 ($30) for a standard ticket and £24 ($48) for first class, and takes 45 minutes.

By bus, you can take the **A6 Airbus** (© 0870/580-8080), which runs regular departures 24 hours a day to many central London locations, and costs £15 ($30). If you prefer the relative privacy of a taxi, you'll pay dearly for the privilege. For a ride to London's West End, a taxi will charge from £85 to £100 ($170–$200). Expect the ride to take around 75 minutes during normal traffic conditions, but beware of Friday afternoons when dense traffic may double your travel time. Our advice: Stick to the Express.

BY TRAIN

Each of London's train stations is connected to the city's vast bus and Underground network, and each has phones, restaurants, pubs, luggage storage areas, and Transport for London Information Centres.

St. Pancras International (http://stpancras.eurostar.com) is the new London hub for Eurostar, replacing Waterloo Station as the arrival point from the Continent. Restored and opened in 2007, it is the point where the high-speed Eurostar pulls into London, connecting England with Belgium and France through the Channel Tunnel.

The station boasts Europe's longest champagne bar, a daily farmer's market, all the Wi-Fi you'll ever need, plus dozens of boutiques—and some of the world's fastest trains. It is also served by six underground tubes, including Victoria, Northern, Piccadilly, Circle, Hammersmith & City, and Metropolitan, as well as seven other rail companies. With such a vast network of transport, you can head virtually anywhere in greater London.

BY CAR

Once you arrive on the English side of the Channel, the M20 takes you directly into London. *Remember to drive on the left.* Two roadways encircle London: The A406 and A205 form the inner beltway; the M25 rings the city farther out. Determine which part of the city you want to enter and follow signposts.

We suggest you confine driving in London to the bare minimum, which means arriving and parking. Because of parking problems and heavy traffic, getting around London by car is not a viable option. Once there, leave your car in a garage and rely on public transportation or taxis. Before arrival in London, call your hotel and inquire if it has a garage (and what the charges are), or ask the staff to give you the name and address of a garage nearby.

VISITOR INFORMATION

The London Tourist Board's **London Visitor Centre,** 1 Lower Regent St., London SW1Y 4XT (© **8701/566-366;** www.visitlondon.com; Tube: Piccadilly Circus), can help you with almost anything, from the most superficial to the most serious. Located within a 10-minute walk from Piccadilly Circus, it deals chiefly with procuring accommodations in all price categories through an on-site travel agency (www.last minute.com), which can also book transit on British Rail or with bus carriers throughout the U.K. There's a kiosk for procuring theater or group tour tickets, a bookshop loaded with titles dealing with travel in the British Isles, a souvenir shop, and a staff that's pleasant, helpful, and friendly. It's open year-round Monday 9:30am to 6:30pm, Tuesday to Friday 9am to 6:30pm, and Sunday 9am to 5pm. Between October and May, Saturday hours are 10am to 4pm, and between June and September, Saturday hours are 9am to 5pm.

A roughly equivalent organization that was conceived to help foreign visitors with their inquiries and confusion about London is the **London Information Centre,** at Leicester Square, W1 (© **020/7292-2333;** www.londoninformationcentre.com; Tube: Leicester Sq.). The London Information Centre is a privately owned, commercially driven organization that may have a vested interest in steering you toward a particular venue.

An option that might help you navigate your way through the logistics of one of the world's biggest cities involves your call to © **0800/LONDON** for city information and to book sometimes discounted rates for London hotels, theaters, sightseeing tours, and airport transfers. A sales staff is available daily from 8am to midnight.

LONDON'S NEIGHBORHOODS IN BRIEF

The West End Neighborhoods

Mayfair Bounded by Piccadilly, Hyde Park, and Oxford and Regent streets, this is the most elegant, fashionable section of London, filled with luxury hotels, Georgian town houses, and swank shops. Grosvenor Square (pronounced *Grov*-nor) is nicknamed "Little America," home to the American embassy and a statue of Franklin D. Roosevelt; Berkeley Square (*Bark*-ley) was made famous by the song "A Nightingale Sang in Berkeley Square." At least once you'll want to dip into this exclusive section. One curiosity of Mayfair is **Shepherd Market,** a tiny village of pubs, two-story inns, book and food stalls, and restaurants, sandwiched among Mayfair's greatness. Mayfair is London's toniest address for hotels, as the prices indicate. If you stay here, you'll be in the very heart of London, with all the great shops on Bond Street and the Cork Street galleries near at hand. Even if you don't lodge here, come for long walks of discovery.

Marylebone First-timers to London head to Marylebone (*Mar*-le-bone) to explore Madame Tussauds or walk along Baker Street in the make-believe footsteps of Sherlock Holmes. The streets form a near-perfect grid, with major ones running north-south from Regent's Park toward Oxford Street. Marylebone Lane and High Street retain some of their former village atmosphere, but this is otherwise a now rather anonymous area. At Regent's Park, you can visit Queen Mary's Gardens or, in summer, see Shakespeare performed in an open-air theater. In addition to exploring, you can also lodge here at often half the price you'd pay in Mayfair.

St. James's Often called "Royal London," St. James's is home to Elizabeth II, who lives at the neighborhood's most famous address, Buckingham Palace. The neighborhood begins at Piccadilly Circus and moves southwest, incorporating Pall Mall, the Mall, St. James's Park, and Green Park; it's "frightfully convenient," as the English say, enclosing many of London's leading department stores. One must-see is Fortnum & Mason, at 181 Piccadilly, the world's most luxurious grocery store. Other than the queen, Prince Charles and the duchess of Cornwall are residents. The district is even more courtly and graceful than Mayfair.

Piccadilly Circus & Leicester Square Piccadilly Circus is the very center of London—its gaudy living room. The circus isn't Times Square yet, but its traffic, neon, and jostling crowds do nothing to make it fashionable. If you want a little more grandeur, retreat to the Regency promenade of exclusive shops, the Burlington Arcade, designed in 1819.

A bit more tawdry is Leicester Square, a center of theaters, restaurants, movie palaces, and nightlife. Once a chic address, it changed forever in the Victorian era when four towering entertainment halls were opened (even Queen Victoria saw a circus here). In time, the old palaces changed from stage to screen; three still show films. The district is known more for fun and amusement than hotels.

Soho These densely packed streets in the heart of the West End are famous for a gloriously cosmopolitan mix of people and trades. A decade ago, much was heard about the decline of Soho, when the thriving sex industry threatened to engulf it. That destruction has now largely been halted. Respectable businesses have returned, and chic restaurants and shops prosper; it's now the heart of London's expanding gay colony. But Soho wouldn't be Soho without a few sex shops and porn theaters. Surprisingly, it has a few of the poshest and most expensive hotels in London, attracting fashionistas and movie stars who want to be right in the heart of the theater district.

Soho starts at Piccadilly Circus and spreads out, basically bordered by Regent Street, Oxford Street, Charing Cross Road, and the theaters of Shaftesbury Avenue. Carnaby Street, a block from Regent Street, was the center of the universe in the swinging '60s and appears to be rising again. Across Shaftesbury Avenue, a busy street lined with theaters, is London's **Chinatown**, centered on Gerrard Street: small, authentic, and packed with excellent restaurants. But Soho's heart—with marvelous French and Italian delicatessens, fine butchers, fish stores, and wine merchants—is farther north, on Brewer, Old Compton, and Berwick streets; Berwick is also a wonderful open-air fresh-food market. To the north of Old Compton Street, Dean, Frith, and Greek streets have fine little restaurants, pubs, and clubs. The British movie industry is centered at Wardour Street.

Bloomsbury This district, a world in itself, lies northeast of Piccadilly Circus, beyond Soho. It is, among other things, the academic heart of London; you'll find the University of London, several other colleges, and many bookstores. Despite its student population, this neighborhood is fairly staid. Its reputation has been fanned by such writers as Virginia Woolf, who lived within its bounds and became one of the unofficial leaders of a group of artists and writers known as "the Bloomsbury Group."

The heart of Bloomsbury is **Russell Square,** and the streets jutting off from the square are lined with hotels and B&Bs. Most visitors come to the neighborhood to visit the British Museum, one of the world's greatest repositories of treasures. The British Telecom Tower (1964) on Cleveland Street is a familiar landmark. If you're hotel shopping, not just sightseeing, Bloomsbury is a solid, respectable address and lined with moderately priced and affordable small hotels that have none of the glamour of such places as Mayfair or Chelsea.

Nearby is **Fitzrovia,** bounded by Great Portland, Oxford, and Gower streets. Goodge Street, with its many shops and pubs, forms the heart of the "village." Once a major haunt of artists and writers—this was the stamping ground of Ezra Pound and George Orwell, among others—the bottom end of Fitzrovia is a virtual extension of Soho, with a cluster of Greek restaurants.

Kings Cross Long a seedy area in the heart of London, Kings Cross is facing a massive regeneration program. Millions of pounds are going into its decaying infrastructure. The area is still far from chic, but was given renewed importance with the arrival of Eurostar, the Channel Tunnel Rail Link coming into St. Pancras instead of Waterloo. Because of this change in venue, it's estimated that some 50 million passengers will pass through Kings Cross annually. Six tubes now convene underneath Kings Cross station, and it is the number-one connection hub enabling visitors to get to and from Gatwick and Heathrow airports.

St. Pancras Alongside Kings Cross, St. Pancras International is the new transport hub for Eurostar, bringing renewed life to this once-decaying part of London. The station is to London what Penn Station was to New York, the finest architectural icon of the Age of Steam. British poet John Betjeman called the 1868 structure, with its gargoyles and Gothic Revival towers, "too beautiful and too romantic to survive."

Today the glamorous and vastly restored station is a dazzling entry point into Britain for those passengers arriving on Eurostar from the Continent. Stay tuned for hotel, shopping, and restaurant developments to blossom around the station. For more information, contact ✆ **020/7843-4250** (www.stpancras.com).

Holborn The old borough of Holborn, abutting the City to the west, takes in the heart of legal London—the city's barristers, solicitors, and law clerks call it home. A 14-year-old Dickens was once employed as a solicitor's clerk at Lincoln's Inn Fields. Old Bailey has stood for English justice through the years (Fagin went to the gallows from this site in *Oliver Twist*). Everything here seems steeped in history. Even as you're quenching your thirst with a half pint of bitter at the Viaduct Tavern (126 Newgate St.; Tube: St. Paul's), you learn the pub was built near the notorious Newgate Prison (which specialized in death by pressing) and was named after Holborn Viaduct, the world's first overpass.

Covent Garden & the Strand The flower, fruit, and "veg" market is long gone, but memories of Professor Higgins and Eliza Doolittle linger on. **Covent Garden** now contains the city's liveliest group of restaurants, pubs, and cafes outside of Soho, as well as some of the city's hippest shops—including the world's only Dr. Marten's Super Store. The restored marketplace, with its glass and iron roofs, has been called a "magnificent example of urban recycling." Covent Garden is traditionally London's theater area, and Inigo Jones's St. Paul's Covent Garden is known as the actors' church. The Theatre Royal

Drury Lane was where Charles II's mistress Nell Gwynne made her debut in 1665. Some of London's poshest and most daring contemporary—but also superexpensive—hotels have opened in "the garden" in recent years.

Beginning at Trafalgar Square, the **Strand** runs east into Fleet Street and borders Covent Garden to the south. Flanked with theaters, shops, hotels, and restaurants, it runs parallel to the River Thames; to walk it is to follow the footsteps of Mark Twain, Henry Fielding, James Boswell, William Thackeray, and Sir Walter Raleigh. The Savoy Theatre helped make Gilbert and Sullivan household names.

Westminster The seat of the British government since the days of Edward the Confessor and dominated by the Houses of Parliament and Westminster Abbey, this area runs along the Thames to the east of St. James's Park. **Trafalgar Square,** at the area's northern end and one of the city's major landmarks, remains a testament to England's victory over Napoleon in 1805, and the paintings in the **National Gallery** will restore your soul. Whitehall is the main thoroughfare, linking Trafalgar Square with Parliament Square. You can visit Churchill's Cabinet War Rooms; no. 10 Downing St., the world's most famous street address, home to Britain's prime minister; and **Westminster Abbey,** one of the world's great Gothic churches.

Westminster encompasses **Victoria,** an area that takes its unofficial name from bustling Victoria Station, known as "the gateway to the Continent." As a hotel district, many affordable and often budget hotels cluster around Victoria Station. These are not the quietest or the most glamorous hotels in London but they are serviceable, affordable, and convenient without any of the grandeur or poshness of Belgravia,

Chelsea, or Mayfair. Westminster also has a few first-class hotels in rather staid palaces for those willing to spend more pounds.

The City & Environs

The City When Londoners speak of "the City," they don't mean all of London; they mean the original square mile that's now the British version of Wall Street. The buildings of this district are known all over the world: the Bank of England, the London Stock Exchange, and Lloyd's of London. This was the origin of Londinium, as it was called by its Roman conquerors. Despite its age, the City doesn't easily reveal its past; much of it has been swept away by the Great Fire of 1666, the German bombs of 1940, the IRA bombs of the early 1990s, and the zeal of modern developers. Still, it retains its medieval character; one of its landmarks is **St. Paul's Cathedral,** the masterpiece of Sir Christopher Wren, which stood virtually alone among the rubble after the Blitz. Since the millennium, many very expensive hotels have opened in the City, catering to those who need to be near the financial center. Otherwise, the City is far too removed from the heart of London for the visitor more intent on sightseeing.

London's journalistic hub since William Caxton printed the first book in English, **Fleet Street** has been abandoned by all of the London tabloids for the Docklands development across the river.

The City of London still prefers to function on its own, separate from the rest of the city; in keeping with its independence, it maintains its own **Information Centre** at St. Paul's Churchyard, EC4 (© **020/7332-1456**). It's open daily from 9:30am to 5:30pm.

Docklands In the last 2 decades, this area—bordered roughly by Tower Bridge to the west and London City Airport and the Royal Docks to the east—has witnessed an ambitious redevelopment. Thames-side warehouses have been converted to Manhattan-style lofts, and the neighborhood has attracted many businesses, including most of the Fleet Street newspapers, as well as museums, entertainment complexes, shops, and an ever-growing list of restaurants.

Canary Wharf, on the Isle of Dogs, is the heart of Docklands; a 240m-high (800-ft.) tower designed by César Pelli, the tallest building in the United Kingdom, dominates this huge 29-hectare (72-acre) site. The Piazza is lined with shops and restaurants. On the south side of the river at Surrey Docks, the Victorian warehouses of **Butler's Wharf** have been converted by Sir Terence Conran into offices, workshops, houses, shops, and restaurants; Butler's Wharf is also home to the Design Museum.

To get to Docklands, take the Underground to Bank and pick up the **Docklands Light Railway** (© **020/7222-1234;** www.tfl.gov.uk/dlr), which operates Monday to Friday 5:30am to 1am, Saturday 5am to 1am, and Sunday 6:40am to midnight.

The East End Traditionally one of London's poorest districts, it was nearly bombed out of existence by the Nazis. Hitler, in the words of one commentator at the time, created "instant urban renewal." The East End extends from the City Walls east encompassing Stepney, Bow, Poplar, West Ham, Canning Town, and other districts. The East End has always been filled with legend and lore. It's the home of the Cockney, London's most colorful characters. To be a true Cockney, it's said that you must have been born "within the sound of Bow Bells," a reference to a church, St. Mary-le-Bow, rebuilt by Sir Christopher Wren in 1670. Many immigrants to London have found a home here.

South Bank Although not officially a district like Mayfair, South Bank is the setting today for the **South Bank Arts Centre,** now the largest arts center in western Europe and still growing. Reached by Waterloo Bridge, it lies across the Thames from the Victoria Embankment. Culture buffs flock to its galleries and halls, including the National Theatre, Queen Elizabeth Hall, Royal Festival Hall, and Hayward Gallery. It's also the setting of the National Film Theatre. Neighborhoods nearby are Elephant & Castle and **Southwark,** home to the grand Southwark Cathedral. To get here, take the Tube to London Bridge.

Central London Beyond the West End

Knightsbridge One of London's most fashionable neighborhoods, Knightsbridge is a top residential and shopping district, just south of Hyde Park. **Harrods,** on Brompton Road, is its chief attraction. Right nearby, Beauchamp Place (*Beech*-am) is a Regency-era, boutique-lined shopping street with a scattering of fashionable restaurants. Knightsbridge, former stamping ground of Princess Di, is one of the great and central locations of London, with several pricey hotels. For the serious shopper, there could be no more idyllic address in London.

Belgravia South of Knightsbridge, this area has long been the aristocratic quarter of London, rivaling Mayfair in grandness. Although it reached the pinnacle of its prestige during the reign of Queen Victoria, it's still a chic address; the duke and duchess of Westminster, one of England's richest families, still live at Eaton Square. Its centerpiece is Belgrave Square, built between 1825 and 1835. When the town houses were built, the aristocrats followed—the duke of Connaught, the earl of Essex, even Queen Victoria's mother, the

duchess of Kent. Chopin, on holiday in 1837, was appropriately impressed: "And the English! And the houses! And the palaces! And the pomp, and the carriages! Everything from soap to the razors is extraordinary." It's better for walking and exploring than living. There are few hotels in the district and not a lot to do at night. We prefer livelier Chelsea for our address.

Chelsea This stylish Thames-side district lies south of Belgravia. It begins at Sloane Square, where flower sellers hustle their flamboyant blooms year-round. The area has been a favorite of writers and artists, including such names as Oscar Wilde, George Eliot, James Whistler, J. M. W. Turner, Henry James, and Thomas Carlyle. Mick Jagger and Margaret Thatcher have been more recent residents, and the late Princess Diana and the "Sloane Rangers" of the 1980s gave it even more fame.

Its major boulevard is **King's Road,** where Mary Quant launched the miniskirt in the '60s and where the English punk look began. King's Road runs the entire length of Chelsea; it's at its liveliest on Saturday. The hip-hop of King's Road isn't typical of otherwise upmarket Chelsea, an elegant village filled with town houses and little mews dwellings that only successful stockbrokers and solicitors can afford to occupy. Although a hike from the center, Chelsea is sprinkled with a few discreet hotels of charm and grace. It has one major drawback: There are few Tube connections, but plenty of buses.

On the Chelsea/Fulham border is **Chelsea Harbour,** a luxury development of apartments and restaurants with a private marina. You can spot its tall tower from far away; the golden ball on top moves up and down to indicate tide level.

Kensington This Royal Borough lies west of Kensington Gardens and Hyde

Park and is traversed by two of London's major shopping streets, Kensington High Street and Kensington Church Street. Since 1689, when asthmatic William III fled Whitehall Palace for Nottingham House (where the air was fresher), the district has enjoyed royal associations. In time, Nottingham House became Kensington Palace, and the royals grabbed a chunk of Hyde Park to plant their roses. Queen Victoria was born here. "KP," as the royals say, was the home of Princess Diana and her two young princes for a time. Kensington Gardens is now open to the public.

Southeast of Kensington Gardens and Earl's Court, primarily residential **South Kensington** is often called "museumland" because it's dominated by a complex of museums and colleges—set upon land bought with the proceeds from Prince Albert's Great Exhibition, held in Hyde Park in 1851—that include the **Natural History Museum, Victoria and Albert Museum,** and **Science Museum;** nearby is **Royal Albert Hall.** South Kensington is also home to some fashionable restaurants and town-house hotels. One of the district's chief curiosities is the **Albert Memorial;** for sheer excess, the Victorian monument is unequaled in the world. Both Kensington and South Kensington, though away from the center, have some of the choicest hotels in London, although they are priced rather high. These beautiful, urban neighborhoods free you from some of the horrendous congestion of such districts as Piccadilly Circus. Many streets are quiet at night, and much of a neighborhood feel remains.

Earl's Court Earl's Court lies below Kensington, bordering the western half of Chelsea. For decades a staid residential district, Earl's Court now attracts a new and younger crowd (often gay), particularly at night, to its pubs, wine bars, and coffeehouses. It's a popular base for budget travelers (particularly Australians), thanks to its wealth of B&Bs and budget hotels, and to its convenient access to central London: A 15-minute Tube ride takes you into the heart of Piccadilly, via either the District or Piccadilly lines.

Once regarded as the boondocks, nearby **West Brompton** is seen today as an extension of central London. It lies directly south of Earl's Court (take the Tube to West Brompton) and directly southeast of West Kensington. It also has many good restaurants, pubs, and taverns, as well as some budget hotels.

Notting Hill Increasingly fashionable Notting Hill is bounded on the north by Bayswater Road and on the east by Kensington. Hemmed in on the north by West Way and on the west by the Shepherd's Bush ramp leading to the M40, it has many turn-of-the-20th-century mansions and small houses sitting on quiet, leafy streets, plus a growing number of hot restaurants and clubs. Gentrified in recent years, it's becoming an extension of central London. This is one of the hippest and hottest districts of London and has a few scattered and select hotels of charm and grace. If you're staid, stay in St. James's or Mayfair, but if you're Nicole Kidman you can hang out here.

On the north end, across Notting Hill, west of Bayswater, is the increasingly hip neighborhood known as **Notting Hill Gate;** its Portobello Road is home to one of London's most famous street markets. The area Tube stops are Notting Hill Gate, Holland Park, and Ladbroke Grove.

Nearby **Holland Park** is a stylish residential neighborhood visited chiefly by the chic guests of Halcyon Hotel, one of the grandest of London's small hotels.

Paddington & Bayswater Centering on Paddington Station, north of Kensington Gardens and Hyde Park, Paddington is one of the major centers in London, attracting budget travelers who fill up the B&Bs in Sussex Gardens and Norfolk Square. After the first railway was introduced in London in 1836, it was followed by a circle of sprawling railway termini, including Paddington Station, which spurred the growth of this middle-class area, now blighted in parts.

Just south of Paddington, north of Hyde Park, and abutting more fashionable Notting Hill to the west, is **Bayswater,** a sort of unofficial area filled with a large number of B&Bs attracting budget travelers. Inspired by Marylebone and elegant Mayfair, a relatively prosperous set of Victorian merchants built homes for their families in this area. These districts are for the frugal hotel shopper unconcerned about a chic address.

Farther Afield

Greenwich Some 6.5km (4 miles) from the city, Greenwich—ground zero for use in the reckoning of terrestrial longitudes—enjoyed its heyday under the Tudors. Henry VIII and both of his daughters, Mary I and Elizabeth I, were born here. Greenwich Palace, Henry's favorite, is long gone,

though; today's visitors come to this lovely port village for nautical sights along the Thames, including the 1869 tea clipper *Cutty Sark.*

Hampstead This residential suburb of north London, beloved by Keats and Hogarth, is a favorite spot for weekending Londoners. Notables from Sigmund Freud to John Le Carré have lived here, and it remains one of the most desirable districts in the greater London area to call home. Its centerpiece is **Hampstead Heath,** nearly 323 hectares (800 acres) of rolling meadows and woodlands with panoramic views; it maintains its rural atmosphere though engulfed by cityscapes on all sides. The hilltop village is filled with cafes, tearooms, and restaurants, as well as pubs galore, some with historic pedigrees.

Highgate With Hampstead, Highgate in north London is another choice residential area, particularly on or near Pond Square and along Highgate High Street. It was long a desirable place to live. Londoners used to flock to its taverns and pubs for "exercise and harmless merriment"; some still do. Today, most visitors come to see moody **Highgate Cemetery,** London's most famous cemetery, the final resting place of such famous figures as Karl Marx and George Eliot.

2 Getting Around

Remember that cars drive on the left and vehicles have the right of way in London over pedestrians. Wherever you walk, always look both ways before stepping off a curb.

BY PUBLIC TRANSPORTATION

The London Underground and the city's buses operate on the same system of six fare zones. The fare zones radiate in rings from the central zone 1, which is where most visitors spend the majority of their time. Zone 1 covers the area from Liverpool Street in the east to Notting Hill in the west, and from Waterloo in the south to Baker Street, Euston, and Kings Cross in the north. To travel beyond zone 1, you need a multizone ticket. Note that all single one-way, round-trip, and 1-day pass tickets are valid only on the day of purchase. Tube and bus maps should be available at any Underground station. You can download them before your trip from the excellent **London Transport (LT)** website

www.tfl.gov.uk/tfl. There are also **LT Information Centres** at several major Tube stations: Euston, Kings Cross, Oxford Circus, St. James's Park, Liverpool Street Station, and Piccadilly Circus, as well as in the British Rail stations at Euston and Victoria and in each of the terminals at Heathrow Airport. Most of them are open daily (some close Sun) from at least 9am to 5pm. A 24-hour public-transportation information service is also available at ✆ **020/7222-1234.**

DISCOUNT PASSES   If you plan to use public transportation a lot, investigate the range of fare discounts available. **Travelcards** offer unlimited use of buses, Underground, Docklands Light Railway, and National Rail services in greater London for any period ranging from a day to a year. Travelcards are available from Underground ticket offices, LT Information Centres, main post offices in the London area, many newsagents, and some newsstands. Children age 10 and younger generally travel free on the Tube and buses.

The **1-Day Travelcard** allows you to go anywhere throughout greater London. For travel anywhere within zones 1 and 2, the cost is £6.80 ($14) for adults or £3.40 ($6.80) for children 5 to 15. The **Off-Peak 1-Day Travelcard,** which is valid after 9:30am on weekdays, is even cheaper. For two zones, the cost is £5.30 ($11) for adults and £3.30 ($6.60) for children 5 to 15.

The system now features a **3-Day Travelcard,** allowing adults to travel within zones 1 and 2 for £17 to £22 ($34–$44), and allowing children to go for £8.70 to £9.50 ($17–$19).

1-Week Travelcards cost adults £24 ($48) and children £12 ($24) for travel in zones 1 and 2.

Consider purchasing the **Oyster card** (www.oystercard.com), a travel discount card that's all the rage. You can prepay for single fares, which cost considerably less than a paper ticket—usually about half the price. Oysters are valid on the Tube, DLR, tram, and National Rail services within your chosen zones and across the entire London bus network. For 24-hour information, call the Oyster hot line at ✆ **0871/2301100.** The card has a daily price cap, meaning you never pay more than £3 ($6) regardless of how many trips you make in 1 day. You can buy an Oyster card at any ticket office.

THE UNDERGROUND

The Underground, or Tube, is the fastest and easiest way to get around. All Tube stations are clearly marked with a red circle and blue crossbar. Routes are conveniently color-coded.

If you have British coins or a credit card, you can get your ticket at a vending machine. Otherwise, buy it at the ticket office. You can transfer as many times as you like as long as you stay in the Underground. Children 4 and younger travel free if accompanied by an adult.

Slide your ticket into the slot at the gate and pick it up as it comes through on the other side and hold on to it—it must be presented when you exit the station at your destination. If you're caught without a valid ticket, you'll be fined £20 ($40) on the spot. If you owe extra money, you'll be asked to pay the difference by the attendant at the exit. The Tube runs roughly from 5am to 12:30am Monday to Saturday and 7:30am to 10:30pm Sunday. After that you must take a taxi or night bus to your destination. For information on the London Tube system, call the **London Underground** at ✆ **020/7222-1234,** but expect to stay on hold for a good while before a live person comes on the line. Information is also available on **www.tfl.gov.uk**.

The Jubilee Line Extension has been extended eastward to serve the growing suburbs of the southeast and the Docklands area. This east-west axis helps ease traffic on some of London's most hard-pressed Underground lines. The line also makes it much easier to reach Greenwich.

BY BUS

The comparably priced bus system is almost as good as the Underground and gives you better views of the city. To find out about current routes, pick up a free bus map at one of London Transport's Travel Information Centres, listed above. The map is available in person only, not by mail. You can also obtain a map at **www.tfl.gov.uk**.

As with the Underground, fares vary according to distance traveled. Generally, bus fares are £2 to £3 ($4–$6). If you want your stop called out, simply ask the conductor or driver. To speed up bus travel, passengers have to purchase tickets before boarding. Drivers no longer collect fares on board. Some 300 roadside ticket machines serve stops in central London—in other words, it's "pay as you board." You'll need the exact fare, however, as ticket machines don't make change.

Buses generally run 24 hours a day. A few night buses have special routes, running once an hour or so; most pass through Trafalgar Square. Keep in mind that night buses are often so crowded (especially on weekends) that they are unable to pick up passengers after a few stops. You may find yourself waiting a long time. Consider taking a taxi. Call the 24-hour **hot line** (✆ **020/7222-1234**) for schedule and fare information.

BY TAXI

London cabs are among the most comfortable in the world. You can pick one up either by heading for a cab rank or by hailing one in the street. (The taxi is available if the yellow taxi sign on the roof is lit.) To **call a cab**, phone ✆ **0871/871-8710**.

The meter starts at £2.20 ($4.40), with increments of £2 ($4) per mile thereafter, based on distance or time. Surcharges are imposed after 8pm and on weekends and public holidays. All these tariffs include VAT; plan to tip 10% to 15%.

If you call for a cab, the meter starts running when the taxi receives instructions from the dispatcher, so you could find that the meter already reads a few pounds more than the initial drop of £2.20 ($4.40) when you step inside.

Minicabs are also available, and they're often useful when regular taxis are scarce or when the Tube stops running. These cabs are meterless, so you must negotiate the fare in advance. Unlike regular cabs, minicabs are forbidden by law to cruise for fares. They operate from sidewalk kiosks, such as those around Leicester Square. If you need to call one, try **Brunswick Chauffeurs/Abbey Cars** (✆ **020/8969-2555**) in west London or **Newham Minicars** (✆ **020/8472-1400**) in south London. Minicab kiosks can be found near many Tube or BritRail stops, especially in outlying areas.

If you have a complaint about taxi service or if you leave something in a cab, contact the **Public Carriage Office,** 15 Penton St., N1 9PU (✆ **0845/602-7000** or 020/7222-1234; Tube: Angel Station). If it's a complaint, you must have the cab number, which is displayed in the passenger compartment.

BY CAR

Don't drive in congested London. It is easy to get around without a car; traffic and parking are nightmares; and, to top it off, you'd have to drive from what you normally consider the passenger seat on the wrong side of the road. It all adds up to a big headache. Another disincentive is that you will have to pay a "Congestion Charge" of £8 ($16) to drive in most of central London between 7am and 6pm, Monday to Friday. Larger gas-guzzling cars will be charged £25 ($50).

BY BICYCLE

One of the most popular bike-rental shops is **On Your Bike,** 52–54 Tooley St., London Bridge, SE1 (© 020/7378-6669; www.onyourbike.com; Tube: London Bridge), open Monday to Friday 7:30am to 7pm, Saturday 10am to 6pm, and Sunday 11am to 5pm. The first-class mountain bikes, with high seats and low-slung handlebars, cost £12 ($24) for the first day and £8 ($16) for each day thereafter, or £35 ($70) per week, and require a 1 pence deposit on a credit card, so they will have your credit card number.

FAST FACTS: London

American Express The main office is at the American Express Travel Service at 78 Brompton Rd., Knightsbridge SW (© 020/761-7905; Tube. Knightsbridge).

Area Code London's area code is **020.** Within the city limits, you don't need to dial it; use only the eight-digit number. If you're calling London from home before your trip, the country code for England is **44.** It must precede the London area code. When you're calling London from outside Britain, drop the "0" in front of the local area code.

Babysitters If your hotel can't recommend a sitter, call **Sitters** (© 0800/38-900-38 or 020/7935-3000; www.babysitter.co.uk). Call or check their website for rates and membership information.

Dentist For dental emergencies, call **Eastman Dental Hospital** (© 020/7915-1000; Tube: Kings Cross).

Doctor Call © **999** in a medical emergency. Some hotels have physicians on call for emergencies. For nonemergencies, try **Medical Express,** 117A Harley St., W1 (© 020/7499-1991; www.medicalexpressclinic.com; Tube: Regent's Park). A private British clinic, it's not part of the free British medical establishment. The clinic is open Monday to Friday 9am to 6pm and Saturday 10am to 2pm.

Emergencies In London, for police, fire, or an ambulance, dial © **999.**

Hospitals The following offer emergency care in London, 24 hours a day, with the first treatment free under the National Health Service: **Royal Free Hospital,** Pond Street (© 020/7794-0500; Tube: Belsize Park), and **University College Hospital,** 235–250 Euston Rd., NW1 (© 0845/46-47; Tube: Great Portland St.). Many other London hospitals also have accident and emergency departments.

Internet Access If you've brought your laptop, the quest will be easier, since many hotels are wired; rates run from £10 to £20 ($20–$40) a day, although £12 ($24) is probably the average. Countless Internet cafes and coin-operated kiosks can be found around town. Libraries are reserved for residents, so you can't rely on them. The most common Internet cafe chain is **easyInternetcafe** (www.easyinternetcafe.com). Fifteen locations are around town, with West End locations in the basement of the following Burger Kings: Piccadilly Circus (46 Regent St., W1, Tube: Piccadilly Circus; 358 Oxford St., W1, Tube: Bond St.; 9–16 Tottenham Court Rd., W1, Tube: Tottenham Court Rd.; and east of Trafalgar Square, 456–459 Strand, WC2, Tube: Charing Cross).

Maps If you plan to explore London in any depth, you'll need a detailed street map with an index, not one of those superficial overviews given away at many hotels and tourist offices. The best ones are published by Falk, and they're available at most newsstands and nearly all bookstores. And no Londoner is without a *London A to Z,* the ultimate street-by-street reference, available at bookstores and newsstands everywhere.

Police In an emergency, dial ℂ **999** (no coins are needed).

Post Office The main post office is at 24–28 William IV St., WC2 (ℂ **020/7484-9307;** Tube: Charing Cross). Hours for stamps and postal services are Monday to Friday 8:30am to 6:30pm and Saturday 9am to 5:30pm. Other post office branches are open Monday to Friday from 9am to 5:30pm and Saturday from 9am to 12:30pm. Many post office branches are closed for an hour at lunch.

Telephone For **directory assistance** for London, dial ℂ **118212** for a full range of services; for the rest of Britain, dial ℂ **118118.** See also "Area Code" above.

3 Where to Stay

Since the 21st century began, more than 10,000 hotel rooms have opened to the public in London. The downside is that most of these hotels are in districts far from the city center and are of the no-frills budget-chain variety. In spite of these bandbox modern horrors sprouting up, some hoteliers wisely decided to adapt former public or institutional buildings rather than start from scratch.

London boasts some of the most famous hotels in the world—temples of luxury such as Claridge's, the Dorchester, and the Ritz. The problem is that London has too many of these high-priced hotels (and many cheap budget options) and not enough moderately priced options.

Even at the luxury level, you may be surprised at what you don't get. Many of the stately Victorian and Edwardian gems are so steeped in tradition that they lack many modern conveniences standard in other luxury hotels around the world. Some have modernized with a vengeance, but others retain amenities from the Boer War era. However, the cutting-edge hotels are not necessarily superior; they frequently lack the personal service and spaciousness that characterize the grand old hotels.

It's also harder to get a hotel room, particularly an inexpensive one, during July and August. Inexpensive hotels are also tight in June, September, and October. If you arrive without a reservation, begin looking for a room as early in the day as possible. Many West End hotels have vacancies, even in peak season, between 9 and 11am, but by noon they are often booked.

If you're looking for budget options, don't despair. London has some good-value places in the lower price ranges, and we've included the best of these. An affordable option is a bed-and-breakfast. The following reliable services will recommend and arrange a B&B room for you: The **London Bed and Breakfast Agency Limited** (ℂ **020/7586-2768;** fax 020/7586-6567; www.londonbb.com) is a reputable agency that can provide inexpensive accommodations in selected private homes for £37 to £60 ($74–$120) per person per night, based on double occupancy (although some accommodations will cost a lot more); and **London B&B** (ℂ **800/872-2632** in the U.S.; fax 619/531-1686; www.londonbandb.com) offers B&B accommodations in private family residences or unhosted apartments. Homes are inspected for quality and comfort, amenities, and convenience.

Where to Stay in London

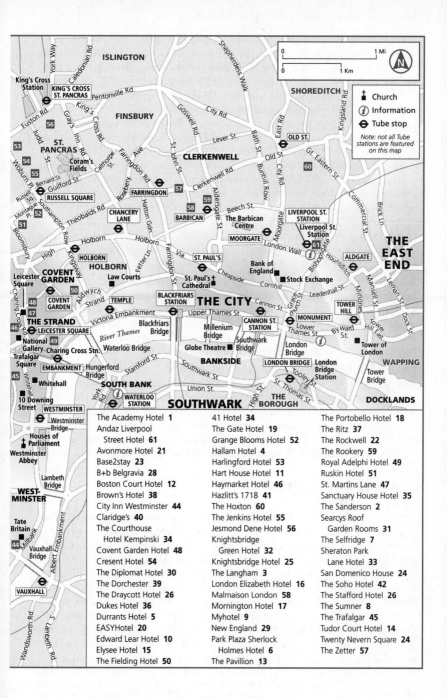

The Academy Hotel **1**
Andaz Liverpool
  Street Hotel **61**
Avonmore Hotel **21**
Base2stay **23**
B+b Belgravia **28**
Boston Court Hotel **12**
Brown's Hotel **38**
City Inn Westminster **44**
Claridge's **40**
The Courthouse
  Hotel Kempinski **34**
Covent Garden Hotel **48**
Cresent Hotel **54**
The Diplomat Hotel **30**
The Dorchester **39**
The Draycott Hotel **26**
Dukes Hotel **36**
Durrants Hotel **5**
EASYHotel **20**
Edward Lear Hotel **10**
Elysee Hotel **15**
The Fielding Hotel **50**

41 Hotel **34**
The Gate Hotel **19**
Grange Blooms Hotel **52**
Hallam Hotel **4**
Harlingford Hotel **53**
Hart House Hotel **11**
Haymarket Hotel **46**
Hazlitt's 1718 **41**
The Hoxton **60**
The Jenkins Hotel **55**
Jesmond Dene Hotel **56**
Knightsbridge
  Green Hotel **32**
Knightsbridge Hotel **25**
The Langham **3**
London Elizabeth Hotel **16**
Malmaison London **58**
Mornington Hotel **17**
Myhotel **9**
New England **29**
Park Plaza Sherlock
  Holmes Hotel **6**
The Pavillion **13**

The Portobello Hotel **18**
The Ritz **37**
The Rockwell **22**
The Rookery **59**
Royal Adelphi Hotel **49**
Ruskin Hotel **51**
St. Martins Lane **47**
Sanctuary House Hotel **35**
The Sanderson **2**
Searcys Roof
  Garden Rooms **31**
The Selfridge **7**
Sheraton Park
  Lane Hotel **33**
San Domenico House **24**
The Soho Hotel **42**
The Stafford Hotel **26**
The Sumner **8**
The Trafalgar **45**
Tudor Court Hotel **14**
Twenty Nevern Square **24**
The Zetter **57**

Instead of B&Bs, some savvy visitors prefer long-term options, including self-catering accommodations or else vacation or apartment rentals. One of the best establishments for arranging this type of rental is **Coach House London Rentals** ✹✹, 2 Tunly Rd., London SW17 7QJ (℃ **020/8133-8332;** fax 020/8181-6152; www.rentals. chslondon.com). The agency has more than 75 properties it represents, ranging from modest flats for couples to spacious homes that can sleep up to 12. The minimum length of a stay is 5 nights, and a car can be sent to the airport to pick you up.

For the upmarket traveler, the aptly named **Uptown Reservations,** 8 Kelso Place, London W8 5QD (℃ **020/7937-2001;** fax 020/7937-6660; www.uptownres.co.uk), features attractive, comfortably furnished accommodations in elegant private homes in swanky districts of the city. A substantial breakfast is included in the price, and you share your digs with the hosts themselves, many of whom are artists, diplomats, businesspeople, or, in some rare cases, lords of the realm who need extra money.

Amazing discounts, seemingly unavailable elsewhere, are offered by **Visit Hotels.com,** 37B New Cavendish St., London W1G 8JR (℃ **08704/352-422;** fax 08704/325-423; www.visithotels.com). Sometimes discounts on a room can range up to 70%.

A NOTE ABOUT PRICES   Unless otherwise noted, published prices are rack rates for rooms with a private bathroom. Many include breakfast (usually continental) and a 10% to 15% service charge. The British government also imposes a VAT (value-added tax) that adds 17.5% to your bill. This is not included in the prices quoted in the guide. Always ask for a better rate, particularly at the first-class and deluxe hotels (B&Bs generally charge a fixed rate). Parking rates are per night.

RATE REGULATIONS   All hotels, motels, inns, and guesthouses in Britain with four bedrooms or more (including self-catering accommodations) must display notices listing minimum and maximum overnight charges in a prominent place in the reception area or at the entrance, and prices must include any service charge and may include VAT. It must be made clear whether these items are included; if VAT isn't included, then it must be shown separately. If meals are included, this must be stated. If prices aren't standard for all rooms, then only the lowest and highest prices need be given.

IN & AROUND THE CITY
VERY EXPENSIVE

Andaz Liverpool Street Hotel ✹✹   In 2007, a new and untested branch of the Hyatt group (Andaz) transformed one of the East End's most venerable hotels into a glossy and very upscale monument to relaxed chic. Strategically positioned at the junction of two trendy, arts-conscious neighborhoods (Shoreditch and Hoxton) and the financial district, it managed to gracefully incorporate respect for the cutting-edge arts with allegiance to old-fashioned British pomp and circumstance. The original hotel dates from 1884, when it was designed by architect Charles Barry, best known for his work on the Houses of Parliament. The hotel's exterior is abloom in all its Victorian glory, complete with a stained-glass dome. Bedrooms are supremely comfortable, with state-of-the-art bathrooms and color schemes of dark red and white.

40 Liverpool St., London EC2M 7QN. ℃ **800/228-9000** or 020/7961-1234. Fax 020/7618-5001. www.hyatt.com or www.london.liverpoolstreet.andaz.com. 267 units. £415–£455 ($830–$910) double; from £595–£720 ($1,190–$1,440) suite. AE, DC, MC, V. Tube: Liverpool St. Station. **Amenities:** 4 restaurants; 5 bars; health club; tour desk; business center; room service; massage; laundry service; dry cleaning. *In room:* A/C, TV, Wi-Fi, minibar, hair dryer, iron, safe.

EXPENSIVE

Malmaison London ✻✻   Who could imagine that this used to be a dreary nursing home? Talk about recycling. The Victorian mansion block overlooks a green cobbled square and is the first London showcase for the U.K.-only hotel chain that is known for opening up winning hotels with clever contemporary designs, state-of-the-art facilities, and, as always, a chic little brasserie serving French classics. On the southern rim of once dreary, now trendy, Clerkenwell in East London, Malmaison is awash in dark teakwood; tall, glowing floor lamps; a highly polished European staff; tasteful fabrics in neutral shades; and a portrait and bust in the lobby of Napoleon and Josephine, who spent many a "wanton night" at the original Château Malmaison outside Paris. The darkwood guest rooms are individually designed and larger than average for central London.

18–21 Charterhouse Sq., London EC1M 6AH. ✆ 020/7012-3700. Fax 020/7012-3702. www.malmaison-london. com. 97 units. £235–£270 ($470–$540) double; from £305 ($610) suite. AE, MC, V. Tube: Barbican or Farringdon. **Amenities:** Restaurant; bar; health club; room service; laundry service; dry cleaning. *In room:* A/C, TV, high-speed Internet, CD player, CD library, minibar, beverage maker, iron, trouser press.

The Rookery ✻ (Finds)   When this hotel opened in the late 1990s, it salvaged the last three remaining then-derelict antique houses in Clerkenwell, a neighborhood midway between the West End and the City. The result is a setting that's permeated with a sense of Johnson and Boswell's London, an oasis of crooked floors, labyrinthine hallways, and antique accessories and furnishings that manage to be simultaneously fun and functional. According to a spokesperson, "We went out of our way to make the floors creak," as part of its charm. Bedrooms are charming and quirky, furnished with carved 18th- and 19th-century bed frames, and lace or silk draperies. Bathrooms contain Edwardian-era fittings, including claw-foot bathtubs. Overall, this place is quirky, eccentric, and abundantly laden with a sense of the antique.

Peter's Lane, Cowcross St., London EC1M 6DS. ✆ 020/7336-0931. Fax 020/7336-0932. www.rookeryhotel.com. 33 units. £210–£295 ($420–$590) double; £395–£495 ($790–$990) suite. AE, DC, MC, V. Tube: Farringdon. **Amenities:** Breakfast room; room service; laundry service; dry cleaning. *In room:* A/C, TV, Wi-Fi, minibar, safe.

The Zetter ✻✻✻   Heaven will be a letdown after this. Imagine hall vending machines dispensing champagne or espresso makers providing complimentary *café* on every floor. This converted Victorian warehouse between the financial district and the West End features seven rooftop studios with patios and panoramic views of the London skyline, among other lures, including a sky-lit atrium flooding its core with natural light. Many of the features and "scars" of the original structure were retained, as tradition was blended with a chic, urban modern. Bedrooms, ranging from small to midsize, are spread across five floors. These accommodations open onto balconies that circle the atrium. Unplastered brick walls reach up to "floating" ceilings and customized wallpaper panels. Secondhand furnishings are set beside classic modern pieces. Designers achieved their goal of "a great bed, a great shower, and state-of-the-art in-room technology."

St. John's Sq., 86–88 Clerkenwell Rd., London EC1M 5RJ. ✆ 020/7324-4445. Fax 020/7324-4445. www.thezetter. com. 59 units. Mon–Thurs £155–£330 ($310–$660) double; Fri–Sun £132–£330 ($264–$660) double. AE, DC, MC, V. Tube: Farringdon. **Amenities:** Restaurant; bar; room service; in-room spa treatments. *In room:* A/C, TV/DVD, high-speed Internet, CD player, safe.

INEXPENSIVE

The Hoxton ✻ (Value)   Custom-built in 2006 in the Shoreditch neighborhood near London's financial district, the Hoxton has a stated aim of avoiding hotel rip-offs. It came up with many innovative policies—for example, instead of getting gouged if you make a phone call from your room, you are charged only 5p (10¢) a minute for calls to Canada and the United States, and you'll find "supermarket prices" at the minimarket in the lobby. The main investor and figurehead, Sinclair Beecham, founder of Britain's popular Prêt-a-Manger fast-food chain, bases his price structure on policies in effect at budget airlines, offering frequent promotions to the rates noted below. Everything is simplified here: The "Lite Pret" breakfast—a bag containing freshly squeezed orange juice, granola, yogurt, and a banana—is hung on your doorknob. Bedrooms are functional and rather small but tastefully furnished, each with either queen-size or two single beds.

81 Great Eastern St., London EC2A 3HU. © 020/7550-1000. Fax 020/7550-1090. www.hoxtonhotels.com. 205 units. £59–£89 ($118–$178) double. Rates include Light Pret breakfast. AE, DC, MC, V. Tube: Old St. **Amenities:** Grill; bar; access to nearby gym (£5/$10). *In room:* TV, Wi-Fi, fridge, hair dryer.

MAYFAIR
VERY EXPENSIVE

Brown's Hotel 🐾🐾 Almost every year a hotel sprouts up trying to evoke an English-country-house ambience with Chippendale and chintz; this quintessential townhouse hotel watches these competitors come and go, and it always comes out on top. Brown's was founded by James Brown, a former manservant to Lord Byron, who knew the tastes of well-bred gentlemen and wanted to create a dignified, clublike place for them. He opened its doors in 1837, the same year Queen Victoria took the throne.

Brown's occupies 14 historic houses just off Berkeley Square. Its guest rooms, completely renovated, vary considerably in decor, but all show restrained taste in decoration and appointments; even the wash basins are antiques. Accommodations range in size from small to extra spacious; some suites have four-poster beds.

30 Albemarle St., London W1S 4BP. © 020/7493-6020. Fax 020/7493-9381. www.brownshotel.com. 117 units. £450 ($900) double; from £1,400 ($2,800) suite. AE, DC, MC, V. Off-site parking £53 ($106). Tube: Green Park. **Amenities:** Restaurant; bar; health club; spa; business center; room service; laundry service; same-day dry cleaning. *In room:* A/C, TV, high-speed Internet, minibar, hair dryer, safe.

Claridge's 🐾🐾🐾 That once-fading 1812 beauty has experienced a rebirth, and its staid image has changed. *Dynasty* diva Joan Collins may have staged her latest marriage here, but now Kate Moss is spotted in the hip bar, Elizabeth Hurley strolls through the lobby, and Gordon Ramsay—Britain's most talked-about and controversial chef (and also the best)—is loud-mouthing it in the kitchen.

If you want to live in the total lap of luxury, at an even tonier address than the Connaught and the Dorchester, make it Claridge's. Much of the Art Deco style of the 1930s remains, although there are other distinctive styles as well, ranging from modern to neoclassical. The hotel's strong sense of tradition and old-fashioned "Britishness" are also intact, in spite of the gloss and the hip clientele. Afternoon tea at Claridge's remains a quintessentially English tradition. The accommodations here are the most diverse in London, ranging from the costly and stunning Brook Penthouse—complete with a personal butler—to the less expensive, so-called superior queen rooms with queen-size beds.

Brook St., London W1A 2JQ. © 020/7629-8860. Fax 020/7499-2210. www.claridges.co.uk. 203 units. £479–£629 ($958–$1,258) double; from £1,500 ($3,000) suite. AE, DC, MC, V. Parking £50 ($100). Tube: Bond St. **Amenities:** 3 restaurants; 2 bars; health club; spa; business services; salon; room service; babysitting; laundry service; dry cleaning. *In room:* A/C, TV, fax, Wi-Fi, minibar, beverage maker, hair dryer, safe.

The Dorchester ★★★   One of London's best hotels, it has all the elegance of the Connaught, but without the upper-crust attitude that can verge on snobbery. Few hotels have the time-honored experience of "the Dorch," which has maintained a tradition of fine comfort and cuisine since it opened in 1931. Breaking from the neoclassical tradition, the most ambitious architects of the era designed a building of reinforced concrete clothed in terrazzo slabs. The Dorchester boasts guest rooms outfitted with Irish linen sheets on comfortable beds, plus all the electronic gadgetry you'd expect, and double- and triple-glazed windows to keep out noise, along with plump armchairs, cherrywood furnishings, and, in many cases, four-poster beds piled high with pillows.

53 Park Lane, London W1A 2HJ. © 800/727-9820 in the U.S., or 020/7629-8888. Fax 020/9629-8080. www.the dorchester.com. 244 units. £465–£510 ($930–$1,020) double; from £710 ($1,420) suite. AE, DC, MC, V. Parking £40 ($80). Tube: Hyde Park Corner or Marble Arch. **Amenities:** 3 restaurants; bar; health club; spa; tour desk; car-rental desk; courtesy car; business services and center; small shopping arcade; 2 salons; room service; babysitting; laundry service; same-day dry cleaning. *In room:* A/C, TV/DVD, fax, high-speed Internet, CD player, minibar, hair dryer, safe.

EXPENSIVE

The Selfridge ★   The location, right next door to Selfridges Department Store's food hall off Oxford Street, is wonderful, especially for shoppers. In fact, the hotel's seven floors look as if they are part of the department store. This mammoth hotel is a member of the Thistle hotel chain and caters to an even mix of business and leisure travelers. Ignore the drab entrance; the hotel brightens considerably in the second-floor reception room, with its wingback chairs, antique art, pine-paneled walls, and a rustic bar whose half-timbered decor was brought and installed piece by piece from an English barn that stood in the Middle Ages. The rooms are hardly the finest in this part of town, but they are usually affordable, especially if you snag one of the promotional offerings. Accommodations are well maintained, nicely decorated, tranquil, and generally spacious. *Tip:* Try for a room facing Orchard Street, as these are larger. Also, the best rooms are the premium units on floors three to five.

Orchard St., London W1H 6JS. © 0870/333-9117. Fax 0870/333-9217. www.thistle.co.uk. 294 units. £139–£162 ($278–$324) double; from £229 ($458) suite. AE, DC, MC, V. Parking £35 ($70). Tube: Bond St. **Amenities:** 2 restaurants; bar; room service; babysitting; laundry service; same-day dry cleaning. *In room:* A/C, TV, Wi-Fi, coffeemaker, hair dryer, safe (in some).

Sheraton Park Lane Hotel ★★   Since 1924, this has been the most traditional of the Park Lane mansions, even more so than the Dorchester. The hotel was sold in 1996 to the Sheraton Corporation, which continues to upgrade it but maintains its quintessential British style. Its Silver Entrance remains an Art Deco marvel that has been used as a backdrop in many films, including the classic BBC miniseries *Brideshead Revisited.*

Overlooking Green Park, the hotel offers luxurious accommodations that are a good deal—well, at least for pricey Park Lane. Many suites have marble fireplaces and original marble bathrooms. The rooms have all benefited from impressive refurbishment. The most tranquil rooms open onto a street in the rear. Rooms opening onto the court are dark. In the more deluxe rooms, you get better views.

Piccadilly, London W1J 7BX. © 800/325-3535 in the U.S., or 020/7499-6321. Fax 020/7499-1965. www.starwood. com/sheraton. 302 units. £159–£350 ($318–$700) double; from £300 ($600) suite. AE, DC, MC, V. Parking £40 ($80). Tube: Hyde Park Corner or Green Park. **Amenities:** 2 restaurants; bar; health club; business center; room service; laundry service; same-day dry cleaning. *In room:* A/C (in most rooms), TV, Wi-Fi, minibar, hair dryer, iron, safe (in most).

MARYLEBONE

VERY EXPENSIVE

The Langham 🏵🏵 After it was bombed in World War II, this well-located hotel languished as dusty office space for the BBC until the early 1990s, when it was painstakingly restored. The Langham's public rooms reflect the power and majesty of the British Empire at its apex. Guest rooms are somewhat less opulent but are still attractively furnished and comfortable, featuring French Provincial furniture and red oak trim. The hotel is within easy reach of Mayfair and Soho restaurants and theaters, and shopping on Oxford and Regent streets. Plus, Regent's Park is just blocks away.

1C Portland Place, London W1B 1JA. © **800/223-6800** or 020/7636-1000. Fax 020/7323-2340. www.langhamhotels. co.uk. 425 units. £350–£470 ($700–$940) double; from £470 ($940) suite; £490–£795 ($980–$1,590) club room. AE, DC, MC, V. Tube: Oxford Circus. **Amenities:** 2 restaurants; bar; Edwardian-style palm court; indoor heated pool; health club; spa; sauna; tour desk; courtesy car; business center; room service; massage; babysitting; laundry service; same-day dry cleaning. *In room:* A/C, TV, minibar, beverage maker, hair dryer, safe.

EXPENSIVE

Durrants Hotel 🏵 This historic hotel off Manchester Square (established in 1789) with its Georgian-detailed facade is snug, cozy, and traditional—almost like a poor man's Brown's (p. 122). We find it to be one of the most quintessentially English of all London hotels. You could invite the queen to Durrants for tea. Over the 100 years that they have owned the hotel, the Miller family has incorporated several neighboring houses into the original structure. A walk through the pine-and-mahogany-paneled public rooms is like stepping back in time: You'll even find an 18th-century letter-writing room. The rooms are rather bland except for elaborate cove moldings and comfortable furnishings, including good beds. Some are air-conditioned, and some are, alas, small. Bathrooms are tiny, with tub/shower combinations.

26–32 George St., London W1H 5BJ. © **020/7935-8131**. Fax 020/7487-3510. www.durrantshotel.co.uk. 92 units. £205 ($410) double; £210 ($420) family room for 3; from £340 ($680) suite. AE, MC, V. Tube: Bond St. or Baker St. **Amenities:** Restaurant; bar; room service; babysitting; laundry service; same-day dry cleaning. *In room:* A/C (in most), TV, high-speed Internet, hair dryer, safe (in most).

Park Plaza Sherlock Holmes Hotel It's not located at that legendary address, 221B Baker St., but it's nearby. The converted boutique hotel was once part of Bedford College for Women and later the YWCA. Former tenants wouldn't know the place today. Modern portraits of the world's most famous detective are on display, but the decor is contemporary. Bedrooms come in a wide range of sizes and styles, ranked superior, executive, or studio. Most preferred, at least by us, is a trio of loft suites. Guests gather in Sherlock's Bar & Grill for good British beer and food.

108 Baker St., London W1U 6LJ. © **020/7486-6161**. www.parkplaza.com/londonuk_sherlockholmes. 119 units. £189 ($378) double; £239 ($478) studio; £239–£319 ($478–$638) suite. AE, MC, V. Tube: Baker St. **Amenities:** Restaurant; bar; gym; spa; laundry service. *In room:* A/C, Wi-Fi, minibar, hair dryer, safe.

MODERATE

Hallam Hotel This heavily ornamented stone-and-brick Victorian—one of the few on the street to escape the Blitz—is just a 5-minute stroll from Oxford Circus. It's the property of brothers Grant and David Baker, who maintain it well. The hotel is warm and friendly, and the central location that you get for these prices can't be beat. The guest rooms are comfortably furnished with good beds. Several of the twin-bedded rooms are quite spacious and have adequate closet space.

12 Hallam St., Portland Place, London W1N 5LF. © **020/7580-1166.** Fax 020/7323-4527. www.hallamhotel.com. 25 units. £100 ($200) double. Rates include English breakfast. AE, DC, MC, V. Tube: Oxford Circus. **Amenities:** Bar. *In room:* TV, minibar, coffeemaker, hair dryer.

Hart House Hotel 🏃 *Kids*

Hart House is a long-enduring favorite with Frommer's readers. In the heart of the West End, this well-preserved historic building (one of a group of Georgian mansions occupied by exiled French nobles during the French Revolution) lies within easy walking distance of many theaters. The rooms—done in a combination of furnishings, ranging from Portobello antique to modern—are spick-and-span, each one with a different character. Favorites include no. 7, a triple with a big bathroom and shower. Ask for no. 11, on the top floor, if you'd like a brightly lit aerie. Housekeeping rates high marks here, and each bedroom is comfortably appointed with chairs, an armoire, a desk, and a large chest of drawers. Hart House has long been known as a good, safe place for traveling families. Many of its rooms are triples. Larger families can avail themselves of special family accommodations with connecting rooms.

51 Gloucester Place, Portman Sq., London W1U 8JF. © **020/7935-2288.** Fax 020/7935-8516. www.harthouse.co.uk. 15 units. £125 ($250) double; £145 ($290) triple; £175 ($350) quad. Rates include English breakfast. MC, V. Tube: Marble Arch or Baker St. **Amenities:** Babysitting. *In room:* TV, coffeemaker, hair dryer.

The Sumner 🏃 *Finds*

This town-house hotel, part of an 1820s Georgian terrace, has blossomed into one of the finest boutique town-house hotels in central London. It retains much of its original architectural allure when it was a private Georgian residence. The standard rooms are midsize and attractively furnished, but you can also rent deluxe rooms with artwork and better furnishings. All the guest rooms are designer -decorated and luxuriously appointed, and there is also an elegant sitting room with a working fireplace and timber flooring.

54 Upper Berkeley St., Marble Arch, London W1H 7QR. © **020/7723-2244.** Fax 087/0705-8767. www.the sumner.com. 20 units. £125–£160 ($250–$320) double. Rates include buffet breakfast. AE, MC, V. Tube: Marble Arch. *In room:* A/C, TV, Wi-Fi, fridge, hair dryer.

INEXPENSIVE

Boston Court Hotel

Upper Berkeley is a classic street of B&Bs; in days of yore, it was home to Elizabeth Montagu (1720–1800), "queen of the bluestockings," who defended Shakespeare against attacks by Voltaire. Today, it's a good, safe, respectable retreat at an affordable price. This unfrilly hotel offers accommodations in a centrally located Victorian-era building within walking distance of Oxford Street shopping and Hyde Park. The small rooms have been redecorated with a no-nonsense decor.

26 Upper Berkeley St., Marble Arch, London W1H 7QL. © **020/7723-1445.** Fax 020/7262-8823. www.boston courthotel.co.uk. 15 units, 4 with shower only. £70–£75 ($140–$150) double with shower only; £80–£85 ($160–$170) double with bathroom; £90–£95 ($180–$190) triple with bathroom. Rates include continental breakfast. MC, V. Tube: Marble Arch. **Amenities:** Laundry service. *In room:* TV, fridge, coffeemaker, hair dryer.

Edward Lear Hotel

This popular hotel, situated 1 block from Marble Arch, is made all the more desirable by the bouquets of fresh flowers in its public rooms. It occupies a pair of brick town houses dating from 1780. The western house was the London home of 19th-century artist and poet Edward Lear, famous for his nonsense verse, and his illustrated limericks adorn the walls of one of the sitting rooms. Steep stairs lead up to cozy rooms, which range from spacious to broom-closet size. Bedrooms are looking better than ever following a wholesale renovation in 2007. If you're looking for classiness, know that the bacon on your plate came from the same butcher used by the queen. One major drawback to the hotel: This is a very noisy part of town. Rear rooms are quieter.

28–30 Seymour St., London W1H 7JB. © 020/7402-5401. Fax 020/7706-3766. www.edlear.com. 32 units, 18 with bathroom. £80 ($160) double without bathroom, £83 ($166) with shower only, £85 ($170) with bathroom; £72–£85 ($144–$170) triple without bathroom, £74–£99 ($148–$198) with shower only. Rates include English breakfast and tax. AE, MC, V. Tube: Marble Arch. *In room:* TV, coffeemaker.

ST. JAMES'S
VERY EXPENSIVE

The Ritz ✦✦✦   Built in French Renaissance style and opened by César Ritz in 1906, this hotel overlooking Green Park is synonymous with luxury. Gold-leafed molding, marble columns, and potted palms abound, and a gold-leafed statue, *La Source,* adorns the fountain of the oval-shaped Palm Court. After a major restoration, the hotel is better than ever: New carpeting and air-conditioning have been installed in the guest rooms, and an overall polishing has recaptured much of the Ritz's original splendor. Still, this Ritz lags far behind the much grander one in Paris (with which it is not affiliated). The Belle Epoque guest rooms, each with its own character, are spacious and comfortable. Many have marble fireplaces, elaborate gilded plasterwork, and a decor of soft pastel hues. A few rooms have their original brass beds and marble fireplaces. Corner rooms are grander and more spacious.

150 Piccadilly, London W1J 9BR. © 877/748-9536 in the U.S., or 020/7493-8181. Fax 020/7493-2687. www.theritz london.com. 136 units. £340 ($680) double; from £620 ($1,240) suite. Children 15 and younger stay free in parent's room. AE, DC, MC, V. Parking £54 ($108). Tube: Green Park. **Amenities:** 2 restaurants (including the Palm Court); bar; exercise room; spa; business services; room service; massage; babysitting; laundry service; same-day dry cleaning. *In room:* A/C, TV, fax, high-speed Internet, minibar, hair dryer, safe.

EXPENSIVE

Dukes Hotel ✦✦✦   Dukes provides elegance without ostentation in what was presumably someone's *Upstairs, Downstairs* town house. Along with its nearest competitors, the Stafford and 22 Jermyn Street, it caters to those looking for charm, style, and tradition in a hotel. It stands in a quiet courtyard off St. James's Place; turn-of-the-20th-century gas lamps help put you into the proper mood before entering the front door. Each well-furnished guest room is decorated in the style of a particular English period, ranging from Regency to Edwardian. It's a lot cozier, more intimate, and even more clubbish than the Stafford, and Dukes is more tranquil since it's set in its own gas-lit alley.

35 St. James's Place, London SW1A 1NY. © 800/381-4702 in the U.S., or 020/7491-4840. Fax 020/7493-1264. www.dukeshotel.co.uk. 90 units. £300–£420 ($600–$840) double; from £660 ($1,320) suite. AE, DC, MC, V. Parking £55 ($110). Tube: Green Park. **Amenities:** Restaurant; bar; health club; spa; tour desk; business services; room service; babysitting; laundry service; same-day dry cleaning. *In room:* A/C, TV, Wi-Fi, minibar, hair dryer, safe.

The Stafford Hotel ✦✦✦   Famous for its American Bar, its St. James's address, and the warmth of its Edwardian decor, the Stafford competes well with Dukes for a tasteful, discerning clientele. All the guest rooms are individually decorated, reflecting the hotel's origins as a private home. Many singles contain queen-size beds. Some of the deluxe units offer four-posters that will make you feel like Henry VIII. Much has been done to preserve the original style of these rooms, including preservation of the original A-beams on the upper floors. You can bet that no 18th-century horse ever slept with the electronic safes, stereo systems, and quality furnishings (mostly antique reproductions) that these rooms feature. Units on the top floor are small. In 2007, 26 luxury junior and master suites were added in the Stafford Mews, each filled with antiques and luxury facilities.

16–18 St. James's Place, London SW1A 1NJ. ⓒ **800/525-4800** in the U.S., or 020/7493-0111. Fax 020/7493-7121. www.thestaffordhotel.co.uk. 107 units. £260–£470 ($520–$940) double; from £495 ($990) suite. AE, DC, MC, V. No parking. Tube: Green Park. **Amenities:** Restaurant; American bar; gym; business services; room service; babysitting; laundry service; same-day dry cleaning. *In room:* A/C, TV, fax, Wi-Fi, CD player, hair dryer, safe.

TRAFALGAR SQUARE
EXPENSIVE

The Trafalgar 🌂🌂   In the heart of landmark Trafalgar Square, this is Hilton's first boutique hotel in London. The facade of this 19th-century structure was preserved, while the guest rooms inside were refitted to modern standards. Because of the original architecture, many of the rooms are uniquely shaped and sometimes offer split-level layouts. Large windows open onto panoramic views of Trafalgar Square. The decor in the rooms is minimalist, and comfort is combined with simple luxury. The greatest view of London's cityscape is from the Hilton's rooftop garden.

2 Spring Gardens, Trafalgar Sq., London SW1A 2TS. ⓒ **800/774-1500** in the U.S., or 020/7870-2900. Fax 020/ 7870-2911. www.thetrafalgar.com. 129 units. £259–£330 ($518–$660) double. AE, DC, MC, V. Parking £30 ($60). Tube: Charing Cross. **Amenities:** Restaurant; bar; gym; spa; courtesy car; business services; room service; laundry service; same-day dry cleaning. *In room:* A/C, TV/DVD and DVD library, CD player and CD library, minibar, beverage maker, hair dryer, iron, safe.

SOHO
EXPENSIVE

The Courthouse Hotel Kempinski 🌂🌂   Guests from Oscar Wilde to Mick Jagger have passed through the doors of this historic courthouse. But today, under the German hotel chain Kempinski, the hospitality is better than ever. In a spectacular reclamation of an existing structure, the hotel retains many aspects of its landmark building, including original Robert Adams fireplaces. A bar has been installed inside three of the original prison cells. The judges' bench, witness stand, and dock still occupy center stage in Silk, the hotel's deluxe dining room. The location is among the best in London, opposite the department store Liberty's and Carnaby Street, just off Regent Street.

Bedrooms are midsize to spacious, each comfortably and tastefully decorated, with 13 suites. The best rooms are in the new wing that was built on the site of a former police station. Our favorite retreat here is the roof terrace, where light meals and cocktails are served.

19–21 Great Marlborough St., London W1F 7HL. ⓒ **800/426-3135** in the U.S., or 020/7297-5555. Fax 020/ 7297-5566. www.courthouse-hotel.com. 116 units. £290–£390 ($580–$780) double; from £550 ($1,100) suite. AE, DC, MC, V. Tube: Oxford Circus. **Amenities:** 2 restaurants; bar; roof terrace; indoor pool; gym; spa; room service; laundry service; same-day dry cleaning. *In room:* A/C, TV, high-speed Internet, minibar, safe.

Haymarket Hotel 🌂🌂🌂   This is a chic upmarket hotel in London for those who want to avoid the grandes dames. Next to the historic Haymarket Theatre, the hotel is ideal for theatergoers. Like all Firmdale hotels, it makes a bold statement with colors of turquoise, fuchsia, mango, and even acid green. Although completely modernized and perhaps the most sophisticated small hotel of London, many satisfying proportions of the original 19th-century John Nash architecture remains. Original works of art and antiques are used, and the bedrooms are sumptuously elegant with fine linens and the latest amenities. There's even an indoor pool lounge.

1 Suffolk Place, London SW1Y 4BP. ℂ **020/7470-4000.** Fax 020/7470-4004. www.firmdale.com. 50 units. £250–£325 ($500–$650) double; £455 ($910) junior suite. AE, DC, MC, V. Tube: Tottenham Court Rd. **Amenities:** Restaurant; bar; indoor pool; gym; room service; laundry service. *In room:* A/C, TV/DVD, Wi-Fi, CD player, hair dryer, safe.

Hazlitt's 1718 🌟🌟 *Finds*   This gem, housed in three historic homes on Soho Square, is one of London's best small hotels. Built in 1718, the hotel is named for William Hazlitt, who founded the Unitarian Church in Boston and wrote four volumes on the life of his hero, Napoleon.

Hazlitt's is a favorite with artists, actors, and models. It's eclectic and filled with odds and ends picked up around the country at estate auctions. Some find its Georgian decor a bit spartan, but the 2,000 original prints hanging on the walls brighten it considerably. Many bedrooms have four-poster beds; some of the floors dip and sway, and there's no elevator, but it's all part of the charm. It has just as much character as the Fielding Hotel (p. 131) but is a lot more comfortable. Some rooms are a bit small, but most are spacious, all with state-of-the-art appointments. Accommodations in the back are quieter but perhaps too dark.

6 Frith St., London W1D 3JA. ℂ **020/7434-1771.** Fax 020/7439-1524. www.hazlittshotel.com. 23 units. £265 ($530) double; £300 ($600) suite. AE, DC, MC, V. Tube: Leicester Sq. or Tottenham Court Rd. **Amenities:** Room service; babysitting; laundry service; same-day dry cleaning. *In room:* A/C, TV, Wi-Fi, minibar, hair dryer, safe.

The Sanderson 🌟🌟🌟   Ian Schrager, the king of New York hip, has brought Tenth Avenue in Manhattan to London. For his latest London hotel, Schrager secured the help of talented partners Philippe Starck and Andra Andrei to create an "ethereal, transparent urban spa," in which walls are replaced by glass and sheer layers of curtains. The hotel, located in a former corporate building near Oxford Street, north of Soho, comes with a lush bamboo-filled roof garden, a large courtyard, and spa. That's not all—Alain Ducasse, arguably the world's greatest chef, directs its restaurant. The accommodations are cutting edge. Although the transformation of this building into a hotel has been remarkable, the dreary grid facade of aluminum squares and glass remains. Your bed is likely to be an Italian silver-leaf sleigh attended by spidery polished stainless-steel night tables and draped with a fringed pashmina shawl.

50 Berners St., London W1T 3NG. ℂ **800/697-1791** or 020/7300-1400. Fax 020/7300-1401. www.sandersonlondon. com. 150 units. £285–£460 ($570–$920) double; from £615 ($1,230) suite. AE, DC, MC, V. Tube: Oxford Circus or Tottenham Court Rd. **Amenities:** Restaurant; 2 bars; health club; spa; business services; room service; in-room massage; babysitting; laundry service; same-day dry cleaning. *In room:* A/C, TV/DVD, Wi-Fi, CD player, minibar, hair dryer, safe.

The Soho Hotel 🌟🌟🌟   A former parking garage in the heart of bustling Soho just became our favorite nest in London. When it's time to check out, we never want to leave. British hoteliers Kit and Tim Kemp have come up with a stunner here. At night we have a cocoonlike feeling entering this luxury lair in a cul-de-sac off Dean Street. The theaters of Shaftesbury are only a block or two away, as is the Ivy restaurant.

All the extremely spacious bedrooms are individually designed in granite and oak. There are four penthouses on the fifth floor with tree-lined terraces opening onto panoramic sweeps of London. All the famous Kemp touches can be found, from boldly striped furnishings to deep bathtubs for a late-night soak. The glitterati, mostly actors and filmmakers, can be seen hanging out at the bar.

4 Richmond Mews, London W1D 3DH. ℂ **020/7559-3000.** Fax 020/7559-3003. www.firmdalehotels.com. 91 units. £255–£315 ($510–$630) double; from £370 ($740) suite. AE, MC, V. Tube: Oxford Circus or Piccadilly Circus. **Amenities:** Restaurant; bar; exercise room; gym; salon; room service; 2 private cinemas. *In room:* A/C, TV/DVD, Wi-Fi, CD player, minibar, hair dryer, safe.

BLOOMSBURY

EXPENSIVE

The Academy Hotel ⭐   The Academy is in the heart of London's publishing district. If you look out your window, you see where Virginia Woolf and other literary members of the Bloomsbury Group passed by every day. Many original architectural details were preserved when these three 1776 Georgian row houses were joined. The hotel was substantially upgraded in the 1990s, with a bathroom added to every bedroom (whether there was space or not). Grace notes include glass panels, colonnades, and intricate plasterwork on the facade. With overstuffed armchairs and half-canopied beds, rooms sometimes evoke English-country-house living, but that of the poorer relations. Guests who have been here before always request rooms opening on the garden in back and not those in front with ducted fresh air, though the front units have double-glazing to cut down on the noise. *Warning:* If you have a problem with stairs, know that no elevators rise to the four floors.

21 Gower St., London WC1E 6HG. ℃ 020/7631-4115. Fax 020/7636-3442. www.theetoncollection.com. 49 units. £140–£165 ($280–$330) double; £180 ($360) suite. AE, DC, MC, V. Tube: Tottenham Court Rd., Goodge St., or Russell Sq. **Amenities:** Bar; room service; laundry service; same-day dry cleaning. *In room:* A/C, TV, Wi-Fi, CD player, minibar, beverage maker, hair dryer, iron, trouser press, safe.

Grange Blooms Hotel ⭐   This restored 18th-century town house has a pedigree: It stands in what were formerly the grounds of Montague House (now the British Museum). Even though it's in the heart of London, the house has a country-home atmosphere, complete with fireplace, period art, and copies of *Country Life* in the magazine rack. Guests take morning coffee in a walled garden overlooking the British Museum. In summer, light meals are served. The small- to medium-size bedrooms are individually designed with traditional elegance, in beautifully muted tones.

7 Montague St., London WC1B 5BP. ℃ 020/7323-1717. Fax 020/7636-6498. www.grangehotels.com. 26 units. £135–£160 ($270–$320) double. AE, DC, MC, V. Tube: Russell Sq. **Amenities:** Restaurant; bar; courtesy car; room service; laundry service; dry cleaning. *In room:* TV, minibar, coffeemaker, hair dryer, trouser press.

Myhotel ⭐ *(Finds*   Creating shock waves among staid Bloomsbury hoteliers, Myhotel is a London row house on the outside with an Asian *moderne*-style interior. It is designed according to feng shui principles—the ancient Chinese art of placement that utilizes the flow of energy in a space. The rooms have mirrors, but they're positioned so you don't see yourself when you first wake up—feng shui rule number one (probably a good rule, feng shui or no feng shui). Rooms are havens of comfort, taste, and tranquillity. Excellent sleep-inducing beds are found in all rooms. Tipping is discouraged, and each guest is assigned a personal assistant responsible for his or her happiness. Aimed at today's young, hip traveler, Myhotel lies within a short walk of Covent Garden and the British Museum.

11–13 Bayley St., Bedford Sq., London WC1B 3HD. ℃ 020/7667-6000. Fax 020/7667-6044. www.myhotels.co.uk. 78 units. £189–£265 ($378–$530) double; from £319 ($638) suite. AE, DC, MC, V. Tube: Tottenham Court Rd. or Goodge St. **Amenities:** Restaurant; bar; exercise room; car at discounted rate; room service; babysitting; laundry service; same-day dry cleaning. *In room:* A/C, TV, Wi-Fi, beverage maker, hair dryer, trouser press (in some), safe.

MODERATE

Harlingford Hotel *(Value*   This hotel comprises three town houses built in the 1820s and joined around 1900 with a bewildering array of staircases and meandering hallways. Set in the heart of Bloomsbury, it's run by a management that seems genuinely concerned about the welfare of its guests, unlike the management at many of the neighboring hotel rivals. (They even distribute little mincemeat pies to their guests during the Christmas holidays.) Double-glazed windows cut down on the street noise, and all the bedrooms are comfortable and inviting. The most comfortable rooms are on the second and third levels, but expect to climb some steep English stairs (there's no elevator). Avoid the rooms on ground level, as they are darker and have less security. You'll have use of the tennis courts in Cartwright Gardens.

61–63 Cartwright Gardens, London WC1H 9EL. ⓒ 020/7387-1551. Fax 020/7387-4616. www.harlingfordhotel. com. 43 units. £99 ($198) double; £110 ($220) triple; £115 ($230) quad. Rates include English breakfast. AE, MC, V. Tube: Russell Sq., Kings Cross, or Euston. **Amenities:** Use of tennis courts in Cartwright Gardens. *In room:* TV, coffeemaker, hair dryer.

INEXPENSIVE

Crescent Hotel   Although Ruskin and Shelley no longer pass by, the Crescent still stands in the heart of academic London. The private square is owned by the City Guild of Skinners (who are furriers, as you might have guessed) and guarded by the University of London, whose student residential halls are across the street. You have access to the gardens and private tennis courts belonging to the City Guild of Skinners. The hotel owners view the Crescent as an extension of their home and welcome you to its comfortably elegant Georgian surroundings, which date from 1810. Some guests have been returning for 4 decades. Bedrooms range from small singles with shared bathrooms to more spacious twin and double rooms with private bathrooms.

49–50 Cartwright Gardens, London WC1H 9EL. ⓒ 020/7387-1515. Fax 020/7383-2054. www.crescenthotelof london.com. 27 units, 18 with bathroom (some with shower only, some with tub and shower). £97 ($194) double with bathroom; £120 ($240) family room. Rates include English breakfast. MC, V. Tube: Russell Sq., Kings Cross, or Euston. **Amenities:** Use of tennis courts in Cartwright Gardens; babysitting. *In room:* TV, Wi-Fi, coffeemaker.

The Jenkins Hotel ⓕ *Value*   Followers of the Agatha Christie TV series *Poirot* will recognize this Cartwright Gardens residence—it was featured in the series. The antiques are gone and the rooms are small, but some of the original charm of the Georgian house remains—enough so that the London *Mail on Sunday* proclaimed it one of the "10 best hotel values" in the city. All the rooms have been redecorated in traditional Georgian style, and many have been completely refurbished. The location is great, near the British Museum, theaters, and antiquarian bookshops. There are some drawbacks: no lift and no reception or sitting room. But this is a place where you can settle in and feel at home.

45 Cartwright Gardens, London WC1H 9EH. ⓒ 020/7387-2067. Fax 020/7383-3139. www.jenkinshotel.demon. co.uk. 14 units. £89 ($178) double; £105 ($210) triple. Rates include English breakfast. MC, V. Tube: Russell Sq., Kings Cross, or Euston. **Amenities:** Use of tennis courts in Cartwright Gardens; use of washer/dryer. *In room:* TV, fridge, coffeemaker, hair dryer, safe.

Ruskin Hotel   Although the hotel is named for author John Ruskin, the ghosts of other literary legends who lived nearby haunt you: Mary Shelley plotting her novel, *Frankenstein,* and James Barrie fantasizing about *Peter Pan.* This hotel has been managed for 2 decades by a hardworking family and enjoys a repeat clientele. Management keeps the place spick-and-span, though you shouldn't expect a decorator's flair. The furnishings, though well polished, are a bit worn. Double-glazing in the front blots out the noise, but we prefer the cozily old-fashioned chambers in the rear, as they open onto a park. Sorry, no elevator. *Note:* Prices here are kept low because only a half-dozen rooms have a private bathroom.

23–24 Montague St., London WC1B 5BH. ⓒ 020/7636-7388. Fax 020/7323-1662. 33 units, 6 with bathroom. £67 ($134) double without bathroom, £75 ($150) with bathroom; £93 ($186) triple without bathroom, £108 ($216) with bathroom. Rates include English breakfast. AE, DC, MC, V. Tube: Russell Sq., Holborn, or Tottenham Court Rd. *In room:* Coffeemaker, hair dryer.

KINGS CROSS
INEXPENSIVE
Jesmond Dene Hotel   Well-maintained and cozy bedrooms are found at this well-run B&B in the rapidly gentrifying area of Kings Cross. For those who plan to use this terminus, this is a good, convenient choice for transportation, including Eurostar to Paris. All the small bedrooms have been refurbished and are comfortable and tasteful.

27 Argyle St., Kings Cross, London WC1H 8EP. (C) 020/7837-4654. Fax 020/7833-1633. www.jesmonddenehotel. co.uk. 23 rooms, 20 with private bathroom. £60 ($120) double without bathroom, £80 ($160) with bathroom; £85–£100 ($170–$200) triple; £120 ($240) quad. AE, DC, MC, V. Tube: Kings Cross. **Amenities:** Breakfast room. *In room:* TV, Wi-Fi.

COVENT GARDEN
VERY EXPENSIVE
Covent Garden Hotel ★★★   This former hospital building lay neglected for years until it was reconfigured in 1996 by hot hoteliers Tim and Kit Kemp—whose flair for interior design is legendary—into one of London's most charming boutique hotels in one of the West End's hippest shopping neighborhoods. *Travel + Leisure* called this hotel 1 of the 25 hottest places to stay in the *world*. It remains so. Behind a bottle-green facade reminiscent of a 19th-century storefront, the hotel has a welcoming lobby outfitted with elaborate inlaid furniture and elegant draperies, plus a charming restaurant. Upstairs, accessible via a dramatic stone staircase, soundproof bedrooms are furnished in English style with Asian fabrics, many adorned with hand-embroidered designs. The hotel has a decorative trademark—each room has a clothier's mannequin.

10 Monmouth St., London WC2H 9HB. (C) 800/553-6674 in the U.S., or 020/7806-1000. Fax 020/7806-1100. www.firmdale.com. 58 units. £275–£320 ($550–$640) double; £375–£995 ($750–$1,990) suite. AE, DC, MC, V. Tube: Covent Garden or Leicester Sq. **Amenities:** Restaurant; bar; small exercise room; tour desk; business services; salon; room service; massage; babysitting; laundry service; same-day dry cleaning; video library. *In room:* A/C, TV/DVD, Wi-Fi, CD player, minibar, hair dryer, safe.

St. Martins Lane ★★★   "Eccentric and irreverent, with a sense of humor," is how Ian Schrager describes his cutting-edge Covent Garden hotel, which he transformed from a 1960s office building into a chic enclave. This was the first hotel that Schrager designed outside the United States, after a string of successes from New York to West Hollywood. The mix of hip design and a sense of cool have been imported across the pond. Whimsical touches abound. For example, a string of daisies replaces DO NOT DISTURB signs. Rooms are all white, but you can use the full-spectrum lighting to make them any color. Floor-to-ceiling windows in every room offer a panoramic view of London.

45 St. Martins Lane, London WC2N 4HX. (C) 800/697-1791 in the U.S., or 020/7300-5500. Fax 020/7300-5501. www.stmartinslane.com. 204 units. £495 ($990) double; from £630 ($1,260) suite. AE, DC, MC, V. Tube: Covent Garden or Leicester Sq. **Amenities:** Restaurant; 2 bars; gym; spa services from nearby spa on request; courtesy car; business center; room service; babysitting; laundry service; same-day dry cleaning; video library. *In room:* A/C, TV, Wi-Fi, minibar, hair dryer, safe.

MODERATE
The Fielding Hotel ★ *Finds*   One of London's more eccentric hotels, this rickety walk-up is cramped, quirky, and quaint, and an enduring favorite of some. Luring media types, the hotel is named after novelist Henry Fielding of *Tom Jones* fame, who

lived in Broad Court. It lies on a pedestrian street still lined with 19th-century gas lamps. The Royal Opera House is across the street, and the pubs, shops, and restaurants of lively Covent Garden are just beyond the front door. Rooms are small but charmingly old-fashioned and traditional. Some units are redecorated or at least "touched up" every year, though floors dip and sway, and the furnishings and fabrics, though clean, have known better times. With a location like this, in the heart of London, the Fielding keeps guests coming back; in fact, some love the hotel's claustrophobic charm. Children 12 and younger are not welcome; occasionally the staff makes adult patrons feel the same.

4 Broad Court, Bow St., London WC2B 5QZ. © 020/7836-8305. Fax 020/7497-0064. www.the-fielding-hotel.co.uk. 24 units. £105–£125 ($210–$250) double. AE, DC, MC, V. Tube: Covent Garden. *In room:* TV, coffeemaker.

INEXPENSIVE

Royal Adelphi Hotel   If you care most about being in a central location, consider the Royal Adelphi. Close to Covent Garden, the theater district, and Trafalgar Square, it's an unorthodox choice away from the typical B&B stamping grounds. London has far better B&Bs, but not in this part of town. Although the bedrooms call to mind London's swinging 1960s heyday, accommodations are decently maintained and comfortable, with good beds. Plumbing, however, is a bit creaky, and the lack of air-conditioning can make London feel like summer in the Australian outback during the city's few hot days.

21 Villiers St., London WC2N 6ND. © 020/7930-8764. Fax 020/7930-8735. www.royaladelphihotel.co.uk. 47 units, 34 with bathroom. £70 ($140) double without bathroom, £92 ($184) with bathroom; £120 ($240) triple with bathroom. Rates include continental breakfast and tax. AE, DC, MC, V. Tube: Charing Cross or Embankment. **Amenities:** Bar. *In room:* TV, coffeemaker, hair dryer.

WESTMINSTER/VICTORIA
EXPENSIVE

City Inn Westminster ✦   Next door to Tate Britain and Parliament, this purpose-built inn with a vast array of rooms is at the nexus of elite London. The River Thames and London Eye are within a short walk. The lobby is graced with stone, oak, and leather chairs, and the on-site restaurant specializes in game and salmon, as befits the hotel's Scottish ownership. The best accommodations are the 67 City Club rooms or the 16 suites, but all units are comfortable with a fresh, light, and contemporary design. Business clients predominate during the week, but on weekends rates are often slashed to bargain prices. Ask about this when booking. Try, if possible, for a guest room opening onto the Thames or else views of Parliament. Rooms are soundproof with 18 inches of concrete between each unit. You can drink and dine in the City Café restaurant and bar with its alfresco terrace, and the stylish Millbank Lounge bar is a popular rendezvous point at night.

30 John Islip St., London SW1P 4DD. © 020/7630-1000. Fax 020/7233-7575. www.cityinn.com. 460 units. £225 ($450) double; £265 ($530) city club room; from £289 ($578) suite. AE, DC, MC, V. Tube: Pimlico or Westminster. **Amenities:** Restaurant; 2 bars; gym; room service. *In room:* A/C, TV/DVD, high-speed Internet, CD player, hair dryer, minibar, beverage maker, iron.

41 Hotel ✦✦✦ *Finds*   This relatively unknown but well-placed gem offers the intimate atmosphere of a private club combined with a high level of personal service. Completely self-contained, it occupies the fifth (top) floor of the building whose lower floors contain an also-recommended hotel, the Rubens at the Palace Hotel. 41 Hotel is best suited to couples or those traveling alone—especially women. Public areas feature an abundance of mahogany, antiques, fresh flowers, and rich fabrics. Read, relax, or watch TV in the library-style lounge, where a complimentary continental breakfast and afternoon snacks are served each day. Guest rooms are individually sized, but all feature elegant black-and-white color schemes and magnificent beds with Egyptian-cotton linens.

41 Buckingham Palace Rd., London SW1W OPS. © **877/955-1515** in the U.S. or Canada, or 020/7300-0041. Fax 020/7300-0141. www.41hotel.com. 30 units. £295–£345 ($590–$690) double; £495–£695 ($990–$1,390) suite. Rates include continental breakfast, afternoon snacks, and evening canapés. AE, DC, MC, V. Tube: Victoria. **Amenities:** Bar; lounge; access to nearby health club; business center; room service; massage; babysitting; laundry service; dry cleaning. *In room:* A/C, TV, fax, high-speed Internet, CD player, iPod docking station, minibar, beverage maker, hair dryer, iron, safe.

MODERATE
New England A family-run business for nearly a quarter of a century, this hotel shut down at the millennium for a complete overhaul. Today it's better than ever and charges an affordable price. Its elegant 19th-century exterior conceals a completely bright and modern interior. On a corner in the Pimlico area, which forms part of the City of Westminster, the hotel is neat and clean and one of the most welcoming in the area—it justly prides itself on its clientele of "repeats." It's also one of the few hotels in the area with an elevator.

20 St. George's Dr., London SW1V 4BN. © **020/7834-1595.** Fax 020/7834-9000. www.newenglandhotel.com. 20 units. £119–£139 ($238–$278) double; £139 ($278) triple; £159 ($318) quad. Rates include breakfast. MC, V. Tube: Victoria. *In room:* TV, Wi-Fi, hair dryer.

Sanctuary House Hotel ✿ Only in the new London, where hotels are bursting into bloom like daffodils, would you find a hotel so close to Westminster Abbey. And a pub hotel, no less, with rooms on the upper floors above the tavern. The building was converted by Fuller Smith and Turner, a traditional brewery in Britain. Accommodations have a rustic feel, but they have first-rate beds. Downstairs, a pub/restaurant, part of the Sanctuary, offers old-style British meals that have ignored changing culinary fashions. "We like tradition," one of the perky staff members told us. "Why must everything be trendy? Some people come to England nostalgic for the old. Let others be trendy." Actually, the food is excellent if you appreciate the roast beef, Welsh lamb, and Dover sole that pleased the palates of Churchill and his contemporaries. Naturally, there's always plenty of brew on tap.

33 Tothill St., London SW1H 9LA. © **020/7799-4044.** Fax 020/7799-3657. www.fullershotels.com. 34 units. £99–£175 ($198–$350) double. AE, DC, MC, V. Tube: St. James's Park. **Amenities:** Restaurant; pub; room service; laundry service; dry cleaning. *In room:* A/C, TV, coffeemaker, hair dryer, trouser press.

IN & AROUND KNIGHTSBRIDGE
EXPENSIVE
Knightsbridge Hotel ✿✿ (Value The Knightsbridge Hotel attracts visitors from all over the world seeking a small, comfortable hotel in a high-rent district. It's fabulously located, sandwiched between fashionable Beauchamp Place and Harrods, with many of the city's top theaters and museums close at hand. Built in the early 1800s as a private town house, this place sits on a tranquil, tree-lined square, free from traffic. Two of London's premier hoteliers, Kit and Tim Kemp, who have been celebrated for their upmarket boutique hotels, have gone more affordable with a revamp of this hotel in the heart of the shopping district. All the Kemp "cult classics" are found here, including such luxe touches as granite-and-oak bathrooms, the Kemps' famed honor bar,

and Frette linens. The hotel has become an instant hit. Most bedrooms are spacious and furnished with traditional English fabrics. The best rooms are nos. 311 and 312 at the rear, each with a pitched ceiling and a small sitting area.

10 Beaufort Gardens, London SW3 1PT. ℂ 020/7584-6300. Fax 020/7584-6355. www.firmdalehotels.com. 44 units. £195–£280 ($390–$560) double; from £330 ($660) suite. AE, DC, MC, V. Tube: Knightsbridge. **Amenities:** Self-service bar; room service; babysitting; laundry service; same-day dry cleaning. *In room:* TV/DVD, Wi-Fi, CD player, minibar, hair dryer, safe.

MODERATE
Knightsbridge Green Hotel ✦
Repeat guests from around the world view this dignified 1890s structure as their home away from home. In 1966, when it was converted into a hotel, the developers kept its wide baseboards, cove moldings, high ceilings, and spacious proportions. Even without kitchens, the well-furnished suites come close to apartment-style living. Most rooms are spacious, with adequate storage space. Bedrooms are decorated with custom-made colors and are often individualized—one has a romantic sleigh bed. This is a solid choice for lodging, just around the corner from Harrods.

159 Knightsbridge, London SW1X 7PD. ℂ 020/7584-6274. Fax 020/7225-1635. www.thekghotel.co.uk. 28 units. £150–£175 ($300–$350) double; from £175 ($350) suite. AE, DC, MC, V. Tube: Knightsbridge. **Amenities:** Room service; laundry service; same-day dry cleaning. *In room:* A/C, TV, Wi-Fi, beverage maker, hair dryer, trouser press, safe.

30 Pavilion Road ✦ *Finds*
Searcy, one of London's best catering firms, operates this recycled surprise: an old pumping station that has been turned into a hotel that's only a hop, skip, and a jump from Harrods and the boutiques of Sloane Street. At this Knightsbridge oasis, you press a buzzer and are admitted to a freight elevator that carries you to the third floor. Upstairs, you'll encounter handsomely furnished rooms with antiques, tasteful fabrics, comfortable beds (some with canopies), and often a sitting alcove. Some of the tubs are placed right in the room instead of in a separate unit. Check out the rooftop garden.

30 Pavilion Rd., London SW1X 0HJ. ℂ 020/7584-4921. Fax 020/7823-8694. www.30pavilionroad.co.uk. 10 units. £180 ($360) double. Rates include continental breakfast. AE, DC, MC, V. Tube: Knightsbridge. **Amenities:** Room service; babysitting; laundry service; dry cleaning. *In room:* A/C, TV, Wi-Fi.

CHELSEA
EXPENSIVE
The Draycott Hotel ✦✦✦
Everything about this place, radically upgraded into a government five-star rating, reeks of British gentility, style, and charm. So attentive is the staff that past clients, who have included John Malkovich, Pierce Brosnan, and Gerard Depardieu, are greeted like old friends when they enter by a staff that manages to be both hip and cordial. The hotel took its present-day form when a third brick-fronted town house was added to a pair of interconnected town houses that had been functioning as a five-star hotel since the 1980s. That, coupled with tons of money spent on English antiques, rich draperies, and an upgrade of those expensive infrastructures you'll never see, including security, have transformed this place into a gem. Bedrooms are each outfitted differently, each with haute English style and plenty of fashion chic. As a special feature, the hotel serves complimentary drinks—tea at 4pm daily, champagne at 6pm, and hot chocolate at 9:30pm.

26 Cadogan Gardens, London SW3 2RP. ℂ 800/747-4942 or 020/7730-6466. Fax 020/7730-0236. www.draycott hotel.com. 35 units. £230–£290 ($460–$580) double; £370 ($740) suite. AE, DC, MC, V. Tube: Sloane Sq. **Amenities:** Bar; access to nearby spa and fitness club; room service; laundry service; dry cleaning. *In room:* A/C, TV/DVD, Wi-Fi, CD player, minibar.

San Domenico House ★★   This "toff" (dandy) address, a redbrick Victorian-era town house that has been tastefully renovated in recent years, is located in Chelsea near Sloane Square. It combines valuable 19th-century antiques with modern comforts. Our favorite spot here is the rooftop terrace; with views opening onto Chelsea, it's ideal for a relaxing breakfast or drink. Bedrooms come in varying sizes, ranging from small to spacious, but all are opulently furnished with flouncy draperies, tasteful fabrics, and sumptuous beds. Many rooms have draped four-poster or canopied beds and, of course, antiques.

29 Draycott Place, London SW3 2SH. ⓒ 800/324-9960 in the U.S., or 020/7581-5757. Fax 020/7584-1348. www.sandomenicohouse.com. 16 units. £225–£255 ($450–$510) double; £285 ($570) suite. AE, DC, MC, V. Tube: Sloane Sq. **Amenities:** Airport transportation (w/prior arrangement); business services; room service; babysitting; laundry service; same-day dry cleaning. *In room:* A/C, TV, high-speed Internet, minibar, hair dryer.

BELGRAVIA
MODERATE
The Diplomat Hotel ★ *Finds*   Part of the Diplomat's charm is that it is a small and reasonably priced hotel located in an otherwise prohibitively expensive neighborhood. Only minutes from Harrods Department Store, it was built in 1882 as a private residence by noted architect Thomas Cubbitt. The registration desk is framed by the sweep of a partially gilded circular staircase; above it, cherubs gaze down from a Regency-era chandelier. The staff is helpful, well mannered, and discreet. The high-ceilinged guest rooms are tastefully done in Victorian style. You get good—not grand—comfort here. Rooms are a bit small and usually furnished with twin beds.

2 Chesham St., London SW1X 8DT. ⓒ 020/7235-1544. Fax 020/7259-6153. www.thediplomathotel.co.uk. 26 units. £125–£170 ($250–$340) double. Rates include English buffet breakfast. AE, DC, MC, V. Tube: Sloane Sq. or Knightsbridge. **Amenities:** Snack bar; business services; babysitting; laundry service; same-day dry cleaning. *In room:* TV, coffeemaker, hair dryer, trouser press.

INEXPENSIVE
B + b Belgravia ★★   In its first year of operation (2005), this elegant town house won a top Gold Award as "the best B&B in London." It richly deserves it. Design, service, quality, and comfort paid off. The prices are also reasonable, the atmosphere in this massively renovated building is stylish, and the location grand: just a 5-minute walk from Victoria Station. The good-size bedrooms are luxuriously furnished. In the guest lounge with its comfy sofas, an open fire burns on nippy nights. There is also a DVD library, and tea and coffee are served 24 hours a day. The full English breakfast in the morning is one of the finest in the area.

64–66 Ebury St., Belgravia, London SW1W 9QD. ⓒ 020/7259-8570. Fax 020/7259-8591. www.bb-belgravia.com. 17 units. £107 ($214) double; £147 ($294) family room. Rates include a full English breakfast. AE, MC, V. Tube: Victoria Station. **Amenities:** Communal lounge; breakfast room. *In room:* TV, high-speed Internet.

KENSINGTON
EXPENSIVE
The Rockwell ★★★ *Finds*   One of London's latest hotels proves that high style doesn't always come with a high price tag in London. This independently owned bastion of deluxe comfort occupies a converted Georgian manse in South Kensington. Its bedrooms are tricked out with oak furnishings and Neisha Crosland wallpaper, each crafted to combine traditional English aesthetics with modern design. The bedrooms themselves are large and inviting and dressed with the finest of Egyptian cotton, feather pillows, and Merino wool blankets. Each room has a bespoke solid oak cupboard and

desk. Rooms are bright and airy with large windows and simple lines. Preferred are the garden units with their own private patios. On-site is the trendy One-Eight-One bistro whose menu is based on English fare given a contemporary twist. Yes, they serve lavender ice cream.

181 Cromwell Rd., London SW5 0SF. ⓒ 020/7244-2000. Fax 020/7244-2001. www.therockwell.com. 40 units. £160–£180 ($320–$360) double. AE, DC, MC, V. Tube: Earls Court or Gloucester Rd. **Amenities:** Restaurant; bar; access to nearby gym; room service; laundry service. In room: A/C, TV, Wi-Fi, minibar, safe.

INEXPENSIVE

Avonmore Hotel ⚃ Finds   The refurbished Avonmore is easily accessible to West End theaters and shops, yet it's located in a quiet neighborhood, only 2 minutes from the West Kensington stop on the District Line. This privately owned place—a former National Award winner as the best private hotel in London—boasts wall-to-wall carpeting in each tastefully decorated room. Bathrooms are well maintained, equipped either with a bathtub or shower. The owner, Margaret McKenzie, provides lots of personal service. An English breakfast is served in a cheerful room, and a wide range of drinks are available in the cozy bar.

66 Avonmore Rd., London W14 8RS. ⓒ 020/7603-4296. Fax 020/7603-4035. www.avonmorehotel.co.uk. 9 units. £85–£110 ($170–$220) double; £95–£130 ($190–$260) triple. Rates include English breakfast. AE, MC, V. Tube: West Kensington. **Amenities:** Bar; room service. In room: TV, Wi-Fi, minibar, coffeemaker, hair dryer.

Base2stay Value   Down in Kensington a new concept in hotels has emerged, offering great value by providing "a synthesis" of what guests really need and use—minus the frills. What you get are stylish, comfortably furnished accommodations with small kitchenettes. The cheapest rooms contain bunk beds for two, and suites can be made by way of interconnecting rooms. Living may be stripped to the basics, but this is no hostel, as there is a 24-hour reception service as well as daily maid service.

25 Courtfield Gardens, London SW5 0PG. ⓒ 800/511-9821 in the U.S., or 020/7491-2948. www.base2stay.com. 67 units. £95 ($190) bunk beds for 2; £119 ($238) double; £189 ($378) deluxe units for 4 guests. AE, MC, V. Tube: Earls Court. In room: A/C, TV, high-speed Internet, kitchenette.

EASYHotel Value   This hotel runs on the principle that guests would rather have smaller hotel rooms and pay less. If you're claustrophobic, this hotel is definitely not for you. The rooms are 6 to 7m (65–75 sq. ft.), with most of the space taken up by standard double beds. If you can get a room with a window, do so because it makes a big difference. Just off Cromwell Road between South Kensington and Earls Court, Easy offers all doubles with cramped bathrooms containing a shower. There are flatscreen TVs in every unit, but a £5 ($10) fee is assessed to use the set. One staff member is permanently on-site, but no services are offered. Housekeeping service costs an optional £10 ($20) per day, there is no elevator, and checkout time is 10am. Instead of phoning the hotel, all EASYHotel bookings are taken by credit card through its website.

14 Lexham Gardens, Kensington, London W8 5JE. www.easyhotel.com. 34 units. £30–£50 ($60–$100) double. MC, V. Tube: South Kensington or Earls Court. In room: A/C, TV.

NOTTING HILL
EXPENSIVE

The Portobello Hotel ⚃   On an elegant Victorian terrace near Portobello Road, two 1850s-era town houses have been combined to form a quirky property that has its devotees. We remember these rooms when they looked better, but they still have plenty of character. Who knows what will show up in what nook? Perhaps a Chippendale, a claw-foot tub, or a round bed tucked under a gauze canopy. Try for no. 16, with a full-tester bed facing the garden. Some of the cheaper rooms are so tiny that they're basically garrets, but others have been combined into large doubles. An elevator goes to the third floor; after that, it's the stairs. Since windows are not double-glazed, request a room in the quiet rear. Some rooms are air-conditioned. Service is erratic at best, but this is still a good choice.

22 Stanley Gardens, London W11 2NG. (𝄯 020/7727-2777. Fax 020/7792-9641. www.portobello-hotel.co.uk. 24 units. £190–£270 ($380–$540) double; £242–£452 ($484–$904) suite. Rates include continental breakfast. AE, MC, V. Tube: Notting Hill Gate or Holland Park. **Amenities:** 24-hr. restaurant and bar in basement; nearby gym; business services; room service; massage; laundry service; same-day dry cleaning. *In room:* A/C (some rooms), TV, minibar, beverage maker, hair dryer.

MODERATE

The Gate Hotel   This antiques-hunters' favorite is the only hotel along the length of Portobello Road—and because of rigid zoning restrictions, it will probably remain the only one for years to come. It was built in the 1820s as housing for farmhands at the now-defunct Portobello Farms and has functioned as a hotel since 1932. It has two cramped but cozy bedrooms on each of its three floors. Be prepared for some *very* steep English stairs. Rooms are color coordinated, with a bit of style, and have such extras as full-length mirrors and built-in wardrobes. Housekeeping is excellent. Especially intriguing are the wall paintings that show the original Portobello Market: Every character looks like it is straight from a Dickens novel. The on-site manager can direct you to the attractions of Notting Hill Gate and nearby Kensington Gardens, both within a 5-minute walk.

6 Portobello Rd., London W11 3DG. (𝄯 020/7221-0707. Fax 020/7221-9128. www.gatehotel.co.uk. 7 units. £80–£100 ($160–$200) double; £120–£150 ($240–$300) triple. Rates include continental breakfast (served in room). AE, MC, V. Tube: Notting Hill Gate or Holland Park. **Amenities:** Room service. *In room:* TV, minibar, beverage maker, hair dryer, iron.

PADDINGTON & BAYSWATER

MODERATE

London Elizabeth Hotel 🐦   This elegant Victorian town house is ideally situated, overlooking Hyde Park. Amid the buzz and excitement of central London, the hotel's atmosphere is an oasis of charm and refinement. Even before the hotel's recent £3-million ($6-million) restoration, it oozed character. Individually decorated rooms range from executive to deluxe and remind us of staying in an English country house. Deluxe rooms are fully air-conditioned, and some contain four-poster beds. Executive units usually contain one double or twin bed. Some rooms have special features such as Victorian antique fireplaces. Suites are pictures of grand comfort and luxury—the Conservatory Suite boasts its own veranda, part of the house's original 1850 conservatory.

Lancaster Terrace, Hyde Park, London W2 3PF. (𝄯 800/721-5566 in the U.S., or 020/7402-6641. Fax 020/7224-8900. www.londonelizabethhotel.co.uk. 49 units. £165–£180 ($330–$360) double; £275 ($550) suite. Rates include buffet breakfast. AE, DC, MC, V. Parking £12 ($24). Tube: Lancaster Gate or Paddington. **Amenities:** Restaurant; bar; room service; laundry service; same-day dry cleaning. *In room:* A/C (in some), TV, Wi-Fi, hair dryer.

Mornington Hotel 🐦   Affiliated with Best Western, the Mornington brings a touch of northern European hospitality to the center of London. Just north of Hyde Park and Kensington Gardens, the hotel has a Victorian exterior and a Scandinavian-inspired decor. The area isn't London's most fashionable, but it's close to Hyde Park and convenient to Marble Arch, Oxford Street shopping, and the ethnic restaurants of Queensway. Renovated guest rooms are tasteful and comfortable. Every year we get our annual Christmas card from "the gang," as we refer to the hotel staff—and what a helpful crew they are.

12 Lancaster Gate, London W2 3LG. (✆ 800/633-6548 in the U.S., or 020/7262-7361. Fax 020/7706-1028. www.bw-morningtonhotel.co.uk. 66 units. £144–£156 ($288–$312) double. Rates include Scandinavian and English breakfast. AE, DC, MC, V. Parking £25 ($50). Tube: Lancaster Gate. **Amenities:** Bar; courtesy car; business center; laundry service; same-day dry cleaning. *In room:* TV, coffeemaker.

The Pavilion 🎖 *Finds*   Until the early 1990s, this was a rather ordinary-looking B&B. Then a team of entrepreneurs with ties to the fashion industry took over and redecorated the rooms with sometimes wacky themes, turning it into an idiosyncratic little hotel. The result is a theatrical and often outrageous decor that's appreciated by the many fashion models and music-industry folks who regularly make this their temporary home in London. Rooms are, regrettably, rather small, but each has a distinctive style. Examples include a kitschy 1970s room ("Honky-Tonk Afro"), an Asian bordello–themed room ("Enter the Dragon"), and even rooms with 19th-century ancestral themes. One Edwardian-style room, a gem of emerald brocade and velvet, is called "Green with Envy."

34–36 Sussex Gardens, London W2 1UL. (✆ 020/7262-0905. Fax 020/7262-1324. www.pavilionhoteluk.com. 30 units. £100 ($200) double; £120 ($240) triple. Rates include continental breakfast. AE, MC, V. Parking £10 ($20). Tube: Edgeware Rd. *In room:* TV, beverage maker.

INEXPENSIVE

Elysee Hotel   Finding an inexpensive hotel in central London grows harder by the year. However, this affordable choice is a good bet for the frugal traveler, facing Hyde Park and lying on Craven Terrace, famous for its Mitre Pub, location of two Woody Allen movies. Privately owned and recently renovated, it offers comfortable but very basic bedrooms. For those who can pay more, we recommend the more spacious and better furnished standard rooms. Guests unwind in the refurbished lounge and bar. Single, double, twin, and family rooms (sleeping up to 6) are available.

25–26 Craven Terrace, London W2 3EL. (✆ 020/7402-7633. Fax 020/7402-4193. www.hotelelysee.co.uk. 55 units. £70–£94 ($140–$188) double; £110–£119 ($220–$238) triple; £130–£140 ($260–$280) quad. MC, V. Parking nearby £15 ($30). Tube: Lancaster Gate. **Amenities:** Bar; lounge. *In room:* TV, Wi-Fi, beverage maker, hair dryer, safe.

Tudor Court Hotel   Originally built in the 1850s and much restored and altered, this Victorian structure is now a boutique hotel of tranquillity and comfort, lying only a 3-minute walk from Paddington Station. It is a standout in a section of less desirable hotels. Bedrooms are midsize, completely restored, and comfortably furnished, with a choice of single, double (or twin), triple, and family rooms available. Rooms without bathrooms have a wash basin, with facilities right outside the door. The hotel's maintenance and affordable price make this one a winner—that, plus a helpful staff.

10–12 Norfolk Sq., London W2 1RS. (✆ 020/7723-6553. Fax 020/7723-0727. www.tudorc.demon.co.uk. 36 units, 19 with bathroom. £69 ($138) double without bathroom, £89 ($178) with bathroom; £79 ($158) triple without bathroom, £99 ($198) with bathroom. Rates include English breakfast. AE, DC, MC, V. Limited street parking. Tube: Paddington. **Amenities:** Breakfast room. *In room:* TV.

EARLS COURT
MODERATE

Twenty Nevern Square 🎖 *Finds*   Many of the affordable hotels around Earls Court are seedy, but not this restored hotel, a stately red-brick Victorian house with a distinctly Asian feeling, from the lounge's porcelain vases and ornate bird cages to the heavy silk draperies. The most elegant of the accommodations is the Pasha Suite, which has luxurious silk draperies printed with a peacock design. Some of the smaller rooms are made to feel much smaller by the heavy furniture, most of which was shipped in from Indonesia. Several of the bedrooms feature private terraces, and most of these are at the lower end of the price scale shown below.

20 Nevern Sq., Earls Court, London SW5 9PD. © **020/7565-9555.** Fax 020/7565-9444. www.twentynevernsquare. co.uk. 23 units. £89–£195 ($178–$390) double; £159–£250 ($318–$500) suite. AE, MC, V. Tube: Earls Court. **Amenities:** Bar; cafe; access to nearby gym; room service; laundry service; dry cleaning. *In room:* TV, Wi-Fi, CD player, hair dryer, trouser press, safe.

4 Where to Dine

London is one of the great food capitals of the world. Both its veteran and upstart chefs have fanned out around the globe for culinary inspiration and have returned with innovative dishes, flavors, and ideas that London diners have never seen before—or at least not at such unprecedented rates. These chefs are pioneering a new style of Modern English cooking, which is forever changing yet comfortingly familiar in many ways. They've committed to centering their dishes on local ingredients from field, stream, and air, and have become daringly innovative with traditional recipes—too much so in the view of some critics, who don't like fresh mango over their blood pudding.

Traditional English cooking has made a comeback, too. The dishes that English mums have been forever feeding their reluctant families are fashionable again. Yes, we're talking English soul food: bangers and mash, Norfolk dumplings, nursery puddings, cottage pie—the works. This may be a rebellion against the excessive minimalism of the nouvelle cuisine that ran rampant over London in the 1980s, but who knows? Maybe it's just plain old nostalgia. Pigs' noses with parsley-and-onion sauce may not be your idea of cutting-edge cuisine, but Simpson's-in-the-Strand (p. 151) is serving it for breakfast.

If you want a lavish meal, London is a good place to eat it. Some of the world's top restaurants call the city home. For those who don't want to break the bank, we include many affordable restaurants where you can dine well. You'll find that London's food revolution has infiltrated every level of the dining scene—even the lowly pub has entered London's culinary sweepstakes. Believe the unthinkable: At certain pubs, you can now dine better than in many restaurants. In some, standard pub grub has given way to Modern English and Mediterranean-style fare; in others, oyster bars have taken hold.

MAYFAIR
VERY EXPENSIVE
Alain Ducasse at the Dorchester ⋆⋆ FRENCH In 2007, the maestro of upper-strata French cuisine reached across the Channel and planted a bulkhead in England with the establishment of this ultrachic corner of gastronomy. Outfitted in tones of pastels and grays, it's rather startlingly arranged around a circular central table for six, which is surrounded with a translucent silk curtain and illuminated with a "waterfall" of illuminated fiber-optic cables. Collectively, it seems to conceal the patrons in a gauzy cloud. What, pray, does someone order in an environment this rarified? Consider prawns wrapped in a hot and spicy cocoon of seaweed; steamed crayfish with hearts of artichoke, served in a potato and truffle shell; steamed halibut with yogurt, spicy condiments, and beans; or a filet of beef Rossini-style, with seared foie gras, root veggies, and Perigueux sauce. Can you expect to see the maestro himself whipping up

Where to Dine in London

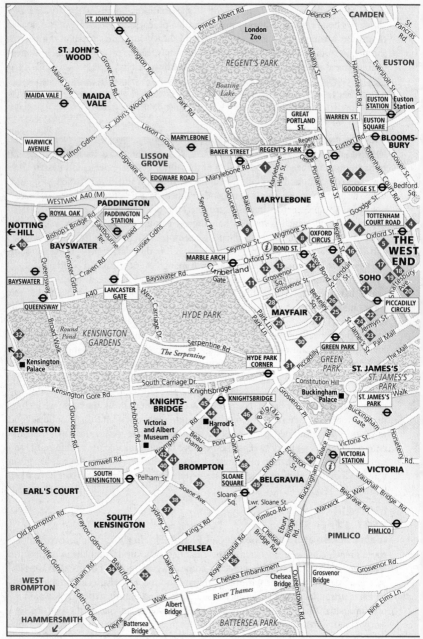

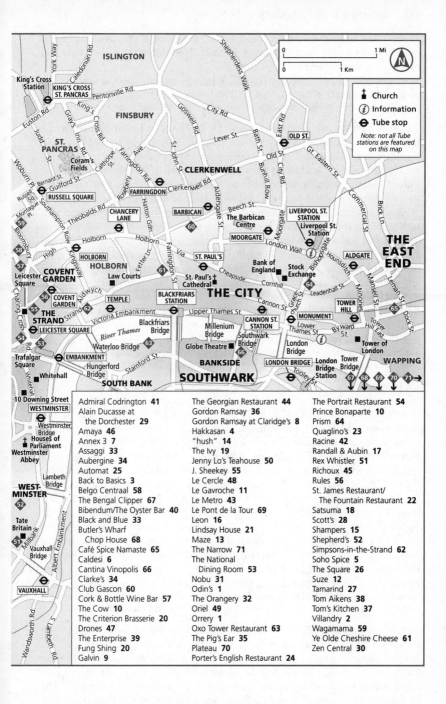

ISLINGTON

King's Cross Station
KING'S CROSS ST. PANCRAS
Pentonville Rd.
York Way
Caledonian Rd.
Euston Rd.
Grays Inn Rd.
King's Cross Rd.
Goswell Rd.
City Rd.
Shepherdess Walk
East Rd.

FINSBURY

Lever St.
Bath St.
Bunhill Row
OLD ST.
Old St.
City Rd.
Gt. Eastern St.
Commercial St.
Brick Ln.

ST. PANCRAS
Woburn Pl.
Bernard St.
Russell Sq.
Guilford St.
Coram's Fields
Calthorpe St.
Rosebery Ave.
St. John St.
Farringdon Rd.

CLERKENWELL

Clerkenwell Rd.
Aldersgate St.
Beech St.
Bunhill Row
Moorgate
Bishopsgate

FARRINGDON

Montague Pl.
Southampton Row
Russell Square
Bloomsbury
Theobalds Rd.
CHANCERY LANE
Hatton Gdn.
BARBICAN
The Barbican Centre
60
MOORGATE
London Wall
LIVERPOOL ST. STATION
Liverpool St. Station

THE EAST END

Mansell St.
Leman St.

High Holborn
Holborn
HOLBORN
HOLBORN
Law Courts
Fetter Ln.
Farringdon St.
Via.
ST. PAUL'S
61
St. Paul's Cathedral
Cheapside
Bank of England
Cornhill
Stock Exchange
64
Leadenhall St.
Houndsditch
Minories
ALDGATE

Leicester Square
COVENT GARDEN
COVENT GARDEN
56
Aldwych
TEMPLE
BLACKFRIARS STATION
Blackfriars Bridge
Upper Thames St.
THE CITY
Cannon St.
CANNON ST. STATION
MONUMENT
Lower Thames St.
TOWER HILL
Tower Hill East
65
Dock St.

Charing Cross
THE STRAND
LEICESTER SQUARE
54
53
Strand
Victoria Embankment
River Thames
Waterloo Bridge
63
Millenium Bridge
Globe Theatre
Southwark Bridge
66
London Bridge
By Ward St.
Tower of London
WAPPING

Trafalgar Square
EMBANKMENT
Whitehall
Hungerford Bridge
Stamford St.
SOUTH BANK
BANKSIDE
SOUTHWARK
Tooley St.
LONDON BRIDGE
London Bridge Station
Tower Bridge
67 68 69 70 71 →

10 Downing Street
WESTMINSTER
Westminster Bridge
Houses of Parliament
Westminster Abbey
Lambeth Bridge

WEST-MINSTER

Tate Britain
51
Vauxhall Bridge
Millbank
Albert Embankment
Wandsworth Rd.
Lambeth Rd.
VAUXHALL

52

0   1 Mi
0   1 Km
N

✝ Church
ⓘ Information
⊖ Tube stop
Note: not all Tube stations are featured on this map

sauces in the kitchen? It's unlikely, since he's farmed many of the day-to-day operations to his long-term disciple, Jocelayn Herland. Nonetheless, he keeps a tight rein on the place from other parts of his empire.

On the lobby level of the Dorchester Hotel, Park Lane. ℂ **020/7629-8866**. Reservations required 2 weeks in advance. Set-price menus £75 ($150) for 3 courses, £95 ($190) for 4 courses, £150 ($300) for 7 courses. AE, DC, MC, V. Tues–Fri noon–1:45pm; Tues–Sat 6:30–9:45pm. Tube: Green Park, Hyde Park Corner, or Marble Arch.

Gordon Ramsay at Claridge's ✮✮✮ EUROPEAN   Gordon Ramsay is the hottest chef in London today. He now rules at the staid, traditional hotel of Claridge's, legendary since 1860 when Queen Victoria stopped by for tea with the Empress Eugenie. The famed Art Deco dining room still retains many of its original architectural features, but the cuisine is hardly the same. Most definitely Victoria wasn't served an *amuse-bouche* of pumpkin soup dribbled with truffle oil and studded with truffles.

Although the menu changes frequently, a memorable culinary highlight began with such starters as crispy Gloucester pork belly with sautéed langoustines, purée of Savoy cabbage, and quail's eggs. Whoever thought celeriac risotto with toasted pine nuts and Parmesan-Reggiano could taste so good? Dishes, including steamed line-caught sea bass with roasted salsify and vanilla jus, or braised Cornish turbot with Oscietra caviar and coriander sauce, are constantly changing and always inventive. A rich, meaty dish is West Country pork cheeks cooked in honey and cloves and served with braising juices. Desserts are similarly surprising—peanut-butter parfait with milk mousse and cherry sauce or assiette of pineapple three ways (ravioli, bavarois, and tatin).

Brook St., W1. ℂ **020/7499-0099**. Reservations required as far in advance as possible. Fixed-price lunch £30 ($60); à la carte menu £65 ($130); 6-course fixed-price dinner £75 ($150). AE, DC, MC, V. Mon–Fri noon–2:45pm and 5:45–11pm; Sat noon–3pm and 5:45–11pm; Sun noon–3pm and 6–10:30pm. Tube: Bond St.

Le Gavroche ✮✮✮ FRENCH   Although challengers come and go, this luxurious "gastro-temple" remains the number-one choice in London for classical French cuisine. It may have fallen off briefly in the early 1990s, but it's fighting its way back to stellar ranks. There's always something special coming out of the kitchen of Michel Roux, Jr., the son of the chef who founded the restaurant in 1966. The service is faultless, and the ambience formally chic without being stuffy. The menu changes constantly, depending on the fresh produce that's available and the current inspiration of the chef. But it always remains classically French, though not of the "essentially old-fashioned bourgeois repertoire" that some critics suggest. Signature dishes honed over years of unswerving practice include the town's grandest cheese soufflé (Soufflé Suissesse); warm foie gras with crispy, cinnamon-flavored crepes; and Scottish filet of beef with port-wine sauce and truffled macaroni. Depending on availability, game is often served as well. A truly Gallic dish is the cassoulet of snails with frog thighs or the mousseline of lobster in a champagne sauce.

43 Upper Brook St., W1. ℂ **020/7408-0881**. Fax 020/7491-4387. Reservations required as far in advance as possible. Main courses £30–£50 ($60–$100); fixed-price lunch £48 ($96); *Le Menu Exceptional* £95 ($190) without wine, £150 ($300) with wine. AE, MC, V. Mon–Fri noon–2pm; Mon–Sat 6:30–11pm. Tube: Marble Arch.

The Square ✮✮✮ FRENCH   Hip, chic, casual, sleek, and modern, the Square still doesn't scare Le Gavroche as a competitor for first place on London's dining circuit, but it is certainly a restaurant to visit on a serious London gastronomic tour. Chef Philip Howard delivers the goods at this excellent restaurant. You get creative, personalized cuisine in a cosseting atmosphere with abstract modern art on the walls. The chef has a magic touch, with such concoctions as a starter of terrine of partridge with smoked foie gras and pear with cider jelly, or else a lasagna of Cornish crab with a champagne foam. For a main course we urge you to try the peppered aged rib-eye of Ayrshire beef with smoked shallots, Tuscan snails, and a red-wine sauce, or else the roast saddle of hare with port-glazed endive. The fish dishes, such as steamed turbot with buttered langoustine claws and poached oysters, are always fresh, and Bresse pigeon is as good as it is in its hometown in France.

6–10 Bruton St., W1. ℭ 020/7495-7100. Reservations required. Fixed-price lunch £25–£30 ($50–$60), dinner £65 ($130). AE, DC, MC, V. Mon–Fri noon–3pm; Mon–Sat 6:30–10:45pm; Sun 6:30–10pm. Tube: Bond St. or Green Park.

EXPENSIVE

hush CONTINENTAL   It's charming, it's trendy, and it's a retreat with lots of attractive people and not a tourist in sight; hush is one of a number of outdoor restaurants in a cul-de-sac. The terrace outside on a summer day seats up to 60 and offers some of London's best alfresco dining. On the ground floor expect a chic decor with a combination of lightwood tables and limestone floors, the color provided by "warm" spice colors. The well-chosen menu features traditional brasserie food—in this case, such items as smoked haddock fishcakes, lobster and chips with garlic butter, and most definitely the Hush Hamburger, which some critics have hailed as the best in London. Start with Andalusian gazpacho or a meze platter (a selection of Greek hors d'oeuvres). Such classic dishes are offered as sautéed calves' liver or Toulouse sausages with creamed potatoes and a mustard sauce. The desserts are hard to resist, especially the champagne jelly with mixed berries or the lemon cheesecake with raspberries.

8 Lancashire Court, Brook St., W1. ℭ 020/7659-1500. Reservations recommended. Main courses £15–£29 ($30–$58); fixed-price menus £23–£27 ($46–$54). AE, DC, MC, V. Restaurant daily noon–3pm and 6:30–11pm. Brasserie Mon–Fri 7:30am–11pm; Sat noon–11pm; Sun noon–4pm. Bar daily 11am–midnight. Tube: Bond St.

Maze ✸✸ INTERNATIONAL   Gordon Ramsay may be the leading chef of London, but our nomination for the most promising chef is Jason Atherton, a one-time protégé of Ramsay. Atherton learned his master's secrets and has plenty of creative culinary imagination all on his own. One reviewer claimed Atherton combined "Spain's progressive technique with Gallic voluptuousness and a dash of British wit." And so he does. His combinations may sound a bit bizarre, but the resulting flavors and ingredients taste sublime.

He's a chef that appeals to "grazers" (that is, those diners liking a series of small plates or tapas). The changing seasons are reflected by what rests on your plate. In a New York–inspired interior by the American architect David Rockwell, Atherton enthralls with dish after dish. Take his starters: Go for the Orkney scallops roasted with spices and served with a peppered golden raisin purée, or else the foie gras marinated in pinot noir. For a main, we'd recommend the roasted partridge with plum preserves or the roast Scottish filet of beef with Landes foie gras and an ox-cheek cottage pie.

10–13 Grosvenor Sq., W1. ℭ 020/7107-0000. Reservations required. Fixed-price lunch £29–£43 ($58–$86); main dishes (small platters) £15–£30 ($30–$60). AE, DC, MC, V. Daily noon–2:30pm and 6–10:30pm. Tube: Bond St.

Nobu ✸✸ JAPANESE/SOUTH AMERICAN   London's innovative restaurant, a celebrity haunt, owes much to its founders, actor Robert De Niro and Chef Nobu Matsuhisa. The kitchen staff is brilliant and as finely tuned as their New York counterparts. The sushi chefs create gastronomic pyrotechnics. Those on the see-and-be-seen circuit don't seem to mind the high prices that go with these incredibly fresh dishes. Elaborate preparations lead to perfectly balanced flavors. Where else can you find an excellent sea urchin tempura? Salmon tartare with caviar is a brilliant appetizer. Follow with a perfectly done filet of sea bass in a sour bean paste or soft-shell crab rolls. The squid pasta is sublime, as is the incredibly popular sukiyaki. Cold sake arrives in a green bamboo pitcher.

In the Metropolitan Hotel, 19 Old Park Lane, W1. ℂ 020/7447-4747. Reservations required 1 month in advance. Main courses £15–£24 ($30–$48); sushi and sashimi £5–£11 ($10–$22) per piece; fixed-price lunch £25 ($50), dinner £70 ($140). AE, DC, MC, V. Mon–Fri noon–2:15pm; Sat–Sun 12:30–2:30pm; Mon–Thurs 6–10:15pm; Fri–Sat 6–11pm; Sun 6–9:45pm. Tube: Hyde Park Corner.

Scott's 🏵🏵 SEAFOOD   In business after a long slumber, Scott's has regained its position as one of London's great seafood restaurants. Opened as an oyster warehouse in 1851 by a young fishmonger, John Scott, the restaurant first earned its fame at its haymarket site where it resided until 1968. Now filled with cosmopolitan glitter in Mayfair, it doesn't rest on its long-ago fame but has made its reputation anew.

Once a favorite of Ian Fleming, creator of the James Bond character, it was the setting in the '50s and '60s where he discovered the dry martini—"shaken, not stirred." It is dear to the seafood lover's heart, from market-fresh Dover sole to "cockles and mussels." Always ask about the fresh catch of the day, or else order filet of halibut with chervil butter or Scottish lobster thermidor. For meat eaters there's rib steak or braised pork cheeks.

20 Mount St., W1. ℂ 020/7495-7309. Reservations required. Main courses £16–£40 ($32–$80). AE, DC, MC, V. Mon–Sat noon–10:30pm; Sun noon–10pm. Tube: Green Park or Bond St.

Tamarind 🏵 INDIAN   In favor with critics as well as the lunchtime business crowd, Tamarind is the most popular Indian restaurant in Mayfair. The basement dining room has gold pillars and a tandoor window so that you can watch the chefs pull their flavorful dishes from the ovens. Chef Alfred Prasad leads a culinary brigade from Delhi that maintains the style of cooking they knew at home. The team selects the best, freshest ingredients in the markets each day. The kitchen prides itself on nouvelle dishes but also excels at traditional Indian fare. The monkfish marinated in saffron and yogurt is delectable, and the mixed kabob platter, with all the kabobs cooked in a charcoal-fired tandoor, is extraordinary—these chefs are the kings of kabobs. Your best bet for a curry? Opt for the prawns in a five-spice mixture. Vegetarians will find refuge here, especially if they go for the *dal Bukhari,* a black-lentil specialty of northwest India.

20 Queen St., W1. ℂ 020/7629-3561. Reservations required. Main courses £16–£26 ($32–$52); fixed-price dinner menu £24 ($48); 3-course fixed-price lunch £22 ($44). AE, DC, DISC, MC, V. Sun–Fri noon–2:45pm; Mon–Sat 6–11:30pm; Sun 6:30–10:30pm. Tube: Green Park.

MODERATE

Zen Central CANTONESE/INDIAN/SZECHUAN   Movie stars always seem to have an advance scouting party informing them of the best places to dine in a foreign city. So when we heard that Eddie Murphy and Tom Cruise were heading here, we followed. We didn't spot any stars, but we found a designer-chic Mayfair restaurant with a cool, dignified decor in black and white. Mirrors cover much of the interior. (Maybe that's why movie stars like it?)

Served by a competent staff, the cuisine is first-rate. Start with the soft-shell crabs cooked in a crust of salt. The steamed sea bass is perfectly cooked and, for extra flavor, served with a black-bean sauce. Pork chops with lemon grass have a Thai flavor, and the baked lobster with crushed roast garlic and slivers of tangerine peel is worth a trip from anywhere. Vegetarian meals are also available. The chef's braised fish cheeks, sharks' fins, and bird's-nest soup serve up flavors enjoyed in China.

20 Queen St., W1. ℂ 020/7629-8103. Reservations recommended. Main courses £11–£20 ($22–$40); fixed-price menu £35 ($70). AE, DC, MC, V. Daily 12:15–11:15pm. Tube: Green Park.

INEXPENSIVE

Automat AMERICAN   The famous faces who flocked to this Mayfair eatery when it opened aren't seen too much anymore, but a clientele of Yankees patronizes the modern precincts, enjoying everything from macaroni and cheese to a soft-shell po' boy sandwich with fries. Some of the best U.S. beef in London is also offered, including New York strip sirloin. London food critics have called it "Mayfair's slice of the Big Apple," after digging into the crab cakes with guacamole or the chili con carne. Salad is a wedge of iceberg lettuce with blue-cheese dressing. Perhaps the most popular item on the menu is the Automat Hamburger with fries.

33 Dover St., W1. ℂ 020/7499-3033. Reservations recommended. Main courses £12–£17 ($24–$34). AE, DC, MC, V. Mon–Fri 7–11am and noon–3pm; Sat–Sun 11am–4pm; Mon–Sat 6–11pm. Tube: Green Park.

Leon 𝕽 (Value MEDITERRANEAN   Its biggest fans call it "gourmet fast food." While gourmet it is not, this is a great place to just sit and eat without being rushed during a day of shopping on Oxford Street. It does what its nearby competitors don't do: It produces fresh, wholesome food at affordable prices. Everything is freshly cooked and that means certain dishes may be variable, but we find ourselves returning in spite of a flaw here and there. Everything on the menu is fresh, often organic. The salads, chicken nuggets, and hearty stews are good. The nuggets are made with succulent breast meat and doused in a creamy yogurt-and-garlic sauce. Even the chili con carne is different. It's a bowl of spicy, tender minced beef with black kidney beans, and is served with a fluffy organic brown rice speckled with pumpkin, sunflower, and sesame seeds, and accompanied by a tasty cabbage and beet slaw. Your drink of choice might be a ginger and carrot juice. Save room for the chocolate brownie "zinged" up with orange zest and swaddled in sinful scoops of ice cream made from Jersey cream. Leon is also the best place in the area for breakfast—try the organic porridge.

35 Great Marlborough St., W1. ℂ 020/7437-5280. Reservations not required. Breakfast from £4.50 ($9); main courses £5.10–£6.50 ($10–$13). AE, MC, V. Mon–Fri 8am–10:30pm; Sat 9:30am–10:30pm; Sun 10:30am–6:30pm. Tube: Oxford Circus.

Suze PACIFIC RIM   The owners of this wine bar attach equal importance to their food and to their impressive wine list. On the ground floor, you can enjoy fine wines along with a well-chosen selection of bar food. Upon arrival, a basket of homemade bread, along with olives, goat cheese, salami, and roasted peppers, is placed before you. The menu has been upgraded and made more sophisticated and appealing. Begin perhaps with the timbale of plum tomato and peppercorn mousse with an avocado salad, or else New Zealand green shell mussels with lime leaf, coriander, and ginger broth. For a main we'd suggest fresh Australian fish with chips and a salad, or New Zealand lamb filet with a vegetable medley.

41 N. Audley St., W1 (between Upper Brook and Oxford sts.). ℂ 020/7491-3237. Reservations recommended. Main courses £12–£22 ($24–$44). AE, MC, V. Mon–Sat noon–11pm. Tube: Bond St.

ST. JAMES'S
MODERATE

Quaglino's 𝕽 CONTINENTAL   Come here for fun, not culinary subtlety and finesse. In 1993, noted restaurateur and designer Sir Terence Conran brought this restaurant—first established in 1929 by Giovanni Quaglino—into the postmodern age with a vital new decor. Menu items have been criticized for their quick preparation and standard format; but considering that on some nights up to 800 people might show up, the marvel is that this place functions as well as it does. That's not to say there isn't an occasional delay. The menu changes often, but your choice of an appetizer might include wild mushroom and truffle soup or else a goat-cheese tart with caramelized onions. You can settle for an old favorite for a main dish—haddock and chips—or else go for the whole roasted sea bass with braised fennel. Their oyster selection is one of the best in central London. Although some diners shy away from organ meats these days, the English still order calves' liver with bacon here. Desserts are mostly favorites such as apple and blackberry crumble or sticky toffee pudding with walnut ice cream. *Note:* A mezzanine with bar features live jazz every night and Sunday at lunch.

16 Bury St., SW1. ℭ **020/7930-6767.** Reservations recommended. Main courses £11–£32 ($22–$64); fixed-price menu (available only for lunch and pretheater dinner from 5:30–6:30pm) 2 courses £17 ($34), 3 courses £19 ($38). AE, DC, MC, V. Daily noon–3pm; Mon–Thurs 5:30pm–midnight; Fri–Sat 5:30pm–1am; Sun 5:30–11pm. Tube: Green Park.

PICCADILLY CIRCUS & LEICESTER SQUARE
EXPENSIVE

Fung Shing ⭐⭐ CANTONESE   In a city where the competition is stiff, Fung Shing emerges as London's finest Cantonese restaurant. Firmly established as a culinary landmark, it dazzles with classic and nouvelle Cantonese dishes. Look for the seasonal specials. Some of the dishes may be a bit experimental—notably stir-fried fresh milk with scrambled egg white—but you'll feel right at home with the soft-shell crab sautéed in a light batter and served with tiny rings of red-hot chili and deep-fried garlic. Chinese gourmets come here for the fried intestines; you may prefer the hotpot of stewed duck with yam. The spicy sea bass and the stir-fried crispy chicken are worthy choices. There are more than 150 dishes from which to choose, and most are moderate in price.

15 Lisle St., WC2. ℭ **020/7437-1539.** Reservations required. Main courses £8–£26 ($16–$52). AE, DC, MC, V. Daily noon–11:30pm. Tube: Leicester Sq.

The Ivy ⭐⭐ MODERN ENGLISH/INTERNATIONAL   Effervescent and sophisticated, the Ivy is the dining choice of visiting theatrical luminaries and has been intimately associated with the theater district ever since it opened in 1911. With its ersatz 1930s look and tiny bar near the entrance, this place is fun and hums with the energy of London's glamour scene. The kitchen has a solid appreciation for fresh ingredients and a talent for preparation. Some appetizers may be a bit much, like wild rabbit salad with black pudding, whereas others are more appealing, such as Bang Bang chicken. The crispy duck and watercress salad is another favorite. For years, the 14-ounce Dover sole has been enjoyed by celebrities and wannabes alike. Mains feature a chargrilled fish of the day, and carnivores take to the sautéed veal kidneys or the escalope of veal Holstein. The Ivy Hamburger continues to appear on the menu. Desserts are familiar, including chocolate pudding soufflé or rhubarb sponge pudding with custard.

1–5 West St., WC2. ℭ **020/7836-4751.** Reservations required. Main courses £8–£40 ($16–$80); Sat–Sun fixed-price lunch £27 ($54). AE, DC, MC, V. Mon–Sat noon–3pm; Sun noon–3:30pm; daily 5:30pm–midnight (last order). Tube: Leicester Sq.

J. Sheekey ⭐ SEAFOOD   English culinary tradition lives on at this fish joint, long a favorite of West End actors. The jellied eels that delighted Laurence Olivier and Vivien Leigh are still here, along with an array of fresh oysters from the coasts of

Ireland and Brittany, plus that Victorian favorite, fried whitebait. Sheekey's fish pie is still on the menu, as is Dover sole. The old "mushy" peas still appear, but the chefs also offer the likes of steamed organic sea beet. Opt for the traditional dishes or specials based on the fresh catch of the day. The double chocolate pudding soufflé is a delight, and many favorite puddings remain.

28–32 St. Martin's Court, WC2. ℂ 020/7240-2565. Reservations recommended. Main courses £10–£36 ($20–$72). AE, DC, MC, V. Mon–Sat noon–3pm and 5:30pm–midnight; Sun noon–3:30pm and 6pm–midnight. Tube: Leicester Sq.

MODERATE
Cork & Bottle Wine Bar 👍👍 *Value* INTERNATIONAL Don Hewitson, a connoisseur of fine wines for more than 30 years, presides over this trove of blissful fermentation. The ever-changing wine list features an excellent selection of Beaujolais Crus from Alsace, 30 selections from Australia, 30 champagnes, and a good selection of California labels. If you want something to wash down, the most successful dish is a raised cheese-and-ham pie, with a cream cheese–like filling and crisp, well-buttered pastry—not your typical quiche. There's also chicken and apple salad, black pudding, Mediterranean prawns with garlic and asparagus, lamb in ale, and a Thai chicken wings platter.

44–46 Cranbourn St., WC2. ℂ 020/7734-7807. Reservations not accepted after 6:30pm. Fixed-price menu £11–£14 ($22–$28); main courses £8–£13 ($16–$26). AE, DC, MC, V. Mon–Sat 11am–11:30pm; Sun noon–10:30pm. Tube: Leicester Sq.

SOHO
EXPENSIVE
Lindsay House 👍👍 MODERN ENGLISH As in an old-fashioned speak-easy, you ring the doorbell for admittance to a Regency town house deep in Soho. Unfolding before you are gilded mirrors and bare wooden floors. The staircase delivers you to one of two floors. Irish-born Chef Richard Corrigan is one of the most inventive chefs in London, with creative offerings changing daily based on market availability. What inspires Corrigan at the market is what will end up on your plate at night. You might start with smoked eel and foie gras terrine, or else crispy frogs' legs and watercress. For your main course, expect such delights as loin of rabbit roasted and stuffed with chorizo, or else stuffed pigs' trotters with sweetbreads and morels. Desserts are also a pleasant surprise, including a lime soufflé with mascarpone sorbet.

21 Romilly St., W1. ℂ 020/7439-0450. Reservations recommended. 3-course lunch £56 ($112); £68 ($136) tasting menu with wine; £68 ($136) vegetarian menu. AE, DC, MC, V. Mon–Fri noon–2:30pm; Mon–Sat 6–11pm. Tube: Leicester Sq.

MODERATE
Annex 3 👍 FRENCH If you're hanging with Beyoncé or Scarlett Johansson, you might take either of them to this kitschy but chic rendezvous for either whimsical cocktails or sophisticated, well-crafted French food. One patron called the decor a "psychedelic Christmas show," but the food, prepared with market-fresh ingredients, is first-rate, including such starters as a homemade terrine with pickled red cabbage or a salad of chicory and bitter greens in a Roquefort dressing. Exceptional products and a finely honed technique are evident in such mains as rainbow trout on braised fennel or seared duck breast with lentils and an orange jus. For dessert, few items top the dark-chocolate parfait with white-chocolate cream. The location is on the fringe of Soho.

16 Little Portland St. ℂ 020/7631-0700. Reservations required. 2 courses £25 ($50); 3 courses £29 ($58). AE, MC, V. Mon–Sat 7pm–midnight. Tube: Tottencourt Rd.

The Criterion Brasserie ✦ FRENCH/MODERN ENGLISH   Designed by Thomas Verity in the 1870s, this palatial neo-Byzantine mirrored marble hall is a glamorous backdrop for a superb cuisine, served under a golden ceiling, with theatrical peacock-blue draperies. The menu is wide ranging, offering everything from Paris brasserie food to "nouvelle-classical," a combination of classic French cooking techniques with some of the lighter, more experimental leanings of modern French cuisine. The food is excellent but falls short of sublime. Start with beef carpaccio in a mustard dressing or else spaghetti with clams and chili peppers, to be followed by such fish as wild sea bass with a shellfish fondue or else roast suckling pig in applesauce.

224 Piccadilly, W1. ⓒ 020/7930-0488. Main courses £16–£25 ($32–$50); 2-course fixed-price lunch £15 ($30), 3 courses £18 ($36). AE, MC, V. Mon–Sat noon–2:30pm and 5:30–11:30pm; Sun noon–3:30pm and 5:30–10:30pm. Tube: Piccadilly Circus.

Hakkasan ✦ Finds CHINESE   Asian mystique and pastiche are found in this offbeat restaurant in a seedy alley off Tottenham Court Road. This is another London venture created by Alan Yau, who became a citywide dining legend because of his Wagamama noodle bars. Come here for great dim sum and tantalizing cocktails. Feast on such dishes as *har gau* (steamed prawn dumplings) and strips of tender barbecued pork. The spring roll is refreshing with the addition of fried mango and a delicate prawn-and-scallop filling. Steamed scallop *shumai* (dumplings) with *tobiko* caviar are fresh and meltingly soft. Desserts in most of London's Chinese restaurants are hardly memorable, but the offerings here are an exception to that rule, especially the layered banana sponge with chocolate cream.

8 Hanway Place. ⓒ 020/7927-7000. Reservations recommended. Main courses £10–£68 ($20–$136). AE, MC, V. Lunch Mon–Fri noon–3pm, Sat noon–5pm; dinner Mon–Wed 6–11:30pm, Thurs–Sat 6–11:30pm, Sun 6–11pm. Tube: Tottenham Court Rd.

Randall & Aubin ✦ Finds SEAFOOD   Past the sex boutiques of Soho you stumble upon this real discovery, whose consultant is TV chef Ed Baines, an ex-Armani model who turned this butcher shop into a cool, hip champagne-and-oyster bar. The impressive shellfish display of the night's goodies is the "bait" used to lure you inside. Chances are you won't be disappointed. Loch Fyne oysters, lobster with chips, panfried fresh scallops—the parade of seafood we've sampled here has in each case been genuinely excellent. The *soupe de poisson* (fish soup) is the best in Soho, or else you might want one of the hors d'oeuvres such as delightful Japanese-style fish cakes or fresh Cornish crab. Yes, they still have Sevruga caviar for lotto winners. For the rare meat-only eater, there is a limited array of dishes such as a perfectly roasted chicken on the spit that has been flavored with fresh herbs. The lemon tart with crème fraîche rounds out a perfect meal.

16 Brewer St., W1. ⓒ 020/7287-4447. Reservations not accepted. Main courses £8–£12 ($16–$24). AE, DC, MC, V. Daily 10am–11pm. Tube: Piccadilly Circus or Leicester Sq.

INEXPENSIVE

Satsuma JAPANESE   This funky Japanese canteen is all the rage in London. The clean lines, stark white walls, and long wooden tables suggest an upmarket youth hostel. But patrons come for good food at reasonable prices. The restaurant is ideal for a pretheater visit. Your meal comes in a lacquered bento box on a matching tray. Try the chicken teriyaki or fresh chunks of tuna and salmon. The dumplings are excellent, as is the miso soup. A specialty is the large bowl of seafood ramen, with noodles swimming in a well-seasoned broth studded with mussels, scallops, and prawns. Tofu steaks are a delight, as are udon noodles with wok-fried chicken and fresh vegetables. You can finish with deep-fried tempura ice cream.

56 Wardour St., W1. © 020/7437-8338. Reservations not accepted. Main courses £6–£15 ($12–$30). AE, DC, MC, V. Mon–Tues noon–11pm; Wed–Thurs noon–11:30pm; Fri–Sat noon–midnight; Sun noon–10:30pm. Tube: Piccadilly Circus or Leicester Sq.

Shampers CONTINENTAL   This is a favorite of West End wine-bar aficionados. In addition to the street-level wine bar serving snacks, there's a more formal basement-level restaurant. In either venue, you can order such main dishes as grilled calves' liver with bacon, chips, and salad; pan-fried large prawns with ginger, garlic, and chili; and platters of cheeses. Salads are popular, including spicy chicken salad or the grilled eggplant salad with tomato, avocado, buffalo mozzarella, and pesto. The platter of Irish mussels cooked in a cream-and-tarragon sauce is everybody's favorite. The restaurant is now open in the evening, but the wine bar also serves an extensive menu, offering fresh squid, tuna steak, pan-fried tiger prawns, free-range chicken, and other tasty specialties. There is also a daily specials menu.

4 Kingly St. (between Carnaby and Regent sts.), W1. © 020/7437-1692. Reservations recommended. Main courses £9–£15 ($18–$30). AE, DC, MC, V. Restaurant and wine bar Mon–Sat noon–11pm. Closed Dec 24–Jan 2. Tube: Oxford Circus or Piccadilly Circus.

Soho Spice INDIAN   This is one of central London's most stylish Indian restaurants, combining a hip atmosphere with the flavors and scents of southern India. You might opt for a drink at the cellar bar before heading to the street-level dining room, decorated in saffron, cardamom, bay, and pepper hues. A staff member dressed in similarly vivid apparel will propose a wide array of choices, including slow-cooked Indian tandoori specials that feature lamb, chicken, fish, or vegetables with combinations of spices. The à la carte menu offers a variety of courses, including *jhinga hara pyaz,* spicy queen prawns with fresh spring onions; and *paneer pasanda,* cottage cheese slices stuffed with spinach and served with almond sauce. The cuisine will satisfy traditionalists but also has a modern flair.

124–126 Wardour St., W1. © 020/7434-0808. Reservations required. Main courses £10–£15 ($20–$30). AE, V. Mon–Tues noon–midnight; Wed–Sat noon–3am; Sun noon–10:30pm. Tube: Tottenham Court Rd.

TRAFALGAR SQUARE
MODERATE
The National Dining Rooms ENGLISH   In the National Gallery, this dining choice lies over the foyer of the Sainsbury Wing, providing a panoramic view of fabled Trafalgar Square. Classic dishes using market-fresh ingredients go into the starters such as warm watercress mousse with braised pearl onions or smoked mackerel pâté with apple and chicory. Try main dishes such as monkfish, mullet, and mussel stew or else baked lemon chicken with Savoy cabbage and creamed potatoes. The cheese selection from Great Britain is amazing in its variety, everything from traditionally aged Stilton to soft goat cheese from the Cotswolds. Finish off with one of the freshly baked cakes such as layered chocolate or walnut and banana. There is a **cafe** offshoot in the basement of the main building, which is a good choice for sandwiches, pastas, soups, and pastries.

In the National Gallery, Trafalgar Sq., WC2. © 020/7747-2525. Reservations not required. 2-course menu £25 ($50); 3 courses £30 ($60). AE, MC, V. Thurs–Tues 10am–5:30pm; Wed 10am–8:45pm. Tube: Charing Cross.

The Portrait Restaurant ✿ MODERN ENGLISH   This rooftop restaurant is a sought-after dining ticket on the fifth floor of the National Portrait Gallery's Ondaatje Wing. Along with the view (Nelson's Column, the London Eye, Big Ben, and the like), you get superb meals. Patrons usually go for lunch, not knowing that the chefs also cook on Thursday and Friday nights. In spring, there's nothing finer than the green English asparagus. All the main courses are filled with flavor. The high quality of the produce really shines through in such dishes as roast breast of guinea fowl with truffles and wild mushrooms, or pan-fried filet of Scotch salmon with bacon-and-onion potato cakes. For your "pudding," nothing is finer than steamed chestnut and honey pudding with toffee and pecan sauce. Chefs aren't afraid of simple preparations, mainly because they are assured of the excellence of their products. The wine list features some organic choices.

In the National Portrait Gallery, Trafalgar Sq., WC2. ✆ 020/7312-2490. Reservations recommended. Main courses £14–£29 ($28–$58). AE, MC, V. Daily 11:45am–2:45pm; Thurs–Fri 5:30–8:30pm. Tube: Leicester Sq. or Charing Cross.

BLOOMSBURY
MODERATE
Back to Basics ✿✿ SEAFOOD   Ursula Higgs's bistro draws discerning palates seeking some of the freshest seafood in London. When the weather's fair, you can dine outside. Otherwise, retreat inside to a vaguely Parisian setting with a blackboard menu and checked tablecloths. The fish is served in large portions, and you can safely forgo an appetizer unless you're ravenous. More than a dozen seafood dishes are offered; the fish can be broiled, grilled, baked, or poached, but frying is not permitted. In other words, this is no fish and chippie. Start with a bowl of tasty, plump mussels or sea bass flavored with fresh basil–and–chili oil. Brill appears with green-peppercorn butter, and plaice is jazzed up with fresh ginger and soy sauce. For the meat eater, there is a T-bone steak or roast chicken. Also try the pastas and the vegetarian dishes. Freshly made salads accompany most meals, and an excellent fish soup is offered daily. For dessert, try the bread pudding or the freshly made apple pie.

21A Foley St., W1. ✆ 020/7436-2181. Reservations recommended. Main courses £11–£17 ($22–$34). AE, DC, MC, V. Mon–Sat noon–3pm and 6–10:30pm. Tube: Oxford Circus or Goodge St.

INEXPENSIVE
Wagamama JAPANESE   This noodle joint, in a basement just off New Oxford Street, is noisy and overcrowded, and you'll have to wait in line for a table. It calls itself a "nondestination food station" and caters to some 1,200 customers a day. Many dishes are built around ramen noodles with your choice of chicken, beef, or salmon. Try the tasty *gyoza,* light dumplings filled with vegetables or chicken. Vegetarian dishes are available, but skip the so-called Korean-style dishes.

4 Streatham St., WC1. ✆ 020/7323-9223. Reservations not accepted. Main courses £7–£11 ($14–$22). AE, MC, V. Mon–Sat noon–11pm; Sun noon–10pm. Tube: Tottenham Court Rd.

COVENT GARDEN & THE STRAND
EXPENSIVE
Rules ✿ TRADITIONAL ENGLISH   If you're looking for London's most quintessentially British restaurant, eat here. London's oldest restaurant was established in 1798 as an oyster bar; today, the antler-filled Edwardian dining rooms exude nostalgia. You can order such classic dishes as Irish or Scottish oysters, jugged hare, and mussels. Game and fish dishes are offered from mid-August to February or March, including wild Scottish salmon; wild sea trout; wild Highland red deer; and game

birds such as grouse, snipe, partridge, pheasant, and woodcock. As a finale, the "great puddings" continue to impress.

35 Maiden Lane, WC2. © **020/7836-5314.** Reservations recommended. Main courses £17–£30 ($34–$60). AE, DC, MC, V. Mon–Sat noon–11:30pm; Sun noon–10:30pm. Tube: Covent Garden.

Simpson's-in-the-Strand ★★ *Kids* TRADITIONAL AND MODERN ENGLISH
Simpson's is more of an institution than a restaurant. Long a family favorite with lots of large tables, it has been in business since 1828, and as a result of a recent £2-million ($4-million) renovation, it's now better than ever with its Adam paneling, crystal, and an army of grandly formal waiters serving traditional English fare. The owners object to the word "menu" here—"too French." It's called "bill of fare." Men and women can now dine together. Before 1904 such an "outrage" was forbidden. Through the years the dress code has become more relaxed—in other words, Elizabeth Taylor in trousers would no longer be forbidden to enter. Famous diners of yesterday include everyone from Charles Dickens to Charles Chaplin, and the restaurant is often used as a film setting, including one for Alfred Hitchcock's *Sabotage.* Most diners agree that Simpson's serves the best roasts in London, an array that includes roast sirloin of beef; roast saddle of mutton with red-currant jelly; roast Aylesbury duckling; and steak, kidney, and mushroom pie.

100 The Strand (next to the Savoy Hotel), WC2. © **020/7836-9112.** Reservations required. Main courses £22–£30 ($44–$60); 3-course fixed-price pretheater dinner £16–£20 ($32–$40); breakfast from £16 ($32). AE, DC, MC, V. Mon–Fri 7:15–10:30am; Mon–Sat 12:15–2:45pm and 5:45–10:45pm; Sun noon–2:45pm and 5:45–9pm. Tube: Charing Cross or Embankment.

MODERATE
Belgo Centraal BELGIAN
Chaos reigns supreme in this cavernous basement, where mussels *marinières* with fries, plus 100 Belgian beers, are the raison d'être. Take a freight elevator past the busy kitchen and into a converted cellar, divided into two large eating areas. One section is a beer hall seating about 250; the menu here is the same as in the restaurant, but you don't need reservations. The restaurant side has three nightly seatings: 5:30, 7:30, and 10pm. Although heaps of fresh mussels are the big attraction, you can opt for fresh Scottish salmon, roast chicken, a perfectly done steak, or one of the vegetarian specialties. Gargantuan plates of wild boar sausages arrive with *stoemp*—Belgian mashed spuds and cabbage. Belgian stews, called *waterzooï,* are also served.

50 Earlham St., WC2. © **020/7813-2233.** Reservations required for the restaurant. Main courses £9–£18 ($18–$36). AE, DC, MC, V. Mon–Thurs noon–11pm; Fri–Sat noon–11:30pm; Sun noon–10:30pm. Closed Christmas. Tube: Covent Garden.

Porters English Restaurant ★★ *Kids* TRADITIONAL ENGLISH
The seventh earl of Bradford serves "real English food at affordable prices." He succeeds notably—and not just because Lady Bradford turned over her carefully guarded recipe for banana-and-ginger steamed pudding. This comfortable, two-storied restaurant is family-friendly, informal, and lively. Porters specializes in classic English pies, including Old English fish pie, lamb and apricot, and, of course, bangers and mash. The overwhelming favorite is steak, Guinness, and mushroom pie. Main courses are so generous—and accompanied by vegetables and side dishes—that you hardly need appetizers. They have also added grilled English fare to the menu, including sirloin and lamb steaks and marinated chicken. Porters is famous for its mouthwatering puddings. Where can you find a good spotted dick these days? It's a steamed syrup sponge

cake with sultanas (raisins). Another favorite is a dark-chocolate-chip pudding made with steamed chocolate sponge, chocolate chips, and chocolate custard. Even the ice cream is homemade. The bar does quite a few exotic cocktails, as well as beers, wine, or English mead. A traditional English tea is served from 2:30 to 5:30pm.

17 Henrietta St., WC2. ☎ 020/7836-6466. Reservations recommended. Main courses £11–£17 ($22–$34); fixed-price lunch and pretheater menu £12 ($24); fixed-price dinner menu £23 ($46). AE, MC, V. Mon–Sat noon–11:30pm; Sun noon–10:30pm. Tube: Covent Garden or Leicester Sq.

WESTMINSTER/VICTORIA
EXPENSIVE

Shepherd's TRADITIONAL ENGLISH   Some observers claim that many of the inner workings of the English government operate from the precincts of this conservative, likable restaurant. Set in the shadow of Big Ben, it enjoys a regular clientele of barristers, members of Parliament, and their constituents from far-flung districts. So synchronized is this place to the goings-on at Parliament that a Division Bell rings in the dining room, calling MPs back to the House of Commons when it's time to vote. Even the decor is designed to make them feel at home, with leather banquettes, sober 19th-century accessories, and a worthy collection of European portraits and landscapes.

The menu reflects years of English culinary tradition, and dishes are prepared intelligently, with fresh ingredients. In addition to the classic roast, dishes include a cream-based mussel stew; hot salmon-and-potato salad with dill dressing; salmon and prawn fish cakes in spinach sauce; and roast leg of lamb with mint sauce.

Marsham Court, Marsham St. (at the corner of Page St.), SW1. ☎ 020/7834-9552. Reservations recommended. Fixed-price menu: 2 courses £24 ($48), 3 courses £27 ($54). AE, DC, MC, V. Mon–Fri 12:15–2:45pm and 6:30–11pm (last order at 11pm). Tube: Pimlico or St. James's.

MODERATE

Rex Whistler ★★ *Value* MODERN ENGLISH   The Tate Britain's restaurant is particularly attractive to wine fanciers. It offers what may be the best bargains for superior wines anywhere in Britain. Bordeaux and burgundies are in abundance, and the management keeps the markup between 40% and 65%, rather than the 100% to 200% added in most restaurants. In fact, the prices here are lower than they are in most wine shops. Wine begins at £15 ($30) per bottle, or £4 ($8) per glass. Oenophiles frequently come for lunch. The restaurant offers an English menu that changes about every month. Dishes might include pheasant casserole, pan-fried skate with black butter and capers, and vegetarian selections. One critic found the staff and diners as traditional "as a Gainsborough landscape." Access to the restaurant is through the museum's main entrance on Millbank.

Tate Britain, Millbank, SW1. ☎ 020/7887-8825. Reservations recommended. Main courses £15 ($30); breakfast from £4.75 ($9.50); afternoon tea £6.95 ($14). AE, DC, MC, V. Mon–Fri 11:30am–3pm; Sat–Sun 10am–3pm; daily 3:30–5pm for afternoon tea. Tube: Pimlico. Bus: 77 or 88.

INEXPENSIVE

Jenny Lo's Teahouse CANTONESE/SZECHUAN   London's noodle dives don't get much better than this. Before its decline, Ken Lo's Memories of China offered the best Chinese dining in London. The late Ken Lo, whose grandfather was the Chinese ambassador to the court of St. James, made his reputation as a cookbook author. Jenny Lo is Ken's daughter, and her father taught her many of his culinary secrets. Belgravia matrons and young professionals come here for perfectly prepared, reasonably priced fare. Ken Lo cookbooks contribute to the dining room decor of black refectory tables set with paper napkins and chopsticks. Opt for such fare as a vermicelli rice noodle dish (a large plate of noodles topped with grilled chicken breast and Chinese mushrooms) or white noodles with minced pork. Rounding out the menu are stuffed Peking dumplings, chili-garnished spicy prawns, and wonton soup with slithery dumplings. The black bean–seafood noodle dish is a delight, as is the chili-beef soup.

14 Eccleston St., SW1 9LT. © 020/7259-0399. Reservations not accepted. Main courses £6.50–£10 ($13–$20). No credit cards. Mon–Fri noon–3pm; Mon–Sat 6–10pm. Tube: Victoria Station.

THE CITY

For locations of the restaurants below, refer to the map "Where to Dine in London," earlier in this chapter.

EXPENSIVE

Prism 🎖🎖 MODERN ENGLISH   This restaurant attracts London's movers and shakers, at least those with demanding palates. In the former Bank of New York, Harvey Nichols—known for his chic department store in Knightsbridge—took this 1920s neo-Grecian hall and installed Mies van der Rohe chairs in chrome and lipstick-red leather. In this setting, traditional English dishes from the north are given a light touch—try the tempura of Whitby cod, or cream of Jerusalem artichoke soup with roasted scallops and truffle oil. For a first course, try a salad composed of flecks of Parmesan cheese seasoning savoy cabbage and Parma ham. The menu reveals the chef has traveled a bit—note such dishes as Moroccan spiced chicken livers served with a lemon-and-parsley couscous.

147 Leadenhall St., EC3. © 020/7256-3875. Reservations required. Main courses £18–£24 ($36–$48). AE, DC, DISC, MC, V. Mon–Fri 11:30am–3pm and 6–10pm. Tube: Bank or Monument.

MODERATE

Café Spice Namaste 🎖🎖 INDIAN   This is our favorite Indian restaurant in London, where the competition is stiff. It's cheerfully housed in a landmark Victorian hall near Tower Bridge, just east of the Tower of London. The Parsi chef, Cyrus Todiwala, is a former resident of Goa (a Portuguese territory absorbed by India long ago), where he learned many of his culinary secrets. He concentrates on southern and northern Indian dishes, with a strong Portuguese influence. Chicken and lamb are prepared a number of ways, from mild to spicy hot. As a novelty, Todiwala occasionally even offers a menu of emu dishes; when marinated, the meat is rich and spicy and evocative of lamb. Emu is not the only dining oddity here. Ever have ostrich gizzard kabob, alligator tikka, or minced moose, bison, or blue boar? Many patrons journey here just for the complex chicken curry known as *xacutti*.

16 Prescot St., E1. © 020/7488-9242. Reservations required. Main courses £12–£19 ($24–$38). AE, DC, MC, V. Mon–Fri noon–3pm and 6:15–10:30pm; Sat 6:30–10:30pm. Tube: Tower Hill.

Club Gascon 🎖🎖 *Finds* FRENCH   This slice of southwestern France serves such tasty treats as foie gras, Armagnac, and duck confit. Chef Pascal Aussignac is all the rage in London, ever since he opened his bistro next to the meat market in Smithfield. He dedicates his bistro to his favorite ingredient: foie gras. Foie gras appears in at least nine different incarnations on the menu, and most of the first-class ingredients are imported from France. His menu is uniquely divided into these categories—the Salt Route, Ocean, and Kitchen Garden. The best way to dine here is to arrive in a party of four or five and share the small dishes, each harmoniously balanced and full of flavor. Each dish is accompanied by a carefully selected glass of wine. After a foie gras pig-out, proceed to such main courses as a heavenly quail served with pear and rosemary honey. A cassoulet of morels and truffles transforms a plain but perfectly cooked steak.

57 W. Smithfield, EC1. ℂ **020/7796-0600.** Reservations required. Main courses £9–£20 ($18–$40). AE, MC, V. Mon–Fri noon–2pm and 7–10pm; Sat 7–10:30pm. Tube: Barbican.

INEXPENSIVE

Ye Olde Cheshire Cheese *Kids* TRADITIONAL ENGLISH   The foundation of this carefully preserved building was laid in the 13th century, and it holds the most famous of the old City chophouses and pubs. Established in 1667, it claims to be the spot where Dr. Samuel Johnson (who lived nearby) entertained admirers with his acerbic wit. Charles Dickens and other literary lions also patronized the place. Later, many of the ink-stained journalists and scandalmongers of 19th- and early-20th-century Fleet Street made it their watering hole. You'll find five bars and two dining rooms here. The house specialties include Ye Famous Pudding (steak, kidney, mushrooms, and game) and Scottish roast beef with Yorkshire pudding and horseradish sauce. Sandwiches, salads, and standby favorites such as steak-and-kidney pie are also available, as are dishes such as Dover sole. The Cheshire is the best and safest venue to introduce your children to an English pub.

Wine Office Court, 145 Fleet St., EC4. ℂ **020/7353-6170.** Main courses £8–£10 ($16–$20). AE, DC, MC, V. Meals: Mon–Fri noon–10pm; Sat noon–2:30pm and 6–9:30pm; Sun noon–2:30pm. Drinks and bar snacks: Mon–Sat 11am–11pm; Sun noon–6pm. Tube: St. Paul's or Blackfriars.

DOCKLANDS
EXPENSIVE

Butler's Wharf Chop House ✦ TRADITIONAL ENGLISH   Of the four restaurants housed in Butler's Wharf (other Butler's Wharf restaurants are listed below), this one is the closest to Tower Bridge. It maintains its commitment to moderate prices. The Chop House was modeled after a large boathouse, with banquettes, lots of exposed wood, flowers, candles, and windows overlooking Tower Bridge and the Thames. Dishes are largely adaptations of English recipes such as fish and chips with mushy peas or steak-and-kidney pudding with oysters, even roast pork loin with applesauce. The bar, among other offerings, features several English wines, plus a half-dozen French clarets by the jug.

36E Shad Thames, SE1. ℂ **020/7403-3403.** Reservations recommended. Main courses £14–£26 ($28–$52); 2-course fixed-price lunch £22 ($44), 3 courses £26 ($52). AE, DC, MC, V. Mon–Fri noon–3pm; Sat–Sun noon–4pm; Mon–Sat 6–11pm (6–10pm May–Oct); Sun 6–10pm. Tube: Tower Hill or London Bridge.

Le Pont de la Tour ✦ INTERNATIONAL   Built in the mid–19th century as a warehouse, Le Pont de la Tour is another of Terrence Conran's restaurants. From its windows, diners and shoppers enjoy sweeping views of some of the densest river traffic in Europe.

The **Bar and Grill's** live piano music (on evenings and weekends) together with a wide choice of wines and cocktails creates one of the most convivial atmospheres in the area. Although such dishes as ham-and–foie gras terrine and langoustines mayonnaise are featured, the culinary star is a heaping platter of fresh shellfish—perfect when shared with a friend, accompanied by a bottle of wine.

In bold contrast is the large, more formal room known simply as the **Restaurant.** Filled with burr oak furniture and decorated with framed lithographs of early-20th-century Parisian cafe society, it offers excellent food and a polite but undeniable

English reserve. The menu may list such temptations as roast rabbit wrapped in herbs with pancetta and a mustard vinaigrette, or whole roast-buttered lobster with herbs. One especially winning selection is best end of lamb, with a black olive–and–herb crust in a red-pepper sauce. All the fish is excellent, but none better than the Dover sole, which can be ordered grilled or meunière.

36D Shad Thames, Butler's Wharf, SE1. © 020/7403-8403. Reservations highly recommended in the Bar and Grill; recommended in the Restaurant. Bar and Grill main courses £12–£30 ($24–$60), fixed-price lunch menu £14–£18 ($28–$36); restaurant main courses £9–£15 ($18–$30), 3-course fixed-price lunch menu £30 ($60). AE, DC, MC, V. Bar and Grill Mon–Fri noon–3pm and 6–11pm; Sat noon–11pm; Sun noon–10:30pm. Restaurant daily noon–3pm and 6–11pm. Tube: Tower Hill or London Bridge.

MODERATE

The Bengal Clipper ✿ INDIAN   This former spice warehouse by the Thames serves what it calls "India's most remarkable dishes." The likable and often animated restaurant is outfitted with cream-colored walls, tall columns, and modern artwork inspired by the Moghul Dynasty's depictions of royal figures, soaring trees, and well-trained elephants. Seven windows afford sweeping views over the industrialized Thames-side neighborhood, and live piano music plays in the background. The cuisine includes many vegetarian choices derived from the former Portuguese colony of Goa and the once-English colony of Bengal. There is a zestiness and spice to the cuisine, but it's never overpowering.

A tasty specialty is stuffed *murgh masala,* a tender breast of chicken with potatoes, onions, and apricots. The duckling (off the bone) comes in a tangy sauce with a citrus bite. One of the finest dishes we tasted in North India is served here and has lost nothing in the transfer: marinated lamb simmered in cream with cashew nuts.

Shad Thames, Butler's Wharf, SE1. © 020/7357-9001. Reservations recommended. Main courses £9–£15 ($18–$30); set menu £10 ($20; available July–Apr); Sunday buffet £7.75 ($16). AE, DC, MC, V. Mon–Sat noon–2:30pm and 6–11:30pm; Sun noon–4pm and 6–11pm. Tube: Tower Hill.

SOUTH BANK
EXPENSIVE

Plateau FRENCH   Entrepreneur Terence Conran has succeeded again with the opening of this trendsetting restaurant at Canary Wharf, serving a modern French cuisine. The chef proudly boasts that he appeals to both high- and lowbrow palates—and so he does, succeeding admirably. The atmosphere is retro chic with Harry Bertoia chrome chairs and Eero Saarinen tables. The location is on the fourth floor at the top of the Canada Place building, with panoramic views of London. There are two different dining sections divided by a semi-open-to-view kitchen. One is a chic bar and grill, the other a more formal restaurant, each with its own terrace.

In the bar and grill, partake of food enjoyed in the 1920s and 1930s, notably Colchester native oysters followed by Billingsgate fish pie. The upgraded cuisine in the main restaurant is quite sumptuous—a foie gras terrine with champagne jelly followed by such main courses as venison stew with spaetzle and savoy cabbage.

Canada Place, Canary Wharf, E14. © 020/7715-7100. Reservations recommended. Bar and grill main courses £11–£28 ($22–$56); restaurant main courses £21–£30 ($42–$60), fixed-price menus (dinner only) £35–£40 ($70–$80). AE, DC, MC, V. Bar and grill Mon–Sat noon–11pm; Sun noon–4pm. Restaurant Mon–Fri noon–3pm; Mon–Sat 6–10:30pm; Sun noon–4pm. Tube: Canary Wharf.

MODERATE

Cantina Vinopolis ✿ *Finds* CONTINENTAL   Not far from the re-created Globe Theatre of Shakespeare's heyday, this place has been called a "Walk-Through Wine

Atlas." In the revitalized Bankside area, south of the Thames near Southwark Cathedral, this bricked, walled, and high-vaulted brasserie was converted from long-abandoned Victorian railway arches. Inside you can visit both the Vinopolis Wine Gallery and the Cantina Restaurant. Although many come here just to drink the wine, the food is prepared with quality ingredients (very fresh), and the menu is sensibly priced. Start with a bit of heaven such as the pea and ham soup. Dishes are full of flavor and never overcooked. Pan-fried snapper, with crushed new potatoes and salsa verde, won us over. A rump of lamb was tender and perfectly flavored and served with a polenta cake. Many of the dishes have the good country taste of a trattoria you'd find in the countryside of southern Italy. Naturally, the wine list is the biggest in the U.K.

1 Bank End, London Bridge, SE1. (C) 020/7940-8333. Reservations required. Main courses £13–£23 ($26–$46); 3-course fixed-price menu £32 ($64). AE, DC, MC, V. Mon–Sat noon–3pm and 6–10:30pm; Sun noon–4pm. Tube: London Bridge.

Oxo Tower Restaurant ✿ INTERNATIONAL   In the South Bank complex, on the eighth floor of the Art Deco Oxo Tower Wharf, you'll find this dining sensation. It's operated by the department store Harvey Nichols. Down the street from the rebuilt Globe Theatre, this 140-seat restaurant could be visited for its view alone, but the cuisine is also stellar. You'll enjoy a sweeping view of St. Paul's Cathedral and the City, all the way to the Houses of Parliament. The decor is chic 1930s-style.

The cuisine, under Chef David Sharland, is rich and prepared with finesse. Menu items change based on the season and the market. Count on a modern interpretation of British cookery, as well as the English classics. The fish is incredibly fresh here. The whole sea bass for two is delectable, as is the roast rump of lamb with split pea, mint purée, and balsamic vinegar sauce. We were also impressed with the roast filet of plaice with olive oil and truffle cabbage cream.

22 Barge House St., South Bank, SE1. (C) 020/7803-3888. Main courses £19–£28 ($38–$56); 3-course fixed-price lunch £32 ($64). AE, DC, MC, V. Mon–Sat noon–2:30pm and 6–11pm; Sun noon–3pm and 6:30–10pm. Tube: Blackfriars or Waterloo.

KNIGHTSBRIDGE
EXPENSIVE
Amaya ✿ INDIAN   This chic restaurant, a hot dining ticket, is credited with introducing the small-plates concept to Indian food. Dishes are shared, hopefully with a party of friends. This is no mere curry house, but an ambitious restaurant with skilled chefs standing over grills and tandoor ovens, in the eye-catching open kitchen. After devouring the rock oysters in a ginger-studded coconut sauce, we knew we were in for a special meal. Our table shared grilled baby eggplant sprinkled with mango powder. Chicken tikka is one of the signature dishes, the lamb chops are fork tender, and the lobster beautifully spiced. Vegetarians delight in the tandoor-cooked broccoli in a yogurt sauce or artichoke biryani (basmati rice cooked with spices) baked in a pastry-sealed pot. For dessert, try the fresh pomegranate granita, which is sugar-free.

Halkin Arcade, Motcomb St., Knightsbridge SW1. (C) 020/7823-1166. Reservations required. Main courses £9.50–£28 ($19–$56); set lunch £17 ($34), dinner £25 ($50). AE, DC, MC, V. Mon–Sat 12:30–2:15pm and 6–11:15pm; Sun 12:45–2:45pm and 6–10:30pm. Tube: Knightsbridge.

MODERATE
Black and Blue ✿ STEAK/ENGLISH   The atmosphere is marvelously informal, the prices affordable, and the steaks of high quality, each from a traditionally reared, grass-fed Scottish cow. Take your pick—Scottish sirloin, rib-eye, T-bone. We especially

like the *cote de boeuf,* a hefty rib of beef for two to share. The sauces served with the steaks are divine. Burgers, chargrilled chicken, and fish dishes are also on offer on the changing menu, even freshly made salads and platters for the vegetarian.

215–217 Kensington Church St., W8. ⓒ 020/7727-0004. Reservations required. Main courses £9–£25 ($18–$50). MC, V. Mon–Thurs noon–11pm; Fri–Sat noon–11:30pm. Tube: Notting Hill Gate.

Drones 🦶 CONTINENTAL   Britain's wonder chef Marco Pierre White took this once-famous but stale restaurant and has once again turned it into a chic dining venue, decorated with black-and-white photographs of famous people lining the wall. Redesigned by David Collins, it is now referred to as "the Ivy of Belgravia," drawing a similar theatrical crowd. The food and Art Deco ambience are delightful, as is the staff. Food is fresh and delicately prepared, including such favorites as cauliflower cream soup with truffles and sea scallops, or smoked haddock and rice pudding. All the delectable meat and fish dishes are prepared with consummate care and served with a certain finesse. Always expect some unusual flavor combination, such as oxtail *en daube* with a rutabaga purée and a bourguignon garnish. For dessert, a summer specialty is gelée of red fruits with a raspberry-syrup drizzle.

1 Pont St., SW1. ⓒ **020/7235-9555.** Reservations required. Main courses £14–£25 ($28–$50); 2-course fixed-price menu £15 ($30), 3 courses £18 ($36). AE, MC, V. Mon–Sat noon–2:30pm and 6–11pm; Sun noon–4pm. Tube: Knightsbridge.

Racine FRENCH   The chef, Henry Harris, may be as English as they get, but the cuisine at this bustling French brasserie puts you across the Channel in Paris. Francophiles flock to this bistro with its wooden floors, dark-leather banquettes, and black-and-white-clad waiters. Seasonal dishes are featured on the ever-changing menu composed by Harris, who serves what he loves to cook and eat. That means such bistro favorites as rabbit in mustard sauce or salad lyonnaise, even *ris de veau* (sweetbreads) with wild mushrooms or sauerkraut Alsacienne. A veal head is served in the classic sauce ravigote. Expect true, robust flavors and a minimum of pretentiousness.

239 Brompton Rd., SW3. ⓒ 020/7584-4477. Main courses lunch £13–£23 ($26–$46), dinner £13–£33 ($26–$66); set lunch £19 ($38) for 2 courses, £21 ($42) for 3 courses. MC, V. Daily noon–3pm and 6–10:30pm. Tube: Knightsbridge.

INEXPENSIVE
Le Metro INTERNATIONAL   Located just around the corner from Harrods, Le Metro draws a fashionable crowd to its basement precincts. The place serves good, solid, reliable food prepared with flair. The menu changes frequently. You might choose the homemade soup of the day with freshly baked bread or the twice-baked cheese soufflé with an arugula salad as your starting point. For a main, opt for such dishes as salmon fish cakes with horseradish mayonnaise or else pork, leek, and herb sausages with red-onion gravy.

28 Basil St., SW3. ⓒ 020/7589-6286. Main courses £9–£11 ($18–$22). AE, DC, MC, V. Mon–Sat 8am–10pm; Sun 8am–4pm. Tube: Knightsbridge.

CHELSEA
VERY EXPENSIVE
Aubergine 🦶🦶 FRENCH   "Eggplant" is luring savvy diners down to the lower reaches of Chelsea where Chef William Drabble took over from the renowned Gordon Ramsay. Although popular with celebrities, the restaurant remains unpretentious and refuses to pander to the whims of the rich and famous. (Madonna was once refused a late-night booking!)

Every dish is satisfyingly flavorsome, from warm salad of truffled vegetables with asparagus purée to roasted monkfish served with crushed new potatoes, roasted leeks, and red-wine sauce. Starters continue to charm and delight palates, ranging from ravioli of crab with mussels, chili, ginger, and coriander *nage* to terrine of foie gras with confit of duck and pears poached in port. Also resting on your Villeroy & Boch eggplant plate might be mallard with a celeriac fondant, or assiette of lamb with a thyme-scented jus. Another stunning main course is a tranche of sea bass with bouillabaisse potatoes. There are only 14 tables, so bookings are imperative.

11 Park Walk, SW10. (C) 020/7352-3449. Reservations required and accepted as many as 4–8 weeks in advance. 3-course fixed-price lunch £29 ($58), dinner £64 ($128); menu gourmand £130 ($260). AE, DC, MC, V. Mon–Fri noon–2:15pm; Mon–Sat 7–11pm. Tube: South Kensington.

Gordon Ramsay ★★★ *Finds* FRENCH   One of the city's most innovative and talented chefs is Gordon Ramsay. All of London is rushing to sample Mr. Ramsay's wares, and he has had to turn away some big names. The queen hasn't been denied a table yet, but that's only because she hasn't called.

Every dish from this kitchen is gratifying, reflecting subtlety and delicacy without any sacrifice to the food's natural essence. Try, for example, Ramsay's celebrated cappuccino of white beans with grated truffles. His appetizers are likely to dazzle: salad of crispy pigs' trotters with calves' sweetbreads, fried quail eggs and a cream vinaigrette, or foie gras three ways—sautéed with quince, *mi-cuit* with an Earl Grey consommé, or pressed with truffle peelings. From here, you can grandly proceed to the main courses, including oven-roasted pigeon from Anjou wrapped in Parma ham with foie gras or else pan-fried filets of John Dory with crab and caviar.

68 Royal Hospital Rd., SW3. (C) 020/7352-4441. Reservations essential (1 month in advance). Fixed-price 3-course lunch £40 ($80), 3-course dinner £85 ($170), 7-course dinner £110 ($220). AE, DC, MC, V. Mon–Fri noon–2:30pm and 6:30–11pm. Tube: Sloane Sq.

EXPENSIVE

Le Cercle ★★ FRENCH   The owners of Club Gascon have come up with another winner in this chic subterranean dining room, a sort of Chelsea speak-easy. At last Sloane Street has a restaurant that is to food what the boulevard has long been to fashion. Service may not be the most efficient, and the noise level is at times deafening, but the food is absolutely amazing. You make your menu selection among an occasional famous face and a lot of lesser mortals.

For us, the best dish was tuna carpaccio with crispy pork cubes. The French-styled dishes are served as tapas-size portions. The menu is divided into seven sections according to principal ingredients. The waitstaff suggests three portions of these small plates before choosing one of the delectable desserts. The milk-fed Pyrenean lamb is meltingly tender. The chefs turn out one of the most succulent cuts of beef in London—it appears as *onglet* on the menu. Particularly memorable was the duck and fig combo and the chestnut risotto. For dessert, the chocolate fondant may arguably be the best served in London. It's served with vanilla and pepper (you heard right) ice cream. As for the cheese selection, one habitué described them to us as "top dog."

1 Wilbraham Place, SW1. (C) 020/7901-9999. Reservations required. Fixed-price lunch (noon–3pm Tues–Sat) £15–£19 ($30–$38); French tapas £5–£12 ($10–$24). AE, MC, V. Tues–Sat noon–10:45pm (snacks only 3–6pm). Tube: Sloane Sq.

Tom's Kitchen ★ BRITISH   Down in Chelsea, a former pub has been stylishly converted into this chic restaurant, which from the moment of its opening attracted a loyal following of the local smart set. Today a bright, bustling brasserie, with an open kitchen in back, it's the dream come true for Tom Aikens, who is assisted by his twin brother, Rob. Stop in for breakfast if you crave brioche French toast with caramelized apples, cinnamon ice cream, and maple syrup. Or else make a luncheon rendezvous to tuck in Tom's seductive fish and chips.

27 Cale St., SW3. ℭ 020/7349-0202. Reservations required. Main courses lunch £12–£24 ($24–$48), dinner £13–£42 ($26–$84). AE, MC, V. Mon–Fri 7–10am, noon–3pm, and 6pm–midnight; Sat 10am–3pm and 6pm–midnight; Sun 11am–3pm and 6pm–midnight. Tube: Fulham Broadway.

INEXPENSIVE

Oriel FRENCH   Right on the corner of Sloane Square in the heart of Chelsea, this brasserie has long been a favorite of shoppers hitting the boutiques along Kings Road. The upstairs is in the French-brasserie style, rather classic with large mirrors and high ceilings. The atmosphere downstairs is more informal, and there are a few sidewalk tables for those who want to check out the Chelsea scene. If you arrive early for coffee and newspaper reading, you could mistake Oriel for a Parisian cafe. The food is fine but not excellent, including such brasserie standards as tuna niçoise or steak and *pommes frites.* Other dishes include steak au poivre with a very peppery sauce, or perhaps a traditional béarnaise. Mussels marinara is another classic dish, and the salads are always freshly tossed. Vegetarians won't go hungry here either.

50–51 Sloane Sq., SW1. ℭ 020/7730-2804. Reservations not required. Main courses £11–£15 ($22–$30). AE, DC, MC, V. Mon–Sat 8:30am–11pm; Sun 9am–10pm. Tube: Sloane Sq.

The Pig's Ear ✿ *Finds* ENGLISH   The staff are still talking about the surprise visit of Prince William—he may be heir to one of the world's most fabled fortunes, but at the end of the evening here he split the bill among his friends, paying only his fair share at this, one of the best gastro-pubs in Chelsea. It might be called the Pig's Ear, but it's really the silk purse when it comes to food. Start with such dishes as Jerusalem artichoke soup with truffle oil, or chicken livers flavored with sherry vinegar. Other dishes include seared tuna with black olives and chicory or else foie gras ballantine with an onion marmalade. In honor of its namesake, the chefs deep-fry pigs' ears. Filet of sea bass appears with beet and baby leeks, and a roast wood pigeon is stuffed with garlic-laced portobello mushrooms. The atmosphere is friendly and unpretentious in either the ground-floor pub area or in the wood-paneled restaurant upstairs.

35 Old Church St. ℭ 020/7352-2908. Reservations required in restaurant. Main courses £7.25–£18 ($15–$36). AE, DC, MC, V. Mon–Sat noon–11pm; Sun noon–10:30pm. Tube: Sloane Sq.

KENSINGTON & SOUTH KENSINGTON
VERY EXPENSIVE

Tom Aikens ✿✿✿ CONTINENTAL   The amazingly skilled Tom Aikens is one of the truly top-flight Gallic chefs of London. Aikens certainly was trained well, working in Paris under Joël Robuchon during the time he was proclaimed as France's greatest chef. Aikens also ran the prestigious Pied-à-Terre in London. In elegant surroundings in chic Knightsbridge, the food is basically a modern interpretation of high French cuisine, with a great deal of flourish and some very elaborately worked dishes.

Regardless of the contrast in ingredients, main courses show harmony and cohesion, as exemplified by the poached sea bass with saffron risotto and a bouillabaisse sauce. Everything sounds like an unlikely combination, but the end result is most satisfying. The menu's most voluptuous side is evoked by braised suckling pig with roasted fresh almonds, apple purée, and a pork lasagna.

43 Elystan St., Knightsbridge, SW3. © 020/7584-2003. Reservations required. Fixed-price lunch £29 ($58), dinner £65 ($130); tasting menu £80 ($160). AE, DC, MC, V. Mon–Fri noon–2:30pm and 6:45–11pm. Tube: South Kensington.

EXPENSIVE

Bibendum/The Oyster Bar ☆ FRENCH/MEDITERRANEAN   In trendy Brompton Cross, this still-fashionable restaurant occupies two floors of a garage that's now an Art Deco masterpiece. Though its heyday came in the early 1990s, the white-tiled room with stained-glass windows, lots of sunlight, and a chic clientele is still an extremely pleasant place. The eclectic cuisine, known for its freshness and simplicity, is based on what's available seasonally. Dishes might include roast pigeon with celeriac purée and apple sauté, rabbit with artichoke and parsley sauce, or grilled lamb cutlets with a delicate sauce. Some of the best dishes are for splitting between two people, including Bresse chicken flavored with fresh tarragon and grilled veal chops with truffle butter. Simpler meals and cocktails are available in the **Oyster Bar** on the building's street level. The bar-style menu stresses fresh shellfish presented in the traditional French style, on ice-covered platters adorned with strands of seaweed.

81 Fulham Rd., SW3. © 020/7581-5817. Reservations required in Bibendum; not accepted in Oyster Bar. Main courses £18–£25 ($36–$50); 2-course fixed-price lunch £24 ($48), 3 courses £29 ($58); cold seafood platter in Oyster Bar £57 ($114) for 2. AE, DC, MC, V. Bibendum Mon–Fri noon–2:30pm and 7–11:30pm; Sat 12:30–3pm and 7–11:30pm; Sun 12:30–3pm and 7–10:30pm. Oyster Bar daily noon–10pm. Tube: South Kensington.

Clarke's ☆ MODERN ENGLISH   Sally Clarke is one of the finest chefs in London, and this is one of the hottest restaurants around. *Still.* She opened it in the Thatcher era, and it's still going strong. In this excellent restaurant, everything is bright and modern, with wood floors, discreet lighting, and additional space in the basement where tables are more spacious and private. Some people are put off by the fact that there is only a fixed-price menu, but the food is so well prepared that diners rarely object to what ends up in front of them. The menu, which changes daily, emphasizes chargrilled foods with herbs and seasonal veggies. You might begin with an appetizer salad of blood orange with red onions, watercress, and black olive–anchovy toast; then follow that with roasted breast of chicken with black truffle, crisp polenta, and arugula.

124 Kensington Church St., W8. © 020/7221-9225. Reservations recommended. Main courses lunch £14–£16 ($28–$32); 3-course dinner £43 ($86), 4 courses £50 ($100); Sat brunch £10–£14 ($20–$28). AE, DC, MC, V. Mon–Fri 12:30–2pm and 7–10pm; Sat 11am–2pm and 7–10pm. Tube: High St. Kensington or Notting Hill Gate.

MODERATE

Admiral Codrington ☆ *Finds* CONTINENTAL/MODERN ENGLISH   Once a lowly pub, this stylish bar and restaurant is now all the rage. The exterior has been maintained, but the old "Cod," as it is affectionately known, has emerged to offer plush dining with a revitalized decor by Nina Campbell and a glass roof that rolls back on sunny days. The bartenders still offer a traditional pint, but the sophisticated menu features such delectable fare as grilled calves' liver and crispy bacon, or pan-fried rib-eye with a truffled horseradish cream. Opt for the charbroiled tuna with eggplant caviar and a red-pepper vinaigrette.

17 Mossop St., SW3. © 020/7581-0005. Reservations recommended. Main courses £15–£30 ($30–$60). AE, MC, V. Mon–Sat 11:30am–midnight; Sun noon–10:30pm. Tube: South Kensington.

The Enterprise EUROPEAN/TRADITIONAL ENGLISH   The Enterprise's proximity to Harrods attracts both regulars and out-of-town shoppers. Although the joint swarms with singles at night, during the day it attracts the ladies who lunch.

With banquettes, white linen, and fresh flowers, you won't mistake it for a lowly boozer. The kitchen serves respectable traditional English fare as well as European favorites. Featured dishes include fried salmon cakes with butter spinach, golden calamari, and grilled steak with fries and salad. The juicy, properly aged, flavorful entrecôte slice of beef is about the best you can find in London.

35 Walton St., SW3. ✆ 020/7584-3148. Reservations accepted for lunch only Mon–Fri. Main courses £14–£15 ($28–$30). AE, MC, V. Mon–Fri noon–3pm and 6–10:30pm; Sat–Sun noon–3:30pm and 6–10pm. Tube: South Kensington or Knightsbridge.

MARYLEBONE
EXPENSIVE

Odin's 𝕊 INTERNATIONAL   Set adjacent to its slightly less expensive twin, Langan's Bistro, Odin's features ample space between tables and an eclectic decor that includes evocative paintings and Art Deco accessories. As other restaurants nearby have come and gone, the cookery here remains solid and reliable. The standard of fresh ingredients and well-prepared dishes is always maintained. The menu changes with the seasons: Typical fare may include forest mushrooms in brioche, braised leeks glazed with mustard and tomato sauce, roast duck with applesauce and sage-and-onion stuffing, or roast filet of sea bass with a juniper cream sauce.

27 Devonshire St., W1. ✆ 020/7935-7296. Reservations required. 2-course fixed-price lunch or dinner £29 ($58), 3 courses £33 ($66). AE, DC, MC, V. Mon–Fri 12:30–2:30pm; Mon–Sat 6:30–11pm. Tube: Regent's Park.

Orrery 𝕊𝕊 FRENCH/INTERNATIONAL   With ingredients imported from France, this is one of London's classic French restaurants. Sea bass from the shores of Montpellier, olive oil from Maussane-les-Alpilles, mushrooms from the fields of Calais, and poultry from Bresse—they all turn up on a highly refined menu, the creation of Chef Andre Garret. On the second floor of the Conran Shop in Marylebone, Orrey changes its menu seasonally to take advantage of the best produce. Garret is a purist in terms of ingredients. Our favorites among his first-rate dishes are Bresse pigeon with savoy cabbage and mushroom ravioli, or duckling with an endive tatin and *cèpe* (flap mushrooms) sauce. Everything has a brilliant, often whimsical touch, as evoked by the sautéed leeks in pumpkin oil. We ended with a cheese plate featuring a Banton goat cheese so fresh that it oozed onto the plate. Enjoy summer evenings on a fourth-floor terrace while drinking and ordering light fare from the bar menu.

55 Marylebone High St., W1. ✆ 020/7616-8000. Reservations required. Main courses £27–£56 ($54–$112); 3-course fixed-price lunch £25 ($50). AE, DC, MC, V. Daily noon–3pm; Sun–Wed 6:30–10:30pm; Thurs–Sat 6:30–11pm. Tube: Baker St.

MODERATE

Assaggi 𝕊 *Finds* ITALIAN   You wouldn't think of heading to the second floor of a very ordinary pub in Bayswater for fine Italian cuisine, but we urge you to do so in this case to sample Chef Nino Sassu's take on Italian classics, especially those from the south. Serious London foodies have discovered its low-key venue, and flock here for food prepared with flair and passion, using market-fresh and top-quality ingredients.

The chef sets out to prove that straightforward dishes can often be the best when simply handled. Grilled Mediterranean vegetables in virgin olive oil and fresh herbs are an always winning appetizer, followed by such mains as grilled sea bass or filet of pork with black truffles. The menu is short but long on flavor if you try such dishes as a butter-and-sage ravioli, tender calves' liver, or panna cotta.

39 Chepstow Place, W2. ✆ 020/7792-9033. Reservations required. Main courses £18–£24 ($36–$48). AE, MC, V. Mon–Sat 12:30–2:30pm and 7:30–11pm. Tube: Bayswater.

Galvin ✮ FRENCH   Evoking the fabled bistros of Paris, this Gallic-inspired *bistro de luxe* has brought foodies to the once gastro wasteland along Baker Street. Chris and Jeff Galvin, two brothers, provide straightforward French cuisine at a decent price (at least for London). The French classics appear in full-flavored combinations using the finest of seasonal ingredients. In an unpretentious setting, you can dine on a superb *soupe de poisons* (fish soup) or a classic endive salad with Roquefort, pear, and walnuts. That old-fashioned starter, salad of poached lamb's tongue with sauce ravigote, also appears on the menu. For robust eaters, there is an array of such dishes as roasted veal brains in *beurre noisette,* part of a platter that also includes roast rump of veal and melt-in-the-mouth braised cheeks.

6 Baker St., W1. ✆ 020/7935-4007. Reservations required. Main courses £13–£18 ($26–$36); fixed-price menu £18 ($36). AE, MC, V. Mon–Sat noon–2:30pm and 6–11pm; Sun noon–9:30pm. Tube: Baker St.

Villandry ✮ CONTINENTAL/INTERNATIONAL   Food lovers and gourmands flock to this food store, delicatessen, and restaurant, where racks of the world's finest meats, cheeses, and produce are displayed and changed virtually every hour. The best of the merchandise is whimsically transformed into the restaurant's menu choices. The setting is an oversize Edwardian-style storefront north of Oxford Circus. The inside is a kind of minimalist temple dedicated to the glories of fresh produce and esoteric foodstuffs. Ingredients here change so frequently that the menu is rewritten twice a day—during our latest visit, it proposed such perfectly crafted dishes as breast of duck with fresh spinach and a gratin of baby onions; and pan-fried turbot with deep-fried celery, artichoke hearts, and hollandaise sauce.

170 Great Portland St., W1. ✆ 020/7631-3131. Reservations recommended. Main courses £19–£22 ($38–$44). AE, MC, V. Restaurant Mon–Sat noon–3pm and 6–10:30pm; Sun 11:30am–4pm. Food store Mon–Sat 8am–10pm; Sun 10am–4pm. Tube: Great Portland St.

NOTTING HILL GATE
MODERATE
The Cow ✮ *Finds* MODERN ENGLISH   You don't have to be a young fashion victim to enjoy the superb cuisine served here (although many of the diners are). This increasingly hip Notting Hill watering hole looks like an Irish pub, but the accents you'll hear are "trustafarian" rather than street-smart Dublin. With a pint of Fuller's or London Pride, you can linger over the modern European menu, which changes daily but is likely to include ox tongue poached in milk; mussels in curry and cream; or a mixed grill of lamb chops, calves' liver, and sweetbreads. The seafood selections are delectable. The Cow Special—a half-dozen Irish rock oysters with a pint of Guinness or a glass of wine for £11 ($22)—is the star of the show. A raw bar downstairs serves other fresh seafood choices.

89 Westbourne Park Rd., W2. ✆ 020/7221-0021. Reservations required. Main courses £16–£20 ($32–$40). MC, V. Daily noon–midnight. Tube: Westbourne Grove.

INEXPENSIVE
Prince Bonaparte INTERNATIONAL   This offbeat restaurant serves great pub grub in what used to be a grungy boozer before Notting Hill Gate became fashionable. Now pretty young things show up, spilling onto the sidewalk when the evenings are warm. The pub is filled with mismatched furniture; and CDs of jazz and lazy blues

Eating at Authentic Chippies

Déclassé or not, Britain's national dish of fish and chips was called "the good companions" by Sir Winston Churchill. Introduced to London by Murano Jews, this dish has been Britain's fast food since the mid–19th century. Those slightly limp chips (fries to Americans) burst open with flavor with a squirt of malt vinegar, and each dish is accompanied by a "wally," in chippy vernacular (a pickled gherkin). Britons consume some 300 million fish-and-chips meals per year. The staunchest of devotees claim that the fish has to be cooked in beef drippings, but there is much disagreement on that in recent years.

We always head for **Rock & Sole Plaice,** 47 Endell St., WC2 (✆ **0871/426-3380;** Tube: Covent Garden), for our fish-and-chips fix. The cooks here prefer to fry the fish, such as sweet, delicate lemon sole, in clean peanut oil instead of beef drippings. This is London's oldest chippy, having existed under one name or another since 1871. Fish here is cooked in a puffy, ale-colored batter. Count on spending from £10 to £15 ($20–$30) for a dinner, served Monday to Saturday 11:30am to 10:30pm and Sunday noon to 10pm.

Another authentic choice is the **Golden Hind,** 73 Marylebone Lane (✆ **0871/ 3327-803;** Tube: Bond St.), tucked away on this side street since 1914. Fresh fish arrives daily from the port of Grimsby on the western coast. Locals claim that "haddock is for heroes, cod for zeroes," so haddock is the way to go here. It's concealed in a thin batter (not overpuffed like most chippies). A dinner ranges from £6.50 to £15 ($13–$30), and service is Monday to Friday noon to 3pm and Monday to Saturday 6 to 10pm.

---

fill the air, competing with the babble. It may seem at first that the staff doesn't have its act together, but once the food arrives, you won't care—the dishes served here are very good. The menu roams the world for inspiration: Moroccan chicken with couscous is as good or better than any you'll find in Marrakech, and the seafood risotto is delicious.

80 Chepstow Rd., W2. ✆ 020/7313-9491. Reservations not required. Main courses £8–£10 ($16–$20). AE, MC, V. Mon–Sat noon–10:30pm. Tube: Notting Hill Gate or Westbourne Park.

LIMEHOUSE
INEXPENSIVE

The Narrow ✿ (Finds) MODERN BRITISH London's most celebrated chef, Gordon Ramsay, has launched an East End gastro-pub standing on a bend of the Thames in the Limehouse district. Warmed by open fires, the restaurant and pub are chicly decorated in nautical navy and white. The menu is a modernized version of a nostalgic English kitchen—for example, such delights "on toast" as soft herring roes or deviled lamb's kidneys. In how many places today can you find braised Gloucester pig cheeks with mashed neeps (turnips)? Other tempting mains include whole baked gilthead bream with fennel and watercress and a Hereford sirloin with portobello mushrooms and anchovy butter. For dessert, there's a good version of the famous Bakewell Tart.

44 Narrow St., E14. ✆ 020/7592-7950. Reservations required for the restaurant. Main courses £10–£13 ($20–$26); bar snacks £1.50–£7 ($3–$14). AE, MC, V. Mon–Fri 11:30am–3pm and 6–10:30pm; Sat noon–10pm; Sun noon–9pm. Tube: Limehouse.

5 Afternoon Tea

Everyone should indulge in a formal afternoon tea at least once while in London. This relaxing, drawn-out, civilized affair usually consists of three courses, all elegantly served on delicate china: first, dainty finger sandwiches (with the crusts cut off, of course); then fresh-baked scones served with jam and deliciously decadent clotted cream (the rich, thick cream is also known as Devonshire cream); and lastly, an array of bite-size sweets. All the while, an indulgent server keeps the pot of your choice fresh at hand. Sometimes ports or aperitif are on offer for your final course. A quintessential English experience . . . here are a few of our favorite places to indulge.

COVENT GARDEN & THE STRAND
MAYFAIR
St. James Restaurant & The Fountain Restaurant   This pair of tea salons functions as a culinary showplace for London's most prestigious grocery store, Fortnum & Mason. The more formal of the two, the St. James, on the store's fourth floor, is a pale green-and-beige homage to formal Edwardian taste. More rapid and less formal is the Fountain Restaurant, on the street level, where a sense of tradition and manners is very much a part of the dining experience, but in a less opulent setting. There is no longer an "official" afternoon tea at the Fountain, but you can order pots of tea plus food from an à la carte menu that includes sandwiches, scones, and the like.

In Fortnum & Mason, 181 Piccadilly, W1. The Fountain ✆ 020/7973-4140; St. James 020/7734-8040, ext. 2241. St. James afternoon tea £22–£30 ($44–$60), champagne afternoon tea £24–£32 ($48–$64); the Fountain à la carte menu £3–£28 ($6–$56). AE, DC, MC, V. St. James Mon–Sat noon–7pm; Sun noon–5pm. The Fountain Mon–Sat 8:30am–8pm. Tube: Piccadilly Circus.

KNIGHTSBRIDGE
The Georgian Restaurant   For as long as anyone can remember, tea at Harrods has been a distinctive feature of Europe's most famous department store. A flood of visitors is gracefully herded into a high-volume but elegant room. Many come here for the ritual of the tea service, as staff members haul silver pots and trolleys laden with pastries and sandwiches through the cavernous dining hall.

On the 4th floor of Harrods, 87–135 Brompton Rd., SW1. ✆ 020/7225-6800. Reservations recommended. High tea £20 ($40) or £30 ($60) with Harrods champagne, per person. AE, DC, MC, V. Daily 3:30–5:30pm (last order). Tube: Knightsbridge.

Richoux   There's an old-fashioned atmosphere at Richoux, established in the 1920s. You can order four hot scones with strawberry jam and whipped cream or choose from a selection of pastries. Of course, tea is obligatory; always specify lemon or cream, one lump or two. A full menu, with fresh salads, sandwiches, and burgers, is served all day. There are three other locations, open Monday to Friday 8am to 11pm, Saturday 8am to 11:30pm. There's a branch at the bottom of Bond Street, 172 Piccadilly (✆ 020/7493-2204; Tube: Piccadilly Circus or Green Park); one at 41A S. Audley St. (✆ 020/7629-5228; Tube: Green Park or Hyde Park Corner); and one at 3 Circus Rd. (✆ 020/7483-4001; Tube: St. John's Wood).

86 Brompton Rd. (opposite Harrods), Knightsbridge, SW3. ✆ 020/7584-8300. Full tea £17 ($34). AE, MC, V. Mon–Sat 8am–9pm; Sun 10am–9pm. Tube: Knightsbridge.

KENSINGTON
The Orangery ✿ *Finds*   In its way, the Orangery is the most amazing place for afternoon tea in the world. Set 46m (150 ft.) north of Kensington Palace, it occupies a

long, narrow garden pavilion built in 1704 by Queen Anne. In homage to her original intentions, rows of potted orange trees bask in sunlight from soaring windows, and tea is served amid Corinthian columns, ruddy-colored bricks, and a pair of Grinling Gibbons woodcarvings. There are even some urns and statuary that the royal family imported from Windsor Castle. The menu includes soups and sandwiches, with a salad and a portion of upscale potato chips known as kettle chips. The array of different teas is served with high style, accompanied by fresh scones with clotted cream and jam, and Belgian chocolate cake.

In the gardens of Kensington Palace, W8. (C) **020/7376-0239.** Reservations not accepted. Pot of tea only £1.95–£2.25 ($3.90–$4.50); cakes and puddings £2.50–£6 ($5–$12); afternoon tea £12–£35 ($24–$70); champagne tea £18 ($36). MC, V. Daily 3–5pm. Tube: High St. Kensington or Queensway.

6

Exploring London

London is more eclectic and electric than it's been in years. Some even think it has surpassed New York for sheer energy, outrageous fashion, trendy restaurants, and a nightlife that's second to none.

But the cool youth culture that grabs headlines is not all there is to London today. What makes the city so fascinating is its cultural diversity. It seems that half the world is flocking there, not just from the far-flung former colonies of the once-great British Empire, but also from Algeria, Argentina, China, and Senegal. With their talent and new ideas, these transplants are transforming a city once maligned as drab and stuffy. In London today, where everything's changing, only the queen appears the same. (After she's gone, even the House of Windsor may be in for a shake-up.)

Though London is more open and dynamic than it has been since 1969, problems exist here, as elsewhere, that all the happening restaurants and pricey boutiques in the world can't obliterate. The gulf between rich and poor continues to widen, and violent crime, once relatively rare, is on the rise.

In this chapter, we can explore only a fraction of what's exciting in London. We went in search of what's causing the hottest buzz in shopping and nightlife, but we also provide plenty of detail about London's time-tested treasures: ancient monuments, literary shrines, walking tours, Parliament debates, royal castles, waxworks, palaces, cathedrals, and royal parks.

1 The Top Attractions

As a rule, and unless otherwise stated in the listings below, children's prices at London attractions apply to those aged 16 and younger. You must be 60 years of age or older to obtain available senior discounts at some attractions. For students to get available discounted admissions, they must have a valid student ID card.

Tower of London ★★★ *Kids*   This ancient fortress continues to pack in the crowds with its macabre associations with the legendary figures imprisoned and/or executed here. There are more spooks here per square foot than in any other building in the whole of haunted Britain. Headless bodies, bodiless heads, phantom soldiers, icy blasts, clanking chains—you name them, the Tower's got them. Centuries after the last head rolled on Tower Hill, a shivery atmosphere of impending doom still lingers over the Tower's mighty walls. Plan on spending a lot of time here.

The Tower is actually an intricately patterned compound of structures built throughout the ages for varying purposes, mostly as expressions of royal power. The oldest is the **White Tower,** begun by William the Conqueror in 1078 to keep London's native Saxon population in check. Later rulers added other towers, more walls, and fortified gates, until the buildings became like a small town within a city. Until the reign of James I (beginning in 1603), the Tower was also one of the royal residences. But above all, it was a prison for distinguished captives.

Every stone of the Tower tells a story—usually a gory one. In the **Bloody Tower,** according to Shakespeare, Richard III's henchmen murdered the two little princes (the sons of Edward IV). On the walls of the **Beauchamp Tower,** you can still read the last messages scratched by despairing prisoners. Through **Traitors' Gate** passed such ill-fated, romantic figures as Robert Devereux, the second earl of Essex and a favorite of Elizabeth I. A plaque marks the eerie place at **Tower Green** where two wives of Henry VIII, Anne Boleyn and Catherine Howard, plus Sir Thomas More, and the 4-day queen, Lady Jane Grey, all lost their lives.

The Tower, besides being a royal palace, a fortress, and a prison, was also an armory, a treasury, a menagerie and, in 1675, an astronomical observatory. Reopened in 1999, the White Tower holds the **Armouries,** which date from the reign of Henry VIII, as well as a display of instruments of torture and execution that recall some of the most ghastly moments in the Tower's history. In the Jewel House, you'll find the Tower's greatest attraction, the **Crown Jewels.** Here, some of the world's most precious stones are set into robes, swords, scepters, and crowns. The Imperial State Crown is the most famous crown on earth; made for Victoria in 1837, it's worn today by Queen Elizabeth II when she opens Parliament. Studded with some 3,000 jewels (principally diamonds), it includes the Black Prince's Ruby, worn by Henry V at Agincourt. The 530-carat Star of Africa, a cut diamond on the Royal Scepter with Cross, would make Harry Winston turn over in his grave. You'll have to stand in long lines to catch just a glimpse of the jewels as you and hundreds of others scroll by on moving sidewalks, but the wait is worth it.

The presumed prison cell of Sir Thomas More is open to the public. More left this cell in 1535 to face his executioner after he'd fallen out with King Henry VIII over the monarch's desire to divorce Catherine of Aragon, the first of his six wives. More is believed to have lived in the lower part of the Bell Tower during the last 14 months of his life, although some historians doubt this claim.

A **palace** inhabited by King Edward I in the late 1200s stands above Traitors' Gate. It's the only surviving medieval palace in Britain. Guides at the palace are dressed in period costumes, and reproductions of furniture and fittings, including Edward's throne, evoke the era, along with burning incense and candles.

With the opening of a visitor center and the restoration of the Tower's 13th-century wharf, the attraction is more user-friendly than ever before. To the west of the Tower is Tower Hill Square, designed by Stanton Williams, with a series of pavilions housing ticketing facilities, a gift shop, and a cafeteria.

Oh, yes—don't forget to look for the ravens. Six of them (plus two spares) are all registered as official Tower residents. According to a legend, the Tower of London and the kingdom will stand as long as those black, ominous birds remain, so to be on the safe side, one of the wings of each raven is clipped.

One-hour guided tours of the entire compound are given by the Yeoman Warders (also known as Beefeaters) every half-hour daily, starting at 9:30am, from the Middle Tower near the main entrance. The last guided walk starts about 3:30pm in summer, 2:30pm in winter—weather permitting, of course.

You can attend the nightly **Ceremony of the Keys,** the ceremonial locking up of the Tower by the Yeoman Warders. For free tickets, write to the Ceremony of the Keys,

What to See & Do in London

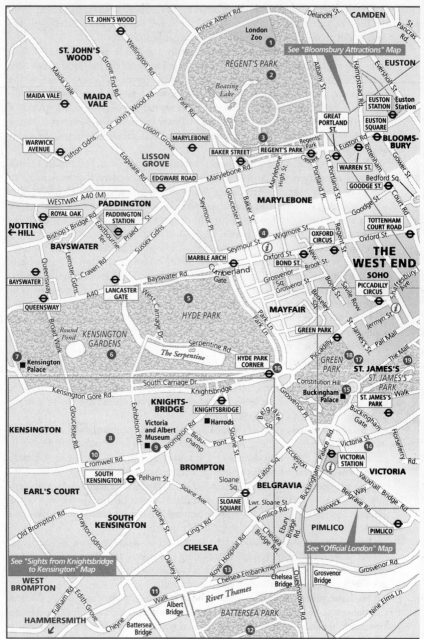

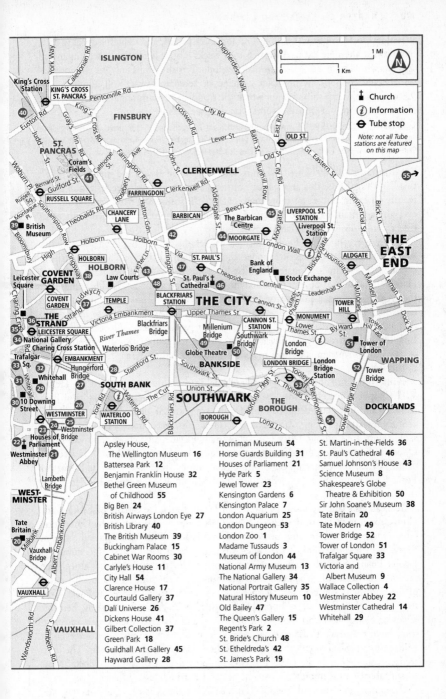

Church	✝
Information	ⓘ
Tube stop	⊖

Note: not all Tube stations are featured on this map

Apsley House,
The Wellington Museum **16**
Battersea Park **12**
Benjamin Franklin House **32**
Bethel Green Museum
of Childhood **55**
Big Ben **24**
British Airways London Eye **27**
British Library **40**
The British Museum **39**
Buckingham Palace **15**
Cabinet War Rooms **30**
Carlyle's House **11**
City Hall **54**
Clarence House **17**
Courtauld Gallery **37**
Dalí Universe **26**
Dickens House **41**
Gilbert Collection **37**
Green Park **18**
Guildhall Art Gallery **45**
Hayward Gallery **28**

Horniman Museum **54**
Horse Guards Building **31**
Houses of Parliament **21**
Hyde Park **5**
Jewel Tower **23**
Kensington Gardens **6**
Kensington Palace **7**
London Aquarium **25**
London Dungeon **53**
London Zoo **1**
Madame Tussauds **3**
Museum of London **44**
National Army Museum **13**
The National Gallery **34**
National Portrait Gallery **35**
Natural History Museum **10**
Old Bailey **47**
The Queen's Gallery **15**
Regent's Park **2**
St. Bride's Church **48**
St. Etheldreda's **42**
St. James's Park **19**

St. Martin-in-the-Fields **36**
St. Paul's Cathedral **46**
Samuel Johnson's House **43**
Science Museum **8**
Shakespeare's Globe
Theatre & Exhibition **50**
Sir John Soane's Museum **38**
Tate Britain **20**
Tate Modern **49**
Tower Bridge **52**
Tower of London **51**
Trafalgar Square **33**
Victoria and
Albert Museum **9**
Wallace Collection **4**
Westminster Abbey **22**
Westminster Cathedral **14**
Whitehall **29**

Waterloo Block, Tower of London, London EC3N 4AB, and request a specific date, but also list alternate dates. At least 6 to 8 weeks' notice is required. Accompany all requests with a stamped, self-addressed envelope (British stamps only) or two international reply coupons. With ticket in hand, a Yeoman Warder will admit you at 9:35pm. Frankly, we think it's not worth the trouble you go through to see this rather cheesy ceremony, but we know some who disagree with us.

Tower Hill, EC3. ℂ **0870/751-5175.** www.tower-of-london.org.uk. Admission £16 ($32) adults, £13 ($26) students and seniors, £9.50 ($19) children ages 5–15, family ticket £45 ($90), free for children 4 and under. Mar–Oct Tues–Sat 9am–5:30pm, Sun–Mon 10am–5:30pm; Nov–Feb Tues–Sat 9am–4:30pm, Sun–Mon 10am–4:30pm. Tube: Tower Hill.

Westminster Abbey 🏛🏛🏛   With its identical square towers and superb archways, this Early English Gothic abbey is one of the greatest examples of ecclesiastical architecture on earth. But it's far more than that: It's the shrine of a nation, the symbol of everything Britain has stood for and stands for, and the place in which most of its rulers were crowned and where many lie buried.

Nearly every figure in English history has left his or her mark on Westminster Abbey. Edward the Confessor founded the Benedictine abbey in 1065 on this spot overlooking Parliament Square. The first king crowned in the abbey may have been Harold, in January 1066, but the man who defeated him at the Battle of Hastings later that year, William the Conqueror, had the first recorded coronation in the abbey on Christmas Day in that year. The coronation tradition has continued to the present day, although Edward V and Edward VIII were never crowned. The essentially Early English Gothic structure existing today owes more to Henry III's plans than to those of any other sovereign, although many architects, including Wren, have contributed to the abbey.

Built on the site of the ancient Lady Chapel in the early 16th century, the **Henry VIII Chapel** is one of the loveliest in Europe, with its fan vaulting, Knights of Bath banners, and Torrigiani-designed tomb for the king himself, near which hangs a 15th-century Vivarini painting, *Madonna and Child.* Also here, ironically buried in the same tomb, are Catholic Mary I and Protestant Elizabeth I (whose archrival, Mary, Queen of Scots, is entombed on the other side of the Henry VII Chapel). In one end of the chapel, you can stand on Cromwell's memorial stone and view the **Royal Air Force Chapel** and its Battle of Britain memorial window, unveiled in 1947 to honor the Royal Air Force.

You can also visit the most hallowed spot in the abbey, the **Shrine of Edward the Confessor** (canonized in the 12th c.). Near the tomb of Henry V is the Coronation Chair, made at the command of Edward I in 1300 to display the mystical Stone of Scone (which some think is the sacred stone mentioned in Genesis and known as Jacob's Pillar). Scottish kings were once crowned on the stone (it has since been returned to Scotland). When you enter the transept on the south side and see a statue of the Bard, with one arm resting on a stack of books, you've arrived at **Poets' Corner.** Shakespeare himself is buried at Stratford-upon-Avon, but resting here are Chaucer, Samuel Johnson, Tennyson, Browning, and Dickens; there's even an American, Henry Wadsworth Longfellow, as well as monuments to just about everybody: Milton, Keats, Shelley, Henry James, T. S. Eliot, George Eliot, and others. The most stylized monument is Sir Jacob Epstein's sculptured bust of William Blake. More recent tablets commemorate Dylan Thomas and Lord Laurence Olivier.

Statesmen and men of science—Disraeli, Newton, Charles Darwin—are also interred in the abbey or honored by monuments. Near the west door is the 1965 memorial to Sir Winston Churchill. In the vicinity of this memorial is the **Tomb of the Unknown Warrior,** commemorating the British dead of World War I.

Although most of the Abbey's statuary commemorates notable figures of the past, 10 new statues were unveiled in 1998. Placed in the Gothic niches above the West Front door, these statues honor 10 modern-day martyrs drawn from every continent and religious denomination. Designed by Tim Crawley and carved under his general direction from French Richemont limestone, the sculptures include Elizabeth of Russia, Janani Luwum, and Martin Luther King, representatives of those who have sacrificed their lives for their beliefs.

Off the Cloisters, the **College Garden** is the oldest garden in England, under cultivation for more than 900 years. Established in the 11th century as the abbey's first infirmary garden, this was once a magnificent source of fruits, vegetables, and medicinal herbs. Five of the trees in the garden were planted in 1850 and they continue to thrive today. Surrounded by high walls, flowering trees dot the lawns, and park benches provide comfort where you can hardly hear the roar of passing traffic. The garden is only open Tuesday to Thursday April to September 10am to 6pm and October to March 10am to 4pm.

Insider's tip: Far removed from the pomp and glory is the **Abbey Treasure Museum,** which displays a real bag of oddities in the undercroft, or crypt, part of the monastic buildings erected between 1066 and 1100. You'll find royal effigies that were used instead of the real corpses for lying-in-state ceremonies because they smelled better. You'll see the almost lifelike effigy of Admiral Nelson (his mistress arranged his hair) and even that of Edward III, his lip warped by the cerebral hemorrhage that felled him. Other oddities include Henry V's funeral armor, a unique corset from Elizabeth I's effigy, and the Essex Ring that Elizabeth I gave to her favorite (Robert Devereux, Earl of Essex) when she was feeling good about him.

On Sundays the abbey is open for services only and all are welcome. The rest of the church is open unless a service is being conducted. For times of services, phone the **Chapter Office** (℃ **020/7222-5152**).

Broad Sanctuary, SW1. ℃ 020/7222-5152. www.westminster-abbey.org. Admission £10 ($20) adults; £7 ($14) for students, seniors, and children 11–18; £24 ($48) family ticket; free for children 10 and younger. Mon–Tues and Thurs–Fri 9:30am–3:45pm; Wed 9:30am–6pm; Sat 9:30am–2:45pm. Tube: Westminster or St. James's Park.

Houses of Parliament & Big Ben ⟨⟨ The Houses of Parliament, along with their trademark clock tower, Big Ben, are the ultimate symbols of London. They're the strongholds of Britain's democracy, the assemblies that effectively trimmed the sails of royal power. Both the House of Commons and the House of Lords are in the former royal Palace of Westminster, which was the king's residence until Henry VIII moved to Whitehall. The current Gothic Revival buildings date from 1840 and were designed by Charles Barry. (The earlier buildings were destroyed by fire in 1834.) Assisting Barry was Augustus Welby Pugin, who designed the paneled ceilings, tiled floors, stained glass, clocks, fireplaces, umbrella stands, and even the inkwells. There are more than 1,000 rooms and 3km (1¾ miles) of corridors. The clock tower at the eastern end houses the world's most famous timepiece. **"Big Ben"** refers not to the clock tower itself, but to the largest bell in the chime, which weighs close to 14 tons and is named for the first commissioner of works, Sir Benjamin Hall.

You may observe debates for free from the **Stranger's Galleries** in both houses. Sessions usually begin in mid-October and run to the end of July, with recesses at Christmas and Easter. The chances of getting into the House of Lords when it's in session are generally better than for the more popular House of Commons. Although we can't promise you the oratory of a Charles James Fox or a William Pitt the Elder, the debates in the House of Commons are often lively and controversial (seats are at a premium during crises).

For years, London tabloids have portrayed members of the House of Lords as a bunch of "Monty Pythonesque upper-class twits," with one foreign secretary calling the House of Lords "medieval lumber." Today, under Gordon Brown's Labour government, the House of Lords is being shaken up as lords lose their inherited posts. Panels are studying what to do with this largely useless house, its members often descendants of royal mistresses and ancient landowners.

Those who'd like to book a tour can do so, but it takes a bit of work. Both houses are open to the general public for guided tours only for a limited season in July and August. The palace is open Monday, Tuesday, Friday, and Saturday from 9:15am to 4:30pm during those times. All tour tickets cost £12 ($24) adult; £8 ($16) for seniors, students, and children 15 and younger; and £30 ($60) family ticket. Children 3 years old and younger may enter free. For advance tickets call © **08709/063773** (www. parliament.uk/visiting/visiting.cfm).

If you arrive just to attend a session, these are free, but you need a card of introduction. Foreign and Commonwealth visitors should apply to their embassy or High Commission in the U.K. for a card of introduction, which will normally permit entry during the early afternoon. Embassies and High Commissions may issue no more than four cards on any day, so visitors from certain countries may find cards are booked for several weeks ahead. Please note that such cards do not guarantee entry. Quite often, it will not be possible to admit their bearers until *after* Prime Minister's Question Time. British embassies abroad do not issue such cards.

With your card of introduction in hand, you line up at Stephen's Gate, heading to your left for the entrance into the Commons or to the right for the Lords. The London daily newspapers announce sessions of Parliament.

Insider's tip: The hottest ticket and the most exciting time to visit is during Prime Minister's Question Time on Wednesdays, which is only from noon to 12:30pm, but which must seem like hours to Gordon Brown, who is on the hot seat. It's not quite as thrilling as it was back when Margaret Thatcher exchanged barbs with the MPs (members of Parliament), but still worth a viewing.

Across the street is the **Jewel Tower** ⚔, Abingdon Street (© **020/7222-2219**), one of only two surviving buildings from the medieval Palace of Westminster. It was constructed in 1365 as a place where Edward III could stash his treasure-trove. The tower hosts an exhibition on the history of Parliament and makes for a great introduction to the inner workings of the British government. The video presentation on the top floor is especially informative. A touch-screen computer allows visitors to take a virtual tour of both houses of Parliament. The tower is open daily from 10am to 5pm April to October and 10am to 4pm November to March. Admission is £2.90 ($5.80) for adults, £2.20 ($4.40) for students and seniors, and £1.50 ($3) for children.

Westminster Palace, Old Palace Yard, SW1. House of Commons © 020/7219-4272; House of Lords © 020/7219-3107. www.parliament.uk. Free admission. Mid-Oct to Aug Mon–Tues 9am–noon; Wed 9–9:20am; Fri 3:30–5pm. Both houses are open for tours (see above). Join line at St. Stephen's entrance. Tube: Westminster.

British Museum ⚔⚔⚔   Set in scholarly Bloomsbury, this immense museum grew out of a private collection of manuscripts purchased in 1753 with the proceeds of a lottery. It grew and grew, fed by legacies, discoveries, and purchases, until it became one of the most comprehensive collections of art and artifacts in the world. It's impossible to take in this museum in a day.

The overall storehouse splits basically into the national collections of antiquities; prints and drawings; coins, medals, and bank notes; and ethnography. Even on a cursory first visit, be sure to see the Asian collections (the finest assembly of Islamic pottery outside the Islamic world), the Chinese porcelain, the Indian sculpture, and the prehistoric and Romano-British collections. Special treasures you might want to seek out on your first visit include the **Rosetta Stone,** in the Egyptian Room, whose discovery led to the deciphering of hieroglyphics; the **Elgin Marbles,** a series of pediments, metopes, and friezes from the Parthenon in Athens, in the Duveen Gallery; and the legendary **Black Obelisk,** dating from around 860 B.C., in the Nimrud Gallery. Other treasures include the contents of Egyptian royal tombs (including mummies); fabulous arrays of 2,000-year-old jewelry, cosmetics, weapons, furniture, and tools; Babylonian astronomical instruments; and winged lion statues (in the Assyrian Transept) that guarded Ashurnasirpal's palace at Nimrud. The exhibits change throughout the year, so if your heart is set on seeing a specific treasure, call to make sure it's on display.

Insider's tip: If you're a first-time visitor, you will, of course, want to concentrate on some of the fabled treasures previewed above. But what we do is duck into the British Museum several times on our visits to London, even if we have only an hour or two, to see the less heralded but equally fascinating exhibits. We recommend wandering rooms 33 and 34, and 91 to 94, to take in the glory of Asia, covering Taoism, Confucianism, and Buddhism. The Chinese collection is particularly strong. Sculpture from India is as fine as anything at the Victoria and Albert. The ethnography collection is increasingly beefed up, especially the Mexican Gallery in room 33C, which traces that country's art from the 2nd millennium B.C. to the 16th century A.D. A gallery for the North American collection is also open nearby. Another section of the museum is devoted to the **Sainsbury African Galleries** ✿, one of the finest collections of African art and artifacts in the world, featuring changing displays selected from more than 200,000 objects. Finally, the museum has opened a new Money Gallery in room 68, tracing the story of money. You'll learn that around 2000 B.C. in Mesopotamia, money was grain and that printed money came into being in the 10th century in China.

For information on the British Library, see p. 186.

Great Russell St., WC1. ✆ 020/7323-8299. www.britishmuseum.org. Free admission. Sat–Wed 10am–5:30pm; Thurs–Fri 10am–8:30pm. Tube: Holborn, Tottenham Court Rd., Goodge St., or Russell Sq.

Buckingham Palace ✿✿ *Kids*

This massive, graceful building is the official residence of the queen. The redbrick palace was built as a country house for the notoriously rakish duke of Buckingham. In 1762, King George III, who needed room for his 15 children, bought it. It didn't become the official royal residence, though, until Queen Victoria took the throne; she preferred it to St. James's Palace. From George III's time, the building was continuously expanded and remodeled, faced with Portland stone, and twice bombed (during the Blitz). Located in a 16-hectare (40-acre) garden, it's 108m (354 ft.) long and contains 600 rooms. You can tell whether the queen is at home by checking to see if the Royal Standard is flying from the mast outside. For most of the year, you can't visit the palace without an official invitation. Since 1993, though, much of it has been open for tours during an 8-week period in August and September, when the royal family is usually vacationing outside London. Elizabeth II agreed to allow visitors to tour the State Room, the Grand Staircase, the Throne Room, and other areas designed by John Nash for George IV, as well as the Picture Gallery, which displays masterpieces by Van Dyck, Rembrandt, Rubens, and others. You have to buy a timed-entrance ticket the same day you tour the palace. Tickets go on sale at 9am, but rather than lining up at sunrise with all the other tourists—this is one of London's most popular attractions—phone to book with a credit card and give yourself a few more hours of sleep.

Buckingham Palace's most famous spectacle is the vastly overrated **Changing of the Guard** (daily Apr–July and on alternating days for the rest of the year). The new guard, marching behind a band, comes from either the Wellington or Chelsea barracks and takes over from the old guard in the forecourt of the palace. The ceremony begins at 11:30am, although it's frequently canceled because of bad weather, state events, and other harder-to-fathom reasons. We like the Changing of the Guard at Horse Guards better (p. 182) because you can actually see the men marching and you don't have to battle such tourist hordes. However, few first-time visitors can resist the Buckingham Palace Changing of the Guard. If that's you, arrive as early as 10:30am and claim territorial rights to a space in front of the palace. If you're not firmly anchored here, you'll miss much of the ceremony.

At end of the Mall (on the road running from Trafalgar Sq.). ℂ **020/7766-7300.** www.royalcollection.org.uk. Palace tours £15 ($30) adults, £14 ($28) 61 and older and students, £8.50 ($17) 16 and younger, family ticket £39 ($78), free for ages 4 and younger; Changing of the Guard free. July 26–Sept 24 (dates can vary), and additional dates may be added. Daily 9:45am–6pm. Changing of the Guard daily Apr–July at 11:30am and alternating days for the rest of the year at 11am. Tube: St. James's Park, Green Park, or Victoria.

Tate Britain ✹✹✹ Fronting the Thames near Vauxhall Bridge in Pimlico, the Tate looks like a smaller and more graceful relation of the British Museum. The most prestigious gallery in Britain, it houses the national collections, covering British art from the 16th century to the present day, as well as an array of international works. In the spring of 2000, the Tate moved the bulk of its 20th- and 21st-century art to the **Tate Modern** (see below). This split helped to open more display space at the Tate Britain, but the collection here is still much too large to be displayed all at once; so the works on view change from time to time.

The older works include some of the best of Gainsborough, Reynolds, Stubbs, Blake, and Constable. William Hogarth is well represented, particularly by his satirical *O the Roast Beef of Old England* (known as *The Gate of Calais*). You'll find the illustrations of William Blake, the incomparable mystical poet, including such works as *The Book of Job, The Divine Comedy,* and *Paradise Lost.* The collection of works by J. M. W. Turner is the Tate's largest collection of works by a single artist—Turner himself willed most of his paintings and watercolors to the nation.

Also on display are the works of many major 19th- and 20th-century painters, including Paul Nash, Matisse, Dalí, Modigliani, Munch, Bonnard, and Picasso. Truly remarkable are the several enormous abstract canvases by Mark Rothko, the group of paintings and sculptures by Giacometti, and the paintings by one of England's best-known modern artists, Francis Bacon. Sculptures by Henry Moore and Barbara Hepworth are also occasionally displayed.

Insider's tip: After you've seen the grand art, don't hasten away. Drop into the Tate Gallery Shop for some of the best art books and postcards in London. The gallery sells whimsical T-shirts with art masterpieces on them. Those ubiquitous Tate Gallery canvas bags seen all over London are sold here, as are the town's best art posters (all make great souvenirs). Invite your friends for tea at the Coffee Shop with its excellent cakes and pastries, or lunch at the Tate Gallery Restaurant. You'll get to enjoy good food, **Rex Whistler** art, and the best and most reasonably priced wine list in London.

Millbank, SW1. ℂ 020/7887-8008. www.tate.org.uk. Free admission; special exhibitions sometimes incur a charge of £7–£11 ($14–$22). Daily 10:30am–5:50pm. Tube: Pimlico.

Tate Modern ✮✮✮   In a transformed Bankside Power Station in Southwark, this museum, which opened in 2000, draws some two million visitors a year to see the greatest collection of international 20th-century art in Britain. How would we rate the collection? At the same level of the Pompidou in Paris, with a slight edge over New York's Guggenheim. Of course, New York's Museum of Modern Art remains in a class of its own. Tate Modern is also viewer-friendly, with eye-level hangings. All the big painting stars are here, a whole galaxy ranging from Dalí to Duchamp, from Giacometti to Matisse and Mondrian, from Picasso and Pollock to Rothko and Warhol. The Modern is also a gallery of 21st-century art, displaying new and exciting art.

You can cross the Millennium Bridge, a pedestrian-only walk from the steps of St. Paul's, over the Thames to the new gallery. Or else you can take the **Tate to Tate** boat (ℂ 020/7887-8888), which takes art lovers on an 18-minute journey across the Thames from the Tate Britain to the Tate Modern, with a stop at the London Eye and the Saatchi Gallery. A ticket costs £4.30 ($8.60), £2.15 ($4.30) for children 15 and under, £11 ($22) for families. Leaving from Millbank Pier, this catamaran is decorated by the trademark colorful dots of that *enfant terrible* artist Damien Hirst.

The Tate Modern makes extensive use of glass for both its exterior and interior, offering panoramic views. Galleries are arranged over three levels and provide different kinds of space for display. Instead of exhibiting art chronologically and by school, the Tate Modern, in a radical break from tradition, takes a thematic approach. This allows displays to cut across movements.

Bankside, SE1. ℂ 020/7887-8888. www.tate.org.uk. Free admission. Sun–Thurs 10am–6pm; Fri–Sat 10am–10pm. Tube: Southwark or Blackfriars.

National Gallery ✮✮✮   This stately neoclassical building contains an unrivaled collection of Western art spanning 7 centuries—from the late 13th to the early 20th—and covering every great European school. For sheer skill of display and arrangement, it surpasses its counterparts in Paris, New York, Madrid, and Amsterdam.

The largest part of the collection is devoted to the Italians, including the Sienese, Venetian, and Florentine masters. They're now housed in the Sainsbury Wing, which was designed by noted Philadelphia architects Robert Venturi and Denise Scott Brown and opened by Queen Elizabeth II in 1991. On display are such works as Leonardo's *Virgin of the Rocks;* Titian's *Bacchus and Ariadne;* Giorgione's *Adoration of the Magi;* and unforgettable canvases by Bellini, Veronese, Botticelli, and Tintoretto. Botticelli's *Venus and Mars* is eternally enchanting. The Sainsbury Wing is also used for large temporary exhibits.

Of the early Gothic works, the Wilton Diptych (French or English school, late 14th c.) is the rarest treasure; it depicts Richard II being introduced to the Madonna and Child by John the Baptist and the Saxon kings, Edmund and Edward the Confessor. Then there are the Spanish giants: El Greco's *Agony in the Garden* and portraits by Goya and Velázquez. The Flemish-Dutch school is represented by Bruegel, Jan van Eyck, Vermeer, Rubens, and de Hooch; the Rembrandts include two of his immortal self-portraits. None of van Eyck's art creates quite the stir that the **Arnolfini Portrait** does. You probably studied this painting from 1434 in your Art History 101 class. The stunning work depicts Giovanni di Nicolao Arnolfini and his wife (who is not pregnant as is often thought; she is merely holding up her full-skirted dress in the contemporary fashion). There's also an immense French Impressionist and post-Impressionist collection that includes works by Manet, Monet, Degas, Renoir, and Cézanne. Particularly charming is the peep-show cabinet by Hoogstraten in one of the Dutch rooms: It's like spying through a keyhole.

British and modern art are the specialties of the Tate galleries (see listings above), but the National Gallery does have some fine 18th-century British masterpieces, including works by Hogarth, Gainsborough, Reynolds, Constable, and Turner.

Guided tours of the National Gallery are offered twice daily at 11:30am and 2:30pm. A Gallery Guide soundtrack is also available. A portable CD player provides audio information on paintings of your choice with the mere push of a button. Although this service is free, contributions are appreciated.

Insider's tip: The National Gallery has a computer information center where you can design your own personal tour map for free. The computer room, located in the Micro Gallery, includes a dozen hands-on workstations. The online system lists 2,200 paintings and has background notes for each work. Using a touch-screen computer, you can design your own personalized tour by selecting a maximum of 10 paintings you would like to view. Once you have made your choices, you print a personal tour map with your selections.

North side of Trafalgar Sq., WC2. ℂ 020/7747-2885. www.nationalgallery.org.uk. Free admission. Thurs–Tues 10am–6pm; Wed 10am–9pm. Tube: Charing Cross or Leicester Sq.

Kensington Palace ✹ *Kids* Once the residence of British monarchs, Kensington Palace hasn't been the official home of reigning kings since George II. William III and Mary II acquired it in 1689 as an escape from the damp royal rooms along the Thames. Since the end of the 18th century, the palace has housed various members of the royal family, and the State Apartments are open for tours.

It was here in 1837 that a young Victoria was awakened with the news that her uncle, William IV, had died and she was now the queen of England. You can view a collection of Victoriana, including some of her memorabilia. In the apartments of Queen Mary II is a striking 17th-century writing cabinet inlaid with tortoiseshell. Paintings from the Royal Collection line the walls. A rare 1750 lady's court dress and splendid examples of male court dress from the 18th century are on display in rooms adjacent to the State Apartments, as part of the Royal Ceremonial Dress Collection, which features royal costumes dating as far back as 200 years.

Kensington Palace was the London home of the late Princess Margaret and is the current home of the duke and duchess of Kent. The palace was also the home of Diana, Princess of Wales, and her two sons. (Harry and William now live with their father at St. James's Palace.) The palace is probably best known for the millions of flowers placed in front of it during the days following Diana's death.

Warning: You don't get to see the apartments where Princess Di lived or where both Di and Charles lived until they separated. Many visitors think they'll get to peek at these rooms and are disappointed. Charles and Di lived on the west side of the palace, still occupied today by minor royals.

The **Kensington Gardens** are open to the public for leisurely strolls through the manicured grounds and around the Round Pond. One of the most famous sights is the controversial Albert Memorial, a lasting tribute not only to Victoria's consort, but also to the questionable taste of the Victorian era. There's a wonderful afternoon tea offered in the Orangery (p. 164).

The Broad Walk, Kensington Gardens, W8. © 0870/7515-170. Admission £12 ($24) adults, £10 ($20) seniors and students, £6 ($12) children 5–15, £33 ($66) family ticket. Mar–Oct daily 10am–6pm; Nov–Feb daily 10am–5pm. Tube: Queensway or Notting Hill Gate; High St. Kensington on south side.

St. Paul's Cathedral ✦✦✦   During World War II, newsreel footage reaching America showed St. Paul's Cathedral standing virtually alone among the rubble of the City, its dome lit by fires caused by bombings all around it. That the cathedral survived at all is a miracle, since it was badly hit twice during the early years of the bombardment of London. But St. Paul's is accustomed to calamity, having been burned down three times and destroyed by invading Norsemen. It was during the Great Fire of 1666 that the old St. Paul's was razed, making way for a new structure designed by Sir Christopher Wren and built between 1675 and 1710. The cathedral is architectural genius Wren's ultimate masterpiece.

The classical dome of St. Paul's dominates the City's square mile. The golden cross surmounting it is 110m (361 ft.) above the ground; the golden ball on which the cross rests measures 2m (6½ ft.) in diameter, though it looks like a marble from below. In the interior of the dome is the Whispering Gallery, an acoustic marvel in which the faintest whisper can be heard clearly on the opposite side. Sit on one side, have your traveling companions sit on the opposite side, and whisper away. You can climb to the top of the dome for a 360-degree view of London. From the Whispering Gallery a second steep climb leads to the **Stone Gallery,** opening onto a panoramic view of London. Another 153 steps take you to the **Inner Golden Gallery,** situated at the top of the inner dome. Here an even more panoramic view of London unfolds.

St. Paul's Churchyard, EC4. © 020/7246-8350. www.stpauls.co.uk. Cathedral and galleries £9.50 ($19) adults, £8.50 ($17) seniors and students, £3.50 ($7) children 6–16, £23 ($46) family ticket, free for children 5 and younger; guided tours £3 ($6) adults, £2.50 ($5) students and seniors, £1 ($2) children; recorded tours £3.50 ($7), free for children 5 and younger. Cathedral (excluding galleries) Mon–Sat 8:30am–4pm; galleries Mon–Sat 9:30am–4pm. No sightseeing Sun (services only). Tube: St. Paul's, Mansion House, Cannon St., or Blackfriars.

Clarence House ✦✦   From 1953 until her death in 2002, the Queen Mother lived at Clarence House in a wing of St. James's Palace. It was constructed between 1825 and 1927 to the designs of John Nash. Today it is the official residence of the Prince of Wales and is open to the public only during a specified period of the year (see below). The present Queen Elizabeth and the duke of Edinburgh lived here following their marriage in 1947.

After the death of the Queen Mother, the house was refurbished and redecorated, with antiques and art added from the royal collection. Visitors are taken on a guided tour of five of the staterooms, where much of the queen's collection of works of art and furniture is on display, along with pieces added by Prince Charles. The Queen Mother had an impressive collection of 20th-century British art, including works by John Piper, Augustus John, and Graham Sutherland. She also was known for her superb collection of Fabergé and English porcelain and silver, especially pieces from her family collection (the Bowes-Lyon family).

Stable Yard Gate, SW1. © 020/7766-7303. www.royal.collection.org.uk. Admission £7.50 ($15) adults, £6.50 ($13) seniors and students, £4 ($8) ages 5–16, free for children 4 and younger. Aug 1–Sept 30 (dates subject to change; call first) daily 10am–5:30pm. Tube: Green Park or St. James's Park.

Victoria and Albert Museum ★★★ The Victoria and Albert is the greatest decorative-arts museum in the world. It's also one of the liveliest and most imaginative museums in London—where else would you find the quintessential "little black dress"—made famous by Coco Chanel—in the permanent collection?

The medieval holdings include such treasures as the Early English Gloucester Candlestick; the Byzantine Veroli Casket, with its ivory panels based on Greek plays; and the Syon Cope, a unique embroidery made in England in the early 14th century. An area devoted to Islamic art houses the Ardabil Carpet from 16th-century Persia.

The V&A boasts the largest collection of Renaissance sculpture outside Italy. A highlight of the 16th-century collection is the marble group *Neptune with Triton* by Bernini. The cartoons by Raphael, which were conceived as designs for tapestries for the Sistine Chapel, are owned by the queen and are on display here. A most unusual, huge, and impressive exhibit is the Cast Courts, life-size plaster models of ancient and medieval statuary and architecture.

The museum has the greatest collection of Indian art outside India, plus Chinese and Japanese galleries. In complete contrast are suites of English furniture, metalwork, and ceramics, and a superb collection of portrait miniatures, including the one Hans Holbein the Younger made of Anne of Cleves for the benefit of Henry VIII, who was again casting around for a suitable wife. The Dress Collection includes a representation of corsets through the ages that's sure to make you wince. There's also a remarkable collection of musical instruments.

V&A has opened 15 modern galleries—the **British Galleries** ★★★—telling the story of British design from 1500 to 1900. No other museum in the world houses such a diverse collection of British design and decorative art. From Chippendale to Morris, all of the top British designers are featured in some 3,000 exhibits, ranging from the 5m-high (16-ft.) Melville Bed (1697) with its luxurious wild-silk damask and red-velvet hangings, to 19th-century classics such as furniture by Charles Rennie Mackintosh. One of the most prized possessions is the "Great Bed of Ware," mentioned in Shakespeare's *Twelfth Night*. Also on exhibit is the wedding suite of James II. And don't miss the V&A's most bizarre gallery, Fakes and Forgeries. The impostors here are amazingly authentic—in fact, we'd judge some of them as better than the Old Masters themselves. The interactive displays hold special interest. Learning about heraldry is far more interesting when you're designing your own coat of arms.

In the winter of 2004, V&A opened a suite of five renovated painting galleries that were originally built in 1850. A trio of these galleries focuses on British landscapes as seen through the eyes of Turner, Constable, and others. Constable's oil sketches were donated by his daughter, Isabel, in 1888. Another gallery showcases the bequest of Constantine Ionides, a Victorian collector, with masters such as Botticelli, Delacroix, Degas, Tintoretto, and Ingres. There's even a piano here designed by the famous Edward Burne-Jones, which once belonged to Ionides's brother.

Cromwell Rd., SW7. ☎ 020/7942-2000. www.vam.ac.uk. Free admission. Temporary exhibitions often £10 ($20). Daily 10am–5:45pm (until 10pm every Wed and the last Fri of each month). Tube: South Kensington.

Trafalgar Square One of the landmark squares of London, Trafalgar Square honors one of England's great military heroes, Horatio Viscount Nelson (1758–1805), who died at the Battle of Trafalgar. Although he suffered from seasickness all his life, he went to sea at the age of 12 and was an admiral at the age of 39. Lord Nelson was a hero of the Battle of Calvi in 1794 where he lost an eye, the Battle of Santa Cruz in 1797 where he lost an arm, and the Battle of Trafalgar in 1805 where he lost his life.

Frommer's Favorite London Experiences

Cruising London's Waterways (Tube: Charing Cross). In addition to the Thames, London is riddled with an antique canal system, complete with towpath walks, bridges, and wharves. Replaced by the railroad, the system was forgotten until recently rediscovered by a new generation. An urban renewal effort has restored the system, with bridges painted and repaired, and towpaths cleaned up. See "Organized Tours," later in this chapter.

Viewing the Turners at the Tate. Upon his death in 1851, J. M. W. Turner bequeathed his personal collection of 19,000 watercolors and some 300 paintings to the people of Britain. He wanted his finished works, some 100 paintings, displayed under one roof. Today at the Tate, you get not only Turner but also glimpses of the Thames through the museum's windows. How appropriate—the artist lived and died on its banks in Chelsea and painted the river in its many changing moods.

Enjoying a Traditional Afternoon Tea. Nothing is more typically British, and it's a great way to spend an afternoon. We suggest our favorite places for tea on p. 164.

Rowing on the Serpentine. When the weather is right, we like to head to this 17-hectare (41-acre) artificial lake, dating from 1730 and located in Hyde Park. A stream was dammed to create the lake, whose name derives from its winding, snakelike shape. At the Boathouse, you can rent a boat by the hour. With the right companion, it's one of the most idyllic ways to spend a sunny London afternoon.

Wandering through Covent Garden. George Bernard Shaw got his inspiration for *Pygmalion* here, where the character of Eliza Doolittle sold violets to wealthy operagoers and became a household name around the world. The old fruit-and-vegetable market, with its Cockney cauliflower peddlers and butchers in blood-soaked aprons, is long gone. But what's left is just as interesting: Covent Garden today is London's best example of urban renewal. An antiques market is in the piazza on Monday, a crafts market Tuesday through Saturday.

Spending a Night at a West End Theater. London is the theatrical capital of the world. The live stage offers a unique combination of variety, accessibility, and economy—and a look at next year's Broadway hit.

Crawling the London Pubs. With some 5,000 pubs within the city limits, you would be crawling indeed if you tried to have a drink in each of them. Enough traditional ones remain, especially in central London, to make it worthwhile to go on a crawl, perhaps fortifying yourself with a ploughman's lunch or a plate of shepherd's pie. Our favorites include **Grenadier** (p. 224), **Salisbury** (p. 225), and **Red Lion** (p. 226).

The square today is dominated by a 44m (145-ft.) granite column, the work of E. H. Baily in 1843. The column looks down Whitehall toward the Old Admiralty, where Lord Nelson's body lay in state. The figure of the naval hero towers 5m (17 ft.)

high, not bad for a man who stood 1.5m (5 ft. 4 in.) in real life. The capital is of bronze cast from cannons recovered from the wreck of the *Royal George*. Queen Victoria's favorite animal painter, Sir Edward Landseer, added the four lions at the base of the column in 1868. The pools and fountains were not added until 1939, the last work of Sir Edwin Lutyens.

Political demonstrations still take place at the square and around the column, which has the most aggressive pigeons in London. These birds will even land on your head or perform less desirable stunts. Actually, the birds are part of a long feathery tradition, for this site was once used by Edward I (1239–1307) to keep his birds of prey. Called "Longshanks," he came here often before he died of dysentery in 1307. Richard II, who ruled from 1377 to 1399, kept goshawks and falcons here, too. By the time of Henry VII, who ruled from 1485 to 1509, the square was used as the site of the royal stables. Sir Charles Barry, who designed the Houses of Parliament, created the present square in the 1830s.

Trafalgar Square has become more user-friendly. A grand staircase has replaced the street between the square and the National Gallery. That's not all: Pedestrian crossings on the other streets enveloping the square make approaching it on foot less risky. Before, you were likely to get run over by a speeding vehicle. Of course, the summer fun of concerts, street entertainment, and open-air cafe-sitting will continue.

To the southeast of the square, at 36 Craven St., stands a house once occupied by Benjamin Franklin when he was a general of the Philadelphia Academy (1757–74). On the north side of the square rises the National Gallery, constructed in the 1830s. In front of the building is a copy of a statue of George Washington by J. A. Houdon.

Trafalgar Sq., WC2. www.london.gov.uk/mayor/trafalgar_square/visit. Tube: Charing Cross.

National Portrait Gallery 🏛🏛

In a gallery of remarkable and unremarkable portraits (they're collected for their subjects rather than their artistic quality), a few paintings tower over the rest, including Sir Joshua Reynolds's first portrait of Samuel Johnson ("a man of most dreadful appearance"), Nicholas Hilliard's miniature of handsome Sir Walter Raleigh, a full-length of Elizabeth I, and a Holbein cartoon of Henry VIII. There's also a portrait of William Shakespeare (with a gold earring) by an unknown artist that bears the claim of being the "most authentic contemporary likeness" of its subject. One of the most famous pictures in the gallery is the group portrait of the Brontë sisters (Charlotte, Emily, and Anne) by their brother, Bramwell. An idealized portrait of Lord Byron by Thomas Phillips is also on display.

The later-20th-century portraiture includes major works by such artists as Warhol and Hambling. Some of the more flamboyant personalities of the past 2 centuries are on show: T. S. Eliot; Disraeli; Macmillan; Sir Richard Burton (the explorer, not the actor); Elizabeth Taylor; and our two favorites, G. F. Watts's famous portrait of his great actress wife, Ellen Terry, and Vanessa Bell's portrait of her sister, Virginia Woolf. A portrait of the late Princess Diana is on the Royal Landing, and this painting seems to attract the most viewers.

In 2000, Queen Elizabeth opened the Ondaatje Wing of the gallery, increasing the gallery's exhibition space by more than 50%. The splendid Tudor Gallery features portraits of Richard III and Henry VII, Richard's conqueror in the Battle of Bosworth in 1485. There's also a portrait of Shakespeare that the gallery acquired in 1856. Rooms lead through centuries of English monarchs, with literary and artistic figures thrown in. It took a decade but the top-floor Regency Galleries cover the period from the start of the French Revolution to 1832, with portraits of such luminaries as Napoleon, Admiral Nelson, Jane Austen, and the duke of Wellington. A Balcony Gallery taps into the cult of celebrity, displaying more recent figures whose fame has lasted longer than Warhol's 15 minutes. These include everybody from Mick Jagger to Joan Collins and, of course, the Baroness Thatcher.

The Gallery operates a cafe and art bookshop.

St. Martin's Place, WC2. (C) 020/7306-0055. www.npg.org.uk. Free admission; fee charged for certain temporary exhibitions. Sat–Wed 10am–6pm; Thurs–Fri 10am–9pm. Tube: Charing Cross or Leicester Sq.

Tower Bridge ✦✦ This is one of the world's most celebrated landmarks and possibly the most photographed and painted bridge on earth. Despite its medieval appearance, Tower Bridge was built in 1894.

In 1993, the Tower Bridge Exhibition opened inside the bridge to commemorate its century-old history; it takes you up the north tower to high-level walkways between the two towers with spectacular views of St. Paul's, the Tower of London, and the Houses of Parliament. You're then led down the south tower and into the bridge's original engine room, containing the Victorian boilers and steam engines that used to raise and lower the bridge for ships to pass. Exhibits in the bridge's towers use animatronic characters, video, and computers to illustrate the history of the bridge.

At Tower Bridge, SE1. (C) 020/7403-3761. www.towerbridge.org.uk. Tower Bridge Experience £6 ($12) adults, £4.50 ($9) students and seniors, £3 ($6) children 5–15, £14 ($28) family ticket, free for children 4 and younger. Tower Bridge Experience Apr–Sept daily 10am–6:30pm; off season daily 9:30am–6pm. Closed Christmas Eve and Christmas Day. Tube: Tower Hill, London Bridge, or Fenchurch St.

2 More Attractions

OFFICIAL LONDON

Whitehall ✦, the seat of the British government, grew up on the grounds of Whitehall Palace and was turned into a royal residence by Henry VIII, who snatched it from its former occupant, Cardinal Wolsey. Whitehall extends south from Trafalgar Square to Parliament Square. Along it you'll find the Home Office, the Old Admiralty Building, and the Ministry of Defence.

Visitors today can see the **Cabinet War Rooms** ✦, the bombproof bunker suite of rooms, just as they were when abandoned by Winston Churchill and the British government at the end of World War II. You can see the Map Room with its huge wall maps, the Atlantic map a mass of pinholes (each hole represents at least one convoy). Next door is Churchill's bedroom-cum-office, which has a bed and a desk with two BBC microphones on it for his famous speech broadcasts that stirred the nation. Between 1945 and 2003, parts of this underground bunker were closed to the public. Today, however, you can view nine more Cabinet War Rooms, including the Chief of Staff map room. You can also see Churchill's private kitchen and dining room as well as Mrs. Churchill's bedroom. There's everything here from a pencil cartoon of Hitler to a mousetrap in the kitchen to the original chamber pots under the beds (they had no flush toilets).

The **Transatlantic Telephone Room,** its full title, is little more than a broom closet, but it housed the Bell Telephone Company's special scrambler phone, called *Sigsaly,* and it was where Churchill conferred with Roosevelt. Visitors are provided with a step-by-step personal sound guide, providing a detailed account of each room's function and history.

Also in the war rooms is the **Churchill Museum,** the world's first major museum dedicated to the life of Sir Winston Churchill. It explores in various exhibits and photographs the saga of Britain's wartime prime minister. The opening marked the 40th anniversary of the prime minister's death. The museum through its memorabilia introduces the visitors to the private man but also traces his development as a world leader.

The entrance to the War Rooms is by Clive Steps at the end of King Charles Street, SW1 (© **020/7930-6961;** www.iwm.org.uk/cabinet; Tube: Westminster or St. James's), off Whitehall near Big Ben. Admission £11 ($22) adults, £9 ($18) seniors and students, and free for children 15 and younger. The rooms are open daily 9:30am to 6pm.

At the Cenotaph (honoring the dead of both World Wars I and II), look down **Downing Street** to the modest little town house at no. 10, flanked by two bobbies. It is no longer possible to walk down the street because of security reasons. You can only peer through the gates. Walpole was the first prime minister to live here; Churchill was the most famous. But Margaret Thatcher was around longer than any of them.

Nearby, north of Downing Street, is the **Horse Guards Building** ⚘, Whitehall (no phone; Tube: Westminster), now the headquarters of the horse guards of the Household Division and London District. There has been a guard change here since 1649, when the site was the entrance to the old Palace of Whitehall. You can watch the Queen's Life Guards ceremony at 11am Monday to Saturday and 10am Sunday. You can also see the hourly smaller **Changing of the Guard,** when mounted troopers are changed. And at 4pm, you can watch the evening inspection, when 10 unmounted troopers and 2 mounted troopers assemble in the courtyard.

Across the street is Inigo Jones's **Banqueting House,** Palace of Whitehall, Horse Guards Avenue (© **0870/751-5178;** www.hrp.org.uk; Tube: Westminster or Embankment), site of the execution of Charles I. William and Mary accepted the crown of England here, but they preferred to live at Kensington Palace. The Banqueting House was part of Whitehall Palace, which burned to the ground in 1698, but the ceremonial hall escaped razing. Its most notable feature today is an allegorical ceiling painted by Peter Paul Rubens. Admission to the Banqueting House is £4.50 ($9) adults, £3.50 ($7) seniors and students, and £2.25 ($4.50) children 15 and younger. It's open Monday to Saturday 10am to 5pm (last admission 4:30pm). Banqueting House often closes on short notice, so it's best to call before going.

LEGAL LONDON

The smallest borough in London, bustling Holborn (pronounced *Ho*-burn) is often referred to as Legal London, home of the city's barristers, solicitors, and law clerks. It also embraces the university district of Bloomsbury. Holborn, which houses the ancient **Inns of Courts**—Gray's Inn, Lincoln's Inn, Middle Temple, and Inner Temple—was severely damaged during World War II bombing raids. The razed buildings were replaced with modern offices, but the borough retains pockets from its former days.

At the 60 or more **Law Courts** presently in use on the Strand, all civil and some criminal cases are heard. Designed by G. E. Street, the neo-Gothic buildings (1874–82) have more than 1,000 rooms and 5.5km (3½ miles) of corridors. Sculptures of Christ, King Solomon, and King Alfred grace the front door; Moses is depicted at the back. Admission is free, and courts are open during sessions Monday

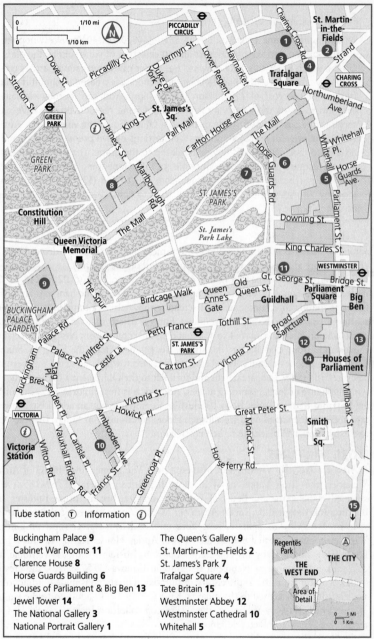

0	1/10 mi
0	1/10 km

PICCADILLY CIRCUS

St. Martin-in-the-Fields

Charing Cross Rd.

National Portrait Gallery **1**

Strand

The National Gallery **3**

Trafalgar Square **4**

CHARING CROSS

Dover St.

Piccadilly St.

Jermyn St.

Duke of York St.

Lower Regent St.

Haymarket

Northumberland Ave.

Stratton St.

King St.

St. James's Sq.

Pall Mall

Carlton House Terr.

The Mall

Whitehall Pl.

Whitehall

GREEN PARK

St. James's St.

Horse Guards Rd.

Horse Guards Ave.

GREEN PARK

Marlborough Rd.

Clarence House **8**

ST. JAMES'S PARK

Horse Guards Building **6**

St. James's Park **7**

Whitehall **5**

Parliament St.

Constitution Hill

The Mall

St. James's Park Lake

Downing St.

Queen Victoria Memorial

King Charles St.

Buckingham Palace **9**

The Spur

WESTMINSTER

Cabinet War Rooms **11**

Gt. George St.

Bridge St.

BUCKINGHAM PALACE GARDENS

Birdcage Walk

Queen Anne's Gate

Old Queen St.

Guildhall

Parliament Square

Big Ben

Buckingham Palace Rd.

Palace St.

Wilfred St.

Castle La.

Petty France

ST. JAMES'S PARK

Tothill St.

Broad Sanctuary

Houses of Parliament **13**

Stag Pl.

Bres

senden Pl.

Victoria St.

Caxton St.

Westminster Abbey **12**

Houses of Parliament **14**

Millbank St.

VICTORIA

Howick Pl.

Victoria St.

Great Peter St.

Smith Sq.

Victoria Station

Wilton Rd.

Vauxhall Bridge Rd.

Carlisle Pl.

Ambrosden Ave.

Francis St.

Westminster Cathedral **10**

Monck St.

Horseferry Rd.

Greencoat Pl.

Tate Britain **15**

Tube station	ⓣ	Information	ⓘ

Regent's Park

THE CITY

THE WEST END

Area of Detail

0   1 Mi
0   1 Km

Finds **A City of Wine**

At **Vinopolis,** 1 Bank End, Park Street, SE1 (© **0870/241-4040;** www.vinopolis.
co.uk), you can partake of London's largest selection of wine sold by the glass.
On the South Bank, this "city of wine" lies under cavernous railway arches created in Victoria's era. The bacchanalian attraction was created in a multimedia
format, at the cost of £23 million ($46 million). You can journey virtually
through some of the earth's most prestigious wine regions, driving a Vespa
through the Tuscan countryside or taking a "flight" over the vineyards of Australia. The price of entrance includes free tastings of five premium wines, and
an on-site shop sells almost any item related to the grape. The site also boasts
a good restaurant (see Cantina Vinopolis, p. 155). Depending on the ticket and
package purchased, admission ranges from £18 to £28 ($36–$56). Hours are
Monday, Thursday, Friday, and Saturday noon to 9pm, Wednesday and Sunday
noon to 6pm.

---

through Friday from 10am to 4:30pm. No cameras, tape recorders, video cameras, or
cellphones are allowed during sessions (Tube: Holborn or Temple).

The court known as the **Old Bailey,** on Newgate Street, EC4 (© **020/7248-3277**),
replaced the infamous Newgate Prison, once the scene of public hangings and other
forms of "public entertainment." It's fascinating to watch the bewigged barristers presenting their cases to the high court judges. Entry is strictly on a first-arrival basis, and
guests line up outside. Courts 1 to 4, 17, and 18 are entered from Newgate Street, and
the balance from Old Bailey (the street). To get here, take the Tube to Temple,
Chancery Lane, or St. Paul's. Travel east on Fleet Street, which along the way becomes
Ludgate Hill. Cross Ludgate Circus and turn left to the Old Bailey, a domed structure
with the figure of Justice standing atop it. Admission is free; children 13 and younger
are not admitted, and ages 14 to 16 must be accompanied by an adult. No cameras,
tape recorders, or cellphones are allowed. Hours are Monday to Friday 10am to 1pm
and 2 to 5pm. The best time to line up is 9am.

MORE MUSEUMS

Apsley House, the Wellington Museum ⓕ   The former town house of Arthur
Wellesley, the "Iron Duke" of Wellington, the British general (1769–1852) who
defeated Napoleon at the Battle of Waterloo and later became prime minister, this
building was designed by Robert Adam (1728–92). Adam pioneered the neoclassical
style in Britain, with light, elegant lines unbound by strict classical proportion.
Wellington once retreated behind the walls of Apsley House, fearing an attack from
Englishmen outraged by his autocratic opposition to reform. In the vestibule is a
colossal marble statue of Napoleon by Antonio Canova (1757–1822), the greatest
Italian sculptor from the 18th century until today. The statue is nude—ironic to say
the least. It was presented to the duke by King George IV. In addition to the famous
Waterseller of Seville by Velázquez, the Wellington collection includes works by Cor-
reggio, Jan Steen, and Pieter de Hooch.

Insider's tip: Apsley House has some of the finest silver and porcelain pieces in
Europe. Grateful to Wellington for saving their thrones, European monarchs endowed
him with treasures. Head for the Plate and China Room on the ground floor. The

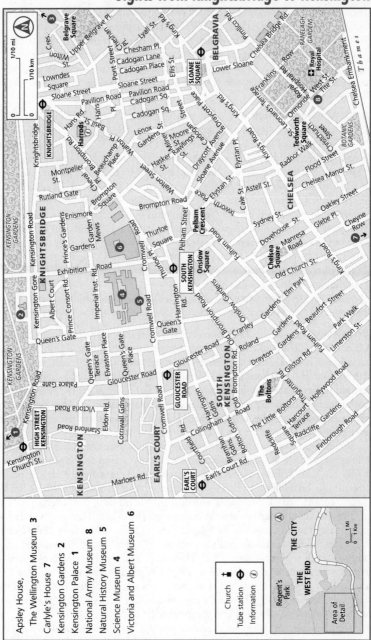

Sights from Knightsbridge to Kensington

Apsley House,
The Wellington Museum **3**
Carlyle's House **7**
Kensington Gardens **2**
Kensington Palace **1**
National Army Museum **8**
Natural History Museum **5**
Science Museum **4**
Victoria and Albert Museum **6**

Church
Tube station
Information

Regent's Park

THE CITY

THE WEST END

Area of Detail

0 | 1 Mi
0 | 1 Km

Sèvres Egyptian service was intended as a divorce present from Napoleon to Josephine, but she refused it. Eventually Louis XVII of France presented it to Wellington. The Portuguese Silver Service in the dining room was created between 1812 and 1816: It has been hailed as the single greatest artifact of Portuguese neoclassical silver.

149 Piccadilly, Hyde Park Corner, W1. (C) 020/7499-5676. Admission £5.30 ($11) adults, £4 ($8) seniors and students, £2.60 ($5.20) children 15 and under. Apr–Oct Tues–Sun 10am–5pm; Nov–Mar Tues–Sun 10am–4pm. Tube: Hyde Park Corner.

Benjamin Franklin House 🅐   The only surviving home of Benjamin Franklin in London opened as a museum in 2006. Off Trafalgar Square, the modest four-story brick building was Franklin's home between 1757 and 1775. He was a diplomat on behalf of the American colonists. Curators call the house "the first de facto U.S. Embassy." The building was also the site of many of Franklin's scientific experiments. It was here that he invented bifocal glasses and created the ethereal-sounding musical instrument, the glass armonica. Mozart and Beethoven later created music on this armonica. Franklin lived here in "serene comfort and affection," often having a full household of friends or relatives. Among other attractions, visitors can view the parlor where Franklin—a great fan of fresh air—sat "air bathing" naked by the open windows. The museum stages a "Historical Experience" every 45 minutes throughout the day. Visitors are taken through the various rooms by actors presenting a re-creation of Franklin's last night in London.

36 Craven St., WC2. (C) 020/7930-6601. www.benjaminfranklinhouse.org. Admission £9 ($18) adults; £6 ($12) children, seniors, and students. Mon and Wed–Sun 10am–5pm (closed Mon Oct–May). Tube: Trafalgar Sq.

British Library 🅐🅐★   In 1996, one of the world's great libraries moved its collection of some 12 million books, manuscripts, and other items from the British Museum to its very own home in St. Pancras. Here you get modernistic beauty rather than the fading glamour and the ghosts of Karl Marx, William Thackeray, and Virginia Woolf of the old library at the British Museum. You are also likely to get the book you want within an hour instead of 3 days. Academics, students, writers, and bookworms from the world over come here. On one visit, we sat next to a student researching the history of pubs.

The bright, roomy interior is far more inviting than the rather dull redbrick exterior suggests (the writer Alain de Botton likened the exterior to a supermarket). Still, Colin St. John Wilson, the architect, says he has been delighted by the positive response to his building. The most spectacular room is the Humanities Reading Room, constructed on three levels with daylight filtered through the ceiling.

The fascinating collection includes such items of historic and literary interest as two of the four surviving copies of the *Magna Carta* (1215), a Gutenberg Bible, Nelson's last letter to Lady Hamilton, and the journals of Captain Cook. Almost every major author—Dickens, Jane Austen, Charlotte Brontë, Keats, and hundreds of others—is represented in the section devoted to English literature. Beneath Roubiliac's 1758 statue of Shakespeare stands a case of documents relating to the Bard, including a mortgage bearing his signature and a copy of the First Folio of 1623. There's also an unrivaled collection of stamps and stamp-related items.

Using headphones set around the room, you can hear thrilling audio snippets such as James Joyce reading a passage from *Finnegans Wake*. Curiosities include the earliest known tape of a birdcall, dating from 1889. Particularly intriguing is an exhibition called "Turning the Pages," where you can, for example, electronically read a complete

Leonardo da Vinci notebook by putting your hands on a special computer screen that flips from one page to another. There is a copy of *The Canterbury Tales* from 1410, and even manuscripts of *Beowulf* (ca. 1000). On display are reproductions of illuminated texts, including the *Codex Sinaitticus* and *Codex Alexandrius,* 3rd-century Greek gospels. In the Historical Documents section are letters by everybody from Henry VIII to Napoleon, from Elizabeth I to Churchill. In the music displays, you can seek out original sheet music by Beethoven, Handel, Stravinsky, and Lennon and McCartney. An entire day spent here will only scratch the surface.

Walking tours of the library cost £8 ($16) for adults and £6.50 ($13) for seniors, students, and children. They are conducted Monday, Wednesday, and Friday at 3pm, and Saturday at 10:30am and 3pm. Library tours that include a visit to one of the reading rooms take place on Sundays and bank holidays at 10:30am and 3pm (£8/$16 adults, £6.50/$13 for seniors and students). Reservations can be made up to 2 weeks in advance.

96 Euston Rd., NW1. ℭ 020/7412-7332. www.bl.uk. Free admission. Mon and Wed–Fri 9:30am–6pm; Tues 9:30am–8pm; Sat 9:30am–5pm; Sun 11am–5pm. Tube: Kings Cross/St. Pancras or Euston.

City Hall   On the South Bank of the Thames adjacent to Tower Bridge, the mayor of London and the London Assembly got a new home in 2002. A gleaming, egg-shaped building, a 10-story steel-and-glass structure, was dedicated by Her Majesty. The new home for city government has become London's latest—some say, most controversial—landmark. Half of City Hall is open to the public who'd like to come in and look around. The views from its rooftop gallery are worth the trek over to the South Bank. An exhibition space highlights changing cultural exhibits, and there is also a cafe on-site.

The Queen's Walk, SE1. ℭ 020/7983-4100. www.london.gov.uk. Free admission. Visitor information desk Mon–Fri 9am–5pm. Cafe Mon–Fri 8am–8pm. Tube: London Bridge.

Courtauld Gallery   The nucleus of this collection was acquired by Samuel Courtauld, who died in 1947 leaving his collection to the University of London. Today it houses the biggest collection of Impressionist and post-Impressionist paintings in Britain, with masterpieces by Monet, Manet, Degas, Renoir, Cézanne, van Gogh, and Gauguin. The gallery also has a superb collection of Old Master paintings and drawings, including works by Rubens and Michelangelo; early Italian paintings, ivories, and majolica; the Lee collection of Old Masters; and early-20th-century English, French, and British paintings.

The galleries on the second floor display a series of paintings and sculptures, some 100 pieces of art from the late 19th and 20th centuries, including an outstanding grouping of Fauve paintings along with art by everybody from Matisse to Dufy, as well as a remarkable series of paintings and drawings by Kandinsky. We come here at least once every season to revisit one work in particular: Manet's exquisite *A Bar at the Folies-Bergère* ✪. Many of the paintings are displayed without glass, giving the gallery a more intimate feeling than most. This gallery is but one of three major attractions at Somerset House. For information about the other attractions, such as the Gilbert Collection, see below.

Somerset House, the Strand, WC2. ℭ 020/7848-2526. www.courtauld.ac.uk. Admission £5 ($10) adults, £4 ($8) seniors and students, free for children 17 and younger. Daily 10am–6pm (last admission 5:30pm). Tube: Temple, Covent Garden, Charing Cross, or Holborn.

Dalí Universe ☆ *Finds*   Next to the London Eye, this exhibition is devoted to the remarkable Spanish artist, Salvador Dalí (1904–89), and is one of London's newest attractions. Featuring more than 500 works of art, including the Mae West Lips sofa, the exhibitions are divided into a trio of themed areas: Sensuality and Femininity, Religion and Mythology, and Dreams and Fantasy. Showcased are important Dalí sculptures, rare graphics, watercolors, and even furnishings and jewelry. You can feast on such surreal works as Dalí's monumental oil painting for the Hitchcock movie *Spellbound,* or view a series of original watercolors and collages including the mystical Tarot Cards and see the world's largest collection of rare Dalí graphics, illustrating themes from literature.

County Hall Gallery, Riverside Building, South Bank, SE1. ℂ 0870/744-7485. www.daliuniverse.com. Admission £12 ($24) adults, £10 ($20) children 12–16, family ticket £30 ($60), free for ages 11 and younger. Daily 10am–6:30pm. Tube: Waterloo or Westminster.

Gilbert Collection ☆☆☆ *Finds*   In 2000, Somerset House became the permanent home for the Gilbert Collection of decorative arts, one of the most important bequests ever made to England. Sir Arthur Gilbert made his gift of gold, silver, mosaics, and gold snuffboxes to the nation in 1996, at which time the value was estimated at £75 million ($150 million). The collection of some 800 objects in three fields is among the most distinguished in the world. The array of mosaics is among the most comprehensive ever gathered, with Roman and Florentine examples dating from the 16th to the 19th centuries. The gold and silver collection, arguably better than the one at the V&A, has exceptional breadth, ranging from the 15th to the 19th centuries, spanning India to South America. It is strong in masterpieces of great 18th-century silversmiths, such as Paul de Lamerie. Such exhibits as the Maharajah pieces, the "Gold Crown," and Catherine the Great's Royal Gates are fabulous. The gallery also displays one of the most representative collections of gold snuffboxes in the world, with some 200 examples. Some of the snuffboxes were owned by Louis XV, Frederick the Great, and Napoleon.

Somerset House, the Strand, WC2. ℂ 020/7420-9400. www.gilbert-collection.org.uk. Admission £5 ($10) adults, £4 ($8) seniors, free for ages 17 and younger. Daily 10am–6pm. Tube: Temple, Covent Garden, Charing Cross, or Embankment.

Guildhall Art Gallery ☆   In 1999, Queen Elizabeth opened this £70-million ($140-million) gallery, a continuation of the original gallery, launched in 1886, burned down in a severe air raid in May 1941. Many famous and much-loved pictures, which for years were known only through temporary exhibitions and reproductions, are once again available for the public to see in a permanent setting in the City. The gallery can display only 250 of the 4,000 treasures it owns at a time. A curiosity is the huge double-height wall built to accommodate Britain's largest independent oil painting, John Singleton Copley's *The Defeat of the Floating Batteries at Gibraltar, September 1782.* The Corporation of London in the City owns these works and has been collecting them since the 17th century. The most popular art is in the Victorian collection, including such well-known favorites as Millais's *My First Sermon* and *My Second Sermon,* and Landseer's *The First Leap.* There is also a large landscape of Salisbury Cathedral by John Constable. Since World War II, all paintings acquired by the gallery have concentrated on London subjects. Included in your admission price is entrance to the ruins of the only Roman amphitheater discovered in London. It was unearthed in 1988.

Guildhall Yard, EC2. ℂ 020/7332-3700. Admission £2.50 ($5) adults, £1 ($2) seniors and students, free for children 15 and younger; free Fri and after 3:30pm on every other day. Mon–Sat 10am–5pm; Sun noon–4pm. Tube: Bank, St. Paul's, Mansion House, or Moorgate.

Hayward Gallery

Opened by Elizabeth II in 1968, this gallery presents a changing program of major contemporary and historical exhibits. It's managed by the South Bank Board, which also includes Royal Festival Hall, Queen Elizabeth Hall, and the Purcell Room. Every exhibition is accompanied by a variety of educational activities, including tours, workshops, lectures, and publications. The gallery closes between exhibitions, so call before crossing the Thames.

Belvedere Rd., South Bank, SE1. ℂ 08703/800400. www.hayward.org.uk. Admission varies but usually £7.50 ($15) adults, £6 ($12) students and seniors, free for children 11 and younger; half-price Mon. Hours subject to change, depending on the exhibit: Thurs and Sat–Mon 10am–6pm; Fri 10am–9pm; Tues–Wed 11am–8pm. Tube: Waterloo or Embankment.

Madame Tussauds *(Overrated (Kids*

Madame Tussauds is not so much a wax museum as an enclosed amusement park. A weird, moving, sometimes terrifying (to children) collage of exhibitions, panoramas, and stage settings, it manages to be most things to most people, most of the time.

Madame Tussaud attended the court of Versailles and learned her craft in France. She personally took the death masks from the guillotined heads of Louis XVI and Marie Antoinette (which you'll find among the exhibits). She moved her original museum from Paris to England in 1802. Her exhibition has been imitated in every part of the world, but never with the realism and imagination on hand here. Madame herself molded the features of Benjamin Franklin, whom she met in Paris. All the rest—from George Washington to John F. Kennedy and Mary, Queen of Scots, to Sylvester Stallone—have been subjects for the same painstaking (and often breathtaking) replication.

In the well-known Chamber of Horrors—a kind of underground dungeon—are all kinds of instruments of death, along with figures of their victims. The shadowy presence of Jack the Ripper lurks in the gloom as you walk through a Victorian London street. Present-day criminals are portrayed within the confines of prison. The latest attraction to open here is "The Spirit of London," a musical ride that depicts 400 years of London's history, using special effects that include audio-animatronic figures that move and speak. Visitors take "time-taxis" that allow them to see and hear "Shakespeare" as he writes and speaks lines, to be received by Queen Elizabeth I, and demonstrate the feel and smell of the Great Fire of 1666 that destroyed London.

We've seen these changing exhibitions so many times over the years that we feel they're a bit cheesy, but we still remember the first time we were taken here as kids. We thought it fascinating back then.

Insider's tip: To avoid the long lines, sometimes more than an hour in summer, call in advance and reserve a ticket for fast pickup at the entrance. If you don't want to bother with that, be aggressive and form a group of nine people waiting in the queue. A group of nine or more can go in almost at once through the "group door." Otherwise, go when the gallery first opens or late in the afternoon when crowds have thinned.

Marylebone Rd., NW1. ℂ 0870/999-0293. www.madame-tussauds.com. Admission £23 ($46) adults, £20 ($40) seniors, £19 ($38) children 15 and younger. **Note:** Admission prices can go higher or lower during the year. Mon–Fri 9:30am–5:30pm; Sat–Sun 9am–6pm. Tube: Baker St.

Museum of London 🎯★★ In the Barbican District near St. Paul's Cathedral, the Museum of London allows visitors to trace the city's history from prehistoric times to the postmodern era through relics, costumes, household effects, maps, and models. Anglo-Saxons, Vikings, Normans—they're all here, displayed on two floors around a central courtyard. The exhibits are arranged so that visitors can begin and end their chronological stroll through 250,000 years at the museum's main entrance, and exhibits have quick labels for museum sprinters, more extensive ones for those who want to study, and still more detail for scholars. It's an enriching experience for everybody—allow at least an hour for a full (but still quick) visit.

You'll see the death mask of Oliver Cromwell; the Great Fire of London in living color and sound; reconstructed Roman dining rooms with kitchen and utensils; cell doors from Newgate Prison, made famous by Charles Dickens; and an amazing shop counter with pre–World War II prices on the items. But the *pièce de résistance* is the Lord Mayor's coach, built in 1757 and weighing 3 tons. Still used each November in the Lord Mayor's Procession, this gilt-and-red horse-drawn vehicle is like a fairy-tale coach. Also on-site is the World City Gallery, which occupies an entire floor whose 2,000 exhibits and artifacts trace life in London between 1789 and 1914, the beginning of World War I.

You can reach the museum, which overlooks London's Roman and medieval walls, by going up to the elevated pedestrian precinct at the corner of London Wall and Aldersgate, 5 minutes from St. Paul's.

150 London Wall, EC2. ✆ 0870/444-3851. www.museumoflondon.org.uk. Free admission. Mon–Sat 10am–5:50pm; Sun noon–5:50pm. Tube: St. Paul's or Barbican.

National Army Museum ★ *Kids* The National Army Museum occupies a building adjoining the Royal Hospital, a home for retired soldiers. Whereas the Imperial War Museum is concerned with wars of the 20th century, the National Army Museum tells the colorful story of British armies from 1485 on. Here you'll find uniforms worn by British soldiers in every corner of the world, plus weapons and other gear, flags, and medals. Even the skeleton of Napoleon's favorite charger is here. Also on display are Florence Nightingale's jewelry, the telephone switchboard from Hitler's headquarters (captured in 1945), and Orders and Medals of HRH the Duke of Windsor. A more recent gallery, "The Rise of the Redcoats," contains exhibitions detailing the life of the British soldier from 1485 to 1793. Included in the exhibit are displays on the English Civil War and the American War of Independence.

Royal Hospital Rd., SW3. ✆ 020/7730-0717. www.national-army-museum.ac.uk. Free admission. Daily 10am–5:30pm. Closed Jan 1, Good Friday, 1st Mon in May, and Dec 24–26. Tube: Sloane Sq.

Natural History Museum ★★ *Kids* This is the home of the national collections of living and fossil plants, animals, and minerals, with many magnificent specimens on display. The zoological displays are quite wonderful; though not up to the level of the Smithsonian in Washington, D.C., they're definitely worthwhile and exciting exhibits designed to encourage people of all ages to learn about natural history. The Mineral Gallery displays marvelous examples of crystals and gemstones. Visit the Meteorite Pavilion, which exhibits fragments of rock that have crashed into the earth, some from the farthest reaches of the galaxy. What attracts the most attention is the dinosaur exhibit, displaying 14 complete skeletons. In the exhibition "Earth Today and Tomorrow," visitors are invited to explore the planet's dramatic history from the big bang to its inevitable death.

The latest development here is the Darwin Centre, dedicated to the great natural-ist Charles Darwin. The center reveals the museum's scientific work with specimens, research, and outreach activities. You're given an insider's look that answers such ques-tions as how specimens are collected today (ethical considerations as well). These are not just specimens in a bottle. You learn, for example, how mosquito DNA helps sci-entists track down the spread of malaria, or about the alien habitat of the deep sea and the strange animals that inhabit these murky depths. Behind-the-scenes free tours (ages 9 and older only) are given of the museum daily; you should book immediately upon entering the museum if you're interested.

Cromwell Rd., SW7. (○ 020/7942-5000. www.nhm.ac.uk. Free admission. Mon–Sat 10am–5:50pm; Sun 11am–5:50pm. Tube: South Kensington.

The Queen's Gallery 🌟🌟   The refurbished gallery at Buckingham Palace reopened to the public in 2002 in time for the Golden Jubilee celebration of Queen Elizabeth II. Visitors going through the Doric portico entrance will find three times as much space as before. John Nash designed the original building in 1831, but it was destroyed in a Nazi air raid in 1940. The gallery is dedicated to changing exhibitions of the wide-ranging treasure-trove that forms the Royal Collection. Anticipate special exhibitions of paintings, prints, drawings, watercolors, furniture, porcelain, minia-tures, enamels, jewelry, and other works of art. At any given time, expect to see such artistic peaks as Van Dyck's equestrian portrait of Charles I, the world-famous *Lady at the Virginal* by Vermeer, a dazzling array of gold snuff boxes, paintings by Monet from the collection of the late Queen Mother, personal jewelry, and studies by Leonardo da Vinci.

Buckingham Palace, SW1. (○ 020/7766-7301. www.royalcollection.org.uk. Admission £8 ($16) adults, £7 ($14) stu-dents and seniors, £4 ($8) children 5–16, free for children 4 and younger. Daily 10am–5:30pm. Tube: Hyde Park Cor-ner, Green Park, or Victoria.

Science Museum 🌟🌟🌟 *Kids*   This museum traces the development of science and industry and their influence on everyday life. These scientific collections are among the largest, most comprehensive, and most significant anywhere. On display are Stephenson's original rocket and the tiny prototype railroad engine; you can also see Whittle's original jet engine and the *Apollo 10* space module. The King George III Collection of scientific instruments is the highlight of a gallery on science in the 18th century. Health Matters is a permanent gallery on modern medicine. The museum has two hands-on galleries, as well as working models and video displays.

Insider's tip: A large addition to this museum explores such topics as genetics, dig-ital technology, and artificial intelligence. Four floors of a new Wellcome Wing shel-ter half a dozen exhibition areas and a 450-seat IMAX theater. One exhibition explores everything from drug use in sports to how engineers observe sea life with robotic submarines. On an upper floor, visitors can learn how DNA was used to iden-tify living relatives of the Bleadon Man, a 2,000-year-old Iron Age Man. On the third floor is the computer that Tim Berners-Lee used to design the World Wide Web out-side Geneva, writing the first software for it in 1990.

Note also the marvelous interactive consoles placed strategically in locations throughout the museum. These display special itineraries, including directions for get-ting to the various galleries for families, teens, adults, and those with special interests.

Exhibition Rd., SW7. (○ 0870/870-4868. www.sciencemuseum.org.uk. Free admission. Daily 10am–6pm. Closed Dec 24–26. Tube: South Kensington.

Sir John Soane's Museum ⭐ This is the former home of Sir John Soane (1753–1837), an architect who rebuilt the Bank of England (not the present structure). With his multiple levels, fool-the-eye mirrors, flying arches, and domes, Soane was a master of perspective and a genius of interior space (his picture gallery, for example, is filled with three times the number of paintings a room of similar dimensions would be likely to hold). William Hogarth's satirical series, *The Rake's Progress,* includes his much-reproduced *Orgy* and *The Election,* a satire on mid-18th-century politics. Soane also filled his house with paintings and classical sculpture. On display is the sarcophagus of Pharaoh Seti I, found in a burial chamber in the Valley of the Kings. Also exhibited are architectural drawings from the collection of 30,000 in the Soane Gallery.

13 Lincoln's Inn Fields, WC2. ⓒ 020/7405-2107. www.soane.org. Free admission (donations invited). Tues–Sat 10am–5pm; 1st Tues of each month 6–9pm. Tours given Sat at 11am; £5 ($10) tickets distributed at 10:30am, first-come, first-served (group tours by appointment only). Tube: Holborn.

Wallace Collection ⭐⭐ *(Finds)* Located in a palatial setting (the modestly described "town house" of the late Lady Wallace), this collection is a contrasting array of art and armaments. The collection is evocative of the Frick Museum in New York and the Musée d'Jacque André in Paris. The art collection (mostly French) includes works by Watteau, Boucher, Fragonard, and Greuze, as well as such classics as Frans Hals's *Laughing Cavalier* and Rembrandt's portrait of his son Titus. The paintings of the Dutch, English, Spanish, and Italian schools are outstanding. The collection also contains important 18th-century French decorative art, including furniture from a number of royal palaces, Sèvres porcelain, and gold boxes. The European and Asian armaments, on the ground floor, are works of art in their own right: superb inlaid suits of armor, some obviously for parade rather than battle, with more businesslike swords, halberds, and magnificent Persian scimitars.

Manchester Sq., W1. ⓒ 020/7563-9500. www.wallacecollection.org. Free admission (some exhibits require admission). Daily 10am–5pm. Tube: Bond St. or Baker St.

LITERARY LANDMARKS

See the discussion of Hampstead Village, later in this chapter, for details on Keats House. See "The Top Attractions" section, earlier in this chapter, for details on Poets' Corner in Westminster Abbey.

Born in London in 1882, the author Virginia Woolf lived and worked in **Bloomsbury,** and she wrote many of her works in London. Virginia spent her formative years at 22 Hyde Park Gate, off Kensington High Street, west of Royal Albert Hall. After the death of her father, the family left Kensington for Bloomsbury and settled in the area around the British Museum (upper-class Victorians at that time, however, didn't view Bloomsbury as "respectable"). From 1905, they lived first at 46 Gordon Sq., east of Gower Street and University College. It was here that the nucleus of the soon-to-be celebrated Bloomsbury Group was created, which would in time embrace Clive Bell (husband of Vanessa) and Leonard Woolf, who was to become Virginia's husband. Later, Virginia lived at 29 Fitzroy Sq., west of Tottenham Court Road, in a house once occupied by George Bernard Shaw. During the next 2 decades, Virginia resided at several more addresses in Bloomsbury, including on Brunswick Square, Tavistock Square, and Mecklenburg Square; these homes have either disappeared or been altered beyond recognition. During this time, the Bloomsbury Group reached out to include artists Roger Fry and Duncan Grant, and Virginia became friends with economist Maynard

What to See & Do in Bloomsbury

British Airways
   London Eye **12**

British Library **1**

British Museum **3**

Courtauld Gallery **7**

Dalí Universe **11**

Dickens House **4**

Gilbert Collection **8**

Hayward Gallery **13**

National Gallery **6**

Percival Davied
   Foundation of
   Chinese Art **2**

St. Bride's Church **10**

Samuel Johnson's
   House **9**

Shakespeare's
   Globe theatre &
   Exhibition **15**

Sir John Soane's
   Museum **5**

Tate Modern **14**

Church ✝
Tube station ⊖

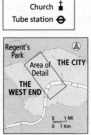

Regent's Park

THE CITY

Area of Detail

THE WEST END

0   1 Mi
0   1 Km

Keynes and author E. M. Forster. At Tavistock Square (1924–39) and at Mecklenburg Square (1939–40), she operated Hogarth Press with Leonard. She published her own early work here, as well as T. S. Eliot's *The Waste Land*. To escape from urban life, Leonard and Virginia purchased Monk's House in the village of Rodmell between Lewes and Newhaven in Sussex. Here, they lived until 1941 when Virginia drowned herself in the nearby Ouse. Her ashes were buried in the garden at Monk's House.

Carlyle's House   From 1834 to 1881, Thomas Carlyle, author of *The French Revolution,* and Jane Baillie Welsh Carlyle, his noted letter-writing wife, resided in this modest 1708 terraced house. Furnished essentially as it was in Carlyle's day, the house is located about three-quarters of a block from the Thames, near the Chelsea Embankment along King's Road. The most interesting room is the not-so-soundproof "soundproof" study in the sky-lit attic. It's filled with Carlyle memorabilia—his books, a letter from Disraeli, personal effects, a writing chair, and even his death mask.

24 Cheyne Row, SW3. © 020/7352-7087. Admission £4.50 ($9) adults, £2.30 ($4.60) children 5–16, free for children 5 and younger. Wed–Sun and bank holidays 2–5pm. Closed Nov–Mar 13. Tube: Sloane Sq. or South Kensington.

Dickens House   Here in Bloomsbury stands the simple abode in which Charles Dickens wrote *Oliver Twist* and finished *The Pickwick Papers* (his American readers actually waited at the dock for the ship that brought in each new installment). The place is almost a shrine: It contains his study, manuscripts, and personal relics, as well as reconstructed interiors. During Christmas week (including Christmas Day), the museum is decorated in the style of Dickens's first Christmas there. During Christmas, the raised admission prices of £10 ($20) for adults and £5 ($10) for children include hot mince pies and a few glasses of "Smoking Bishop," Dickens's favorite hot punch, as well as a copy of the museum's guidebooks.

48 Doughty St., WC1. © 020/7405-2127. www.dickensmuseum.com. Admission £5 ($10) adults, £4 ($8) students and seniors, £3 ($6) children, £14 ($28) family ticket. Mon–Sat 10am–5pm; Sun 11am–5pm. Tube: Russell Sq., Chancery Lane, or Holborn.

Samuel Johnson's House 🏚🏚   Dr. Johnson and his copyists compiled a famous dictionary in this Queen Anne house, where the lexicographer, poet, essayist, and fiction writer lived from 1748 to 1759. Although Johnson also lived at Staple Inn in Holborn and at a number of other places, the Gough Square house is the only one of his residences remaining in London. The 17th-century building has been painstakingly restored, and it's well worth a visit.

17 Gough Sq., EC4. © 020/7353-3745. www.drjohnsonshouse.org. Admission £4.50 ($9) adults, £3.50 ($7) students and seniors, £1.50 ($3) children, £10 ($20) family ticket, free for children 10 and younger. Oct–Apr Mon–Sat 11am–5pm; May–Sept Mon–Sat 11am–5:30pm. Tube: Blackfriars, Chancery Lane, Temple, or Holborn. Walk up New Bridge St. and turn left onto Fleet St.; Gough Sq. is tiny and hidden, north of Fleet St.

Shakespeare's Globe Theatre & Exhibition 🏚   A re-creation of what was probably the most important public theater ever built, it's on the exact site where many of Shakespeare's plays opened. The late American filmmaker, Sam Wanamaker, worked for some 20 years to raise funds to re-create the theater as it existed in Elizabethan times, thatched roof and all. A fascinating exhibit tells the story of the Globe's construction, using the materials (including goat hair in the plaster), techniques, and craftsmanship of 400 years ago. The new Globe isn't an exact replica: It seats 1,500 patrons, not the 3,000 who regularly squeezed in during the early 1600s, and this thatched roof has been specially treated with a fire retardant. Guided tours are offered throughout the day.

21 New Globe Walk, Southwark, SE1. © 020/7902-1500. www.shakespeares-globe.org. Admission £9 ($18) adults, £7.50 ($15) seniors and students, £6.50 ($13) children 15 and younger. Oct–Apr daily 10am–7:30pm; May–Sept daily 9am–noon and 12:30–5pm. Tube: Mansion House or London Bridge.

LANDMARK CHURCHES

Many of the churches listed below offer free **lunchtime concerts;** it's customary to leave a small donation. A full list of churches offering lunchtime concerts is available from the **London Visitor Centre,** 1 Lower Regent St., London SW1Y 4XT (© **8701/ 566-366;** www.visitlondon.com; Tube: Piccadilly Circus).

St. Martin–in-the-Fields ⊀, overlooking Trafalgar Square, WC2 (© **020/7766-1100;** www.stmartin-in-the-fields.org; Tube: Charing Cross), is the Royal Parish Church. The first known church on the site dates from the 13th century, but the present classically inspired church, with its famous steeple, dates from 1726. From St. Martin's vantage position in the theater district, it has drawn many actors to its door—none more notable than Nell Gwyn, the mistress of Charles II. On her death in 1687, she was buried in the crypt. Throughout the war, many Londoners rode out uneasy nights in the crypt while Blitz bombs rained down overhead. One bomb, in 1940, blasted out all the windows. Today, the crypt has a pleasant restaurant, a bookshop, and a gallery. It is home to London's original **Brass Rubbing Centre** (© **020/7930-9306**), which is open Monday to Wednesday 10am to 7pm, Thursday to Saturday 10am to 10pm, and Sunday noon to 7pm.

St. Bride's Church ⊀, on Fleet Street (© **020/7427-0133;** www.stbrides.com; Tube: Blackfriars), known as the church of the press, is a remarkable landmark: The current church is the eighth one that has stood here. Its spire has four octagonal tiers capped by an obelisk that's topped off with a ball and vane. This soaring confection (70m/234 ft. tall) reportedly inspired the wedding cakes of a pastry cook who lived on Fleet Street in the late 17th century. The crypts are now a museum.

St. Etheldreda's, Britain's oldest Roman Catholic church, lies at 14 Ely Place, Holborn Circus, EC1 (© **020/7405-1061;** www.stetheldreda.com; Tube: Farringdon or Chancery Lane), leading off Charterhouse Street at Holborn Circus. Built in 1251, it was mentioned by the Bard in both *Richard II* and *Richard III.* One of the survivors of the Great Fire of 1666, the church was built by, and property of, the diocese of Ely. The church has a distinguished musical tradition, with 11am Latin Mass on Sunday.

The spectacular brick-and-stone **Westminster Cathedral,** 42 Francis St., SW1 (© **020/7798-9055;** www.westminstercathedral.org.uk; Tube: Victoria), is headquarters of the Roman Catholic church in Britain. Done in high Byzantine style, it's massive; 100 different marbles compose the richly decorated interior. Mosaics emblazon the chapels and the vaulting of the sanctuary. If you climb to the top of the 82m-tall (273-ft.) campanile, you'll be rewarded with a sweeping view over Victoria and Westminster.

HANGING "AROUND" IN LONDON

The world's largest observation wheel, the **British Airways London Eye** ⊀, Millennium Jubilee Gardens (© **0870/5000-600;** www.ba-londoneye.com; Tube: Westminster or Waterloo), opened in 2000. It is the fourth-tallest structure in London, offering panoramic views that extend for some 40km (25 miles), if the weather's clear. Passengers are carried in 32 "pods" that make a complete revolution every half-hour. Along the way you'll see some of London's most famous landmarks from a bird's-eye view.

Built out of steel by a European consortium, it was conceived and designed by London architects Julia Barfield and David Marks, who claim inspiration from the Statue of Liberty in New York and the Eiffel Tower in Paris. Some 3.5 million visitors ride the Eye every year.

The Eye lies close to Westminster Bridge (you can hardly miss it). Tickets for the ride are £13 ($26) for adults, £10 ($20) for seniors and students, and £6.50 ($13) for children 5 to 15. Hours are October to May daily 10am to 8pm and June to September daily 10am to 9pm.

3 London's Parks & Gardens

London has the greatest system of parklands of any large city on the globe. Not as rigidly laid out as the parks of Paris, London's are maintained with a loving care and lavish artistry that puts their American equivalents to shame.

The largest—and one of the world's biggest—is **Hyde Park** ⊕, W2. With the adjoining Kensington Gardens, it covers 252 hectares (636 acres) of central London with velvety lawn interspersed with ponds, flower beds, and trees. Hyde Park was once a favorite deer-hunting ground of Henry VIII. Running through the width is a 17-hectare (41-acre) lake known as the Serpentine. Rotten Row, a 2.5km (1½-mile) sand track, is reserved for horseback riding and on Sunday attracts some skilled equestrians.

At the northeastern corner of Hyde Park, near Marble Arch, is **Speaker's Corner** (www.speakerscorner.net), where anyone can speak. The only rules: You can't blaspheme, be obscene, or incite a riot. The tradition actually began in 1855—before the legal right to assembly was guaranteed in 1872—when a mob of 150,000 gathered to attack a proposed Sunday Trading Bill. Orators from all over Britain have been taking advantage of this spot ever since. The corpse of Oliver Cromwell was hung up here in a cage for the public to gape at or throw rotten eggs at. The king wanted to warn others against what might happen to them if they wished to abolish the monarchy.

Lovely **Kensington Gardens,** W2, blending with Hyde Park, border on the grounds of Kensington Palace. These gardens are home to the celebrated statue of Peter Pan, with the bronze rabbits that toddlers are always trying to kidnap. The Albert Memorial is also here, and you'll recall the sea of flowers and tributes left here after the death of Diana, Princess of Wales.

East of Hyde Park, across Piccadilly, stretch **Green Park** ⊕ and **St. James's Park** ⊕, W1, forming an almost-unbroken chain of landscaped beauty. This is an ideal area for picnics, and one that you'll find hard to believe was once a festering piece of swamp near a leper hospital. There is a romantic lake, stocked with a variety of ducks and pelicans, descendants of the pair that the Russian ambassador presented to Charles II in 1662.

Regent's Park ⊕⊕⊕, NW1, covers most of the district by that name, north of Baker Street and Marylebone Road. Designed by 18th-century genius John Nash to surround a palace of the prince regent that never materialized, this is the most classically beautiful of London's parks. The core is a rose garden planted around a small lake alive with waterfowl and spanned by humped Japanese bridges. The open-air theater and London Zoo are here, and, as in all local parks, hundreds of deck chairs are on the lawns for sunbathers. The deck-chair attendants, who collect a small fee, are mostly college students on vacation.

The **London Zoo** ⊕ (© **020/7722-3333;** www.londonzoo.co.uk) is more than 150 years old. Run by the Zoological Society of London, the 15-hectare (36-acre) garden houses some 8,000 animals, including some of the rarest species on earth. It has waned in popularity the last few years, but a recent campaign won the zoo corporate sponsorship that is funding a modernization program. Zoo admission is £13 ($26) adults, £12 ($24) students and seniors, £10 ($20) children 3 to 15, £41 ($82) family ticket (two adults and two children or one adult and three children). Hours are March to October daily 10am to 5:30pm, November to February 10 daily 10am to 4:30pm, and February 11 to the end of February daily 10am to 4:30pm. Take the Tube to Camden Town or bus no. 274 or C2.

Battersea Park, SW11 (© **020/8871-7530;** www.batterseapark.org), is a vast patch of woodland, lakes, and lawns on the south bank of the Thames, opposite Chelsea Embankment between Albert Bridge and Chelsea Bridge. Formerly known as Battersea Fields, the present park was laid out between 1852 and 1858 on an old dueling ground. The park, which measures 1km (⅔ mile) on each of its four sides, has a lake for boating, a fenced-in deer park with wild birds, and fields for tennis and football (soccer). There's even a children's zoo. The park's architectural highlight is the Peace Pagoda, built of stone and wood. The park, open daily from dawn until dusk, is not well serviced by public transportation. The nearest Tube is in Chelsea on the right bank (Sloane Sq.); from there it's a brisk 15-minute walk. If you prefer the bus, take no. 137 from the Sloane Square station, exiting at the first stop after the bus crosses the Thames.

4 Sights on the Outskirts

HAMPSTEAD HEATH & VILLAGE ✿

Located about 6.5km (4 miles) north of the center of London, **Hampstead Heath,** a 320-hectare (800-acre) expanse of high heath surrounded entirely by London, is a chain of continuous park, wood, and grassland. On a clear day you can see St. Paul's Cathedral and even the hills of Kent south of the Thames. For years, Londoners have come here to fly kites, sun worship, fish the ponds, swim, picnic, or jog. In good weather, it's also the site of big 1-day fairs. At the shore of Kenwood Lake, in the northern section, is a concert platform devoted to symphony performances on summer evenings. In the northeast corner, in Waterlow Park, ballets, operas, and comedies are staged occasionally at the Grass Theatre in June and July.

When the Underground came to **Hampstead Village** (Tube: Hampstead) in 1907, its attraction as a place to live became widely known, and writers, artists, architects, musicians, and scientists—some from the City—came to join earlier residents. D. H. Lawrence, Rabindranath Tagore, Percy Bysshe Shelley, Robert Louis Stevenson, and Kingsley Amis once lived here; John Le Carré still does.

The Regency and Georgian houses in this village are just 20 minutes by Tube from Piccadilly Circus. Along Flask Walk, a pedestrian mall, is a palatable mix of historic pubs, toyshops, and chic boutiques. The original village, on the side of a hill, still has old roads, alleys, steps, courts, and groves to be strolled through.

Fenton House This National Trust property is on the west side of Hampstead Grove, just north of Hampstead Village. Built in 1693, its paneled rooms contain furniture and pictures; 18th-century English, German, and French porcelain; and an outstanding collection of early keyboard musical instruments.

Windmill Hill, NW3. © 020/7435-3471. Admission £5.20 ($10) adults, £2.60 ($5.20) children, £13 ($26) family ticket. Mar Sat–Sun 2–5pm; Apr–Oct Sat–Sun 11am–5pm, Wed–Fri 2–5pm. Closed Nov–Feb. Tube: Northern Line to Hampstead.

Freud Museum After Sigmund Freud and his family left Nazi-occupied Vienna as refugees, he lived, worked, and died in this spacious three-story house in northern

London. In view are rooms with original furniture, letters, photographs, paintings, and the personal effects of Freud and his daughter, Anna. In the study and library, you can see the famous couch and Freud's large collection of Egyptian, Roman, and Asian antiquities.

20 Maresfield Gardens, NW3. ℂ 020/7435-2002. www.freud.org.uk. Admission £5 ($10) adults, £3 ($6) full-time students and seniors, free for children 11 and younger. Wed–Sun noon–5pm. Tube: Jubilee Line to Finchley Rd.

Highgate Cemetery   A stone's throw east of Hampstead Heath, Highgate Village has a number of 16th- and 17th-century mansions and small cottages, lining three sides of the now-pondless Pond Square. Its most outstanding feature, however, is this beautiful cemetery, laid out around a huge, 300-year-old cedar tree and laced with serpentine pathways. The cemetery was so popular and fashionable in the Victorian era that it was extended on the other side of Swain's Lane in 1857. The most famous grave is that of Karl Marx, who died in Hampstead in 1883; his grave, marked by a gargantuan bust, is in the eastern cemetery. In the old western cemetery—accessible only by guided tour, given hourly on weekends—are scientist Michael Faraday and poet Christina Rossetti.

Swain's Lane, N6. ℂ 020/8340-1834. http://highgate-cemetery.org. Western cemetery guided tour £5 ($10); eastern cemetery admission £3 ($6). Western cemetery Mar–Oct guided tours Mon–Fri at 2pm, Sat–Sun hourly 11am–4pm; Nov–Feb tours Sat–Sun hourly 11am–3pm. Eastern cemetery Apr–Oct Mon–Fri 10am–5pm, Sat–Sun 11am–5pm; Nov–Mar Mon–Fri 10am–4pm, Sat–Sun 11am–3:30pm. Both cemeteries closed at Christmas and during funerals. Tube: Northern Line to Archway, then walk or take bus no. 143, 210, or 271.

Keats House 🟊🟊   The poet lived here for only 2 years, but that was nearly half of his creative life; he died of tuberculosis in Rome at the age of 25 (in 1821). In Hampstead, Keats wrote some of his most celebrated odes, including "Ode on a Grecian Urn" and "Ode to a Nightingale." His Regency house possesses the manuscripts of his last sonnet ("Bright star, would I were steadfast as thou art") and a portrait of him on his deathbed in a house on the Spanish Steps in Rome.

Keats Grove, NW3. ℂ 020/7435-2062. www.cityoflondon.gov.uk/keats. Admission £3.50 ($7) adults, £1.75 ($3.50) students and seniors, free for children 15 and younger. Tues–Sun 1–5pm. Tube: Northern Line to Hampstead or Belsize Park.

Kenwood House 🟊🟊   Kenwood House was built as a gentleman's country home and was later enlarged and decorated by the famous Scottish architect Robert Adam, starting in 1764. The house contains period furniture and paintings by Turner, Frans Hals, Gainsborough, Reynolds, and more.

Hampstead Lane, NW3. ℂ 020/8348-1286. www.english-heritage.org.uk. Free admission. Apr–Oct daily 11am–5pm; Nov–Mar daily 11am–4pm. Tube: Northern Line to Golders Green, then bus no. 210.

HAMPTON COURT
Hampton Court Palace 🟊🟊🟊   The 16th-century palace of Cardinal Wolsey can teach us a lesson: Don't try to outdo your boss, particularly if he happens to be Henry VIII. The rich cardinal did just that, and he eventually lost his fortune, power, and prestige, and ended up giving his lavish palace to the Tudor monarch. Henry took over, even outdoing the Wolsey embellishments. The Tudor additions included the Anne Boleyn gateway, with its 16th-century astronomical clock that tells the high-water mark at London Bridge. From Clock Court, you can see one of Henry's major contributions, the aptly named Great Hall, with its hammer-beam ceiling. Also added by Henry were the tiltyard (where jousting competitions were held), a tennis court, and a kitchen.

To judge from the movie *A Man for All Seasons*, Hampton Court had quite a retinue to feed. Cooking was done in the Great Kitchen. Henry cavorted through the various apartments with his wife of the moment—from Anne Boleyn to Catherine Parr (the latter reversed things and lived to bury her erstwhile spouse). Charles I was imprisoned here at one time and managed to temporarily escape his jailers.

Although the palace enjoyed prestige and pomp in Elizabethan days, it owes much of its present look to William and Mary—or rather to Sir Christopher Wren, who designed and had built the Northern or Lion Gates, intended to be the main entrance to the new parts of the palace. The fine wrought-iron screen at the south end of the south gardens was made by Jean Tijou around 1694 for William and Mary. You can parade through the apartments today, filled as they were with porcelain, furniture, paintings, and tapestries. The King's Dressing Room is graced with some of the best art, mainly paintings by Old Masters on loan from Queen Elizabeth II. Finally, be sure to inspect the royal chapel (Wolsey wouldn't recognize it). To confound yourself totally, you may want to get lost in the serpentine shrubbery maze in the garden, also the work of Wren. More and more attention is focusing on improving and upgrading the famous gardens here—the formal gardens are among the last surviving examples of garden methods and designs from several important periods of history.

The 24-hectare (60-acre) gardens—including the Great Vine, King's Privy Garden, Great Fountain Gardens, Tudor and Elizabethan Knot Gardens, Board Walk, Tiltyard, and Wilderness—are open daily year-round from 7am until dusk (but not later than 9pm) and can be visited free except for the Privy Garden. A garden cafe and restaurant are in the Tiltyard Gardens.

Hampton Court, on the north side of the Thames and 21km (13 miles) west of London, is easily accessible. Frequent trains run from Waterloo Station (Network Southeast) to **Hampton Court Station** (© **0845/748-4950**). Once at the station, buses will take you the rest of the way to the palace. If you're driving from London, take the A308 to the junction with the A309 on the north side of Kingston Bridge over the Thames.

East Molesey, Surrey. © **0870/752-7777**. www.hrp.org.uk. Palace admission £13 ($26) adults, £11 ($22) students and seniors, £6.50 ($13) children 5–15, family ticket £36 ($72), free for children 4 and younger; general gardens free admission; south and east formal gardens £4.50 ($9) adults, £3 ($6) students and seniors, £2.30 ($4.60) children without palace ticket during summer months. Cloisters, courtyards, state apartments, great kitchen, cellars, and Hampton Court exhibition Mar–Oct daily 10am–6pm, Nov–Feb daily 10am–4:30pm; gardens year-round daily 7am–dusk (no later than 9pm).

KEW 🏵🏵🏵

About 15km (9 miles) southwest of central London, Kew is home to one of the best-known botanical gardens in Europe. It's also the site of **Kew Palace** 🏵🏵 (© **0870/751-5179**), former residence of George III and Queen Charlotte. A dark redbrick structure, it is characterized by its Dutch gables. The house was constructed in 1631, and at its rear is the Queen's Garden in a very formal design and filled with plants thought to have grown here in the 17th century. The interior is very much an elegant country house of the time, fit for a king, but not as regal as Buckingham Palace. You get the feeling that someone could have actually lived here as you wander through the dining room, the breakfast room, and upstairs to the queen's drawing room where musical evenings were staged. The rooms are wallpapered with designs actually used at the time. Perhaps the most intriguing exhibits are little possessions once owned by royal occupants here—everything from snuffboxes to Prince Frederick's gambling debts. The palace is open March 24 to October 28 daily 10am to 5pm, charging an admission of £5 ($10). The most convenient way to get to Kew is to take the **District Line** Tube to the Kew Gardens stop, on the south bank of the Thames. Allow about 30 minutes.

Royal Botanic Gardens, Kew ⭐⭐⭐   These world-famous gardens offer thousands of varieties of plants. But Kew Gardens, as it's known, is no mere pleasure garden— it's essentially a vast scientific research center that happens to be beautiful. The gardens, on a 121-hectare (300-acre) site, encompass lakes, greenhouses, walks, pavilions, and museums, along with examples of the architecture of Sir William Chambers. Among the 50,000 plants are notable collections of ferns, orchids, aquatic plants, cacti, mountain plants, palms, and tropical water lilies.

No matter what season you visit, Kew always has something to see, from the first spring flowers through to winter. Gigantic hothouses grow species of shrubs, blooms, and trees from every part of the globe, from the Arctic Circle to tropical rainforests. Attractions include a newly restored Japanese gateway in traditional landscaping, as well as exhibitions that vary with the season. The newest greenhouse, the Princess of Wales Conservatory (beyond the rock garden), encompasses 10 climatic zones, from arid to tropical; it has London's most thrilling collection of miniature orchids. The Marianne North Gallery (1882) is an absolute gem, paneled with 246 different types of wood that the intrepid Victorian artist collected on her world journeys; she also collected 832 paintings of exotic and tropical flora, all displayed on the walls. The Visitor Centre at Victoria Gate houses an exhibit telling the story of Kew, as well as a bookshop.

Kew. ⓒ 020/8332-5655. www.rbgkew.org.uk. Admission £13 ($26) adults, £10 ($20) students and seniors, free for children 16 and younger. Apr–Aug Mon–Fri 9:30am–6pm, Sat–Sun 9:30am–7pm; Sept–Oct daily 9:30am–5:30pm; Nov–Jan daily 9:30am–3:45pm; Feb–Mar daily 9:30am–5pm. Tube: District Line to Kew Gardens.

GREENWICH ⭐⭐⭐

When London overwhelms you, and you'd like to escape for a beautiful, sunny afternoon on the city's outskirts, make it Greenwich.

Greenwich Mean Time is the basis of standard time throughout most of the world, and Greenwich has been the zero point used in the reckoning of terrestrial longitudes since 1884. But this lovely village—the center of British seafaring when Britain ruled the seas—is also home of the Royal Naval College, the National Maritime Museum, and the Old Royal Observatory. In dry dock at Greenwich Pier is the historic clipper ship *Cutty Sark*, which was heavily damaged by fire in May 2007; a 4-year restoration project is planned.

ESSENTIALS

GETTING THERE   The fastest way to get to Greenwich is to take the Tube in central London to Waterloo Station, where you can take a fast train to Greenwich Station.

The Tube is for speed, taking only 15 minutes, but if you'd like to travel the 6.5km (4 miles) to Greenwich the way Henry VIII did, you still can. In fact, getting to Greenwich is half the fun. The most appealing way involves boarding any of the frequent ferryboats that cruise along the Thames at intervals that vary from every halfhour (in summer) to every 45 minutes (in winter). Boats that leave from Charing Cross Pier (Tube: Embankment) and Tower Pier (Tube: Tower Hill) are run by **Catamaran Cruises, Ltd.** (ⓒ 020/7987-1185). Depending on the tides and the carrier you select, travel time varies from 50 to 75 minutes each way. Passage is £5.60 to £6.80 ($11–$14) one-way.

VISITOR INFORMATION The **Greenwich Tourist Information Centre** is at 2 Cutty Sark Gardens (© **0870/0082000**); it's open daily from 10am to 5pm. The Tourist Information Centre conducts **walking tours** of Greenwich's major sights. Tours cost £5 ($10) for adults and £4 ($8) for students, seniors, and children; depart daily at 12:15 and 2:15pm; and last 1¼ to 1½ hours. Advance reservations aren't required, but you may want to phone in advance to find out any last-minute schedule changes.

SEEING THE SIGHTS

The **National Maritime Museum, Old Royal Observatory,** and **Queen's House** stand together in a beautiful royal park, high on a hill overlooking the Thames. All three attractions are free to get into and open daily from 10am to 5pm (until 6pm in summer). For more information, call © **020/8858-4422** or visit **www.nmm.ac.uk**.

From the days of early seafarers to 20th-century sea power, the **National Maritime Museum** ✪✪ illustrates the glory that was Britain at sea. The cannon, relics, ship models, and paintings tell the story of a thousand naval battles and a thousand victories, as well as the price of those battles. Look for some oddities here—everything from the dreaded cat-o'-nine-tails used to flog sailors until 1879 to Nelson's Trafalgar coat, with the fatal bullet hole in the left shoulder clearly visible. In time for the millennium, the museum spent £20 million ($40 million) in a massive expansion that added 16 new galleries devoted to British maritime history and improved visitor facilities.

Old Royal Observatory ✪ is the original home of Greenwich Mean Time. It has the largest refracting telescope in the United Kingdom and a collection of historic timekeepers and astronomical instruments. You can stand astride the meridian and set your watch precisely by the falling time-ball. Sir Christopher Wren designed the Octagon Room. Here the first royal astronomer, Flamsteed, made his 30,000 observations that formed the basis of his *Historia Coelestis Britannica*. Edmond Halley, he of the eponymous Halley's Comet, succeeded him. In 1833, the ball on the tower was hung to enable shipmasters to set their chronometers accurately.

Designed by Inigo Jones, **Queen's House** ✪✪ (1616) is a fine example of this architect's innovative style. It's most famous for the cantilevered tulip staircase, the first of its kind. Carefully restored, the house contains a collection of royal and marine paintings and other objets d'art.

The **Wernher Collection at Ranger's House** ✪✪, Chesterfield Walk (© **020/ 8853-0035;** www.english-heritage.org.uk), is a real find and one of the finest and most unusual 19th-century mixed-art collections in the world. Acquired by a German diamond dealer, Sir Julius Wernher, the collection contains some 650 exhibits, some dating as far back as 3 B.C. It's an eclectic mix of everything, including jewelry, bronzes, ivory, antiques, tapestries, porcelain pieces, and classic paintings. Hanging on the walls of the gallery are rare works by such old masters as Hans Memling and Filippino Lippi, along with portraits by such English painters as Reynolds and Romney. One salon is devoted to the biggest collection of Renaissance jewelry in Britain. Look also for the carved medieval, Byzantine, and Renaissance ivories, along with Limoges enamels and Sèvres porcelain. The most unusual items are enameled skulls and a miniature coffin complete with 3-D skeleton. Don't expect everything to be beautiful—Wernher's taste was often bizarre. Admission is £5.50 ($11) adults, £4.10 ($8.20) seniors and students,

£2.80 ($5.60) children, free for children 4 and younger. The attraction is open only March 1 to September Sunday to Wednesday 10am to 5pm.

Nearby is the **Royal Naval College** ✸✸, King William Walk, off Romney Road (✆ **020/8269-4747**; www.greenwichfoundation.org.uk). Designed by Sir Christopher Wren in 1696, it occupies 4 blocks named after King Charles, Queen Anne, King William, and Queen Mary. Formerly, Greenwich Palace stood here from 1422 to 1640. It's worth stopping in to see the magnificent Painted Hall by Thornhill, where the body of Nelson lay in state in 1805, and the Georgian chapel of St. Peter and St. Paul. It's open daily from 10am to 5pm; admission is free.

5 Especially for Kids

The London Tourist Board offers a website—Kidslovelondon.com—providing both a fun and educational guide for planning time in the capital. The site boasts interactive quizzes, up-to-date information on what's hot, and children's reviews of London attractions, with tips on everything from walking with "dinosaurs" to cool places to eat.

London has fun places for kids of all ages. In addition to what's listed below, kids love **Madame Tussauds,** the **Science Museum,** the **Natural History Museum,** the **Tower of London,** and the **National Maritime Museum** in Greenwich, all discussed earlier in this chapter.

Bethnal Green Museum of Childhood   This branch of the Victoria and Albert specializes in toys. The variety of dolls alone is staggering; some have such elaborate period costumes that you don't even want to think of the price tags they would carry today. With the dolls come dollhouses, from simple cottages to miniature mansions, complete with fireplaces, grand pianos, kitchen utensils, and carriages. You'll also find optical toys, marionettes, puppets, a considerable exhibit of soldiers and war toys from both world war eras, trains and aircraft, and a display of clothing and furniture relating to the social history of childhood.

Cambridge Heath Rd., E2. ✆ **020/8983-5200.** www.museumofchildhood.org.uk. Free admission. Daily 10am–5:45pm. Tube: Central Line to Bethnal Green.

Horniman Museum   This century-old museum set in 6.5 hectares (16 acres) of landscaped gardens is quirky, funky, and fun. The collection was accumulated by Frederick Horniman, a Victorian tea trader. A full range of events and activities takes place here, including storytelling and art-and-crafts sessions for kids, along with workshops for adults. The museum owns some 350,000 objects ranging from a gigantic, overstuffed walrus to such oddities as oversize model insects. There are also displays of live insects and a small aquarium constructed in waterfall-like tiers. The torture chair thought to have been an original used at the Spanish Inquisition was proven to be a fake, but the instruments are genuine.

100 London Rd., Forest Hill, SE23. ✆ **020/8699-1872.** www.horniman.ac.uk. Free admission except for temporary exhibitions. Museum daily 10:30am–5:30pm; library Wed–Sat 10:30am–5pm, Sun 2–5:30pm; gardens Mon–Sat 7:30am–dusk, Sun 8am–dusk. Tube: London Bridge.

London Aquarium ✸   One of the largest aquariums in Europe, this South Bank attraction boasts 350 species of fish, everything from British freshwater species to sharks that once patrolled the Pacific. Observe the bountiful riches of the coral reefs of the Indian Ocean and what lurks in the murky depths of the Atlantic and Pacific oceans, including an array of eels, sharks, piranhas, rays, jellyfish, and other denizens of the deep. You ford a freshwater stream into a mangrove swamp to reach a tropical rainforest. The seawater, incidentally, is just normal Thames water mixed with 8 tons of salt at a time.

County Hall, Westminster Bridge Rd., SE1. (℃) 020/7967-8000. www.londonaquarium.co.uk. Admission £13 ($26) adults, £11 ($22) students and seniors, £9.75 ($20) ages 3–14, £44 ($88) family ticket. Sept–July daily 10am–6pm; Aug daily 10am–7pm. Closed Christmas Day. Tube: Waterloo.

The London Dungeon   This ghoulish place was designed to chill the blood while reproducing the conditions of the Middle Ages. Set under the arches of London Bridge Station, the dungeon is a series of tableaux more grisly than those at Madame Tussauds. The rumble of trains overhead adds to the atmosphere, and tolling bells bring a constant note of melancholy; dripping water and caged rats make for even more atmosphere. Naturally, it offers a burning at the stake as well as a torture chamber with racking, branding, and fingernail extraction, and a spine-chilling "Jack the Ripper Experience." The special effects were originally conceived for major film and TV productions. They've recently added a new show called "Boat Ride to Hell." You're sentenced to death (by actors, of course) and taken on a boat ride to meet your fate. If you survive, a Pizza Hut is on-site, and a souvenir shop sells certificates that testify you made it through the works. New for 2007, "Extremis: Drop Ride to Doom" is a thrill attraction that simulates a hanging (only without those pesky nooses): When the trapdoor opens, you plummet down into the dark. Visitors to the dungeon should use discretion with young children.

28–34 Tooley St., SE1. (℃) 020/7403-7221. www.thedungeons.com. Admission £20 ($40) adults, £16 ($32) students and seniors, £14 ($28) children 5–14, free for children 4 and younger. Nov 1–Mar 18 daily 10:30am–5pm; Mar 19–Apr 3 daily 9:30am–5:30pm; Apr 4–May 27 daily 10am–5pm; May 28–Oct daily 10am–7:30pm. Tube: London Bridge.

6 Organized Tours

BUS TOURS

For the first-timer, the quickest and most economical way to bring the big city into focus is to take a bus tour. One of the most popular is the **Original London Sight-seeing Tour,** which passes by all the major sights in just about 1½ hours. The tour—which uses a traditional double-decker bus with live commentary by a guide—costs £19 ($38) for adults, £12 ($24) for children 15 and younger, free for those 4 and younger. The tour allows you to hop on or off the bus at any point in the tour at no extra charge.

Departures are from convenient points within the city; you can choose your departure point when you buy your ticket. Tickets can be purchased on the bus or at a discount from any London Transport or London Tourist Board Information Centre. Most hotel concierges also sell tickets. For information or phone purchases, call (℃) 020/8877-1722. It's also possible to book online at **www.theoriginaltour.com**.

Big Bus Company Ltd., Waterside Way, London SW17 ((℃) **020/7233-9533;** www.bigbus.co.uk), operates a 2-hour tour in summer, departing frequently between 8:30am and 4:30pm daily from Marble Arch by Speakers Corner, Green Park by the Ritz Hotel, and Victoria Station (Buckingham Palace Rd. by the Royal Westminster Hotel). Tours cover the highlights—18 in all—ranging from the Houses of Parliament and Westminster Abbey to the Tower of London and Buckingham Palace (exterior looks only), accompanied by live commentary. The cost is £22 ($44) for adults, £10

($20) for children. A 1-hour tour follows the same route but covers only 13 sights. Tickets are valid all day; you can hop on and off the bus as you wish.

WALKING TOURS

The **Original London Walks,** 87 Messina Ave., P.O. Box 1708, London NW6 4LW (℗ 020/7624-3978; www.walks.com), the oldest established walking-tour company in London, is run by an Anglo-American journalist/actor couple, David and Mary Tucker. Their hallmarks are variety, reliability, reasonably sized groups, and—above all—superb guides. The renowned crime historian Donald Rumbelow, the leading authority on Jack the Ripper and author of the classic guidebook *London Walks,* is a regular guide, as are several prominent actors (including classical actor Edward Petherbridge). Walks are regularly scheduled daily and cost £6 ($12) for adults, £5 ($10) for students and seniors; children 14 and younger go free. Call for a schedule; no reservations are needed.

RIVER CRUISES

A trip up or down the river gives you an entirely different view of London from the one you get from land. You see how the city grew along and around the Thames and how many of its landmarks turn their faces toward the water. Several companies operate motor launches from the Westminster piers (Tube: Westminster), offering panoramic views of one of Europe's most historic waterways en route.

Thames River Services, Westminster Pier, Victoria Embankment, SW1 (℗ 020/ 7930-4097; www.westminsterpier.co.uk), concerns itself only with downriver traffic from Westminster Pier to such destinations as Greenwich. The most popular excursion departs for Greenwich (a 50-min. ride) at half-hour intervals between 10am and 4pm daily in April, May, September, and October, and between 10am and 5pm from June to August; from November to March, boats depart from Westminster Pier at 40-minute intervals daily from 10:40am to 3:20pm. One-way fares are £7.20 ($14) for adults, £6 ($12) for seniors, and £3.60 ($7.20) for children 15 and younger. Round-trip fares are £9.40 ($19) for adults, £8 ($16) for seniors, £4.70 ($9.40) for children. A family ticket for two adults and as many as three children 14 and younger costs £21 ($42) one-way, £25 ($50) round-trip.

Westminster Passenger Association (Upriver) Ltd., Westminster Pier, Victoria Embankment, SW1 (℗ 020/7930-2062 or 020/7930-4721; www.wpsa.co.uk), offers the only riverboat service upstream from Westminster Bridge to Kew, Richmond, and Hampton Court, with regular daily sailings from the Monday before Easter until the end of October on traditional riverboats, all with licensed bars. Trip time, one-way, can be as little as 1½ hours to Kew and between 2½ and 4 hours to Hampton Court, depending on the tide. Cruises from Westminster Pier to Hampton Court via Kew Gardens leave daily at 10:30, 11:15am, and noon. Round-trip tickets are £20 ($40) for adults, £13 ($26) for seniors, £9.75 ($20) for children ages 4 to 14, and £49 ($98) for a family ticket; one child 3 or younger accompanied by an adult goes free.

7 Shopping

THE TOP SHOPPING STREETS & NEIGHBORHOODS

Several key streets offer some of London's best retail stores—or simply one of everything—compactly located in a niche or neighborhood so that you can just stroll and shop.

THE WEST END   The West End includes the Mayfair district and is home to the core of London's big-name shopping. Most of the department stores, designer shops, and multiples (chain stores) have their flagships in this area.

The key streets are **Oxford Street** for affordable shopping (start at Marble Arch Tube station if you're ambitious, or Bond St. station if you just want to see some of it) and **Regent Street,** which intersects Oxford Street at Oxford Circus (Tube: Oxford Circus).

While there are several branches of the private label department store **Marks & Spencer,** their Marble Arch store (on Oxford St.) is the flagship and worth shopping for their high-quality goods. There's a grocery store in the basement and a home-furnishings department upstairs.

Regent Street has fancier shops—more upscale department stores (including the famed **Liberty of London**), and specialty dealers—and leads all the way to Piccadilly.

In between the two, parallel to Regent Street, is **Bond Street.** Divided into New and Old, Bond Street (Tube: Bond St.) also connects Piccadilly with Oxford Street and is synonymous with the luxury trade. Bond Street has had a revival and is the hot address for all the international designers; **Donna Karan** has not one, but two shops here. Many international hotshots have digs surrounding hers, from **Chanel** and **Ferragamo** to **Versace.**

Burlington Arcade (Tube: Piccadilly Circus), the famous glass-roofed, Regency-style passage leading off Piccadilly, looks like a period exhibition and is lined with intriguing shops and boutiques. The small, smart stores specialize in fashion, jewelry, Irish linen, cashmere, and more. If you linger in the arcade until 5:30pm, you can watch the beadles in their black-and-yellow livery and top hats ceremoniously put in place the iron grills that block off the arcade until 9am the next morning, at which time they just as ceremoniously remove them to mark the start of a new business day. Also at 5:30pm, a hand bell called the Burlington Bell is sounded, signaling the end of trading.

Just off Regent Street (actually tucked right behind it) is **Carnaby Street** (Tube: Oxford Circus), which is also having a comeback. While it no longer dominates the world of pace-setting fashion as it did in the 1960s, it's still fun for teens who may need cheap souvenirs, a purple wig, or a little something in leather. A convenient branch of **Boots the Chemists** is also here.

For a total contrast, check out **Jermyn Street,** on the far side of Piccadilly, a tiny 2-block-long street devoted to high-end men's haberdashers and toiletries shops; many have been doing business for centuries. Several hold royal warrants, including **Turnbull & Asser,** where HRH Prince Charles has his pj's made.

The West End leads to the theater district and to two more shopping areas: the still-not-ready-for-prime-time **Soho,** where the sex shops are slowly being turned into cutting-edge designer shops, and **Covent Garden,** which is a masterpiece unto itself. The marketplace has eaten up the surrounding neighborhood so that even though the streets run a little higgledy-piggledy and you can easily get lost, it's fun to just wander and shop.

KNIGHTSBRIDGE & CHELSEA   This is the second-most famous of London's retail districts and the home of **Harrods** (Tube: Knightsbridge). A small street nearby, **Sloane Street,** is chockablock with designer shops; **Cheval Place,** in the opposite direction, is also lined with designer resale shops.

Walk toward Museum Row, and you'll soon find **Beauchamp Place** (pronounced *Beech*-am; Tube: Knightsbridge). The street is only a block long, but it features the kinds of shops where young British aristos buy their clothing.

Head out at the **Harvey Nichols** end of Knightsbridge, away from Harrods, and shop your way through the designer stores on Sloane Street (**Hermès, Armani, Prada,** and the like), then walk past Sloane Square and you're in an altogether different neighborhood: Chelsea.

King's Road (Tube: Sloane Sq.), the main street of Chelsea, which starts at Sloane Square, will forever remain a symbol of London in the swinging '60s. Today, the street is still frequented by young people, but with fewer Mohawks, "Bovver boots," and Edwardian ball gowns than before. More and more, King's Road is a lineup of markets and "multistores," large or small conglomerations of indoor stands, stalls, and booths in one building or enclosure.

Chelsea doesn't begin and end with King's Road. If you choose to walk the other direction from Harrods, you connect to a part of Chelsea called **Brompton Cross,** another hip and hot area for designer shops made popular when Michelin House was rehabbed by Sir Terence Conran for the **Conran Shop.**

Also seek out **Walton Street,** a tiny little snake of a street running from Brompton Cross back toward the museums. About 2 blocks of this 3-block street are devoted to fairy-tale shops for m'lady where you can buy aromatherapy from **Jo Malone,** needlepoint, or costume jewelry, or meet with your interior designer, who runs a small shop of objets d'art.

Finally, don't forget all those museums right there in the corner of the shopping streets. They all have great gift shops.

KENSINGTON & NOTTING HILL **Kensington High Street** is the new hangout of the classier breed of teen who has graduated from Carnaby Street and is ready for street chic. While a few staples of basic British fashion are on this strip, most of the stores feature items that stretch; are very, very short; or are very, very tight. The Tube station here is High Street Kensington.

From Kensington High Street, you can walk up **Kensington Church Street,** which, like Portobello Road, is one of the city's main shopping avenues for antiques. Kensington Church Street dead-ends into the Notting Hill Gate Tube station, which is where you would arrive for shopping on **Portobello Road.** The dealers and the weekend market are 2 blocks beyond.

THE DEPARTMENT STORES

Contrary to popular belief, Harrods is not the only department store in London. The British invented the department store, and they have lots of them—mostly in Mayfair, and each with its own customer profile.

Fenwick of Bond Street Fenwick (the "w" is silent), dating from 1891, is a stylish fashion store that offers an excellent collection of designer women's wear, ranging from moderately priced ready-to-wear items to more expensive designer fashions. A wide range of lingerie in all price ranges is also sold. 63 New Bond St., W1. © 020/7629-9161. www.fenwick.co.uk. Tube: Bond St.

Fortnum & Mason The world's most elegant grocery store is a British tradition dating from 1707. This store exemplifies the elegance and style you would expect from an establishment with three royal warrants (meaning that they supply goods to the royal family). Enter and be transported to another world of deep-red carpets, crystal chandeliers, spiraling wooden staircases, and unobtrusive, tail-coated assistants.

The grocery department is renowned for its impressive selection of the finest foods from around the world—the best champagne, the most scrumptious Belgian chocolates, and succulent Scottish smoked salmon. Wander through the four floors and inspect the bone china and crystal cut glass, find the perfect gift in the leather or stationery departments, or reflect on the changing history of furniture and ornaments in the antiques department. Dining choices include **St. James Restaurant** and **The Fountain Restaurant** (p. 164). Fortnum & Mason offers exclusive and specialty ranges for the home, as well as beauty products and fashions for both women and men. 181 Piccadilly, W1. © 020/ 7734-8040. www.fortnumandmason.com. Tube: Piccadilly Circus.

Harrods   An institution as firmly entrenched in English life as Buckingham Palace and the Ascot Races, Harrods is an elaborate emporium, at times as fascinating as a museum. The sheer range, variety, and quality of merchandise are dazzling. If you visit only one store in all of England, make it Harrods, even if you're just looking.

The fifth floor is devoted to sports and leisure, with a wide range of equipment and attire. Toy Kingdom is on the fourth floor, along with children's wear. The Egyptian Hall, on the ground floor, sells crystal from Lalique and Baccarat, plus porcelain. You'll also find a men's grooming room, an enormous jewelry department, and a fashion-forward department for younger customers. In the basement, you'll find a bank, a theater-booking service, and a travel bureau. Harrods Shop for logo gifts is on the ground floor. When you're ready for a break, you have a choice of 28 restaurants and bars. Best of all are the Food Halls, stocked with a huge variety of foods and several cafes. Harrods began as a grocer in 1849, still the heart of the business. 87–135 Brompton Rd., Knightsbridge, SW1. © 020/8479-5100. www.harrods.com. Tube: Knightsbridge.

John Lewis   Trends come and go but this department store remains one of the most traditional outlets in London. Their motto is that they are never knowingly undersold, and they mean that. We've always found great bargains at this store, most recently in a clearance sale of fine earthenware by Royal Stafford. Whatever you're looking for, ranging from mauve Egyptian towels to clothing and jewelry, it's likely to be for sale here. 300 Oxford St., W1. © 020/7629-7711. www.johnlewis.com. Tube: Oxford Circus.

Liberty   This major British department store is celebrated for its Liberty Prints: top-echelon, carriage-trade fabrics, often in floral patterns, prized by decorators for adding a sense of English tradition to a room. The front part of the store on Regent Street isn't particularly distinctive, but don't be fooled: Some parts of the place have been restored to Tudor-style splendor that includes half-timbering and lots of interior paneling. Liberty houses six floors of fashion, china, and home furnishings, as well as the famous Liberty Print fashion fabrics, upholstery fabrics, scarves, ties, luggage, and gifts. 210–220 Regent St., W1. © 020/7734-1234. www.liberty.co.uk. Tube: Oxford Circus.

SOME CLASSIC LONDON FAVORITES

ANTIQUES   See also "The Markets," below. Portobello Road is really the prime hunting ground.

At the **Antiquarius Antiques Centre,** 131–141 King's Rd., SW3 (© 020/7351-5353; www.antiquarius.co.uk; Tube: Sloane Sq.), more than 120 dealers offer specialized merchandise, such as antique and period jewelry, silver, first-edition books, boxes, clocks, prints, and paintings, with an occasional piece of antique furniture. You'll find a lot of items from the 1950s. Open Monday to Saturday 10am to 6pm; closed Sunday.

Alfies Antique Market, 13–25 Church St., NW8 (© 020/7823-3900; www. alfiesantiques.com; Tube: Marylebone or Edgware Rd.), is the biggest and one of the best-stocked conglomerates of antiques dealers in London, all crammed into the premises of what was built before 1880 as a department store. It contains more than 370 stalls, showrooms, and workshops scattered across 3,251 sq. m (35,000 sq. ft.) of floor space. Open Tuesday to Saturday 10am to 6pm; closed Sunday to Monday. A whole antiques district has grown up around Alfies along Church Street.

ARTS & CRAFTS   Hailed by *The Times of London* as "the best place to see contemporary art in north London," **Camden Arts Centre** ♠, Arkwright Road, NW3 (✆ 020/7472-5500; www.camdenartscentre.org), opened after a multimillion-dollar refurbishment. Today it invites you to its cafe, bookstore, studios, and exhibition galleries, where the displays are frequently changed.

Gabriel's Wharf, 56 Upper Ground, SE1 (✆ 020/7401-2255; www.gabriels wharf.co.uk; Tube: Blackfriars, Southwark, Waterloo, or Embankment), is a South Bank complex of shops, restaurants, and bars open Tuesday through Sunday from 11am to 6pm (dining and drinking establishments open later). Lying 2 minutes by foot from Oxo Tower Wharf, it is filled with some of the most skilled of London craftspeople, turning out original pieces of sculpture, jewelry, ceramics, art, and fashion. From food to fashion, from arts to crafts, it awaits you here. The place is a lot of fun to poke around in.

BATH & BODY   Branches of the **Body Shop** are seemingly everywhere. Check out the one at 374 Oxford St., W1 (✆ 020/7409-7868; www.thebodyshop.com. Tube: Bond St.). Prices are much lower in the United Kingdom than in the United States.

Boots the Chemists has branches all over Britain. A convenient branch is at 490 Oxford St., W1C (✆ 020/7491-8546; www.boots.com; Tube: Marble Arch). The house brands of beauty products are usually the best, be they Boots' products (try the cucumber facial scrub), Boots' versions of the Body Shop (two lines, Global and Naturalistic), or Boots' versions of Chanel makeup (called No. 7).

Stock up on essential oils, or perhaps dream pillows, candles, sachets of letters of the alphabet, and aromatherapy fans at **Culpeper the Herbalist,** 8 The Market, Covent Garden, WC2 (✆ 020/7379-6698; www.culpeper.co.uk).

Floris, 89 Jermyn St., SW1 (✆ 0845/702-3239; www.florislondon.com; Tube: Greek Park), stocks a variety of toilet articles and fragrances in floor-to-ceiling mahogany cabinets, which are architectural curiosities in their own right, dating from the Great Exhibition of 1851.

Lush, 11 The Piazza, Covent Garden (✆ 020/7240-4570; www.lush.co.uk; Tube: Covent Garden), sells the most intriguing handmade cosmetics in London. This outlet is always launching something new, such as its latest soap, "Rock Star," looking very pink and smelling like a Creamy Candy Bubble Bar. Tam O'Santa is an allspice, sandalwood, and frankincense bubble bath; and the selection goes on and on, the products made of fresh fruit and vegetables, the finest essential oils, and safe synthetics—no animal ingredients.

The Victorian perfumery called **Penhaligon's,** 41 Wellington St., WC2 (✆ 020/ 7621-3444; www.penhaligons.co.uk; Tube: Covent Garden), offers a large selection of perfumes, after-shaves, soaps, and bath oils for women and men. Gifts include antique-silver scent bottles and leather traveling requisites.

FASHION, PART I: THE TRUE BRIT   Every internationally known designer worth his or her weight in Shantung has a boutique in London, but the best buys are on the sturdy English styles that last forever.

The name **Burberry,** 157–167 Regent St., SW1 (✆ 020/7806-1328; www. burberry.com; Tube: Piccadilly Circus), has been synonymous with raincoats ever since Edward VII publicly ordered his valet to "bring my Burberry" when the skies threatened. An impeccably trained staff sells the famous raincoats, along with excellent men's shirts, sportswear, knitwear, and accessories. Raincoats are available in women's sizes and styles as well. Prices are high, but you get quality and prestige.

The finest name in men's shirts, **Hilditch & Key,** 37 and 73 Jermyn St., SW1 (© 020/7734-4707; www.hilditchandkey.co.uk; Tube: Piccadilly Circus or Green Park), has been in business since 1899. The two shops on this street both offer men's clothing (including a bespoke shirt service) and women's ready-made shirts. Hilditch also has an outstanding tie collection. Shirts go for half-price during the twice-yearly sales. Men fly in from all over the world for them.

FASHION, PART II: THE CUTTING EDGE Currently the most cutting-edge shopping street in London is **Conduit Street,** W1, in Mayfair (Tube: Oxford Circus). Once known for its dowdy display of international airline offices, it is now London's smartest street for fashion. Trendy shops are opening between Regent Street and the "blue-chip" boutiques of New Bond Street even as we speak. Current stars include **Vivienne Westwood,** 44 Conduit St., W1 (© 020/7924-4747; www.viviennewestwood. com), who has overcome her punk origins to become the grande dame of English fashion.

Other famous designers with boutiques on Conduit Street include **Krizia,** 25 Conduit St., W1 (© 020/7491-4987; www.krizia.net); **Yohji Yamamoto,** 14–15 Conduit St., W1 (© 020/7491-4129; www.yohjiyamamoto.co.jp); and **Issey Miyake,** 52 Conduit St., W1 (© 020/7851-4620; www.isseymiyake.com).

The **Library,** 268 Brompton Rd., SW3 (© 020/7589-6569; Tube: South Kensington or Knightsbridge), in spite of its name, is a showcase for some of the best of the young designers for men. It's very cutting edge without dipping into the extremities of male fashion. The Library is famous for having introduced Helmut Lang to London, but now features such designers as Fabrizio del Carlo, Kostas Murkudis, and even Alexander McQueen.

FASHION, PART III: VINTAGE & SECONDHAND CLOTHING A London institution since the 1940s, **Pandora,** 16–22 Cheval Place, SW7 (© 020/7589-5289; Tube: Knightsbridge), stands in fashionable Knightsbridge, a stone's throw from Harrods. Several times a week, chauffeurs drive up with bundles packed anonymously by the gentry of England. One woman voted best dressed at Ascot several years ago was wearing a secondhand dress acquired here. Prices are generally one-third to one-half the retail value. Outfits are usually no more than two seasons old.

For the best in original street wear from the '50s, '60s, and '70s, **Pop Boutique,** 6 Monmouth St., WC2 (© 020/7497-5262; www.pop-boutique.com; Tube: Covent Garden), is tops. Right next to the chic Covent Garden Hotel, it has fabulous vintage wear at affordable prices.

Note: There's no value-added tax (VAT) refund on used clothing.

FURNITURE **David Linley Furniture,** 60 Pimlico Rd., SW1 (© 020/7730-7300; www.davidlinley.com; Tube: Sloane Sq.), is a showcase for the remarkable furniture of the Viscount Linley, a designer who bears a resemblance to his mother, the late Princess Margaret. He designs pieces of furniture of a complex nature, both in terms of design and structure. For example, one of his designs, the Apsley House Desk, is made of French walnut with ebony and nickel-plated detailing, containing secret drawers. The desk is rimmed with a miniature of the neoclassical Apsley House.

The director at the Victoria and Albert Museum has predicted that Linley's furnishings and accessories will become the designs of the antiques of the future.

HOME DESIGN & HOUSEWARES   At the **Conran Shop,** Michelin House, 81 Fulham Rd., SW3 (℃ **020/7589-7401;** www.conranshop.co.uk; Tube: South Kensington), you'll find high style at reasonable prices from the man who invented it all for Britain: Sir Terence Conran. It's great for gifts, home furnishings, and tabletop knickknacks—or just for gawking. The **Couverture Shop,** 310 King's Rd., SW3 (℃ **020/7795-1200;** www.couverture.co.uk; Tube: Sloane Sq.), is an emporium of the unexpected, with original products for both adults and children as well as the home. It's strongest on what they call "bedroom must-haves," embracing bed linen, throws, cushions, and the like. Vintage finds along with designer pieces—often handmade—are also sold.

SHOES   Shoes for both men and women are stocked at **Natural Shoe Store,** 21 Neal St., WC2 (℃ **020/7836-5254;** www.thenaturalshoestore.com; Tube: Covent Garden), which also does repairs for some labels. The selection includes all comfort and quality footwear, from Birkenstock to the best of the British classics.

TOYS   **Hamleys,** 188–196 Regent St., W1 (℃ **0800/2802-444;** www.hamleys. com; Tube: Oxford Circus), is the finest toyshop in the world—more than 35,000 toys and games on seven floors of fun and magic. A huge selection is offered, including soft, cuddly stuffed animals, as well as dolls, radio-controlled cars, train sets, model kits, board games, outdoor toys, and computer games. A small branch is also at Heathrow Airport.

THE MARKETS

THE WEST END   **Covent Garden Market** ✦ (℃ **020/7836-9136;** www.covent gardenmarket.com; Tube: Covent Garden), the most famous market in all of England, offers several markets Monday to Saturday from 10am to 6pm—we think it's most fun to come on Sunday from 11am to 6pm when more vendors are set up and street entertainment is at its peak. It can be a little confusing until you dive in and explore. **Apple Market** is the bustling market in the courtyard, where traders sell—well, everything. Many of the items are what the English call collectible nostalgia: a wide array of glassware and ceramics, leather goods, toys, clothes, hats, and jewelry. Some of the merchandise is truly unusual. Many items are handmade, with some of the craftspeople selling their own wares—except on Monday, when antiques dealers take over. Some goods are new, some are very old. Out back is **Jubilee Market** (℃ **020/7836-2139**), also an antiques market on Monday. Tuesday to Sunday, it's sort of a fancy hippie market with cheap clothes and books. Out front there are a few tents of cheap stuff, except on Monday.

The indoor market section of Covent Garden Market (in a superbly restored hall) is one of the best shopping venues in London. Specialty shops sell fashions and herbs, gifts and toys, books and dollhouses, cigars, and much more. There are bookshops and branches of famous stores (Hamleys, the Body Shop), and prices are kept moderate.

St. Martin–in-the-Fields Market (Tube: Charing Cross) is good for teens and hipsters who are interested in imports from India and South America, crafts, and local football (soccer) souvenirs. It's located near Trafalgar Square and Covent Garden; hours are Monday through Saturday from 11am to 5pm and Sunday from noon to 5pm.

Berwick Street Market (Tube: Oxford Circus or Tottenham Court Rd.) may be the only street market in the world that's flanked by two rows of strip clubs, porno stores, and adult-movie dens. Don't let that put you off. Humming 6 days a week in the scarlet heart of Soho, this array of stalls and booths sells the best and cheapest fruit and vegetables in town. It also hawks ancient records, tapes, books, and old magazines, any of which may turn out to be a collector's item one day. It's open Monday to Saturday 8am to 5:30pm.

On Sunday mornings along **Bayswater Road,** artists hang their work on the railings along the edge of Hyde Park and Kensington Gardens for more than 1.5km (1 mile). If the weather's right, start at Marble Arch and walk. You'll see the same thing on the railings of Green Park along Piccadilly on Saturday afternoon.

NOTTING HILL **Portobello Market** (Tube: Notting Hill Gate) is a magnet for collectors of virtually anything. It's mainly a Saturday happening, from 6am to 5pm. You needn't be here at the crack of dawn; 9am is fine. Once known mainly for fruit and vegetables (still sold here throughout the week), in the past 4 decades Portobello has become synonymous with antiques. But don't take the stallholder's word for it that the fiddle he's holding is a genuine Stradivarius left to him in the will of his Italian great-uncle; it might just as well have been "nicked" from an East End pawnshop.

The market is divided into three major sections. The most crowded is the antiques section, running between Colville Road and Chepstow Villas to the south. (*Warning:* There's a great concentration of pickpockets in this area.) The second section (and the oldest part) is the "fruit and veg" market, lying between Westway and Colville Road. In the third and final section is a flea market, where Londoners sell bric-a-brac and lots of secondhand goods they didn't really want in the first place. But looking around still makes for interesting fun.

Note: Some 90 antiques-and-art shops along Portobello Road are open during the week when the street market is closed. This is actually a better time for the serious collector to shop because you'll get more attention from dealers, and you won't be distracted by the organ grinder.

SOUTH BANK Open on Fridays only, **New Caledonian Market** is commonly known as the **Bermondsey Market** because of its location on the corner of Long Lane and Bermondsey Street (Tube: London Bridge, then bus no. 78 or walk down Bermondsey St.). The market is at the extreme east end, beginning at Tower Bridge Road. It's one of Europe's outstanding street markets for the number and quality of the antiques and other goods. The stalls are well known, and many dealers come into London from the country. Prices are generally lower here than at Portobello and the other markets. It gets started at 5am—with the bargains gone by 9am—and closes at noon. Bring a torch (flashlight) if you go in the wee hours.

8 London After Dark

Weekly publications such as *Time Out* and *Where* carry full entertainment listings, including information on restaurants and nightclubs. You'll also find listings in daily newspapers, notably the *Times* and the *Telegraph.*

THE THEATER

In London, you'll have a chance to see the world-renowned **English theater** on its home ground. Matinees are on Wednesday (Thurs at some theaters) and Saturday. Theaters are closed on Sunday. It's impossible to describe all of London's theaters in this space, so below are listed just a few from the treasure-trove.

GETTING TICKETS

To see specific shows, especially hits, purchase your tickets in advance. The best method is to buy your tickets from the theater's box office, which you can do over the phone using a credit card. You'll pay the theater price and pick up the tickets the day of the show. You can also go to a ticket agent, especially for discount tickets such as those sold by the **Society of London Theatre** (© 020/7557-6700; www.official londontheatre.co.uk) on the southwest corner of Leicester Square, open Monday to Saturday 10am to 7pm and Sunday noon to 3pm. A £2 ($4) service fee is charged. You can purchase all tickets here, although the booth specializes in half-price sales for shows that are undersold. These tickets must be purchased in person—not over the phone. For phone orders, you have to call **Ticketmaster** at © 0870/060-2340.

For tickets and information before you go, try **Keith Prowse,** 234 W. 44th St., Ste. 1000, New York, NY 10036 (© 800/669-8687 or 212/398-1468; www.keithprowse. com). Their London office (which operates under the name of both Global Tickets and First Call Tickets) is at the British Visitors Center, 1 Regent St., SW1 Y4XT (© 0870/ 906-3860). They'll mail your tickets, fax a confirmation, or leave your tickets at the appropriate production's box office. Instant confirmations are available for most shows. A booking and handling fee of up to 20% is added to the price of all tickets.

Applause Theatre and Entertainment Service, 311 W. 43rd St., Ste. 601, New York, NY 10036 (© 800/451-9930 or 212/307-7050; fax 212/397-3729; www. applause-tickets.com), can sometimes get you tickets when Prowse can't. In business for some 2 decades, it is a reliable and efficient company.

Another option is **Theatre Direct International** (**TDI;** © 800/BROADWAY [276-2392] or 212/541-8457 in the U.S. only; www.broadway.com). TDI specializes in providing London fringe theater tickets but also has tickets to major productions, including those at the Royal National Theatre and the Barbican. The service allows you to arrive in London with your tickets or have them held for you at the box office.

If you're staying at a first-class or deluxe hotel with a concierge, you can also call and arrange tickets before you arrive, putting them on a credit card.

London theater tickets are priced quite reasonably when compared with the United States. Prices vary greatly depending on the seat—from £25 to £85 ($50–$170). Sometimes gallery seats (the cheapest) are sold only on the day of the performance, so you'll have to head to the box office early in the day and return an hour before the performance to queue up because they're not reserved seats.

Many of the major theaters offer reduced-price tickets to students on a standby basis, but not to the general public. When available, these tickets are sold 30 minutes prior to curtain. Line up early for popular shows, as standby tickets go fast and furious. Of course, you must have a valid student ID.

Warning: Beware of scalpers who hang out in front of theaters with hit shows. Many report that scalpers sell forged tickets, and their prices are outrageous.

THE MAJOR COMPANIES & THEATERS

One of the world's finest theater companies, the **Royal Shakespeare Company** ✮✮✮ performs at various theaters throughout London. Check its website at **www.rsc. org.uk** for current shows and venues or call © 0844/800-1110 Monday to Saturday 9am to 8pm. The theater troupe performs in London during the winter months, naturally specializing in the plays of the Bard. In summer, it tours England and abroad.

Cadogan Hall   Nestled in the heart of Chelsea, this decommissioned church, the first Christian Science church in the world, founded in 1893, has been turned into a concert hall for the Royal Philharmonic Orchestra. Completely restored and massively altered, the building now boasts a 900-seat auditorium and all the acoustics of the 21st century. The box office is open Monday to Saturday from 10am to 7pm and Sunday from 10am to 7pm performance days only. 5 Sloane Terrace, SW1. ℂ 020/7730-4500. www.cadoganhall.com. Tickets vary according to the event. Tube: Sloane Sq.

Open-Air Theatre   This outdoor theater is in Regent's Park; the setting is idyllic, and both seating and acoustics are excellent. Presentations are mainly of Shakespeare, usually in period costume. Its theater bar, the longest in London, serves both drink and food. In the case of a rained-out performance, tickets are offered for another date. The season runs from June to mid-September Monday to Saturday at 8pm, plus Wednesday, Thursday, and Saturday matinees at 2:30pm. Inner Circle, Regent's Park, NW1. ℂ 020/7935-5756. www.openairtheatre.org. Tickets £10–£33 ($20–$66). Tube: Baker St.

Royal Court Theatre   This theater has always been a leader in producing provoca-tive, cutting-edge, new drama. In the 1950s, it staged the plays of the angry young men, notably John Osborne's then-sensational *Look Back in Anger;* earlier it debuted the plays of George Bernard Shaw. The theater is home to the English Stage Company, formed to promote serious stage writing. Box office hours are Monday to Saturday from 10am to 6pm. Sloane Sq., SW1. ℂ 020/7565-5000. www.royalcourttheatre.com. Tickets £10–£25 ($20–$50); call for the latest information. Tube: Sloane Sq.

Royal National Theatre   Home to one of the world's greatest stage companies, the Royal National Theatre is not one but three theaters—the Olivier, reminiscent of a Greek amphitheater with its open stage; the more traditional Lyttelton; and the Cottesloe, with its flexible stage and seating. The National presents the finest in world theater, from classic drama to award-winning new plays, including comedies, musi-cals, and shows for young people. A choice of at least six plays is offered at any one time.

It's also a full-time theater center, with an amazing selection of bars, cafes, restau-rants, free foyer music and exhibitions, short early-evening performances, bookshops, backstage tours, riverside walks, and terraces. You can have a three-course meal in Mezzanine, the National's restaurant; enjoy a light meal in the brasserie-style Terrace cafe; or have a snack in one of the coffee bars. Box office hours are Monday to Satur-day 10am to 8pm. South Bank, SE1. ℂ 020/7452-3000. www.nationaltheatre.org.uk. Tickets £10–£38 ($20–$76); midweek matinees, Sat matinees, and previews cost less. Tube: Waterloo, Embank-ment, or Charing Cross.

Shakespeare's Globe Theatre   In May 1997, the new Globe Theatre—a replica of the Elizabethan original, thatched roof and all—staged its first slate of plays (*Henry V* and *A Winter's Tale*) yards away from the site of the 16th-century theater where the Bard originally staged his work.

Productions vary in style and setting; not all are performed in Elizabethan costume. In keeping with the historic setting, no lighting is focused just on the stage, but flood-lighting is used during evening performances to replicate daylight in the theater—Elizabethan performances took place in the afternoon. Theatergoers sit on wooden benches of yore—in thatch-roofed galleries, no less—but these days you can rent a cushion to make yourself more comfortable. About 500 "groundlings" can stand in the uncovered yard around the stage, just as they did when the Bard was here.

From May to September, the company intends to hold performances Tuesday to Saturday at 2 and 7pm. There will be a limited winter schedule. In any season, the schedule may be affected by weather because this is an outdoor theater. Performances last 2½ to 4 hours, depending on the play.

For details on the exhibition that tells the story of the painstaking re-creation of the Globe, as well as guided tours of the theater, see p. 194. New Globe Walk, Bankside, SE1. ✆ 020/7902-1400 for box office. www.shakespeares-globe.org. Tickets £5 ($10) for groundlings, £15–£32 ($30–$64) for gallery seats; exhibition tickets £9 ($18) adults, £7.50 ($15) seniors and students, £6.50 ($13) ages 5–15. Tube: Mansion House or Blackfriars.

Theatre Royal Drury Lane   Drury Lane is one of London's oldest and most prestigious theaters, crammed with tradition—not all of it respectable. This, the fourth theater on this site, dates from 1812; the first was built in 1663. Nell Gwynne, the rough-tongued Cockney lass who became Charles II's mistress, used to sell oranges under the long colonnade in front. Nearly every star of London theater has taken the stage here at some time. It has a wide-open repertoire but leans toward musicals, especially long-running hits. Guided tours of the backstage area and the front of the house are given most days at 10:15am, noon, 2:15, and 4:45pm. The box office is open Monday to Saturday from 10am to 8pm. Evening performances are held Monday to Saturday at 7:30pm, with matinees on Wednesday and Saturday at 2:30pm. Catherine St., Covent Garden, WC2. ✆ 0870/890-0149. www.theatre-royal.com. Tickets £27–£60 ($54–$120). Tube: Covent Garden.

THE REST OF THE PERFORMING ARTS SCENE

Currently, London supports five major orchestras—the **London Symphony,** the **Royal Philharmonic,** the **Philharmonia Orchestra,** the **BBC Symphony,** and the **BBC Philharmonic**—several choirs, and many smaller chamber groups and historic instrument ensembles. Look for the **London Sinfonietta,** the **English Chamber Orchestra,** and, of course, the **Academy of St. Martin in the Fields.** Performances are in the South Banks Arts Centre and the Barbican. Smaller recitals are at Wigmore Hall and St. John's Smith Square.

Barbican Centre (home of the London Symphony Orchestra and more)
The largest art and exhibition center in western Europe, the roomy and comfortable Barbican complex is the perfect setting for enjoying music and theater. Barbican Hall is the permanent home address of the London Symphony Orchestra, as well as host to visiting orchestras and performers of all styles, from classical to jazz, folk, and world music.

In addition to its hall and two theaters, Barbican Centre encompasses the Barbican Art Gallery, the Curve Gallery, and foyer exhibition spaces; Cinemas One and Two, which show recently released mainstream films and film series; the Barbican Library, a general lending library that places a strong emphasis on the arts; the Conservatory, one of London's largest greenhouses; and restaurants, cafes, and bars. The box office is open Monday to Saturday from 9am to 8pm. Silk St., EC2. ✆ 020/7638-8891. www. barbican.org.uk. Tickets depend on the event. Tube: Barbican or Moorgate.

London Coliseum (home of the English National Opera)   Built in 1904 as a
variety theater and converted into an opera house in 1968, the London Coliseum is the city's largest theater. For its 100th birthday, the renowned opera house received a $75-million restoration fit for a diva. Today not only is the Edwardian splendor restored, but there are roomier foyers, plus a two-story lobby and bar with views of Trafalgar Square. The 2,358-seat Coliseum still remains the largest proscenium theater

in England. One of two national opera companies, the English National Opera performs a range of works here, from classics to Gilbert and Sullivan to new experimental works. All performances are in English. The Opera presents a repertory of 18 to 20 productions 5 or 6 nights a week for 10 months of the year (the theater is dark mid-July to mid-Sept). The theater also hosts touring companies. Although balcony seats are cheaper, many visitors seem to prefer the upper circle or dress circle. The box office is open Monday to Saturday from 10am to 6pm. London Coliseum, St. Martin's Lane, WC2. ℭ **0870/145-0200.** www.eno.org. Tickets from £10 ($20) balcony, £26–£81 ($52–$162) upper or dress circle or stalls; about 100 discount balcony tickets sold on the day of performance from 10am. Tube: Charing Cross or Leicester Sq.

Royal Albert Hall Opened in 1871 and dedicated to the memory of Victoria's consort, Prince Albert, this circular building holds one of the world's most famous auditoriums. With a seating capacity of 5,200, it's a popular place to hear music by stars. Occasional sporting events (especially boxing) figure strongly here, too.

Since 1941, the hall has hosted the BBC Henry Wood Promenade Concerts, known as "the Proms," an annual series that lasts for 8 weeks between mid-July and mid-September. The Proms, incorporating a medley of rousing, mostly British orchestral music, have been a British tradition since 1895. Although most of the audience occupies reserved seats, true aficionados usually opt for standing room in the orchestra pit, with close-up views of the musicians on stage. Newly commissioned works are often premiered here. The final evening is the most traditional; the rousing favorites "Jerusalem" or "Land of Hope and Glory" echo through the hall. After its 8-year restoration, the Albert Hall now allows tours every 30 minutes, starting at 10:30am Friday to Tuesday and ending at 2:30pm, at a cost of £7.50 ($15). Limited to only 15 participants, tours take in such sights as the Queen's Box and the Royal Retiring Room used by royals during intermission. Those on tour are also shown the Royal Albert Hall organ with it 9,999 pipes. The box office is open daily 9am to 9pm. Kensington Gore, SW7 2AP. ℭ **020/7589-8212.** www.royalalberthall.com. Tickets £5–£150 ($10–$300), depending on the event. Tube: South Kensington.

The Royal Opera House (home of the Royal Ballet and the Royal Opera) The Royal Ballet and the Royal Opera are at home again in this magnificently restored theater. Opera and ballet aficionados hardly recognize the renovated place, with its spectacular public spaces, including the Floral Hall (a chamber-music venue), a rooftop restaurant, and bars and shops. The entire northeast corner of one of London's most famous public squares has been transformed, finally realizing Inigo Jones's original vision for this colonnaded plaza.

Performances of the Royal Opera are usually sung in the original language, but supertitles are projected. The Royal Ballet, which ranks with top companies such as the Kirov and the Paris Opera Ballet, performs a repertory with a tilt toward the classics, including works by its earlier choreographer-directors Sir Frederick Ashton and Sir Kenneth MacMillan. The box office is open Monday to Saturday from 10am to 8pm. Bow St., Covent Garden, WC2. ℭ **0871/663-2587.** www.royalopera.org. Tickets £6–£185 ($12–$370). Tube: Covent Garden.

Sadler's Wells Theatre This is a premier venue for dance and opera. It occupies the site of a series of theaters, the first built in 1683. In the early 1990s, the turn-of-the-20th-century theater was mostly demolished, and construction began on an innovative new design completed at the end of 1998. The turn-of-the-century facade has been retained, but the interior has been completely revamped with a stylish cutting-edge theater design. The new theater offers classical ballet, modern dance of all degrees of "avant-garde-ness," and children's theatrical productions, including a Christmas ballet. Performances are usually at 7:30pm. The box office is open Monday to Saturday from 9am to 8:30pm. Rosebery Ave., EC1. ℭ 020/7863-8096. www.sadlers-wells.com. Tickets £10–£50 ($20–$100). Tube: Northern Line to Angel.

Southbank Centre   Three of the most acoustically perfect concert halls in the world were erected here between 1951 and 1964: the Royal Festival Hall, the Queen Elizabeth Hall, and the Purcell Room, all located in this complex. Together, the halls present more than 1,200 performances a year, including classical music, ballet, jazz, popular music, and contemporary dance. Also here is the internationally renowned Hayward Gallery (p. 189).

The Southbank Centre, which usually opens daily at 10am, offers an extensive array of things to see and do, including free exhibitions in the foyers and occasional free lunchtime music at 12:30pm. On Friday, "Commuter Jazz" in the foyer from 5:15 to 6:45pm is free. The Poetry Library is open Tuesday to Sunday 11am to 8pm, and shops display a selection of books, records, and crafts. Food and drink are also served at various venues. The box office is open daily from 9am to 8pm. On the South Bank, SE1. Box office ℭ 08703/800400. www.rfh.org.uk. Tickets £8–£60 ($16–$120). Tube: Waterloo or Embankment.

Wigmore Hall   An intimate auditorium, Wigmore Hall offers an excellent series of voice recitals, piano and chamber music, early and baroque music, and jazz. A cafe/bar and restaurant are on the premises; a cold supper can be preordered if you are attending a concert. Performances are held nightly in addition to the "Sunday Morning Coffee Concerts" and Sunday concerts at 11:30am or 4pm. The box office is open Monday to Saturday 10am to 7pm and Sunday from 10:30am to 5pm. 36 Wigmore St., W1. ℭ 020/7935-2141. www.wigmore-hall.org.uk. Tickets £10–£35 ($20–$70). Tube: Bond St. or Oxford Circus.

OUTSIDE CENTRAL LONDON

Kenwood Lakeside Concerts   These band and orchestral concerts on the north side of Hampstead Heath have been a British tradition for more than half a century. In recent years, laser shows and fireworks have been added to a repertoire that includes everything from rousing versions of the *1812 Overture* to jazz to operas such as *Carmen*. The final concert of the season always features some of the "Pomp and Circumstance" marches of Sir Edward Elgar. Music drifts across the lake to serenade wine-and-cheese parties on the grass. Concerts take place in July and August, Saturday at 7:30pm. The box office is open Monday to Saturday from 9:30am to 6:30pm. Kenwood, Hampstead Lane, Hampstead Heath, London NW3 7JR. ℭ 0870/890-0146. www.picnic concerts.com. Tickets £23 ($46) for lawn seats, £30 ($60) for reserved deck chairs. Discounts of 13% for students and persons older than 60. Tube: Northern Line to Golders Green or Archway, then bus no. 210, a 30–45-min. jaunt to the north of London.

THE CLUB & MUSIC SCENE
COMEDY

The Comedy Store   This is London's showcase for established and rising comic talent. Inspired by comedy clubs in the U.S., the club has given many comics their start, and today a number of them are established TV personalities. Even if their names are unfamiliar, you'll enjoy the spontaneity of live comedy before a British audience. Visitors must be 18 and older; dress is casual. Reserve through **Ticketmaster** (ℭ 0870/060-2340); the club opens 1½ hours before each show. *Insider's tip:* Go on Tuesday when the humor is more cutting edge. Tuesday to Sunday, doors open at 6:30pm and the show starts at 8pm; on Friday and Saturday, an extra show starts at midnight (doors open at 11pm). 1A Oxendon St., off Piccadilly Circus, SW1. © 0844/847-1728. www.the comedystore.co.uk. Cover £16 ($32). Tube: Leicester Sq. or Piccadilly Circus.

LIVE MUSIC

The Bull & Gate   Outside central London, and smaller, cheaper, and often more animated and less touristy than many of its competitors, the Bull & Gate is the unofficial headquarters of London's pub rock scene. Indie and relatively unknown rock bands are served up in back-to-back handfuls at this somewhat battered Victorian pub. The place attracts a young crowd, mainly in their 20s. If you like spilled beer, this is off-the-beaten-track London at its most authentic. Bands that have played here and later ascended to fame on Europe's club scene have included Madness, Blur, and Pulp. There's music nightly from 8pm to midnight. 389 Kentish Town Rd., NW5. © 020/ 8826-5000. www.bullandgate.co.uk. Cover from £5 ($10). Tube: Northern Line to Kentish Town.

Shepherd's Bush Empire   Located in an old BBC television theater with great acoustics, this is a major venue for big-name pop and rock stars. Announcements appear in the local press. There's a seating capacity of 2,000. The spot mostly attracts fans in their 20s. The box office is open Monday to Friday from noon to 4pm, but you can book 24 hours through **Ticketweb** at © 0870/771-2000. Shepherd's Bush Green, W12. © 020/8354-3300. www.shepherds-bush-empire.co.uk. Ticket prices vary according to show. Tube: Hammersmith & City Line to Shepherd's Bush or Goldhawk Rd.

Sound   In the heart of London, this 700-seat venue has booked the big acts, everybody from Sinéad O'Connor to Puff Daddy to the Spice Girls. Sound functions as a restaurant and bar every night, with limited live music and a DJ until 11pm; after 11pm, the mood changes, the menu is simplified to include only bar snacks, and the site focuses much more heavily on live music and dancing. The music program is forever changing; call to see what's on at the time of your visit and to reserve tickets. Crowds and age levels can vary here depending on what act is featured. Reservations are recommended for dinner, but reservations after 11pm are not accepted. The box office is open Monday to Saturday 10am to 6pm. 1 Leicester Sq., W1. © 020/7287-1010. www.soundlondon.com. Free admission until 9pm daily; £8 ($16) 9–10pm, £10–£12 ($20–$24) 10–11pm, £15 ($30) from 11pm. Tube: Leicester Sq.

Windmill ★★   It's the music that lures devotees to the back streets of Brixton. This unpretentious club, whose reputation went from ground zero to great, is now hailed as one of the top 10 music venues in the U.K. Entry is cheap, and so is the beer. The staff is friendly, the atmosphere candlelit. The beer garden overflows with a hip, young crowd of Londoners and foreigners come to hear every group from the Black Lips to Die! Die! Die! Sounds embrace psycho beats, punk, goth rock, and music as yet unlabeled. This place is open Monday to Saturday from 8pm to 2am. 22 Blenheim Gardens, SW2. © 020/8671-0700. www.windmillbrixton.co.uk. Cover £3–£5 ($6–$10). Tube: Brixton.

TRADITIONAL ENGLISH MUSIC

Cecil Sharpe House   CSH was the focal point of the folk revival in the 1960s, and it continues to treasure and nurture folk music and dance. You'll find a whole range of traditional music and dance here, with different evenings devoted to, among others, Irish set dances, English barn dances (similar to American square dances), dances from Louisiana's Cajun country, even reenactment of 18th-century quadrilles.

Although many of the regular patrons of this bar and dance club know these arcane dances by heart, they're usually charitable toward quick-learning and agile newcomers who can pick up the steps and the beat quickly. Call to see what's happening on the nights that you're in town. The box office is open Monday to Friday 9:30am to 5:30pm. 2 Regent's Park Rd., NW1. ✆ 020/7485-2206. Tickets £5–£15 ($10–$30). Tube: Northern Line to Camden Town.

JAZZ & BLUES

Ain't Nothin' But Blues Bar   This club, which bills itself as the only true blues venue in town, features local acts and occasional touring American bands. On weekends, prepare to wait in line for a while. Open Monday to Wednesday 6pm to 1am, Thursday 6pm to 2am, Friday 6pm to 3am, Saturday 2pm to 3am, and Sunday 3pm to midnight. 20 Kingly St., W1. ✆ 020/7287-0514. www.aintnothinbut.co.uk. Cover £5 ($10). Free Sun–Wed, Thurs before 9:30pm, Fri–Sat before 8:30pm. Tube: Oxford Circus or Piccadilly Circus. From the Oxford Circus Tube stop, walk south on Regent St., turn left on Great Marlborough St., and then make a quick right on Kingly St.

100 Club   Although less plush and expensive than some jazz clubs, 100 Club is a serious contender on the music front, with presentations of some remarkably good jazz. Its cavalcade of bands includes the best British jazz musicians and some of their Yankee brethren. Rock, R&B, and blues are also on tap. Serious devotees of jazz from ages 20 to 45 show up here. Open Monday to Thursday and Sunday 7:30 to 11:30pm; Friday noon to 3pm and 8:30pm to 2am; and Saturday 7:30pm to 1am. *Note:* These hours are subject to change. 100 Oxford St., W1. ✆ 020/7636-0933. www.the100 club.co.uk. Cover £7–£13 ($14–$26). Club members get a £1 ($2) discount Sat nights. Tube: Tottenham Court Rd. or Oxford Circus.

Pizza Express   Don't let the name fool you: This restaurant/bar serves some of the best jazz in London by mainstream artists, along with thin-crust Italian pizza. You'll find local bands or visiting groups, often from the United States. The place draws an equal mix of Londoners and visitors in the 20-to-40 age bracket. Although the club has been enlarged, it's still important to reserve ahead of time. The restaurant is open daily from 11:30am to midnight; jazz plays from 7:30 to 11pm. 10 Dean St., W1. ✆ 020/ 7734-3220. www.pizzaexpresslive.com. Cover £15–£22 ($30–$44). Tube: Tottenham Court Rd.

Ronnie Scott's Jazz Club   Inquire about jazz in London, and people immediately think of Ronnie Scott's, the European vanguard for modern jazz. Only the best English and American combos, often fronted by top-notch vocalists, are booked here. The programs make for an entire evening of cool jazz. In the heart of Soho, Ronnie Scott's is a 10-minute walk from Piccadilly Circus along Shaftesbury Avenue. In the Main Room, you can watch the show from the bar or sit at a table, at which you can order dinner. The Downstairs Bar is more intimate; among the regulars at your elbow may be some of the world's most talented musicians. The club is open Monday to Saturday 6pm to 3am, Sunday 6pm to midnight. Reservations are recommended. 47 Frith St., W1. ✆ 020/7439-0747. www.ronniescotts.co.uk. Cover nonmembers £26 ($52), members 10% off. Tube: Leicester Sq. or Piccadilly Circus.

606 Club   Located in a discreet basement in Chelsea, the 606, a jazz supper club in the boondocks of Fulham, presents live music nightly. Predominantly a venue for modern jazz, its styles range from traditional to contemporary. Local musicians and some very big names play here, whether at planned gigs or informal jam sessions after they finish shows elsewhere in town. Because of license requirements, patrons can order alcohol only with food. Locals show up here along with a trendy crowd from more posh neighborhoods in London. Open Monday to Wednesday 7:30pm to 1am; Thursday to Saturday 8pm to 1:30am; selected Sundays noon to 4pm and 8pm to midnight. 90 Lots Rd., SW10. ℂ 020/7352-5953. www.606club.co.uk. Cover Mon–Thurs £8 ($16), Fri–Sat £12 ($24), Sun lunch £8 ($16), Sun night £10 ($20). Bus: 11, 19, 22, 31, 39, C1, or C3. Tube: Earl's Court.

DANCE, DISCO & ECLECTIC

Bar Rumba   Despite its location on Shaftesbury Avenue, this Latin bar and music club could be featured in a book of underground London. A hush-hush address, it leans toward radical jazz-fusion on some nights and phat funk on other occasions. It boasts two full bars and a different musical theme every night. All the music here is live. On weeknights you have to be 18 or older; on Saturday and Sunday, nobody younger than 21 is allowed in. 36 Shaftesbury Ave., W1. ℂ 020/7287-6933. www.barrumba. co.uk. Cover £5–£10 ($10–$20). Free Sat before 10pm. Tube: Piccadilly Circus.

Cargo   This watering hole in ultratrendy Hoxton draws a smart urban crowd from their expensive West End flats. Its habitués assure us it's the place to go for a "wicked time" and great live bands. If there are no bands on a particular night, then great DJs dominate the club. Music and dancing start at 6pm and the joint is jumping by 9:30pm nightly. It's fun and funky, with two big arched rooms, fantastic acoustics, and a parade of videos. As for the patrons, the bartender characterized it just right: "We get the freaks and the normal people." Open Monday to Thursday noon to 1am, Friday noon to 3am, Saturday 6pm to 3am, and Sunday 1pm to midnight. Kingsland Viaduct, 83 Rivington St., Shoreditch, EC2. ℂ 020/7739-3440. www.cargo-london.com. Cover £8–£13 ($16–$26) after 10pm. Tube: Liverpool St.

The Cross   In the backwaters of Kings Cross, this club has been hot since 1993. Hipsters come here to dance in the space's industrial-looking brick-lined vaults. Music runs the gamut from acid rock to Caribbean/African fusion to Jamaican soca. This place is shadowy, sweaty, raunchy, and sometimes down-and-dirty. Call to find out who's performing. Open Friday and Saturday from 10pm to 6am. The Arches, Kings Cross Goods Yard, York Way, N1. ℂ 0845/371-4489. www.thecross.co.uk. Cover £10–£20 ($20–$40). Tube: Kings Cross.

Egg ⚿   There's a wild party going on here for serious clubbers drawn to the somewhat seedy location across from Kings Cross. Spread over three floors, the joint is warehouse-style, with music that embraces everything from electro-disco beats to house (its specialty). Egg is a leading contender in London's underground scene, complete with a large garden and balcony terrace. Sexy clubbers—both gay and straight—show up for such events as "Playtime" on Friday nights. Open Friday 10pm to 6am and Saturday from 10pm until noon on Sunday. 200 York Way, N7. ℂ 020/7609-8364. www. egglondon.net. Tube: Kings Cross.

The End   This club is better than ever after its enlargement. You'll find a trio of large dance floors, along with four bars and a chill-out area. Speaker walls will blast you into orbit. The End is the best club in London for live house and garage music. It draws both straight and gay Londoners. "We can't tell the difference anymore," the club owner confessed, "and who cares anyway?" From its drinking fountain to its swanky toilets, the club is alluring. Dress for glam and to be seen on the circuit. Some big names in London appear on the weekends to entertain. Open Monday and Wednesday 9pm to 3am, Tuesday 6pm to 3am, Thursday 8pm to 3am, Friday 6pm to 3:30am, Saturday 9pm to 3:30am, and Sunday 9pm to 1:30am. 18 W. Central St., WC1. ℂ 020/7419-9199. www.endclub.com. Cover £5–£20 ($10–$40). Tube: Tottenham Court Rd.

Fabric   While other competitors have come and gone, Fabric continues to draw crowds since opening in 1999. Its main allure is that it has a license for 24-hour music and dancing from Thursday to Sunday night. This is one of the most famous clubs in the increasingly trendy East London sector. On some crazed nights, at least 2,500 members of young London, plus a medley of international visitors, crowd into this mammoth place. It has a trio of dance floors, bars wherever you look, unisex toilets, chill-out beds, and even a roof terrace. Live acts are presented every Friday, with DJs reigning on weekends. You'll hear house, garage, soca, reggae, and whatever else is on the cutting edge of London's underground music scene at the time. Open Thursday and Friday 9:30pm to 5am, Saturday 10pm to 7am. 77A Charterhouse St., EC1. 𝄞 **020/ 7336-8898.** www.fabriclondon.com. Cover £12–£16 ($24–$32). Tube: Farringdon.

Ministry of Sound   Removed from the city center, this club-of-the-hour remains hot, hot, hot. With a large bar and huge sound system, it blasts garage and house music for the energetic crowds that pack the two dance floors. If music and lights in the rest of the club have gone to your head, you can chill in the lounge. *Note:* The cover charge is stiff, and bouncers decide who is cool enough to enter, so slip into your grooviest and most glamorous club gear. Open Friday 10pm to 5am and Saturday 11pm to 7am. Student night is Tuesday 10pm to 4am. 103 Gaunt St., SE1. 𝄞 **44/870-060- 0010.** www.ministryofsound.com. Cover £12–£20 ($24–$40). Tube: Northern Line to Elephant & Castle.

Notting Hill Arts Club   This is one of the hippest nighttime venues in London, with the action taking place in a no-frills basement in increasingly fashionable Notting Hill Gate. Yes, that was Liam Gallagher you spotted dancing with Courtney Love. To justify the name of the club, art exhibitions are sometimes staged here. Most of the clients are younger than 35, and they come from a wide range of backgrounds—from Madonna to Ziggy Marley wannabes. The music is eclectic, varying from night to night—jazz, salsa, hip-hop, indie, and so on. Open Monday to Friday from 6pm to 2am, Saturday 4pm to 2am, and Sunday 4pm to 1am. Bands perform Monday to Thursday, Saturday, and Sunday. 21 Notting Hill Gate, W11. 𝄞 **020/7460-4459.** www.notting hillartsclub.com. Cover £5–£11 ($10–$22). Tube: Notting Hill Gate.

Vibe Bar   As more and more of hip London heads east, bypassing even Clerkenwell for Hoxton, Vibe has been put on the map. The *Evening Standard* named it among the top five DJ bars in London. The paper compared it to an "expensively distressed pair of designer jeans." It's a nightspot operated by Truman Brewery. In summer the action overflows onto a courtyard. Patrons check their e-mail, lounge on comfortable couches, and listen to diverse music such as reggae, Latin, jazz, R&B, Northern Soul, African, or hip-hop. Hours are Sunday to Thursday 1:30 to 11:30pm, Friday and Saturday 5pm to 1am. 91 Brick Lane, E1. 𝄞 **020/7426-0491.** www.vibe-bar.co.uk. Cover free to £5 ($10) sometimes assessed after 6pm. Tube: Liverpool St.

Zoo Bar   The owners spent millions of pounds outfitting this club in the slickest, flashiest, and most psychedelic decor in London. If you're looking for a true Euro nightlife experience replete with gorgeous au pairs and trendy Europeans, this is it. Zoo Bar upstairs is a menagerie of mosaic animals beneath a glassed-in ceiling dome. Downstairs, the music is intrusive enough to make conversation futile. Clients range in age from 18 to 35; androgyny is the look of choice. Hours are daily 4pm to 3am. 13–17 Bear St., WC2. 𝄞 **020/7839-4188.** www.zoobar.co.uk. Cover £2–£10 ($4–$20) after 10pm. Tube: Leicester Sq.

THE GAY & LESBIAN SCENE

Time Out also carries listings on gay and lesbian clubs. Another good place for finding out what's hot and hip is **Prowler Soho**, 3–7 Brewer St., Soho, W1 (℗ **020/7734-4031;** Tube: Piccadilly Circus), the largest gay lifestyle store in London. (You can also buy anything from jewelry to CDs and books, fashion, and sex toys.) It's open until 10pm Monday to Saturday, Sunday noon to 8pm. On the Web, **www.gingerbeer. co.uk** is the best site for lesbians to find out what's going on in London, and the magazine that all bona fide lesbians read is *G3* (www.g3magazine.co.uk).

Admiral Duncan   Gay men and their friends go here to drink, have a good time, and make a political statement. British tabloids shocked the world in 1999 when they reported that this pub had been bombed, with three people dying in the attack. Within 6 weeks, the pub reopened its doors. We're happy to report that the bar is better than ever, now also attracting nongays showing their support. 54 Old Compton St., W1. ℗ **020/7437-5300.** Tube: Piccadilly Circus or Leicester Sq.

The Box   Adjacent to one of Covent Garden's best-known junctions, Seven Dials, this sophisticated Mediterranean-style bar attracts all kinds of men. In the afternoon, it is primarily a restaurant, serving meal-size salads, club sandwiches, and soups. Food service ends abruptly at 5pm, after which the place reveals its core: a cheerful, popular rendezvous for London's gay and counterculture crowds. The Box considers itself a "summer bar," throwing open doors and windows to a cluster of outdoor tables at the slightest hint of sunshine. Open Monday to Saturday 11am to 11:30pm and Sunday 11am to 11pm. 32–34 Monmouth St. (at Seven Dials), WC2. ℗ **020/7240-5828.** www. boxbar.com. Tube: Leicester Sq.

Candy Bar   This is the most popular lesbian bar in London at the moment. It has an extremely mixed clientele, ranging from butch to femme and from young to old. There are a bar and a club downstairs. Design is simple, with bright colors and lots of mirrors upstairs and darker, more flirtatious decor downstairs. Men are welcome as long as a woman escorts them. Open Monday to Thursday 5 to 11:30pm, Friday and Saturday 5pm to 2am, and Sunday 5 to 11pm. 4 Carlisle St., W1. ℗ **020/7494-4041.** Cover Fri £5 ($10), Sat £6 ($12). Tube: Tottenham Court Rd.

The Edge   Few bars in London can rival the tolerance, humor, and sexual sophistication found here. The first two floors are done up with decorations that, like an English garden, change with the seasons. Dance music can be found on the crowded, high-energy lower floors. Three menus are featured: a funky daytime menu, a cafe menu, and a late-night menu. Dancers hit the floors starting around 7:30pm. Clientele ranges from flamboyantly gay to hetero pub-crawlers. One downside: A reader claims the bartenders water the drinks. Open Monday to Saturday noon to 1am and Sunday 2 to 11:30pm. 11 Soho Sq., W1. ℗ **0044/207-439-1313.** Tube: Tottenham Court Rd.

First Out Café Bar   First Out prides itself on being London's first (est. 1986) all-gay coffee shop. Set in a 19th-century building whose wood panels have been painted the colors of the gay-liberation rainbow, the bar and cafe are not particularly cruisy. Cappuccino and whisky are the preferred libations, and an exclusively vegetarian menu includes curry dishes, potted pies in phyllo pastries, and salads. Don't expect a raucous atmosphere—some clients come here with their grandmothers. Look for the bulletin board with leaflets and business cards of gay and gay-friendly entrepreneurs. Open Monday to Saturday 10am to 11pm and Sunday 11am to 10:30pm. 52 St. Giles High St., W1. ℗ **020/7240-8042.** Tube: Tottenham Court Rd.

G.A.Y. Name notwithstanding, the clientele here is mixed, and on a Saturday night this could be the most rollicking club in London. You may not find love here, but you could discover a partner for the evening. Patrons have been known to strip down to their briefs or shorts. A mammoth place, this club draws a young crowd to dance beneath its mirrored disco balls. Open Monday, Thursday, Friday 11pm to 4am, Saturday 10:30pm to 5am. London Astoria, 157 Charing Cross Rd., WC2. ℂ 020/7434-9592. www. g-a-y.co.uk. Cover £1–£15 ($2–$30). Tube: Tottenham Court Rd.

Heaven This club, housed in the vaulted cellars of Charing Cross Railway Station, is a London landmark. Heaven is one of the biggest and best-established gay venues in Britain. Painted black and reminiscent of an air-raid shelter, the club is divided into at least four areas, connected by a labyrinth of catwalk stairs and hallways. Each room offers a different type of music, from hip-hop to rock. Heaven also has theme nights, which are frequented at different times by gays, lesbians, or a mostly heterosexual crowd. Thursday in particular seems open to anything, but on Saturday it's gays only. Call before you go. Open Monday 10pm to 6:30am, Wednesday 10:30pm to 3am, Friday 11pm to 6am, and Saturday 10:30pm to 5am. The Arches, Villiers, and Craven sts., WC2. ℂ 020/7930-2020. www.heaven-london.com. Cover £12–£15 ($24–$30). Tube: Charing Cross or Embankment.

THE BAR & PUB SCENE
OUR FAVORITE BARS

Absolut Icebar You might say that this watering hole is the coolest joint in town. The temperature is always kept at 5°F (–15°C) year-round, with everything inside made out of crystal-clear ice from the Torne River in Sweden. You've got to make a reservation to chill out for 40 minutes, and you're given a silver cape and hood to wear for the experience. Inside you're offered a vodka cocktail to warm your soul. Open Monday to Wednesday 3:30 to 11pm, Thursday 3:30 to 11:45pm, Friday 3:30pm to 12:30am, Sat 12:30pm to 12:20am, and Sunday 3:30 to 10:15pm. 31–33 Heddon St., W1. ℂ 020/7478-8910. www.belowzerolondon.com. Cover Mon–Wed and Sun £12 ($24); Thurs–Sat £15 ($30). Tube: Oxford Circus.

Annex 3 On the fringe of Soho and in spite of its kitschy decor, this is one of the hottest bars in London. Its decor has been compared to a psychedelic Christmas show, but its cocktail menu is among the finest in town. Some of the concoctions are based on recipes served in the West Indies in the 1800s. Fortunately, Millionaire Cocktail, one of the bartender's specialties, doesn't require you to be that. Open Monday to Thursday 6pm to midnight, Friday 5:30pm to 1am, Saturday 6pm to 1am, and Sunday 6pm until midnight. 6 Little Portland St., Fitzrovia, W1. ℂ 020/7631-0700. Tube: Oxford Circus.

Bartok ⟨★⟩ ⟨Finds⟩ It's been around for about a decade, but still isn't very well known—and it should be. The hippest bar is Camden, specializing in classical music (of all things) and named for the Hungarian composer, Bela Bartok. It's been called the ultimate chill-out bar in London, ideal for a romantic evening regardless of your sexual persuasion. Crystal chandeliers and the flicker of candle set the rather decadent, hedonistic mood. Visitors sprawl out on tapestry-covered couches, enjoying actual conversation, the music, the food, the drink, and each other. Open Monday to Thursday 5pm to 3am, Friday 5pm to 4am, Saturday 1pm to 4am, and Sunday 1pm to 3am. 78–79 Chalk Farm Rd. (opposite the Roundhouse), NW1. ℂ 020/7916-0595. Tube: Chalk Farm.

Beach Blanket Babylon   Come here if you're looking for a hot singles bar that attracts a crowd in their 20s and 30s. This Portobello joint is very cruisy. The decor is a bit wacky, no doubt designed by an aspiring Salvador Dalí who decided to make it a fairy-tale grotto (or was he going for a medieval dungeon look?). It's close to the Portobello Market. Friday and Saturday nights are the hot, crowded times for bacchanalian revelry. Open daily noon to midnight. 45 Ledbury Rd., W11. ℗ 020/7229-2907. www. beachblanket.co.uk. Tube: Notting Hill Gate.

Cantaloupe   This bustling pub and restaurant is hailed as the bar that jump-started the increasingly fashionable Shoreditch scene. Businesspeople commuting from their jobs in the City mix with East End trendoids in the early evening at what has been called a "gastro-pub/preclub bar." The urban beat is courtesy of the house DJ. The restaurant and tapas menus are first-rate. Open Thursday to Saturday noon to midnight, Sunday to Wednesday noon to 11pm. 35 Charlotte Rd., Shoreditch, EC2. ℗ 020/7729-5566. Tube: Old St.

Lab ⌘   Perhaps the best mixologists in London are found right in the heart of the city at this '70s kitsch-inspired cocktail bar, where bartenders will whip you up the best Feijon Flip or Red Hot Chili Pepper in town. Come here for the ultimate in intoxication, hanging out in an interior of leather and Formica spread over two floors. A thick cocktail book lies on every table; if you're in London long enough you may want to work your way through all the drinks from the classic to house specialties. In a glam, glossy setting, DJs keep the mood relaxed. Open Monday to Saturday 4pm to midnight and Sunday 4 to 10:30pm. 12 Old Compton St., W1. ℗ 020/7437-7820. www.lab-townhouse.com. Tube: Leicester Square.

The Lobby Bar & the Axis Bar   These bars are found in one of London's best deluxe hotels. We advise that you check out the dramatic visuals of both bars before selecting your preferred nesting place. The Lobby Bar occupies what was built in 1907 as the grand, high-ceilinged reception area for one of London's premier newspapers. If the Lobby Bar setting doesn't appeal, take a look at the travertine, hardwood, and leather-sheathed bar in the Axis restaurant. Many fashionistas younger than 40 frequent this bar. The Lobby Bar is open Monday to Saturday 9am to midnight, Sunday 8am to 6:30pm; the Axis bar is open Monday through Saturday from 5:45 to 11pm. In the Hotel One Aldwych, 1 Aldwych, WC2. ℗ 020/7300-1000. Tube: Covent Garden.

Match EC1   This epicenter for the fashionable 20s-to-30s set in London has put the *P* in partying in the once-staid Clerkenwell district. Drinkers sit on elegant sofas or retreat to one of the cozy booths for a late snack. The bar claims to be the home of the Cosmopolitan cocktail, which swept across the drinking establishments of New York. The bartenders make some of the best drinks in London but warn you "there is no such thing as a chocolate martini." Open Monday to Thursday 11am to midnight, Friday 11am to 2am, and Saturday 6pm to 2am. 45–47 Clerkenwell Rd., EC1. ℗ 020/7250-4002. Tube: Farringdon.

The Phoenix Artist Club   What's something so old it's new again? This is where Laurence Olivier made his stage debut in 1930, although he couldn't stop giggling even though the play was a drama. Live music is featured, but it's the hearty welcome, the good beer, and the friendly patrons from ages 20 to 50 who make this rediscovered theater bar worth a detour. It's open to the general public from 5 to 8pm only— it's "members only" after 8pm, but if it's relatively quiet at that time, the club will also admit nonmembers. 1 Phoenix St., WC2. ℗ 020/7836-1077. Tube: Tottenham Court Rd.

LONDON'S MOST EVOCATIVE PUBS

Belgravia

Grenadier Tucked away in a mews, the Grenadier is one of London's reputedly haunted pubs, the ghost here being an 18th-century British soldier. Aside from the poltergeist, the basement houses the original bar and skittles alley used by the duke of Wellington's officers. The scarlet front door of the one-time officers' mess is guarded by a scarlet sentry box and shaded by a vine. The bar is nearly always crowded. Lunch and dinner are offered daily—even on Sunday, when it's a tradition to drink bloody marys (made from a well-guarded recipe) here. In the stalls along the side, you can order good-tasting fare based on seasonal ingredients. Well-prepared dishes include pork Grenadier, beef Wellington, and a chicken-and-Stilton roulade. Snacks such as fish and chips are available at the bar. 18 Wilton Row, SW1. ☎ 020/7235-3074. Tube: Hyde Park Corner.

Bloomsbury

Museum Tavern Across the street from the British Museum, this pub (ca. 1703) retains most of its antique trappings: velvet, oak paneling, and cut glass. It lies right in the center of the University of London area and is popular with writers, publishers, and researchers from the museum. Supposedly, Karl Marx wrote while dining here. Traditional English food is served: shepherd's pie, sausages cooked in English cider, turkey-and-ham pie, ploughman's lunch, and salads. Several English ales, cold lagers, cider, Guinness, wines, and spirits are available. Food and coffee are served all day. The pub gets crowded at lunchtime. 49 Great Russell St., WC1. ☎ 020/7242-8987. Tube: Holborn or Tottenham Court Rd.

The City

Bow Wine Vaults Bow Wine Vaults has existed since long before the wine-bar craze began in the 1970s. One of the most famous in London, the bar attracts cost-conscious diners and drinkers to its vaulted cellars for such traditional fare as deep-fried Camembert, lobster ravioli, and a mixed grill, along with fish. The cocktail bar is popular with the after-work crowd (weekdays 11:30am–11pm). More-elegant meals, served in the street-level dining room, include Thai green mussels in curry sauce, escallop of veal Milanese garnished with pasta, and haddock Monte Carlo. Wines from around the world are available; the last time we were there, the wine of the day was a Chilean chardonnay. 10 Bow Churchyard, EC4. ☎ 020/7248-1121. www.bowwinevaults.com. Tube: Mansion House, Bank, or St. Paul's.

Jamaica Wine House This was one of the first coffeehouses in England and, reputedly, the Western world. For years, merchants and sea captains came here to transact deals over rum and coffee. Nowadays, the two-level house dispenses coffee, beer, ale, lager, and fine wines, among them a variety of ports. The oak-paneled bar is on the street level and attracts crowds of investment bankers. You can order standard but filling dishes such as a ploughman's lunch and toasted sandwiches. 12 St. Michael's Alley, off Cornhill, EC3. ☎ 020/7929-6972. Tube: Bank.

Ye Olde Watling Ye Olde Watling was rebuilt after the Great Fire of 1666. On the ground level is a mellow pub. Upstairs is an intimate restaurant where, sitting at trestle tables under oak beams, you can dine on simple English main dishes for lunch. The menu varies daily, with such choices and reliable standbys as fish and chips, lasagna, fish cakes, and usually a vegetarian dish. All are served with two vegetables or salad, plus rice or potatoes. 29 Watling St., EC4. ☎ 020/7653-9971. Tube: Mansion House.

Covent Garden

Lamb & Flag   Dickens once frequented this pub, and the room has changed little from the days when he prowled the neighborhood. The pub has an amazing and scandalous history. Poet and author Dryden was almost killed by a band of thugs outside its doors in December 1679, and the pub gained the nickname the "Bucket of Blood" during the Regency era (1811–20) because of the bare-knuckled prizefights here. Tap beers include Courage Best and Directors, Old Speckled Hen, John Smiths, and Wadworths 6X. 33 Rose St., off Garrick St., WC2. ℂ 020/7497-9504. Tube: Leicester Sq.

Nags Head   This Nags Head is one of London's most famous Edwardian pubs. In days of yore, patrons had to make their way through a fruit-and-flower market to drink here. Today, the pub is popular with young people. The draft Guinness is very good. Lunch (served noon–4pm) is typical pub grub: sandwiches, salads, pork cooked in cider, and garlic prawns. Snacks are available all afternoon. 10 James's St., WC2. ℂ 020/7836-4678. Tube: Covent Garden.

East End (Wapping)

Prospect of Whitby   One of London's most historic pubs, Prospect was founded in the days of the Tudors, taking its name from a coal barge that made trips between Yorkshire and London. Come here for a tot, a noggin, or whatever it is you drink, and soak up the atmosphere. The pub has got quite a pedigree. Writer Dickens and diarist Samuel Pepys used to drop in, and painter Turner came here for weeks at a time studying views of the Thames. In the 17th century, the notorious Hanging Judge Jeffreys used to get drunk here while overseeing hangings at the adjoining Execution Dock. Tables in the courtyard overlook the river. You can order a Morlands Old Speckled Hen from a hand-pump or a malt whisky. 57 Wapping Wall, E1. ℂ 020/7481-1095. Tube: Wapping.

Holborn

Cittie of Yorke   This pub boasts the longest bar in all of Britain, rafters ascending to the heavens, and a long row of immense wine vats, all of which give it the air of a great medieval hall—appropriate because a pub has existed at this location since 1430. Samuel Smith's is on tap. 22 High Holborn, WC1. ℂ 020/7242-7670. Tube: Holborn or Chancery Lane.

Knightsbridge

Nag's Head   This Nag's Head (not to be confused with the more renowned one at 10 James's St.; see above) is on a back street a short walk from the Berkeley Hotel. Previously a jail dating from 1780, it's said to be the smallest pub in London. In 1921, it was sold for £12 and 6p. Have a drink up front or wander to the tiny bar in the rear. For food, you might enjoy "real ale sausage" (made with pork and ale), shepherd's pie, or the quiche of the day, all served by the welcoming staff. A cosmopolitan clientele— newspaper people, musicians, and travelers—patronizes this warm, cozy pub. The pub touts itself as an "independent," or able to serve any "real ale" they choose because of their lack of affiliation. 53 Kinnerton St., SW1. ℂ 020/7235-1135. Tube: Hyde Park.

Leicester Square

Salisbury   An original gin palace, Salisbury's cut-glass mirrors reflect the faces of English stage stars (and hopefuls) sitting around the curved buffet-style bar. A less prominent place to dine is the old-fashioned wall banquette with its copper-topped tables and Art Nouveau decor. The pub's specialties, home-cooked pies set out in a buffet cabinet with salads, or fish and chips, are quite good and inexpensive. 90 St. Martin's Lane, WC2. ℂ 020/7836-5863. Tube: Leicester Sq.

Mayfair

Shepherd's Tavern   One of the focal points of the all-pedestrian shopping zone of Shepherd's Market, this pub occupies an 18th-century town house amid a warren of narrow, cobble-covered streets behind Park Lane. The street-level bar is cramped but congenial. Many of the regulars recall this tavern's popularity with the pilots of the Battle of Britain. Bar snacks include simple plates of shepherd's pie, and fish and chips. More-formal dining is available upstairs in the cozy, cedar-lined Georgian-style restaurant. The classic British menu probably hasn't changed much since the 1950s, and you can always get honey-roasted ham or roast beef with Yorkshire pudding. 50 Hertford St., W1. ✆ 020/7499-3017. Tube: Green Park.

Notting Hill Gate

Ladbroke Arms   Previously honored as London's "Dining Pub of the Year," Ladbroke Arms is that rare pub known for its food. A changing menu includes roast cod filet with lentils and salsa verde; and aged bone-in rib steak with mustard, peppercorn, and herb-and-garlic butter. With background jazz and rotating art prints, the place strays from the traditional pub environment. This place makes for a pleasant stop and a good meal. The excellent Eldridge Pope Royal is on tap, as well as John Smiths, Courage Directors, and several malt whiskies. 54 Ladbroke Rd., W11. ✆ 020/7727-6648. Tube: Notting Hill Gate.

St. James's

Red Lion   This Victorian pub, with its early-1900s decorations and 150-year-old mirrors, has been compared to Manet's painting *A Bar at the Folies-Bergère* (on display at the Courtauld Gallery). You can order premade sandwiches, and on Saturday, homemade fish and chips are served. Wash down your meal with Ind Coope's fine ales or the house's special beer, Burton's, a brew made of spring water from the Midlands town of Burton-on-Trent. 2 Duke of York St. (off Jermyn St.), SW1. ✆ 020/7321-0782. Tube: Piccadilly Circus.

Soho

Dog & Duck   This snug little joint, a Soho landmark, is the most intimate pub in London. A wide mixture of ages and persuasions flock here, usually chatting amiably. Publicans here stock an interesting assortment of English beers, including Tetleys, Fuller London, and Timothy Taylor Landlord. In autumn, customers will ask for Addlestone's Cider. The cozy upstairs bar is also open. 18 Bateman St. (corner of Frith St.), W1. ✆ 020/7494-0697. Tube: Tottenham Court Rd. or Leicester Sq.

Southwark

George   The existing structure was built in 1877 to replace the original pub, which was destroyed in the Great Fire of 1666. That pub's accolades date from 1598, when it was reviewed as a "faire inn for the receipt of travelers." The present pub was built in the typical "traditional Victorian" style, with stripped oak floors, paneled walls, a curved bar counter, brass ceiling lights, and windows with etched and cut glass. Three huge mirrors decorate the walls. It's still a great place to enjoy Flowers Original, Boddingtons, and London Pride Abbot on tap. 77 Borough High St., SE1. ✆ 020/7407-2056. Tube: Northern Line to London Bridge or Borough.

Trafalgar Square

Sherlock Holmes   The Sherlock Holmes was the gathering spot for the Baker Street Irregulars, a once-mighty clan of mystery lovers who met to honor the genius of Sir Arthur Conan Doyle's famous fictional character. Upstairs, you'll find a re-creation of the living room at 221B Baker St. and such "Holmesiana" as the serpent from *The Speckled Band* and a faux beast's head from *The Hound of the Baskervilles.* In the upstairs dining room, you can order complete meals with wine. Downstairs is mainly for drinking, but there's a good snack bar with cold meats, salads, cheeses, and wine and ales sold by the glass. 10 Northumberland St., WC1. *C* **020/7930-2644.** www.sherlockholmes pub.com. Tube: Charing Cross or Embankment.

7

The Thames Valley:
Royal Windsor & Regal Oxford

The historic Thames Valley and Chiltern Hills lie so close to London that you can easily reach them by car, train, or Green Line coach. In fact, you can explore this area during the day and return to London in time to see a West End show.

The second-most visited historic site in England is **Windsor Castle,** 34km (21 miles) west of London. If you base yourself in Windsor, you can spend another day exploring some of the sights on its periphery, including **Eton** (which adjoins Windsor), **Runnymede,** and **Windsor Great Park.**

If your visit coincides with the spring social sporting season, you can head to Ascot or Henley-on-Thames for the famous social sporting events: Ascot and the Royal Regatta.

Some great historic homes and gardens in the area include Woburn Abbey, Hatfield House, Hughenden Manor, Mapledurham House, and Wellington Ducal Estate. If your time is severely limited, the two most important country mansions to visit are **Woburn Abbey** and **Hatfield House.** Woburn Abbey could consume an entire day, whereas you can visit Hatfield in a half-day.

It's not just the historic homes that make the Home Counties intriguing to visit; the land of river valleys and gentle hills makes for wonderful drives. The beech-clad Chilterns are at their most beautiful in spring and autumn. This 64km (40-mile) chalk ridge extends in an arc from the Thames Valley to the old Roman city of St. Albans in Hertfordshire. The whole region is popular for boating holidays on its 322km (200-mile) network of canals.

Oxfordshire is a land of great mansions, old churches of widely varying architectural styles, and rolling farmland. Certainly your main reason for visiting Oxfordshire is to explore the university city of **Oxford,** about an hour's ride from London by car or train. It's not a good day trip, though, as it has too much to see and do. Plan to spend the night; the next morning you can visit Blenheim Palace, England's answer to Versailles.

1 Windsor & Eton ✦

34km (21 miles) W of London

Were it not for the castle, Windsor might still be a charming Thames town to visit. But because it is the home of the best-known asset the royal family possesses, it is over-run in summer by tourists who all but obscure the town's charm.

The good news is that after the disastrous fire of 1992, Windsor Castle is restored, though some of the new designs for it have been called a "Gothic shocker" or "ghastly." Actually, in spite of some media criticism, a remarkable activity in restoration went on, as woodcarvers, gilders, and plasterers followed the same techniques

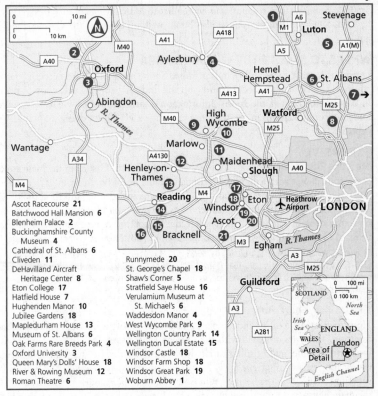

0   10 mi
0   10 km

N

Ascot Racecourse **21**
Batchwood Hall Mansion **6**
Blenheim Palace **2**
Buckinghamshire County
    Museum **4**
Cathedral of St. Albans **6**
Cliveden **11**
DeHavilland Aircraft
    Heritage Center **8**
Eton College **17**
Hatfield House **7**
Hughenden Manor **10**
Jubilee Gardens **18**
Mapledurham House **13**
Museum of St. Albans **6**
Oak Farms Rare Breeds Park **4**
Oxford University **3**
Queen Mary's Dolls' House **18**
River & Rowing Museum **12**
Roman Theatre **6**

Runnymede **20**
St. George's Chapel **18**
Shaw's Corner **5**
Stratfield Saye House **16**
Verulamium Museum at
    St. Michael's **6**
Waddesdon Manor **4**
West Wycombe Park **9**
Wellington Country Park **14**
Wellington Ducal Estate **15**
Windsor Castle **18**
Windsor Farm Shop **18**
Windsor Great Park **19**
Woburn Abbey **1**

their predecessors did in the Middle Ages, when William the Conqueror built the castle. Queen Elizabeth opened the state apartments in November 1997 following a $62-million project that returned most of the ruined part of the castle to its original condition. Windsor Castle remains Britain's second-most visited historic building, behind the Tower of London, attracting 1.2 million visitors a year.

ESSENTIALS

GETTING THERE   More than a dozen trains per day make the 30-minute trip from Waterloo or Paddington Station in London (you'll have to transfer at Slough to the Slough-Windsor shuttle train). The cost is £7.70 ($15) round-trip. Call ✆ **0845/748-4950** or visit **www.networkrail.co.uk** for more information.

   Green Line coach no. 702 (✆ **0870/608-7261;** www.greenline.co.uk) from Victoria Station in London takes about 1¼ hours. A same-day round-trip costs between £8.20 and £10 ($16 and $20), depending on the time of day and week. The bus drops you near the parish church, across the street from the castle.

   If you're driving from London, take the M4 west.

VISITOR INFORMATION   A **Tourist Information Centre** is at Booking Hall, Windsor Royal Shopping Center (✆ **01753/743900;** www.windsor.gov.uk). It is open April to June daily 10am to 5pm; July and August Monday to Saturday 10am to

5:30pm, Sunday 10am to 5pm; and September to March Monday to Saturday 10am to 5pm, Sunday 10am to 4pm. It also books walking tours for the Oxford guild of guides.

WHERE TO STAY IN THE WINDSOR AREA

During the Ascot races and Windsor Horse Show, reservations are necessary far in advance. Unlike such towns as Oxford, you will find a not-so-great collection of B&Bs in Windsor. In a pinch, the Tourist Information Centre (see above) will book you into budget accommodations in the area but will charge £5 ($10) for doing so, plus a 10% deposit.

EXPENSIVE

Mercure Castle Windsor ⚜   In the shadow of Windsor Castle, on the main street, is this solid choice with a dignified Georgian facade. It was originally built in the 15th century to shelter the workers laboring on the town's foundations and royal buildings. The grounds behind the hotel once served as the stable yard for Windsor Castle, but now they contain a modern wing, where the bedrooms are much more sterile than those in the main building. Some rooms have four-poster beds.

18 High St., Windsor, Berkshire SL4 1LJ. ℭ 01753/851577. Fax 01753/856-930. www.mercure.com. 108 units. £165–£210 ($330–$420) double; £290–£310 ($580–$620) suite. AE, DC, MC, V. Children 12 and younger stay free in parent's room. **Amenities:** Restaurant; bar; room service; laundry service. *In room:* A/C, TV, Wi-Fi, minibar, beverage maker, hair dryer, trouser press.

The Oakley Court Hotel ⚜⚜   Built beside the Thames (a 20-min. drive from Heathrow) by a Victorian industrialist, the Oakley Court is imbued with a sense of tradition. Today it's affiliated with the Queen's Moat House hotel chain. The building's jutting gables and bristling turrets have lent themselves to the filming of several horror movies, including *The Rocky Horror Picture Show* and *Dracula*. The hotel is far superior to choices in the heart of Windsor. Although the grandest public areas are in the main house, most rooms are in a trio of well-accessorized modern wings that ramble through the estate's 14 hectares (35 acres) of parks and gardens. Some rooms offer four-poster beds and views of the River Thames.

Windsor Rd., Water Oakley, Windsor, Berkshire SL4 5UR. ℭ 01753/609988. Fax 01628/637011. www.oakleycourt. com. 118 units. £136–£184 ($272–$368) double (weekends with breakfast); £170–£229 ($340–$458) double (Mon–Fri with breakfast). AE, DC, MC, V. Take the river road, A308, 5km (3 miles) from Windsor toward Maidenhead. **Amenities:** Restaurant; bar; health club; indoor heated swimming pool; gym; Jacuzzi; sauna/steam room; boat rentals; room service; babysitting; laundry service; dry cleaning. *In room:* A/C, TV, Wi-Fi, minibar, beverage maker, hair dryer, trouser press, safe.

Runnymede Hotel & Spa ⚜⚜   Because of the dearth of top-of-the-line hotels within Windsor itself, more and more guests are seeking out this hotel and spa on the lovely banks of the Thames between Windsor and Staines. A privately owned hotel, the complex lies only 30 minutes by train from London just off the A30. The spa is one of the finest in the greater London and greater Windsor area, offering personalized exercise programs and healthcare treatments plus a splendid neoclassical-style pool. Bedrooms are fairly spacious and beautifully designed. The contemporary Left Bank restaurant is one of the finest in the area, opening onto the Thames and designed around an aquatic theme, with a trio of aquariums and an open seafood bar.

Windsor Rd., Egham, Surrey TW20 0AG. ℭ 01784/436171. Fax 01784/436340. www.runnymedehotel.com. 180 units. Mon–Thurs £265 ($530) double; Fri–Sun £170–£200 ($340–$400) double. Rates include breakfast. AE, MC, V. Take Rte.

A308 out of Windsor, a 15-min. drive. **Amenities:** Restaurant; bar; indoor pool; 3 tennis courts; spa; room service; babysitting; laundry service; dry cleaning. *In room:* A/C, TV, Wi-Fi, minibar, beverage maker, hair dryer, trouser press.

Sir Christopher Wren's House Hotel ⓧ

Designed by Christopher Wren in 1676 as his home, this former town house occupies a prime position on the Thames, just a 3-minute walk from the castle. Wren's oak-paneled former study is equipped with his Empire desk, a fireplace, and shield-back Hepplewhite chairs. The bay-windowed main drawing room opens onto a garden and a riverside flagstone terrace for after-dinner coffee and drinks. Rooms come in a wide range of sizes; some have fine old furniture and a full-canopied bed, others have a half-canopied bed. Several bedrooms overlook the river. Room no. 2, Wren's bedroom, is said to be haunted. In 2008, the hotel opened the finest spa in the shire.

Thames St., Windsor, Berkshire SL4 1PX. ⓒ **01753/861354.** Fax 01753/860172. www.sirchristopherwren.co.uk. 96 units. £230 ($460) double; £320 ($640) suite. AE, DC, MC, V. Parking £10 ($20). **Amenities:** Restaurant; bar; gym; spa; sauna; concierge; secretarial services; room service; babysitting; laundry service; dry cleaning. *In room:* TV, Wi-Fi, beverage maker, hair dryer, trouser press.

MODERATE

Royal Adelaide Hotel   This landmark Georgian building is opposite the famous Long Walk leading to Windsor Castle, 5 minutes away. Named for Queen Adelaide, who visited the premises during her reign, thereby dubbing it "royal," all its well-furnished rooms have recently been refurbished. Though small, bathrooms have sufficient shelf space and many have tub/shower combinations.

46 King's Rd., Windsor, Berkshire SL4 2AG. ⓒ **01753/863916.** Fax 01753/830682. www.theroyaladelaide.com. 42 units. £79–£135 ($158–$270) double. Rates include English breakfast. AE, MC, V. **Amenities:** Restaurant; bar; room service; babysitting. *In room:* TV, Wi-Fi, beverage maker, hair dryer, iron, trouser press, safe.

Ye Harte & Garter Hotel

On Castle Hill opposite Windsor Castle is the old Garter Inn. Named for the Knights of the Garter and used as the setting for scenes in Shakespeare's *The Merry Wives of Windsor,* the Garter burned down in the 1800s and was rebuilt as part of one hostelry that included the Harte. From the front rooms, you can watch the guards marching up High Street every morning on their way to change the guard at the castle. The renovated rooms are comfortable and rather functionally furnished, though they vary greatly in size. More expensive are the Windsor rooms, which have front views and Jacuzzis.

31 High St., Windsor, Berkshire SL4 1PH. ⓒ **01753/863426.** Fax 01753/830527. www.harteandgarter.com. 79 units. £175 ($350) double; £185 ($370) suite. AE, DC, MC, V. **Amenities:** 2 restaurants; bar; laundry service; dry cleaning. *In room:* TV, Wi-Fi, beverage maker, hair dryer, trouser press.

INEXPENSIVE

Langton House ⓥalue   The best B&B near the castle is run by welcoming hosts, Paul and Sonja Fogg, who have converted a Victorian town house that dates from 1890 when it housed Queen Victoria's government officials. Lying only a 5-minute walk from the castle, the large, double-fronted Victorian house is built of dark red brick. In later life, it was a nursing home before it was turned into a B&B, offering comfortably furnished, midsize bedrooms, each with private bathroom equipped with a shower stall.

46 Alma Rd., Windsor, Berkshire S14 3HA. ⓒ **01753/858299.** www.langtonhouse.co.uk. 4 units. £80–£90 ($160–$180) double. Rates include English breakfast. AE, MC, V. **Amenities:** Breakfast room. *In room:* TV, Wi-Fi, hair dryer.

WHERE TO DINE IN WINDSOR & ETON

Many visitors prefer to dine in Eton; most of the restaurants and fast-food places along the main street of Windsor, in front of the castle, serve dreary food.

You'll find good, cheap food at the **Waterman's Arms,** Brocas Street (© **01753/ 861-001**), just over the bridge to Eton. Founded in 1542, it's a student favorite. Featured are four varieties of fish and chips, including cod, haddock, plaice, and skate. Platters cost £8 to £9 ($16–$18). Meat pies and other main dishes are also served. Our favorite is the beef and Guinness. Special English roast dinners, including beef and lamb, are offered on Sunday, costing £7.95 to £11 ($16–$22). It's open daily 11:30am to 11:30pm. MasterCard and Visa are accepted.

Antico ⟨*Value*⟩ ITALIAN   Eton's finest Italian restaurant, Antico serves Mediterranean food in a formal setting. People have been dining here for 200 years, though not from an Italian menu. On your way to the tiny bar, you pass a cold table, displaying hors d'oeuvres and cold meats. With many fish dishes, such as grilled fresh salmon, Dover sole, or sea bass, and a wide selection of pastas, the food is substantial and filling—a good value, but rarely exciting.

42 High St., Eton. © **01753/863977.** Reservations strongly recommended. Main courses £12–£20 ($24–$40); 3-course fixed-price lunch menu £13 ($26). AE, MC, V. Mon–Sat 12:30–2:30pm and 7–11pm. Closed bank holidays.

Crooked House Tea Rooms ⭐ ⟨*Finds*⟩ CONTINENTAL   Historically called Market Cross House, this is a charming old relic from 1687. It acquired its tilt after it was restructured in 1718. A mixture of original and unseasoned timber resulted in its much-photographed crooked look. A secret passage from its cellar leads directly to Windsor Castle, suggesting an unknown but intriguing connection. Next to the Crooked House is the shortest street in Britain, measuring 15m (51 ft.). It's called Queen Charlotte Street. The Tea Rooms serves the best Cornish clotted cream tea in the area, along with a "High Tea." It also offers a variety of light lunches and fresh homemade soups throughout the day.

51 High St., Eton. © **01753/857534.** Reservations not needed. Light lunches £5.50–£7.50 ($11–$15); high tea £7–£16 ($14–$32). MC, V. Daily 10am–6pm.

Gilbey's Bar and Restaurant MODERN ENGLISH/CONTINENTAL   Just across the bridge from Windsor, this charming place is located on Eton's main street, among the antiques shops. Furnished with pinewood tables and simple chairs, a glassed-in conservatory is out back. A brigade of seven chefs turns out quite good Modern English dishes. Begin with one of the well-prepared soups. Main dishes include pan-fried skate wing with a champagne or chili-and-caper risotto. For dessert, try the delicious white-and-dark mousse with amaretto cream.

82–83 High St., Eton. © **01753/854921.** Reservations recommended. Main courses £13–£20 ($26–$40); fixed-price menu £14 ($28). AE, MC, V. Sun–Thurs noon–2:30pm and 6–9:30pm; Fri–Sat noon–2:30pm and 6–10:30pm.

The Oak Leaf Restaurant at the Oakley Court Hotel ⭐⭐ INTERNATIONAL   In the mid-1990s, this chic London restaurant, known for its delectable food and sophisticated clientele, moved from central London to this new setting beside the Thames. Today, under the supervision of chef Damien Bradley, the reincarnated Oak Leaf serves a modern cuisine that may include a parfait of duck livers with a confit of red onions and mandarin oranges, or a pâté of Scottish salmon with creamed leeks served with broad beans and a red-wine shallot sauce.

Windsor Rd., Water Oakley, Windsor. ✆ **01753/609988.** Reservations recommended. Main courses £16–£28 ($32–$56); table d'hôte lunch and dinner £32 ($64). AE, DC, MC, V. Sun–Fri 12:30–2pm; Mon–Fri 7–9:30pm; Sat 7–10pm; Sun 7–9pm.

Strok's MODERN ENGLISH/CONTINENTAL   This restaurant, located near the castle, is Windsor's most elegant and charming, possessing garden terraces, a conservatory, and a dining room designed a bit like a greenhouse. Chef Philip Wild selects an individual garnish to complement each well-prepared dish. For starters, try the tower of smoked salmon and asparagus. For a main course, enjoy the rosettes of spring lamb with beans, artichokes, and an herb Yorkshire pudding, or a seafood platter of lobster, king prawns, crab, mussels, and shrimps. A variety of vegetarian dishes are also offered. At dinner, a pianist entertains.

In Sir Christopher Wren's House Hotel, Thames St., Windsor. ✆ **01753/442422.** Main courses £18–£23 ($36–$46). AE, DC, MC, V. Daily 12:30–2:15pm and 6:30–10pm.

ON THE OUTSKIRTS
The Fat Duck ✸✸✸ MODERN   In the post–nouvelle cuisine era, the self-taught master chef Heston Blumenthal is hailed by many British food critics as running the "hottest and most exciting restaurant in the country." Who said that ice cream can't be made of crab, or that mashed potatoes can't be mixed with lime jelly? The grain-mustard ice cream and the red-cabbage gazpacho were firsts for us—and a delight. Don't become unduly alarmed—not all dishes are this experimental. Starters include the likes of goat cheese and roasted pepper with shaved truffle salad or game terrine with parsnips, spring onion spaghetti, and grape jelly. Delectable main dishes include grilled swordfish with a butternut mash and red-wine sauce; or filet of beef with pan-fried foie gras, wild mushroom flan, and beet balsamic jus.

1 High St., Bray. ✆ **01628/580333.** Reservations required. Dinner menus £80–£98 ($160–$196); set lunch £35 ($70). AE, DC, DISC, MC, V. Tues–Sat noon–1:45pm and 7–9:45pm; Sun noon–3pm. Leave the motorway at exit 4. On the roundabout, take the exit to Maidenhead (A404M/M4) and follow the dual Carriage Way to the roundabout at the M4. Take the 1st left exit to Maidenhead Central. At the 2nd roundabout, take the exit to Bray and Windsor (A308). Continue for 1km (a half-mile) and turn left at the sign to Bray Village (B3028). After entering the village, continue past the bottleneck; the Fat Duck is on the right-hand side adjacent to the Hinds Head Hotel.

CASTLE HILL SIGHTS
Jubilee Gardens   To celebrate Queen Elizabeth's Jubilee, the .8-hectare (2-acre) Jubilee Gardens were created inside the castle's main entrance. Filled with trees, roses, and flowering shrubs, they were created by Tom Stuart-Smith, a Chelsea Flower Show gold medalist. The gardens are the first established at Windsor Castle since the days of George IV in the 1820s. The gardens extend from the main gates of Windsor to St. George's Gate on Castle Hill. Color is provided by broad swaths of woodland perennials. White rambling roses clothing the old stone walls are particularly romantic.

Same hours and admission as Windsor Castle (see below).

Queen Mary's Dolls' House *Kids*   A palace in perfect miniature, the Doll's House was given to Queen Mary in 1923. It was a gift of members of the royal family, including the king, along with contributions made by some 1,500 tradesmen, artists, and authors. The house, designed by Sir Edwin Lutyens, was created on a scale of 1 to 12. It took 3 years to complete. Every item is a miniature masterpiece; each room is exquisitely furnished, and every item is made exactly to scale. Working elevators stop on every floor, and there is running water in all five bathrooms.

Castle Hill. ℂ **01753/831118** for recorded information. Admission is included in entrance to Windsor Castle. Mar–Oct daily 9:45am–5:15pm; Nov–Feb daily 9:45am–4:15pm. As with Windsor Castle, it's best to call ahead to confirm opening times.

St. George's Chapel ✿✿✿ A gem of the Perpendicular style, this chapel shares the distinction with Westminster Abbey of being a pantheon of English monarchs (Victoria is a notable exception). The present St. George's was founded in the late 15th century by Edward IV on the site of the original Chapel of the Order of the Garter (Edward III, 1348). You first enter the nave, which contains the tomb of George V and Queen Mary, designed by Sir William Reid Dick. Off the nave in the Urswick Chapel, the Princess Charlotte memorial provides an ironic touch; if she had survived childbirth in 1817, she, and not her cousin Victoria, would have ruled the British Empire. In the aisle are tombs of George VI and Edward IV. The latest royal burial in this chapel was an urn containing the ashes of the late Princess Margaret. The Edward IV "Quire," with its imaginatively carved 15th-century choir stalls, evokes the pomp and pageantry of medieval days. In the center is a flat tomb, containing the vault of the beheaded Charles I, along with Henry VIII and his third wife, Jane Seymour.

Castle Hill. ℂ **01753/848888**. www.stgeorges-windsor.org. Admission is included in entrance to Windsor Castle. Mon–Sat 10am–4:15pm, last admission 4pm. Closed for a few days in June and Dec.

Windsor Castle ✿✿✿ William the Conqueror first ordered a castle built on this location, and since his day it has been a fateful spot for English sovereigns: King John cooled his heels at Windsor while waiting to put his signature on the Magna Carta at nearby Runnymede; Charles I was imprisoned here before losing his head; Queen Bess did some renovations; Victoria mourned her beloved Albert, who died at the castle in 1861; the royal family rode out much of World War II behind its sheltering walls; and when Queen Elizabeth II is in residence, the royal standard flies. With 1,000 rooms, Windsor is the world's largest inhabited castle.

The apartments display many works of art, armor, three Verrio ceilings, and several 17th-century Gibbons carvings. Several works by Rubens adorn the King's Drawing Room. In the relatively small King's Dressing Room is a Dürer, along with Rembrandt's portrait of his mother and Van Dyck's triple portrait of Charles I. Of the apartments, the grand reception room, with its Gobelin tapestries, is the most spectacular.

George IV's elegant **Semi-State Chambers** ✿✿ are open only from the end of September until the end of March. They were created by the king in the 1820s as part of a series of royal apartments designed for his personal use. Seriously damaged in 1992 by fire, they have been returned to their former glory, with lovely antiques, paintings, and decorative objects. The Crimson Drawing Room is evocative of the king's flamboyant taste, with its crimson silk damask hangings and sumptuous art.

It is recommended that you take a free guided tour of the castle grounds, including the Jubilee Gardens. Guides are very well informed and recapture the rich historical background of the castle.

In our opinion, the Windsor **Changing of the Guard** ✿ is a more exciting experience than the London exercises. The guard marches through the town whether the court is in residence or not, stopping the traffic as it wheels into the castle to the tunes of a full regimental band; when the queen is not here, a drum-and-pipe band is mustered. From April to July, the ceremony takes place Monday to Saturday at 11am. In winter, the guard is changed every 48 hours Monday to Saturday. It's best to call ℂ **020/7766-7304** for a schedule.

Castle Hill. ℂ **01753/83118**. www.royalcollection.org.uk. Admission £14 ($28) adults, £13 ($26) students and seniors, £8 ($16) children 16 and younger, £37 ($74) family of 4 (2 adults and 3 children 16 and younger). Mar–Oct daily 9:45am–5:15pm; Nov–Feb daily 9:45am–4:15pm. Last admission 1 hr. before closing. Closed for periods in Apr, June, and Dec when the royal family is in residence.

Windsor Farm Shop 🌟 *Finds*   Had any of the queen's jars of jam lately, maybe her homemade pork pie, or a bottle of her special brew? If not, head for this outlet, selling produce from her estates outside Windsor, including pheasants and partridges bagged at royal shoots. The cream, yogurt, ice cream, and milk come from the two Royal Dairy farms. The meat counter is especially awesome, with its cooked hams and massive ribs of beef. The steak-and-ale pies are especially tasty. You can also purchase 15-year-old whisky from Balmoral Castle in Scotland. Stock up on the queen's vittles and head for a picnic in the area.

Datchet Rd., Old Windsor. ℂ **01753/623800**. www.windsorfarmshop.co.uk. Free admission. Mon–Sat 9am–5pm; Sun 10am–4pm.

NEARBY ETON COLLEGE 🌟🌟

Eton is home of what is arguably the most famous public school (Americans would call it a private school) in the world. From Windsor Castle's ramparts, you can look down on the river and onto the famous playing fields of Eton.

To get here, take a train from Paddington Station, go by car, or take the Green Line bus to Windsor. If you go by train, you can walk from the station to the campus. By car, take the M4 to exit 5 to go straight to Eton.

Insider's tip: Parking is likely to be a problem, so we advise turning off the M4 at exit 6 to Windsor; you can park here and take an easy stroll past Windsor Castle and across the Thames Bridge. Follow Eton High Street to the college.

Eton College (ℂ **01753/671000;** www.etoncollege.com) was founded by 18-year-old Henry VI in 1440. Some of England's greatest men, notably the duke of Wellington, have played on these fields. Twenty prime ministers were educated here, as well as such literary figures as George Orwell, Aldous Huxley, Ian Fleming, and Percy Bysshe Shelley, who, during his years at Eton (1804–10), was called "Mad Shelley" or "Shelley the Atheist" by his fellow pupils. Prince William, second in line to the throne, was a student here. If it's open, take a look at the Perpendicular chapel, with its 15th-century paintings and reconstructed fan vaulting.

The history of Eton College since its inception in 1440 is depicted in the **Museum of Eton Life,** Eton College (ℂ **01753/671000**), located in vaulted wine cellars under College Hall, which were originally used as a storehouse by the college's masters. The displays, ranging from formal to extremely informal, include a turn-of-the-20th-century boy's room, schoolbooks, and canes used by senior boys to apply punishment.

Admission to the school and museum is £4.20 ($8.40) for adults and £3.45 ($6.90) for seniors and children 14 and younger. You can also take guided tours for £5.50 ($11) adults or £4.50 ($9) seniors and children. Eton College is open to the public from March 25 to April 20 and July 2 to September 5 daily 10:30am to 4:30pm, and April 21 to July 1 and September 6 to October 1 daily from 2:30 to 4:30pm. *Note:* These dates vary every year and Eton may close for special occasions. It's best to call.

MORE TO DO IN & AROUND WINDSOR

Windsor is largely Victorian, with lots of brick buildings and a few remnants of Georgian architecture. In and around the castle are two cobblestone streets, Church and

Market, which have antiques shops, silversmiths, and pubs. After lunch or tea, you can stroll along the 5km (3-mile) aptly named **Long Walk.**

Savill Garden, Wick Lane, Englefield Green, Egham, and Surrey are all in **Windsor Great Park** ⚘ (© **01753/860222;** www.thecrownestate.co.uk), which is signposted from Windsor, Egham, and Ascot. Started in 1932, the 14-hectare (35-acre) garden is one of the finest. The display starts in spring with rhododendrons, camellias, and daffodils beneath the trees; then throughout the summer are spectacular displays of flowers and shrubs presented in a natural and wild state. It's open daily year-round (except at Christmas) from 10am to 6pm (to 4pm in winter). There is no admission charge, except for the Savill Garden. From March to October admission prices are £7 ($14) adults, £6.50 ($13) seniors, and £3.50 ($7) ages 6 to 16; November to February it's £5 ($10) adults, £4.50 ($9) seniors, and £2 ($4) for children. Family tickets range from £12 to £18 ($24–$36), and kids 5 and under go in free. The location is 8km (5 miles) from Windsor along the A30; turn off at Wick Road and follow the signs to the gardens. The nearest rail station is at Egham; you'll need to take a taxi a distance of 5km (3 miles). A self-service restaurant and gift shop is on-site.

Adjoining Savill Garden are the **Valley Gardens,** full of shrubs and trees in a series of wooded natural valleys running to the water. It's open daily year-round; entrance to the gardens is free, though parking is £3 ($6) per vehicle.

On the B3022 Bracknell/Ascot Road, outside Windsor, **LEGOLAND** (© **0870/ 504-0404;** www.lego.com/legoland), a 61-hectare (150-acre) theme park, opened in 1996. Although a bit corny, it's fun for the entire family. Attractions, spread across five main activity centers, include Duplo Gardens, offering a boat ride, puppet theater, and waterworks, plus a Miniland, showing European cities or villages re-created in minute detail from millions of Lego bricks. Enchanted Forest has treasure trails, a castle, and animals created from Lego bricks. Dragon Knight's Castle takes you back to the days of knights and dragons and includes a blazing dragon roller coaster. The park is open daily from 10am to 5pm from mid-March to October (until 7pm during school holidays). Admission varies through the season, starting at £34 ($68) for adults, £26 ($52) for seniors and children 3 to 15 (free for children 2 and younger).

Only 5km (3 miles) south of Windsor is **Runnymede,** the 75-hectare (188-acre) meadow on the south side of the Thames, in Surrey, where it's believed that King John put his seal on the Great Charter after intense pressure from his feudal barons and lords. Runnymede is also the site of the John F. Kennedy Memorial, an acre of ground given to the United States by the people of Britain. The memorial, a large block of white stone, is clearly signposted and reached after a short walk. The pagoda that shelters it was placed here by the American Bar Association to acknowledge the fact that American law stems from the English system. The historic site, to which there is free access all year, lies beside the Thames, 1km (½ mile) west of the hamlet of Old Windsor on the south side of the A308. If you're driving on the M25, exit at Junction 13. The nearest rail connection is at Egham, 1km (½ mile) away. Trains depart from London's Waterloo Station and take about 25 minutes.

TOURS OF WINDSOR

The tourist office can put you in touch with a Blue Badge (official) guide to lead you on a **walking tour** of town. The cost depends upon the number of people and the length of the tour. Advance booking is essential.

The best way to see the area around Windsor is from the water. Informative **boat tours** depart from Windsor's main embarkation point along Windsor Promenade,

Barry Avenue, for a 40-minute round-trip to Boveney Lock. The cost is £4.90 ($9.80) for adults, £2.45 ($4.90) for children. You can also take a 2-hour tour through the Boveney Lock and up past stately private riverside homes, the Bray Film Studios, Queens Eyot, and Monkey Island for £7.80 ($16) for adults, £3.90 ($7.80) for children. Of all the tours offered, we find this one the most scenic, insightful, and evocative. There's also a 45-minute tour from Runnymede on board the *Lucy Fisher*, a replica of a Victorian paddle steamer. You pass Magna Carta Island, among other sights. This tour costs £4.90 ($9.80) for adults, £2.45 ($4.90) for children. In addition, longer tours between Maidenhead and Hampton Court are offered. The boats offer light refreshments and have a well-stocked bar, plus the decks are covered in case of an unexpected shower. Tours are operated by **French Brothers, Ltd.,** Clewer Boathouse, Clewer Court Road, Windsor (℡ **01753/851900;** www.boat-trips.co.uk).

SHOPPING

For a survey of the best antiques for sale in Windsor, walk through the shops on **High Street, King Edward Court,** and **Peascod Street.**

Windsor Royal Station, the shopping center at the main railway station (℡ **01753/ 797070**), has a concentration of shops, often with London connections such as Liberty's Department Store.

If you're not going to Scotland, head for the **Edinburgh Woollen Mill,** 10 Castle Hill (℡ **01753/855151**), with the finest selection of Scottish knitwear and tartans in Windsor. A colorful traditional English perfumery, **Woods of Windsor,** Queen Charlotte Street (℡ **01753/868125**), dates from 1770. It offers soaps, shampoos, scented drawer liners, and hand and body lotions, all prettily packaged in pastel-flower and bright old-fashioned wraps. At **Billings & Edmonds,** 132 High St., Eton (℡ **01753/ 861348**), you may think you've blundered into a time warp. This distinctive clothing store supplies school wear, suits made to order, and a complete line of cuff links, shirts, ties, and accessories. **Asquith's Teddy Bear Shop,** 33 High St., Eton (℡ **01753/ 831200**), appeals to your inner child with every bear imaginable, including Winnie and Paddington. Bear clothes from dungarees to Eton College uniforms mix with more than 500 teddy bears in stock. The store also sells furniture for the bears.

WINDSOR AFTER DARK

Except for pub life, it's fairly quiet. The major cultural venue is **Theatre Royal,** Thames Street (℡ **01753/853888;** www.theatreroyalwindsor.co.uk), with a tradition of putting on plays that goes back 2 centuries. The theater is one of the finest regional theaters in England, often drawing first-rate actors or stars from London's West End. During the 6 weeks preceding Christmas, a series of pantomimes are presented. The box office is open Monday to Saturday 10am to 8pm (call the phone number above for bookings). Performances are Monday to Saturday at 8pm, with matinees on Thursday at 2:30pm and Saturday at 4:45pm. Tickets cost between £10 and £106 ($20–$212).

SIDE TRIPS FROM WINDSOR

If you have time to spare, you can take any number of fascinating excursions. But if you can squeeze in only one, make it Hughenden Manor (see below).

HUGHENDEN MANOR: DISRAELI CALLED IT HOME

Hughenden Manor ✹✹   This country manor not only gives insight into the age of Victoria but also acquaints us with a remarkable man: Benjamin Disraeli, one of the most enigmatic figures of 19th-century England. At age 21, "Dizzy" anonymously published his five-volume novel, *Vivian Grey*. In 1839, he married an older widow for her money, though they apparently developed a most harmonious relationship. He entered politics in 1837 and continued writing novels, his later ones meeting with more acclaim.

In 1848, Disraeli acquired Hughenden Manor, a country house that befitted his fast-rising political and social position. He served briefly as prime minister in 1868, but his political fame rests on his stewardship as prime minister from 1874 to 1880. He became friends with Queen Victoria, who in 1877 paid him the rare honor of a visit. In 1876, Disraeli became earl of Beaconsfield; he died in 1881. Instead of being buried at Westminster Abbey, he preferred the simple little graveyard of Hughenden Church.

Today, Hughenden houses an odd assortment of memorabilia, including a lock of Disraeli's hair, letters from Victoria, and a portrait of Lord Byron.

High Wycombe. ⓒ 01494/755573. www.nationaltrust.org.uk. Admission £7 ($14) adults, £3.50 ($7) children, £18 ($36) family ticket; garden only £2.90 ($5.80) adults, £2.10 ($4.20) children. Mar–Oct Wed–Sun 1–5pm. Closed Nov–Feb and Good Friday. From Windsor take M4 (toward Reading), then A404 to A40. Continue north of High Wycombe on A4128 for about 2.5km (1½ miles). From London (Heathrow Airport), catch coach A40 (operated by Carousel Buses) to High Wycombe, then board a Beeline bus (High Wycombe–Aylesbury no. 323 or 324).

WEST WYCOMBE 🍿

Snuggled in the Chiltern Hills 48km (30 miles) west of London and 24km (15 miles) northwest of Windsor, the village of West Wycombe still has an atmosphere of the early 18th century. The thatched roofs have been replaced by tiles, and some of the buildings have been rebuilt, but the village is still 2 centuries removed from the present day.

From Windsor, take the M4 (toward Reading), then the A404 to the A40. Signs to follow en route include MAIDENHEAD, MARLOW, and OXFORD. If you previously visited Hughenden Manor, the village of West Wycombe lies immediately to the west. Public transportation is awkward, but the Chiltern Line from London stops at High Wycombe, from which you can catch a bus from the station to West Wycombe or hail a taxi.

A visit to West Wycombe wouldn't be complete without a tour of **West Wycombe Park,** seat of the Dashwood family. Now owned by the National Trust, it's of both historical and architectural interest. The house is one of the best examples of Palladian-style architecture in England. The interior is lavishly decorated with paintings and antiques from the 18th century.

In the mid–18th century, Sir Francis Dashwood began an ambitious building program at West Wycombe. His strong interest in design led Sir Francis to undertake a series of monuments and parks that are still among the finest in the country.

Sir Francis also commissioned the excavation of a cave on the estate to serve as a meeting place for the notorious Hellfire Club, which spent its time partying and drinking. The cave is about 1km (a half-mile) long, filled with stalactites and stalagmites, and dotted with statues.

The house and grounds are open April to May Sunday to Thursday 2 to 6pm, June to August Sunday to Thursday 2 to 6:30pm. Admission is £6 ($12) for adults, £3 ($6) for children, and £15 ($30) for a family ticket. If you wish to visit only the grounds (Apr–Aug), the cost is £3 ($6). The caves are open daily April to October 11am to 5:30pm; off-season hours are only on Saturday and Sunday 11am to 5:30pm. Admission is £5 ($10) for adults, £4 ($8) for seniors and children. The cave tour includes stops for talks about former Hellfire members; it lasts 30 minutes. For more information, call the West Wycombe Estate Office at West Wycombe (© **01494/513569**) or the caves at © **01494/533739** (www.hellfirecaves.co.uk).

Other sights include the **Church of St. Lawrence,** perched on West Wycombe Hill and topped by a huge golden ball. Parts of the church date from the 13th century; its interior was copied from a 3rd-century Syrian sun temple. The view from the hill is worth the trek up. Near the church stands the **Dashwood Mausoleum,** built in a style derived from Constantine's Arch in Rome.

After your tour, head for **George & Dragon,** High Street (© **01494/464414;** www.george-and-dragon.co.uk), for a pint or a good, inexpensive lunch. In a building that dates from 1720, this former coaching inn has a cheerful log fire, a comfortable-size bar (which gets crowded on weekends), and an impressive oak staircase with its own ghost. A separate room is open to children, as well as a children's play area and a garden for dining outside. If you want to stay over, eight cozily furnished rooms with private bathroom, phone, TV, beverage maker, and hair dryer cost £75 ($150) for a double, or £80 ($160) for a four-poster room, including breakfast.

CLIVEDEN: FORMER HOME OF LADY ASTOR

Cliveden 🎕🎕   Now a National Trust property, Cliveden, former home of Lady Astor, stands on a constructed terrace of mature gardens high above the Thames. The estate's original mansion and sweeping lawns were created by William Winde in 1666 for the second duke of Buckingham. Later, the father of King George III reared his sons here. After a fire in 1795, Sir Charles Barry, the architect of the Houses of Parliament, converted the house into its present gracefully symmetrical form. A soaring clock tower was added to one side as a later Victorian folly. When the house was sold by the duke of Southerland to the Astors in 1893, Queen Victoria lamented the passage. The house remained part of the Astor legacy, a repository of a notable collection of paintings and antiques, until 1966.

The surrounding **gardens** have a distinguished variety of plantings, ranging from Renaissance-style topiary to meandering forest paths with vistas of statuary and flowering shrubs. Garden features are a glade garden, a magnificent parterre, and an amphitheater where "Rule Britannia" was played for the first time. There are 150 hectares (375 acres) of gardens and woodland to explore.

16km (10 miles) northwest of Windsor. © 01628/605069. Admission to house and grounds £7.50 ($15) for adults, £3.70 ($7.40) for children, family ticket £19 ($38). Grounds mid-Mar to Oct daily 11am–6pm, Nov–Dec 11am–4pm; house Apr–Oct Thurs and Sun 3–5:30pm (3 rooms of the mansion are open to the public, as is the Octagon Temple, with its rich mosaic interior). The estate is reached by private car. From Windsor, follow M4 toward Reading to the junction at no. 7 (direction Slough West). At the roundabout, turn left onto A4, signposted MAIDENHEAD. At the next roundabout, turn right, signposted BURNHAM. Follow the road for 4km (2½ miles) to a T junction with B476. The main gates to Cliveden are directly opposite.

Where to Stay & Dine

Cliveden House 🎕🎕🎕   Lady Astor's former estate is one of the most beautiful and luxurious hotels in England. Often acclaimed as "Hotel of the Year" by various rating services in England, this majestic property was home to a prince of Wales and a scattering of dukes before the Astors moved in. It was also a setting for the infamous Profumo scandal of the 1960s that shook the empire.

Rooms—named for famous guests who've stayed here, including T. E. Lawrence and Charlie Chaplin—are sumptuous, each furnished in impeccable taste. The bathrooms with deep marble tubs are among the finest we've seen in England. Less preferred are recently added rooms in the Clutton Wing. Nothing (except perhaps renting Lady Astor's bedroom itself) is more elegant here than walking down to the river and boarding a hotel boat for a champagne cruise before dinner. In the morning you can go horseback riding on the 150-hectare (371-acre) estate along the riverbank.

Cliveden, Taplow, Maidenhead, Berkshire SL6 0JF. (℗) 01628/668561. Fax 01628/661837. www.clivedenhouse.co.uk. 39 units. £415–£535 ($830–$1,070) double; from £640 ($1,280) suite. Rates include English breakfast. AE, DC, MC, V. **Amenities:** 3 restaurants; bar; 2 heated pools (1 indoor, 1 outdoor); 3 tennis courts (1 indoor, 2 outdoor); squash court; health club; spa w/steam rooms; billiard room; room service; babysitting; laundry service; dry cleaning. *In room:* A/C (in some rooms), TV, hair dryer, safe.

THE COTTAGE WHERE MILTON WROTE *PARADISE LOST*

The modern residential town of **Gerrards Cross** is often called the Beverly Hills of England, as it attracts many wealthy Londoners, among others. To the north of it is **Chalfont St. Giles,** where poet John Milton lived during the Great Plague in 1665. To reach it, take the A355 north from Windsor for 74km (46 miles), bypassing Beaconsfield until you come to the signposted cutoff for Chalfont St. Giles to the east.

Chalfont St. Giles today is a typical English village, though its history goes back to Roman times. The charm of the village is in its center, with shops, pubs, and cafes clustered around the green and the village pond.

The 16th-century **John Milton's Cottage,** Chalfont St. Giles (℗) **01494/872313;** www.miltonscottage.org), is the site where the great poet completed *Paradise Lost* and started *Paradise Regained.* Its four rooms contain many relics and exhibits devoted to Milton. It is open March to October Tuesday to Sunday 10am to 1pm and 2 to 6pm, costing adults £4 ($8) and children 14 and younger £2 ($4).

2 Ascot

45km (28 miles) W of London

While following the royal buckhounds through Windsor Forest, Queen Anne decided to have a racecourse on Ascot Heath. The first race meeting at Ascot, which is directly south of Windsor at the southern end of Windsor Great Park, was held in 1711. Since then, the Ascot Racecourse has been a symbol of high society, as pictures of the royal family enjoying the races there, including the queen and Prince Philip, have been flashed around the world. Ladies: Be sure to wear a hat.

GETTING THERE

Trains travel between Waterloo in London and Ascot Station, which is about 10 minutes from the racecourse. The trip takes about 1 hour, and trains arrive roughly every 30 minutes during the day. For rail information, call (℗) **0845/748-4950** or visit **www.nationalrail.co.uk**.

Buses frequently depart from London's Victoria Coach Station. Call (℗) **0870/580-8080** for more information, or visit **www.nationalexpress.com**.

If you're driving from Windsor, take the A332 west.

WHERE TO STAY & DINE

The entire town of Ascot and its racecourse don't even appear in budget guides to England. If you are a frugal traveler you can visit just for the day, returning to London or elsewhere for the night. Ascot is known for some superb, but pricey, inns, catering only to the well-heeled horsey set. If you want an affordable room, ask for one of the least expensive accommodations at the Brockenhurst (see below).

Brockenhurst *(Value* A small, tastefully refurbished 1905 Edwardian hotel of charm and distinction, Brockenhurst is conveniently situated near shops and the train station. Bedrooms are generally spacious. Well-appointed and well-maintained rooms are mostly modern, though some contain antiques. Classy and reasonably priced, this is a very good alternative to the pricey Royal Berkshire or Berystede.

Brockenhurst Rd., S. Ascot, Berkshire SL5 9HA. (C) **01344/621912.** Fax 01344/873252. www.brockenhurst.com. 20 units. £100–£120 ($200–$240) double. Rates include continental breakfast. AE, MC, V. Free parking. **Amenities:** Restaurant; bar; babysitting; laundry service. *In room:* TV, coffeemaker, hair dryer, trouser press.

Macdonald Berystede Hotel & Spa ⭐ This hotel just south of Ascot is a Victorian fantasy of medieval towers, steeply pitched roofs, and a landscaped garden. Drawing racegoers and businesspeople, it also caters to conferences (at which time it's best avoided). With their high ceilings and chintz, rooms evoke a private country house. The best rooms are in the main house and are more spacious and better decorated. Most of the other rooms are in a more modern annex with less character. For optimum sunshine and more room, try to book room no. 360 or 369. A roof terrace has been installed for summer dining.

Bagshot Rd., Sunninghill Ascot, Berkshire SL5 9JH. (C) **0870/400-81111** or 01344/623311, or 888/892-0038 in the U.S. Fax 01344/872301. www.berystede.com. 126 units. £210 ($420) double; from £268 ($536) suite. AE, DC, MC, V. Free parking. Take A330 2.5km (1½ miles) south of Ascot. **Amenities:** Restaurant; bar; indoor swimming pool; health club; spa; room service; babysitting; laundry service; dry cleaning. *In room:* A/C, TV, Wi-Fi, minibar, beverage maker, hair dryer, iron, trouser press, safe.

The Royal Berkshire ⭐⭐ This is a prestigious and elegant hotel with a rich history. Built in Queen Anne style in 1705, it housed the Churchill family for many years. The stylish rooms are divided between the main house and an annex. All rooms are spacious with thick carpeting and large comfortable beds. While the annex rooms are exceedingly comfortable and well furnished, they aren't equal to those in the main building. If you want the character of old England, opt for the main building.

London Rd., Sunninghill, Ascot, Berkshire SL5 0PP. (C) **01344/623322.** Fax 01344/627100. www.ramadajarvis.co.uk. 63 units. £140–£200 ($280–$400) double; £195–£275 ($390–$550) suite. AE, DC, MC, V. Free parking. Take A322 3km (2 miles) northeast of Ascot. **Amenities:** Restaurant; bar; indoor heated pool; 2 outdoor tennis courts; health club; spa; sauna; room service; babysitting; laundry service; dry cleaning. *In room:* TV, high-speed Internet, fridge, beverage maker, hair dryer, trouser press.

ASCOT RACECOURSE ⭐

Ascot Racecourse, High Street ((C) **0870/722-7227;** www.ascot.co.uk), England's largest and most prestigious course, is open throughout the year. The facility hosts 27 days of racing yearly. The highlight of the Ascot social season is the **Royal Meeting** (or **Royal Week**), when many women wear fancy hats and white gloves. Excellent racing also takes place on De Beers Diamond Day (fourth Sat in July) and during the Festival at Ascot (last Fri, Sat, and Sun in Sept), when the prize money usually exceeds £1 million ($2 million) per event.

You can buy tickets for one of three distinctly different observation areas, known as "enclosures." These include the Members Enclosure, which, during the Royal Meeting (5 days in June), is known as the Royal Enclosure. Also available are the Tattersalls Enclosure, largest of the three; and the Silver Ring, which does not enjoy direct access to the paddocks and has traditionally been the site of most of Ascot's budget seating. Except during the Royal Meeting, newcomers can usually secure viewing space in the Member's Enclosure, but only if they call ahead to confirm that space is available.

Finds Golf, Goldfinger & Posh Decadence

One of Europe's greatest hotels lies only 30 minutes from London's West End and in close proximity to Ascot and Windsor. It's **Stoke Park Club,** Park Road, Stoke Poges, Buckinghamshire SL2 4PG (© **01753/717171;** www.stokepark club.com). Golfers from all over the world flock to the 27-hole golf course designed by celebrated architect Harry Shapland Colt. James Bond defeated Goldfinger on its 18th green in 1964. Each bedroom or suite is individually decorated with antiques, paintings, and original prints, and all bedrooms feature fireplaces. Some bedrooms open onto balconies. Double rooms range from £285 to £345 ($570–$690) per night. The hotel has three indoor tennis courts, six Wimbledon-standard grass tennis courts, and four all-weather tennis courts; a gym; a spa; an indoor heated pool that incorporates two underwater massage areas with hydroseat Jacuzzis; and a steam room.

General admission prices range from £54 to £60 ($108–$120). Children 16 and younger are admitted free (except for the Royal Enclosure) if accompanied by an adult, and there is free supervised day care for children 7 and younger.

Beginning January 1 every year, you can arrange advance bookings for guaranteed seating in the most desirable areas during the most popular races. Write for tickets to the Secretary's Office, Ascot Racecourse, Ascot, Berkshire SL5 7JN, or book at www.ascot.co.uk. Credit cards are accepted at © **0870/727-1234.** Car parking is free except on June 22 and July 27 (both 2009 dates), and during the Festival Meeting in September.

3 Henley-on-Thames & the Royal Regatta

56km (35 miles) W of London

At the eastern edge of Oxfordshire, Henley-on-Thames, a small town and resort on the river at the foothills of the Chilterns, is the headquarters of the **Royal Regatta,** held annually in late June and early July. Henley, which lies on a stretch of the Thames that's known for its calm waters, unobstructed bottom, and predictable currents, is a rower's mecca. The regatta, which dates from the first years of Victoria's reign, is the major competition among international oarsmen and oarswomen, who find it both challenging and entertaining.

The Elizabethan buildings, tearooms, and inns along the town's High Street will live up to your preconception of an English country town. Henley-on-Thames is an excellent stopover en route to Oxford, though its fashionable inns are far from cheap.

ESSENTIALS

GETTING THERE Trains depart from London's Paddington Station but require a change at the junction in Twyford. More than 20 trains make the journey daily; the trip takes about 40 minutes. For rail information, call © **0845/748-4950** or visit **www.nationalrail.co.uk.**

About 10 buses depart every day from London's Victoria Coach Station for Reading. From Reading, take local bus no. 421 to Henley. These buses depart every hour. Call **0870/580-8080** for more information, or visit **www.nationalexpress.com.**

If you're driving from London, take the M4 toward Reading to Junction 819, then head northwest on the A4130.

VISITOR INFORMATION   The **Tourist Information Centre** is at Benson Lane, Crownmarsh Gifford Road (℗ **01491/823000;** www.visithenley-on-thames.co.uk). Winter hours are Monday to Saturday 10am to 3pm. Summer hours are Monday to Saturday 10am to 4pm.

An entire book could be written about these government-funded national trails—and indeed one has. It's the *National Trail Guide* by David Sharp (published by Aurum Press), detailing every twist and turn of the river.

WHERE TO STAY

It's impossible to find a room during the Royal Regatta, unless you've made reservations months in advance.

Hotel du Vin ★★   This riverside town has been invaded by the Hotel du Vin chain, which has taken a former Brakspears Brewery and imaginatively converted it into a fine example of industrial recycling. What has emerged is the poshest hotel in the area. Each of the beautifully furnished rooms, with their solid oak pieces and Shaker simplicity, is named after a vineyard. The decorator ordered that all the walls be painted in a "toast color," and installed thick wall-to-wall carpeting, with "dreamboat beds." Fine Egyptian linens and spectacular power showers in the bathrooms are further allures.

New St., Henley-on-Thames, Oxfordshire RG9 2BP. ℗ **01491/848400.** Fax 01491/848401. www.hotelduvin.co.uk. 43 units. £145–£195 ($290–$390) double; £210–£295 ($420–$590) suite. AE, DC, MC, V. Parking £15 ($30). **Amenities:** Restaurant; bar; billiards room; room service; laundry service. *In room:* TV, Wi-Fi, minibar, hair dryer.

Lenwade Guest House *Value*   Built in the early 1900s, this semidetached Victorian guesthouse is owned and operated by Jacquie and John Williams. Entering from a small courtyard filled with flowering vines and lush foliage, you'll see a 1.5m (5-ft.) stained-glass window thought to depict Joan of Arc. Another memorable detail is the winding staircase with its original handrails. The small to midsize bedrooms are individually decorated and comfortably furnished.

The Thames: Liquid History

Stretching for 289km (180 miles), **Thames Path** ★★ is one of more than a dozen government-protected national trails in England. You can choose any part of this river for exploration, our favorite being the "secret" section between Kelmscott and Oxford. Between the two towns, you will find 48km (30 miles) of lonely meadowlands of grazing sheep and cattle. You'll come across a stone-built bridge leading to a Thames-side pub with a mellow atmosphere. The Thames Valley has more than 60 river-bordering marinas and boatyards. The best deals are made with **Kris Cruisers** in Datchet (℗ **01753/543930;** www. kriscruisers.co.uk). The outfitter rents the largest fleet of fully equipped cruisers on the Thames, boats containing between two and eight berths. From Datchet you can travel upstream to Windsor and Eton or on to such towns as Maidenhead. Heading downstream you can visit such attractions as Runnymede, with its associations with the Magna Carta.

3 Western Rd., Henley-on-Thames, Oxfordshire RG9 1JL. ©/fax **01491/573468.** www.w3b-ink.com/lenwade. 4 units. £75 ($150) double. Rates include English breakfast. No credit cards. Free parking. **Amenities:** Breakfast room. *In room:* TV, Wi-Fi, beverage maker, hair dryer, iron.

Red Lion Hotel 🔓 This wisteria-covered coaching inn (ca. 1531) near Henley offers a guest list that reads like a hall of fame: Johnson and Boswell, George IV (who, it is said, consumed 14 mutton chops one night), and Charles I. You can book the room in which Princess Grace stayed when her brother Jack was competing in the Royal Regatta in 1947. Most of the well-furnished rooms overlook the Thames. Bedrooms are midsize to spacious. The three most expensive rooms sport four-poster beds.

Hart St., Henley-on-Thames, Oxfordshire RG9 2AR. © **01491/572161.** Fax 01491/410039. www.redlionhenley. co.uk. 26 units. £165–£175 ($330–$350) double. AE, MC, V. Free parking. **Amenities:** Restaurant; bar; room service; babysitting; laundry service; dry cleaning. *In room:* TV, Wi-Fi, beverage maker, hair dryer, trouser press.

WHERE TO DINE

Argyll ENGLISH/SCOTTISH This very Scottish pub, complete with tartan carpeting and framed prints of Scottish soldiers, is a popular lunch spot with locals. The homemade meals are the main attraction. They serve hearty portions of steak-and-kidney pie, shepherd's pie, and other favorites.

15 Market Place. © **01491/573400.** Main courses and platters £3.75–£13 ($7.50–$26). AE, MC, V. Sun–Thurs 10am–midnight; Fri–Sat 10am–1am.

THE HENLEY ROYAL REGATTA 🔓🔓

The Henley Royal Regatta, held the first week in July, is one of the country's premier racing events. For a close-up view from the Stewards' Enclosure, you'll need a guest badge, only obtainable through a member—in other words, you have to know someone to obtain special privileges. However, admission to the Regatta Enclosure is open to all. Entry fees are £30 to £80 ($60–$160). Information is available by writing to the Secretary, Henley Royal Regatta, Henley-on-Thames, Oxfordshire RG9 2LY (© **01491/572153;** www.hrr.co.uk).

During the annual 5-day event, up to 100 races are organized each day, with starts scheduled as frequently as every 5 minutes. This event is open only to all-male crews of up to nine at a time. In late June, rowing events for women are held at the 3-day Henley Women's Regatta.

If you want to float on the waters of the Thames yourself, stop by the town's largest and oldest outfitter, **Hobbs & Sons, Ltd.,** Station Road Boathouse (© **01491/ 572035;** www.hobbs-of-henley.com), established in 1870. Open daily from April to October from 8:30am to 5:30pm, Hobbs has an armada of watercraft including rowboats that rent for £10 to £13 ($20–$26) per hour. Motorboats can be rented for £20 to £50 ($40–$100) per hour. Prices include fuel. On the premises, a chandlery shop sells virtually anything a boat crew could need, as well as T-shirts and boaters' hats.

MUSEUM CELEBRATING THE THAMES

River & Rowing Museum *Finds* This museum celebrates the Thames and those oarsmen and oarswomen who row upon it. Opened by Queen Elizabeth in 1998, the museum, designed by English architect David Chipperfield, is the finest of its kind in Britain. A short walk south of Henley Bridge, it opens onto the banks of the Thames. The Rowing Gallery follows the saga of rowing from the days of the Greeks. It's all here: models of arctic whaleboats in the 1700s, elaborate Venetian gondolas fit for a doge, and coastal lifeboats that pulled many a victim from the cold waters of the

North Sea. In a more modern exhibit, you'll find the boat in which British oarsmen captured the gold medal in the Olympic Games at Atlanta in 1996. The museum reaches out to embrace the saga of the Thames itself, as well as the history of the regatta in Henley.

Mill Meadows. ⓒ 01491/415600. www.rrm.co.uk. Admission £3.50 ($7) adults; £2.50 ($5) ages 3–16; £10 ($20) family ticket for 4, £12 ($24) for 5, and £13 ($26) for 6. May–Aug daily 10am–5:30pm; Sept–Apr daily 10am–5pm.

SIDE TRIPS FROM HENLEY
A ROMANTIC BOAT TRIP TO A HISTORIC HOME
Mapledurham House *(Finds)*   The Blount family mansion lies beside the Thames in the unspoiled village of Mapledurham. In the house, you'll see the Elizabethan ceilings and the great oak staircase, as well as the portraits of the two beautiful sisters with whom the poet Alexander Pope, a frequent visitor here, fell in love. The family chapel, built in 1789, is a fine example of modern Gothic architecture. Cream teas with homemade cakes are available at the house. On the grounds, the last working water mill on the Thames still produces flour.

The most romantic way to reach this lovely old house is to take the boat that leaves the promenade next to Caversham Bridge at 2pm on Saturday, Sunday, and bank holidays from Easter to September. The journey upstream takes between 30 and 80 minutes, and the boat leaves Mapledurham again at 5pm for the return trip to Caversham, giving you plenty of time to walk through the house. The round-trip boat ride from Caversham costs £6 ($12) for adults and £4.50 ($9) for children. An additional landing fee of £2 ($4) adults and £1 ($2) for children is charged. You can get further details about the boat from **Thames Rivercruise Ltd.,** Pipers Island, Bridge Street, Caversham Bridge, Reading (ⓒ **01189/481088;** www.thamesrivercruise.co.uk).

Mapledurham. ⓒ 01189/723350. www.mapledurham.co.uk. Admission to house and mill £6.50 ($13) adults, £3 ($6) children 5–14, free for children 4 and younger. Sat–Sun and bank holidays 2–5:30pm. Closed Oct–Easter. From Henley-on-Thames, head south along A4155 toward Reading; at the junction with A329, head west; Mapledurham is signposted from this road. Or, take the boat trip described above.

THE WELLINGTON DUCAL ESTATE
Stratfield Saye House *(Kids)*   This combined house and country park provides tangible evidence of the fortune of the duke of Wellington and his descendants. The complex's centerpiece is the Stratfield Saye House, the home of the dukes of Wellington since 1817, when the 17th-century house was bought for the Iron Duke to celebrate his victory over Napoleon at the Battle of Waterloo. A grateful Parliament granted a large sum of money for its purchase. Many memories of the first duke remain in the house, including his billiard table, battle spoils, and pictures. The funeral carriage that once rested in St. Paul's Cathedral crypt is on display. In the gardens is the grave of Copenhagen, the charger ridden to battle at Waterloo by the first duke. There are also extensive landscaped grounds, together with a tearoom and gift shop.

If you're looking for greenery and lovely landscaping, you'll find it 5km (3 miles) away, on the opposite side of the A33 highway, at the **Wellington Country Park.**

1.5km (1 mile) west of Reading, beside A33 to Basingstoke. ⓒ 01256/882882. www.stratfield-saye.co.uk. Mon–Fri £7 ($14) adults, £6 ($12) students and seniors, £4 ($8) children; Sat–Sun £8 ($16) adults, £7 ($14) students, £5 ($10) children. Mar 20–24 and July 3–28 daily 11:30am–3:30pm. From Henley, head south along A1455.

Wellington Country Park *(Kids)* *(Finds)*   Under the same administration as Stratfield Saye, this favorite place for locals to picnic and stroll has a nice lake and miles of well-maintained walking paths. But a handful of attractions are inside as well: The park contains a riding school, a miniature steam railway, a deer park, and the Thames Valley Time Trail, a walk-through series of exhibits related to the geology of the region and the dinosaurs that once inhabited it.

Riseley, Reading, Berkshire RG7 1SP. © 01189/326444. www.wellington-country-park.co.uk. Admission £6 ($12) adults, £5 ($10) seniors and children 3–15, free for children 2 and younger. Park and exhibits Feb–Nov daily 10am–5:30pm.

MARLOW: RETREAT OF *THE COMPLEAT ANGLER*

This Thames-side town, 56km (35 miles) northwest of London and 13km (8 miles) east of Henley-on-Thames, is a miniature version of the better-known Henley. To reach it from Henley, take Route 4155 and just follow the signs. Many prefer its more pastoral look to the larger Henley.

Along this middle reach of the Thames is some of the most beautiful rural scenery in England, a land of green fields and deep woods, of stately mansions and parks. It was in these surroundings that Izaak Walton wrote his immortal work on fishing, *The Compleat Angler,* published in 1655. On the south bank of the river facing Marlow itself stood the inn in which he stayed. That inn still stands and is named after his work.

Where to Stay

Frankly, Marlow attracts mainly well-heeled fishermen who like to stay at the **Compleat Angler** (see below), a very pricey hotel because of its associations with Izaak Walton. If you're a frugal traveler and find yourself trapped in the area for the night, you can discover reasonable but hardly spectacular accommodations at **Glade End,** 2 Little Marlow Rd., Marlow, Buckinghamshire S17 1HD (© **01628/471334;** www. gladeend.com), where doubles go for £110 ($220) a night.

The Compleat Angler Hotel ★★

This hotel of charm and character blends architectural eras, including Queen Anne, Regency, Georgian, and Victorian. It occupies an emerald swath of lawns stretching down to the banks of the Thames. It's had a long and distinguished list of guests, including Percy Shelley and his wife, Mary, along with Dame Nellie Melba (for whom the peach dessert was named), J. M. Barrie (author of *Peter Pan*), and F. Scott Fitzgerald. The hotel is a well-organized and impeccably polite center of English chintz, predictably elegant bars, and very fine dining. Each room is outfitted like a private country home, with antiques or reproductions and plush, comfortable beds. The more expensive rooms look out on the Thames. The finest accommodations are in a modern wing with balconies overlooking the rushing weir. Modern bathrooms with separate showers are the order of the day.

Marlow Bridge, Bisham Rd., Marlow, Buckinghamshire SL7 1RG. © 01628/484444. Fax 01628/486388. www. compleatangler-hotel.co.uk. 64 units. £160–£260 ($320–$520) double; £290–£415 ($580–$830) suite. AE, DC, MC, V. **Amenities:** 2 restaurants; bar; room service; babysitting; laundry service; dry cleaning. *In room:* A/C, TV, minibar, beverage maker, hair dryer, iron, trouser press, safe.

Where to Dine

The Vanilla Pod ★★ FRENCH/ENGLISH   Michael Macdonald has struck out on his own with this absolutely delightful dining choice. In a tasteful dining room, known for its fine service, a truly excellent cuisine is offered on a menu that changes monthly to take advantage of the best produce in any season. Our starters on a visit were memorable, especially the endive tatin with foie gras and citrus sauce, or the carpaccio of beet with goat cheese and aged balsamic vinegar. We moved on to delight in a filet of venison with parsnip purée and a licorice sauce (don't knock it 'til you've tried it), and roasted squab with peppered apricots and a turnip compote. For dessert, we finished off with chocolate soup (that's right) and pistachio ice cream.

31 West St. ℂ **01628/898101.** Reservations required (as far in advance as possible). 2-course lunch £16 ($32), 3 courses £20 ($40); 3-course dinner £40 ($80); 7-course gourmand dinner £45 ($90). AE, MC, V. Tues–Sat noon–2pm and 7–10pm. Closed 2 weeks around Easter.

4 Oxford: The City of Dreaming Spires ⭐⭐

87km (54 miles) NW of London; 87km (54 miles) SE of Coventry

A walk down the long sweep of the High, one of the most striking streets in England; a mug of cider in one of the old student pubs; the sound of May Day dawn when choristers sing in Latin from Magdalen Tower; students in traditional gowns whizzing past on rickety bikes; towers and spires rising majestically; nude swimming at Parson's Pleasure; the roar of a cannon launching the bumping races; a tiny, dusty bookstall where you can pick up a valuable first edition—romantic Oxford is still here, but to get to it, you have to experience the bustling and crowded city that is also Oxford. You may be surprised by a never-ending stream of polluting buses and the fast-flowing pedestrian traffic. Surrounding the university are suburbs that keep growing, and not in a particularly attractive manner.

At any time of the year, you can enjoy a tour of the colleges. The Oxford Tourist Information Centre (see below) offers guided walking tours daily throughout the year. Just don't mention the other place (Cambridge), and you shouldn't have any trouble. Comparisons between the two universities are inevitable: Oxford is better known for the arts, Cambridge more for the sciences.

The city predates the university—in fact, it was a Saxon town in the early part of the 10th century. By the 12th century, Oxford was growing in reputation as a seat of learning, at the expense of Paris, and the first colleges were founded in the 13th century. The story of Oxford is filled with conflicts too complex and detailed to elaborate upon here. Suffice it to say, the relationship between town and gown wasn't as peaceful as it is today. Riots often flared, and both sides were guilty of abuses. Nowadays, the young people of Oxford take out their aggressiveness in sporting competitions.

Ultimately, the test of a great university lies in the caliber of the people it turns out. Oxford can name-drop a mouthful: Roger Bacon, Sir Walter Raleigh, John Donne, Sir Christopher Wren, Samuel Johnson, William Penn, John Wesley, William Pitt, Matthew Arnold, Lewis Carroll, Harold Macmillan, Graham Greene, A. E. Housman, T. E. Lawrence, and many others. Women were not allowed until 1920, but since then many have graduated from Oxford and gone on to fame—Indira Gandhi and Margaret Thatcher both graduated from Somerville College.

ESSENTIALS

GETTING THERE Trains from Paddington Station reach Oxford in 1½ hours. Five trains run every hour. A cheap, same-day round-trip ticket costs £18 ($36). For more information, call ℂ **0845/748-4950** or visit **www.networkrail.co.uk.**

Stagecoach (ℂ **01865/772250;** www.stagecoachbus.com) operates the Oxford Tube, with buses leaving London at the rate of three to five per hour, costing £12 ($24) one-way or £10 ($20) if you're a student.

If you're driving, take the M40 west from London and just follow the signs. Traffic and parking are a disaster in Oxford. However, there are four large park-and-ride parking lots on the north, south, east, and west of the city's ring road, all well marked.

Parking is 60p ($1.20) per car. From 9:30am on and all day Saturday, you pay £2 ($4) for a round-trip ticket for a bus ride into the city, which drops you off at St. Aldate's Cornmarket or Queen Street to see the city center. The buses run every 8 to 10 minutes in each direction. There is no service on Sunday. The parking lots are on the Woodstock road near the Peartree traffic circle, on the Botley road toward Farringdon, on the Abingdon road in the southeast, and on the A40 toward London.

VISITOR INFORMATION   The **Oxford Tourist Information Centre** is at 15–16 Broad St. (© **01865/252200;** www.oxford.gov.uk/index.cfm). The center sells a comprehensive range of maps, brochures, and souvenir items, as well as the famous Oxford University T-shirt. Guided walking tours leave from the center daily (see "Exploring the City," later in this chapter). The center is open Monday to Saturday 9:30am to 5pm, and Sunday and bank holidays in summer 10am to 1pm and 1:30 to 3:30pm.

GETTING AROUND   The **Oxford Bus Company,** 395 Cowley Rd. (© **01865/ 785400;** www.oxfordbus.co.uk), has green Park-and-Ride buses that leave from four parking lots in the city using the north-south or east-west routes. A round-trip ticket costs £2 ($4). Their Airline buses are blue and travel to Heathrow and Gatwick. A one-way ticket from Oxford to Heathrow costs £18 ($36) for adults, £9.30 ($19) for children aged 5 to 15. A one-way ticket from Oxford to Gatwick costs £22 ($44) for adults, £11 ($22) for children aged 5 to 15. The company's red local buses cover 15 routes in all suburbs, with a day pass allowing unlimited travel for £3.30 ($6.60). Weekly and monthly passes are available.

The competition, **Stagecoach,** Unit 4, Horsepath, Cowley (© **01865/772250;** www.stagecoachbus.com/oxfordshire), uses blue-and-cream minibuses and coaches colored red, blue, and orange. City buses leave from Queen Street in Oxford's city center. A 1-day ticket that allows unlimited travel within Oxford city (called Dayrider) costs £3.30 ($6.60).

WHERE TO STAY

Accommodations in Oxford are limited, though motels have sprouted on the outskirts of town—good for those who want modern amenities. If you have a car, you may want to consider country houses or small B&Bs on the outskirts. Bedrooms, albeit expensive ones, are also provided at Le Manoir aux Quat' Saisons (p. 252).

The **Oxford Tourist Information Centre** (© **01865/252200**), operates a year-round room-booking service for a £5 ($10) fee, plus a 10% refundable deposit. If you'd like to seek lodgings on your own, the center has a list of accommodations, maps, and guidebooks.

EXPENSIVE

Macdonald Randolph Hotel ✲   Since 1864, the Randolph has overlooked St. Giles, the Ashmolean Museum, and the Cornmarket. The hotel is an example of how historic surroundings can be combined with modern conveniences to make for elegant accommodations. The lounges, though modernized, are cavernous enough for dozens of separate and intimate conversational groupings. The furnishings are traditional. Some rooms are quite large; others are a bit cramped. The double-glazing on the windows appears inadequate to keep out the noise of midtown traffic. We'd opt first for the more stylish and intimate Old Parsonage (see below) before checking in here.

Oxford

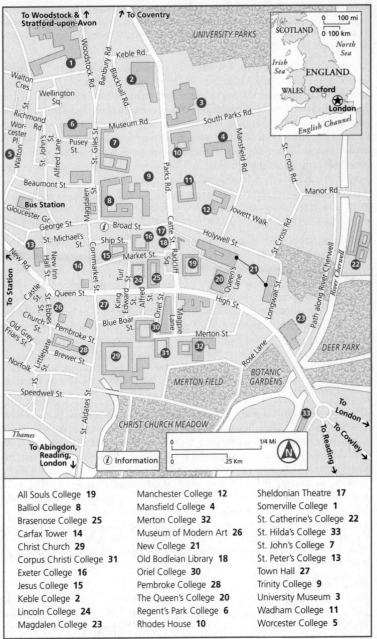

All Souls College **19**
Balliol College **8**
Brasenose College **25**
Carfax Tower **14**
Christ Church **29**
Corpus Christi College **31**
Exeter College **16**
Jesus College **15**
Keble College **2**
Lincoln College **24**
Magdalen College **23**

Manchester College **12**
Mansfield College **4**
Merton College **32**
Museum of Modern Art **26**
New College **21**
Old Bodleian Library **18**
Oriel College **30**
Pembroke College **28**
The Queen's College **20**
Regent's Park College **6**
Rhodes House **10**

Sheldonian Theatre **17**
Somerville College **1**
St. Catherine's College **22**
St. Hilda's College **33**
St. John's College **7**
St. Peter's College **13**
Town Hall **27**
Trinity College **9**
University Museum **3**
Wadham College **11**
Worcester College **5**

Beaumont St., Oxford, Oxfordshire OX1 2LN. © **0870/8304812.** Fax 01865/791678. www.randolph-hotel.com. 151 units. £175–£300 ($350–$600) double; from £400 ($800) suite. AE, DC, MC, V. Parking £23 ($46). Bus: 7. **Amenities:** Restaurant; 2 bars; concierge; room service; babysitting; laundry service; dry cleaning. *In room:* TV, CD player, minibar, coffeemaker, hair dryer, trouser press.

Malmaison Oxford Castle 🌟🌟 *Finds*

In a TripAdvisor poll of the top 10 quirkiest hotels in the world, the Malmaison in Oxford made the list. Formerly it was for inmates detained at Her Majesty's pleasure, and many aspects of prison life, including barred windows, have been retained. In a converted Victorian building, guest rooms are remodeled "cells" that flank two sides of a large central atrium, a space that rises three stories and is crisscrossed by narrow walkways like in one of those George Raft prison movies of the '30s. The former inmates never had it so good—great beds, mood lighting, power showers, satellite TV, and serious wines. In spite of its former origins, this is a stylish and comfortable place to stay.

3 Oxford Castle, Oxford OXI 1AY. © **01865/268400.** Fax 01845/3654247. www.malmaison.com. 94 units. £160 ($320) double; £290 ($580) suite. AE, DC, MC, V. Parking (prebooking required) £20 ($40). **Amenities:** 2 restaurants; bar; gym; room service; laundry service; dry cleaning. *In room:* TV/DVD, Wi-Fi, CD player, minibar, beverage maker.

Old Bank Hotel 🌟🌟

The first hotel created in the center of Oxford in 135 years, the Old Bank opened late in 1999 and immediately surpassed the traditional favorite, the Randolph (not reviewed), in style and amenities. Located on Oxford's main street and surrounded by some of its oldest colleges and sights, the building dates back to the 18th century and was indeed once a bank. The hotel currently features a collection of 20th-century British art handpicked by the owners. The bedrooms are comfortably and elegantly appointed, often opening onto views. A combination of velvet and shantung silk-trimmed linen bedcovers gives the accommodations added style.

92–94 High St., Oxford OX1 4BN. © **01865/799599.** Fax 01865/799598. www.oldbank-hotel.co.uk. 42 units. £175–£210 ($350–$420) double; £325 ($650) suite. AE, DC, MC, V. Free parking. Bus: 7. **Amenities:** Restaurant; bar; room service; babysitting; laundry service; dry cleaning. *In room:* A/C, TV, high-speed Internet, CD player, beverage maker, hair dryer, safe.

Old Parsonage Hotel 🌟🌟

This extensively renovated hotel, near St. Giles Church and Keble College, looks like an extension of one of the ancient colleges. Originally a 13th-century hospital, it was restored in the early 17th century. In the 20th century, a modern wing was added, and in 1991 it was completely renovated and made into a first-rate hotel. This intimate old hotel is filled with hidden charms such as tiny gardens in its courtyard and on its roof terrace. In this tranquil area of Oxford, you feel like you're living at one of the colleges yourself. The rooms are individually designed but not large; each of them opens onto the private gardens.

1 Banbury Rd., Oxford OX2 6NN. © **01865/310210.** Fax 01865/311262. www.oldparsonage-hotel.co.uk. 30 units. £160–£200 ($320–$400) double; £250 ($500) suite. AE, DC, MC, V. Free parking. Bus: 7. **Amenities:** Restaurant; bar; car and limo service for hire; room service; laundry service; dry cleaning. *In room:* A/C, TV, high-speed Internet, hair dryer, trouser press.

MODERATE

Bath Place Hotel 🌟🌟 *Finds*

Its owners took these 17th-century weavers' cottages and converted them into a small inn of charm and grace, one of the "secret addresses" of Oxford. Bath Place lies on a cobbled alleyway off Holywell Street in the center of Oxford between New College and Hertford College. Flemish weavers built the cottages around a tiny flagstone courtyard. The Turf Tavern, adjacent to the hotel, is the oldest in Oxford. The site has had a notorious history, especially when it was known as the Spotted Cow, as a center for illicit gambling, bear baiting, and cockfighting. Thomas Hardy mentioned the cottages in his novel *Jude the Obscure*. The address became a secret hideaway for the married Richard Burton and his "mistress," Elizabeth Taylor, when he was acting at the Oxford Playhouse. Completely refurbished to a high standard, the inn today offers comfortable and well-appointed bedrooms.

4–5 Bath Place, Oxford OX1 3SU. 🕐 **01865/791812.** Fax 01865/791834. www.bathplace.co.uk. 13 units. £100–£145 ($200–$290) double; £175 ($350) family suite. Rates include continental buffet or room-service breakfast. AE, DC, MC, V. Free parking. **Amenities:** Room service. *In room:* TV, minibar, beverage maker.

Mercure Eastgate Hotel 🕐

The Eastgate, built on the site of a 1600s structure, stands within walking distance of Oxford College and the city center. Recently refurbished, it offers modern facilities while somewhat retaining the atmosphere of an English country house. The bedrooms are well worn but still cozy and range in size from small to medium.

73 The High St., Oxford, Oxfordshire, OX1 4BE. 🕐 **0870/400-8201.** Fax 01865/791681. www.accorhotels.com. 63 units. £120–£160 ($240–$320) double. AE, DC, MC, V. Parking £13 ($26). Bus: 3, 4, 7, or 52. **Amenities:** Bar; room service; babysitting; laundry service; dry cleaning. *In room:* A/C, TV, minibar, beverage maker, hair dryer, iron, trouser press.

The Oxford Hotel

This is a good choice if you have a car; it's 3km (2 miles) north of the city center and hidden from traffic at the junction of A40 and A34. It attracts a lot of business travelers, but also visitors, and is a good base for exploring not only Oxford but also the Cotswolds, which are within easy reach. The M40 motorway is just a 13km (8-mile) drive away. Rooms are motel-like, with modern, contemporary furnishings that are comfortable and spacious.

Godstow Rd., Wolvercote Roundabout, Oxford, Oxfordshire OX2 8AL. 🕐 **01865/489988.** Fax 01865/489952. www.paramount-hotels.co.uk. 149 units. £105–£179 ($210–$358) double; £200–£289 ($400–$578) suite. AE, DC, MC, V. Free parking. Bus: 6. **Amenities:** Restaurant; bar; indoor heated pool; 2 squash courts; fitness center; spa; sauna; room service; laundry service; dry cleaning. *In room:* A/C, TV, Wi-Fi, beverage maker, hair dryer, trouser press, safe.

Weston Manor 🕐🕐

This 5.2-hectare (13-acre) manor has existed since the 11th century; portions of the present building date from the 14th and 16th centuries. The estate is the ancestral home of the earls of Abingdon and Berkshire. It was also an abbey until Henry VIII abolished the abbeys and assumed ownership of the property. Of course, there are ghosts: Mad Maude, the naughty nun who was burned at the stake for her "indecent and immoral" behavior, returns to haunt the Oak rooms. Most of the rooms are spacious and furnished with antiques (often four-poster beds). Bedrooms are divided between the main house and a former coach house that was skillfully converted into well-equipped guest rooms. Regardless of location, each bedroom is first-rate and extremely comfortable

Weston-on-the-Green, Oxfordshire OX25 3QL. 🕐 **01869/350621.** Fax 01869/350901. www.westonmanor.co.uk. 35 units. £121–£215 ($242–$430) double; £225 ($450) suite. Rates include English breakfast. AE, MC, V. Free parking. Drive 9.5km (6 miles) north of Oxford on A34. **Amenities:** Restaurant; bar; outdoor heated pool; room service. *In room:* A/C, TV, beverage maker, hair dryer, iron.

INEXPENSIVE

Dial House 🕐*Value*   Three kilometers (2 miles) east of the heart of Oxford, beside the main highway leading to London, is this country-style house originally built between 1924 and 1927. Graced with mock Tudor half-timbering and a prominent blue-faced sundial (from which it derives its name), it has cozy and recently renovated rooms. The owners, the Morris family, serve only breakfast in their bright dining room.

25 London Rd., Headington, Oxford, Oxfordshire OX3 7RE. ℂ **01865/425100.** Fax 01865/427388. www.oxford city.co.uk/accom/dialhouse. 8 units. £60–£75 ($120–$150) double; £75–£95 ($150–$190) family room. Rates include English breakfast. AE, MC, V. Free parking. Bus: 2, 7, 7A, 7B, or 22. *In room:* TV, beverage maker, hair dryer, safe, no phone.

The Galaxie Hotel   When it was built about a century ago, this redbrick hotel served as a plush private mansion for a prosperous local family. This little hotel is better than ever following a refurbishment when a conservatory lounge was added. Each of the well-maintained bedrooms is well furnished to a high standard. Although no meals other than breakfast are served, the hotel is within a short walk of at least five restaurants and two pubs. A public bus runs down Banbury Road to the center of Oxford.

180 Banbury Rd., Oxford, Oxfordshire OX2 7BT. ℂ **01865/515688.** Fax 01865/556824. www.galaxie.co.uk. 32 units, 28 with bathroom. £96–£125 ($192–$250) double. Rates include English breakfast. MC, V. Limited street parking. **Amenities:** Breakfast room; lounge. *In room:* TV, Wi-Fi, hair dryer, beverage maker.

Green Gables Guest House   This hotel was originally a large Edwardian private residence of a local toy manufacturer. Today's hosts, among the best in Oxford, continue to make improvements to this property. Many of the bedrooms are quite large, all in spick-and-span condition. The breakfast room is bright and inviting. Trees screen the house from the main road, and parking for eight cars is available.

326 Abingdon Rd., Oxford, Oxfordshire OX1 4TE. ℂ **01865/725870.** Fax 01865/723115. www.greengables.uk.com. 11 units. £72 ($144) double; £90–£100 ($180–$200) family room. Rates include English breakfast. AE, MC, V. Free parking. 1.6km (1 mile) south of Oxford on A4144. **Amenities:** Breakfast room; lounge. *In room:* TV, beverage maker.

Victoria House Hotel *Value*   Just minutes from the colleges, this centrally located hotel is one of the best deals for the price in the heart of Oxford, where everything is relatively expensive. You don't get glamour but you are offered renovated bedrooms in a sort of no-frills atmosphere. Many businesspeople not on expense accounts check in here during the week. A lot of university students gather in the basement of the hotel at the on-site bar, which features a resident DJ on weekends.

29 George St., Oxford OX1 2AY. ℂ **01865/727400.** Fax 01865/727402. www.victoriahouse-hotel.co.uk. 14 units. £85–£95 ($170–$190) double. Extra bed £15 ($30). AE, DC, MC, V. Parking £10 ($20). **Amenities:** Breakfast-only restaurant; bar. *In room:* TV, hair dryer.

WHERE TO DINE
VERY EXPENSIVE

Le Manoir aux Quat' Saisons ✸✸✸ MODERN FRENCH   Some 19km (12 miles) southeast of Oxford, Le Manoir aux Quat' Saisons offers the finest cuisine in the Midlands. The gray-and-honey-colored stone manor house, originally built by a Norman nobleman in the early 1300s, has attracted many famous visitors. Today, the restaurant's connection with France has been masterfully revived by the Gallic owner and chef, Raymond Blanc. His reputation for comfort and cuisine attracts guests from as far away as London. The menu is adjusted to take advantage of the best produce in any season. The best-loved dishes at Le Manoir are smoked haddock soup with sea bass tartare and caviar as a starter, followed by Cornish red mullet with a fricassee of squid. Longtime favorites are roast suckling pig in its own juices and roasted Anjou squab with a celeriac sauerkraut in a juniper-berry sauce. For a sweet finish, bite into a pastry filled with caramelized apples and honey and served with a ginger ice cream.

Accommodations are also available. Each very pricey room—rates are £400 ($800) for a double, from £850 ($1,700) for a suite—is decorated with luxurious beds and linens, ruffled canopies, and antique reproductions.

Church Rd., Great Milton, Oxfordshire. ✆ 800/845-4274 in the U.S., or 01844/278881. Fax 01844/278847. www. manoir.com. Reservations required. Main courses £40–£45 ($80–$90); lunch *menu du jour* £49 ($98); lunch or dinner *menu gourmand* £95 ($190). AE, DC, MC, V. Daily 12:15–2:30pm and 7:15–9:30pm. Take exit 7 off M40 and head along A329 toward Wallingford; look for signs for Great American Milton Manor about 1.6km (1 mile) after.

EXPENSIVE

Cherwell Boathouse Restaurant ✿ FRENCH/MODERN ENGLISH An Oxford landmark on the River Cherwell, this restaurant is owned by Anthony Verdin, who is assisted by a young crew. With an intriguing fixed-price menu, the cooks change the fare every 2 weeks to take advantage of the availability of fresh vegetables, fish, and meat. There is a very reasonable, even exciting, wine list. The kitchen is often cited for its "sensible combinations" of ingredients. The success of the main dishes is founded on savory treats such as grilled quail with garlic-and-oregano dressing; pan-fried medallions of beef with a shallot-and-truffle sauce, and chargrilled loin of pork with a chorizo-laced butter. A special treat is the grilled gray mullet with ratatouille accompanied by a basil-and-chili sauce. For dessert, indulge in the lemon-and-almond roulade. The style is sophisticated yet understated, with a heavy reliance on quality ingredients that are cooked in such a way that natural flavors are always preserved.

Bardwell Rd. ✆ 01865/552746. www.cherwellboathouse.co.uk. Reservations recommended. Main courses £16–£18 ($32–$36); fixed-price dinner from £25 ($50); Mon–Fri set lunch £23 ($46), express lunch £13–£16 ($26–$32). AE, MC, V. Daily noon–2:30pm and 6–9:30pm. Closed Dec 24–30. Bus: Banbury Rd.

Rosamund the Fair ✿ *Finds* CONTINENTAL/ENGLISH This establishment accurately bills itself as Oxfordshire's cruising restaurant, a weekend retreat. A purpose-built narrow boat restaurant, this floating dining room cruises the Oxford Canal in and around Banbury; as you dine, say hello to the swans. The chefs might get by with the novelty of it all, but they also serve a sublime cuisine. The boat seats 20 people who for 2½ hours enjoy the dinner and the cruise. Between courses you can go on deck and admire the view. A typical menu includes such starters as mango, avocado, and papaya salad with a lime-and-yogurt dressing, followed by sea bream with deep-fried leeks and a lime-butter sauce; or you might select ravioli with a salmon-and-chervil mousse with champagne sauce—a delightful choice—followed by a best end of lamb with a mustard-hollandaise glaze and rosemary jus.

Tooley's, Banbury Museum, Spiceball Park Rd., Banbury. ✆ 01295/278690. www.rosamundthefair.co.uk. Reservations required. Fixed-price menu £55 ($110) per person. MC, V. Sat 7–10:45pm; Sun noon–2:30pm. Closed Jan.

MODERATE

Browns *(Value* ENGLISH/CONTINENTAL Oxford's busiest and most bustling English brasserie suits all groups, from babies to undergraduates to grandmas. A 10-minute walk north of the town center, it occupies the premises of five Victorian shops whose walls were removed to create one large, echoing, and very popular space. A thriving bar trade (where lots of people seem to order Pimm's) makes the place an evening destination in its own right. A young and enthusiastic staff serves traditional English cuisine. Your meal may include meat pies, hot salads, burgers, pastas, steaks, or poultry. Afternoon tea here is a justly celebrated Oxford institution. Reservations are not accepted, so if you want to avoid a delay, arrive here during off-peak dining hours.

5–11 Woodstock Rd. ✆ 01865/511995. Main courses £9.50–£22 ($19–$44). AE, MC, V. Mon–Wed 9am–11pm; Thurs–Sat 9am–11:30pm; Sun 9am–10:30pm. Bus: 2 or 7.

Gee's Restaurant ✿ MEDITERRANEAN/INTERNATIONAL This restaurant, in a spacious Victorian glass conservatory, was converted from what for 80 years was the leading florist of Oxford. Its original features were retained by the owners, also of the Old Parsonage Hotel (p. 250), who have turned it into one of the most nostalgic and delightful places to dine in the city. Based on fine ingredients and a skilled preparation, the meals are likely to include pan-fried venison with carrot-and-beet purée, whole roasted partridge with red-wine jus, or homemade semolina gnocchi with baby spinach, goat cheese, and pine nuts. A good dessert choice is the lemon tart with blackberries.

61 Banbury Rd. ⓒ 01865/553540. Reservations recommended. Main courses £15–£26 ($30–$52); 2-course fixed-price menu £22 ($44), 3 courses £25 ($50); set lunch and pretheater menu £16–£19 ($32–$38). AE, MC, V. Mon–Fri noon–10:30pm; Sat–Sun 11am–10:30pm.

Le Petit Blanc 𝕉 FRENCH/MEDITERRANEAN   The biggest culinary news in Oxford is the return of Raymond Blanc with another Le Petit Blanc. (A previous one proved disappointing.) Monsieur Blanc is a wiser restaurateur now, and this buzzing brasserie is doing just fine. A former piano shop has been converted into a stylish place offering a menu that promises something for every palate. Here you can get a taste of the famous chef's creations without the high prices of his famed Le Manoir aux Quat' Saisons. The menu is more straightforward here, with a large emphasis on fresh ingredients. The food is based on authentic provincial French cuisine, complemented by Mediterranean and Asian accents. Enticing you will be an appetizer such as a Roquefort soufflé with a pear-and-walnut salad, followed by Loch Duart salmon and fish cakes. The desserts are first-rate, especially the raspberry soufflé.

71–72 Walton St. ⓒ 01865/510999. Reservations recommended. Main courses £11–£16 ($22–$32); 2-course fixed-price lunch £12 ($24); set dinner £15 ($30). AE, MC, V. Mon–Fri noon–2:45pm and 5:30–10:30pm; Sat noon–11pm; Sun noon–10pm.

INEXPENSIVE

Al-Salam 𝕉 *Value* LEBANESE   Some Oxford students think this place offers the best food value in the city, and because it's a bit less expensive (and a bit less formal) than its major competitor (the also-recommended Al-Shami; see below), we tend to agree. You'll dine within one of three sand-colored dining rooms, each separated from the other with antique (and very solid) wooden doors. Ironically, the newest of the three rooms looks as if it's the oldest, thanks to stone-built arches and a commitment to the kinds of raw materials (wood and masonry) that would have been available in Lebanon a century ago. The menu depends on what's available in the marketplace, and the chef's skill is reflected in such dishes as king prawns sautéed with a garlic-and-tomato sauce, or spicy lamb with a chili-and-onion sauce. Long lines can form at the door, especially on Friday and Saturday. The location is 2 minutes from both the bus and train stations.

6 Park End St. ⓒ 01865/245710. Reservations recommended. Main courses £7.50–£12 ($15–$24). MC, V. Daily noon–midnight.

Al-Shami LEBANESE   Bearing the archaic name for the city of Damascus, this Lebanese restaurant is a bit more formal than its also-recommended competitor, Al-Salam (see above). It contains two separate dining rooms: one with blessings from the Koran stenciled in calligraphic patterns under the coves, the other with pale beige walls and lots of wood paneling. Expect a clientele of local residents, with probably fewer students than you're likely to find at Al-Salam, and a formally dressed, Arabic- and English-speaking staff wearing black trousers, bow ties, and white vests. Many diners don't go beyond the appetizers because they comprise more than 40 delectable hot and cold selections—everything from falafel to a salad made with lamb's brains. Charcoal-grilled chopped lamb, chicken, or fish constitute most of the main-dish selections. Desserts are chosen from the cart, and vegetarian meals are also available.

25 Walton Crescent. (C) **01865/310066.** Reservations recommended. Main courses £6.20–£12 ($12–$24). MC, V. Daily noon–midnight.

THE PUB SCENE

These places are all good choices for affordable meals, too.

The **Head of the River,** Abingdon Road at Folly Bridge, near the Westgate Centre Mall ((C) **01865/721600**), is operated by the family brewery Fuller Smith and Turner. It's a lively place offering true traditional ales and lagers, along with good sturdy fare. In summer, guests sit by the river and can rent a punt or a boat with an engine. Twelve rooms, all with bathrooms and overlooking the river, are available for £60 to £85 ($120–$170), including breakfast, newspaper, and parking.

At the **Eagle and Child,** 49 Saint Giles St. ((C) **01865/302925**), literary history suffuses the dim, paneled alcoves and promotes a sedate atmosphere. For at least a quarter of a century, it was frequented by the likes of C. S. Lewis and J. R. R. Tolkien. In fact, *The Chronicles of Narnia* and *The Hobbit* were first read aloud at this pub. Known as the "Bird and Baby," this hallowed ground still welcomes the local dons, and the food is good. It's a settled, quiet place to read the newspapers and listen to classical music on CDs.

The **King's Arms,** 40 Holywell St. ((C) **01865/242369**), hosts a mix of students, gays, and professors. One of the best places in town to strike up a conversation, the pub, owned by Young's Brewery, features six of the company's ales along with visiting lagers and bitters that change periodically.

EXPLORING THE CITY

The best way to get a running commentary on the important sights is to take a 2-hour **walking tour** through the city and the major colleges. The tours leave daily from the Oxford Tourist Information Centre at 11am, 1pm, and 2pm. Tours costs £6.50 ($13) for adults and £3 ($6) for children 15 and younger; the tours do not include New College or Christ Church. There are two tours that leave the Oxford Tourist Information Centre on Saturday at 10:30am and 1:30pm; these tours include admission to Christ Church. They cost £7.50 ($15) adults, £3.50 ($7) children 15 and younger. Call (C) **01865/252200** for more information.

For a good orientation, hour-long, open-top bus tours around Oxford are available from **City Sightseeing Oxford** ((C) **01865/790522;** www.citysightseeingoxford.com), whose office is at the railway station (tours also start from the railway station; other pickup points are Sheldonian Theatre, Gloucester Green Bus Station, and Pembroke College). Buses leave every 10 to 15 minutes daily. Tickets are good for the day. Tours run daily from 9:30am to 3:40pm November to February, daily from 9:30am to 4:40pm in March, and daily 9:30am to 6:30pm April to October. The cost is £12 ($23) for adults, £9.50 ($19) for students and seniors, £6 ($12) for children 5 to 14 years old; a family ticket for two adults and three children is £31 ($62). Children 4 and younger get to ride free. Tickets can be purchased from the driver and are valid for 24 hours.

The **Tourist Information Centre,** 15–16 Broad St. ((C) **01865/252200**), offers a ghost tour, which explores Oxford's ghoulish and gory past. The office also has a number of walking tours, with the ghost tour available Friday and Saturday evenings June to October from 7:45pm, covering the dark alleyways around the ancient schools. The cost is £5 ($10) for adults and £3 ($6) for children; tickets are available at the office during the day. Day tours begin at 10am daily, including Christmas.

EXPLORING OXFORD UNIVERSITY

Many Americans arriving at Oxford ask, "Where's the campus?" If a local looks amused when answering, it's because Oxford University, in fact, is made up of 35 colleges sprinkled throughout the town. To tour all of these would be a formidable task. It's best to focus on just a handful of the better-known colleges.

A word of warning: The main business of a university is, of course, to educate—and this function at Oxford has been severely hampered by the number of visitors who disturb the academic work of the university. So visiting is restricted to certain hours and small groups of six or fewer. Furthermore, visitors are not allowed at all in certain areas, but the tourist office will be happy to advise you when and where you may take in the sights of this great institution.

AN OVERVIEW For a bird's-eye view of the city and colleges, climb **Carfax Tower** ⑂, located in the center of the city. This structure is distinguished by its clock and figures that strike on the quarter-hour. Carfax Tower is all that remains from St. Martin's Church, where William Shakespeare once stood as godfather for William Davenant, who also became a successful playwright. A church stood on this site from 1032 until 1896. The tower used to be higher, but after 1340 it was lowered, following complaints from the university to Edward III that townspeople threw stones and fired arrows at students during town-and-gown disputes. Admission is £2 ($4) for adults, £1 ($2) for children. The tower is open year-round, except for from Christmas Eve to January 1. April to October, hours are 10am to 4pm daily. Off-season hours are Monday to Saturday 10am to 3pm. Children 4 and younger are not admitted. For information, call ⓒ **01865/792653.**

CHRIST CHURCH ⑂⑂ *Kids* Begun by Cardinal Wolsey as Cardinal College in 1525, Christ Church (ⓒ **01865/276150;** www.chch.ox.ac.uk), known as the House, was founded by Henry VIII in 1546. Facing St. Aldate's Street, Christ Church has the largest quadrangle of any college in Oxford. Tom Tower houses Great Tom, an 18,000-pound bell. It rings at 9:05pm nightly, signaling the closing of the college gates. The 101 times it peals originally signified the number of students in residence at the time the college was founded. Although the student body has grown significantly, Oxford traditions live forever. There are some portraits in the 16th-century Great Hall, including works by Gainsborough and Reynolds. There's also a separate portrait gallery.

The college chapel was constructed over a period of centuries, beginning in the 12th century. (Incidentally, it's not only the college chapel but also the cathedral of the diocese of Oxford.) The cathedral's most distinguishing features are its Norman pillars

---

Moments **A Nostalgic Walk**

Our favorite pastime here is to take **Addison's Walk** through the water meadows. The stroll is named after a former Oxford alumnus, Joseph Addison, the 18th-century essayist and playwright noted for his contributions to *The Spectator* and *The Tatler.*

Moments **Punting the River Cherwell**

Punting on the River Cherwell remains the favorite outdoor pastime in Oxford. At Punt Station, **Cherwell Boathouse**, Bardwell Road (© **01865/515978**; www. cherwellboathouse.co.uk), you can rent a punt (flat-bottom boat maneuvered by a long pole and a small oar) for £12 to £14 ($24–$28) per hour, plus a £60 to £70 ($120–$140) deposit. Similar charges are made for punt rentals at **Magdalen Bridge Boathouse**, Bardwell Road (© **01865/515979**). Punts are rented from mid-March to mid-October daily 10am until dusk. Hours of operation seem to be rather informal, however, and you're not always guaranteed that someone will be here to rent you a boat, even if the punt itself is available.

---

and the vaulting of the choir, dating from the 15th century. In the center of the great quadrangle is a statue of Mercury mounted in the center of a fishpond. Many scenes from the Harry Potter films have been shot with the cloisters, quads, and staircases of Christ Church standing in for Hogwarts, making this a popular stop for kids of all ages. You can visit the college and cathedral between 9am and 5pm, though times vary (1–5pm Sun). It's best to call before you visit. The entrance fee is £4.90 ($9.80) for adults and £3.90 ($7.80) for children.

MAGDALEN COLLEGE Pronounced *Maud*-lin, Magdalen College, High Street (© **01865/276000**; www.magd.ox.ac.uk), was founded in 1458 by William of Waynflete, bishop of Winchester and later chancellor of England. Its alumni range from Wolsey to Wilde. Opposite the botanic garden, the oldest in England, is the bell tower, where the choristers sing in Latin at dawn on May Day. Charles I, his days numbered, watched the oncoming Roundheads from this tower. Visit the 15th-century chapel, in spite of many of its latter-day trappings. Ask when the hall and other places of special interest are open. The grounds of Magdalen are the most extensive of any Oxford college; there's even a deer park. From July to September it is open daily noon to 6pm; from October to June daily 1 to 6pm. Admission is £3 ($6) adults; £2 ($4) seniors, students, and children.

MERTON COLLEGE 🎭🎭 Founded in 1264, Merton College, Merton Street (© **01865/276310**; www.merton.ox.ac.uk), is among the three oldest colleges at the university. It stands near Corpus Christi College on Merton Street, the sole survivor of Oxford's medieval cobbled streets. Merton College is noted for its library, built between 1371 and 1379 and said to be the oldest college library in England. Though a tradition once kept some of its most valuable books chained, now only one book is secured in that manner to illustrate that historical custom. One of the library's treasures is an astrolabe (an astronomical instrument used for measuring the altitude of the sun and stars) thought to have belonged to Chaucer. You pay £2 ($4) to visit the ancient library as well as the Max Beerbohm Room (the satirical English caricaturist who died in 1956). Call ahead for information. The library and college are open Monday to Friday 2 to 4pm, and Saturday and Sunday 10am to 4pm. It's closed for 1 week at Easter and Christmas and on weekends during the winter.

NEW COLLEGE New College, Holywell Street (© **01865/279555**; www.new.ox. ac.uk), was founded in 1379 by William of Wykeham, bishop of Winchester and later lord chancellor of England. His college at Winchester supplied a constant stream of students. The first quadrangle, dating from before the end of the 14th century, was the initial quadrangle to be built in Oxford and formed the architectural design for the other colleges. In the antechapel is Sir Jacob Epstein's remarkable modern sculpture of Lazarus and a fine El Greco painting of St. James. One of the treasures of the college is a crosier (pastoral staff of a bishop) belonging to the founding father. Don't miss the beautiful garden outside the college, where you can stroll among the remains of the old city wall. It's an evocative, romantic site. The college (entered at New College Lane) can be visited from Easter to October daily between 11am and 5pm, and in the off season daily between 2 and 4pm. Admission is £2 ($4) from Easter to October and free off season.

THE OLD BODLEIAN LIBRARY ☆☆   This famed library on Catte Street (© **01865/ 277000;** www.bodley.ox.ac.uk) was launched in 1602, initially funded by Sir Thomas Bodley. It is home to some 50,000 manuscripts and more than five million books. Over the years the library has expanded from the Old Library complex to other buildings, including the Radcliffe Camera next door. The easiest way to visit the library is by taking a guided tour, leaving from the Divinity School across the street from the main entrance. In summer there are four tours Monday to Friday and two on Saturday; in winter, two tours leave per day. Call for specific times.

SHOPPING

Golden Cross, an arcade of first-class shops and boutiques, lies between Cornmarket Street and the Covered Market (or between High and Market sts.). Parts of the colorful gallery date from the 12th century. Many buildings remain from the medieval era, along with some 15th- and 17th-century structures. The market also has a reputation as the Covent Garden of Oxford, with live entertainment on Saturday mornings in summer. In the arcade shops is a diverse selection of merchandise, including handmade Belgian chocolates, clothing for both women and men, and luxury leather goods.

In its way, **Alice's Shop,** 83 St. Aldate's (© **01865/723793**), played an important role in English literature. Set within a 15th-century building that has housed some kind of shop since 1820, it functioned as a general store (selling brooms, hardware, and the like) during the period that Lewis Carroll, at the time a professor of mathematics at Christ Church College, was composing *Alice in Wonderland.* It is believed to have been the model for important settings within the book. Today, the place is a favorite stopover of Lewis Carroll fans from as far away as Japan, who gobble up commemorative pencils, chess sets, party favors, bookmarks, and in rare cases original editions of some of Carroll's works.

(*Finds* A Pokey Home for Old Masters

Almost overlooked by the average visitor is an unheralded little gem known as **Christ Church Picture Gallery** (© **01865/276-172;** www.chch.ox.ac.uk), entered through the Canterbury Quad. Here you come across a stunning collection of Old Masters, mainly from the Dutch, Flemish, and Italian school, including works by Michelangelo and Leonardo da Vinci. The gallery is open May to September Monday to Saturday from 10:30am to 5pm, Sunday 2 to 5pm. From October to April hours are Monday to Saturday 10:30am to 1pm and daily 2 to 4:30pm. Admission is £2 ($4) for adults or £1 ($2) for students and seniors.

Tips   A Quiet Oasis

The oldest botanic garden in Great Britain, the **Botanic Gardens** (✆ **01865/286690;** www.botanic-garden.ox.ac.uk) opposite Magdalen, were first planted in 1621 on the site of a Jewish graveyard from the early Middle Ages. Bounded by a curve of the Cherwell, they still stand today and are the best place in Oxford to escape the invading hordes. The Botanic Gardens are open March to October daily 9am to 5pm (until 6pm May–Aug); November to February Monday to Friday 9am to 4:30pm (last admission 45 min. before closing). Admission is £3 ($6) for adults, £2.50 ($5) for students, and free for children 11 and younger.

The **Bodleian Library Shop,** Old School's Quadrangle, Radcliffe Square, Broad Street (✆ **01865/277091**), specializes in Oxford souvenirs, from books and paperweights to Oxford banners and coffee mugs.

Castell & Son (The Varsity Shop), 13 Broad St. (✆ **01865/244000;** www.varsity shop.co.uk), is the best outlet in Oxford for clothing emblazoned with the Oxford logo or heraldic symbol. Choices include both whimsical and dead-on-serious neckties, hats, T-shirts, pens, beer and coffee mugs, and cuff links. It's commercialized Oxford, but it's still got a sense of relative dignity and style. A second location is at 109–114 High St. (✆ **01865/249491**).

OXFORD AFTER DARK
THE PERFORMING ARTS

Highly acclaimed orchestras playing in truly lovely settings mark the Music at Oxford series at the **Oxford Playhouse Theatre,** Beaumont Street (✆ **01865/305305;** www.oxfordplayhouse.com). The autumn season runs from mid-September to December, the winter season from January to April, and the spring–summer season from May to early July. Tickets range from £5 to £37 ($10–$74). Classical music is performed by outstanding groups such as the European Union Chamber Orchestra, the Canterbury Musical Society, the Bournemouth Symphony, and the Guild Hall String Ensemble of London. All performances are held in the Sheldonian Theatre, a particularly attractive site, designed by Sir Christopher Wren, with paintings on the ceiling. The Playhouse Box Office is open Monday to Saturday 9:30am to 6pm (or to half an hour after the start of an evening performance) and from at least 2 hours before a performance on Sunday.

New Theatre (formerly the Apollo), George Street (✆ **01865/320760** for administration, or call Ticketmaster ✆ **0844/8471585** for bookings), is Oxford's primary theater. Tickets are £15 to £49 ($30–$98). A continuous run of comedy, ballet, drama, opera, and even rock contributes to the variety. The Welsh National Opera often performs, and the Glyndebourne Touring Opera appears regularly. Advance booking is highly recommended, though some shows may have tickets the week of the performance. The box office is open Monday to Saturday 10am to 8pm (to 6pm if there is no evening performance).

THE CLUBS: BLUES, JAZZ & CELTIC ROCK

As a sign of the times, **Freud,** 119 Walton St. (✆ **01865/311171**), has turned an 18th-century church, stained-glass windows and all, into a jazz and folk club with an expansive array of drink choices. There is no cover charge, and hours are Tuesday noon to 11pm and Wednesday to Sunday noon to 2am.

Finds   Pubs with a Pedigree

Every college town the world over has a fair number of bars, but few can boast local watering holes with such atmosphere and history as Oxford.

A short block from the High, overlooking the north side of Christ Church College, the **Bear Inn,** 6 Alfred St. (© **01865/721783**), is an Oxford landmark, built in the 13th century and mentioned time and time again in English literature. The Bear brings together a wide variety of people in a relaxed way. You may talk with a raja from India, a university don, or a titled gentleman who's the latest in a line of owners that goes back more than 700 years. Some former owners developed an astonishing habit: clipping neckties. Around the lounge bar you'll see the remains of thousands of ties, which have been labeled with their owners' names.

Even older than the Bear is the **Turf Tavern,** 7 Bath Place (off Holywell St.; © **01865/243235**), on a very narrow passageway near the Bodleian Library. The pub is reached via St. Helen's Passage, which stretches between Holywell Street and New College Lane. (You'll probably get lost, but any student worth his beer can direct you.) Thomas Hardy used the place as the setting for *Jude the Obscure.* It was "the local" of the future U.S. president Bill Clinton during his student days at Oxford. In warm weather, you can choose a table in any of the three separate gardens that radiate outward from the pub's central core. For wintertime warmth, braziers are lighted in the courtyard and in the gardens. A food counter set behind a glass case displays the day's fare—salads, soups, sandwiches, and so on. Local ales (including one named Headbanger, with a relatively high alcohol content) are served, as well as a range of wines.

Just outside of town, hidden away some 4km (2½ miles) north of Oxford, the **Trout Inn,** 195 Godstow Rd., Wolvercote (© **01865/302071**), is a private world where you can get ale and beer and standard fare. Have your drink in one of the historic rooms, with their settles (wooden benches), brass, and old prints, or go out in sunny weather to sit on a stone wall. On the grounds are peacocks, ducks, swans, and herons that live in and around the river and an adjacent weir pool; they'll join you if you're handing out crumbs. Take an arched stone bridge, architecture with wildly pitched roofs and gables, add the Thames River, and you have the Trout. The Smoking Room, the original 12th-century part, complements the inn's relatively "new" 16th-century bars. Daily specials are featured. Hot meals are served all day in the restaurant; salads are featured in summer, and there are grills in winter. On your way there and back, look for the view of Oxford from the bridge. Take bus no. 6A, 6B, or 6C to Wolvercote, and then walk 1km (a half-mile); it's also fun to bike here from Oxford. Open hours are Sunday 11am to 10:30pm, Monday to Saturday 11am to 11pm.

OFS, 40 George St. (© **01865/297170**), covers all the bases, including live entertainment, a bar, theater, art museum, and a science museum called Curiosity, with a light show and other exhibits. Music cover charges begin at 11pm and are £5 ($10).

Offerings change nightly but include 1970s disco, blues, jazz, and local bands. It's open daily 9pm to 2am.

Zodiac, 190 Crowley Rd. (*©* **01865/420042**), presents everything from easy listening to Celtic rock. The cover varies from £5 to £15 ($10–$30), depending on the group featured. It's usually open from about 7pm to 2am daily. Club ownership is shared by some major English bands, and local and big-name bands are featured along with DJs, so call ahead to be sure of what you're getting.

Castle Tavern, 24 Paradise St. (*©* **01865/201510**), is the best-known gay bar in Oxford, and you can meet fellow gays here, enjoying the pub grub and beer. Should you tire of it, head down the street to **Jolly Farmers**, 20 Paradise St. (*©* **01865/ 793759**), with its rear courtyard. For such a university town with such a large gay population, you'd think there would be more clubs for gays. But many of the Oxford clubs stage "gay nights," and these soirees keep the juices flowing. Flyers advertising what's happening are distributed at both pubs recommended above.

5 Woodstock & Blenheim Palace

100km (62 miles) NW of London; 13km (8 miles) NW of Oxford

The small country town of Woodstock, birthplace in 1330 of the Black Prince, ill-fated son of King Edward III, lies on the edge of the Cotswolds. Some of the stone houses here were constructed when Woodstock was the site of a royal palace. This palace had so suffered the ravages of time that its remains were demolished when Blenheim Palace was built. Woodstock was once the seat of a flourishing glove industry.

ESSENTIALS

GETTING THERE   Take the train to Oxford (see "Essentials," earlier in this chapter). The Gloucester Green bus (no. 20 or 120A) leaves Oxford about every 30 minutes during the day. The trip takes a little more than a half-hour. Call **Stagecoach** (*©* **01865/772250;** www.stagecoachbus.com) for details. If you're driving, take the A44 from Oxford.

VISITOR INFORMATION   The **Tourist Information Centre** is at the Oxfordshire Museum, Park Street (*©* **01993/813276**), open Monday to Saturday from 10am to 5pm and Sunday from 2 to 5pm in winter, Monday to Saturday 9:30am to 5:30pm and Sunday 1 to 5pm in summer.

WHERE TO STAY & DINE

The Bear Hotel ★★   The Bear Hotel is one of the six oldest coaching inns in England, dating from the 13th century. The half-stone structure is located in the center of Woodstock. Richard Burton and Elizabeth Taylor, at the height of their tempestuous romance in the 1960s, stayed in the Marlboro Suite, an attractively decorated sitting room plus a bedroom and bathroom. According to legend, one of the chambers of the hotel is haunted. Rooms come in a variety of sizes and styles, but each offers grand comfort and a mix of modern luxuries with antiques; nine of the rooms contain four-poster beds. Blazing hearth fires are found throughout the hotel when the days and nights are cool.

Park St., Woodstock, Oxfordshire OX20 1SZ. *©* 0870/400-8202. Fax 01993/813380. www.bearhotelwoodstock.co.uk. 54 units. £150–£174 ($300–$348) double; £224–£264 ($448–$528) suite. AE, DC, MC, V. **Amenities:** Restaurant; bar; room service; babysitting; laundry service; dry cleaning. *In room:* TV, CD player, minibar, coffeemaker, hair dryer, iron, trouser press.

Feathers ⟨☆⟩   Just a short walk from Blenheim Palace, Feathers dates from the 17th century and has been an inn since the 18th century. The bedrooms in this beautifully furnished hotel are individually decorated. Some units have draped awnings over the beds. The two lounges have wood fires. A multitude of stuffed birds (from which the house took its name) adorn the bar; from here you can go into the delightful garden in the courtyard.

Market St., Woodstock, Oxfordshire OX20 1SX. ⟨𝒞⟩ **01993/812291.** Fax 01993/813158. www.feathers.co.uk. 20 units. £165–£195 ($330–$390) double; £225–£275 ($450–$550) suite. Rates include English breakfast. AE, DC, MC, V. **Amenities:** Restaurant; bar; room service; babysitting; laundry service. *In room:* TV, hair dryer.

A FAVORITE LOCAL PUB

Star Inn, 22 Market Place (⟨𝒞⟩ **01993/811373**), has three locally brewed real ales from which to choose: Tetley's, Wadworth's 6X, and Marston's Pedigree. You can enjoy the requisite bar munchies as well as full dinners. The management boasts that its half-shoulder of lamb is the tenderest around because of the slow-cooking process.

ONE OF ENGLAND'S MOST MAGNIFICENT PALACES

Blenheim Palace ⟨☆☆☆⟩ *(Kids)*   The extravagantly baroque Blenheim Palace is England's answer to Versailles. Blenheim is the home of the 11th duke of Marlborough, descendant of the first duke John Churchill, once an on-again, off-again favorite of Queen Anne's. In his day (1650–1722), the first duke became the supreme military figure in Europe. Fighting on the Danube near a village named Blenheim, Churchill defeated the forces of Louis XIV, and the lavish palace of Blenheim was built for the duke as a gift from the queen. It was designed by Sir John Vanbrugh, who was also the architect of Castle Howard; the landscaping was created by Capability Brown. The palace is loaded with riches: antiques, porcelain, oil paintings, tapestries, and chinoiserie. North Americans know Blenheim as the birthplace of Sir Winston Churchill. The room in which he was born is included in the palace tour, as is the Churchill exhibition: four rooms of letters, books, photographs, and other relics. Today, the former prime minister lies buried in Bladon Churchyard, near the palace.

Insider's tip: **Marlborough Maze,** 540m (1,800 ft.) from the palace, is the largest symbolic hedge maze on earth, with an herb and lavender garden, a butterfly house, and inflatable castles for children. Also, be sure to look for the castle's gift shops, tucked away in an old palace dairy. Here you can purchase a wide range of souvenirs, handicrafts, and even locally made preserves.

⟨𝒞⟩ **01993/811091.** www.blenheimpalace.com. Admission £14–£16 ($28–$32) adults, £11–£14 ($22–$28) students and seniors, £7.50–£9.75 ($15–$20) children 5–15, £18–£43 ($36–$86) family ticket, free for children 4 and younger. Daily 10:30am–5:30pm. Last admission 4:45pm. Closed mid-Dec to mid-Feb (except for park).

6 Aylesbury

74km (46 miles) NW of London; 35km (22 miles) E of Oxford

Aylesbury has retained much of its ancient charm and character, especially along the narrow Tudor alleyways and in the 17th-century architecture of the houses in the town center. Among the more ancient structures is St. Mary's Church, which dates from the 13th century and features an unusual spirelet. The 15th-century King's Head Public House, a National Trust property, has seen many famous faces in its time, including Henry VIII, who was a frequent guest while he was courting Anne Boleyn.

The market, which has been an integral part of the town since the 13th century, is still a thriving force in Aylesbury life, with markets held on Wednesday, Friday, and

Saturday, and a flea market on Tuesday. During the 18th and 19th centuries, ducks were the most famous commodity of the Aylesbury market. The pure white ducks were a delicacy for the rich and famous of London and were much desired for their dinner tables. The demand for the Aylesbury duck declined in the 20th century, though not before the breed became threatened with extinction. Today, however, most ducks found on restaurant menus are raised elsewhere, and the threat to the Aylesbury duck has subsided. The ivory fowl are now enjoyed more for their beauty than their flavor.

ESSENTIALS

GETTING THERE   Aylesbury is 1 hour and 12 minutes by train from London's Marylebone Station, or 25 minutes off the M25 via the A41. For rail information, call ℭ **0845/748-4950** or visit **www.nationalrail.co.uk**.

VISITOR INFORMATION   The **Aylesbury Tourist Information Centre,** Kings Head Passage, off Market Square (ℭ **01296/330559**), is open April to October 9:30am to 5pm Monday to Saturday. From November to March, hours are Monday to Saturday 10am to 4:30pm.

WHERE TO STAY & DINE

Hartwell House ★★★   One of England's great showcase country estates and a member of Relais & Châteaux, Hartwell House lies just 3km (2 miles) southwest of Aylesbury (the nearest rail station) on the A418, and about 32km (20 miles) from Oxford. It stands on 36 hectares (90 acres) of landscaped parkland. As you enter the house, you can enjoy a medley of architectural styles, ranging from the 16th through the 18th centuries. The home was built for the Hampden and Lee families, ancestors of the Confederacy's General Robert E. Lee. You can wander from the morning room to the oak-paneled bar, pausing in the library where a former tenant, the exiled Louis XVIII, signed the document returning him to the throne of France. Rooms are as regal as the prices. The stellar accommodations literally ooze with comfort, charm, and character, even those recently built in a converted stable block.

Oxford Rd., Aylesbury, Buckinghamshire HP17 8NR. ℭ **01296/747444.** Fax 01296/747450. www.hartwell-house. com. 46 units. £280–£490 ($560–$980) double; £390–£800 ($780–$1,600) suite. AE, MC, V. **Amenities:** 2 restaurants; bar; heated indoor pool; 2 tennis courts; health club; whirlpool; sauna; steam room; salon; room service; laundry service; dry cleaning. *In room:* TV, Wi-Fi, hair dryer, trouser press.

West Lodge Hotel   Close to Aylesbury, this Victorian hotel on the A41 outdoes all others in the area with its facilities, the best of which must be its own hot-air balloon. The comfortable rooms are furnished with nice extras and private shower-only bathrooms. For dinner, Montgolfier is a French restaurant located across the street named after the brothers who made the first successful hot-air balloon flight in 1783.

45 London Rd., Aston Clinton, Aylesbury HP22 5HL. ℭ **01296/630362.** Fax 01296/630151. www.westlodge.co.uk. 9 units. £80–£90 ($160–$180) double. Rates include breakfast. AE, MC, V. **Amenities:** Restaurant; bar; Jacuzzi; sauna; room service. *In room:* TV, Wi-Fi, beverage maker, hair dryer, trouser press.

SEEING THE SIGHTS

Following in the footsteps of the Rothschilds (see Waddesdon Manor, below), many wealthy Victorian merchants built mansions in and around Aylesbury, and many of these half-timbered examples of regal domestic architecture still stand. If you aren't busy spending money at the market, you may want to stroll through the town to see the houses and buildings that line the streets. **Hickman's Almshouses** and the

Prebendal Houses are structures that date from the 17th century; you can walk by after enjoying tea at St. Mary's Church, which is just down the road.

Buckinghamshire County Museum *(Kids)*   This museum is located in two buildings, a house and a grammar school, both dating from the 18th century. The latest addition to the museum is the Roald Dahl Children's Gallery. Dahl's children's books, especially *Charlie and the Chocolate Factory* and *James and the Giant Peach,* come to life as visitors ride in the Great Glass Elevator or crawl inside the Giant Peach. Hands-on exhibits don't stop upon entering the main museum, however. Innovative displays focusing on the cultural heritage of Buckinghamshire are interactive and touchable. Advance arrangements are necessary for the Children's Gallery because of the large number of school groups that visit.

Church St. (✆) **01296/331441.** www.buckscc.gov.uk/museum. Free admission to main museum. Children's Gallery £4 ($8); free for 2 and younger. Mon–Sat 10am–5pm; Sun 2–5pm.

Oak Farms Rare Breeds Park *(Kids)*   While in the area, you'll of course want to see the famous Aylesbury ducks; this is the best place to catch sight of the once-threatened species. The traditional working farm is home to a variety of animals, from sheep to pigs, many of which are rare breeds. Guests can hand-feed the animals their special food, take a picnic of their own, and enjoy a nature trail.

Off A41 on the way to Broughton. (✆) **01296/415709.** Admission £3 ($6) adults, £2 ($4) ages 16 and younger. Daily 10am–5:30pm. Closed Nov to mid-Feb.

Waddesdon Manor *(★)*   Built by Baron Ferdinand de Rothschild in the 1870s, the manor features French Renaissance architecture and a variety of French furniture, carpets, and porcelain. Eighteenth-century artwork by several famous English and Dutch painters is exhibited, and, of course, you can view wine cellars. In the surrounding gardens, an aviary houses exotic birds. On the premises are a restaurant and a gift shop, both featuring a vast assortment of Rothschild wines.

Bicester Rd. (✆) **01296/653226.** www.waddesdon.org.uk. Admission to house and grounds £10–£15 ($20–$30) adults, £6–£11 ($12–$22) children 5–15, family ticket £14–£18 ($28–$36), free for children 4 and younger; grounds only £5.50–£7 ($11–$14) adults, £2.75–£3.50 ($5.50–$7) children 5–16, free for children 4 and younger. House Mar–Oct Wed–Fri noon–4pm, Sat–Sun 11am–4pm; grounds and aviary Jan to mid-Mar Sat–Sun 10am–5pm, mid-Mar to Dec Wed–Sun 10am–5pm. Audio guide can be rented at the entrance for £2 ($4). Bus: 16 or 17.

AYLESBURY AFTER DARK

Hobgoblin, 14 Kingsbury Sq. ((✆) **01296/415100**), is a pub housed in a structure from 1742. Among on-tap offerings are house ales, Hobgoblin and Wychwood, as well as John Smith's, and there is also a full bar. Snack food is available, as are such distractions as pool tables, TVs, and video games. Sunday nights are karaoke.

7 St. Albans *(★)*

43km (27 miles) NW of London; 66km (41 miles) SW of Cambridge

Some 2,000 years old, today's cathedral city of St. Albans was named after a Roman soldier who was the first Christian martyr in England. Medieval pilgrims made the trek to visit the shrine of St. Alban, and visitors today still find the ancient cathedral city and the surrounding countryside inspiring.

Peter Rabbit was created in this county by Beatrix Potter, and George Bernard Shaw found inspiration in the view from his countryside home near Ayot St. Lawrence. As you explore St. Albans and nearby attractions, you'll tread in the footsteps of Queen Elizabeth I and Henry VIII, who passed through before you.

Although today industry has crept in and greater London keeps getting greater and greater, St. Albans is situated at the center of what was known as "the market basket of England." The 1,000-year-old tradition of the street market continues as merchants of every kind set up colorful stalls to display their goods. Held on Wednesday and Saturday, it's one of the largest in the southeast.

ESSENTIALS

GETTING THERE   St. Albans is easily reached from London. The rail connection, ThamesLink, takes you from London's King Cross to St. Albans in just 20 minutes. From London, Green Line coach no. 724 also runs to St. Albans frequently (Green Line buses to St. Albans depart only from Heathrow airport). For rail information, call ℂ **0845/748-4950** or visit **www.nationalrail.co.uk**. For bus information, dial ℂ **0870/608-2608** or visit **www.stagecoachbus.com**.

If you're driving, take the M25 Junction 21A or 22; M1 Junctions 6, 7, or 9; and A1 (M) Junction 3.

VISITOR INFORMATION   The **Tourist Information Centre** is at the Town Hall, Market Place (ℂ **01727/864511**). Its hours are Monday to Saturday 10am to 5pm, Sunday 10am to 4pm.

WHERE TO STAY

The Black Lion Inn   This is the nicest pub hotel in the area and one of the best bargains. A former bakery built in 1837, it lies in the most colorful part of town, St. Michael's Village, where bustling coaches from London once arrived. Bedrooms are simple and plain and, although a bit cramped, are well maintained. Free Wi-Fi is available in the reception area and bar.

St. Michael's Village, 198 Fishpool St., St. Albans, Hertfordshire AL3 4SB. ℂ **01727/848644**. Fax 01727/859243. www.theblacklioninn.com. 16 units, 14 with bathroom. £70 ($140) double; £85 ($170) family room. AE, MC, V. **Amenities:** Breakfast room; bar; babysitting; laundry service. *In room:* TV, coffeemaker, hair dryer, trouser press.

St. Michael's Manor ★★   Set on 2 hectares (5 acres) of beautifully maintained lakeside gardens, the manor dates from 1586 but was recently upgraded and refurbished. Constructed on medieval fortifications, the hotel stands in award-winning gardens with an abundance of wildlife. It's hard to imagine you're in a city. Rooms are individually decorated with fine antique pieces. Each has a certain charm with no bad choice among them. Rooms are stocked with everything from mineral water to a teddy bear to sleep with. The manor also has a superb restaurant, the Terrace Room (with an ornate Victorian conservatory overlooking the floodlit lawns).

St. Michael's Village, Fishpool St., St. Albans, Hertfordshire AL3 4RY. ℂ **01727/864444**. Fax 01727/848909. www.stmichaelsmanor.com. 30 units. £180–£335 ($360–$670) double. Special weekend rate £145–£335 ($290–$670) double. Rates include English breakfast. AE, MC, V. **Amenities:** Restaurant; bar; room service; laundry; dry cleaning. *In room:* A/C, TV/DVD, high-speed Internet, beverage maker, hair dryer.

Sopwell House ★★★   This place is in a neck-to-neck competition with St. Michael's Manor (see above), though Sopwell has more facilities. A private mansion from the days of George III, at one time it belonged to Lord Louis Mountbatten and has seen its share of royal heads. Converted into a hotel of taste, charm, and character, it occupies nearly a dozen acres 3km (2 miles) southeast of the city center. Avoid it if it's hosting a conference, but at other times you can enjoy the grace of an English country house. From the drawing room to the library, public rooms are elegant and comfy. Some of the bedrooms are equipped with four-poster beds and have a traditional feel, whereas others are more contemporary. Regardless, the decor is tasteful, rather chic, and handsomely coordinated.

Cottonmill Lane, St. Albans, Hertfordshire AL1 2HQ. (℗) **01727/864477.** Fax 01727/844741. www.sopwellhouse. co.uk. 129 units. Mon–Thurs £185–£217 ($370–$434) double, £229–£275 ($458–$550) suite; Fri–Sun £169–£205 ($338–$410) double, £216–£275 ($432–$550) suite. AE, DC, MC, V. **Amenities:** 2 restaurants; 2 bars; indoor heated pool; gym; spa; salon; room service; babysitting; laundry service. *In room:* A/C (in some rooms), TV, beverage maker, hair dryer, trouser press, safe (in some).

WHERE TO DINE

The Restaurant ⊕ FRENCH/ENGLISH   Consistently serving the best food in the area, this restaurant lies beneath a glass roof that's pierced with a trio of magnolias whose branches gracefully arch into the open air outside. The ambience is light, elegant, upscale, and inviting, partly because of the formal and well-trained staff, and partly because the food is more sophisticated and prepared with more flair than anywhere else in town. You may begin with an award-winning version of seared scallops with chili-and-lime salsa. Main courses change with Chef Ian Pennet's inspiration, but we enjoyed the roasted filet of lamb with cream sauce.

Also on premises is a terrace bar that's open daily (only in summer) from 11am to 11pm. The food it serves is a lot more down-home, and also a lot cheaper.

In the Sopwell House Hotel, Cottonmill Lane. (℗) **01727/864477.** Reservations highly recommended. Main courses £12–£24 ($24–$48). AE, DC, MC, V. Tues–Fri and Sun noon–2:30pm; Mon–Sat 7–10pm; Sun 7–9:30pm.

EXPLORING THE TOWN

The Association of Honorary Guides, a trained group of local volunteers, provides **guided walks** costing £2 to £5 ($4–$10). These include a tour of the ancient Roman city of Verulamium and the Medieval Town, a ghost walk, and a coaching-inn walking tour. In addition to prebooked tours, free public guided walks are available on several Sundays; the tour begins at 11:15am and 3pm at the Tourist Information Centre. Tours are not always conducted regularly, so it's best to call in advance. Guides are also available on Sunday at the Verulamium Museum and Roman Theatre at 2:30pm to give short talks on a number of topics concerning the Romans and their time in the area. You can get full details from the Tourist Information Centre (see above).

Cathedral of St. Albans ⊕, Holywell Hill and High Street (℗ **01727/860780;** www.stalbanscathedral.org.uk), is still known as "the Abbey" to locals, though Henry VIII dissolved it as such in 1539. Construction of the cathedral began in 1077; it is one of England's early Norman churches. The bricks, especially visible in the tower, came from Verulamium, an old Roman city located at the foot of the hill. The nave and west front date from 1235.

The new chapter house, the first modern structure built beside a great medieval cathedral in the country, was opened by the queen in 1982. The building houses an information desk, gift shop, and restaurant. There is also a video detailing the history of the cathedral that you can view for free (donations appreciated).

The cathedral and chapter house are generally open daily from 9am to 5:45pm. In addition to church services, organ recitals are often open to the public. The church's choir can sometimes be heard rehearsing, if they're not on tour.

Verulamium Museum at St. Michael's ⊕ (℗ **01727/751810;** www.stalbans museums.org.uk) stands on the site of the ancient Roman city of the same name. Here you'll view some of the finest Roman mosaics in Britain as well as re-created Roman rooms. Part of the Roman town hall, a hypocaust (an ancient design for heating rooms), and the outline of houses and shops are still visible in the park that surrounds the museum. The museum is open year-round Monday to Saturday 10am to 5:30pm and Sunday 2 to 5:30pm; admission is £3.30 ($6.60) for adults, £2 ($4) for seniors and children, and £8 ($16) for a family ticket. By car, Verulamium is 15 to 20 minutes from Junction 21A on the M25; it is also accessible from Junction 9 or 6 on the M1; follow the signs for St. Albans and the Roman Verulamium. A train to St. Albans City Station will put you within 3km (2 miles) of the museum.

Just a short distance from Verulamium is the **Roman Theatre** (© 01727/835035; www.romantheatre.co.uk). The structure is the only theater of the period that is open to visitors in Britain. You can tour the site daily between 10am and 5pm (4pm in winter). Admission is £2 ($4) for adults, £1.50 ($3) for students and seniors, and £1 ($2) for children.

Museum of St. Albans, Hatfield Road (© 01727/819340; www.stalbansmuseums. org.uk), details the history of St. Albans from the departure of the Romans to the present day. It's open Monday through Saturday from 10am to 5:30pm and Sunday from 2 to 5:30pm. Admission is £3.30 ($6.60) for adults, £2 ($4) for seniors and children, and £8 ($16) for a family ticket. Located in the city center, it's a 5-minute walk from St. Albans City Station.

Batchwood's 18-hole golf course is one of the finest public courses in the country. The Batchwood Indoor Tennis Centre, which has four indoor courts plus outdoor courts, has professional coaches available for all play levels. Both the golf and the tennis center are located on the grounds of the **Batchwood Hall Mansion** on Batchwood Drive (© 01727/856596).

SHOPPING

The twice-weekly **street market,** held every Wednesday and Saturday on St. Peters Street, is defined by its frantic pace. In contrast, modern off-street precincts and small specialty shops in St. Albans combine to create a unique, laid-back atmosphere the rest of the week.

The **Past Times Shop,** 33 Market Place (© 0871/7162723), sells items that cover 12 historic eras. Here you'll find books on historic places, jewelry, clothes, and CDs featuring music from a variety of time periods.

For antiques, visit **By George,** 23 George St. (© 01727/853032). St. Albans's largest antiques center, the building also houses a tearoom and crafts arcade.

THEATER PERFORMANCES

St. Albans's nightlife centers on theater. The Company of Ten, with its base at the **Abbey Theatre,** Westminster Lodge, Holywell Hill (© 01727/857861; www.abbey theatre.org.uk), is one of the leading amateur dramatic companies in Britain. The troupe presents 10 productions each season in either the well-equipped main auditorium or a smaller studio. Performances begin at 8pm; tickets cost from £6 to £8 ($12–$16). The box office is open Monday to Saturday 10:30am to 7pm.

The **Maltings Arts Theatre,** in the Maltings Shopping Centre (© 01727/ 844222), presents performances based on literature—from Shakespeare to modern novels. Plays are generally presented only once and begin at 8:30pm on Thursday, Friday, and Saturday (there is a children's show at 3pm). Tickets are £6.50 to £12 ($13–$24). The theater box office is open Monday to Saturday 11am to 5pm.

SIDE TRIPS FROM ST. ALBANS

DeHavilland Aircraft Heritage Center   This is the oldest aircraft museum in Britain. The hall where De Havilland Aircraft Company developed the "Mosquito," known as the most versatile aircraft of World War II, is no longer open to the public. However, the museum displays more than 20 types of aircraft, including modern military and civil jets, along with aircraft engines and other memorabilia. Several of the displays are hands-on.

On the grounds of Salisbury Hall, on the south side of the main M25 London–St. Albans Rd. ⓒ 01727/822051. www.dehavillandmuseum.co.uk. Admission £5 ($10) adults; £3 ($6) seniors, students with ID, and children 5–16; £13 ($26) family ticket; free for children 5 and younger. Mar–Oct Tues, Thurs, and Sat 2–5:30pm; Sun and bank holidays 10:30am–5:30pm. Closed Nov–Feb. Take M25 Junction 22 at London Colney 8km (5 miles) south of St. Albans. The museum is on B556.

Hatfield House ⓡⓡⓡ   Hatfield was a part of the lives of both Henry VIII and Elizabeth I. In the old palace, begun in 1497, Elizabeth romped and played as a child. Though Henry was married to her mother, Anne Boleyn, at the time of Elizabeth's birth, the marriage was later nullified. (Anne lost her head; Elizabeth, her legitimacy.) Henry stashed away his oldest daughter, Mary Tudor, at Hatfield. But when Mary became queen of England and set about earning the dubious distinction of "Bloody Mary," she found Elizabeth to be a problem and kept her for a while in the Tower of London, eventually letting her return to Hatfield. In 1558, Elizabeth learned of her succession to the throne of England while at Hatfield.

Only the banqueting hall of the original Tudor palace remains; the rest of the house is Jacobean. The brick-and-stone structure that exists today has much antique furniture and many tapestries and paintings, as well as three often-reproduced portraits, including the ermine and rainbow portraits of Elizabeth I. The Great Hall is suitably medieval, complete with a minstrel's gallery. One of the rarest exhibits is a pair of silk stockings, said to have been worn by Elizabeth herself, the first woman in England to don such apparel. The park and the gardens are also worth exploring. Luncheons and teas are available from 11am to 5:30pm in the converted coach house.

Elizabethan banquets are staged with much gaiety and music in the banqueting hall of the Old Palace on Fridays. Guests are invited to drink in an anteroom, and then join the long tables for a feast of five courses with continuous entertainment from a group of Elizabethan players, minstrels, and jesters. Wine is included in the cost of the meal, but predinner drinks are not. The menu isn't particularly medieval, and you're granted the (modern-day) luxury of knives and forks. The entertainment is a bit cheesy and the banquets are very touristy, but they are packed every night.

The cost of the banquet is from £49 ($98). *Warning:* Prices fluctuate frequently. For current prices, reservations, and more information, call either the number listed below or ⓒ **01707/262055,** or go online to www.hatfield-house.co.uk.

9.5km (6 miles) east of St. Albans on A414. ⓒ 01707/287010 for information. www.hatfield-house.co.uk. Admission £10 ($20) adults, £9 ($18) seniors, £4.50 ($9) for persons 15 and younger. House daily noon–5pm; park and gardens daily 11am–5:30pm. Closed Oct to Good Friday. From St. Albans, take A414 east and follow the brown signs that lead you directly to the estate. By bus, take the university bus from St. Albans City Station. Hatfield House is directly across from Hatfield Station.

Shaw's Corner ⓕ*finds*   George Bernard Shaw lived here from 1906 to 1950. The utilitarian house, with its harsh brickwork and rather comfortless interior, is practically as he left it at his death. In the hall, for example, his hats are still hanging, as if ready for him to don one. Shaw wrote 6 to 8 hours a day, even when he'd reached his 90s.

Evidence of his longtime relationship with the written word is obvious; one of his old typewriters is still in position. Shaw, of course, was famous for his eccentricities, his vegetarianism, and his longevity. And, of course, he was famed for his vast literary output, the most well known of which remains *Pygmalion,* on which the musical *My Fair Lady* was based.

Off Hill Farm Lane, in the village of Ayot St. Lawrence. (€) **01438/820307.** Admission £4.50 ($9) adults, £2.25 ($4.50) children. Wed–Sun and bank holidays 1–5pm. Closed Nov to early Mar. From St. Albans, take B651 to Wheathampstead. Pass through the village, go right at the roundabout, and take the 1st left turn; 1.5km (1 mile) up on the left is Brides Hall Lane, which leads to the house.

8 Woburn Abbey: England's Great Georgian Manor (★(★(★

71km (44 miles) N of London

Aside from Windsor Castle, the most visited attraction in the Home Counties is Woburn Abbey, which is so spectacular you should try to visit even if you have to miss all the other historic homes described in this chapter. The great 18th-century Georgian mansion has been the traditional seat of the dukes of Bedford for more than 3 centuries.

WHERE TO STAY

Bell Hotel and Inn   This 17th-century inn is a mixture of Tudor, Georgian, and Victorian architecture. Its modernized bedrooms are small to midsize, each tastefully and comfortably furnished. The inn is convenient for touring Woburn Abbey and the safari park. A good, filling English breakfast greets you in the morning.

21 Bedford St., Woburn, Bedfordshire MK17 9QB. (€) **01525/290280.** Fax 01525/290017. www.bellinn-woburn.com. 24 units. £95 ($190) double; £105 ($210) four-poster double. Rates include English breakfast. AE, MC, V. **Amenities:** Restaurant; bar; room service; laundry service; dry cleaning. *In room:* TV, beverage maker.

The Inn at Woburn (★   After visiting the abbey, head here for food and lodging at the gates of the estate. This Georgian coaching inn has a checkered history that blends old and new. Tastefully modernized, it preserves a certain mellow charm. Guests are housed in one of several well-furnished and beautifully maintained rooms, which have been refurbished. A more modern block provides "executive bedrooms," which don't have the charm of the older units but are more up-to-date and comfortable.

1 George St., Woburn, Bedfordshire MK17 9PX. (€) **01525/290441.** Fax 01525/290432. www.theinnatwoburn.com. 57 units. £135–£165 ($270–$330) double; £190–£205 ($380–$410) suite. Children 15 and younger stay free in parent's room. AE, DC, MC, V. **Amenities:** Restaurant; bar; room service; laundry service. *In room:* TV, minibar, coffeemaker, hair dryer, trouser press, safe.

WHERE TO DINE

The Black Horse ENGLISH/INTERNATIONAL   Our favorite pub in Woburn opened in 1824 as a coaching inn, and it retains a dark, woodsy interior evocative of that era. It sits behind a stucco-sheathed Georgian facade on the town's main street. Simple pub platters at lunch accompany the ales and lagers served, which include "filled baguettes" (sandwiches on French bread). Steaks, lasagna, a ploughman's lunch of bread and cheese, and spicy soups inspired by Thai recipes are also served. In a separate room you can order more substantial restaurant fare, including fresh fish such as Dover sole grilled with lemon butter or salmon with dill in a white-wine sauce.

1 Bedford St. (€) **01525/290210.** Main courses £9.50–£13 ($19–$26). AE, DISC, MC, V. Daily noon–3pm and 6–9:45pm.

The Magpies Hotel ENGLISH   After your visit to Woburn Abbey (see below), head here for food and drink. This is a small, family-run pub housed in a 16th-century former coaching inn near the Woburn Golf Club. The beers of choice are Ruddles Best, Webster's, and Marston's Pedigree. The food is simple but good and filling fare, including well-stuffed sandwiches and a ploughman's lunch of bread and cheese. More substantial meals include steaks, roast duck breast with buttered leek cabbage, mussels in white wine, and cod fried in a beer batter. There is also a separate room for dining, plus a courtyard with tables where guests can eat and drink outside in fair weather.

Bedford St. ⓒ 01525/290219. Bar lunches and sandwiches £6.95–£8.50 ($14–$17); Sun roast dinners £6.95–£13 ($14–$26). MC, V. Fri noon–2pm; Sat noon–2:30pm; Sun 11:30am–2:30pm; Tues–Sat 6:30–9:30pm.

Paris House 🐾🐾 CONTINENTAL/FRENCH   This reconstructed timbered house stands in a park where you can see deer grazing. The black-and-white building originally stood in Paris where it was constructed for the Great Exhibition 1878, but it was torn down and transplanted, timber by timber, to Woburn. Since 1983, it has been the domain of Bedfordshire's finest chef, Peter Chandler, the first English apprentice of the legendary Roux brothers. Chandler has brought his own innovative touch to the dishes served here. He still regularly visits France for new ideas and is known for his use of the freshest of seasonal ingredients. Try his delectable marinated Cajun prawns, delicately spiced savory, or duck confit in a black currant–and–orange sauce. The chef is rightly known for his *tulipe en fantaisie*, a sugar fantasy with fruit and ice cream.

Woburn Park (3.5km/2¼ miles southeast of Woburn on A4012). ⓒ 01525/290692. www.parishouse.co.uk. Reservations required. Fixed-price dinner £60 ($120), lunch £30 ($60). AE, MC, V. Tues–Sun noon–2pm; Tues–Sat 7–9:30pm.

TOURING THE ESTATE

Woburn Abbey   In the 1950s, the present duke of Bedford opened Woburn Abbey to the public to pay off his debt of millions of pounds in inheritance taxes. In 1974, he turned the estate over to his son and daughter-in-law, the marquess and marchioness of Tavistock, who reluctantly took on the business of running the 75-room mansion. And what a business it is, today drawing hundreds of thousands of visitors a year and employing more than 300 people to staff the shops and grounds.

Its state apartments are rich in furniture, porcelain, tapestries, silver, and a valuable art collection, including paintings by Van Dyck, Holbein, Rembrandt, Gainsborough, and Reynolds. One of the most notable paintings is the Armada Portrait of Elizabeth I. Her hand rests on the globe, as Philip's invincible armada perishes in the background.

Queen Victoria and Prince Albert visited Woburn Abbey in 1841; Victoria's dressing room displays a fine collection of 17th-century paintings from the Netherlands. Among the oddities and treasures at Woburn Abbey are a grotto of shells, a Sèvres dinner service (gift of Louis XV), and a chamber devoted to memorabilia of "the Flying Duchess," the wife of the 11th duke of Bedford, a remarkable woman who disappeared on a solo flight in 1937 (coincidentally, the same year as Amelia Earhart). The duchess was 72 years old at the time.

Today, Woburn Abbey is surrounded by a 1,214-hectare (3,000-acre) deer park, including the famous Père David deer herd, which was originally from China and saved from extinction at Woburn. **Woburn Safari Park** has lions, tigers, giraffes, camels, monkeys, Przewalski's horses, bongos, and other animals.

1km (a half-mile) southeast of the village of Woburn, which is 21km (13 miles) southwest of Bedford. (©) 01525/ 290333. www.woburnabbey.co.uk. Admission £9.50–£16 ($19–$32) adults, £8.50–£15 ($17–$30) seniors, £8.50–£13 ($17–$26) children. House Apr–Sept daily 11am–5pm, to 3pm in winter; park daily 10am–4:30pm. In summer, travel agents can book you on organized coach tours out of London. Otherwise, if driving, take M1 north to Junction 12 or 13, where directions are signposted.

NEARBY SHOPPING & AFTERNOON TEA

In a wonderful old building, **Town Hall Antiques,** Market Place (© **01525/ 290950**), is a treasure-trove of collectibles and antiques, including Early English porcelain and pieces from the 1940s. Some unusual commemorative items are also sold, such as an array of Victorian, Georgian, and Edwardian memorabilia. There's something here to suit a wide range of pocketbooks, including clocks, Victorian jewelry, brass, copper, "kitchenalia," paintings (originals and reproductions), guns, and swords.

At teatime, head to **Capriocoli,** 15 Market Place (© **01525/290464**); it's inside a B&B with low-beamed ceilings that add to its intimacy and charm. A pot of tea with clotted cream and cake is £6 ($12). Baked goods include scones (chocolate, lemon, and Victoria sponge), Italian pastries, and cake (carrot, coffee, and fruit), as well as daily specials. The tearoom is open Tuesday to Sunday, but it's a good idea to call on weekends between January and Easter as it may be closed if business is slow.

8

Kent, Surrey & Sussex: The Garden of England

South and southeast of London are the shires (counties) of Kent, Surrey, and East and West Sussex. Traditionally, this is a playground used by Londoners for quick holiday breaks, often weekend jaunts.

In **Kent, Canterbury** is the major highlight and makes the best base for exploring the area. Another convenient option is **Dover,** Britain's historic gateway to the Continent and famed for its white cliffs. Though Kent is on London's fringe, it's far removed in spirit and scenery. Since the days of the Tudors, cherry blossoms have enlivened the fertile landscape. Orchards and hop fields abound, earning Kent its title, "garden of England"—in England, that's tough competition. Kent suffered severe destruction during World War II, as it was the alley over which the Luftwaffe flew in its Blitz of London. But despite much devastation, it's still filled with interesting old towns and castles.

In fact, Kent has some of Europe's grandest mansions. If time is limited, seek out the big four: **Knole,** one of the largest private houses of England, a great example of Tudor architecture; **Hever Castle,** dating from the end of the 13th century, a gift from Henry VIII to the "great Flanders mare," Anne of Cleves; **Penshurst Place,** a magnificent English Gothic mansion and one of the outstanding country houses of Britain; and lovely **Leeds Castle,** near Maidstone, dating from A.D. 857. Although it doesn't compare with these grand castles, **Chartwell**

also merits a visit because of the man who used to call it home: Sir Winston Churchill. For more advice on how to tour these homes, refer to "Kent's Country Houses, Castles & Gardens," later in this chapter.

With the continuing expansion of London's borders, it's a wonder that the tiny county of **Surrey** hasn't been gobbled up and turned into a sprawling suburb. Yet its countryside remains unspoiled, though many people commute from here to London (only about 45–60 min. away).

If King Harold hadn't loved **Sussex** so much, English history might have been changed forever. Had the brave Saxon waited longer in the north, he could have marshaled more adequate reinforcements before striking south to meet the Normans. But Duke William's soldiers were ravaging the countryside he knew so well, and Harold rushed down to counter them.

Harold's enthusiasm for Sussex is understandable. The landscape rises and falls like waves. The county is known for its woodlands, from which came the timbers to build England's mighty fleet in days gone by. The shires lie south of London and Surrey, bordering Kent in the east, Hampshire in the west, and opening directly onto the English Channel, where the coast is dotted with seaside towns.

Like other sections in the vulnerable south of England, Sussex was the setting of some of the most significant events in

English history. Apart from the Norman landings at **Hastings,** the most life-changing transformation occurred in the 19th century, as middle-class Victorians flocked to the seashore, pumping new spirit into **Brighton** and even old Hastings.

The old towns and villages of Sussex, particularly **Rye** and **Winchelsea,** are far more intriguing than the seaside resorts. No Sussex village is lovelier than **Alfriston** (and the innkeepers know it, too); **Arundel** is noted for its castle; and the cathedral city of **Chichester** is a mecca for theater buffs. The old market town of **Battle** was the setting for the Battle of Hastings in 1066.

Where to base yourself in Sussex? The best option is Brighton because it has a wide choice of hotels, restaurants, and nightclubs. There's more excitement here at "London by the Sea" than at Hastings. If you're seeking old-English charm and village life, head instead to Alfriston or Rye.

1 Canterbury ⟨★⟨★⟨★

90km (56 miles) SE of London

Under the arch of the ancient West Gate journeyed Chaucer's knight, solicitor, nun, squire, parson, merchant, miller, and others—spinning tales. They were bound for the shrine of Thomas à Becket, archbishop of Canterbury, who was slain by four knights of Henry II on December 29, 1170. (The king later walked barefoot from Harbledown to the tomb of his former friend, where he allowed himself to be flogged in penance.) The shrine was finally torn down in 1538 by Henry VIII, as part of his campaign to destroy the monasteries and graven images. But Canterbury, by then, had already become an attraction.

The medieval Kentish city on the River Stour is the ecclesiastical capital of England. Once completely walled, many traces of its old fortifications remain. Canterbury was inhabited centuries before the birth of Jesus Christ. Although its most famous incident was the murder of Becket, the medieval city witnessed other major events in English history, including Bloody Mary's order to burn nearly 40 victims at the stake. Richard the Lion-Hearted returned this way from crusading, and Charles II passed through on the way to claim his crown.

Canterbury "pilgrims" continue to arrive today, except now they're called day-trippers and they overrun the city and its monuments. Because it lay in the pathways of bombers heading for London during the Nazi Blitz of 1941, historic Canterbury suffered enormous damage to its center. After the war, there was some attempt at restoration, but the city no longer has its wonderful prewar medieval look. Yet there is much still left to intrigue today's visitor, who can easily spend a day there. The city has an active university life—mainly students from Kent—and an enormous number of pubs. Its High Street is filled with shoppers in from the country. We suggest exploring Canterbury in the early morning or the early evening, after the busloads have departed.

ESSENTIALS

GETTING THERE   Frequent train service arrives from Victoria, Charing Cross, Waterloo, and London Bridge stations. The journey takes 1½ hours. For rail information, call ⟨ **0845/748-4950** or visit **www.nationalrail.co.uk**.

The bus from Victoria Coach Station takes 1½ to 2 hours and leaves every hour. For schedules, call ⟨ **0870/580-8080** or visit **www.nationalexpress.com**.

If you're driving from London, take the A2, then the M2. Canterbury is signposted all the way. The city center is closed to cars, but it's only a short walk from several parking areas to the cathedral.

VISITOR INFORMATION   A few doors from St. Margaret's Church, the **Canterbury Tourist Information Centre,** 12–13 Sun St., Canterbury CT1 2HX (© **01227/ 378100;** www.canterbury.co.uk), is generally open Monday to Saturday 10am to 5pm (closes at 4pm off season).

GETTING AROUND BY BIKE   Using your credit card as a security deposit, you can also arrange rentals at **Downland Cycle Hire,** St. Stephens Rd. (© **01227/ 479643;** www.downlandcycles.co.uk), which charges from £12 ($24) per day.

WHERE TO STAY

In spite of all its fame as a tourist destination, Canterbury still lacks a really first-class hotel. What you get isn't bad, but it's not state-of-the-art.

MODERATE

ABode Canterbury 🏵🏵   This hotel has been around since the end of Victoria's reign, with a recorded history dating from 1588. But never in its life has it been such a fine bastion of comfort and class as following its takeover by the ABode hotel chain. Lying inside the ancient city walls and within minutes of the cathedral, ABode's location is one of the best in town. All the bedrooms accent luxury with comfortable, tasteful furnishings. Rooms are amusingly ranked "desirable" (impossible to resist); "enviable" (sinfully self-indulgent), and "fabulous" (the ultimate in ABode luxury). Michael Caine's restaurant in the hotel is Canterbury's finest choice for dining (p. 277).

High St., Canterbury, Kent CT1 2RX. © **01227/766266.** Fax 01227/784874. www.abodehotels.co.uk. 72 units. £110–£180 ($220–$360) double; from £295 ($590) suite. AE, DC, MC, V. Parking £5 ($10). **Amenities:** Restaurant; bar; minigym; room service; babysitting; laundry service. *In room:* TV/DVD, Wi-Fi, coffeemaker, hair dryer, iron.

The Chaucer Hotel 🏵   Located on a historic street, the Chaucer Hotel is in a Georgian house a few minutes' walk from the cathedral. Comfortably furnished rooms lie at the end of a labyrinth of stairs, narrow hallways, and doors. (The hotel staff carries your luggage and parks your car.) The best rooms, with views over Canterbury rooftops and the cathedral, are nos. 60, 61, and 65. All rooms, however, are named in a wonderfully quirky way that honors former archbishops as well as some of Chaucer's racier pilgrims. Units range from midsize to most spacious, each chamber evoking a country inn. The most elegant room is no. 20, the honeymoon chamber with a Henry VIII–style four-poster bed. If you'd like to share a room with a ghost, book no. 62.

63 Ivy Lane (off Lower Bridge St.), Canterbury, Kent CT1 1TU. © **01227/464427.** Fax 01227/450397. www.swallowhotels.com/hotels/chaucer-hotel. 42 units. £90–£120 ($180–$240) double. AE, MC, V. Free parking. **Amenities:** Restaurant; bar; secretarial services; room service; babysitting; laundry service; dry cleaning. *In room:* A/C, TV, minibar, coffeemaker, hair dryer, iron, trouser press.

Ebury Hotel 🏵 *Value*   One of the finest small inns in Canterbury, this gabled Victorian house stands on .8 hectares (2 acres) of gardens at the city's edge, easy walking distance from the city center. Built in 1850, it's composed of two separate houses that were joined several years ago; the management also rents flats on a weekly basis. The accommodations are roomy and pleasantly decorated. The rooms, ranging from small to medium, are constantly being refurbished. *Note:* Rooms fill up quickly, so it's important to reserve in advance.

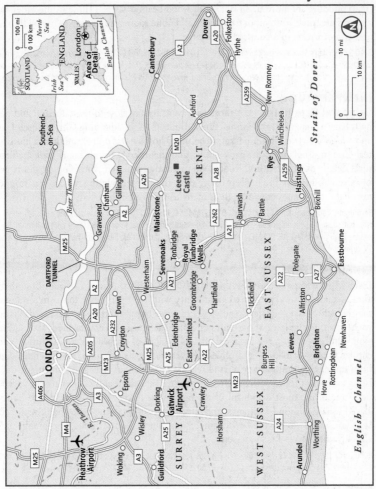

65–67 New Dover Rd., Canterbury, Kent CT1 3DX. ☎ **01227/768433**. Fax 01227/459187. www.ebury-hotel.co.uk. 15 units. £95–£145 ($190–$290) double; £115–£145 ($230–$290) family room. Rates include English breakfast. AE, MC, V. Free parking. Closed Dec 23 to mid-Jan. Follow the signs to A2, Dover Rd., on left-hand side, south of the city. **Amenities:** Restaurant; bar; heated indoor pool; Jacuzzi; room service; laundry service; dry cleaning. *In room:* TV, Wi-Fi, coffeemaker, hair dryer, iron, trouser press.

Falstaff Hotel   Just 360m (1,200 ft.) from the West Station, this classic Canterbury choice, complete with a flagstone-covered courtyard, retains its sense of history. Next to the Westgate Tower, it has a parking lot and easy access to the M2 and the M20. Many of the small, cozy rooms evoke old England with their polished oak tables, leaded glass windows, and original ceiling beams; most have solid modern furniture. Some units are large enough to accommodate small families. Accommodations in the main building are more traditional with wood beams, whereas those in the other two annexes are more contemporary in styling. Public rooms are as cozy as the bedrooms, and you can relax in a comfortable lounge.

8–10 St. Dunstan's St., Canterbury, Kent CT2 8AF. (℗ **01227/462138**. Fax 01227/463525. www.foliohotels.com. 46 units. £80–£160 ($160–$320) double. Rates include breakfast. AE, DC, MC, V. Free parking. **Amenities:** Restaurant; bar; lounge; room service; laundry service; dry cleaning. In room: TV, Wi-Fi, coffeemaker, hair dryer, trouser press.

INEXPENSIVE
Cathedral Gate Hotel For those who want to stay close to the cathedral and perhaps have a view of it, this is the choice. Built in 1438, adjoining Christchurch Gate and overlooking the Buttermarket, this former hospice was one of the first fashionable teahouses in England in the early 1600s, and the interior reveals many little architectural details of that century. Rooms are modestly furnished, with sloping floors and massive oak beams. You'll sleep better than the former pilgrims who often stopped over here, sometimes crowding in as many as six to eight in a bed.

36 Burgate, Canterbury, Kent CT1 2HA. (℗ **01227/464381**. Fax 01227/462800. www.cathgate.co.uk. 25 units, 12 with bathroom (shower only). £58–£70 ($116–$140) double without bathroom, £98 ($196) with bathroom. Rates include English breakfast. AE, DC, MC, V. Parking £5 ($10) nearby. **Amenities:** Restaurant; bar; room service. In room: TV, coffeemaker, hair dryer.

WHERE TO DINE
Café Mauresque ★ (Finds) SPANISH/MOROCCAN A touch of exotica and the aura of the souk are brought to Canterbury with the opening of this cafe/restaurant that not only serves the best sandwiches in town but also offers the best tapas. Sandwiches feature the likes of Serrano lamb and manchego cheese flavored with saffron aioli. You can also order such delights as a salad of barbecued squid stuffed with chorizo, cherry tomatoes, and olives. A *salon de thé*, or tea salon, also operates daily from midday to 5pm, serving a good selection of delicious tarts and homemade cakes along with mint tea or coffee. As to be expected, couscous and tagines are the specialties. One of the most delightful of the tagines we discovered was duck with honey-glazed squash, almonds, sultanas, and cinnamon, although the lamb shank with baby eggplant and dates flavored with ginger was almost as delectable. The orange-and-almond cake makes a tasty dessert.

8 Butchery Lane. (℗ **01227/464300**. Reservations recommended. Main courses £9.50–£15 ($19–$30); tapas £2.75–£4 ($5.50–$8); lunch sandwiches £5.25–£7.50 ($11–$15). AC, DC, MC, V. Daily noon–10pm.

Duck Inn (Finds) ENGLISH/MEDITERRANEAN Once called the Woodsmen Arms, this restaurant is known as the Duck Inn because of its low door. (As you entered, the clientele would shout "Duck!"). It's set within a 16th-century building that once belonged to the grandmother of novelist Ian Fleming, author of the James Bond series (he composed the first draft of *You Only Live Twice* within its garden). From its kitchens emerge a combination of old-fashioned English country fare—steak-and-kidney pudding, cod filets with chips, and Mediterranean food such as mussels in white wine and pesto-flavored pasta. Blackboards list the various, and frequently changing, specials of the day. In summer, the garden offers seating outdoors, but throughout the rest of the year, most visitors prefer the timbered nostalgia-laden interior.

Pett Bottom, near Bridge. (℗ **01227/830354**. Reservations recommended. Main courses £7–£15 ($14–$30). AE, DC, MC, V. Mon–Fri noon–3pm and 6pm–midnight; Sat–Sun noon–midnight. Drive 8km (5 miles) outside Canterbury near the village of Bridge on the road to Dover.

Michael Caine's Restaurant at ABode ✿✿✿ ENGLISH/CONTINENTAL   At long last Canterbury has a deluxe restaurant serving a light, elegant cuisine. The beautifully designed restaurant forms the centerpiece of the town's front-ranking hotel. Although modernized, it maintains a classic elegance. The chefs secure the best of local ingredients from the "Garden of England," as Kent is called. Their larder also branches out to include Sussex beef and Romney Marsh lamb plus shellfish from Whitstable (especially those delectable oysters). The chef's food is not overly adorned to destroy natural flavors. Appetizers include herb-crusted filet of halibut with lyonnaise potatoes or fresh green-bean soup scented with smoked bacon and white truffle oil, followed by such mains as roast sirloin of Kentish beef with a wild mushroom purée or roast monkfish with a leek fondue in a chive-butter sauce.

High St. ✆ 01277/826684. www.abodehotels.co.uk. Reservations required. Main courses £19–£22 ($38–$44). AE, DC, MC, V. Mon–Sat noon–2:30pm and 7–10pm; Sun 12:30–2:30pm.

Osteria Posillipo ✿ ITALIAN   This trattoria is a bastion of zesty Italian cookery. Some dishes are standard, including the pastas, beef, and veal found on most Italian menus, but the daily specials have a creative flair and are based on the freshest ingredients available that day. Some of the best starters include fresh mussels in white-wine sauce or bruschetta topped with garlic, basil, and fresh tomatoes. Among the tasty mains are lamb in a red-wine sauce or fresh salmon and king prawns in a lemon sauce.

16 The Borough. ✆ 01227/761471 or 01227/784924. Reservations recommended, especially at lunch. Main courses £8.50–£15 ($17–$30). AE, DC, MC, V. Daily noon–3pm and 6–11pm. Closed last 2 weeks in Aug.

SEEING THE SIGHTS

Canterbury Cathedral ✿✿✿   The foundation of this splendid cathedral dates from A.D. 597, but the earliest part of the present building is the great Romanesque crypt built around A.D. 1100. The monastic quire erected on top of this at the same time was destroyed by fire in 1174, only 4 years after the murder of Thomas à Becket on a dark December evening in the northwest transept, which is still one of the most famous places of pilgrimage in Europe. The destroyed quire was immediately replaced by a magnificent early Gothic one, the first major expression of that architectural style in England.

Frankly, the exterior of the cathedral is more impressive than the interior, which is surprising since this is the mother church of Anglican Christianity and the seat of the archbishop of Canterbury. The landmark 72m (235-ft.) **Bell Harry Tower** ✿✿, completed in 1505, is the most distinctive feature of the building. You enter through the ornate **Christ Church Gate** ✿ from the early 16th century.

Inside, you wander into a stage setting that evokes T. S. Eliot's play *Murder in the Cathedral.* Our favorite architectural fantasies are the fan-vaulted colonnades of the **Great Cloister** ✿ on the northern flank of the building. From the cloister you can enter the **Chapter House,** with its magnificent web of intricate tracery from the 1300s. This architectural ensemble supports the roof and a wall of stained glass, depicting scenes from Becket's tragic life.

Perpendicular arches support intricate fan vaulting from the 1400s at the crossing of the nave and transepts, creating architectural drama under the Bell Harry Tower. Look for the slender shafts of columns that rise without interruption into the high vault.

The lofty aisles were meant to provoke awe in the Canterbury pilgrim. Abundant light floods in from windows designed to create an air of tranquillity, although that is shattered by the thousands of visitors who descend every day.

The cathedral is noteworthy for its medieval tombs of royal personages, such as King Henry IV and Edward the Black Prince. Prince Edward of England was the eldest son of Edward III and the father of Richard II. Prince Edward was one of England's ablest military commanders during the Hundred Years' War. His nickname was probably derived from the color of his armor, but nobody knows for sure. To the later Middle Ages belong the great 14th-century nave and the Bell Harry Tower. The cathedral stands on spacious precincts amid the remains of the buildings of the monastery—cloisters, chapter house, and Norman water tower—which have survived intact from Henry VIII's Dissolution.

Becket's shrine was destroyed by the Tudor king, but the site of that tomb is in Trinity Chapel, near the high altar. The saint is said to have worked miracles, and the cathedral has some rare stained glass depicting those feats.

But the most miraculous event is that the windows escaped Henry VIII's agents of destruction as well as Hitler's bombs. The windows were removed as a precaution at the beginning of the war. During the war, a large area of Canterbury was flattened, but the main body of the church was unharmed. However, the cathedral library was damaged during a German air raid in 1942. The replacement windows of the cathedral were blown in, which proved the wisdom of having the medieval glass safely stored away.

Insider's tip: We prefer to visit the cathedral at Evensong, when you can hear beautiful cathedral music played. Performances are Monday to Friday at 5:30pm and Saturday and Sunday at 3:15pm. Admission is free for Evensong, but you must tell the warder at the gate that you'd like to attend a performance; otherwise you'll be charged an entrance fee. You can also rent an audio tour—one of the best of any cathedral in England—costing £3.50 ($7) for adults or £2.50 ($5) for students and seniors. The informative tour on audio lasts 40 minutes.

11 The Precincts. ✆ 01227/762862. www.canterbury-cathedral.org. Admission £6.50 ($13) adults; £5 ($10) students, seniors, and children. Guided tours £4 ($8) adults, £3 ($6) students and children. Easter–Sept 30 Mon–Sat 9am–5pm; Oct 1–Easter Monday–Sat 9am–4:30pm; year-round Sun 12:30–2pm. No guided tours on Sun.

OTHER ATTRACTIONS

Canterbury Roman Museum   This museum is located beneath street level and is constructed around actual archaeological excavations. Interactive computer shows and the actual handling of Roman artifacts bring the past to life for all ages. The Roman town of Durovernum Cantiacorum was established shortly after Emperor Claudius's invasion of the area in A.D. 43 and continued to flourish for nearly 400 years. Visitors can follow the archaeologists' detective work through an excavated Roman house site containing patterned mosaics that were discovered after the wartime bombing. Other exhibits include the reconstruction of a Roman market place.

Butchery Lane. ✆ 01227/785575. Admission £3.10 ($6.20) adults; £1.90 ($3.80) students, seniors, and children; £7.80 ($16) family ticket. Year-round Mon–Sat 10am–5pm; June–Oct Sun 1:30–5pm. Last entry time is 4pm. Closed Christmas week and Good Friday.

The Canterbury Tales *(Overrated*   This is a rather cheesy, yet very popular, commercial attraction. You might give it a try if you're hard up for something to do. Visitors are handed headsets with earphones, which give oral recitations of five of Chaucer's *Canterbury Tales* and the murder of St. Thomas à Becket. Audiovisual aids bring famous characters to life, and stories of jealousy, pride, avarice, and love are recounted. The sideshow re-creates the pilgrimages of Chaucerian England through a series of

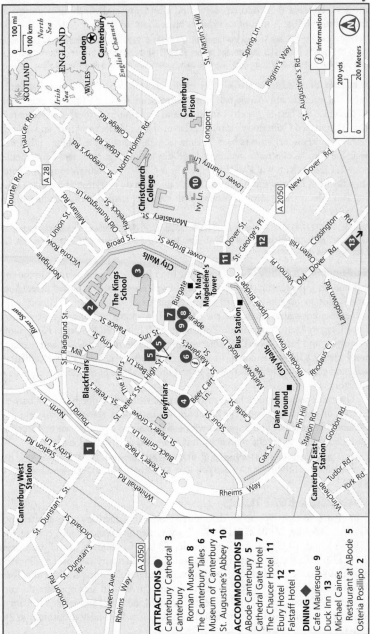

Canterbury

ATTRACTIONS ●
Canterbury Cathedral **3**
Canterbury
Roman Museum **8**
The Canterbury Tales **6**
Museum of Canterbury **4**
St. Augustine's Abbey **10**

ACCOMMODATIONS ■
ABode Canterbury **5**
Cathedral Gate Hotel **7**
The Chaucer Hotel **11**
Ebury Hotel **12**
Falstaff Hotel **1**

DINING ◆
Cafe Mauresque **9**
Duck Inn **13**
Michael Caines
    Restaurant at ABode **5**
Osteria Posillipo **2**

medieval tableaux that children might find a bit scary, and which older visitors may find a little boring. A tour of all exhibits takes about an hour.

23 St. Margaret's St. (off High St., near the cathedral). © 01227/479227. www.canterburytales.org.uk. Admission £7.50 ($15) adults, £6.50 ($13) students and seniors, £5.50 ($11) children 5–16, free for children 4 and younger. Mar–June and Sept–Oct daily 10am–5pm; July–Aug daily 9:30am–5pm; Nov–Feb daily 10am–4:30pm.

Museum of Canterbury *Kids*   Set in the ancient Poor Priests' Hospital with its medieval interiors and soaring oak roofs, the museum features award-winning displays to showcase the best of the city's treasures and lead visitors through crucial moments that have shaped Canterbury's history. State-of-the-art video, computer, and hologram technology transport visitors back in time to such events as the Viking raids and the wartime Blitz. Collections include a huge display of pilgrim badges from medieval souvenir shops. Kids will love the Rupert Bear Gallery, a children's museum centered on a toy bear, Rupert, and his chums. Little ones can do everything here, from watching Paul McCartney videos to playing with toy giant snakes, even attending Rupert's tea party.

Stour St. © 01227/475202. Admission £3.40 ($6.80) adults; £2.20 ($4.20) students, seniors, and children; £8.70 ($17) family ticket. Year-round Mon–Sat 10:30am–5pm; June–Sept Sun 1:30–5pm. Last entry time is 4pm. Closed Christmas week and Good Friday.

St. Augustine's Abbey *★★*   One of the most historic religious centers in the country, only its ruins remain, mostly at ground level. Augustine was buried here. (Augustine is not to be confused with the also-famous St. Augustine of Hippo, who is sometimes known as "Augustine the African.") In an attempt to convert the Saxons, Pope Gregory I sent Augustine to England in 597. Ethelbert, the Saxon King, allowed Augustine and his followers to build a church outside the city walls, and it endured until Henry VIII tore it down. In its day, the abbey church rivaled the cathedral in size, and enough of the ruins remain to conjure the whole of the cloister, church, and refectory.

The ruins are in a grassy field, so the average visitor who doesn't have a particular interest or who doesn't know the history may want to look elsewhere. Adjacent to the remains are the abbey buildings that were converted into a royal palace by Henry VIII and used briefly by several monarchs, including Elizabeth I and Charles I.

Corner of Lower Chantry Lane and Longport Rd. © 01227/767345. Admission £3.90 ($7.80) adults, £2.90 ($5.80) students and seniors, £2 ($4) children. Apr–Sept daily 10am–6pm; Oct–Mar Wed–Sun 10am–4pm. Closed Dec 24–26 and Jan 1.

WALKING & BOAT TOURS

From Easter to early November, daily guided tours of Canterbury are organized by the **Guild of Guides** (© 01227/459779; www.canterbury-walks.co.uk), costing £4.50 ($9) for adults, £4 ($8) students and seniors, £3 ($6) for children 11 and younger, and £15 ($30) for a family ticket. The cold stones of Canterbury take on new life as you take this tour, often conducted by witty and insightful guides. Meet at the Tourist Information Centre at 34 St. Margaret's St., in a pedestrian area opposite the cathedral. In 2009 tours leave July 2 to September 8 Monday to Saturday at 11:30am and 2pm; September 10 to October 28 and April 1 to July 1 Monday to Saturday at 2pm. On Sundays year-round tours leave at 2pm.

From just below the Weavers House, boats leave for half-hour **trips on the river** with commentary on the history of the buildings you pass. We recommend these boat tours, even if you've taken the walking tour. They can be a lot of fun, and you get to see Canterbury from a different perspective—that is, from the water. Admission costs £6 ($12) for adults, £5 ($10) for seniors and students, and £4 ($8) for children. Tours leave April to October daily 10am to 5pm, with departures every 15 to 20 minutes. For more information call **Canterbury Historic River Tours** at $©$ **07790/534744.**

HORSEBACK RIDING
The **Bursted Manor Riding Centre** in Pett Bottom ($©$ **01227/830568;** www.bursted manor.co.uk) is open Tuesday to Sunday 9am to 6pm. The last lesson is at 6pm on weekdays and 5pm on Saturday and Sunday. A 1-hour group lesson or hack ride is available for £39 ($78). The location is 4.5km (2¾ miles) southeast of Canterbury.

SHOPPING
Handmade pottery (vases, mugs, and teapots in earth colors of blues, greens, and browns) is sold at **Canterbury Pottery,** 38A Burgate, just before Mercury Lane ($©$ **01227/452608;** www.canterburypottery.co.uk). It is sturdy ware that wears well, including house-number plates that take 2 weeks to complete but can be mailed to your home.

Put on your tweed jacket and grab your pipe for a trip to a secondhand **Chaucer Bookshop,** 6–7 Beer Cart Lane ($©$ **01227/453912;** www.chaucer-bookshop.co.uk), with first editions (both old and modern), out-of-print books, special leather-bound editions, and a large selection of local history books.

CANTERBURY AFTER DARK
Gulbenkian Theatre, University of Kent, Giles Lane ($©$ **01227/769075;** www. kent.ac.uk/gulbenkian), is open from 11am to 5pm during school terms and 5:30 to 9pm on Saturday and Sunday, and offers a potpourri of jazz and classical productions, dance, drama, comedy, and a mix of new and student productions. The highlight of the theater season occurs at Cricket Week during the first week of August. Tickets cost £7 to £20 ($14–$40). The location is too far from the center of Canterbury to walk to—you need to drive or take a taxi.

Kids The World of Charles Dickens Lives Again
In the town of Chatham, where Charles Dickens spent part of his childhood, **Dickens World** has opened at Leviathan Way ($©$ **01634/890-421;** www.dickens world.co.uk). The town also holds a Dickens Festival every summer to honor the author of *A Christmas Carol.*

At this theme park the cobbled streets of Victorian England are peopled once again by pickpockets, wenches, rogues, and runaways, but it's all in fun. Visitors will have a chance to see the Ghost of Christmas Past in Ebenezer Scrooge's haunted house, be hectored by a schoolmaster at Dotheboxs Hall, and peer into the fetid cells of the notorious Newgate Prison. Expect more than whiff of kitsch, and know that Dickens purists will be offended.

The location is 35 miles southwest of London following the A2/M2; exit at Junction 1, 3, or 4. Trains from Victoria Station also lead to Chatham Station, where a shuttle bus will take you to the theme park for £1 ($2). Open daily 10am to 5pm, the park charges £13 ($25) for adults or £7.50 ($15) for children.

Marlowe Theatre, the Friars (© **01227/787787;** www.marlowetheatre.com), is Canterbury's only commercial playhouse. It's open year-round and offers drama, jazz and classical concerts, and contemporary and classical ballet. Tickets cost from £10 to £38 ($20–$75). The box office at Marlowe Theatre is open Monday to Saturday 10am to 9pm (Tues from 10:30am), and until 7pm on nonperformance nights. Most shows begin at 7:30pm.

A favorite local pub, **Alberry's Wine Bar,** 38 St. Margaret's St. (© **01227/452378**), offers a clubby atmosphere every night with a DJ spinning hip-hop, drum and bass, or chart music. The cover is £5 ($10) after 9pm Tuesday to Friday or the same fee after 10pm on weekends.

A laid-back student hangout, the **Cherry Tree,** 10 White Horse Lane (© **01227/451266**), offers a wide selection of beers, including Bass Ale on draft, Cherry Tree ale, three traditional lagers, and four bitters. The atmosphere is clubby, filled with casual conversation.

2 The White Cliffs of Dover

122km (76 miles) SE of London; 135km (84 miles) NE of Brighton

In Victoria's day, Dover was popular as a seaside resort; today it's known as a port for cross-Channel car and passenger traffic between England and France (notably Calais). Because it was one of England's most vulnerable and easy-to-hit targets during World War II, repeated bombings destroyed much of its harbor. The opening of the Channel Tunnel (Chunnel) in 1994 renewed Dover's importance.

Unless you're on your way to France or want to use Dover as a base for exploring the surrounding countryside, you can skip a visit here. Dover is rather dull except for those white cliffs. Even its hotels are second-rate; many people prefer to stay in Folkestone, about 16km (10 miles) to the southwest.

ESSENTIALS

GETTING THERE   Frequent trains run from Victoria Station or Charing Cross Station in London, daily from 5am to 10pm. You arrive at Priory Station, off Folkestone Road. During the day, two trains per hour depart from Canterbury East Station heading for Dover. For rail information, call © **0845/748-4950** or visit **www.national rail.co.uk**.

Frequent buses leave throughout the day—daily from 7am to 11:45pm—from London's Victoria Coach Station bound for Dover. Call © **0870/580-8080** for schedules or visit **www.nationalexpress.com**. The local bus station is on Pencester Road (no phone). Stagecoach provides daily bus service between Canterbury and Dover.

If you're driving from London, head first to Canterbury (see "Essentials," in section 1), then continue along the A2 southeast until you reach Dover, on the coast.

VISITOR INFORMATION   The **Tourist Information Centre** is on Old Town Gaol Street (© **01304/205108;** www.whitecliffscountry.org.uk). June, July, and August it's open daily 9am to 5:30pm; September to April open hours are Monday to Friday 9am to 5:30pm, Saturday and Sunday 10am to 4pm.

WHERE TO STAY

Best Western Churchill Hotel   Dover's most consistently reliable hotel is this interconnected row of town houses built to overlook the English Channel in the 1830s. After World War I, the premises were transformed into a hotel, and in 1994 it was completely refurbished. It offers a seafront balcony, a glass-enclosed front veranda, and tranquil rooms. Ranging from small to spacious, many rooms offer uninterrupted views of the coast of France. The hotel lies close to the eastern and western docks and the Hoverport for travel to and from France and Belgium.

Waterloo Crescent, Dover Waterfront, Dover, Kent CT17 9BP. ℂ 800/780-7234 in the U.S., or 01304/203633. Fax 01304/216320. www.bw-churchillhotel.co.uk. 81 units. £93 ($186) double; £108 ($216) executive double; £103 ($206) family. AE, DC, MC, V. **Amenities:** Restaurant; bar; health club w/sauna; salon; room service; laundry service; dry cleaning. *In room:* TV, high-speed Internet (in some rooms); minibar (in some rooms), coffeemaker, hair dryer, iron, trouser press.

Ramada Dover   Situated 5km (3 miles) north of Dover's Center, within a semi-industrial maze of superhighways and greenbelts, the court was originally custom-built as a motel in the 1970s. Bedrooms are carefully positioned so that most of them overlook lawns (and a view of the motorway), fields, and a children's playground next door. Each room is functional and comfortable.

Singledge Lane, Whitfield, near Dover CT16 3LF. ℂ 01304/821230. Fax 01304/825576. www.ramadainternational. com. 68 units. £70–£90 ($140–$180) double. AE, MC, V. Lies adjacent to the Whitfield exit of the A2 motorway. **Amenities:** Restaurant; bar; gym; room service; babysitting; laundry service; dry cleaning. *In room:* TV, Wi-Fi, minibar, coffeemaker, hair dryer, iron.

Wallett's Court ✺ *(Finds)*   Surrounded by fields and gardens in a tiny hamlet 2.5km (1½ miles) east of Dover, this is our preferred stopover in the area. Rebuilt in the Tudor style in the 1400s, it rests on a foundation dated from the time of the Norman Conquest of England. In 1975, the property was in seriously dilapidated condition until members of the Oakley family bought and restored it. The setting, near cliff tops overlooking the English Channel, is savored by bird-watchers and hill climbers. Each carefully restored bedroom features a different decorative theme, with the more expensive ones containing four-poster beds. Some lie within a barn that was comfortably converted into living quarters. Richly accessorized, each has a vivid Edwardian country-house motif and lots of mementos.

West Cliffe, St. Margaret's at Cliffe, Dover, Kent CT15 6EW. ℂ 01304/852424. Fax 01304/853430. www.walletts court.com. 16 units. Sun–Fri £129 ($258) double, Sat £209 ($418) double; Sun–Fri £169 ($338) suite, Sat £249 ($498) suite. Rates include English breakfast every day and dinner on Sat. AE, MC, V. Closed Dec 24–27. Follow A258 for 2.5km (1½ miles) east from the center of Dover (signposted DEAL). Wallett's Court is signposted off A258. **Amenities:** Restaurant (see Wallett's Court review, below); bar; indoor heated pool; outdoor tennis court; health club; spa; room service; babysitting; laundry service; dry cleaning. *In room:* TV/DVD, Wi-Fi, CD player, coffeemaker, hair dryer, iron.

WHERE TO DINE

Wallett's Court ✺ ENGLISH/INTERNATIONAL   One of the most appealing restaurants in the area lies within a half-timbered Jacobean-era manor house, grandly restored over 15 years. Within a dining room that's exemplary for its sense of history, you can enjoy dishes that change with the season—spring lamb, lobster and Dover sole in summer, or game in the autumn and winter months. For starters, try the caramelized Rye Bay scallops and medallions of wild rabbit with bay leaf (flavored with orange and cardamom), or else seared yellowfin tuna carpaccio with red chard, mango, lime, and chili. Some of the most delicious mains include pan-fried suckling pig with ouzo-flamed prunes and thyme-flavored mashed potatoes; or else try the poached filets of dealfish with langoustines.

West Cliffe, St. Margaret's at Cliffe (in Wallett's Court hotel). ℂ 01304/852424. Reservations recommended. 3-course fixed-price menu £40 ($80). AE, DC, MC, V. Tues–Sat 7–9pm; Sun noon–2pm and 7–9pm. Closed 1 week at Christmas.

EXPLORING DOVER

Your best view of the famous **white cliffs** ✸✸✸ is when arriving at Dover by ferry or hovercraft from Calais. Otherwise, walk out to the end of the town's Prince of Wales pier, the largest of the town's western docks. From there, the cliffs loom above you. Or drive 8km (5 miles) east to the pebble-covered beaches of the fishing hamlet of Deal. A local fisher may take you on an informal boat ride.

Deal Castle ✸   Deal Castle is .5km (a quarter-mile) south of the Deal town center, 8km (5 miles) from Dover. A defensive fort built around 1540, it's the most spectacular example of the low, squat forts constructed by Henry VIII. Its 119 gun positions made it the most powerful of his defense forts. Centered on a circular keep surrounded by two rings of semicircle bastions, the castle was protected by an outer moat. The entrance was approached by a drawbridge with an iron gate. The castle was damaged by bombs during World War II but has since been restored to its earlier form. The admission price includes audio tours.

On the seafront. ✆ **01304/372762.** Admission £4 ($8) adults, £3 ($6) seniors, £2 ($4) children. Daily 10am–6pm. Closed Oct–Mar.

Dover Castle ✸✸✸   Rising nearly 120m (400 ft.) above the port is one of the oldest and best-known castles in England. Its keep was built at the command of Becket's fair-weather friend, Henry II, in the 12th century. The ancient castle was called back to active duty as late as World War II. The Pharos on the grounds is a lighthouse built by the Romans in the first half of the 1st century. The Romans first landed at nearby Deal in 54 B.C., but after 6 months they departed and didn't return until nearly 100 years later, in A.D. 43, when they stayed and occupied the country for 400 years. The castle houses a military museum and a film center, plus "Live and Let's Spy," an exhibition of World War II spying equipment. Audio tours of the castle are included in admission price.

Castle Hill. ✆ **01304/211067.** Admission £10 ($21) adults, £8.20 ($16) students and seniors, £5.20 ($10) children ages 5–15, free for children age 4 and under. Thurs–Mon 10am–4pm (last tour at 3pm).

Roman Painted House ✸✸   This 1,800-year-old Roman structure, called Britain's "buried Pompeii," has exceptionally well-preserved walls and an under-floor heating system. It's famous for its unique Bacchic murals. Brass-rubbing is also offered. You'll find it in the town center near Market Square.

New St. ✆ **01304/203279.** Admission £2 ($4) adults, 80p ($1.60) seniors and children 16 and younger. Apr–Sept Tues–Sat 10am–5pm; July–Aug Mon–Sat 10am–5pm; year-round Sun 2–5pm.

Secret War Time Tunnels ✸ *Finds*   These secret tunnels, used during the evacuation of Dunkirk in 1940 and the Battle of Britain, can now be explored on a 40-minute guided tour. The tunnels were originally excavated to house cannons to be used (if necessary) against an invasion by Napoleon. Some 60m (200 ft.) below ground, they were the headquarters of Operation Dynamo, when more than 300,000 troops from Dunkirk were evacuated. On once forbidden ground to all but those with the strongest security clearance, you can stand in the very room where Ramsey issued orders; experience the trauma of life in an underground operating theater; and look out over the English Channel from the hidden, cliff-top balcony, just as Churchill did during the Battle of Britain.

Dover Castle, Castle Hill. ✆ **01304/211067.** Admission included in Dover Castle price (see above). Last tour leaves 1 hr. before castle closing time.

3 The Ancient Seaport of Rye ✮✮

100km (62 miles) SE of London

"Nothing more recent than a Cavalier's Cloak, Hat and Ruffles should be seen on the streets of Rye," said Louis Jennings. This ancient town, formerly an island, flourished in the 13th century. In its early days, **Rye** was a smuggling center, its residents sneaking in contraband from the marshes to stash away in little nooks.

But the sea receded from Rye, leaving it perched like a giant whale out of water, 3km (2 miles) from the Channel. Attacked several times by French fleets, Rye was practically razed in 1377. But it rebuilt successfully, in full Elizabethan panoply. When Queen Elizabeth I visited in 1573, she was so impressed that she bestowed upon the town the distinction of Royal Rye. This has long been considered a special place and, over the years, has attracted famous people, such as novelist Henry James.

Its narrow cobblestone streets twist and turn like a labyrinth, and jumbled along them are buildings whose sagging roofs and crooked chimneys indicate the town's medieval origins. The town overflows with sites of architectural interest.

Neighboring Winchelsea has also witnessed the water's ebb. Its history traces from Edward I and has experienced many dramatic moments, such as sacking by the French. In the words of one 19th-century writer, Winchelsea is "a sunny dream of centuries ago." The finest sight of this dignified residential town is a badly damaged 14th-century church with a number of remarkable tombs.

ESSENTIALS

GETTING THERE   From London, the Southeastern Line offers trains south from Charing Cross or Cannon Street Station, with a change at Ashford, before continuing on to Rye. You can also go via Tunbridge Wells with a change in Hastings. Trains run every hour during the day, arriving at the Rye Train Station off Cinque Ports Street. The trip takes 1½ to 2 hours. Call ✆ **0845/748-4950** or visit www.nationalrail.co.uk for schedules and information.

You'll need to take the train to get to Rye, but once there you'll find buses departing every hour on the hour for many destinations, including Hastings. Various bus schedules are posted on signs in the parking lot. For bus information on connections in the surrounding area, call ✆ **0870/608-2608.**

If you're driving from London, take the M25, M26, and M20 east to Maidstone, going southeast along the A20 to Ashford. At Ashford, continue south on the A2070.

VISITOR INFORMATION   The **Rye Tourist Office** is in the Heritage Centre on the Strand Quay (✆ **01797/226696**). It's open from April to the end of October daily 10am to 5pm; November to December and March daily 10am to 4pm, and January and February daily 10am to 3pm. The Heritage Centre houses a free exhibition and is also home to **Story of Rye,** a sound-and-light show depicting more than 700 years of Rye's history. Adults pay £3 ($6), students and seniors £1.50 ($3), children £1 ($2), and families £7 ($14).

WHERE TO STAY

Durrant House Hotel   This beautiful Georgian house, restored in 2003, is set on a quiet residential street at the end of Market Street. The charm and character of the hotel are enhanced by a cozy lounge with an arched, brick fireplace. The renowned artist Paul Nash lived next door until his death in 1946; in fact, his celebrated view, as seen in his painting *View of the Rother*, can be enjoyed from the River Room, a four-poster bedroom suite. Bedrooms range from small to medium in size; some of them are big enough for families and others have four-poster beds. At one time, the house was used as a relay station for carrier pigeons; these birds brought news of the victory at Waterloo.

2 Market St. (off High St.), Rye, East Sussex TN31 7LA. © 01797/223182. Fax 01797/226940. www.durranthouse. com. 6 units. £90 ($180) double; £105 ($210) four-poster room. Rates include English breakfast. MC, V. **Amenities:** Lounge; babysitting. *In room:* TV, coffeemaker, hair dryer.

The George ✪

This coaching inn enjoys a long history dating from 1575. In the 18th century, it drew a diverse clientele: some traveling by horse-drawn carriage, others by boat between London and France. The half-timbered architecture charms a visitor like no other small inn in the region (except the Mermaid, which has an even more antique atmosphere; see below). Some of the timbers may be from the wreck of an English ship broken up in Rye Harbour after the defeat of the Spanish Armada. Bedrooms have been refurbished and modernized, each room individually designed with custom furniture and Italian linens.

High St., Rye, East Sussex TN31 7JT. © 01797/222114. Fax 01797/224065. www.thegeorgeinrye.com. 24 units. £125–£175 ($250–$350) double; £225 ($450) suite. Rates include English breakfast. AE, DC, MC, V. **Amenities:** Restaurant; bar; room service; babysitting; laundry service; dry cleaning. *In room:* TV/DVD, high-speed Internet, coffeemaker, hair dryer, trouser press.

Hope Anchor Hotel

At the end of a cobblestone street, on a hill dominating the town, stands this 17th-century hostelry, which enjoys panoramic views of the surrounding countryside and overlooks the Strand Quay, where impressive yachts can be seen at their moorings. Oak beams and open fires in winter make this a most inviting place to spend a few days. Bedrooms are comfortable, ranging from small to midsize; two feature four-poster beds and have been refurbished. The most expensive unit is the Admiral Apartment, which is luxurious and spacious with a large drawing room and deluxe bathroom.

Watchbell St., Rye, East Sussex TN31 7HA. © 01797/222216. Fax 01797/223796. www.thehopeanchor.co.uk. 15 units. £110–£165 ($220–$330) double; £160–£210 ($320–$420) suite. Rates include English breakfast. AE, MC, V. **Amenities:** Restaurant; bar; room service; babysitting; laundry service; dry cleaning. *In room:* TV, Wi-Fi (in most rooms), coffeemaker, hair dryer.

The Mermaid Inn ✪✪

The Mermaid Inn is one of the most famous of the old smugglers' inns of England, known to that band of cutthroats, the real-life Hawkhurst Gang, as well as to Russell Thorndike's fictional character, Dr. Syn. (One of the rooms, in fact, is called Dr. Syn's Bedchamber and is connected to the bar by a secret staircase, stowed away in the thickness of the wall.) This place, with its Elizabethan associations and traditional touches, remains one of the most romantic old-world inns in Sussex. The most sought-after rooms are in the building overlooking the cobblestone street. Five units have four-poster beds. The accommodations vary considerably in shape and size, some quite large, others a bit cramped, as befits a building of this age. Comfort is the keynote, regardless of room assignment. Six units are spacious enough for a small family.

Mermaid St. (between West St. and the Strand), Rye, East Sussex TN31 7EY. © 01797/223065. Fax 01797/225069. www.mermaidinn.com. 31 units. £80–£110 ($160–$220) per person double with breakfast, £110–£140 ($220–$280) with breakfast and dinner. AE, DC, MC, V. **Amenities:** Restaurant; bar; room service; babysitting; laundry service; dry cleaning. *In room:* TV, hair dryer, beverage maker.

White Vine House ★ *(Finds)*   The winner of several awards for the beauty of its small front garden and the quality of its restoration, this charming house dates from 1568. Restored from an almost derelict shell in 1987 and recently refurbished by its owners, the creeper-clad inn carefully maintains the Georgian detailing of the formal public rooms and the Tudor-style wall and ceiling beams of the bedrooms. The restored bedrooms are light and airy, furnished mostly in white and cream with period furniture. In 2005, the oak panels in the restaurant and bar were restored for the first time since the inn was built.

High St., Rye, East Sussex TN31 7JF. (C) 01797/224748. Fax 01797/223599. www.whitevinehouse.co.uk. 7 units. £125–£165 ($250–$330) double; £185 ($370) family room. Rates include English breakfast. AE, DC, MC, V. **Amenities:** Restaurant; bar. *In room:* TV, coffeemaker.

WHERE TO DINE

Our preferred spot for teatime is the **Swan Cottage Tea Rooms,** 41 The Mint, High Street ((C) **01797/222423**), dating from 1420 and situated on the main street. This black-and-white half-timbered building is one of the most historic in town. We gravitate to the room in the rear because of its big brick fireplace. Delectable pastries and freshly made cakes await you along with a selection of teas, including Darjeeling, Earl Grey, Pure Assam, and others.

Flushing Inn ★ SEAFOOD/ENGLISH   The best restaurant in Rye, this 16th-century inn has preserved the finest of the past, including a wall-size fresco dating from 1544 that depicts a menagerie of birds and heraldic beasts. A rear dining room overlooks a flower garden. A special feature is the Sea Food Lounge Bar, where sandwiches and plates of seafood are available. Start with some tangy mussels in a cream-and–white wine sauce and follow perhaps with Rye Bay Dover sole pan-fried or on the bone. A whole steamed lobster comes in a garlic-butter sauce.

4 Market St. (C) 01797/223292. Reservations recommended. Fixed-price lunch £19 ($38), dinner £27–£37 ($54–$74); seafood main courses £9–£37 ($18–$74). DC, MC, V. Wed–Sun noon–1:30pm and 7–8:30pm. Closed 1st 2 weeks in Jan and 1st 2 weeks in June.

The Landgate Bistro MODERN ENGLISH   People come from miles around to dine in this pair of interconnected Georgian shops whose exteriors are covered with "mathematical tiles" (18th-c. simulated brick, applied over stucco facades to save money). Inside, Martin Peacock and Nilla Westin make everything from scratch, including their sourdough bread and ice cream, using local ingredients whenever possible. The bistro has the largest list of starters in town, delectable items such as a leek and Roquefort tart or else turbot and salt codfish cakes. The fresh fish brought in by the local fleet is the most popular item to order, especially Dover sole. You might also feast on duck breast in cider or wild rabbit with sherry. The Romoney Marsh lamb shank in red wine is another winning dish.

5–6 Landgate. (C) 01797/222829. Reservations required on weekends. Main courses £10–£16 ($20–$32); set-price menu Tues–Thurs £15 ($30) for 2 courses, £18 ($36) for 3 courses. AE, DC, MC, V. Tues–Fri and Sun before bank holidays 7–9:30pm; Sat 7–10pm. (Closing time may vary.)

EXPLORING THE AREA

In Rye, the old town's entrance is **Land Gate,** where a single lane of traffic passes between massive, 12m-high (40-ft.) stone towers. The top of the gate has holes through which boiling oil used to be poured on unwelcome visitors, such as French raiding parties.

Rye has had potteries for centuries, and today is no exception, with a number of outlets in town. The best potteries include **Rye Pottery,** Wishward Street (✆ **01797/ 223038**), and **David Sharp Ceramics,** the Mint (✆ **01797/222620**). The town also abounds in antiques and collectibles shops and new and used bookstores.

Lamb House   Henry James lived at Lamb House from 1898 to 1916. Many James mementos are scattered throughout the house, which is set in a walled garden. Its previous owner joined the gold rush in North America but perished in the Klondike, and James was able to buy the freehold for a modest £2,000 ($4,000). Some of his well-known books were written here. In *English Hours,* James wrote: "There is not much room in the pavilion, but there is room for the hard-pressed table and tilted chair—there is room for a novelist and his friends."

West St. (at the top of Mermaid St.). ✆ **01892/890651.** Admission £3.50 ($7) adults, £1.80 ($3.60) children. Thurs and Sat 2–6pm. Closed Dec–Mar.

Rye Castle Museum   This stone fortification was constructed around 1250 by King Henry III to defend the coast against attack by the French. For 300 years it was the town jail but has long since been converted into a museum that documents the town history. In 1996, the medieval Ypres Tower was restored.

3 East St., Rye. ✆ **01797/226728.** www.ryemuseum.co.uk. East St. site (main site) admission £2.50 ($5) adults, £2 ($4) students and seniors, free for children 15 and younger; Ypres Tower £2.95 ($5.90) adults, £2.50 ($5) students and seniors, free for children 15 and younger; combined ticket to both sites £5 ($10) adults, £4 ($8) students and seniors. East St. site Apr–Oct Sat–Sun 10:30am–1pm, Thurs–Mon 2–5pm; Ypres Tower Apr–Oct Thurs–Mon 10:30am–1pm and 2–5pm, Nov–Mar Sat–Sun 10:30am–3pm.

St. Mary's Parish Church   One notable historical site is the mid-12th-century church with its 16th-century clock flanked by two gilded cherubs (known as Quarter Boys because of their striking of the bells on the quarter-hour). The church is often referred to as "the Cathedral of East Sussex" because of its expansive size and ornate beauty. If you're brave, you can climb a set of wooden stairs and ladders to the bell tower of the church for an impressive view.

Church Sq. ✆ **01797/224935.** Admission to tower £2 ($4) adults, £1 ($2) children. Contributions appreciated to enter the church. June–Aug daily 9am–6pm; off season daily 9am–4pm.

Smallhythe Place *(Finds)*   On the outskirts of Winchelsea, this was for 30 years the country house of Dame Ellen Terry, the English actress acclaimed for her Shakespearean roles, who had a long theatrical association with Sir Henry Irving; she died in the house in 1928. This timber-framed structure, known as a "continuous-jetty house," was built in the first half of the 16th century and is filled with Terry memorabilia—playbills, props, makeup, and a striking display of costumes. An Elizabethan barn, adapted as a theater in 1929, is open for viewing on most days.

Smallhythe (on B2082 near Tenterden, about 9.5km/6 miles north of Rye). ✆ **01580/762334.** Admission £5 ($10) adults, £2.50 ($5) children, £13 ($26) family ticket. 2009 hours: Mar 3–18 Sat–Sun 11am–5pm; Mar 19–Oct 28 Mon–Wed and Sat–Sun 11am–5pm. Take bus no. 312 from Tenterden or Rye.

4 1066 & All That: Hastings ★★★ & Battle ★★

Hastings: 72km (45 miles) SW of Dover; 101km (63 miles) SE of London. Battle: 55km (34 miles) NE of Brighton; 88km (55 miles) SE of London

The world has seen bigger skirmishes, but few are as well remembered as the Battle of Hastings in 1066. When William, duke of Normandy, landed on the Sussex coast and lured King Harold (already fighting Vikings in Yorkshire) south to defeat, the destiny of the English-speaking people was changed forever.

The actual battle occurred at what is now Battle Abbey (13km/8 miles away), but the Norman duke used Hastings as his base of operations. You can visit the abbey, have a cup of tea in Battle's main square, and then be off, as the rich countryside of Sussex is much more intriguing than this sleepy market town.

Present-day Hastings is a little seedy and run-down. If you're seeking an English seaside resort, head for Brighton instead.

ESSENTIALS

GETTING THERE   Daily trains run hourly from London's Charing Cross Station to Hastings. The trip takes 1½ to 2 hours. The train station at Battle is a stop on the London-Hastings rail link. For rail information, call ℭ **0845/748-4950** or visit **www.nationalrail.co.uk**.

Hastings is linked by bus to Maidstone, Folkestone, and Eastbourne, which has direct service with scheduled departures. **National Express** operates regular daily service from London's Victoria Coach Station. If you're in Rye or Hastings in summer, several frequent buses run to Battle. For information and schedules, call ℭ **0870/580-8080** or visit **www.nationalexpress.com**.

If you're driving from the M25 ring road around London, head southeast to the coast and Hastings on the A21. To get to Battle, cut south to Sevenoaks and continue along the A21 to Battle via the A2100.

VISITOR INFORMATION   In Hastings, the **Hastings Information Centre** is at Queen's Square, Priory Meadow (ℭ **0845/2741001**; www.visithastings.com). It's open Monday to Friday from 8:30am to 6:15pm, Saturday 9am to 5pm, and Sunday 10:30am to 4:30pm.

In Battle, the **Tourist Information Centre** at Battle Abbey Gatehouse (ℭ **01424/773721**; www.1066country.com) is open April to September daily 9:30am to 5:30pm, October daily 10am to 5pm, and November through March daily from 10am to 4pm.

WHERE TO STAY
IN HASTINGS

Beauport Park Hotel ✦   This hotel has a cozy country-house aura and is more intimate and hospitable than the Royal Victoria (reviewed below). Originally the private estate of General Murray, former governor of Quebec, the building was destroyed by fire in 1923 and rebuilt in the old style. It's surrounded by beautiful gardens; the Italian-style grounds in the rear feature statuary and flowering shrubbery. Rooms range from midsize to large; some are fitted with elegant four-poster beds. The self-contained Forest Lodge is equipped with a double, twin, children's room, living area, sauna, and kitchen.

Battle Rd. (A2100), Hastings, East Sussex TN38 8EA. ℭ **01424/851222.** Fax 01424/852465. www.beauportpark hotel.co.uk. 25 units. £130–£150 ($260–$300) double; £170 ($340) suite. Rates include English breakfast. AE, DC, MC, V. Head 5.5km (3½ miles) northwest of Hastings, to the junction of A2100 and B2159. **Amenities:** 2 restaurants; bar; indoor heated pool; 9-hole golf course; tennis court; gym; spa; sauna; room service; laundry service; dry cleaning. *In room:* TV, coffeemaker, hair dryer, iron, trouser press.

Best Western Royal Victoria ✦   This seafront hotel, constructed in 1828, offers the most impressive architecture in town and the best accommodations in Hastings or

St. Leonards. It has welcomed many famous visitors, including its namesake, Queen Victoria herself. Many of the elegant and comfortably appointed rooms have separate lounge areas and views of the English Channel and Beachy Head. Many of the bedrooms are extremely large; all of them look as if Laura Ashley traipsed through, as evoked by dozens of half-tester beds in English chintz. Some of the accommodations are large enough for families, and a number of them are duplexes.

Marina, St. Leonards, Hastings, East Sussex TN38 0BD. ℂ 800/780-7234 in the U.S., or 01424/445544. Fax 01424/721995. www.bestwestern.co.uk. 52 units. £90–£140 ($180–$280) double. Children 15 and younger stay free in parent's room. Rates include English breakfast. AE, DC, MC, V. **Amenities:** Restaurant; 3 bars; room service; laundry service; dry cleaning. *In room:* TV, Wi-Fi, coffeemaker, hair dryer, iron, trouser press, safe.

Eagle House Hotel ☆ One of the best hotels in the area, this three-story mansion, originally built in 1860 as a palatial private home, lies in a residential section about a 10-minute walk from the beaches (it's adjacent to St. Leonards Shopping Centre). The well-furnished bedrooms come in various shapes and sizes.

12 Pevensey Rd., St. Leonards, East Sussex TN38 0JZ. ℂ 01424/430535. Fax 01424/437771. www.eaglehousehotel. co.uk. 18 units. £61 ($122) double. Rates include English breakfast. AE, DC, MC, V. **Amenities:** Restaurant; bar; lounge; room service. *In room:* TV, coffeemaker, hair dryer.

Parkside House A 15-minute walk north of Hastings's center, in a neighborhood of legally protected architecture and wildlife, this bed-and-breakfast hotel dates from 1880, when it was built of brick and slate. Views from many of the windows overlook a private garden and a duck pond in Alexander Park, a greenbelt that's said to be the largest municipal park in southeast England. Brian Kent, the owner, offers comfortable and well-maintained small- to medium-size bedrooms. Guests have access to the hotel's modest inventory of recorded films.

59 Lower Park Rd., Hastings, East Sussex TN34 2LD. ℂ 01424/433096. Fax 01424/421431. 5 units. £65 ($130) double. Rates include English breakfast. AE, MC, V. **Amenities:** Breakfast room; lounge; laundry service. *In room:* TV, coffeemaker, hair dryer.

IN BATTLE

Powder Mills Hotel ☆ *Finds* Near Battle Abbey and adjacent to the fabled battlefield of 1066, this restored Georgian house sits on 81 hectares (200 acres). On-site was a thriving gunpowder industry, which operated for 2 centuries beginning in 1676. The name of the hotel honors that long-ago tradition. Privately owned by Douglas and Julie Cowpland, the property has attracted such distinguished guests as the duke of Wellington. It's also said to be haunted by a lady dressed in white. Bedrooms are spacious and tastefully furnished, mostly with antiques and various period pieces. Some rooms offer four-poster beds. Grace notes include log fires on winter evenings, a drawing room, a music room, and the Orangery Restaurant with its colonial-style wicker seating.

Powdermill Lane, Battle, East Sussex TN33 0SP. ℂ 01424/775511. Fax 01424/774540. www.powdermillshotel.com. 40 units. £130–£160 ($260–$320) double; from £195 ($390) suite. Rates include English breakfast. AE, DC, MC, V. **Amenities:** Restaurant; bar; outdoor pool; room service; babysitting; laundry service; dry cleaning. *In room:* TV, Wi-Fi, beverage maker, trouser press.

EXPLORING THE HISTORIC SITES

Battle Abbey ☆ *Kids* King Harold, last of the Saxon kings, fought bravely here, not only for his kingdom but also for his life. As legend has it, he was killed by an arrow through the eye, and his body was dismembered. To commemorate the victory,

William the Conqueror founded Battle Abbey; some of the construction stone was shipped from his lands at Caen in northern France.

During the Dissolution of the Monasteries from 1538 to 1539 by King Henry VIII, the church of the abbey was largely destroyed. Some buildings and ruins, however, remain in what Tennyson called "O Garden, blossoming out of English blood." The principal building still standing is the Abbot's House, which is leased to a private school for boys and girls and is open to the general public only during summer holidays. Of architectural interest is the gatehouse, which has octagonal towers and stands at the top of Market Square. All the north Precinct Mall is still standing, and one of the most interesting sights of the ruins is the ancient Dorter Range, where the monks once slept.

The town of Battle flourished around the abbey; even though it has remained a medieval market town, many of the old half-timbered buildings have regrettably lost much of their original character because of stucco plastering carried out by past generations.

This is a great place for the kids. A themed play area is here, and at the gate, a daily activity sheet is distributed. You can relax with a picnic or stroll in the parkland that once formed the monastery grounds.

At the south end of Battle High St. (a 5-min. walk from the train station). ℭ **01424/773792**. £6.30 ($13) adults, £4.70 ($9.40) students and seniors, £3.20 ($6.40) children, £16 ($32) family ticket. Apr–Sept daily 10am–6pm; Oct–Mar daily 10am–4pm.

Hastings Castle ✹✹   In ruins now, the first of the Norman castles built in England sprouted on a western hill overlooking Hastings, around 1067. The fortress was unfortified by King John in 1216 and was later used as a church. Owned by the Pelham dynasty from the latter 16th century to modern times, the ruins have been turned over to Hastings. There is now an audiovisual presentation of the castle's history, including the famous battle of 1066. From the mount, you'll have a good view of the coast and promenade.

Castle Hill Rd., West Hill. ℭ **01424/444412**. Admission £3.75 ($7.50) adults, £3.10 ($6.20) seniors, £2.70 ($5.40) children, £12 ($24) family ticket. Easter–Sept daily 10am–5pm; Oct–Easter Sat daily 11am–3pm. Take the West Hill Cliff Railway from George St. to the castle for £1.60 ($3.20) adults, £1 ($2) children.

5 Royal Tunbridge Wells

58km (36 miles) SE of London; 53km (33 miles) NE of Brighton

Dudley Lord North, courtier to James I, is credited with the accidental discovery in 1606 of the mineral spring that led to the creation of a fashionable resort, Royal Tunbridge Wells. Over the years, "Chalybeate Spring" became known for its curative properties, the answer for everything from too many days of wine and roses to failing sexual prowess. It's still possible to take the waters today.

The spa resort reached its peak in the mid–18th century under the foppish patronage of Beau Nash (1674–1761), a dandy and final arbiter on how to act, what to say, and even what to wear (for example, he got men to remove their boots in favor of stockings). Tunbridge Wells continued to enjoy a prime spa reputation up through the reign of Queen Victoria, who used to vacation here as a child, and in 1909, Tunbridge Wells received its Royal status.

Today, the spa is long past its zenith. But the town is a pleasant place to stay—it can be used as a base for exploring the many historic homes in Kent (see "Kent's

Country Houses, Castles & Gardens," below); it's very easy, for example, to tour Sissinghurst and Chartwell from here.

The most remarkable feature of the town itself is the **Pantiles** ⊛, a colonnaded walkway for shoppers, tea drinkers, and diners, built near the wells. If you walk around town, you'll see many other interesting and charming spots. Entertainment is presented at the **Assembly Hall** (www.assemblyhalltheatre.co.uk) and **Trinity Arts Centre** (www.trinitytheatre.net).

ESSENTIALS

GETTING THERE   Two to three trains per hour leave London's Charing Cross Station during the day bound for Hastings, going via the town center of Royal Tunbridge Wells. The trip takes 50 minutes. For **rail information,** call ℂ **0845/748-4950** or visit **www.nationalrail.co.uk**.

If you're driving, after reaching the ring road around London, continue east along the M25, cutting southeast at the exit for the A21 to Hastings.

VISITOR INFORMATION   The **Tourist Information Centre,** Old Fish Market, the Pantiles (ℂ **01892/515675;** www.visittunbridgewells.com), provides a full accommodations list and offers a reservations service. The office is open 9am to 5pm Monday to Saturday and 10am to 4pm on Sunday (10am–5pm May–Aug).

WHERE TO STAY

Bethany House   One of the best B&Bs in town is run by Martin and Corinna Perry, who offer spacious bedrooms, each comfortably and tastefully furnished, and each individually designed. They provide quality extras such as chocolates, fresh fruits, flowers, magazines, and a small library of books. Their breakfast is one of the finest in town, featuring items such as freshly baked croissants and porridge with honey and whisky.

170 St. Johns Rd., Tunbridge Wells, Kent TN4 9UY. ℂ **01892/684363.** Fax 01892/521503. www.bethanyhouse twells.co.uk. 3 units. £75–£85 ($150–$170) double. MC, V. **Amenities:** Breakfast room. *In room:* TV, beverage maker, hair dryer, trouser press.

The Spa Hotel (Kids)   Standing on 6 hectares (15 acres), this building dates from 1766. Once a private home, it was converted to a hotel in 1880 and remains the town's leading hotel. The kind of old-fashioned place where guests check in for long stays, bedrooms are of various sizes and shapes, as was typical in the 19th century. Bedrooms are individually furnished, some with four-poster beds, and many offer panoramic vistas. The hotel offers a few activity options for kids, including a special pony-riding paddock.

Mt. Ephraim, Royal Tunbridge Wells, Kent TN4 8XJ. ℂ **800/528-1234** in the U.S., or 01892/520331. Fax 01892/510575. www.spahotel.co.uk. 70 units. £150–£170 ($300–$340) double; £210 ($420) suite. AE, DC, MC, V. From the Pantiles, take Major Yorke Rd. Free parking. **Amenities:** Restaurant; bar; lounge; dance studio; indoor heated pool; lighted tennis court; health club; sauna; room service; babysitting; laundry service; dry cleaning. *In room:* TV, Wi-Fi, beverage maker, hair dryer, iron, trouser press, safe.

WHERE TO DINE

Thackeray's House   ENGLISH/FRENCH   You'll get a bit of history and the finest food in town, as this 1660 house was once inhabited by novelist William Makepeace Thackeray, who wrote *Tunbridge Toys* here. Owner/Chef Richard Phillips has created an elegant atmosphere, backed by attentive service, for his specialties. Care goes into all his dishes, and many have flair. Flavors and textures are beautifully balanced in such dishes as butter-poached lobster with a saffron linguine or medallions of roast monkfish with

Parma ham. For starters try the venison carpaccio with beet or layers of oak-smoked salmon with young spinach and a lime crème fraîche.

85 London Rd. (at the corner of Mt. Ephraim Rd.). © **01892/511921.** Reservations required. Main courses £20–£29 ($40–$58); 2-course fixed-price lunch £16 ($32), 3 courses £17 ($34). AE, MC, V. Tues–Sun noon–2:30pm; Tues–Sat 6:30–10:30pm.

6 Kent's Country Houses, Castles & Gardens

Many of England's finest country houses, castles, and gardens are in Kent, where you'll find the palace of **Knole,** a premier example of English Tudor or half-timbered architecture; **Hever Castle,** the childhood home of Anne Boleyn and later the home of William Waldorf Astor; **Leeds Castle,** a spectacular castle with ties to America; and **Penshurst Place,** a stately home that was a literary salon of sorts during the first half of the 17th century. Kent also has a bevy of homes that once belonged to famous men but have since been turned into intriguing museums, such as **Chartwell,** where Sir Winston Churchill lived for many years, and Down House, where Charles Darwin wrote *On the Origin of Species.* Here you can amble down the same path the naturalist trod every evening.

It would take at least a week to see all of these historic properties—more time than most visitors have. When you make your choices, keep in mind that Knole, Hever, Penshurst, Leeds, and Chartwell are the most deserving of your attention.

We have found the guided tours to some of Kent's more popular stately homes too rushed and too expensive to recommend. Each attraction can be toured far more reasonably on your own. Because public transportation into and around Kent can be awkward, we advise driving from London, especially if you plan to visit more than one place in a day. Accordingly, this section is organized as you may drive it from London. However, if it's possible to get to an attraction via public transportation, we include that information in the individual listings below.

ATTRACTIONS

Chartwell ⊛   Sir Winston Churchill's home from 1922 until his death, though not as grand as his birthplace (Blenheim Palace; p. 262), Chartwell has preserved its rooms as the Conservative politician left them—maps, documents, photographs, pictures, personal mementos, and all. Two rooms display gifts that the prime minister received from people all over the world. A selection of many of his well-known uniforms includes his famous "siren-suits" and hats. Many of Churchill's paintings are displayed in a garden studio. You can see the garden walls that the prime minister built with his own hands and the pond where he sat to feed the Golden Orfe. A restaurant on the grounds serves food on days when the house is open.

Near the town of Edenbridge. © **01732/868381.** Admission to house, garden, and studio £11 ($22) adults, £5.40 ($11) children, £27 ($54) family ticket. Mar 17–June and Sept–Oct Wed–Sun 11am–5pm; July–Aug Tues–Sun 11am–5pm. If driving from London, head east on M25, taking the exit to Westerham. Drive 3km (2 miles) south of Westerham on B2026 and follow the signs.

Down House   Here stands the final residence of the famous naturalist Charles Darwin. In 1842, upon moving in, he wrote, "House ugly, looks neither old nor new." Nevertheless, he lived there "in happy contentment" until his death in 1882. The drawing room, dining room, billiard room, and old study have been restored to the way they were when Darwin was working on his famous, and still controversial, book *On the Origin of Species,* first published in 1859. The garden retains its original landscaping and a glass house, beyond which lies the Sand Walk or "Thinking Path," where Darwin took his daily solitary walk.

On Luxted Rd., in Downe. (C) **01689/859119.** Admission £7.20 ($14) adults, £5.40 ($11) students and seniors, £3.60 ($7.20) children. Apr–June and Sept–Oct Wed–Sun 11am–5pm; July–Aug daily 11am–5pm; Nov–Dec 16 and Mar 1–20 Wed–Sun 11am–4pm. From Westerham, get on A233 and drive 9km (5½ miles) south of Bromley to the village of Downe. Down House is .5km (¼ mile) southeast of the village. From London's Victoria Station, take a train (available daily) to Bromley South, then go to Downe by bus no. 146 (Mon–Sat only) or to Orpington by bus no. R2.

Groombridge Place Gardens   These formal gardens, with a vineyard and woodland walks, date from the 17th century. Part of the complex includes an Enchanted Forest, an ancient woodland in which the artist Ivan Hicks designed a series of "interactive" gardens, using natural objects, native wildflowers, mirrors, and glass to create a mysterious, surreal ambience. The White Rose Garden is compared favorably to that at fabled Sissinghurst. The English Knot Garden is based on paneling in the drawing room of an English country house. In the Fern Valley, huge Jurassic plants are as old as time. At the center is Groombridge Place, built on the site of a 12th-century castle and one of the most beautiful moated manor houses in England. Sir Christopher Wren, or so it is believed, helped with the architecture. The palace was built in 1662 by one of the courtiers to King Charles II, Philip Packer. Sir Arthur Conan Doyle was a regular visitor to the house to take part in séances, and the manor was the setting for the Sherlock Holmes mystery *The Valley of Fear.*

The gardens are often visited after an exploration of Knole near Sevenoaks. After leaving Sevenoaks, you can take Route A21 southeast until you reach the junction of Route A26 south. Follow this route until you see the signposted cutoff heading west to the little village of Groombridge and its gardens.

Groombridge. (C) **08192/861444.** www.groombridge.co.uk. Admission £8.95 ($18) adults, £7.45 ($15) seniors and children 3–12, £30 ($60) family ticket. Last 2 weekends of Mar and Apr–Nov 3 daily 10am–5:30pm.

Ightham Mote ⭑   Dating from 1320, Ightham Mote was extensively remodeled in the early 16th century, and remodeling is still going on. The chapel, with its painted ceiling, timbered outer wall, and ornate chimneys, reflects the Tudor period. You'll cross a stone bridge over a moat to its central courtyard. From the Great Hall, known for its magnificent windows, a Jacobean staircase leads to the old chapel on the first floor, where you go through the solarium, which has an oriel window, to the Tudor chapel.

Unlike many other ancient houses in England that have been occupied by the same family for centuries, Ightham Mote passed from owner to owner, with each family leaving its mark on the place. When the last private owner, an American who was responsible for a lot of the restoration, died, he bequeathed the house to the National Trust, which chose to keep the Robinson Library laid out as it was in a 1960 edition of *Homes & Gardens.*

Mote Rd., Ivy Hatch. (C) **01732/810378.** Admission £9.50 ($19) adults, £4.75 ($9.50) children, £24 ($48) family ticket. Sun–Mon and Wed–Fri 10:30am–5:30pm. Closed Nov–Mar. Drive 9.5km (6 miles) east of Sevenoaks on A25 to the small village of Ivy Hatch; the estate is 4km (2½ miles) south of Ightham; it's also signposted from A227.

Knole ⭑⭑   Begun in the mid–15th century by Thomas Bourchier, archbishop of Canterbury, and set in a 404-hectare (1,000-acre) deer park, Knole is one of the largest private houses in England and is one of the finest examples of pure English Tudor–style architecture.

Henry VIII liberated the former archbishop's palace from the church in 1537. He spent considerable sums of money on Knole, but history records only one visit (in

1541) after extracting the place from the reluctant Archbishop Cranmer. It was a royal palace until Queen Elizabeth I granted it to Thomas Sackville, first earl of Dorset, whose descendants have lived here ever since. (Virginia Woolf, often a guest of the Sackvilles, used Knole as the setting for her novel *Orlando*.)

The house covers 2.8 hectares (7 acres) and has 365 rooms, 52 staircases, and seven courts. The elaborate paneling and plasterwork provide a background for the 17th- and 18th-century tapestries and rugs, Elizabethan and Jacobean furniture, and collection of family portraits. If you want to see a bed that's to die for, check out the state bed of James II in the King's Bedroom.

8km (5 miles) north of Tunbridge, at the Tunbridge end of the town of Sevenoaks. ✆ 01732/462100. Admission to house £8.50 ($17) adults, £4.25 ($8.50) children, £21 ($42) family ticket; gardens £2 ($4) adults, £1 ($2) children. House mid-Mar to Oct Wed–Sun noon–4pm, bank holiday Mon noon–4pm; gardens every Wed of the month late Mar to late Oct 11am–4pm (last admission at 3:30pm); park daily to pedestrians and to cars only during house hours. To reach Knole from Chartwell, drive north to Westerham, pick up A25, and head east for 13km (8 miles). Frequent train service is available from London (about every 30 min.) to Sevenoaks, and then you can take the connecting hourly bus service or a taxi, or walk the remaining 2.5km (1½ miles) to Knole.

Squerryes Court   Built in 1681, this manor house has been owned by the Warde family for the last 250 years. At one time, British General James Wolfe, who commanded forces in the bombardment of Quebec, lived here with his family. The house still contains pictures and relics of General Wolfe's family. The Warde family has restored the formal gardens, dotting banks surrounding the lake with spring bulbs, herbaceous borders, and old roses to retain its beauty year-round, and returned rooms to their original uses. You can enjoy the fine collection of Old Master paintings from the Italian, 17th-century Dutch, and 18th-century English schools, along with antiques, porcelain, and tapestries, all acquired or commissioned by the family in the 18th century. General Wolfe received his commission on the grounds of the house— the spot is marked by a cenotaph.

1km (½ mile) west of the center of Westerham (10 min. from exit 6 or exit 5 on M25). ✆ 01959/562345. www.squerryes.co.uk. Admission to house and garden £6.50 ($13) adults, £6 ($12) students and seniors, £3.50 ($7) children 15 and younger, £14 ($28) family ticket; garden only £4 ($8) adults, £3.50 ($7) seniors, £2 ($4) children 15 and younger, £7.50 ($15) family ticket. Apr 1–Sept 30 Wed–Thurs, Sun, and bank holiday Mon house 1–5:30pm, grounds 11:30am–5:30pm (last entry 4:30pm). Take A25 just west of Westerham and follow the signs.

TOURING LEEDS CASTLE: "THE LOVELIEST IN THE WORLD" ✫✫✫

Once described by Lord Conway as the loveliest castle in the world, Leeds Castle (✆ 01622/765400; www.leeds-castle.com) dates from A.D. 857. Originally constructed of wood, it was rebuilt in 1119 in its present stone structure on two small islands in the middle of the lake; it was an almost impregnable fortress before the importation of gunpowder. Henry VIII converted it to a royal palace.

The castle has strong ties to America through the sixth Lord Fairfax who, as well as owning the castle, owned 2 million hectares (5 million acres) in Virginia and was a close friend and mentor of the young George Washington. The last private owner, the Hon. Lady Baillie, who restored the castle with a superb collection of fine art, furniture, and tapestries, bequeathed it to the Leeds Castle Foundation. Since then, the royal apartments, known as Les Chambres de la Reine (the queen's chambers), in the Gloriette, the oldest part of the castle, have been open to the public. The Gloriette, the last stronghold against attack, dates from Norman and Plantagenet times, with later additions by Henry VIII.

Within the surrounding parkland is a wildwood garden and duckery where rare swans, geese, and ducks abound. This is the best place for country walks in this part of England. The redesigned aviaries contain a superb collection of birds, including parakeets and cockatoos. Dog lovers will enjoy the Dog Collar Museum at the gatehouse, with a unique collection of collars dating from the Middle Ages. A 9-hole golf course is open to the public. The Culpepper Garden is a delightful English-country flower garden. Beyond are the castle greenhouses, with the maze centered on a beautiful underground grotto and the vineyard recorded in William the Conqueror's survey document, the Domesday Book (1086), which is once again producing Leeds Castle English white wine.

From March 21 to September the park is open daily 10am to 5pm, the castle 10:30am to 6pm; off season, the park is open daily 10am to 3pm, the castle 10:30am to 4pm. The castle and grounds are closed on the last Saturday in June and the first Saturday in July before open-air concerts. Admission to the castle and grounds is £14 ($28) for adults, £11 ($22) for students and seniors, and £8 ($16) for children 4 to 15. Car parking is free, with a free ride on a fully accessible minibus available for those who cannot manage the 1km (half-mile) or so walk from the parking area to the castle.

Trains run frequently from London's Victoria Station to Maidstone, 58km (36 miles) to the southeast. The best way to go is by National Express coach, departing from Victoria Coach Station at 9am and arriving at the castle at 10:25am, costing £18 ($36) for adults, £13 ($26) for children. Seats must be booked in advance (© **0870/ 5808080** or **www.nationalexpress.com**). If you're driving from London's ring road, continue east along the M26 and the M20. The castle is 6.5km (4 miles) east of Maidstone at the junction of the A20 and the M20 London-Folkestone roads.

Snacks, salads, cream teas, and hot meals are offered daily at a number of places on the estate, including Fairfax Hall, a restored 17th-century tithe barn, and the Terrace Restaurant, which provides a full range of hot and cold meals.

MORE KENT ATTRACTIONS

Hever Castle & Gardens 🍀🍀 Hever Castle dates from 1270, when the massive gatehouse, the outer walls, and the moat were first constructed. Some 200 years later, the Bullen (or Boleyn) family added a comfortable Tudor dwelling house inside the walls. Hever Castle was the childhood home of Anne Boleyn, the second wife of Henry VIII and mother of Queen Elizabeth I.

In 1903, William Waldorf Astor acquired the estate and invested time, money, and imagination in restoring the castle, building the Tudor Village, and creating the gardens and lakes. The Astor family's contribution to Hever's rich history can be appreciated through the castle's collections of furniture, paintings, and objets d'art, as well as the quality of its workmanship, particularly in the woodcarving and plasterwork.

The gardens are ablaze with color throughout most of the year. The spectacular Italian Garden contains statuary and sculpture dating from Roman to Renaissance times. The formal gardens include a walled Rose Garden, fine topiary work, and a maze. There's a 14-hectare (35-acre) lake and many streams, cascades, and fountains.

Hever Castle, Hever, near Edenbridge, Kent TNG 7NG. © 01732/865224. www.hevercastle.co.uk. Admission to castle and gardens £11 ($22) adults, £8.80 ($18) students and seniors, £5.70 ($11) children ages 5–14, £27 ($54) families (2 adults, 2 children); garden only £8.40 ($17) adults, £7.20 ($14) students and seniors, £5.40 ($11) children ages 5–14, £22 ($44) families, free for children 4 and younger. Gardens daily 11am–5pm; castle daily noon–5pm; closes at 4pm Mar, 3pm Nov–Dec 23 (castle only in Dec). Closed Jan–Feb. Follow the signs northwest of Royal Tunbridge Wells; it's 5km (3 miles) southeast of Edenbridge, midway between Sevenoaks and East Grinstead, and 30 min. from exit 6 of M25.

Penshurst Place ⟨★★⟩ ⟨*Kids*⟩   Stately Penshurst Place is one of Britain's outstanding country houses, as well as one of England's greatest defended manor houses, standing in a peaceful rural setting that has changed little over the centuries. In 1338, Sir John de Pulteney, four times lord mayor of London, built the manor house whose Great Hall still forms the heart of Penshurst. The boy king, Edward VI, presented the house to Sir William Sidney, and it has remained in that family ever since. In the first half of the 17th century, Penshurst was known as a center of literature and attracted such personages as Ben Jonson, who was inspired by the estate to write one of his greatest poems.

The **Nether Gallery,** below the **Long Gallery** with its suite of ebony-and-ivory furniture from Goa, houses the Sidney family collection of armor. You can also see the splendid state dining room. In the Stable Wing is a toy museum, with playthings from past generations. On the grounds are nature and farm trails plus an adventure playground for children.

9.5km (6 miles) west of Tunbridge. ⟨✆⟩ **01892/870307.** www.penshurstplace.com. Admission to house and grounds £7.50 ($15) adults, £7 ($14) students and seniors, £5 ($10) children 5–16, £21 ($42) family ticket; grounds only £6 ($12) adults, £5.50 ($11) students and seniors, £4.50 ($9) children 5–16, family ticket £18 ($36); free for children 4 and younger. Daily house noon–4pm, grounds 10:30am–6pm (Sat–Sun only in Mar). Closed Nov–Feb. From M25 Junction follow A21 to Tunbridge, leaving at the Tunbridge (north) exit; then follow the brown tourist signs. The nearest mainline station is Tunbridge.

Sissinghurst Castle Garden ⟨★★⟩   These spectacular gardens, which are situated between surviving parts of an Elizabethan mansion, were created by one of England's most famous and dedicated gardeners, Bloomsbury writer Vita Sackville-West, and her husband, Harold Nicolson. In spring, the garden is resplendent with flowering bulbs and daffodils in the orchard.

The white garden reaches its peak in June. The large herb garden, a skillful montage that reflects her profound plant knowledge, has something to show all summer long, and the cottage garden, with its flowering bulbs, is at its finest in the fall. It is also possible to visit the library and study of Vita Sackville-West from April to October 15 Monday, Tuesday, and Friday noon to 5:30pm and Saturday and Sunday 10am to 5:30pm. Meals are available in the Granary Restaurant. The garden area is flat, so it is wheelchair accessible; note, however, that only two wheelchairs are allowed at a time.

Sissinghurst, near Cranbrook, Kent TN17 2AB. ⟨✆⟩ **01580/710700.** Admission £7.80 ($16) adults, £3.60 ($7.20) children, £20 ($40) family ticket. Mid-Mar to Oct Mon–Tues and Fri–Sun 11am–6:30pm. The garden is 85km (53 miles) southeast of London and 24km (15 miles) south of Maidstone. It's most often approached from Leeds Castle, which is 6.5km (4 miles) east of Maidstone at the junction of A20 and M20 London-Folkestone roads. From this junction, head south on B2163 and A274 through Headcorn. Follow the signposts to Sissinghurst.

7 Historic Mansions & Gardens in Dorking & Guildford

Dorking, birthplace of Lord Laurence Olivier, lies on the Mole River at the foot of the North Downs. Within easy reach are some of the most scenic spots in the shire, including Silent Pool, Box Hill, and Leith Hill.

The guildhall in **Guildford,** a country town on the Wey River, has an ornamental projecting clock that dates from 1683. Charles Dickens claimed that High Street, which slopes to the river, was one of the most beautiful in England.

ESSENTIALS
GETTING THERE   Frequent daily train service to Dorking takes 45 minutes from London's Victoria Station or Waterloo Station. The train to Guildford departs London's

Waterloo Station and takes 40 minutes. For information, call © 0845/748-4950 or visit www.nationalrail.co.uk.

National Express operates buses from London's Victoria Coach Station daily, with a stopover at Guildford on its runs from London to Portsmouth. For schedules, call © 0870/580-8080 or visit www.nationalexpress.com. It's usually more convenient to take the train.

If you're driving to Dorking, take the A24 south from London. If you're driving to Guildford from London, head south along the A3.

VISITOR INFORMATION   The Guildford Tourist Information Centre is at 14 Tunsgate (© 01483/444333; www.guildford.gov.uk). It's open October to April Monday to Saturday 9:30am to 5pm, and May to September Monday to Saturday 9am to 5:30pm and Sunday 10am to 4:30pm.

WHERE TO STAY & DINE
IN DORKING
Burford Bridge Hotel ✦   This inn is the best in Dorking, offering stylish living in a rural town. At the foot of beautiful Box Hill, the hotel has many historical associations. Keats completed "Endymion" here in 1817; Wordsworth and Robert Louis Stevenson also visited the hotel. You get the best of both the old and the new, including a tithe barn (ca. 1600). All the guest rooms are refurbished. The grounds include a flowered patio and fountain that are particularly enjoyable in summer.

Box Hill, Dorking, Surrey RH5 6BX. © 01306/884561. Fax 01306/887821. www.burfordbridgehotel.com. 57 units. £115–£135 ($230–$270) double. AE, DC, MC, V. Take A24 2.5km (1½ miles) north of Dorking. **Amenities:** Restaurant; bar; heated outdoor pool; room service; laundry service; dry cleaning. *In room:* TV, Wi-Fi, coffeemaker, hair dryer, iron, trouser press.

White Horse Hotel   Just 16km (10 miles) from Gatwick Airport, this inn is supposed to have been the home of the "Marquis of Granby" in *The Pickwick Papers*. Dickens was known to have frequented the bar parlor. Bedrooms have been refurbished, and all are comfortable and well maintained; a few have four-poster beds. Some units are in a rather sterile modern annex. The inn has a restaurant, as well as the Pickwick Bar, that offers a moderately priced table d'hôte dinner. The hotel also has a rose garden and can arrange a temporary membership in a nearby sports club with its own swimming pool.

High St., Dorking, Surrey, RH4 1BE. © 800/225-5843 in the U.S. and Canada, or 01306/881138. Fax 01306/880386. www.whitehorsedorking.co.uk. 78 units. £110–£160 ($220–$320) double. AE, DC, MC, V. **Amenities:** Restaurant; bar; room service; laundry service; dry cleaning. *In room:* TV, Wi-Fi, coffeemaker, hair dryer, iron, trouser press.

IN GUILDFORD
Holiday Inn   Though part of a chain, the feeling of heritage at this hotel is conveyed by its natural red-elm joinery, marble floors, and landscaped grounds. The bedrooms incorporate both living and sleeping areas. Both business travelers and visitors fill the attractively decorated bedrooms, which are generally midsize. The latest addition to the hotel contains a series of modern rooms that are better appointed and more spacious than the older units.

Egerton Rd., Guildford, Surrey GU2 7XZ. © 0870/400-9036. Fax 01483/302960. www.holiday-inn.com. 168 units. £132–£220 ($264–$440) double. AE, DC, MC, V. Head about 3km (2 miles) southwest of the center of Guildford, just off A3. **Amenities:** Restaurant; bar; indoor heated pool; health club; whirlpool; sauna; salon; room service; babysitting; laundry service; dry cleaning. *In room:* TV, coffeemaker, hair dryer, iron (in some), trouser press (in some), safe (in some).

WHERE TO SHARE A PINT

Weyside, Milford (✆ **01483/568024**), a riverside pub with a terraced garden and large conservatory on the River Wey, offers traditional pub food with homemade specials served daily at lunch and dinner; bar snacks are available all day. A variety of real ales are on tap. Children are welcome until 9pm.

The **White House,** 8 High St. (✆ **01483/302006**), is another riverside pub, with a conservatory overlooking a lovely waterside garden. Pub grub is available at lunch and dinner; sandwiches are offered all day. They serve traditional London ales aged in barrels.

SEEING THE SIGHTS

Loseley House ✿ This beautiful and historic Elizabethan mansion visited by Queen Elizabeth I, James I, and Queen Mary has been featured on TV and in numerous films. Its works of art include paneling from Henry VIII's Nonsuch Palace, period furniture, a unique carved chalk chimney piece, magnificent ceilings, and cushions made by Queen Elizabeth I. Lunches and teas are served in the Courtyard Tearoom daily from 11am to 5pm, and a lunch restaurant serves more substantial meals.

Loseley Park (4km/2½ miles southwest of Guildford). ✆ **01483/304440.** www.loseley-park.com. Admission to house and gardens £7 ($14) adults, £6.50 ($13) students and seniors, £3.50 ($7) children; gardens only £4 ($8) adults, £3.50 ($7) students and seniors, £2 ($4) children. House May–Aug Tues–Thurs and Sun 1–5pm; gardens May–Sept Tues–Sun 11am–5pm.

Polesden Lacey Built in 1824, this former Regency villa houses the Greville collection of antiques, paintings, and tapestries. In the early part of the 20th century it was enlarged to become a comfortable Edwardian country house, home of celebrated hostess Mrs. Ronald Greville, who frequently entertained royalty from 1906 to 1939. The estate has 560 hectares (1,400 acres). Stroll the 18th-century garden, lined with herbaceous borders and featuring a rose garden and beech trees.

Signposted from Great Bookham, off A246 Leatherhead-Guildford Rd. ✆ **01372/452048.** Admission to grounds £6.50 ($13) adults, £3.20 ($6.40) children, £16 ($32) family ticket; admission to house £11 ($21) adults, £5.20 ($10) children, £27 ($54) families. Grounds daily Mar–Oct 11am–5pm, Nov–Feb daily 11am–4pm; house mid-Mar to Oct Wed–Sun and bank holidays 11am–5pm.

Wisley Garden ✿✿ Every season, this 101-hectare (250-acre) garden, one of the great gardens of England, has a profusion of flowers and shrubs, ranging from the alpine meadow carpeted with wild daffodils in spring, to Battleston Hill brilliant with rhododendrons in early summer, to the heather garden's colorful foliage in fall, and a riot of exotic plants in the greenhouses in winter. Model gardens and a landscaped orchid house can also be visited. Mid-2007 saw the opening of the massive Glasshouse, which shelters endangered and delicate plants from three climatic zones. This greenhouse looks onto a manicured man-made lake. This garden is the site of a laboratory where botanists, plant pathologists, and entomologists experiment and assist amateur gardeners. A large gift shop stocks a variety of gardening books.

Wisley (near Ripley, just off M25, Junction 10, on A3 London-Portsmouth Rd.). ✆ **01483/224234.** www.rhs.org.uk. Admission £7.50 ($15) adults, £2 ($4) children 6–16, free for children 5 and younger. Mar–Oct Mon–Fri 10am–6pm, Sat–Sun 9am–6pm; Nov–Feb Mon–Fri 10am–4:30pm, Sat–Sun 9am–4:30pm (last admission 1 hr. before closing).

8 Chichester

50km (31 miles) W of Brighton; 111km (69 miles) SW of London

Chichester might have been just a market town if the Chichester Festival Theatre had not been born there. One of the oldest Roman cities in England, Chichester draws a crowd from all over for its theater. Though it lacks other attractions, the town is a good base for exploring a history-rich part of southern England.

ESSENTIALS

GETTING THERE Trains depart for Chichester from London's Victoria Station once every hour during the day. The trip takes 1½ hours. However, if you visit Chichester to attend the theater, plan to stay over—the last train back to London is at 9pm. For rail information, call ℂ **0845/748-4950** or visit **www.nationalrail.co.uk**.

Buses leave from London's Victoria Coach Station once a day. For schedules, call ℂ **0870/580-8080** or visit **www.nationalexpress.com**.

If you're driving from London's Ring Road, head south on the A3, turning onto the A286 for Chichester.

VISITOR INFORMATION The **Tourist Information Centre**, 29A South St. (ℂ **01243/775888;** www.visitchichester.org), is open October to March Monday 10:15am to 5:15pm and Tuesday to Saturday 9:15am to 5:15pm. From April to September the center is open Monday to Saturday 9:15am to 5:15pm and Sunday 11am to 3:30pm.

WHERE TO STAY IN THE AREA

Millstream Hotel Bosham Lane The Millstream, built in the 1700s to provide food and accommodations for travelers through Sussex from other parts of England, is 8km (5 miles) south of Chichester. The hotel is in the hamlet of Bosham, with its beautiful harbor. Behind a facade of weathered yellow bricks, the hotel exudes a sense of history. The rooms, modern in style, have been redecorated and upgraded.

Bosham Line, Chichester, West Sussex PO18 8HL. ℂ 01243/573234. Fax 01243/573459. www.millstream-hotel. co.uk. 35 units. £142–£186 ($284–$372) double; £192–£212 ($384–$424) suite. Rates include English breakfast. AE, DC, MC, V. Bus: Bosham bus from Chichester. Take the road to the village of Bosham and its harbor, off A27. **Amenities:** Restaurant; bar; room service; babysitting; laundry service; dry cleaning. *In room:* TV, minibar, coffeemaker, hair dryer, iron, trouser press, safe.

Ship Hotel A classic Georgian building, the Ship is only a few minutes' walk from Chichester Cathedral, Chichester Festival Theatre, and many fine antiques shops. Built as a private house in 1790 for Admiral Sir George Murray, it retains an air of elegance and comfort, made all the more so by a wholesale renovation in 2007. A grand staircase leads from its main entrance to the bedrooms, which are named after historic ships. Some rooms have four-poster beds; others are specially designated for families.

North St., Chichester, West Sussex PO19 1NH. ℂ 01243/778000. Fax 01243/788000. www.shiphotelchichester. co.uk. 36 units. £120–£145 ($240–$290) double; £155 ($310) family room; £175 ($350) suite. Rates include English breakfast. AE, DC, MC, V. Free parking. **Amenities:** Restaurant; bar; lounge; limited room service; laundry service; dry cleaning. *In room:* TV, coffeemaker, hair dryer.

The Spread Eagle Hotel ★★ *(finds* This 1430 inn, and the market town of Midhurst, are so steeped in history that the room you sleep in and the pavement you walk on each probably have a thousand tales to tell. Curiosities include the White Room, where smugglers allegedly made a secret passage, and the Queen's Room, from which Elizabeth I watched the revelry on the square during her 1591 visit. The rooms here are medieval in character, with beams, small mullioned windows, and unexpected corners. The most elegant have four-poster antique beds, fireplaces, and 500-year-old wall paneling. The eagle in the lounge is the actual one from the back of Hermann Göring's chair in the Reichstag. It was acquired for its apt illustration of the hotel's name.

South St., Midhurst, West Sussex GU29 9NH. © **01730/816911.** Fax 01730/815668. www.hshotels.co.uk. 39 units. £99–£305 ($198–$610) double. Rates include English breakfast. AE, DC, MC, V. Midhurst bus from Chichester. Free parking. **Amenities:** Restaurant; bar; indoor heated pool; gym; spa; sauna; steam room; salon; room service; laundry service; dry cleaning. *In room:* TV, coffeemaker, hair dryer.

WHERE TO DINE IN THE AREA

If you're on the run and don't want a formal meal, drop in at the **George & Dragon,** 51 North St. (© **01243/785660**). In the heart of the city, this is a family-run bar and restaurant, with a traditional feel.

Comme ça ✦ FRENCH   This is the best French restaurant in town—in fact, the best restaurant, period. The unpretentious decor blends old Victorian and Edwardian prints with objets d'art. The theme continues in the garden room leading through French doors to an enclosed patio and garden. In summer, you'll want to dine out here, although in winter, a log fire in the inglenook fireplace welcomes you to the bar. Try delights of the field or river. Only the finest-quality ingredients are used. All menus have vegetarian dishes, and special dietary requirements can also be catered to. Starters—including pan-fried tiger prawns flambéed with cognac and served in a phyllo basket with a brochette of apple crisps, or else seared scallops in spicy shrimp butter—have harmonious pairings of flavors. Well-crafted main dishes include free-range roasted guinea fowl with Madeira jus and French lentils, or else seared filet of wild sea bass with lemon, olive oil, and herbed potatoes with warm chorizo and a red-pepper vinaigrette.

67 Broyle Rd. (a 10-min. walk from the town center). © **01243/788724.** Reservations required. Main courses £16–£22 ($32–$44); fixed-price 2-course lunch £20 ($40), 3 courses £23 ($46). AE, DC, MC, V. Wed–Sun 11:30am–2pm; Tues–Sat 6–10pm.

Shepherd's Tea Rooms TEA/PASTRIES   Located in a white building with blue trim in the center of town, the tearoom is casual, with a mix of locals and tourists. The interior is simple but nice, with fine china on lace-covered tables. You'll find croissants, scones, and a variety of cakes, plus chocolate éclairs and meringues. Earl Grey, Darjeeling, English Breakfast, and other teas are served.

35 Little London. © **01243/774761.** Afternoon tea £6.95 ($14); cakes, scones, and pastries 80p–£2.50 ($1.60–$5). MC, V. Mon–Fri 9:15am–5pm; Sat 9am–5pm; Sun 10am–4pm.

White Horse ENGLISH/FRENCH   The wine cellar at this informally elegant country restaurant is one of the most comprehensive in Britain, partly because of the careful attention the owners pay to the details of their 18th-century inn, whose patina has been burnished every day since it was built in 1765. The menu is heavy on local game in season, bought from people known by the owners. Among the more delectable mains is a platter on which filet of sole is dressed with seared scallops; another good dish is the pan-fried loin of venison. The chefs also emphasize organic produce.

1 High St., Chilgrove. © **01243/535219.** Reservations required on weekends. Main courses £15–£22 ($30–$44); 2-course fixed-price menu £20–£23 ($40–$46), 3 courses £25 ($50). MC, V. Tues–Sat noon–2pm and 7–9pm; Sun noon–2pm. Closed Dec 25–26. Head 10km (6½ miles) north of Chichester on B2141 to Petersfield.

THE CHICHESTER FESTIVAL THEATRE ✦

Only a 5-minute walk from the Chichester Cathedral and the old Market Cross, the 1,400-seat theater, with its apron stage, stands on the edge of Oaklands Park. It opened in 1962, and its first director was none other than Lord Laurence Olivier. Its reputation has grown steadily, pumping new vigor and life into the former walled city, although originally many irate locals felt the city money could have been better spent on a swimming pool instead of a theater.

Chichester Festival Theatre, built in the 1960s, offers plays and musicals during the summer (Apr–Sept), and in the winter and spring months, orchestras, jazz, opera, theater, ballet, and a Christmas show for the entire family.

The **Minerva,** built in the late 1980s, is a multifunctional cultural center that includes a theater plus dining and drinking facilities. The Minerva Studio Theatre and the Chichester Festival Theatre are managed by the same board of governors but show different programs and different plays.

Theater reservations made over the telephone will be held for a maximum of 4 days (✆ **01243/781312;** www.cft.org.uk). Festival ticket prices range from £10 to £35 ($20–$70).

A RACETRACK

One of the most famous sports-car-racing courses in the world, **Goodwood Motor Circuit** (✆ **01243/755000;** www.goodwood.co.uk), reopened in 1998, near Chichester, and was restored to its look of 50 years ago. The course became dangerous for faster cars and was retired as an active track in the 1960s, as the 4km (2½-mile) circuit was never modernized. Now, that is part of its charm, offering a chance to relive the days when courageous drivers raced Jaguars or Ferraris on tracks enveloped by cornfields and hay bales. The course is now used for special exhibition races featuring historic sports cars from the '50s and '60s. The track can be reached by taking the A3 to Milford and the A283 to Petwork, then the A285 to Halnaker, following the signposts from there. Call to see if any exhibitions are being staged during your visit to the area.

Fishbourne Roman Palace   This is what remains of the largest Roman residence yet discovered in Britain. Built around A.D. 75 in villa style, it has many mosaic-floored rooms and even an under-floor heating system. The gardens have been restored to their original 1st-century plan. The story of the site is told both by an audiovisual program and by text in the museum. Guided tours are offered twice a day. (See what an archaeological dig in July 1996 unearthed.) In 2006, the attraction underwent a multimillion-dollar redevelopment; it now offers a state-of-the-art computer graphic reconstruction of the palace. Roman artifacts are on display in the Discovery Centre.

North of A259, off Salthill Rd. (signposted from Fishbourne; 2.5km/1½ miles from Chichester). ✆ 01243/785859. Admission £6.80 ($14) adults, £5.80 ($12) students and seniors, £3.60 ($7.20) children, £17 ($34) families. Jan Sat–Sun 10am–4pm; Feb daily 10am–4pm; Mar–July and Sept–Oct daily 10am–5pm; Aug daily 10am–6pm; Nov–Dec 10am–4pm (not always open during this time—call first). Buses stop regularly at the bottom of Salthill Rd., and the museum is within a 10-min. walk of British Rail's station at Fishbourne.

Weald & the Downland Open Air Museum   In the beautiful Sussex countryside, historic buildings, saved from destruction, are reconstructed on a 20-hectare (49-acre) downland site. The structures show the development of traditional building from medieval times to the 19th century, in the weald and downland area of southeast England. Exhibits include a Tudor market hall, a working water mill producing stone-ground flour, a blacksmith's forge, plumbers' and carpenters' workshops, a toll cottage, a charcoal burner's camp, and a 19th-century village school. A "new" reception area with shops and offices is set in Longport House, a 16th-century building rescued from the site of the Channel Tunnel.

At Singleton, 9.5km (6 miles) north of Chichester on A286 (the London Rd.). (℗ 01243/811363. www.wealddown. co.uk. Admission £8.25 ($17) adults, £7.25 ($15) seniors, £4.40 ($8.80) students and children 5–15, £23 ($46) family ticket. Apr–Oct daily 10:30am–6pm; Nov–Dec 22 daily 10:30am–4pm; Jan 3–Feb 18 Wed and Sat–Sun 10:30am–4pm; Feb 19–Mar daily 10:30am–4pm. Bus no. 60 from Chichester.

9 Arundel Castle ★★
34km (21 miles) W of Brighton; 93km (58 miles) SW of London

The small town of Arundel in West Sussex nestles at the foot of one of England's most spectacular castles. Without the castle, it would be just another English market town. The town was once an Arun River port, and its residents enjoyed the prosperity of considerable trade and commerce. Today, however, the harbor traffic has been replaced with buses filled with tourists.

ESSENTIALS
GETTING THERE   Trains leave hourly during the day from London's Victoria Station. The trip takes 1¼ hours. For rail information, call (℗ 0845/748-4950 or visit **www.nationalrail.co.uk**.

Most bus connections are through Littlehampton, opening onto the English Channel west of Brighton. From Littlehampton, you can leave the coastal road by taking bus no. 700 (run by Stagecoach Coastline), which runs between Littlehampton and Arundel every 30 minutes (7am–7pm) during the day. If you're dependent on public transportation, the Tourist Information Centre (see below) keeps an update on the possibilities.

If you're driving from London, follow the signs to Gatwick Airport, and from there head south toward the coast along the A29.

VISITOR INFORMATION   The **Tourist Information Centre,** 61 High St. ((℗ 01903/882268), is open from April to October Monday to Saturday 10am to 5pm (until 6pm July–Aug), Sundays 10am to 4pm; off season hours are daily 10am to 3pm.

WHERE TO STAY IN THE AREA
Amberley Castle Hotel ★★ (Finds)   The best place for food and lodging is near the village of Amberley. Joy and Martin Cummings offer accommodations in a 14th-century castle with sections dating from the 12th century. Elizabeth I held the lease on this castle from 1588 to 1603, and Cromwell's forces attacked it during the civil war. Charles II visited the castle on two occasions. Each of the sumptuous rooms, all doubles, is named after a castle in Sussex. All rooms also have a video library. Bedrooms are the ultimate in English-country-house luxury; you can choose from four-poster, twin four-poster, or brass double beds. *Note:* This hotel is a member of Relais & Châteaux.

Amberley, near Arundel, West Sussex BN18 9LT. (℗ 01798/831992. Fax 01798/831998. www.amberleycastle.co.uk. 19 units. £155–£385 ($310–$770) double. AE, DC, MC, V. Take B2139 north of Arundel; the hotel is 2.5km (1½ miles) southwest of Amberley. **Amenities:** 2 restaurants, including Queens Room (see review below); 18-hole golf course; tennis court; bike rental; room service; dry cleaning. *In room:* TV, minibar, coffeemaker, hair dryer, trouser press.

Hilton Avisford Park ★   This is not your usual Hilton. Set in 36 hectares (89 acres) of gardens and lovely parkland, it opens onto England's South Downs. Once it was the home of Baronet Montagu, admiral and friend of Lord Nelson. Now successfully converted into a hotel, it is completely modernized but still keeps some of the allure of its original construction. Bedrooms come in a range of styles, sizes, and designs, and are handsomely laid out. The hotel is also the best equipped in the area, especially if sports are part of your vacation. A first-class restaurant, the Cedar Restaurant, is on-site.

Yapton Lane, Walberton, Arundel, West Sussex BN18 0LS. © 01243/551215. Fax 01243/552485. www.arundel. hilton.com. 139 units. £89–£179 ($178–$358) double; £149–£210 ($298–$420) suite. Rates include breakfast. AE, DC, MC, V. Lies 4.8km (3 miles) west of Arundel on B2132 (off A27). **Amenities:** Restaurant; bar; indoor heated pool; 18-hole golf course; tennis court; squash court; fitness room; salon; business center; room service; babysitting; laundry; valet. *In room:* TV, high-speed Internet (in some), fridge, beverage maker, hair dryer, iron.

Norfolk Arms   A former coaching inn, the Norfolk Arms is on the main street just a short walk from the castle. It's best place to stay if you want to be in the market town itself. The lounges and dining room are in the typically English-country-inn style. The hotel has been restored with many modern amenities blending with the old architecture. The bedrooms are handsomely maintained and furnished, each with personal touches. Rooms vary considerably in size, from small to spacious. Some rooms lie in a separate modern wing overlooking the courtyard. Four bedrooms are large enough for small families.

22 High St., Arundel, West Sussex BN18 9AD. © 01903/882101. Fax 01903/884275. www.norfolkarmshotel.com. 34 units. £129–£144 ($258–$288) double. Children 13 and younger stay free in parent's room. Rates include breakfast. AE, DC, MC, V. Free parking. **Amenities:** Restaurant; 2 bars; room service; laundry service; dry cleaning. *In room:* TV, Wi-Fi, coffeemaker, hair dryer, trouser press.

WHERE TO DINE

China Palace BEIJING/SZECHUAN   The most prominent Chinese restaurant in the region, it has an elaborately carved 17th-century ceiling imported by a former owner from a palace in Italy. Interior decorations include the artfully draped sails from a Chinese junk. It's located across the road from the crenelated fortifications surrounding Arundel's castle. The Beijing and Szechuan cuisine includes such classic dishes as Peking duck, king prawns Kung Pao, and lobster with fresh ginger and spring onions.

67 High St. © 01903/883702. Reservations recommended on weekends. Main courses £8–£10 ($16–$20); fixed-price 3-course dinner for 2 £38–£39 ($76–$78). AE, MC, V. Daily noon–2:15pm and 6pm–midnight.

Queens Room Restaurant ✸✸ ENGLISH/CONTINENTAL   No contest: The best cuisine around Arundel is served at the Amberley Castle Hotel (see above). The chef has raided England's culinary past for inspiration but gives his dishes modern interpretations. We especially admire his use of natural ingredients from the area—wild Southdown rabbit, lavender, lemon thyme, and nettles. The menu changes frequently, though the special menu of the day is always alluring. For starters, enjoy such delights as seared foie gras or roast Anjou quail, followed by such well-crafted mains as local Sussex lamb with suet pudding, perhaps Cornish red mullet with sorrel. For dessert, try the rhubarb milk mousse or the baked spiced fig cake. The staff is attentive and friendly, yet warmly informal, and there's a well-chosen wine list.

In the Amberley Castle Hotel, Amberley, near Arundel. © 01798/831992. Reservations required. Lunch £20 ($40) for 2 courses, £25 ($50) for 3 courses; dinner £43 ($86) for 2 courses, £50 ($100) for 3 courses. AE, DC, MC, V. Daily noon–2pm and 7–9pm.

SEEING THE SIGHTS

Arundel Castle ✸✸   The ancestral home of the dukes of Norfolk, Arundel Castle is a much-restored mansion of considerable importance. Its legend is associated with some of the great families of England—the Fitzalans and the powerful Howards of

Norfolk. This castle received worldwide exposure when it was chosen as the backdrop for *The Madness of King George* (it was "pretending" to be Windsor Castle in the film).

Arundel Castle has suffered destruction over the years, particularly during the civil war, when Cromwell's troops stormed its walls, perhaps in retaliation for the 14th earl of Arundel's (Thomas Howard) sizable contribution to Charles I. In the early 18th century, the castle had to be virtually rebuilt, and in late Victorian times it was remodeled and extensively restored again. Today it's filled with a valuable collection of antiques, along with an assortment of paintings by Old Masters, such as Van Dyck and Gainsborough.

The latest attraction is the opening of the Gate House for the first time. In various rooms you can see exhibits of the civil war that was fought at the castle between 1642 and 1645. Costumed mannequins and an audio presentation bring this former era to life.

Surrounding the castle, in the center off High Street, is a 445-hectare (1,100-acre) park whose scenic highlight is Swanbourne Lake.

On Mill Rd. ✆ **01903/883136.** www.arundelcastle.org. Admission £12 ($24) adults, £9.50 ($19) students and seniors, £7.50 ($15) children 5–16, £32 ($64) family ticket, free for children 4 and younger. Tues–Sun noon–5pm (last admission 4pm). Closed Nov–Mar.

Arundel Cathedral   A Roman Catholic cathedral, the Cathedral of Our Lady and St. Philip Howard, stands at the highest point in town. A. J. Hansom, inventor of the Hansom taxi, built it for the 15th duke of Norfolk. However, it was not consecrated as a cathedral until 1965. The interior includes the shrine of St. Philip Howard, featuring Sussex wrought-iron work.

London Rd. ✆ **01903/882297.** www.arundelcathedral.org. Free admission, but donations appreciated. Daily 9:30am–dusk. From the town center, continue west from High St.

10 Brighton: London by the Sea ★★

84km (52 miles) S of London

Brighton was one of the first of the great seaside resorts of Europe. The prince of Wales (later George IV), the original swinger who was to shape so much of its destiny, arrived in 1783; his presence and patronage gave it immediate status.

Fashionable dandies from London, including Beau Brummell, turned up. The construction business boomed as Brighton blossomed with charming and attractive town houses and well-planned squares and crescents. From the prince regent's title came the voguish word *Regency*, which was to characterize an era, but more specifically refers to the period between 1811 and 1820. Under Victoria, and despite the fact that she cut off her presence, Brighton continued to flourish.

But as the English began to discover more glamorous spots on the Continent, Brighton lost much of its old *joie de vivre.* People began to call it "tatty," and it began to feature the usual run of funfair-type English seaside amusements. Because of its boardwalk and pier world, it still has a Coney Island type of ambience, although much of its historic core has been gentrified. Holiday makers flock here on day trains for a rowdy time spent at "London-by-the-Sea," and this clientele still makes Brighton a bit tawdry.

As Betty Kemp, publican, said, "But that's all right, ducky. We've always been a place where Londoners can slip off for some hanky-panky. Now, who would ever want to change that state of affairs? Brighton will always be the goal of the off-the-record weekender." A huge number of Londoners have moved in (some of whom now commute), and the invasion has made Brighton increasingly lighthearted and sophisticated today.

It also attracts a fair number of gay vacationers, and a beach east of town has been set aside for nude bathers (Britain's first such venture).

ESSENTIALS

GETTING THERE Fast trains (41 a day) leave from Victoria or London Bridge Station, making the trip in 55 minutes. For rail information, call © **0845/748-4950** or visit www.nationalrail.co.uk. Buses from London's Victoria Coach Station take about 2 hours.

If you're driving, the M23 (signposted from central London) leads to the A23, which takes you into Brighton.

VISITOR INFORMATION At the **Tourist Information Centre,** 4–5 Pavilion Buildings (© **0906/711-2255** only in the U.K. at 50p/£1 per min.; www.visit brighton.com) next to the Royal Pavilion shop, you can make hotel reservations, reserve tickets for National Express coaches, and pick up a list of current events. It's open Monday to Saturday 10am to 5pm; from March to October, there are also Sunday hours from 10am to 4pm.

GETTING AROUND **Brighton & Hove Bus and Coach Company** serves both Brighton and Hove with frequent and efficient service. Local fares are only £1.70 ($3.40); and free maps of the company's routes are available at the Tourist Information Centre (see above). You can also call the company directly at © **01273/886200,** or visit **www.buses.co.uk**.

SPECIAL EVENTS If you're here in May, the international **Brighton Festival** (© **01273/709709;** www.brightonfestival.org), the largest arts festival in England, features drama, literature, visual art, dance, and concerts ranging from classical to rock. A festival program is available annually in February for those who want to plan ahead.

WHERE TO STAY

Gay travelers should refer to "Brighton's Gay Scene," later in this section, for a selection of gay-friendly accommodations.

VERY EXPENSIVE

The Grand 🏵🏵🏵 Opening onto the seafront promenade, Brighton's premier hotel, the original Grand was constructed in 1864 and entertained some of the most eminent Victorians and Edwardians. This landmark was massively damaged in a 1984 terrorist attack directed at Margaret Thatcher and other key figures in the British government. Mrs. Thatcher narrowly escaped, though several of her colleagues were killed; entire sections of the hotel looked as if they had been hit by an air raid. Today it's the most elegant Georgian re-creation in town.

You enter via a glassed-in conservatory and register in a grandiose public room. The rooms, of a very high standard, are generally spacious with many extras, including hospitality trays and PlayStations. The sea-view rooms have minibars and new beds and furniture; the deluxe rooms offer separate sitting rooms and views of the English Channel. "Romantic rooms" offer double whirlpool tubs. All standard rooms have been refurbished with new bathrooms.

Kings Rd., Brighton, East Sussex BN1 2FW. © 01273/224300. Fax 01273/224321. www.grandbrighton.co.uk. 200 units. £150–£320 ($300–$640) double; £540–£650 ($1,080–$1,300) suite. Rates include English breakfast. AE, DC, MC, V. Parking £25 ($50). Bus: 1, 2, or 3. **Amenities:** Restaurant; bar; indoor heated pool; gym; spa; Jacuzzi; sauna; salon; room service; babysitting; laundry service; dry cleaning. *In room:* TV, high-speed Internet, minibar, coffeemaker, hair dryer, iron, trouser press, safe.

Brighton

ACCOMMODATIONS ■
Blanch House **20**
Brighton Court
 Craven Hotel **17**
Cowards Guest House **15**
The Grand **6**
Hilton Brighton Metropole **5**
Legends Hotel **19**
Nineteen **11**
Old Ship Hotel **7**
Paskins Hotel **18**
Regency Hotel **2**
Thistle Brighton **8**
Topps Hotel **3**

ATTRACTIONS ●
Brighton Museum & Art Gallery **14**
The Royal Pavilion at Brighton **13**

DINING ◆
Brighton Rocks **12**
Brighton Rocks **16**
China Garden **1**
Due South **4**
English's of Brighton **9**
Location 3 **7**
Terre à Terre **10**

EXPENSIVE

Hilton Brighton Metropole ✦ Originally built in 1889, with a handful of its rooms housed in a postwar addition, the Brighton Metropole is the largest hotel in Brighton and one of the city's top three or four hotels (though not as grand as the Grand or Thistle Brighton). This hotel, with a central seafront location, often hosts big conferences. The refurbished rooms are comfortable and generous in size with roomy sitting areas. The spacious bathrooms include faux marble vanities and tub/shower combos. Each room has a PlayStation game console.

106 King's Rd., Brighton, East Sussex BN1 2FU. ☎ **01273/775432.** Fax 01273/207764. www.hilton.co.uk/brightonmet. 334 units. £225–£300 ($450–$600) double; £310–£385 ($620–$770) suite. AE, DC, MC, V. Parking £14 ($28). Bus: 1, 2, or 3. **Amenities:** Restaurant; 2 bars; nightclub; indoor heated pool; gym; spa; Jacuzzi; sauna; room service; babysitting; laundry service; dry cleaning. *In room:* TV, high-speed Internet, coffeemaker, hair dryer, iron.

Thistle Brighton ✦✦ This relatively modern hotel is one of the finest in the south of England, topped in Brighton only by the Grand. Rising from the seafront promenade, just minutes from the Royal Pavilion, it has been luxuriously designed for maximum comfort. Rooms tend to be large but are often blandly decorated in a sort of international modern style. Each is exceptionally comfortable, with small sitting areas and long desks.

King's Rd., Brighton, East Sussex BN1 2GS. ✆ **0870/3339129.** Fax 0870/3339229. www.thistlehotels.com. 208 units. £160–£190 ($320–$380) double; £282–£460 ($564–$920) suite. Children 16 and younger stay free in parent's room. AE, DC, MC, V. Parking £15 ($30). Bus: 1, 2, or 3. **Amenities:** 2 restaurants; bar; indoor heated pool; health club; spa; sauna; room service; babysitting; laundry service; dry cleaning. *In room:* A/C, TV, Wi-Fi, minibar, coffeemaker, hair dryer, iron, trouser press.

MODERATE

Blanch House ✪ *Finds*   Is it a hotel or is it theater? Only 2 blocks from the sea, this small hotel in a restored Georgian building is known for its very theatrical theme rooms, ranging from Moroccan to "Snowstorm" to our favorite, "the Decadence Suite." For those who got off on the movie of the same name, there is always "Boogie Nights." Rooms have queen- or king-size beds. The bar is one of the hippest in Brighton where the competition is severe, and the on-site restaurant is a gastronomic delight with such offerings as seared pigeon breast with grilled salsify and butternut squash, and a fresh pea-and-mint risotto with honeyed parsnip "pearls."

17 Atlingworth St., Brighton, East Sussex BN2 1PL. ✆ **01273/603504.** Fax 01273/689813. www.blanchhouse.co.uk. 12 units. £100–£160 ($200–$320) double; £190–£230 ($380–$460) suite. Rates include breakfast. AE, DC, MC, V. Parking £8 ($16). **Amenities:** Restaurant; bar. *In room:* TV/DVD, high-speed Internet, coffeemaker, hair dryer.

Nineteen ✪ *Finds*   Only 1 block from the beach, this rather stunning urban hotel lies close to the Brighton Pier. It's located in Kemp Town, a rapidly gentrified and up-and-coming section of Brighton. The hotel is an oasis of pure white, its bedrooms filled with works by contemporary local artists. This artwork is all that breaks the pure white, that and slatted silver blinds and glass beds illuminated by blue lighting. That same subtle blue lighting bathes the rooms in a lovely glow. Everything is as modern as tomorrow, including state-of-the-art bathrooms with tub and shower. Glass brick platforms support the comfortable beds. Guests are invited to make their own snacks in the cellar kitchen.

19 Broad St., Brighton, East Sussex BN2 1TJ. ✆ **01273/675529.** Fax 01273/675531. www.hotelnineteen.co.uk. 8 units. £120–£275 ($240–$550) double. Rates include breakfast. Minimum of 2 nights required for weekend bookings. AE, MC, V. Parking £8 ($16). **Amenities:** Bar; room service. *In room:* TV, Wi-Fi, CD player, hair dryer.

Old Ship Hotel ✪   First used as an inn in 1559, this sea-bordering hotel, a favorite among conference groups, is the largest and best of Brighton's middle-priced choices. The place is proud of its pedigree and was once the site of royal gatherings and society balls. Most of its structure dates from the 1880s; despite many subsequent modernizations, it retains a sense of its late Victorian origins. Nearly two-thirds of the rooms are nicely furnished, with modern bathrooms containing tub/shower combinations; the rest are still somewhat dowdy. The east wing has the most smartly furnished rooms. Brighton's oldest hotel, it has managed to stay abreast of the times in comfort. Prices drop if you stay for more than 1 night.

King's Rd., Brighton, East Sussex BN1 1NR. ✆ **01273/329001.** Fax 01273/820718. www.paramount-hotels.co.uk. 152 units. £150–£220 ($300–$440) double; £320–£370 ($640–$740) suite. Children 11 and younger stay free in parent's rooms. Rates include English breakfast. AE, DC, MC, V. Parking £15 ($30). Bus: 1, 2, or 3. **Amenities:** Restaurant (Location 3, p. 310); bar; room service; babysitting; laundry service; dry cleaning. *In room:* TV, Wi-Fi, coffeemaker, hair dryer, trouser press.

INEXPENSIVE

Paskins Hotel   This well-run eco-friendly hotel is 2 blocks from the sea and a short walk from the Palace Pier and Royal Pavilion. Rates depend on plumbing and furnishings, the most expensive units fitted with four-poster beds. Bedrooms are individually decorated with contemporary styling. Bathrooms, compact but tidily maintained, have shower stalls. Recent upgrading has made this one of the more charming B&Bs in Brighton. A friendly, informal atmosphere prevails; the freshly cooked award-winning English breakfast (vegetarians are specially catered to), served in a cozy room, is one of the best in town.

18–19 Charlotte St., Brighton, East Sussex BN2 1AG. (𝒞 01273/601203. Fax 01273/621973. www.paskins.co.uk. 19 units, 16 with shower. £55–£80 ($110–$160) double without shower; £70–£100 ($140–$200) with shower; £90–£130 ($180–$260) double with four-poster bed. Rates include English breakfast. AE, MC, V. Parking £5 ($10). Bus: 7. **Amenities:** Lounge; breakfast room; room service. *In room:* TV, coffeemaker, hair dryer, iron, trouser press.

Regency Hotel   A block from the sea, this typical 1820 Regency town house, once the home of Jane, dowager duchess of Marlborough and great-grandmother of Sir Winston Churchill, is a skillfully converted family-managed hotel with a licensed bar and modern comforts. Many rooms enjoy window views across the square and out to the sea. Rooms come in a variety of shapes and sizes, but each is well furnished with such extras as bedside radios. The Regency Suite has a half-tester bed (1840) and antique furniture, along with a huge bow window dressed with ceiling-to-floor swagged curtains and a balcony facing the sea and West Pier. The Regency is only a few minutes' walk from the Conference Center and an hour by train or car from Gatwick Airport.

28 Regency Sq., Brighton, East Sussex BN1 2FH. (𝒞 01273/202690. Fax 01273/220438. www.regencyhotel brighton.com. 15 units, all with shower. £65–£120 ($130–$240) double; £110–£180 ($220–$360) Regency Suite. Rates include English breakfast. AE, DC, MC, V. Parking £12 ($24). Bus: 1, 2, 3, 5, or 6. **Amenities:** Breakfast room; bar; lounge; room service; laundry service. *In room:* TV, Wi-Fi, coffeemaker, hair dryer, iron.

Topps Hotel   This cream-colored hotel enjoys a diagonal view of the sea from its position beside the sloping lawn of Regency Square, a half-block from the sea. Each room is differently shaped and individually furnished. Except for the singles, most rooms have fireplaces. All units have well-kept bathrooms with tub/shower combos; try for a unit with four-poster bed and private balcony opening to a view of the sea.

17 Regency Sq., Brighton, East Sussex BN1 2FG. (𝒞 01273/729334. Fax 01273/203679. www.toppshotel.com. 14 units. £85–£150 ($170–$300) double. Rates include English breakfast. AE, DC, MC, V. Parking £9.20–£11 ($18–$22). Bus: 1, 2, 3, 5, or 6. **Amenities:** Room service; laundry service. *In room:* TV, minibar, coffeemaker, hair dryer, iron, trouser press.

IN NEARBY HOVE

Lansdowne Place Hotel   Near the seafront in Hove, 3.2km (2 miles) west of Brighton, the Lansdowne is just a few blocks from the resort's bronze statue of Queen Victoria. Going up marble steps, you register within view of 18th-century antiques. The large, high-ceilinged public rooms emphasize the deeply comfortable chairs and the chandeliers. The bedrooms offer tall windows and stylish furniture. Bedrooms are usually midsize with walnut furnishings, bathrooms are well appointed with a bidet, the bathtubs and sinks have marble basins, and there are even heated towel racks.

Lansdowne Place, Hove, Brighton, East Sussex BN3 1HQ. (𝒞 01273/736266. Fax 01273/729802. www.lansdowne place.co.uk. 84 units. £130–£160 ($260–$320) double; from £220–£350 ($440–$700) suite. AE, DC, MC, V. Bus: 2 or 5. **Amenities:** Restaurant; bar; gym; sauna; spa; room service; babysitting; laundry service; dry cleaning. *In room:* TV, coffeemaker, hair dryer, iron, trouser press.

WHERE TO DINE

The **Mock Turtle Tea Shop,** 4 Pool Valley (𝒞 01273/327380), is a small but busy tearoom that has many locals stopping by to gossip and take their tea. They offer a variety of cakes, flapjacks, tea breads, and light, fluffy scones with homemade preserves. Everything is made fresh daily. The most popular item is the scone with strawberry preserves or whipped cream. They also serve a wide variety of good teas.

MODERATE

China Garden BEIJING/CANTONESE   The menu at the China Garden is large and satisfying. It may not be ready for London, and it's certainly pricey, but it's the brightest in town, with many classic dishes deftly handled by the kitchen staff. Dim sum (a popular luncheon choice) is offered only until 4pm. Try crispy sliced pork Szechuan-style or Peking roast duck with pancakes. We've found that some of the most savory dishes on the menu include delectable soft-shell crab, spicy barbecue spareribs, and a superb salt-and-pepper squid. The location is only 3 blocks from the sea.

88 Preston St. (in the town center off Western Rd.). ℂ 01273/325124. Reservations recommended. Main courses £8.50–£22 ($17–$44). AE, DC, MC, V. Mon–Fri noon–11:30pm; Sat–Sun noon–11:45pm. Closed Dec 25–26.

Due South ✦ MODERN BRITISH   This restaurant has the best green credentials in Sussex. Its chefs seek the very best "organic, free range, and biodynamic" ingredients they can find, most of their foodstuff coming from a 56km (35-mile) radius of Brighton Beach. That means that fresh fish and shellfish are their strong selling points. True to their green philosophy, they keep the decor rather simple—wooden furniture and floors. Their location is under one of the arches of the Brighton Promenade close to the beach.

Their cooking is straightforward and honest, as evoked by such starters as beet soufflé or pan-roasted quail with wilted greens. Their classic, well-prepared cookery is also well represented by such mains as pan-fried guinea fowl breast with chestnuts or their pan-seared loin of venison with celeriac and a truffle purée. The selection of fresh oysters is the best in town. "Puds" are sometimes startlingly original—ever had a Jerusalem artichoke and thyme crème brûlée?

139 Kings Road Arches. ℂ 01273/821218. Reservations recommended. Main courses £13–£22 ($26–$44). AE, MC, V. Daily noon–4pm and 6–10pm.

English's of Brighton SEAFOOD   This popular seafood restaurant occupies a trio of very old fishermen's cottages 1 block from the sea. Owned and operated by the same family since the end of World War II, it sits in the center of town, near Brighton's bus station. The food is solid and reliable—and fresh. Quality ingredients go into creating such starters as classic English potted shrimp or smoked Scottish salmon. Fresh fish such as Dover sole and lobster dominate the main courses. Chefs often dress up the fish with intriguing seasonings, as in the pan-fried scallops with sesame seeds and mild chili peppers. English seafood platters are also served. The upstairs dining area incorporates murals depicting Edwardian dinner and theater scenes. In summer, guests can dine alfresco on the terrace.

29–31 East St. ℂ 01273/327980. Reservations recommended. Main courses £15–£25 ($30–$50); fixed-price menu £15–£25 ($30–$50) for 2 courses, £30 ($60) for 3 courses. AE, DC, MC, V. Mon–Sat noon–10:15pm; Sun 12:30–9:30pm.

Location 3 ENGLISH   A longtime favorite, this restaurant in the Old Ship Hotel (p. 308), in the center of town, enjoys an ideal location on the waterfront. When possible, locally caught fish is on the menu. Come here to savor such dishes as mussels in a fennel-and-black-pepper cream sauce, or grilled cod steak with a homemade tomato sauce. A meat specialty is roast rump of Southdown lamb with confit potatoes. The wine list is excellent. Stop in the adjoining pub for a before- or after-dinner drink.

In the Old Ship Hotel, King's Rd. © **01273/329001.** Reservations recommended. Main courses £10–£22 ($20–$44). AE, DC, MC, V. Daily noon–2pm and 6–9pm. Bus: 1, 2, or 3.

INEXPENSIVE

Bill's Produce Store ☆ *(Finds* MODERN BRITISH   The Bill in the name of this eatery is Bill Collison, who takes great care to support local farmers, preferring them for his supply of varied fruit and vegetable. In what used to be the Brighton bus depot, he has created this successful fresh produce store, deli, and modern dining room that evokes a food market. Eating stops early in the evening, but you can drop in all day long to sample his market-fresh offerings backed up by a selection of organic wines.

The day begins early here with such breakfast offerings as crumpets with blackberry butter or buttermilk pancakes. As the day progresses, the menu offers such temptations as steamed Cornish mussels in beer or a charcuterie plate that features Bill's meats with grilled breads. One of the most tantalizing offerings is a Thai spiced pumpkin and coconut curry.

The Depot, 100 North St. © **01273/692894.** Reservations recommended after 5pm. Main courses £8.95–£16 ($18–$32). AE, MC, V. Mon–Sat 8am–8pm; Sun 10am–4pm.

Brighton Rocks ☆ *(Finds* TAPAS   Brighton grows hipper and hipper, the latest rage being a take on a Cape Cod beach bar, the type that JFK, Jr., might have frequented in days of yore. At this light, spacious, and airy bar, drinks are consumed at a glass-topped bar covering sand, driftwood, shells, and pebbles. The tapas featured here are the best in town, including smoked salmon and crayfish salad, king prawn tempura, sweet-potato wedges, grilled halloumi cheese, stuffed vine leaves, and fresh-baked focaccia. No tapas are served on Sunday evenings, but they do offer traditional English roasts such as pork and beef until 5pm. After that, DJs take over. The opening hours below are when food is served, but the joint itself is open Monday to Thursday noon to 12:30am, Friday and Saturday noon to 1am, and Sunday noon to 11pm. The bar even has its own transport cafe: an old jeep parked outside with a table in the back where patrons can sit and sip their drinks.

6 Rock Place. © **01273/601139.** Reservations not needed. Small plates £3–£8 ($6–$16); 3-course fixed-price menu £31 ($62). AE, DC, MC, V. Mon–Sat noon–3:30pm and 6–10pm; Sun noon–5pm.

Terre à Terre ☆☆ *(Finds* VEGETARIAN/VEGAN   The finest vegetarian restaurant on the south coast of England, this is a truly outstanding choice even if you're a carnivore. You dine in a trio of spacious rooms in vivid colors, and everything has a bustling brasserie aura. Cooks roam the world for inspiration in the preparation of their delectable dishes. Sushi, couscous, pizza—it's all here and does it ever taste good, especially the selection of tapas. To give you an idea of what to expect, good appetizers are goat cheese crostini with onions and pumpkin confit and a green olive mash, or the lentils cooked in wine with mixed greens. For a main course, vegetable soufflés are often featured, as are potatoes mousseline or stuffed deep-fried green olives. Breads are Italian, and the house wine is organic French. Children's meals are available. The location is 1½ blocks from the sea.

71 East St. © **01273/729051.** Reservations recommended. Main courses £12–£15 ($24–$30). AE, DC, MC, V. Tues–Fri noon–10:30pm; Sat noon–11pm; Sun noon–10pm.

THE ROYAL PAVILION

The Royal Pavilion at Brighton ☆☆☆   Among royal residences in Europe, the Royal Pavilion at Brighton, a John Nash version of an Indian mogul's palace, is unique. Ornate and exotic, it has been subjected over the years to the most devastating wit of English satirists and pundits, but today we can examine it more objectively as one of the most outstanding examples of the Asian tendencies of England's Romantic Movement.

Originally a farmhouse, a neoclassical villa was built on the site in 1787 by Henry Holland, but it no more resembled its present appearance than a caterpillar does a butterfly. By the time Nash had transformed it from a simple classical villa into an Asian fantasy, the prince regent had become King George IV, and the king and one of his mistresses, Lady Conyngham, lived in the palace until 1827.

A decade passed before Victoria, then queen, arrived in Brighton. Though she was to bring Albert and the children on a number of occasions, the monarch and Brighton just didn't mix. The very air of the resort seemed too flippant for her. By 1845, Victoria began packing, and the royal furniture was carted off. Its royal owners gone, the Pavilion was in serious peril of being torn down when, by a narrow vote, Brightonians agreed to purchase it. Gradually it was restored to its former splendor, enhanced in no small part by the return of much of its original furniture, including many items on loan from the queen. A new exhibit tours the Royal Pavilion Gardens.

Of exceptional interest is the domed **Banqueting Room,** with a chandelier of bronze dragons supporting lilylike glass globes. In the Great Kitchen, with its old revolving spits, is a collection of Wellington's pots and pans from his town house at Hyde Park Corner. In the **State Apartments,** particularly the domed salon, dragons wink at you, serpents entwine, and lacquered doors shine. The Music Room, with its scalloped ceiling, is a fantasy of water lilies, flying dragons, reptilian paintings, bamboo, silk, and satin.

In the first-floor gallery, look for Nash's views of the Pavilion in its elegant heyday. Other attractions include **Queen Victoria's Apartments,** beautifully re-created, and the impressively restored **South Galleries,** breakfast rooms for George IV's guests. Refreshments are available in the Queen Adelaide Tea Room, which has a balcony overlooking the Royal Pavilion Gardens.

ⓒ 01273/290900. www.royalpavilion.org.uk. Admission £7.70 ($15) adults, £5.90 ($12) students and seniors, £5.10 ($10) children ages 5–15, £21 ($42) family ticket, free for children 4 and younger. Apr–Sept daily 9:30am–5:45pm; Oct–Mar daily 10am–5:15pm. Closed Dec 25–26.

OTHER ATTRACTIONS

Brighton Museum & Art Gallery ★★   After a £10-million ($20-million) redevelopment, one of the great cultural attractions in the southeast of England has opened. In Victorian buildings opposite the Royal Pavilion, the museum is devoted to an eclectic collection of world art and artifacts, ranging from Salvador Dalí's "Mae West's Lips Sofa" to costumes worn at King George IV's coronation in 1821. Employing all the latest museum interpretive techniques, the museum is one of the most user-friendly outside London. The central gallery displays 20th-century decorative art, including furniture by Philippe Starck, works by Lalique and Bugatti, and a host of other luminaries. You'll see everything from Henry Willett's collection of 2,000 pieces of innovative porcelain to Shiro Kuramata's "How High the Moon Chair" from 1986 (it was inspired by the Duke Ellington jazz standard). The Fashion & Style Gallery draws upon Brighton's extensive collections of period costumes. In the museum's World Art Collection, you'll find some 15,000 objects collected from the Americas, Africa, Asia, and the Pacific, ranging from Vietnamese water puppets to a black basalt George Washington bust by Wedgwood.

Royal Pavilion Gardens. (℅ 01273/292882. www.brighton.virtualmuseum.info. Free admission. Tues 10am–7pm; Wed–Sat 10am–5pm; Sun 2–5pm.

SHOPPING

Mall rats head for **Churchill Square,** Brighton's spacious shopping center, which is home to major chain stores. The shopping center runs from Western Road to North Street (about 3km/2 miles long) and offers many inexpensive shops and stalls with great buys on everything from antiques to woolens. On Saturdays, there are many more antiques exhibits and sidewalk stalls. The mall is open Monday to Wednesday 9am to 6pm, Friday and Saturday 9am to 7pm, and Sunday 11am to 5pm.

Regent Arcade, which is located between East Street, Bartholomew Square, and Market Street, sells artwork, jewelry, and other gift items, as well as high-fashion clothing.

Everyone raves about the shopping on the **Lanes.** The Lanes are a close-knit section of alleyways off North Street in Brighton's Old Town; many of the present shops were formerly fishers' cottages. The shopping is mostly for tourists, and while you may fall for a few photo ops, you'll find that the nearby **North Laine**—between the Lanes and the train station—is the area for up-and-coming talent and for alternative retail. Just wander along a street called Kensington Gardens to get the whole effect. Innumerable shops are located in the Lanes that carry antique books and jewelry, and many boutiques are found in converted backyards on Duke Lane just off Ship Street. In the center of the Lanes is Brighton Square, which is ideal for relaxing or people-watching near the fountain on one of the benches or from a cafe-bar.

Bargain hunters head for the **Kemptown Flea Market** on 31A Upper James St. Monday to Saturday 9:30am to 5:30pm and Sunday 10:30am to 5pm. A more famous **flea market** is held in the parking lot of the train station, but only on Sunday 6am to 2pm.

Framework, 26 Kensington Gardens (℅ 01273/818585), has old photographs of the local area, illustrations, prints, and a complete framing service.

In addition to its malls and shopping complexes, Brighton also abounds in specialty shops. One of our favorites is the finest gift shop in Brighton, the **Pavilion Shop,** 4–5 Pavilion Buildings, Brighton (℅ 01273/292798), next to the Royal Pavilion. Here you can purchase gift and home-furnishing items in the style of design schools that created the look (from Regency to Victorian). Books, jams, needlepoint kits, notebooks, pencils, stencil kits, and other souvenirs are also available. Latest British designers for women are showcased at a fashionable store, **Pussy,** 3A Kensington Gardens (℅ 01273/604861).

BRIGHTON AFTER DARK

Brighton offers lots of entertainment options. You can find out what's happening by looking for *What's On,* a single sheet of weekly events posted throughout the town.

One theater offers drama throughout the year: the **Theatre Royal,** New Road (℅ 08700/606650), with pre-London shows. Bigger concerts are held at **Brighton Centre,** Kings Road (℅ 01273/290131; www.brightoncentre.co.uk), a 5,000-seat facility featuring mainly pop-music shows.

Nightclubs also abound. Cover charges range from free admission (most often on early or midweek nights) to £10 ($20), so call the clubs to find out about admission fees and updates in their nightly schedules, which often vary from week to week or season to season.

Audio, 10 Marine Parade (℡ **01273/606906**), home to both gay and straight dancers, has one floor for dancing and offers different music styles on different nights of the week on the second floor.

The hot, hot club on West Street is **Oceana Brighton** (℡ **01273/732627**), a new multiroom complex and the first nightclub in the area to offer an early-evening bar. There are three different venues here under one roof: the Deep Bar, the New York Disco, and the Reykjavik Icehouse. There's disco dancing on Europe's largest illuminated dance floor. Expect to pay a cover of £10 ($20), but this could vary depending on the night.

For a change of pace, **Casablanca,** Middle Street (℡ **01273/321817**), features jazz with an international flavor.

Pubs are a good place to kick off an evening, especially the **Colonnade Bar,** New Road (℡ **01273/328728**), serving drinks for over 100 years. The pub gets a lot of theater business because of its proximity to the Theatre Royal. **Cricketers,** Black Lion Street (℡ **01273/329472**), is worth a stop because it's Brighton's oldest pub, parts of which date from 1549. Drinking lures patrons to **Fortune of War,** 157 King's Rd. (℡ **01273/205065**).

H. J. O'Neil's, 27 Ship St. (℡ **01273/827621**), is an authentic Irish pub located at the top of the Lanes. A stop here will fortify you with traditional Irish pub grub, a creamy pint of Guinness, and a soundtrack of folk music. Of course, they make the best Irish stew in town.

BRIGHTON'S GAY SCENE

After London, Brighton has the most active gay scene in England. Aside from vacationers, it's home to gay retirees and executives who commute into central London by train. The town has always had a reputation for tolerance and humor, and according to the jaded owners of some of the town's 20 or so gay bars, more drag queens live within the local Regency town houses than virtually anywhere else in England.

But the gay scene here is a lot less glittery than in London. And don't assume that the south of England is as chic as the south of France. Its international reputation is growing, but despite that, gay Brighton remains thoroughly English, and at times, even a bit dowdy.

GAY-FRIENDLY PLACES TO STAY

Brighton Court Craven Hotel   This three-story hotel isn't particularly exciting and doesn't have many facilities, but it's the cheapest option we recommend, and it has an atmosphere of casual permissiveness. It's proud of a clientele that's almost 100% gay and mostly male. Breakfasts are served communally, with all the traditional English accompaniments. The bedrooms are rather bare-bones: You stay here for the camaraderie—not grand comfort.

2 Atlingworth St., Brighton BN2 1PL. ℡ **01273/696009.** www.courtcraven.co.uk. 12 units, all with shower. Mon–Thurs £55 ($110) double; Fri–Sun £60 ($120) double. Rates include breakfast. 2-night minimum stay on weekends. MC, V. **Amenities:** Bar. *In room:* TV, coffeemaker.

Cowards Guest House   Originally built in 1807, this five-story, Regency-era house is extremely well maintained. Inside, Jerry and his partner, Cyril (a cousin of the late playwright and bon vivant Noel Coward), welcome only gay men, of all degrees of flamboyance. Don't expect any frills in the conservative, standard rooms, such as those you may find in any modern hotel in England. It offers very few extras, though a number of gay bars and watering holes lie nearby.

Finds A Side Trip to Kipling's Hometown

"Heaven looked after it in the dissolute times of mid-Victorian restoration and caused the vicar to send his bailiff to live in it for 40 years, and he lived in peaceful filth and left everything as he found it," wrote **Rudyard Kipling**.

He was writing of **Bateman's** ⟨ (*℗* **01435/882302**), the 17th-century iron-master's house in the village of Burwash, on the A265, the Lewes-Etching-ham road, some 43km (27 miles) northeast of Brighton, close to the border with Kent. Born in Bombay, India, in 1865, Kipling loved the countryside of Sussex, and the book that best expressed his feelings for the shire is *Puck of Pook's Hill,* written in 1906. The following year he won the Nobel Prize for literature. He lived at Bateman from 1902 until his death in 1936. His widow died 3 years later, leaving the house to the National Trust.

Kipling is known mainly for his adventure stories, such as *The Jungle Book* (1894) and *Captains Courageous* (1897). He is also remembered for his tales about India, including *Kim* (1901). He lived in America after his marriage to Caroline Balestier in 1892. But by 1896, he had returned to the south of England, occupying a house at Rottingdean, a little village on the Sussex Downs, 6.5km (4 miles) east of Brighton. Here he wrote the famous line: "What should they know of England who only England know?" In a steam-driven motorcar, Kipling and Caroline set out to explore Sussex, of which they were especially fond. Though the population of Rottingdean was only that of a small village, they decided at some point that it had become too crowded. In their motorcar one day, they spotted Bateman's, their final home. "It is a good and peaceable place standing in terraced lawns nigh to a walled garden of old red brick, and two fat-headed oasthouses with redbrick stomachs, and an aged silver-grey dovecot on top," Kipling wrote.

The Burwash city fathers invited Kipling to unveil a memorial to the slain of World War I, and he agreed. It's in the center of town at the church. Kipling said that visitors should "remember the sacrifice." Both the church and an inn across the way appear in the section of *Puck of Pook's Hill* called "Hal o' the Draft." The famous writer and son of Anglo-Indian parents died in London and was given an impressive funeral before being buried in Poets' Corner at Westminster Abbey.

The interior of Bateman's is filled with Asian rugs, antique bronzes, and other mementos the writer collected in India and elsewhere. Kipling's library is quite interesting. The house and gardens are open mid-March to October Saturday to Wednesday 11am to 5pm. Admission is £6.20 ($12) for adults, £3.10 ($6.20) for children, and £16 ($32) for a family ticket.

12 Upper Rock Gardens, Brighton BN2 1QE. *℗* **01273/692677.** www.cowardsbrighton.co.uk. 6 units. £70–£80 ($140–$160) double. Rates include full English breakfast. 2-night minimum stay on weekends. AE, MC, V. *In room:* TV, fridge, coffeemaker.

Legends Hotel   Hands-down, this is the largest, busiest, and most fun gay hotel in Brighton. First, it's a bona fide hotel, not a B&B as most of Brighton's other gay-friendly lodgings are. Unlike many of its competitors, it welcomes women, though very few of them tend to be comfortable. Because of the high jinks and raucousness that can float up from the bars below, rooms can be noisy but are nonetheless comfortable, clean, and unfrilly. All units have well-kept bathrooms with shower units. In addition to these rooms, the few luxury boutique doubles are more spacious and furnished more stylishly, with upgraded bathrooms. The staff is happy to camp it up for you before your arrival (adding balloons, champagne, flowers, and streamers), for a fee.

31–32 Marine Parade, Brighton BN2 1TR. © 01273/624462. Fax 01273/624575. www.legendsbrighton.com. 40 units. £60–£80 ($120–$160) double. Rates include breakfast. 2-night minimum stay on weekends. AE, DC, MC, V. **Amenities:** 2 bars. *In room:* TV, coffeemaker, hair dryer.

GAY NIGHTLIFE

A complete, up-to-date roster of the local gay bars is available in any copy of *G-Scene* magazine (© **01273/722457;** www.gscene.com), distributed free in gay hotels and bars throughout the south of England. See also "Brighton After Dark," above, for a few popular dance clubs.

Doctor Brighton's Bar, 16 Kings Rd., the Seafront (© **01273/328765**), is the largest and most consistently reliable choice. The staff expends great energy on welcoming all members of the gay community. In their words, "We get everyone from 18-year-old designer queens to 50-year-old leather queens, and they, along with all their friends and relatives, are welcome." Originally built around 1750, with a checkered past that includes stints as a smuggler's haven and an abortion clinic, it also has more history and more of the feel of an old-time Victorian pub than any of its competitors. It's open Monday to Thursday 2pm to midnight, Friday 2pm to 1am, Saturday 1pm to 1am, and Sunday 1 to 11pm. With no real lesbian bar in town, gay women tend to congregate at Doctor Brighton's.

Two of the town's busiest and most flamboyant gay bars lie within the Legends Hotel (see above). The one with the longer hours is **Legends,** a pubby, clubby bar with a view of the sea that's open to the public daily from 11am to 11pm and to residents of the Legends Hotel and their guests until 3:30am. Legends features cross-dressing cabarets and women vocalists, while tweedy-looking English matrons and diaphanous Edwardian vamps are portrayed with loads of tongue-in-cheek satire and humor. Legends nightclub is a cellar-level denim and leather joint. The bars are open daily 11pm to 3:30am and charge a £5 ($10) cover on the weekend.

The **Marlborough,** 4 Princes St. (© **01273/570028**), has been a staple on the scene for years. Set across from the Royal Pavilion, this Victorian-style pub has a cabaret theater on its second floor. It remains popular with the gay and, to a lesser degree, straight communities. A changing roster of lesbian performance art and both gay and straight cabaret within the second-floor theater is presented.

11 Alfriston ★★ & Lewes ★

97km (60 miles) S of London

Nestled on the Cuckmere River, Alfriston is one of the most beautiful villages of England. It lies northeast of Seaford on the English Channel, near the resort of Eastbourne and the modern port of Newhaven. During the day, Alfriston is overrun by coach tours (it's that lovely and that popular). The High Street, with its old market cross, looks just like what you would always imagine a traditional English village to be. Some of the old houses still have hidden chambers where smugglers stored their loot (alas, the loot is gone). There are also several old inns.

About a dozen miles away along the A27 toward Brighton is the rather somber market town of Lewes. (Thomas Paine lived at Bull House on High St. in what is now a restaurant.) Because the home of the Glyndebourne Opera is only 8km (5 miles) to the east, it's hard to find a place to stay, even in Lewes, during the renowned annual opera festival.

ESSENTIALS

GETTING THERE   Trains leave from London's Victoria Station. Two trains per hour make the 1¼-hour trip daily. For rail information, call ℭ **0845/748-4950** or visit **www.nationalrail.co.uk**. Alfriston has no rail service.

Buses run daily to Lewes from London's Victoria Coach Station, though the 3-hour trip has so many stops that it's better to take the train. Call ℭ **0870/580-8080** for schedules or visit **www.nationalexpress.com**.

A bus runs from Lewes to Alfriston every 90 minutes. It's operated by **Countryliner** (bus no. 125; ℭ **01444/506919**). For bus information and schedules in the area, call ℭ **0870/608-2608.** The bus station at Lewes is on East Gate Street in the center of town.

If you're driving, head east along the M25 (the London Ring Rd.), and cut south on the A26 via East Grinstead to Lewes. Once at Lewes, follow the A27 east to the signposted turnoff for the village of Alfriston.

VISITOR INFORMATION   The **Tourist Information Centre** is in Lewes at 187 High St. (ℭ **01273/483448**). In season, from Easter until the end of October, hours are Monday to Friday 9am to 5pm, Saturday 9:30am to 5:30pm, and Sunday 10am to 2pm. Off-season hours are Monday to Friday from 9am to 5pm and Saturday 10am to 2pm.

WHERE TO STAY
IN ALFRISTON

Dean's Place Hotel   Dean's Place offers English-country-house living at a reasonable price. The place dates from the 1300s, though it has been much improved and architecturally altered over the years. Set in beautifully landscaped gardens, it is a cliché of English country charm with creeper-covered walls. Bedrooms come in a variety of sizes, each comfortably appointed with firm beds. The staff is polite and helpful. The location is convenient for trips to Lewes and Brighton, among other places.

Seaford Rd., Polgate, East Sussex BN26 5TW. ℭ **01323/870248.** Fax 01323/870918. www.deansplacehotel.co.uk. 36 units. £95–£150 ($190–$300) double. Rates include breakfast. AE, MC, V. On the 2nd roundabout after Lewes, take the 3rd exit for Alfriston and Drusilla's Zoo. Pass through Alfriston to the south side. The hotel is on the left-hand side of the road. **Amenities:** Restaurant; bar; outdoor heated pool; putting green; croquet; room service; laundry service. *In room:* TV, coffeemaker, hair dryer, iron.

George Inn   The George dates from 1397, making it one of the oldest inns in the country. It was once a rendezvous for smugglers. The midsize bedrooms are inviting and comfortable; two of them have four-poster beds. All rooms have neatly kept bathrooms equipped with a tub. The George, however, is better known for good food. A garden is in back, but most guests head for the restaurant with its Windsor chairs and beamed ceiling.

High St., Alfriston, East Sussex BN26 5SY. ℂ **01323/870319.** Fax 01323/871384. www.thegeorge-alfriston.com. 6 units. £90–£130 ($180–$260) double. Rates include English breakfast. MC, V. **Amenities:** Restaurant; bar; laundry service. *In room:* A/C, TV/DVD, coffeemaker, hair dryer, no phone.

Riverdale House   Set on a hill overlooking the town, this small B&B is one of the finest in the area. A restored Victorian home, it offers handsomely furnished bedrooms in various sizes. Each comes with a small but well-kept private bathroom with shower. Most rooms open onto lovely countryside views including a well-kept garden in front. Riverdale also has a large conservatory where guests socialize or else enjoy the reading material.

Seaford Rd., Alfriston, East Sussex BN26 5TR. ℂ **01323/871038.** www.riverdalehouse.co.uk. 4 units. £75–£85 ($150–$170) double; £110 ($220) suite. Rates include breakfast. MC, V. **Amenities:** Breakfast room; guest lounge. *In room:* TV/DVD, coffeemaker.

The Star Inn ℱ   The Star Inn—the premier place to stay in Alfriston—occupies a building dating from 1450, though it was originally founded in the 1200s to house pilgrims en route to Chichester and the shrine of St. Richard. Located in the center of the village, its carved front remains unchanged. The lounges are on several levels, a forest of old timbers. We infinitely prefer the rooms in the main building, which have far more character even though they've been altered and renovated over the years. Out back is a more sterile motel wing, with studio rooms. Bedrooms vary in size and style, but each one in the main building is well maintained with an old-world aura.

High St., Alfriston, East Sussex BN26 5TA. ℂ **01323/870495.** Fax 01323/870922. www.star-inn-alfriston.com. 37 units. £98–£138 ($196–$276) double. Rates include breakfast. AE, DC, MC, V. **Amenities:** Restaurant; bar; room service; babysitting; laundry service. *In room:* TV, coffeemaker, hair dryer, iron, trouser press.

IN LEWES

Lewes is blessed with a number of affordable B&Bs, the largest concentration of recommendable ones found along Gundreda Road. The best of these include **Two Chimneys Bed and Breakfast,** 25 Gundreda Rd., Lewes BN7 1PT (ℂ **01273/476079;** www.visitlewesbedandbreakfast.co.uk). Here two guests are charged only £60 ($120) for B&B. A second possibility is the well-recommended **Phoenix House,** 23 Gundreda Rd., Lewes BN7 1PT (ℂ **01273/473250**). B&B costs £65 ($130) a night for two.

Crown Inn   Built around 1760, this is one of the oldest inns in Lewes, a 30-minute ride from Gatwick and 60 minutes from London. Located opposite the town's war memorial, it stands at a traffic circle on the main street. The hotel is considerably refurbished, though still a bit creaky. Pub lunches and dinner are served daily in a Victorian conservatory.

191 High St., Lewes, East Sussex BN7 2NA. ℂ **01273/480670.** Fax 01273/480679. www.crowninn-lewes.co.uk. 8 units, 7 with bathroom. £60 ($120) double without bathroom, £70 ($140) with bathroom; £80 ($160) family room. Rates include English breakfast. MC, V. **Amenities:** Breakfast room; bar. *In room:* TV, coffeemaker, hair dryer.

Shelleys Hotel ℱ   The earl of Dorset owned this 1526 manor house before it was sold to the Shelley family, wealthy Sussex landowners (and relatives of the poet Percy Bysshe Shelley). Radical changes were made to the architecture in the 18th century. A complete refurbishment has turned the hotel into a two-restaurant luxurious country-house retreat. There are traditional details throughout, such as the family coat of arms in the central hall. The standards of the management are reflected in the fine antiques, bowls of flowers, paintings and prints, well-kept gardens and, most important, helpful staff. The bedrooms are personal, individually furnished, usually spacious, and most comfortable.

High St., Lewes, East Sussex BN7 1XS. © 01273/472361. Fax 01273/483152. www.shelleys-hotel.com. 19 units. £180–£200 ($360–$400) double. Children 5 and younger stay free in parent's room. AE, DC, MC, V. **Amenities:** Restaurant; bar; room service; babysitting; laundry service; dry cleaning. *In room:* TV, minibar, coffeemaker, hair dryer, trouser press.

WHERE TO DINE
IN ALFRISTON

Around teatime, head for the **Tudor House,** on Alfriston's High Street (© **01323/ 870891**). The well-lit interior has two tearooms that provide a calm setting for afternoon tea. Cheese, ham-and-cheese, and egg-salad sandwiches and muffins, Danish, scones, and cakes are served. Afternoon tea costs £3.50 to £5 ($7–$10) sandwiches £3 to £4 ($6–$8), and cakes and pastries from £1.50 ($3). It's open daily 10:30am to 4:30pm and Wednesday to Saturday 7 to 9pm.

IN LEWES

The Juggs ENGLISH   In a romantic setting in the South Downs, this old pub serves good food and plenty of beer and ale in the satellite village of Kinston, lying 4.8km (3 miles) southeast of Lewes. A tile-coated 1400s cottage, it is said to be named for a woman called "Juggs," who walked from Brighton with baskets of fresh fish for sale in the countryside. You can still order fresh fish here along with such English specialties as steak-and-kidney pudding and roasts. Look for daily specials as well. For dessert, why not have the homemade chocolate brownie with chocolate fudge sauce?

The Street, Kingston. © 01273/472523. No reservations needed. Main courses £6–£13 ($12–$26). MC, V. Mon–Sat 11am–11pm; Sun noon–10pm.

Pailin *(Kids)* THAI   Spicy-hot Thai food has come to Lewes, though some of the fiery dishes have been toned down for English taste buds. Begin perhaps with the lemon chicken soup with lemon grass, followed by a crab-and-prawn hot pot. A special favorite with locals is the barbecued marinated chicken, which is served with a spicy but delectable sweet-and-sour plum sauce. Vegetarian meals are served, and children are welcome and given small portions at reduced prices.

20 Station St. © 01273/473906. Reservations not needed. Main courses £6–£12 ($12–$24); fixed-price lunch or dinner £15–£19 ($30–$38). AE, DC, MC, V. Tues–Sat noon–3pm and 6–10:30pm. Closed Nov 5 and Dec 25–26.

THE GLYNDEBOURNE OPERA FESTIVAL ⋆

In 1934, a group of local opera enthusiasts established an opera company based in the hamlet of Glyndebourne, which is 2.5km (1½ miles) east of Lewes and 8km (5 miles) northwest of Alfriston. See listings under either of these towns for a selection of places to overnight if you'd like to stay in the area after the performances and not take the train back to London. The festival has been running ever since and is now one of the best regional opera companies in Britain.

In 1994, the original auditorium was demolished, and a dramatic modern glass, brick, and steel structure, designed by noted English architect Michael Hopkins, was built adjacent to some remaining (mostly ornamental) vestiges of the original building. The new auditorium is known for its acoustics.

Operas are presented only between mid-May and late August, and productions tend to be of unusual works. For information, contact the **Glyndebourne Festival,** P.O. Box 2624, Glyndebourne (Lewes), East Sussex BN8 5UW (© **01273/815000;**

www.glyndebourne.co.uk). You can call the box office at © **01273/813813.** Tickets range from £10 to £150 ($20–$300). You can usually get last-minute tickets because of cancellations by season-ticket holders. But if you want to see a specific show, it's a good idea to buy a ticket several months in advance. Credit card orders (Visa and MasterCard) are accepted, and for an additional postage charge, you can have tickets delivered to you. Dress is formal: Many Londoners show up in black tie, which is requested but not required.

To get to the theater from Lewes, take the A26 to the B2192, following the signs to Glynde and Glyndebourne. From Alfriston, follow the hamlet's main street north of town in the direction of the A27, then turn left following signs first to Glynde, then to Glyndebourne. There are also trains from London that are specially scheduled to deliver operagoers to Glyndebourne, and then take them home after the picnic and the performances.

EXPLORING THE TWO TOWNS

Anne of Cleves House   This half-timbered house was part of Anne of Cleves's divorce settlement from Henry VIII, but Anne never lived in the house and there's no proof that she ever visited Lewes. Today it's a museum of local history, cared for by the Sussex Archaeological Society. The museum has a furnished bedroom and kitchen and displays of furniture, local history of the Wealden iron industry, and other crafts.

52 Southover High St., Lewes. © **01273/474610.** Admission £3.50 ($7) adults, £3 ($6) students and seniors, £1.60 ($3.20) children. Mar–Oct Tues–Sat 10am–5pm, Sun–Mon 11am–5pm; Nov–Feb Tues–Sat 10am–5pm. Bus: 123.

Drusilla's Park *Kids*   This fascinating but not-too-large park has a flamingo lake, Japanese garden, and unusual breeds of some domestic animals, among other attractions. The park is perfect for families with children. Check out the newly converted £85,000 ($170,000) bat house, where a family of 20 Rodrigues fruit bats (also called mega bats) have taken up residence. With a wingspan of about 1m (3 ft.) and rich golden brown fur, they are one of the most beautiful and rarest bat species in the world.

About 1.5km (1 mile) outside Alfriston, off A27. © **01323/874100.** www.drusillas.co.uk. Admission £11–£13 ($22–$26) adults, £9.70–£12 ($19–$24) children 2–12, free for children 1 and younger. Daily 10am–5pm (until 4pm in winter). Closed Dec 24–26.

Barbican House Museum   Lewes, of course, matured in the shadow of its Norman castle. Adjacent to the castle is this museum, where a 20-minute audiovisual show is available by advance request. Audio tours of the castle are also available.

169 High St., Lewes. © **01273/486290.** Joint admission ticket to both castle and museum £4.70 ($9.40) adults, £4.20 ($8.40) students and seniors, £2.40 ($4.80) children, £12 ($24) family ticket. Both sites Tues–Sat 10am–5:30pm; Sun–Mon 11am–5:30pm. The castle closes at dusk in the winter. Closed Dec 25–26. Bus: 27, 28, 121, 122, 166, 728, or 729.

A SIDE TRIP FROM LEWES: VIRGINIA WOOLF'S HOME ✿ & THE BLUEBELL RAILWAY

This is gorgeous countryside for walks. If you want some direction in your ramblings, consider the rustic properties below. The most scenic walk you can take is the 4.8km (3-mile) trek south of Lewes (it's signposted) to the village of Rodmell. If you take this walk to call on the former home of Virginia Woolf, you'll be following a trail blazed by other walkers, each a part of the so-called literati Bloomsbury group, the roster including T. S. Eliot, Aldous Huxley, Bertrand Russell, and E. M. Forster.

The small downland village of **Rodmell** lies midway between Lewes and the port of Newhaven on C7. It's known for **Monk's House,** a National Trust property that was bought by Virginia and Leonard Woolf in 1919, and was their home until his death in 1969. Much of the house was furnished and decorated by Virginia's sister, Vanessa Bell, and the artist Duncan Grant.

The house has limited visiting hours: from April to October, and then only on Wednesday and Saturday from 2 to 5:30pm. Admission is £3.30 ($6.60) adults, £1.65 ($3.30) 5 and up, and free for children 4 and younger. A family ticket costs £8.25 ($17). More information is available by calling ℂ **01323/870001.**

Rodmell also has a 12th-century church, a working farm, and a tiny Victorian school still in use. Take Southdown bus no. 123 from the Lewes rail station if you prefer not to walk.

The trail of Virginia Woolf also leads to **Charleston Farmhouse,** along the A27 at Charleston, near Firle, 9.5km (6 miles) east of Lewes (ℂ **01825/720825;** www.charleston.org.uk). This house is the former country residence of Virginia's sister, Vanessa Bell, and the artist Duncan Grant. They were the glittering faces of the artistically influential "Bloomsbury Group" early in the 20th century. Preserved much as they left it, the property is filled with mementos and is open to guided tours on most days. Opening times are April to June and September to October Wednesday and Saturday 11:30am to 6pm, and Thursday, Friday, and Sunday 2 to 6pm; July and August hours are Wednesday to Saturday 11:30am to 6pm, and Sunday 2 to 6pm. Admission is £6.50 ($13) for adults, £4.50 ($9) for children, and £18 ($36) for a family ticket. On Sundays no tours are offered, but visitors are free to explore the house on their own. The trust that runs the property also has changing exhibitions and sponsors an annual literary and arts festival.

The all-steam **Bluebell Railway** starts at Sheffield Park Station near Uckfield in East Sussex (ℂ **01825/722370;** www.bluebell-railway.co.uk), on A275 between East Grinstead and Lewes. The name is taken from the spring flowers that grow alongside the track, running from Sheffield Park to Kingscote. It's a delight for railway buffs, with locomotives dating from the 1870s through the 1950s, when British Railways ended steam operations. You can visit locomotive sheds and a small museum, then later patronize the bookshop or have lunch in a large buffet, bar, and restaurant complex. The round-trip is 1½ hours as the train wanders through a typical English countryside. It costs £9.80 ($20) adults and £4.90 ($9.80) for children 3 to 16 years, with a family ticket going for £28 ($56). Trains run daily from April to September, and Saturday and Sunday the rest of the year.

9

Hampshire & Dorset: Austen & Hardy Country

You're in **Hampshire** and **Dorset,** two shires jealously guarded as special rural treasures. Everybody knows of Southampton and Bournemouth, but less known is the hilly countryside farther inland, which is best previewed in the **New Forest** (p. 337). Discover tiny villages and thatched cottages untouched by the industrial invasion at **Chideock** (p. 353) and **Charmouth** (p. 353).

Jane Austen wrote of Hampshire's firmly middle-class inhabitants. Her six novels, including *Pride and Prejudice* and *Sense and Sensibility,* earned her a permanent place among the pantheon of 19th-century writers and unexpected popularity among 1990s film directors and producers. You can visit her grave in **Winchester Cathedral** and the house where she lived, **Chawton Cottage.**

Hampshire encompasses the **South Downs,** the **Isle of Wight** (Victoria's favorite retreat), and the naval city of **Portsmouth.** More than 36,421 hectares (90,000 acres) of the **New Forest** were preserved by William the Conqueror as a private hunting ground; this vast woodland and heath remains ideal for walking and exploring. We concentrate on two major areas: **Southampton,** for convenience, and **Winchester,** for history.

Dorset is Thomas Hardy country. Born in Dorset in 1840, this celebrated novelist disguised the county of his birth as "Wessex" in his novels. "The last of the great Victorians," as he was called, died in 1928 at age 88. His tomb occupies a position of honor in Westminster Abbey.

One of England's smallest shires, Dorset encompasses the old seaport of **Poole** in the east and **Lyme Regis** (known to Jane Austen) in the west. Dorset is a southwestern county and borders the English Channel. It's known for its cows, and Dorset butter is served at many an afternoon tea. This is mainly a land of farms and pastures, with plenty of sandy heaths and chalky downs.

The most prominent tourist center of Dorset is the Victorian seaside resort of **Bournemouth.** If you don't stay here, you can try a number of Dorset's other seaports, villages, and country towns; we mostly stick to the areas along the impressive coastline.

You'll find the most hotels, but not the greatest charm, at Bournemouth. If you're interested in things maritime, opt for Portsmouth, the premier port of the south and home of HMS *Victory,* Nelson's flagship. For history buffs and Austen fans, Winchester, the ancient capital of England, with a cathedral built by William the Conqueror, makes a good base for exploring the countryside.

The best beaches are at Bournemouth, set among pines with sandy beaches and fine coastal views; and **Chesil Beach,** a 32km-long (20-mile) bank of shingle running from Abbottsbury to the Isle of Portland—great for beachcombing. However, the most natural spectacle is New Forest itself, 375 sq. km (145 sq. miles) of heath and woodland, once the hunting ground of Norman kings.

1 Winchester ★★

116km (72 miles) SW of London; 19km (12 miles) N of Southampton

The most historic city in all of Hampshire, Winchester is big on legends because it's associated with King Arthur and the Knights of the Round Table.

The city is also linked with King Alfred, who is honored today by a statue. King Alfred the Great, born in 849, was crowned king in 871, ruling until his death in 899. He is called "the Great," because he defended Anglo-Saxon England against Viking raids, formulated a code of laws, and fostered a rebirth of religious and scholarly activity.

Of course, Winchester is a mecca for Jane Austen fans. You can visit her grave in Winchester Cathedral (Emma Thompson did, while working on her adapted screenplay of *Sense and Sensibility*), as well as Chawton Cottage, Jane Austen's house, which is 24km (15 miles) east of Winchester.

Its past glory but a memory, Winchester is essentially a market town today, lying on the downs along the Itchen River.

ESSENTIALS

GETTING THERE   Frequent daily train service runs from London's Waterloo Station to Winchester. The trip takes 1 hour. For rail information, call © **0845/748-4950** or visit www.nationalrail.co.uk. Arrivals are at Winchester Station, Station Hill, northwest of the city center. **National Express** buses leaving from London's Victoria Coach Station depart regularly for Winchester during the day. The trip takes 2 hours. Call © **0870/580-8080** or visit **www.nationalexpress.com** for schedules and information.

If you're driving, from Southampton drive north on the A335; from London, take the M3 motorway southwest.

VISITOR INFORMATION   The **Tourist Information Centre,** on Winchester High Street (© **01962/840500;** www.visitwinchester.co.uk), is open from October to April Monday to Saturday 10am to 5pm, and from May to September Monday to Saturday 9:30am to 5:30pm and Sunday 11am to 4pm. Guided walking tours are conducted for £4 ($8) per person, departing from this tourist center. Departure times vary; check with the center once you're there.

WHERE TO STAY

Lainston House ★★★   The beauty of this fine, restored William and Mary redbrick manor house strikes visitors as they approach via a long, curving, tree-lined drive. It's situated on 25 hectares (63 acres) of rolling land and linked with the name Lainston in the Domesday Book. Elegance is keynote inside the stately main house, where panoramically big suites are located. Other rooms, less spacious but also comfortable and harmoniously furnished, are in a nearby 1990 annex. The better units have large dressing areas and walk-in closets. The latest block of beautifully appointed rooms is a series of six converted stables.

Sparsholt, Winchester, Hampshire SO21 2LT. ① **01962/776088.** Fax 01962/776672. www.lainstonhouse.com. 50 units. £225–£325 ($450–$650) double; £425–£625 ($850–$1,250) suite. MC, V. Take B3420 2.5km (1½ miles) north-west of Winchester. Free parking. **Amenities:** Restaurant; bar; lounge; 2 outdoor tennis courts; gym; room service; babysitting; laundry service; dry cleaning. *In room:* TV, hair dryer, safe, Jacuzzi tub (in some).

The Winchester Royal This fine hotel is a comfortable choice. Built at the end of the 16th century as a private house, it was used by Belgian nuns as a convent for 50 years before being turned into a hotel, quickly becoming the center of the city's social life. Only a few minutes' walk from the cathedral, it still enjoys a secluded position. A modern extension overlooks gardens, and all rooms have traditional English styling. Bedrooms in the main house are more traditional than those in the modern wing, but each unit is well appointed.

St. Peter St., Winchester, Hampshire SO23 8BS. ① **800/528-1234** in the U.S., or 01962/840840. Fax 01962/841582. www.thewinchesterroyalhotel.co.uk. 75 units. £149–£169 ($298–$338) double. Rates include English breakfast. AE, DC, MC, V. Free parking. **Amenities:** 2 restaurants; bar; room service; babysitting; laundry service; dry cleaning. *In room:* TV, Wi-Fi, beverage maker, hair dryer, trouser press.

Wykeham Arms ⭐ *(Finds)* Our longtime favorite in Winchester, it lies behind a 200-year-old brick facade in the historic center of town, near the cathedral. Rooms are traditionally furnished with antiques or reproductions and such touches as fresh flowers and baskets of potpourri. Most bedrooms are a bit small but attractively appointed. Six rooms were added in a 16th-century building that faces the original hotel. The annex has the most luxurious accommodations; the rooms are more spacious. The large modern bathrooms are well equipped, each with tub and shower. A large suite with cozy fire-warmed sitting room and upstairs bedroom is also available. Overlooking the Winchester College Chapel, these rooms have the same amenities as the original rooms. *Note:* The hotel does not accept children 13 or younger as guests.

75 Kingsgate St., Winchester, Hampshire SO23 9PE. ① **01962/853834.** Fax 01962/854411. www.accommodating-inns.co.uk/wykeham. 14 units. £115 ($230) double in original building, £130 ($260) double in extension; £150 ($300) suite. Rates include English breakfast. AE, DC, MC, V. Free parking. **Amenities:** Restaurant; bar. *In room:* TV, beverage maker, hair dryer.

WHERE TO DINE

Hotel du Vin & Bistro ⭐ *(Value)* ENGLISH/CONTINENTAL This inn offers both food and lodging, bringing a touch of chic to Winchester. It's a town-house hotel that dates from 1715 and has a walled garden. Gerard Basset and Robin Hutson learned their lessons well at exclusive Chewton Glen (p. 338) before embarking on their own enterprise. The chef, Matt Sussex, delivers some of the finest food in Winchester today. The bistro fare is excellent and a good value. The menu always features regional ingredients: Try the Torbay sole filet served with spinach and potato galette, with a mushroom, white-wine, and cream sauce. Basset has the finest wine list in the county.

You can stay overnight in one of 24 double rooms decorated with a wine theme. The comfortable rooms have good beds, antiques, TVs, and state-of-the-art bathrooms with tub/shower combos, costing from £130 to £190 ($260–$380).

14 Southgate St., Winchester, Hampshire SO23 9EF. ① **01962/841414.** Fax 01962/842458. www.hotelduvin.com. Reservations recommended. Main courses £16–£18 ($32–$36). AE, DC, MC, V. Mon–Fri noon–1:45pm; Sat 12:30–1:45pm; Sun 12:30–2:15pm; Sun–Thurs 7–10pm; Fri–Sat 7–10:30pm.

Old Chesil Rectory ⭐⭐⭐ FRENCH One of the finest restaurants in Hampshire, the 15th-century building, restored over the years, is aglow with half-timbered architecture and whitewashed panels. White candles, white flowers, and white table linen

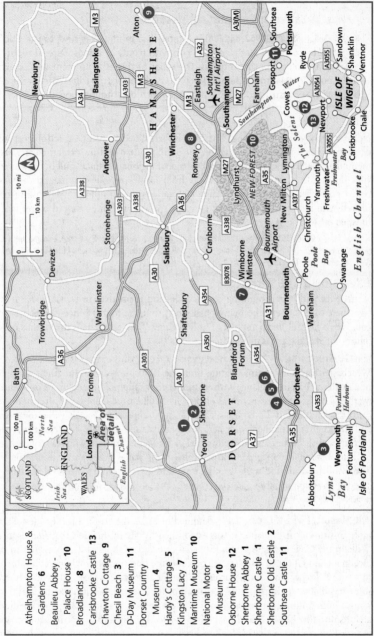

Athelhampton House & Gardens **6**

Beaulieu Abbey - Palace House **10**

Broadlands **8**

Carisbrooke Castle **13**

Chawton Cottage **9**

Chesil Beach **3**

D-Day Museum **11**

Dorset Country Museum **4**

Hardy's Cottage **5**

Kingston Lacy **7**

Maritime Museum **10**

National Motor Museum **10**

Osborne House **12**

Sherborne Abbey **1**

Sherborne Castle **1**

Sherborne Old Castle **2**

Southsea Castle **11**

Finds **A Lager at England's Oldest Bar**

Royal Oak Pub (② **01962/842701**) is located in a passageway next to the God Begot House on High Street. A busy pub with plenty of atmosphere, it reputedly has the oldest bar in England. The cellar of this establishment was originally built in 944 to dispense drink to Winchester's pilgrims; the present building was constructed in 1630 atop the much older foundation.

---

create a lovely mood for dining. The chef, Robert Quehan, turns out refined versions of classic French dishes, made lighter for more modern and discerning palates. The menu is adjusted seasonally to take advantage of regional produce. Full of brawny flavors and heady perfumes, starters range from lobster ravioli with mango to twice-baked goat cheese soufflé. Main dish temptations include filet of Hampshire beef topped with a spicy foie gras, or line-caught sea bass with mussels and oyster sauce, finished off with a fig crème brûlée.

1 Chesil St. ② **01962/851555**. www.chesilrectory.co.uk. Reservations required. Fixed-price 2-course lunch £19 ($38), 3 courses £23 ($46); fixed-price 3-course dinner £49 ($98); 6-course tasting menu £65 ($130). DC, MC, V. Wed–Sat noon–3pm; Tues–Sat 7–10pm.

EXPLORING THE AREA

Winchester and its surrounding countryside lend themselves to walks. Space is too tight here to document the many possibilities, but the tourist office (see above) has compiled a helpful free pamphlet, *The Winchester Walk,* that details the various possibilities for walking tours of their town.

Castle Great Hall 𝕜 This is the only part that remains of the castle first erected in Winchester by the Normans. Dating from the 1200s, it is one of the finest examples of a medieval hall in England, with its timber roof supported on columns of Purbeck marble. The first fortress here was erected by William the Conqueror after he'd subdued England. Henry III rebuilt a castle on its foundation. Once it was a royal seat, and the English Parliament met here for the first time in 1246. The castle played a part in English history, including the trial of Sir Walter Raleigh, who was condemned to death here in 1603 for conspiring against King James I. See an exhibition on the history of the castle and walk through tranquil Queen Eleanor's Medieval Garden.

Castle Hill. ② **01962/846476**. www.hants.gov.uk/greathall. Free admission. Mid-Feb to Oct daily 10am–5pm; Nov to mid-Feb daily 10am–4pm.

The Hospital of St. Cross 𝕜𝕜 Founded in 1132, the hospital is the oldest charitable institution in England. It was established by Henri du Blois, the grandson of William the Conqueror, as a link for social care and to supply life's necessities to the local poor and famished travelers. It continues the tradition of providing refreshments to visitors. Simply stop at the Porter's Lodge for a Wayfarer's Dole, and you'll receive some bread and ale. In the inner courtyard of the hospital, you can see the Brethren's houses from 1450, the refectory, and a church, which is a fine example of medieval architecture (ca. 1250). Inside the church is a lectern from 1510. In the south chapel is a triptych created in the 1530s. The English lyric poet, John Keats, has associations with this hospital. He spent 3 months here in 1818 attending his brother, Tom, who was seriously ill with tuberculosis. After your visit to this complex, you can head east

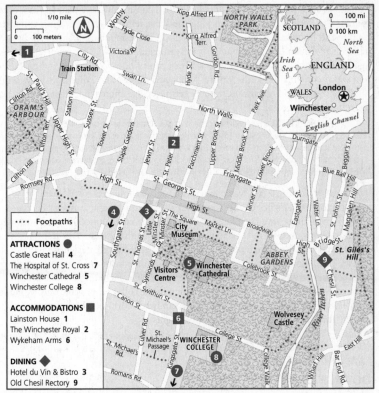

ATTRACTIONS ●
Castle Great Hall **4**
The Hospital of St. Cross **7**
Winchester Cathedral **5**
Winchester College **8**

ACCOMMODATIONS ■
Lainston House **1**
The Winchester Royal **2**
Wykeham Arms **6**

DINING ◆
Hotel du Vin & Bistro **3**
Old Chesil Rectory **9**

to St. Catherine's Hill, rising 78m (255 ft.). Once here, you can enjoy a vista of the town and country and see the ruins of an Iron Age fort and a medieval chapel. On a clear day you can see the hamlet of Chilcomb to the northeast, with its small early Norman church.

Cross Rd. ☏ **01962/851375**. www.cityofwinchester.co.uk/history/html/st_cross.html. Admission £2.50 ($5) adults, £2 ($4) students and seniors, 50p ($1) children. Apr–Oct daily 9:30am–5pm; off season daily 10:30am–3:30pm.

Winchester Cathedral ★★★   This is one of the great churches of England. The present building, the longest medieval cathedral in Britain, dates from 1079, and its Norman heritage is still in evidence. When a Saxon church stood on this spot, St. Swithun, bishop of Winchester and tutor to young King Alfred, suggested modestly that he be buried outside. Following his subsequent indoor burial, it rained for 40 days. The legend lives on: Just ask a resident of Winchester what will happen if it rains on St. Swithun's Day, July 15, and you'll get a prediction of rain for 40 days.

The Perpendicular nave, with its two aisles, is the architectural highlight of the building. The elaborately carved choir stalls from 1308 are England's oldest. The cathedral is graced with a series of beautiful ornamental screens dating from the late 15th century. Other architectural highlights include the Lady Chapel rebuilt by Elizabeth of York at the dawn of the 16th century after her son was baptized in the cathedral. Jane

Austen is buried here; her grave is marked with a commemorative plaque. Also, chests contain the bones of many Saxon kings and the remains of the Viking conqueror Canute and his wife, Emma. The son of William the Conqueror, William Rufus (who reigned as William II), is also buried at the cathedral.

The library houses Bishop Morley's 17th-century book collection, and an exhibition room contains the 12th-century Winchester Bible. The Triforium shows sculpture, woodwork, and metalwork from 11 centuries and affords magnificent views over the rest of the cathedral.

The Close. ℭ **01962/857200.** www.winchester-cathedral.org.uk. Admission to the cathedral £5 ($10) adults, £4 ($8) seniors, £3 ($6) students, free for children 15 and younger; admission to library and Triforium Gallery £1 ($2) adults. Free guided tours year-round 10am–3pm hourly. Crypt is often flooded during winter, but part may be seen from a viewing platform. Cathedral Mon–Sat 8:30am–6pm; Sun 8:30am–5:30pm. Library and Triforium Gallery Apr–Oct Mon 1:30–4pm, Tues–Sat 11am–1pm and 1:30–4pm; Nov–Mar Wed and Sat 11am–3:30pm (Jan–Feb Sat only).

Winchester College ⚐   Winchester College was founded by William of Wykeham, bishop of Winchester and chancellor to Richard II, and was first occupied in 1394. Its buildings have been in continuous use for more than 600 years, making it the oldest continuously open school in England. The structures vary from Victorian Tudor Gothic to the more modern trimmings of the New Hall designed in 1961. The Chapel Hall, kitchens, and the Founder's Cloister date from the 14th century. In the 17th century, buildings were added on the south side, including a schoolroom constructed between 1683 and 1687. Exploration of the college is possible only by guided tour, lasting an hour and covering the Chamber Court, the 14th-century Gothic chapel, and the College Hall, among other sights.

73 Kingsgate St. ℭ **01962/621209.** www.winchestercollege.co.uk. Admission £3.50 ($7) adults, £3 ($6) students and seniors. Guided tours Tues and Thurs 10:45am and noon; Mon, Wed, and Fri–Sat 10:45am, noon, 2:15, and 3:30pm; Sun 2:15 and 3:30pm.

OUTSIDE OF WINCHESTER

Chawton Cottage ⚐   You can see where Jane Austen spent the last 7½ years of her life, her most productive period. In the unpretentious but pleasant cottage is the table on which she penned new versions of three of her books and wrote three more, including *Emma.* You can also see the rector's George III mahogany bookcase and a silhouette likeness of the Reverend Austen presenting his son to the Knights. On display are examples of Austen's needlework and jewelry. In this cottage, Jane Austen became ill in 1816 with what would have been diagnosed by the middle of the 19th century as Addison's disease. She died in July 1817.

The grounds feature an attractive garden where you can picnic and an old bake house with Austen's donkey cart. A bookshop stocks new and secondhand books.

Chawton. ℭ **01420/83262.** http://jane-austens-house-museum.org.uk. Admission £5 ($10) adults, £4 ($8) students and seniors, £1 ($2) children 8–18. June–Aug daily 10am–5pm; Sept–Dec and Mar–May daily 10:30am–4:30pm. Closed Dec 25–26 and Jan–Feb. 1.5km (1 mile) southwest of Alton off A31 and B3006, 24km (15 miles) east of Winchester.

SHOPPING Fill up those empty suitcases at **Cadogan,** 30–31 The Square (ℭ **01962/877399;** www.cadoganandcompany.co.uk), with an upscale and stylish selection of British clothing for both men and women. For a unique piece of jewelry by one of today's most acclaimed designers, stroll into **Carol Darby Jewellery,** 23 Little Minster St. (ℭ **01962/867671**). The oldest book dealer in town is **P&G Wells,** 11 College St. (ℭ **01962/852016;** www.bookwells.co.uk), with new releases and secondhand fiction and nonfiction.

WINCHESTER AFTER DARK

The place to go is the **Porthouse,** Upper Brook Street (✆ **01962/869397;** www. porthousenightclub.com), a pub-cum-nightclub, sprawling across three floors. Different nights have different themes, from funk to pop. After 9pm, a cover charge is imposed, ranging from £1 to £5 ($2–$10), depending on the night.

2 Portsmouth ✦ & Southsea

121km (75 miles) SW of London; 31km (19 miles) SE of Southampton

Virginia, New Hampshire, and Ohio may each have a Portsmouth, but the forerunner of them all is the old port and naval base on the Hampshire coast, seat of the British Navy for 500 years. German bombers in World War II leveled the city, hitting about nine-tenths of its buildings. But the seaport was rebuilt admirably and now aggressively promotes its military attractions. It draws visitors interested in the nautical history of England as well as World War II buffs.

Its maritime associations are known around the world. From Sally Port, the most interesting district in the Old Town, countless naval heroes have embarked to fight England's battles, including on June 6, 1944, when Allied troops set sail to invade occupied France.

Southsea, adjoining Portsmouth, is a popular seaside resort with fine sands, lush gardens, bright lights, and a host of vacation attractions. Many historic monuments are along the stretches of open space, where you can walk on the Clarence Esplanade, look out on the Solent Channel, and view the busy shipping activities of Portsmouth Harbour.

ESSENTIALS

GETTING THERE   Trains from London's Waterloo Station stop at Portsmouth and Southsea Station frequently throughout the day. The trip takes 2 hours. Call ✆ **0845/748-4950** or visit **www.nationalrail.co.uk.**

National Express coaches out of London's Victoria Coach Station make the run to Portsmouth and Southsea every 2 hours during the day. The trip takes 2 hours and 45 minutes. Call ✆ **0870/580-8080** or visit **www.nationalexpress.com** for information and schedules.

If you're driving from London's Ring Road, drive south on the A3.

VISITOR INFORMATION   The **Tourist Information Centre,** at the Hard in Portsmouth (✆ **023/9282-6722;** www.visitportsmouth.co.uk), is open September to June daily 9:30am to 5:15pm, and July and August daily 9:30am to 5:45pm.

WHERE TO STAY

Best Western Royal Beach Hotel   The balconied Victorian facade of this hotel, directly east of Southside Common, rises above the boulevard running beside the sea. Restored by its owners, the hotel's interior decor ranges from contemporary to full-curtained traditional, depending on the room. Each of the bedrooms has been renovated with built-in furniture.

South Parade, Southsea, Portsmouth, Hampshire PO4 0RN. ✆ **023/9273-1281.** Fax 023/9281-7572. www.royal beachhotel.co.uk. 126 units. £65–£125 ($130–$250) double; £165–£225 ($330–$450) suite. Rates include English breakfast. Children 5 and younger stay free in parent's room. AE, DC, MC, V. **Amenities:** Restaurant; bar; room service; laundry service; dry cleaning. *In room:* TV, Wi-Fi (in some), beverage maker, hair dryer, trouser press.

Westfield Hall ✿ *Finds* In the resort of Southsea, two early-20th-century homes near the water have been turned into a hotel with a certain charm and character. One of the most inviting and most comfortable of the little family-run hotels in the area, this highly commendable establishment offers a warm welcome and beautifully maintained and comfortably furnished bedrooms. Many accommodations are graced by large bay windows. Guests enjoy the use of three lounges.

65 Festing Rd., Southsea, Portsmouth, Hampshire PO4 0NQ. 📞 **023/9282-6971.** Fax 023/9287-0200. www.whhotel. info. 26 units. £85 ($170) double. AE, DC, MC, V. Free parking. **Amenities:** Restaurant; bar; 3 lounges. *In room:* TV, Wi-Fi, beverage maker, hair dryer, trouser press.

IN NEARBY WICKHAM

The Old House Hotel ✿ *Finds* A handsome early Georgian (1715) structure, the Old House is surrounded by low, medieval timber structures around the square. The hotel has undergone a classic refurbishment, giving it the look of a proud English country house. The paneled rooms on the ground and first floors of the hotel contrast with the beamed bedrooms on the upper floors, once the servants' quarters. All bedrooms have period furniture, many pieces original antiques, and warm, comfortable beds. Four of the units are called "Garden Suites," although they are rooms, not suites. These accommodations are available in an annex, which is more spacious than those in the main building. Although modern, these so-called suites have some period furniture.

The Square, Wickham, Fareham, Hampshire PO17 5JG. 📞 **01329/833049.** Fax 01329/833672. www.oldhouse hotel.co.uk. 12 units. £85–£150 ($170–$300) double. Rates include continental breakfast. AE, MC, V. Free parking. Bus no. 69 from Fareham. Head 14km (9 miles) west from Portsmouth on M27; exit at no. 10. The village is 3km (2 miles) north of the junction of B2177 and A32. **Amenities:** Restaurant; bar; guest lounge. *In room:* TV, Wi-Fi, beverage maker, hair dryer, trouser press.

WHERE TO DINE

Bistro Montparnasse ✿ ENGLISH/FRENCH Serving the best food in the area, this bistro offers a welcoming atmosphere. Fresh produce is delicately prepared in the well-rounded selection of dishes here. The cooking is familiar fare but well executed. Homemade breads and fresh fish, caught locally, are specialties. Especially recommended is the breast of duck and roast leg of duck with orange and honey flavors, as well as roasted loin of lamb seasoned with thyme, and butter-roasted turbot with scallops and lobster dressing.

103 Palmerston Rd., Southsea. 📞 023/9281-6754. www.bistromontparnasse.co.uk. Reservations recommended. Main courses £12–£17 ($24–$34); 2-course fixed-price dinner £27 ($54), 3 courses £32 ($64). AE, MC, V. Tues–Sat 11:45am–2pm and 7–9:30pm. Southsea bus. Follow the signs to the D-Day Museum, and at the museum turn left and go to the next intersection; the restaurant is on the right.

MARITIME ATTRACTIONS IN PORTSMOUTH

You can buy a ticket that admits you to four attractions: HMS *Victory,* the *Mary Rose,* the HMS *Warrior 1860,* and the Royal Naval Museum. It costs £17 ($33) for adults, £14 ($28) for seniors and children ages 5 to 16, and £48 ($96) for a family ticket (up to two adults, three children). Individual attraction ticket costs are £12 ($24) adult, £10 ($20) senior, £8 ($16) children aged 5 to 15, and £32 ($64) family. Check at the Visitor Centre of the Portsmouth Historic Dockyard (📞 **023/9272-8060**), or you can buy them online at **www.historicdockyard.co.uk**.

HMS *Victory* ✿✿✿ Of major interest is Lord Nelson's flagship, a 104-gun, first-rate ship that is the oldest commissioned warship in the world, launched May 7, 1765. It earned its fame on October 21, 1805, in the Battle of Trafalgar, when the English

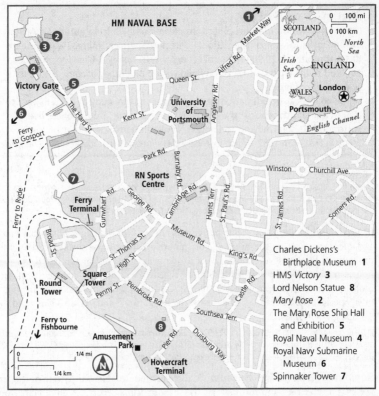

scored a victory over the combined Spanish and French fleets. It was in this battle that Lord Nelson lost his life. The flagship, after being taken to Gibraltar for repairs, returned to Portsmouth with Nelson's body on board (he was later buried at St. Paul's in London).

1–7 College Rd., in Portsmouth Naval Base. ℂ **023/9272-8060.** www.historicdockyard.co.uk. See above for admission prices. Apr–Oct daily 10am–6pm; Nov–Mar daily 10am–5:30pm. Last entry 1½ hr. before closing. Closed Dec 24–26. Use the entrance to the Portsmouth Naval Base through Victory Gate and follow the signs.

The *Mary Rose* Ship Hall and Exhibition ⋆   The *Mary Rose,* flagship of the fleet of King Henry VIII's wooden men-of-war, sank in the Solent Channel in 1545 in full view of the king. In 1982, Prince Charles watched the *Mary Rose* break the water's surface after more than 4 centuries on the ocean floor, not exactly in shipshape condition, but surprisingly well preserved nonetheless. Now the remains are on view, but the hull must be kept permanently wet.

The hull and more than 20,000 items brought up by divers constitute one of England's major archaeological discoveries. On display are the almost-complete equipment of the ship's barber-surgeon, with cabin saws, knives, ointments, and plaster all ready for use; long bows and arrows, some still in shooting order; carpenters' tools; leather jackets; and some fine lace and silk. Close to the Ship Hall is the *Mary Rose* Exhibition, where artifacts recovered from the ship are stored.

Sherlock's on His Way

One of the world's greatest collections of memorabilia from author Sir Arthur Conan Doyle, creator of the fictional detective Sherlock Holmes, was donated to Portsmouth. A 20,000-item collection, worth nearly $4 million, has been donated to the city's Central Library and will go on display at some future date as yet unannounced.

The collection includes a full-size re-creation of the study at 221B Baker St., the fictional address of the detective in London. Doyle once lived in Portsmouth before moving to London. It was in Portsmouth that he wrote *A Study in Scarlet* in 1887, which introduced Holmes and his sidekick, Dr. Watson.

College Rd., Portsmouth Naval Base. ✆ 023/9272-8060. www.historicdockyard.co.uk. See above for admission prices. Apr–Oct daily 10am–6pm; Nov–Mar daily 10am–5:30pm. Last entry 1½ hr. before closing. Closed Dec 24–26. Use the entrance to the Portsmouth Naval Base through Victory Gate and follow the signs.

Royal Naval Museum ☙   The museum is next to Nelson's flagship, HMS *Victory,* and the *Mary Rose,* in the heart of Portsmouth's historic naval dockyard. The only museum in Britain devoted exclusively to the general history of the Royal Navy, it houses relics of Nelson and his associates, together with unique collections of ship models, naval ceramics, figureheads, medals, uniforms, weapons, and other memorabilia. Special displays feature "The Rise of the Royal Navy" and "HMS *Victory* and the Campaign of Trafalgar."

In the dockyard, Portsmouth Naval Base. ✆ 023/9272-7562. www.historicdockyard.co.uk. See above for admission prices. Apr–Oct daily 10am–6pm; Nov–Mar daily 10am–5:30pm. Last entry 1½ hr. before closing. Closed Dec 24–26. Use the entrance to the Portsmouth Naval Base through Victory Gate and follow the signs.

Royal Navy Submarine Museum   Cross Portsmouth Harbour by one of the ferries that bustles back and forth all day to Gosport. Some departures go directly from the station pontoon to HMS *Alliance* for a visit to the submarine museum, which traces the history of underwater warfare and life from the earliest days to the present nuclear age. Within the refurbished historical and nuclear galleries, the principal exhibit is HMS *Alliance,* and after a brief audiovisual presentation, visitors are guided through the boat by ex-submariners.

Haslar Jetty Rd., Gosport. ✆ 023/9252-9217. www.rnsubmus.co.uk. Admission £7 ($14) adults, £5.50 ($11) children and seniors, £17 ($34) family ticket. Apr–Oct daily 10am–5:30pm; Nov–Mar daily 10am–4:30pm. Last tour 1 hr. before closing. Closed Dec 24–25. Bus: 19. Ferry: From the Hard in Portsmouth to Gosport.

Spinnaker Tower ☙☙   Towering over the historic Portsmouth Harbour, this 170m (558-ft.) tower has become one of the biggest attractions of southern England. On a clear day, you can see for 37km (23 miles) in three directions. You can glide to the top in a panoramic lift or else take a high-speed internal lift. The panoramic elevator glides to the top in 90 seconds, the internal elevator in 30 seconds. Sightseers experience the thrill "walking on air," or daring to cross the largest glass floor in Europe. On the top deck, Crow's Nest, visitors are exposed to the elements. In addition to the open-air view, there is a trio of glass-enclosed viewing decks. On-site is the **Tower Café & Bar,** where you can order and enjoy coffee, cakes, and sandwiches while soaking up the view.

Gunwharf Quays. ✆ 023/9285-7520. www.spinnakertower.co.uk. Admission £6.20 ($12) adults, £5 ($10) children 5–15, £5.60 ($11) students and seniors, £21 ($42) family ticket, panoramic lift £2.50 ($5) per person extra. Children 15 and younger must be accompanied by an adult. Sun–Fri 10am–5pm; Sat 10am–10pm.

MORE ATTRACTIONS

Charles Dickens's Birthplace Museum   The 1804 small terrace house, in which the famous novelist was born in 1812 and lived for a short time, has been restored and furnished to illustrate the middle-class taste of the southwestern counties of the early 19th century. It is recommended that you call in advance to see if the museum is indeed open.

393 Old Commercial Rd. (near the center of Portsmouth, off Mile End Rd./M275 and off Kingston Rd.). ✆ 023/9282-7261. www.charlesdickensbirthplace.co.uk. Admission £3.50 ($7) adults, £3 ($6) seniors, £2.50 ($5) children, £9.50 ($19) family ticket, free for children 12 and younger. Daily 10am–5:30pm. Closed Oct–Mar.

D-Day Museum   Next door to Southsea Castle, this museum, devoted to the Normandy landings, displays the Overlord Embroidery, which shows the complete story of Operation Overlord. The appliquéd embroidery, believed to be the largest of its kind (82m/272 ft. long and 1m/3 ft. high), was designed by Sandra Lawrence and took 20 women of the Royal School of Needlework 5 years to complete. A special audiovisual program includes displays such as reconstructions of various stages of the mission. You'll see a Sherman tank in working order, jeeps, field guns, and even a DUKW (popularly called a Duck), an extremely useful amphibious truck that operates on land and sea.

Clarence Esplanade (on the seafront), Southsea. ✆ 023/9282-7261. www.ddaymuseum.co.uk. Admission £6 ($12) adults, £5 ($10) seniors, £4.20 ($8.40) children and students, £17 ($34) family ticket, free for children 4 and younger. Apr–Sept daily 10am–5:30pm; Oct–Mar 10am–5pm. Closed Dec 24–26.

Portchester Castle   On a spit of land on the northern side of Portsmouth Harbour are the remains of this castle, plus a Norman church. Built in the late 12th century by King Henry II, the castle is set inside the **walls** ✪ of a 3rd-century Roman fort built as a defense against Saxon pirates when this was the northwestern frontier of the declining Roman Empire. This is the most complete set of Roman walls remaining in northern Europe. However, the castle itself is long gone. But the central tower remains, and from it you can take in a panoramic view of the harbor and the rocky coast.

On the south side of Portchester off A27 (between Portsmouth and Southampton, near Fareham). ✆ 023/9237-8291. Admission £4 ($8) adults, £3 ($6) seniors, £2 ($4) children 5–15, free for children 4 and younger. Apr–Sept daily 10am–6pm; Oct–Mar daily 10am–4pm.

Southsea Castle   A fortress built of stones from Beaulieu Abbey in 1545 as part of King Henry VIII's coastal defense plan, the castle is now a museum. Exhibits trace the development of Portsmouth as a military stronghold, as well as the naval history and the archaeology of the area. The castle is in the center of Southsea near the D-Day Museum.

Clarence Esplanade, Southsea. ✆ 023/9282-7261. www.southseacastle.co.uk. Admission £3.50 ($7) adults, £3 ($6) seniors, £2.50 ($5) students and children ages 13–18, £9.50 ($19) family ticket, free for children 12 and younger. Daily 10am–5:30pm. Closed Oct–Mar.

SHOPPING

In quay-side Portsmouth, you might turn into a shopaholic. All the big-name outlets are found along **Commercial Road,** especially in the mall called **Cascades Arcade.** It's best to go Thursday, Friday, or Saturday when a historic market takes place here. At least it's worth a browse.

But we prefer to gravitate to the waterside development, **Gunwharf Quays,** with nearly 100 designer outlet shops. Portsmouth is also working to open one of the biggest shopping centers along the southern coast in 2010, with nearly 100 quality outlets.

3 Southampton

140km (87 miles) SW of London; 259km (161 miles) E of Plymouth

For many North Americans, England's number-one passenger port is the gateway to Britain. Southampton is a city of sterile wide boulevards, parks, and dreary shopping centers. During World War II, some 31.5 million men set out from here (in World War I, more than twice that number), and Southampton was repeatedly bombed, destroying its old character. Today, the rather shoddy downtown section represents what happens when a city's architectural focus is timeliness rather than grace, with more to see on the city's outskirts than in the city itself. If you're spending time in Southampton, you may want to explore some of the major sights of Hampshire nearby (New Forest, Winchester, the Isle of Wight, and Bournemouth, in neighboring Dorset).

Its supremacy as a port dates from Saxon times when the Danish conqueror Canute was proclaimed king here in 1017. Southampton was especially important to the Normans and helped them keep in touch with their homeland. Its denizens were responsible for bringing in the bubonic plague, which wiped out a quarter of the English population in the mid–14th century. On the Western Esplanade is a memorial tower to the Pilgrims, who set out on their voyage to the New World from Southampton on August 15, 1620. Both the *Mayflower* and the *Speedwell* sailed from here but were forced by storm damages to put in at Plymouth, where the *Speedwell* was abandoned.

In the spring of 1912, the "unsinkable" White Star liner, the 46,000-ton *Titanic,* sailed from Southampton on its maiden voyage. Shortly before midnight on April 14, while steaming at 22 knots, the great ship collided with an iceberg and sank to the bottom of the icy Atlantic. The sinking of the *Titanic,* subject of the Oscar-winning box office smash of 1997, is one of the greatest disasters in maritime history, as 1,513 people perished.

ESSENTIALS

GETTING THERE   Trains depart from London's Waterloo Station several times daily. The trip takes a little more than an hour. Call © **0845/748-4950** or visit **www.nationalrail.co.uk**.

National Express operates hourly departures from London's Victoria Coach Station. The trip takes 2½ hours. Call © **0870/580-8080,** or visit **www.nationalexpress. com** for information and schedules.

If you're driving, take the M3 southwest from London.

VISITOR INFORMATION   The **Tourist Information Centre,** 9 Civic Centre Rd. (© **023/8033-3333;** www.visit-southampton.co.uk), is open Monday to Saturday 9:30am to 5pm, Sunday and bank holidays 10am to 3:30pm.

WHERE TO STAY

Finding a place to stay right in Southampton isn't as important as it used to be. Very few ships now arrive, and accommodations outside the city are generally better.

Southampton

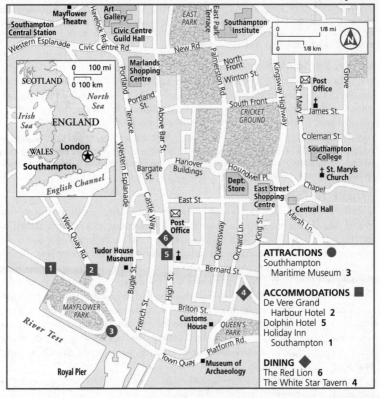

ATTRACTIONS ●
Southhampton
  Maritime Museum **3**

ACCOMMODATIONS ■
De Vere Grand
  Harbour Hotel **2**
Dolphin Hotel **5**
Holiday Inn
  Southampton **1**

DINING ◆
The Red Lion **6**
The White Star Tavern **4**

De Vere Grand Harbour Hotel ✦✦ If you must stay in town and you can afford it, this is the most comfortable place to be. Completed in 1994, the five-story structure, sheathed in granite and possessing a dramatically tilted glass facade, is the most exciting hotel to open in Southampton since World War II. Some 30 of the brightly painted bedrooms have air-conditioning. Most of the bathrooms are filled with luxuries, including tubs, separate walk-in showers, and granite vanities. Bedrooms range from midsize to spacious, with a pair of armchairs and traditional polished wood surfaces, plus snug beds. Some rooms offer balconies; some have waterfront views.

W. Quay Rd., Southampton, Hampshire SO15 1AG. ☎ **023/8063-3033.** Fax 023/8063-3066. www.deveregrand harbour.co.uk. 173 units. £139–£245 ($278–$490) double; £269–£339 ($538–$678) suite. Rates include English breakfast. AE, DC, MC, V. Free parking. **Amenities:** 2 restaurants; 2 bars; indoor pool; gym; spa; Jacuzzi; sauna; steam room; room service; babysitting; laundry service; dry cleaning. *In room:* TV, Wi-Fi, beverage maker, hair dryer, iron, safe.

Dolphin Hotel ✦ If you want tradition, this is your best choice. This bow-windowed Georgian coaching house in the center of the city was Jane Austen's choice, and Thackeray's, too. Even Queen Victoria visited via her horse-drawn carriage. The rooms vary widely in size but are generally spacious and well equipped. You can choose from contemporary rooms, mainly in the 1890s section of the building, or more traditional accommodations found in the 1750s section. Bedrooms are tastefully and comfortably furnished. Three rooms are large enough for families.

35 High St., Southampton, Hampshire SO14 2HN. ℂ **023/8033-9955.** Fax 023/8033-3650. www.thedolphin.co.uk. 65 units. £115–£157 ($230–$314) double; £135–£250 ($270–$500) suite. Children 15 and younger stay free in parent's room. AE, DC, MC, V. Bus: 2, 6, or 8. **Amenities:** Restaurant; 2 bars; room service; laundry service; dry cleaning. *In room:* TV, beverage maker, hair dryer, trouser press.

Holiday Inn Southampton This 10-floor high-rise across from Mayflower Park was built near the new docks to overlook the harbor and is only 5 minutes away from the city center. Rooms are standard but generally spacious, with built-in furniture and picture-window walls, and have recently been refurbished and upgraded to ensure a pleasant stay. It's not big on extras, but what you get is adequate for the price.

Herbert Walker Ave., Southampton, Hampshire SO15 1HJ. ℂ **0870/400-9073.** Fax 023/8033-2510. www.holiday-inn.com. 132 units. £110–£145 ($220–$290) double. AE, DC, MC, V. Free parking. **Amenities:** Restaurant; bar; indoor pool; health club; whirlpool; sauna; room service; laundry service; dry cleaning. *In room:* A/C, TV, high-speed Internet, beverage maker, hair dryer, iron, trouser press.

WHERE TO DINE

The Red Lion ⚐ ENGLISH   One of the few architectural jewels to have survived World War II, this pub traces its roots to the 13th century (as a Norman cellar), but its Henry V Court Room, with high ceilings and rafters, is from Tudor times. The room was the scene of the trial of the earl of Cambridge and his accomplices, Thomas Grey and Lord Scrope, who were condemned to death for plotting against the life of the king in 1415. Today, the Court Room is adorned with coats of arms of the noblemen who were peers of the condemned trio. The Red Lion is a fascinating place for a drink and a chat. Typical pub snacks are served in the bar, whereas in the somewhat more formal restaurant section the well-seasoned specialties include an array of steaks (including sirloin), stews, roasts, and fish platters. Try the rib-eye steak with crushed black peppercorns or the steak-and-kidney pudding, perhaps cod and chips, even a barbecued chicken breast.

55 High St. ℂ **023/8033-3595.** Reservations not needed. Main courses £5.50–£13 ($11–$26); pub snacks £2–£5 ($4–$10). MC, V. Mon–Sat 11am–11pm; Sun noon–10:30pm. Bus: 1, 2, 6, or 8.

The White Star Tavern ENGLISH   This former seafarer's hotel has been stylishly revived and turned into a bar-cum-restaurant where you can dine on "bar bites" or else full-course meals. At this gastro-pub, the cooking is classic English, even such pub classics as wild boar and apple sausage or beer-battered fish. A whole grilled lemon sole appears with anchovy butter. For dessert, try a classic Bakewell tart with cherry ice cream or a selection of local cheese with fruity preserves. If you'd like to stay overnight, you'll find comfortably furnished bedrooms costing from £79 to £149 ($158–$298) in a double.

28 Oxford St. ℂ **023/80821990.** Reservations not needed. Main courses lunch £9.50–£19 ($19–$38), dinner £11–£19 ($22–$38). AE, MC, V. Mon–Thurs noon–2:30pm and 6:30–9:30pm; Fri–Sat noon–3pm and 6–10pm; Sun noon–9pm.

EXPLORING SOUTHAMPTON

Ocean Village and the town quay on Southampton's waterfront are bustling with activity and are filled with pubs, restaurants, and entertainment possibilities.

West Quay Retail Park, the first phase of Southampton's £250-million ($500-million) Esplanade development, has become a major hub for shoppers from the surrounding areas. The central shopping area is pedestrian only, and tree- and shrub-filled planters provide a backdrop for summer flowers and hanging baskets. You can sit and listen to the buskers (street entertainers). For a vast array of shops, try the **Town Quay** (☎ 023/8023-4397) or **Southampton Market** (no phone), but there may be little here to interest the international traveler.

Better shopping on the outskirts is at the **Whitchurch Silk Mill,** 28 Winchester St., Whitchurch (☎ 01256/892065; www.whitchurchsilkmill.org.uk). Admission is £3.50 ($7) for adults, £3 ($6) for students and seniors, £1.75 ($3.50) for children 4 to 16, and £8.75 ($18) for a family ticket. Visitors flock to this working mill, located in colorful surroundings on the River Test. The gift shop sells silk on the roll, ties, scarves, handkerchiefs, jewelry, and souvenirs. Hours are Tuesday to Sunday from 10:30am to 5pm.

Southampton Maritime Museum   This museum is housed in an impressive 14th-century stone warehouse with a magnificent timber ceiling. Its exhibits trace the history of Southampton, including a model of the docks as they looked at their peak in the 1930s. Also displayed are artifacts from some of the great ocean liners whose home port was Southampton.

The most famous of these liners was the fabled *Titanic,* which was partially built in Southampton and sailed from this port on its fateful, fatal voyage. James Cameron's box office smash has increased traffic to the relatively small *Titanic* exhibit at the museum. It features photographs of the crew (many of whom were from Southampton) and passengers, as well as letters from passengers, Capt. Edward Smith's sword, and a video with a dated interview with the fallen captain plus modern interviews with survivors.

The Wool House, Town Quay. ☎ 023/8063-5904. Free admission. Tues–Sat 10am–4pm; Sun 1–4pm.

A SIDE TRIP TO BROADLANDS: HOME OF THE LATE EARL OF MOUNTBATTEN

Broadlands ☆   Broadlands, one of the finest examples of mid-Georgian architecture in England, was the home of the late Earl Mountbatten of Burma, who was assassinated in 1979. Born at Windsor Castle in 1900, Mountbatten was a British admiral and statesman and the last viceroy and first governor-general of an independent India. He lent the house to his nephew, Prince Philip, and Princess Elizabeth as a honeymoon haven in 1947; and in 1981, Prince Charles and Princess Diana spent the first nights of their honeymoon here.

Broadlands is now owned by Lord Romsey, Earl Mountbatten's eldest grandson, who has created a fine exhibition and audiovisual show that depicts the highlights of his grandfather's brilliant career as a sailor and statesman. The house, originally linked to Romsey Abbey, was transformed into an elegant Palladian mansion by Lancelot "Capability" Brown (1715–83), the greatest of all English landscape gardeners.

13km (8 miles) northwest of Southampton in Romsey, on A31. ☎ 01794/505010. www.broadlands.net. Admission £8 ($16) adults, £7 ($14) students and seniors, £4 ($8) children 12–14, free for children 11 and younger. End of June to Sept 1 Mon–Fri 1–5:30pm. Last admission 4pm.

4 The New Forest ★★

153km (95 miles) SW of London; 16km (10 miles) W of Southampton

Encompassing 37,231 hectares (92,000 acres), the New Forest is a large tract created by William the Conqueror, who laid out the limits of this then-private hunting preserve. Successful poachers faced the executioner if they were caught, and those who hunted but missed had their hands severed. Henry VIII loved to hunt deer in the New Forest, but he also saw an opportunity to build up the British naval fleet by supplying oak and other hard timbers to the boatyards at Buckler's Hand on the Beaulieu River.

Today you can visit the old shipyards and the museum at Buckler's Hard (see below), with its fine models of men-of-war, pictures of the old yard, and dioramas showing the building of these ships, their construction, and their launching. Away from the main roads, where signs warn of wild ponies and deer, you'll find a private world of peace and quiet.

ESSENTIALS
GETTING THERE By train, go to Southampton, where you can make rail connections to a few centers in the New Forest. Where the train leaves off, you can make bus connections to all towns and many villages. Southampton and Lymington have the best bus connections to New Forest's villages.

If you're driving, head west from Southampton on the A35.

VISITOR INFORMATION The **New Forest Visitor Centre,** Main Car Park, Lyndhurst (© **023/8028-2269;** www.thenewforest.co.uk), is open daily from 10am to 5pm.

WHERE TO STAY AROUND THE NEW FOREST
VERY EXPENSIVE
Chewton Glen Hotel 𝕶𝕶𝕶 A gracious country house on the fringe of the New Forest, Chewton Glen, within easy reach of Southampton and Bournemouth, is the finest place to stay in southwest England (with princely rates to match). In the old house, a magnificent staircase leads to well-furnished double rooms opening onto views of the spacious grounds. In the new wing, you find yourself on the ground level, with French doors opening onto your own private patio. Accommodations vary widely and come in different shapes, sizes, and periods, but each is equipped with a double or twin bed. Attic accommodations and all newly refurbished rooms contain air conditioners. The best accommodations are the Croquet Lawn Rooms, which open onto the greens and have big private balconies or terraces.

Christchurch Rd., New Milton, Hampshire BH25 6QS. © **800/398-4534** in the U.S., or 01425/275341. Fax 01425/272310. www.chewtonglen.com. 58 units. £299–£517 ($598–$1,034) double; from £485 ($970) suite. AE, DC, MC, V. After leaving the village of Walkford, follow signs off A35 (New Milton–Christchurch Rd.), through parkland. **Amenities:** Restaurant; bar; 3 lounges; 2 pools (1 indoor, 1 outdoor); 9-hole golf course; putting green; 4 tennis courts (2 indoor, 2 outdoor); health club; spa; Jacuzzi; sauna; croquet; billiards; room service; laundry service; dry cleaning. *In room:* A/C in some, TV, Wi-Fi, minibar, hair dryer, trouser press, safe.

EXPENSIVE
Master Builders House Hotel 𝕶𝕶 This hotel is located about 4km (2½ miles) south of Beaulieu, in the historic maritime village of Buckler's Hard. This 17th-century redbrick building was once the home of master shipbuilder Henry Adams, who incorporated many of his shipbuilding techniques into the construction of this lovely old house.

Most of the hotel's comfortable and conservatively decorated accommodations are in a modern wing, built after World War II. If you like the creaky floorboards and charm of old-world England, opt for one of the six old-fashioned bedrooms in the main house. If you want a greater number of luxuries and more space, select a room in the purpose-built annex; these are plainer but better equipped. Bedrooms vary in size and shape.

A Rare Visit to a Rothschild Garden

Unknown to the average visitor to the New Forest, you can explore the private gardens of Edmund and Anne de Rothschild. **Exbury Gardens** 🌟🌟🌟 in the New Forest (℃ **023/8089-1203;** www.exbury.co.uk) is open to the public from mid-March to early November daily 10am to 5:30pm. The highest admission is charged during the summer. Entry ranges from £6.50 to £7.50 ($13–$15) for adults, £6 to £7 ($12–$14) for seniors and students, and costs £1.50 ($3) at all times for ages 3 to 15, with a family ticket costing from £15 to £18 ($30–$36). The 81-hectare (200-acre) garden is celebrated for the Rothschild collection of rhododendrons, azaleas, and camellias, a blooming riot of color in spring. But any season is a delight here, including the flowering displays in summer or the autumnal colors of the maples and deciduous azaleas. Part of the gardens can be toured on a 12 1/4-gauge Steam Railway.

Buckler's Hard, Beaulieu, Hampshire SO42 7XB. ℃ **01590/616253.** Fax 01590/616297. www.themasterbuilders. co.uk. 25 units. £160–£242 ($320–$484) double. Rates include English breakfast. AE, MC, V. **Amenities:** Restaurant; bar; room service; laundry service; dry cleaning. *In room:* TV, beverage maker, hair dryer.

The Montagu Arms 🌟🌟   This hotel has an interesting history; it was built in the 1700s to supply food and drink to the laborers who hauled salt from the nearby marshes to other parts of England. The garden walls were constructed with stones salvaged from Beaulieu Abbey after it was demolished by Henry VIII. The hexagonal column supporting a fountain in the hotel's central courtyard is one of six salvaged, according to legend, from the ruined abbey's nave. Bedrooms are individually decorated in an English-country-house tradition, come in a range of shapes and sizes, and have extras including a trouser press and a writing desk. Many units contain a traditional four-poster bed.

Palace Lane, Beaulieu, New Forest, Hampshire SO42 7ZL. ℃ **01590/612324.** Fax 01590/612188. www.montagu armshotel.co.uk. 22 units. £185–£195 ($370–$390) double; from £215 ($430) suite. Rates include English breakfast. £25 ($50) per extra person in room. AE, DC, MC, V. **Amenities:** 2 restaurants; 2 bars; nearby spa; room service; laundry service; dry cleaning. *In room:* TV, beverage maker, hair dryer, trouser press.

MODERATE

Balmer Lawn Hotel 🌟 *Kids*   This hotel lies about a 10-minute walk from Brockenhurst's center in a woodland location. Built as a private home during the 17th century, it was later enlarged into an imposing hunting lodge. During World War II, it was a military hospital. (In the past decade, many overnight guests have spotted the ghost of one of the white-coated doctors with his stethoscope, roaming the hotel's first floor.) The hotel has a pleasant and humorous staff (who refer to the ghost as "Dr. Eric"). A good range of bedrooms, in all shapes and sizes, all have an individual character. Request a room with a view of the forest. There are three family bedrooms, and children as old as 16 stay free in their parent's room.

Lyndhurst Rd., Brockenhurst, Hampshire SO42 7ZB. ℃ **01590/623116.** Fax 01590/623864. www.balmerlawnhotel. com. 55 units. £135–£235 ($270–$470) double; £270–£305 ($540–$610) family room. Rates include English breakfast. AE, DC, MC, V. Take A337 (Lyndhurst-Lymington Rd.) about 1km (½ mile) outside Brockenhurst. **Amenities:** Restaurant; bar; 2 pools (1 indoor, 1 outdoor); tennis court; 2 squash courts; gym; spa; Jacuzzi; sauna; table tennis; croquet; room service; laundry service; dry cleaning. *In room:* TV, beverage maker, hair dryer, trouser press.

Carey's Manor ★★ *Finds*   This manor house dates from Charles II, who used to come here when it was a hunting lodge. Greatly expanded in 1888, the building became a country hotel in the 1930s. Much improved in recent years, the old house is still filled with character, possessing mellow, timeworn paneling and a carved oak staircase. Most bedrooms, whether in the restored main building or in the garden wing, have balconies. Six rooms contain an old-fashioned four-poster bed, but whether your room does or not, it will still have a firm bed offering cozy comfort. *Note:* Children 9 and younger are not accepted as guests.

Lyndhurst Rd., Brockenhurst, Hampshire SO42 7RH. © **01590/623551.** Fax 01590/622799. www.careysmanor. co.uk. 79 units. £178–£258 ($356–$516) double; from £258 ($516) suite. Rates include English breakfast. AE, DC, MC, V. From the town center, head toward Lyndhurst on A337. **Amenities:** 3 restaurants; bar; indoor pool; gym; spa; Jacuzzi; sauna; solarium; room service; laundry service; dry cleaning. *In room:* TV, Wi-Fi, beverage maker, hair dryer, trouser press.

The Crown Hotel   Though the present building is only 100 years old, a hostelry has been here on the main street of the New Forest village of Lyndhurst for centuries. For generations, it has been a favorite of visitors to the New Forest, who delight in its gardens, where afternoon tea is served, or its roaring fireplace in winter. Bedrooms are most inviting, each furnished in the classic tradition of an English country house, many featuring four-poster beds. Some rooms are more modern, with padded headboards and fine furnishings. A few of the superior rooms can accommodate families.

9 High St., Lyndhurst, Hampshire SO43 7NF. © **023/8028-2922.** Fax 023/8028-2751. www.crownhotel-lyndhurst. co.uk. 38 units. £145–£165 ($290–$330) double; £185 ($370) suite. Rates include English breakfast. Children 15 and younger stay free in parent's room. AE, DC, MC, V. Bus: 56 or 56A. Exit M27 at Junction 1 and drive 5km (3 miles) due south. **Amenities:** Restaurant; bar; room service; babysitting (by arrangement); laundry service; dry cleaning. *In room:* TV, Wi-Fi, beverage maker, hair dryer, iron, trouser press.

Lyndhurst Park Hotel   This large Georgian country house lies on 2 hectares (5 acres) of beautiful gardens. Located at the edge of town where Lyndhurst meets the New Forest, this hotel often attracts conferences. Much of the property remains characteristically rustic, though filled with modern comforts. Bedrooms are medium in size and extremely well kept, often with brass headboards crowning the fine English beds. Bathrooms are tiled and fully carpeted, each with tub and shower.

High St., Lyndhurst, Hampshire SO43 7NL. © **0808/144-9494** or 023/8028-3923. Fax 023/8028-3019. www.lyndhurst parkhotel.co.uk. 59 units. £129–£149 ($258–$298) double. Rates include English breakfast. Children 13 and younger stay free in parent's room. AE, DC, MC, V. Bus: 56. **Amenities:** Restaurant; bar; heated outdoor pool; tennis court; sauna; room service; laundry service. *In room:* TV, Wi-Fi, beverage maker, hair dryer, trouser press.

New Park Manor Hotel ★   This former royal hunting lodge, from the days of William the Conqueror and a favorite of Charles II, is the only hotel in the New Forest itself. Though now a modern country hotel, the original rooms have been preserved, with such features as beams and, in some rooms, open log fires. Since its purchase in 1998 by the Countess von Essen, the hotel has been much improved. Each room has been individually furnished; several rooms and suites have four-poster beds. Most rooms have a view overlooking the forest.

Lyndhurst Rd., Brockenhurst, Hampshire SO42 7QH. © **01590/623467.** Fax 01590/622268. www.newparkmanor hotel.co.uk. 24 units. £175–£315 ($350–$630) double. Rates include breakfast. AE, DC, MC, V. Head 3km (2 miles) north off A337 (Lyndhurst-Brockenhurst Rd.) toward the New Forest Show Ground. **Amenities:** Restaurant; bar; outdoor heated pool; tennis court; spa; horseback riding; croquet lawn; room service; babysitting; laundry service; dry cleaning. *In room:* TV, beverage maker, hair dryer, trouser press.

WHERE TO DINE

Simply Poussin ✦ FRENCH/ENGLISH   Serving the best food in the area, this restaurant is located in what was originally a 19th-century stable and workshop. In summer a conservatory and outdoor dining areas are popular features. To reach it, pass beneath the arched alleyway (located midway between nos. 49 and 55 Brookley Rd.) and enter the stylishly simple premises directed by English-born Chef Alexander Aitken and his wife, Caroline.

Amid a decor accented with framed 19th-century poems and illustrations celebrating poultry, the staff offers fish and game dishes, with ingredients usually fresh from the nearby New Forest. Try "Fruits of the New Forest," individually cooked portions of pigeon, wild rabbit, hare, and venison, encased in puff pastry and served with game sauce. Specialties include whole plaice meunière pan-fried in lemon butter, followed by desserts such as passion-fruit soufflé with sorbet.

The Courtyard, at the rear of 49–55 Brookley Rd., Brockenhurst. ℂ **01590/623063**. www.simplypoussin.co.uk. Reservations recommended 1 month in advance on weekends. Main courses £13–£16 ($26–$32); 2-course set menu £11 ($22), 3 courses £16 ($32). MC, V. Tues–Sat noon–2pm and 7–9:30pm.

SEEING THE SIGHTS

Beaulieu Abbey–Palace House ✦✦   The abbey and house, as well as the National Motor Museum, are on the property of Lord Montagu of Beaulieu (pronounced *Bew*-ley). A Cistercian abbey was founded on this spot in 1204, and you can explore its ruins. The Palace House, surrounded by gardens, was the gatehouse of the abbey before it was converted into a private residence in 1538. Although much was destroyed during the reign of Henry VIII, you can still see an ancient doorway, the cloisters, and the lay brothers' refectory, housing an exhibition depicting monastic life in the abbey through a series of modern embroidered wall hangings. The cloisters are especially inviting and tranquil, planted with fragrant herbs.

National Motor Museum ✦✦, one of the best and most comprehensive automotive museums in the world, with more than 250 vehicles, is on the grounds and is open to the public. Famous autos include four land-speed record holders, among them Donald Campbell's Bluebird. Some of the vehicles used in James Bond movies are on display, as well as those once used by everybody from Eric Clapton to Marlene Dietrich. The collection was built around Lord Montagu's family collection of vintage cars. For further information, contact the visitor reception manager at the John Montagu Building (ℂ **01590/612345**).

Beaulieu, on B3056 in the New Forest (8km/5 miles southeast of Lyndhurst and 23km/14 miles west of Southampton). ℂ **01590/612345**. www.beaulieu.co.uk. Admission £15 ($30) adults, £14 ($28) seniors and students, £9 ($18) children 13–17, £8 ($16) children 5–12, £41 ($82) family ticket (2 adults, 3 children), free for children 4 and younger. May–Sept daily 10am–6pm; Oct–Apr daily 10am–5pm. Closed Dec 25. Buses run from the Lymington bus station Mon–Sat; Sun you'll need a taxi or car.

Maritime Museum ✦   Buckler's Hard, a historic 18th-century village 4km (2½ miles) from Beaulieu on the banks of the River Beaulieu, is where ships for Nelson's fleet were built, including the admiral's favorite, *Agamemnon,* as well as *Eurylus* and *Swiftsure.* The Maritime Museum highlights the village's shipbuilding history as well as Henry Adams, master shipbuilder; Nelson's favorite ship; Buckler's Hard and Trafalgar; and models of Sir Francis Chichester's yachts and items of his equipment. The cottage exhibits re-create 18th-century life in Buckler's Hard—stroll through the New Inn of 1793 and a shipwright's cottage of the same period or look in on the family of a poor laborer.

The walk back to Beaulieu, 4km (2½ miles) on the riverbank, is well marked through the woodlands. During the summer, you can take a 30-minute cruise on the River Beaulieu in the present *Swiftsure,* an all-weather catamaran cruiser.

Buckler's Hard. ⓒ **01590/616203.** Admission to Buckler's Hard and river cruise £7.25 ($15) adults, £6.25 ($13) seniors, £5.75 ($12) children 5–17, £18 ($36) family ticket. Easter–Sept daily 10am–5pm; Oct–Easter daily 10am–4pm.

5 The Isle of Wight ★★

146km (91 miles) SW of London; 6.5km (4 miles) S of Southampton

The Isle of Wight is known for its sandy beaches and its ports, long favored by the yachting set. The island has attracted such literary figures as Alfred Lord Tennyson and Charles Dickens. Tennyson wrote his beloved poem "Crossing the Bar" en route across the Solent from Lymington to Yarmouth. You may want to come just for the day. Some parts are rather tacky, especially Sandown and Shanklin, though other areas out on the island are still tranquil and quite beautiful.

To see Wight at its scenic best, you can walk at least part of a 106km (65-mile) trail called the **Coastal Path** ★★. This footpath links cross-country trails with panoramic views of sea cliffs, the ocean, and the downs. The most scenic part of the trail for those who don't want to walk all of it is the stretch between Shanklin and Ventnor.

The Isle of Wight is compact, measuring 37km (23 miles) from east to west, 21km (13 miles) north to south. **Ryde** is the railhead for the island's transportation system. **Yarmouth** is a busy little harbor providing a mooring for yachts.

Cowes is the premier port for yachting in Britain. Henry VIII ordered the castle built here, but it's now the headquarters of the Royal Yacht Squadron. The seafront and the high cliff road are worth exploring for the scenic views. The port is divided into West Cowes and East Cowes, and separated by the narrow Medina River, which is linked only by a chain ferry called "the floating bridge." Hovercraft are built in the town, which is also the home and birthplace of the well-known maritime photographer Beken of Cowes. In winter, everyone wears oilskins and wellies, leaving a wet trail behind them.

Newport, a bustling market town in the heart of the island, is the capital and has long been a favorite of British royalty. Along the southeast coast are the twin Victorian resorts of **Sandown** and **Shanklin.** Both of these family resorts have a very similar atmosphere, with cafes, shops (rather mediocre), pubs, restaurants, safe bathing, and a mild climate. The pier in Sandown dates from 1879 and provides all-weather amusements such as video games. Shanklin at the southern end of Sandown Bay holds the British annual sunshine record. We suggest you skip Sandown and visit at Shanklin for its old village and a glimpse at **Shanklin Cline,** a fissure in the cliff where you can walk up to see a 12m (40-ft.) waterfall. Farther along the coast, **Ventnor** is called the "Madeira of England" because it rises from the sea in a series of steep hills.

On the west coast are the many-colored sand cliffs of **Alum Bay.** The Needles, three giant chalk rocks, and the Needles Lighthouse are the farther features of interest at this end of the island. If you want to stay at the western end of Wight, consider **Freshwater Bay.**

ESSENTIALS

GETTING THERE   A direct train from London's Waterloo Station to Portsmouth deposits travelers directly at the pier for a ferry crossing to the Isle of Wight; ferries are timed to meet train arrivals. Travel time from London to the arrival point of Ryde on the Isle of Wight (including ferry-crossing time) is 2 hours. One train per hour departs during the day from London to Portsmouth. For rail information, call ℂ **0845/ 748-4950** or visit **www.nationalrail.co.uk**.

Drive to Southampton and take the ferry or leave Southampton and head west along the A35, cutting south on the A337 toward Lymington on the coast, where the ferry crossing to Yarmouth (Isle of Wight) is shorter than the trip from Southampton.

Red Funnel operates a vehicle ferry service from Terminal 1 in Southampton to East Cowes; the trip takes 55 minutes. An inclusive round-trip fare (valid for 5 days) costs £12 ($25) for adults, £9.70 ($19) for seniors, and £6.20 ($12) for children. More popular with train travelers from Waterloo Station in London is a high-speed passenger-only catamaran operating from the Town Quay Terminal 2 in Southampton, going to West Cowes; the trip takes 22 minutes. A round-trip fare costs £18 ($36) for adults, £14 ($28) for seniors, and £9 ($18) for children. For ferry departure times, call ℂ **0844/8449988** or visit **www.redfunnel.co.uk**.

The **Wight Link ferry** (ℂ **0870/5820202**; www.wightlink.co.uk) operates between Portsmouth and Ryde, taking 20 minutes and costing £17 ($34) for adults and £8.50 ($17) for children, round-trip standard return. Daytime departures are every 30 minutes in summer and every 60 minutes in winter.

GETTING AROUND   Visitors can explore the Isle of Wight just for the day on the Island Explorer bus service. Tickets may be purchased on the bus, and you can board or leave the bus at any stop on the island. The price of a Day Rover is £10 ($20) for adults and £5 ($10) for children. It also entitles you to passage on the island's only railway, which runs from the dock at Ryde to the center of Shanklin, a distance of 13km (8 miles). For further information, call **Southern Vectis** at ℂ **0871/2002233** or visit **www.islandbuses.info**.

Our preferred way to get around the island is by bike or moped. Rentals are available at **1st Call**, 15 College Close, Sandown (ℂ **01983/400055**), costing £10 ($20) per day for a bike. Another possibility is **Tav Cycle Sport**, 140 High St. at Ryde (ℂ **01983/812989**), where cycles rent for £12 ($24) for a day. Both outlets are open Monday to Saturday 9am to 5pm.

VISITOR INFORMATION   The **information office** is at 67 High St., Shanklin (ℂ **01983/813818**; www.islandbreaks.co.uk). It's open Monday to Saturday March to October 9:30am to 5pm, Sunday 10am to 4pm, and November to March Tuesday to Saturday 10am to 4:30pm. It's best to call first, as these hours are subject to change.

WHERE TO STAY

Bourne Hall Country House Hotel   Many visitors prefer to base themselves at Shanklin. At Bourne Hall, they receive a warm welcome from the owners, who have one of the area's best-equipped hotels. The hotel stands on nearly 1.2 hectares (3 acres), adjoining open farmland. Bedrooms are furnished in a delightful English-country-house style. Some have been redecorated, and even those that haven't are still in fine shape. Children 15 and younger are not permitted to stay at the hotel.

Luccombe Rd., Shanklin, Isle of Wight PO37 6RR. ℂ **01983/862820.** Fax 01983/865138. www.bournehallhotel. co.uk. 31 units. £120–£170 ($240–$340) bed-and-breakfast; £150–£204 ($300–$408) double including half-board and transfers. AE, DC, MC, V. **Amenities:** Restaurant; bar; 2 pools (1 indoor, 1 outdoor); spa; Jacuzzi; sauna; game room; room service; laundry service. *In room:* TV, CD player, minibar (in some), beverage maker, hair dryer, trouser press (in some).

The George Hotel ★★ The best cuisine and most elegant lodgings are at this former governor's residence dating from the 17th century. Between the quay and the castle, overlooking the Solent, this is a tranquil oasis in this port so beloved by English yachties. The good-size bedrooms are individually decorated, each with style and an eye for comfort. The professionalism of this place is to be applauded. It's leagues ahead of some of the dowdy properties on the island, many of them looking like leftovers from Victoria's era. Even if you aren't a guest, call for a reservation in one of the George's two dining options (see "Where to Dine," below).

Quay St., Yarmouth, Isle of Wright PO41 0PE. © **01983/760331.** Fax 01983/760425. www.thegeorge.co.uk. 17 units. £180–£255 ($360–$510) double. 2-night minimum stay Sat–Sun. Rates include English breakfast. AE, MC, V. Parking £6 ($12). **Amenities:** 2 restaurants; bar; room service; beauty treatments; laundry service. *In room:* A/C, TV, hair dryer.

Hotel Ryde Castle *(Kids)* This historic seafront castle looking onto the Solent makes a fine base for exploring the island. The castle, dating from the 16th century, has been added to over the centuries. Field Marshall Montgomery stayed here before D-day landings. With its crenelated, ivy-clad exterior and its well-kept public rooms, the hotel attracts families as well as single visitors. Bedrooms, small to medium in size, have an inviting aura with traditional British styling. Comfort is the keynote here, and some accommodations have a more romantic aura and a four-poster bed. Most rooms offer sea views. Kids can hang around at the children's play area or look for the friendly ghost rumored to be a hotel resident.

The Esplanade, Ryde, Isle of Wight PO33 1JA. © **01983/563755.** Fax 01983/566906. www.rydecastle.com. 18 units. £105–£130 ($210–$260) double. Rates include English breakfast. AE, DC, MC, V. **Amenities:** Restaurant; bar; room service. *In room:* TV, beverage maker.

St. Catherine's Hotel This hotel lies a few minutes' walk from Sandown's sandy beach, leisure center, and pier complex, with its sun lounges, theater, and Sandown railway station. St. Catherine's was built in 1860 of creamy Purbeck stone and white trim for the dean of Winchester College. A modern extension was added for streamlined and sunny bedrooms, which have duvets, white furniture, and built-in headboards. The brightly redecorated lounge has matching draperies at the wide bay windows, along with card tables and a small library of books.

1 Winchester Park Rd., Sandown, Isle of Wight PO36 8HJ. ©/fax **01983/402392.** www.smoothhound.co.uk/hotels/stcather.html. 19 units. £60 ($120) double. Rates include English breakfast. MC, V. **Amenities:** Restaurant; bar; room service; babysitting. *In room:* TV, beverage maker.

Wight Mouse Inn ★ *(Kids)* The Wight Mouse is a cheerful place to stay. This old coaching inn lies on the most southerly part of the island, where the vegetation is almost tropical. From here, you can see over the Channel to the mainland coast. Though a bit small, each bedroom is prettily decorated in an English-country-house style. Children are warmly welcomed and can burn off energy in MouseWorld, an indoor play area, or at the outdoor playground.

Newport Rd. (B3399; 45m/150 ft. off Military Rd.), Chale, Isle of Wight PO38 2HA. © **01983/730431.** Fax 01983/730043. www.innforanight.co.uk. 8 units. £40–£75 ($80–$150) double. MC, V. **Amenities:** Restaurant; bar. *In room:* TV, beverage maker, hair dryer.

WHERE TO DINE

The Brasserie ★★ CONTINENTAL/FRENCH The most refined cuisine on the island is at the George Hotel (see above). One kitchen services the formal restaurant and the relaxed brasserie. The restaurant is imbued with a rich aura of candlelight and painted panels, and the best view of the Solent is from the sunny brasserie. The restaurant is known for its quality ingredients, deftly handled and beautifully presented in showcase fixed-price dinners. Try such delightful main courses as the free-range duck with endive and a jasmine-tea sauce, or else sea bass with broad beans, sweet potatoes, and gnocchi. Some of the most succulent desserts include passion fruit with banana sorbet or sticky toffee pudding with caramelized pear and tonka-bean ice cream.

In the George Hotel, Quay St., Yarmouth. ⓒ **01983/760331.** Main courses £14–£18 ($28–$36); fixed-price dinner £36–£40 ($72–$80). AE, MC, V. Daily noon–3pm and 7–10pm.

The Hambrough Restaurant ⚐ ENGLISH/CONTINENTAL In this stylish boutique hotel, the restaurant serves a savory cuisine on the southern fringe of the island, opening onto panoramic vistas of the bay at Ventnor. Trained at some of the best restaurants in England, head chef Craig Atchinson is the island's finest, and has become known for his clever use of the great bounty of the English countryside. His salad of baby artichokes, asparagus, truffle shavings, and truffle dressing arguably is the best on island. You might also start with his pressed duck confit with foie gras and poached cherries. You'll also savor such mains as sautéed sea trout, poached and roasted chicken with wild mushrooms, or else tenderloin of pork with an onion-and-sage risotto. A dessert specialty in summer is raspberry soup.

You can also stay overnight here at a charge ranging from £152 to £210 ($304–$420) for two people, rates including dinner, bed, and breakfast.

In the Hambrough Hotel, Hambrough Rd., Ventnor. ⓒ **01983/856333.** Reservations required. 2-course set lunch £15 ($30), 3 courses £18 ($36); 2-course set dinner £30 ($60), 3 courses £39 ($78). DC, MC, V. Wed–Sun noon–2:30pm; Mon and Wed–Sat 7–9:30pm.

EXPLORING THE ISLE OF WIGHT

Carisbrooke Castle ⚐⚐ This fine medieval castle lies in the center of the Isle of Wight. In 1647, during one of the most turbulent periods of English history, Charles I was imprisoned here, far from his former seat of power in London, by Cromwell's Roundheads. On the castle premises is the 16th-century Well House, where, during periods of siege, donkeys took turns treading a large wooden wheel connected to a rope that hauled up buckets of water from a well. Accessible from the castle's courtyard is a museum (ⓒ **01983/523112**) with exhibits pertaining to the social history of the Isle of Wight and the history of Charles I's imprisonment.

Carisbrooke, 2km (1¼ miles) southwest of Newport. ⓒ **01983/523112.** www.carisbrookecastlemuseum.org.uk. Castle and museum £5.60 ($11) adults, £4.20 ($8.40) seniors and students, £2.80 ($5.60) children. Apr–Sept daily 10am–5pm; Oct–Mar daily 10am–4pm. Bus: 91A.

Osborne House ⚐⚐ Queen Victoria's most cherished residence was built at her own expense. Prince Albert, with his characteristic thoroughness, contributed to many aspects of the design of the Italian-inspired mansion, which stands amid lush gardens, right outside the village of Whippingham. The rooms remain as Victoria knew them, down to the French piano she used to play and all the cozy clutter of her sitting room. Grief-stricken at the death of Albert in 1861, she asked that Osborne House be kept as it was, and so it has been. Even the turquoise scent bottles he gave her, decorated with cupids and cherubs, are still in place. In her bedroom at Osborne House, the queen died on January 22, 1901. Within the Italianate gardens, you can visit a museum of royal mementos, a summerhouse, and a Swiss Cottage where the royal children were taught.

1.5km (1 mile) southeast of E. Cowes. ⓒ 01983/200022. House and grounds £9.80 ($20) adults, £7.40 ($15) seniors, £4.90 ($9.80) children 5–15. Apr–Sept daily 10am–5pm; Oct daily 10am–4pm; Nov–Mar Wed–Sun 10am–2:30pm (guided tours only). Closed Dec 25–26 and Jan 1. Bus: 4 or 5.

6 Bournemouth ⓐ

167km (104 miles) SW of London; 24km (15 miles) W of the Isle of Wight

This south coast resort at the doorstep of the New Forest didn't just happen: It was carefully planned and executed—a true city in a garden. Flower-filled, park-dotted Bournemouth is filled with an abundance of architecture inherited from those arbiters of taste, Victoria and her son, Edward. (The resort was discovered back in Victoria's day, when sea bathing became an institution.) Bournemouth's most distinguished feature is its chines (narrow, shrub-filled, steep-sided ravines) along the coastline. For the best view of them, walk along the waterfront promenade appropriately called the **Undercliff** ⓐⓐ.

Bournemouth, along with neighboring Poole and Christchurch, forms the largest urban area in the south of England. It makes a good base for exploring a historically rich part of England; on its outskirts are the New Forest, Salisbury, Winchester, and the Isle of Wight.

ESSENTIALS

GETTING THERE   An express train from London's Victoria Station to Bournemouth takes 2 hours, with frequent service throughout the day. For schedules and information, call ⓒ **0845/748-4950** or visit **www.nationalrail.co.uk**. Arrivals are at the Bournemouth Rail Station, on Holden Surst Road.

Buses leave London's Waterloo Station every 2 hours during the day, heading for Bournemouth. The trip takes 2½ hours. Call ⓒ **0870/580-8080,** or visit **www.nationalexpress.com** for information and schedules.

If you're driving, take the M3 southwest from London to Winchester, then the A31 and the A338 south to Bournemouth.

VISITOR INFORMATION   The **information office** is at Westover Road (ⓒ **08450/511701;** www.bournemouth.co.uk). From September to May, it's open Monday to Saturday from 9:30am to 5:30pm, and from June to August on Sunday from 10am to 5:30pm.

WHERE TO STAY
VERY EXPENSIVE
Bournemouth Highcliff Marriott ⓐⓐ   This 1888 cliff-side hotel is one of the best in Bournemouth, rivaled only by Menzie's Carlton, Langtry Manor, and Royal Bath. The high-ceilinged interior has been tastefully renovated. A funicular elevator takes guests from the hotel to the seaside promenade. Many bedrooms have beautiful views of the sea. Each is traditionally furnished in elegant English style and is located in the main building or in Coast Guard cottages built in 1912. Rooms are generally spacious.

105 St. Michael's Rd., West Cliff, Bournemouth, Dorset BH2 5DU. ⓒ **800/228-9290** in the U.S., or 0102/557702. Fax 01202/293155 www.marriotthotels.com/bohbm. 160 units. £150–£240 ($300–$480) double; from £215 ($430) suite. AE, DC, MC, V. Parking £10 ($20). **Amenities:** Sea Breezes restaurant (p. 349); 2 bars; 2 pools (1 indoor, 1 outdoor); tennis court; gym; whirlpool; sauna; solarium; room service; babysitting; laundry service; dry cleaning. *In room:* A/C, TV, minibar, beverage maker, hair dryer, iron, trouser press.

Langtry Manor Hotel ✦ *Finds*   A much more atmospheric choice and run with a more personal touch than Menzies Carlton and Norfolk Royale, the Red House, as this hotel was originally called, was built in 1877 for Lillie Langtry, a gift from Edward VII to his favorite mistress. The house has all sorts of reminders of its illustrious inhabitants, including initials scratched on a windowpane. The bedrooms, each a double, range from ordinary twins to the Lillie Langtry Suite, Lillie's own room, with a four-poster bed and a double heart-shaped bathtub; or you can rent the Edward VII Suite, furnished as it was when His Royal Highness lived in this spacious room.

26 Derby Rd. (north of Christchurch Rd., A35), East Cliff, Bournemouth, Dorset BH1 3QB. ⓒ **01202/553887.** Fax 01202/290115. www.langtrymanor.co.uk. 27 units. £158–£178 ($316–$356) double; from £198 ($396) suite for 2. Rates include English breakfast. 2-night minimum stay Fri–Sat. AE, MC, V. Free parking. **Amenities:** Restaurant; bar; room service; dry cleaning. *In room:* TV, Wi-Fi, minibar, hair dryer.

Menzies Carlton Hotel ✦   More resort than ordinary hotel, the Carlton sits atop a seaside cliff lined with private homes and other hotels. This Edwardian pile, with panoramic views, is one of the best places to stay in Bournemouth. It exudes a 1920s aura, with rather opulent public rooms. Extensively renovated, most bedrooms are spacious and open onto views of the sea. Many of the rooms have marbled wallpaper, mottled mirrors, and armchairs. On the downside, readers have complained that in some rooms the double-glazing on the windows does little to cut down on the noise.

Meyrick Rd., East Overcliff, Bournemouth, Dorset BH1 3DN. ⓒ **01202/552011.** Fax 01202/299573. www.book menzies.com. 76 units. £130–£215 ($260–$430) double; from £260 ($520) suite. AE, DC, MC, V. Free parking. **Amenities:** Restaurant; bar; 2 heated pools (1 outdoor, 1 indoor); health club; spa; Jacuzzi; sauna; solarium; business services; salon; room service; laundry service; dry cleaning. *In room:* TV, Wi-Fi, beverage maker, hair dryer, trouser press.

The Norfolk Royale ✦✦   One of the oldest and most prestigious hotels in town, a few blocks from the seafront and central shopping area, it recently underwent a major £5-million ($10-million) renovation program, restoring it to its former Edwardian elegance, with a two-tier, cast-iron veranda. Nevertheless, we think it still plays second fiddle to both the Carlton and the Royal Bath. It exudes the atmosphere of a country estate, with formal entrance, rear garden, and fountain shaded by trees. Rooms and suites have been luxuriously appointed with the styles of the period blending with modern comforts.

Richmond Hill, Bournemouth, Dorset BH2 6EN. ⓒ **01202/551521.** Fax 01202/229729. www.norfolk-royale.co.uk. 95 units. £128–£180 ($256–$360) double; £180–£225 ($360–$450) suite. Rates include breakfast. AE, DC, MC, V. Parking £12 ($24). **Amenities:** Restaurant; bar; indoor pool; Jacuzzi; sauna; room service; babysitting; laundry service. *In room:* TV, high-speed Internet, minibar, beverage maker, hair dryer, trouser press, safe.

The Priory Hotel   This hotel lies 3km (2 miles) west of Bournemouth in Wareham, beside the River Frame and near the village church. It has a well-tended garden adorned by old trees. Inside, a paneled bar and a lounge filled with antiques open onto views of the lawn. Rooms are individually decorated (often with fine antiques) and offer much comfort, including such items as mineral water, fruit, and bathrobes; some feature four-poster beds. Some accommodations are in a well-crafted annex. The main building houses the standard and superior doubles, and suites are in the boathouse in the gardens by the river. Boathouse rooms also come with whirlpool tubs. *Note:* Children 13 and younger are not permitted as guests.

Church Green, Wareham, Dorset BH20 4ND. ⓒ **01929/551666.** Fax 01929/554519. www.theprioryhotel.co.uk. 18 units. £215–£290 ($430–$580) double; £315–£345 ($630–$690) suite. Rates include English breakfast. DC, MC, V. Free parking. **Amenities:** 2 restaurants; bar; room service; laundry service; dry cleaning. *In room:* TV, minibar (in some), hair dryer.

Royal Bath Hotel ★★★ This early Victorian version of a French château, with towers and bay windows looking out over the bay and Purbeck Hill, dates from June 28, 1838, the very day of Victoria's coronation. After the adolescent Prince of Wales (later Edward VII) stayed here, the hotel added "Royal" to its name. Over the years, it has attracted notables from Oscar Wilde to Rudolf Nureyev to the great Prime Minister Disraeli. In luxury and style, it is in a neck-and-neck race with the Carlton. It's located in a 1.2-hectare (3-acre) garden where cliff-top panoramas open onto the sea. The mostly spacious bedrooms are furnished with a certain English style and grace, and the larger rooms have sitting areas. Most bedrooms have been refurbished.

Bath Rd., Bournemouth, Dorset BH1 2EW. ✆ 01202/555555. Fax 01202/554158. www.devereroyalbath.co.uk. 140 units. £150–£240 ($300–$480) double; from £265 ($530) suite. Rates include English breakfast. AE, DC, MC, V. Free parking. **Amenities:** 2 restaurants (including Oscars; see review below); bar; indoor heated pool; gym; spa; Jacuzzi; sauna; salon; room service; laundry service; dry cleaning. *In room:* TV, high-speed Internet, minibar, beverage maker, hair dryer, trouser press.

INEXPENSIVE

Mayfield Private Hotel In a residential neighborhood about a 15-minute walk east of Bournemouth's center, this hotel dates from around 1900, when it was built as a private home. A brick house painted white with a garden, it's the domain of the Barling family, whose midsize rooms are attractive and uncomplicated. Guests can request an evening meal.

46 Frances Rd., Bournemouth, Dorset BH1 3SA. ✆/fax 01202/551839. www.mayfieldhotel.com. 8 units. £52–£56 ($104–$112) double. Rates include English breakfast. No credit cards. Closed Dec. Free parking. **Amenities:** Dining room; lounge. *In room:* TV, fridge, beverage maker, hair dryer, trouser press.

The New Westcliff Hotel (Value) This hotel is a 5-minute walk from the town center, near Durley Chine, and was once the luxurious south-coast home of the duke of Westminster, who had it built in 1876. Now run by the Blissert family, the hotel draws lots of repeat business. All rooms are comfortably furnished and well maintained; some have four-posters. As befits a former private home, bedrooms come in various shapes and sizes. There's a large garden and a parking area.

27 Chine Crescent, West Cliff, Bournemouth, Dorset BH2 5LB. ✆ 01202/551062. Fax 01202/315377. www.newwestcliffhotel.co.uk. 53 units. £44–£60 ($88–$120) per person double. Rates include breakfast and dinner. MC, V. Free parking. **Amenities:** Restaurant; 2 bars; indoor heated pool; Jacuzzi; sauna; solarium; game room; theater area w/screening room. *In room:* TV, beverage maker, hair dryer, iron, trouser press.

Wood Lodge Hotel (Value) Lying a short walk from the ocean, this hotel dates from the early 20th century but has been beautifully restored and modernized to receive guests. Many of its original features remain, including stained-glass windows and an old-fashioned staircase. A Victorian presence still permeates, and there are four ground-floor rooms for those who don't like stairs. Many of the accommodations open onto views of the award-winning garden. Breakfasts are a special feature here (ever had kippers with a poached egg?).

10 Manor Rd., East Cliff, Bournemouth, Dorset BH1 3EY. ✆ 01202/290891. Fax 01202/290892. www.woodlodge hotel.co.uk. 15 units. £64–£86 ($128–$172) double. MC, V. **Amenities:** Restaurant; bar. *In room:* TV, Wi-Fi, hair dryer.

WHERE TO DINE

Coriander (Value) MEXICAN This restaurant, located in a pedestrian-only zone, brings south-of-the-Yankee-border flair to staid Bournemouth. All menu items are prepared with fresh ingredients. Homemade soups are a feature here, based on seasonal ingredients, or else you can opt for starters such as tortilla chips and salsa or crispy marinated chicken wings. Even better are the skewered tiger prawns with a sweet-chili salsa. The town's best quesadillas and burritos are served here. House specialties include a Cajun-style gumbo with chorizo and peppers and a Mexican chicken casserole called Coriander Vesuvius.

22 Richmond Hill. © 01202/552202. Reservations required Sat–Sun. Main courses £8–£13 ($16–$26); 2-course fixed-price lunch menu £8.75 ($18), 3 courses £12 ($24). AE, MC, V. Daily noon–10pm.

Oscars ⑤ FRENCH   Sporting Oscar Wilde mementos, Bournemouth's best restaurant is located cliff-side, with panoramic sea views. The chef presents market-fresh ingredients deftly handled by a skilled staff. The excellent appetizers may include a terrine of salmon scallops and king prawns with a saffron and basil jelly. The imaginative main courses may include roasted Dorset lamb with sweet dumplings, or else pan-fried loin of monkfish with crab and flavored with tarragon butter.

In the Royal Bath Hotel, Bath Rd. © 01202/555555. Reservations required. Main courses £13–£23 ($26–$46). AE, DC, MC, V. Daily noon–2pm and 7:30–10pm.

Sea Breezes ENGLISH/FRENCH   This is a smart brasserie-style restaurant and bar that offers some of the best Anglo-French cookery at the resort. With a traditional decor, it is warm and inviting. Its chefs don't muck up the ingredients with a lot of fancy sauces. Food is relatively straightforward, but the preparation is right on target. You might begin with such starters as a duck terrine flavored with coriander and served with a lime salsa, or a bowl of seafood chowder. The chefs also prepare excellent main dishes such as pan-fried sea-bass filet with sautéed mushrooms and chorizo sausage. It's family-friendly, and service is gracious. You can also dine inexpensively at the bar.

In the Bournemouth Highcliff Hotel, 105 St. Michael's Rd., W. Cliff. © 01202/557702. Reservations recommended. Main courses £12–£20 ($24–$40). AE, MC, V. Daily noon–2pm and 6–10pm.

EXPLORING THE AREA

The resort's amusements are varied, and this is a much more upmarket and tasteful resort than jazzy Brighton. It's a bit staid during the day but at night swarms of young people flock to its bars and clubs where brassy, loud sounds pierce the night. At the **Pavilion Theatre,** you can see West End–type productions from London. The **Bournemouth Symphony Orchestra** is justly famous in Europe. And there's the usual run of golf courses, band concerts, variety shows, and dancing.

And, of course, this seaside resort has a spectacular beach—11km (7 miles) of uninterrupted sand stretching from Hengistbury Head to Alum Chine. Most of it is known simply as **Bournemouth Beach,** although its western edge, when it crosses over into the municipality of Poole, is called **Sandbanks Beach.** Beach access is free, and a pair of blue flags will indicate where the water's fine for swimming. The flags also signify the highest standards of cleanliness, management, and facilities. A health-conscious, nonsmoking zone now exists at Durley Chine, East Beach, and Fisherman's Walk. Fourteen full-time lifeguards patrol the shore and the water; they are assisted by volunteers during the busiest summer months. The promenade is traffic-free during the summer. There are two piers, one at Boscombe and the other at Bournemouth.

Amenities at the beach include beach bungalows, freshwater showers, seafront bistros and cafes, boat trips, rowboats, canoes, jet skis, and windsurfers. Cruises run in the summer from Bournemouth Pier to the Isle of Wight.

The traffic-free town center, with its wide avenues, is elegant but by no means stuffy. Entertainers perform on the corners of streets that are lined with boutiques,

---

Finds Exploring Nearby Wareham

This historic town on the Frome River, 3km (2 miles) west of Bournemouth, is an excellent center for touring the South Dorset coast and the Purbeck Hills. See the remains of early Anglo-Saxon and Roman town walls, plus the Saxon church of St. Martin, with its effigy of T. E. Lawrence (Lawrence of Arabia), who died in a motorcycle crash in 1935. His former home, **Clouds Hill** (*©* **01929/ 405616**), lies 11km (7 miles) west of Wareham (1.5km/1 mile north of Bovington Camp) and is extremely small. It's open only from mid-March to October Thursday to Sunday from noon to 5pm. Admission is £4 ($8), free for children 4 and younger.

---

cafes, street furniture, and plenty of meeting places. Specialized shopping is found mainly in the suburbs—Pokesdown for antiques and collectibles, Westbourne for individual designer fashion and home accessories. Victorian shopping arcades can be found in both Westbourne and Boscombe.

The best golf course is **Bournemouth & Meyrick Park Golf Club,** at Meyrick Park (*©* **01202/786000**), one of the South Coast's most beautiful courses. It's laid out across challenging terrain. Greens fees range from £20 to £23 ($40–$46).

BOURNEMOUTH AFTER DARK

A choice of major venues offers great performances year-round. **International Centre's Windsor Hall** hosts leading performers from London, the **Pavilion** puts on West End musicals as well as dancing with live music, and the **Winter Gardens,** the original home and favorite performance space of the world-famous Bournemouth Symphony Orchestra, offers regular concerts. Program and ticket information for all three venues is available by calling *©* **0870/111-3000.**

EN ROUTE TO DORCHESTER: A 17TH-CENTURY MANSION

Kingston Lacy An imposing 17th-century mansion set on 101 hectares (250 acres) of wooded park, Kingston Lacy was the home of the Bankes family for more than 300 years. They entertained such distinguished guests as King Edward VII, Kaiser Wilhelm, Thomas Hardy, and George V. If you have an hour—better yet, 2 hours—the time could be spent exploring this attraction and its grounds. The house displays a magnificent collection of artwork by Rubens, Titian, and Van Dyck, as well as an important collection of Egyptian artifacts.

The present structure replaced Corfe Castle, the Bankes family home that was destroyed in the civil war. During her husband's absence while performing duties as chief justice to King Charles I, Lady Bankes led the defense of the castle, withstanding two sieges before being forced to surrender to Cromwell's forces in 1646 because of the actions of a treacherous follower. The keys to Corfe Castle hang in the library at Kingston Lacy.

At Wimborne Minster, on B3082 (Wimborne-Blandford Rd.), 2.5km (1½ miles) west of Wimborne. *©* 01202/ 883402. Admission to the house, garden, and park £10 ($20) adults, £4 ($8) children, £25 ($50) family ticket; garden only £5 ($10) adults, £2.50 ($5) children, £13 ($26) family ticket. House mid-Mar to Oct Wed–Sun 11am–4pm; garden and park mid-Mar to Oct daily 10:30am–6pm, Nov to mid-Dec Fri–Sun 10:30am–4pm, Feb to mid-Mar Sat–Sun 10:30am–4pm. Closed mid-Dec to Jan.

7 Dorchester: Hardy's Home ✦

193km (120 miles) SW of London; 43km (27 miles) W of Bournemouth

In his 1886 novel *The Mayor of Casterbridge,* Thomas Hardy gave Dorchester literary fame. Actually, Dorchester was notable even in Roman times, when Maumbury Rings, the best Roman amphitheater in Britain, was filled with the sounds of 12,000 spectators screaming for the blood of the gladiators. Today, it's a sleepy market town that seems to go to bed right after dinner.

ESSENTIALS

GETTING THERE   Trains run from London's Waterloo Station each hour during the day. The trip takes 2½ hours. For rail information, call ✆ **0845/748-4950** or visit **www.nationalrail.co.uk.** Dorchester has two train stations, the South Station at Station Approach and the West Station on Great Western Road.

One **National Express** coach a day departs from London's Victoria Coach Station heading for Dorchester. The trip takes 3¾ hours. Call ✆ **0870/580-8080,** or visit **www.nationalexpress.com** for information and schedules.

If driving from London, take the M3 southwest, but near the end take the A30 toward Salisbury to connect with the A354 for the final approach to Dorchester.

VISITOR INFORMATION   The **Tourist Information Centre** is at Unit 11, Antelope Walk (✆ **01305/267992;** www.visit-dorchester.co.uk). It's open from April to October Monday to Saturday 9am to 5pm (also May–Sept Sun 10am–3pm), and November to March Monday to Saturday 9am to 4pm.

WHERE TO STAY & DINE IN & AROUND DORCHESTER

Best Western Kings Arms Hotel   In business for more than 3 centuries, the Kings Arms offers great bow windows above the porch and a swinging sign hanging over the road, a legacy of its days as a coaching inn. It's still the best place to stay within Dorchester's center, though superior lodgings are on the outskirts. An archway leads to the courtyard and parking area at the back of the hotel. All rooms are comfortably furnished; most are small to medium in size and have been modernized while retaining a traditional English aura.

30 High East St., Dorchester, Dorset DT1 1HF. ✆ 01305/265353. Fax 01305/260269. www.bestwestern.co.uk. 37 units. £89 ($178) double. AE, MC, V. **Amenities:** Restaurant; bar; room service. *In room:* TV, Wi-Fi, beverage maker, hair dryer.

Summer Lodge ✦✦✦   In this country-house hotel (a Relais & Châteaux property) 24km (15 miles) north of Dorchester, resident owners Nigel and Margaret Corbett provide care, courtesy, and comfort. Once home to heirs of the earls of Ilchester, the house, in the village of Evershot, now stands on 1.6 hectares (4 acres) of secluded gardens. Evershot appears as Evershed in *Tess of the D'Urbervilles,* and author Thomas Hardy (that name again) designed a wing of the house. In this relaxed, informal atmosphere, bedrooms have views of either the garden or over village rooftops to fields beyond. The hotel is regularly redecorated and recarpeted. Bedrooms are individually decorated and have many comforts. Rooms and suites are split among the main building, a coach house, and three cottages.

Summer Lane, Evershot, Dorset DT2 0JR. ✆ 01935/482000. Fax 01935/482040. www.summerlodgehotel.com. 24 units. £113–£180 (£226–$360) per person double; from £213 ($426) per person suite. Rates include English breakfast, early-morning tea, and newspaper. AE, DC, MC, V. Head north from Dorchester on A37. **Amenities:** Restaurant; bar; indoor pool; tennis court; gym; spa; croquet lawn; room service; laundry service. *In room:* A/C, TV/DVD, Wi-Fi, beverage maker, hair dryer, safe.

Yalbury Cottage Hotel and Restaurant ★ *(Finds)*   This thatch-roofed cottage with inglenooks and beamed ceilings is in a small country village within walking distance of Thomas Hardy's cottage and Stinsford Church. The cottage is some 300 years old and was once home to a local shepherd and the keeper of the water meadows. A mile to the north is Thorncombe Wood (home to badgers, deer, and many species of birds), offering a pleasant stroll and a chance to see Hardy's birthplace, which is tucked in under the edge of the woods. The bedrooms overlook the English country garden beyond, reflecting a mood of tranquillity, and have pinewood furniture in the English cottage style.

Lower Bockhampton, near Dorchester, Dorset DT2 8PZ. ⓒ 01305/262382. Fax 01305/266412. www.yalbury cottage.com. 8 units. £98–£112 ($196–$224) double. Rates include breakfast. MC, V. Head 3km (2 miles) east of Dorchester (A35) and watch for signs to Lower Bockhampton. Closed Sun–Mon Nov–Mar 20. **Amenities:** Restaurant; room service; babysitting; laundry service. *In room:* TV/DVD, beverage maker, hair dryer.

SEEING THE SIGHTS

To learn more about the Victorian author Thomas Hardy, you can join in organized walks that follow in the footsteps of his novels in and around the Dorchester area. They are conducted April to October by the **Thomas Hardy Society** (ⓒ **01305/ 251501;** www.hardysociety.org). These walks and tours take up a full day and are followed by lectures on Hardy and readings of his works, both poetry and prose.

Athelhampton House & Gardens ★★   This is one of England's great medieval houses and the most beautiful and historic in the south, lying a mile east of Puddletown. Thomas Hardy mentioned it in some of his writings but called it Athelhall. It was begun during the reign of Edward IV on the legendary site of King Athelstan's palace. A family home for more than 500 years, it's noted for its 15th-century Great Hall, Tudor great chamber, state bedroom, and King's Room.

Insider's tip: Though many visitors come to see the house, the gardens are even more inspiring. Dating from 1891, they are full of vistas, and their beauty is enhanced by the River Piddle flowing through and by fountains. These walled gardens, winners of the HHA/Christies Garden of the Year award, contain the famous topiary pyramids and two pavilions designed by Inigo Jones. You'll see fine collections of tulips and magnolias, roses, and lilies, and also a 15th-century dovecote. Yes, the gardens were often visited by Thomas Hardy.

On A35, 8km (5 miles) east of Dorchester. ⓒ 01305/848363. www.athelhampton.co.uk. Admission £8.50 ($17) adults, £8 ($16) seniors, £6 ($12) students, free for children 4 and younger. Mar–Oct Sun–Thurs 10:30am–5pm; Nov–Feb Sun 10:30am–5pm. Take the Dorchester-Bournemouth Rd. (A35) east of Dorchester for 8km (5 miles).

Dorset County Museum ★   This museum has a gallery devoted to memorabilia of Thomas Hardy's life. In addition, you'll find an archaeological gallery with displays and finds from Maiden Castle, Britain's largest Iron Age hill fort, plus galleries on the geology, local history, and natural history of Dorset.

High West St. (next to St. Peter's Church). ⓒ 01305/262735. www.dorsetcountymuseum.org. Admission £6 ($12) adults, £5 ($10) seniors and students, 2 accompanied children 5–15 free, additional children £1 ($2), free for children 4 and younger. July–Sept daily 10am–5pm; Oct–June Mon–Sat 10am–5pm. Closed Christmas Day.

Hardy's Cottage   Thomas Hardy was born in 1840 at Higher Bockhampton. His home, now a National Trust property, may be visited. Approach the cottage on foot— it's a 10-minute walk—after parking your vehicle in the space provided in the woods.

Higher Bockhampton (5km/3 miles northeast of Dorchester and 1km/½ mile south of Blandford Rd./A35). ⓒ 01297/ 561900. Admission £3.50 ($7) adults, £1.50 ($3) children. Sun–Thurs 11am–5pm. Closed Nov–Mar.

8 Dorset's Coastal Towns: Chideock, Charmouth & Lyme Regis ★★

Chideock and Charmouth: 253km (157 miles) SW of London, 1.5km (1 mile) W of Bridport; Lyme Regis: 258km (160 miles) SW of London, 40km (25 miles) W of Dorchester

Chideock is a charming village hamlet of thatched houses with a dairy farm in the center. About a mile from the coast, it's a gem of a place for overnight stopovers, and even better for longer stays.

On Lyme Bay, Charmouth, like Chideock, is another winner. A village of Georgian houses and thatched cottages, Charmouth provides some of the most dramatic coastal scenery in West Dorset. The village is west of Golden Cap, which is the highest cliff along the coast of southern England.

Also on Lyme Bay, near the Devonshire border, the resort of Lyme Regis is one of the most attractive centers along the south coast. For those who shun big, commercial resorts, Lyme Regis is ideal—it's a true English coastal town with a mild climate. Seagulls fly overhead, the streets are steep and winding, and walks along Cobb Beach are brisk. The views, particularly of the craft in the harbor, are so photogenic that John Fowles, a longtime resident of the town, selected it as the site for the 1980 filming of his novel *The French Lieutenant's Woman*.

During its heyday, the town was a major seaport. Later, Lyme developed into a small spa, including among its visitors Jane Austen. She wrote her final novel, *Persuasion* (published posthumously and based partly on the town's life), after staying here in 1803 and 1804.

ESSENTIALS

GETTING THERE   The nearest train connection to Chideock and Charmouth is Dorchester (see "Essentials" in the Dorchester section, above). Buses run frequently through the day, west from both Dorchester and Bridport.

To get to Lyme Regis, take the London-Exeter train, getting off at Axminster and continuing the rest of the way by bus. For rail information, call ✆ **0845/748-4950** or visit **www.nationalrail.co.uk**. Bus no. 31 runs from Axminster to Lyme Regis (one bus per hour during the day). There's also **National Express** bus service. Call ✆ **0870/580-8080** or visit **www.nationalexpress.com** for schedules and information.

If you're driving to Chideock and Charmouth from Bridport, continue west along the A35. To get to Lyme Regis from Bridport, continue west along the A35, cutting south to the coast at the junction with the A3070.

VISITOR INFORMATION   In Lyme Regis, the **Tourist Information Centre,** at Guildhall Cottage, Church Street (✆ **01297/442138;** www.westdorset.com), is open November to March Monday to Saturday 10am to 3pm, April to October Monday to Saturday 10am to 5pm.

WHERE TO STAY & DINE
IN CHIDEOCK & CHARMOUTH

Chideock House Hotel ★★ *Finds*   In a village of winners, this 15th-century thatched house is the prettiest. The house was used by the Roundheads in 1645, and ghosts of the village martyrs still haunt it because their trial was held here. Located near the road, behind a protective stone wall, the house has a garden in back; a driveway leads to a large parking area. The beamed lounge, recently face-lifted, has two fireplaces, one an Adam fireplace with a wood-burning blaze on cool days. Bedrooms are individually decorated and vary in size; superior rooms have dressing gowns and toiletries.

Main St., Chideock, Dorset DT6 6JN. © **01297/489242.** Fax 01297/489184. www.chideockhousehotel.com. 9 units, all with bathroom. £75–£88 ($150–$176) double. Rates include English breakfast. £125–£138 ($250–$276) double with half-board (minimum 2 days). AE, MC, V. Bus: 31 from Bridport. **Amenities:** Restaurant; bar. *In room:* TV, beverage maker, hair dryer.

White House ★   The White House is the best place to stay in Charmouth. This Regency home, with its period architecture and bow doors, is well preserved and tastefully furnished. Ian and Liz Simpson took this place, constructed in 1827, and made it comfortable, with touches such as electric kettles in their handsomely furnished bedrooms. Rooms range in size from small to medium and include such extras as complimentary decanters of sherry and homemade shortbread.

2 Hillside, the Street, Charmouth, Dorset DT6 6PJ. © **01297/560411.** Fax 01297/560702. www.whitehouse hotel.com. 8 units. £170–£220 ($340–$440) double. Rates include English breakfast and 5-course table d'hôte. MC, V. Closed Dec–Jan, but open for New Year's Day. Bus: 31 from Bridport. No children 11 and under. **Amenities:** Restaurant; bar; room service; laundry service; dry cleaning. *In room:* TV, beverage maker.

IN LYME REGIS

Hotel Alexandra ★   Built in 1735, this hotel is situated on a hill about 5 minutes from the center of Lyme Regis. Today, it has the best bedrooms and amenities of any inn in town, though it lacks the personal charm of Kersbrook Hotel (see below). In rooms once occupied by such "blue bloods" as Dowager Countess Poulett or Duc du Stacpoole, you sleep in grand comfort in the handsome beds. Most rooms command superb sea views over Lyme Regis and the Cobb. It has been discreetly modernized around its original character.

Pound St., Lyme Regis, Dorset DT7 3HZ. © **01297/442010.** Fax 01297/443229. www.hotelalexandra.co.uk. 26 units. £100–£150 ($200–$300) double. Rates include English breakfast. MC, V. **Amenities:** Restaurant; bar; room service; laundry service; dry cleaning. *In room:* TV, beverage maker, hair dryer.

Kersbrook Hotel ★ *(Finds)*   Built of stone in 1790 and crowned by a thatch roof, the Kersbrook sits on a ledge above the village (which provides a panoramic view of the coast), on .6 hectare (1½ acres) of gardens landscaped according to the original 18th-century plans. The public rooms have been refurnished with antique furniture, re-creating old-world charm with modern facilities. All of the small to medium-size bedrooms have a certain 17th-century charm, with furnishings ranging from antique to contemporary. Rooms are comfortable and tidily maintained.

Pound Rd., Lyme Regis, Dorset DT7 3HX. ©/fax **01297/442596.** www.lymeregis.com/kersbrook-hotel. 10 units. £65–£80 ($130–$160) double. Rates include breakfast. AE, MC, V. **Amenities:** Bar; breakfast room. *In room:* TV, beverage maker, hair dryer, no phone.

The Royal Lion Hotel *(Kids)*   This former coaching inn dates from 1610, growing throughout the years to incorporate oak-paneled bars, lounges, and comfortably up-to-date bedrooms. Situated in the center of town on a hillside climbing up from the sea, the hotel features country-inspired furnishings and such venerable antiques as the half-tester bed regularly used by Edward VII when he was prince of Wales. Bedrooms are divided between the main house, where the traditionally furnished rooms have more character and fireplaces, and a modern wing, where rooms have contemporary furnishings and the added advantage of a private terrace with sea view. Children are welcomed and some of the hotel's family rooms have bunk beds.

Broad St., Lyme Regis, Dorset DT7 3QF. © **01297/445622.** Fax 01297/445859. www.royallionhotel.com. 30 units. £86–£124 ($172–$248) double with breakfast, £124–£162 ($248–$324) double with breakfast and dinner. AE, DC, MC, V. **Amenities:** Restaurant; bar; lounge; indoor pool; gym; Jacuzzi; sauna; game room. *In room:* TV, beverage maker.

EXPLORING THE TOWNS

Chideock and Charmouth are the most beautiful villages in Dorset. It's fun to stroll though them to see the well-kept cottages, well-manicured gardens, and an occasional 18th- or 19th-century church. Charmouth, more than Chideock, boasts a small-scale collection of unusual antiques shops. Both villages are less than a mile from the western edge of **Chesil Beach,** one of the Hampshire coast's most famous (and longest) beaches. Although it's covered with shingle (sharp rocks), and hard on your feet if you go sunbathing, the beach nonetheless provides 8km (5 miles) of sweeping views toward France. Along the stretch you'll find numerous facilities such as toilets and places to order food and drink.

The surrounding area is a fascinating place for botanists and zoologists because of the predominance of blue Lias, a sedimentary rock well suited to the formation of fossils. In 1810, Mary Anning (at the age of 11) discovered one of the first articulated ichthyosaur skeletons. She went on to become one of the first professional fossilists in England. Books outlining walks in the area and the regions where fossils can be studied are available at the local information bureau.

9 Sherborne ⓕ

206km (128 miles) SW of London; 31km (19 miles) NW of Dorchester

A little gem of a town with well-preserved medieval, Tudor, Stuart, and Georgian buildings still standing, Sherborne is in the heart of Dorset, surrounded by wooded hills, valleys, and chalk downs. It was here that Sir Walter Raleigh lived before his fall from fortune.

ESSENTIALS

GETTING THERE   Frequent trains depart from London's Waterloo Station through the day. The trip takes 2 hours. For information, call © **0845/748-4950** or visit **www.nationalrail.co.uk**.

One **National Express** coach departs daily from London's Victoria Coach Station. Call © **0870/580-8080,** or visit **www.nationalexpress.com** for information and schedules.

If you're driving, take the M3 west from London, continuing southwest on the A303 and the B3145.

VISITOR INFORMATION   The **Tourist Information Centre,** on Digby Road (© **01935/815341;** www.sherbornetown.co.uk), is open April to October Monday to Saturday 9am to 5pm, and November to March Monday to Saturday 10am to 3pm.

WHERE TO STAY

Eastbury Hotel ⓕ   This Georgian town-house hotel, Sherborne's best, is situated in its own walled garden near the 8th-century abbey and the two castles. Built in 1740 during the reign of George II, it has a traditional ambience, with its own library of antiquarian books. Beautifully restored, it retains its 18th-century character. Bedrooms are named after flowers and are handsomely maintained and decorated. Rooms are small to medium in size, bright and inviting, and furnished in a traditional way, often graced with fresh flowers; some have four-poster beds. After a restful night's sleep, you can sit outside and enjoy the well-kept garden.

Long St., Sherborne, Dorset DT9 3BY. ℂ 01935/813131. Fax 01935/817296. www.theeastburyhotel.co.uk. 23 units. £120–£160 ($240–$320) double. Rates include English breakfast. AE, MC, V. **Amenities:** Restaurant (see review below); 2 bars; room service; laundry service; dry cleaning. *In room:* TV, beverage maker, hair dryer, trouser press.

The Sherborne Hotel   Built of red brick in 1969, this two-story hotel lies near a school and a scattering of factories and houses. Getting high marks for quality, the Sherborne is more elegant than a typical roadside hotel, with more amenities than may be expected and easy access to the town's historic center. The hotel's bedrooms, small to medium in size, are too functional to be the most glamorous in the area. Eleven of the rooms are spacious enough for small families.

Horsecastles Lane (near A30 and about 1.5km/1 mile west of Sherborne's center), Sherborne, Dorset DT9 6BB. ℂ 01935/813191. Fax 01935/816493. www.sherbornehotel.co.uk. 59 units. £78–£138 ($156–$276) double. Rates include English breakfast. AE, DC, MC, V. **Amenities:** Restaurant; bar; room service. *In room:* TV, beverage maker, hair dryer, trouser press.

WHERE TO DINE

Eastbury Hotel Restaurant   FRENCH/INTERNATIONAL   In a tasteful setting in this previously recommended hotel, this restaurant presents a range of well-prepared dishes based on fresh ingredients and an imaginative, intellectual use of flavors. Get started with such delights as terrine of beef and foie gras, or else roasted wood pigeon with a beet gnocchi, followed by such main courses as loin of venison in an elderberry sauce or roast partridge with a celeriac fondant. The cuisine is backed up by one of the finest wine lists in the area. You can finish with such desserts as spiced pumpkin cake and pistachio ice cream.

Long St. ℂ 01935/813131. Reservations recommended. Main courses lunch £9–£12 ($18–$24), dinner £16–£22 ($32–$44); table d'hôte menu £27–£33 ($54–$66). AE, MC, V. Daily noon–2pm and 7–9:15pm.

EXPLORING SHERBORNE

Sherborne Abbey ⸙⸙   One of the great churches of England, this abbey was founded in A.D. 705 as the Cathedral of the Saxon Bishops of Wessex. In the late 10th century, it became a Benedictine monastery, and since the Reformation it has been a parish church. Famous for its fan-vaulted roof added by Abbot Ramsam at the end of the 15th century, it was the first of its kind erected in England. Inside are many fine monuments, including Purbeck marble effigies of medieval abbots as well as Elizabethan "four-poster" and canopied tombs. The baroque statue of the earl of Bristol stands between his two wives and dates from 1698. A public school occupies the abbey's surviving medieval monastic buildings and was the setting for the classic film *Goodbye, Mr. Chips.*

Abbey Close. ℂ 01935/812452. www.sherborneabbey.com. Free admission; donations for upkeep welcomed. Apr–Sept daily 8am–6pm; Oct–Mar daily 8am–4pm.

Sherborne Castle ⸙   Sir Walter Raleigh built this castle in 1594, when he decided that it would not be feasible to restore the old castle (see below) to suit his needs. This Elizabethan residence was a square mansion; later owners added four Jacobean wings to make it more palatial. After King James I had Raleigh imprisoned in the Tower of London, the monarch gave the castle to a favorite Scot, Robert Carr, banishing the Raleighs from their home. In 1617, it became the property of Sir John Digby, first earl of Bristol, and has been the Digby family home ever since. The mansion was enlarged by Sir John in 1625, and in the 18th century, the formal Elizabethan gardens and fountains of the Raleighs were altered by Capability Brown, who created a serpentine lake between the two castles. The 8 hectares (20 acres) of lawns and pleasure grounds around the 20-hectare (50-acre) lake are open to the public. In the house are fine furniture, china, and paintings by Gainsborough, Lely, Reynolds, Kneller, and Van Dyck, among others.

Cheap St. (off New Rd. 1.5km/1 mile east of the center). (✆ **01935/813182.** www.sherbornecastle.com. Castle and grounds £9 ($18) adults, £8.50 ($17) seniors, free for ages 15 and younger; grounds only £4.50 ($9) adults, free for ages 15 and younger. Apr 1–Oct 31 Tues–Thurs; Sat–Sun and bank holidays 11am–5pm (last admission 4:30pm).

Sherborne Old Castle ✿

The castle was built by the powerful Bishop Roger de Caen in the early 12th century, but it was seized by the crown at about the time of King Henry I's death in 1135 and Stephen's troubled accession to the throne. The castle was given to Sir Walter Raleigh by Queen Elizabeth I. The gallant knight built Sherborne Lodge in the deer park close by (now privately owned). The buildings were mostly destroyed in the civil war, but you can still see a gatehouse, some graceful arcades, and decorative windows.

Castleton, off A30, 1km (½ mile) east of Sherborne. (✆ **01935/812730.** Admission £2.60 ($5.20) adults, £2.10 ($4.20) seniors and students, £1.50 ($3) children 5–16, free for children 4 and younger. Apr–June and Sept daily 10am–5pm; July–Aug daily 10am–6pm; Oct daily 10am–4pm. Closed Nov–Mar. Follow the signs 1.5km (1 mile) east from the town center.

10

Wiltshire & Somerset: Regal Bath & Mysterious Stonehenge

For our look at the "West Countree," we move into Wiltshire and Somerset, two of the most historic shires of England. Once you reach this area of pastoral woodland, London seems far removed. For a total view of the West Country, you can also visit Devon and Cornwall (see chapters 11 and 12).

Most people agree that the West Country, a loose geographical term, begins at **Salisbury,** with its Early English cathedral. Nearby is **Stonehenge,** England's oldest prehistoric monument. (Both Stonehenge and Salisbury are in Wiltshire.) When you cross into Wiltshire, you enter a country of chalky, grassy uplands and rolling plains. Much of the shire is agricultural; a large part is pasture.

Somerset has some of the most beautiful scenery in England. The undulating limestone hills of **Mendip** and the irresistible **Quantocks** are especially lovely in spring and fall. Somerset opens onto the Bristol Channel, with **Minehead** serving as its chief resort. The shire is rich in legend and history, possessing particularly fanciful associations with King Arthur and Queen Guinevere, Camelot, and

Alfred the Great. Its villages are noted for the tall towers of its parish churches.

Somerset also encompasses the territory around the old port of **Bristol** and the old Roman city of **Bath,** known for its abbey and spa water, lying beside the River Avon.

The two best places to base yourself while you explore the area are Bath and Salisbury. From Salisbury, you can visit Stonehenge and **Old Sarum,** the two most fabled ancient monuments in the West Country. Yet some say visiting the stones at **Avebury** is a much more personal experience. And **Glastonbury,** with its once-great abbey that is now a ruined sanctuary, may be one of Britain's oldest inhabited sites. The greatest natural spectacle in the area is **Exmoor National Park,** once an English royal hunting preserve, stretching for 686 sq. km (265 sq. miles) on the north coast of Devon and Somerset. Many terrific country houses and palaces are also in this region, including **Wilton House,** the site of 17th-century staterooms designed by Inigo Jones. The other two major attractions, **Longleat House** and the fabled gardens at **Stourhead,** can be visited in a busy day while you're based at Bath.

1 Salisbury ★★

145km (90 miles) SW of London; 85km (53 miles) SE of Bristol

Long before you enter Salisbury, the spire of its cathedral comes into view—just as John Constable captured it on canvas. The 121m (404-ft.) pinnacle of the Early English and Gothic cathedral is the tallest in England.

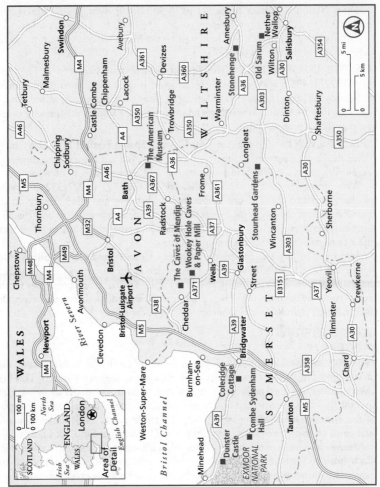

Salisbury, or New Sarum, lies in the valley of the River Avon. Filled with Tudor inns and tearooms, it is the only true city in Wiltshire. It's an excellent base for visitors anxious to explore Stonehenge or Avebury, who, unfortunately, tend to visit the cathedral and then rush on their way. But the old market town is an interesting destination on its own, and if you choose to linger here for a day or two, you find that its pub-to-citizen ratio is perhaps the highest in the country.

ESSENTIALS

GETTING THERE **Network Express trains** depart for Salisbury hourly from Waterloo Station in London; the trip takes 1½ hours. Sprinter trains offer fast, efficient service every hour from Portsmouth, Bristol, and South Wales. Also, direct rail service is available from Exeter, Plymouth, Brighton, and Reading. For rail information, call ② **0845/748-4950** or visit **www.nationalrail.co.uk**.

Three **National Express buses** (© **0870/580-8080**; www.nationalexpress.com) make a 3-hour run daily from London, costing £14 ($28) for a one-way ticket.

If you're driving from London, head west on the M3 to the end of the run, continuing the rest of the way on the A30.

VISITOR INFORMATION   The **Tourist Information Centre** is at Fish Row (© **01722/334956**; www.visitsalisbury.com) and is open October to April Monday to Saturday 9:30am to 5pm; May Monday to Saturday 9:30am to 5pm and Sunday 10:30am to 4:30pm; and June to September Monday to Saturday 9:30am to 6pm and Sunday 10:30am to 4:30pm.

SPECIAL EVENTS   The Salisbury **St. George's Spring Festival** in April is a traditional medieval celebration of the city's patron saint. You can witness St. George slaying the dragon in the Wiltshire mummers play and see acrobats and fireworks.

With spring comes the annual **Salisbury Festival** (© **01722/332977**; www. salisburyfestival.co.uk). The city drapes itself in banners, and street theater—traditional and unusual—is offered everywhere. There are also symphony and chamber music concerts in Salisbury Cathedral, children's events, and much more. It takes place from mid-May to the beginning of June.

At the end of July, you can see the **Salisbury Country and Garden Show,** Hudson's Field (© **01189/478996**), a treat for gardening enthusiasts, with a floral marquee packed with Chelsea exhibits, as well as display gardens created especially for the event. For those members of the family who tire of the gardens, there are also specialty food tastings, crafts sales, and a vintage and classic car show.

WHERE TO STAY
MODERATE

Best Western Red Lion Hotel ★ *Value*   From the 1300s, the Red Lion continues to accommodate wayfarers from London on their way to the West Country. This Best Western–affiliated hotel no longer reigns supreme in town—we prefer the White Hart and the Rose and Crown—but it's a fine choice. Cross under its arch into a courtyard with a hanging, much-photographed creeper, a red lion, and a half-timbered facade, and you'll be transported back to an earlier era. This antiques-filled hotel is noted for its unique clock collection, which includes a skeleton organ clock in the reception hall. Each small to medium-size bedroom is individually furnished and tastefully decorated. Two units are spacious enough for families, and the most expensive rooms have four-poster beds.

4 Milford St., Salisbury, Wiltshire SP1 2AN. © **800/528-1234** in the U.S., or 01722/323334. Fax 01722/325756. www.the-redlion.co.uk. 51 units. £134 ($268) double; £154 ($308) family room. AE, DC, MC, V. **Amenities:** Restaurant; bar; room service; laundry service; dry cleaning. *In room:* TV, Wi-Fi (in some), coffeemaker, hair dryer.

Grasmere House ★ *Kids*   Grasmere House stands near the confluence of the Nadder and Avon rivers on .6 hectares (1½ acres) of grounds. Constructed in 1896 for Salisbury merchants, the house still suggests a family home. The original architectural features were retained as much as possible, including a "calling box" for servants in the dining room. A conservatory restaurant and bar overlooks the cathedral, as do three luxurious rooms. Four rooms are in the original house, with the remainder in a newer wing. Each room has a distinctive character and often opens onto a scenic view. Two accommodations are large enough for families, and the hotel welcomes young children.

70 Harnham Rd., Salisbury, Wiltshire SP2 8JN. © **01722/338388**. Fax 01722/333710. www.grasmerehotel.com. 36 units. £110–£165 ($220–$330) double; £150 ($300) family room. Rates include English breakfast. AE, DC, MC, V. Take

A3094 2.5km (1½ miles) from town center. **Amenities:** Restaurant; bar; room service; laundry service. *In room:* TV, coffeemaker, hair dryer, iron, trouser press.

The Legacy Rose and Crown Hotel ✮✮✮

This half-timbered, 13th-century gem stands with its feet almost in the River Avon; beyond the water, you can see the tall spire of the cathedral. Because of its tranquil location, it's our top choice. From here, you can easily walk over the arched stone bridge to the center of Salisbury in 10 minutes. Old trees shade the lawns and gardens between the inn and the river, and chairs are set out so that you can enjoy the view and count the swans. The inn has both a new and an old wing. The new wing is modern, but the old wing is more appealing, with its sloping ceilings and antique fireplaces and furniture. Bedrooms in the main house range from small to medium in size, though those in the new wing are more spacious and better designed.

Harnham Rd., Salisbury, Wiltshire SP2 8JQ. ✆ **0870/832-9946.** Fax 0870/832-9947. www.legacy-hotels.co.uk. 28 units. £80–£197 ($160–$394) double. Rates include breakfast. AE, DC, MC, V. Take A3094 2.5km (1½ miles) from the center of town. **Amenities:** Restaurant; 2 bars; room service. *In room:* TV, beverage maker, hair dryer, trouser press.

Mercure White Hart ✮✮

Combining the best of old and new, the White Hart is a Salisbury landmark from Georgian times. Its classic facade is intact, with tall columns crowning a life-size hart (stag). The older accommodations are traditional, and a new section has been added in the rear, opening onto a large parking area. New-wing units are tastefully decorated; although rooms in the main building have more style and character, many are quite small. You can enjoy a before-dinner drink, followed by a meal of Modern English fare, in the White Hart Restaurant.

1 St. Johns St., Salisbury, Wiltshire SP1 2SD. ✆ **800/221-4542** in U.S., or 01722/327476. Fax 01722/412761. www.mercure.com. 68 units. £120–£160 ($240–$320) double. Rates include breakfast. AE, DC, MC, V. Free parking. **Amenities:** Restaurant; bar; room service. *In room:* TV, minibar (in some), coffeemaker, hair dryer, iron, trouser press, safe.

INEXPENSIVE

The Beadles ✮✮ *Finds*

A traditional modern Georgian house with antique furnishings and a view of the cathedral, the Beadles offers unobstructed views of the beautiful Wiltshire countryside from its .4-hectare (1-acre) gardens. It's situated in a small, unspoiled English village, 11km (7 miles) from Salisbury, which offers excellent access to Stonehenge, Wilton House, the New Forest, and the rambling moors of Thomas Hardy country. Even the road to Winchester is an ancient Roman byway. Furnished tastefully, this household contains rooms with twins or doubles. Owners David and Anne-Marie Yuille-Baddeley delight in providing information on the area.

Middleton, Middle Winterslow, near Salisbury, Wiltshire SP5 1QS. ✆ **01980/862922.** Fax 01980/863565. www.guest accom.co.uk/754.htm. 3 units. £70 (US$140) double. Rates include English breakfast. MC, V. Turn off A30 at Pheasant Inn to Middle Winterslow. Enter the village, make the 1st right, turn right again, and it's the 1st right after Trevano. **Amenities:** Dining room; tour services. *In room:* TV, coffeemaker, hair dryer.

Cricket Field House Hotel ✮ *Finds*

This snug B&B takes its name from the cricket field it overlooks 3km (2 miles) west of Salisbury. The original structure was a game-keeper's cottage that has been handsomely converted. In its own large garden, the family-run house is comfortably furnished and modernized. Rooms are in both the main house and an equally good pavilion annex. Each unit is decorated and furnished individually.

Wilton Rd., Salisbury, Wiltshire SP2 9NS. ✆ **01722/322595.** www.cricketfieldhousehotel.co.uk. 17 units. £70–£95 (US$140–US$190) double; £80–£130 ($160–$260) family room. Rates include English breakfast. AE, MC, V. On the

A36, 3km (2 miles) west of Salisbury. **Amenities:** Restaurant for guests only; room service; laundry service; dry cleaning. *In room:* TV, Wi-Fi, coffeemaker, hair dryer.

Wyndham Park Lodge

From this appealing Victorian 1880 house, it's an easy walk to the heart of Salisbury and its cathedral, and about a 5-minute walk to a swimming pool and the bus station. The small to midsize rooms are comfortably furnished with Victorian and Edwardian antiques. They have either one double or two twin beds.

51 Wyndham Rd., Salisbury, Wiltshire SP1 3AB. ✆ **01722/416517.** Fax 01722/328851. www.wyndhamparklodge. co.uk. 4 units. £55–£60 ($110–$120) double; £70–£80 ($140–$160) family room for 3. Rates include English breakfast. MC, V. **Amenities:** Breakfast room. *In room:* TV, Wi-Fi, coffeemaker, hair dryer.

A CHOICE IN NEARBY TEFFORT EVIAS

Howard's House ✿ *(Finds)*

Housed in a 17th-century dower house that has been added to over the years, this property set in a medieval hamlet is the most appealing small hotel and restaurant in the area. Much care is lavished on the decor, with fresh flowers in every public room and bedroom. Most bedrooms are spacious in size, and one room is large enough for a family. Some rooms have four-poster beds. The hotel has attractive gardens, and on chilly nights, log fires burn.

Teffont Evias, 14km (9 miles) from Salisbury, Wiltshire SP3 5RJ. ✆ **01722/716392.** Fax 01722/716820. www. howardshousehotel.co.uk. 9 units. £155–£175 ($310–$350) double. Rates include English breakfast. AE, MC, V. Leave Salisbury heading east on the A36 until you reach a roundabout. Take the 1st left leading to the A30. On the A30, continue for 5km (3 miles) coming to the turnoff (B3089) for Barford Saint-Martin. Continue for 6.5km (4 miles) on this secondary road to the town of Teffont Evias, where the hotel is signposted. **Amenities:** Restaurant (see review below); bar; laundry service. *In room:* TV, hair dryer.

WHERE TO DINE

See "Salisbury After Dark," below, for a selection of pubs with affordable fare.

Après LXIX ✿ MODERN ENGLISH

Close to the Salisbury Cathedral, this is the finest dining room within the city itself. It's awakened the sleepy taste buds of Salisbury, which has suffered for decades without a really good first-class restaurant. In a stylish contemporary interior, a Modern English but French-inspired cuisine is served. Ingredients are adjusted on the menu to take advantage of the changing seasons. Try, for example, roasted sea bass with a "mash" of spinach served in a velvety smooth and chive-laced white-butter sauce. One excellent dish is Angus beef served with foie gras and very thick potatoes cooked like french fries. A more delicate offering, but one equally good, is *mille feuille*, "a thousand leaves," in this case, puff pastry filled with wild mushrooms and toasted peanuts. Smoked river eel adds an exotic touch to the menu.

69 New St. ✆ **01722/340000.** Reservations not required. Main courses £8–£14 ($16–$28). AE, MC, V. Mon–Sat noon–2:30pm and 6–9:30pm. Closed Dec 24–Jan 2.

Harper's Restaurant ENGLISH/INTERNATIONAL

The chef-owner of this place prides himself on specializing in homemade and wholesome "real food." The pleasantly decorated restaurant is on the second floor of a redbrick building at the back end of Salisbury's largest parking lot, in the center of town. In the same all-purpose dining room, you can order from two different menus, one with affordable bistro-style platters, including beefsteak casserole with "herby dumplings." A longer menu, with items that take more time to prepare, includes roast Barbury duck breast on a plum-ginger-and-star-anise confit, or local grilled lamb chops with red currant jus.

6–7 Ox Row, Market Sq. ✆ **01722/333118.** www.harpersrestaurant.co.uk. Reservations recommended. Main courses £8.50–£15 ($17–$30); bistro main courses £7.90 ($16). AE, DC, MC, V. Mon–Sat noon–2pm and 6–9:30pm.

Howard's House Hotel Restaurant ℱ INTERNATIONAL   If you'd like to dine in one of the loveliest places in the area and enjoy a refined cuisine at the same time, leave Salisbury and head for this previously recommended hotel (see above). It's a 14km (9-mile) drive to Teffont Evias, but well worth the trip. The village itself is one of the most beautiful in Wiltshire.

The elegantly appointed restaurant showcases a finely honed cuisine prepared with first-class ingredients. The menu changes daily but is likely to feature such starters as Cornish scallop risotto with deep-fried basil or maple-glazed pork belly. Main courses are very appealing with well-balanced flavors, as exemplified by filet of wild sea bass in a saffron broth or filet of Scottish beef with foie gras and truffle jus.

Teffont Evias, near Salisbury. ℂ 01722/716392. Reservations required. 2-course fixed-price lunch £21 ($42), 3 courses £25 ($50); 2-course fixed-price dinner £33 ($66), AE, MC, V. 3 courses £42 ($84). Sun–Wed 12:30–1:30pm; daily 7:30–9pm. For directions, see the Howard's House listing above.

Salisbury Haunch of Venison ENGLISH   Right in the heart of Salisbury, this creaky-timbered chophouse (it dates from 1320) serves excellent dishes, especially English roasts and grills. Stick to its specialties and you'll rarely go wrong. Begin with a tasty warm salad of venison sausages with garlic croutons and then follow with the time-honored roast haunch of venison with parsnips and juniper berries. Other classics are served as well, including sugar-baked Wiltshire ham with bubble-and-squeak (a dish of cabbage and potatoes).

1 Minster St. ℂ 01722/411313. Fixed-price menu £9.90 ($20) served daily noon–2pm and 6–8pm; main courses £7.90–£16 ($16–$32). MC, V. Mon–Sat 11:30am–11pm; Sun noon–10:30pm.

EXPLORING SALISBURY

You can easily see Salisbury by foot, either on your own or by taking a guided daytime or evening walk sponsored by the Salisbury City Guides (ℂ 01722/320349). Tickets are £3.50 ($7) for adults and £1.50 ($3) for children. Check with the Tourist Information Centre about themed walks on Saturday and the Ghost Walk on Friday.

Mompesson House ℱ   This is one of the most distinguished houses in the area. Built by Charles Mompesson in 1701, while he was a member of Parliament for Old Sarum, it is a beautiful example of the Queen Anne style and is well known for its fine plasterwork ceilings and paneling. It also houses a collection of 18th-century drinking glasses. Visitors can wander through a garden and order a snack in the garden tearoom.

Cathedral Close. ℂ 01722/335659. Admission £4.70 ($9.40) adults, £2.30 ($4.60) children 17 and younger, £12 ($24) family. Apr–Oct Sat–Wed 11am–5pm. Closed Nov–Mar.

Salisbury Cathedral ℱℱℱ   You'll find no better example of the Early English pointed architectural style than Salisbury Cathedral. Construction on this magnificent building began as early as 1220 and took only 45 years to complete. (Most of Europe's grandest cathedrals took 300 years to build.) Salisbury Cathedral is one of the most homogenous of all the great European cathedrals.

The cathedral's 13th-century octagonal chapter house possesses one of the four surviving original texts of the Magna Carta, along with treasures from the diocese of Salisbury and manuscripts and artifacts belonging to the cathedral. The cloisters enhance the cathedral's beauty, along with an exceptionally large close. At least 75 buildings are in the compound, some from the early 18th century and others from much earlier.

Insider's tip: The 121m (404-ft.) spire was one of the tallest structures in the world when completed in 1315. In its day, this was far more advanced technology than the world's tallest skyscrapers. Amazingly, the spire was not part of the original design and was conceived and added some 30 years after the rest. The name of the master mason is lost to history. In 1668, Sir Christopher Wren expressed alarm at the tilt of the spire, but no further shift has since been measured. The entire ensemble is still standing; if you trust towering architecture from 700 years ago, you can explore the tower on 1½-hour guided visits costing £5.50 ($11) for adults, £4.50 ($9) for children and seniors. Between March and October there are two to four tours a day depending on demand. From November to February there is only one tour a day at 2:15pm.

The Close, Salisbury. ℭ 01722/555120. www.salisburycathedral.org.uk. Suggested donation £5 ($10), £3.50 ($7) students and seniors, £3 ($6) children, £12 ($24) family. Sept to mid-June Mon–Sat 7:15am–6:15pm; mid-June to Aug Mon–Sat 7:15am–7:15pm; year-round Sun 7:15am–6:15pm.

SIGHTS NEARBY

Old Sarum ⭐   Believed to have been an Iron Age fortification, Old Sarum was used again by the Saxons and flourished as a walled town into the Middle Ages. The Normans built a cathedral and a castle here; parts of the old cathedral were taken down to build the city of New Sarum (Salisbury).

3km (2 miles) north of Salisbury off A345 on Castle Rd. ℭ 01722/335398. www.english-heritage.org.uk/oldsarum. Admission £2.90 ($5.80) adults, £2.20 ($4.40) seniors, £1.50 ($3) children. Apr–June and Sept daily 10am–5pm; July–Aug daily 9am–6pm; Oct daily 10am–4pm; Nov–Feb daily 11am–3pm; Mar daily 10am–4pm. Bus: 3, 5, 6, 7, 8, or 9, every 30 min. during the day from the Salisbury bus station.

Wilton House ⭐⭐   This home of the earls of Pembroke is in the town of Wilton. It dates from the 16th century but has undergone numerous alterations, most recently in Victoria's day, and is noted for its 17th-century staterooms, designed by celebrated architect Inigo Jones. Shakespeare's troupe is said to have entertained here, and Eisenhower and his advisers prepared here for the D-day landings at Normandy, with only the Van Dyck paintings as silent witnesses.

The house is filled with beautifully maintained furnishings and world-class art, including paintings by Rubens, Bruegel, and Reynolds. You can visit a reconstructed Tudor kitchen and Victorian laundry.

On the 8.4-hectare (21-acre) estate are giant cedars of Lebanon trees, the oldest of which were planted in 1630, as well as rose and water gardens, riverside and woodland walks, and a huge adventure playground for children.

5km (3 miles) west of Salisbury on A36. ℭ 01722/746714. www.wiltonhouse.co.uk. Admission (including grounds) £12 ($24) adults, £9.75 ($20) seniors, £6.50 ($13) children 5–15, £30 ($60) family ticket, free for children 4 and younger. Easter–Sept Sun–Fri 10:30am–5:30pm (last entrance at 4:30pm); grounds Sat only. Closed Nov to Easter Sat.

SHOPPING

Many shops in Salisbury are set in beautiful medieval timber-framed buildings. As you wander through the colorful market or walk the ancient streets, you'll find everything from touristy gift shops to unique specialty stores.

Hard-core shoppers and locals gravitate to the **Old George Mall Shopping Centre,** 23B High St. (ℭ **01722/333500**), a short walk from the cathedral. With more than 40 individual shops and High Street stores, you can find the latest fashions as well as household appliances, CDs, toiletries, and greeting cards.

Another place of note, situated within a 14th-century building with hammered beams and some original windows, is **Watsons,** 8–9 Queen St. (ℭ **01722/320311**). This elegant store carries bone china from Wedgwood, Royal Doulton, and Aynsley; Dartington glassware; and a fine line of paperweights.

Salisbury

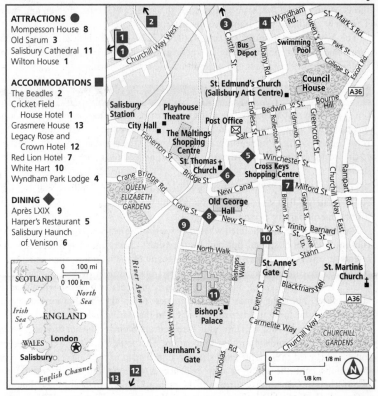

ATTRACTIONS ●
Mompesson House **8**
Old Sarum **3**
Salisbury Cathedral **11**
Wilton House **1**

ACCOMMODATIONS ■
The Beadles **2**
Cricket Field
  House Hotel **1**
Grasmere House **13**
Legacy Rose and
  Crown Hotel **12**
Red Lion Hotel **7**
White Hart **10**
Wyndham Park Lodge **4**

DINING ◆
Après LXIX **9**
Harper's Restaurant **5**
Salisbury Haunch
  of Venison **6**

We always stop in at **Rivermead Books,** 19 North St., Wilton (✆ **01722/741609**), which sells an array of secondhand books, plus some rare first editions. There are more than 23,400 books in stock. We once purchased an autographed murder mystery by Agatha Christie here for a reasonable price.

SALISBURY AFTER DARK

The **Salisbury Playhouse,** Malthouse Lane (✆ **01722/320333** for the box office; www.salisburyplayhouse.com), produces some of the finest theater in the region. Food and drink are available from the bar and restaurant to complete your evening's entertainment.

The **City Hall,** Malthouse Lane (✆ **01722/434434** for the box office; www.city hallsalisbury.co.uk), has a program of events to suit most tastes and ages in comfortable surroundings. A thriving entertainment center, it attracts many of the national touring shows in addition to local amateur events, exhibitions, and sales, thus providing good entertainment at a reasonable price.

The **Salisbury Arts Center,** Bedwin Street (✆ **01722/321744;** www.salisburyarts centre.co.uk), housed within the former St. Edmund's Church, offers a wide range of performing and visual arts. A typical program contains a broad mix of music, contemporary and classic theater, and dance performances, plus cabaret, comedy, and family shows. Regular workshops are available for all ages in arts, crafts, theater, and dance. The lively cafe/bar is a pleasant meeting place.

The **Avon Brewery Inn,** 75 Castle St. (© **01722/416184**), is decorated like a Victorian saloon from the gay 1890s. Its idyllic garden setting overlooks the River Avon. It offers some of the tastiest and most affordable food in town.

2 Prehistoric Britain: Stonehenge (ૠૠૠ & Avebury (ૠૠ

On the doorstep of Salisbury (see above) you can visit two famous prehistoric monuments, all in 1 day if you move fast enough. If you have time to visit only one, there is no contest. Make it Stonehenge, of course, one of the most famous prehistoric sites in the world, composed of earthworks surrounding a circular setting of large standing stones.

Stonehenge (ૠૠૠ This huge circle of lintels and megalithic pillars, believed to be approximately 5,000 years old, is considered by many to be the most important prehistoric monument in Britain.

Some visitors are disappointed when they see that Stonehenge is nothing more than concentric circles of stones. But perhaps they don't understand that Stonehenge represents an amazing engineering feat because many of the boulders, the bluestones in particular, were moved many miles (perhaps from southern Wales) to this site. If you're a romantic, you'll see the ruins in the early glow of dawn or else when shadows fall at sunset. The light is most dramatic at these times, the shadows longer, and the effect is often far more mesmerizing than it is in the glaring light of midday.

The widely held view of 18th- and 19th-century Romantics that Stonehenge was the work of the Druids is without foundation. The boulders, many weighing several tons, are believed to have predated the arrival in Britain of the Celtic culture. Recent excavations continue to bring new evidence to bear on the origin and purpose of Stonehenge. Controversy surrounds the prehistoric site, especially since the publication of *Stonehenge Decoded* by Gerald S. Hawkins and John B. White, which maintains that Stonehenge was an astronomical observatory—that is, a Neolithic "computing machine" capable of predicting eclipses.

Your ticket permits you to go inside the fence surrounding the site that protects the stones from vandals and souvenir hunters. You can go all the way up to a short rope barrier, about 15m (50 ft.) from the stones.

A full circular tour around Stonehenge is possible. A modular walkway was introduced to cross the archaeologically important avenue, the area that runs between the Heel Stone and the main circle of stones. This enables visitors to complete a full circuit of the stones and to see one of the best views of a completed section of Stonehenge as they pass by, an excellent addition to the informative audio tour.

Insider's tip: From the road, if you don't mind the noise from traffic, you can get a good view of Stonehenge without paying admission to go for a close-up encounter. What we like to do is climb **Amesbury Hill,** clearly visible and lying 2.4km (1½ miles) up the A303. From here, you'll get a free panoramic view.

Wilts & Dorset (© **01722/336855;** www.wdbus.co.uk) runs several buses daily (depending on demand) from Salisbury to Stonehenge, as well as buses from the Salisbury train station to Stonehenge. The bus trip to Stonehenge takes 40 minutes, and a round-trip ticket costs £7.50 ($15) for adults, £4.50 ($9) for children ages 5 to 15 (4 and younger ride free), £5.50 ($11) seniors, and £14 ($28) family ticket.

At the junction of A303 and A344/A360. ℂ **01980/623108** for information. www.stonehenge.co.uk. Admission £6.30 ($13) adults, £4.70 ($9.40) students and seniors, £3.20 ($6.40) children, £16 ($32) family ticket. June–Aug daily 9am–7pm; Mar 16–May and Sept–Oct 15 daily 9:30am–6pm; Oct 16–Mar 15 daily 9:30am–4pm. If you're driving, head north on Castle Rd. from the center of Salisbury. At the first roundabout (traffic circle), take the exit toward Amesbury (A345) and Old Sarum. Continue along this road for 13km (8 miles) and then turn left onto A303 in the direction of Exeter. You'll see signs for Stonehenge, leading you up A344 to the right. It's 3km (2 miles) west of Amesbury.

Avebury 👁👁   One of the largest prehistoric sites in Europe, Avebury lies on the Kennet River, 11km (7 miles) west of Marlborough and 32km (20 miles) north of Stonehenge. Some say visiting Avebury, in contrast to Stonehenge, is a more organic experience—you can walk right up and around the stones, as no fence keeps you away. Also, the site isn't mobbed with tour buses.

Visitors can walk around the 11-hectare (28-acre) site at Avebury, winding in and out of the circle of more than 100 stones, some weighing up to 50 tons. The stones are made of sarsen, a sandstone found in Wiltshire. Inside this large circle are two smaller ones, each with about 30 stones standing upright. Native Neolithic tribes are believed to have built these circles.

Wilts & Dorset (ℂ **01722/336855;** www.wdbus.co.uk) has two buses (nos. 5 and 6) that run between the Salisbury bus station and Avebury five times a day Monday through Saturday and three times a day on Sunday. The one-way trip takes 1 hour and 40 minutes. Round-trip tickets are £7.50 ($15) for adults, £5.50 ($11) seniors, £14 ($28) family ticket, and £4.50 ($9) for children ages 5 to 14 (4 and younger ride free).

Also here is the **Alexander Keiller Museum** (ℂ **01672/539250**), which houses one of Britain's most important archaeological collections, including material from excavations at Windmill Hill and Avebury, and artifacts from other prehistoric digs at West Kennet, Long Barrow, Silbury Hill, West Kennet Avenue, and the Sanctuary.

On A361 between Swindon and Devizes (1.5km/1 mile from the A4 London-Bath Rd.). ℂ **01672/539250**. Admission £4.20 ($8.40) adults, £2.10 ($4.20) children, £11 ($22) family ticket. Apr–Oct daily 10am–6pm; Nov–Mar daily 10am–4pm. The closest rail station is at Swindon, 19km (12 miles) away, which is served by the main rail line from London to Bath. For rail information, call ℂ **0845/748-4950** or visit www.nationalrail.co.uk. A limited bus service (no. 49) runs from Swindon to Devizes through Avebury.

3 Bath: Britain's Most Historic Spa Town 👁👁👁

185km (115 miles) W of London; 21km (13 miles) SE of Bristol

In 1702, Queen Anne made the trek from London to the mineral springs of **Bath,** launching a fad that was to make the city the most celebrated spa in England.

The most famous name connected with Bath was the 18th-century dandy Beau Nash, who cut a striking figure as he made his way across the city, with all the plumage of a bird of paradise. This polished arbiter of taste and manners made dueling déclassé. While dispensing (at a price) trinkets to the courtiers and aspirant gentlemen of his day, Beau was carted around in a sedan chair.

The 18th-century architects John Wood the Elder and his son provided a proper backdrop for Nash's considerable social talents. These architects designed a city of stone from the nearby hills, a feat so substantial and lasting that Bath today is the most harmoniously laid-out city in England. During Georgian and Victorian times, this city, on a bend of the River Avon, attracted leading political and literary figures, such as Dickens, Thackeray, Nelson, and Pitt. Canadians may already know that General Wolfe lived on Trim Street, and Australians may want to visit the house at 19 Bennett St., where their founding father, Admiral Phillip, lived. Even Henry Fielding came this way, observing in *Tom Jones* that the ladies of Bath "endeavor to appear as ugly as possible in the morning, in order to set off that beauty which they intend to show you in the evening."

Even before its Queen Anne, Georgian, and Victorian popularity, Bath was known to the Romans as Aquae Sulis. The foreign legions founded the baths here (which you can visit today) to ease rheumatism in their curative mineral springs.

Remarkable restoration and careful planning have ensured that Bath retains its handsome look today. The city suffered devastating destruction from the infamous Baedeker air raids of 1942, when Luftwaffe pilots seemed more intent on bombing historic buildings than on hitting any military targets.

After undergoing major restoration in the postwar era, Bath today has somewhat of a museum look, with the attendant gift shops. Its parks, museums, and architecture continue to draw hordes of visitors, and because of this massive tourist invasion, prices remain high. It's one of the high points of the West Country and a good base for exploring Avebury.

ESSENTIALS

GETTING THERE   Trains leave London's Paddington Station bound for Bath once every half-hour during the day. The trip takes about 1½ hours. For rail information, call ℂ **0845/748-4950** or **visit www.nationalrail.co.uk**.

A **National Express** coach leaves London's Victoria Coach Station every 90 minutes during the day. The trip takes 3½ hours. Coaches also leave Bristol bound for Bath and make the trip in 40 minutes. For schedules and information, call ℂ **0870/580-8080** or visit **www.nationalexpress.com**.

Drive west on the M4 to the junction with the A4, then continue west to Bath.

VISITOR INFORMATION   The **Bath Tourist Information Centre** is at Abbey Chambers, Abbey Church Yard (ℂ **09067/112000** toll call 50p/$1 per minute; www.visitbath.co.uk), next to Bath Abbey. It's open May to September, Monday to Saturday 9:30am to 6pm, Sunday 10am to 4pm; off season, Monday to Saturday 9:30am to 5pm and Sunday 10am to 4pm. It is closed Christmas Day and New Year's Day.

GETTING AROUND   One of the best ways to explore Bath is by bike. Rentals are available at the **Bath & Dundas Canal Company,** Brass Knocker Basin at Monkton Combe (ℂ **01225/722292;** www.bathcanal.com). Daily rentals go for £14 ($28).

SPECIAL EVENTS   Bath's graceful Georgian architecture provides the setting for one of Europe's most prestigious international festivals of music and the arts, the **Bath International Music Festival.** For 15 days in late May and early June each year, the city is filled with more than 1,000 performers. The festival focuses on classical music, jazz, new music, and the contemporary visual arts, with orchestras, soloists, and artists from all over the world. In addition to the main music and art program, the festival offers walks, tours, and talks, plus free street entertainment, a free Festival Club, and opening-night celebrations with fireworks. For information, contact the **Bath Festivals Box Office,** 2 Church St., Abbey Green, Bath BA1 1NL (ℂ **01225/463362;** www.bathmusicfest.org.uk).

WHERE TO STAY
VERY EXPENSIVE

The Bath Priory ✦✦✦   Converted from one of Bath's Georgian houses in 1969, the Priory is situated on .8 hectares (2 acres) of formal and award-winning gardens

Bath

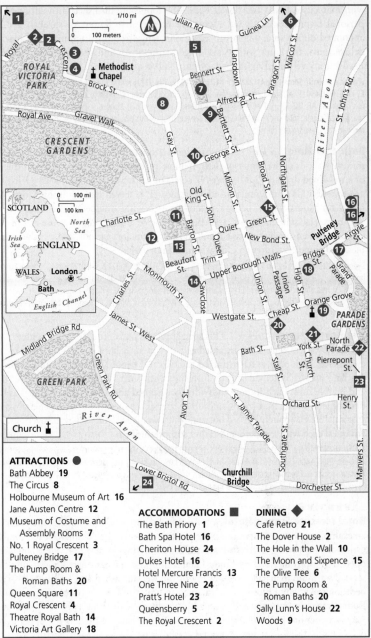

Church ✝

ATTRACTIONS ●
Bath Abbey **19**
The Circus **8**
Holbourne Museum of Art **16**
Jane Austen Centre **12**
Museum of Costume and
 Assembly Rooms **7**
No. 1 Royal Crescent **3**
Pulteney Bridge **17**
The Pump Room &
 Roman Baths **20**
Queen Square **11**
Royal Crescent **4**
Theatre Royal Bath **14**
Victoria Art Gallery **18**

ACCOMMODATIONS ■
The Bath Priory **1**
Bath Spa Hotel **16**
Cheriton House **24**
Dukes Hotel **16**
Hotel Mercure Francis **13**
One Three Nine **24**
Pratt's Hotel **23**
Queensberry **5**
The Royal Crescent **2**

DINING ◆
Café Retro **21**
The Dover House **2**
The Hole in the Wall **10**
The Moon and Sixpence **15**
The Olive Tree **6**
The Pump Room &
 Roman Baths **20**
Sally Lunn's House **22**
Woods **9**

with manicured lawns and flower beds. The rooms are furnished with antiques; our personal favorite is Clivia (all rooms are named after flowers or shrubs), a nicely appointed duplex in a circular turret. Rooms range from medium in size to spacious deluxe units, the latter with views, large sitting areas, and generous dressing areas. Each has a lovely old English bed, often a half-tester.

Weston Rd., Bath, Somerset BA1 2XT. ℭ 01225/331922. Fax 01225/448276. www.thebathpriory.co.uk. 27 units. £245–£360 ($490–$720) standard double; from £425 ($850) suite; from £495 ($990) family room. Rates include English breakfast. AE, DC, MC, V. Free parking. **Amenities:** Restaurant; bar; 2 pools (1 indoor, 1 outdoor); health club; spa; Jacuzzi; sauna; solarium; croquet lawn; room service; babysitting; laundry service; dry cleaning. *In room:* A/C, TV, minibar, hair dryer, trouser press.

Bath Spa Hotel ★★★

This stunning restored 19th-century mansion is a 10-minute walk from the center of Bath. Behind a facade of Bath stone, it lies at the end of a tree-lined drive on 2.8 hectares (7 acres) of landscaped grounds, with a Victorian grotto and a Grecian temple. In its long history, it served many purposes (once as a hostel for nurses) before being returned to its original grandeur. The hotel uses log fireplaces, elaborate moldings, and oak paneling to create country-house charm. The rooms are handsomely furnished, and most of them are spacious. Most beds are doubles, and some even offer an old-fashioned four-poster.

Sydney Rd. (east of the city, off A36), Bath, Somerset BA2 6JF. ℭ 0870/4008222. Fax 01225/444006. www.bathspa-hotel.co.uk. 129 units. £149–£359 ($298–$718) double; £399–£679 ($798–$1,358) suite. Rates include breakfast. AE, MC, V. Free parking. **Amenities:** 2 restaurants; bar; indoor pool; gym; spa; whirlpool; sauna; croquet lawn; salon; room service; laundry service; dry cleaning; valet. *In room:* A/C, TV, Wi-Fi, minibar, coffeemaker, hair dryer, iron, trouser press, safe.

The Royal Crescent ★★★

This special place stands proudly in the center of the famed Royal Crescent. Long regarded as Bath's premier hotel (before the arrival of the even better Bath Spa), it has attracted the rich and famous. The bedrooms, including the Jane Austen Suite, are lavishly furnished with such amenities as four-poster beds and marble tubs. Each room is individually designed and offers such comforts as bottled mineral water, fruit plates, and other special touches. Bedrooms, generally quite spacious, are elaborately decked out with thick wool carpeting, silk wall coverings, and antiques, each with a superb and rather sumptuous bed.

15–16 Royal Crescent, Bath, Somerset BA1 2LS. ℭ 01225/823333. Fax 01225/339401. www.royalcrescent.co.uk. 45 units. £305–£405 ($610–$810) double; from £545 ($1,090) suite. AE, DC, MC, V. Parking £5 ($10). **Amenities:** Restaurant; bar; indoor pool; health club; steam room; sauna; room service; babysitting; laundry service; dry cleaning. *In room:* TV, Wi-Fi, minibar (in some), beverage maker, hair dryer, safe.

EXPENSIVE

Hotel Mercure Francis Hotel ★

An integral part of Queen Square, the Francis is an example of 18th-century taste and style, but we find it too commercial and touristy. Originally consisting of six private residences dating from 1729, the Francis was opened as a private hotel by Emily Francis in 1884 and has offered guests first-class service for more than 100 years. Many of the well-furnished and traditionally styled bedrooms overlook Queen Square, named in honor of George II's consort, Caroline. Rooms range in size from rather small to medium, with either twin or double beds. Accommodations in the older building have more charm, especially the upper floor.

Queen Sq., Bath, Somerset BA1 2HH. ℭ 888/221-4542 in the U.S. and Canada, or 01225/424105. Fax 01225/319715. www.mercure.com. 95 units. £135–£195 ($270–$390) double; £195 ($390) suite. Rates include breakfast. AE, DC, MC, V. Parking £10 ($20). **Amenities:** Restaurant; bar; room service; babysitting; laundry service; dry cleaning. *In room:* A/C in some, TV, Wi-Fi, fridge, hair dryer, iron, trouser press.

Pratt's Hotel ✿ Once the home of Sir Walter Scott, Pratt's dates from the heady days of Beau Nash. Functioning as a hotel since 1791, it has become part of the legend and lore of Bath. Several elegant terraced Georgian town houses were joined together to form this complex with a very traditional British atmosphere. Rooms are individually designed, and as is typical of a converted private home, bedrooms range from small to spacious (the larger ones are on the lower floors). Regardless of their dimensions, the rooms are furnished in a comfortable though utilitarian style.

S. Parade, Bath, Somerset BA2 4AB. ℂ 01225/460441. Fax 01225/448807. www.prattshotel.com. 46 units. £139–£149 ($278–$298) double. Children 13 and younger sharing a room with 2 adults stay free. Rates include English breakfast. AE, DC, MC, V. Parking £12 ($24). **Amenities:** Restaurant; bar; room service; laundry service; dry cleaning. *In room:* TV, coffeemaker, hair dryer, iron, trouser press.

Queensberry ✿ A gem of a hotel, this early Georgian-era town house has been beautifully restored. In our view, it is now among the finest places to stay in a city where the competition for restored town-house hotels is fierce. The Marquis of Queensberry commissioned John Wood the Younger to build this house in 1772. Rooms—often spacious but sometimes medium in size—are delightful, each tastefully decorated with antique furniture and such thoughtful extras as fresh flowers.

Russell St., Bath, Somerset BA1 2QF. ℂ 01225/447928. Fax 01225/446065. www.thequeensberry.co.uk. 29 units. £115–£230 ($230–$460) double; £225–£410 ($450–$820) suite. AE, MC, V. Free parking. **Amenities:** The Olive Tree restaurant (p. 373); bar; room service; babysitting; laundry service; dry cleaning. *In room:* TV, beverage maker, hair dryer.

MODERATE

Apsley House Hotel ✿✿ *Finds* This charming and stately building, just 1.5km (1 mile) west of the center of Bath, dates from 1830, during the reign of William IV. In 1994, new owners refurbished the hotel, filling it with country-house chintzes and a collection of antiques borrowed from the showrooms of an antiques store they own. (Some furniture in the hotel is for sale.) Style and comfort are the keynote here, and all the relatively spacious bedrooms are inviting, appointed with plush beds.

141 Newbridge Hill, Bath, Somerset BA1 3PT. ℂ 01225/336966. Fax 01225/425462. www.apsley-house.co.uk. 11 units. £70–£170 ($140–$340) double; £100–£200 ($200–$400) suite. Rates include English breakfast. AE, MC, V. Free parking. Take A4 to Upper Bristol Rd., fork right at the traffic signals into Newbridge Hill, and turn left at Apsley Rd. **Amenities:** Bar; room service; in-room massage; laundry service; dry cleaning. *In room:* TV, Wi-Fi, coffeemaker, hair dryer, trouser press.

Dukes Hotel A short walk from the heart of Bath, this 1780 building is fresher than ever following a complete restoration. Many of the original Georgian features, including cornices and moldings, have been retained. Rooms, ranging from small to medium, are exceedingly comfortable. All of the bathrooms are small but efficiently arranged and sport tub/shower combinations or just showers. Guests can relax in a refined drawing room or patronize the cozy bar overlooking a garden. The entire setting has been called a "perfect *Masterpiece Theatre* take on Britain," with a fire burning in the grate.

53–54 Great Pulteney St., Bath, Somerset BA2 4DN. ℂ 01225/787960. Fax 01225/787961. www.dukesbath.co.uk. 17 units. £155–£175 ($310–$350) double; £215 ($430) four-poster room; £198 ($396) suite. Rates include continental breakfast. 2-night minimum stay on weekends. AE, MC, V. Bus: 18. **Amenities:** Restaurant; bar; business services; room service; laundry service; dry cleaning. *In room:* TV, minibar (in some), coffeemaker, hair dryer.

Tasburgh House Hotel Set about 1.5km (1 mile) east of Bath center, amid 2.8 hectares (7 acres) of parks and gardens, this spacious Victorian country house dates from 1890. The redbrick structure contains a large glassed-in conservatory, stained-glass windows, and antiques. Bedrooms are tastefully decorated, often with half-tester beds, and most have sweeping panoramic views. Two rooms have four-poster beds. As there is no air-conditioning, windows have to be opened on hot summer nights, which will subject you to a lot of traffic noise. The Avon and Kennet Canal runs along the rear of the property, and guests enjoy summer walks along the adjacent towpath.

Warminster Rd., Bath, Somerset BA2 6SH. ⓒ 01225/425096. www.bathtasburgh.co.uk. 12 units. £120–£140 ($240–$280). Rates include English breakfast. 2-night minimum stay on weekends. MC, V. Free parking. Bus: 4. **Amenities:** Bar; room service; dining room; croquet lawn; laundry service; dry cleaning. *In room:* TV, coffeemaker, hair dryer.

INEXPENSIVE

Badminton Villa   Located about a kilometer (a half-mile) south of the city center, this house dates from 1883. Constructed of honey-colored blocks of Bath stone, it lies on a hillside with sweeping views over the world-famous architecture of Bath. The owners transformed it from a villa in disrepair to one of the most charming small hotels in Bath. Furnishings are an eclectic but unpretentious mix of objects. The small to medium-size bedrooms feature double-glazed windows; there's also a three-tiered garden with patio.

10 Upper Oldfield Park, Bath, Somerset BA2 3JZ. ⓒ 01225/426347. Fax 01225/420393. www.badmintonvilla.co.uk. 4 units. £75–£85 ($150–$170) double; £95–£105 ($190–$210) family room. Rates include English breakfast. MC, V. Free parking. Bus: 14. Children 7 and under not accepted. **Amenities:** Breakfast room. *In room:* TV, Wi-Fi, coffeemaker, hair dryer.

Cheriton House   This elegant 1886 home still offers many of its original architectural adornments, including fireplaces. The owners work hard to make guests comfortable in this home; and the large house is spotlessly clean. Each small to midsize unit is efficiently organized, and there is ongoing refurbishment in the bedrooms. This is really a house for adults, not young children. Only breakfast is served.

9 Upper Oldfield Park, Bath, Somerset BA2 3IX. ⓒ 01225/429862. Fax 01225/428403. www.cheritonhouse.co.uk. 13 units. £72–£110 ($144–$220) double. Rates include English breakfast. MC, V. Free parking. Bus: 14, 14A, or 14B. Children 11 and younger not accepted. **Amenities:** Breakfast room; lounge. *In room:* TV, coffeemaker, hair dryer, iron.

One Three Nine ⚘ *Value*   At the southern side of the city on the A367 road to Exeter (Devon), this Victorian residence from the 1870s is a 10-minute walk from the center of Bath, and minibuses pass by frequently. David and Annie Lanz offer one of the best-value accommodations in the area. The hotel rents elegant and spacious bedrooms, individually furnished and decorated.

139 Wells Rd., Bath, Somerset BA2 3AL. ⓒ 01225/314769. Fax 01225/443079. www.139bath.co.uk. 8 units. £70–£160 ($140–$320) double; £110–£175 ($220–$350) family room. Rates include English breakfast. 2-night minimum stay on weekends. AE, MC, V. Free parking. On approaching Bath, follow A367 Exeter signs but ignore the LIGHT VEHICLES ONLY sign; turn left onto A37/A367 (the Wells Rd.) and follow the black railings uphill (450m/1,500 ft.); when the railings end, turn left into Hayesfield Park, and One Three Nine will be on the right. **Amenities:** Breakfast room; lounge. *In room:* A/C in some, TV, Wi-Fi, coffeemaker, hair dryer.

WHERE TO DINE

The best place for afternoon tea is the **Pump Room & Roman Baths** (p. 376). Another choice, just a 1-minute walk from the Abbey Church and Roman Baths, is **Sally Lunn's House,** 4 N. Parade Passage (ⓒ 01225/461634; www.sallylunns.co.uk), where visitors have been eating for more than 1,700 years. For £6 ($12), you can get the Fantastic Sally Lunn Cream Tea, which includes toasted and buttered scones served with strawberry jam and clotted cream, along with your choice of tea or coffee.

Café Retro, York Street (© **01225/339347**), serves a variety of teas and coffees. You can order a pot of tea for £1.30 ($2.60) or a large cappuccino for £1.90 ($3.80) and add a tea cake for £1.50 ($3).

EXPENSIVE

The Dover House ★★ ENGLISH   The Royal Crescent contains this city's most stunning collection of Georgian architecture. In a discreet hotel, the unmarked door of the Royal Crescent Hotel leads to this on-site restaurant, now hailed as one of the West Country's finest dining choices. With his garden and cozy inside dining room, the chef dazzles the discerning palates of Bath with a series of perfectly prepared and innovative dishes. His contemporary British menu roams the world for inspiration. The setting is romantic, with hand-painted wall coverings and distinctive pottery from Dartington. Through elegant French windows, tables overlook the private gardens. Sterling craftsmanship marks a menu that includes roast cod cheeks with Iberico ham, loin of monkfish with crab linguine, or wild sea bass with a smoked eel tortellini. You might finish with one of the lush desserts such as a hazelnut chocolate teardrop autumn truffle ice cream with Marsala syrup.

15–16 Royal Crescent. © **01225/823333.** Reservations required. Lunch main courses £7.50–£14 ($15–$28); 2-course fixed-price dinner £45 ($90), 3 courses £55 ($110). AE, DC, MC, V. Daily noon–2pm and 7–9:30pm (until 10:30pm Sat).

The Moody Goose ★★★ ENGLISH   For some of the finest food in greater Bath, you have to go outside the center to Midsomer Norton. The kitchen has an absolute passion for fresh ingredients and food cooked to order, and the chefs believe in using produce grown as near home as possible, though the Angus beef comes in from Scotland and the fresh fish from the coasts of Cornwall and Devon. Natural flavors are appreciated here and not smothered in sauces. Even the breads, ice creams, and petits fours are homemade. The kitchen team is expert at chargrilling.

Some of the best-tasting starters include crab salad with tarragon mayonnaise and tomato sorbet, or else a terrine of wood pigeon. Chicken and braised chicory with a raspberry vinaigrette is yet another appetizer. Main courses that we highly recommend include roast quail with spinach, ricotta cake, and a sage cream sauce, or else roast filet of brill with caviar butter and a sweet-potato fondant.

In the Old Priory Hotel, Church Sq., Midsomer Norton, outside Bath. © **01761/416784.** www.moodygoose.co.uk. Reservations required. Main courses £19–£21 ($38–$42); 2-course fixed-price lunch £15 ($30), 3 courses £20 ($40); table d'hôte dinner menu £25 ($50). MC, V. Mon–Sat noon–1:30pm and 7–9:30pm.

The Olive Tree ★ MODERN ENGLISH/MEDITERRANEAN   This is one of the most sophisticated little restaurants in Bath. Head Chef Marc Salmon uses the best local produce, with an emphasis on freshness. The menu is changed to reflect the season, with game and fish being the specialties. You might begin with a tomato tart with goat-cheese fritters or a galatine of wood pigeon, duck, and rainbow chard set off with a spiced gooseberry chutney. You can then proceed to such good-tasting mains as roast rum of West Country lamb with sweetbreads or Aberdeen Angus rib-eye steak with a tarragon gnocchi, or perhaps roast loin of venison with beet in a port-wine sauce.

In the Queensberry Hotel, Russel St. © **01225/447928.** Reservations highly recommended. Main courses £16–£22 ($32–$44). AE, MC, V. Mon–Sat noon–2pm and 7–10pm; Sun noon–2pm and 7–9:30pm.

MODERATE

The Hole in the Wall ★ MODERN ENGLISH/FRENCH   This much-renovated Georgian town house once was hailed as the best restaurant in the West Country.

Because of increased competition, it no longer enjoys such a lofty position, but the food is still good. Menu choices change frequently, according to the inspiration of the chef and the availability of ingredients. Everything is made on-site and from scratch. Start with such choices as steamed River Exe mussels in sweet chili jam or locally kiln-smoked chicken on a seasonal salad bed. From here, you can order such well-crafted mains as a roast pumpkin and sage risotto, or grilled filet of line-caught sea bass with a shallot-and-balsamic dressing. A whole roast partridge is served on savoy cabbage with bread sauce.

16 George St. ⓒ 01225/425242. Reservations recommended for weekdays and required Sat. Main courses £11–£18 ($22–$36); 2-course lunch £10 ($20), 3 courses £14 ($28). MC, V. Daily 11am–2:30pm and 5–10pm.

The Moon and Sixpence INTERNATIONAL   Occupying a stone structure east of Queen Square, the Moon and Sixpence is one of the leading restaurants and wine bars of Bath, although the food here isn't quite as good as that served at more acclaimed choices, including the Hole in the Wall (see above). At lunch, a large cold buffet with a selection of hot dishes is featured in the wine bar section. In the upstairs restaurant overlooking the bar, full service is offered. Main courses may include filet of lamb with caramelized garlic or roast breast of duck with Chinese vegetables. Look for the daily specials on the Continental menu.

6A Broad St. ⓒ 01225/460962. Reservations recommended. Main courses £14–£20 ($28–$40). AE, MC, V. Mon–Sat noon–2:30pm and 5:30–10:30pm; Sun noon–2:45pm and 6–10:30pm.

Woods MODERN ENGLISH/FRENCH/ASIAN   Named after John Wood the Younger, architect of Bath's famous Assembly Room, which lies across the street, this restaurant is run by horse-racing enthusiast David Price and his French-born wife, Claude. A fixed-price menu is printed on paper, whereas the seasonal array of à la carte items is chalked onto a frequently changing blackboard. Good bets include the slow-roasted belly of pork with port-braised cabbage and cinnamon sauce, or else filet of cod with a white-wine, cream, and coriander sauce.

9–13 Alfred St. ⓒ 01225/314812. Reservations recommended. Main courses £12–£20 ($24–$40); 2-course fixed-price lunch £14 ($28), dinner £19 ($38). MC, V. Mon–Sat noon–2:30pm and 6–10:30pm; Sun noon–2pm.

SEEING THE SIGHTS

Stroll around to see some of the buildings, crescents, and squares in town. John Wood the Elder (1704–54) laid out many of the most famous streets and buildings of Bath, including **North and South Parades** and **Queen Square.** His masterpiece is the **Circus** 𝕲𝕲𝕲, built on Barton Fields outside the old city walls. He showed how a row of town houses could be made to look palatial. Fellow architects have praised his "uniform facades and rhythmic proportions." Also of interest is the shop-lined **Pulteney Bridge,** designed by Robert Adam and often compared to the Ponte Vecchio of Florence.

The younger John Wood designed the **Royal Crescent** 𝕲𝕲𝕲, an elegant half-moon row of town houses (copied by Astor architects for their colonnade in New York City in the 1830s). At **No. 1 Royal Crescent** (ⓒ 01225/428126), the interior has been redecorated and furnished by the Bath Preservation Trust to look as it might have toward the end of the 18th century. The house lies at one end of Bath's most magnificent crescents, west of the Circus. Admission is £5 ($10) for adults, £4 ($8) for students and seniors, and £2.50 ($5) for children aged 5 to 16; a family ticket is £12 ($24). The house is open from mid-March to October Tuesday to Sunday 10:30am to 5pm, and November Tuesday to Sunday from 10:30am to 4pm (last admission 30 min. before closing); it is closed Good Friday and December to mid-February.

Free 1¾-hour walking tours are conducted throughout the year by the **Mayor's Honorary Society** (© **01225/477411**). Tours depart from outside the Pump Room in the Abbey churchyard (look for the WALKING TOURS sign) Sunday to Friday at 10:30am and 2pm, Saturday at 10:30am; May to September, another tour is added on Tuesday, Friday, and Saturday at 7pm.

The **Jane Austen Centre**, 40 Gay St. (© **01225/443000;** www.janeausten.co.uk), is located in a Georgian town house on an elegant street where Miss Austen once lived. Exhibits and a video convey a sense of what life was like in Bath during the Regency period. The center is open mid-February to October daily from 10am to 5:30pm, and November to mid-February Sunday to Friday 11am to 4:30pm, Saturday 10am to 5:30pm. Admission is £6.50 ($13) for adults, £4.95 ($9.90) students and seniors, £3.50 ($7) children, and £18 ($36) family ticket.

The American Museum 🏛🏛 Some 4km (2½ miles) outside Bath, get an idea of what life was like in America prior to the mid-1800s. The first American museum established outside the U.S., it sits proudly on extensive grounds high above the Somerset Valley. Among the authentic exhibits shipped over from the States are a New Mexico room, a Conestoga wagon, the dining room of a New York town house of the early 19th century, and (on the grounds) a copy of Washington's flower garden at Mount Vernon. Throughout the summer, the museum hosts various special events, from displays of Native American dancing to very realistic reenactments of the Civil War.

Claverton Manor, Bathwick Hill. © 01225/460503. www.americanmuseum.org. Admission £7.50 ($15) adults, £6.50 ($13) students and seniors, £4 ($8) children 5–16, £20 ($40) family ticket, free for 4 and younger. Late Mar to Oct Tues–Sun noon–5:30pm for the museum. Closed Nov to late Mar. Bus: 18.

Bath Abbey 🏛 Built on the site of a much larger Norman cathedral, the present-day abbey is a fine example of the late Perpendicular style. When Queen Elizabeth I came to Bath in 1574, she ordered a national fund to be set up to restore the abbey. The west front is the sculptural embodiment of a Jacob's Ladder dream of a 15th-century bishop. When you go inside and see its many windows, you'll understand why the abbey is called the "Lantern of the West." Note the superb fan vaulting with its scalloped effect. Beau Nash was buried in the nave and is honored by a simple monument totally out of keeping with his flamboyant character. The Bath Abbey Heritage Vaults opened in 1994 on the south side of the abbey. This subterranean exhibition traces the history of Christianity at the abbey site since Saxon times.

Orange Grove. © 01225/422462. www.bathabbey.org. £2.50 ($5) donation requested, free for children 15 and younger. Abbey Apr–Oct Mon–Sat 9am–6pm; Nov–Mar Mon–Sat 9am–4:30pm; year-round Sun 1–2:30pm (Apr–Oct also 4:30–5:30pm). The Heritage Vaults Mon–Sat 10am–3:30pm (last entrance).

Holburne Museum of Art 🏛 *Finds* This has been called, quite accurately, "one of the most perfect small museums of Europe." It was constructed in 1796 as a building in which to entertain guests to Sydney Gardens, the luminaries including Jane Austen. It was converted into a museum at the turn of the 20th century to display a collection of Sir William Holburne's treasures, such as a bronze nude favored by Louis XIV, along with some of the finest Renaissance majolica or earthenware in England. Also on display are works illuminating the glittering society of 18th-century Bath at its pinnacle, including masterpieces by Thomas Gainsborough such as *The Byam Family,* on indefinite loan. Other choice tidbits from this treasure-trove include the lovely portrait of *The Reverend Carter Thelwall and His Family* by Stubbs and such surprising exhibits as a Steinway piano used by Rachmaninoff for rehearsals of his music. The museum is also the temporary venue of traveling exhibits.

Insider's tip: After your visit to the Holburne Museum, walk behind the building to the **Bath Boating Station** along Forester Road (© **01225/312900;** www.bath boating.co.uk). From April to September you can rent punts or canoes to explore the River Avon. It gives you a unique perspective on one of England's most beautiful cities.

Great Pulteney St. © **01225/466669.** www.bath.ac.uk/holburne. Admission £4.50 ($9) adults, £3.50 ($7) students and seniors, free for children. Tues–Sat 10am–5pm; Sun 11am–5pm. Closed mid-Dec to mid-Feb. Bus: 18.

Museum of Costume and Assembly Rooms 👫👫   Operated by the National
Trust and housed in an 18th-century building, the grand **Assembly Rooms** played host to dances, recitals, and tea parties. Damaged in World War II, the elegant rooms have been gloriously restored and look much as they did when Jane Austen and Thomas Gainsborough attended society events here.

Housed in the same building, the **Museum of Costume** sports one of the best collections of fashion and costume in Europe. A fascinating audio tour escorts visitors through the history of fashion—including accessories, lingerie, and shoes—from the 16th century to the present day. Highlights include a 17th-century "silver tissue" dress; an ultrarestricting whalebone corset; an original suit, once owned by Dame Margot Fonteyn, from Christian Dior's legendary "New Look" collection; and the ultrasheer Versace dress made famous—or infamous—by actress Jennifer Lopez. The museum is also famous for its "Dress of the Year" collection, which highlights notable ideas in contemporary style. Some selections have been notably prescient; its choice for the 1987 dress of the year was by then-unknown designer John Galliano. Only 2,000 of the museum's 30,000 items are on display at any one time, but exhibits change frequently and special themed collections are often presented.

Bennett St. © **01225/477789.** www.museumofcostume.co.uk. Admission (includes audio tour) £6.75 ($14) adults, £5.75 ($12) students and seniors, £4.75 ($9.50) children age 6 and older, £19 ($38) family ticket. Nov–Feb daily 11am–4pm; Mar–Oct daily 11am–5pm. Last admission 1 hr. before closing. Closed Dec 25–26.

The Pump Room 👫 & Roman Baths 👫👫   Founded in A.D. 75 by the Romans,
the baths were dedicated to the goddess Sulis Minerva; in their day, they were an engineering feat. Even today, they're among the finest Roman remains in the country, and they are still fed by Britain's most famous hot-spring water. After centuries of decay, the original baths were rediscovered during Queen Victoria's reign. The site of the Temple of Sulis Minerva has been excavated and is now open to view. The museum displays many interesting objects from Victorian and recent digs (look for the head of Minerva).

Coffee, lunch, and tea, usually with music from the Pump Room Trio, can be enjoyed in the 18th-century pump room, overlooking the hot springs. You can also find a drinking fountain with hot mineral water that tastes horrible.

In the Bath Abbey churchyard, Stall St. © **01225/477785.** www.romanbaths.co.uk. Admission £10–£11 ($20–$22) adults, £8.75 ($18) seniors, £6.50 ($13) children, £29 ($58) family ticket. Apr–June and Sept daily 9am–6pm; July–Aug daily 8am–10pm; Oct–Mar Mon–Sat 9:30am–5:30pm.

Theatre Royal Bath   Theatre Royal, located next to the new Seven Dials development, was restored in 1982 and refurbished with plush seats, red carpets, and a

painted proscenium arch and ceiling; it is now the most beautiful theater in Britain. It has 880 seats, with a small pit and grand tiers rising to the upper circle. Despite all the work, Theatre Royal has no company, depending upon touring shows to fill the house during the 8-week theater season each summer. Beneath the theater, reached from the back of the stalls or by a side door, are the theater vaults, where you will find a bar in one with stone walls. The next vault has a restaurant, serving an array of dishes from soup to light à la carte meals.

A studio theater at the rear of the main building opened in 1996. The theater publishes a list of forthcoming events; its repertoire includes West End shows, among other offerings.

Sawclose. *(C)* **01225/448844.** www.theatreroyal.org.uk. Tickets £10–£30 ($20–$60). Box office Mon–Sat 10am–8pm, Sun noon–8pm; shows Mon–Wed at 7:30pm, Thurs–Sat at 8pm, Wed and Sat matinees at 2:30pm.

Victoria Art Gallery   This relatively unknown gallery showcases the area's best collection of British and European art from the 15th century to the present. Most of the works are on display in the sumptuous Victorian Upper Gallery. The collection includes paintings by artists who have lived and worked in the Bath area, including Gainsborough. Singled out for special attention is the art of Walter Richard Sickert (1860–1942) now that he has been "outed" as the real Jack the Ripper in Patricia Cornwell's bestseller, *Portrait of a Killer: Jack the Ripper—Case Closed.* In the two large modern galleries downstairs, special exhibitions are shown. These exhibitions change every 6 to 8 weeks and are likely to feature displays ranging from cartoons to boat sculpture.

Bridge St. *(C)* **01225/477233.** www.victoriagal.org.uk. Free admission. Tues–Sat 10am–5pm; Sun 1:30–5pm.

SHOPPING

Bath is loaded with markets and fairs, antiques centers, and small shops, with literally hundreds of opportunities to buy (and ship) anything you want (including the famous spa waters, for sale by the bottle). Prices, however, are comparable to London's.

The whole city is basically one long, slightly undulating shopping area. It's not defined by one high street, as are so many British towns—if you arrive by train, don't be put off by the lack of scenery. Within 2 blocks are several shopping streets. The single best day to visit, if you are a serious shopper intent on hitting the flea markets, is Wednesday.

The **Bartlett Street Antiques Centre,** Bartlett Street, encompasses 20 dealers and 50 showcases displaying furniture, silver, antique jewelry, paintings, toys, military items, and collectibles.

Walcot Reclamation, 108 Walcot St. (*(C)* **01225/444404;** www.walcot.com), is Bath's salvage yard. This sprawling and appealingly dusty storeroom of 19th-century architectural remnants is set .5km (a quarter-mile) northeast of the town center. Its 1,858-sq.-m (20,000-sq.-ft.) warehouse offers pieces from demolished homes, schools, hospitals, and factories throughout south England. Mantelpieces, panels, columns, and architectural ornaments are departmentalized into historical eras. Items range from a complete, dismantled 1937 Georgian library crafted from Honduran mahogany to objects costing around £10 ($20) each. Anything can be shipped by a battery of artisans who are trained in adapting antique fittings for modern homes.

The largest purveyor of antique coins and stamps in Bath, the **Bath Stamp & Coin Shop,** 12–13 Pulteney Bridge (*(C)* **01225/463073**), offers hundreds of odd and unusual numismatics. Part of the inventory is devoted to Roman coins, some of which were unearthed in archaeological excavations at Roman sites near Bath.

Near Bath Abbey, the **Beaux Arts Gallery,** 12–13 York St. (© **01225/464850;** www.beauxartsbath.co.uk), is the largest and most important gallery of contemporary art in Bath, specializing in well-known British artists including Ray Richardson, John Bellany, and Nicola Bealing. Closely linked to the London art scene, the gallery occupies a pair of interconnected, stone-fronted Georgian houses. Its half-dozen showrooms exhibit objects beginning at £30 ($60).

The very upscale **Rossiter's,** 38–41 Broad St. (© **01225/462227**), sells very traditional English tableware and home decor items. They'll ship anywhere in the world. Look especially for the display of Moorcraft ginger jars, vases, and clocks, as well as the Floris perfumes.

BATH AFTER DARK

To gain a very different perspective of Bath, you may want to take the **Bizarre Bath Walking Tour** (© **01225/335124;** www.bizarrebath.co.uk), a 1½-hour improvisational tour of the streets during which the tour guides pull pranks, tell jokes, and behave in a humorously annoying manner toward tourgoers and unsuspecting residents. The tour runs nightly at 8pm from Easter to October, no reservations necessary; just show up, ready for anything, at the Huntsman Inn at North Parade Passage. Cost is £7 ($14) for adults, £5 ($10) for students and children.

After your walk, you may need a drink or want to check out the local club and music scene. At the **Bell,** 103 Walcot St. (© **01225/460426;** www.walcotstreet.com), music ranges from jazz and country to reggae and blues on Monday and Wednesday nights and Sunday at lunch and dinner. On music nights, the band performs in the center of the long, narrow 400-year-old room.

SIDE TRIPS FROM BATH

LACOCK: AN 18TH-CENTURY VILLAGE ✿

From Bath, take the A4 about 19km (12 miles) to the A350, then head south to Lacock, a National Trust village showcasing English architecture from the 13th through the 18th centuries.

Unlike many villages that disappeared or were absorbed into bigger communities, Lacock remained largely unchanged because of a single family, the Talbots, who owned most of it and preferred to keep their traditional village traditional. Turned over to the National Trust in 1944, it's now one of the best-preserved villages in all of England with many 16th-century homes, gardens, and churches. Notable is **St. Cyriac Church,** Church Street, a Perpendicular-style church built by wealthy wool merchants between the 14th and 17th centuries.

Lacock Abbey, High Street (© **01249/730459**), founded in 1232 for Augustinian canonesses, was updated and turned into a private home in the 16th century. It fell victim to Henry VIII's Dissolution, when, upon establishing the Church of England, he seized existing church properties to bolster his own wealth. Admission for all church properties is £8.30 ($17) for adults and £4.10 ($8.20) for children; a family ticket costs £21 ($42). It is open from the end of March to October, Monday and Wednesday to Sunday from 1 to 5:30pm. It is closed Good Friday.

While on the grounds, stop by the medieval barn, home to the **Fox Talbot Museum** (© **01249/730459**). Here, William Henry Fox Talbot carried out his early experiments with photography, making the first known photographic prints in 1833. In his honor, the barn is now a photography museum featuring some of those early prints. Daily hours are March to October 11am to 5:30pm; November to February, it is open Saturday and Sunday only 11am to 4pm. Admission is included in the Lacock Abbey fee (listed above); admission to the museum only is £5.10 ($10) adults, £2.50 ($5) children.

Where to Stay

At the Sign of the Angel 🎯 The rooms at this inn, built in the 14th century, are quiet and split between the main building and a 17th-century garden cottage, whose rooms we prefer because they are more spacious and have more style. Each guest room is distinctly decorated with a host of antiques. One room has a magnificently carved Spanish bed that is said to have belonged to Isambard Kingdom Brunel, the famous railway and canal builder. Some rooms in the main building are standard and rather small, others are more spacious—no. 12, for example, has a four-poster bed, and no. 3 is a generously sized superior room with a very large bed. Bathrooms have adequate shelf space and a tub or shower.

Church St., Lacock, Chippenham, Wiltshire SN15 2LB. ✆ **01249/730230.** Fax 01249/730527. www.lacock.co.uk. 6 units. £105–£155 ($210–$310) double. Rates include English breakfast. AE, MC, V. **Amenities:** Restaurant; room service. *In room:* TV, coffeemaker, hair dryer.

Where to Dine

The George Inn *Kids* ENGLISH Housed in a building that has been used as a pub since 1361, the George Inn has been modernized since then but maintains many of its vestiges from the past—uneven floors, a large open fireplace with a dog-wheel once used for spit roasting—and has an extensive garden used as a dining area in the summer, as well as a children's playground. About 30 daily specials are chalked onto a blackboard in addition to a regular menu of fish, meat, and vegetarian dishes. Two of the best desserts—admittedly old-fashioned—are bread-and-butter pudding and sticky toffee pudding.

4 West St. ✆ **01249/730263.** Main courses £6–£13 ($12–$26). AE, MC, V. Mon–Fri noon–2pm and 6–9pm; Sat–Sun noon–9pm.

CASTLE COMBE 🎯🎯

This village was once voted England's prettiest village. The financially disastrous *Dr. Doolittle* was filmed here in 1967, and the 15th-century **Upper Manor House,** used as Rex Harrison's residence in the movie, is its most famous site. Consisting of one street lined with cottages (known simply as "the Street"), it is the quintessential West Country village, easily explored in its entirety during a morning or afternoon, before moving on to your next destination. Located 16km (10 miles) northeast of Bath, Castle Combe is reached by taking the A46 north 9.5km (6 miles) to the A420, then heading east to Ford, following the signs north to Castle Combe. From Lacock, take the A350 north to Chippenham, then get on the A420 west and follow the signs.

Where to Stay & Dine

Manor House Hotel & Golf Club 🎯 The house and accompanying estate date from the 14th century and once served as the baronial seat in Castle Combe. The main building and its accompanying cottages sit regally on 19 hectares (47 acres) of gardens with wooded trails and a lake. The trout-stocked River Bybrook flows south of the manor, and fishing is permitted. Bedrooms come in a variety of sizes, and some have four-poster beds. You can stay either in the main house or in a row of original stone cottages on the grounds. The latter have been upgraded to meet the standards of the main house. Eight rooms are large enough for families.

Castle Combe, Wiltshire SN14 7JW. © **01249/782206.** Fax 01249/782159. www.exclusivehotels.co.uk. 48 units. £235 ($470) double; £295–£800 ($590–$1,600) suite. Rates include English breakfast. AE, MC, V. Free parking. **Amenities:** Restaurant; 2 bars; pool; 18-hole golf course; tennis court; gym; sauna; croquet lawn; room service; babysitting; laundry service; dry cleaning. In room: TV, coffeemaker, hair dryer.

4 Bristol ★★

193km (120 miles) W of London; 21km (13 miles) NW of Bath

Bristol, the largest city in the West Country, is just across the Bristol Channel from Wales and is a good place to base yourself for touring western Britain. This historic inland port is linked to the sea by 11km (7 miles) of the navigable River Avon. Bristol has long been rich in seafaring traditions and has many links with the early colonization of America. In fact, some claim that the new continent was named after a Bristol town clerk, Richard Ameryke. In 1497, John Cabot sailed from Bristol and pioneered the discovery of the northern half of the New World.

Although Bath is much more famous as a tourist mecca, Bristol does have some attractions, such as a colorful harbor life, that makes it at least a good overnight stop in your exploration of the West Country.

ESSENTIALS

GETTING THERE   Bristol Airport (© **0871/334-4444**) is conveniently situated beside the main A38 road, a little more than 11km (7 miles) from the city center.

Rail services to and from the area are among the fastest and most efficient in Britain. **First Great Western** runs very frequent services from London's Paddington Station to each of Bristol's two main stations: Temple Meads in the center of Bristol and Parkway on the city's northern outskirts. The trip takes 1¼ hours. For rail information, call © **0845/000125** or visit **www.firstgreatwestern.co.uk**.

National Express buses depart every hour during the day from London's Victoria Coach Station, making the trip in 2½ hours. For more information and schedules, call © **0870/580-8080** or visit **www.nationalexpress.com**.

If you're driving, head west from London on the M4.

VISITOR INFORMATION   The **Tourist Information Centre** is at the Annex, Wildscreen Walk, Harbourside, Bristol (© **0906/711-2191**; www.visitbristol.co.uk). Hours are Monday to Friday 10am to 5pm, Saturday and Sunday 10am to 6pm.

WHERE TO STAY
EXPENSIVE
Bristol Marriott City Centre ★   In the heart of town at the edge of Castle Park, this modern 11-story hotel is one of Bristol's tallest buildings, far superior to other chains in amenities, style, and comfort. Many improvements have been undertaken since it was a rather ordinary Holiday Inn, and it attracts business travelers as well as foreign tourists. The comfortable rooms are conservatively modern.

2 Lower Castle St., Bristol BS1 3AD. © **800/228-9290** in the U.S. and Canada, or 01179/294281. Fax 01179/276377. www.marriott.com. 301 units. £114–£180 ($228–$360) double. AE, DC, MC, V. Parking £7.50 ($15). Bus: 9. **Amenities:** 2 restaurants; bar; indoor pool; gym; spa; whirlpool; sauna; steam room; room service; babysitting; laundry service; dry cleaning. In room: A/C, TV, Wi-Fi, minibar, coffeemaker, hair dryer, iron, trouser press, safe.

Hotel du Vin ★ Finds   This stylish Anglo-French run hotel is one of Bristol's best examples of recycling. Six 18th-century sugar-refining warehouses, lying in the vicinity of the docklands, were taken over and sensitively restored into this inviting small hotel. Today, you'll find a series of "loft-style" bedrooms with superb beds covered in soft Egyptian linen. Each of the accommodations comes with a well-maintained and state-of-the-art bathroom with what management prefers to call "serious" showers (read: large). As much as possible, the original industrial features of the warehouses have been retained for dramatic effect. Even if you're not a guest, you may want to visit for a drink in the Sugar Bar or a first-class meal in the contemporary French restaurant. For such a small hotel, the wine cellar here is most impressive, and specially staged wine tastings and dinners are frequent events throughout the year.

Narrow Lewin Mead, Bristol, Somerset BS1 2NU. (© **01179/255577.** Fax 01179/251199. www.hotelduvin.com. 40 units. £145–£200 ($290–$400) double; £215–£370 ($430–$740) suite. AE, DC, MC, V. Parking £13 ($25). **Amenities:** Restaurant; 2 bars; billiard room; room service; laundry service; dry cleaning; library. *In room:* A/C, TV, Wi-Fi, minibar, coffeemaker, hair dryer, trouser press, safe.

Mercure Brigstow Hotel ⭐ In a prime position on the Welshback in Bristol, this contemporary hotel opens onto panoramic riverside frontage in the heart of this ancient port. Granted four stars by the government, it offers some of the city's finest bedrooms, most of which are spacious with all the extras provided. Even the bathrooms have plasma TVs so you can bathe and watch your shows. Ellipse, the on-site restaurant, serves fresh and well-prepared food in light and airy surroundings with views of the river.

Welshback, Bristol BS1 4SF. (© **0117/9291030.** Fax 0117/9292030. www.mercure.com. 116 rooms. £149–£165 ($298–$330) double. AE, DC, MC, V. Parking £13 ($26). **Amenities:** Restaurant; bar; use of nearby gym; business center; room service; laundry service; dry cleaning. *In room:* A/C, TV, Wi-Fi, minibar, beverage maker, hair dryer, trouser press, safe.

Ramada Plaza Bristol ⭐ Situated conveniently amid the commercial bustle of the town center, this modern six-story hotel offers a good, safe haven for the night (though some readers have commented that the pealing bells of St. Mary Redcliffe next door have awakened them early in the morning). Bedrooms, furnished in a bland international style, range from small to medium and include mostly double beds.

Redcliffe Way, Bristol, Somerset BS1 6NJ. (© **0844/815-9100.** Fax 01179/255054. www.ramadainternational.com. 201 units. £119–£140 ($238–$280) double; £160–£190 ($320–$380) suite. AE, DC, MC, V. Parking £5 ($10). **Amenities:** Restaurant; bar; indoor pool; health club; Jacuzzi; sauna; steam room; business center; room service; babysitting; laundry service; dry cleaning. *In room:* A/C, TV, high-speed Internet, coffeemaker, hair dryer, iron, trouser press.

INEXPENSIVE

Downlands House This well-appointed Victorian home is on a tree-lined road on the periphery of the Durdham Downs. About 3km (2 miles) from the center of Bristol, it lies on a bus route in a residential suburb. The recently redecorated bedrooms have private, shower-only bathrooms or adequate hallway facilities. It's basic but inviting.

33 Henleaze Gardens, Henleaze, Bristol, Somerset BS9 4HH. (©/fax **01179/621639.** www.downlandshouse.com. 10 units, 7 with bathroom. £55–£60 ($110–$120) double without bathroom; £68–£75 ($136–$150) double with bathroom. Rates include English breakfast. AE, MC, V. Free parking. Bus: 1, 2, 3, or 501. **Amenities:** Breakfast room. *In room:* TV, Wi-Fi, coffeemaker, hair dryer.

Tyndall's Park Hotel This elegant early Victorian house retains many of its original features, including a marble fireplace and ornate plasterwork. Note the fine staircase in the imposing entrance hall. The hotel still observes the old traditions of personal service. There is a Victorian aura in the bedrooms, which range from small to medium, and each is clean and comfortable.

4 Tyndall's Park Rd., Clifton, Bristol BS8 1PG. © 01179/735407. Fax 01179/237965. www.tyndallsparkhotel.co.uk. 15 units. £58 ($116) double. Rates include English breakfast. MC, V. Bus: 8 or 9. **Amenities:** Breakfast room. *In room:* TV, coffeemaker, hair dryer.

WHERE TO DINE

Bell's Diner ⚘ *(Finds* MEDITERRANEAN   This little hideaway serves savory cuisine from the Mediterranean and does so exceedingly well. The daily offerings change frequently, based on the day's shopping for market-fresh ingredients, but what you get is usually well prepared, fresh, and flavorful. In what used to be "the little shop on the corner," this bistro has been installed with tables sitting on hardwood floors, the walls adorned with cityscapes. Most of the recipes are imaginative and sometimes surprising, as in the case of the slow-braised pork belly served with foie gras. The perfectly roasted breast of chicken comes with a delightful accompaniment of black-truffle potatoes, and the grilled tuna is still moist—never dried out—and served with fresh rocket leaves and a tangy tomato confit.

1 York Rd., Montpelier. © 01179/240357. Reservations recommended. Main courses £15–£20 ($30–$40); 8-course fixed-price menu Mon–Thurs £45 ($90). AE, MC, V. Tues–Fri noon–3pm; Mon–Sat 7–10:30pm. Closed 1 week in Dec. Follow A38 north (signposted STOKES CROFT), turning right on Ashley Rd. and taking the next left at Picton St. Picton leads into York Rd.

Byzantium ⚘ ENGLISH/FRENCH   At this restaurant, the decor alone is stunning, with stone, crystal, wood, marble, and glass combined to create an unusual, even offbeat restaurant with rich colors, informal corners, and subtle lighting, plus the sweep of a marble staircase. The cuisine almost could be called fusion though it's mainly modern French. The venue is on two floors, with a cavernous bar/lounge downstairs with padded seats where entertainment is provided—from tango and belly dancing to magicians. The restaurant's "Food Lantern" is unique in Bristol, consisting of a selection of elaborate nibbles served on a two-tier iron slate. For a main course, you are faced with such selections as pork tenderloin roasted with lemon sage, seared filet of sea bass with a white-grape sauce, or filet of lamb in phyllo pastry with a light basil mousse.

2 Portwall Lane. © 01179/221883. www.byzantium.co.uk. Reservations required. Main courses £14–£20 ($28–$40); 3-course dinner £25 ($50). DC, MC, V. Mon–Sat 6:30pm–2am.

EXPLORING THE TOWN

The **Bristol Harbour** ⚘, its rough-and-ready days of the 19th century a memory of the past, is rapidly being recycled as it moves deeper into the 21st century. Beautiful architecture, wonderful hotels, excellent restaurants, and good shopping await visitors today along with bistros, wine bars, and art centers. The harborfront's two major attractions, if you need a goal for your sightseeing, are **At-Bristol** and the **SS *Great Britain*** (see below).

Guided **walking tours** are conducted each Saturday at 11am April to September and last about 2 hours. Walking tours cost £3.50 ($7) per person and depart from the Beetle Statue at Anchor Square. Consult the Tourist Information Centre (see above) for more information.

Clifton Suspension Bridge, spanning the beautiful Avon Gorge, has become the symbol of the city of Bristol. Originally conceived in 1754, it was completed more than 100 years later, in 1864. The architect, Isambard Kingdom Brunel, died 5 years before its completion. His fellow engineers completed the bridge as a memorial to him.

Bristol Cathedral ⚐ Construction of the cathedral, once an Augustinian abbey, began in the 12th century; the central tower was added in 1466. The chapter house and gatehouse are good examples of late Norman architecture.

In 1539, the abbey was closed, and the incomplete nave was demolished. The building was turned into the Cathedral Church of the Holy and Undivided Trinity in 1542. In 1868, plans were drawn up to complete the nave to its medieval design. The architect, G. E. Street, found the original pillar bases, so the cathedral is much as it would have been when it was still the abbey church.

The eastern end of the cathedral, especially the choir, gives the structure a unique place in the development of British and European architecture. The nave, choir, and aisles are all of the same height, making a large hall. Bristol Cathedral is the major example of a "hall church" in Great Britain and one of the finest anywhere in the world.

College Green. ✆ **01179/264879.** www.bristol-cathedral.co.uk. Free admission; £2.50 ($5) donation requested. Mon–Fri 8am–6pm; Sat 8am–5:30pm; Sun 7:30am–5pm. Bus: 8 or 9.

SS *Great Britain* In Bristol, the world's first iron steamship and luxury liner has been restored to its 1843 appearance. This vessel, which weighs 3,443 tons, was designed by Isambard Kingdom Brunel, a Victorian engineer. Incidentally, in 1831 (at the age of 25), Brunel began the Bristol landmark Clifton Suspension Bridge over the 76m-deep (250-ft.) Somerset Gorge at Clifton (see above).

City Docks, Great Western Dock. ✆ **01179/260680.** www.ssgreatbritain.org. Admission £11 ($22) adults, £8 ($16) seniors, £5.50 ($11) children, £29 ($58) family ticket. Apr–Oct daily 10am–5pm; Nov–Mar daily 10am–3:30pm. Last admission an hour before closing. Bus: 500 (from city center).

St. Mary Redcliffe Church ⚐⚐ The parish church of St. Mary Redcliffe is one of the finest examples of Gothic architecture in England. Queen Elizabeth I, on her visit in 1574, is said to have described it as "the fairest, goodliest, and most famous parish church in England." Thomas Chatterton, the boy poet, called it "the pride of Bristol and the western land." The American Chapel (St. John's Chapel) houses the tomb and armor of Admiral Sir William Penn, father of Pennsylvania's founder.

12 Colston Parade. ✆ **01179/291487.** www.stmaryredcliffe.co.uk. Free admission; donations are welcome. Apr–Oct Mon–Sat 8:30am–5pm; Nov–Mar Mon–Sat 9am–4pm; Sun year-round 8am–7:30pm.

SHOPPING

The biggest shopping complex is **Broadmead,** mainly pedestrianized with branches of all High Street stores, plus cafes and restaurants. Many specialty shops are found at **Clifton Village,** in a Georgian setting where houses are interspaced with parks and gardens. Here you'll find a wide array of shops selling antiques, arts and crafts, and designer clothing. Even if you don't purchase anything, you'll enjoy strolling about the old, tree-shaded streets. Less impressive than Clifton Village, and only if you have the time, is **St. Nicholas Markets,** which opened in 1745. They are still going strong, selling antiques, memorabilia, handcrafted gifts, jewelry, and haberdashery. The **West End** is another major shopping area, taking in Park Street, Queen's Road, and Whiteladies Road. These streets are known for clothing outlets, bookstores, and unusual gift items from around the world, as well as wine bars and restaurants. The best market for antiques is the **Bristol Antique Centre,** at Brunel Rooms, Broad Plain, which is open daily, including Sunday.

BRISTOL AFTER DARK

On a cultural note, **Bristol Old Vic,** King Street (© **01179/877877;** www.bristol-old-vic.co.uk), is the oldest working theater in the country, known for its performances (often Shakespeare) that were first launched in 1766. The theatrical grouping uses different theaters for its shows; some performances are staged at other venues such as the new Vic Studio and the Basement Theatre. Music lovers gravitate to the performances at **St. George's,** Great George Street, off Park Street (© **01179/294929;** www.stgeorgesbristol.co.uk), a converted church from the 1700s. Today instead of gospel you will hear everything from jazz concerts to classical musical performances. At lunch, concerts are a regular feature.

Bath may be more stiff and formal, but Bristol clubs and pubs are more laid-back, drawing more working-class Brits than yuppies. One of the best pubs along King Street is **Trow,** 5 King St. (© **01179/260783**), with its mellow West Country ambience.

Acid jazz and other types of music rain down in **Thelka** (© **01179/293301**), a converted freight steamer moored on the Grove. The other leading venue for jazz is the **Bebop Club** at the Bear, Hotwell Road (© **01179/877796**). The leading comedy club is **Jester's,** 142 Cheltenham Rd. (© **01179/096655;** www.jesterscomedyclub. co.uk). Covers range from £5 to £20 ($10–$40) but can vary depending on the entertainment offered.

5 Wells ✶✶ & the Caves of Mendip ✶

198km (123 miles) SW of London; 34km (21 miles) SW of Bath

To the south of the Mendip Hills, the cathedral town of Wells is a medieval gem. Wells was a vital link in the Saxon kingdom of Wessex—important long before the arrival of William the Conqueror. Once the seat of a bishopric, it was eventually toppled from its ecclesiastical hegemony by the rival city of Bath. But the subsequent loss of prestige has paid off handsomely for Wells today: After experiencing the pinnacle of prestige, it fell into a slumber—and much of its old look was preserved.

Many visitors come only for the afternoon or morning, look at the cathedral, then press on to Bath for the evening. But though it's rather sleepy, Wells's old inns make a tranquil stopover.

ESSENTIALS

GETTING THERE Wells has good bus connections with surrounding towns and cities. Take the train to Bath (see "Bath: Britain's Most Historic Spa Town," earlier in this chapter) and continue the rest of the way by First Bristol bus no. 173. Departures are every hour Monday through Saturday and every 2 hours on Sunday. Bus no. 376 runs between Bristol and Glastonbury every hour daily, with a stop at Wells each way. Call © **01179/553231** or 08456/020156 for schedules and information.

If you're driving, take the M4 west from London, cutting south on the A4 toward Bath and continuing along the A39 into Wells.

VISITOR INFORMATION The **Tourist Information Centre** is at the Town Hall, Market Place (© **01749/672552**), and is open daily November to March from 10am to 4pm and April to October from 9:30am to 5:30pm.

WHERE TO STAY

The Crown ✶ This is one of the oldest and most historic hotels in the area, a tradition for overnighting since medieval times. William Penn was thrown in jail here in

1695. The charge? Preaching without a license. The landmark status building lies at the medieval Market Place in the heart of Wells, overlooking the splendid cathedral. The building still retains much of its 15th-century character, although the bedrooms are completely up-to-date—in fact, furnished with a Nordic contemporary style. For more tradition, ask for one of a quartet of rooms graced with four-posters.

Market Place, Wells, Somerset BA5 2RP. (℃ **01749/673457.** Fax 01749/679792. www.crownatwells.co.uk. 15 units. £90 ($180) double; £110 ($220) suite. AE, MC, V. **Amenities:** Restaurant; pub; babysitting. *In room:* TV, coffeemaker, hair dryer, no phone.

The Swan Hotel ✦   Set behind a stucco facade on one of the town's main streets, this place was originally built in the 15th century as a coaching inn. Today, facing the west front of Wells Cathedral, it is the best of the inns within the town's central core. Rooms vary in style and size; a third of them have four-poster beds. The spacious and elegant public rooms stretch out to the left and right of the entrance. Both ends have a blazing and baronial fireplace and beamed ceilings.

11 Sadler St., Wells, Somerset BA5 2RX. (℃ **800/528-1234** in the U.S. and Canada, or 01749/836300. Fax 01749/836301. www.bhere.co.uk. 50 units. £134–£170 ($268–$340) double. Rates include English breakfast. AE, DC, MC, V. Free parking. **Amenities:** Restaurant; bar; room service; laundry service. *In room:* TV, beverage maker, hair dryer, trouser press.

White Hart   Opposite the cathedral, this is the best-located hotel in Wells. A former coaching inn, it dates from the 15th century. The Swan is more comfortable and remarkable, but the White Hart is an enduring favorite nonetheless. The creaky old bedrooms lie in the main house, or you can stay in more modern surroundings in a converted stable block where horses and coaches from London were housed in olden times. Each bedroom is comfortably and tastefully furnished.

Sadler St., Wells, Somerset BA5 2RR. (℃ **01749/672056.** Fax 01749/671074. www.whitehart-wells.co.uk. 15 units. £99–£110 ($198–$220) double; £119–£130 ($238–$260) triple. Rates include English breakfast. AE, MC, V. Free parking. **Amenities:** Restaurant; bar; room service; laundry service. *In room:* TV, coffeemaker, hair dryer, trouser press.

WHERE TO DINE
The City Arms ENGLISH   The former city jail, 2 blocks from the bus station, is now a pub with an open courtyard furnished with tables, chairs, and umbrellas. In summer it's a mass of flowers. Full meals may include homemade soup of the day followed by fresh salmon, lamb in burgundy sauce, or stuffed quail in Cointreau sauce. From the charcoal grill you can order rump steak or chicken with Stilton cheese, and longtime favorites include beef Wellington or steak-kidney-and-ale pie. Vegetarian dishes are also offered. Upstairs is an Elizabethan timbered restaurant. The food is a notch above the typical pub grub.

69 High St. (℃ **01749/673916.** Reservations recommended. Main courses £7–£17 ($14–$34). AE, MC, V. Daily 9am–10pm (closes at 9pm Sun).

SEEING THE SIGHTS
After a visit to the **Wells Cathedral,** walk along its cloisters to the moat-surrounded **Bishop's Palace.** The Great Hall, built in the 13th century, is in ruins. Finally, the street known as the **Vicars' Close** is one of the most beautifully preserved streets in Europe.

Easily reached by heading west out of Wells, the Caves of Mendip are two exciting natural attractions: the great caves of Cheddar and Wookey Hole (see below).

Cheddar Showcaves & Gorge ★★ A short distance from Bath, Bristol, and Wells is the village of Cheddar, home of cheddar cheese. It lies at the foot of Cheddar Gorge, within which lie the Cheddar Caves, underground caverns with impressive formations. The caves are more than a million years old, including Gough's Cave, with its cathedral-like caverns, and Cox's Cave, with its calcite sculptures and brilliant colors. The Crystal Quest is a dark walk "fantasy adventure" taking you deep underground, and in the Cheddar Gorge Heritage Centre, you'll find a 9,000-year-old skeleton. You can also climb Jacob's Ladder for cliff-top walks and Pavey's Lookout Tower for views over Somerset—on a clear day you may even see Wales.

Adults and children older than 12 years of age can book an "Adventure Caving" expedition for £16 ($32) adults and £13 ($26) children 11 to 17, which includes overalls, helmets, and lamps. Other attractions include local craftspeople at work, ranging from the glass blower to the sweets maker.

Cheddar, Somerset. ✆ 01934/742343. www.cheddarcaves.com. Admission £14 ($28) adults, £9 ($18) children 5–15, £37 ($74) family ticket, free for 4 and younger. July–Aug daily 10am–5:30pm; Oct–June daily 10:30am–5pm. Closed Dec 24–25. From A38 or M5, cut onto A371 to Cheddar.

Wells Cathedral ★★★ Begun in the 12th century, this is a well-preserved example of Early English architecture. The medieval sculpture (six tiers of statues) of its west front is without equal. The western facade was completed in the mid–13th century. The landmark central tower was erected in the 14th century, with the fan vaulting attached later. A unique feature of this cathedral is the so-called **"scissor arch"** ★. An amazing feat of engineering, these inverted arches can be seen at the east end of the nave. The scissor arch of striking beauty was built together with similar arches at the northern and southern sides of the crossing from 1338 to 1348 when the west piers of the crossing tower began to sink. The arches strengthened the top-heavy structure and prevented the central tower from collapsing. It was the master mason, William Joy, who devised this ingenious solution, which has done the job nicely for 6½ centuries.

Much of the stained glass dates from the 14th century. The fan-vaulted Lady Chapel, also from the 14th century, is in the Decorated style. To the north is the vaulted chapter house, built in the 13th century but restored. Look also for a medieval astronomical clock in the north transept.

In the center of town, Chain Gate. ✆ 01749/674483. www.wellscathedral.org.uk. Free admission but donations appreciated: £5.50 ($11) adults, £4 ($8) seniors, £2.50 ($5) students and children. Apr–Sept daily 7am–7pm; Oct–Mar daily 7am–6pm.

Wookey Hole Caves & Paper Mill ★ Just 3km (2 miles) west of Wells, you'll first come upon the source of the Axe River. In the first chamber of the caves, as legend has it, is the Witch of Wookey turned to stone. These caves are believed to have been inhabited by prehistoric people at least 60,000 years ago. A tunnel, opened in 1975, leads to the chambers unknown previously and at one time accessible only to divers.

Leaving the caves, follow a canal path to the mill, where paper has been made by hand since the 17th century. Here, the best-quality handmade paper is made by skilled workers according to the tradition of their ancient craft. You can purchase fine handmade stationery direct from the paper mill at an on-site shop, featuring artists' paper pads, greeting cards (some of which are Celtic), and boxed stationery. Also in the mill are "hands-on vats" (where visitors can try making a sheet of paper), and an Edwardian Penny Pier Arcade where you can exchange new pennies for old ones to play the original machines. Other attractions include the Magical Mirror Maze and an enclosed passage of multiple image mirrors.

Wookey Hole, near Wells. © **01749/672243.** www.wookey.co.uk. 2-hr. tour £13 ($26) adults; £9.50 ($19) seniors, students, and children 14 and younger; £38 ($76) family ticket. Apr–Oct daily 10am–5pm; Nov–Mar daily 10:30am–4pm. Closed Dec 20–27. Follow the signs from the center of Wells for 3km (2 miles). Bus: 172 from Wells.

6 Glastonbury Abbey ★★

219km (136 miles) SW of London; 42km (26 miles) S of Bristol; 9.5km (6 miles) SW of Wells

Glastonbury may be one of the oldest inhabited sites in Britain. Excavations have revealed Iron Age lakeside villages on its periphery (some of the discoveries that were dug up can be seen in a little museum on High St.). After the destruction of its once-great abbey, the town lost prestige; today it is just a market town with a rich history. The ancient gatehouse entry to the abbey is a museum, and its principal exhibit is a scale model of the abbey and its community buildings as they stood in 1539, at the time of the Dissolution.

Where Arthurian myth once held sway, now exists a subculture of mystics, spiritualists, and hippies, all drawn to the kooky legends whirling around the town. Glastonbury is England's New Age center, where Christian spirituality blends with druidic beliefs. The average visitor arrives just to see the ruins and the monuments, but the streets are often filled with people trying to track down Jesus, if not Arthur and Lancelot.

ESSENTIALS

GETTING THERE   Connections are awkward when traveling to Glastonbury by public transportation. No direct train service runs to Glastonbury. You can, however, take a train from London's Paddington Station to Bristol's Temple Meads Train Station (trip time: 1 hr., 40 min.), where you can catch a bus into Glastonbury. Buses run twice an hour from this train station; trip time is 1¼ hours.

One **National Express** bus a day (no. 403) leaves London's Victoria Coach Station at 7pm and arrives in Glastonbury at 10:50pm. For more information and schedules, call © **0870/580-8080** or visit **www.nationalexpress.com.**

If you're driving, take the M4 west from London, then cut south on the A4 via Bath to Glastonbury.

VISITOR INFORMATION   The **Tourist Information Centre** is at the Tribunal, 9 High St. (© **01458/832954;** www.glastonburytic.co.uk). It's open October to March, Sunday to Thursday 10am to 4pm, and Friday and Saturday 10am to 4:30pm; April to September hours are 10am to 5pm Sunday to Thursday, 10am to 5:30pm Friday and Saturday.

WHERE TO STAY

George & Pilgrims ★   One of the few pre-Reformation hostelries still left in England, this inn in the center of town once offered hospitality to Glastonbury pilgrims. Its facade looks like a medieval castle, with stone-mullioned windows with leaded glass. Some rooms were formerly monks' cells; others have four-poster beds, veritable carved monuments of oak. You may be given the Henry VIII Room, from which the king watched the burning of the abbey in 1539. Rooms come in a variety of shapes and sizes, as befits a hotel of this vintage. Some bedrooms have been refurbished.

1 High St., Glastonbury, Somerset BA6 9DP. © **01458/831146.** Fax 01458/832252. www.thegeorgeandpilgrim. co.uk. 14 units. £85–£100 ($170–$200) double. Rates include English breakfast. AE, MC, V. Free parking. **Amenities:** The Brasserie restaurant (see below); bar; room service; laundry service; dry cleaning. In room: TV, coffeemaker, hair dryer, trouser press.

Number 3 Hotel   This small property, adjoining the Glastonbury ruins, is housed in a Georgian structure in which Winston Churchill once resided. The double rooms are all tastefully and individually decorated. The bathrooms are small but well organized with adequate shelf space and tub/shower combinations.

3 Magdalene St., Glastonbury, Somerset BA6 9EW. © **01458/832129.** Fax 01458/834227. www.numberthree.co.uk. 5 units. £110–£120 ($220–$240) double. Rates include continental breakfast. AE, DC, MC, V. Closed Nov–Feb. **Amenities:** Breakfast room; laundry service. In room: TV, coffeemaker.

WHERE TO DINE

The Brasserie ENGLISH/CONTINENTAL   This is a solid, reliable choice in a town not known for its dining. A reasonably priced à la carte menu with the chef's special of the day is posted on blackboards. The food consists of brasserie-style classics such as slow-roasted belly of pork or rack of lamb, and always plenty of fresh fish. The menu changes frequently and the chefs specialize in organic ingredients.

In the George & Pilgrims hotel, 1 High St. © **01458/831146.** Reservations recommended. Main courses £12–£15 ($24–$30). AE, MC, V. Wed–Sun noon–2:30pm and 7–9:30pm.

SEEING THE SIGHTS

Glastonbury Abbey ★★   Though no more than a ruined sanctuary today, Glastonbury Abbey was once one of the wealthiest and most prestigious monasteries in England. It provides Glastonbury's claim to historical greatness, an assertion augmented by legendary links to such figures as Joseph of Arimathea, King Arthur, and Queen Guinevere.

Joseph of Arimathea, a biblical, perhaps mythical figure, is said to have journeyed to what was then the Isle of Avalon with the Holy Grail in his possession. According to tradition, he buried the chalice at the foot of the conical Glastonbury Tor (a high, craggy hill), and a stream of blood burst forth. You can scale this more than 150m-high (500-ft.) hill today, on which rests a 15th-century tower.

Joseph, so it goes, erected a church of wattle in Glastonbury. (The town, in fact, may have had the oldest church in England, as excavations have shown.) And at one point, the saint is said to have leaned against his staff, which was immediately transformed into a fully blossoming tree; a cutting alleged to have survived from the Holy Thorn remains on the grounds—it blooms at Christmas time. Some historians trace this particular story back to Tudor times.

Another famous chapter in the story, popularized by Tennyson in the Victorian era, holds that King Arthur and Queen Guinevere were buried on the abbey grounds. In 1191, the monks dug up the skeletons of two bodies on the south side of the Lady Chapel, said to be those of the king and queen. In 1278, in the presence of Edward I, the bodies were removed and transferred to a black marble tomb in the choir. Both the burial spot and the shrine are marked today.

A large Benedictine Abbey of St. Mary grew out of the early wattle church. St. Dunstan, who was born nearby, was the abbot in the 10th century and later became archbishop of Canterbury. Edmund, Edgar, and Edmund "Ironside," three early English kings, were buried at the abbey.

In 1184, a fire destroyed most of the abbey and its vast treasures. It was eventually rebuilt, after much difficulty, only to be dissolved by Henry VIII. Its last abbot, Richard Whiting, was hanged at Glastonbury Tor. Like the Roman forum, the abbey was used as a stone quarry for years.

Today, you can visit the ruins of the chapel, linked by an Early English "Galilee" to the nave of the abbey. The best-preserved building on the grounds is a 14th-century octagonal Abbot's Kitchen, where oxen were once roasted whole to feed the wealthier pilgrims.

Magdalene St. ℂ 01458/832267. www.glastonburyabbey.com. Admission £4.50 ($9) adults, £4 ($8) students and seniors, £3 ($6) children 5–16, £13 ($26) family ticket. Dec–Jan daily 10am–4:30pm; Feb daily 10am–5pm; Mar daily 9:30am–5:30pm; Apr–May and Sept daily 9:30am–6pm; June–Aug daily 9am–6pm; Oct daily 9:30am–5pm; Nov daily 9:30am–4:30pm.

Somerset Rural Life Museum The history of the Somerset countryside since the early 19th century is chronicled here. Its centerpiece is the abbey barn, built around 1370. The magnificent timbered room, stone tiles, and sculptural details (including the head of Edward III) make it special. Exhibits in a Victorian farmhouse illustrate farming in Somerset during the "horse age" as well as domestic and social life in Victorian times. In summer, you can watch demonstrations of butter making, weaving, basketwork, and many other traditional craft and farming activities that are rapidly disappearing.

Abbey Farm, Chilkwell St. ℂ 01458/831197. www.somerset.gov.uk/museums. Free admission. Apr–Oct Tues–Fri 10am–5pm, Sat–Sun 2–6pm; Nov–Mar Tues–Sat 10am–5pm. Closed New Year's Day, Good Friday, and Dec 25–28.

7 Longleat House ✦ & Stourhead Gardens ✦✦

If you're driving, you can visit both Longleat and Stourhead in 1 busy day. Follow the directions to Longleat given below, then drive 9.5km (6 miles) down the B3092 to Stourton, a village just off the highway, 5km (3 miles) northwest of Mere (A303), to reach Stourhead.

Longleat House and Safari Park ✦ A magnificent Elizabethan house built in the early Renaissance style, Longleat House was owned by the seventh marquess of Bath. On first glimpse, it's romantic enough, but once you've been inside, it's hard not to be dazzled by the lofty rooms and their exquisite paintings and furnishings.

The house is quite grand, but the attractions that have opened around it are a bit of a cheesy tourist trap, although thousands of visitors are fascinated by the extra amusements.

From the Elizabethan Great Hall and the library to the State Rooms and the grand staircase, the house is filled with all manner of beautiful things. The walls of the State Dining Room are adorned with fine tapestries and paintings, whereas the room itself has displays of silver and plate. The library represents the finest private collection in the country. The Victorian kitchens are open, offering a glimpse of life "below the stairs" in a well-ordered country home. Various exhibitions are mounted in the stable yard.

Adjoining Longleat House is **Longleat Safari Park.** The park hosts several species of endangered wild animals, including rhinoceroses and elephants, which are free to roam the surroundings. Here you can walk among giraffes, zebras, camels, and llamas, and view lions and tigers, as well as England's only white tiger, from your car. You can also ride on a safari boat around the park's lake to see gorillas and to feed sea lions. You can see the park by train for a railway adventure or visit the tropical butterfly garden. The park provides plenty of theme-park amusements as well, including an Adventure Castle, *Doctor Who* exhibition, and the world's longest maze, the **Maze of Love.**

Warminster, Wiltshire. ℂ **01985/844400.** www.longleat.co.uk. Admission to Longleat House £10 ($20) adults, £6 ($12) children; Safari Park £11 ($22) adults, £8 ($16) seniors and children; special exhibitions and rides require separate admission tickets; passport tickets for all attractions £22 ($44) adults, £16 ($32) seniors and children 4–14. Longleat House Apr–Oct Mon–Fri 10am–5pm, Sat–Sun 10am–5:30pm; Nov–Mar Sat–Sun 11am–3pm. Park Apr–Oct 31 Mon–Fri 10am–4pm (last admission), Sat–Sun 10am–5pm; weekends only in Mar. From Bath or Salisbury, take the train to Warminster; then take a taxi to Longleat (about 10 min.). Driving from Bath, take A36 south to Warminster; then follow the signposts to Longleat House. From Salisbury, take A36 north to Warminster, following the signposts to Longleat House.

Stourhead ✮✮ In a country of superlative gardens and gardeners, Stourhead is the most celebrated example of 18th-century English landscape gardening. More than that, it's a delightful place to wander—among its trees, flowers, and colorful shrubs are tucked bridges, grottoes, and temples. Although Stourhead is a garden for all seasons, it is at its most idyllic in summer when rhododendrons are in full bloom.

A neoclassical house, Stourhead was built in the 18th century by the Hoare banking family, who created 40 hectares (100 acres) of prime 18th-century landscaped gardens. Henry Hoare II (1705–85), known as "Henry the Magnificent," contributed to the development of the landscape of this estate.

The **Temple of Flora** was the first building in the garden, designed by the architect Henry Flitcroft in 1744. The **Grotto,** constructed in 1748, is lined with tufa, a water-worn limestone deposit. The springs of the Stour flow through the cold bath, where a lead copy of the sleeping Ariadne lies. The **Pantheon** was built in 1753 to house Rysbrack's statues of Hercules and Flora and other classical figures. In 1765, Flitcroft built the **Temple of Apollo,** the route that takes the visitor over the public road via a rockwork bridge constructed in the 1760s. The art-filled house at Stourhead, designed by Colen Campbell, a leader in the neoclassical revival, was built for Henry Hoare I between 1721 and 1725.

Henry Hoare II's 18th-century redbrick folly, **Alfred's Tower,** is another feature at Stourhead. It sits 48m (160 ft.) above the borders of Wiltshire, Somerset, and Dorset and has 221 steps. The **Obelisk** was built between 1839 and 1840 of Bath stone and replaced the original of Chilmark stone constructed by William Privet for Henry Hoare in 1746.

Stourhead Estate Office, Stourton. ℂ **01747/841152.** Mid-Mar to Oct admission for garden and house £11 ($22) adults, £5.50 ($11) children, £26 ($52) family ticket; Nov–Feb garden only £6.60 ($13) adults, £3.60 ($7.20) children, £16 ($32) family ticket. House mid-Mar to Oct Fri–Tues 11:30am–4:30pm (last admission 4pm). Garden year-round daily 9am–7pm. A direct bus from Bath runs only on the 1st Sat of each month. Getting to Stourhead by public transportation is very difficult if you don't have a car. You can take the train from Bath to Frome, a 30-min. trip. From here it's still 16km (10 miles) away. Most visitors without a car take a taxi from Frome to Stourhead.

8 Dunster ✮✮ & Exmoor National Park ✮✮

296km (184 miles) W of London; 5km (3 miles) SE of Minehead

The village of Dunster, in Somerset, lies near the eastern edge of Exmoor National Park. It grew up around the original Dunster Castle, constructed as a fortress for the de Mohun family, whose progenitor came to England with William the Conqueror. The village, about 6.5km (4 miles) from the Cistercian monastery at Cleeve, has an ancient priory church and dovecote, a 17th-century gabled yarn market, and little cobbled streets dotted with whitewashed cottages.

ESSENTIALS

GETTING THERE   The best route by rail is to travel to Minehead via Taunton, which is easily reached on the main London-Penzance line from Paddington Station in London. For rail information, call $©$ **0845/748-4950** or visit **www.nationalrail. co.uk**. From Minehead, a taxi or bus takes you to Dunster.

At Taunton, you can take one of the seven **First Somerset** coaches ($©$ **0845/ 6064446;** www.firstgroup.com) leaving hourly Monday through Saturday, with only one coach on Sunday. Trip time is 1 hour and 10 minutes. Buses (no. 28 or 398) from Minehead stop in Dunster Village at the rate of one per hour.

If driving from London, head west along the M4, cutting south at the junction with the M5 until you reach the junction with the A39, going west to Minehead. Before your final approach to Minehead, cut south to Dunster along the A396.

VISITOR INFORMATION   Dunster doesn't have an official tourist office, but **Exmoor National Park Visitor Centre** is at Dunster Steep ($©$ **01643/821835**), 3km (2 miles) east of Minehead. It's open from Easter to October daily 10am to 5pm, plus limited hours in winter (call ahead).

WHERE TO STAY IN THE AREA

Luttrell Arms 😊😊   A hostelry for weary travelers has been on this site for more than 600 years. Simply the best choice around, this hotel is the outgrowth of a guesthouse the Cistercian abbots at Cleeve had built in the village of Dunster. It was named for the Luttrell lords of the manor, who bought Dunster Castle and the property attached to it in the 14th century. It has, of course, been updated with modern amenities, but from its stone porch to the 15th-century Gothic hall with hammer-beam roof, it still retains a feeling of antiquity. Bedrooms range in size and are attractively decorated in keeping with the hotel's long history; five of them have four-poster beds. Rooms in a section called the "Latches" are cottagelike in style, with tight stairways and narrow corridors. One room is big enough for use by a family.

32–36 High St., Dunster, Somerset TA24 6SG. $©$ **01643/821555.** Fax 01643/821567. www.luttrellarms.co.uk. 28 units. £104–£137 ($208–$274) double. Rates include breakfast. AE, MC, V. Free parking. **Amenities:** Restaurant; bar; room service; babysitting. *In room:* TV, coffeemaker, hair dryer, trouser press.

EXPLORING THE AREA

Dunster Castle 😊😊   Dunster Castle is on a tor from which you can see Bristol Channel. It stands on the site of a Norman castle granted to William de Mohun of Normandy by William the Conqueror shortly after the conquest of England. The 13th-century gateway, built by the de Mohuns, is all that remains of the original fortress. In 1376, the castle and its lands were bought by Lady Elizabeth Luttrell; her family owned it until it was given to the National Trust in 1976, together with 12 hectares (30 acres) of surrounding parkland.

The first castle was largely demolished during the civil war. The present Dunster Castle is a Jacobean house constructed in the lower ward of the original fortifications in 1620, then rebuilt in 1870 to look like a castle. From the terraced walks and gardens, you'll have good views of Exmoor and the Quantock Hills.

On A396 (just off A39). © **01643/821314.** Admission to castle and grounds £7.80 ($16) adults, £4 ($8) children, £19 ($38) family ticket; grounds only £4.30 ($8.60) adults, £2.20 ($4.40) children, £11 ($22) family ticket. Castle Mar–July and Sept–Oct Sat–Wed 11am–4pm; July–Aug Sat–Wed 11am–5pm; closed Nov–Feb. Grounds Mar and Nov–Dec daily 11am–4pm; Apr–Oct daily 10am–5pm; closed Jan–Feb. Bus: 28 or 38 from Minehead.

Exmoor National Park 🏵🏵 Between Somerset and Devon, along the northern coast of England's southwest peninsula, is Exmoor National Park, an unspoiled plateau of lonely moors. One of the smallest but most cherished national parks in Britain, it includes the wooded valleys of the rivers Exe and Barle, the Brendon Hills, a sweeping stretch of rocky coastline, and such sleepy but charming villages as **Culbone, Selworthy, Parracombe,** and **Allerford.** Bisected by a network of heavily eroded channels for brooks and streams, the park is distinctive for lichen-covered trees, gray-green grasses, gorse, and heather. The moors reach their highest point at Dunkery Beacon, 512m (1,707 ft.) above sea level.

Although the park boasts more than 1,127km (700 miles) of walking paths, most visitors stay on the **coastal trail** that winds around the bays and inlets of England's southwestern peninsula or along some of the shorter **riverside trails.** Of all the trails, our favorite is the **Somerset and North Devon Coastal Path** 🏵🏵. It begins in the resort of Minehead in the east and goes along the coast all the way to Bude in the west. Few visitors have time to walk this entire coast, but if you leave Minehead in the morning you will have seen the path's most beautiful scenery by nightfall. For more information, contact the **South West Coast Path Association** at © **01752/896237.**

The park's administrative headquarters is located in a 19th-century workhouse in the village of Dulverton, in Somerset, near the park's southern edge, where you can pick up the "Exmoor Visitor" brochure, listing events, guided walks, and visitor information. A program of walking tours is offered at least five times a week; tours cost from £3 to £5 ($6–$10) per person, depending on the length of the walk. Children 15 and younger and students go for free. Themes include Woodland Walks, Moorland Walks, Bird-Watching Excursions, and Deer Spottings. Most of the tours last from 4 to 6 hours. Wear sturdy shoes and rain gear.

Dulverton, Somerset TA22 9HL. © **01398/323665.** www.exmoor-nationalpark.gov.uk. Free admission. Visitor center daily 10:30am–3pm.

NEARBY SIGHTS
Coleridge Cottage The hamlet of Nether Stowey is on the A39, north of Taunton, across the Quantock Hills to the east of Exmoor. The cottage is at the west end of Nether Stowey on the south side of the A39. Here you can visit the home of Samuel Taylor Coleridge, where he penned "The Rime of the Ancient Mariner." During his 1797-to-1800 sojourn here, he and his friends, William Wordsworth and sister Dorothy, enjoyed exploring the Quantock woods. The parlor and reading room of his National Trust property are open to visitors.

35 Lime St., Nether Stowey, near Bridgwater. © **01278/732662.** Admission £3.90 ($7.80) adults, £1.90 ($3.80) children. Apr–Sept Thurs–Sun 2–5pm. From Minehead, follow A39 east about 48km (30 miles), following the signs to Bridgwater. About 13km (8 miles) from Bridgwater, turn right, following signs to Nether Stowey.

Combe Sydenham Hall 🏵 This hall was the home of Elizabeth Sydenham, wife of Sir Francis Drake, and it stands on the ruins of monastic buildings that were associated with nearby Cleeve Abbey. Here you can see a cannonball that legend says halted the wedding of Lady Elizabeth to a rival suitor in 1585. The gardens include

Lady Elizabeth's Walk, which circles ponds originally laid out when the knight was courting his bride-to-be. The valley ponds fed by spring water are full of rainbow trout (ask about getting fly-fishing lessons). You can also take a woodland walk to Long Meadow, with its host of wildflowers. Also to be seen are a deserted hamlet, whose population reputedly was wiped out by the Black Death, and a historic corn mill. In the hall's tearoom, smoked trout and pâté are produced on oak chips, as in days of yore, and there's a shop and working bakery.

Monksilver. ℂ 01984/656284. Admission £6 ($12) adults, £3 ($6) children. Country park Easter–Sept Sun–Fri 9am–5pm. Courtroom and gardens May–Sept Mon and Wed–Thurs 1:30pm guided tours only. From Dunster, drive on A39, following signs pointing to Watchet and/or Bridgwater. On the right, you'll see a minor zoo, Tropiquaria, at which you turn right and follow the signs pointing to Combe Sydenham.

11

Devon: Red Cliffs, Moors & Plymouth Pilgrims

The great patchwork-quilt area of southwest England, part of the "West Countree," abounds in cliff-side farms, rolling hills, foreboding moors, semitropical plants, and fishing villages that provide some of the finest scenery in England. You can pony trek across moor and woodland, past streams and sheep-dotted fields; or you can soak up atmosphere and ale at a local pub. For more details on how this is accomplished, see "Exploring the Moors" (p. 406).

The British approach **Devon** with the same kind of excitement normally reserved for hopping over to the Continent. Especially along the coastline, the names of the seaports, villages, and resorts are synonymous with holidays in the sun: Torquay, Clovelly, and Lynton-Lynmouth. Devon is a land of jagged coasts—the red cliffs in the south face the English Channel. In South Devon, the coast from which Drake and Raleigh set sail, tranquillity prevails; and on the bay-studded coastline of North Devon, pirates and smugglers found haven.

Almost every village is geared to accommodate visitors. But many small towns and fishing villages don't allow cars; these towns have parking areas on the outskirts, with a long walk to reach the center of the harbor area. From mid-July to mid-September, the most popular villages are quite crowded, so make reservations for a place to stay well in advance.

Along the south coast, the best bases from which to explore the region are **Exeter, Plymouth,** and **Torquay.** Along the north coast, we suggest **Lynton-Lynmouth.** The area's most charming village (with very limited accommodations) is **Clovelly.** The greatest natural spectacle is **Dartmoor National Park,** northeast of Plymouth, a landscape of gorges and moors filled with gorse and purple heather—home of the Dartmoor pony.

If you're taking the bus around North Devon, First Devon offers an unlimited-use ticket for specific areas. Rates are £3.60 ($7.20) adults, £3 ($6) children for 1 day. You can plan your journeys from the maps and timetables available at any **First Devon and Cornwall** office when you purchase your ticket (© **0870/6082608;** www.firstgroup.com). For information about other tours, contact **Stagecoach Devon Ltd.,** Paris Street, Exeter, Devon EX1 2JP (© **01392/427711;** www.stagecoach.bus.com). This bus line covers a wider area of Devon, charging £6 ($12) for adults and £4 ($8) for children.

1 Exeter ★★

324km (201 miles) SW of London; 74km (46 miles) NE of Plymouth

Exeter was a Roman city founded in the 1st century A.D. on the banks of the River Exe. Two centuries later it was encircled by a mighty stone wall, traces of which remain

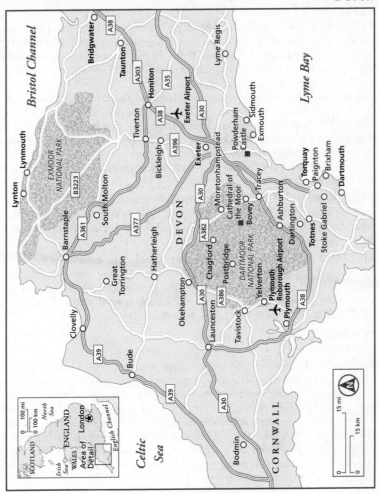

today. Conquerors and would-be conquerors, especially Vikings, stormed the fortress in later centuries; none was more notable than William the Conqueror, who brought Exeter to its knees on short notice.

Under the Tudors, the city grew and prospered. Sir Walter Raleigh and Sir Francis Drake were just two of the striking figures who strolled through Exeter's streets. In May 1942, the Germans bombed Exeter, destroying many of its architectural treasures. The town was rebuilt, but the new, impersonal-looking shops and offices can't replace the Georgian crescents and the black-and-white-timbered buildings with their plastered walls. Fortunately, much was spared, and Exeter still has its Gothic cathedral, a renowned university, some museums, and several historic houses.

Exeter is a good base for exploring both Dartmoor and Exmoor national parks, two of the finest England has to offer. It's also a good place to spend a day, with a lot to do in what's left of the city's old core.

ESSENTIALS

GETTING THERE   Trains from London's Paddington Station depart every hour during the day. The trip takes 2½ hours. For rail information, call © **0845/7000125** or visit **www.firstgreatwestern.co.uk**. Trains also run every 20 minutes during the day between Exeter and Plymouth; the trip takes 1 hour. Trains often arrive at Exeter St. David's Station at St. David's Hill.

A **National Express** coach departs from London's Victoria Coach Station every 2 hours during the day; the trip takes 4½ hours. You can also take Stagecoach bus no. X38 or 39 between Plymouth and Exeter. During the day, two coaches depart per hour for the 1-hour trip. For information and schedules, call © **0870/580-8080** or visit **www.nationalexpress.com**.

If you're driving from London, take the M4 west, cutting south to Exeter on the M5 (junction near Bristol).

VISITOR INFORMATION   The **Tourist Information Centre** is at the Civic Centre, Paris Street (© **01392/265700;** fax 01392/265260). It's open from September to June Monday to Saturday 9am to 5pm, and in July and August Monday to Saturday 9am to 5pm and Sunday 10am to 4pm.

SPECIAL EVENTS   A classical music lover's dream, the **Exeter Festival,** usually held the first 2 weeks in July, includes more than 150 events, ranging from concerts and opera to lectures. Festival dates and offerings vary from year to year, and more information is available by contacting the **Exeter Festival Office,** Civic Center (© **01392/265198;** www.exeter.gov.uk/festival).

WHERE TO STAY

EXPENSIVE

Buckerell Lodge Hotel   This country house originated in the 12th century, but it has been altered and changed beyond recognition over the years. The latest refurbishment occurred in 2007 when the rooms were painted in neutral tones of mauve, taupe, and cream. The exterior is a symmetrical and severely dignified building with a Regency feel. Often hosting business travelers, it's also a tourist favorite, especially in summer. The bedrooms, in a range of styles and sizes, are well decorated and nicely equipped. The best rooms are the executive accommodations in the main house, though most bedrooms are in a more sterile modern addition. Two units are large enough to accommodate families.

Topsham Rd., Exeter, Devon EX2 4SQ. © **01392/221111.** Fax 01392/424333. www.activehotels.com. 54 units. £129–£165 ($258–$330) double. AE, DC, MC, V. Free parking. Bus: S, T, or R. Take B3182 1.5km (1 mile) southeast, off Junction 30 of M5. **Amenities:** Restaurant; bar; room service; laundry service. *In room:* TV, Wi-Fi, coffeemaker, hair dryer, iron, trouser press.

Royal Clarence/ABode Exeter Hotel ⋆ *Kids*   Just a 2-minute walk from the rail station, this hotel offers far more tradition and style than the sometimes better-rated and more recently built Southgate at Southernhay East, or the Thistle on Queen Street (see below). It dates from 1769 and escaped the Nazi Blitz. Just a step away from the cathedral, it offers individually furnished rooms in categories classified as comfortable, desirable, enviable, and fabulous. Five rooms are large enough for families; some rooms have four-poster beds.

A great two-star Michelin chef (Michael Caines) and a top-notch hotelier of south England (Andrew Brownsword) have joined in partnership to run this hotel. A chic little nook, the Moët et Chandon Champagne & Cocktail Bar, has been added.

Honiton: The World of Antique Lace

In Honiton, 26km (16 miles) northwest of Exeter, lace has been made since 1560, and many of its connoisseurs hail it as the world's highest-quality lace. Much in demand in the 17th and 18th centuries by rich families, the cottage industry is still flourishing at the **Honiton Lace Shop** ✹✹, 44 High St. (© **01404/ 42416**). The shop sells and displays antique lace from the 16th to the early 20th centuries. The outlet also sells lace-making equipment for both beginners and experienced lace makers. Demonstrations (no set times) are scheduled from June to August—always call for an appointment.

Cathedral Yard, Exeter, Devon EX1 1HD. © **01392/319955**. Fax 01392/439423. www.abodehotels.co.uk/exeter. 53 units. £130–£175 ($260–$350) double; £185–£250 ($370–$500) suite. AE, DC, MC, V. Parking £6 ($12). **Amenities:** Restaurant; cafe; 2 bars; gym; spa; room service; babysitting; laundry service; dry cleaning. *In room:* A/C, TV/DVD, coffeemaker, hair dryer, trouser press, safe.

Thistle Exeter   Though its history is far less impressive than the **Royal Clarence/Abode Exter Hotel** (see above), this great, old-fashioned, rambling Victorian hotel is also a traditional choice for those who want to stay in the center of town. Its small to medium bedrooms are comfortably furnished in a modern style.

Queen St. (opposite the central train station), Exeter, Devon EX4 3SP. © **0870/333-9133**. Fax 0870/333-9233. www. thistlehotels.com. 90 units. £110–£170 ($220–$340) double; £215–£250 ($430–$500) suite. AE, DC, MC, V. Parking £5 ($10). **Amenities:** Restaurant; bar; room service. *In room:* TV, Wi-Fi, coffeemaker, hair dryer, safe (in some).

MODERATE

Barcelona ✹ *Finds*   A former hospital devoted to the treatment of eye problems, this hip, modern, and rather tony hotel was created from an old redbrick pile. The big corridors used for wheeling patients and the giant elevators are still here, but everything else is new. Many adornments and artifacts from past decades, notably the '50s and '60s, have been put in place. The bedrooms are rather luxurious, each tastefully furnished. Expect bold spreads and carpets in geometric patterns, large windows, and the original parquet floors. On Friday and Saturday, live jazz and blues are played in the cocktail bar.

Magdalen St., Exeter, Devon EX2 4HY. © **01392/281000**. Fax 01392/281001. www.aliashotels.com/barcelona. 46 units. £119–£140 ($238–$280) double. Children stay free in parent's room. AE, MC, V. Free parking. **Amenities:** Restaurant; bar; lounge; room service; laundry service; dry cleaning. *In room:* TV, Wi-Fi, coffeemaker, hair dryer.

Gipsy Hill Hotel *Kids*   Affiliated with Best Western, this late Victorian country house stands on the eastern edge of the city and is close to the airport. (It's especially convenient if you're driving, as it's within easy reach of the M5.) Bedrooms, ranging from small to medium, are comfortably appointed; some have four-poster beds. Five accommodations are large enough for families. Bedrooms have more tradition and ambience in the main house, and the other 17 rooms are located in an annex.

Gipsy Hill Lane, via Pinn Lane, Monkerton, Exeter, Devon EX1 3RN. © **01392/465252**. Fax 01392/464302. www.gipsy hillhotel.co.uk. 37 units. £70–£100 ($140–$200) double. AE, DC, MC, V. Free parking. **Amenities:** Restaurant; bar; room service; babysitting. *In room:* TV, Wi-Fi, coffeemaker, hair dryer, trouser press.

St. Olaves Court Hotel ✹   This is our favorite place to stay in town. The location is ideal, within a short walk of the cathedral—you can hear the church bells. A Georgian mansion, it was constructed in 1827 by a rich merchant as a home. The house has been discreetly furnished, in part with antiques, and decorated with sporting prints. Each of the bedrooms is tastefully decorated; some have four-poster beds.

Mary Arches St. (off High St.), Exeter, Devon EX4 3AZ. (℅ **800/544-9993** in the U.S., or 01392/217736. Fax 01392/413054. www.olaves.co.uk. 15 units. £115–£125 ($230–$250) double; £145 ($290) family room; £155 ($310) suite. Rates include English breakfast. MC, V. Free parking. **Amenities:** Restaurant (see review for the Treasury below); bar; room service. *In room:* TV, coffeemaker, hair dryer.

White Hart Hotel   In the center of town, this inn, a coaching inn in the 15th century, is one of the oldest in the city. Oliver Cromwell stabled his horses here. The hotel is a mass of polished wood, slate floors, oak beams, and gleaming brass and copper. The rooms, which combine old and new, are housed in either the old wing or a more impersonal modern one. Six rooms are large enough for families, and each comes with a bathroom equipped with a tub/shower combination.

66 South St., Exeter, Devon EX1 1EE. (℅ **01392/279897.** Fax 01392/250159. www.roomattheinn.info. 55 units. Mon–Thurs £70 ($140) double, Fri–Sun £60 ($120) double; family rooms year-round £90 ($180). Rates include English breakfast. AE, DC, MC, V. Free parking. **Amenities:** Restaurant; bar; laundry service. *In room:* TV, Wi-Fi, coffeemaker, hair dryer, trouser press.

INEXPENSIVE
Park View Hotel   This hotel lies near the heart of town and the train station. A landmark Georgian house, it offers comfortably but plainly furnished rooms, ranging in size from small to medium. The decor is regularly upgraded. The public bathrooms available to other guests are convenient and well maintained. Guests take their breakfast in a cozy room opening onto the hotel's garden. Breakfast is the only meal served, but the staff will prepare a packed lunch for touring.

8 Howell Rd., Exeter, Devon EX4 4LG. (℅ **01392/271772.** Fax 01392/253047. www.parkviewexeter.co.uk. 13 units, 10 with bathroom. £55 ($110) double without bathroom, £65 ($130) with bathroom. Rates include English breakfast. MC, V. Free parking. **Amenities:** Breakfast room; TV lounge. *In room:* TV, coffeemaker.

Woodbine Guesthouse (¥ (Value   In the heart of Exeter, near the landmark clock tower, this is one of the cathedral city's best-run guesthouses. The hosts are friendly, the rooms are comfortable and well furnished, and the English breakfast is ample fortification for the day. The house was built in the mid-Victorian era, but is not old-fashioned—it was completely modernized and furnished in a contemporary style. The location is an easy walk from the Exeter Coach and Bus Station, and some guest rooms open onto a city park. Rooms are named after flowers, such as jasmine. We like the Honeysuckle, decorated in yellow, gold, and antique cream with deep-red accents. Luxuries include a power shower and under-floor heating in the bathroom.

1 Woodbine Terrace, Exeter, Devon, EX4 4LJ. (℅ **01392/203302.** Fax 01392/254162. www.woodbineguesthouse. co.uk. 5 units. £64 ($128) double. Rates include English breakfast. AE, MC, V. Free parking. **Amenities:** Breakfast room. *In room:* TV, Wi-Fi, coffeemaker.

WHERE TO DINE
Michael Caines at ABode Exeter (¥(¥ FRENCH   Exeter at long last offers a restaurant worthy of itself, with an aura of smart, sophisticated brasserie. Try to get a table near one of the bay windows overlooking the cathedral. As is obvious by the name, Michael Caines, a skilled chef is in charge of the overall operation. Excellent, not deluxe, raw materials are purchased and turned into an impressive array of dishes beautifully prepared and served. The dishes we've sampled have been filled with flavor and perfectly spiced. For a starter, Cornish lobster appears with avocado, watermelon, and cherry tomatoes, or else you can sample the foie gras with mango relish. Some

enticing mains include roast partridge with a pumpkin fondant or else line-caught sea bass in red-wine butter.

Cathedral Yard. © **01392/223638**. Reservations required. Main courses £20–£25 ($40–$50); 2-course fixed-price lunch menu £13 ($26), 3 courses £18 ($36); 2-course table d'hôte menu £20 ($40), 3 courses £25 ($50). AE, DC, MC, V. Mon–Sat noon–2pm and 7–10pm.

The Ship Inn _Finds_ ENGLISH   Often visited by Sir Francis Drake, Sir Walter Raleigh, and Sir John Hawkins, this restaurant still provides tankards of real ale, lager, and stout. Real ale, as every Brit knows, means that the yeast in the drink is still present at the point of consumption—that is, it is unfiltered. A large selection of snacks are offered in the bar every day, whereas the restaurant upstairs provides more substantial English fare. At either lunch or dinner, you can order French onion soup, whole grilled lemon sole, five different steaks, and more. Portions are large, as in Elizabethan times.

St. Martin's Lane. © **01392/272040**. Reservations recommended. Restaurant main courses £6–£12 ($12–$24); pub platters £3–£8 ($6–$16). MC, V. Daily noon–9pm.

The Treasury Restaurant 🍴 CONTINENTAL   At one of Exeter's finest restaurants, guests enjoy before-dinner drinks in a paneled bar that overlooks a verdant garden. The menu reflects the sophisticated palate of the congenial owners. Always anticipate something savory, often in unusual yet harmonious combinations of flavors. A West Country sirloin steak appears with prunes and ale sauce, and the delectable chicken breasts are served with a tarragon-laced white-wine-and-cream sauce, with a side of wild-mushroom lasagna. Veggies can order saffron risotto with baby vegetables and Parmesan cream.

In the St. Olaves Court Hotel, Mary Arches St. © **01392/217736**. Reservations recommended. Main courses £15–£20 ($30–$40). DC, MC, V. Daily noon–2pm and 7–9:30pm.

EXPLORING EXETER

Exeter Cathedral 🗝🗝   The Roman II Augusta Legion made its camp on the site where the Cathedral Church of Saint Peter now stands in Exeter. It has been occupied by Britons, Saxons, Danes, and Normans. The English Saint Boniface, who converted northern Germany to Christianity, was trained here in A.D. 690. The present cathedral structure was begun around 1112, and the twin Norman towers still stand. Between the towers runs the longest uninterrupted true Gothic vault in the world, at a height of 20m (66 ft.) and a length of 90m (300 ft.). It was completed in 1369, and is the finest existing example of Decorated Gothic architecture (see "Gothic Architecture [1150–1550]" in chapter 2). The Puritans destroyed the cathedral cloisters in 1655, and a German bomb finished off the twin chapels of St. James and St. Thomas in May 1942. Now restored, it's one of the prettiest churches anywhere. Its famous choir sings evensong Monday to Friday at 5:30pm and again at 3pm on Saturday and Sunday. On school holidays, visiting choirs perform.

1 The Cloisters. © **01392/285983**. www.exeter-cathedral.org.uk. Free admission; a donation of £3.50 ($7) is requested of adults. Daily 9:30am–5pm.

Exeter Guildhall   This colonnaded building on the main street is the oldest municipal building in the kingdom—the earliest reference to the guildhall is in a deed from 1160. The Tudor front that straddles the pavement was added in 1593. Inside you'll find a fine display of silver, plus a number of paintings. The ancient hall is paneled in oak. This is a working building, so hours of operation are not guaranteed.

High St. © **01392/665500**. Free admission. Mon–Fri 10:30am–1pm and 2–4pm. It's best to call before visiting.

Moments **A Relic from William the Conqueror**

Just off "the High," at the top of Castle Street, stands an impressive **Norman Gatehouse** from William the Conqueror's castle. Though only the gatehouse and walls survive, you can enjoy the panoramic view and surrounding gardens, and contemplate all the invasions that have assaulted Exeter, from the Romans to the Nazi bombers of World War II.

Powderham Castle ⭐ This private house is occupied by the countess and earl of Devon, who let Ismail Merchant and James Ivory use their home as a setting for *The Remains of the Day*, starring Anthony Hopkins and Emma Thompson. It was built in the late 14th century by Sir Philip Courtenay, sixth son of the second earl of Devon, and his wife, Margaret, granddaughter of Edward I. Their magnificent tomb is in the south transept of Exeter Cathedral. The castle has many family portraits and fine furniture, including a remarkable clock that plays full tunes at 4 and 8pm, and midnight; some 17th-century tapestries; and a chair used by William III for his first council of state at Newton Abbot. The chapel dates from the 15th century, with hand-hewn roof timbers and carved pew ends.

In Powderham, Kenton. ℂ **01626/890243**. www.powderham.co.uk. Admission £8.50 ($17) adults, £7.50 ($15) seniors, £6.50 ($13) ages 5–14, free for children 4 and younger, family ticket £24 ($48). Sun–Fri 10am–5:30pm. Closed Nov–Mar. Take the A379 Dawlish Rd. 13km (8 miles) south of Exeter; the castle is signposted.

SHOPPING

Exeter has long been famous for its silver. If you seek, ye shall find old Exeter silver, especially spoons, sold in local stores. **Brufords,** 17 Guildhall, Queen Street (ℂ **01392/254901**), sells modern silver and jewelry.

You can find a number of antiques dealers in Exeter, many on the Quay off Western Way. The **Quay Gallery Antiques Emporium** (ℂ **01392/213283**) houses 10 dealers who sell furniture, porcelain, metalware, and other collectibles. The **Antique Centre** on the Quay (ℂ **01392/493501**) has 20 dealers.

The **Edinburgh Woollen Mill,** 23 Cathedral Yard (ℂ **01392/412318**), carries a large selection of woolen goods, including kilts, Aran jumpers, tartan travel rugs, and quality wool suits for women and trousers for men.

A daily market on Sidwell Street is Exeter's version of a flea market.

EXETER AFTER DARK

Exeter is a lively university town offering an abundance of classical concerts and theater productions, as well as clubs and pubs.

An abundance of concerts, opera, dance, and film can be found year-round at the **Exeter Phoenix,** Bradninch Place, Gandy Street (ℂ **01392/667080;** www.exeter phoenix.org.uk), and Exeter University's **Northcott Theatre,** Stocker Road (ℂ **01392/493493;** www.northcott-theatre.co.uk), which is also home to a professional theater company.

On the club scene, head to **Riva,** the Quay (ℂ **01392/211347**), a two-story club that attracts a young crowd. The upstairs bar, Riva VIP, has a lounge area and VIP room decorated with blue and lit by red lights. In the downstairs bar the aura is more

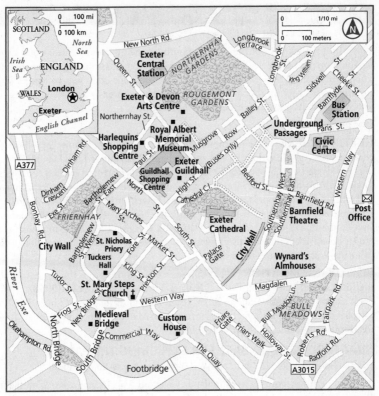

rustic, with exposed bricks, slate floors, and rich browns and reds. Monday is student night; Tuesday is gay night; on other nights, pop music, rhythm and blues, and disco take over. Riva is open Monday 9pm to 2am, Tuesday 10pm to 2am, Thursday 9pm to 2am, and Friday and Saturday 10pm to 3am. The cover charge varies from free to £5 ($10).

Well House Tavern, Cathedral Close (© 01392/223611), is part of the Royal Clarence/ABode Exeter (p. 396). It's housed in a building believed to have been constructed in the 14th century, though the Roman well in the basement predates that estimate. The tavern is said to be haunted—though the ghost, who wears a flowing white dress and is affectionately called Alice, is said to be good-spirited when she appears. Join Alice and the other regulars for a pint or a light meal.

Featuring a great view of the canal, **Double Locks,** Canal Banks (© 01392/256947), welcomes a varied crowd, largely students. It features live music (jazz, rock, and blues) with no cover charge, and you can get traditional pub grub to go with your pint. Though spaciously spread through a Georgian mansion, the **Imperial Pub,** New North Road (© 01392/434050), is friendly to frugal travelers, with the cheapest brand-name beer in town, starting at £2 ($4), and a fast-food menu.

2 Dartmoor National Park ★/★

343km (213 miles) SW of London; 21km (13 miles) W of Exeter

This national park lies northeast of Plymouth, stretching from Tavistock and Oke-hampton on the west to near Exeter in the east, a granite mass that sometimes rises to a height of 600m (1,968 ft.) above sea level. The landscape offers vistas of gorges with rushing water, spiny shrubs, and purple heather ranged over by Dartmoor ponies—a foreboding landscape for the experienced hiker only.

ESSENTIALS

GETTING THERE   Take the train from London to Exeter, then use local buses to connect you with the various villages of Dartmoor. **Transmoor Link,** a public transport bus service, usually operates throughout the summer, an ideal way to get onto the moor. Information on the Transmoor Link and on the bus link between various towns and villages on Dartmoor is available from the **Travel Line** (✆ **0870/608-2608**).

If you're driving, Exeter is the most easily reached gateway. From here, continue west on the B3212 to such centers as Dartmoor, Chagford, Moretonhampstead, and North Bovey. From these smaller towns, tiny roads—often not really big enough for two cars—cut deeper into the moor.

VISITOR INFORMATION   The main source of information is the **Tourist Information Centre,** Town Hall, Bedford Square, Tavistock (✆ **01822/612938**). It will book accommodations within an 80km (50-mile) radius for free. It's open April to October daily 9:30am to 5pm. From November to March, it's open on Monday, Tuesday, Friday, and Saturday 10am to 4:30pm.

CHAGFORD: A GOOD BASE FOR EXPLORING THE PARK ★

351km (218 miles) SW of London; 21km (13 miles) W of Exeter; 32km (20 miles) NW of Torquay

At 180m (590 ft.) above sea level, romantic Chagford is an ancient town. With moors all around, it's a good base for exploring the often forlorn yet enchanting north Dartmoor. You're in Sir Francis Drake country now. Chagford overlooks the Teign River and is itself overlooked by the high granite tors (high craggy hills). There's good fishing in the Teign. From Chagford, the most popular excursion is to Postbridge, a village with a prehistoric clapper bridge. This ancient form of bridge, found on the moors of Dartmoor and Exmoor, is formed by large flat slabs of granite supported on stone piers.

To get here, take a train to Exeter, and then catch a bus to Chagford (Stagecoach bus no. 173). If you're driving from Exeter, drive west on the A30, then south on the A382 to Chagford.

WHERE TO STAY & DINE

Bovey Castle ★★★   The grandest address in Devon is an elegant 1906 estate within the national park that still pursues such "gentlemanly pursuits" as trout fishing, archery, and falconry. The golf course's revamped links were first laid out in 1926. Although the hotel had been completely restored, the halcyon Edwardian era lives on in the decor from the Palm Court dining room to the Art Deco artwork and vintage travel posters. Luxury abounds at this castle, which seems to await the arrival any minute of Agatha Christie, or at least Hercule Poirot. The spacious bedrooms are the epitome of comfort, taste, and elegance. For those seeking the ultimate retreat, there is the North Lodge with an exquisite home standing in private gardens. The accommodations are virtual staterooms, the epitome of English country living.

Moments **A Cuppa & an Homage to Lorna Doone**

At teatime, drop in at **Whiddons,** High Street (© **01647/433406**), serving freshly baked scones and delectable cucumber sandwiches. After tea, visit the nearby Church of St. Michael, where a spurned lover killed Mary Whiddon on her wedding day (later fictionalized in R. D. Blackmore's classic *Lorna Doone*).

North Bovey, Devon TQ13 8RE. © **01647/445016.** Fax 01647/445020. www.boveycastle.com. 63 units. £225–£445 ($450–$890) double; from £595 ($1,190) suite. AE, DC, MC, V. **Amenities:** Restaurant; bar; 2 pools (1 indoor, 1 outdoor); 18-hole golf course; 2 outdoor tennis courts; spa; gym; archery center; children's farm; equestrian center; falconry; fly-fishing; business services; room service; laundry service; dry cleaning; movie theater. *In room:* A/C, TV, Wi-Fi, minibar, beverage maker, hair dryer, safe.

Easton Court Bed and Breakfast *Finds* Established in the 1920s, this Tudor house, standing in 1.6 hectares (4 acres) of gardens and paddocks, is a longtime favorite of the literati and theatrical celebrities. Best known as the place where Evelyn Waugh wrote *Brideshead Revisited,* the atmosphere here is very English country house: ancient stone house with thatched roof, inglenook where log fires burn, and high-walled flower garden. Bedrooms are snug and comfortable, ranging in size from small to medium. Rooms are appointed with comfortable English beds where the greats of yesteryear slept; some have four-posters. Most rooms open onto views.

Easton Cross, Chagford, Devon TQ13 8JL. © **01647/433469.** www.easton.co.uk. 5 units. £64–£75 ($128–$150) double. Rates include English breakfast. MC, V. Take A382 2.5km (1½ miles) northeast of Chagford. No children 10 or younger. **Amenities:** Guest lounge. *In room:* TV, CD player, coffeemaker, hair dryer.

Gidleigh Park Hotel *★★★* This Tudor-style hotel, a Relais & Châteaux member, is country house supreme, the finest and most elegant place to stay in the Dartmoor area. On 1.8 hectares (4½ acres) the hotel lies in the Teign Valley, opening onto panoramic vistas of the Meldon and Nattadon Hills. Its owners, Andrew and Christina Brownsword, have renovated and refurnished the house with flair and imagination, often inspired by the Devon Arts and Crafts movement; they've also converted the top floor into bedrooms. An extension also offers completely up-to-date and elegant accommodations. Most of the bedrooms are on the second floor and are reached by a grand staircase. Bedrooms are roomy and furnished in the most elegant English-country-house tradition. Half-canopies usually crown the sumptuous English beds. The hotel has a two-bedroom, two-bathroom thatched cottage across the river.

Gidleigh Park (3km/2 miles outside town), Chagford, Devon TQ13 8HH. © **01647/432367.** Fax 01647/432574. www.gidleigh.com. 23 units, 1 cottage. £440–£1,200 ($880–$2,400) double; £700–£940 ($1,400–$1,880) cottage. Rates include English breakfast, morning tea, and dinner. AE, DC, MC, V. To get here from Chagford Sq., turn right onto Mill St. at Lloyds Bank. After 135m (450 ft.), turn right and go down the hill to the crossroads. Cross straight over onto Holy St., following the lane passing Holy St. Manor on your right and shifting into low gear to negotiate 2 sharp bends on a steep hill. Over Leigh Bridge, make a sharp right turn into Gidleigh Park. A 1km (½-mile) drive will bring you to the hotel. **Amenities:** Restaurant; bar; putting green; tennis court; bowling green; croquet lawn; in-room massage and other spa treatments; babysitting; laundry service. *In room:* TV, Wi-Fi, hair dryer.

EXPLORING THE AREA

Castle Drogo *★ Kids* This massive granite castle, in the hamlet of Drewsteignton, 27km (17 miles) west of Exeter, was designed and built between 1910 and 1930 by architect Sir Edwin Lutyens, then at the height of his powers, for his client, Julius Drewe, who was a self-made millionaire whose chain of Home & Colonial Stores enabled him to retire very rich in 1899 at the age of 33. It was the last private country house built in the United Kingdom on a grand scale. Though constructed of granite and castellated and turreted like a medieval castle from the age of chivalry, it was never intended to be a military stronghold. The castle occupies a bleak but dramatic position high above the River Teign, with views sweeping out over the moors.

The tour covers an elegant series of formal rooms designed in the tradition of the Edwardian age. Two restaurants and a buffet-style tearoom are on premises. Serving standard English fare, these restaurants are more for convenience than any grand cuisine. But the food is at least first-class cafeteria fare, prepared with fresh ingredients.

Insider's tip: The castle is so overpowering it's easy to forget the secluded gardens. But they are wonderful, including a sunken lawn enclosed by raised walkways, a circular croquet lawn (sets are available for rent), geometrically shaped yew hedges, and a children's playroom based on a 1930s residence.

Drewsteignton, 6.5km (4 miles) northeast of Chagford and 9.5km (6 miles) south of the Exeter-Okehampton Rd. (A30). ⓒ **01647/433306.** Admission (castle and grounds) £7.40 ($15) adults, £3.70 ($7.40) children, £19 ($38) family ticket; grounds only £4.75 ($9.50) adults, £2.60 ($5.20) children. House Mar–Oct Wed–Mon 11am–5pm, Dec 1–23 Sat–Sun noon–4pm; grounds Mar–Oct daily 10:30am–5:30pm, Nov–Dec 23 Fri–Sun 11am–4pm. Closed Jan–Feb. Take A30 and follow the signs.

Sir Francis Drake's House ⚡   Constructed in 1278, Sir Francis Drake's House was originally a Cistercian monastery. The monastery was dissolved in 1539 and became the country seat of sailors Sir Richard Grenville and, later, Sir Francis Drake. The house remained in the Drake family until 1946, when the abbey and grounds were given to the National Trust. The abbey is now a museum, with exhibits including Drake's drum, banners, and other artifacts. There is also an audiovisual presentation about the history of the house.

Buckland Abbey, Yelverton. ⓒ **01822/853607.** Admission £7.40 ($15) adults, £3.70 ($7.40) children, £19 ($38) family ticket. Mid-Mar to Oct Fri–Wed 10:30am–5:30pm; Nov to mid-Mar Sat–Sun 2–5pm. Last admission 45 min. before closing. Go 5km (3 miles) west of Yelverton off A386.

CHAGFORD AFTER DARK

The local watering hole is **Globe Inn,** High Street (ⓒ **01647/433485;** www.globeinn chagford.co.uk), which puts up wayfarers the way it has done since the 16th century when stagecoach passengers used to stop by for the night. In the center of town, it is also the most popular pub in the area, drawing locals and visitors to its two bars and restaurants, where daily specials and traditional English dishes such as roasts are served. If you have too much of the local brew, you can stay over in a family room or else one of two doubles at a cost of £25 ($50) per person nightly.

OTHER TOWNS IN & AROUND DARTMOOR

Some 21km (13 miles) west of Exeter, the peaceful little town of **Moretonhampstead** is perched on the edge of Dartmoor. Moretonhampstead contains several 17th-century colonnaded almshouses and a Market Cross, a carved stone structure used for centuries to mark the site of the local market, which is still around.

The much-visited Dartmoor village of **Widecombe-in-the-Moor** is only 11km (7 miles) northeast of Moretonhampstead. Widecombe also has a parish church worth visiting. Called the **Cathedral of the Moor,** with a roster of vicars beginning in 1253, the house of worship in a green valley is surrounded by legends. When the building was restored, a wall plate was found bearing the badge of Richard II (1377–99), the figure of a white hart (an old word for stag). As a personal badge of Richard II, the symbol of the hart was derived from the coat of arms of his mother, who was called Joan, "the Fair Maid of Kent." The town is very disappointing, tacky, and unkempt in spite of its fame.

Let yourself drift back in time to the days when craftspeople were the lifeblood of thriving communities. Basket weavers, wood-turners, and potters are among the traditional crafters that you can still see in the area. In the Dartmoor National Park in West Devon, you'll find that The **Yelverton Paperweight Centre,** Leg O'Mutton (✆ **01822/854250;** www.paperweightcentre.co.uk), presents an impressive display of more than 800 glass paperweights for sale along with paintings of Dartmoor scenes. It's open April to October daily 10:30am to 5pm.

WHERE TO STAY & DINE IN THE AREA

The Castle Inn A good stopover on the road between Okehampton and Tavistock, this inn dates from the 12th century, when it was built next to Lydford Castle. With its pink facade and row of rose trellises, it is the hub of the village. The owners have maintained the character of the roomy old rustic lounge. One room, the Snug, has a group of high-backed oak benches arranged in a circle. Bedrooms are not large but are attractively furnished, often with mahogany and marble Victorian pieces.

Lydford, near Okehampton (1.5km/1 mile off A386), Devon EX20 4BH. ✆ **01822/820241.** Fax 01822/820454. 8 units. £65–£90 ($130–$180) double. MC, V. **Amenities:** Restaurant; bar. *In room:* TV, coffeemaker.

Cherrybrook Hotel This is a small family-run hotel in the center of the Dartmoor National Park, on the high moor but within easy driving distance of Exeter and Plymouth. It was built in the early 19th century by a prince regent's friend who received permission to enclose a large area of the Dartmoor forest for farming. The lounge and bar with their beamed ceilings and slate floors are a reminder of those times. Ann and Roy Daniels rent small to medium-size rooms with a traditional decor, often with a granite fireplace. A different group of bedrooms is redecorated each year, and bathrooms contain a shower stall.

On B3212 between Postbridge and Two Bridges, Yelverton, Devon PL20 6SP. ✆/fax **01822/880260.** www.cherrybrook-hotel.co.uk. 7 units. £99 ($198) double with English breakfast, £129 ($258) with breakfast and dinner. MC, V. Closed Dec 22–Jan 2. **Amenities:** Restaurant; bar; lounge. *In room:* TV, coffeemaker, hair dryer.

Holne Chase Hotel ✦ *Kids* The hotel on 28 hectares (70 acres) is a white-gabled country house, 5km (3 miles) northwest of the center of town, within sight of trout- and salmon-fishing waters. You can catch your lunch and take it back to the kitchen to be cooked. Though the mood of the moor predominates, Holne Chase is surrounded by trees, lawns, and pastures—a perfect setting for walks along the Dart. The house is furnished in period style; a stable block has been converted into four sporting lodges. Rooms come in various shapes, sizes, and styles; some have their original fireplaces and four-poster beds, ideal for a romantic interlude. If assigned a room in the stable, don't be disappointed, as they are really delightful split-level suites. All the comforts of English country living are found here. Seven rooms are large enough for families.

Tavistock Rd., Ashburton (between the Holne Bridge and New Bridge), Devon TQ13 7NS. ✆ **01364/631471.** Fax 01364/631453. www.holne-chase.co.uk. 16 units. £160–£180 ($320–$360) double; £200–£210 ($400–$420) suite. Rates include English breakfast. MC, V. **Amenities:** Restaurant; bar; room service; babysitting; laundry service. *In room:* TV, coffeemaker, hair dryer.

Lewtrenchard Manor On the northwest edges of Dartmoor, near the oft-visited Okehampton, this 17th-century Jacobean house has a certain charm and grace. There has been a manor of some sort on this property since 1086 when it was mentioned in the Domesday Book. It was at one time the residence of Victorian hymn writer Rev. Sabine Baring Gould (hardly a household name today). It is set in a garden open to the general public as part of the National Gardens Scheme, and you can take several scenic walks. As typical of its time, the house features oak paneling, leaded windows, beautifully detailed ceilings, and antiques. Rooms come in various shapes and sizes, but each is exceedingly comfortable. Five bedrooms are more contemporary and stylish than the existing rooms, yet still in keeping with the Jacobean style.

Lewdown, Devon EX20 4PN. ℰ **01566/783222.** Fax 01566/783332. www.lewtrenchard.co.uk. 14 units. £155–£225 ($310–$450) double; £240–£270 ($480–$540) suite. Rates include English breakfast. AE, DC, MC, V. **Amenities:** Restaurant; bar; room service; laundry service. *In room:* TV, hair dryer.

EXPLORING THE MOORS

This region is as rich in myth and legend as anywhere else in Britain. Crisscrossed with about 805km (500 miles) of bridle paths and hiking trails and covering about 932 sq. km (360 sq. miles)—466 sq. km (180 sq. miles) of which comprise Dartmoor National Park—the moors rest on a granite base with numerous rocky outcroppings.

The **Dartmoor National Park Authority (DNPA)** runs **guided walks** of varying difficulty, ranging from 1½ to 6 hours for a trek of some 14 to 19km (9–12 miles). All you have to do is turn up suitably clad at your selected starting point. The country is rough, and on the high moor you should always make sure you have good maps, a compass, and suitable clothing and shoes. Details are available from DNPA information centers or from the DNPA headquarters (ℰ **01822/890414;** www.dartmoor-npa.gov.uk), High Moorland Visitor Centre, Tavistock Road, Princetown (near Yelverton) PL20 6QF. Information centers are open daily Easter through October 10am to 5pm; most (including the High Moorland Visitor Centre) are open daily off season 10am to 4pm. Guided tours cost £3 ($6) for a 2-hour walk, £4.50 ($9) for a 3-hour walk, £5 ($10) for a 4-hour walk, and £6 ($12) for a 6-hour walk. These prices are subsidized by the national park services.

Throughout the area are stables where you can arrange for a day's trek across the moors. For **horseback riding** in Dartmoor, there are too many establishments to list. All are licensed, and you are accompanied by an experienced rider/guide. The moor can be dangerous because sudden fogs descend on the treacherous marshlands without warning. Prices are around £15 ($30) per hour. Most riding stables are listed in a useful free publication, *The Dartmoor Visitor,* which also provides details on guided walks, places to go, accommodations, local events, and articles about the national park. *The Dartmoor Visitor* is obtainable from DNPA information centers and tourist information centers or by mail. Send an International Reply Coupon to the DNPA headquarters (address above).

Some of the best Dartmoor riding is provided by **Skaigh Stables** at Belstone (ℰ **01837/840917**), 1.6km (1 mile) from the A30 Exeter-Okehampton road. Rides go over dramatic moorland in England's largest wilderness. Morning or afternoon rides are offered from mid-April until the end of September, with 2-hour rides beginning at £32 ($64) per person. We're also fond of the **Doone Valley Stables,** Oare, Lynton (ℰ **01598/741234;** www.doonevalleytrekking.co.uk), set in the heart of the beautiful Doone Valley and offering escorted rides, especially picnic rides.

3 Torquay ⟨★⟩

359km (223 miles) SW of London; 37km (23 miles) SE of Exeter

The resort of Torquay—the birthplace of mystery writer Agatha Christie—opens onto 35km (22 miles) of rocky coastline with 18 poor-to-fair beaches set against a backdrop of the red cliffs of Devon, with many sheltered pebbly coves. The entire area is filled with parks and gardens often planted with subtropical vegetation. At night, concerts, theatrical productions from London's West End, often-corny British vaudeville shows, and old-fashioned ballroom dancing keep the vacationers and many honeymooners entertained.

Torquay is more upscale than Brighton. Because of its easy commute from London, Brighton attracts a lot of tawdry "London-by-the-Sea" crowds, whereas Torquay, as a destination unto itself, draws a well-heeled clientele seeking a more tranquil seaside holiday.

ESSENTIALS

GETTING THERE Frequent trains run throughout the day from London's Paddington Station to Torquay, whose station is at the town center on the seafront. The trip takes 2½ hours. For rail information, call ⟨€⟩ **0845/7484950** or visit **www.nationalrail.co.uk**.

National Express coach links from London's Victoria Coach Station leave every 2 hours during the day for the 5-hour trip to Torquay. For information and schedules, call ⟨€⟩ **0870/580-8080** or visit **www.nationalexpress.com**.

If you're driving from Exeter, head west on the A38, veering south at the junction with the A380.

VISITOR INFORMATION The **Tourist Information Centre** is at Vaughan Parade (⟨€⟩ **01803/2112111**); open June to September Monday to Saturday from 9:30am to 5:30pm and Sunday from 10am to 4pm, and October to May Monday to Saturday 9:30am to 5pm.

WHERE TO STAY

EXPENSIVE

The Imperial ⟨★★★⟩ This leading government-rated five-star hotel in the West Country dates from 1866, but a major refurbishing has kept it abreast of the times and way ahead of its competition. It sits on 2.2 hectares (5½ acres) of subtropical gardens opening onto rocky cliffs, with views of the Channel. You'll follow the example of some of the characters of Agatha Christie if you check in here. She called it the Esplanade in *The Rajah's Emerald,* the Castle in *Partners in Crime,* and the Majestic in *Peril at End House.* Inside is a world of soaring ceilings, marble columns, and ornate plasterwork—enough to make a former visitor, Edward VII, feel at home. Rooms are studies in grand living, with beautiful reproduction pieces, striped wallpaper, and upholstered seating. Many have private balconies suspended high above a view.

Park Hill Rd., Torquay, Devon TQ1 2DG. ⟨€⟩ **01803/294301.** Fax 01803/298293. www.paramount-hotels.co.uk. 169 units. £119–£245 ($238–$490) double; £195–£370 ($390–$740) suite. Rates include English breakfast, use of sporting facilities, and dancing in the ballroom Mon–Sat. AE, DC, MC, V. Parking £7 ($14). **Amenities:** 2 restaurants; bar; 2 heated pools (indoor, outdoor); 2 tennis courts; 2 squash courts; health club; spa; sauna; steam room; solarium; salon; room service; laundry service; dry cleaning. *In room:* TV, Wi-Fi, minibar, coffeemaker, hair dryer, safe.

Orestone Manor ⚑ Sometimes the best way to enjoy a bustling seaside resort is from afar, nestled in a country home. Orestone Manor is in nearby Maidencombe, a small village north of Torquay. In one of the loveliest valleys in South Devon, this gabled manor house, constructed in the early 19th century as a private home, enjoys a tranquil rural setting, situated on .8 hectare (2 acres) of well-landscaped gardens. All of the bedrooms are handsomely furnished. The gable rooms are a bit small but some offer sea views; all the superior rooms have sea views and complimentary sherry. Because this was once a country lodge, all the bedrooms have an individual character and aren't just square boxes.

Rockhouse Lane, Maidencombe, Torquay, Devon TQ1 4SX. ✆ 01803/328098. Fax 01803/328336. www.orestone. co.uk. 12 units. £135–£225 ($270–$450) double. Rates include English breakfast. AE, DC, MC, V. Free parking. Closed 2 weeks in Jan. Drive 5.5km (3½ miles) north of Torquay on A379. **Amenities:** Restaurant; bar; outdoor pool; room service; babysitting; laundry service; dry cleaning. *In room:* TV, Wi-Fi, coffeemaker, hair dryer.

Palace Hotel ⚑ In Torquay, only the Imperial is better. This 1921 hotel was built when life was experienced on a grand scale, an attitude reflected by spacious public rooms with molded ceilings and columns. With its recent improvements, the hotel has entered the 21st century in a premier position. Luxurious through and through, the bedrooms are well furnished. The hotel occupies 10 choice hectares (25 acres) of real estate in Torquay, sweeping down to Anstey's Cove.

Babbacombe Rd., Babbacombe, Torquay, Devon TQ1 3TG. ✆ 01803/200200. Fax 01803/299899. www.palace torquay.co.uk. 141 units. £138–£236 ($276–$472) double; £256–£296 ($512–$592) suite for 2. Rates include English breakfast. AE, DC, MC, V. Free parking. From the town center take B3199 east. Bus: 32. **Amenities:** Restaurant; 2 bars; 2 pools (1 indoor, 1 outdoor); putting green; 9-hole golf course; 6 tennis courts; 2 squash courts; fitness room; sauna; croquet; room service; babysitting; laundry service; dry cleaning. *In room:* TV, minibar, coffeemaker, hair dryer, trouser press.

INEXPENSIVE

Colindale This hotel is a good choice, centrally located, opening onto King's Garden, a 5-minute walk from Corbyn Beach and a 3-minute walk from the railway station. Rooms are cozily furnished, in a range of sizes and shapes, each in a Victorian style. Colindale is one of a row of attached brick Victorian houses, with gables and chimneys.

20 Rathmore Rd., Chelston, Torquay, Devon TQ2 6NY. ✆ 01803/293947. www.colindalehotel.co.uk. 8 units. £60–£65 ($120–$130) double; £65–£75 ($130–$150) superior room. Rates include English breakfast. MC, V. Free parking. Children 10 and under not accepted. **Amenities:** Breakfast room; TV lounge; bar. *In room:* TV, coffeemaker, hair dryer.

Fairmount House Hotel ⚑ *Finds* Standing on a perch overlooking the Cockington Valley, this little haven of tranquillity is far removed from the bustle of the resort, lying in the residential valley of Chelston, on the periphery of Torquay. A converted Victorian building has been turned into a winning little B&B, with its gardens facing south. Torquay Harbour is within easy reach, and the sea is less than .6km (1 mile) away. The family home, complete with cellars and servants' quarters, dates from the turn of the 20th century. The aura is more of a large family home than a hotel. A highlight is the Victorian Conservatory Bar, with French doors opening onto the sun-trap patio that is sheltered from the wind. Bedrooms are midsize and tastefully furnished. Two garden rooms have a tub and shower. An evening dinner can be arranged in advance.

Herbert Rd., Chelston, Torquay, Devon TQ2 6RW. ✆/fax 01803/605446. www.fairmounthousehotel.co.uk. 8 units. £50–£70 ($100–$140) double. Rates include breakfast. MC, V. Free parking. **Amenities:** Restaurant; bar. *In room:* TV, beverage maker, hair dryer, no phone.

WHERE TO DINE

Capers Restaurant ★ INTERNATIONAL   This intimate, French-style bistro lies at Lisbourne Square, just off the main artery, Babbacombe Road. Torquay is not renowned for its dining, but this serious little restaurant is a bright note in a culinary wasteland. Families are among the regular patrons. The chef-owner, Antonia Rios, shops for the freshest of regional produce, when available, and serves locally caught fish and shellfish. The sauces that go with the fish are a harmonious match to the catch of the day. Tempting mains include poached lobster in garlic butter and a savory beef stroganoff laced with brandy and cream. A selection of vegetarian dishes is also available.

7 Lisbourne Sq. (C) **01803/291177**. www.caperstorquay.co.uk. Reservations required. Main courses £10–£22 ($20–$44). AE, MC, V. Tues–Sat 6:30–10pm.

Mulberry House ★ *Value* TRADITIONAL ENGLISH   Lesley Cooper is an inspired cook, and she'll feed you well in her little dining room, seating some two dozen diners at midday. The restaurant is situated in one of Torquay's Victorian villas, facing a patio of plants and flowers, with outside tables for summer lunches. Vegetarians will find comfort here in the eggplant and mozzarella baked in a tomato coulis, and others can feast on Lesley's filet of beef with pink peppercorns and strawberry crisps or chicken baked in its own juices. Fish is caught locally and varies daily. Traditional roasts draw the Sunday crowds. The choice is wisely limited so that everything served will be fresh.

You can even stay here in one of three bedrooms, each comfortably furnished and well kept, with private bathrooms. Bed-and-breakfast rates, from £30 ($60) per person daily, make this one of the best bargains of the whole area. *Note:* The restaurant serves only hotel guests Monday and Tuesday between 7 and 9pm.

1 Scarborough Rd. (C) **01803/213639**. www.mulberryhousetorquay.co.uk. Reservations required. 2-course meal £21 ($42); 3-course meal £24 ($48); 4-course meal £27 ($54). MC, V. Fri–Sun noon–2pm; Wed–Sat 7–9pm. Bus: 32. From the Seafront, turn up Belgrave Rd.; Scarborough Rd. is the 1st right.

PALM TREES & ISADORA DUNCAN

This area is known for offering one of the balmiest climates in Britain. It's so temperate, because of its proximity to the Gulf Stream, that subtropical plants such as palm trees and succulents thrive.

Oldway Mansion   You'll see the conspicuous consumption of England's Gilded Age here. The mansion was built in 1874 by Isaac Merritt Singer, founder of the sewing-machine empire. His son, Paris, enhanced its decor, massive Ionic portico, and 6.8 hectares (17 acres) of Italianate gardens. The mansion's eclectic decor includes a scaled-down version of the Hall of Mirrors in the Palace of Versailles. During its Jazz Age heyday, Oldway served as a rehearsal space and performance venue for Isadora Duncan, who was having a not-very-discreet affair with Paris.

Torbay Rd., in Preston, near Paignton (a short drive south of the center of Torquay on the main Paignton-Torquay Rd.). (C) **01803/207933**. Free admission. Year-round Mon–Fri 9am–5pm; Sun 2–5pm in summer.

TORQUAY AFTER DARK

Seven theaters in town, all open year-round, offer everything from Gilbert and Sullivan and tributes to Sinatra and Nat King Cole to Marine Band concerts and comedy shows. Among the most active are the **Palace Theatre,** Palace Avenue, Paignton ((C) **01803/665800**), and the **Princess Theatre,** Torbay Road ((C) **08702/414120**).

A Walk Across South Devon

The 56km-long (35-mile) **John Musgrave Heritage Trail** ★★, launched in early 2006, starts at Maidencombe near Torquay and winds its way across some of the most beautiful tracts of land in South Devon. A highlight of the trip is crossing the Dart River on the Dittisham Ferry (pedestrians only) to Greenway, once home to Agatha Christie. The path continues uphill after you get off the ferry, taking in panoramic views of the river. It comes to an end at Brixham Harbour.

Fifteen area nightclubs cater to everyone from teeny-boppers to gays, but dancing rules the town, and there's virtually nowhere to catch live club acts. Among the better dance clubs are **Bohemia,** Torwood Street (① 01803/292079), attracting ages 20 to 30 to its Thursday-to-Sunday house music, with a cover charge varying from £3 to £9 ($6–$18).

4 Totnes ★

361km (224 miles) SW of London; 19km (12 miles) NW of Dartmouth

One of the oldest towns in the West Country, Totnes rests quietly in the past, seemingly content to let the Torquay area remain in the vanguard of the building boom. On the River Dart, upstream from Dartmouth, Totnes has several historic buildings, notably the ruins of a Norman castle, an ancient guildhall, and the 15th-century Church of St. Mary. In the Middle Ages, the town was encircled by walls; the North Gate serves as a reminder of that period.

ESSENTIALS

GETTING THERE   Totnes is on the main London-Plymouth line. Trains leave London's Paddington Station once an hour throughout the day, the trip taking 2¾ hours. For rail information, call ① **08457/000125** or visit **www.firstgreatwestern. co.uk**.

If you're driving from Torquay, head west on the A385.

Between the months of May and October many visitors approach Totnes by river steamer from Dartmouth. Contact **Dart Pleasure Craft,** 5 Lower St., River Link (① **01803/834488;** www.riverlink.co.uk), for information.

VISITOR INFORMATION   The **Tourist Information Centre** is at the Town Mill, Coronation Road (① **01803/863168;** www.totnesinformation.co.uk). It's open year-round Monday to Saturday 9:30am to 5pm.

WHERE TO STAY IN THE TOTNES AREA

The Cott Inn ★ (Finds)   Built in 1320, this hotel is the second-oldest inn in England. It's a low, rambling two-story building of stone, cob, and plaster, with a thatched roof and 1m-thick (3-ft.) walls. The owners rent low-ceilinged double rooms upstairs, with modern conveniences. The refurbished rooms come in all shapes and sizes. The inn is a gathering place for the people of Dartington, and you'll feel the pulse of English country life here.

Dartington, near Totnes (on the old Ashburton-Totnes Turnpike), S. Devon TQ9 6HE. ① 01803/863777. Fax 01803/866629. www.thecottinn.co.uk. 7 units. £80 ($160) double. Rates include breakfast. MC, V. Bus: X80 travels from Totnes to Dartington, but most people take a taxi for the 2.5km (1½-mile) journey. **Amenities:** Restaurant; bar. *In room:* TV, coffeemaker, hair dryer.

Orchard House ⭐ *Value*   Lying between Totnes and Kingsbridge, this is a delightful little choice. It takes its name from the location, which is within an old cider orchard. It's a real find for those who appreciate the charms of bucolic Devon. The house enjoys a tranquil location among mature gardens. The bedrooms are beautifully furnished, and each has a private bathroom with shower. Bathrooms are large and airy with elegant toiletries provided. Local produce is used in the English cooked breakfasts.

Horner, Halwell, near Totnes, Devon TQ9 7LB. © **01548/821448.** www.orchard-house-halwell.co.uk. 3 units. £50–£55 ($100–$110) double. Rates include breakfast. No credit cards. Closed Nov–Feb. Get off the A38 at the Buckfastleigh Totnes junction and follow the road into Totnes. Upon entering the town, turn right for Kingsbridge (A381) and drive to Habertonford. After passing a garage, take the 2nd right for 2.5km (1½ miles), turning right at the sign marked HORNER. Take the next right. Orchard House is the 2nd house on the left. **Amenities:** Breakfast room. *In room:* TV, beverage maker, hair dryer, no phone.

Royal Seven Stars Hotel   A historic former coaching inn in the center of Totnes, this hotel largely dates from 1660. The hotel overlooks a square in the town center, near the banks of the River Dart. The interior courtyard, once used for horses and carriages, is now enclosed in glass, with an old pine staircase. Decorated with antiques, paintings, and the hotel's own heraldic shield, the courtyard forms an inviting entrance to the inn. The bedrooms have been modernized and have built-in furniture. Two rooms have four-poster beds.

The Plains, Totnes, S. Devon TQ9 5DD. © **01803/862125.** Fax 01803/867925. www.royalsevenstars.co.uk. 16 units. £99–£130 ($198–$260) double. Rates include English breakfast. AE, MC, V. **Amenities:** Restaurant; 2 bars; room service. *In room:* TV, Wi-Fi, coffeemaker, hair dryer.

WHERE TO DINE

When it's teatime, **Greys Dining Room,** 96 High St. (© **01803/866369**), sets out its fine silver and china to welcome you in an atmosphere of wood paneling and antiques. About 40 different teas along with homemade cakes and scones will invite you to extend the afternoon.

The Royal Seven Stars Restaurant ENGLISH   For the kind of cuisine that pleased Grandpa, this old coaching inn delivers quite well. You can order à la carte at lunch, but only a set menu is offered at night. Start perhaps with the homemade chicken liver pâté with mango- and cinnamon-flavored chutney or else the local mussels in a sauce of white wine, herbs, and garlic. Main dish favorites include Devon rack of lamb in a red-wine jus or pan-fried Devon duck breast with a red-currant jus. Vegetables of the day are fresh and well prepared. Finish in the British manner with blue Stilton cheese or a fruit pie with clotted cream. The adjoining Saloon bar has a wide range of ales, wine, and spirits.

In the Royal Seven Stars Hotel. © **01803/862125.** Reservations recommended. Main courses £12–£17 ($24–$34). AE, MC, V. Daily noon–2:30pm and 6:30–9:30pm.

EXPLORING TOTNES

You need spend no more than 2 hours or so exploring the major monuments outlined below. With any time remaining, you can visit the **Buckfast Butterflies & Dartmoor Otter Sanctuary,** Buckfastleigh (© **01364/642916;** www.ottersandbutterflies.co.uk), which is open only from April to October daily 10am to 5:30pm. Admission is £6.50 ($13) for adults, £5.95 ($12) seniors, and £4.95 ($9.90) for children 11 and younger. On display are exotic butterflies and moths from around the world along with beautiful birds in landscaped gardens. Three different species of otter are on display, along with native British otter.

The Elizabethan Museum   This 16th-century home of a wealthy merchant houses furniture, costumes, documents, and farm implements of the Elizabethan age. One room is devoted to local resident Charles Babbage (1792–1871), a mathematician and inventor. He invented a calculating machine whose memory capacity categorized it as an early version of the computer. His other inventions included the ophthalmoscope, a speedometer, and the cowcatchers later used to nudge cows off the tracks of railways around the world.

70 Fore St. ℂ **01803/863821.** Admission £1.50 ($3) adults, £1 ($2) seniors, 50p ($1) children. Mon–Fri 10:30am–5pm. Closed Nov to mid-Mar.

Totnes Castle   Crowning the hilltop at the northern end of High Street, this castle was built by the Normans shortly after their conquest of England. It's one of the best examples of motte-and-bailey construction remaining in the United Kingdom. Although the outer walls survived, the interior is mostly in ruins.

Castle St. ℂ **01803/864406.** Admission £2.40 ($4.80) adults, £1.80 ($3.60) students and seniors, £1.20 ($2.40) children. Apr–June and Sept daily 10am–5pm; July–Aug daily 10am–6pm; Oct daily 10am–4pm. Closed Nov–Mar.

Totnes Guildhall   This symbol of Totnes, originally built as a priory (monastery) in 1553, contains an old gaol (jail), a collection of civic memorabilia, and the table Oliver Cromwell used to sign documents during his visit to Totnes in 1646.

Ramparts Walk. ℂ **01803/862147.** Admission £1 ($2) adults, 25p (50¢) children. Mon–Fri 10:30am–1:30pm and 2–4pm. Closed Oct–Mar.

5 Dartmouth ★★

380km (236 miles) SW of London; 56km (35 miles) SE of Exeter

At the mouth of the Dart River, this ancient seaport is home of the Royal Naval College. Traditionally linked to England's maritime greatness, Dartmouth sent out the young midshipmen who saw to it that "Britannia ruled the waves." You can take a river steamer up the Dart to Totnes. The Dart is Devon's most beautiful river. Dartmouth's 15th-century castle was built during the reign of Edward IV. The town's most noted architectural feature is the Butter Walk, a row of 17th-century houses standing on granite pillars. A Flemish influence, acquired through trade during the Middle Ages, is evident in some of the houses.

ESSENTIALS

GETTING THERE   Dartmouth is not easily reached by public transport. Trains run to Totnes and Paignton. Buses run hourly between Totnes and Dartmouth. Call ℂ **0870/608-2608,** or visit **www.stagecoachbus.com** for schedules.

If you're driving from Exeter, take the A38 southwest, cutting southeast to Totnes on the A381; then follow the A381 to the junction with the B3207.

Riverboats make the 16km (10-mile) run from Totnes to Dartmouth, but these trips depend on the tide and operate only from Easter to the end of October. See "Essentials," in the Totnes section above, for details on obtaining boat schedules.

VISITOR INFORMATION   The **Tourist Information Centre** is at the Engine House, Mayors Avenue (ℂ **01803/834224;** www.discoverdartmouth.com), and is open April to October Monday to Saturday 9:30am to 5:30pm, and Sunday 10am to 2pm; off-season hours are Monday to Saturday 9:30am to 4:30pm.

WHERE TO STAY

The inns and hotels of Dartmouth are expensive. The tourist office keeps a list of guesthouses providing affordable bed-and-breakfast. Our favorites include the **Hill View House,** 76 Victoria Rd., Dartmouth, Devon TQ6 9DZ (℃/fax **01803/839372;** www.hillviewdartmouth.co.uk). The well-run guesthouse offers five stylishly furnished, midsize bedrooms, each with a bathroom containing a tub or shower. The five-story restored late-Victorian house lies near the town center and waterfront. Charges range from £57 to £82 ($114–$164) for a double, with breakfast included. Diners Club, MasterCard, and Visa are accepted.

Another good choice is a small family-run guesthouse, **Capritia,** 69 Victoria Rd., Dartmouth, Devon TQ6 9RX (℃ **01803/833419;** www.capritia.co.uk), offering four small to midsize, but comfortably furnished, bedrooms ranging from £65 to £70 ($130–$140; no credit cards) for a double, including breakfast. Rooms have TVs, Wi-Fi, small fridges, beverage makers, and hair dryers.

A final possibility is **Cladda,** 90 Victoria Rd. (℃ **01803/835957;** fax 01803/835803; www.cladda-guesthouse.co.uk), a 1km (half-mile) walk from the center. There are six units, including two suites. Rates, which include a full English breakfast, are £70 ($140) for a double, and £125 ($250) for a suite (no credit cards). Suites are in a building next to the main house; each has a lounge and kitchen.

Dart Marina Hotel ✪   This hotel—the town's "second choice"—sits at the edge of its own marina, within a 3-minute walk from the center of town. It was originally built as a clubhouse for local yachties late in the 19th century and was then enlarged and transformed into a hotel just before World War II. It does not have as much charm or character as the Royal Castle. The bar, the riverside terrace, and each bedroom afford a view of yachts bobbing at anchor in the Dart River. Bedrooms on the third floor enjoy the best views and are the most contemporary, with neutral tones. Some have French windows opening onto small balconies; others have a small terrace with chaise longues and chairs. The more traditional rooms downstairs are decorated in a simpler English-country-house style, and some also have small balconies. Families will appreciate the contemporary apartments that sleep four.

Sandquay, Dartmouth, Devon TQ6 9PH. ℃ **01803/832580.** Fax 01803/835040. www.dartmarinahotel.com. 50 units. £155–£245 ($310–$490) double; £235–£275 ($470–$550) suite for 2; £190–£385 ($380–$770) apt for 4. Rates include breakfast. AE, MC, V. Free parking. **Amenities:** 2 restaurants; bar; indoor heated pool; gym; spa; Jacuzzi; steam room; room service. *In room:* A/C (in some), TV, minibar (in some), coffeemaker, hair dryer, trouser press, safe (in some).

Royal Castle Hotel ✪   A coaching inn on the town quay since 1639, this is the leading choice in Dartmouth. The Royal Castle has hosted Sir Francis Drake, Queen Victoria, Charles II, and Edward VII. Horse-drawn carriages (as late as 1910) dispatched passengers in a carriageway, now an enclosed reception hall. The glassed-in courtyard, with its winding wooden staircase, has the original coaching horn and a set of 20 antique spring bells connected to the bedrooms. Three rooms open off the covered courtyard, and the rambling corridors display antiques. River-view rooms are the most sought-after. Three rooms are air-conditioned, and eight units offer a Jacuzzi. Five rooms contain a four-poster bed, and each is individually decorated, although all reflect the age of the building. Four accommodations are large enough for families.

11 The Quay, Dartmouth, Devon TQ6 9PS. ℃ **01803/833033.** Fax 01803/835445. www.royalcastle.co.uk. 25 units. £130–£199 ($260–$398) double. Rates include English breakfast. AE, MC, V. Free parking. **Amenities:** Restaurant; 2 bars; room service; babysitting; laundry service; dry cleaning. *In room:* A/C (in some), TV, coffeemaker, hair dryer, safe.

WHERE TO DINE

Horn of Plenty ✿ INTERNATIONAL   As you drive from Tavistock to Calling-ton, a small sign points north along a leafy drive to a solid Regency house built by the duke of Bedford in the early 1800s as a private home on 2 hectares (5 acres) of grounds. Today's owners operate what the French call a *restaurant avec chambres;* after a day of touring the country, hotel guests enjoy well-prepared dinners at the award-winning restaurant. High-caliber starters range from pan-fried scallops with king prawn and an apple-and-coriander-laced pasta, or else roast pigeon wrapped in potato and served on a foie gras salad with a port-and-red-wine dressing. For tempting mains, opt for the pan-fried sea bass on a bed of new potatoes; it's served with a saffron-laced white-wine sauce. After dining, ascend to 1 of the 10 spacious, warm, and elegant bed-rooms that have been installed over the old stables of the house. With a full English breakfast included, doubles range from £160 to £250 ($320–$500).

In the Tamar View House, Gulworthy, Tavistock, Devon PL19 8JD. ✆ **01822/832528.** www.thehornofplenty.co.uk. Reservations recommended. 3-course fixed-price lunch £27 ($54); 3-course fixed-price dinner Mon £28 ($56), Tues–Sun £45 ($90). AE, MC, V. Daily noon–2pm and 7–9pm.

Kendricks (Value) BRITISH/INTERNATIONAL   One of the most reliable local eateries, patronized by visitors and locals alike, is this restaurant set in the heart of the historic port district. Local ingredients are used whenever possible in market-fresh dishes that range from succulent ribs to sizzling fajitas. On a windy day, the home-made soup with freshly baked bread is a favorite, though you can also begin with any-thing from nachos to goat-cheese salad with marinated olives. Steaks from rump to filet are a West Country feature, and we enjoy the rack of succulent pork ribs. Other main dish specialties include blackened salmon filets and the chef's own jambalaya with chicken and prawns (based on an old New Orleans recipe).

29 Fairfax Place. ✆ **01803/832328.** Reservations recommended. Main courses £7.95–£15 ($16–$30). MC, V. Daily 6:30–10pm.

The New Angel ✿✿ CONTINENTAL   The best and most stylish restaurant in town stands in a half-timbered building with a heavily carved facade, rising on the harbor front. The cookery is both innovative and well executed, more akin to the cre-ative cuisine of the Continent than the traditional food of England. Michelin-starred Chef John Burton-Race has moved into town, awakening the sleepy local taste buds. Fish is brought in from the local boats and purchased from Devon fishermen. Burton-Race creates his menu from the best and freshest produce of the day. Redolent of rich, subtly intermingled flavors are such dishes as roasted breast of duckling with poached white peaches or braised Dartmouth lobster with a tomato-and-basil-butter sauce.

The New Angel also offers accommodations—six well-furnished and quite com-fortable bedrooms, including one suite, from £130 to £150 ($260–$300) a night.

2 S. Embankment. ✆ **01803/839425.** www.thenewangel.co.uk. Reservations required. Main courses £10–£29 ($20–$58). AE, MC, V. Tues–Sun noon–2:30pm; Tues–Sat 6:30–10:30pm. Closed Jan.

A FAVORITE LOCAL PUB

Just a 2-minute walk from Bayard's Cove is one of our favorite pubs, the **Cherub,** 13 Higher St. (✆ **01803/832571;** www.the-cherub.co.uk). It was originally built in 1380 as the harbor master's house. Today this charming pub is a great place to drink and dine on simple traditional British platters and bar snacks. There's a more formal dining room upstairs that serves a number of fish dishes, steaks, lamb, and duck.

EXPLORING DARTMOUTH

Many visitors come to Dartmouth for the bracing salt air and a chance to explore the surrounding marshlands, which are rich in bird life and natural beauty. The way to do this is to book a cruise aboard **River Link,** which departs Dartmouth daily in summer with departures starting at 8:30am, heading for Totnes (see earlier in this chapter). To book tickets, look for the kiosk at Dartmouth Embankment (© **01803/834488**). The cruise lasts about an hour, costing £8.50 ($17) for adults, £7.50 ($15) for seniors, and £5.50 ($11) for children 11 and younger.

The town's most historic and interesting church is **St. Petrox,** on Castle Road, a 17th-century Anglican monument with an ivy-draped graveyard whose tombstones evoke the sorrows of Dartmouth's maritime past. The church is open daily from 7am to dusk.

It's also worth walking through **Bayard's Cove,** a waterfront, cobbled, half-timbered neighborhood that's quite charming. Set near the end of Lower Street, it prospered during the 1600s thanks to its ship-repair services. In 1620, its quays were the site for repairs of the Pilgrims' historic ships, the *Speedwell* and the *Mayflower,* just after their departure from Plymouth.

Dartmouth Castle Originally built during the 15th century, the castle was later outfitted with artillery and employed by the Victorians as a coastal defense station. A tour of its bulky ramparts and somber interiors provides insight into the changing nature of warfare throughout the centuries, and you'll see sweeping views of the surrounding coast and flatlands.

Castle Rd. (1km/½ mile south of the town center). © 01803/833588. Admission £3.90 ($7.80) adults, £2.90 ($5.80) seniors, £2 ($4) children. Apr–June and Sept daily 10am–5pm; July–Aug daily 10am–6pm; Oct daily 10am–4pm; Nov–Mar 23 Sat–Sun 10am–4pm.

Dartmouth Museum This is the region's most interesting maritime museum, focusing on the British Empire's military might of the 18th century. Built between 1635 and 1640, it's set amid an interconnected row of 17th-century buildings—the Butter Walk—whose overhanging, stilt-supported facade was originally designed to provide shade for the butter, milk, and cream sold there by local milkmaids. Today, the complex houses the museum, as well as shops selling wines, baked goods, and more.

The Butterwalk. © 01803/832923. Admission £1.50 ($3) adults, £1 ($2) seniors, 50p ($1) children. Apr–Oct Mon–Sat 10am–4pm; Nov–Mar Mon–Sat noon–3pm.

6 Plymouth ★★

390km (242 miles) SW of London; 259km (161 miles) SW of Southampton

The historic seaport of Plymouth is more romantic in legend than in reality. But this was not always so—during World War II, greater Plymouth lost at least 75,000 buildings to Nazi bombs. The heart of present-day Plymouth, including the municipal civic center on the Royal Parade, has been entirely rebuilt; however, the way it was rebuilt is the subject of much controversy. Instead of reconstructing half-timbered Elizabethan buildings, many property owners preferred the concrete bunker approach.

For the old part of town, you must go to the Elizabethan section, known as the **Barbican,** and walk along the quay in the footsteps of Sir Francis Drake (once the mayor of Plymouth). From here, in 1577, Drake set sail on his round-the-world voyage. The Barbican also holds special interest for visitors from the United States as the final departure point of the Pilgrims in 1620. The two ships, *Mayflower* and *Speedwell,* that sailed from Southampton in August of that year put into Plymouth after suffering storm damage. The *Speedwell* was abandoned as unseaworthy; the *Mayflower* made the trip to the New World alone.

ESSENTIALS

GETTING THERE   Plymouth Airport (✆ **01752/204090**) lies 6.5km (4 miles) from the center of the city. **Air Southwest** (✆ **0870/241-8202;** www.airsouthwest. com) has direct service from the London airport, Gatwick, to Plymouth.

Frequent trains run from London's Paddington Station to Plymouth in 3¼ to 4 hours. For rail information, call ✆ **08457/000125** or visit **www.firstgreatwestern. co.uk.** The **Plymouth Train Station** lies on North Road, north of the Plymouth Center. Western National Bus no. 83/84 runs from the station to the heart of Plymouth.

National Express has frequent daily bus service between London's Victoria Coach Station and Plymouth. The trip takes 5¼ hours. Call ✆ **0870/580-8080** for schedules and information, or visit **www.nationalexpress.com**.

If you're driving from London, take the M4 west to the junction with the M5 going south to Exeter. From Exeter, head southwest on the A38 to Plymouth.

VISITOR INFORMATION   The **Tourist Information Centre** is at the Mayflower, in the Barbican (✆ **01752/306330;** www.visitplymouth.co.uk). It is open from Easter to October Monday to Saturday 9am to 5pm, and Sunday 10am to 4pm, and off season Monday to Friday 9am to 5pm, and Saturday 10am to 4pm,

WHERE TO STAY

Astor Hotel   This appealing and restored hotel is better than ever following massive improvements. It was once the private home of a sea captain during the Victorian era. The best rooms are the so-called executive suites with four-poster beds, and even better are the bridal suites with both four-poster and a Jacuzzi. Of course, you don't have to be a honeymooner to book any of these. Even the mostly midsize standard rooms are exceedingly comfortable. You don't need to leave the premises at night as there is a cozy lounge bar and a first-class restaurant serving both a traditional British and an international cuisine.

14–22 Elliott St., the Hoe, Plymouth, Devon PL1 2PS. ✆ **01752/225511.** Fax 01752/251994. www.astorhotel.co.uk. 62 units. £70–£160 ($140–$320) double; £100–£200 ($200–$400) family room; £125–£400 ($250–$800) suite. Rates include English breakfast. AE, DC, MC, V. Free parking overnight, £2.50 ($5) permit parking nearby. **Amenities:** Restaurant; 2 bars; room service; laundry service. *In room:* TV, coffeemaker, trouser press.

Duke of Cornwall Hotel ✪   This Best Western hotel is a Victorian Gothic building that survived World War II bombings. Constructed in 1863, it was regarded by Sir John Betjeman as the finest example of Victorian architecture in Plymouth. The refurbished bedrooms are comfortable and well maintained. Four rooms contain antique four-poster beds, and six units are large enough for families.

Millbay Rd., Plymouth, Devon PL1 3LG. ✆ **800/780-7234** in the U.S., or 01752/275850. Fax 01752/275854. www.thedukeofcornwallhotel.com. 72 units. £104–£160 ($208–$320) double; from £150 ($300) suite. Rates include English breakfast. AE, DC, MC, V. Free parking. **Amenities:** Restaurant (see review below); bar; room service; babysitting; laundry service; dry cleaning. *In room:* TV, coffeemaker, hair dryer, trouser press.

Holiday Inn Plymouth ✪   One of the most distinguished hotels in the West Country, overlooking the harbor and the Hoe, this chain-run hotel is a midget high-rise. It is the town's finest address, superior to the long-standing Duke of Cornwall. The good-size rooms are well furnished with long double beds and have wide picture windows; compact bathrooms come with tub/shower combos. The decor is tasteful, in neutral browns and creams, and the overall atmosphere is casual and comfortable.

Armada Way, Plymouth, Devon PL1 2HJ. *(C)* **888/465-4329** in the U.S., or 0870/2250301. Fax 01752/673816. www.holidayinn.co.uk. 211 units. £99–£155 ($198–$310) double. AE, DC, MC, V. Parking £3.50 ($7). **Amenities:** Restaurant; 2 bars; indoor pool; health club; spa; sauna; solarium; salon; room service; babysitting; laundry service; dry cleaning. *In room:* A/C, TV, minibar (in executive rooms), coffeemaker, hair dryer, iron, trouser press, safe (in some).

WHERE TO DINE

The **Plymouth Arts Centre Restaurant,** 38 Looe St. (*(C)* **01752/202616**), offers one of the most filling and down-home vegetarian meals in town. Prices range from £3.50 to £9 ($7–$18), and it's also ideal for a snack. You can even see a movie downstairs if you'd like. Food is served Monday 10am to 5pm and Tuesday to Saturday 10am to 8:30pm.

Duke of Cornwall Hotel Restaurant 🐾 MODERN BRITISH   This landmark hotel dining room is one of the finest in the area. Lit by a Victorian chandelier, your menu is illuminated in an elegant setting. Traditional and classic favorites are included on the menu, but the taste is definitely contemporary English. High-quality ingredients are seriously and professionally cooked. Bold—but never outrageous—combinations of flavors are reflected by starters such as goat cheese with crispy pancetta and maple syrup, or smoked salmon with a halibut gâteau, cucumber "ribbons," and sweet chili vinaigrette. Among the main courses, we especially like the chargrilled rib-eye steak flavored with brandy and a peppercorn glaze, as well as the chicken breast stuffed with sun-dried tomatoes and fresh basil with an herb pesto. For dessert, finish off with a white chocolate and pistachio confection drizzled with bitter chocolate syrup. Service is first class, and there's also a good wine list.

Millbay Rd. *(C)* **01752/275850.** Reservations recommended. Main courses £13–£15 ($26–$30). AE, DC, MC, V. Daily 7–10pm.

Tanners 🐾🐾 ENGLISH/MEDITERRANEAN   Plymouth's leading restaurant lies in a character-filled 15th-century house, reputedly the oldest in town, with mullioned windows, exposed stone, antique tapestries, and even an illuminated water well. In spite of the old surroundings near the Theatre Royal and the City's Guildhall, the cuisine is contemporary with much use made of market-fresh ingredients. Chris and James Tanner, who welcome you to this citadel of fine cuisine, are often seen on TV food programs in Britain. As befits a port city, you get plenty of fish. Depending on the chef's mood or the time of year, tempting starters include seared local mackerel with a superb lobster risotto, or else roasted wood pigeon with vanilla-flavored shallots and a sherry vinegar reduction. For a main, taste the likes of seared filet of brill with smoked salmon croquettes or else roast partridge in a fresh thyme sauce.

Prysten House, Finewell St. *(C)* **01752/252001.** www.tannersrestaurant.com. Reservations required. 2-course lunch £15 ($30), 3 courses £20 ($40); Mon–Thurs 2-course dinner £26 ($52), 3 courses £32 ($64); Fri–Sat 5-course dinner £37 ($74). AE, DC, MC, V. Tues–Fri noon–2:30pm; Sat noon–2pm; Tues–Sat 7–9pm.

SEEING THE SIGHTS

To commemorate the spot from which the *Mayflower* sailed for the New World, a white archway, erected in 1934 and capped with the flags of Great Britain and the United States, stands at the base of Plymouth's West Pier, on the Barbican. Incorporating a granite monument that was erected in 1891, the site is referred to as both the *Mayflower* **Steps** and the **Memorial Gateway.**

The **Barbican** is a mass of narrow streets, old houses, and quay-side shops selling antiques, brass work, old prints, and books. It's a perfect place for strolling and browsing through shops at your leisure.

Fishing boats still unload their catches at the wharves, and passenger-carrying ferryboats run short harbor cruises. The best way to view Plymouth, in our opinion, is to take one of the boat trips outlined below. You not only get to see Plymouth from a nautical perspective, but you get to experience an added thrill by knowing that this was the pilgrims' last view of England before departing for the New World. A trip includes views from the water of Drake's Island in the sound, the dockyards, naval vessels, and the Hoe—a greenbelt in the center of the city that opens onto Plymouth Harbour. A cruise of Plymouth Harbour costs £7 ($14) for adults and £4.50 ($9) for children. Departures are April to October, with cruises leaving every half-hour from 10am to 4pm daily. These **Tamar Cruising** and **Cremyll Ferry** cruises are booked at Cremyll Quay, Torpoint (© **01752/822105**).

National Marine Aquarium 🐟 The best aquarium in the United Kingdom stands near the center of the harbor area, displaying both freshwater and seawater fish, even a shark theater. At least three times a week visitors can watch in awe as the sharks feed, putting on a gruesome *Jaws*-like show. You can actually walk under the sharks in their holding tank. Fearing many sea creatures are being destroyed, the institution also engages in such work as a breeding program for sea horses. There are many other exhibits as well.

Rope Walk, Coxside. © 01752/600301. www.national-aquarium.co.uk. Admission £9.50 ($19) adults, £8 ($16) students and seniors, £5.75 ($12) children ages 4–15, £27 ($54) family ticket, free for children 3 and younger. Apr–Oct daily 10am–6pm; Nov–Mar daily 10am–5pm.

Plymouth Gin Distillery One of Plymouth's oldest surviving buildings, this is where the Pilgrims met before sailing for the New World. Plymouth Gin has been produced here for 200 years on a historic site that dates from a Dominican monastery built in 1425. Public guided tours (including a tasting) are offered, and a Plymouth Gin Shop is on the premises.

Black Friars Distillery, 60 Southside St. © 01752/665292. www.plymouthgin.com. Admission £6 ($12) adults, free for children with paying adult. Nov to day before Easter daily 9am–5pm; day after Easter to Oct daily 9am–5:30pm. Closed Christmas and Easter. Bus: 54.

Prysten House Built in 1490 as a town house close to St. Andrew's Church, this is now a church house and working museum. Reconstructed in the 1930s with American help, it displays a model of Plymouth in 1620 and tapestries depicting the colonization of America. At the entrance is the gravestone of the captain of the U.S. brig *Argus*, who died on August 15, 1813, after a battle in the English Channel.

Finewell St. © 01752/661414. Admission £1 ($2) adults, 50p ($1) children. Mon–Sat 10am–4pm.

7 Clovelly ⭐⭐

386km (240 miles) SW of London; 18km (11 miles) SW of Bideford

This is the most charming of all Devon villages and one of the main attractions of the West Country. Starting at a great height, the village cascades down the mountainside. Its narrow, cobblestone High Street makes driving impossible. You park your car at the top and make the trip on foot; supplies are carried down by donkeys. Every step of the way provides views of tiny cottages, with their terraces of flowers lining the main street. The village fleet is sheltered at the stone quay at the bottom.

The major sight of Clovelly is Clovelly itself. Victorian author Charles Kingsley once said, "It is as if the place had stood still while all the world had been rushing and rumbling past it." The price of entry to the village (see below) includes a guided tour of a fisherman's cottage as it would have been at the end of the 1800s. For the same price, you can also visit the **Kingsley Exhibition.** Author of *Westward Ho!,* Kingsley lived in Clovelly while his father was curate at the church. This exhibition traces the story of his life. He was also a social reformer, which led him to write his enduring children's classic, *The Water Babies.*

Right down below the Kingsley Exhibition—and our shopping note for the town—is a **craft gallery** where you have a chance to see and buy a wide variety of works by local artists and craftspeople. Once you've reached the end, you can sit and relax on the quay, taking in the views and absorbing Clovelly's unique atmosphere from this tiny, beautifully restored 14th-century quay.

Once you've worked your way to the bottom, how do you get back up? You can climb back up the steep cobbled streets to the top and the parking lot. Or you can go to the rear of the Red Lion Inn and line up for a Land Rover. In summer, the line is often long.

Insider's tip: To avoid the tourist crowd, stay out of Clovelly from around 11am until teatime. When the midday congestion is at its height, visit nearby villages such as Bucks Mills (5km/3 miles to the east) and Hartland Quay (6.5km/4 miles to the west).

ESSENTIALS

GETTING THERE   From London's Paddington Station, trains depart for Exeter frequently. At Exeter, you transfer to a train headed for the end destination of Barnstaple. Travel time from Exeter to Barnstaple is 1¼ hours. For rail information, call *©* **0845/7484950** or visit **www.nationalrail.co.uk**. From Barnstaple, passengers transfer to Clovelly by bus.

From Barnstaple, about one bus per hour, operated by either the Red Bus Company or the Filers Bus Company, goes to Bideford. The trip takes 40 minutes. At Bideford, connecting buses (with no more than a 10-min. wait between arrival and departure) continue on for the 30-minute drive to Clovelly. Two Land Rovers make continuous round-trips to the Red Lion Inn from the top of the hill. The Clovelly Visitor Centre (see below) maintains up-to-the-minute transportation information about getting to Clovelly, depending on your location.

If driving from London, head west on the M4, cutting south at the junction with the M5. At the junction near Bridgewater, continue west along the A39 toward Lynton. The A39 runs all the way to the signposted turnoff for Clovelly.

VISITOR INFORMATION   Go to the **Clovelly Visitor Centre** (*©* **01237/ 431781**), where you'll pay £4.95 ($9.90) for adults and £3.25 ($6.50) for kids 7 to 16, or £15 ($30) for a family ticket, for the cost of parking, use of facilities, entrance to the village, and an audiovisual theater admission, offering a multiprojector show tracing the story of Clovelly from 2000 B.C. Also included in the price is a tour of a fisherman's cottage and admission to the **Kingsley Exhibition** (see above). It's open Monday to Saturday 9am to 5:30pm April to June and October, daily 11am to 3:30pm November to March, and daily 9am to 6:30pm July to September. If you're booked into one of the inns in the village, you don't have to pay the entrance fee.

WHERE TO STAY & DINE

New Inn   About halfway down High Street is the village pub, a good meeting place at sundown. It offers the best lodgings in the village, in two buildings on opposite sides of the steep street (but only a 3.5m/12-ft. leap between balconies). Each room is relatively small but comfortable, and two are large enough for a family. If you're driving, you can park in the lot at the entrance to the town. It's advisable to pack a smaller overnight bag because your luggage will have to be carried down (but is returned to the top by donkey).

High St., Clovelly, North Devon EX39 5TQ. © **01237/431303.** Fax 01237/431636. www.newinn-clovelly.co.uk. 19 units, 8 with bathroom. £80 ($160) double without bathroom, £94 ($188) with bathroom. Rates include English breakfast. AE, MC, V. **Amenities:** Restaurant; bar. *In room:* TV, coffeemaker, trouser press.

Red Lion At the bottom of the steep cobbled street, right on the stone seawall of the little harbor, Red Lion occupies the prime position in the village. Rising three stories with gables and a courtyard, it's actually an unspoiled country inn, where life centers on an antique pub and village inhabitants, including sea captains, who gather to satisfy their thirst over pints of ale. Most rooms look directly onto the sea with spectacular views, and they have been refurbished. Many are small, but two are spacious enough for a family.

The Quay, Clovelly, Devon EX39 5TF. © **01237/431237.** Fax 01237/431044. www.redlion-clovelly.co.uk. 11 units. £103–£141 ($206–$282) double. Rates include English breakfast. AE, MC, V. **Amenities:** Restaurant; bar. *In room:* TV, coffeemaker, hair dryer.

EN ROUTE TO LYNTON-LYNMOUTH: A STAY ON A WORKING FARM

Halmpstone Manor ⭐ *Finds* In the countryside, this working farm is operated by Charles and Jane Stanbury. Originally built in the 11th century as a manor house with 22 rooms, the structure has diminished in size because of two fires that occurred in the 15th and 16th centuries. The edifice was rebuilt in 1701 in its present form, with 15th-century paneling located in the dining room and high ceilings in the four-poster bedrooms. Family heirlooms are scattered throughout, and all the spacious bedrooms are a regal statement of English taste, luxuriously furnished with either four-poster or brass and coronet beds.

Chittlehampton Rd., Bishop's Tawton, Barnstaple, N. Devon EX32 0EA. © **01271/830321.** Fax 01271/830826. www.halmpstonemanor.co.uk. 5 units. £100 ($200) double; £140 ($280) suite. Rates include English breakfast and afternoon tea. MC, V. From Clovelly, take A39 east for 30–45 min., turning off the A39 when you see signs for Chittlehampton. About 3km (2 miles) after the turnoff, you'll see signs pointing to Halmpstone Manor. **Amenities:** Restaurant; bar. *In room:* TV, coffeemaker, hair dryer, trouser press.

8 Lynton-Lynmouth ⭐

332km (206 miles) W of London; 95km (59 miles) NW of Exeter

Our favorite places to stay along the rugged northern coast of Devon are the twin Victorian villages of Lynton and Lynmouth. The harbor town is **Lynmouth,** and the higher town is **Lynton,** rising 183m (600 ft.) over the port. The two villages are linked by a cliff railway (see below for details).

Artists such as Gainsborough have long been attracted to the area for its scenic views. He called Lynmouth "the most delightful place for a landscape painter this country can boast." Other artists and writers have been drawn to the area, including Shelley, who honeymooned here with his 16-year-old bride, Harriet Westbrook. He wrote *Queen Mab* here.

Summer visitors come here to take boat trips along the Exmoor Coast and to explore the surrounding wooded valleys with waterfalls. From the North Devon cliffs, you can see some of the greatest **views** in the West Country, looking across the Bristol Channel to the Welsh coast.

ESSENTIALS

GETTING THERE   The town is rather remote, and the local tourist office recommends that you rent a car to get here. However, local daily trains from Exeter arrive at Barnstaple. For rail information, call ℭ **0845/7484950** or visit **www.national rail.co.uk**.

From Barnstaple, bus service is provided to Lynton at a frequency of about one every hour. Call ℭ **01598/752225** for schedules.

If you're driving, take the M4 west from London to the junction with the M5, then head south to the junction with the A39. Continue west on the A39 to Lynton-Lynmouth.

VISITOR INFORMATION   The **Tourist Information Centre** is at the Town Hall, Lee Road (ℭ **01598/752225;** www.lynton-lynmouth-tourism.co.uk), and is open from Easter to October Monday to Saturday 9:30am to 5pm, Sunday 10am to 4pm, and from November to Easter Monday to Saturday 10am to 4pm, Sunday 10am to 2pm.

WHERE TO STAY & DINE

Hewitt's at the Hoe   Hewitt's is named for Sir Thomas Hewitt, who helped construct the funicular railway that links the twin resorts. In the 1860s, he also built a home for himself, and today that place is one of the most successful small hotels in Lynton. Situated on some 11 hectares (27 acres), it opens onto the beautiful vistas of Lynmouth Bay (best enjoyed while seated on a sunny terrace). The old house is filled with architectural character, as exemplified by its grand staircase, time-mellowed paneling, antiques, and stained-glass windows. All rooms are comfortably appointed. The hotel is "for all seasons" and has a country-house atmosphere. It's a perfect Agatha Christie set, enhanced by a pianist who plays in the lobby nightly from 6:30 to 8pm.

The Hoe, North Walk, Lynton, Devon EX35 6HJ. ℭ **01598/752293.** Fax 01598/752489. www.hewittshotel.co.uk. 5 units. £120–£160 ($240–$320) double; from £370 ($740) serviced apt for 3 (per week). AE, MC, V. Free parking. **Amenities:** Restaurant; bar; Jacuzzi; room service; laundry service; dry cleaning. *In room:* TV, minibar, coffeemaker, hair dryer, trouser press.

The Rising Sun 👁👁   Bask in the wonder and warmth of an inn that has been in business for more than 600 years. Following a renovation under the direction of an international designer from London, the bedrooms and bathrooms look more glamorous and romantic than ever, many with four-poster beds. Stylish and tasteful fabrics were used extensively to give the rooms more elegance. Behind the inn, halfway up the cliff, a tiny garden brightens with flowers in summer. The owner also has rooms available nearby in Shelley's Cottage, where the poet honeymooned in 1812. *Note:* The hotel discourages children 6 and younger from staying here.

The Harbourside, Lynmouth, N. Devon EX35 6EG. ℭ **01598/753223.** Fax 01598/753480. www.risingsunlynmouth. co.uk. 16 units, 1 cottage. £120–£150 ($240–$300) double; £160 ($320) Shelley's Cottage for 2. Rates include English breakfast. MC, V. Parking £5 ($10). **Amenities:** Restaurant; bar; room service; laundry service. *In room:* TV, coffeemaker, hair dryer.

St. Vincent House 👁   This charming guesthouse was built by a master mariner in 1834 and has since been sensitively converted to receive guests. Captain Thomas Green fought alongside Admiral Nelson at the Battle of St. Vincent off the west coast of Portugal—hence, the name of the house. All the well-furnished and comfortable bedrooms were named after victorious battleships. Many of the original features of the seaman's home, including a beautiful Regency spiral staircase, have been retained. Belgian Jean-Paul Saltpetier and his partner, Linda Cameron, will house and feed you well. In the traditional guest lounge, visitors enjoy an open fire on chilly nights.

Castle Hill, Lynton, Devon EX35 6JA. (℃ **01598/752244.** Fax 01598/752244. www.st-vincent-hotel.co.uk. 7 units. £35–£38 ($70–$76) per person double. No credit cards. Free parking. Closed Nov–Easter. **Amenities:** Restaurant; lounge; garden. *In room:* TV, beverage maker, hair dryer.

Shelley's Hotel ⚘ Established more than 2 centuries ago, "Mrs. Hooper's Lodgings" was where the Romantic poet brought his child bride, Harriet Westbrook, in 1812. Today it's been transformed into a remarkable little hotel of charm and grace. (Shelley left without paying his bill, incidentally.) In the center of the village, the hotel, opening onto views of Lynmouth Bay, has been tastefully restored and individually decorated, some of its handsomely furnished bedrooms with their own private conservatory and balcony. Big windows make the rooms bright when the sun is shining, and the staff is most helpful and welcoming.

8 Watersmeet Rd., Lynmouth EX35 6EP. (℃ **01598/753219.** Fax 01598/753751. www.shelleyshotel.co.uk 11 units. £90–£130 ($180–$260) double. MC, V. Parking £2 ($4). **Amenities:** Breakfast room; bar; laundry service. *In room:* TV, beverage maker, hair dryer.

Tors Hotel Set high on a cliff, the Tors Hotel opens onto a view of the coastline and the bay. It was built in 1895 in the fashion of a Swiss château, with more than 40 gables, Tyrolean balconies jutting out to capture the sun (or the moon), and some 30 chimneys. The interior has been modernized, and much attention has been lavished on the comfortable bedrooms, five of which are large enough for families. The superior rooms all have sea views. All rooms contain well-maintained bathrooms with tub/shower combos.

Tors Park, Lynmouth, Lynton, N. Devon EX35 6NA. (℃ **01598/753236.** Fax 01598/752544. www.torslynmouth.co.uk. 31 units. £112–£144 ($224–$288) double; £250 ($500) suite. Rates include English breakfast. AE, DC, MC, V. Free parking. Closed Jan–Feb. **Amenities:** Restaurant; bar; heated outdoor pool; room service; laundry service. *In room:* TV, coffeemaker, hair dryer.

Victoria Lodge This elegant hotel, west of Church Hill, is imbued with a Victorian theme throughout, following a complete refurbishing and redecorating. It's known locally for its comfort and cuisine. Each centrally heated bedroom is decorated in a Victorian motif; some deluxe units have four-poster beds. The hotel is not suitable for children 11 and younger. The cuisine is a fairly standard blend of English and Continental; vegetarian and special diets can be honored.

Lee Rd., Lynton, Devon EX35 6BS. (℃/fax **01598/753203.** www.victorialodge.co.uk. 9 units. £70–£140 ($140–$280). Rates include English breakfast. MC, V. Free parking. Closed Nov–Mar. **Amenities:** Breakfast room; lounge; bar. *In room:* TV, beverage maker, hair dryer, no phone.

SEEING THE SIGHTS

Lynton is linked to its twin, Lynmouth, by the most celebrated **railway** in Devon, the **Lynton & Lynmouth Cliff Railway** (℃ **01598/753486;** www.cliffrailwaylynton. co.uk). The century-old train uses no electricity and no power. Instead, the railway covers the differences in distance and altitude by means of a complicated network of cables and pulleys, allowing cars to travel up and down the face of the rocky cliff. The length of the track is 259m (862 ft.) with a gradient of 1 inch, which gives it a vertical height of approximately 150m (500 ft.). The two passenger cars are linked together with two steel cables, and the operation of the lift is on the counterbalance system, which is simply explained as a pair of scales where one side, when weighted by a water ballast, pulls the other up. The train carries about 40 passengers at a time for £2.75 ($5.50) adults, £1.75 ($3.50) children, each a round-trip ticket. Trains depart daily from March to October, at 2- to 5-minute intervals, from 10am to 5pm. In peak summer season, trains often run until 8 or 9pm. From November to February, the line is shut down.

For hikers, the area abounds in trails, the most dramatic being west along North Walk, a 1.6km (1-mile) trail leading to the **Valley of the Rocks** ✿, a grouping of rugged rock formations rising from a grass-covered valley to peaks of bare sandstone and shale, said to have been carved during the Ice Age by the harsh winds from the Bristol Channel. Locals have given names to many of these rocks, including "the Devil's Cheesewring." The centerpiece of the formation is Castle Rock, known for its resident herd of wild goats.

To learn more about the best hikes in the area, go to the tourist office (see above) and pick up a copy of a bulletin, *Walking in North Devon,* outlining the best walks in North Devon with the most varied scenery. Over the years we have taken most of these walks, our favorite being the **Lyn Gorge** ✿, stretching for 8km (5 miles). This walk begins at the Hillsford Bridge on the A39 south of Lynmouth. Details of all these walks can be downloaded at **www.devon-holiday.co.uk/walks.html**.

12

Cornwall: The Ancient Duchy

The ancient duchy of **Cornwall** is in the extreme southwestern part of England, often called "the toe." This peninsula is a virtual island—culturally if not geographically. Encircled by coastline, it abounds in rugged cliffs, hidden bays, fishing villages, sandy beaches, and sheltered coves where smuggling was once rampant. Though many of the seaports with hillside cottages resemble towns on the Mediterranean, Cornwall retains its own distinctive flavor.

The ancient land had its own language until about 250 years ago, and some of the old words (*pol* for pool, *tre* for house) still survive. The Cornish dialect is more easily understood by the Welsh than by those who speak the queen's English.

We suggest basing yourself at one of the smaller fishing villages, such as **East** or **West Looe, Polperro,** or **Mousehole,** where you'll experience the true charm of the duchy. Many of the villages, such as

St. Ives, are artists' colonies. Except for St. Ives and **Port Isaac,** some of the best places lie on the southern coast, often hyped as the **Cornish Riviera.** However, the north coast has its own peculiar charm as well. The majestic coastline is studded with fishing villages and hidden coves for swimming, which are best seen at the East or West Looe and especially at Polperro, which are the most evocative. Visit these little ports even if you have to skip the rest. A little farther west is **Land's End,** where England actually comes to an end. And the **Isles of Scilly,** 43km (27 miles) off the Cornish coast, have only five islands inhabited out of more than 100. Here you'll find the **Abbey Gardens of Tresco,** 297 hectares (735 acres) with 5,000 species of plants. Finally, a trip to this region is incomplete without a visit to **Tintagel Castle,** linked with the legends of King Arthur, Lancelot, and Merlin.

1 The Fishing Villages of Looe & Polperro ⊛

Looe: 425km (264 miles) SW of London, 32km (20 miles) W of Plymouth; Polperro: 463km (271 miles) SW of London, 9.5km (6 miles) SW of Looe, 42km (26 miles) W of Plymouth

The ancient twin towns of **East and West Looe** are connected by a seven-arched stone bridge that spans the Looe River. Houses on the hills are stacked one on top of the other in terrace fashion. In each fishing village are good accommodations.

The old fishing village of **Polperro,** surrounded by cliffs, is one of the handsomest villages in Cornwall, with parts of it harkening back to the 17th century. The village is reached by a steep descent from the top of a hill from the main road. You can take the 7km (4½-mile) cliff walk from Looe to Polperro, but the less adventurous will want to drive. However, in July and August you're not allowed to take cars into town unless you have a hotel reservation, in order to prevent traffic bottlenecks. A large parking area charges according to the length of your stay. For those unable to walk, a horse-drawn bus will take visitors to the town center.

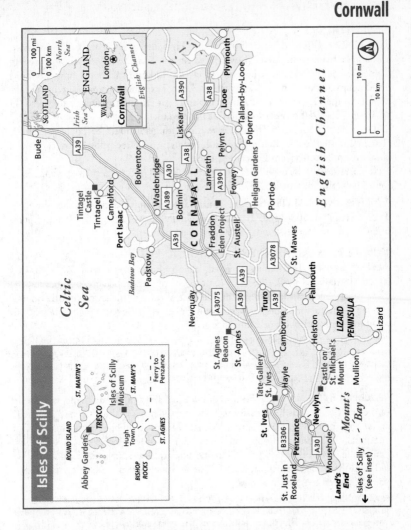

The neighboring settlements of **Lanreath** and **Pelynt** are two Cornish villages with accommodations for those seeking lodgings outside Polperro. Like many Cornish villages, they're steeped in legend—ghosts, headless horses, and the like—and actually date back to the Domesday Book of 1086. The tiny villages are relatively devoid of attractions and sustain themselves by farming and summer tourists.

Fishing and sailing are two of the major sports in the area, and the sandy coves, as well as **East Looe Beach,** are spots for sea bathing. Beyond the towns are cliff paths and chalky downs worth a ramble. Looe is noted for its shark fishing, but you may prefer simply walking the narrow, crooked medieval streets of East Looe, with its old harbor and 17th-century guildhall.

ESSENTIALS

GETTING THERE   Daily trains run from Plymouth to Looe, and rail connections can also be made from Exeter (Devon) and Bristol (Somerset). Most visitors drive to Polperro, but the nearest main-line station is at Liskeard, 3½ hours from London's Paddington Station, with a branch line to Looe. Taxis meet incoming trains to take visitors to the various little villages in the area. For rail information in the area, call *C* **0845/748-4950** or visit **www.nationalrail.co.uk**.

Local bus companies have various routings from Plymouth to Looe. Ask at the Tourist Information Centre in Plymouth for a schedule (see below). You can take a local bus to Polperro from Liskeard or Looe.

If you're driving to Looe from Plymouth, take the A38 west, then the B3253. To get to Polperro, follow the A387 southwest from Looe.

VISITOR INFORMATION   The **Tourist Information Centre** is at the Guildhall, Fore Street (*C* **01503/262072**), and is open daily April to September 10am to 5pm, and October to March Monday to Friday 10am to noon.

WHERE TO STAY & DINE IN & AROUND LOOE

Barclay House   This family-operated, country-house hotel stands on a wooded hillside surrounded by 2.4 hectares (6 acres) of private woodlands overlooking the Looe River Valley, but it's also just on the edge of town at the entrance to Looe, and about a 5-minute walk from the harbor and the center of the resort. Units are spacious and fitted with soft twins or a king-size bed.

St. Martins Rd. (the main Plymouth-Looe Rd., B3253), E. Looe, Cornwall PL13 1LP. *C* **01503/262929**. www.barclay house.co.uk. 10 units, 8 cottages. £90–£110 ($180–$220) double; £275–£1,375 ($550–$2,750) cottage per week. Rates (except cottages) include English breakfast. AE, MC, V. **Amenities:** Restaurant; bar; lounge; outdoor heated pool; room service; babysitting. *In room:* TV, coffeemaker, hair dryer.

Fieldhead Hotel *(Kids)*   The Fieldhead, built in 1896 as a private home, is now one of the area's best hotels. Commanding a view of the sea, it is situated on .8 hectare (2 acres) of gardens. The rooms have a high standard of traditional furnishings and are continually maintained. Rooms are warm and inviting; most of them open onto panoramic views of St. George's Island and the bay. *Note:* Families like not only the kid-friendly management here, but also the location in a garden setting where even young children can play in safety.

Portuan Rd., Hannafore, W. Looe, Cornwall PL13 2DR. *C* **01503/262689**. Fax 01503/264114. www.fieldheadhotel.co.uk. 16 units. £73–£150 ($146–$300) double. Rates include English breakfast. AE, MC, V. **Amenities:** Restaurant; bar; lounge; outdoor heated pool; room service; laundry service. *In room:* TV, coffeemaker, hair dryer, iron.

The Talland Bay Hotel *(R)*   A country house dating from the 16th century, situated on 1 hectare (2½ acres), this hotel is the domain of George and Mary Granville, who will direct you to local beaches and the croquet lawn. Its rectangular swimming pool is ringed with flagstones and a semitropical garden. Views from the tastefully furnished bedrooms include the sea and rocky coastline. Some bedrooms are in a comfortable annex.

Talland-by-Looe, Porthallow 1, Cornwall PL13 2JB. *C* **01503/272667**. Fax 01503/272940. www.tallandbayhotel.co.uk. 23 units. Nov–Apr £155–£210 ($310–$420) double; May–June and Sept–Oct £190–£245 ($380–$490) double; July–Aug £200–£255 ($400–$510) double; year-round from £235 ($470) suite. Rates include English breakfast and dinner. MC, V. Take A387 6.5km (4 miles) southwest of Looe. **Amenities:** Restaurant; bar; lounge; heated outdoor pool; putting green; lawn tennis; croquet; room service; babysitting; laundry service. *In room:* TV, coffeemaker, hair dryer, safe.

The Well House 🎿 *Kids*   Well House is one of those *restaurants avec chambres* found occasionally in the West Country, and it's one of the best. Located 5km (3 miles) from Liskeard, it has 2 hectares (5 acres) of gardens opening onto vistas of the Looe Valley. It offers beautifully furnished bedrooms, with many thoughtful extras, such as fresh flowers. Two beautiful terrace rooms are at the garden level. Most rooms have a twin bed or else a large double. Families are welcomed into extra-large rooms; especially popular is the hotel's family suite, with one large double bedroom plus a twin-bedded unit.

St. Keyne, Liskeard, Cornwall PL14 4RN. © 01579/342001. Fax 01579/343891. www.wellhouse.co.uk. 9 units. £145–£170 ($290–$340) double; £205–£245 ($410–$490) family suite. Rates include English breakfast. MC, V. From Liskeard, take B3254 to St. Keyne, 5km (3 miles) away. **Amenities:** Restaurant; bar; heated outdoor pool; tennis court; croquet lawn; room service. *In room:* TV, hair dryer, trouser press.

WHERE TO STAY IN NEARBY PELYNT & LANREATH

Jubilee Inn 🎿   Built in the 16th century, this inn takes its name from Queen Victoria's Jubilee celebration, when it underwent restoration. It's a comment on, rather than a monument to, the past. A glass-enclosed circular staircase, built to serve as a combined tower and hothouse, takes you to the bedrooms. All but the three newest rooms have excellent 19th-century furnishings. Most rooms are midsize, though two are large enough for families.

Jubilee Hill, Pelynt (6.5km/4 miles from Looe, 5km/3 miles from Polperro), Cornwall PL13 2JZ. © 01503/220312. Fax 01503/220920. 11 units. £50–£70 ($100–$140) double. Rates include English breakfast. MC, V. **Amenities:** Restaurant; bar. *In room:* TV, coffeemaker, hair dryer.

The Punch Bowl Inn 🎿   Opened in 1620, the Punch Bowl has since served as a courthouse, coaching inn, and rendezvous for smugglers. Today its bedrooms (all with four-poster beds) provide old-fashioned comfort. One of the kitchens here is one of the few licensed in Britain as a bar. Many bedrooms are quite small, though they come in various shapes and sizes, each with a small, compact bathroom.

Lanreath, Cornwall PL13 2NX. © 01503/220778. 9 units. £60–£70 ($120–$140) double. Rates include English breakfast. MC, V. From Polperro, take B3359 north. **Amenities:** Restaurant; bar; lounge. *In room:* TV, coffeemaker, no phone.

Cornwall's Geodesic Domed Eden

At first you think some spaceship filled with aliens has invaded sleepy old Cornwall. A second look reveals one of England's newest and most dramatic attractions, the **Eden Project** 🎿🎿, Bodelva, St. Austell (© **01726/811911**; www.edenproject.com), a 48km (30-mile) drive west of Plymouth. This sprawling attraction presents plants from the world over. It's open March 26 to October 29 daily 9am to 6pm (last admission at 4:30pm); October 30 to March 25 daily 10am to 4:30pm (last admission at 3pm). Admission is £14 ($28) for adults, £10 ($20) for seniors, £7 ($14) for students, £5 ($10) for children 5 to 18, or £35 ($70) for a family ticket (two adults, three children 5–15). The project lies 9.5km (6 miles) from the St. Austell train station, to which it is linked by frequent buses.

WHERE TO DINE IN POLPERRO

The Kitchen SEAFOOD   This pink cottage halfway to the harbor from the parking area was once a wagon-builder's shop. It's now a restaurant offering good English cooking; everything is homemade from fresh ingredients. The menu changes seasonally and features local fresh fish. Typical dishes include Fowey sea trout with lemon-and-herb butter and breast of duckling with blueberry-and-Drambuie sauce. Many vegetarian dishes are offered as main courses.

The Combes. © 01503/272780. Reservations required. Main courses £18–£22 ($36–$44). MC, V. Wed–Sun 10am–4pm. Closed Jan.

Nelson's Restaurant SEAFOOD   Situated in the lower reaches of Polperro, near the spot where the local river meets the sea, this is the only structure in town specifically built as a restaurant. It features succulent preparations of regional fish and shellfish that arrive fresh from local fishing boats. The menu changes daily but usually includes fresh crab, Dover sole, fresh lobster, and many other exotic fish. Fresh meat, poultry, and game, all from local suppliers, are also available and are beautifully prepared. A lower deck features a cafe/bar and bistro. A comprehensive wine list boasts some fine vintages.

Saxon Bridge. © 01503/272366. Reservations recommended. Main courses £7–£22 ($14–$44). MC, V. Tues–Sun 6:30pm to last customer; Sun 10:30am–2pm. Closed mid-Jan to mid-Feb.

2 St. Mawes ⭐

483km (300 miles) SW of London; 3km (2 miles) E of Falmouth; 29km (18 miles) S of Truro

Overlooking the mouth of the Fal River, St. Mawes is sheltered from northern winds, and subtropical plants can grow here. From the town quay, you can take a boat to Frenchman's Creek and Helford River, as well as other places (see below). St. Mawes is noted for its sailing, boating, fishing, and yachting, and half a dozen sandy coves lie within a 15-minute drive from the port. The town, built on the Roseland Peninsula, makes for scenic walks because of its colorful cottages and sheltered harbor.

GETTING THERE

Trains leave London's Paddington Station for Truro several times a day. The trip takes 4½ to 5 hours. For schedules and information, call © **0845/748-4950** or visit **www.nationalrail.co.uk**. Passengers transfer at Truro to one of the two buses that make the 45-minute bus trip from Truro to St. Mawes. It's much easier to take a taxi from either Truro or, even better, from the village of St. Austell, which is the train stop before Truro.

Buses leave London's Victoria Coach Station three times a day for Truro. The bus takes 7½ hours. For schedules and information, call © **0870/580-8080** or visit **www.nationalexpress.com**.

If you're driving, to reach St. Mawes, turn left off the A390 (the main road along the southern coast of Cornwall), at a junction 6.5km (4 miles) past St. Austell, onto the Tregony road, which will take you into St. Mawes.

A ferry travels to St. Mawes from both Falmouth and Truro, but schedules are erratic, varying with the tides and the weather conditions.

WHERE TO STAY & DINE

Hotel Tresanton ⭐⭐   Laura Ashley and the designer of an ocean liner must have joined forces to create this country-house hotel, which lies above the sea overlooking

Finds The Lost Gardens of Heligan

Seeing **Heligan Gardens** 𝒶𝒶 is like traveling back in time to Victoria's day. Europe's largest garden restoration project sprawls over 32 hectares (80 acres) of pure enchantment, with award-winning gardens. Near the fishing village of Mevagissey, these gardens "slept" for nearly 7 decades before they were rediscovered and restored.

In summer the gardens are open from 10am to 6pm (they close at 5pm off season). Admission is £8.50 ($17) for adults, £7.50 ($15) for seniors, £5 ($10) for ages 5 to 16, free for 4 and younger. A family ticket sells for £24 ($48). For more information, call ℭ **01726/845100** or check out **www.heligan.com**.

the fishing harbor. Tresanton has quickly replaced Idle Rocks and Rising Sun as the premier address in town. The whole place casts an aura of a chic house party, 1930s-style, and even includes a movie theater where screenings are held. A glamorous hotel, Tresanton offers a combination of beautiful old and new furnishings in its spacious, airy bedrooms. The views from the bedrooms are among the most panoramic on the coast, which you'll want to explore on long walks above *Rebecca*-like cliffs. The preferred units are nos. 22 through 27, each with its own terrace overlooking the churning waters.

St. Mawes, Cornwall TR2 5DR. ℭ **01326/270055.** Fax 01326/270053. www.tresanton.com. 29 units. £185–£315 ($370–$630) double; £310–£450 ($620–$900) suite. Rates include English breakfast. Minimum 2-night stay Sat–Sun. AE, MC, V. Free parking. **Amenities:** Restaurant; bar; lounge; children's playroom; room service; massage; babysitting; laundry service. *In room:* TV, hair dryer, safe.

The Idle Rocks Hotel *Kids*   The second-best place to stay in St. Mawes is this solid old building, right on the seawall, sporting gaily colored umbrellas and tables all along the terrace. Water laps at the wall, and the site opens onto views over the river and the constant traffic of sailboats and dinghies. Most rooms have sea or river views; the 17 units in the main hotel building charge higher rates. Four rooms tout balconies and four-poster beds. Families flock here for the bustling harbor view, which kids love, and for the number of extra-large, comfortably appointed rooms.

Harbourside, St. Mawes, Cornwall TR2 5AN. ℭ **0844/502-7587.** Fax 0871/903-2987. www.idlerocks.co.uk. 27 units. £148–£328 ($296–$656) double. Rates include half-board. AE, MC, V. Parking £5 ($10). **Amenities:** Restaurant; bar; lounge; room service; babysitting; laundry service; dry cleaning. *In room:* TV, coffeemaker, hair dryer.

The Rising Sun 𝒶   Converted from four 17th-century fishing cottages, with a flower-draped flagstone terrace out front, this colorful seafront inn in the center of town exudes charm. Known as one of Cornwall's best inns, it offers recently refurbished bedrooms that are functional and cozy. The small to midsize bedrooms are graced with specially commissioned watercolors by local artists.

The Square, St. Mawes, Cornwall TR2 5DJ. ℭ **01326/270233.** Fax 01326/270198. www.risingsunstmawes.co.uk. 8 units. £120–£160 ($240–$320) double. Children ages 4–15 receive 50% discount. Rates include English breakfast. MC, V. Free parking. **Amenities:** Restaurant; bar; lounge; room service; laundry service. *In room:* TV, coffeemaker, hair dryer.

3 Penzance ⭒

451km (280 miles) SW of London; 124km (77 miles) SW of Plymouth

This little harbor town, which Gilbert and Sullivan made famous, is at the end of the so-called Cornish Riviera. It's noted for its moderate climate (it's one of the first towns in England to blossom with spring flowers), and for the summer throngs that descend for fishing, sailing, and swimming. Overlooking Mount's Bay, Penzance is graced in places with subtropical plants including palm trees.

Those characters in *The Pirates of Penzance* were not entirely fictional. The town was raided by Barbary pirates, destroyed in part by Cromwell's troops, sacked and burned by the Spaniards, and bombed by the Germans. In spite of its turbulent past, it offers tranquil resort living today.

The most westerly town in England, Penzance is a good base for exploring Land's End; the Lizard Peninsula; St. Michael's Mount; the old fishing ports and artists' colonies of St. Ives, Newlyn, and Mousehole; and even the Isles of Scilly.

ESSENTIALS

GETTING THERE Ten express trains leave daily from Paddington Station in London for Penzance; the trip takes 5½ hours. Call ℭ **0845/748-4950** or visit **www. nationalrail.co.uk**.

Five buses per day, run by **National Express** (ℭ **0870/580-8080;** www.national express.com), leave from London's Victoria Station heading for Penzance (trip time: 8½–9 hr.). The buses have toilets and reclining seats.

By car, you can drive southwest across Cornwall on the A30 all the way to Penzance; the trip takes between 5 and 6 hours.

VISITOR INFORMATION The **Tourist Information Centre** is on Station Approach (ℭ **01736/362207**). It's open Easter to September daily 9am to 5pm; October to Easter, hours are Monday to Friday 9am to 5pm.

WHERE TO STAY

Abbey Hotel This small-scale hotel occupies a stone-sided house that was erected in 1660 on the site of a 12th-century abbey that was demolished by Henry VIII. It's situated on a narrow side street on raised terraces that overlook the panorama of Penzance Harbour. Behind the hotel is a medieval walled garden that was part of the original abbey. Bedrooms are furnished with English-country-house flair.

Abbey St., Penzance, Cornwall TR18 4AR. ℭ **01736/366906**. Fax 01736/351163. www.theabbeyonline.com. 6 units. Low season £105–£145 ($210–$290) double, £150–£190 ($300–$380) suite; summer £130–£180 ($260–$360) double, £190–£240 ($380–$480) suite. Rates include English breakfast. AE, MC, V. **Amenities:** Restaurant; bar; room service; laundry service. *In room:* TV, coffeemaker, hair dryer.

Camilla House Hotel ⭒ This comfortable, nicely furnished house is located near the town promenade, within walking distance of shops and restaurants. A local mariner built this house for his family in 1836. The small to midsize bedrooms will give you the feeling of being "at home." Susan and Simon Chapman are most helpful in providing information for attractions in Penzance and surrounding areas. They're also agents for the Skybus (airplane) and *Scillonian III* (ferry), and book day trips to the Isles of Scilly. A delicious English breakfast is served in a charming dining room.

12 Regent Terrace, Penzance, Cornwall. ℭ/fax **01736/363771**. www.camillahouse-hotel.co.uk. 8 units. £75–£85 ($150–$170) double. Rates include English breakfast. AE, MC, V. Free parking. Closed Jan 9–29. **Amenities:** Dining room; bar; lounge. *In room:* TV, beverage maker, hair dryer, no phone.

Finds   Escape to an Oasis: Trengwainton Garden

Just 3.2km (2 miles) west of Penzance you'll discover **Trengwainton Garden** ✿, west of Heamoor off the Penzance-Morvah Road (© **01736/ 363148**), a woodland garden of trees and shrubs on a 40-hectare (98-acre) plot overlooking Mount's Bay. Allow at least an hour to explore this property, with its flourishing collection of camellias, magnolias, and rhododendrons. Because of the mild climate, the garden site is famed for its series of walled gardens, with sloping beds that contain tender species not found elsewhere in the United Kingdom. Along a stream you'll find feathery bamboos and Australian tree ferns on its banks, along with lilies and other water-loving plants. This National Trust property is open February 11 to November 4; admission is £5.20 ($10) for adults, £2.60 ($5.20) for children 11 and younger, and £13 ($26) for a family pass.

Ennys ✿ *(Finds)*   Once a flower farm, Ennys produces mainly vegetables today. Owned by Gill and Jill Charlton, this Cornish granite farmhouse has a slate roof; its front section dates back to the 17th century, and other portions are thought to be much older. The bedrooms are furnished in an old-fashioned farmhouse style with patchwork quilts and four-poster beds. The family suites are in a converted barn on the premises. The hostess prepares an afternoon Cornish-style cream tea.

St. Hilary, Penzance, Cornwall TR20 9BZ. © **01736/740262**. Fax 01736/740055. www.ennys.co.uk. 5 units. £85–£125 ($170–$250) double; £115–£180 ($230–$360) family suite. Rates include English breakfast and afternoon tea. MC, V. **Amenities:** Dining room; outdoor heated pool; tennis court. *In room:* TV, Wi-Fi, beverage maker, hair dryer, no phone.

Tarbert Hotel   This dignified granite-and-stucco house lies about a 2-minute walk northwest of the town center. Some of the small to midsize rooms retain original high ceilings and elaborate cove moldings. Each room has comfortable furniture. Improvements include a new reception area, a completely refurbished bar, and a patio.

11–12 Clarence St., Penzance, Cornwall TR18 2NU. © **01736/363758**. Fax 01736/331336. www.tarbert-hotel.co.uk. 12 units. £65–£95 ($130–$190) double; £125 ($250) family room. Rates include English breakfast. AE, MC, V. **Amenities:** Restaurant; bar; laundry service. *In room:* TV, Wi-Fi, beverage maker, hair dryer, safe.

WHERE TO DINE

The **Nelson Bar,** in the Union Hotel on Chapel Street in Penzance (© **01736/ 362319**), is known for its robust pub grub and collection of Nelsoniana. It's the spot where the admiral's death at Trafalgar was first revealed to the English people. Lunch and dinner are served daily.

Harris's Restaurant ✿ FRENCH/ENGLISH   Down a narrow cobblestone street off Market Jew Street, this warm, candlelit place has a relaxed atmosphere and is your best bet for a meal. A beacon of light against the culinary bleakness of Penzance, Harris's offers dining in two small rooms. The seasonally adjusted menu emphasizes local produce, including seafood and game. On any given night, you might enjoy such well-crafted dishes as whole steamed lobster with lime-butter sauce or steamed John Dory with a saffron sauce.

46 New St. ℂ **01736/364408.** Reservations recommended. Main courses £16–£30 ($32–$60). AE, MC, V. Mon–Sat noon–2pm and 7–10pm. Closed 3 weeks in winter.

The Turk's Head 🎌🎌 ENGLISH/INTERNATIONAL   Dating from 1233, this inn, said to be the oldest in Penzance, serves the finest food of any pub in town. In summer, drinkers overflow into the garden. The interior is decorated in a mellow style, as befits its age, with flatirons and other artifacts hanging from the inn's timeworn beams. Meals include fishermen's pie, local seafood, chicken curry, and prime quality steaks including rib-eye. See the chalkboards for the daily specials.

49 Chapel St. ℂ **01736/363093.** Reservations not needed. Main courses £7.50–£16 ($15–$32); bar snacks £4–£9 ($8–$18). AE, MC, V. Mon–Sat 11am–2:30pm and 6–10pm; Sun noon–2:30pm and 6–9pm. From the rail station, turn left just past Lloyd's Bank.

SEEING THE SIGHTS AROUND PENZANCE

Unlike some tacky places along the Cornish coast, which are overrun with cheesy shops selling cheap souvenirs, Penzance maintains a bit of a regal air in spite of its hordes of summer visitors. Of course, it has a vast array of antiques stores hustling their wares, often trinkets more than genuine antiques, but it can be a lot of fun nonetheless.

At night in summer, young people flock to the fun-loving, often rowdy, pubs to begin drinking lager in time to enjoy some of the most spectacular sunsets in the West Country.

Frankly, if you're from Miami, the waters for swimming will always be too cold for you. But for the average visitor, the best temperatures are in July and the first 2 weeks in August. After that time passes, find other pastimes with which to amuse yourself.

Castle on St. Michael's Mount 🎌🎌   Rising about 75m (250 ft.) from the sea, St. Michael's Mount is topped by a part medieval, part 17th-century castle. It's 5km (3 miles) east of Penzance and is reached at low tide by a causeway. At high tide, the mount becomes an island, reached only by motor launch from Marazion. In winter, you can go over only when the causeway is dry.

A Benedictine monastery, the gift of Edward the Confessor, stood on this spot in the 11th century. The castle now has a collection of armor and antique furniture. A

⟨**Finds** **A Fishing Village & Artists' Colony**

From Penzance, a 3.2km (2-mile) promenade leads to **Newlyn** 🎌, another fishing village—second largest in the country—and a port of infinite charm on Mount's Bay. Artist Stanhope Forbes (1857–1947) founded an art school in Newlyn in 1899, and the village has been an artists' colony ever since, attracting both the serious painter and the Sunday sketcher. If you're in Newlyn at lunchtime, fish is, of course, what to order. For the tastiest fish and chips in town, head for **Tolcarne Inn,** Tolcarne Place (ℂ **01736/363074**). Under a beamed ceiling from 1717, the main room for dining evokes a Cornish pub, with paintings by local artists on display. If you don't want fish and chips, opt for the Newlyn fish pie or, better yet, the fresh crab. Main dishes cost from £5.50 to £15 ($11–$30) and MasterCard and Visa are accepted. It's open daily 10:30am to 3:30pm and 6:30 to 11:30pm. A bus runs throughout the day linking Penzance with Newlyn. We suggest you walk to Newlyn, then take the bus back to Penzance if you're tired.

tea garden is on the island, as well as a National Trust restaurant, both open in summer. The steps up to the castle are steep and rough, so wear sturdy shoes. To avoid disappointment, call the number listed below to check on the tides, especially during winter. Allow 3 hours for a visit.

On St. Michael's Mount, Mount's Bay. © **01736/710507**. Admission £6.40 ($13) adults, £3.20 ($6.40) children, £16 ($32) family ticket. Mar 16–Nov 2 Sun–Fri 10:30am–5pm; guided tours off season Tues–Fri at 11am and 2pm. Bus no. 2 or 2A from Penzance to Marazion, the town opposite St. Michael's Mount. Parking £2 ($4).

Minack Theatre ★★★   One of the most unusual theaters in southern England, this open-air amphitheater was cut from the side of a rocky Cornish hill near the village of Porthcurno, 14km (9 miles) southwest of Penzance. Its legendary creator was Rowena Cade, an arts enthusiast and noted eccentric, who began work on the theater after World War I by physically carting off much of the granite from her chosen hillside. On the premises, an exhibition hall showcases Cade's life and accomplishments.

Up to 750 visitors at a time can sit directly on grass- or rock-covered ledges, sometimes on cushions if they're available, within sightlines of both the actors and a sweeping view out over the ocean. Experienced theatergoers sometimes bring raincoats for protection against the occasional drizzle. Theatrical events are staged by repertory theater companies that travel throughout Britain, and performances are likely to include everything from London's visiting Royal Shakespeare Company to musical comedy. The productions staged here are the most professional and polished of any theater in the West Country; many come direct from critical acclaim in London's West End.

Porthcurno. © **01736/810694**. www.minack.com. Theater tickets £7–£8.50 ($14–$17) adults, £4–£5.50 ($8–$11) children; tour tickets £3.50 ($7) adults, £2.50 ($5) seniors, £1.40 ($2.80) children 12–15, free for 11 and younger. Exhibition hall Apr–May 21 daily 9:30am–5:30pm; May 22–Sept 16 Sat–Tues and Thurs 9:30am–5:30pm; Sept 17–Oct daily 10am–5pm; Nov–Easter daily 10am–4pm. Performances held May 21–Sept 16, matinees Wed and Fri at 2pm, evening shows Mon–Fri at 8pm. From Penzance take A30 heading toward Land's End; after 5km (3 miles), bear left onto B3283 and follow the signs to Porthcurno.

4 The Isles of Scilly ★

43km (27 miles) SW of Land's End

Off the Cornish coast, the **Isles of Scilly,** a cluster of small granite masses, are warmed by the Gulf Stream to the point where semitropical plants thrive. In some winters they never see signs of frost. They're the first landfall most oceangoing passengers see on journeys from North America. Charles, the Prince of Wales (who is the duke of Cornwall as well), makes regular visits to Scilly.

Five inhabited and more than 100 uninhabited islands are in the group. Some are only a few square miles, whereas others, such as the largest, St. Mary's, encompass some 77 sq. km (30 sq. miles). Three of these islands—Tresco, St. Mary's, and St. Agnes—attract visitors from the mainland. Early flowers are the main export and tourism is the main industry.

The islands experience some of the harshest winds of winter, raging in from the Atlantic, but in summer they are the fairest isles in the queen's kingdom. Unlike the rest of Britain, there is subtropical vegetation here, a mass of flowers from early spring to fall. Some are cultivated, as the English do so well, but others grow wild.

The Isles contain the best and most unspoiled beaches in Cornwall, and there are so many of them that you are likely to have a beach for yourself. We'd go to the Isles just to enjoy the swarms of seabirds flying in here from the Atlantic, perhaps enjoying a well-deserved rest.

The Isles are relatively flat. On any island, we'd recommend a stroll along the coast. In fact, we've walked around many of these islands, which are small enough so this can be easily accomplished.

The islands were largely shaped by a turbulent Atlantic. Lashing waves created natural "sculptures" out of the granite. The farms remaining on these islands evoke small holdings of the late 19th century in Britain. Fields are protected from the winds by hardy trees introduced here, which grew in a climate warmed by the Gulf Stream.

Fishing is a big activity, especially lobster, crayfish, and crabs pulled up in traditional "inkwell pots." The islands are studded with burial chambers, standing stones, and a few remains of former windmills, lighthouses, deserted cottages, and smugglers' hide-outs.

The Isles of Scilly figured prominently in the myths and legends of ancient Greece and Rome; in Celtic legend, they were inhabited entirely by holy men. More ancient burial mounds are on these islands than anywhere else in southern England, and artifacts have clearly established that people lived here more than 4,000 years ago.

St. Mary's is the capital, with about seven-eighths of the total population of all the islands, and it's here that the ship from the mainland docks at Hugh Town. However, if you'd like to make this a day visit, we recommend the helicopter flight from Penzance to Tresco, the neighboring island, where you can enjoy a day's walk through 297 hectares (735 acres), mostly occupied by the Abbey Gardens.

ESSENTIALS

GETTING THERE   You can fly by plane or helicopter. **Isles of Scilly Skybus Ltd.** (© 0845/7105555; www.islesofscilly-travel.co.uk) operates 2 to 20 flights per day, depending on the season, between Penzance's Land's End Airport and Hugh Town on St. Mary's Island. Flight time on the eight-passenger fixed-wing planes is 15 minutes each way. The round-trip fare is £80 ($160) for a same-day return or £100 to £125 ($200–$250) if you plan to stay overnight.

A helicopter service run by **British International Helicopters,** Penzance Heliport Eastern Green (© 01736/363871 for recorded information; www.islesofscillyhelicopter. com), operates, weather permitting, up to 26 helicopter flights, Monday through Saturday, between Penzance, St. Mary's, and Tresco. Flight time is 20 minutes from Penzance to either island. A same-day round-trip fare is £104 ($208), £120 to £154 ($240–$308) if you choose to stay overnight. A bus, whose timing coincides with the departure of each flight, runs to the heliport from the railway station in Penzance for £2 ($4) per person each way.

The rail line ends in Penzance (see "Getting There," in section 3, above).

Slower, but more cadenced and contemplative, is a ship leaving from the **Isles of Scilly Travel Centre,** on Quay Street in Penzance (© 0845/710-5555; www.islesof scilly-travel.co.uk). It departs at least 6 days a week between April and October, requiring 2 hours and 40 minutes for the segment between Penzance and Hugh Town, with an additional 20 or so minutes for the second leg of the trip, which is from Hugh Town to Tresco. It departs Monday to Friday at 9:15am, returning from St. Mary's at 4:30pm. Saturday departures usually follow the Monday-to-Friday timing, but not always, as the managers sometimes add a second Saturday sailing to accommodate weekend holidaymakers, depending on the season. Between November 6 and April 7 there is no service. Depending on the time of year, a same-day round-trip ticket from Penzance to St. Mary's costs £36 ($72) for adults and £18 ($36) for children 15 and younger. If you choose to spend the night, the trip costs £46 ($92) each way (£23/$46 for children 15 and younger).

VISITOR INFORMATION   St. Mary's Tourist Information Office, at High Street, St. Mary's (© **01720/422536;** www.simplyscilly.co.uk), is open November to March Monday to Friday 9am to 5pm; from April to October, hours are Monday to Friday 8:30am to 6pm, Saturday from 8:30am to 5pm, and Sunday from 9am to 2pm.

ST. MARY'S

St. Mary's is made for walking, biking, and exploring—casual, relaxed sightseeing, nothing too demanding. The attraction of the island is its natural beauty. It is 5km (3 miles) across at its widest point, but its coastline stretches for 15km (9 miles). We've spent an entire day just wandering this beautiful, cove-studded coastline. If along the way you stop to chat with a local Scillonian fisherman, so much the better.

Hugh Town, the main settlement, deserves at least an hour or two of your time. It was constructed on a sandbar that lies between the principal part of St. Mary's and a hill in the west, called the **Garrison.** Constructed in the mid-1700s, a **guard gate** here gives access to the **Star Castle Hotel** (see below). We recommend a stroll inside the ramparts for one of the **greatest views** ★★ of the Scilly Islands.

From Hugh Town you can see the island's highest point, **Telegraph Tower,** rising 48m (158 ft.). This is a memorable walk, and you can also pass on the way a stone burial chamber, **Bants Carn,** dating from the 3rd century B.C.

To get around St. Mary's, cars are available but hardly necessary. The **Island Bus Service** charges £1.50 ($3) for adults from one island point to another; children ride for half fare. Bicycles are one of the most practical means of transport. **St Mary's Bicycle Hire,** the Strand, St. Mary's (©/fax **01720/422289**), is the only bike-rental outfit. They stock "shopper's cycles" with 3 speeds, hybrid bikes with 6 to 12 speeds, and 18-speed mountain bikes. All are available at prices ranging from £6 to £8 ($12–$16) daily; a £12 ($24) deposit is required.

For the best selections of island crafts, visit **Phoenix Stained Glass Studio,** Portmellon Industrial Estate, St. Mary's (© **01720/422900**). At this studio, you can watch original artifacts being made into stained glass. The shops also sell a wide assortment of gifts, including jewelry and leaded lights and souvenirs.

Isles of Scilly Perfumery, Porthloo Studios, St. Mary's (no phone), a 10-minute walk from the center of Hugh Town, is packed with intriguing gifts, made from plants grown on the Isles—everything from a delicate shell-shaped soap to fine fragrances, cosmetics, potpourri, and other accessories.

Isles of Scilly Museum, on Church Street in St. Mary's (© **01720/422337;** www.iosmuseum.org), illustrates the history of the Scillies from 2500 B.C., with drawings, artifacts from wrecked ships, and assorted relics discovered on the islands. A locally themed exhibit changes annually. It's open from Easter to September Monday to Saturday 10am to 4:30pm; off season, hours are Monday to Saturday 10am to noon. Admission is £2.50 ($5) for adults, £1.50 ($3) seniors and students, and 50p ($1) for children.

WHERE TO STAY

Star Castle Hotel ★ 𝐾𝑖𝑑𝑠   This hotel, built as a castle in 1593 to defend the Isles of Scilly against Spanish attacks, offers views out to sea, and over town and harbor. A young prince of Wales (later King Charles II) took shelter here in 1643 when he was being hunted by Cromwell and his parliamentary forces. The 18 rooms in the garden annex are extra-large units opening directly onto the gardens. Eight double rooms and four single rooms are in the castle. The rooms in the castle are full of more character, including 10 rooms with four-poster beds and beamed ceilings, although the garden apartments are more spacious and comfortable. Seventeen rooms are large enough for families.

The Garrison, St. Mary's, Isles of Scilly TR21 0TA. © **01720/422317.** Fax 01720/422343. www.star-castle.co.uk. 34 units. £80–£144 ($160–$288) per person double; £96–£164 ($192–$328) per person suite. Rates include half-board. MC, V. Closed late Dec to early Feb. **Amenities:** 2 restaurants; bar; lounge; indoor pool; tennis court; game room; room service; laundry service. *In room:* TV, coffeemaker, hair dryer.

WHERE TO DINE
Chez Michel FRENCH   The finest dining outside the hotels is found at this warm and cozy 24-seat restaurant. The cooks emphasize fresh ingredients, whatever the season. In the heart of town, the restaurant sells beer and wine. Lunches are fairly light, including such standards as a Cornish crab sandwich or a fresh lobster salad made from seafood harvested right off the shores. At night, fare is more elaborate. Count on such delights as Cornish beef filet with white-mushroom sauce or baked and crusted fresh sea bass. The breast of duckling with cranberry sauce is also delicious.

Parade, Hugh Town, St. Mary's. © **01720/422871.** Reservation required for dinner. Lunch £6.50–£10 ($13–$20); dinner £13–£22 ($26–$44). No credit cards. Year-round Tues, Thurs, and Sat 10am–2pm; summer Mon–Sat 6:30–11pm; winter Sat 6:30pm–closing.

TRESCO
No cars or motorbikes are allowed on Tresco, but you can rent bikes by the day; the hotels use a special wagon towed by a farm tractor to transport guests and luggage from the harbor.

Abbey Gardens (★ (Finds   The gardens are the most outstanding feature of Tresco, started by Augustus Smith in the mid-1830s. When he began his work, the area was a barren hillside, a fact visitors now find hard to believe.

The gardens are a nature lover's dream, with more than 5,000 species of plants from 80 different countries. The old abbey, or priory, now in ruins, was allegedly founded by Benedictine monks in the 11th century, though some historians date it from A.D. 964. Of special interest in the gardens is Valhalla, a collection of nearly 60 figureheads from ships wrecked around the islands; the gaily painted figures from the past have a rather eerie quality, each one a ghost with a different story to tell.

If time remains after you visit the gardens, you can explore the meadows and coastal fields that surround these gardens. There is no particular trail to follow. Just wander at leisure through the fields and across paths made by others who blazed these trails before you. You can walk along the dunes, which are often thick with heather, enjoying the wildflowers, the birds that fly overhead, and maybe some shell collecting. The seabirds are so fearless that they'll land within a foot or so of you, looking for a handout.

© **01720/424108.** www.tresco.co.uk. Admission £9 ($18), free for 15 and under. Daily 10am–4pm.

WHERE TO STAY & DINE
The island's pub is the **New Inn** (see below) where you can also overnight. In a spectacular setting overlooking the ocean, the pub lies on New Grimsby Harbour, some 50m (164 ft.) from the water. In summer drinks and food can be enjoyed in the patio garden, with its direct access to the harbor. The food to order, of course, is locally caught fish, including prawns and, our favorite, white crab, but you can also enjoy

John Dory, Cornish sea bass, and monkfish. The pub is open daily from 10am to 3pm and 6 to 11pm; meals are served from noon to 3pm and 6 to 9pm. Main courses cost from £6 to £18 ($12–$36).

Island Hotel Tresco 𝆕 *Kids*   This is the finest hotel in the Scillies, located at Old Grimsby Harbour near the northeastern shore of Tresco. It was established in 1960 when a late-19th-century stone cottage was enlarged with conservatory-style windows and a series of long and low extensions. Today, the plant-filled interior feels almost Caribbean. Some rooms overlook the sea; others face inland. All are comfortably furnished with easy chairs and storage spaces. Bedrooms range from medium to spacious, and nearly two dozen of them are large enough for families. The hotel is noted for its subtropical garden.

Old Grimsby, Tresco, Isles of Scilly, Cornwall TR24 0PU. © 01720/422883. Fax 01720/423008. www.tresco.co.uk. 48 units. £130–£275 ($260–$550) per person double; £180–£360 ($360–$720) per person suite. Rates include breakfast and dinner. MC, V. Closed Nov to early Feb. **Amenities:** Restaurant; bar; outdoor heated pool; tennis court; croquet lawn; game room; room service; babysitting; laundry service. *In room:* TV, coffeemaker, hair dryer.

New Inn   An interconnected row of 19th-century fishermen's cottages and shops, the New Inn is situated at the center of the island, beside its unnamed main road. The rooms are tastefully decorated in a modern style in blue and creamy yellow hues; each features matching twin or double beds, and the more expensive units offer sea views.

Tresco, Isles of Scilly, Cornwall TR24 0QQ. © 01720/422844. Fax 01720/423200. www.tresco.co.uk. 15 units. £140–£210 ($280–$420) double. Rates include English breakfast. MC, V. **Amenities:** Restaurant; pub; 2 bars; outdoor heated pool; tennis court; laundry service. *In room:* TV, coffeemaker, hair dryer.

ST. AGNES 𝆕

St. Agnes lies farther southwest than any other community in Britain and, luckily, remains relatively undiscovered. Much of the area is preserved by the Nature Conservancy Council. Because the main industries are flower farming and fishing, it has little pollution; visitors can enjoy clear waters that are ideal for snorkeling and diving. Call **David Peacock** at © 01720/422704 (www.st-agnes-boating.co.uk) about boating and snorkeling possibilities. Little traffic moves on single-track lanes crossing the island; the curving sandbar between St. Agnes and its neighbor, the island of Gugh, is one of the best beaches in the archipelago. The coastline is diverse and idyllic for long walks along a relatively flat, shrub-dotted landscape. A coastal trail leads to any number of sandy coves, granite outcroppings, flower-studded heaths and meadows, and even a freshwater pool. Sunsets are romantic and are followed by a brilliant showcase of the night sky.

The widest choice of boat trips of the Scilly Isles is offered by the **St. Mary's Boatmen's Association** (© 01720/423999; www.scillyboating.co.uk). In summer boats heading for St. Agnes leave St. Mary's at 10:15 and 11:45am and 2pm, returning at 2:12, 4, and 4:45pm. A day trip costs £7 ($14).

Many places in Britain claim to be unspoiled, but St. Agnes actually is, measuring about 1.6km (1 mile) across a somewhat flat terrain broken in parts by green hills. In the western part of the island are granite outcroppings, and the scenery here is much wilder than in the east, with sandy coves and rock pools. Beachcombers in the sands can find beads from 17th-century shipwrecks. The island is known for its daffodils in the spring; its birds, butterflies, and wildflowers in the summer; and its migrant birds, including many rare species, in the fall.

WHERE TO STAY

Coastguards   The home of Wendy Hick opens onto excellent views of the sea from its location at St. Warna's Cove. Accommodations are midsize bedrooms that are simply but pleasantly and comfortably furnished. One has a shower stall, the other a full tub. Housekeeping is very good here, and the welcome is warm. The food, mainly seafood, is also good.

St. Agnes, Isles of Scilly, Cornwall TR22 0PL. © **01720/422373.** 2 units. £88 ($176) per person. Rates include half-board. No credit cards. Closed Nov–Apr. *In room:* TV, coffeemaker.

THE LOCAL PUB

The **Turks Head** at St. Agnes (© **01720/422434**) dates from the 1890s, when it was constructed as a boathouse. Prominently located a few steps from the pier, it serves the best beer and ales on island, along with other drinks. It's the second building after the arrival point of the ferryboats from St. Mary's. It's open daily 10:30am to 4:30pm and 6:30 to 11pm.

---

5 Mousehole ⟨★ & Land's End ⟨★

Mousehole: 5km (3 miles) S of Penzance; Land's End: 14km (9 miles) W of Penzance

Reached by traveling through some of Cornwall's most beautiful countryside, Land's End is literally the end of Britain. The natural grandeur of the place has been somewhat marred by theme park–type amusements, but the view of the sea crashing against rocks remains undiminished. If you want to stay in the area, you can find accommodations in Mousehole, a lovely Cornish fishing village. If you visit in July and August, you'll need reservations far in advance, as Mousehole doesn't have enough bedrooms to accommodate the summer hordes.

GETTING THERE

From London, journey first to Penzance (see "Getting There," in section 3, earlier in this chapter), then take a local bus for the rest of the journey (bus no. 6 to Mousehole and bus no. 1 to Land's End). There is frequent service throughout the day.

If you're driving from Penzance, take the B3315 south for 15 minutes.

MOUSEHOLE

The Cornish fishing village of Mousehole (pronounced *Mou*-sel) attracts hordes of visitors, who, fortunately, haven't changed it too much. The cottages still sit close to the harbor wall, the fishermen still bring in the day's catch, the salts sit around smoking tobacco talking about the good old days, and the lanes are as narrow as ever. About the most exciting thing to happen here was the arrival in the late 16th century of the Spanish galleons, whose sailors sacked and burned the village. In a sheltered cove of Mount's Bay, Mousehole today has developed as the nucleus of an artists' colony.

If you'd like to go fishing yourself, you can call **Tom Arnull** at © **01736/756162;** he can hook you up with rock and beach angling. Otherwise, call **S. Farley** (© **01736/731154**), who can arrange charter boat fishing.

There is no great attraction to visit in Mousehole other than the village itself. You can spend an hour or two strolling its narrow streets and passing by its quaint, stone-built cottages. Walks always end at the quay where you can look at the boats at harbor. Perhaps you can have lunch here and be on your way or at the end of the day you can walk 1.6km (1 mile) south of the village to **Spaniards' Point** where the Iberian raiders landed to pillage the countryside, laying devastation to the Cornish landscape. It's a beautiful walk as you take in a rugged seascape and landscape.

WHERE TO STAY

The Old Coastguard 🌟🌟   The best views in the area are to be enjoyed in this former lookout for the Coast Guard. It has been skillfully converted into a seacoast inn serving some of the best food in the area. Guest rooms are split between the main building and the Lodge, a newer annex down the hill, and rooms are comparable in style and quality for both buildings. Picture windows look out on the bay in many rooms, all of which are decorated in a modern style with beech and pine furniture. The best units open onto sea views enjoyed from a private balcony or terrace. The on-site restaurant prides itself on fresh produce, especially fish brought into Newlyn Harbour.

The Parade, Mousehole, Cornwall TR19 6PR. ℂ 01736/731222. Fax 01736/731720. www.oldcoastguardhotel.co.uk. 20 units. £90–£170 ($180–$340) double. Rates include English breakfast. AE, MC, V. **Amenities:** Restaurant; bar. *In room:* TV, beverage maker.

The Ship Inn   This charming pub and inn is located on the harbor in this fishing village. The exterior has a stone facade, and the interior has retained much of the original rustic charm with its black beams and paneling, granite floors, built-in wall benches, and the requisite nautical motif decorating its two bars. The rooms, offering views of the harbor and the bay, have window seats. The rooms are simply furnished and tend to be small but are cozy.

S. Cliff, Mousehole, Penzance, Cornwall TR19 6QX. ℂ 01736/731234. 7 units. £65–£70 ($130–$140) double. Rates include English breakfast. MC, V. **Amenities:** Restaurant; 2 bars. *In room:* TV, coffeemaker, hair dryer.

WHERE TO DINE

The most substantial meals are served at the restaurant of the **Ship Inn** (see above). If you're looking for a quick bite, head for **Pam's Pantry,** 3 Mill Lane (ℂ **01736/ 731532**), a small, cheerful cafe that specializes in locally caught fish. Accepting cash only, this hole in the wall features Newlyn crab in salads, soups, and well-stuffed sandwiches. You can also stop in for a Cornish cream tea for £5 ($10) with main courses going for £5 to £10 ($10–$20). Sandwiches to go and pizzas are also sold. Our favorite dessert is the homemade apple pie with clotted cream. Pam's is open daily 9am to 6:30pm.

The Cornish Range 🌟 ENGLISH/MEDITERRANEAN   Hidden away on a narrow street in Old Town, this restaurant—the finest in the area—was converted from an 18th-century cottage that processed pilchards (sardines). Filled with local paintings, this rustic, intimate eatery has a vaguely Mediterranean aura with its wooden tables and chairs. A daily changing menu is based on fresh, seasonal produce, much of it harvested from the sea by the fishermen off the coast of Newlyn. Fresh fruits and vegetables come from Cornish farms. Dishes are well balanced in flavors and enticingly prepared, including such starters as Mediterranean fish soup or potted Newlyn crab with dill crème fraîche and melted Gruyère. To follow, try Newlyn crab and pea risotto with poached salmon and a citrus crème fraîche or else pan-fried wild sea bass filets with a chorizo risotto cake and king prawns. The inn also rents out three comfortable bedrooms, each beautifully furnished with a private bathroom, costing £80 to £100 ($160–$200) in a double.

6 Chapel St. ℂ 01736/731488. www.cornishrange.co.uk. Reservations required. Main courses £13–£19 ($26–$38). MC, V. Daily 10:45am–2:15pm and 6–9:30pm.

LAND'S END

Craggy Land's End is where England comes to an end. America's coast is 5,299km (3,291 miles) west of the rugged rocks that tumble into the sea beneath Land's End.

Once here you'll see coastal footpaths allowing you to walk along the cliffs for dramatic **views** ★★ of the crashing sea on the rocks below. These paths are constantly being eroded and new ones built. In an attempt to prevent future erosion, the paths are protected by "hedges"—really granite walls covered with turf.

Meeting at Land's End are the northern and southern sections of the **Cornish Coastal Footpath.** This is the center of the longest continuous footpath in Britain, going from the coast at Poole Harbour to Dorset and Somerset and on to the Bristol Channel. In all, this is a walk of 804km (500 miles), but the most dramatic and spectacular scenery is found at Land's End.

WHERE TO STAY & DINE

Land's End Hotel   This hotel is situated in a complex of buildings rising from the rugged landscape at the end of the main A30 road, the very tip of England. The hotel has a panoramic cliff-top position and is exposed to the wind and sea spray. The rooms are attractively furnished and well maintained. Accommodations range from small to spacious, especially the premier or family rooms. Three contain four-poster beds and offer sea views.

Land's End, Sennen, Cornwall TR19 7AA. ℂ **01736/871844.** Fax 01736/871599. www.landsendhotel.co.uk. 33 units. £80–£164 ($160–$328) double. Rates include breakfast. AE, MC, V. **Amenities:** Restaurant; bar; room service; laundry service. *In room:* TV, coffeemaker, hair dryer, iron, trouser press.

6 The Artists' Colony of St. Ives ★★

514km (319 miles) SW of London; 34km (21 miles) NE of Land's End; 16km (10 miles) NE of Penzance

This north-coast fishing village, with its sandy beaches, narrow streets, and well-kept cottages, is England's most famous artists' colony. The artists settled in many years ago and have integrated with the fishermen and their families. They've been here long enough to have developed several schools or "splits," and they almost never overlap—except in the pubs. The old battle continues between the followers of the representational and the devotees of the abstract in art, with each group recruiting young artists all the time. In addition, potters, weavers, and other craftspeople all work, exhibit, and sell in this area.

St. Ives becomes virtually impossible to visit in August, when you're likely to be trampled underfoot by busloads of tourists, mostly the English themselves. However, in spring and early fall the pace is much more relaxed.

ESSENTIALS

GETTING THERE   There is frequent service throughout the day between London's Paddington Station and the rail terminal at St. Ives. The trip takes 5½ hours. Trains are not direct; it's necessary to change at St. Erth, which is just a 10-minute ride from St. Ives. Call ℂ **0845/748-4950** or visit **www.nationalrail.co.uk** for schedules and information.

Two coaches a day run from London's Victoria Coach Station to St. Ives. The trip takes 8½ hours. Call ℂ **0870/580-8080** or visit **www.nationalexpress.com** for schedules and information.

If you're driving, take the A30 across Cornwall, heading northwest at the junction with the B3306, heading to St. Ives on the coast. During the summer, many streets in the center of town are closed to vehicles. You may want to leave your car in the Lelant Saltings Car Park, 5km (3 miles) from St. Ives on the A3074, and take the regular train service into town, an 11-minute journey. Departures are every half-hour. It's free to all car passengers and drivers, and the parking charge is £8 to £12 ($16–$24) per day. You can also use the large Trenwith Car Park, close to the town center, for £4 ($8), and then walk down to the shops and harbor or take a bus that costs £1 ($2) per person.

VISITOR INFORMATION   The **Tourist Information Centre** is at the Guildhall, Street-an-Pol (© **01736/796297;** www.stives-cornwall.co.uk). From October to May, hours are Monday to Friday 9am to 5pm and Saturday 10am to 1pm. From June to September, hours are Monday to Friday 9am to 5:30pm, Saturday 9am to 5pm, and Sunday 10am to 4pm.

WHERE TO STAY

The Garrack Hotel *Value*   This small vine-covered hotel, once a private home, commands a panoramic view of St. Ives and Porthmeor Beach from its .8-hectare (2-acre) knoll at the head of a narrow lane. This is one of the friendliest and most efficiently run midprice hotels on the entire coast, and each room is furnished in a warm, homey manner. Most units are midsize, but three rooms are large enough to accommodate families.

Burthallan Lane, Higher Ayr, St. Ives, Cornwall TR26 3AA. © 01736/796199. Fax 01736/798955. www.garrack.com. 18 units. Low season £120–£180 ($240–$360) double; summer £136–£198 ($272–$396) double. Rates include English breakfast. AE, DC, MC, V. Free parking. Take B3306 to the outskirts of St. Ives; after passing a gas station on the left, take the 3rd road left toward Porthmeor Beach and Ayr and after 180m (600 ft.) look for the hotel sign. **Amenities:** Restaurant (see review below); 2 bars; lounge; indoor pool; health club; spa; sauna; room service; laundry service. *In room:* TV, coffeemaker, hair dryer.

Pedn-Olva Hotel   The panoramic view of the bay afforded from its restaurant and most rooms is the outstanding feature of this establishment. It was built in the 1870s as the home of the paymaster for the local mines, before being transformed into a hotel in the 1930s. The rooms are furnished in a modern style, with comfortable twin or double beds. Seven of the rooms are in a less desirable annex where the chambers are more sterile and lack the character of the main building. Five rooms are large enough for families. There are sun terraces with lounges, umbrellas, and a swimming pool for those who don't want to walk down the rocky path to Porthminster Beach. If you crave solitude, however, scramble down the rocks to sunbathe just above the gentle rise and fall of the sea.

The Warren, St. Ives, Cornwall TR26 2EA. © 01736/796222. Fax 01736/797710. www.pednolva.co.uk. 30 units. £150–£170 ($300–$340) double; £220 ($440) suite. Rates include English breakfast. AE, MC, V. Parking £6 ($12). **Amenities:** Restaurant; bar; outdoor heated pool; coin-op laundry. *In room:* TV, coffeemaker, hair dryer, iron.

Porthminster Hotel *&*   This leading Cornish Riviera resort, the town's best address, stands on the main road into town amid a beautiful garden and within easy walking distance of Porthminster Beach. Large and imposing, the Porthminster is a traditional choice for visitors to St. Ives. With its 1894 Victorian architecture, it is warm and inviting. The spacious rooms are well furnished, although with a bland decor. Over the years the bedrooms have been considerably upgraded, and the standard of comfort is high here.

The Terrace, St. Ives, Cornwall TR26 2BN. © 01736/795221. Fax 01736/797043. www.porthminster-hotel.co.uk. 43 units. £60–£125 ($120–$250) per person double; £125–£150 ($250–$300) per person suite. Rates include half-board. AE, DC, MC, V. Free parking. Closed 2 weeks in Jan. **Amenities:** Restaurant; bar; 2 pools (1 indoor, 1 outdoor); tennis court; gym; spa; sauna; solarium; room service; massage; laundry service. *In room:* TV, coffeemaker, hair dryer.

Primrose Valley Hotel ★ *Finds*   This Edwardian villa has been stylishly converted to receive guests from its position in a residential cul-de-sac across the railroad tracks from Porthminster Beach. The furnishings are contemporary, everything from soft Italian leather chairs to oak tables. As befits a house of its age, the bedrooms vary in size, and four of them open onto views of the sea, two from covered balconies. The owners believe that breakfast is the most important meal of the day, and they obtain quality foodstuffs from local suppliers. The morning meal is always cooked by one of the partners.

Porthminster Beach, St. Ives, Cornwall TR26 2ED. ℂ **01736/794939.** www.primroseonline.co.uk. 10 units. £85–£155 ($170–$310) double; £175–£225 ($350–$450) suite. Rates include breakfast. AE, MC, V. Limited free parking. No children 8 and younger. **Amenities:** Restaurant; bar. *In room:* TV, Wi-Fi.

WHERE TO DINE

The Garrack Restaurant ENGLISH/INTERNATIONAL   The dining room at the Garrack Hotel produces excellent cuisine and, whenever possible, uses fresh ingredients from its own garden. The hotel dining room, which is open to nonguests, offers a set dinner, plus a cold buffet or snacks at the bar. The menu features some of the best English dishes, such as slow-roasted pork belly with Bramley apple purée; pan-roasted filet of hake with a pea pesto, or roast sirloin of beef in a tarragon jus. Live lobsters swim in the seawater tank—until they're removed for preparation and cooked to order. Cheese and dessert trolleys are at your service.

In the Garrack Hotel, Burthallan Lane, Higher Ayr. ℂ **01736/796199.** Reservations recommended. Main courses £12–£20 ($24–$40); fixed-price 2-course menu £22 ($44), 3 courses £25 ($50), 4 courses £28 ($56). AE, DC, MC, V. Daily 6:30–9pm.

The Sloop Inn ENGLISH/INTERNATIONAL   Proud of its long history (it dates from at least 1312), this stone-and-slate building contains the busiest and most visible pub in St. Ives, located on the harborfront in the town center. Most clients come to drink at one of the three different bar areas amid comfortably battered furnishings. If you're hungry, however, place your order at one of the bars and someone will bring your food to your table. Menu items include ploughman's lunches of cheese and bread, platters of roast chicken or ham, sandwiches, chili, fish and chips, bangers and mash, and lasagna. The kitchen also offers a large selection of locally caught fish, and the eatery is known for its homemade fish pie. The seafood chowder is another excellent choice. The aim seems more to fill you up rather than tantalize your palate.

The Wharf. ℂ **01736/965584.** Bar meals £4–£10 ($8–$20). DC, MC, V. Kitchen daily noon–3pm and 5–9:30pm. Pub daily 10am–midnight.

SEEING THE SIGHTS

Barbara Hepworth Museum and Garden ★   Dame Barbara Hepworth lived at Trewyn from 1949 until her death in 1975 at the age of 72. In her will she asked that her working studio be turned into a museum where future visitors could see where she lived and created her world-famous sculpture. Today, the museum and garden, now an extension of London's Tate, are virtually just as she left them. On display are about 47 sculptures and drawings, covering the period from 1928 to 1974, as well as photographs, documents, and other Hepworth memorabilia. You can also visit her workshops, housing a selection of tools and some unfinished carvings.

Barnoon Hill. ℂ **01736/796226.** www.tate.org.uk/stives/hepworth. Admission £4.75 ($9.50) adults, £2.75 ($5.50) students, free for seniors and children 17 and younger. Mar–Oct daily 10am–5:20pm; Nov–Feb Tues–Sun 10am–4:20pm or dusk if earlier.

Tate Gallery St. Ives 𝕂𝕂   This branch of London's famous Tate Gallery exhibits changing groups of work from the Tate Gallery's preeminent collection of St. Ives painting and sculpture, dating from about 1925 to 1975. The gallery is administered jointly with the Barbara Hepworth Museum (see above). The collection includes works by artists associated with St. Ives, including Alfred Wallis, Ben Nicholson, Barbara Hepworth, Naum Gabo, Peter Lanyon, Terry Frost, Patrick Heron, and Roger Hilton. All artists shown here had a decisive effect on the development of painting in the United Kingdom in the second half of the 20th century. About 100 works are on display at all times.

Boasting dramatic sea views, the museum occupies a spectacular site overlooking Porthmeor Beach, close to the home of Alfred Wallis and to the studios used by many of the St. Ives artists.

Porthmeor Beach. ℭ 01736/796226. www.tate.org.uk/stives. Admission £5.75 ($12) adults, £3.25 ($6.50) students, free for seniors and children 17 and younger. Mar–Oct daily 10am–5:20pm; Nov–Feb Tues–Sun 10am–4:20pm. Closes occasionally to change displays; call for dates.

EN ROUTE TO PORT ISAAC

The stretch of coastline between St. Ives and Port Isaac doesn't have the charm of Cornwall's eastern coast. The fastest way to get to Port Isaac is to take the A30 northeast. However the B3301, hugging close to the Atlantic Ocean, is the more scenic route.

Heading north along the B3301, your first stop will be the estuary town of **Hayle,** once known for its tin and copper mines, but now a beach resort with miles of sand fronting the often wind-tossed Atlantic. Going north from here, the first attraction is **St. Agnes Beacon** (it's signposted). This is the most panoramic belvedere along this wild stretch of north Cornish coastline. At a height of 191m (627 ft.), you can see all the way from Trevose Head in the northeast to St. Michael's Mount in the southwest—that is, if the weather's clear. It's often rainy and cloudy.

The first town of any importance is **Newquay,** a resort with sandy beaches at the foot of the cliffs, opening onto a sheltered bay. Taking its name from a "new" quay built in 1439, it attracts everyone from young surfers to elderly ladies who check into B&Bs along the harbor for long stays. Newquay is a rather commercial town, lacking the charm of St. Ives or Port Isaac, but its beaches attract families in summer. At night, pubs fill up with surfers ready to party.

If you'd like to stay over in Newquay, we recommend the **Hotel Bristol,** Narrowcliff (ℭ **800/528-1234** in the U.S., or 01637/875181; fax 01637/879347; www.hotelbristol.co.uk). This redbrick hotel overlooking the beach has 74 well-furnished rooms that cost £130 to £160 ($260–$320) for doubles, including English breakfast. This friendly and inviting place is popular with families. Facilities include an indoor swimming pool, sauna, game room, beauty salon, and solarium; American Express, Diners Club, MasterCard, and Visa are accepted.

Back on the road again, the next important stop is **Padstow.** This town has a long and ancient history. It reached its heyday in the 19th century when it was an important port. Unfortunately, ships became too big to pass the sandbar (called "the Doom Bar") at the estuary mouth. Walk along its quay-lined harbor and explore its narrow streets. At the end of the quay stands **St. Petroc's Church** and **Prideaux Place,** a Tudor house with 18th-century battlements.

Try to arrive in Padstow in time for lunch because a restaurant—simply called the **Seafood Restaurant** 𝕂, at Riverside (ℭ **01841/532700**)—offers the best cuisine

---

Finds **An Escape to Brigadoon**

One of the loveliest spots in the west of England is **St. Just in Roseland** ⭐⭐, a tiny hamlet of stone cottage terraces and a church dating from the 1200s. Locals call it their Garden of Eden because of its subtropical foliage, including rhododendrons and magnolias. There are even palm trees—in England, no less.

---

along this stretch of coastline. Here, Rick Stein selects the best "fruits of the sea," which he crafts into French-influenced dishes such as Monkfish Goan Curry and Dover sole with stir-fried garlic, sorrel, and asparagus. Stein also rents 14 rooms above the restaurant, bistro, and coffee shop for £135 to £230 ($270–$460) double per night including breakfast; two have private balconies opening onto harbor views. The bar is open all day; lunch is served from noon to 2pm and dinner is served from 7 to 10pm; MasterCard and Visa are accepted.

7 Port Isaac ⭐

428km (265 miles) SW of London; 23km (14 miles) SW of Tintagel; 14km (9 miles) N of Wadebridge

Port Isaac remains the most unspoiled fishing village on the north Cornish coastline, in spite of large numbers of summer visitors. By all means, wander through its winding, narrow lanes, gazing at the whitewashed fishing cottages with their rainbow trims.

ESSENTIALS

GETTING THERE Bodmin is the nearest railway station. It lies on the main line from London (Paddington Station) to Penzance (about a 4-hr. trip). Call ✆ **0845/ 748-4950** or visit www.nationalrail.co.uk. Many hotels will send a car to pick up guests at the Bodmin station, or you can take a taxi. If you take a bus from Bodmin, you'll have to change buses at Wadebridge, and connections are not good. Driving time from Bodmin to Port Isaac is 40 minutes.

A bus from Wadebridge goes to Port Isaac about six times a day. It's maintained by Western Greyhound (✆ **01637/871871**). Wadebridge is a local bus junction to many other places in the rest of England.

If you're driving from London, take the M4 west, then drive south on the M5. Head west again at the junction with the A39, continuing to the junction with the B3267, which you follow until you reach the signposted cutoff for Port Isaac.

WHERE TO STAY & DINE

Port Gaverne Hotel ⭐ Built in the 17th century as a coastal inn for fishermen needing a rest from their seagoing labors, Port Gaverne, 1km (a half-mile) east of Port Isaac, today caters to vacationing families and couples. It's the port's best bet for food and lodgings. The small to midsize bedrooms are traditionally furnished. Its painted facade is draped with vines. Clusters of antiques and early photographs of Cornwall add somewhat homey touches.

Port Gaverne, Port Isaac, Cornwall PL29 3SQ. ✆ **01208/880244.** Fax 01208/880151. www.chycor.co.uk/hotels/ port-gaverne-inn/index.htm. 16 units. £95–£110 ($190–$220) double. Rates include English breakfast. MC, V. Free parking. **Amenities:** Restaurant; bar; coin-op laundry. *In room:* TV, coffeemaker, hair dryer.

Slipway Hotel ⭐ Built in 1527, with major additions made in the early 1700s, this waterside building has seen more uses than any other structure in town, serving as everything from fishing cottages to the headquarters of the first bank here. The building was also once a lifeboat station for rescuing sailors stranded on stormy seas. The cozy bedrooms have compact bathrooms.

The hotel is also known for its restaurant where ultrafresh seafood is the chef's specialty. Its main dining room contains a minstrel's gallery and lies adjacent to a popular bar frequented by both visitors and locals. At lunch, sandwiches, fish and chips, and seafood pancakes are served. Dinner is more elaborate, featuring fish directly from the nets of local fisherman. *Note:* The hotel's steep and narrow staircases are not suitable for young kids or persons with limited mobility.

The Harbour Front, Port Isaac, Cornwall PL29 2RH. © **01208/880264.** Fax 01208/880408. www.portisaachotel.com. 10 units. £90–£130 ($180–$260) double; £130–£170 ($260–$340) suite. Rates include English breakfast. AE, MC, V. No parking. Closed Jan to mid-Feb. **Amenities:** Restaurant; bar; lounge. *In room:* TV, coffeemaker, hair dryer.

8 Tintagel Castle: King Arthur's Legendary Lair ★★

425km (264 miles) SW of London; 79km (49 miles) NW of Plymouth

Even if you don't buy into the legend of King Arthur, a visit is recommended to Tintagel, a little village 9.7km (6 miles) northwest of Camelford, which is said to have been the legendary Camelot. Once at Tintagel, signs point the way to the splendid ruins of **Tintagel Castle,** allegedly the site of King Arthur's birth.

Whether the tales of Arthurian chivalry and the famous Round Table are true or not, we'd come here just for the views, some of the most dramatic coastal scenery in the West Country. Steep cliffs and a rugged sea combine to paint a powerful portrait, and it's fun climbing up and down the cliffs, but only at low tide.

The 13th-century ruins of the castle that stand here—built on the foundations of a Celtic monastery from the 6th century—are popularly known as King Arthur's Castle. They stand 90m (300 ft.) above the sea on a rocky promontory, and to get to them you must take a long, steep, tortuous walk from the parking lot. In summer, many visitors make the ascent to Arthur's Lair, up 100 rock-cut steps. You can also visit Merlin's Cave at low tide. Once you reach Merlin's Cave, the site might not be so much—after all, it's only a cave, although one of legendary status. But the climb along the steep cliffs to reach it provides the thrill.

The castle is 1km (a half-mile) northwest of Tintagel. It's open April to September daily 10am to 6pm, October daily 10am to 5pm, and November to March daily 10am to 4pm. Admission is £4.50 ($9) for adults, £3.40 ($6.80) for students and seniors, and £2.30 ($4.60) for children. For information, call © **01840/770328** or go to **www.english-heritage.org.uk.**

ESSENTIALS

GETTING THERE   The nearest railway station is in Bodmin, which lies on the main rail line from London to Penzance. From Bodmin, you'll have to take a taxi for 30 minutes to get to Tintagel (there's no bus service from Bodmin to Tintagel). For railway inquiries, call © **0845/748-4950** or visit **www.nationalrail.co.uk.**

If you're driving, from Exeter, head across Cornwall on the A30, continuing west at the junction with the A395. From this highway, various secondary roads lead to Tintagel.

VISITOR INFORMATION   In Truro, the **Municipal Building,** Boscawen Street (© **01872/274555**), has tourist information and is open from April to October, Monday to Friday 9am to 5:30pm and Saturday 9am to 5pm; from November to March, it's open Monday through Friday from 9am to 5pm.

WHERE TO STAY & DINE IN TINTAGEL

Bossiney House Hotel   The hotel, in its inviting location, is comfortable and in a fairly tranquil and idyllic setting. Bedrooms have a streamlined, modern feel, accompanied by small bathrooms with a combination tub/shower (or else a shower stall). The hotel offers one of the best restaurants in the area, serving excellent Cornish cuisine based on fresh regional produce and especially seafood caught along the coast.

Bossiney Rd., Bossiney, Tintagel, Cornwall PL34 0AX. ⓒ **01840/770240.** Fax 01840/770501. www.bossineyhouse. co.uk. 19 units. £68–£80 ($136–$160) double. Rates include English breakfast. AE, MC, V. Closed Dec 22–28. Take B3263 1km (½ mile) northeast of Tintagel. **Amenities:** Restaurant; bar; indoor pool; 9-hole putting green; sauna; solarium. *In room:* TV, Wi-Fi, coffeemaker, hair dryer.

Trevigue Farm ⓐ *Finds*   Owned by the National Trust, this working dairy farm, whose tenants are Ken and Janet Crocker, is located cliff-side, offering access to a beach called the Strangles, where swimming is best experienced during a rising tide. The hotel is housed in two stone buildings: two bedrooms in the 16th-century farmhouse and two in a separate house with views of a wooded valley. Accommodations are cozy and tidy. Although only one bedroom contains a TV, there is a cozy sitting room with television for all guests to enjoy, a log fire, and a wealth of books. Meals feature English fare with a mixture of international dishes.

Crackington Haven, Bude, Cornwall EX23 0LQ. ⓒ/fax **01840/230418.** www.trevigue.co.uk. 4 units. £60–£72 ($120–$144) double. Rates include English breakfast. MC, V. Closed Dec 25. No children 11 or under. **Amenities:** Restaurant (Thurs–Sat only); lounge. *In room:* TV (in 1 unit), beverage maker.

13

The Cotswolds: Honey Stone & "Wool Churches"

Between Oxford and the River Severn, about a 2-hour drive west of London, the pastoral **Cotswolds** occupy a stretch of grassy limestone hills, deep ravines, and barren plateaus known as *wolds,* Old English for "God's high open land." Ancient villages with names such as **Stow-on-the-Wold, Wotton-under-Edge,** and **Moreton-in-Marsh** dot this bucolic area, most of which is in Gloucestershire, with portions in Oxfordshire, Wiltshire, and Worcestershire.

Made rich by wool from their sheep, the landowners here invested in some of the finest domestic architecture in Europe, distinctively built of honey-brown **Cotswold stone.** The gentry didn't neglect spiritual duties, for some of the simplest Cotswold hamlets have churches that, in style and architectural detail, seem far beyond their modest means. Since Cotswold wool was once sold all over the world and wealthy merchants used some of the money to build these churches, they are sometimes referred to as "wool churches."

You'll also see some **thatched cottages** in the Cotswolds. More common are Cotswold roof shingles fashioned from split slabs of stone, which required massive buttressing from medieval carpenters as a means of supporting the weight of the roof. Buildings erected since the 1700s, however, usually have slate roofs.

Mobbed by tourists, overrun **Broadway,** with its 16th-century stone houses and cottages, is the most popular base for touring this area, but we suggest you also head

for **Bibury, Painswick,** or other small villages to capture the true charm of the Cotswolds. You'll find the widest range of hotels and facilities in **Cheltenham,** once one of England's most fashionable spas, with a wealth of Regency architecture. And families may head to **Birdland,** in Bourton-on-the-Water, where you can see some 1,200 birds of 361 different species.

Biking the country roads of the Cotswolds is one of the best ways to experience the quiet beauty of the area. For a self-guided tour (but with a lot of help), you can hook up with **Cotswold Country Cycles** (© **01386/438706;** cotswoldcountrycycles.com), whose tours are designed to take you off the beaten track. Accommodations are arranged in advance, often at manor houses or historic homes. A typical tour price is a 3-day, 2-night adventure called "Simply Cotswolds," starting at £205 ($410) per person. A simpler option is offered by **Hartwells Cycle-Hire** (© **01451/820405;** www.hartwells.supanet.com), which rents bikes for £10 ($20) a day from its base on Bourton-on-the-Water.

The Cotswolds is also one of the most famous regions of England for hiking. With such a large area in which to ramble, it's a good idea to know where you are (and aren't) welcome. The **Cotswold Voluntary Wardens Service,** Shire Hall, Gloucester (© **01451/862000;** www.cotswoldsaonb.org.uk), offers free brochures highlighting trails and paths.

The **Wayfarers,** 174 Bellevue Ave., Newport, RI 02840 (© **800/249-4620;** www.thewayfarers.com), sponsors about six Cotswold walks a year from May to October. The cost of a 6-day tour is $3,495 (£1,748) per person, and includes all meals and snacks, first-class accommodations with private bathrooms along the route, and admission to attractions.

To explore on your own, you can get info from the **Cheltenham Tourist Information Centre,** 77 The Promenade (© **01242/522878;** www.visitcheltenham. gov.uk). Be sure to buy a copy of the Cotswold Way map.

Offering both self-guided and guided tours, **Cotswold Walking Holidays,** Festival House, Jessop Avenue in Cheltenham (© **01242/633680;** www.cotswoldwalks. com), is the leading purveyor of walking holidays in the region. Footpaths in general are well maintained, and this outfitter can show you the way to the best of them. Each night along the way you can stay in a good standard B&B in a Cotswold village with a wide range of pubs and restaurants. Route instructions and maps are provided. Your luggage will be transported from place to place each day. With B&B arranged, 3-night tours begin at £185 ($370) per person.

If you want to experience the Cotswolds in a nutshell and don't have a lot of vacation time, our favorite walk is "The Great Cotswold Ramble" (p. 468).

Warning to motorists: The Cotswolds in the past decades has experienced an overwhelming rise in both population and tourism. The narrow roads are sometimes impossibly overcrowded, and parking is difficult even in the smallest of villages.

1 Tetbury

182km (113 miles) W of London; 42km (27 miles) NE of Bristol

In the rolling Cotswolds, Tetbury was out of the tourist mainstream until the heir to the British throne and his beautiful bride, Lady Di, took up residence at the Macmillan Place, a Georgian building situated on nearly 141 hectares (350 acres). Then, crowds came here to catch a glimpse of Prince Charles riding horses and Princess Di shopping. (Today, folks keep an eye out for Charles and his second wife, Camilla Parker-Bowles.) Though it can't be seen from the road, the nine-bedroom Windsor mansion, **Highgrove,** is 2.5km (1½ miles) southwest of Tetbury on the way to Westonbirt Arboretum. If you continue out of town on the A433 toward Bath, the first big gate on the right is the entrance to Highgrove. Unlike Buckingham Palace, it can't be visited on most occasions. Actually, it can be visited, but only by an organized group. There is a waiting list of between 3 and 4 years. Any interested party can apply in writing to the **Prince of Wales Office,** St. James's Palace, London, SW1A 1AA.

Tetbury itself has a 17th-century market hall and a number of antiques shops and boutiques. The town's inns weren't cheap before royalty moved in, and the prices certainly have not dropped since then.

ESSENTIALS

GETTING THERE Frequent daily trains run from London's Paddington Station to Kemble, 11km (7 miles) east of Tetbury. For more information and schedules, call © **0845/748-2950** or visit **www.nationalrail.co.uk.** You can then take a bus from there to Tetbury.

National Express buses leave London's Victoria Coach Station with direct service to Cirencester, 16km (10 miles) northeast of Tetbury. For information, call © **0870/ 580-8080** or visit **www.nationalexpress.co.uk.** Several buses a day connect Cirencester to Tetbury.

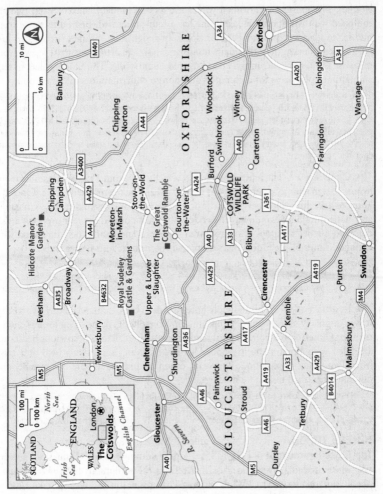

If you're driving from London, take the M40 northwest to Oxford, continuing along the A40 to the junction with the A429. Drive south to Cirencester, where you connect with the A433 southwest into Tetbury.

VISITOR INFORMATION The **Tourist Information Centre** in Tetbury, 33 Church St. (© **01666/503552;** www.tetbury.org), is open March to October Monday to Saturday 9:30am to 4:30pm, and November to February Monday to Saturday 9:30am to 2:30pm.

WHERE TO STAY

Calcot Manor ⭐⭐ *Kids*   Though the Close in town has a more refined atmosphere (see below), this inn is the finest place on the outskirts. The thick stone walls of the main house shelter a flowering terrace where tea and drinks are served in good weather. The rooms are furnished with antiques and modern conveniences; two are equipped with whirlpool tubs, and one has a four-poster bed. Bedrooms range from midsize to spacious, and some rooms, specially designed for families, are located in a refurbished granary near the main house and have small refrigerators. Views from many of the rooms encompass the Cotswold countryside. The building has indoor and outdoor play areas for children in addition to child monitors in each room.

Calcot, near Tetbury, Gloucestershire GL8 8YJ. © 01666/890391. Fax 01666/890394. www.calcotmanor.co.uk. 35 units. £265–£325 ($530–$650) double; £301–£325 ($602–$650) family room; £422–£460 ($844–$920) family suite. Rates include early morning tea, English breakfast, and dinner. AE, DC, MC, V. Free parking. Take A4135 5.5km (3½ miles) west of Tetbury. **Amenities:** 2 restaurants; pub; indoor heated pool; tennis court; gym; spa; sauna; steam room; room service; babysitting; laundry service. *In room:* TV, fridge (family rooms and suites only), beverage maker, hair dryer, iron, trouser press.

The Close ✿✿✿   The refurbished Close, which dates from 1596 and takes its name from a Cistercian monastery that was on this site, is the town's premier inn. Once the home of a wealthy wool merchant, the house was built of Cotswold stone, with gables and stone-mullioned windows. The ecclesiastical windows in the rear overlook a garden with a reflecting pool. Most rooms are spacious and handsomely furnished with antiques. Three of the individually decorated rooms have four-poster beds.

8 Long St., Tetbury, Gloucestershire GL8 8AQ. © 01666/502272. Fax 01666/504401. www.theclose-hotel.com. 15 units. £120–£180 ($240–$360) double. Rates include English breakfast. AE, MC, V. Free parking. **Amenities:** Restaurant (see review below); bar; room service; laundry service; dry cleaning. *In room:* TV, beverage maker, hair dryer, trouser press.

The Snooty Fox ✿   This desirable hotel stands in the commercial heart of Tetbury. It was originally a 16th-century coaching inn. Despite its name, it's a lot less snooty than the Close and is a popular local rendezvous. The small to very spacious bedrooms are filled with English-country-house luxury, including sumptuous beds and fresh fruit. Two rooms have antique beds with canopies, and the rest are comfortably and tastefully furnished in a more modern style.

Market Place, Tetbury, Gloucestershire GL8 8DD. © 01666/502436. Fax 01666/503479. www.snooty-fox.co.uk. 12 units. £70–£170 ($140–$340) double; £165–£210 ($330–$420) four-poster double. Rates include English breakfast. AE, DC, MC, V. Parking £2 ($4). **Amenities:** Restaurant; bar; room service. *In room:* TV, beverage maker, hair dryer, trouser press.

WHERE TO DINE

The Close Restaurant ✿ ENGLISH   This is a dining room of distinction, set with exquisite porcelain, silver, and glass that reflects the sumptuous but discreet atmosphere and friendly service. While sipping champagne on the terrace, take time to peruse the imaginative menu, which is complemented by the town's best wine list.

The à la carte menu is seasonally adjusted to take advantage of market-fresh ingredients. Main courses are likely to feature local venison, pan-fried sea bream, or filet of Scottish salmon. Braised lamb shank comes with sautéed forest mushrooms, and lobster is steamed and served with a saffron beurre blanc. Desserts sometimes reach back in England's culinary attic for inspiration, such as a parsnip-and-Cotswold-honey soufflé with whisky and lime ice.

In the Close, 8 Long St. © 01666/502272. Reservations recommended. Main courses £16–£22 ($32–$44); fixed-price dinner £30 ($60). AE, MC, V. Daily 12:30–2:30pm and 7–9:30pm.

EXPLORING THE TOWN

Everything in Tetbury is conveniently located in the center of the village; you can easily spend a morning wandering in and out of the many antiques shops and gazing up at the old houses.

Antiquing the 'Wolds

If ever there were an English fantasy, it's to drive the country back roads of the Cotswolds, stay in a manor house hotel, and spend your days browsing the antiques shops, densely packed into these old market towns.

The **Cotswold Art and Antique Dealers' Association (CADA)** publishes a free brochure of members and will happily guide you toward shippers and even hotels. Established in the mid-1970s, and with about 45 active dealers scattered throughout the region, it offers valuable help in organizing your antiques-buying assault on a region known for its decorative treasures. Write to the Secretary, CADA, Broadwell House, Sheep Street, Stow-on-the-Wold, Gloucestershire GL54 1JS, England (📞 **07789/968319;** www.cotswolds-antiques-art.com).

The **Parish Church of St. Mary the Virgin,** built between 1777 and 1781, has been hailed as the best Georgian Gothic church in the country. Extensive restoration has returned the interior to its original 18th-century appearance, and the spire is among England's tallest. For information, call 📞 **01666/502333;** it's more than likely the vicar himself will come on the line.

One of the finest examples of a Cotswold-pillared market house is the 1655 **Market House of Tetbury.** It's still in use, hosting one of the most interesting markets in the Cotswolds, in the antique stalls of its meeting hall. Try to schedule a Wednesday morning visit here to sift through the bric-a-brac.

After the market, head for **Chipping Steps.** The Chipping (market) was for centuries the site of "mop fairs," where farmhands and domestic staff offered themselves for employment. Many surrounding buildings have medieval origins.

Another place to explore is **Gumstoll Hill,** one of Tetbury's most ancient streets and now famous for its annual Woolsack Races.

Tetbury Police Museum, Old Courthouse, 63 Long St., situated in the former police station and magistrates court, is worth a peek. The old cells house a collection of relics from centuries of Cotswold law enforcement. The hours are Monday to Friday 10am to 3pm.

Chavenage House   The drama started with Colonel Nathaniel Stephens, who owned the house during the English Civil War and met an unfortunate demise while living here. He was persuaded by Cromwell, a relative by marriage, to vote for the impeachment of King Charles. This angered Stephens's daughter to the point that she cursed him. Soon after, Stephens died, and it is rumored that his ghostly form can be seen being driven away from Chavenage by a headless coachman wearing royal vestments. The house has been a location shoot for several BBC television productions, including Agatha Christie's *Hercule Poirot.* Aside from its fine Cromwell-era tapestries, furniture, and artifacts, this Elizabethan country house is worth a visit for its rich history and legends.

3km (2 miles) northwest of Tetbury. 📞 **01666/502329.** Fax 01453/836778. www.chavenage.com. Admission (including guided tour) £6 ($12) adults, £3 ($6) children. May–Sept Thurs and Sun 2–5pm; also open on Easter and bank holiday Mon.

2 Cirencester ⊛

143km (89 miles) W of London; 26km (16 miles) S of Cheltenham; 27km (17 miles) SE of Gloucester; 58km (36 miles) W of Oxford

Cirencester is the unofficial capital of the Cotswolds. In the Middle Ages, it flourished as the center of the great Cotswold wool industry. Dating from the 17th and 18th centuries, many well-preserved old stone houses are still intact, some having bow-fronted shops of the type familiar to Charles Dickens.

Once known as Corinium, the town had five roads converging here during the Roman occupation. In size, it ranked second only to London. Today, it is chiefly a market town and a good base for touring. We prefer to visit the **Market Place** in the center of town on Monday or Friday morning when the people from the country flock to town to hawk their produce. (And don't worry about how to pronounce *Cirencester*. Even the English disagree. Say *Siren*-cess-ter and you'll be close enough.)

ESSENTIALS

GETTING THERE   Cirencester has no railway station, but trains depart several times a day from London's Paddington Station for the 80-minute trip to Kemble, which is 6.5km (4 miles) southwest of Cirencester. You may have to transfer trains at Swindon. For schedules and information, call ☎ **0845/748-4950** or visit **www.nationalrail.co.uk**. From Kemble, a bus travels to Cirencester four to five times a day.

National Express buses leave London's Victoria Coach Station with direct service to Cirencester. For schedules and information, call ☎ **0870/580-8080** or visit **www.nationalexpress.co.uk**.

If driving from London, take the M40 northwest to Oxford, continuing along the A40 to the junction with the A429, which you'll take south to Cirencester.

VISITOR INFORMATION   The **Costwold Visitors Centre** is located in the Corinium Museum at Park Street (☎ **01285/654180**). Year-round hours are Monday to Saturday from 10am to 5pm, Sunday 2 to 5pm.

WHERE TO STAY & DINE IN & AROUND CIRENCESTER

Tatyan's, 27 Castle St. in Cirencester (☎ **01285/653529**), is a great place to dine. It serves Peking, Hunan, and Szechuan specialties, with nearly a dozen prawn dishes on the large menu. For a pint, head for the town favorite, the **Crown,** 17 W. Market Place (☎ **01285/653206**), a friendly pub enjoyed by locals and students alike, with out-of-towners predominating in summer. The place boasts a 400-year-old tradition of serving ale and victuals on this site, and it has the most convivial nightlife in town.

Barnsley House ⊛⊛⊛ *(Finds*   The gardens here, surrounding a 17th-century manor house, were always one of the major attractions of the Cotswolds. They were created by the late Rosemary Verey, the garden writer. Following her death in 2001, the property has been turned into a small inn of charm and grace. Although old-fashioned outside, its interiors are of the 21st century, with strong Italian and French influences. Each unit is individually designed with elegant, comfortable furnishings and such surprise features as complimentary chocolates, 2.1m (7-ft.) beds, and chilled champagne. The food is among the finest in the area.

Barnsley, Cirencester, Gloucestershire GL7 5EE. ☎ 01285/740000. Fax 01285/740925. www.barnsleyhouse.com. 9 units. £290–£400 ($580–$800) double; £340–£490 ($680–$980) suite. Rates include continental breakfast. 2-night minimum stay Sat–Sun. AE, MC, V. Lies 6.4km (4 miles) northeast of Cirencester on the B4425. **Amenities:** Restaurant; bar; hydrotherapy pool; tennis court; spa; sauna; steam room; croquet lawn; room service; babysitting; laundry service; dry cleaning. *In room:* A/C, TV, minibar, hair dryer.

The Fleece Hotel   It was on this site that Charles II hid out, posing as a servant to the house mistress, Jane Lane, in 1651, with Cromwell's troops in hot pursuit. The half-timbered facade here hints at origins as an Elizabethan coaching inn, but it was enlarged by the Georgians and today has had many modernizations. The comfortable small to midsize rooms feature old-fashioned hints of yesteryear, including quilts. Two rooms are large enough for families, and two have four-poster beds.

Market Place, Cirencester, Gloucestershire GL7 2NZ. ℂ 01285/658507. Fax 01285/651017. www.fleecehotel.co.uk. 28 units. £115–£137 ($230–$274) double. Rates include English breakfast. Children 15 and younger stay free in same room with up to 2 paying adults. AE, MC, V. **Amenities:** Restaurant; bar; room service. *In room:* TV, beverage maker, hair dryer, iron, trouser press, safe.

The Pear Tree at Purton 𝕏 *Finds*   This English country hotel/restaurant, on 3 hectares (7½ acres), offers individually styled rooms in various shapes and sizes, each equipped with extras such as sherry and mineral water. All accommodations (three with four-poster beds) have views of the traditional Victorian garden and countryside; some executive rooms have whirlpool tubs. Rooms are named for characters associated with the village of Purton—Anne Hyde, for example, mother of Queen Mary and Queen Anne. Bathrooms are well supplied, each with a tub/shower combination. The Cotswold stone house was formerly the vicarage for the twin-towered parish Church of St. Mary.

Church End, Purton, near Swindon, Wiltshire SN5 4ED. ℂ 01793/772100. Fax 01793/772369. www.peartreepurton. co.uk. 17 units. £110–£140 ($220–$280) double; £140–£180 ($280–$360) suite. Rates include English breakfast. AE, DC, MC, V. Closed Dec 26–30. Purton is 13km (8 miles) southeast of Cirencester, 5km (3 miles) from Junction 16 of M4, and 8km (5 miles) from Swindon. From Cirencester, follow Rte. B419 in the direction of Swindon. Turn left when signs point to Cricklade, and from here, follow the signs to Purton. **Amenities:** Restaurant; bar; croquet lawn; room service; laundry service; dry cleaning. *In room:* TV, Wi-Fi, hair dryer, trouser press, safe.

Stratton House Hotel 𝕏   Built in several stages throughout the 18th century, with a modern wing added in the 1990s, this inviting country house is part Jacobean and part Georgian. It is surrounded by beautiful grounds with a walled garden and herbaceous borders. The rooms are large and well furnished (the "cozy" rooms being the smallest of the lot); some have four-poster beds. Two-thirds of the units lie within the most modern wing—designer-decorated, with an aura evoking a traditional private English country house.

Gloucester Rd., Cirencester, Gloucestershire GL7 2LE. ℂ 01285/651761. Fax 01285/640024. www.strattonhousehotel. co.uk. 40 units. £135–£145 ($270–$290) double. Rates include English breakfast. AE, DC, MC, V. Take A417 2km (1¼ miles) northwest of Cirencester. **Amenities:** Restaurant; bar; room service. *In room:* TV, beverage maker, hair dryer, trouser press.

EXPLORING CIRENCESTER

Cirencester has some of the greatest walks and scenic views of any town in the Cotswolds. You don't have to go miles out of town to enjoy a stroll—they are easily reached from the center at Market Place. On the grounds of the Church of St. John the Baptist (see below), attractive trees and shrubs highlight a well-manicured landscape. You can see swans and wild fowl on the River Churn and the lake, even remnants of the town's Roman walls. For a great stroll, take 1.6km-long (1 mile) riverside walk along the Churn from Barton Lane to the Abbey Grounds.

For more walks, head south from Market Place for 4.8km (3 miles) to **Cotswold Water Park,** a 1,214-hectare (3,000-acre) setting of parkland and woodland walks. Pedestrian access is from Cecily Hill (no vehicles). This is Britain's largest water park, with more than 133 lakes created by extracting gravel. Known for its wildlife, the park is filled with picnic tables and barbecue sites, along with a network of footpaths. Concessions here will hook you up with sailing, fishing, canoeing, cycling, kayaking, horseback riding, and water-skiing. All equipment needed is for rent on-site. Swimming is possible June to September. The park is signposted off B4696, Shorncote (© 01285/861459; www.waterpark.org). Entrance to the park June to August Monday to Friday is £3 ($6) for adults, rising to £4 ($8) on Saturday and Sunday; the rest of the year it's £1 ($2) for adults. Children pay 50p ($1) April to September; from October to March, children enter free.

Brewery Arts Centre The living heart of this arts complex is the workshop area of 15 resident crafts workers, who produce everything from baskets to chandeliers. Other components of the center include three galleries featuring both craft and fine-art exhibitions, a theater, education classes, a shop selling the best in British crafts, and a coffeehouse.

Brewery Court © 01285/657181. www.breweryarts.org.uk. Free admission. Mon–Fri 10am–5pm; Sat 9:30am–5:30pm.

Church of St. John the Baptist A church may have stood here in Saxon times, but the present building overlooking the Market Place in the town center dates from Norman times and Henry I. In size, it appears more like a cathedral than a mere parish church, with a variety of styles, largely Perpendicular, as in the early-15th-century tower. Among the treasures inside are a 15th-century "wineglass" pulpit and a silver-gilt cup given to Queen Anne Boleyn 2 years before her execution. In the Trinity Chapel, you can rub some great 15th-century brasses.

Market Place. © 01285/654552. Free admission; donations invited. Mon–Fri 10am–1pm.

Corinium Museum ★★ This museum houses one of the finest collections of archaeological remains from the Roman occupation, found locally in and around Cirencester. Mosaic pavements excavated on Dyer Street in 1849 and other mosaics are the most important exhibits. Provincial Roman sculpture, including such figures as Minerva and Mercury, pottery, and artifacts salvaged from long-decayed buildings, provide a link with the remote civilization that once flourished here. The museum has been completely modernized to include full-scale reconstructions and special exhibitions on local history and conservation.

Park St. © 01285/655611. www.cotswold.gov.uk. Admission £3.90 ($7.80) adults, £2.90 ($5.80) seniors, £2 ($4) students and children, £9 ($18) family ticket. Mon–Sat 10am–5pm; Sun 2–5pm.

SHOPPING

For antiques in Cirencester, try **William H. Stokes,** the Cloisters, 6–8 Dollar St. (© 01285/653907), which specializes in furniture, tapestries, and other items from the 16th and 17th centuries.

The arts complex known as the **Brewery Arts Centre** (see above) has 15 independent workshops of area craftspeople ranging from jewelers and weavers to basket makers. Three galleries and a crafts shop recognized by the Crafts Council sell many of the artists' wares.

3 Painswick ★

6.5km (4 miles) N of Stroud; 172km (107 miles) W of London; 16km (10 miles) SW of Cheltenham; 24km (15 miles) NW of Cirencester

This sleepy stone-built Cotswold wool town vies with Bibury for the title of the most beautiful in the Cotswolds. Painswick is a dream of England of long ago, the perfect escape from a string of dull market towns too often encountered. Its mellow gray stone houses and inns date from as early as the 14th century.

A visit to Painswick at any time of the year would be idyllic, in spite of the day-trippers and tourist buses, but there are two special occasions that make it an especially wonderful destination. One is the town's Victorian Market Day in early July. You can contact the **Tourist Information Centre** (see below) for the exact day, which is announced in the late spring. The other big occasion is the Clipping Feast (see "Special Events," below).

ESSENTIALS

GETTING THERE   Trains depart London's Paddington Station several times a day for Stroud, the nearest railway station, 5km (3 miles) away. The trip takes from 1½ to 2 hours, and you may have to change trains at Swindon. For rail information, call © **0845/748-4950** or visit **www.nationalrail.co.uk**. From Stroud, buses run to Painswick, some as frequently as every hour. Many taxis also wait at the Stroud railway station.

If you're driving from Cirencester, continue west along the A419 to Stroud, then head north on the A46 to Cheltenham and Painswick.

VISITOR INFORMATION   The Painswick **Tourist Information Centre** is at the Painswick Library, Stroud Road (© **01452/813552**), and is open Monday to Saturday from 10am to 5pm. These hours are true at least in theory, but the staff volunteers manning the office don't always show up. In that case, you can visit the more reliably open tourist office at Stroud, located in Subscription Rooms, George Street (© **01453/760960**).

SPECIAL EVENTS   The **Clipping Feast** of Painswick, also known as the Clipping Ceremony, is an unusual, early-medieval ceremony that anthropologists think may have begun in the dim Celtic prehistory of Britain. Every September, a month that coincides with the harvest ceremonies of pagans, adults and as many children as can be mustered hold hands in a circle around St. Mary's Anglican Church. The circle moves first one way, then the other, and the participants sing hymns and pray out loud in a celebration of thanksgiving. Participants and observers come from all over the region to take part in this important rite.

On **Victorian Market Day,** locals dressed in Victorian attire come into town from the neighboring villages. Shoppers meander through the streets, absorbing the festive atmosphere and purchasing handicrafts and other gifts. Food, based on old-fashioned recipes, is sold at various kiosks.

Contact the Tourist Information Centre (see above) for the exact day and schedule of these events.

WHERE TO STAY & DINE

Cardynham House ♠ (Value)   Adjacent to St. Mary's Church, this small but choice house dates from 1498. It was later enlarged thanks to beams that were salvaged from the remains of a wrecked ship from the Spanish Armada. The owner has outfitted the interior with lots of cozy accessories that fit in well with a stylish hodgepodge of cabinets, wide floorboards, and an intricate network of ceiling beams. Bedrooms are cozy, each with a different theme (Arabian Nights and Medieval Garden are good examples). All of the accommodations feature four-poster or half-tester beds. One of them is a bit larger than the others and enjoys exclusive access to a 5m (16-ft.) indoor swimming pool. The Dovecote room is good for families.

Local produce is deftly handled at the on-site restaurant, the Bistro, which is open Tuesday to Saturday nights for dinner and Tuesday to Sunday for lunch. Roast beef with all the trimmings is a feature at the Sunday lunch, and tender Cotswold lamb appears frequently on the menu.

The Cross, Painswick, Gloucestershire GL6 6XX. ℂ **01452/814006.** Fax 01452/812321. www.cardynham.co.uk. 9 units. £69–£210 ($138–$420) double. Rates include breakfast. Minimum stay of 2 nights Fri–Sun. AE, MC, V. Parking £2.50. **Amenities:** Restaurant; lounge. *In room:* TV, beverage maker, hair dryer.

Cotswold 88 ⟨★★⟩   If Henry VII or even Elizabeth I were passing through the village today, they might be horrified at what has happened to the old Painswick Hotel, a former vicarage encircled by terraces of formal gardens. This mansion behind the Painswick parish church has been completely renovated. Today it retains its old architectural features but has been completely modernized inside, sort of what you might expect to see in a rock star's country manor. The bedrooms have been updated with a very modern and slightly crazy interior decor, decorated with works by photo artists David Hiscock and Leigh Bowery. Its restaurant and bar is the hippest in town.

Kemps Lane, Painswick, Gloucestershire GL6 6YB. ℂ **01452/813688.** Fax 01452/814059. www.cotswolds88hotel. com. 18 rooms. £140–£225 ($280–$450) double; £411–£464 ($822–$928) suite. AE, MC, V. **Amenities:** Restaurant; bar; spa services; room service; babysitting; laundry service. *In room:* TV, Wi-Fi, hair dryer, safe.

EXPLORING THE TOWN

The charm of this town comes from its mellow Cotswold architecture with stone-built houses. Funded by wealthy farmers and merchants in the era when fluffy wool was called "white gold," the houses of Painswick represent a peak in English domestic architecture. The architecture is best seen by walking around **New Street** in the center of the village. This has to be one of the most misnamed streets in England, as it dates from 1450 and there isn't anything new about it.

Painswick Rococo Garden ⟨★⟩, B4073, .8km (½ mile) north of Painswick (ℂ **01452/ 813204;** www.rococogarden.co.uk), is a rare English garden and is a throwback to the flamboyant English rococo period, which lasted only from 1720 to 1760. Today the garden is best known for its spectacular display of snowdrops that appear in the early spring, sometimes when snow is still on the ground. On certain summer evenings, Shakespeare's plays are performed in the garden. Admission is £5.50 ($11) adults, £4.50 ($9) seniors, £2.75 ($5.50) children 5 to 16, and £15 ($30) family ticket (two adults, two children); visits are possible from mid-January until October daily 11am to 5pm.

St. Mary's Church, the centerpiece of the village, was originally built between 1377 and 1399, and it was reconstructed into its present form in 1480. Its churchyard contains 99 massive yew trees, each of which is at least 200 years old. Local

---

⟨*Finds*⟩ **Owlpen Manor: A Journey to Yesterday**

As beautiful as Painswick is, nearby is a place even lovelier. The hamlet of **Owlpen Manor** lies immediately to the south of Painswick, off the beaten track. This fairy-tale hamlet is administered by Nicholas Mander, a descendant of Sir Geoffrey and Lady Mander, fabled pre-Raphaelite patrons of the arts. The manor house here is open from May to September on Tuesday, Thursday, and Sunday only from 2 to 5pm, charging £5.25 ($11) for adults, £2.25 ($4.50) for children ages 4 to 14; a family ticket goes for £15 ($30). For information about visits to the manor or grounds, or rentals of the cottages, call ℂ **01453/860261** or visit **www.owlpen.com.**

legend states that no matter how hard well-meaning gardeners have tried, they've never been able to grow more than 99 of them.

159km (99 miles) NW of London; 14km (9 miles) NE of Gloucester; 69km (43 miles) W of Oxford

Legend has it that the Cheltenham villagers discovered a mineral spring by chance when they noticed pigeons drinking from a spring and observed how healthy they were (the pigeon has been incorporated into the town's crest). King George III arrived in 1788 and launched the town's career as a spa. Today many British look upon it as a staid, safe place for retirement, the town attracting mainly well-heeled conservatives, some of the women looking like Margaret Thatcher did in the 1980s.

Cheltenham remains one of England's most fashionable spas; many visitors come just to see its gardens. The architecture is mainly Regency, with lots of ironwork, balconies, and verandas. Attractive parks and open spaces of greenery make the town especially inviting. The main street, the Promenade, is one of the most beautiful thoroughfares in the Cotswolds. Rather similar are Lansdowne Place and Montpellier Parade (with caryatids separating the stores). Montpelier Walk contains more than 30 statues adorning its storefronts.

ESSENTIALS

GETTING THERE   Twenty-one trains depart daily from London's Paddington Station for the 2¼-hour trip. You may have to change trains at Bristol or Swindon. For information, call ℗ **0845/748-4950** or visit **www.nationalrail.co.uk**. Trains between Cheltenham and Bristol take an hour, with continuing service to Bath.

National Express offers 10 buses daily from London's Victoria Coach Station to Cheltenham. The ride takes about 2½ to 3 hours. For schedules and information, call ℗ **0870/580-8080** or visit **www.nationalexpress.co.uk**.

If you're driving from London, head northwest on the M40 to Oxford, continuing along the A40 to Cheltenham.

VISITOR INFORMATION   The **Tourist Information Centre,** 77 The Promenade (℗ **01242/522878;** www.visitcheltenham.com), is open Monday to Saturday from 9:30am to 5:15pm. On Wednesday mornings, it opens at 10am.

SPECIAL EVENTS   The **International Festival of Music** and the **Festival of Literature** take place each year in July and October, respectively, and attract internationally acclaimed performers and orchestras. There are other festivals as well—a folk festival in February, a jazz festival in May, and a science festival in June. For details, call ℗ **01242/227979** or visit **www.cheltenhamfestivals.co.uk**.

WHERE TO STAY

Beaumont House ⚑ *(Finds*   One of the best-rated B&Bs in the area, this house is set in a lovely garden a short walk from the town center and convenient to local shops and restaurants. Its owners have made significant improvements and today its renovated bedrooms are among the best in the area—indeed, they've won awards. No accommodations are alike, ranging from small singles to luxurious and spacious rooms suitable for families. Comfort and style combine with a warm welcome to make this a desirable choice—and the price is right, too.

56 Shurdington Rd., Cheltenham, Gloucestershire GL53 0JE. ℗ **01242/223311.** Fax 01242/520044. www.bh hotel.co.uk. 16 units. £96–£164 ($192–$328) double; £201 ($402) suite. Rates include breakfast. AE, MC, V. **Amenities:** Breakfast room. *In room:* TV, Wi-Fi, beverage maker, hair dryer, safe.

Central Hotel   Within easy reach of Cheltenham's range of attractions, this hotel consists of a pair of stone houses that were originally built in the 1700s and then combined. Today, it's a family-run hotel, with a street-level public house. The comfortable bedrooms are conservatively modern with everything you need, including a kitchen for self-catering.

7–9 Portland St., Cheltenham, Gloucestershire GL52 2NZ. ℂ 0870/240-7113. Fax 01242/524789. www.central hotelcheltenham.co.uk. 23 units. £50–£55 ($100–$110) double; £60 ($120) family room. MC, V. **Amenities:** Restaurant; bar; laundry service. *In room:* TV, kitchen, fridge, beverage maker, hair dryer.

The Greenway ✸✸   An elegant and beautifully furnished former Elizabethan manor house from the 1540s in a garden setting, this is an ivy-clad Cotswold showpiece. Restored with sensitivity, Greenway rents rooms in both its main house and a converted coach house. Bedrooms, midsize to spacious, are sumptuously outfitted. This is the best English-country-house living in the area.

Shurdington, near Cheltenham, Gloucestershire GL51 4UG. ℂ 01242/862352. Fax 01242/862780. www.the-greenway. co.uk. 21 units. £175–£220 ($350–$440) double; £250–£300 ($500–$600) suite. Rates include English breakfast and early-morning tea and coffee. AE, DC, MC, V. Take A46 less than 6.5km (4 miles) southwest of Cheltenham. **Amenities:** Restaurant; bar; room service; massage; laundry service; dry cleaning. *In room:* TV, hair dryer.

Hotel de la Bere   This 16th-century Cotswold-stone building stands near the Cheltenham racecourse and until its takeover by a nationwide chain a few years ago, it had been owned by the de la Bere family for 3 centuries. Converted into a hotel in 1972, it retains its original charm. All rooms are furnished to preserve their individual character. Five rooms have double four-poster beds.

Southam, Cheltenham, Gloucestershire GL52 3NH. ℂ 01242/545454. Fax 01242/236016. www.foliohotels.com. 57 units. £110–£140 ($220–$280) double. AE, DC, MC, V. Take B4632 5km (3 miles) northeast of town, following the signs to Prestbury. **Amenities:** Restaurant; bar; tennis court; squash court; room service; laundry service; dry cleaning. *In room:* TV, beverage maker, hair dryer, trouser press.

Hotel on the Park ✸✸   In what was formerly an 1830s private villa, this is one of the most talked-about hotels in town. It is located among similar terraced buildings in the once-prominent village of Pittville Spa, 1km (a half-mile) north of Cheltenham's town center. Owned and operated by Darryl and Joanne Gregory, who undertook most of the Regency-inspired interior design, it has received several awards. Each bedroom is named after a prominent 19th-century visitor who came here shortly after the villa was built. Comfortable and high-ceilinged, the rooms have stylish accessories and a tasteful assortment of antique and reproduction furniture. Bedrooms are beautifully appointed, with thoughtful extras such as sherry and mineral water.

Evesham Rd., Cheltenham, Gloucestershire GL52 2AH. ℂ 01242/518898. Fax 01242/511526. www.hotelonthepark. com. 12 units. £139–£220 ($278–$440) double. AE, DC, MC, V. **Amenities:** Restaurant; bar; room service; library; drawing room. *In room:* TV, Wi-Fi, beverage maker, hair dryer.

Kandinsky ✸   This Georgian inn has been dramatically modernized and is today a stylish stopover in this spa town. Fashionable, teak designer furnishings decorate the modern accommodations, which are both tasteful and comfortable with attractive little bathrooms with showers. Large potted plants and a choice of antiques grace the public lounges, and throw rugs cover many of the floors. The on-site Café Paradiso serves the best antipasti in town, along with other Continental offerings; it's like a cool 1950s bar, where entertainment is often presented.

Bayshill Rd., Montpellier, Cheltenham, Gloucestershire GL50 3AS. © **01242/527788.** Fax 01242/226412. www. aliaskandinsky.com. 48 units. £120–£145 ($240–$290) double; £150 ($300) suite. AE, DC, MC, V. **Amenities:** Restaurant; bar; cafe/nightclub; use of nearby health club. *In room:* TV, Wi-Fi, beverage maker, hair dryer.

Lypiatt House ✿ *Value*   This beautifully restored Victorian home stands in the Montpellier area, the most fashionable part of Cheltenham. A hotel of ambience and character, it offers a large elegant drawing room with a colonial-style conservatory and "honesty bar." The bedrooms are beautifully furnished and of generous size. The friendly owners are the most helpful in town.

Lypiatt Rd., Cheltenham, Gloucestershire GL50 2QW. © **01242/224994.** Fax 01242/224996. www.lypiatt.co.uk. 10 units. £80–£90 ($160–$180) double. Rates include English breakfast. AE, MC, V. **Amenities:** Bar; laundry service. *In room:* TV, beverage maker.

WHERE TO DINE

Le Champignon Sauvage ✿✿✿ FRENCH   This is among the culinary highlights of the Cotswolds. David Everitt-Matthias, a chef of considerable talent, limits the selection of dishes each evening for better quality control. Some evenings his imagination roams a bit, so dining here is usually a pleasant surprise. You may begin with light cauliflower soup flavored with cumin. Main courses may include braised lamb dumplings with roasted carrots and shallots. On a more daring level, you can sample roast partridge with caramelized chicory and Puy lentils, or pumpkin risotto with pork belly and artichoke foam. Dessert choices include iced licorice parfait with damson sorbet, and baked caramel cheesecake with caramelized banana.

24–26 Suffolk Rd. © **01242/573449.** www.lechampignonsauvage.co.uk. Reservations required. 2-course fixed-price meal £39 ($78), 3 courses £48 ($96), 4 courses £56 ($112). AE, DC, MC, V. Tues–Sat 12:30–1:30pm and 7:30–9pm. Closed 2 weeks in June, 1 week in Dec.

Le Petit Blanc ✿ FRENCH   Already a bit of a dining legend in Oxford, this off-spring long ago invaded Cheltenham. Under the guidance of Master Chef Raymond Blanc, a celebrity chef whose more famous, and more expensive, gastronomic restaurant is known throughout England, this is a *brasserie de luxe,* with a decor inspired by turn-of-the-20th-century Paris, modern paintings, a row of unusual sculpture that runs up the middle, and a hip and knowledgeable staff. Cuisine is beautifully presented and prepared with the freshest of the day's available ingredients. Some of the finest examples include such starters as Loch Fyne mussels with white-wine-and-cream sauce or a truffle-flavored chicken liver parfait, followed by such mains as crab and salmon fishcakes or filet of seared haddock and shellfish in a creamy wine sauce.

Next to the Queen's Hotel, the Promenade. © **01242/266800.** www.lepetitblanc.co.uk. Reservations recommended. Main courses lunch £18–£21 ($36–$42), dinner £8.50–£22 ($17–$44); fixed-price 2-course menu £12 ($24). AE, DC, MC, V. Mon–Fri noon–2:45pm and 5:30–10:30pm; Sat noon–11pm; Sun noon–10pm.

EXPLORING THE TOWN

Cheltenham Art Gallery & Museum   This gallery houses one of the foremost collections of the Arts and Crafts movement, notably the fine furniture of William Morris and his followers. One section is devoted to Edward Wilson, Cheltenham's native son, who died with Captain Scott in the Antarctic in 1912. The gallery is located near Royal Crescent and the Coach Station.

Clarence St. © **01242/237431.** www.cheltenhammuseum.org.uk. Free admission; donations welcome. Mon–Sat 10am–5:20pm. Closed bank holidays.

Everyman Theatre   Cheltenham is the cultural center of the Cotswolds, a role solidified by the Everyman Theatre. Designed in the 1890s as an opera house by Frank Matcham, Victorian England's leading theater architect, it retains its ornate cornices, sculpted ceilings, and plush velvets despite extensive renovations to its stage and lighting facilities. The theater has begun to attract some of England's top dramatic companies. Shakespeare, musicals, comedies, and other genres are performed in the small (658 seats) but charming hall.

Regent St. (℃ 01242/572573. www.everymantheatre.org.uk. Admission £8–£28 ($16–$56), depending on the event. Box office Mon–Sat 9:30am–8:30pm (until 6pm in Aug), and from 2 hr. before the performance on Sun.

Pittville Pump Room   Cheltenham Waters are the only natural, consumable alkaline waters in Great Britain and are still drunk at one of the spa's finest Regency buildings. The Pittville Pump Room is open Sundays from the end of May until the end of September for a host of activities, including lunch, afternoon cream teas, live classical music, landau carriage rides around the city, and brass bands playing in Pittville Park.

East Approach Dr., Pittville Park. (℃ 01242/523852. Free admission; donations welcome. Wed–Mon 10am–4pm. From the town center, take Portland St. and Evesham Rd.

SHOPPING

Start in the **Montpellier quarter** for individual boutiques and craft and specialty shops, and then continue to the nearby **Suffolk quarter** to find most of Cheltenham's antiques stores.

An enjoyable short stroll to the **Promenade** takes you by stores featuring attractive clothing and shoes, as well as several bookstores. From the Promenade, take Regent Street to **High Street,** which is mostly pedestrian-only, and you'll find several brand-name department stores in the **Beechwood Shopping Centre.**

The **weekly market** is in the Henrietta Street car park on Thursday. Weather permitting, the market is open from 9am to 2pm.

The **Courtyard,** on Montpellier Street in the heart of the Montpellier quarter, has become an award-winning shopping mall that offers a fun blend of shops specializing in unique fashion, furniture, and gift items. A good mix of restaurants, cafes, and wine bars rounds out the mall.

Cavendish House, the Promenade (℃ **01242/521300**), is a long-established shopping landmark.

CHELTENHAM AFTER DARK

The major venue for entertainment is the **Everyman Theatre** (see above), which is the premier sightseeing attraction of Cheltenham. You'll find a lot more theater at the **Playhouse,** Bath Road (℃ **01242/522852;** www.playhousecheltenham.org), which presents new local, amateur productions of drama, comedy, dance, and opera staged at the dizzying pace of every 2 weeks. Tickets are £6 to £18 ($12–$36).

Otherwise, the best center for nocturnal affairs is **Moda,** 33–35 Albion St. (℃ **01242/570583**), which is entered from High Street. It offers three floors of fun, with loud music blaring everything from R&B to hits from the Reagan era. Cover ranges from £3 to £5 ($6–$10), but it's most often free if you enter before 10pm. Moda is open Monday and Wednesday to Saturday 9pm to 3am.

A SIDE TRIP TO SUDELEY CASTLE ★

Royal Sudeley Castle and Gardens   This 15th-century structure is one of England's finer stately homes. It has a rich history that begins in Saxon times, when the village was the capital of the Mercian kings. Later, Catherine Parr, the sixth wife of Henry VIII, lived and died here. Her tomb is in a chapel on the grounds, which include a host of formal gardens like the Queen's Garden, now planted with old-world roses and dating from the time of Catherine Parr. While exploring the gardens, you're sure to see the waterfowl and flamboyant peacocks that call Sudeley home. For the past 30 years, Lady Ashcombe, an American by birth, has owned the castle and welcomed visitors from the world over. The castle houses many works of art by Constable, Turner, Rubens, and Van Dyck, among others, and has several permanent exhibitions, magnificent furniture and glass, and many artifacts from the castle's past. In the area to the right of the keep, as you enter the castle, workshops are devoted to talented local artisans who continue to use traditional techniques to produce stained glass, textiles, wood and leather articles, and marbled paper. The admission prices given below are for exhibitions and the gardens. To actually tour the private apartments costs another £15 ($30) per person. These "connoisseur tours" are available Tuesday to Thursday at 11am and 1 and 3pm, including the stone-built drawing room, the library, and the billiard room.

In the village of Winchcombe (9.5km/6 miles northeast of Cheltenham). *C* **01242/602308.** www.sudeleycastle. co.uk. Admission £7.20 ($14) adults, £6.20 ($12) seniors, £4.20 ($8.40) children 5–15, £21 ($42) family ticket. Castle Apr–Oct daily 10:30am–5pm (last entry at 4:30pm); gardens and grounds Mar–Oct daily 10:30am–5:30pm. From Cheltenham, take the regular bus to Winchcombe and get off at Abbey Terrace. Then walk the short distance along the road to the castle. If you're driving, take B4632 north out of Cheltenham, through Prestbury, and up Cleve Hill to Abbey Terrace, where you can drive right up to the castle.

5 Bibury ✦ ✦

138km (86 miles) W of London; 48km (30 miles) W of Oxford; 42km (26 miles) E of Gloucester

On the road from Burford to Cirencester, Bibury is one of the loveliest spots in the Cotswolds. In fact, the utopian romancer of Victoria's day, poet William Morris, called it England's most beautiful village. In the Cotswolds, it is matched only by Painswick for its scenic village beauty and purity. Both villages are still unspoiled by modern intrusions.

GETTING THERE

About five trains per day depart London's Paddington Station for the 1-hour, 20-minute trip to Kemble, the nearest station, 21km (13 miles) south of Bibury. Some will require an easy change of train in Swindon (the connecting train waits across the tracks). For information, call *C* **0845/748-4950** or visit **www.nationalrail.co.uk**. No buses run from Kemble to Bibury, but most hotels will arrange transportation if you ask in advance.

Ten buses leave London's Victoria Coach Station daily for Cirencester, 11km (7 miles) from Bibury. For information, call *C* **0870/580-8080** or visit **www.national express.co.uk**. With no connecting buses into Bibury, local hotels will send a car, and taxis are available.

If driving from London, take the M4 to exit 15, head toward Cirencester, then follow the A33 (on some maps this is still designated as the B4425) to Bibury.

WHERE TO STAY & DINE

Bibury Court Hotel ✦ *Finds* You can feel the history when you stay at this Jacobean manor house, built by Sir Thomas Sackville in 1633 (parts of it date from Tudor times). The house was a residence until it was turned into a hotel in 1968. The structure is built of Cotswold stone, with many gables, huge chimneys, and a formal graveled entryway. Many rooms have four-poster beds, original oak paneling, and antiques. Bedrooms are furnished in old English style but have modern comforts.

Bibury, Gloucestershire GL7 5NT. ℂ **01285/740337.** Fax 01285/740660. www.biburycourt.co.uk. 18 units. £150–£190 ($300–$380) double; £230 ($460) suite. Rates include continental breakfast. AE, DC, MC, V. **Amenities:** 2 restaurants; bar; croquet lawn; room service. *In room:* TV, beverage maker, hair dryer, trouser press.

The Swan 🐦🐦 Well managed, upscale, and discreet, this hotel and restaurant is the finest in the village. It originated as a riverside cottage in the 1300s, but was greatly expanded through the centuries. Much of the interior is outfitted in a traditional, warm-toned design evocative of a discreetly upscale stately home, with tartan-patterned and flowered fabrics, and autumn-inspired colors. The bedrooms are outfitted with antique furniture and an individualized decor. Each contains an elegant bed—some are four-posters—with soft linens. There are three modern and luxurious suites located a short walk from the main building, each with its own landscaped garden and containing such extras as an iPod/MP3 docking station.

Bibury, Gloucestershire GL7 5NW. ℂ **01285/740695.** Fax 01285/740473. www.swanhotel.co.uk. 18 units. £145–£265 ($290–$530) double; £245–£280 ($490–$560) 2-bedroom suite for 4; £255–£295 ($510–$590) garden suite. Rates include English breakfast. AE, DC, MC, V. **Amenities:** 2 restaurants; bar; room service; laundry service. *In room:* TV, beverage maker, hair dryer, trouser press.

EXPLORING THE TOWN

On the banks of the tiny Coln River, Bibury is noted for **Arlington Row,** a group of 17th-century gabled cottages protected by the National Trust. Originally built for weavers, these houses are its biggest and most photographed attraction, but it's rude to peer into the windows, as many do, because people still live here.

To get a view of something a bit out of the ordinary for the Cotswolds, check out **St. Mary's Parish Church.** As the story goes, the wool merchants who had the power and money in the area were rebuilding the churches. However, they did not finish the restoration to St. Mary's, and, as a result, much of the original Roman-style architecture has been left intact. The 14th-century Decorated-style windows have even survived the years. This is an often-overlooked treasure. The so-called "Decorated" style was given to the second period of English Gothic architecture, mainly from the late 13th to the mid–14th centuries, when adornments became more elaborate and stone construction lighter and more spacious.

6 Burford ⋆

122km (76 miles) NW of London; 32km (20 miles) W of Oxford

Built of Cotswold stone and serving as a gateway to the area, the unspoiled medieval town of Burford is largely famous for its Norman church (ca. 1116) and its High Street lined with coaching inns.

Burford was one of the last of the great wool centers, the industry bleating out its last breath during Queen Victoria's day. Be sure to photograph the bridge across the River Windrush where Queen Elizabeth I once stood. As the antiques shops along High Street testify, Burford today is definitely equipped for visitors.

The River Windrush, which toward Burford is flanked by willows and meadows, passes beneath the packhorse bridge and goes around the church and away through more meadows. Strolling along its banks is one of the most delightful experiences in the Cotswolds.

ESSENTIALS

GETTING THERE   Many trains depart from London's Paddington Station to Oxford, a 1-hour trip. For information, call ℂ **0845/748-4950** or visit **www.firstgreat western.co.uk**. From Oxford, passengers walk a short distance to the entrance of the Taylor Institute, from which about three or four buses per day make the 30-minute run to Burford.

If you're driving from Oxford, head west on the A40 to Burford.

VISITOR INFORMATION   The **Tourist Information Centre** is at the Old Brewery on Sheep Street (ℂ **01993/823558**) and is open November to February Monday to Saturday 10am to 4:30pm, and March to October Monday to Saturday 9:30am to 5:30pm.

WHERE TO STAY

Bay Tree Hotel 🌟🌟   This is the best and most atmospheric of Burford's many interesting old inns. The house was built for Sir Lawrence Tanfield, the unpopular lord chief baron of the exchequer to Elizabeth I. The house has oak-paneled rooms with stone fireplaces and a high-beamed hall with a minstrel's gallery. Modern comforts have been discreetly installed in the tastefully furnished rooms, some of which have four-poster beds. Some of the accommodations are in a comfortable annex, though the chambers in the main building—nine in all—have more character. Try to get a room overlooking the terraced gardens at the rear of the house.

12–14 Sheep St., Burford, Oxfordshire OX18 4LW. ℂ **01993/822791**. Fax 01993/823008. www.cotswold-inns-hotels. co.uk. 21 units. £165–£205 ($330–$410) double; £215–£250 ($430–$500) suite. Rates include English breakfast. AE, DC, MC, V. **Amenities:** Restaurant; bar; room service; babysitting; laundry service; dry cleaning. *In room:* TV, beverage maker, hair dryer.

Golden Pheasant Hotel 🌟   This inn is housed in what was once the 15th-century home of a prosperous wool merchant. It began serving food and drink in the 1730s when it was used both to brew and serve beer. Today, it's one of the best places to stay in town (though it lacks the rich furnishings of the best, the Bay Tree Hotel; see above). Like many of its neighbors, the Golden Pheasant is capped with a slate roof and fronted with hand-chiseled stones. The cozy accommodations come in a range of sizes, many a bit small, and one room has a four-poster bed. Each, though, is stylishly appointed with period furniture. One room is large enough for a family.

91 High St., Burford, Oxfordshire OX18 4QA. ℂ **01993/823223**. Fax 01993/822621. www.goldenpheasant-burford. co.uk. 12 units. £85–£110 ($170–$220) double. Rates include English breakfast. MC, V. **Amenities:** Restaurant; bar. *In room:* TV, beverage maker, hair dryer, iron, trouser press.

The Lamb Inn 🌟🌟   This thoroughly Cotswold house, solidly built in 1430, offers thick stone walls, mullioned and leaded windows, many chimneys and gables, and a slate roof now mossy with age. Vying with the Bay Tree in antique furnishings, it opens onto a stone-paved rear garden, with a rose-lined walk and a shaded lawn. The bedrooms are a mixture of today's comforts and antiques, and prices depend on how recently the room was furnished. Rooms vary in size, and each has a compact bathroom with a tub/shower combination (one has a shower stall). The public living rooms have heavy oak beams, stone floors, window seats, Oriental rugs, and fine antiques. An excellent restaurant (see review below) is on-site.

Sheep St., Burford, Oxfordshire OX18 4LR. ℂ **01993/823155**. Fax 01993/822228. www.lambinn-burford.co.uk. 15 units. Sun–Thurs £145–£195 ($290–$390) double; Fri–Sat £165–£255 ($330–$510) double. Rates include English breakfast. MC, V. **Amenities:** Restaurant; bar; room service; laundry service. *In room:* TV, beverage maker, hair dryer.

WHERE TO DINE

After you've browsed through the antiques shops, head to **Burford House** (© 01993/ 823151) for tea. This old Cotswold favorite serves nonresidents Monday to Saturday from 10:30am to 5pm. Freshly baked goods, including flans, scones, cakes, and muffins, will tempt you.

Lamb Inn Restaurant MODERN   A meal in this pretty pillared restaurant is the perfect way to cap off a visit to Burford. Good pub lunches dominate the agenda at midday; dinners are formal, candlelit affairs. The evening menu is beautifully cooked and served. You might begin with Jerusalem artichoke soup with a smoked bacon boudin and follow with pan-fried sea bass with an open prawn ravioli in a sun-dried tomato sauce. The pub here attracts folks from all walks of life. They seem to adore its mellow atmosphere and charm. Guinness, cider, and a carefully chosen collection of ales, including a local brew, Wadworth Hook Norton Ale, are on tap.

Sheep St., in the Lamb Inn. © **01993/823155.** Reservations recommended for dinner. 3-course dinner £33 ($66); lunch platters £9–£13 ($18–$26). MC, V. Daily noon–2:30pm and 7–9:30pm.

SEEING THE SIGHTS

Approaching Burford from the south, you'll experience one of the finest views of any ancient market town in the country. The main street sweeps down to the River Windrush, past an extraordinary collection of houses of various styles and ages. Burford's ancient packhorse bridge still does duty at the bottom of the hill. Hills opposite provide a frame of fields, trees, and, with luck, panoramic skies.

Though the wool trade has long vanished, most of Burford remains unchanged in appearance, with old houses in the High Street and nearby side streets. Nearly all are built of local stone. Like many Cotswold towns, Burford has a Sheep Street, with many fine stone-built houses covered with roofs of Stonesfield slate. Burford Church (ca. 1175) is almost cathedral-like in proportion. It was enlarged throughout succeeding centuries until the decline of the wool trade. Little has changed here since about 1500.

Traders and vendors still set up their stalls under the Tolsey on Friday, where, from the 12th century, the guild has collected tolls from anyone wishing to trade in the town. It still stands at the corner of Sheep Street. On the upper floor is the minor Tolsey Museum, where you can see a medieval seal bearing Burford's insignia, the "rampant cat."

On High Street in Burford, you'll find several antiques shops, including **Manfred Schotten Antiques,** the Crypt, 109 High St. (© **01993/822302**). Sporting antiques and collectibles, they also carry library and club furniture. **Jonathan Fyson Antiques,** 50–52 High St. (© **01993/823204**), carries English and Continental furniture and porcelain, glass, and brass items. At the Burford Roundabout, on Cheltenham Road, **Gateway Antiques** (© **01993/823678**) has a variety of items displayed in large showrooms. English pottery, metalware, and 19th-century furniture dominate the inventory. Unique arts and crafts items and interesting decorative objects are fun to browse through, even if you don't buy.

Three kilometers (2 miles) south of Burford on the A361 lies the **Cotswold Wildlife Park** (© **01993/823006;** www.cotswoldwildlifepark.co.uk). The 65 hectares (160 acres) of gardens and forests around this Victorian manor house have been transformed into a jungle of sorts, with a Noah's Ark consortium of animals ranging from voracious ants to rare Asiatic lions, rhinos, and leopards. Children can romp around the farmyard and the adventure playground. A narrow-gauge railway runs from April to October, and there are extensive picnic areas plus a cafeteria. The park is open March to September daily 10am to 4:30pm, and October to February daily 10am to 3:30pm (last entry 1 hr. before closing). Admission is £9.50 ($19) for adults, £7 ($14) for seniors and children 3 to 16, and free for children 2 and younger.

And before you leave Burford, we suggest a slight detour to **Swinbrook,** a pretty village by the River Windrush immediately to the east. It's best known as the one-time home of the fabled Mitford sisters. Visit the local parish church to see the grave of writer Nancy Mitford and the impressive tiered monuments to the Fettiplace family.

7 Bourton-on-the-Water ✶

137km (85 miles) NW of London; 58km (36 miles) NW of Oxford

This is the quintessential Cotswold village, with history dating from the Celts. Today it's overrun with tourists in summer. Residents fiercely protect the heritage of 15th- and 16th-century architecture, though their town is singled out for nearly every bus tour that rolls through the Cotswolds. Populated in Anglo-Saxon times, Bourton-on-the-Water developed into a strategic outpost along the ancient Roman road, Fosse Way, which traversed Britain from the North Sea to St. George's Channel. During the Middle Ages, its prosperity came from wool, which was shipped all over Europe. During the Industrial Revolution, when the greatest profits lay in finished textiles, it became a backwater as a producer of raw wool—albeit with the happy result for us that it never "modernized."

This scenic Cotswold village on the banks of the Windrush River has earned the title of "Venice of the Cotswolds," with its mellow stone houses, its village greens on the banks of the water, and its bridges. Don't expect gondoliers, however. This makes a good stopover, if not for the night, at least as a place to enjoy a lunch and a rest along the riverbanks. Afterward, you can take a peek inside St. Lawrence's Church in the center of the village. Built on the site of a Roman temple, it has a crypt from 1120 and a tower from 1784. You can also visit this lovely spot as part of a fine walking tour (see the box, "The Great Cotswold Ramble," below).

GETTING THERE

Trains go from London's Paddington Station to nearby Moreton-in-Marsh, a trip of 1½ hours. For information, call © **0845/748-4950** or visit **www.firstgreatwestern. co.uk**. From here, take a Pulhams Bus Company coach (© **01451/820369**) 9.5km (6 miles) to Bourton-on-the-Water. Trains also run from London to Cheltenham and Kingham; while somewhat more distant than Moreton-in-Marsh, both have bus connections to Bourton-on-the-Water.

National Express buses run from Victoria Coach Station in London to both Cheltenham and Stow-on-the-Wold. For schedules and information, call © **0870/580-8080** or visit **www.nationalexpress.co.uk**. Pulhams Bus Company operates about four buses per day from both towns to Bourton-on-the-Water.

If you're driving from Oxford, head west on the A40 to the junction with the A429 (Fosse Way). Take it northeast to Bourton-on-the-Water.

WHERE TO STAY & DINE

Chester House Hotel   This 300-year-old Cotswold-stone house, built on the banks of the Windrush River, is conveniently located in the center of town. The main building and its adjoining row of stables were converted into this comfortable hotel;

the stables were completely renovated and turned into small to midsize bedrooms. Bathrooms are small and compact but with adequate shelf space.

Victoria St., Bourton-on-the-Water, Cheltenham, Gloucestershire GL54 2BU. ✆ **01451/820286.** Fax 01451/820471. www.chesterhousehotel.com. 22 units. £70–£90 ($140–$180) double; £90–£100 ($180–$200) family room. Rates include continental or English breakfast. AE, MC, V. Closed Jan. **Amenities:** Restaurant; bar. *In room:* TV, Wi-Fi, beverage maker, hair dryer.

Dial House Hotel ✿   Our top choice in town, this 1698 house is constructed from yellow Cotswold stone and stands in the heart of the village center. Mr. and Mrs. Adrian Campbell-Howard, your hosts, offer not only a nostalgic retreat but some of the best cuisine in the area. Set on .6 hectare (1½ acres) of manicured gardens, the house overlooks the River Windrush. Each room has an individual character, and some boast four-poster beds. Two of the rooms, as charming as those in the main building, are in a converted coach house. All rooms have well-kept bathrooms with shower units and Penhaligon toiletries. Log fires burn on chilly nights, and there are two small dining rooms, one with an inglenook fireplace.

The Chestnuts, High St., Bourton-on-the-Water, Gloucestershire GL54 2AN. ✆ **01451/822244.** Fax 01451/810126. www.dialhousehotel.com. 14 units. £110–£180 ($220–$360) double; £190 ($380) suite. Rates include English breakfast. MC, V. **Amenities:** Restaurant; bar; croquet lawn; room service. *In room:* TV, Wi-Fi, beverage maker, hair dryer.

The Old Manse Hotel ✿ *Finds*   An architectural gem, this hotel sits in the center of town by the river that wanders through the village green. Built of Cotswold stone in 1748, with chimneys, dormers, and small-paned windows, it has been frequently modernized. Rooms are midsize and cozy, much like something you'd find in the home of your favorite great-aunt.

Victoria St., Bourton-on-the-Water, Cheltenham, Gloucestershire GL54 2BX. ✆ **01451/820082.** Fax 01451/810381. www.oldmansehotel.com. 15 units. £75–£125 ($150–$250) double. Rates include English breakfast. AE, DC, MC, V. **Amenities:** Restaurant; bar. *In room:* TV, beverage maker, hair dryer.

Old New Inn   The Old New Inn, originally built in 1793, is a landmark in the village. On the main street, overlooking the river, it's a good example of Queen Anne design (see the Model Village at the Old New Inn, below). Hungry or tired travelers are drawn to old-fashioned comforts and cuisine of this most English inn. Rooms are comfortable, with homey furnishings and soft beds. Some rooms are spacious, especially if they have a four-poster bed, but most are small and lie in a cottage annex.

High St., Bourton-on-the-Water, Cheltenham, Gloucestershire GL54 2AF. ✆ **01451/820467.** Fax 01451/810236. www.theoldnewinn.co.uk. 9 units. £76 ($152) double. Rate includes English breakfast. MC, V. **Amenities:** Restaurant; 3 bars. *In room:* TV, beverage maker, hair dryer.

A TINY VILLAGE, THE BIRDS, VINTAGE CARS & MORE

Within the town are a handful of minor museums, each of which was established from idiosyncratic collections amassed over the years by local residents. They include the **Bourton Model Railway Exhibition and Toy Shop** (✆ **01451/820686;** www.bourtonmodel railway.co.uk) and the **Cotswold Motor Museum** (✆ **01451/821255;** www.cotswold-motor-museum.com).

Birdland *Kids*   This handsomely designed attraction sits on 3.4 hectares (8½ acres) of field and forests on the banks of River Windrush, about 1.6km (1 mile) east of Bourton-on-the-Water. It houses about 500 birds, including three species of penguins. Other feathered friends include pelicans, storks, flamingos, cranes, parrots, toucans, kookaburras, and pheasants. Birdland has a picnic area and a children's playground in a wooded copse.

Rissington Rd. (✆) **01451/820480.** www.birdland.co.uk. Admission £5.25 ($11) adults, £4.25 ($8.50) seniors, £3.25 ($6.50) children 4–14, £16 ($32) family ticket, free for children 3 and younger. Apr–Oct daily 10am–6pm; Nov–Mar daily 10am–4pm (last admission 1 hr. before closing).

Cotswold Perfumery   This permanent perfume exhibition details the history of the perfume industry and also focuses on its production. Perfumes are made on the premises and sold in the shop. Flacons of these fragrances range from £2 to £35 ($4–$70) each, depending on their size. The price of admission includes a 45-minute factory tour, but it's always best to call in advance as they do not always have staff available to conduct such a tour.

Victoria St. (✆) **01451/820698.** www.cotswold-perfumery.co.uk. Admission £5 ($10) adults, £3.50 ($7) children ages 4–16. Mon–Sat 9:30am–5pm; Sun 10:30am–5pm. Closed Dec 25–26.

The Model Village at the Old New Inn *Kids*   Beginning in the 1930s, a local hotelier, Mr. Morris, whiled away some of the doldrums of the Great Depression by constructing a scale model (1:9) of Bourton-on-the-Water as a testimony to its architectural charms. This isn't a tiny and cramped display set behind glass—the model is big enough that you can walk through this near-perfect and most realistic model village.

High St. (✆) **01451/820467.** www.theoldnewinn.co.uk/village.htm. Admission £3 ($6) adults, £2.75 ($5.50) seniors, £2.50 ($5) children. Daily 10am–5:45pm in summer; daily 10am–3:45pm in winter.

---

8 Upper & Lower Slaughter ⭐

3km (2 miles) N of Bourton-on-the-Water; 6.5km (4 miles) SW of Stow-on-the-Wold

Midway between Bourton-on-the-Water and Stow-on-the-Wold (below) are two of the prettiest villages in the Cotswolds: Upper and Lower Slaughter. Don't be put off by the name—"Slaughter" is actually a corruption of *de Sclotre,* the name of the original Norman landowner. Houses here are constructed of honey-colored Cotswold stone, and a stream meanders right through the street, providing a home for free-wandering ducks, which beg scraps from kindly passersby. Upper Slaughter has a fine example of a 17th-century Cotswold manor house.

The **Old Mill,** in Lower Slaughter (✆ **01451/820052;** www.oldmill-lowerslaughter.com), is a sturdy 19th-century stone structure built on the River Eye with the sole purpose of grinding out flour. The river still turns the massive water wheel that powers this Victorian flourmill today. Visitors can enjoy an ice-cream parlor and tearoom while visiting the mill. Entrance to the mill costs £1.25 ($2.50) for adults, 50p ($1) for children.

GETTING THERE

Lower Slaughter and Stow-on-the-Wold are 6.5km (4 miles) apart. From Stow, take the A429 (the Main Fosse Way) and follow signs to Cirencester and Bourton-on-the-Water. Turn off the highway when you see signs to Upper and Lower Slaughter. The road will then divide, and you can pick which hamlet you want to head to.

To reach Lower Slaughter from Bourton-on-the-Water, head west along Lansdowne Road, turning right (north) onto A436; after a short distance you'll see a signpost pointing left into Lower Slaughter along an unmarked road.

WHERE TO STAY & DINE

Lords of the Manor Hotel ⭐⭐⭐   A 17th-century house set on several acres of rolling fields, the Lords of the Manor offers gardens with a stream featuring brown trout. A quintessentially British hotel of great style and amenities, it's a showplace. It

The Great Cotswold Ramble

A walking tour between the villages of Upper and Lower Slaughter, with an optional extension to Bourton-on-the-Water, is one of the most memorable in England. Between the Slaughters, it's about 1.6km (1 mile) each way, or 4km (2½ miles) from Upper Slaughter to Bourton-on-the-Water; the walk can take 2 to 4 hours.

A well-worn footpath known as **Warden's Way** meanders beside the edge of the swift-moving River Eye. From its well-marked beginning in Upper Slaughter's central car park, the path passes sheep grazing in meadows, antique houses crafted from local honey-colored stone, stately trees arching over ancient millponds, and footbridges that have endured centuries of foot traffic and rain.

The rushing river powers a historic mill on the northwestern edge of Lower Slaughter. In quiet eddies, you'll see ample numbers of waterfowl and birds, such as wild ducks, gray wagtails, mute swans, coots, and Canada geese.

Most visitors turn around at Lower Slaughter, but Warden's Way continues another 2.5km (1½ miles) to Bourton-on-the-Water by following the Fosse Way, route of an ancient Roman footpath. Most of it, from Lower Slaughter to Bourton-on-the-Water, is covered by tarmac; it's closed to cars but ideal for walking or biking. You're legally required to close each of the several gates that stretch across the footpath.

Warden's Way will introduce you to Bourton-on-the-Water through the hamlet's northern edges. The first landmark you'll see will be the tower of St. Lawrence's Anglican Church. From the base of the church, walk south along the Avenue (one of the hamlet's main streets) and end your Cotswold ramble on the Village Green, directly in front of the War Memorial.

You can follow this route in reverse, but parking is more plentiful in Upper Slaughter than in Lower Slaughter.

may be modernized, but it successfully maintains the quiet country-house atmosphere of 300 years ago. Half the rooms are in a converted old barn and granary, and many have lovely views. Each offers a high standard of comfort and elegant beds with sumptuous linens.

Upper Slaughter, near Bourton-on-the-Water, Gloucestershire GL54 2JD. (C) **01451/820243.** Fax 01451/820696. www.lordsofthemanor.com. 27 units. £170–£320 ($340–$640) double; £290–£320 ($580–$640) suite. Rates include half-board. AE, DC, MC, V. Take A429 29km (18 miles) north of Cheltenham. **Amenities:** Restaurant; bar; room service; laundry service. *In room:* TV/DVD, iPod docking station, minibar, hair dryer, safe.

Lower Slaughter Manor ✪✪✪   This hotel dates from 1658, when it was owned by Sir George Whitmore, high sheriff of Gloucestershire. It remained in the same family until 1964 when it was sold as a private residence. Today, it's one of the great inns of the Cotswolds, though its charms are matched in every way by Lords of the Manor. Standing on its own private grounds, it has spacious and sumptuously furnished rooms, some with four-poster beds. Bedrooms in the main building have more old

English character, although those in the annex are equally comfortable and include the same luxuries.

Lower Slaughter, near Cheltenham, Gloucestershire GL54 2HP. ℂ 01451/820456. Fax 01451/822150. www.lower slaughter.co.uk. 19 units. £230–£375 ($460–$750) double; £525 ($1,050) suite. Rates include English breakfast. AE, DC, MC, V. Take A429 turnoff at the sign for the Slaughters, and drive 1km (½ mile); manor is on right as you enter the village. No children 11 or younger. **Amenities:** Restaurant; lounge; tennis court; room service; laundry service; dry cleaning. *In room:* TV, high-speed Internet, hair dryer.

9 Stow-on-the-Wold ⓐ

14km (9 miles) SE of Broadway; 16km (10 miles) S of Chipping Campden; 6.5km (4 miles) S of Moreton-in-Marsh; 34km (21 miles) S of Stratford-upon-Avon

As you pass through Shakespeare's "high wild hills and rough uneven ways," you arrive at Stow-on-the-Wold, its very name evoking the elusive spirit of the Cotswolds, one of the greatest sheep-rearing districts of England. Lying 240m (800 ft.) above sea level, it stands on a plateau where "the cold winds blow," or so goes the old saying. This town prospered when Cotswold wool was demanded the world over. Stow-on-the-Wold may not be the cognoscenti's favorite—Chipping Campden takes that honor—but it's even more delightful as it has a real Cotswold town atmosphere.

The town lies smack in the middle of the Fosse Way, one of the Roman trunk roads that cut a swath through Britain. Kings have passed through here, including Edward VI, son of Henry VIII, and they've bestowed their approval on the town. Stagecoaches stopped off here for the night on their way to Cheltenham.

A 14th-century cross stands in the large Market Square, where you can still see the stocks where "offenders" in the past were jeered at and punished by the townspeople who threw rotten eggs at them. The final battle between the Roundheads and the Royalists took place outside Stow-on-the-Wold, and mean old Cromwell incarcerated 1,500 Royalist troops in St. Edward's Market Square.

The square today teems with pubs and outdoor cafes. But leave the square at some point and wander at leisure along some of the narrowest alleyways in Britain. When the summer crowds get you down, head in almost any direction from Stow to surrounding villages that look like sets from a Merchant Ivory film.

ESSENTIALS

GETTING THERE   Several trains run daily from London's Paddington Station to Moreton-in-Marsh (see below). For schedules and information, call ℂ **0845/748-4950** or visit **www.firstgreatwestern.co.uk**. From Moreton-in-Marsh, Pulhams Bus Company makes the 10-minute ride to Stow-on-the-Wold.

If driving from Oxford, take the A40 west to the junction with the A424, near Burford. Head northwest along the A424 to Stow-on-the-Wold.

VISITOR INFORMATION   The **Tourist Information Centre** is at Hollis House, the Square (ℂ **01451/831082**). It's open Easter to October Monday to Saturday 9:30am to 5:30pm; from November to mid-February, hours are Monday to Saturday 9:30am to 4:30pm; and from mid-February to Easter, it's open Monday to Saturday 9:30am to 5pm.

WHERE TO STAY & DINE

Fosse Manor Hotel   Though lacking the charm of the Grapevine (see below), Fosse Manor is at least the second best in town, even more inviting than the Stow Lodge. The hotel lies near the site of an ancient Roman road that used to bisect England. Its stone walls and neo-Gothic gables are almost concealed by strands of ivy. From some of the high stone-sided windows, you can enjoy a view of a landscaped garden with a sunken lily pond and old-fashioned sundial. Inside, the interior is conservatively modern, with homey bedrooms. Some are large enough for a family; others have a four-poster bed. Six bedrooms, equal in comfort to those in the main building, are located in a converted coach house on the grounds.

Fosse Way, Stow-on-the-Wold, Cheltenham, Gloucestershire GL54 1JX. ✆ 01451/830354. Fax 01451/832486. www. fossemanor.co.uk. 22 units. £130–£175 ($260–$350) double, £225 ($450) junior suite; half-board £175–£225 ($350– $450) double, £275 ($550) suite. Rates include English breakfast. Children 9 and younger stay free when sharing with a paying adult. AE, DC, MC, V. Take A429 2km (1¼ miles) south of Stow-on-the-Wold. **Amenities:** Restaurant; bar; lounge; room service; laundry service; dry cleaning. *In room:* TV, beverage maker, hair dryer, trouser press.

The Grapevine Hotel ★ (Value)   Facing the village green, the Grapevine mixes urban sophistication with reasonable prices, rural charm, and intimacy. It's the best inn in town, although it doesn't have the charm and grace of Wyck Hill House on the outskirts (see below). It was named after the ancient vine whose tendrils shade and shelter the beautiful conservatory restaurant. Many of the bedrooms have been redecorated, and each varies in size—some quite small—but comfort is the keynote here. Ten rooms are in a comfortably appointed annex and lack the character of the stone-sided walls and crooked floors in the main building.

Sheep St., Stow-on-the-Wold, Cheltenham, Gloucestershire GL54 1AU. ✆ 01451/830344. Fax 01451/832278. www. vines.co.uk. 22 units. £140–£160 ($280–$320) double. Rates include breakfast. AE, DC, MC, V. **Amenities:** 2 restaurants; bar; room service; laundry service; dry cleaning. *In room:* TV, minibar (in some), beverage maker, hair dryer, trouser press (in some).

Stow Lodge Hotel   Stow Lodge dominates the marketplace but is set back far enough to avoid too much noise. Its gardens, honeysuckle growing over the stone walls, diamond-shaped windows, gables, and many chimneys capture the best of country living, even though you're right in the heart of town. The ample, well-furnished rooms vary in size; one has a four-poster bed. The main building has more character, though some equally comfortable rooms are in a converted coach house (most on the ground floor). Room nos. 17 and 18—the smallest in the hotel—share a private bathroom.

The Square, Stow-on-the-Wold, Cheltenham, Gloucestershire GL54 1AB. ✆ 01451/830485. Fax 01451/831671. www. stowlodge.com. 20 units. £78–£136 ($156–$272) double. Rates include English breakfast. MC, V. Closed Dec 16–Jan 25. Children 4 and younger not allowed. **Amenities:** Restaurant; bar; room service; laundry service. *In room:* Ceiling fan, TV, beverage maker, hair dryer.

Wyck Hill House ★★★   This is sleepy old Stow's pocket of posh. Parts of this otherwise Victorian country house on 40 hectares (100 acres) of grounds and gardens date from 1720, when its stone walls were first erected. It was discovered in the course of recent restoration that one wing of the manor house rests on the foundations of a Roman villa. The interior adheres to 18th-century authenticity with room after room leading to paneled libraries and Adam sitting rooms. The well-furnished bedrooms are in the main hotel, in the coach-house annex, or in the Orangery, a building erected in the 1980s whose larger-than-usual bedrooms are outfitted in a vaguely Mediterranean theme. Some rooms offer four-poster beds and views of the surrounding countryside.

A424 Burford Rd., Stow-on-the-Wold, Cheltenham, Gloucestershire GL54 1HY. ✆ 01451/831936. Fax 01451/ 832243. www.wyckhillhouse.com. 54 units. £185–£225 ($370–$450) double; £245–£265 ($490–$530) suite. Rates include English breakfast. AE, MC, V. Drive 4km (2½ miles) south of Stow-on-the-Wold on A424. **Amenities:** Restaurant; bar; spa; sauna; steam room; croquet lawn; room service; laundry service. *In room:* TV, Wi-Fi, beverage maker, hair dryer, trouser press, safe.

ANTIQUES HEAVEN

Don't be fooled by the village's sleepy, country setting: Stow-on-the-Wold has developed over the last 20 years into the antiques buyer's highlight of Britain and has at least 60 merchandisers scattered throughout the village and its environs.

Set within four showrooms inside an 18th-century building on the town's main square, **Anthony Preston Antiques, Ltd.,** the Square (© **01451/831586**), specializes in English and French furniture, including some large pieces such as bookcases, and decorative objects that include paperweights, lamps, paintings on silk, and small objects designed to add a glossy accent to carefully contrived interior decors.

Located on Church Street, **Baggott Church Street, Ltd.** (© **01451/830370**), is the smaller, and perhaps more intricately decorated, of two shops founded and maintained by a local antiques merchant, Duncan ("Jack") Baggott, a frequent denizen at estate sales of country houses throughout Britain. The shop contains four showrooms loaded with furniture and paintings from the 17th to the 19th centuries.

Covering about half a block in the heart of town, **Huntington's Antiques Ltd.,** Church Street (© **01451/830842**), contains one of the largest stocks of quality antiques in England. Wander at will through 10 ground-floor rooms, then climb to the second floor where a long gallery and a quartet of additional showrooms bulge with refectory tables, unusual cupboards, and all kinds of finds.

10 Moreton-in-Marsh ⦿

134km (83 miles) NW of London; 6.5km (4 miles) N of Stow-on-the-Wold; 11km (7 miles) S of Chipping Campden; 27km (17 miles) S of Stratford-upon-Avon

This is no swampland as the name implies. Marsh derives from an old word meaning "border," so you won't be wading through wetlands to get here. Moreton is a real Cotswold market town that is at its most bustling on Tuesday morning when farmers and craftspeople from the surrounding area flood the town to sell their wares and produce.

An important stopover along the old Roman road, Fosse Way, as well as an important layover for the night for stagecoach passengers, Moreton-in-Marsh has one of the widest High Streets in the Cotswolds. Roman legions trudged through here centuries ago, but today visitors and antiques shops have replaced them.

The town is still filled with records of its past, including a market hall on High Street built in Victorian Tudor style in 1887, and Curfew Tower on Oxford Street dating from the 17th century. Its bell was rung daily until the late 19th century.

For a fascinating lesson on birds of prey, stop by the **Cotswold Falconry Centre,** Batsford Park (© **01386/701043;** www.cotswold-falconry.co.uk). It's open daily from mid-February to mid-November from 10:30am to 5:30pm. Flying displays are daily at 11:30am, 1:30pm, 3pm, and 4:30pm. Admission is £6 ($12) for adults, £5 ($10) seniors and students, and £2.50 ($5) for children 4 to 14 (free for kids 3 and younger).

GETTING THERE

Trains run from London's Paddington Station to Moreton-in-Marsh, a nearly 2-hour trip. For schedules and information, call © **0845/748-4950** or visit **www.firstgreat western.co.uk**.

If you're driving from Stow-on-the-Wold, take the A429 north.

WHERE TO STAY & DINE

The Bell Inn _Value_ This is a coaching inn from the 1700s. It has been well restored and is now a traditional and welcoming Cotswold inn. In summer, guests can enjoy a pint or two in the old courtyard or join the locals in the large bar. Under beamed ceilings, bedrooms are comfortably and tastefully furnished in an old English styling, each with a small bathroom with shower. *Note:* The hotel publicizes that it caters to those with disabilities, and while there are no entrance ramps, the entrance door is wide and there are some specially equipped bathrooms.

High St., Moreton-in-Marsh, Gloucestershire GL56 0AF. © **01608/651688.** Fax 01608/652195. www.bellinncotswold. co.uk. 5 units. £90 ($180) double; £100–£125 ($200–$250) suite. Rates include English breakfast. DC, MC, V. **Amenities:** Restaurant; pub. *In room:* TV, Wi-Fi (in some), beverage maker, no phone.

The Falkland Arms ★ *Finds* Immerse yourself in old England with a meal or an overnight at this historic Cotswold village dating from the 1500s when it was known as the Horse & Groom. The original settle along with flagstone floors and an inglenook fireplace make this a warm, inviting place—that and the extensive range of malt whiskies. An on-site restaurant (reservations essential) offers an imaginative menu daily based on market-fresh ingredients. A spiral stone staircase leads to the cozy accommodations, with brass bedsteads and white covers. Rooms are beautifully furnished and look out over the countryside and the village green.

Great Tew, Oxfordshire OX7 4DB. © **01608/683653.** Fax 01608/683656. www.falklandarms.org.uk. 5 units. £85–£115 ($170–$230) double. Rates include breakfast. AE, MC, V. Lies 7.4km (12 miles) east of Moreton-in-Marsh. Take A44 to Chipping Norton, then follow A361 to B4022. No children 15 and younger. **Amenities:** Restaurant; pub. *In room:* TV, no phone.

Manor House Hotel ★ The town's best hotel, the Manor House comes complete with its own ghost, a secret passage, and a moot room used centuries ago by local merchants to settle arguments over wool exchanges. On the main street, it's a formal yet gracious house, and its rear portions reveal varying architectural periods of design. Inside are many living rooms, one especially intimate with leather chairs and a fireplace-within-a-fireplace, ideal for drinks and swapping "bump-in-the-night" stories. The cozy rooms are tastefully furnished, often with antiques or fine reproductions. Many have fine old desks set in front of window ledges, with a view of the garden.

High St., Moreton-in-Marsh, Gloucestershire GL56 0LJ. © **01608/650501.** Fax 01608/651481. www.cotswold-inns-hotels.co.uk. 38 units, 1 family suite. £135–£220 ($270–$440) double; £245–£285 ($490–$570) suite. Rates include English breakfast. AE, MC, V. **Amenities:** Restaurant; bar; room service; babysitting; laundry service; dry cleaning. *In room:* TV, coffeemaker, hair dryer, iron, trouser press, safe.

Redesdale Arms Though the Manor House is better appointed and more comfortable, this is one of the largest and best-preserved coaching inns in Gloucestershire. Originally established around 1774 as the Unicorn Hotel, it functioned around 1840 as an important link in the Bath-Lincoln stagecoach routes, offering food and accommodations to both humans and horses during the arduous journey. Since then, the inn has been considerably upgraded, with modernized and comfortably furnished bedrooms, but much of the old-fashioned charm remains intact. The small to midsize bedrooms are appointed with either twin or double beds. Six executive rooms were added in a new building made of Cotswold stone. These units contain four-poster beds but are designed in a more modern style than the existing rooms.

High St., Moreton-in-Marsh, Gloucestershire GL56 0AW. © **01608/650308.** Fax 01608/651843. www.redesdalearms. com. 18 units. £75–£105 ($150–$210) double; £100–£150 ($200–$300) suite. Rates include breakfast. MC, V. **Amenities:** Restaurant; bar; lounge; room service; laundry service; dry cleaning. *In room:* TV, beverage maker, hair dryer, trouser press.

The White Hart Royal Hotel A mellow old Cotswold inn graced by Charles I in 1644, the White Hart provides modern amenities without compromising the personality of yesteryear. It long ago ceased being the town's premier inn but is still a comfortable place to spend the night. The well-furnished rooms all have a few antiques mixed with basic 20th-century pieces. Much of the original character of the bedrooms remains intact, but you get comfort here, not a lot of style.

High St., Moreton-in-Marsh, Gloucestershire GL56 0BA. ✆ 01608/650731. Fax 01608/650880. 18 units. £55–£70 ($110–$140) double. Rates include English breakfast. AE, MC, V. **Amenities:** Restaurant; bar. *In room:* TV, beverage maker.

11 Broadway ✦

24km (15 miles) SW of Stratford-upon-Avon; 150km (93 miles) NW of London; 24km (15 miles) NE of Cheltenham

The showcase village of the Cotswolds, if you don't mind the summer coach tours, Broadway is the most overrun village in the Cotswolds. Many prime attractions of the Cotswolds, including Shakespeare Country, are nearby. Flanked by honey-colored stone buildings, its **High Street** is a gem, remarkable for its harmonious style and design from a point overlooking the lovely Vale of Evesham. Once you've toured the main street and walked up and down it once, you've done Broadway. More adventurous visitors will want to settle in one of the less overrun towns—**Chipping Campden** nearby would be ideal (see below).

ESSENTIALS

GETTING THERE Rail connections are possible from London's Paddington Station via Oxford. The nearest railway stations are at Moreton-in-Marsh (11km/7 miles away) or at Evesham (8km/5 miles away). For schedules and information, call ✆ 0845/600-0880 or visit **www.firstgreatwestern.co.uk**. Frequent buses arrive from Evesham, but you have to take a taxi from Moreton.

If you're driving from Oxford, head west on the A40, then take the A434 to Woodstock, Chipping Norton, and Moreton-in-Marsh.

VISITOR INFORMATION The **Tourist Information Centre** is at Unit 14, Russel Square (✆ 01386/852937). The office is open year-round Monday to Friday 10am to 5pm, and Sunday 2 to 5pm.

WHERE TO STAY

The Broadway Hotel ✦✦   On the village green and one of the most colorful places in Broadway, this converted 15th-century house keeps its old-world charm while providing modern comforts. The recently refurbished rooms are tastefully and comfortably furnished. One room has a four-poster bed. Some guests seek out the more private bedrooms on the ground floor of a separate building, with its direct access to the garden.

The Green, Broadway, Worcestershire WR12 7AA. ✆ 01386/852401. Fax 01386/853879. www.cotswold-inns-hotels. co.uk. 19 units. £140–£180 ($280–$360) double; £180–£200 ($360–$400) suite. Rates include English breakfast. AE, DC, MC, V. **Amenities:** Restaurant; bar; room service; laundry service. *In room:* TV, beverage maker, hair dryer.

Buckland Manor Hotel ✦✦✦   The Lygon Arms (see below) reigned supreme in Broadway for so long that people thought it had squatters' rights to the title of top inn in town, both for food and lodging. But along came Buckland Manor on the town's outskirts, topping the Lygon Arms in every way, especially in cuisine. This imposing slate-roofed manor house is ringed with fences of Cotswold stone. The core of the manor house was erected in the 13th century, with wings added in succeeding centuries. Leaded windows in the rooms overlook gardens and grazing land with cattle and sheep. Some of the large bedrooms have four-poster beds and fireplaces.

Buckland, near Broadway, Worcestershire WR12 7LY. ✆ **01386/852626.** Fax 01386/853557. www.bucklandmanor. com. 13 units. £260–£460 ($520–$920) double. Rates include early-morning tea and English breakfast. AE, MC, V. Take B4632 about 3km (2 miles) south of Broadway, into Gloucestershire. No children 11 or younger. **Amenities:** Restaurant; bar; putting green; tennis court; room service; laundry service; dry cleaning. *In room:* TV, high-speed Internet, hair dryer.

Dormy House ✦   This manor house, high on a hill above the village, boasts views in all directions. Its panoramic position has made it a favorite place whether you're seeking a meal, afternoon tea, or lodgings. Halfway between Broadway and Chipping Campden, it was created from a sheep farm. The owners transformed it, furnishing the 17th-century farmhouse with a few antiques. They also brought glamour to an old adjoining timbered barn, converted into two executive suites and eight deluxe doubles. Bowls of fresh flowers adorn tables and alcoves throughout the hotel.

Willersey Hill, Broadway, Worcestershire WR12 7LF. ✆ 01386/852711. Fax 01386/858636. www.dormyhouse.co.uk. 48 units. £165–£205 ($330–$410) double; £205 ($410) four-poster room; £230 ($460) suite. Rates include English breakfast. AE, DC, MC, V. Closed Dec 24–29. Take A44 3km (2 miles) southeast of Broadway. **Amenities:** Restaurant (see the Dining Room review below); bar; putting green; gym; sauna; steam room; game room; croquet lawn; room service; babysitting; laundry service. *In room:* TV, high-speed Internet, beverage maker, hair dryer, trouser press.

The Lygon Arms ✦✦✦   Despite the challenge of Buckland Manor (see above), this many-gabled structure with mullioned windows still basks in its reputation as one of the great old English inns. It opens onto a private rear garden, with 1.2 hectares (3 acres) of lawns, trees, and borders of flowers, stone walls with roses, and nooks for sipping tea or sherry. The oldest portions date from 1532 or earlier, and additions have been made many times since then. King Charles I reputedly drank with his friends in one of the oak-lined chambers, and later, his enemy Oliver Cromwell slept here the night before the Battle of Worcester. Today, many, but not all, of the bedrooms are in the antique style; a comfortable annex added in the 1970s offers more of a modern feel.

High St., Broadway, Worcestershire WR12 7DU. ✆ **01386/852255.** Fax 01386/858611. www.thelygonarms.co.uk. 77 units. £150–£350 ($300–$700) double; from £350 ($700) suite. Rates include English breakfast. AE, DC, MC, V. **Amenities:** 2 restaurants; bar; cafe; indoor heated pool; health club; spa; sauna; steam room; room service; massage; laundry service. *In room:* TV, high-speed Internet (in some), hair dryer, trouser press, safe.

The Olive Branch Guest House *Value*   In the heart of an expensive village, this is a terrific bargain. The house, dating from the 16th century, retains its old Cotswold architectural features. Behind the house is a large-walled English garden and parking area. Guests are given a discount for purchases at the owners' attached antiques shop. Furnishings are basic but comfortable. One family room can accommodate up to four people and one room has a four-poster bed.

78 High St., Broadway, Worcestershire WR12 7AJ. ✆ **01386/853440.** Fax 01386/859070. www.theolivebranch-broadway.com. 8 units, 7 with bathroom. £75–£88 ($150–$176) double with bathroom. Rates include English breakfast. MC, V. **Amenities:** Breakfast room; lounge. *In room:* TV, minibar (in some), beverage maker, hair dryer.

Windrush House *Value*   In high-priced Broadway, Evan and Judith Anderson have opened an affordable B&B. They provide handsomely furnished and most comfortable bedrooms in a tranquil setting, even though it's near the busy center of town. They have fully renovated and upgraded an old house, vastly improving it to receive guests. Bedrooms are completely modernized and most inviting. The Andersons welcome you with a drink and a slice of homemade cake.

Station Rd., Broadway, Worcestershire WR12 7DE. ✆ **01386/853577.** Fax 01386/852850. www.broadway-windrush. co.uk. 4 units. £85 ($170) double. Rates include breakfast. AE, DC, MC, V. **Amenities:** Breakfast room. *In room:* TV, beverage maker, hair dryer.

WHERE TO DINE

The best place in Broadway for a cup of tea is **Tisanes,** the Green (© **01386/ 852112**), offering perfectly blended teas with a variety of sandwiches and salads. Within the town itself, the finest cuisine is served at the previously recommended Lygon Arms (see above), which has both a formal dining room, the Great Hall, plus a less formal brasserie, Goblets. A classic British and French cuisine is featured. Dine on such fare as roast squab in Madeira sauce or Cornish turbot with fresh, handmade noodles and a drizzle of red-pepper pesto.

The Dining Room ★ MODERN Set 3km (2 miles) from the center of Broadway, beside the highway to Moreton-in-Marsh and Oxford, this is one of the most charming and well-managed restaurants in the region. Elegant, though not as formal and stuffy as some competitors, the setting is as pastoral as a painting by Constable. Roger Chanti is perhaps the best chef in town, turning out a finely honed cuisine based on market-fresh ingredients. His appetizers are made with a sharp culinary skill, as best represented by seared scallops with a celeriac purée or terrine of pork belly with smoked garlic and lentils. We especially savor his main courses such as chargrilled beef with oxtail pudding or pan-fried turbot in a bouillabaisse sauce.

In Dormy House, off A44, Willersey Hill, Broadway. © **01386/852711.** Reservations recommended. Main courses £20–£25 ($40–$50); fixed-price dinner £36 ($72); fixed-price Sun lunch £27 ($54). AE, DC, MC, V. Daily 7–9:30pm.

SEEING THE SIGHTS

Broadway's **High Street** ★★ is one of the most beautiful in England—perhaps the most beautiful, if the summer tour buses and hordes of visitors don't run you down. Many of its striking facades date from 1620 or a century or two later. The most famous facade is that of the **Lygon Arms** (see above), a venerable old inn that been serving wayfarers since 1532. Even if you're not staying here, you may want to visit for a meal or a drink.

You may also seek out **St. Eadurgha's Church,** a place of Christian worship for more than 1,000 years. It's located just outside Broadway on Snowshill Road and is open most days, though with no set visiting hours. If it's closed at the time of your visit, a note on the porch door will tell you what house to go to for the key. Occasional Sunday services are held here.

On the outskirts of Broadway stands the **Broadway Tower Country Park** on Broadway Hill (© **01386/852390;** www.broadway-cotswolds.co.uk/tower.html), a "folly" created by the fanciful mind of the sixth Earl of Coventry. Today, you can climb this tower on a clear day for a panoramic vista of 12 shires. It's the most sweeping view in the Cotswolds. The tower is open from April to October daily 10:30am to 5pm, and November to March Saturday and Sunday 10:30am to 3:30pm. Admission is £3.80 ($7.60) for adults, £2.30 ($4.60) for children, and £10 ($20) for a family ticket. You can also bring the makings for a picnic here and spread them out for your lunch in designated areas.

Five kilometers (3 miles) south of Broadway, a final attraction is **Snowshill Manor,** at Snowshill (© **01386/852410;** www.nationaltrust.org.uk), a house that dates mainly from the 17th century. The village of Snowshill itself is one of the most unspoiled in the Cotswolds. It was once owned by an eccentric, Charles Paget Wade, who collected virtually everything he could between 1900 and 1951. Queen Mary once remarked that Wade himself was the most remarkable artifact among his entire flea market. You'll find a little bit of everything here: Flemish tapestries, toys, lacquer cabinets, narwhal tusks, mousetraps, and cuckoo clocks—a glorious mess, like a giant attic of the 20th century. The property, owned by the National Trust, is open April to October Wednesday to Sunday noon to 5pm. Admission is £7.70 ($15) for adults, £3.90 ($7.80) for children, and £20 ($40) for a family ticket. Garden admission is £4.20 ($8.40) adults, £2.10 ($4.20) children, and £11 ($22) family ticket.

12 Chipping Campden ★★

58km (36 miles) NW of Oxford; 19km (12 miles) S of Stratford-upon-Avon; 150km (93 miles) NW of London

The wool merchants have long departed, but the architectural legacy of honey-colored stone cottages—financed by their fleecy "white gold"—remains to delight the visitor today. Try to tie in a stopover here as you rush from Oxford to Stratford-upon-Avon.

On the northern edge of the Cotswolds, it opens onto the dreamy Vale of Evesham that you've seen depicted in a thousand postcards. Except for the heavy traffic in summer, the main street still looks as it did centuries ago—in fact, the noted British historian G. M. Trevelyan called it "the most beautiful village street now left in the island." And so it is even today. You can tie in a stop here on the same day you visit Broadway, lying 6.5km (4 miles) to the west.

Arriving through beautiful Cotswold landscapes, you come upon this country town, whose landmark is the soaring tower of the Church of St. James. You'll see it for miles around. Constructed in the Perpendicular style by the town's wool merchants in the 15th century, it is one of the finest churches in the Cotswolds.

The town's long High Street is curved like Oxford's, and it's lined with stone houses dating from the 16th century. A hundred years later, Chipping Campden was one of the richest wool towns of England. The Campden Trust, a determined group of dedicated conservationists, has preserved the town the way it should be.

Of special interest is the Silk Mill, Sheep Street, open Monday to Friday 9am to 5pm, Saturday 9am to noon. The Guild of Handicrafts was established here in 1902, practicing such skills as bookbinding and cabinetmaking. It folded in 1920 but has been revived today with a series of craft workshops.

ESSENTIALS

GETTING THERE   Trains depart from London's Paddington Station for Moreton-in-Marsh, a 1½- to 2-hour trip. For schedules and information, call ✆ **0845/748-4950** or visit **www.firstgreatwestern.co.uk**. A bus operated by Castleway's travels the 11km (7 miles) from Moreton-in-Marsh to Chipping Campden five times a day. Many visitors opt for a taxi from Moreton-in-Marsh to Chipping Campden.

The largest and most important nearby bus depot is Cheltenham, which receives service several times a day from London's Victoria Coach Station. For schedules and information, call ✆ **0870/580-8080** or visit **www.nationalexpress.co.uk**.

If you're driving from Oxford, take the A40 west to the junction with the A424. Follow it northwest, passing by Stow-on-the-Wold. The route becomes the A44 until you reach the junction with the B4081, which you take northeast to Chipping Campden.

VISITOR INFORMATION   The **Tourist Information Centre** is at the Old Police Station, High Street (✆ **01386/841206;** www.visitchippingcampden.com). It's open daily 10am to 5:30pm in summer, and 10am to 5pm off season.

WHERE TO STAY
EXPENSIVE
Charingworth Manor Hotel ✦✦✦   In nearby Charingworth, this elegant country home is the showpiece of the area, more luxurious than Cotswold House (see below) in town. A manor has stood on this spot since the time of the Domesday Book. The present Tudor-Jacobean house, in honey-colored stone with slate roofs, has 22 hectares (55 acres) of grounds. In the 1930s, it hosted such illustrious guests as T. S. Eliot. Its old-world charm has been preserved, in spite of modernization. Each spacious room is luxuriously furnished with antiques and English fabrics. Many of the period rooms have four-poster beds. Guests can also wander through a lovely garden.

Charingworth, near Chipping Campden, Gloucestershire GL55 6NS. ✆ 01386/593555. Fax 01386/593353. www. classiclodges.co.uk. 26 units. £180 ($360) double; £295 ($590) suite. Rates include English breakfast. AE, DC, MC, V. Take B4035 5km (3¼ miles) east of Chipping Campden. **Amenities:** Restaurant; bar; indoor heated pool; tennis court; gym; sauna; steam room; solarium; billiards room; room service; laundry service. *In room:* TV, hair dryer, trouser press, safe.

The Cotswold House Hotel ✦✦   This is the best place to stay in town. A stately, formal Regency house dating from 1800, right in the heart of the village opposite the old wool market, Cotswold House sits amid .6 hectare (1½ acres) of tended, walled gardens with shaded seating. An Old Grammar School Suite is furnished with antiques and paintings, and ideal for a honeymoon retreat. Many guests prefer one of the more secluded Garden Cottages, each beautifully furnished, with more luxurious appointments than the main house bedrooms. Many guests opt for Montrose House, with elegant bedrooms. For a good English meal, try the hotel's Hicks Brasserie (see review below).

The Square, Chipping Campden, Gloucestershire GL55 6AN. ✆ 01386/840330. Fax 01386/840310. www.cotswold house.com. 30 units. £150–£295 ($300–$590) double; £395–£725 ($790–$1,450) cottage or suite. Rates include English breakfast. AE, MC, V. **Amenities:** 2 restaurants; 2 bars; room service; babysitting; laundry service. *In room:* A/C in suites, TV/DVD, high-speed Internet, minibar, beverage maker, hair dryer, trouser press.

Malt House ✦   In the little hamlet bordering Chipping Campden, this classic Cotswold cottage has a well-manicured garden set against a backdrop of orchards. With its paneled walls, exposed beams, and leaded windows, it's a Cotswold cliché. From Chipping Campden you can walk to the Malt House in just 20 minutes. The midsize bedrooms have been beautifully furnished, each with a private bathroom with shower. Deep sofas and roaring fires greet you in winter, with a terrace for afternoon tea being a summer allure. Three bedrooms have their own entrances from the garden.

Broad Campden, Gloucestershire GL55 6UU. ✆ 01386/840295. Fax 01386/841334. www.malt-house.co.uk. 7 units. £132–£140 ($264–$280) double; £155 ($310) suite. AE, MC, V. Take the B4081 south of Chipping Campden for 2km (1¼ miles). **Amenities:** Breakfast room. *In room:* TV, beverage maker, hair dryer, iron.

Noel Arms Hotel   Long before more elegant country houses came along, this old coaching inn was famous, and it still is, with a history dating from the 14th century. Charles II rested here in 1651 after his defeat at the Battle of Worcester. Tradition is kept alive in the decor, which includes fine antiques, muskets, swords, and shields. Twelve rooms date from the 14th century; the others, comfortably furnished and well appointed, are housed in a modern wing built of Cotswold stone. Those bedrooms in the older part of the hotel are the most stylish—one has an exquisitely carved four-poster bed—although rooms in the more modern annex are more spacious.

High St., Chipping Campden, Gloucestershire GL55 6AT. ✆ 01386/840317. Fax 01386/841136. www.noelarms hotel.com. 26 units. £130–£220 ($260–$440) double. Rates include English breakfast. AE, DC, MC, V. **Amenities:** Restaurant; 2 bars; room service; laundry service. *In room:* TV, beverage maker, hair dryer, trouser press.

INEXPENSIVE

Cornerways Bed and Breakfast *Value*   Lying a 2-minute walk from the famous High Street, this family-run B&B is one of the best in the area. Its rooms are attractively and comfortably furnished—each spacious with pine beds. One is a family room with one king-size and two singles and the other is a triple with one double and one single. Breakfast is not only substantial here but a delight, with homemade jams.

George Lane, Chipping Campden GL55 6DA. ☎ **01386/841307.** www.cornerways.info. 2 units. £65 ($130) double. Rates include English breakfast. No credit cards. *In room:* TV, beverage maker, hair dryer.

Holly House Bed & Breakfast *Finds*   Offering good value, this mellow old place lies in the quaint village of Ebrington, just 3.2km (2 miles) east of Chipping Campden. On beautiful grounds, it is a warm, inviting choice with a flower-filled garden. All the midsize rooms are attractively and comfortably furnished, the ground floor units with their own private entrance. The owners provide maps outlining walks along the many footpaths that surround the village. Serving good food, the local pub, Ebrington Arms, is only a 2-minute walk away.

Ebrington, Gloucestershire GL55 6NL. ☎ **01386/593213.** Fax 01386/593181. www.hollyhousebandb.co.uk. 3 units. £60–£70 ($120–$140) double; £80–£100 ($160–$200) family room. Rates include English breakfast. No credit cards. **Amenities:** Breakfast room. *In room:* TV, beverage maker.

WHERE TO DINE

Hicks Brasserie ENGLISH   You can eat a whole day's meals here. The owners of Chipping Campden's most elegant hostelry oversee a staff serving seasonal dishes. You can get going with such tantalizing appetizers as fish cakes with a caper balsamic dressing or perhaps a salad of green beans, artichokes, and toasted pine nuts. These starters can be followed by such well-crafted mains as duck leg confit with wild mushrooms or pan-fried cod with new potatoes. A delight is the braised shank of Lighthorne lamb in a red-wine jus.

In the Cotswold House Hotel, the Square. ☎ **01386/840330.** Reservations recommended. Main courses £12–£25 ($24–$50). AE, MC, V. Daily 9am–9:30pm.

The Kings ENGLISH/CONTINENTAL   The Kings offers a full restaurant and pub within it. Try to visit for the best bar snacks in town. You'll be tempted by artichokes and Stilton dressing, baked eggs, crab with Gruyère cheese and cream, fresh filet of mackerel in mustard-cream sauce, or more prosaic soups and pâtés. Some of the best main courses are seared tuna steak with a mango salsa or else filet of pan-fried Pollack with a prawn and saffron-flavored chowder. The kitchen does its best to add zest and flavor to the food. The Kings also rents out a dozen midsize to spacious bedrooms, each comfortably furnished with a private bathroom, costing £100 to £165 ($200–$330).

The Square. ☎ **01386/840256.** www.thekingsarmshotel.com. Reservations recommended. Main courses £15–£20 ($30–$40). AE, MC, V. Restaurant daily noon–2:30pm and 6:30–9:30pm. Pub daily 11:30am–11pm.

SEEING THE SIGHTS

In 1907, American horticulturist Major Lawrence Johnstone created **Hidcote Manor Garden** ✪✪, 6.5km (4 miles) northeast of Chipping Campden and 14km (9 miles) south of Stratford-upon-Avon (☎ **01386/438333**). Set on 4 hectares (10 acres), this masterpiece is composed of small gardens, or rooms, that are separated by a variety of hedges, old roses, rare shrubs, trees, and herbaceous borders. March to September, the garden is open Saturday to Wednesday from 10am to 5:30pm (also open Fri July–Aug); it closes at 5pm in October. Last admission is 1 hour before closing. Admission is £8 ($16) for adults, £4 ($8) for children, and £20 ($40) family ticket.

At the studio of **D. I. Hart Silversmiths,** the Guild, the Silk Mill, Sheep Street (© **01386/841100**), silver is expertly smithed by descendants of George Hart (born in the 1890s), an original member of the Guild of Handicraft, in the original Ashbee workshop. **Robert Welch Studio Shop,** Lower High Street (© **01386/840522**), is where William and Rupert Welch have been crafting silverware, stainless steel, and cutlery within an organization established more than 50 years ago. **Martin Gotrel,** the Square (© **01386/841360**), designs fine contemporary and traditional jewelry.

If antiques and antiques hunting are your passion, visit **School House Antiques,** High Street (© **01386/841474**), or the **Barn Antiques Centre,** Long Marston on the Stratford-upon-Avon Road (© **01789/721399**). For new, secondhand, and antiquarian books, look up **Campden Bookshop,** High Street (© **01386/840944**), or **Draycott Books,** 2 Sheep St. (© **01386/841392**).

14

Shakespeare Country & the Heart of England

After London, Shakespeare Country is the most popular destination in England. The main attraction is that foremost tourist town, Stratford-upon-Avon, birthplace of Shakespeare and one of the great meccas for writers, readers, and playgoers from around the world.

Shakespeare's hometown is the best center for touring this part of England. You'll want to take in some theater while in Stratford-upon-Avon and branch out for day trips—notably to **Warwick Castle** in nearby Warwick, to **Kenilworth Castle,** and to **Coventry Cathedral.**

And then you have the heart of England at your doorstep. The adventure can begin in nearby **Birmingham,** England's second-largest city. Though abandoned warehouses and bleak factories remain, this industrial city, like the rest of England, is being spruced up. From here, you can branch out to any number of lovely old market towns and bucolic spots. There are the scenic **Malverns,** the historic town of **Shrewsbury,** and **Worcester,** of Royal Worcester Porcelain fame. Those who are truly passionate about porcelain flock to the fabled potteries to visit towns like **Stoke-on-Trent.** Here, factory and outlet shops sell Wedgwood, Portmeirion, and other fine brands of English tableware at a discount.

1 Stratford-upon-Avon ★★

147km (91 miles) NW of London; 64km (40 miles) NW of Oxford; 13km (8 miles) S of Warwick

Crowds of tourists overrun this market town on the River Avon during the summer. In fact, today, Stratford aggressively hustles its Shakespeare connection—everybody seems to be in business to make a buck off the Bard. However, the throngs dwindle in winter, when you can at least walk on the streets and seek out the places of genuine historical interest.

Aside from the historic sites, the major draw for visitors is the **Royal Shakespeare Theatre,** where Britain's foremost actors perform during a long season that lasts from April to November. Other than the theater, Stratford is rather devoid of any rich cultural life, and you may want to rush back to London after you've seen the literary pilgrimage sights and watched a production of *Hamlet.* But Stratford-upon-Avon is also a good center for trips to Warwick Castle, Kenilworth Castle, and Coventry Cathedral (later in this chapter).

ESSENTIALS

GETTING THERE The journey from London to Stratford-upon-Avon takes about 2¼ hours, and a round-trip ticket costs £28 to £69 ($56–$138) depending on the train. For schedules and information, call ☎ **0845/748-4950,** or go to **www. nationalrail.co.uk**. The train station at Stratford is on Alcester Road.

Warwickshire: Shakespeare Country

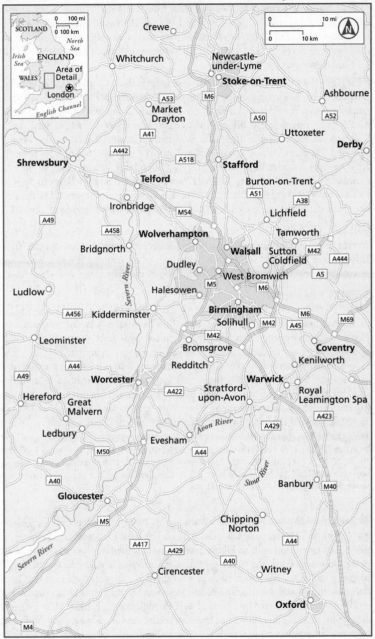

Four **National Express** buses a day leave from London's Victoria Station, with a trip time of 3¼ hours. A single-day round-trip ticket costs £17 ($34). For schedules and information, call ⒸⒸ **0870/580-8080** (www.nationalexpress.co.uk).

If you're driving from London, take the M40 toward Oxford and continue to Stratford-upon-Avon on the A34.

VISITOR INFORMATION The **Tourist Information Centre,** Bridgefoot, Stratford-upon-Avon, Warwickshire CV37 6GW (ⒸⒸ **0870/160-7930;** www.shakespeare-country.co.uk), provides any details you may wish to know about the Shakespeare houses and properties, and will assist in booking rooms (see "Where to Stay," below). Call and ask for a copy of their free *Shakespeare Country Holiday* guide. They also operate a Thomas Cook currency-exchange office (ⒸⒸ **01789/269750**). It's open April to September Monday to Saturday 9am to 5:30pm and Sunday 10am to 4pm, and October to March Monday to Saturday 9am to 5pm and Sunday 10am to 3pm.

To contact **Shakespeare Birthplace Trust,** which administrates many of the attractions, call the Shakespeare Centre (ⒸⒸ **01789/204016;** www.shakespeare.org.uk).

WHERE TO STAY

During the long theater season, you'll need reservations way in advance. The **Tourist Information Centre** (ⒸⒸ **0870/160-7930**), part of the national "Book-a-Bed-Ahead" service, will help find accommodations for you in the price range you're seeking.

VERY EXPENSIVE

Menzies Welcombe Hotel Spa & Golf Club 𝕮𝕮𝕮   For a formal, historic hotel in Stratford, there's nothing better than the Welcombe. One of England's great Jacobean country houses, this hotel is a 10-minute ride from the heart of Stratford-upon-Avon. Its key feature is an 18-hole golf course. It's surrounded by 63 hectares (156 acres) of grounds and has a formal entrance on Warwick Road, a winding driveway leading to the main hall. Bedrooms are luxuriously furnished in traditional Jacobean style, with fine antiques and elegant fabrics. Most bedrooms are seemingly big enough for tennis matches, but those in the garden wing, although comfortable, are small. Some of the bedrooms are sumptuously furnished with elegant four-posters.

Warwick Rd., Stratford-upon-Avon, Warwickshire CV37 0NR. ⒸⒸ **01789/295252**. Fax 01789/414666. www.menzies-hotels.co.uk. 78 units. £195–£245 ($390–$490) double; £245–£470 ($490–$940) suite. Rates include English breakfast. AE, DC, MC, V. Free parking. Take A439 2km (1¼ miles) northeast of the town center. **Amenities:** 2 restaurants; bar; indoor heated pool; golf course; tennis court; gym; aerobics studio; spa; business center; room service; laundry service; dry cleaning. *In room:* TV, Wi-Fi, hair dryer, iron.

EXPENSIVE

Macdonald Alveston Manor Hotel 𝕮𝕮   This Tudor manor is perfect for theatergoers—it's just a 5-minute walk from the theaters. The hotel has a wealth of chimneys and gables, and everything from an Elizabethan gazebo to Queen Anne windows. Mentioned in the Domesday Book, the building predates the arrival of William the Conqueror. The rooms in the manor will appeal to those who appreciate the old-world charm of slanted floors, overhead beams, and antique furnishings. Some triples or quads are available in the modern section, connected by a covered walk through the rear garden. Most rooms here are original and have built-in walnut furniture and a color-coordinated decor. You can live in luxury in the original rooms with their walnut furniture or be assigned a rather routine standard twin that, though comfortable, will lack romance.

Clopton Bridge (off B4066), Stratford-upon-Avon, Warwickshire CV37 7HP. ⒸⒸ **800/225-5843** in the U.S. and Canada, or 0870/400-8181. Fax 01789/414095. www.macdonaldhotels.co.uk. 114 units. £142–£210 ($284–$420) double; £172–£250 ($344–$500) suite. Rates include breakfast. AE, MC, V. Free parking. **Amenities:** Restaurant; bar; indoor heated pool; gym; spa; sauna; room service; babysitting; laundry service; dry cleaning. *In room:* TV, beverage maker, hair dryer, iron.

MODERATE

Best Western Grosvenor Hotel   A pair of Georgian town houses, built in 1832 and 1843, join together to form this hotel, which is one of the second-tier choices in Stratford, on equal footing with the Thistle Stratford-upon-Avon (see below). In the center of town, with lawns and gardens to the rear, it is a short stroll from the inter-section of Bridge Street and Waterside, allowing easy access to the Avon River, Ban-croft Gardens, and the Royal Shakespeare Theatre. There is a rambling ground floor that has tremendous character—it reminds us of an elegant English country house, with small intimate lounges and open fires. Bedrooms are midsize to spacious, each personally designed with a high standard of tasteful modern furnishings. Rooms are not overly adorned or stylish, but they're snug and cozy.

12–14 Warwick Rd., Stratford-upon-Avon, Warwickshire CV37 6YT. (©) **01789/269213.** Fax 01789/266087. www.bwgh.co.uk. 73 units. £100–£175 ($200–$350) double; £165 ($330) suite. AE, MC, V. Free parking. **Amenities:** Restaurant; bar; access to nearby recreation center; room service; babysitting; laundry service. *In room:* TV, Wi-Fi (in most), beverage maker, hair dryer, iron, trouser press, safe (in some).

Holiday Inn Stratford (★)   This first-class hotel stands on ample landscaped lawns on the banks of the River Avon near Clopton Bridge. Although it lacks the charm of the Macdonald Alveston Manor, as far as amenities go, this modern hotel is on the same level as the Welcombe. It's one of the flagships of Queens Moat Houses, a British hotel chain, built in the early 1970s, although it's actually run by the Holiday Inn peo-ple. Every room has a high standard of comfort.

Bridgefoot, Stratford-upon-Avon, Warwickshire CV37 6YR. (©) **0870/225-4701.** Fax 01789/298589. www.moathousehotels.com. 259 units. £70–£135 ($140–$270) double; £95–£215 ($190–$430) suite. AE, DC, MC, V. Parking £5 ($10). **Amenities:** Restaurant; bar; indoor heated pool; exercise room; spa; salon; Jacuzzi; sauna; solarium; game room; room service; laundry service; dry cleaning. *In room:* A/C, TV, Wi-Fi, beverage maker, hair dryer, trouser press.

Legacy Falcon   This inn blends the very old and the very new. The black-and-white timbered inn was licensed a quarter of a century after Shakespeare's death; connected to its rear by a glass passageway is a more sterile bedroom extension added in 1970. In the heart of Stratford, the inn faces the Guild Chapel and the New Place Gardens. The recently upgraded rooms in the older section have oak beams, diamond leaded-glass windows, antiques, and good reproductions. In the inn's intimate Merlin Lounge, you'll find an open copper-hooded fireplace where fires are stoked under beams salvaged from old ships.

Chapel St., Stratford-upon-Avon, Warwickshire CV37 6HA. (©) **0870/832-9905.** Fax 0870/832-9906. www.legacy-hotels.co.uk. 84 units. £90–£150 ($180–$300) double; from £165 ($330) suite. AE, DC, MC, V. Free parking. **Amenities:** 2 restaurants; 2 bars; room service. *In room:* TV, beverage maker, hair dryer, trouser press.

Mercure Shakespeare Hotel (★★)   Filled with historical associations, the original core of this hotel, dating from the 1400s, has seen many additions in its long life. Qui-eter and plusher than the Falcon (see above), it is equaled in the central core of Strat-ford only by the Macdonald Alveston Manor (see above). Residents relax in the post-and-timber-studded public rooms, within sight of fireplaces and playbills from 19th-century productions of Shakespeare's plays. Bedrooms are named in honor of noteworthy actors, Shakespeare's plays, or Shakespearean characters. The oldest are capped with hewn timbers, and all have modern comforts. Even the newer accommodations are at least 40 to 50 years old and have rose-and-thistle patterns carved into many of their exposed timbers. Bathrooms range in size.

Chapel St., Stratford-upon-Avon, Warwickshire CV37 6ER. ✆ 888/892-0038 in the U.S., or 01789/294997. Fax 01789/415411. www.mercure.com. 74 units. £100–£180 ($200–$360) double; from £130 ($260) suite. Rates include buffet breakfast. Children 12 and younger stay free in parent's room. AE, DC, MC, V. Parking £5 ($10). **Amenities:** Restaurant; bar; room service; laundry service; dry cleaning. *In room:* A/C, TV, minibar (in some), beverage maker, hair dryer, iron.

Thistle Stratford-upon-Avon ✿   Theatergoers flock to this Georgian-town-house-style hotel, located across the street from the entrance to the Royal Shakespeare and Swan theaters. The hotel's redbrick main section dates from the Regency period, although over the years a handful of adjacent buildings were included in the hotel and an uninspired modern extension was added. Today, the interior has a well-upholstered lounge and bar, a covered garden terrace, and comfortable but narrow bedrooms. Though small, rooms have a sitting area with a couple of armchairs and round side tables, plus twin beds (for the most part). Some rooms are graced with four-poster beds.

44 Waterside, Stratford-upon-Avon, Warwickshire CV37 6BA. ✆ 0870/333-9146. Fax 0870/333-9246. www.stratford thistle.co.uk. 63 units. £70–£225 ($140–$450) double. AE, DC, MC, V. Parking £5 ($10). **Amenities:** Restaurant; bar; room service; laundry service; dry cleaning. *In room:* TV, beverage maker, hair dryer, trouser press.

White Swan   This cozy, intimate hotel, housed in Stratford's oldest building, is one of the most atmospheric in Stratford. In business for more than a century before Shakespeare appeared on the scene, it competes successfully with the Legacy Falcon (see above) in offering an ancient atmosphere. The gabled medieval front would present the Bard with no surprises, but the modern comforts inside would surely astonish him. Many of the rooms have been well preserved despite the addition of modern conveniences. Paintings dating from 1550 hang on the lounge walls. All bedrooms are well appointed.

Rother St., Stratford-upon-Avon, Warwickshire CV37 6NH. ✆ 01789/297022. Fax 01789/268773. www.pebblehotels. com. 41 units. £85 ($170) double. Rates include English breakfast. AE, DC, MC, V. Parking £5 ($10). **Amenities:** Restaurant; bar (p. 489); room service. *In room:* TV, beverage maker, hair dryer, trouser press.

INEXPENSIVE

Heron Lodge ✿ *Value*   Bob and Chris Heaps run one of the better B&Bs in Stratford, their lodge lying a kilometer (½ mile) outside the heart of town. Their midsize bedrooms have individual character, and the furnishings are both tasteful and comfortable. They still practice the old-fashioned custom of an afternoon "cuppa" served in their conservatory. Like Penryn House (see below), the Heaps serve one of the town's best breakfasts, using local products when available.

260 Alcester Rd., Stratford-upon-Avon, Warwickshire CV37 9JQ. ✆ 01789/299169. www.heronlodge.com. 5 units. £56–£70 ($112–$140) double. Rates include English breakfast. MC, V. Free parking. *In room:* TV, beverage maker, hair dryer, no phone.

Moonraker Guest House ✿ *Finds*   Privately owned and personally managed by Ruth and Morris Masaaki, this is a delightful choice and a discovery, lying midway between Anne Hathaway's House Cottage and Shakespeare's birthplace. Each bedroom is comfortably and attractively furnished. A luxury suite is available with a bedroom, lounge, and kitchenette, plus two more suites, each having two rooms. Among the amenities are four-poster beds, a lounge area, and garden patios. A hearty English breakfast is followed by toast and homemade marmalade and jams.

40 Alcester Rd., Stratford-upon-Avon, Warwickshire CV37 9DB. ⓒ/fax **01789/268774**. www.moonrakerhouse.com. 7 units. £70–£85 ($140–$170) double. Rates include English breakfast. MC, V. Free parking. 2 min. by car from the heart of town on A422. **Amenities:** Breakfast room; garden patio. *In room:* TV, beverage maker, hair dryer.

Penryn House *☆* *Value*   The location is convenient and the price is right at this B&B, where hosts Anne and Robert Dawkes are among the most welcoming in town. Their bedrooms are a bit small but well furnished and comfortable. They justifiably take special pride in their breakfasts right down to their superb "Harvest of Arden" English apple juice. Free-range Worchestershire eggs are served along with fresh seasonal fruit and locally produced bacon and sausage. They even prepare a vegetarian breakfast if requested. The location is close to the rail station, Anne Hathaway's Cottage, and the heart of town.

126 Alcester Rd., Stratford-upon-Avon, Warwickshire CV37 9DP. ⓒ **01789/293718**. Fax 01789/266077. www.penryn guesthouse.co.uk. 7 units. £65–£85 ($130–$170) double. Rates include English breakfast. MC, V. Free parking. **Amenities:** Breakfast room; laundry service. *In room:* TV, Wi-Fi, hair dryer.

Salamander Guest House   This 1906 Edwardian house is a 5-minute walk from the town center just off B439 (Evesham Rd.). One of the better guesthouses in the area, the homelike Salamander fronts a woodsy park. The owners rent comfortable, attractive rooms, including one for families.

40 Grove Rd., Stratford-upon-Avon, Warwickshire CV37 6PB. ⓒ/fax **01789/205728**. www.salamanderguesthouse. co.uk. £38–£60 ($76–$120) double. Rates include English breakfast. MC, V. Free parking. Bus: X16. **Amenities:** Breakfast room; babysitting. *In room:* TV, beverage maker, hair dryer (on request), no phone.

Victoria Spa Lodge   This B&B is old-fashioned and atmospheric. Opened in 1837, the year Queen Victoria ascended the throne, this was the first establishment to be given her name, and it is still going strong. The lodge was originally a spa frequented by the queen's eldest daughter, Princess Vicky. The accommodating hosts offer tastefully decorated, comfortable bedrooms.

Bishopton Lane (2.5km/1½ miles north of the town center where A3400 intersects A46), Stratford-upon-Avon, Warwickshire CV37 9QY. ⓒ **01789/267985**. Fax 01789/204728. www.victoriaspa.co.uk. 7 units. £70 ($140) double. Rates include English breakfast. MC, V. Free parking. **Amenities:** Breakfast room. *In room:* TV, beverage maker, hair dryer.

A NEARBY PLACE TO STAY

Ettington Park Hotel *☆☆☆*   This Victorian Gothic mansion is one of the most sumptuous retreats in Shakespeare Country. It opened as a hotel in 1985 but has a history that spans 9 centuries. The land is a legacy of the Shirley family, whose 12th-century burial chapel is near the hotel. Like a grand private home, the hotel boasts baronial fireplaces and a conservatory. Adam ceilings, stone carvings, and ornate staircases have been beautifully restored. A modern wing, assembled with the same stone and neo-Gothic carving of the original house, stretches toward a Renaissance-style arbor entwined with vines. In the spacious and elegant bedrooms, the most up-to-date comforts are concealed behind antique facades. The best units are deluxe doubles, which are larger than the standard units and open onto garden views. Some rooms have old-fashioned four-posters.

Alderminster, Warwickshire CV37 8BU. ⓒ **0845/0727454**. Fax 0845/0727455. www.handpicked.co.uk. 48 units. £149–£210 ($298–$420) double; from £259 ($518) suite. Rates include English breakfast. AE, DC, MC, V. Free parking. Drive 8km (5 miles) south along A3400 just past Alderminster, then take 2nd left (signposted) into Ettington Park. **Amenities:** Restaurant; bar; indoor heated pool; tennis court; spa; whirlpool; sauna; croquet lawn; room service; babysitting; laundry service; dry cleaning; library. *In room:* TV, Wi-Fi, beverage maker, hair dryer, iron, trouser press.

WHERE TO DINE

After visiting the birthplace of Shakespeare, pop across the street for tea at **Brasserie, Henley Street** (© **01789/262189**). This airy tearoom is tremendously popular, but the very attentive staff more than compensates for the throngs of patrons. Choose from an array of tea blends, cream teas, and various cakes, pastries, and tea cakes—all freshly baked in their own kitchen.

EXPENSIVE TO MODERATE

Callands ℱ INTERNATIONAL   The chefs still admire traditional British cookery, but they are also innovative at this dining spot that attracts both discerning locals and visitors. A relaxed mood prevails at this popular bistro, which scores with its pleasingly simple decor and capable service. Whenever possible, the cookery is based on local farm products, and, like the Mediterranean kitchen, the chefs pay particular homage to fresh vegetables, even serving a plate of grilled vegetables doused in lemon oil and flavored with rosemary, with an accompaniment of saffron-laced couscous. Pastas are a special feature, especially the cheese-studded tagliatelle with almond pesto and pumpkin, even candied eggplant added for good measure. The "puds" are made fresh daily, some of the happy tastes remembered from your childhood.

13–14 Meer St. © **01789/269304**. Reservations recommended. Main courses £12–£18 ($24–$36); fixed-price lunch £19 ($38), dinner £24 ($48). AE, MC, V. Tues–Sat noon–2pm and 6–10:30pm.

Lambs ℱ CONTINENTAL/ENGLISH   A stone's throw from the Royal Shakespeare Theatre, this cafe-bistro is housed in a building dating from 1547 (and with connections to Lewis Carroll). For a quick, light meal or pretheater dinner, it's ideal. The menu changes monthly. Begin with such starters as an English muffin with smoked haddock and creamed leeks, or else Serrano ham with fresh figs and a basil salad. Then you can tuck into such mains as filet of Scottish beef with portobello mushrooms or else rack of Cornish lamb with dauphinoise potatoes, perhaps roast Gressingham duck with Puy lentils. For dessert, why not the dark-chocolate truffle cake with white-chocolate ice cream? Look to the blackboard for daily specials. The chef takes chances (no doubt inspired by trips to the Continent), and it's a nice departure from the bland tearoom food served for decades in Stratford.

12 Sheep St. © **01789/292554**. www.lambsrestaurant.co.uk. Reservations required for dinner Fri–Sat. Main courses £11–£19 ($22–$38); fixed-price menu £15 ($30) for 2 courses, £20 ($40) for 3 courses. DC, MC, V. Mon 5:30–10pm; Tues–Sat noon–2pm and 5–10pm; Sun noon–2:30pm.

Malbec ℱℱ BRITISH/FRENCH   Many savvy local foodies cite this as the best restaurant in Stratford-upon-Avon, and we're inclined to agree. The chef and owner, Simon Malin, offers market-fresh and unpretentious cuisine in fashionable surroundings. His produce is fresh, his seasonings on target, and his imagination active. On the ground floor is an intimate restaurant of character, and on the lower level is a charming cellar with vaulted ceilings and flagstone floors. You'll be impressed with such starters as sautéed lamb's kidneys with thyme-roasted onions or crispy fried squid with almond and a roasted-pepper dipping sauce. You might also savor such mains as rump of local lamb with a butternut-squash gnocchi or free-range pork belly with chorizo sausages and butter beans. Desserts are made fresh daily. How about champagne-laced rhubarb with whipped vanilla shortcake?

6 Union St. © **01789/269106**. Reservations required. Main courses £15–£18 ($30–$36). AE, MC, V. Daily noon–2pm; Mon–Sat 7–9:30pm.

Marlowe's Restaurant ENGLISH   Many famous actors appearing in Shakespeare plays have made their way here for dinner, including Paul Schofield, Vanessa Redgrave, Sir Ralph Richardson, and Sir John Gielgud. You can dine formally in the Elizabethan Room or more casually in the Bistro. A large bar in winter has a fireplace blazing with logs, and it opens into a splendid oak-paneled room. In summer there is a spacious courtyard for alfresco dining. Starters are a harmonious blend of flavors, including terrine of guinea fowl and oyster mushrooms with sherry and a red-onion marmalade. Among the fish dishes, grilled sea bass emerges from the kitchen with roasted fennel and a tomato fondue, or else you can opt for one of the chargrilled dishes such as a filet steak with pan-fried mushrooms and grilled tomatoes. Drunken duck has been a longtime specialty here. It's marinated in gin, red wine, and juniper berries before it's roasted in the oven.

18 High St. © **01789/204999.** Reservations recommended. Main courses £8–£14 ($16–$28). AE, MC, V. Elizabethan Room Mon–Sat 5:30–10:30pm; Sun 7–9pm. Bistro daily noon–2:15pm and 5:30–11pm.

The One Elm ENGLISH   This is a convenient stopover because of its long hours of food service. Guests enjoy its pub atmosphere, ground-floor restaurant, or its courtyard for dining and drinking. The cooks pride themselves on serving dishes fresh from their suppliers, including free-range chicken and eggs and high-quality Scottish beef. You can see these chefs at work in an open kitchen, so you know they are preparing everything to order. A special feature is the Elm's "Deli Board," featuring all sorts of antipasti and charcuterie, such as a hot chorizo-and-butter-bean salad. Both starters and mains are an appetizing array of market freshness. Begin with shredded beef samosa or else smoked Scottish salmon with horseradish blinis. Among the most enticing main dishes are fish cakes of salmon and smoked haddock with sautéed spinach or else whole roast black bream with kumquat potatoes. A Catalan fish stew is made from the catch of the day.

1 Guild St. © **01789/404919.** Reservations not needed. Main courses £9–£14 ($18–$28). MC, V. Mon–Sat 11am–10pm; Sun noon–3pm and 6:30–9:30pm.

The Quarto's Restaurant ☆ FRENCH/ITALIAN/TRADITIONAL ENGLISH   This restaurant enjoys the best location in town—it's in the Royal Shakespeare Theatre itself—with glass walls providing an unobstructed view of the swans on the Avon. You can partake of an intermission snack of smoked salmon and champagne or dine by flickering candlelight after the performance. Many dishes are definitely old English; others reflect a Continental touch. You can revel in such appetizers as Stilton with a cucumber-and-red-pepper salad enhanced with a walnut dressing, or else sample the ham terrine with parsley dressing and an apple-and-onion marmalade. The chef has learned his craft well as reflected by such main dishes as seared tuna with fresh thyme and baby spinach with a mango and lime chutney. Or else you might try the chicken with smoked bacon and apricots, served with savoy cabbage and a tarragon-cream sauce.

In the Royal Shakespeare Theatre, Waterside. © **01789/403415.** Reservations recommended. Main courses £11–£17 ($22–$34). AE, MC, V. Thurs and Sat 11:30am–2:30pm; Mon–Sat 5:30–11pm. Closed when theater is shut down.

Sorrento ☆ ITALIAN   For a taste of Italy, visit this family-run restaurant, where Jackie and Tony de Angelis welcome you at a location only a 4-minute walk from the Shakespeare Theatre. Guests seated on leather furniture enjoy a predinner aperitif in the lounge before heading into the stylish yet informal restaurant itself. Everything is cooked to order using market-fresh ingredients, so you need to allow time for each dish to be prepared. In summer those dishes may be enjoyed alfresco on the patio.

A selection of well-chosen Italian wines complements the meal, which might begin with such starters as the chef's homemade chicken liver pâté or else a roast-pepper-and-artichoke salad dressed with olive oil, basil, and capers. The pastas are among the best in town. Salmon and lemon sole are united in a white-wine sauce with capers and garlic. The filet steak is flamed in brandy and served in a creamy sauce of black peppercorns, or else you can order strips of chicken breast with mixed peppers and mushrooms.

8 Ely St. ✆ 01789/297999. Reservations recommended. Main courses £13–£17 ($26–$34); set lunch £8.90 ($18) for 2 courses, £13 ($26) for 3 courses. MC, V. Tues–Wed 11:30am–1:45pm; Mon–Sat 5–10:30pm.

Thai Boathouse ✸ THAI   The only restaurant set on the Avon, this charming choice is reached by crossing Clopton Bridge toward Oxford and Banbury. The second-floor dining room opens onto vistas of the river. This restaurant, originally established 4 decades ago in Bangkok, has brought spice and zest to Stratford's lazy restaurant scene. The decor comes from Thailand itself, with elephants, woodcarvings, and Buddhas adorning the restaurant. Seasonal specialties such as wild duck and pheasant are a special feature of the menu. Fresh produce, great skill in the kitchen, and exquisite presentations are the hallmarks of this restaurant. Sample a selection of authentic Thai appetizers before going on to the delectable main courses, which include stir-fried mixed seafood with fresh chili and sweet Thai basil, or else chicken stir-fried with sweet peppers, pineapple, and onion in a sweet-and-sour sauce.

Swan's Nest Lane. ✆ 01789/297733. Reservations recommended. Main courses £6–£12 ($12–$24); fixed-price menus £21–£26 ($42–$52). MC, V. Sun–Fri noon–2:30pm; daily 5:30–10:30pm.

INEXPENSIVE

The Oppo INTERNATIONAL   Located in the heart of Stratford within a 16th-century building, this refreshingly unpretentious restaurant serves up good bistro cooking at reasonable prices. The menu often includes local farm products. Salmon fish cakes are served on a bed of spinach with a sorrel sauce, and pork filet is slow roasted with fondant potatoes. The most exotic item on the menu is chicken roasted with banana in lime butter and served with basmati rice and a mild curry sauce.

13 Sheep St. ✆ 01789/269980. Reservations recommended. Main courses £9–£18 ($18–$36). DC, MC, V. Daily noon–2pm; Mon–Sat 5–10pm; Sun 6–9:30pm.

Russons INTERNATIONAL   Because the theater is a short stroll away, this is a great place for a preshow meal. The restaurant is housed in a 400-year-old building and the two simply furnished dining rooms both feature inglenook fireplaces. The menu changes monthly, reflecting the availability of seasonal ingredients. Fresh seafood is the specialty here, with different choices every day. Daily specials are posted on a blackboard and include shoulder of lamb, Norfolk duck, and numerous vegetarian dishes. Finish with one of the delicious homemade desserts.

8 Church St. ✆ 01789/268822. Reservations recommended. Lunch and pretheater main courses £6.50–£11 ($13–$22); dinner main courses £9.50–£18 ($19–$36). AE, MC, V. Tues–Sat noon–2pm and 5:15–9pm.

The Vintner ENGLISH/CONTINENTAL   In a timber-framed structure little altered since its construction in the late 15th century, the Vintner may very well be the place where William Shakespeare went to purchase his wine. It derives its name from John Smith, who traded as a wine merchant (vintner) during the 1600s. Close to the Shakespeare Theatre, the Vintner is both a cafe/bar and a restaurant owned by the same family for 5 centuries; its location makes it ideal for a pretheater lunch or supper. When possible, fresh local produce is used. Good-tasting mains include breast of chicken with mango and slow-roasted lamb shank with parsley mashed potatoes. Escalopes of pork filet are made more enticing by caper butter, and a rib-eye comes in a peppercorn sauce. For dessert, try that British nursery favorite, toffee pudding with vanilla ice cream.

4–5 Sheep St. ℂ 01789/297259. Reservations not needed. Main courses £8.95–£18 ($18–$36). DC, MC, V. Mon–Sat 10am–11pm; Sun 10am–9:30pm.

THE BEST PLACES FOR A PINT

The Black Swan ("the Dirty Duck") ★★ ENGLISH   Affectionately known as the Dirty Duck, this has been a popular hangout for Stratford players since the 18th century. The wall is lined with autographed photos of its many famous patrons. Typical English grills, among other dishes, are featured in the Dirty Duck Grill Room, though no one has ever accused it of serving the best food in Stratford. You'll have a choice of a dozen appetizers, most of which would make a meal themselves. In fair weather, you can have drinks in the front garden and watch the swans glide by on the Avon.

Waterside. ℂ 01789/297312. Reservations required for dining. Main courses £9–£15 ($18–$30); bar snacks £4–£8 ($8–$16). AE, DC, MC, V (in restaurant only). Restaurant daily noon–10pm. Bar daily 11am–1am.

The Garrick Inn ENGLISH   Near Harvard House, this black-and-white timbered Elizabethan pub has an unpretentious charm. The front bar is decorated with tapestry-covered settles, an old oak refectory table, and an open fireplace that attracts the locals. The back bar has a circular fireplace with a copper hood and mementos of the triumphs of the English stage. The specialty is homemade pies such as steak and kidney or chicken and mushroom. Wild boar and venison are other specialties.

25 High St. ℂ 01789/292186. Main courses £5–£11 ($10–$22). MC, V. Meals Mon–Sat noon–10pm; Sun noon–9pm. Pub Mon–Thurs 11am–11pm; Fri–Sat 11am–midnight; Sun noon–10:30pm.

The White Swan ENGLISH   In the town's oldest building is this atmospheric pub, with cushioned leather armchairs, oak paneling, and fireplaces. You're likely to meet amiable fellow drinkers, who revel in a setting once enjoyed by Will Shakespeare himself when it was known as the Kings Head. At lunch, you can partake of hot dishes of the day, along with fresh salads and sandwiches. Typical mains include a warm brie salad with tomatoes and walnuts, or else salmon with savoy cabbage and potatoes. You can also enjoy the chef's fried chicken served with a red-wine sauce.

In the White Swan hotel, Rother St. ℂ 01789/297022. Bar snacks £2–£7 ($4–$14); main courses £7–£18 ($14–$36). AE, DC, MC, V. Daily noon–9pm.

THE ROYAL SHAKESPEARE THEATRE

On the banks of the Avon, the **Royal Shakespeare Theatre (RST),** Waterside, Stratford-upon-Avon CV37 6BB (ℂ **01789/403444;** www.rsc.org.uk), is a major showcase for the Royal Shakespeare Company and seats 1,500 patrons. The theater's season runs from April to November and typically features five Shakespearean plays. The company has some of the finest actors on the British stage. *Warning:* The theater is undergoing restoration, with its Art Deco exterior remaining but a new thrust stage being built inside. Expect a gala opening sometime in 2010. During the work, the company will perform at a new theater, the **Courtyard,** near the RST.

You usually need **ticket reservations,** with two successive booking periods, each one opening about 2 months in advance. You can pick these up from a North American or English travel agent. A small number of tickets are always held for sale on the day of a performance, but it may be too late to get a good seat if you wait until you arrive in Stratford. Tickets can be booked through **Keith Prowse** (© **800/669-8687** in North America, or 0870/840-1111 in England; www.keithprowse.com).

You can also call the **theater box office** directly (© **0844/800-1110**) and charge your tickets. The box office is open Monday to Saturday 9am to 8pm, although it closes at 6pm on days when there are no performances. Seat prices range from £5 to £45 ($10–$90). You can make a credit card reservation and pick up your tickets on the performance day, but you must cancel at least 1 full week in advance to get a refund.

SEEING THE SIGHTS

Besides the attractions on the periphery of Stratford, many Elizabethan and Jacobean buildings are in town, a number of them administrated by the **Shakespeare Birthplace Trust** (© **01789/204016;** www.shakespeare.org.uk). One ticket—costing £15 ($30) adults, £13 ($26) for seniors and students, and £7.20 ($14) for children—lets you visit the five most important sights. You can also buy a family ticket to all five sights (good for two adults and three children) for £38 ($76)—a good deal. Pick up the ticket if you're planning to do much sightseeing (obtainable at your first stopover at any one of the Trust properties).

Guided tours of Stratford-upon-Avon are conducted by **City Sightseeing,** Civic Hall, Rother Street. In summer, open-top double-decker buses depart every 15 minutes daily from 9:30am to 6pm. You can take a 1-hour ride without stops, or you can get off at any or all of the town's five Shakespeare properties. Though the bus stops are clearly marked along the historic route, the most logical starting point is the sidewalk in front of the Pen & Parchment Pub, at the bottom of Bridge Street. Tour tickets are valid all day so you can hop on and off the buses as many times as you want. The tours cost £10 ($20) for adults, £8 ($16) for seniors or students, and £5 ($10) for children 5 to 15 (children 4 and younger ride for free). A family ticket sells for £25 ($50). Tour frequency depends on the time of year; call for information.

Anne Hathaway's Cottage ⚘   Before she married Shakespeare, Anne Hathaway lived in this thatched, wattle-and-daub cottage in the hamlet of Shottery, 1.6km (1 mile) from Stratford. It's the most interesting and the most photographed of the Trust properties. The Hathaways were yeoman farmers, and their descendants lived in the cottage until 1892. As a result, it was never renovated and provides a rare insight into the life of a family in Shakespearean times. The Bard was only 18 when he married Anne, who was much older. Many original furnishings, including the courting settle (the bench on which Shakespeare is said to have wooed Anne) and various kitchen utensils, are preserved inside the house. After visiting the house, take time to linger in the garden and orchard.

Cottage Lane, Shottery. © **01789/292100.** Admission £6 ($12) adults, £5 ($10) seniors and students, £3 ($6) children, £14 ($28) family ticket (2 adults, 3 children). Nov–Mar daily 10am–4pm; Apr–May and Sept–Oct Mon–Sat 9:30am–5pm, Sun 10am–5pm; June–Aug Mon–Sat 9am–5pm, Sun 9:30am–5pm. Closed Dec 23–26. Take a bus from Bridge St. or walk via a marked pathway from Evesham Place in Stratford across the meadow to Shottery.

Hall's Croft   This house is on Old Town Street, not far from the parish church, Holy Trinity. It was here that Shakespeare's daughter Susanna probably lived with her husband, Dr. John Hall. Hall's Croft is an outstanding Tudor house with a walled garden, furnished in the style of a middle-class home of the time. Dr. Hall was widely respected and built up a large medical practice in the area. Fascinating exhibits illustrate the theory and practice of medicine in Dr. Hall's time.

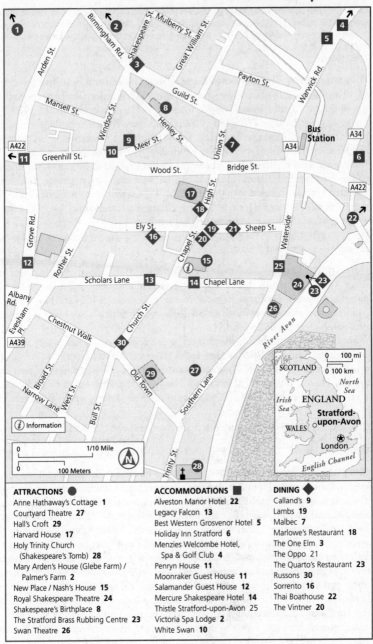

Stratford-upon-Avon

ATTRACTIONS ●
Anne Hathaway's Cottage **1**
Courtyard Theatre **27**
Hall's Croft **29**
Harvard House **17**
Holy Trinity Church
(Shakespeare's Tomb) **28**
Mary Arden's House (Glebe Farm) /
Palmer's Farm **2**
New Place / Nash's House **15**
Royal Shakespeare Theatre **24**
Shakespeare's Birthplace **8**
The Stratford Brass Rubbing Centre **23**
Swan Theatre **26**

ACCOMMODATIONS ■
Alveston Manor Hotel **22**
Legacy Falcon **13**
Best Western Grosvenor Hotel **5**
Holiday Inn Stratford **6**
Menzies Welcombe Hotel,
Spa & Golf Club **4**
Penryn House **11**
Moonraker Guest House **11**
Salamander Guest House **12**
Mercure Shakespeare Hotel **14**
Thistle Stratford-upon-Avon **25**
Victoria Spa Lodge **2**
White Swan **10**

DINING ◆
Calland's **9**
Lambs **19**
Malbec **7**
Marlowe's Restaurant **18**
The One Elm **3**
The Oppo **21**
The Quarto's Restaurant **23**
Russons **30**
Sorrento **16**
Thai Boathouse **22**
The Vintner **20**

Old Town St. (near Holy Trinity Church). ℂ **01789/292107**. Admission £4 ($8) adults, £3.50 ($7) seniors and students, £2 ($4) children, £11 ($21) family ticket (2 adults, 3 children). Nov–Mar daily 11am–4pm; Apr–May daily 11am–5pm; June–Aug Mon–Sat 9:30am–5pm, Sun 10am–5pm; Sept–Oct daily 11am–5pm. Closed Dec 23–28. To reach Hall's Croft, walk west from High St., which becomes Chapel St. and Church St. At the intersection with Old Town St., go left.

Harvard House   The most ornate home in Stratford, Harvard House is a fine example of an Elizabethan town house. Rebuilt in 1596, it was once the home of Katherine Rogers, mother of John Harvard, founder of Harvard University. In 1909, the house was purchased by a Chicago millionaire, Edward Morris, who presented it as a gift to the famous American university. Today, following a restoration, it has reopened as a Museum of British Pewter. The museum displays trace the use of pewter from the Roman era until modern times. Pewter, as you learn, used to be the most common choice for household items. Even kiddie toys were made from pewter. Highlights include a tankard engraved with the images of William and Mary, a teapot inspired by the Portland Vase, and a rare bell-based Elizabethan candlestick. Two "hands-on" activities allow children to examine original items.

High St. ℂ **01789/204507**. £2.75 ($5.50) adults, free for children. May–June and Sept–Oct Fri–Sun noon–5pm; July–Aug Wed–Sun noon–5pm.

Holy Trinity Church (Shakespeare's Tomb)   In an attractive setting near the River Avon is the parish church where Shakespeare is buried ("and curst be he who moves my bones"). The Parish Register records his baptism in 1564 and burial in 1616 (copies of the original documents are on display). The church is one of the most beautiful parish churches in England.

Shakespeare's tomb lies in the chancel, a privilege bestowed upon him when he became a lay rector in 1605. Alongside his grave are those of his widow, Anne, and other members of his family. You can also see the graves of Susanna, his daughter, and those of Thomas Nash and Dr. John Hall. Nearby on the north wall is a bust of Shakespeare that was erected approximately 7 years after his death—within the lifetime of his widow and many of his friends.

Old Town St. ℂ **01789/266316**. Free admission to church; Shakespeare's tomb £1.50 ($3) adults, 50p ($1) students. Apr–Sept Mon–Sat 8:30am–6pm, Sun 12:30–5pm; Mar and Oct Mon–Sat 9am–5pm, Sun 12:30–5pm; Nov–Feb Mon–Sat 9am–4pm, Sun 12:30–5pm. Walk 4 min. past the Royal Shakespeare Theatre with the river on your left.

Mary Arden's House (Glebe Farm)/Palmer's Farm 🦌   So what if millions of visitors have been tricked into thinking this timber-framed farmhouse with its old stone dovecote and various outbuildings was the girlhood home of Shakespeare's mother, Mary Arden? It's still one of the most intriguing sights outside Stratford, even if local historian Dr. Nat Alcock discovered in 2000 that the actual childhood home of Arden was the dull-looking brick-built farmhouse, Glebe Farm, next door. Glebe Farm has now been properly renamed Mary Arden's House. It was all the trick of an 18th-century tour guide, John Jordan, who decided Glebe Farm was too unimpressive to be the home of the Bard's mother, so he told tourists it was this farmstead instead. What was known for years as "Mary Arden's House" has been renamed Palmer's Farm. Actually, this farm wasn't constructed until the late 16th century, a little late to be Mary Arden's actual home. After the name confusion, local authorities have converted Palmer's Farm into a working farm. Visitors can tour the property seeing firsthand how a farming household functioned in the 1570s—yes, cows to be milked, bread to be baked, and vegetables cultivated in an authentic 16th-century manner. In the barns, stable, cowshed, and farmyard is an extensive collection of farming implements illustrating life and work in the local countryside from Shakespeare's time to the present.

Wilmcote. ✆ **01789/293455**. Admission £7 ($14) adults, £6 ($12) students and seniors, £3.50 ($7) children, £18 ($36) family ticket, free for children 4 and younger. Nov–Mar daily 10am–4pm; Apr–May and Sept–Oct daily 10am–5pm; June–Aug daily 9:30am–5pm. Closed Dec 23–26. Take A3400 (Birmingham) for 5.5km (3½ miles).

New Place/Nash's House   Shakespeare retired to New Place in 1610 (a prosperous man by the standards of his day) and died here 6 years later. Regrettably, the house was torn down, so only the garden remains. A mulberry tree planted by the Bard was so popular with latter-day visitors to Stratford that the garden's owner chopped it down. It is said that the mulberry tree that grows here today was planted from a cutting of the original tree. You enter the gardens through Nash's House (Thomas Nash married Elizabeth Hall, a granddaughter of the poet). Nash's House has 16th-century period rooms and an exhibition illustrating the history of Stratford. The popular Knott Garden adjoins the site and represents the style of a fashionable Elizabethan garden.

Chapel St. ✆ **01789/292325**. Admission £4 ($8) adults, £3.50 ($7) seniors and students, £2 ($4) children, £11 ($22) family ticket (2 adults, 3 children). Nov–Mar daily 11am–4pm; Apr–May and Sept–Oct daily 11am–5pm; June–Aug Mon–Sat 9:30am–5pm, Sun 10am–5pm. Closed Dec 23–26. Walk west down High St.; Chapel St. is a continuation of High St.

Shakespeare's Birthplace ⚜   The son of a glover and whittawer (leather worker), the Bard was born on St. George's Day, April 23, 1564, and died on the same date 52 years later. Filled with Shakespeare memorabilia, including a portrait and furnishings of the writer's time, the Trust property is a half-timbered structure, dating from the early 16th century. The house was bought by public donors in 1847 and preserved as a national shrine. You can visit the living room, the bedroom where Shakespeare was probably born, a fully equipped kitchen of the period (look for the "babyminder"), and a Shakespeare museum, illustrating his life and times. Later, you can walk through the garden. You won't be alone: It's estimated that some 660,000 visitors pass through the house annually.

Built next door to commemorate the 400th anniversary of the Bard's birth, the modern **Shakespeare Centre** serves both as the administrative headquarters of the Birthplace Trust and as a library and study center. An extension houses a visitor center, which acts as a reception area for those coming to the birthplace.

Henley St. (in the town center near the post office, close to Union St.). ✆ **01789/204016**. Admission £8 ($16) adults, £7 ($14) students and seniors, £4 ($8) children, £21 ($42) family ticket (2 adults, 3 children). Nov–Mar Mon–Sat 10am–4pm, Sun 10:30am–4pm; Apr–May and Sept–Oct daily 10am–5pm; June–Aug Mon–Sat 9am–5pm, Sun 9am–5pm. Closed Dec 23–26.

The Stratford Brass Rubbing Centre   This is a brass-rubbing center, where medieval and Tudor brasses illustrate the knights and ladies, scholars, merchants, and priests of a bygone era. The Stratford collection includes a large assortment of exact replicas of brasses. Entrance is free, but visitors are charged depending on which brass they choose to rub. According to size, the cost ranges from £2 ($4) to make a rubbing of a small brass, to a maximum of £20 ($40) for a rubbing of the largest brass.

The Royal Shakespeare Theatre Summer House, Avon Bank Gardens. ✆ **01789/297671**. www.stratfordbrassrubbing. co.uk. Free admission. Mar–Oct daily 10am–6pm; Nov–Feb daily 11am–4pm.

SHOPPING

Among the many tacky tourist traps are some quality shops, including the ones described below.

Set within an antique house with ceiling beams, the **Shakespeare Bookshop,** 39 Henley St. (© **01789/292176**), across from the Shakespeare Birthplace Centre, is the region's premier source for textbooks and academic treatises on the Bard and his works. It specializes in books for every level of expertise on Shakespearean studies, from picture books for junior high school students to weighty tomes geared to anyone pursuing a Ph.D. in literature.

Everything in the **Pickwick Gallery,** 32 Henley St. (© **01789/294861**), is a well-crafted work of art produced by copper or steel engraving plates, or printed by means of a carved wooden block. Hundreds of botanical prints, landscapes, and renderings of artfully arranged ruins, each suitable for framing, can be purchased. Topographical maps of regions of the United Kingdom are also available if you're planning on doing any serious hiking.

Other shopping bets include the **Antique Market** along Ely Street, with some 50 or more stalls selling porcelain, silver, jewelry, and Shakespeare memorabilia. **Antique Arms & Armour,** Poet's Arbour on Sheep St. (© **01789/293453**), has the best collection of antique swords and armor, some of it looking like old props from previous Shakespeare productions.

2 Warwick: England's Finest Medieval Castle

148km (92 miles) NW of London; 13km (8 miles) NE of Stratford-upon-Avon

Most visitors come to this town just to see Warwick Castle, the finest medieval castle in England. Some combine it with a visit to the ruins of Kenilworth Castle (see below), but the historic center of ancient Warwick has a lot more to offer.

Warwick cites Ethelfleda, daughter of Alfred the Great, as its founder. But most of its history is associated with the earls of Warwick, a title created by the son of William the Conqueror in 1088. The story of those earls—the Beaumonts and the Beauchamps (such figures as "Kingmaker" Richard Neville)—makes for an exciting episode in English history. A devastating fire swept through the heart of Warwick in 1694, but a number of Elizabethan and medieval buildings still survive, along with some fine Georgian structures from a later date.

ESSENTIALS

GETTING THERE Trains run frequently between Stratford-upon-Avon and Warwick. A one-way ticket costs around £4.50 ($9). Call © **0845/748-4950** for schedules and information.

One **Stagecoach** bus, the 16, departs Stratford-upon-Avon every hour during the day. The trip takes roughly half an hour. Call the **tourist office** (© **0870/160-7930**) for schedules. **National Express** (© **0870/580-8080;** www.nationalexpress.com) runs four buses daily from the Riverside bus station in Stratford-upon-Avon to Puckerings Lane in Warwick for £1.50 ($3). Take the A46 if you're driving from Stratford-upon-Avon.

VISITOR INFORMATION The **Tourist Information Centre** is at the Court House, Jury Street (© **01926/492212;** www.warwick-uk.co.uk), and is open daily from 9:30am to 4:30pm (it's closed Dec 24–26 and Jan 1).

WHERE TO STAY

Many people prefer to stay in Warwick and commute to Stratford-upon-Avon, though the accommodations here are not as special as those at Stratford.

The Glebe at Barford ☆ *Finds*   This 1820s rectory to the Church of St. Peter has been welcoming wayfarers to either Stratford-upon-Avon or Warwick since it was successfully converted into a small country-house hotel in 1948. The church still stands adjacent to the hotel's grounds. In recent years, much redecorating and many modern facilities have been added, including the Cedars Conservatory Restaurant looking out onto the gardens. A small swimming pool with hydro-jets has been added as well. Each of the bedrooms has been individually designed, with either a tented ceiling, a four-poster, or a coronet-style bed. The hotel lays only a 10-minute drive from the center of Warwick.

Church St., Barford, Warwickshire CV35 8BS. Ⓒ **01926/624218.** Fax 01926/624625. www.glebehotel.co.uk. 39 units. £140–£150 ($280–$300) double; £175 ($350) Shakespeare Suite (with Jacuzzi corner bathroom). Rates include full English breakfast. AE, DC, MC, V. Free parking. **Amenities:** Restaurant; bar; heated indoor heated pool; fitness center; spa; hot tub; sauna; solarium. *In room:* TV, high-speed Internet, beverage maker, hair dryer.

Hilton Warwick ☆   Though outside of town, the Hilton is the best choice in the area. Lying at the junction of a network of highways, it's popular with business travelers and hosts many conferences for local companies. But tourists also find that its comfort and easy-to-find location make it a good base for touring Warwick and the surrounding regions. It's a low-rise modern design with a series of interconnected bars, lounges, and public areas. Room furnishings are bland but comfortable.

Warwick Bypass (A429 Stratford Rd.), Warwick, Warwickshire CV34 6RE. Ⓒ **800/445-8667** in the U.S. and Canada, or 01926/499555. Fax 01926/410020. www.hilton.co.uk. 181 units. £100–£150 ($200–$300) double. AE, DC, MC, V. Take A429 3km (2 miles) south of Warwick or 11km (7 miles) north of Stratford-upon-Avon to the Junction 15 lying off the M40 from London. **Amenities:** Restaurant; cafe; bar; indoor heated pool; health club; sauna; steam room; room service; babysitting; laundry service; dry cleaning. *In room:* A/C (in deluxe rooms), TV, high-speed Internet, beverage maker, hair dryer, iron, trouser press.

Lord Leycester Hotel   This affordable choice lies within walking distance of the castle and the other historic buildings of Warwick. In 1726, this manor house belonged to Lord Archer of Umberslade; in 1926, it was finally turned into this modest hotel. The rooms are small but offer reasonable comfort for the price with decent double or twin beds.

17 Jury St., Warwick, Warwickshire CV34 4EJ. Ⓒ **01926/491481.** Fax 01926/491561. www.lord-leycester.co.uk. 48 units. £80–£98 ($160–$196) double. Rates include English breakfast. AE, DC, MC, V. **Amenities:** 2 restaurants; bar; room service. *In room:* TV, Wi-Fi, beverage maker, hair dryer, trouser press.

Tudor House Inn & Restaurant   At the edge of town, on the main road from Stratford-upon-Avon to Warwick Castle, is a 1472 timbered inn. It's one of the few buildings to escape the fire that destroyed High Street in 1694. Off the central hall are two large rooms, each of which could be the setting for an Elizabethan play. All the simply furnished bedrooms have washbasins, and two contain doors only 1m (3 ft.) high. In the corner of the lounge is an open, turning staircase.

90–92 West St. (opposite the main Warwick Castle car park, 1km/½ mile south of town on A429), Warwick, Warwickshire CV34 6AW. Ⓒ **01926/495447.** Fax 01926/492948. 10 units, 8 with bathroom. £70–£90 ($140–$180) double. Rates include English breakfast. DC, MC, V. **Amenities:** Restaurant; bar. *In room:* TV, beverage maker, hair dryer.

WHERE TO DINE

For a break from sightseeing, it's hard to beat the ancient ambience of tea at **Brethren's Kitchen,** Lord Leycester Hospital (Ⓒ **01926/491422**). This tearoom is part of a 16th-century hospital the earl established in the year 1571. It has cool stone floors and wonderful exposed oak beams. Indian, Chinese, and herbal teas are all available, as well as scones with fresh cream, sponge cake, and fruit cake. It's closed between November and March and on Mondays but open on bank holidays.

Catalan (Value) MEDITERRANEAN   It's the castle that draws you to Warwick, not the cuisine, but this bistro is notable for serving affordable food that is both good-tasting and prepared with fresh ingredients. If you come for lunch, you'll be greeted with a Spanish tapas menu that is both experimental and tasteful. There's also lighter fare such as sandwiches, panini, and salads. Dinner is more elaborate, such as loin of monkfish wrapped with pancetta and roasted with fresh herbs or a braised lamb shank with Spanish saffron and a rich shallot and port jus.

6 Jury St. © 01926/498930. www.cafecatalan.com. Reservations recommended. Main courses £13–£19 ($26–$38); Mon–Fri 2-course fixed-price lunch £10 ($20). AE, MC, V. Mon–Fri noon–3pm; Mon and Wed–Thurs 6–9:30pm; Fri 6–10pm; Sat noon–10pm; Sun noon–9:30pm.

Findon's Restaurant MODERN BRITISH   The building is authentically Georgian, constructed in 1700. You'll dine surrounded by original stone floors and cupboards, within a setting for only 43 diners in snug comfort. Michael Findon, owner and sometime chef, works hard at orchestrating a blend of traditional and modern British cuisine. Starters to tempt you include a salad of prosciutto, melon, and fresh fig with Parmesan shavings. It's served with a strawberry and mango dressing. You can also order a home-cured organic salmon starter with an orange-and-coriander-flavored salad. Some of the best main dishes include Cornish lamb with zucchini, spring onion, and a ginger-flavored ragout. For meat eaters there is an aged rib-eye steak with caramelized red onion, plum tomatoes, fresh basil, and a red-wine sauce. A heavenly dessert is the apple, almond, and raisin tartlet flavored with amaretto and mascarpone.

7 Old Sq. © 01926/411755. Reservations recommended. Main courses £11–£16 ($22–$32); Mon–Fri 2-course fixed-price meal £16 ($32). MC, V. Mon–Sat 6:30–9:30pm.

Rose & Crown BRITISH   This former coaching inn has been modernized and turned into the best city dining pub in Warwick, with large leather sofas and low tables by an open fire. Order a Wells & Youngs Bombardier ale while you peruse the carefully chosen menu. Many locals start with the homemade soup of the day with crusty bread, though you may prefer a caramelized balsamic-and-red-onion tart with goat cheese. No starter is as tasty as the crab and lime fritters with a chili dressing. For mains, try the aged Aberdeenshire rump steak with peppercorn butter or the whole roasted sea bass with shrimp and vegetable Thai broth. An old-fashioned sherry trifle is offered for dessert.

30 Market Place. © 01926/411117. Reservations recommended at night. Main courses £8.75–£15 ($18–$30). MC, V. Daily noon–2:30pm and 6:30–10pm (until 9:30pm Sun).

SEEING THE SIGHTS

Lord Leycester Hospital   The great fire spared this group of half-timbered almshouses at the West Gate. The buildings were erected around 1400, and the hospital was founded in 1571 by Robert Dudley, earl of Leicester, as a home for old soldiers. It's still used by ex-service personnel and their spouses. On top of the West Gate is the attractive little chapel of St. James, dating from the 12th century but renovated many times since. Nathaniel Hawthorne wrote of his visits to the gardens in 1855 and 1857; the gardens were restored based on the observations he made in his writings. If you visit in the spring, you can see some 4,000 tulips in bloom.

High St. © 01926/491422. Admission £4.90 ($9.80) adults, £4.40 ($8.80) seniors, £3.90 ($7.80) children. Easter Sat to Oct Tues–Sun 10am–5pm; Nov–Easter Tues–Sun 10am–4pm.

St. John's House Museum   At Coten End, not far from the castle gates, this early-17th-century house has exhibits on Victorian domestic life. A schoolroom is furnished with original 19th-century furniture and equipment. During the school term, Warwickshire children dress in period costumes and learn Victorian-style lessons. Groups of children also use the Victorian parlor and the kitchen. Because it's impossible to display more than a small number of items at a time, a study room is available where you can see objects from the reserve collections. The costume collection is a particularly fine one, and visitors can study the drawings and photos that make up the costume catalog. These facilities are available for viewing by appointment only. Upstairs is a military museum, tracing the history of the Royal Warwickshire Regiment from 1674 to the present.

St. John's, at the crossroads of the main Warwick-Leamington Rd. (A425/A429) and the Coventry Rd. (A429). ℂ 01926/412132. Free admission. Tues–Sat and bank holidays 10am–5pm; May–Sept also Sun 2:30–5pm.

St. Mary's Church   Destroyed in part by the fire of 1694, this church, with rebuilt battlemented tower and nave, is among the finest examples of late-17th- and early-18th-century architecture. The Beauchamp Chapel, spared from the flames, encases the Purbeck marble tomb of Richard Beauchamp, a well-known earl of Warwick who died in 1439 and is commemorated by a gilded bronze effigy. Even more powerful than King Henry V, Beauchamp has a tomb that's one of the finest remaining examples of the Perpendicular Gothic style from the mid–15th century. The tomb of Robert Dudley, earl of Leicester, a favorite of Elizabeth I, is against the north wall. The Perpendicular Gothic choir dates from the 14th century; the Norman crypt and chapter house are from the 11th century.

21 Church St. ℂ 01926/403940. www.saintmaryschurch.co.uk. Free admission; donations accepted. Apr–Oct daily 10am–6pm; Nov–Mar daily 10am–4:30pm. All buses to Warwick stop at Old Sq., 2 blocks from the church.

Warwick Castle 🟢🟢🟢   Perched on a rocky cliff above the River Avon in the town center, a stately late-17th-century mansion is surrounded by a magnificent 14th-century fortress, the finest medieval castle in England. Even 3 hours may not be enough time to see everything. Surrounded by gardens, lawns, and woodland, where peacocks roam freely, and skirted by the Avon, Warwick Castle was described by Sir Walter Scott in 1828 as "that fairest monument of ancient and chivalrous splendor which yet remains uninjured by time."

Ethelfleda, daughter of Alfred the Great, built the first significant fortifications here in 914. William the Conqueror ordered the construction of a motte-and-bailey castle in 1068, 2 years after the Norman Conquest. The mound is all that remains today of the Norman castle, which Simon de Montfort sacked in the Barons' War of 1264.

The Beauchamp family, the most illustrious medieval earls of Warwick, is responsible for the appearance of the castle today; much of the external structure remains unchanged from the mid–14th century. When the castle was granted to Sir Fulke Greville by James I in 1604, he spent £20,000 (an enormous sum in those days) converting the existing castle buildings into a luxurious mansion. The Grevilles have held the earl of Warwick title since 1759.

The staterooms and Great Hall house fine collections of paintings, furniture, arms, and armor. The armory, dungeon, torture chamber, ghost tower, clock tower, and Guy's tower create a vivid picture of the castle's turbulent past and its important role in the history of England.

The private apartments of Lord Brooke and his family, who in recent years sold the castle to Tussaud's Group, are open to visitors. They house a display of a carefully reconstructed Royal Weekend House Party of 1898. The major rooms contain wax portraits of important figures of the time, including a young Winston Churchill. In the Kenilworth bedroom, a likeness of the Prince of Wales, later King Edward VII, reads a letter. The duchess of Marlborough prepares for her bath in the red bedroom. Among the most lifelike of the figures is a uniformed maid bending over to test the temperature of the water running into a bathtub.

You can also see the Victorian rose garden, a re-creation of an original design from 1868 by Robert Marnock. Near the rose garden is a Victorian alpine rockery and water garden.

Warwick Castle. ℭ **0870/442-2000.** www.warwick-castle.co.uk. Admission £14–£19 ($28–$38) adults, £10–£17 ($20–$34) students and seniors, £9–£12 ($18–$24) children 4–16, £40–£56 ($80–$112) family ticket, free for children 3 and younger. Apr–Sept daily 10am–6pm; Oct–Mar daily 10am–5pm. Closed Dec 25.

3 Kenilworth Castle ★★

164km (102 miles) NW of London; 8km (5 miles) N of Warwick; 21km (13 miles) N of Stratford-upon-Avon

The big attraction in the village of Kenilworth, an otherwise dull English market town, is Kenilworth Castle—and it's reason enough to stop here.

ESSENTIALS
GETTING THERE   InterCity train lines make frequent and fast connections from London's Paddington and Euston stations to either Coventry or Stratford-upon-Avon. For information, call ℭ **0845/748-4950** or go to **www.nationalrail.co.uk.** Midland Red Line buses make regular connections from both towns to Kenilworth.

If you're driving from Warwick, take the A46 toward Coventry.

VISITOR INFORMATION   The **Tourist Information Centre** is in the village at the Kenilworth Library, 11 Smalley Place (ℭ **01926/748900**). It's open Monday and Thursday 9:30am to 7pm; Tuesday and Friday 9am to 5:30pm; Wednesday 10:30am to 5:30pm; and Saturday 9am to 4pm. On the Web, a valuable resource is **www. kenilworthweb.com**.

WHERE TO STAY
Clarendon House Hotel   Located in the old part of Kenilworth, the oak tree around which the original alehouse was built in 1430 still supports the roof of the building today. The bedrooms vary greatly in size, but each is tastefully decorated with a comfortable bed—usually a double or twins, though there are two four-posters.

6–8 Old High St., Kenilworth, Warwickshire CV8 1LZ. ℭ **01926/857668.** Fax 01926/850669. www.clarendonhouse-hotel.com. 20 units. £60–£81 ($120–$162) double; £125 ($250) family suite. Rates include English breakfast. AE, DC, MC, V. Free parking. **Amenities:** Restaurant; bar. *In room:* TV, beverage maker, hair dryer, iron.

WHERE TO DINE
Restaurant Bosquet ✦ FRENCH   This narrow, stone-fronted town house from the late Victorian age is a culinary oasis. It's owned and operated by French-born Bernard Lignier, who does the cooking, and his English wife, Jane, who supervises the dining room. The à la carte menu changes every 2 months and might include such well-crafted dishes as boneless roast squab stuffed with mushrooms or wild venison served on a purée of parsnips with a game sauce. The best starter is foie gras served with a sweet-wine-and-grape sauce.

97A Warwick Rd. ℂ **01926/852463.** Reservations recommended. Main courses £20 ($40); 3-course lunch or dinner £31 ($62). AE, MC, V. Tues–Fri noon–2pm; Tues–Sat 7–9:30pm. Closed 1 week for Christmas and last 3 weeks in Aug.

THE MAGNIFICENT RUINS OF KENILWORTH CASTLE ⭐⭐

Kenilworth Castle (ℂ **01926/852078;** www.english-heritage.org.uk) was built by Geoffrey de Clinton, a lieutenant of Henry I. At one time, its walls enclosed an area of 4.3 hectares (7 acres), but it is now in magnificent ruins. Caesar's Tower, with its 5m-thick (16-ft.) walls, is all that remains of the original structure.

Edward II was forced to abdicate at Kenilworth in 1327 before being carried off to Berkeley Castle in Gloucestershire, where he was undoubtedly murdered. In 1563, Elizabeth I gave the castle to her favorite, Robert Dudley, earl of Leicester. He built the gatehouse, which the queen visited on several occasions. After the civil war, the Roundheads were responsible for breaching the outer walls and towers and blowing up the north wall of the keep. This was the only damage inflicted following the earl of Monmouth's plea that it be "[s]lighted with as little spoil to the dwelling house as might be."

The castle is the subject of Sir Walter Scott's romance, *Kenilworth.* In 1957, Lord Kenilworth presented the decaying castle to England and limited restoration has since been carried out. The castle is open March to August daily 10am to 6pm, September and October daily 10am to 5pm, and November to February daily 10am to 4pm; it's closed January 1 and December 24 to December 26. Admission is £6 ($12) adults, £4.50 ($9) seniors, £3 ($6) children 5 to 16, and free for children 4 and younger; a family ticket costs £15 ($30).

4 Coventry ⭐

161km (100 miles) NW of London; 32km (20 miles) NE of Stratford-upon-Avon; 29km (18 miles) SE of Birmingham; 84km (52 miles) SW of Nottingham

Coventry has long been noted in legend as the ancient market town through which Lady Godiva took her famous ride in the buff. A real Lady Godiva actually existed in the 11th century and was the wife of Leofric, earl of Mercia, one of England's most powerful noblemen. She was a benefactor to the poor and urged her husband to reduce their tax burden, which he agreed to do at a price. He made her a bet. If she'd ride naked through Coventry market at midday, he would in return abolish all local taxes save those on horses. On the appointed day, she rode naked through the market, unashamed of her nudity, and the taxes were duly removed. As such, she rode into legend, and that's the naked truth. The myth goes that a Coventry tailor was struck blind after looking at Lady Godiva, giving rise to the term "Peeping Tom."

Coventry today is a Midlands industrial city. The city was partially destroyed by German bombers during World War II, but the restoration is miraculous.

ESSENTIALS

GETTING THERE   Trains run every half-hour from London's Euston Station to Coventry (trip time: 1¼ hr.). For schedules and information, call ℂ **0845/748-4950,** or go to **www.nationalrail.co.uk**.

From London's Victoria Coach Station, 12 buses run daily between 6am and 1am for the 2¼-hour trip, costing £15 ($30). From Stratford-upon-Avon, four **National Express** buses, with a trip time of 1 hour, travel to Pool Meadow bus station, at Fairfax Street in Coventry. A single-day round-trip ticket costs £3.50 ($7). For schedules and information, call ℂ **0870/580-8080,** or visit **www.nationalexpress.com**.

VISITOR INFORMATION   The **Coventry Tourist Office,** 4 Priory Row (© 024/
7622-7264), is open from Easter to mid-October Monday to Friday 10am to 5pm,
Saturday 10am to 4:30pm, and Sunday 10am to 12:30pm and 1:30 to 4:30pm; mid-
October to Easter, hours are Monday to Friday 9:30am to 4:30pm, Saturday 10am to
4:30pm, and Sunday 10am to 12:30pm and 1:30 to 4:30pm. On the Web, **www.visit
coventry.co.uk** is a valuable resource.

TOURING COVENTRY CATHEDRAL ✿✿✿

Consecrated in 1962, Sir Basil Spence's controversial **Coventry Cathedral,** 7 Priory
Row (© 024/7652-1200; www.coventrycathedral.org.uk), is the city's main attraction. The cathedral is on the same site as the 14th-century Perpendicular building, and
you can visit the original tower. Many locals maintain that the structure is more likely
to be appreciated by the foreign visitor because Brits are more attached to traditional
cathedral design. Some visitors consider the restored site one of the most poignant and
religiously evocative modern churches in the world.

Outside is Sir Jacob Epstein's bronze masterpiece, *St. Michael Slaying the Devil.*
Inside, the outstanding feature is the 21m-high (70-ft.) altar tapestry by Graham
Sutherland, said to be the largest in the world. The floor-to-ceiling abstract stained-
glass windows are the work of the Royal College of Art. The West Screen (an entire
wall of stained glass installed during the 1950s) depicts rows of stylized saints and
prophets with angels flying among them.

In the undercroft of the cathedral is a visitor center, the Walkway of Holograms,
whose otherwise plain walls are accented with three-dimensional images of the Stations of the Cross, created with reflective light. One of the most evocative objects here
is a charred cross wired together by local workmen from burning timbers that crashed
to the cathedral's floor during the Nazi bombing. An audiovisual exhibit on the city
and church includes the fact that 450 aircraft dropped 40,000 firebombs on the city
in 1 day.

The cathedral is open daily from 9am to 5pm; the tower is open during summer
months when staff availability permits. A donation of £3.50 ($7) per person is sug-
gested for adults for entrance to the cathedral; tower admission is £2.50 ($5) adults,
£1 ($2) children 5 to 15.

5 Birmingham ✦

193km (120 miles) NW of London; 40km (25 miles) N of Stratford-upon-Avon

England's second-largest city may lay claim fairly to the title "Birthplace of the Industrial Revolution." It was here that James Watt first used the steam engine with success
to mine the Black Country. Watt and other famous 18th-century members of the
Lunar Society regularly met under a full moon in the nearby Soho mansion of manufacturer Matthew Boulton. Together, Watt, Boulton, and other "lunatics," as Joseph
Priestly, Charles Darwin, and Josiah Wedgwood cheerfully called themselves,
launched the revolution that thrust England and the world into the modern era.

Today, this brawny, unpretentious metropolis still bears some of the scars of industrial excess and the devastation of the Nazi Luftwaffe bombing during World War II.
But an energetic building boom has occurred recently, and Brummies have nurtured
the city's modern rebirth by fashioning Birmingham into a convention city that hosts
80% of all trade exhibitions in the country.

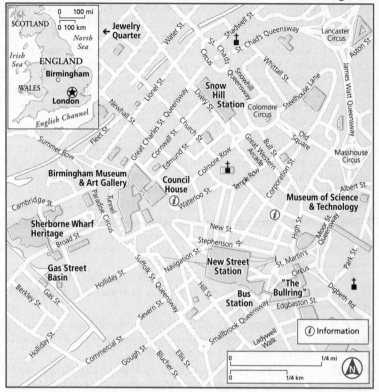

Birmingham has worked diligently in recent decades to overcome the blight of overindustrialization and poor urban planning. New areas of green space and the city's cultivation of a first-rate symphony and ballet company, as well as art galleries and museums, have all made Birmingham more appealing.

Though not an obvious tourist highlight, Birmingham serves as a gateway to England's north. With more than one million inhabitants, Birmingham has a vibrant nightlife and restaurant scene. Its three universities, 2,428 hectares (6,000 acres) of parks and nearby pastoral sanctuaries, and restored canal walkways also offer welcome quiet places.

ESSENTIALS
GETTING THERE

BY PLANE Three major international carriers fly transatlantic flights directly to **Birmingham International Airport (BHX)** from four North American gateways. Newark Airport is the only U.S. airport that offers flights directly to Birmingham, with **Continental Airlines** (© 800/5233273; www.continental.com) making the flight every evening (twice a day May–Sept).

In Canada, **Air Transat** (© 866/847-1112; www.airtransat.ca) departs from Toronto-Pearson every Friday, March to September, for direct flights to Birmingham. **Air India** (© 800/223-7776 in the U.S., or 800/625-6424 in Canada; www.airindia.com) also flies from Toronto-Pearson to Birmingham every Monday, Wednesday, Friday, Saturday, and Sunday. On Wednesdays, **Flyglobespan** (© **800/663-8614;** www.flyglobespan. com) leaves Toronto-Hamilton for Birmingham.

Direct air service between Birmingham and London is almost nonexistent. Many air carriers, however, maintain a virtual air-shuttle service between London airports and nearby Manchester, which is a 1½-hour trip to Birmingham via ground transport. For example, British Airways (BA) operates 12 daily flights from London's Heathrow to Manchester and seven daily flights from London's Gatwick. BA runs about the same number of return flights daily from Manchester to London.

Birmingham's airport lies about 13km (8 miles) southeast of the Birmingham City Centre and is easily accessible by public transportation. **AirRail Link** offers a free shuttle bus service every 10 minutes from the airport to the Birmingham International Rail Station and National Exhibition Centre (NEC). **InterCity** train services operate a shuttle from the airport to New Street Station in the City Centre, just a 15-minute trip.

BY TRAIN InterCity offers half-hourly train service (Mon–Fri) between London's Euston Station and Birmingham, a 90-minute rail trip. Regular train service is also available from London's Euston Station. Trains depart every 2 hours for Birmingham. Birmingham's New Street Station in the City Centre and the airport's International Station link the city to the national rail network.

Trains leave Manchester's Piccadilly Station nearly every hour for Birmingham. The trip takes 90 minutes. Call © **0845/748-4950,** or go to **www.nationalrail.co.uk** for train schedules and current fares.

BY BUS **National Express** (© **0870/580-8080;** www.nationalexpress.com) provides regular bus service, as frequent as every half-hour, between Birmingham and London (2¾-hr. trip), Manchester, and regional towns.

BY CAR From London, the best route is via the M40, which leads onto the M42, the motorway that circles south and east of Birmingham. Once on the M42, any of the roads from junctions 4 to 6 will lead into the center of Birmingham.

The drive takes about 2 to 2½ hours from London, depending on traffic conditions. Parking is available at locations throughout Birmingham.

VISITOR INFORMATION The **Birmingham Convention & Visitor Bureau (BCVB),** 150 New St., in the City Centre (© **0870/2250127;** www.beinbirmingham. com), is open Monday to Saturday 9:30am to 5:30pm, Sunday 10:30am to 4:30pm. The BCVB assists travelers in arranging accommodations, obtaining theater or concert tickets, and planning travel itineraries.

GETTING AROUND Birmingham's City Centre hosts a number of attractions within easy walking distance. **Centro** (© **0121/200-2700;** www.centro.org.uk) provides information on all local bus and rail services within Birmingham and the West Midlands area. For bus use only, a **Day Saver Pass** costs £3.40 ($6.80) for one adult and is an economical way to use the Centro bus system. For the metro and buses, a weekly **Centro Card** costs from £16 to £22 ($32–$44) depending on what zones you travel. Exact change is required on one-way local bus and train trips. Taxis queue at various spots in the City Centre, rail stations, and the National Exhibition Centre. Travelers can also ring up a radio-cab operator such as **TOA Taxis** at (© **0121/4278888**).

WHERE TO STAY
EXPENSIVE

Jonathans' Hotel and Restaurant 🐸 *Finds*   Filled with Victorian antiques, this hotel takes you back to the 1880s. The location is within a classic 19th-century country-house hotel, 8km (5 miles) from New Street Station in the center of Birmingham. The bedrooms, all suites, are spacious and furnished with antiques and quaint Victoriana; some rooms have four-poster beds, and some have fireplaces. On-site is a Victorian restaurant serving traditional British food and an Indian restaurant offering tantalizing Indian fusion dishes.

16–26 Wolverhampton Rd., Oldbury, Birmingham B68 0HL (at the crossroads of A456 and A4123, just off exit 2 or 3 on the M5). © 0121/429-3757. Fax 01214/343-107. www.jonathans.co.uk. 45 suites. £85–£125 ($170–$250) standard suite; £125–£140 ($250–$280) executive or luxury suite. AE, MC, V. Free parking. **Amenities:** 2 restaurants; bar; room service; laundry service; dry cleaning. *In room:* TV, beverage maker, hair dryer, iron, trouser press.

Malmaison 🐸🐸 *Finds*   This string of oh-so-chic hotels that stretches from London to Edinburgh has now invaded Birmingham, bringing a touch of class. The "fab" hotel occupies part of "the Mailbox," a converted 1960s Royal Mail Sorting Office with a panoramic canal-side setting. Bedrooms have the latest designs and are sleekly modern and invitingly comfortable—great beds, slinky lights, bathrooms with tub and power showers, and *luxe* toiletries along with CD players and libraries. You can relax in Le Petit Spa, called Birmingham's "sexiest," or else work out in Gymtonic.

1 Wharfside St., Birmingham B1 1RD. © 0121/246-5000. Fax 0121/246-5002. www.malmaison.com. 189 units. £160–£180 ($320–$360) double; £270–£495 ($540–$990) suite. AE, DC, MC, V. Parking £18 ($36). **Amenities:** Restaurant; bar; gym; spa; room service; laundry service; dry cleaning. *In room:* A/C, TV, high-speed Internet, CD player, CD library, minibar, beverage maker, hair dryer, iron.

New Hall 🐸🐸🐸   A 12th-century manor, reputedly the oldest in England, has been converted into a luxurious country-house hotel residing outside the city of Birmingham. The location is in a leafy suburb where a tree-lined drive leads to 10 hectares (26 acres) of gardens and this moated manor at a point 11km (7 miles) northeast of the center. This is one of the best places in England for a romantic escape. All the bedrooms are furnished sumptuously and luxuriously, with all the modern amenities. Most of the well-accessorized guest rooms are in a more contemporary addition. The public rooms are even more gracious, especially the 16th-century oak-paneled dining room where an award-winning chef serves an innovative Continental cuisine. The public rooms are lit by 18th-century chandeliers and a stone fireplace is from the 17th century.

Walmley Rd., Sutton Colffield, Birmingham B76 1QX. © 0121/378-2442. Fax 0121/378-4637. www.newhalluk. com. 60 units. £135–£170 ($270–$340) double; £201–£236 ($402–$472) suite. AE, DC, MC, V. Free parking. **Amenities:** Restaurant; bar; indoor heated pool; 9-hole golf course; tennis court; fitness center; spa; hot tub; sauna; room service; in-room massage. *In room:* TV, Wi-Fi, beverage maker, hair dryer, iron, safe (in some).

MODERATE

Apollo Hotel   A 5-minute drive from City Centre, this hotel offers comfortable modern rooms, a restaurant, an Internet kiosk, and a location convenient to the convention centers and the countryside. Rooms are often a bit cramped, but all are equipped with twin or double beds. Bathrooms are small but tidily organized, but make sure to ask whether yours has a shower or tub, as the rooms vary. Double-glazed windows cut down noise. The suites are a good value here, as they incorporate a minibar, private kitchen, and their own dining and lounge facilities.

Hagley Rd., Edgbaston, Birmingham B16 9RA. © 0121/455-0271. Fax 0121/456-2394. www.apollobirmingham.com. 126 units. Mon–Thurs £45–£85 ($90–$170); Fri–Sun £35–£55 ($70–$110) double. AE, DC, MC, V. Free parking. Take exit

3 from M5, or exit 6 from M6. **Amenities:** Restaurant; bar; room service; laundry service; dry cleaning. *In room:* TV, Wi-Fi, beverage maker, hair dryer, trouser press.

Awentsbury Hotel University and Pebble Mill Studio visitors will find this lodging—installed in a restored 1882 house—convenient and comfortable. The place is kept spick-and-span, and the rooms, while not stylish, are acceptable in every other way. Two of the units are large enough for families. Eleven units have small bathrooms with a shower stall; otherwise, there are enough corridor bathrooms so you'll rarely have to wait.

21 Serpentine Rd., Selly Park, Birmingham B29 7HU. ©/fax **0121/472-1258.** www.awentsbury.com. 16 units. £56 ($112) double without bathroom; £64 ($128) with bathroom; £72 ($144) family room. Rates include English breakfast. AE, DC, MC, V. Free parking. Take A38 from City Centre for about 3km (2 miles), turn left at Bournebrook Rd., then take the 1st right onto Serpentine Rd. *In room:* TV, beverage maker.

City Inn ★ (Value A favorite of the business traveler, this is a vast hotel with a large atrium with bright rugs and blond-wood furnishings. In the heart of Brindley Place, it offers modern design. Bedrooms are midsize and a bit peas-in-the-pod, but well kept, stylish, and comfortable. An on-site restaurant is one of the best in the city for hotel dining.

1 Brunswick Sq., Brindley Place, Birmingham B1 2HW. © **0121/643-1003.** Fax 0121/643-1005. www.cityinn.com. 238 units. £84–£180 ($168–$360) double. AE, DC, MC, V. Parking £11 ($22). **Amenities:** Restaurant; bar; gym; room service. *In room:* A/C, TV/DVD, DVD library, high-speed Internet, CD player, beverage maker, hair dryer, iron, trouser press.

Copperfield House Hotel This red-brick Victorian Gothic house rests on a steep slope on a residential street. Rooms are midsize for the most part, nos. 3, 4, and 10 being the most desirable, thanks to garden views and large, well-outfitted bathrooms. Each unit is well maintained and comfortably furnished.

60 Upland Rd., Selly Park, Birmingham B29 7JS. © **0121/472-8344.** Fax 0121/415-5655. www.copperfieldhousehotel. fsnet.co.uk. 17 units. £70–£90 ($140–$180) double; £85–£105 ($170–$210) family room. Rates include English breakfast. AE, MC, V. Free parking. The hotel is reached via the M5, Junction 4 to the A38 and the City Centre. Turn left at Priory Rd., then right at the 1st light on A441 and right again at Upland Rd. **Amenities:** Restaurant. *In room:* A/C, TV, beverage maker, hair dryer.

Novotel Birmingham Centre In the city center, this is a well-run chain hotel that offers good, comfortable rooms that have a bit of style. It's a handy choice because many of Birmingham's hotels are booked all week. Bedrooms, midsize for the most part, are in the motel style. The on-site brasserie serves affordable food made with fresh ingredients, and the Canal Boat Bar is a popular rendezvous. All in all, especially considering the moderate prices, this isn't a bad choice.

70 Broad St., Birmingham B1 2HT. © **0121/643-2000.** Fax 0121/643-9786. www.novotel.com. 148 units. £69–£165 ($138–$330) double. Children stay free in parent's room. AE, MC, V. Free parking. **Amenities:** Restaurant; bar; gym; Jacuzzi; sauna; room service; laundry service; dry cleaning. *In room:* A/C, TV, Wi-Fi, minibar, beverage maker, hair dryer, iron, safe.

INEXPENSIVE

Elmdon Lodge (Value One of the most comfortable—and affordable—guesthouses lies in south Birmingham in the suburb of Acocks Green, which is linked by public transportation to the center of the city. The guesthouse lies only a 5-minute walk from the Acocks Green rail station. A welcoming, family-run hotel, Elmdon is filled with bedrooms that are comfortably furnished in a homelike style. Rooms come in various sizes and configurations, from single to family rooms and triples, each with a small private bathroom with shower. Guests meet fellow guests in the breakfast lounge. The hotel stands in a landscaped garden, which also has a private car park.

20–24 Elmdon Rd., Acocks Green, Birmingham B27 6LH. © 0121/7066968. Fax 0121/6285566. www.elmdon lodge.co.uk. 18 units. £55–£70 ($110–$140) double; £70–£80 ($140–$160) family; £75 ($150) triple. Rates include English breakfast. AE, MC, V. Free parking. **Amenities:** Breakfast lounge. *In room:* TV, Wi-Fi (in some), beverage maker.

Premier Inn Birmingham Central East Lying between the M6 motorway and the City Centre, this is a modern, well-kept, and well-run lodge. It is a chain hotel and offers substantially comfortable though rather standard bedrooms. For the motorist just passing through Birmingham or spending only a night, it might be ideal. The hotel also has an affordable on-site restaurant so you don't have to drive into the center of Birmingham at night.

Richard St., Waterlinks, Birmingham B7 4AA. © 0870/2383312. Fax 0121/333-6490. www.premierinn.com. 60 units. £58–£62 ($116–$124) double. AE, MC, V. Free parking. **Amenities:** Restaurant; bar. *In room:* A/C, TV, beverage maker, hair dryer.

WHERE TO DINE

Bank 𝄞 *Kids* FRENCH/BRITISH You are likely to enjoy your finest meal at this relatively new restaurant, which is winning friends among the more discriminating palates of Birmingham. Affiliated with its even more famous sibling in London, chefs work feverishly in the open-plan kitchen. Start perhaps with seared scallops with asparagus or a confit of duck leg with a sesame-and-honey dressing. For a main dish, you can sample such superb choices as ricotta gnocchi with roasted eggplant, zucchini, and Parma ham, or the roast marinated duck breast with potato Rösti and blueberry jus. Desserts include a classic English bread-and-butter pudding or a passion-fruit mousse. Bank features the best children's menu in town.

4 Brindley Place. © 0845/658-7878. Reservations recommended. Main courses £12–£18 ($24–$36); fixed-price 2-course meal £13 ($26), 3 courses £15 ($30); children's menu £5.95 ($12). AE, DC, MC, V. Mon–Fri 7:30–10:30am and noon–3pm; Mon–Thurs 5:30–11pm; Fri–Sat 5:30–11:30pm; Sat 11:30am–3pm; Sun 11:30am–3:30pm and 5–10pm.

Chung Ying CHINESE More than 400 flavor-filled items are on this predominantly Cantonese menu (40 dim sum items alone). Samples include pan-cooked Shanghai dumplings, stuffed crispy duck packed with crabmeat, steamed eel in bean sauce, and a variety of tasty casseroles. Specialties include deep-fried stuffed crab claws or steamed beef dumplings. A delight is the steamed whole sea bass with ginger and spring onion. To go really authentic and sample some of the dishes the local Chinese community likes, try fried frogs' legs with bitter melon, steamed pork pie with dried or fresh squid, or fish cakes.

Chung Ying Garden, another restaurant owned by the same proprietor, is at 17 Thorpe St. (© **0121/666-6622**).

16–18 Wrottesley St., City Centre. © 0121/622-5669. Main courses £7–£15 ($14–$30). AE, DC, MC, V. Daily noon–11:30pm.

Le Petit Blanc 𝄞 MODERN FRENCH Gallic owner Raymond Blanc made his fame with Le Manoir aux Quat' Saisons outside Oxford. Since that time his empire has expanded, now taking in the city of Birmingham. In his latest outpost, he brings not haute cuisine but a brasserie-style regional French menu to Birmingham, and does so exceedingly well. It's one of your best bets for dining in the city. The setting is sophisticated and modern, with polished metal, lots of plate glass, and blond woods. You get not only an excellent cuisine, but fine service and good value for the money.

The cookery is competent, the presentation a strong point, and the ingredients first-rate. Dip into such delights as chicken stuffed with flap mushrooms and served with a wild-mushroom risotto, or else sample calves' liver with smoked bacon, or perhaps fish cakes made with salmon and crab. The most tantalizing appetizers include Burgundian snails in garlic butter or steamed Loch Fyne mussels with a creamy white-wine sauce.

9 Brindley Place ⓒ 0121/633-7333. www.lepetitblanc.co.uk. Reservations highly recommended. Main courses £8.50–£22 ($17–$44). AE, MC, V. Mon–Fri noon–2:45pm and 5:30–10:30pm; Sat noon–11pm; Sun noon–10pm.

Maharaja INDIAN   Set a few doors down from the Birmingham Hippodrome, this rather good restaurant specializes in Mughlai and north Indian dishes. Dining is on two floors, with framed fragments of Indian printed cloth on the walls. The menu features such dishes as lamb *dhansak* (cubes of lamb in thick lentil sauce), chicken *patalia* (chicken cooked in spices, herbs, and fruit), and prawn Madras. The most popular dish is tandoori fish marinated in yogurt, garlic, and spices. They also serve chili Madras with tomatoes, almonds, and lemon. The kitchen's balanced use of spices, herbs, and other flavorings lends most dishes an aromatic but delicate taste.

23 Hurst St., near the Hippodrome. ⓒ 0121/622-2641. Main courses £8–£14 ($16–$28). AE, DC, MC, V. Mon–Sat noon–2pm and 6–11pm.

Shimla Pinks ⭑⭑ SOUTH ASIAN   In India this restaurant's name refers to "bright young things," but in Birmingham it stands for the finest Indian cuisine in this part of England. A carefully selected menu featuring mostly Indian and Sri Lankan dishes is served by a very courteous staff in this relaxed, elegant restaurant. Main dish specialties include lamb Karahi (braised in spicy masala of garlic with ginger, onions, and tomatoes). Chicken tikka masala comes in a smooth and creamy sauce, and lamb roganjosh is a rich, spicy dish. Another favorite is king prawns in a tomato-and-onion masala. The restaurant also functions as a dance club. Special buffets complement the main menu, ranging from the two-course gourmet banquet at £25 ($50) to the four-course royal banquet at £50 ($100). Parking is available on Tennent Street behind the restaurant.

214 Broad St., City Centre. ⓒ 0121/633-0366. Main courses £8–£12 ($16–$24). AE, MC, V. Mon–Fri 11am–3pm and 6–11pm; Sat–Sun 6–11:30pm.

EXPLORING BIRMINGHAM

Stephenson Place, at the intersection of New and Corporation streets, is a good starting point for sampling the attractions of City Centre. A 5-minute stroll along New Street leads to Victoria Square, where **Council House,** Victoria Square (ⓒ **0121/ 303-2040**), the city's most impressive Victorian building, anchors the piazza. Built in 1879, it is still the meeting place for the Birmingham City Council and an impressive example of the Italian Renaissance style. It's open for viewing Monday through Thursday from 9am to 5pm and on Friday from 9am to 4pm. The chamber can only be seen by guided tour, which must be arranged in advance.

Along Broad Street is the **Gas Street Basin** (ⓒ 0121/236-9811). Operated by Second City Canal Cruises, it forms the hub of the 3,220km (2,000-mile) canal network that runs in all directions from Birmingham to Liverpool, London, Nottingham, and Gloucester. From the Basin, you can take a cruise along the canals or just walk by the towpaths.

Just a 10-minute walk from City Centre is the **Jewelry Quarter** at 75–79 Vyse St. (ⓒ **0121/554-3598**). This complex includes more than 100 jewelry shops. The skill

---

Moments **"Bucket Dining" Kashmiri-Style**

A growing phenomenon, which we can only call the **Birmingham Balti Experience,** may interest those who love spicy food. *Balti* literally means bucket, but it refers to a Kashmiri style of cooking over a fast, hot flame. With the city's large Kashmiri population, there are now many *baltihouses* in Birmingham, most of which are bare-bones, BYOB affairs. One of the better ones is **Celebrity Balti,** 44 Broad St. (© **0121/643-8969;** www.celebritybalti.co.uk), close to the Convention Centre, which is open daily from 6pm to midnight.

---

of the jeweler's craft can be viewed at the Discovery Centre's restored Smith and Pepper factory displays, or by visiting shop workbenches that still produce most of the jewelry made in Britain. A unique time capsule of the ancient craft of jewelry making and working with precious metals, the quarter offers bargain hunters the opportunity to arrange repairs, design a custom piece, or just browse. Admission to the **Museum of the Jewelry Quarter** is free; it's open April to October Tuesday to Sunday 11:30am to 4pm and November to March Tuesday to Saturday 11:30am to 4pm.

Barber Institute of Fine Arts 🏵🏵   Don't be put off by the stark, stone-and-brick building that houses the Barber Institute collection. Some critics consider it the finest small art museum in England and the equal of any museum outside London. The choice selection of paintings includes works by Bellini, Botticelli, Bruegel, Canaletto, Delacroix, Gainsborough, Gauguin, Guardi, Murillo, Renoir, Rubens, Turner, van Gogh, and Whistler.

University of Birmingham (just off Edgbaston Park Rd., near the University's East Gate, 4km/2½ miles south of City Centre). © **01214/147333.** www.barber.org.uk. Free admission. Mon–Sat 10am–5pm; Sun noon–5pm. Bus: 61, 62, or 63 from City Centre.

Birmingham Museum and Art Gallery 🏵   Known chiefly for its collection of pre-Raphaelite paintings (including works by Ford Maddox Brown, Dante Gabriel Rossetti, Edward Burne-Jones, and Holman Hunt), the gallery also houses exceptional paintings by English watercolor masters from the 18th century. There is also a museum section with an Egyptian mummy, plus tools and artifacts 400,000 years old. The BMAG is instantly recognized by its "Big Brum" clock tower.

Chamberlain Sq. © **0121/303-2834.** www.bmag.org.uk. Free admission; varying charges for special exhibitions. Mon–Thurs and Sat 10am–5pm; Fri 10:30am–5pm; Sun 12:30–5pm.

The Black Country Living Museum   Much of the area immediately surrounding Birmingham is called the Black Country (after the black smoke that billowed over the area during the iron-working era). That period is best preserved at the Black Country Living Museum in Dudley, a town about 16km (10 miles) northwest of Birmingham. The museum occupies a sprawling landscape in the South Staffordshire coal fields, an early forge of the Industrial Revolution, and re-creates what it was like to work and live in the Black Country of the 1850s. An electric tramway takes visitors to a thick underground coal seam, and trolleys move through a reconstructed industrial village with a schoolhouse, anchor forge, working replica of a 1712 steam engine, and trade shops.

Tipton Rd., Dudley (5km/3 miles north of Junction 2 exit on M5). © **0121/557-9643.** www.bclm.co.uk. Admission £12 ($24) adults, £9.75 ($20) seniors, £6.50 ($13) children, £33 ($66) family ticket. Mar–Oct daily 10am–5pm; Nov–Feb Wed–Sun 10am–4pm.

Blakesley Hall   Modern houses live outside its gates, but once inside the grounds of Blakesley Hall you are transported back in time some 400 years. Blakesley is a restored Tudor farmhouse from 1590. The half-timbered structure is typical of building once common in the West Midlands. Its original architectural features, including a herringbone floor, are still intact. The Great and Little Parlours on the ground floor have been restored. Oak furnishings include carved, panel-back armchairs, long refectory tables, and other period pieces. Many artifacts from the era are on display, including pewter goblets and candlesticks. In the painted bedchamber, paintings on the walls from 1590 were uncovered after having been hidden for centuries.

Blakesley Rd., Yardley. (0121/464-2193. www.bmag.org.uk. Free admission. Apr 1–Oct 28 Tues–Sun 11:30am–4pm.

Sherborne Wharf Heritage Narrowboats   One of the best ways to see Birmingham is by water, a series of artificial canals created as the "motorways" of their day during the Industrial Revolution of the 18th century. These waters, still in good shape after 2 centuries or more, cut across deep valleys on high aqueducts and embankments. Boats sailed on them carrying finished products or raw materials. Departures of sightseeing boats are from the International Convention Centre Quayside, taking you on 1-hour tours of Birmingham from the water. The city scenically passes in review before you.

Heritage Marina (near the junction of Macclesfield and Trent & Mersey Canals in Scholar Green). (0121/ 455-6163. www.shergornewharf.co.uk. Tickets £5.50 ($11) for adults, £4.50 ($9) seniors, and £4.25 ($8.50) children. Departures daily Easter–Oct at 11:30am, 1, 2:30, and 4pm (call off season, as tours are conducted on weekends at 1 and 2:30pm only if weather permits.)

Thinktbank at Millennium Point (Kids)   This museum and science attraction is both educational and fun, appealing to adults and kids alike. It examines the past, presents today's technology, and explores future breakthroughs that might occur scientifically. Science and history meet in 10 different galleries where you can have close encounters with the exhibits, which are spread across four floors. Children can do everything from grabbing a handful of polar bear blubber to taking control of a digger. Various sections deal with such subjects as "Medicine Matters," exploring surgical instruments and health in general. Nature is uncovered in the "Wild Life" section, as you learn how scientists study the wild world and how animals adapt to change. "Futures" gives you a look into a living tomorrow. An IMAX theater plays educational movies.

Curzon St. (0121/202-2222. www.thinktank.ac. Admission £7.75 ($16) adults; £5.75 ($12) seniors, students, and children 3–15. Daily 10am–5pm. Call for IMAX schedule.

SHOPPING

In addition to exploring the **Jewelry quarter** (see above), Birmingham is a great town for shopping. There are more than 700 retail stores, and many people in the Midlands come here just to shop, especially along **Cannon Street** and **New Street** with recently opened top-brand designer stores. The city's **Mailbox** complex at Wharfside Street ((0121/632-1000) was once used to sort the mail. But now it's become a gargantuan shopping center, with such department stores as Harvey Nichols moving in. Emporio Armani, DKNY, Hugo Boss, Jaeger, and Crabtree & Evelyn call the Mailbox home. It also houses 12 restaurants, a spa, salons, and the upscale Malmaison hotel. In the heart of town, the **Bullring** ((0121/632-1500), near St. Martin's Square, has been developed into Europe's largest city-center retail area, based around the historic street patterns of the city and linking New Street and High Street. It's more affordable and less classy than its cousin the Mailbox, with such U.S. mainstays as H&M, Gap, FCUK, and Footlocker.

The reinvention of "Brum" (as Britain's much-maligned second city is nicknamed) is reflected by the opening of a grand department store, **Selfridges,** Bullring Centre (© **0800/123400**). As a fashion emporium, its architecture was appropriately inspired by a dress. The curvaceous complex is adorned with 15,000 aluminum disks a la Paco Rabanne's 1960 chain-mail frocks.

BIRMINGHAM AFTER DARK
THE PERFORMING ARTS

Connected to the Convention Centre, **Symphony Hall,** at Broad Street (© **0121/ 780-3333;** www.symphonyhall.co.uk), has been hailed as an acoustical gem since its completion in 1990. Home to the **City of Birmingham Symphony Orchestra,** it also hosts special classical music events.

The **National Indoor Arena,** King Edward's Road (© **0870/730-0196;** www.nec group.co.uk), seats 13,000 and is a favorite site for jazz, pop, and rock concerts; sporting events; and conventions.

The **Birmingham Repertory Theatre** on Broad Street at Centenary Square (© **0121/ 236-4455;** www.birmingham-rep.co.uk), houses one of the top companies in England. Some of the world's greatest actors have performed with the repertory company over the years, including Lord Olivier, Albert Finney, Paul Scofield, Dame Edith Evans, and Kenneth Branagh. The widely known "Rep" comprises the **Main House,** which seats 800 theatergoers, and the **Door,** a more intimate 120-seat venue that often stages new and innovative works. The box office is open from Monday through Saturday 10am to 8pm on performance days, 10am to 6pm on nonperformance days. Tickets cost £10 to £25 ($20–$50).

Midlands Arts Centre (MAC) in Cannon Hill Park (© **0121/440-3838;** www. macarts.co.uk) is close to the Edgbaston Cricket Ground and reached by car or bus (no. 1, 45, or 47). The MAC houses three performance areas and stages a lively range of drama, dance, and musical performances, as well as films. The box office is open daily from 9am to 8:45pm.

The **Alexandra Theatre,** Station Street (© **0870/607-7533;** www.alexandratheatre. org.uk), hosts national touring companies, including productions from London's West End. The theater serves as a temporary home to many of England's touring companies. Contact the box office for show details.

Note: Tickets for all Birmingham theaters are available through Birmingham visitor offices.

The restored **Birmingham Hippodrome,** Hurst Street (© **0870/730-1234;** www. birminghamhippodrome.com), is home to the **Birmingham Royal Ballet** and visiting companies from around the world. It hosts a variety of events, from the Welsh National Opera to musicals to dance. The box office is open Monday to Saturday from 9:30am to 8:30pm.

CLUBS & PUBS

Boho Rooms, 52 Gas St., along the City Centre canal (© **0121/643-2572**), is a converted warehouse with a bar and two nightclubs. **Liberty's,** 184 Hagley Rd. (© **0121/ 454-4444**), is a large, fashionable club, complete with champagne bar, vodka bar, and other smaller bars; it's open Friday and Saturday nights.

Goose O.V.T., 561 Bristol Rd. (© **0121/472-3186**), one of the largest pubs in England, is popular with university students. One local fan says it's "good for dodgy music." Another laments that while it is "generally a good pub, there are vast numbers of wasted students."

Otherwise, Broad Street has become the center of nightlife in Birmingham. Just walk up and down the street and pick your favorites. We like **Revolution,** Broad Street (© **0121/665-6508**), a vodka bar drawing a hip collection of the younger-than-40 crowd.

Birmingham has a thriving gay and lesbian community, most of them seemingly packed at night into the **Nightingale** on Kent Street (© **0121/62266943**), nick-named "the Gale." With its five bars and two frenzied dance floors, it is the "Queer as Folk" choice. There's also a jazz lounge. The cover is £3 ($6), but this can vary. It's open Tuesday to Thursday 9pm to 2am, Friday 7pm to 4am, Saturday 7pm to 6am, and Sunday 7pm to 2am.

6 Worcester ⟨★

200km (124 miles) NW of London; 42km (26 miles) SW of Birmingham; 98km (61 miles) N of Bristol

The River Severn flows through the heart of Worcester, a world-famous porcelain cen-ter. Most of the world today knows of the town for lending its name to the famous tangy sauce found in millions of households.

Between the two cathedral cities of Hereford and Worcester, the ridge of the Malverns rises from the Severn Plain. To sample the lush river scenery of the River Wye Valley, in which Worcester lies, you might want to head for the Malverns (see below), a more scenic and beautiful center than Worcester itself. Nonetheless, there is a bevy of sights in Worcester to occupy your time if you have some to spare. You can usually "do" the attractions of Worcester in a full morning or an afternoon. The bridge over the Severn offers the best view of the 900-year-old Worcester Cathedral, with its 60m-high (200-ft) tower.

ESSENTIALS

GETTING THERE   Regular trains depart London's Paddington or Euston Station for Worcester, arriving about 2¼ hours later. For schedules and information, call © **0845/748-4950.**

Two **National Express** buses leave throughout the day from London's Victoria Coach Station and make the 4-hour journey to Worcester. For schedules and informa-tion, call © **0870/580-8080** (www.nationalexpress.com).

Driving from London, take the M5 to Junction 7 toward Worcester. Give yourself about 3 hours. From Hereford, it's a short drive to Worcester. Just take the A449 42km (26 miles) west.

VISITOR INFORMATION   The **Worcester Tourist Information Centre,** in the Guildhall on High Street (© **01905/726311;** www.visitworcester.com), is open from 9:30am to 5pm Monday to Saturday.

WHERE TO STAY

Diglis House Hotel ⟨★   This is the town's best choice. Set within gardens at the edge of the Severn River, this mansion was built in the 1700s as a guesthouse for visitors to the nearby cathedral. Later, it was the family home of the noted landscape architect Benjamin Williams Leader, whose paintings of bucolic England have graced many English Christmas cards. The building's interior was upgraded to country-house hotel standards. Bedrooms, though small, are arranged cozily and comfortably, each fitted with twin or double beds.

Severn St., Worcester WR1 2NF. ℂ **01905/353518.** Fax 01905/767772. www.diglishousehotel.co.uk. 30 units. £90–£120 ($180–$240) double; £110–£160 ($220–$320) junior suite. Rates include English breakfast. AE, DC, MC, V. Free parking. **Amenities:** Restaurant; bar; room service; laundry service; dry cleaning. *In room:* TV, beverage maker, hair dryer.

The Elms Hotel 🌟 *Kids*   This is one of the most impressive hotels in the region, built in 1710 by Gilbert White, a disciple of Sir Christopher Wren. It is chic, fun, sophisticated, and international, and lies on the outskirts of Worcester. Surrounded by 4 hectares (10 acres) of field, park, and forest, it offers what some visitors consider a fantasy version of the best of England, complete with mahogany or walnut 18th- and 19th-century antiques, an intriguing collection of clocks and oil paintings, and log-burning fireplaces. The frequently redecorated bedrooms come in various shapes and sizes, and feature twin or double beds. The Elms welcomes families more than any other hotel in the area. If you notify the staff in advance, a member will round up all your baby needs in advance, from food to "nappies" (diapers to Americans).

On A443 (3km/2 miles west of Abberley, near Worcester), Worcester WR6 6AT. ℂ **01299/896666.** Fax 01299/896804. www.theelmshotel.com. 21 units. £150–£330 ($300–$660) double; £237–£360 ($474–$720) suite. Rates include half-board. AE, DC, MC, V. Free parking. Take A443 for 9.5km (6 miles) west of Worcester, following the signs to Tenbury Wells. **Amenities:** Restaurant; bar; spa; tennis court; croquet lawn; room service; babysitting; laundry service; dry cleaning. *In room:* TV, hair dryer.

Fownes Hotel   A 5-minute walk west of Worcester's cathedral, this hotel occupies the industrial-age premises of the Fownes Glove Factory (ca. 1892). A civic monument and source of income for many local residents until glove wearing went out of fashion, it was converted in the 1980s into Worcester's most interesting large hotel. Public rooms are attractively outfitted and are unified by a decorating theme that includes gilt-edged photographs of the hotel during its glove-making heyday. Bedrooms are cozy and furnished in a conservative English style that includes the wide or tall many-paned windows of the factory's original construction.

City Walls Rd., Worcester WR1 2AP. ℂ **01905/613151.** Fax 01905/23742. www.fownesgroup.co.uk. 61 units. £99–£145 ($198–$290) double; £135–£180 ($270–$360) suite. Rates include English breakfast. Children 14 and younger stay free in same room as 2 paying adults. AE, DC, MC, V. Free parking. **Amenities:** Restaurant; bar; room service; laundry service; dry cleaning. *In room:* TV, beverage maker, hair dryer, trouser press.

WHERE TO DINE

Across from the cathedral, the **Pub at Ye Old Talbot Hotel,** Friar Street (ℂ **01905/23573;** www.yeoldetalbot.tablesir.com), contains lots of Victorian nostalgia and old-fashioned wood paneling that has been darkened by generations of cigarette smoke and spilled beer. It offers predictable pub grub that's a bit better than expected, especially when it's accompanied with a pint of the house's half-dozen ales on tap. The restaurant on-site is called the Black Pear Bistro, where the decor is more modern than in the pub. Here you can order lamb's liver in a red-wine sauce or slow-cooked tender leg of duck on a bed of green lentils. Half a roast chicken is another favorite. It's served with seasonal vegetables and a tarragon mayonnaise.

One of Worcester's most whimsical restaurant pubs is the **Little Sauce Factory,** London Road (ℂ **01905/350159**). The entire place is a takeoff on Worcester's famous sauce, with posters advertising food flavorings, all the accessories of an old-fashioned kitchen, and an enormous ceiling map of Britain in ceramic tiles.

Benedictos ITALIAN   Set within 180m (600 ft.) of the cathedral in a half-timbered, 16th-century Elizabethan building, this restaurant has an ambience that's a lot more international and suave than the very English exterior suggests. The town's best antipasti selection features such delights as mussels sautéed in white wine, fresh toma-toes, and black olives, or a fresh daily homemade soup. Pastas are succulent, especially the homemade cannelloni filled with fresh spinach and ricotta, and the penne with salmon and a cream sauce. The chefs also have a winning way with oven-baked duck breast served in a rich orange and brandy sauce, or else filet of lemon sole with a light prawn sauce. Salmon is cooked in a white-wine sauce and served with creamy mussels and prawns.

34 Sidbury St. (℗ 01905/21444. Reservations recommended. Main courses £13–£18 ($26–$36). AE, MC, V. Mon–Sat noon–2pm and 6–10:30pm.

SEEING THE SIGHTS

One of the best ways to see Worcester is from the river aboard one of the 2-hour cruise trips offered by **Worcester River Cruises,** 37 The Tything (℗ **01905/611060**). A cream tea cruise costs £13 ($26). These cruises operate from 10am to midnight daily April to October.

If you're interested in shopping, you might want to take a stroll down **Friar Street,** taking in the eclectic collection of individual timber-framed and brick shops. **G. R. Pratley & Sons,** Shambles (℗ **01905/22678**), offers a smorgasbord of glass, china, and earthenware.

Bygones of Worcester, 3 College Precincts and Cathedral Square (℗ **01905/ 23132**), is actually two shops packed with an intriguing collection of antiques and odds and ends. Wander through this store to find furnishings for your home that range from the bizarre to the decorative and fanciful—all from cottages and castles in England.

The Commandery   Originally the 11th-century Hospital of St. Wulstan, the Com-mandery was transformed over the years into a sprawling 15th-century, medieval tim-ber-framed building that served as the country home of the Wylde family. This was the headquarters of King Charles II during the Battle of Worcester in 1651, the last battle in the English Civil War. The Great Hall has a hammer-beam roof and a min-strel's gallery. England's premier **Civil War Centre** is now situated here. This exciting, interactive, and hands-on museum marvelously incorporates life-size figures, sound systems, and videos to take you through the bloody and turbulent years of England's civil war. You can even try on helmets, handle weapons, and pick up cannon balls. The Commandery also has canal-side tearooms, a picnic area, and a Garden of Fragrance.

109 Sidbury St. (℗ 01905/361821. Admission £5.25 ($11) adults, £3.50 ($7) children and seniors. Mon–Sat 10am–5pm; Sun 1:30–5pm. The Commandery is a 3-min. walk from Worcester Cathedral.

Royal Worcester Porcelain Factory ⋆   This factory has been achieving its goal of creating "ware of a form so precise as to be easily distinguished from other English porcelain" since its founding in 1751. It produces a unique range of fine china and porcelain that remains unsurpassed throughout the world. Behind-the-scenes tours last about an hour and do not accept children 10 and younger, very elderly visitors, or persons with disabilities, because of safety regulations.

The **Retail and Seconds Shops** at the factory are open to all and offer a unique chance to buy the beauty of Royal Worcester at bargain prices. Many of the pieces are marked as seconds, but most of the time you won't be able to tell why. The **Worces-ter Porcelain Museum** is also located at the factory and houses the world's largest col-lection of Worcester Porcelain.

Severn St. ☏ **01905/746000**. www.worcesterporcelainmuseum.org.uk. Museum admission £5 ($10) adults; £4.25 ($8.50) seniors, students, and children. Factory tours available Mon–Fri at 11:30am, 1:30pm, and 2:30pm; cost is £5 ($10) adults, £4.25 ($8.50) seniors, students, and children. Call ahead to reserve. Ticket for tour and museum £9 ($18) adults; £8 ($16) seniors, students, and children. Museum Mar–Nov Mon–Sat 10am–5pm, Sun 11am–5pm; Dec–Feb Mon–Sat 10am–4pm, Sun 11am–5pm.

Sir Edward Elgar's Birthplace Museum   This charming and inviting redbrick country cottage, stable, and coach house is set on well-tended grounds. Elgar, one of England's greatest composers, was born in this early-19th-century house on June 2, 1857. Today, the cottage houses a unique collection of manuscripts and musical scores, photographs, and other personal memorabilia. Just yards from the cottage, a new visitor center introduces you to the man and his music, even showing film clips of the composer with his beloved dogs. Sir Elgar wrote, among other pieces, *The Enigma Variations* and the *Dream of Gerontius*.

Crown E. Lane, Lower Broadheath. ☏ **01905/333224**. www.elgarfoundation.org. Admission £5 ($10) adults, £4.50 ($9) seniors, £3 ($6) students, £2 ($4) children, £12 ($24) family ticket. Year-round daily 11am–5pm. Closed Dec 23–Jan 31. Drive out of Worcester on A44 toward Leominster. After 3km (2 miles), turn off to the right at the sign. The house is 1km (½ mile) on the right.

Worcester Cathedral ☏☏   Historically speaking, the most significant part of Worcester Cathedral is its crypt, a classic example of Norman architecture that dates from 1084. It contains the tombs of King John, whose claim to fame is the Magna Carta, and Prince Arthur, the elder brother of Henry VIII. Both tombs can be found near the high altar. The 12th-century chapter house is one of the finest in England and, along with the cloisters, evokes the cathedral's rich monastic past. The cathedral is also known for a distinguished history of fine choral music, and, rotating with the cathedrals of Gloucester and Hereford, hosts the oldest choral festival in Europe, the Three Choirs Festival.

College Yard at High St. ☏ **01905/28854**. www.cofe-worcester.org.uk/cathedral. Free admission; adults asked for a £3 ($6) donation. Daily 7:30am–6pm.

7 The Malverns

195km (127 miles) NW of London; 55km (34 miles) SW of Birmingham

Once part of the ancient and formidable kingdom of Mercia, the beautiful and historic Malvern Hills lie just west of Worcester, rising suddenly from the Severn Valley and stretching for 14km (9 miles). This tranquil area offers 13km (8 miles) of hiking trails. The towns are especially famous for their healing waters, refreshing air, and country vistas.

Six townships cling to the Malvern Hills, making this an outstanding place to strike out for easy day hikes while in Worcester or Hereford. You can wander through Great Malvern, Malvern Link, West Malvern, Weldon, Malvern Wells, Little Malvern, and several other hamlets in a day's stroll. Great Malvern is resplendent with Victorian grandeur, much of which was gained from its importance as a 19th-century spa resort. The town has the largest priory church in the area, dating from the 15th century and boasting some fine stained-glass windows, as well as a great Gothic tower. The monks' stalls have superb misericords and medieval titles. The greatest and most beloved singer of the 19th century—the wildly talented "Swedish Nightingale," Jenny Lind—as well as that century's greatest English composer, Sir Edward Elgar, called this area home.

The Malvern Hills provide a breathtaking backdrop for hiking and biking. You can take in immense views, eastward to the Cotswolds and westward to the Wye Valley and the Welsh mountains, while exploring the most beautiful countryside in England. The Malverns Tourist Information Centre (see below) can provide you with detailed maps and route descriptions.

Our favorite walk in the **Malvern Hills** ⚹⚹ begins directly to the south of Great Malvern. As you leave town, you can see the ruins of an Iron Age fort high on a ridge. If you head here, you'll enjoy a magnificent vista of the countryside, with the Black Mountains looming to the west. A hike along this ridge, starting at Chase End Hill, with a return trip, takes about 4½ hours. But you will have experienced some of the best scenery the Malverns have to offer. The trail is well maintained.

St. Wulstan's Church, 3km (2 miles) west of Great Malvern on the Ledbury Road, is where the composer Sir Edward Elgar is buried with his wife and daughter. You'll find a bronze bust of the composer in Priory Park, and he lived at Craeglea on the Malvern Wells Road and at Forli in Alexandra Road, where he composed the *Enigma Variations, Sea Pictures,* and the *Dreams of Gerontius.*

ESSENTIALS

GETTING THERE   From London, trains leave every 2 hours from Paddington Station via Worcester for the 2½-hour trip to Great Malvern. For schedules and information, call ℂ **0845/748-4950.**

Two **National Express** buses depart daily from Victoria Coach Station in London, arriving in Great Malvern 4 hours later. One bus stops at Birmingham, making the journey 5½ hours. Call ℂ **0870/580-8080,** or go to **www.nationalexpress.com** for more information.

If you're driving from London, take the M5 to the A4104 west, then the A449 north toward Great Malvern. Depending on traffic, the drive takes about 2 hours.

VISITOR INFORMATION   The **Malverns Tourist Information Centre,** 21 Church St., Malvern, Worcestershire WR14 2AA (ℂ **01684/892289;** www.malvernhills.gov.uk), is open daily from 10am to 5pm (Dec–Mar Sun 10am–4pm).

WHERE TO STAY

Best Western Foley Arms   Home to one of the town's most bustling pubs, this is the oldest hotel in Malvern, with a Georgian pedigree from 1810 when it welcomed the affluent and exhausted for curative sessions at the nearby spa. Princess Mary of Teck, the grandmother of Queen Elizabeth II, liked the hotel so much she left her coat of arms, which can be seen over the rotating doors leading into this Georgian coaching hotel. Close to the town center, it rises from a very steep hillside, which makes it inconvenient for mobility-impaired guests, but also gives it glorious views over the Severn River to the edge of the Cotswolds from many of its bedroom windows. Rooms contain old, usually antique, furniture and heavy draperies; they have all the modern conveniences but offer old-fashioned character.

14 Worcester Rd., Malvern, Worcestershire WR14 4QS. (ℂ **01684/573397.** Fax 01684/569665. www.foleyarmshotel. com. 28 units. £116–£142 ($232–$284) double. AE, DC, MC, V. **Amenities:** Restaurant; bar; access to nearby pool and gym; room service; babysitting; laundry service; dry cleaning. *In room:* TV, beverage maker, hair dryer, iron, trouser press.

The Cotford Hotel *(Kids)*   A 5-minute walk east of Malvern's town center, on an acre of lawns and rock gardens, this towering and stately home dates from 1851 when it was built as the local bishop's residence. Constructed of Cotswold stone and accented with lavish gingerbread, it retains a vaguely ecclesiastical air despite the modern-day furnishings. Views extend over the garden through elaborate windows carved from wood to resemble Gothic tracery. The main appeal of the place derives from its monumental historic premises, the warm welcome, and such Victorian touches as the tile-floored wide entrance hallway. The bedrooms, usually midsize, have been much improved in recent years, with excellent beds. Several rooms have been specifically set aside for families.

Graham Rd., Malvern, Worcestershire WR14 2HU. © 01684/572427. Fax 01684/572952. www.cotfordhotel.co.uk. 15 units. £95–£105 ($190–$210) double; £140 ($280) family room. Rates include full English breakfast. AE, DC, MC, V. Free parking. **Amenities:** Restaurant; bar; access to nearby pool and sauna; room service; laundry service; dry cleaning. *In room:* TV, high-speed Internet, beverage maker, hair dryer.

The Cottage in the Wood ✦ There is indeed a cottage in the woods associated with this hotel (it contains four cozy bedrooms and dates from the 17th c.). But most of the inn occupies a nearby Georgian house from the late 1700s. Originally built for the semi-retired mother of the lord of a neighboring estate, it's referred to as "the Dower House" and is appropriately outfitted in an attractive Laura Ashley style. The bedrooms are small, but this place is so charming and offers such panoramic views that most visitors don't mind. The place is exceedingly well furnished with thoughtfully equipped bedrooms. Rooms in the Pinnacles are the most modern, though the bedrooms are still decorated in the English-country-house style.

Holywell Rd., Malvern Wells, Great Malvern, Worcestershire WR14 4LG. © 01684/588860. Fax 01684/560662. www. cottageinthewood.co.uk. 31 units. £99–£189 ($198–$378) double. Rates include full English breakfast. AE, MC, V. Free parking. After leaving Great Malvern on A449, turn right just before the B4209 turnoff on the opposite side of the road. The inn is on the right. **Amenities:** Restaurant (see review below); bar; room service; babysitting. *In room:* TV, beverage maker, hair dryer.

WHERE TO DINE

The Cottage in the Wood MODERN BRITISH An 18th-century, Georgian-style dower's house, on a steeply sloping, wooded plot of land with panoramic views over the Herefordshire countryside, the site manages to be elegant, cozy, and nurturing at the same time, thanks to the hard work and charm of resident owners John and Sue Pattin. With the help of their son, chef Dominic Pattin, they offer modern adaptations of traditional British favorites. Offered are such imaginative appetizers as roast quail with apricot chutney. Among the more tempting mains are Herefordshire beef filet served with a pearl barley risotto or braised pork belly with glazed apples. The best desserts are always the homemade ice creams. *Note:* The accommodations on the property are reviewed above.

Holywell Rd., Malvern Wells. © 01684/575859. Reservations recommended. Main courses £11–£23 ($22–$46); fixed-price Sun lunch £22 ($44). AE, MC, V. Daily 12:30–2pm; Mon–Sat 7–9:30pm; Sun 7–9pm.

8 Hereford ✦

214km (133 miles) NW of London; 82km (51 miles) SW of Birmingham

Situated on the Wye River, the city of Hereford is a bustling market town today, known as the center of a great cattle industry. Its white-faced Hereford breed has spread to nearly every continent.

Hereford was the birthplace of both David Garrick—the actor, producer, and dramatist who breathed life back into London theater in the mid–18th century—and Nell Gwynne, an actress who was the mistress of Charles II. Dating from 1080, the red sandstone Hereford Cathedral (see below) contains an eclectic mix of architectural styles from Norman to Perpendicular.

Surrounded by pristine countryside, including orchards and lush pasturelands, Hereford is home to some of the finest cider around, best sampled in one of the city's traditional and atmospheric pubs.

Except for the cathedral, the town is rather drowsy. The cathedral lies on the northern bank of the Wye River, with a number of shopping streets fanning out from it. Our favorite part for walks is along the banks of the Wye on the southern fringe of Hereford, where you can see the Wye Bridge from the Middle Ages, and also the neighboring Greyfriars Bridge, dating from the 12th century. Find a spot along these riverbanks on a summer day for a picnic.

ESSENTIALS

GETTING THERE   By train from London's Paddington Station, Hereford is a 3-hour trip. For schedules and information, call ℂ 0845/748-4950.

To make the 4-hour-plus trip by bus from London, you'll need to catch one of the three daily direct **National Express** buses from Victoria Coach Station. Others make stops in Gloucester and Heathrow Airport. For schedules and information, call ℂ **0870/580-8080** or visit **www.nationalexpress.com**.

The trip to Hereford makes a scenic 3-hour drive from London. Take the M5 to either Ledbury or Romp-on-Wye, then turn onto the A49 toward Hereford.

VISITOR INFORMATION   Hereford's **Tourist Information Centre** (ℂ 01432/268430) is located at 1 King St. and is open Monday to Saturday 9am to 5pm and on Sunday 10am to 4pm in summer.

WHERE TO STAY

The Green Dragon ⊛   The Green Dragon is the oldest, most historic hotel in Hereford, and it's the best. In 1857, this attractive inn, situated near the cathedral, had already been in business for 300 years when the then-owners decided to replace its front with the stately neoclassical facade you see today. Rooms are scattered over three upper floors and have all the high ceilings, thick walls, and squeaky floors you'd expect from an old treasure like this. Each has reasonably modern furnishings and is comfortably appointed.

Broad St., Herefordshire HR4 9BG. ℂ **0870/400-8113.** Fax 01432/352139. www.greendragon-hereford.co.uk. 83 units. £70–£100 ($140–$200) double. Rates include English breakfast. AE, DC, MC, V. Free parking. **Amenities:** Restaurant (see Shires Restaurant review, below); bar; lounge; room service. *In room:* TV, beverage maker, hair dryer, trouser press.

Three Counties Hotel   This hotel is set 1.5km (1 mile) south of Hereford's center on the opposite bank of the River Wye. This hotel has a distinctive hip-roofed, barnlike design that's more common in central Europe than England. You can't miss its prominent tawny-colored tile roof from a distance. The hotel caters to business travelers and bus tours. Rooms are monochromatic and modern, nothing fussy. Comfort is the keynote, and some of the bedrooms are suitable for persons with disabilities. Not all of the rooms are in the main building; some lie in separate buildings opening onto the parking lot.

Belmont Rd. (Hwy. A465), Herefordshire HR2 7BP. ℂ **01432/299955.** Fax 01432/275114. www.threecountieshotel. co.uk. 60 units. £89–£103 ($178–$206) double. Rates include English breakfast. AE, DC, MC, V. Free parking. **Amenities:** Restaurant; bar; room service; laundry service; dry cleaning. *In room:* TV, beverage maker, hair dryer, trouser press (in most).

WHERE TO DINE

Café @ All Saints ⊛ VEGETARIAN/SEAFOOD   This coffee bar and restaurant is Hereford's number-one spot for casual dining. It occupies the west end of a local medieval church right in the center of Hereford. The cooks here serve a simple, daily changing lunch menu combined with an all-day feature of coffee, homemade bread, cakes, and sandwiches. How about ordering the roast peppers, new potatoes, and goat cheese gratin with purple sprouting broccoli? You might also select salmon with a sorrel hollandaise, or else go for the Catalan casserole thickened with an almond-and-garlic piccada and served with basmati rice. The pan-fried mackerel filet appears with "melted" onions and black olives.

All Saints Church, High St. ℂ 01432/370415. Reservations not needed. Main courses £3.25–£7.95 ($6.50–$16); sandwiches £4.45 ($8.90). MC, V. Mon–Sat 8am–5pm. Occasional evening dinners with live music.

Shires Restaurant ENGLISH/FRENCH   Set on the street level of the town's most historic and prestigious hotel, this restaurant is sheathed with very old paneling, some of it from the 17th century, carved from Herefordshire oak. Everyone in town considers it the stateliest restaurant around, suitable for formal family celebrations. Main courses at lunchtime are selected from an all-English carvery table, where a uniformed attendant will carve from roasted joints of beef, turkey, or ham, garnished with all the traditional fixings. Dinners are more French in their flavor and are conducted with as much fanfare as anything else. The menu changes frequently but count on traditional British food, including salmon and asparagus terrine and vegetables. For a main, the grilled lamb cutlets are savory, as is the steak-and-mushroom pie.

In the Green Dragon hotel, Broad St. ℂ 0870/400-8113. Dinner main courses £7–£10 ($14–$20). AE, MC, V. Daily 6:30–9:30pm.

A FAVORITE LOCAL PUB

The **Orange Tree,** 16 King St. (ℂ **01432/267698**), a consistently popular pub, attracts beer lovers and tipplers from across the county. Nothing is particularly unusual about this woodsy pub (mostly a place to soak up local color), but its beers on tap include Buddington's and a changing roster of ales and lagers sent on spec from local breweries, sometimes as part of local sales promotions.

EXPLORING THE TOWN

Shopping can be had within a labyrinth of historic buildings known collectively as **High Town.** Limited only to pedestrians, it's enhanced with street performers and visiting entertainers. Principal shopping streets include Widemarsh Street, Commercial Road, St. Owen's Street, and the most charming and artfully old-fashioned of them all, Church Street.

Also near the town center is **Hereford Market,** evoking West Country street fairs of old with its cornucopia of collectibles and junk displayed in an open-air setting. It's conducted throughout the year, every Wednesday and Saturday morning from 10am to 4pm. Wednesdays include a livestock market, where you'll find cattle, as well as fruits, vegetables, and meats. The area literally pulsates with life as vendors sell items ranging from sweatshirts and saucepans to paintings and pet food.

Andrew Lamputt, 28 St. Owen St. (ℂ **01432/274961**), is the place to pick up the perfect silver gift. It boasts an extensive array of quality silverware and fine gold jewelry, and maintains a stable of skilled craftspeople that restore old pieces.

Cider Museum and King Offa Cider Brandy Distillery   This museum tells the story of traditional cider making from its heyday in the 17th century to modern factory methods. The King Offa Distillery has been granted the first new license to distill cider in the United Kingdom in more than 250 years; visitors can see it produced from beautiful copper stills brought from Normandy. The museum shop sells cider, cider brandy, cider brandy liqueur, and Royal Cider, the real wine of old England, as well as a good selection of gifts and souvenirs. On-site is a tea-and-coffee shop.

21 Ryelands St. (a 5-min. walk from the city center and .5km/¼ mile from City Ring Rd. on A438 to Brecon). (*© 01432/354207. www.cidermuseum.co.uk. Admission £3 ($6) adults, £2.50 ($5) seniors, £2 ($4) students and children. Apr–Oct Tues–Sat 10am–5pm; Nov–Mar Tues–Sat 11am–3pm.

Hereford Cathedral ⋆⋆   This is one of the oldest cathedrals in England (its cornerstone was laid in 1080). The cathedral is primarily Norman and includes a 13th-century Lady Chapel erected in 1220, as well as a majestic "Father" Willis organ, one of the finest in the world.

Exhibited together in the new library building at the west end of the Hereford Cathedral are two of Hereford's unique and priceless historical treasures: the Mappa Mundi of 1290, which portrays the world oriented around Jerusalem, and a 1,600-volume library of chained books, with some volumes dating from the 8th century. The cathedral also contains the Diocesan Treasury and the St. Thomas à Becket Reliquary.

Hereford City Centre. (*© 01432/374202. www.herefordcathedral.org. Free admission and tours. Admission for exhibitions at Mappa Mundi and Chained Library exhibition £4.50 ($9) adults, £3.50 ($7) children and seniors, £10 ($20) family ticket (2 adults, 3 children), free for children 4 and younger. Cathedral Mon–Sat 7:30am–5:30pm, Sun 8am–3:30pm; exhibits Mon–Sat 10am–4:30pm, Sun 11am–3:30pm (Apr 16–Oct 31 only).

The Old House   This is a completely restored Jacobean-period museum with 17th-century furnishings on three floors. The painstakingly restored half-timbered building was constructed in 1621 and includes a kitchen, hall, and rooms with four-poster beds.

High Town. (*© 01432/260694. Free admission. Apr–Sept Tues–Sat 10am–5pm, Sun 10am–4pm; Oct–Mar Tues–Sat 10am–5pm.

9 Ludlow ⋆

261km (162 miles) NW of London; 47km (29 miles) S of Shrewsbury

An outpost on the Welsh border during Norman times, this mellow town on the tranquil Teme River is often referred to as "the perfect historic town." Indeed, a tremendous amount of history whispers through its quiet lanes and courts, all lined with Georgian and Jacobean timbered buildings. The two little princes who died in the Tower of London lived here, and it was once the refuge of Henry VIII's first wife, Catherine of Aragon. You can still visit the church where the unhappy queen prayed. The town's most colorful street is the Broad, which rises from the old Ludford Bridge to Broadgate, the last remains of a wall erected in the Middle Ages. Be sure to visit the Buttercross on Broad Street, a private house and the most picturesque old home in Ludlow, having been designed in 1743 by William Baker. Also worth checking out is A. E. Housman's grave in the town cemetery.

ESSENTIALS

GETTING THERE   Trains run hourly from Paddington Station in London to Ludlow, with a transfer at Newport. It's approximately a 3-hour journey. For schedules and information, call (*© 0845/748-4950.**

National Express buses depart London's Victoria Coach Station for Shrewsbury, where you must change to the local line to reach Ludlow. It's a slow journey, approximately 5½ hours, but for those who are still interested, call (*© 0870/580-8080** (www.nationalexpress.com) for the current schedule.

By car, it's a much shorter, 3-hour drive. Follow the M25 out of London to the M40 at Oxford. Take the M40 to Bromsgrove. Once at Bromsgrove, follow the M42 until Kidderminster. From here, take the A456 to Ludlow.

VISITOR INFORMATION The **Ludlow Tourist Information Centre,** Castle Street (✆ **01584/875053;** www.ludlow.org.uk), is open November to March, Monday to Saturday 10am to 5pm; in April to October it's also open on Sunday 10:30am to 5pm.

SPECIAL EVENTS The 2-week **Ludlow Festival,** held annually in late June and early July, is one of England's major arts festivals. The centerpiece is an open-air Shakespeare performance within the Inner Bailey of Ludlow Castle. Orchestral concerts, historical lectures, readings, exhibitions, and workshops round out the festival. From March onward, a schedule can be obtained from the box office. Write to the Ludlow Festival box office, Castle Square, Ludlow, Shropshire SY8 1AY, enclosing a self-addressed stamped envelope; call ✆ **01584/872150;** or visit **www.ludlowfestival. co.uk**. The box office is open Monday to Saturday beginning in early May.

WHERE TO STAY

Dinham Hall Hotel Not to be confused with a less desirable competitor, Ludlow's Dinham Weir Hotel, the Dinham Hall Hotel rises in severe gray-stoned dignity, across the road from Ludlow Castle. Especially popular with participants of the Ludlow Festival, it offers a kind of Georgian-era, stately ambience. Built in 1792 by the earl of Mortimer, it served through the 1960s and 1970s as a dormitory for the nearby public boys' school. Many of the comfortable but very simple bedrooms bear the names of that school's former headmasters. The hotel enjoys a well-deserved reputation for the quality of its bedrooms, two of which are in a converted cottage. Some of the rooms have four-poster beds.

Dinham by the Castle, Ludlow, Shropshire SY8 1EJ. ✆ **01584/876464.** Fax 01584/876019. www.dinhamhall.co.uk. 13 units. £140–£190 ($280–$380) double; £240 ($480) suite. Rates include English breakfast. AE, MC, V. **Amenities:** Restaurant; bar; room service; laundry service. *In room:* TV, hair dryer, trouser press.

The Feathers Hotel ★★ The *New York Times* hailed this as "the most handsome inn in the world," and after a glance at its lavishly ornate half-timbered facade, you may agree. Built as a private home in 1603 and enlarged many times since, it boasts a winning combination of formal, high-style plasterwork ceilings and rustic, Elizabethan half-timbering and exposed stone, especially in the pub and restaurant. Only the suite and a few of the rooms have exposed Tudor-style beams; others are traditional and conservative, without the medieval vestiges of the building's exterior. Twelve rooms have recently been refurbished in an old Georgian style. Some of the spacious rooms have massive headboards skillfully fashioned from antique overmantels or mirror frames. Some rooms have four-poster beds and two are suitable for families.

The Bull Ring, Ludlow, Shropshire SY8 1AA. ✆ **01584/875261.** Fax 01584/876030. www.feathersatludlow.co.uk. 40 units. £125–£195 ($250–$390) double. Rates include breakfast. AE, DC, MC, V. **Amenities:** Restaurant; bar; room service. *In room:* TV, high-speed Internet, beverage maker, hair dryer, trouser press.

WHERE TO DINE

Les Marches MODERN BRITISH/FRENCH This well-recommended and rather stylish restaurant has an ambitious menu that usually succeeds with flair. The oak-paneled dining room evokes the grand age of private dinner parties. Menu items are prepared by Olivier Bossut or his assistants, with straightforward but intelligent use of fresh ingredients. The skill of the chef is reflected by such dishes as a cassoulet of quail with Spanish white beans or a duo of duck breast with wild sea bass. The wine list boasts more than 300 selections.

In the Overton Grange Hotel, Overton, near Ludlow. ℂ **01584/873500.** Reservations required for nonguests. Fixed-price menus £43–£60 ($86–$120). MC, V. Mon–Sat 7–9pm.

Mr. Underhill's at Dinham Weir ★★★ BRITISH/MEDITERRANEAN   Serious foodies think nothing of journeying here from Oxford or Birmingham for dinner. Weekends see many Londoners arriving at the place for a serious bite-down. Chris Bradley, the chef and owner, turned this threadbare inn, which looked like Fawlty Towers, into a charming inn beneath the ruins of an 11th-century castle overlooking an English garden above a dam on the River Teme. In summer, tables are placed outside in the garden.

Since the menu changes every night, you don't know what you'll be served. For one of your most memorable meals in England, you might start with a chestnut custard with crispy smoked duck and follow with a monkfish-studded pasta enlivened with cèpe mushrooms. Venison flavored with elderberry thyme appears in a red-wine sauce, and roasted rack and shoulder of lamb is married to sorrel, mint, and baby spinach. Other mains include a pavé of halibut on shredded vegetables with the startling addition of coconut. For dessert, why not try the iced plum sponge cake with star anise ice cream?

Many diners choose to overnight here, and we recommend you follow their example. The B&B rate is £140 to £190 ($280–$380), rising to £235 to £290 ($470–$580) in a suite.

Dinham Weir. ℂ **01584/874431.** www.mr-underhills.co.uk. Reservations required. Fixed-price 7-course dinner £45 ($90). MC, V. Wed–Sun 7–11pm.

A FAVORITE LOCAL PUB

The town's most atmospheric and evocative pub, the **Church Inn,** Church Street, Buttercross (ℂ **01584/872174;** www.thechurchinn.com), is everybody's favorite source for beer, gossip, and good cheer. Beer, mead, and wine have flowed here since at least 1446, and according to some historians, even earlier. Meals are served daily from noon to 3:30pm and 6:30 to 9pm. Whether you eat informally in the bar or head for the more formal restaurant, the food and prices are exactly the same: Main courses range from £7 to £12 ($14–$24). Cuisine is straightforward, British, and rib-sticking, with traditional pub grub such as steak-and-kidney pie, fried prawns, and omelets. The owners proudly proclaim that they only use fresh local produce. The bar is open Monday to Saturday 11am to 11pm, and Sunday noon to 10:30pm.

EXPLORING THE TOWN

Whitcliffe Common, a public park, was the common land of Ludlow during the Middle Ages. From here, you can enjoy panoramic views of Ludlow as you stroll. Leave town by one of two bridges across the River Teme and follow any of a number of paths through the Common.

A **flea market** is held on Castle Square on alternate Sundays throughout the year from 9am to approximately 4pm. In addition, the town is filled with traditional family businesses; of particular interest are the many antiques, book, arts-and-crafts, and gift shops. The **Marches Pottery,** 45 Mill St. (ℂ **01584/878413**), produces a wide selection of hand-thrown tableware and individual pieces decorated with subtle Chinese glazes, including a host of terra-cotta flowerpots.

Ludlow Castle 🜚   This Norman castle was built around 1094 as a frontier outpost to keep out the as-yet-unconquered Welsh. The original castle, or the inner bailey, was encircled in the early 14th century by a very large outer bailey and transformed into a medieval palace by Roger Mortimer, the most powerful man in England at the time. After the War of the Roses, the castle was turned into a royal residence, and Edward IV sent the Prince of Wales and his brother (the "Princes in the Tower") to live here in 1472. It was also the seat of government for Wales and the Border Counties. Catherine of Aragon and Mary Tudor and her court also spent time in this 900-year-old home. Norman, medieval, and Tudor architectural styles can be found throughout the castle. Many of the original buildings still stand, including the Chapel of St. Mary Magdalene, with one of England's last remaining circular naves. Excellent views of the castle can be spied from the banks of the River Teme.

Castle Sq., Ludlow Town Centre. ℭ 01584/873355. www.ludlowcastle.com. Admission £4 ($8) adults, £3.50 ($7) seniors, £2 ($4) children, £11 ($22) family ticket. Jan Sat–Sun 10am–4pm; Feb–Mar and Oct–Dec daily 10am–4pm; Apr–July and Sept daily 10am–5pm; Aug daily 10am–7pm. Last admission 30 min. before closing time.

Ludlow Museum 🄺🄸🄳🅂   This museum tells the story of Ludlow town: the construction of its castle 900 years ago, the prosperity gained from wool and agriculture during the Middle Ages, and its rise in political importance. The museum also houses natural history displays; the Norton Gallery contains "Reading the Rocks," an exhibit that celebrates Ludlow's unique contribution to international geology. There are several hands-on, interactive displays, including a video microscope that lets you examine geological specimens. Visitors can also try on helmets used in England's civil war. It's a great place for kids.

Castle Sq. ℭ 01584/7813666. Free admission. Apr–Oct Mon–Sat 10:30am–1pm and 2–5pm; June–Aug also Sun 10:30am–1pm and 2–5pm.

Secret Hills 🜚   This center depicts the geology, ecology, history, and culture of Shropshire. Engulfed by meadows and topped off with a green grass roof, the center in particular honors resident writers, such as Mary Webb who wrote *Gone to Earth*, published in 1917. Webb is still known today in the area as much so as the Brontë sisters who still haunt the Yorkshire Moors. Jennifer Jones filmed the story as a 1950 movie, retitled *Wild Heart* in the U.S. Another writer, A. E. Housman, is also honored by the exhibit. But what caught our attention more than any other exhibit is the life-size model of a Shropshire mammoth.

Shropshire Hills Discovery Centre, School Rd., Craven Arms. ℭ 01588/676000. Admission £4.50 ($9) adults, £4 ($8) students and seniors, £3 ($6) children, £14 ($28) family ticket. Apr–Oct daily 10am–5:30pm; Nov–Mar daily 10am–4:30pm. Last admission 1 hr. before closing time. Lies beside A49 on the southern outskirts of Craven Arms, 11km (7 miles) northwest of Ludlow.

10 Shrewsbury 🄲

264km (164 miles) NW of London; 63km (39 miles) SW of Stoke-on-Trent; 77km (48 miles) NW of Birmingham

The finest Tudor town in England, Shrewsbury is noted for its black-and-white buildings of timber and plaster, including Abbot's House (dating from 1450), and the tall gabled Ireland's Mansion (ca. 1575) on High Street. These houses were built by the powerful and prosperous wool traders, or drapers. Charles Dickens wrote of his stay in Shrewsbury's Lion Hotel, "I am lodged in the strangest little rooms, the ceilings of which I can touch with my hands. From the windows I can look all downhill and slantwise at the crookedest black-and-white houses, all of many shapes except straight shapes." The town also has a number of Georgian and Regency mansions, some old bridges, and handsome churches, including the Abbey Church of Saint Peter and St. Mary's Church.

ESSENTIALS

GETTING THERE   Shrewsbury-bound trains depart London's Euston Station daily every half-hour. You change trains in Birmingham with a total travel time of about 3 hours. For information, call ✆ **0845/748-4950.**

Four **National Express** buses depart daily from London's Victoria Coach Station for the 5-hour trip, two with stopovers in Birmingham. For information, call ✆ **0870/ 580-8080** (www.nationalexpress.com).

By car from London, the drive is 2½ hours; take the M1 to the M6 to the M54 to reach the A5, which will take you directly to Shrewsbury.

VISITOR INFORMATION   The **Shrewsbury Tourist Information Centre,** the Square (✆ **01743/281200;** www.visitshrewsbury.com), is open from 9:30am to 5:30pm Monday to Saturday and from 10am to 4pm Sunday, from May to September. From October to April, its hours are from 10am to 5pm Monday to Saturday.

WHERE TO STAY

Albright Hussey Hotel ✪✪   Its unusual name derives from the feudal family (the Husseys) who occupied it between 1292 and the 1600s. Today, it's one of the best examples of an elaborate Tudor timber-frame building in Shrewsbury. The brick-and-stone wing was added around 1560. The interior has all the old-world charm and eccentricities you could hope for, including oak panels, fireplaces large enough to roast an ox, and a moated garden with several pairs of fiercely territorial black swans. Most furnishings date from the early 19th century, contrasting well with dozens of beams that have been artfully exposed in the ceilings and walls of bedrooms and public areas. Five rooms have four-poster beds. Rooms in the main house have more character, though those in the new wing are slightly more spacious with more up-to-date furnishings.

Ellesmere Rd., Shrewsbury, Shropshire SY4 3AF. ✆ **01939/290571.** Fax 01939/291143. www.albrighthussey.co.uk. 26 units. £95–£130 ($190–$260) double; £160–£190 ($320–$380) suite. Rates include English breakfast. AE, DC, MC, V. Free parking. 4km (2½ miles) northeast of Shrewsbury along A528. **Amenities:** Restaurant; bar; room service; babysitting; laundry service; dry cleaning. *In room:* TV, Wi-Fi, beverage maker, hair dryer, trouser press.

The Lion   Housed on the site of a 17th-century coaching inn that claims to have origins in the 14th century, this is easily the most evocative hotel in Shrewsbury itself. The rooms have been enlarged, and the setting has been lavishly gentrified with lots of patterned chintz and modern luxuries. Only the suite contains artfully gnarled oaken beams—other rooms are comfortable as well and are being refurbished in a style evocative of the 17th century. Beds are exceedingly comfortable.

Wyle Cop, Shrewsbury, Shropshire SY1 1UY. ✆ **0870/609-6167.** Fax 01743/352744. www.english-inns.co.uk/lion hotel-shrewsbury. 59 units. £59–£81 ($118–$162) double. AE, DC, MC, V. Free parking. **Amenities:** Restaurant; bar; room service. *In room:* TV, Wi-Fi, beverage maker, hair dryer, trouser press.

WHERE TO DINE

The Peach Tree ✪ *(finds* BRITISH/EUROPEAN/ASIAN   Its name derives from the hundreds of ripe peaches, peach trees, and peach boughs that someone laboriously stenciled onto the walls. The setting dates from the 15th century, when this was a weaver's cottage adjacent to the abbey. The food is based on solid, time-tested recipes made with fresh ingredients and loads of European savoir-faire. It's some of the best in town. The menu is split into Asian, Shropshire, and Italian themes. For a starter, try the basil-infused chicken liver pâté with shallot jam. Among the most delightful of the main courses is Thai red curry or else chicken or king prawns flavored with chili, lemon grass, ginger, garlic, cilantro, and coconut cream. An enticing loin of pork is sage flavored and served with a pear Calvados reduction. Another favorite is smoked salmon and prawn pasta in a dill-cream sauce with pecorino shavings.

21 Abbey Foregate. © 01743/355055. www.thepeachtree.co.uk. Reservations recommended on weekends. Main courses £8–£20 ($16–$40). AE, DC, MC, V. Daily 9am–10pm (last order).

SEEING THE SIGHTS

Many tales and stories are locked within Shrewsbury's winding narrow streets and black-and-white buildings. The best way to learn this local lore is to take one of the many walking or bus tours hosted by official Shrewsbury guides. Special themed walking tours such as "Ghosts," "Brother Cadfael," and the "Civil War" are also available. A typical tour starts in the town center and lasts 1½ hours. Tickets can be purchased from the Tourist Information Centre (see above).

Attingham Park   This elegant classical house set on 100 hectares (250 acres) of woodlands and landscaped deer park is graced with superbly decorated staterooms, including a red dining room and blue drawing room. Treasures of the house include Regency silver used at 19th-century ambassadorial receptions and elegant Italian furniture. A tearoom and gift shop on the grounds make a pleasant stop before or after you've toured the house.

Shrewsbury. © 01743/708162. www.nationaltrust.org.uk. House admission £6.40 ($13) adults, £3.20 ($6.40) children, £16 ($32) family ticket; park and grounds £3.60 ($7.20) adults, £1.80 ($3.60) children, £9 ($18) family ticket. House Mar Sat–Sun 1–4pm, Apr–Oct Fri–Tues 1–5:30pm; park Mar–Oct daily 10am–5:30pm, Nov–Feb daily 9am–5pm. Attingham Park lies 4km (2½ miles) southeast of Shrewsbury in Atcham on the B4380. Turn into the estate at the entrance opposite the Mytton and Mermaid Hotel.

Shrewsbury Abbey   Founded in 1083, Shrewsbury Abbey became one of the most powerful Benedictine monasteries in England. It's the setting of the Brother Cadfael tales, a series of mysteries written by Ellis Peters that have been adapted for television. The church remains in use to this day, and visitors can see displays devoted to the abbey's history as well as the remains of the 14th-century shrine of St. Winefride.

Abbey Foregate. © 01743/232723. www.shrewsburyabbey.com. Free admission; donations of £2 ($4) requested for the Abbey Fund. Daily 10am–4:30pm. Shrewsbury Abbey is just off of Robertson Way and Monk Moor Rd. at Judith Butts Lane.

Shrewsbury Castle   Built in 1083 by a Norman earl, Roger de Montgomery, this castle was designed as a powerful fortress to secure the border with Wales. The Great Hall and walls were constructed during the reign of Edward I, but 200 years ago, Thomas Telford extensively remodeled the castle. Today, it houses the Shropshire Regimental Museum, which includes the collections of the King's Shropshire Light Infantry, the Shropshire Yeomanry, and the Shropshire Royal Horse Artillery. These collections represent more than 300 years of regimental service and include a lock of Napoleon's hair and an American flag captured during the seizure and burning of the White House during the War of 1812.

Castle St. © 01743/361196. Admission £2.50 ($5) adults, £1.30 ($2.60) seniors, free for students and children 15 and younger. In 2009: Sept 10–Dec 22 and Feb 13–May 26 Tues–Sat 10am–4pm; May 27–Sept 9 Mon–Sat 10am–5pm, Sun 10am–4pm. Closed Dec 23–Feb 12.

SHREWSBURY AFTER DARK

Quench your thirst or have a bite to eat at the **Lion & Pheasant Hotel** bar, 49–50 Wyle Cop (© **01743/236288**), where in colder months, an inviting firelight ambience presides. Or check out the **Boat House Pub,** New Street ((© **01743/231658**), located beside a beautiful old park on the River Severn. In summer, they open up the terrace overlooking the river, and it becomes a popular date place. Couples enjoy a healthy selection of beers and ales, along with a tasty pub grub that ranges from soup and sandwiches to pies.

The **Buttermarket Nightclub** (© **01743/241455**), set in the old butter market on Howard Street, caters to the older-than-25 crowd. Other clubs include the **Liquid Diva,** Ravens Meadows (© **01743/289022**).

The **Music Hall,** the Square (© **01743/281281**; www.musichall.co.uk), hosts musicals, plays, and concerts year-round. Tickets range from £6 to £24 ($12–$48).

11 Ironbridge

217km (135 miles) NW of London; 58km (36 miles) NW of Birmingham; 29km (18 miles) SE of Shrewsbury

If you're looking for pretty, bucolic England, the name of Ironbridge might turn you off. But it's a rather charming tree-lined village filled with natural beauty, even though it was one of the birthplaces of the Industrial Revolution. It is also a World Heritage Site. Today it has a cluster of museums documenting its manufacturing history from its 19th-century heyday. There are also plenty of gift shops and other stores in town selling souvenirs to remind you of your visit.

Ironbridge, located in the Ironbridge Gorge, is famous for kicking off an early stage of the Industrial Revolution. Indeed, this stretch of the Severn River valley has been an important industrial area since the Middle Ages because of its iron and limestone deposits. But the event that clinched this area's importance came in 1709, when the Quaker ironmaster, Abraham Darby I, discovered a method for smelting iron by using coke as a fuel, instead of charcoal. This paved the way for the first iron rails, boats, wheels, aqueducts, and bridges, cast in Coalbrookdale in 1779. So momentous was this accomplishment that the area, originally called Coalbrookdale, was renamed Ironbridge. The area literally buzzed with the new transportation and engineering innovations that soon followed.

ESSENTIALS

GETTING THERE   Trains leave Euston heading for Birmingham every 30 minutes. Once at the Telford Central Station, take a bus or taxi into Ironbridge. The entire journey takes about 2½ hours. For schedules and information, call © **0845/748-4950** or go to **www.nationalrail.co.uk**.

Four **National Express** buses daily depart London's Victoria Coach Station, arriving in Telford about 4 hours later. Two of those are direct; the others make a stop in Birmingham. Call © **0870/580-8080,** or visit **www.nationalexpress.com** for information. Local buses that leave Telford for the 20-minute ride to Ironbridge include nos. 9, 39, 76, 77, 96, and 99.

If you're driving from London, take the M1 to the M6 to the M54, which leads directly to Ironbridge.

VISITOR INFORMATION   The **Ironbridge Gorge Tourist Information Centre,** the Toll House, Bower Yard (© **01952/884391;** www.shropshiretourism.info/ironbridge), is open Monday to Friday 10am to 5pm and Saturday and Sunday 9am to 5pm.

WHERE TO STAY

Best Western Valley Hotel This hotel was originally built as a private home around 1750. This riverside inn was enlarged over the years into the sprawling, light-brown brick design you see today. The high-ceilinged interior contains hints of its original grandeur, including a worthwhile restaurant, the Chez Maw (see below). Fifteen of the hotel's rooms lie within the original stable and are accessible via a glass-roofed courtyard. Although rooms in the main house usually have more panoramic views, many visitors prefer the coziness of the former stables. All rooms are well maintained and modern; some have four-poster beds.

Ironbridge, Telford, Shropshire TF8 7DW. ℂ 800/528-1234 in the U.S., or 01952/432247. Fax 01952/432308. www.thevalleyhotel.co.uk. 44 units. £140–£150 ($280–$300) double. Rates include breakfast. AE, DC, MC, V. **Amenities:** Restaurant; 2 bars; room service; laundry service. *In room:* TV, Wi-Fi, beverage maker, hair dryer, trouser press.

Bridge House Set 2.5km (1½ miles) west of Ironbridge, on the outskirts of the hamlet of Buildwas, this ivy-draped, half-timbered coaching inn is from 1620. Resident proprietor Janet Hedges will tell you unusual stories about the house, such as the 365 nails (one for every day of the year) that hold together the planks of the front door, which comes from the abbey and probably dates from the 1300s. Rooms are genteel and comfortable, sometimes with touches of Edwardian drama (lavishly draped beds, in some cases). Others have exposed beams, and all have creaking floors and uneven walls that testify to the age of the building. Rooms are small and snug, and each is individually decorated.

Buildwas Rd., Telford, Shropshire TF8 7BN. ℂ 01952/432105. Fax 01952/432105. 4 units. £75 ($150) double; £95 ($190) family unit. Rates include breakfast. MC, V. Closed for 2 weeks at Christmas. *In room:* TV, beverage maker, hair dryer.

Library House ✦ *Finds* This restored landmark, parts of which date back to 1752, has been used for many purposes, including a doctor's surgery and even the village library, from which the B&B takes its name. Breakfast is served in a room with a rich collection of copper. The breakfast is the best in the area, and the house was in the running for the Automobile Association's best breakfast award. The delightful bedrooms are individually designed and decorated, and named after such famous writers as Eliot, Austen, Milton, and Chaucer. All guest bedrooms have their own teddy bears if you want to cuddle up. There is also a pretty terraced garden.

11 Severn Bank, Ironbridge, Telford, Shropshire TF8 7AN. ℂ 01952/432299. Fax 01952/433967. www.libraryhouse. com. 4 units. £70 ($140) double; £90 ($180) family rooms. No credit cards. **Amenities:** Breakfast room; garden. *In room:* TV/DVD, beverage maker, hair dryer, no phone.

WHERE TO DINE

Restaurant Chez Maw BRITISH The name refers to Arthur Maw, long-ago owner of the house and founder of a nearby factory that produced decorative tiles during the 19th century. Prized examples of his ceramic creations line the reception area and the monumental staircase. Outfitted with crisp napery, Windsor-style chairs, and a high ceiling, the restaurant serves updated British food. The cooking is inspired by the bounty of the enveloping countryside—try the tenderloin of pork with sage-flavored apples or else pan-seared sea trout with smoked garlic. The breast of Gressingham duck comes with honey-roasted apples and pears. For dessert, nothing quite equals the dark chocolate and Bailey's torte with chocolate ice cream and a milk-chocolate sauce.

In the Best Western Valley Hotel. ℂ 01952/432247. Reservations required for nonguests. Main courses £13–£20 ($26–$40). AE, DC, MC, V. Daily noon–2pm; Mon–Sat 7–9:30pm; Sun 7–9pm.

A FAVORITE LOCAL PUB

A rebuilt Victorian pub, complete with a chicken coop in the backyard? Yes, it's the **New Inn,** in the Blists Hill Museum complex (© **01952/586063**). It's gimmicky in its re-creation of yesterday, complete with gas lamps, sawdust floors, and friendly staff sporting vintage Victorian garb. You'll find a good selection of ales; hearty, rib-sticking home-cooked meals; and plenty of pub games.

EXPLORING THE AREA

The Ironbridge Valley plays host to seven main museums and several smaller ones, collectively called the **Ironbridge Gorge Museums** ★★, Ironbridge, Telford (© **01952/ 433522** Mon–Fri, or 01952/432166 Sat–Sun; www.ironbridge.org.uk). Museums include the **Coalbrookdale Museum and Darby Houses,** with its Darby Furnace of Iron and sound-and-light display, as well as restored 19th-century homes of the Quaker ironmasters; the **Ironbridge,** with its original tollhouse; **Jackfield Tile Museum,** where you can see demonstrations of tile-pressing, decorating, and firing; **Blists Hill Victorian Town** ★★, with its re-creation of a 19th-century village; **Coalport China Museum and Tar Tunnel** ★★, which includes a tour of an underground mine; **Broseley Pipeworks,** a 50-year-old abandoned tobacco pipe-making factory; and **Enginiuty,** a children's interactive exhibit that allows them to become engineers for a day. Since it is unlikely that you will have time for everything, we recommend that you visit Blists Hill Victorian Town and the Coalport China Museum, even if you have to skip all the rest. A passport ticket to all museums in Ironbridge Gorge is £14 ($28) for adults, £13 ($26) for seniors, £9.50 ($19) for students and children, and £46 ($92) for families (two adults, three children). The sites are open Monday to Friday from 9am to 5pm and weekends from 10am to 5pm. The Tar Tunnel, Darby Houses, and Broseley Pipeworks are closed from November to March.

You can also find some good shopping here. You can buy Coalport china at the **Coalport China Museum** and decorative tiles at the **Jackfield Tile Museum.** Another place worth visiting is just beyond the Jackfield Museum: **Maws Craft Centre** (© **01952/ 883030;** www.mawscraftcentre.co.uk) is the site of 20 workshops situated in an old Victorian tile works beside the River Severn. Here, you can browse for glass sculptures, dollhouses, original Celtic art, pictures with frames made while you wait, jewelry, and stained glass. There's also a tearoom on-site that's open for lunch and afternoon tea.

12 Stoke-on-Trent: The Potteries

261km (162 miles) NW of London; 74km (46 miles) N of Birmingham; 95km (59 miles) NW of Leicester; 66km (41 miles) S of Manchester

Unless you have an abiding interest in pottery, you may want to skip commercial Stoke-on-Trent, one of author Arnold Bennett's famous *Five Towns* that he described so vividly. Kilns were busy here in the 14th century, long before Josiah Wedgwood (1730–95), England's most distinguished potter, arrived. Most of the great kilns have disappeared, but there is much that remains to interest visitors. The town and its architecture still reflect the dreary Victorian era, but few visitors take note as they hop from one pottery to another, seeking their favorite patterns.

Although it has been created in the area since 2000 B.C., it wasn't until the Romans rolled through in A.D. 46 that the first pottery kiln was set up at Trent Vale. Now it's **Stoke-on-Trent,** a loose confederation of six towns (Tunstall, Burslem, Stoke, Fenton,

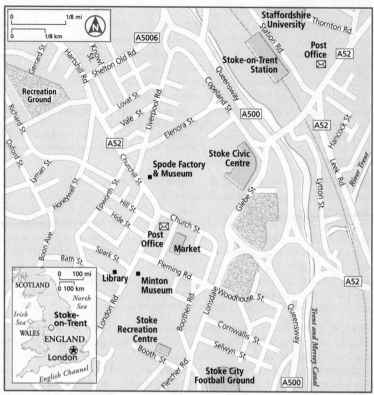

Longton, and Hanley, the most important town) covering an 11km (7-mile) area, that's the real center of the pottery trade. During the Industrial Revolution, the area known collectively as Stoke-on-Trent became the world's leading producer of pottery, and today it is a tourist attraction.

ESSENTIALS

GETTING THERE It's a direct train ride of 1½ hours to Stoke-on-Trent from London's Euston Station. Trains make half-hourly departures daily. For schedules and information, call ℭ **0845/748-4950** or go to **www.nationalrail.co.uk**.

Seven direct **National Express** buses leave London's Victoria Coach Station daily for the 4- to 5-hour trip to Stoke. Many others make a detour to Birmingham. For information, call ℭ **0870/580-8080** (www.nationalexpress.com).

By car from London, drive along the M1 to the M6 to the A500 at Junction 15. It will take you 2 to 3 hours by car.

VISITOR INFORMATION The **Stoke-on-Trent Tourist Information Centre,** Bagnall Street, Cultural Quarter, Stoke-on-Trent (ℭ **01782/236000;** www.visitstoke.co.uk), is open Monday to Saturday 9:15am to 5:15pm. You can pick up a "China Experience" visitor map, noting most potteries, shops, and museums in the area.

WHERE TO STAY & DINE

Best Western Stoke-on-Trent Moat House ⚔ This is the town's leading hotel, built in the 18th century as the home of Josiah Wedgwood. A four-story annex wing, which houses the bulk of the accommodations, has been joined to the historic core by a glass-sided corridor. The result is a modern, chain-style hotel that retains a sense of history, which its hardworking staff strives to maintain. All the midsize rooms have been redecorated and furnished to a comfortable standard.

Etruria Hall, Festival Way, Etruria, Stoke-on-Trent, Staffordshire ST1 5BQ. ℂ 0870/225-4601. Fax 01782/206101. www.bestwestern.com. 147 units. £119–£140 ($238–$280) double; £169–£190 ($338–$380) suite. Rates include breakfast and dinner. AE, DC, MC, V. Free parking. **Amenities:** Restaurant; 2 bars; indoor heated pool; health club; whirlpool; sauna; room service; laundry service; dry cleaning. *In room:* A/C, TV, high-speed Internet, beverage maker, hair dryer, iron, trouser press, safe.

George Hotel This is one of the most upscale, formal, and dignified hotels in town, the kind of place where the mayor would invite some cronies or a businessperson might bring an important client. Built in 1929 of red brick, it rises three floors above the hamlet of Burslem, one of the six villages that make up the Stoke-on-Trent district. Public areas are outfitted with traditional furniture and large 19th-century oil paintings of the town and region. The conservative but comfortable bedrooms are well furnished and generally spacious.

Swan Sq., Burslem, Stoke-on-Trent ST6 2AE. ℂ 01782/577544. Fax 01782/837496. www.georgehotelstoke.com. 39 units. £60–£85 ($120–$170) double. Rates include English breakfast. AE, DC, MC, V. Free parking. **Amenities:** Restaurant; bar; room service; laundry service; dry cleaning. *In room:* TV, beverage maker, hair dryer, trouser press.

Haydon House Hotel This imposing late-Victorian house is the home of the Machin family. They've added a collection of built-in mahogany furniture to the bedrooms and reconfigured their home and their lives to welcome overnight guests. You'll find many of the original Victorian fittings, an unusual collection of clocks, and many modern amenities that will make your stay comfortable in the tastefully furnished bedrooms. Suites have efficiently arranged kitchenettes and private entrances and are usually rented for a full week.

1–9 Haydon St., Basford, Stoke-on-Trent, Staffordshire ST4 6JD. ℂ 01782/711311. Fax 01782/717470. www.haydon-house-hotel.co.uk. 23 units. £60–£65 ($120–$130) double; £275 ($550) per week suite. AE, DC, MC, V. Free parking. **Amenities:** Restaurant; bar; room service; laundry service; dry cleaning. *In room:* TV, beverage maker, hair dryer, trouser press.

HISTORY FIRST: TWO WORTHWHILE MUSEUMS

The Gladstone Pottery Museum ⚔ This is the only complete Victorian pottery factory that has been restored as a museum, with craftspeople providing daily demonstrations in original workshops. Various galleries depict the rise of the Staffordshire pottery industry, tile history, and so on (check out the toilets of all shapes, sizes, colors, and decoration). There are great hands-on opportunities for plate painting, pot throwing, and ornamental-flower making.

Uttoxeter Rd. at Longton. ℂ 01782/319232. www.stoke.gov.uk/museums. Admission £5.95 ($12) adults, £4.95 ($9.90) seniors and students, £4.50 ($9) children, £18 ($36) family ticket. Daily 10am–5pm (last admission at 4pm).

The Potteries Museum and Art Gallery ⚔ Start here for an overview of Stoke-on-Trent history. It houses departments of fine arts, decorative arts, natural history, archaeology, and social history. It also has one of the largest and finest collections of ceramics in the world. It's a great place for training your eyes before exploring the factories and shops of Stoke-on-Trent.

Bethesda St., Hanley. ✆ **01782/232323**. www.stoke.gov.uk/museums. Free admission. Nov–Feb Mon–Sat 10am–4pm, Sun 1–4pm; Mar–Oct Mon–Sat 10am–5pm, Sun 2–5pm.

TOURING & SHOPPING THE POTTERIES

With more than 40 factories in Stoke-on-Trent—all with gift shops and seconds shops on-site—you need to be in shape for this adventure. In fact, some have several shops, selling everything from fine china dinner services to hand-painted tiles.

Seconds are always a great bargain. They're still high-quality pieces with imperfections that only the professional eye can detect. But don't expect bargains on top-of-the-line pieces. Shops discount their best wares once in a while, but most of the time, prices for first-quality items are the same here as they are in London, elsewhere in England, or in America.

During the big January sales in London, many department stores, including Harrods, truck in seconds from the factories in Stoke, so if you're in London then, you don't have to visit here to bring home a bargain.

Each factory discussed below offers shipping and can help you with the value-added tax (VAT) refund. Expect your purchases to be delivered within 1 to 3 months.

Moorcroft Pottery   Moorcroft is a welcome change from the work of the pottery world's more famous names. It was founded in 1898 by William Moorcroft, who produced his own special brand of pottery and was his own exclusive designer until his death in 1945. Decoration is part of the first firing here, giving it a higher quality of color and brilliance than, say, Spode, creating floral designs in bright, clear colors (think of it as the Art Nouveau of the pottery world). There is much to admire and buy in the factory seconds shop. There is always someone around to explain the various processes and to show you around the museum, with its collections of early Moorcroft. Tours are not suitable for kids 10 and younger.

W. Moorcroft, Sandbach Rd., Burslem. ✆ **01782/214345**. www.moorcroft.com. Tours (must be booked 2 weeks in advance) £4.50 ($9) adults, £3.50 ($7) seniors, £2.50 ($5) children 11–16. Factory tours Mon and Wed–Thurs 11am and 2pm, Fri 11am. Museum and shop Mon–Fri 10am–5pm, Sat 9:30am–4:30pm. A taxi from the Stoke-on-Trent train station will run about £8 ($16). If you're driving from London, follow M1 north to M6. Take it north to Junction 15, which becomes A500. Follow the signs.

Spode 🍴   The oldest English pottery company operating on the same site, since 1770, and the birthplace of fine bone china, Spode offers regular factory tours lasting about 1½ hours and connoisseur tours lasting 2½ hours. In the **Craft Centre,** visitors can see demonstrations of engraving, lithography, hand painting, printing, and clay casting. An unrivaled collection of Spode's ceramic masterpieces is on display in the **Spode Museum.** The Blue Italian Restaurant cooks up refreshments and lunch—all served on Spode's classic blue tableware, Blue Italian. The Factory Shop sells seconds at reduced prices.

Church St., Stoke-on-Trent. ✆ **01782/744011**. www.spode.co.uk. Free admission for Spode Visitor Centre and Museum. Basic factory tour £4.50 ($9) adults; £4 ($8) children 12 and older, students, and seniors. Connoisseur factory tour £7.50 ($15) adults; £6.50 ($13) children 12 and older, students, and seniors. Visitor Centre Mon–Sat 9am–5pm; Sun 10am–4pm. Tours Mon–Fri at 10am, 1:30, and 3pm. Tours must be booked weeks in advance. Spode is a 10-min. walk from the Stoke-on-Trent train station. If you're driving from London, follow M1 north until you reach M6. Take it north to Junction 15, which becomes A500. Follow the signs for Stoke.

Wedgwood Visitor Centre 🍴   The visitor center includes a demonstration hall to watch clay pots being formed on the potter's wheel and witness plates being turned and fired, then painted. Highly skilled potters and decorators are happy to answer your questions. An art gallery and gift shop showcase samples of factory-made items that also can be purchased. (Note that the prices at this shop are the same as those found elsewhere.) Tours don't have to be booked in advance, but the staff prefers that you do so. Leave 2 hours for a full tour. The Centre's **Wedgwood Museum** covers 3 centuries of design and features living displays, including Josiah Wedgwood's Etruria factory and the company's Victorian showroom. Other room settings can also be seen at the museum. The Josiah Wedgwood Restaurant is the perfect place to relax with a cup of coffee or enjoy a full meal. Wedgwood seconds, which are available at reduced prices, are not sold at the center but are available at the **Wedgwood Group Factory Shop,** King Street, Fenton (© **01782/316161**).

Barlaston. © **01782/282986.** www.thewedgwoodstory.com. Admission £8.25 ($17) adults; £6.25 ($13) seniors, students, and children; £28 ($56) family ticket (2 adults, 3 children). Mon–Fri 9am–5pm; Sat–Sun 10am–5pm. Tours year-round Mon–Thurs 9:30am–3:30pm; Fri 9:30–11am. Take a taxi from the Stoke-on-Trent train station, a 9.5km (6-mile) trip that will cost around £10 ($20). If you're driving from London, head north along M1 until you reach M6. Continue north to Junction 14, which becomes A34. Follow A34 to Barlaston and follow the signs to Wedgwood.

15

Cambridge & East Anglia:
Fens & the Norfolk "Broads"

The four essentially bucolic counties of **East Anglia** (Essex, Suffolk, Norfolk, and Cambridgeshire) were once an ancient Anglo-Saxon kingdom dominated by the Danes. In part, the region is a land of heaths, fens, marshes, and inland lagoons known as "broads." Many old villages and market towns abound. East Anglia is a place in which to experience the outdoors, and many walkers, cyclists, and boaters are drawn to the area. See individual towns for suggestions about how to come into a close encounter with the countryside.

Suffolk and Essex are Constable Country and boast some of England's finest landscapes. Many visitors drive through Essex on the way to **Cambridge.** Though close to London and industrialized in places, this land of rolling fields has rural areas and villages, many on the seaside. Essex stretches east to the English Channel.

The easternmost county of England, Suffolk is a refuge for artists, just as it was in the day of its famous native sons, Constable and Gainsborough, who preserved its landscapes on canvas. Though a fast train can whisk visitors from London to East Suffolk in approximately 1½ hours,

its fishing villages, historic homes, and national monuments remain off the beaten track for most tourists. To capture the true charm of Suffolk, you must explore its little market towns and villages. Beginning at the Essex border, we head toward the North Sea, highlighting the most scenic villages as we move eastward across the shire.

Seat of the dukes of Norfolk, **Norwich** is less popular, but those who venture toward the North Sea are rewarded with some of England's most beautiful scenery. An occasional dike or windmill reminds you of the Netherlands. From here you can branch out and visit the **Broads,** a network of waterways.

The resort town of **Wroxham,** capital of the Broads, is easily reached from Norwich, only 13km (8 miles) to the northeast. Motorboats regularly take parties on short trips from Wroxham. Some of the best scenery of the Broads is on the periphery of Wroxham. From Norwich you can also make a trip to **Sandringham,** the country home of four generations of British monarchs.

1 Cambridge: Town & Gown ★★★

89km (55 miles) N of London; 129km (80 miles) NE of Oxford

The university town of Cambridge is a collage of images: the Bridge of Sighs; spires and turrets; drooping willows; dusty secondhand bookshops; carol singing on Christmas Eve in King's College Chapel; dancing until sunrise at the May balls; Elizabethan madrigals; narrow lanes upon which Darwin, Newton, and Cromwell once walked;

the "Backs" where the college lawns sweep down to the River Cam; tattered black robes of hurrying upperclassmen flying in the wind.

Along with Oxford, Cambridge is one of Britain's ancient seats of learning. In many ways their stories are similar, particularly the age-old conflict between town and gown. Cambridge can name-drop with the best of them, citing alumni such as Isaac Newton, John Milton, and Virginia Woolf. Cambridge continues to graduate many famous scientists such as physicist Stephen Hawking, author of *A Brief History of Time*.

In the 1990s, Cambridge became known as a high-tech outpost, or "a silicon fen," if you will. High-tech ventures continue to base themselves here to produce new software—start-up companies produce £2 billion ($4 billion) a year in revenues. Even Bill Gates, in 1997, financed an £80-million ($160-million) research center here, claiming that Cambridge was becoming "a world center of advanced technology."

ESSENTIALS

GETTING THERE   Trains depart frequently from London's Liverpool Street and Kings Cross stations, arriving an hour later. For inquiries, call © **0845/748-4950.** A one-way ticket costs £19 to £32 ($38–$64).

National Express buses leave hourly from London's Victoria Coach Station for the 2-hour trip to Drummer Street Station in Cambridge. A one-way ticket costs £10 ($20). For schedules and information, call © **0870/580-8080.**

If you're driving from London, head north on the M11.

GETTING AROUND   The center of Cambridge is made for pedestrians, so park your car at one of the car parks (rates increase as you approach the city center) and stroll the widely dispersed colleges. Follow the courtyards through to the Backs (the college lawns) and walk through to Trinity (where Prince Charles studied) and St. John's colleges, where you'll find the Bridge of Sighs.

Another popular way of getting around is by bicycle. **Station Cycles** (© **01223/ 307125;** www.stationcycles.co.uk) has bikes for rent for £6 ($12) per half-day, £8 ($16) per day, or £18 ($36) per week. A deposit of £50 ($100) is required. Call in advance to reserve a bike; at that time you'll be told the address at which to pick up the bike. The shop is open Monday to Friday 8am to 6pm, Saturday 9am to 5pm, and Sunday 10am to 4pm.

Stagecoach, 100 Cowley Rd. (© **01223/423-578**), services the Cambridge area with a network of buses, with fares ranging in price from 65p to £3 ($1.30–$6) for a day pass. The local tourist office has bus schedules.

VISITOR INFORMATION   In back of the guildhall, the **Cambridge Tourist Information Centre,** Wheeler Street (© **0871/2268006;** www.visitcambridge.org), has a wide range of information, including data on public transportation and sightseeing attractions. Year-round, the office is open Monday to Friday 10am to 5:30pm and Saturday 10am to 5pm; April to September, the office is also open Sunday 11am to 4pm.

City Sightseeing at Cambridge Railway Station (© **01223/457574**) on the concourse of the railway station, sells brochures and maps. Also available is a full range of tourist services, including accommodations booking. It's open in summer daily from 8:45am to 7pm (closes at 5pm off season). Guided tours of Cambridge leave the center daily.

SPECIAL EVENTS   Cambridge's artistic bent peaks at the end of July during the **Cambridge Folk Festival** (www.cambridgefolkfestival.co.uk). Event tickets are generally from £9 to £15 ($18–$30).

East Anglia

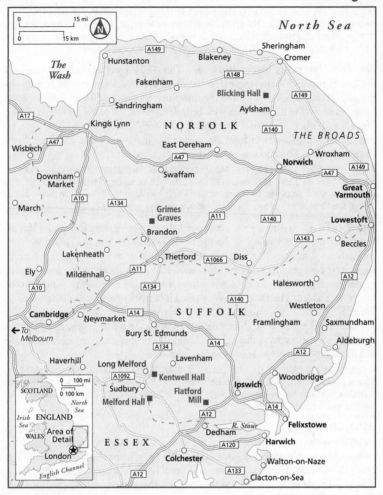

WHERE TO STAY
EXPENSIVE

Cambridge Garden ✸✸ This modern hotel sits between the riverbank and a cobblestone street in the oldest part of town, a short stroll from the principal colleges. (Because of its riverside location, we prefer it over its nearest competitor, the De Vere University Arms, which is in the center of town; see below.) It offers ample parking. You can rent punts at a boatyard next door. Visitors can relax on comfortable sofas and chairs in the bars and lounge. The soundproof bedrooms have wooden nightstands, adequate desk space, and private balconies. The expensive units (premium rooms) are very spacious with large sitting areas with face-to-face sofas. The river-view rooms are the most desirable. The hotel has a series of outdoor terraces where drinks and afternoon tea are served in nice weather.

Granta Place, Mill Lane, Cambridge, Cambridgeshire CB2 1RT. © **01223/259988**. Fax 01223/316605. www. moathousehotels.com. 122 units. £199–£239 ($398–$478) double. AE, DC, MC, V. Free parking. **Amenities:** Restaurant; bar; indoor heated pool; health club; Jacuzzi; sauna; steam room; business center; salon; room service; laundry service; dry cleaning. *In room:* A/C, TV, Wi-Fi, minibar, beverage maker, hair dryer, iron, safe.

De Vere University Arms Hotel ✦ This 1834 hotel maintains much of its antique charm and many original architectural features despite modernization over the years. Near the city center and the university, it offers suitable bedrooms. Rooms range from small to midsize, each with bedside controls; the premium rooms also have slippers and robes. Many of the bedrooms have been recently refurbished; eight have four-poster beds. Rooms in front are smaller but more up-to-date and have double-glazed windows. Three rooms are suitable for families.

Regent St., Cambridge, Cambridgeshire CB2 1AD. © **01223/273000**. Fax 01223/273037. www.devereonline.co.uk. 120 units. £140–£160 ($280–$320) double; £190 ($380) suite. Rates include English breakfast. AE, DC, MC, V. Parking £12 ($24). Bus: 1. **Amenities:** Restaurant; bar; room service; babysitting; laundry service; dry cleaning. *In room:* TV, high-speed Internet, minibar, beverage maker, hair dryer, iron, trouser press, safe.

Hotel Felix ✦✦ Although it lies about 1.6km (1 mile) from the center, this contemporary hotel has shot up to the top of the heap as the best in Cambridge. Set in more than 1.2 hectares (3 acres) of landscaped gardens, its stylish design and tasteful decor have brought luxury to the often staid accommodations of this university city. A chic boutique hotel, the Felix arises from a Victorian mansion to which two new wings were added. The *Daily Telegraph* called it "a work of art," and the *Sunday Times* hailed it as "one of the country's choicest boltholes." We like the way the Felix, Cambridge's first designer hotel, harmoniously blended the old and new, all while maintaining a cozy atmosphere throughout. Imbued with specially commissioned modern art, the bedrooms have wide beds and unfussy decor.

Whitehouse Lane, Huntingdon Rd., Cambridge CB3 0LX. © **01223/277977**. Fax 01223/277973. www.hotelfelix.co.uk. 52 units. £175–£215 ($350–$430) double; from £265 ($530) suite. Rates include breakfast. AE, DC, MC, V. Free parking. **Amenities:** Restaurant; bar; room service; access to health club; laundry service; dry cleaning. *In room:* TV, Wi-Fi, CD player, minibar, hair dryer, trouser press.

MODERATE

Arundel House Occupying one of the most desirable sites in Cambridge, this hotel consists of six interconnected identical Victorian row houses—all fronted with dark-yellow local bricks. In 1994, after two additional houses were purchased, the hotel was enlarged, upgraded, and expanded into the well-maintained hostelry you'll see today. Though not as well appointed as the University Arms or the Felix (see above), it competes successfully with the Gonville (see below) and has the best cuisine of the hotels. Rooms overlooking the River Cam and Jesus Green cost more, as do those on lower floors (there's no elevator). All rooms are simple but comfortable, with upholstered chairs and carpeting.

53 Chesterton Rd., Cambridge, Cambridgeshire CB4 3AN. © **01223/367701**. Fax 01223/367721. www.arundel househotels.co.uk. 103 units. £95–£140 ($190–$280) double; £120–£150 ($240–$300) family bedroom. Rates include continental breakfast. AE, DC, MC, V. Free parking. Bus: 1 or 3. **Amenities:** Restaurant (see review below); bar; laundry service; dry cleaning. *In room:* A/C, TV, beverage maker, hair dryer.

Gonville Hotel This hotel and its grounds are opposite Parker's Piece park, only a 5-minute walk from the center of town. The Gonville has been much improved in recent years and is better than ever, although not yet the equal of the Hotel Felix (see above). It's like an ivy-covered country house, with shade trees and a formal car entry. The recently refurbished rooms are comfortable and modern in style.

Gonville Place, Cambridge, Cambridgeshire CB1 1LY. ⓒ **800/780-7234** in the U.S. and Canada, or 01223/366611. Fax 01223/315470. www.gonvillehotel.co.uk. 73 units. £130–£149 ($260–$298) double. AE, DC, MC, V. Free parking. **Amenities:** Restaurant; bar; room service; laundry service; dry cleaning. *In room:* TV, Wi-Fi, beverage maker, hair dryer, iron, trouser press, safe.

Holiday Inn Cambridge

Located a short walk from a small artificial lake, which the bedrooms overlook, this modern two-story hotel is vaguely influenced by the designs of nearby country houses. There's a grassy courtyard partially enclosed by the hotel's wings. Public rooms with peak ceilings are furnished with scattered clusters of sofas and chairs. The small yet comfortable bedrooms have large windows with pleasant views.

Lakeview, Bridge Rd., Lakeview Bridge, Impington, Cambridge, Cambridgeshire CB4 9PH. ⓒ **888/465-4329** in the U.S. and Canada, or 08704/009015. Fax 01223/233426. www.holiday-inn.com. 161 units. £80–£185 ($160–$370) double. AE, DC, MC, V. Free parking. Bus: 104, 105, or 106. Drive 3km (2 miles) north of Cambridge on B1049 (Histon Rd.) to A45 intersection. **Amenities:** Restaurant; bar; indoor heated pool; health club; Jacuzzi; sauna; steam room; business center; salon; room service; babysitting; laundry service; dry cleaning. *In room:* TV, minibar (in some), beverage maker, hair dryer, safe.

Menzies Cambridge Hotel & Golf Course

This place offers the best sports facilities in the Cambridge area. Built around 1977, it has comfortable bedrooms with tub/shower combinations and nice views, a putting green, and an 18-hole championship golf course where greens fees range from £45 ($90) Monday to Friday to £60 ($120) Saturday and Sunday. There's a restaurant in the hotel, although the food is just standard stuff. Meals are also served daily in the bar.

Huntingdon Rd., Bar Hill, Cambridge, Cambridgeshire CB3 8EU. ⓒ **01954/249988.** Fax 01954/780010. www.menzies-hotels.co.uk. 136 units. £89–£205 ($178–$410) double. Children 15 and younger stay free in parent's room. AE, DC, MC, V. Free parking. Take A14 9km (5½ miles) northwest of the town center. **Amenities:** Restaurant; 2 bars; indoor heated pool; golf course; 2 tennis courts; health club; sauna; steam room; room service; laundry service; dry cleaning. *In room:* TV, Wi-Fi, beverage maker, hair dryer, trouser press.

INEXPENSIVE

Hamilton Hotel (Value

One of the better and more reasonably priced of the small hotels of Cambridge, this redbrick establishment lies about 1.6km (1 mile) northeast of the city center, close to the River Cam. Well run and modestly accessorized, the hotel stands on a busy highway, but there's a parking area out back. The well-furnished bedrooms contain reasonably comfortable twin or double beds. Bathrooms are compact with shower stalls. The hotel has a small, traditionally styled licensed bar, offering standard pub food and snacks.

156 Chesterton Rd., Cambridge, Cambridgeshire CB4 1DA. ⓒ **01223/365664.** Fax 01223/314866. www.hamiltonhotel cambridge.co.uk. 25 units. £55–£80 ($110–$160) double. Rates include English breakfast. AE, DC, MC, V. Free parking. Bus: 3 or 3A. **Amenities:** Bar. *In room:* TV, Wi-Fi, beverage maker, hair dryer.

Regent Hotel

This is one of the most desirable of Cambridge's reasonably priced small hotels. Right in the city center, overlooking Parker's Piece park, the house was built in the 1840s as the original site of Newnham College. It became a hotel when the college outgrew its quarters. Bedrooms are on the small side but are redecorated frequently in traditional Georgian style.

41 Regent St., Cambridge, Cambridgeshire CB2 1AB. ⓒ **01223/351470.** Fax 01223/464937. www.regenthotel.co.uk. 22 units. £109–£140 ($218–$280) double. Rates include continental breakfast. AE, DC, MC, V. Parking £10 ($20). Closed Dec 22–Jan 2. Bus: 1. **Amenities:** Bar. *In room:* A/C, TV, high-speed Internet, beverage maker, hair dryer, trouser press.

WHERE TO DINE

Drop down into the cozy **Rainbow Vegetarian Cafe,** King's Parade, across from King's College (© **01223/321551**), for coffee, a slice of fresh-baked cake, or a meal from their selection of whole-food and vegetarian offerings. A main-course lunch or dinner goes for only £7.95 ($16). It is open Tuesday to Saturday 10am to 10pm. The cafe lies at the end of a lily-lined path.

VERY EXPENSIVE

Midsummer House ★★ *Finds* MEDITERRANEAN   Located in an Edwardian-era cottage near the River Cam, the Midsummer House is a real find. We prefer to dine in the elegant conservatory, but you can also find a smartly laid table upstairs. The fixed-price menus are wisely limited, and quality control and high standards are much in evidence here. Daniel Clifford is the master chef, and he has created such special-ties as filet of beef Rossini with braised winter vegetables and sauce Perigourdine; and roast squab pigeon, *pomme* Anna, *tarte tatin* of onions, caramelized endives, and jus of morels.

Midsummer Common. © **01223/369299.** Reservations required. 2-course set lunch £45 ($90); 3-course fixed-price dinner £60 ($120). AE, MC, V. Tues–Sat noon–2pm and 7–10pm.

MODERATE

Arundel House Restaurant ★ ENGLISH/FRENCH/VEGETARIAN   One of the best and most acclaimed restaurants in Cambridge is in a hotel overlooking the River Cam and Jesus Green, a short walk from the city center. Winner of many awards, it's noted not only for its excellence and use of fresh produce, but also for its good value. The decor is warmly inviting with Sanderson curtains, Louis XV–uphol-stered chairs, and spacious tables. The menu changes frequently, and you can dine both à la carte or from the set menu. Perhaps you'll sample such dishes as filet of plaice in lime-and-basil butter or grilled salmon wrapped in Parma of ham. Medallions of pork are sautéed with sweet peppers and served in a Dijon-mustard-and-cream sauce, and supreme of chicken appears with wild mushrooms in a cream-and-brandy sauce.

In the Arundel House hotel, 53 Chesterton Rd. © **01223/367701.** Reservations required. Main courses £10–£19 ($20–$38); 2-course fixed-price menu £17 ($34), 3 courses £21 ($42). AE, DC, MC, V. Daily 7:30–10am, 12:15–1:45pm, and 6:30–9:30pm. Bus: 3 or 5.

Browns ★ *Value* CONTINENTAL/ENGLISH   After wowing them at Oxford, Browns now lures Cambridge students in equal numbers. The building lies opposite the Fitzwilliam Museum and was constructed in 1914 as the outpatient department of a hospital dedicated to Edward VII; that era's grandeur is apparent in the building's neoclassical colonnade. Today, it's the most lighthearted place for dining in the city, with wicker chairs, high ceilings, pre–World War I woodwork, and a long bar covered with bottles of wine. The extensive bill of fare includes pastas, scores of fresh salads, several selections of meat and fish (from charcoal-grilled leg of lamb with rosemary to fresh fish in season), hot sandwiches, and the chef's daily specials. If you drop by in the afternoon, you can also order thick milkshakes or natural fruit juices. In fair weather, outdoor seats are prized possessions.

23 Trumpington St. (5 min. from King's College and opposite the Fitzwilliam Museum). © **01223/461655.** Reservations not accepted on weekends. Main courses £9–£16 ($18–$32). AE, MC, V. Mon–Sat 10am–11pm; Sun 11:30am–10:30pm. Bus: 2.

Cotto ★ BRITISH/CONTINENTAL   This innovative restaurant lies above a small deli-bakery, attracting a youthful clientele to its contemporary, wood-filled interior decorated with modern paintings for sale. Its success stems from its "no frills, no choice" three-course fixed-price dinners. That menu is based on quality ingredients freshly cooked to order. A typical evening meal might begin with carpaccio of Cornish monkfish, follow with a soup of wood-roasted Fenland spaghetti squash with pesto. For a main, perhaps slow-roasted Suffolk partridge might appear with a beet salad, followed by a selection of cheese and poached prunes. For dessert, perhaps a tart of Willingham pear and almond. Much of the produce that goes into these meals comes from local organic farmers. Lunch is less elaborate, featuring such dishes as Pollock and leek fish cakes or roasted pigeon breast. You can also try Cotto for breakfast (have a slice of their sourdough bread).

183 East Rd. ℂ 01223/302010. Reservations recommended for dinner. Fixed-price dinner £30 ($60); lunch main courses £7.50–£12 ($15–$24). AE, MC, V. Mon–Thurs 8:30am–3:30pm; Fri–Sat 6–10pm.

Twenty Two ⊛ CONTINENTAL/ENGLISH   One of the best in Cambridge, this restaurant is located in a quiet district near Jesus Green and is a secret jealously guarded by the locals. The homelike but elegant Victorian dining room offers an ever-changing fixed-price menu based on fresh market produce. Owner David Carter uses time-tested recipes along with his own inspirations, offering creations such as white-onion soup with toasted goat cheese or sautéed breast of chicken on braised celery with thyme jus.

22 Chesterton Rd. ℂ 01223/351880. Reservations required. Fixed-price menu £28 ($56). AE, MC, V. Tues–Sat 7–9:30pm.

INEXPENSIVE

Charlie Chan CHINESE   Most people say that this is the finest Chinese restaurant in Cambridge, and we agree. We've always found Charlie Chan reliable and capable, which is remarkable given its huge menu. Downstairs is a long corridor-like restaurant, with pristine decor. The ambience is more lush in the Blue Lagoon upstairs. Most of the dishes here are inspired by the traditional cuisine of Beijing. The specialties we've most enjoyed include an aromatic and crispy duck, lemon chicken, and prawns with garlic and ginger. Most of the dishes are affordably priced except for the expensive shellfish specialties, especially lobster.

14 Regent St. ℂ 01223/361763. Reservations recommended. Main courses £6–£35 ($12–$70). AE, MC, V. Daily noon–5pm and 6–11pm.

The Green Man ENGLISH   Named in honor of Robin Hood, this 400-year-old inn is the most popular pub for outings from Cambridge. It's located on A604, 3km (2 miles) south of Cambridge in the hamlet of Grantchester, made famous by poet Rupert Brooke (see "Punting on the Cam," below). Even if you haven't heard of Brooke, you may enjoy a late afternoon wandering through the old church and then heading, as everybody does, to the Green Man. In winter, a crackling fire welcomes the weary, but in summer it's more tempting to retreat to the beer garden, from which you can stroll to the edge of the River Cam. Place your order at the counter; a server will bring your food to your table. The fare ranges from fish cakes in a Thai curry sauce to chicken Kiev and even traditional English pies and bangers and mash, as well as various vegetarian choices.

59 High St., Grantchester. ℂ 01223/841178. Reservations recommended. Main courses £5–£16 ($10–$32). MC, V. Restaurant Mon–Sat noon–2:30pm and 6:30–9:30pm; Sun noon–2:30pm. Pub Mon–Sat noon–2:30pm and 5:30–11pm; Sun noon–3pm. Bus: 118 from Cambridge.

ORGANIZED TOURS

The **Cambridge Tourist Information Centre** (earlier in this chapter) sponsors 2-hour walking tours, taking in the highlights of the city, costing £8 to £15 ($16–$30) for adults or £4.50 to £7.50 ($9–$15) for children 6 to 11, and free for children 5 and younger. Call for opening times.

City Sightseeing, on the concourse of Cambridge Railway Station (© 01708/866000), offers daily guided tours of Cambridge via open-top, double-decker buses. In summer, they depart every 15 minutes from 9:30am to 4pm from Silver Street. Departures are curtailed off season depending on demand. The tour can be a 1-hour ride, or you can get off at any of the many stops and rejoin the tour whenever you wish. Tickets are valid all day. The fare is £10 ($20) for adults, £7 ($14) for seniors and students, £5 ($10) for children 6 to 11, and free for kids 5 and younger. A family ticket for £25 ($50) covers two adults and up to three children.

EXPLORING THE UNIVERSITY

Oxford University predates Cambridge, but by the early 13th century, scholars began coming here, too. Eventually, Cambridge won partial recognition from Henry III, rising or falling with the approval of subsequent English monarchs. Cambridge consists of 31 colleges for both men and women. Colleges are closed for exams from mid-April until the end of June.

The following listing is only a sample of the colleges. If you're planning to be in Cambridge a while, you may also want to visit **Magdalene College,** on Magdalene Street, founded in 1542; **Pembroke College,** on Trumpington Street, founded in 1347; **Christ's College,** on St. Andrew's Street, founded in 1505; and **Corpus Christi College,** on Trumpington Street, which dates from 1352.

KING'S COLLEGE ✶✶   The adolescent Henry VI founded King's College on King's Parade (© 01223/331100; www.kings.cam.ac.uk) in 1441. Most of its buildings today date from the 19th century, but the construction of its crowning glory, the **Perpendicular King's College Chapel** ✶✶✶, began in the Middle Ages. Owing to the whims of royalty, the chapel wasn't completed until the early 16th century.

Henry James called King's College Chapel "the most beautiful in England." Its most striking features are its magnificent fan vaulting, all in stone, and its great windows, most of which were fashioned by Flemish artisans between 1517 and 1531 (the west window dates from the late Victorian period). The chapel also boasts Rubens's *Adoration of the Magi* and an ornamental screen from the early 16th century. The chapel is famous for its choir and musical concerts. You can call the college (phone number above) for concert dates and times.

Tips **Caution: Students at Work**

Because of disturbances caused by the influx of tourists, Cambridge limits visitors, or excludes them altogether, from various parts of the university. In some cases, a small entry fee is charged. Small groups of up to six people are generally admitted with no problem; you can inquire with the local tourist office about visiting hours. All colleges are closed during exams and graduation, on Easter and all bank holidays, and other times without notice.

Cambridge

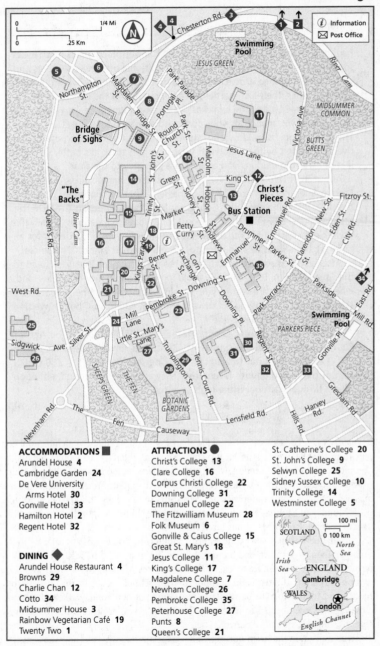

0 1/4 Mi
0 .25 Km

Information
Post Office

Chesterton Rd.

Swimming Pool

JESUS GREEN

Northampton St.

Magdalen St.

Park Parade

Portugal Pl.

Bridge St.

Park/Round Church St.

Bridge of Sighs

St. John's St.

Green St.

Jesus Lane

Malcolm St.

Hobson St.

Sidney St.

King St.

Christ's Pieces

MIDSUMMER COMMON

Victoria Ave

BUTTS GREEN

Fitzroy St.

New Sq.

Eden St.

City Rd.

"The Backs"

River Cam

Queen's Rd.

West Rd.

Trinity St.

Market

Petty Curry

Benet St.

Corn Exchange St.

Andrews St.

Bus Station

Emmanuel St.

Drummer St.

Parker St.

Clarendon St.

Emmanuel Rd.

Kings Parade

Pembroke St.

Downing St.

Downing Pl.

Park Terrace

Parkside

East Rd.

Mill Rd.

Mill Lane

Little St. Mary's Lane

Trumpington St.

Tennis Court Rd.

Regent St.

Swimming Pool

PARKERS PIECE

Gonville Pl.

Gresham Rd.

Sidgwick

Ave. Silver St.

SHEEPS GREEN

THE FEN

BOTANIC GARDENS

Newnham Rd.

The Fen

Causeway

Lensfield Rd.

Hills Rd.

Harvey Rd.

ACCOMMODATIONS ■
Arundel House **4**
Cambridge Garden **24**
De Vere University Arms Hotel **30**
Gonville Hotel **33**
Hamilton Hotel **2**
Regent Hotel **32**

DINING ◆
Arundel House Restaurant **4**
Browns **29**
Charlie Chan **12**
Cotto **34**
Midsummer House **3**
Rainbow Vegetarian Café **19**
Twenty Two **1**

ATTRACTIONS ●
Christ's College **13**
Clare College **16**
Corpus Christi College **22**
Downing College **31**
Emmanuel College **22**
The Fitzwilliam Museum **28**
Folk Museum **6**
Gonville & Caius College **15**
Great St. Mary's **18**
Jesus College **11**
King's College **17**
Magdalene College **7**
Newham College **26**
Pembroke College **35**
Peterhouse College **27**
Punts **8**
Queen's College **21**

St. Catherine's College **20**
St. John's College **9**
Selwyn College **25**
Sidney Sussex College **10**
Trinity College **14**
Westminster College **5**

SCOTLAND
North Sea
Irish Sea
ENGLAND
Cambridge
WALES
London
English Channel

0 100 mi
0 100 km

⌒Moments Punting on the Cam

Punting on the River Cam in a wood-built, flat-bottomed boat (which looks somewhat like a Venetian gondola) is a traditional pursuit of students and visitors to Cambridge. Downstream, you pass along the ivy-covered "backs" of the colleges, their lush gardens sweeping down to the Cam.

People sprawl along the banks of the Cam on a summer day to judge and tease you as you maneuver your punt with a pole about 4.5m (15 ft.) long. The river's floor is muddy, and many a student has lost his pole in the riverbed shaded by the willows. If your pole gets stuck, it's better to leave it sticking in the mud instead of risking a plunge into the river.

About 3km (2 miles) upriver lies Grantchester, immortalized by Rupert Brooke. Literary types flock to Grantchester, either by punting or by taking the path following the River Granta for less than an hour to Grantchester Meadows (the town lies about 1.6km/1 mile from the meadows). When the town clock stopped for repairs in 1985, its hands were left frozen "for all time" at 10 minutes to 3, in honor of Brooke's famed sonnet "The Soldier."

After so much activity, you're bound to get hungry or thirsty, so head to the **Green Man** (p. 537), a 400-year-old inn named in honor of Robin Hood, where a crackling fire warms you in cold weather and summer features a back beer garden, leading off toward the river, where your punt is waiting to take you back to Cambridge.

Scudamore's Boatyards, Granta Place (© 01223/359750), by the Anchor Pub, has been in business since 1910. Punts and rowboats rent for £14 to £18 ($28–$36) per hour (maximum of six persons per punt). A £80 ($160) cash or credit card deposit is required. They are open year-round, although March through October is the high season.

Insider's tip: For a classic view of the chapel, you can admire the architectural complex from the rear, which is an ideal picnic spot along the river. To acquire the makings of a picnic, head for the vendors who peddle inexpensive food, including fresh fruit, at **Market Square,** open Monday to Saturday 9:30am to 4:30pm. You can also get the makings of a picnic at a major grocery store, **Sainsbury's,** 44 Sidney St. (© 01223/366891), open Monday to Saturday 8am to 10pm and Sunday 11am to 5pm. E. M. Forster came here to contemplate scenes for his novel *Maurice.*

The chapel is open during college term, Monday to Friday 9:30am to 3:30pm, Saturday 9:30am to 3:15pm, and Sunday 1:15 to 2:15pm and 5 to 5:30pm. During the term, the public is welcome to attend choral services Monday to Saturday at 5:30pm and on Sunday at 10:30am and 3:30pm. During school vacations, the chapel is open to visitors Monday to Saturday 9:30am to 4:30pm and on Sunday 10am to 5pm; it is closed from December 23 to January 1. It may be closed at other times for recording sessions, broadcasts, and concerts.

An exhibition in the seven northern side chapels shows why and how the chapel was built. Admission to the college and chapel, including the exhibition, is £4.50 ($9) for adults, £3 ($6) for students and seniors, and free for children 11 and younger.

EMMANUEL COLLEGE   On St. Andrew's Street, Emmanuel (© **01223/334200;** www.emma.cam.ac.uk) was founded in 1584 by Sir Walter Mildmay, a chancellor of the exchequer to Elizabeth I. John Harvard, of the American university that bears his name in another city called Cambridge, studied here. You can stroll around Emmanuel's attractive gardens and visit the chapel designed by Sir Christopher Wren, consecrated in 1677. Both the chapel and college are open daily during sunlight hours.

Insider's tip: Harvard men and women, and those who love them, can look for a memorial window in Wren's chapel dedicated to John Harvard, an alumnus of Emmanuel who lent his name to that other university.

PETERHOUSE COLLEGE   On Trumpington Street, Peterhouse College (© **01223/ 338200;** www.pet.cam.ac.uk) attracts visitors because it's the oldest Cambridge college, founded in 1284 by Hugh de Balsham, the bishop of Ely. Of the original buildings, only the hall remains. It was restored in the 19th century and has stained-glass windows by William Morris. The chapel, called Old Court, dates from 1632 and was renovated in 1754. Ask to enter at the porter's lodge.

Insider's tip: Almost sadly neglected, the Little Church of St. Mary's next door was the college chapel until 1632. Pay it the honor of a visit.

QUEENS' COLLEGE ★★   On Silver Street, Queens' College (© **01223/335511;** www.quns.cam.ac.uk) is the loveliest of Cambridge's colleges. Dating back to 1448, it was founded by two English queens, Margaret of Anjou, the wife of Henry VI, and Elizabeth Woodville, the wife of Edward IV. Its second cloister is the most interesting, flanked by the early-16th-century half-timbered President's Lodge.

Admission is £2 ($4) for adults, free for children 11 and younger accompanied by parents. A printed guide is issued. From October 27 to March 14, hours are daily 1:45 to 4:30pm; March 15 to May 18 Monday to Friday 11am to 3pm, Saturday and Sunday 10am to 4:30pm; May 19 to June 21 closed; June 22 to September 28 daily 10am to 4:30pm; September 29 to October 26 Monday to Friday 10:45am to 4:30pm, Saturday and Sunday 10am to 4:30pm. Entry and exit is by the old porter's lodge in Queens' Lane only. The old hall and chapel are usually open to the public when not in use.

Insider's tip: Queens' College's wide lawns lead down to the "Backs" (the backs of the colleges), where you can stroll, sit, or go punting. Take in Mathematical Bridge, best viewed from the Silver Street bridge, dating from 1902.

ST. JOHN'S COLLEGE ★★   On St. John's Street, this college (© **01223/338600;** www.joh.cam.ac.uk) was founded in 1511 by Lady Margaret Beaufort, mother of Henry VII, who had launched Christ's College a few years earlier. The impressive gateway bears the Tudor coat of arms, and the Second Court is a fine example of late Tudor brickwork. The college's best-known feature is the Bridge of Sighs crossing the Cam. Built in the 19th century, it was patterned after the covered bridge in Venice. It connects the older part of the college with New Court, a Gothic Revival on the opposite bank, where there is an outstanding view of the famous "backs." The Bridge of Sighs is closed to visitors but can be seen from neighboring Kitchen Bridge. Wordsworth was an alumnus of this college. Visitors are admitted from March 3 to October 28 daily 10am to 5:30pm; it is also open Saturday and Sunday in November and again in February at the hours given. Admission is £2.80 ($5.60) for adults, £1.70 ($3.40) for seniors and children 12 to 17, free for children 11 and younger. Visitors are welcome to attend choral services in the chapel.

Insider's tip: The Bridge of Sighs links the old college with an architectural "folly" of the 19th century, the elaborate New Court, which is a crenelated neo-Gothic fantasy. It's adorned with a "riot" of pinnacles and a main cupola. Students call it "the wedding cake."

TRINITY COLLEGE ✦✦   On Trinity Street, Trinity College (not to be confused with Trinity Hall; ✆ **01223/338400;** www.trin.cam.ac.uk) is the largest college in Cambridge. It was founded in 1546 by Henry VIII, who consolidated a number of smaller colleges that had existed on the site. The courtyard is the most spacious in Cambridge, built when Thomas Neville was master. Sir Christopher Wren designed the library.

Insider's tip: What's fun to do here is to contemplate what went on here before you arrived. Pause at Neville's Court where Isaac Newton first calculated the speed of sound. Take in the delicate fountain of the Great Court where Lord Byron used to bathe naked with his pet bear. Why a bear? The university forbade students from having dogs, but there was no proviso for bears. Years later, Vladimir Nabokov walked through that same courtyard dreaming of the young lady he would later immortalize as *Lolita*. For admission to the college, apply at the porter's lodge. Trinity College is open to visitors March to November Monday to Friday from 10am to 5pm. There's a charge of £2.20 ($4.40) adults, £1.30 ($2.60) seniors and children, and £4.40 ($8.80) for families.

CAMBRIDGE'S OTHER ATTRACTIONS

Fitzwilliam Museum ✦✦   This is one of Britain's finest museums, founded by the bequest of the seventh viscount Fitzwilliam of Merrion to the University of Cambridge in 1816. The permanent collections contain remarkable antiquities from ancient Egypt, Greece, and Rome. Galleries display Roman and Romano-Egyptian art along with Western-Asiatic exhibits. The Fitzwilliam's Applied Arts section showcases English and European pottery and glass, as well as furniture, clocks, armor, fans, rugs and samplers, Chinese jades, and ceramics from Japan and Korea. The museum also has married a rare ancient and medieval coin collection with a host of medals created from the Renaissance onward. The Fitzwilliam is best loved for its collection of paintings, which includes masterpieces by Simone Martini, Titian, Veronese, Rubens, Van Dyck, Canaletto, Hogarth, Gainsborough, Constable, Monet, Degas, Renoir, Cézanne, and Picasso. There is also a fine collection of other 20th-century art, miniatures, drawings, watercolors, and prints. The Fitzwilliam stages occasional musical events, including evening concerts, in Gallery III. Throughout the year, it plays host to some of the best lectures in England.

Trumpington St., near Peterhouse. ✆ **01223/332900.** www.fitzmuseum.cam.ac.uk. Free admission, donations appreciated; guided tours £6 ($12) per person. Tues–Sat 10am–5pm, Sun noon–5pm; tours Sat 2:45pm. Closed Jan 1, Good Friday, May Day, and Dec 24–31.

Great St. Mary's   Closely associated with events of the Reformation because the leaders of the movement (Erasmus, Cranmer, Latimer, and Ridley) preached here, this university church was built mostly in 1478 on the site of an 11th-century church. The cloth that covered the hearse of King Henry VII is on display in the church. There is a fine view of Cambridge from the top of the tower.

King's Parade. ✆ **01223/741716.** Admission to tower £2 ($4) adults, £1 ($2) children. Tower summer Mon–Sat 9:30am–5pm, Sun 12:30–5pm; church daily 9am–6pm.

SHOPPING

Forage around the shops lining St. John's Street, Trinity Street, King's Parade, and Trumpington Street.

Primavera, 10 King's Parade (© **01223/357708**), is a showplace of British crafts, featuring pottery, glass, ceramics, jewelry, ironwork, and fabric crafts ranging from ties to wall hangings. Be sure to explore the basement exhibition of paintings and crafts items.

A posh area of extremely chic, small, and exclusive shops runs between Market Square and Trinity Street and is called **Rose Crescent.** Here, you can buy leather goods, smart women's clothing, and fine hats as well as jewelry and a host of very expensive gift items.

Another well-defined shopping district is comprised of Bridge, Sidney, St. Andrew's, and Regent streets.

For book lovers, Cambridge's bookstores will truly delight you. **Heffers of Cambridge** is a huge book, stationery, and music store with six branches, all of which can be contacted through one central phone number (© **01223/568568**). The main store, at 20 Trinity St., carries academic books; an art-and-graphics shop has an address of 15–21 King St.; and the music store at 19 Trinity St. features classical, popular, and choral college music. Heffers also has a shop in the mall at Grafton Centre that carries new fiction and nonfiction titles.

David G., 16 St. Edward's Passage (© **01223/354619**), hawks secondhand books, publishers' overruns at reduced prices, and antiquarian books. **Waterstone,** 22 Sydney St. (© **01223/351688**), deals exclusively in new books on a variety of subjects. The **Haunted Bookshop,** 9 St. Edward's Passage (© **01223/312913**), specializes in out-of-print children's books and first editions.

CAMBRIDGE AFTER DARK

Nightlife in this university city revolves around the new and improved complex, **Cambridge Leisure Park** (© **01223/511511**), lying behind the Cambridge Station. The complex features a multiscreen cinema, a bowling alley, numerous chain restaurants, and bars, some of which offer live entertainment. Saturday night is the big blast here, attracting hundreds of university students. There is also a theater presenting comedy, drama, and even children's shows.

You can take in a production where Emma Thompson and other well-known thespians got their start at the **Amateur Dramatic Club,** Park Street near Jesus Lane (© **01223/359547,** or 01223/300085 for box office; www.cuadc.org). It presents two student productions nightly, Tuesday through Saturday, with the main show tending toward classic and modern drama or opera, and the late show being of a comic or experimental nature. The theater is open nearly year-round, closing in September, and tickets run from £3.50 to £8 ($7–$16).

The most popular Cantabrigian activity is the **pub-crawl** (www.cambridge-pubs. co.uk). With too many pubs in the city to list, you may as well start at Cambridge's oldest pub, the **Pickerel,** on Magdalene Street (© **01223/355068**), dating from 1432. English pubs don't get more traditional than this. If the ceiling beams or floorboards groan occasionally—well, they've certainly earned the right over the years. Real ales on tap include Bulmer's Traditional Cider, Old Speckled Hen, Theakston's 6X, Old Peculiar, and Best Bitter. The **Maypole,** Portugal Place at Park Street (© **01223/ 352999**), is the local hangout for actors from the nearby ADC Theatre. Known for cocktails and not ales, you can still get a Tetley's 6X or Castle Eden.

The **Eagle,** Benet Street off King's Parade (✆ **01223/505020**), will be forever famous as the place where Nobel Laureates Watson and Crick first announced their discovery of the DNA double helix. Real ales include Icebreaker and local brewery Greene King's Abbott, so make your order and raise a pint to the wonders of modern science.

To meet up with current Cambridge students, join the locals at the **Anchor,** Silver Street (✆ **01223/353554**), or **Tap and Spiel (the Mill),** 14 Mill Lane, off Silver Street Bridge (✆ **01223/357026**), for a pint of Greene King's IPA or Abbott. The crowd at the Anchor spills out onto the bridge in fair weather, whereas the Tap and Spiel's clientele lays claim to the entire riverside park.

For a gay and lesbian hangout, your best bet is to head for **Five Bells,** 126 Newmarket St. (✆ **01223/314019**), especially on a Friday or Saturday night when the joint is packed. In summer the action overflows into the garden in the rear. You might also check out **Fleur-de-Lys,** 73 Humberstone Rd. (✆ **01223/470401**), which features everything from drag shows to striptease, dance music, and karaoke.

For musical entertainment, you can find out who's playing by checking out fliers posted around town or by reading the *Varsity.* The **Corn Exchange,** Wheeler Street and Corn Exchange (✆ **01223/357851**), hosts everything from classical concerts to bigger-name rock shows. The **Graduate,** 16 Chesterton Rd. (✆ **01223/301416**), is a pub located in a former movie theater.

Entertainment in some form can be found nightly at the **Junction,** Clifton Road, near the train station (✆ **01223/511511**), where an eclectic mix of acts takes the stage weeknights to perform all genres of music, comedy, and theater, and DJs take over on the weekend. Cover charges vary from £5 to £19 ($10–$38), depending on the event.

Ballare, Lion Yard (✆ **01223/364222**), a second-story club, has a huge dance floor and plays everything from house to the latest pop hits, Monday to Saturday 9pm until 2am. Sometimes they even DJ the old-fashioned way, by taking requests. The cover charge ranges from £3 to £8 ($6–$16), depending on what night you're here.

2 Ely

113km (70 miles) NE of London; 26km (16 miles) N of Cambridge

Ely Cathedral is the top attraction in the fen country, outside of Cambridge. After you've seen the cathedral, you can safely be on your way; Ely is simply a sleepy market town that can't compete with the life and bustle found at Cambridge.

ESSENTIALS

GETTING THERE Ely is a major railway junction served by express trains to Cambridge. Service is frequent from London's Kings Cross. For schedules and information, call ✆ **0845/748-4950** or visit **www.nationalrail.co.uk**.

Stagecoach buses run frequently between Cambridge and Ely. Call ✆ **01223/423578** for schedules and information.

If you're driving from Cambridge, take the A10 north.

VISITOR INFORMATION The **Tourist Information Centre** is at Oliver Cromwell's House, 29 St. Mary's St. (✆ **01353/662062;** www.ely.org.uk); it's open April through October daily 10am to 5:30pm, and November to March Monday to Friday 11am to 4pm, Saturday 10am to 5pm, and Sunday 11:15am to 4pm.

WHERE TO STAY

Lamb Hotel   Right in the center of town, this hotel is a former 14th-century coaching inn. In the shadow of the cathedral, this hotel offers renovated bedrooms furnished traditionally but with modern comfort. Each contains a good English bed, usually king-size or twin. Bathrooms offer adequate shelf space and tub/shower combinations. In the 1400s, this place was known as the "Holy Lambe," a stopping-off spot for wayfarers, often pilgrims, passing through East Anglia. Rather standard English meals are served.

2 Lynn Rd., Ely, Cambridgeshire CB7 4EJ. ℭ 01353/663574. Fax 01353/662023. www.thelamb-ely.com. 31 units. £65–£125 ($130–$250) double. Rates include English breakfast. AE, DC, MC, V. Free parking. Bus: 109. **Amenities:** Restaurant; bar; room service; laundry service; dry cleaning. *In room:* TV, beverage maker, hair dryer, trouser press.

WHERE TO DINE

Around the corner from St. Mary's Church is **Steeplegate,** 16–18 High St. (ℭ **01353/664731**), a tearoom and craft shop with wooden tables and ancient windows. There are tea selections plus light lunch items, scones, and creamy gâteaux. After tea, venture downstairs to the craft shop and have a look at the variety of handmade pottery, glass, and baskets.

An unusual choice is the **Almonry Restaurant & Tea Rooms in the College,** Ely Cathedral, High Street (ℭ **01353/666360**). Housed in the medieval college buildings on the north side of the cathedral, this is a comfortable tearoom with table service in a beautiful 12th-century undercroft licensed to sell drinks. You can take your tea out to a garden seat in good weather. It is open for late-morning coffee, lunches, and afternoon teas. Meals start at £7 ($14).

Boathouse 🍴 BRITISH/CONTINENTAL   This is the best gastro-pub-cum-restaurant in town, housed in a converted boathouse that opens onto Great Ouse. The cookery is generous and personal, menus showcasing modern dishes with authentic country roots. The lunch menu features dishes not usually found at midday, including pigeon with chicory and a pine-nut salad, or a snail, leek, and Gruyère gratin. At night you can kick off with such starters as smoked loin of venison or crab cakes with ginger mayonnaise. Main courses are likely to feature pork belly with honey-glazed baby onions in a cider sauce, or else sea bass with shellfish potato cakes and fried leeks. For dessert, few items equal the honey-and-hazelnut mousse.

5 Annesdale. ℭ 01353/664388. Reservations recommended. Main courses lunch £10–£15 ($20–$30), dinner £10–£19 ($20–$38). AE, MC, V. Daily noon–2:30pm and 6–9:30pm.

The Old Fire Engine House 🍴 *Finds* ENGLISH   It's worth a special trip to this converted fire station in a walled garden, within a building complex that includes an art gallery. Soups are served in huge bowls, accompanied by coarse-grained crusty bread. Main dishes include lamb noisettes in pastry with tomato and basil, jugged hare, casseroled pheasant, and rabbit with mustard and parsley. Two especially good dishes include casserole of pigeon and beef braised in both port wine and Guinness. In summer, you can dine outside in the garden and even order a cream tea.

25 St. Mary's St. (opposite St. Mary's Church). ℭ 01353/662582. Reservations required. Main courses £14–£18 ($28–$36). MC, V. Daily 12:30–2pm and 3:30–5:30pm; Mon–Sat 10:30–11:30am and 7:30–9pm. Bus: 109.

SEEING THE SIGHTS

Ely Cathedral 🍴🍴   The near-legendary founder of this cathedral was Etheldreda, the wife of a Northumbrian king who established a monastery on the spot in 673. The present structure dates from 1081. Visible for miles around, the landmark octagonal lantern is the crowning glory of the cathedral. Erected in 1322 following the collapse of the old tower, it represents a remarkable engineering achievement. Four hundred tons of lead and wood hang in space, held there by timbers reaching to the eight pillars.

You enter the cathedral through the Galilee West Door, a good example of the Early English style of architecture. The lantern tower and the Octagon are the most notable features inside, but visit the Lady Chapel, too. Although its decor has deteriorated over the centuries, it's still a handsome example of the Perpendicular style, having been completed in the mid–14th century. The entry fee goes to help preserve the cathedral. Monday through Saturday, guided tours gather at 11:15am and 2:15pm in the off season; in the summer, tours occur throughout the day.

At the Brass Rubbing Centre, a large selection of replica brass is available for you to rub. These can produce remarkable results for wall hangings or special gifts. It's open year-round in the North Aisle, outside the Cathedral Shop.

ⓒ **01353/667735.** www.cathedral.ely.anglican.org. Admission £5.20 ($10) adults, £4.50 ($9) students and seniors, free for children 11 and younger. Apr–Oct daily 7am–7pm; Nov–Mar Mon–Sat 7:30am–6pm, Sun 7:30am–5pm.

Ely Museum   A gallery presents a chronological history of Ely and the Ely Isle from the Ice Age to the present day. Displays include archaeology, social history, rural life, local industry, and military history, as well as a tableau of the debtor's cell and condemned cell, which are also on view.

The Old Gaol, Market St. ⓒ **01353/666655.** www.elymuseum.org.uk. Admission £3 ($6) adults; £2.50 ($5) children, students, and seniors; free for children 6 and younger. Summer Mon–Sat 10:30am–5pm, Sun 1–5pm; winter Mon and Wed–Sat 10:30am–4pm, Sun 1–4pm. Closed Dec 20–Jan 2.

Grimes Graves   This is the largest and best-preserved group of Neolithic flint mines in Britain; they produced the cutting edges of spears, arrows, and knives for prehistoric tribes throughout the region. Because of its isolated location within sparsely populated, fir-wooded countryside, it's easy to imagine yourself transported back through the millennia.

A guardian will meet you near the well-signposted parking lot. After determining that you are not physically impaired, he or she will open one or several of the mineshafts, each of which requires a descent down an almost-vertical 9m (30-ft.) ladder (a visit here is not recommended for very young children, elderly travelers, or those with disabilities). Because the tunnel and shaft have been restored and reinforced, it's now possible to see where work took place during Neolithic times. Although it's not essential, many archaeologists, professional and amateur, bring their own flashlights with them. The mines, incidentally, are situated close to the military bases that housed thousands of American Air Force personnel during World War II.

On B1107, 4km (2¾ miles) northeast of Brandon, Norfolkshire. ⓒ **01842/810656.** www.english-heritage.org.uk. Admission £2.90 ($5.80) adults; £1.50 ($3) students, seniors, and children 5–15; £7.30 ($15) family ticket; free for children 4 and younger. Mar and Oct Thurs–Mon 10am–5pm; Apr–Sept daily 10am–6pm. Take A134 for 11km (7 miles) northwest of Thetford, then transfer to B1107.

Oliver Cromwell's House   This restored house was owned by the Puritan Oliver Cromwell, a name hardly beloved by the royals, even today. He rose to fame as a military and political leader during the English Civil Wars of 1642 to 1649, which led to the execution of Charles I and the replacement of the monarchy by the Commonwealth, the designation for England until the monarchy was restored. In 1653, Cromwell was declared lord protector, and the local farmer was the most powerful man in the land until his death in 1658. Exhibitions, displays, and period rooms offer insight into Cromwell's character and 17th-century domestic life. A tourist center is also located here.

29 St. Mary's St. (next to St. Mary's Church). ⓒ **01353/662062.** www.ely.org.uk/tic.htm. Admission £4 ($8) adults, £3.60 ($7.20) seniors and students, £2.95 ($5.90) children, £12 ($24) family ticket. Apr–Oct daily 10am–5:30pm; off season Sun–Fri 11am–4pm, Sat 10am–5pm.

3 Newmarket

100km (62 miles) NE of London; 21km (13 miles) NE of Cambridge

This old Suffolk town has been famous as a horse-racing center since the time of James I. Visitors can see Nell Gwynne's House, but mainly they come to visit Britain's first and only equestrian museum.

GETTING THERE

Trains depart from London's Liverpool Street Station every 45 to 60 minutes for Cambridge (see earlier in this chapter). In Cambridge, passengers change trains and head in the direction of Mildenhall. Three stops later, they arrive at Newmarket.

About eight National Express buses leave London's Victoria Coach Station for Norwich every day, stopping at Stratford, Stansted, and (finally) Newmarket along the way. For schedules and information, call ⓒ **0870/580-8080** or visit **www.national express.com**.

If you're driving from Cambridge, head east on the A133.

WHERE TO STAY & DINE

Heath Court Hotel   A member of the Queen's Moat House hotel chain, this brick-fronted hotel is near the Gallops, the exercise area for the stables at the Newmarket Heath racetrack, about a 5-minute walk from the center of town. Built in the mid-1970s, it's a favorite of the English horse-racing world and is fully booked during the racing season. Its public rooms are decorated in an appropriate country-elegant style, including oil portraits of horses and souvenirs of the racing life in its bar and restaurant. The bedrooms are well appointed, conservatively modern, and comfortable. Most of the units are spacious and, in the more expensive units, called executive rooms, there are also bathrobes and small refrigerators.

Moulton Rd., Newmarket, Suffolk CB8 8DY. ⓒ **800/780-7234** in the U.S. and Canada, or **01638/667171.** Fax 01638/ 666533. www.heathcourt-hotel.co.uk. 43 units. £110–£145 ($220–$290) double; £145–£195 ($290–$390) studio; £165–£235 ($330–$470) family room; £250–£290 ($500–$580) suite. Extra bed £40 ($80). Rates include English breakfast. AE, DC, MC, V. Free parking. **Amenities:** Restaurant; bar; room service; laundry service. *In room:* A/C, TV, Wi-Fi, beverage maker, hair dryer, trouser press, safe.

Swynford Paddocks ⓚ   This well-appointed country house, one of the finest in the area, is situated on a 24-hectare (60-acre) stud farm surrounded by beautiful grounds. Once a retreat of Lord Byron, he wrote many of his works at the foot of a now-felled beech. The house then became the home of Lord and Lady Halifax until 1976, when it was converted into a luxury hotel. Many guests use it as a base for exploring both Newmarket and Cambridge. Each spacious bedroom, opening onto scenic views, is decorated with a special character; some have four-poster beds and are quite romantic. For extra-special occasions, try for a suite of rooms or the two sumptuous four-poster rooms.

Six Mile Bottom, Cambridgeshire CB8 0UE. ⓒ **01638/570234.** Fax 01638/570283. www.swynfordpaddocks.com. 15 units. £135–£175 ($270–$350) double. Prices double during races. Rates include English breakfast. AE, DC, MC, V. Free parking. Take A1304 9.5km (6 miles) southwest of Newmarket. **Amenities:** 2 restaurants; bar; room service; laundry service; dry cleaning. *In room:* TV, beverage maker, hair dryer, trouser press.

OFF TO THE RACES

Britain's most prestigious racecourse lies at **Newmarket,** a small country town whose main tourist draw is the series of warm-weather horse races with origins dating from the days of James I and Charles II. Charles II was so enthusiastic about racing that he frequently ordered most of his Restoration-era court up from London to attend the races.

The headquarters of British racing, and the venue where precedents and policies are hammered out before being applied to the more formal venue of Ascot, Newmarket is the only racecourse in Britain with two separate racetracks.

The more bucolic of these is the July Race Course, where races are held during the heat and glare of June, July, and August. It's the site of the prestigious July Cup. The Rowley Mile, smaller than the other course, is known for its rows of beech trees that shade the saddling boxes and promenade grounds, as well as the thatched roofs that add an old-English charm to ornamental entryways and some of the showcase buildings used by investors, owners, and fans. The grandstands have conventional roofs shielding fans from the sun and the rain.

The more industrial-looking racetrack is the Rowley Mile, used during the racing season's cooler months (mid-Apr to late May and early Sept to Nov 2). Dress codes are less strictly observed here than at the July Race Course, where men wear jackets and ties, but the venue at Rowley Mile attracts a bigger and brasher crowd. At the Rowley Mile, prestigious races such as the Guineas Races, the Cesarewitch Handicap, and the Champion Stakes are run.

The two courses lie within 1km (a half-mile) of each other and share the same administration. For information, contact the **Clerk of the Course,** Westfield House, the Links, Newmarket, Suffolk CB8 0TG (✆ **01638/663482;** www.newmarketrace courses.co.uk).

National Horseracing Museum   Visitors can see the history of horse racing over 300 years in this museum housed in the old subscription rooms, early-19th-century betting rooms. There are fine paintings of famous horses, paintings on loan from Queen Elizabeth II, and copies of old parliamentary acts governing races. A 53-minute audiovisual presentation shows races and racehorses.

To make history come alive for visitors, they also offer equine tours of this historic town. Guides take you to watch morning gallops on the heath where you'll see bronzes of horses from the past.

99 High St. ✆ 01638/667333. www.nhrm.co.uk. Admission £5.50 ($11) adults, £4.50 ($9) seniors, £3 ($6) children. Mar 18–Nov 2 daily 11am–4pm (opens 10am on race days); off season Mon–Sat 10am–4:30pm.

The National Stud   Next to Newmarket's July Race Course, 3km (2 miles) southwest of the town, this place is home to some of the world's finest horses and a renowned breeding stud operation. A tour lasting about 75 minutes lets you see many mares and foals, plus top-class stallions. Reservations for tours must be made at the National Stud office or by phoning the number given below.

July Race Course. ✆ 01638/666789. www.nationalstud.co.uk. Admission £6.50 ($13) adults; £5 ($10) seniors, students, and children. Mar–Sept race day only. Guided tours daily 11:15am and 2:30pm. Closed Dec–Feb.

4 Bury St. Edmunds ✯

127km (79 miles) NE of London; 43km (27 miles) E of Cambridge; 19km (12 miles) N of Lavenham

Bury St. Edmunds is "a handsome little town, of thriving and cleanly appearance." That's how Charles Dickens described it in *Pickwick Papers,* and it remains true. This historic town, founded around the powerful Benedictine Abbey in 1020, derives its name from St. Edmund, king of the East Angles in the mid–9th century. In the Abbey Church, the barons of England united and forced King John to sign the Magna Carta in 1214. Though it's sometimes hard to tell, Bury is filled with many original medieval buildings. (Many buildings were given face-lifts in the 17th and 18th c.; it's only when you step inside that their medieval roots become clear.) During the 18th century, this market town was quite prosperous and had a thriving cloth-making industry. The large number of fine Georgian buildings bear testament to the wealth of the day.

Upon the Vikings' arrival to the area, they dubbed it "the Summer Country." And, indeed, the summer, when the town bursts into bloom, is the best time to visit. Most of the historic sites and gardens open for the season on Easter.

ESSENTIALS

GETTING THERE   Trains leave regularly from either Liverpool Street Station or Kings Cross Station in London; however, none are direct. Leaving from Liverpool Street, you will change at Ipswich. And from Kings Cross Station, you'll have to switch trains at Cambridge. The trip takes approximately 1½ hours. For schedules and information, call ℂ **0845/748-4950** or visit **www.nationalrail.co.uk**.

National Express runs several direct buses every day from London's Victoria Coach Station, which reach Bury in 2 hours. For schedules and information, call ℂ **0870/ 580-8080** or visit **www.nationalexpress.com**.

By car, take the M11 north out of London. As you near Cambridge, get on the A45 and continue on to Bury. The drive takes about 1½ hours.

It's also possible to get here by train or bus from Cambridge. Regular trains leave from the Cambridge Rail Station and arrive about 45 minutes later in Bury St. Edmunds. **Stagecoach Bus Company** runs five buses a day to Bury from the Drummer Street Bus Station in Cambridge; it's a 1-hour ride. Call ℂ **01223/423578** for information and schedules. By car from Cambridge, simply take the A45 directly. It's a 45-minute drive.

VISITOR INFORMATION   The **Bury St. Edmunds Tourist Information Centre,** 6 Angel Hill (ℂ **01284/764667;** www.stedmundsbury.gov.uk), is open November to Easter, Monday to Friday 10am to 4pm and Saturday 10am to 1pm; and from Easter to October, Monday to Saturday 9:30am to 5:30pm, Sunday 10am to 3pm.

SPECIAL EVENTS   The **Bury St. Edmunds Festival** (ℂ **01284/757630;** www.bury festival.co.uk) is held annually in May. The 17-day festival includes performances from leading ensembles and soloists ranging from classical to contemporary. Exhibitions, talks, walks, films, plays, and a fireworks display are integral parts of this internationally renowned festival.

WHERE TO STAY

The Angel Hotel ✰   Originally a 1452 coaching inn, the hotel received an exterior face-lift during the Georgian era, and its front facade is now completely covered with lush ivy. The location is ideal for sightseeing and shopping, as both are only a short walk from the hotel. Look out the window of any of the front-facing rooms, and you'll see the romantic Abbey Gardens. Each of the rooms is individually decorated with antique furnishings and some have four-poster beds. No. 36 is one of the more popular rooms with its four-poster bed, bold peach-colored walls (a shade you can almost taste), and armchairs. Ten of the bedrooms have been recently refurbished.

Angel Hill, Bury St. Edmunds, Suffolk IP33 1LT. ✆ **01284/714000.** Fax 01284/714001. www.theangel.co.uk. 76 units. £137 ($274) double; £197 ($394) suite. AE, DC, MC, V. Free parking. **Amenities:** 2 restaurants; bar; room service; babysitting; laundry service; dry cleaning. *In room:* A/C (in some rooms), TV, Wi-Fi, beverage maker, hair dryer, iron, trouser press.

Ramada Bury St. Edmunds   This standard, rather ordinary hotel, built relatively recently, is located 10 minutes from Bury on the A14 motorway. The grassy grounds are landscaped, and there is a sunny patio for dining alfresco. All the rooms are decorated in the same bland style with landscape pictures and an armchair or two, along with an accompanying desk. Because of the proximity to the motorway, the windows are double-paned to reduce traffic noise and to help guests get a better night's rest.

Symonds Rd., Bury St. Edmunds, Suffolk IP32 7DZ. ✆ **800/2-RAMADA** (800/272-6232) in the U.S., or 01284/760884. Fax 01284/755476. www.ramada.com. 66 units. Sun–Thurs £87 ($174) double; Fri–Sat £75 ($150) double. AE, DC, MC, V. Free parking. **Amenities:** Restaurant; bar; room service; laundry service; dry cleaning. *In room:* TV, Wi-Fi, beverage maker, hair dryer, trouser press, safe.

Ravenwood Hall 🕍🕍 *Finds*   Located 5km (3 miles) outside of town, this Tudor hall dates from the 1500s and is set in a peaceful 2.8-hectare (7-acre) park with well-manicured lawns, gardens, and forest. This rustic country place has a magnificent fireplace that is the focal point of the restaurant, where diners enjoy an à la carte menu. The individually decorated rooms are full of atmosphere. If you're a fancier of fine beds, check out the Oak Room with its four-poster bed and the bridal suite with its brass bed. Some rooms are in the main house, others in a converted stable mews; all are equally comfortable.

Rougham, Bury St. Edmunds, Suffolk IP30 9JA. ✆ **01359/270345.** Fax 01359/270788. www.ravenwoodhall.co.uk. 14 units. £120–195 ($240–$390) double. Rates include breakfast. AE, DC, MC, V. Free parking. **Amenities:** Restaurant; bar; outdoor heated pool; outdoor tennis court; room service; babysitting; laundry service. *In room:* TV, beverage maker, hair dryer, safe.

WHERE TO DINE

Maison Bleue SEAFOOD   This restaurant is the town's best. The open and airy dining room has a nautical theme, in keeping with the fresh seafood that's served. The same menu is available for both lunch and dinner and changes regularly with the seasons. A sublime main course is the whole grilled sea bass marinated with lime, lemon grass, and pink peppercorns. We also revel in the layered gâteau of poached salmon and sliced king scallop with a butter sauce flavored with parsley and fresh shallots. As another treat, the half grilled lobster and pan-fried Black Tiger prawns are topped with garlic butter.

31 Churchgate St. ✆ **01284/760623.** Reservations recommended for dinner. Main courses £11–£23 ($22–$46); fixed-price lunch £18 ($36); 3-course fixed-price dinner £27 ($54). AE, MC, V. Tues–Sat noon–2:30pm and 7–9:30pm (until 10pm Fri–Sat).

EXPLORING THE TOWN

For a bit of easy and always interesting sightseeing, take one of the hour-long **guided walks** around Bury St. Edmunds. Choices include a "Blue Badge Guided Tour" and theme tours with Bury's historical monk, Brother Jocelin, or with gravedigger William Hunter. Tours leave from the Tourist Information Centre (see above) where tickets can also be purchased.

The normally quiet town center is a hub of hustle and bustle on Wednesday and Saturday mornings when the market arrives. Weather permitting, hours are approximately from 9am to 4pm. You'll find a pleasing mix of family-run businesses and High Street names for shopping in and around town and its pedestrian zones.

Several parks are located just outside of town. Our two favorite parks are listed below. If you have kids in tow, make it **West Stow Country Park,** which has more man-made attractions. But if it's unspoiled nature you seek, a series of relatively easy and quite romantic walks, head for **Nowton Park,** which will give you the best view and the most evocative scenery of what the Suffolk landscape looks like. The **West Stow Anglo-Saxon Village** (✆ **01284/728718**) is part of West Stow Country Park. This reconstructed village is built on the excavated site of an ancient Anglo-Saxon village, and period reenactments take place throughout the year. The park is open daily from 9am to 5pm in winter, 9am to 8pm in summer. Admission is free. The village is open year-round from 10am to 5pm. Admission is £5 ($10) for adults and £4 ($8) for children. Family tickets are also available for £15 ($30).

Nowton Park ✦ (✆ **01284/763666**) is 2.5km (1½ miles) outside of Bury on 81 hectares (200 acres) of Suffolk countryside. Landscaped a century ago, the park is typically Victorian and has many country-estate features. In the springtime, walk the avenue of lime trees with its masses of bright yellow daffodils. Marked walking paths snake through the park. Depending on the path, walks take between 20 and 75 minutes. It's open daily from 8:30am to dusk; free admission.

The Abbey ✦✦   The Abbey Visitor Centre is a good starting point for a visit to the entire abbey precinct. (The abbey itself is in ruins today and sits in the middle of the Abbey Gardens.) The Visitor Centre is housed in the west front of the abbey's remains and uses a clever series of displays to give the visitor an idea of what life was like in this powerful abbey from its beginnings in 1020 to its dissolution in 1539.

A tour of the Abbey Gardens is led by medieval monk Brother Jocelin; book it through the town's Tourist Information Centre at ✆ **01284/764667.**

Samson's Tower. ✆ **01284/757490** for Visitor Centre. Free admission. Visitor Centre Easter–Oct daily 10am–5pm; Abbey Gardens and ruins year-round Mon–Sat 7:30am to a half-hour before dusk, Sun 9am to a half-hour before dusk.

Ickworth House   This National Trust property was built in 1795 and contains an impressive rotunda, staterooms, and art collections of silver and paintings. An Italian garden surrounds the house, and all is set in a peaceful, landscaped park.

5km (3 miles) south of Bury at Horringer. ✆ **01284/735270.** www.nationaltrust.org.uk. Admission £7.50 ($15) adults, £3 ($6) children, family ticket £18 ($36). In 2009: Mar 17–Sept 30 Fri–Tues 1–5pm; Oct 1–Nov 4 Fri–Tues 1–4:30pm.

Moyse's Hall Museum   Located in one of England's last surviving Norman stone houses, this museum has nationally important archaeological collections and local artifacts.

Cornhill. ✆ **01284/706183.** www.stedmundsbury.gov.uk/sebc/visit/moyses-hall.cfm. Admission £2.60 ($5.20) adults, £2.10 ($4.20) seniors and children. Mon–Fri 10:30am–4:30pm; Sat–Sun 11am–4pm.

St. Edmundsbury Cathedral   This 16th-century church has a magnificent font, beautiful stained-glass windows, and a display of 1,000 embroidered kneelers.

Angel Hill. ✆ **01284/754933.** www.stedscathedral.co.uk. Free admission but suggested donation of £3 ($6) for adults, 50p ($1) for children. Daily 8am–6pm.

St. Mary's Church   St. Mary's was built on the site of a Norman church in 1427. Note its impressive roof and nave. It is also where Henry VIII's sister, Mary "the Tudor Rose," is buried.

Angel Hill. ✆ **01284/754680.** www.stmarystpeter.net. Free admission. Call the church to arrange a tour.

BURY ST. EDMUNDS AFTER DARK

Throughout the centuries, Bury has enjoyed a well-deserved reputation as a small center of arts and entertainment. The **Theatre Royal,** Westgate Street, is the oldest purpose-built theater in England. Its Georgian building has been lovingly and richly restored to its original grandeur. Programs include opera, dance, music, and drama from the best touring companies. Tickets are £8.50 to £35 ($17–$70) and can be purchased at the **box office** (© **01284/759505;** www.theatreroyal.org).

Stop by the 17th-century pub **Dog and Partridge,** 29 Crown St. (© **01284/764792**), and see where the bar scenes from the BBC hit series *Lovejoy* were filmed while you sample one of the region's Greene King Ales. Also try wiggling your way into the **Nutshell,** corner of the Traverse and Abbeygate Street (© **01284/764867**). This pub has been notoriously dubbed the smallest pub in all of England and is a favorite tourist stop. The **Masons Arms,** 14 Whiting St. (© **01284/753955**), features more of a family atmosphere and welcomes children. Home-cooked food is served along with a standard selection of ales. There's a patio garden in use in summer.

A SIDE TRIP TO SUDBURY

Thirty-two kilometers (20 miles) south of Bury St. Edmunds along the A134 is Sudbury, a town that has prospered through the ages thanks to its sheep (the wool industry) and prime location along the banks of the River Stour. A handful of medieval half-timbered buildings and Georgian homes attest to the town's ripe old age. Its most famous native son is Thomas Gainsborough, who was born in 1727 and went on to become one of England's most beloved painters.

His birthplace, **Gainsborough's House,** 46 Gainsborough St. (© **01787/372958;** www.gainsborough.org), is a museum and arts center that has many of his works of art on display. Visitors will notice that several different architectural styles make up the house, and there is a walled garden in back worth seeing. It's open from Monday to Saturday from 10am to 5pm and bank holiday Sundays and Mondays from 2 to 5pm. Admission is £4 ($8) adults, £3.20 ($6.40) seniors, £1.50 ($3) children ages 5 to 18 and students, but it is free during the month of December (and year-round for children 4 and younger).

WHERE TO STAY

Hotel Elizabeth The Mill ★ *Finds* As its name implies, this four-story hotel is located in the shell of an old mill. In fact, the River Stour, which runs under the hotel, still turns the mill's 5m (16-ft.) water wheel, now encased in glass and on display in the hotel's restaurant and bar. Rooms vary in size; some have heavy oak beams and massive columns, but all are outfitted with comfortable furnishings. You may even be able to watch the local cows occasionally pass by the water's edge, as many of the rooms have a river or mill pond view. *Note:* The hotel has no elevator.

Walnut Tree Lane, Sudbury CO10 1BD. © **01787/375544.** Fax 01787/373027. www.elizabethhotels.co.uk. 56 units. £105–£120 ($210–$240) double; £130 ($260) suite. AE, DC, MC, V. Free parking. **Amenities:** Restaurant; bar; room service; laundry service. *In room:* TV, beverage maker, hair dryer, iron.

5 Lavenham ★

106km (66 miles) NE of London; 56km (35 miles) SE of Cambridge

Once a great wool center, Lavenham is the classic Suffolk village, beautifully preserved today. It features a number of half-timbered Tudor houses washed in the characteristic Suffolk pink. The town's wool-trading profits are apparent in its guildhall, on the triangular main "square." Inside, exhibits on Lavenham's textile industry show how yarn was spun, then "dyed in the wool" with woad (the plant used by ancient Picts to dye themselves blue), following on to the weaving process. Another display shows how half-timbered houses were constructed.

The Church of St. Peter and St. Paul, at the edge of Lavenham, has interesting carvings on the misericords and the chancel screen, as well as ornate tombs. This is one of the "wool churches" of the area, built by pious merchants in the Perpendicular style with a landmark tower.

ESSENTIALS

GETTING THERE Trains depart London's North Street Station at least once an hour, sometimes more often, for Colchester, where they connect quickly to the town of Sudbury. For information, call ✆ **0845/748-4950** or visit **www.nationalrail.co. uk**. From Sudbury, **Chambers & Sons, Ltd.** (✆ **01787/227233;** www.chambers coaches.co.uk) has about nine daily buses making the short run to Lavenham. The trip from London takes between 2 and 2½ hours.

National Express buses depart from London's Victoria Coach Station, carrying passengers to the town of Bury St. Edmunds, some 14km (9 miles) from Lavenham. For information, call ✆ **0870/580-8080** or visit **www.nationalexpress.com**. From Bury St. Edmunds, you can take another bus on to Lavenham. The trip takes about 2½ hours.

If you're driving from Bury St. Edmunds, continue south on the A134 toward Long Melford, but cut southeast to Lavenham at the junction with the A1141.

VISITOR INFORMATION The **Tourist Information Centre** is on Lady Street (✆ **01787/248207**) and is open Easter to October 31 daily 10am to 4:45pm; March and November, Saturday hours are 11am to 5pm.

WHERE TO STAY

Lavenham Priory ⭐ *(Finds* The Tudor age lives again in this building dating from the 13th century and once owned by Benedictine monks. In time the mansion became the property of the earls of Oxford before being sold to rich cloth merchants. Today it's been restored to its appearance during its Elizabethan period. The timber-framed house has been beautifully restored and sensitively modernized to offer guests grand comfort. An oak Jacobean staircase leads to the bedchambers featuring four-posters, Tudor wall paintings, and oak floors. Each room is furnished individually. You can enjoy a chair by an inglenook fireplace or order a summer breakfast in the herb garden. The hotel stands in 1.2 hectares (3 acres) of grounds in the center of the village.

Water St., Lavenham, Suffolk CO10 9SH. ✆ 01787/247404. Fax 01787/248472. www.lavenhampriory.co.uk. 6 units. £98–£128 ($196–$256); £138 ($276) suite. Rates include breakfast. MC, V. **Amenities:** Sitting room; breakfast lounge. *In room:* TV, beverage maker.

The Swan ⭐⭐⭐ This lavishly timbered inn, with the best accommodations in Suffolk, is one of the oldest and best-preserved buildings in a relatively unspoiled village. It has been so successful that it has expanded into an adjoining ancient wool hall, which provides a high-ceilinged guesthouse and raftered, second-story bedrooms opening onto a tiny cloistered garden. The bedrooms vary in size, according to the eccentricities of the architecture. Most have beamed ceilings and a mixture of traditional pieces that blend well with the old. The more expensive rooms feature four-poster beds.

High St., Lavenham, Sudbury, Suffolk CO10 9QA. ✆ 01787/247477. Fax 01787/248286. www.theswanatlavenham. co.uk. 49 units. £180–£254 ($360–$508) double; £230–£270 ($460–$540) suite. Rates include breakfast and dinner.

AE, DC, MC, V. **Amenities:** Restaurant; bar; lounge; room service; laundry service. *In room:* TV, minibar, beverage maker, hair dryer, iron, trouser press, safe.

WHERE TO DINE

The Great House Hotel ✦ FRENCH   With its Georgian facade and location near the marketplace, the Great House is the town's finest place to dine, a quintessentially French hotel in a beautiful English town. The interior is also attractively decorated, with Laura Ashley prints, an inglenook fireplace, and old oak beams. Assisted by his wife, Martine, owner Régis Crépy does double duty as the *chef de cuisine*. He is an inventive, quixotic cook, as reflected by such dishes as roasted rack of English lamb with rosemary jus or grilled marinated filet of red mullet with braised chicory. Another specialty is grilled saddle of venison in red-wine-and-cranberry sauce.

The house also rents five elegantly decorated suites for £85 to £180 ($170–$360) for a double, including an English breakfast. The units have TVs, phones, and private bathrooms or showers.

Market Place. ℗ **01787/247431.** Fax 01787/248007. Reservations recommended. Tues–Sat fixed-price dinner £26 ($52); Tues–Sat fixed-price lunch £17 ($34), Sun £26 ($52); snacks £3–£10 ($6–$20). AE, MC, V. Tues–Sun noon– 2:30pm; Tues–Sat 7–9:30pm. Closed Jan.

SHOPPING & TEATIME

Shoppers from all over East Anglia flock to **Timbers,** 12 High St. (℗ **01787/ 247218**), a center housing 24 dealers specializing in antiques and collectibles, including books, toys, military artifacts, glass, porcelain, and much more. It's open daily.

After strolling the medieval streets of Lavenham, stop by **Tickle Tink Tea Rooms,** 17 High St. (℗ **01787/248438**). This two-story timber-frame home was built by the son of a priest in 1530 and provides an ample dose of history for patrons to absorb while sipping any one of a selection of teas that are served with English breakfast, sandwiches, or cake.

6 Two Stately Homes in Long Melford

98km (61 miles) NE of London; 55km (34 miles) SE of Cambridge

Long Melford has been famous since the days of the early cloth makers. Like Lavenham, it attained prestige and importance during the Middle Ages. Of the old buildings remaining, the village church is often called "one of the glories of the shire." Along its 5km-long (3-mile) High Street is an array of one of the greatest concentrations of antiques shops in Europe. There are many private homes erected by wealthy wool merchants in the area, the two stateliest being Melford Hall and Kentwell Hall, recommended below.

ESSENTIALS

GETTING THERE   Trains run from London's Liverpool Street Station toward Ipswich and on to Marks Tey. Call ℗ **0845/748-4950,** or visit **www.nationalrail.co. uk** for information. Here, you can take a shuttle train going back and forth between that junction and Sudbury. From the town of Sudbury, it's a 5km (3-mile) taxi ride to Long Melford.

From Cambridge, take a Stagecoach bus (℗ **01223/423578;** www.stagecoachbus. com) to Bury St. Edmunds, then change for the final ride into Long Melford. These buses run about once an hour throughout the day and early evening.

If driving from Newmarket, continue east on the A45 to Bury St. Edmunds, but cut south on the A134 (toward Sudbury) to Long Melford.

VISITOR INFORMATION   There is a **Tourist Information Centre** in the Town Hall, Sudbury (© **01787/881320**), that's open Monday to Friday 9am to 5pm and Saturday 10am to 4:45pm (until 2:45pm during winter).

WHERE TO STAY

Black Lion   The Bull (see below) has the edge, but this place is doing something right, as an inn has stood here since the 12th century. Fourteenth-century documents mention it as the spot where drinks were dispensed to revolutionaries during one of the peasants' revolts. The present building dates from the early 1800s and has been richly restored by its owners. All rooms are of a high standard with antique furnishings. The Black Lion overlooks one of the loveliest village greens in Suffolk.

The Green, Long Melford, Suffolk CO10 9DN. © **01787/312356**. Fax 01787/374557. www.blacklionhotel.net. 10 units. £150–£195 ($300–$390) double. Rates include English breakfast. AE, MC, V. **Amenities:** Restaurant; bar; room service; babysitting; laundry service. *In room:* TV, beverage maker, hair dryer, iron, safe.

Bull Hotel ⚐   Here is an opportunity to experience life in one of the great old inns of East Anglia. Built by a wool merchant in 1540, this is Long Melford's finest hotel and its best-preserved building, with lots of improvements and modernizations added over the years. The rooms here are a mix of the old and the new. The interior and exterior of the hotel have been refurbished, and the beds are usually king-size or twins. A medieval weavers' gallery and an open hearth with Elizabethan brickwork have been incorporated into the hotel's design.

Hall St., Long Melford, Sudbury, Suffolk CO10 9JG. © **01787/378494**. Fax 01787/880307. www.thebull-hotel.com. 27 units. £120–£140 ($240–$280) double; £140–£160 ($280–$320) suite. 2-night minimum stay Sat–Sun. AE, DC, MC, V. **Amenities:** Restaurant; bar; room service. *In room:* TV, beverage maker, hair dryer, iron, trouser press.

WHERE TO DINE

Scutchers Bistro ENGLISH   This upscale bistro earns favorable recommendations from many locals. The building was erected in stages between the 1600s and the 1800s and was named after the workers (scutchers) who, in olden days, rendered flax into linen. As the Scutchers Arms, it was a favorite pub—until the owners painted its facade bright yellow and filled its heavily beamed interior with vivid Mediterranean colors. The food here has been considerably improved and upgraded, as evoked by such dishes as filet of wild halibut on a prawn and chive risotto with a lobster sauce or grilled filet of plaice with an herb crust in a lemon-butter sauce. Especially tasty is the loin filet of Suffolk lamb with mint gravy.

Westgate St. © **01787/310200**. Reservations recommended. Main courses £12–£23 ($24–$46). AE, MC, V. Tues–Sat noon–2pm and 7–9:30pm.

A TUDOR MANSION & BEATRIX POTTER'S ANCESTRAL HOME

Kentwell Hall   At the end of an avenue of linden trees, the redbrick Tudor mansion called Kentwell Hall, surrounded by a broad moat, has been restored by its owners, Mr. and Mrs. Patrick Phillips. A 15th-century moat house, interconnecting gardens, a brick-paved maze, and a costume display are of interest. There are also rare-breed farm animals here. Two gatehouses are constructed in 16th-century style. The hall hosts regular re-creations of Tudor domestic life, including events during the weeks of June 16 to July 7 when admission prices tend to escalate slightly.

On A134 between Sudbury and Bury St. Edmunds. (℃ **01787/310207**. www.kentwellhall.co.uk. Admission £7.75 ($16) adults, £6.75 ($14) seniors, £5 ($10) children. Consult website or call ahead for opening days and hours because of special-event schedules. The entrance is north of the green in Long Melford on the west side of A134, about 1km (½ mile) north of Melford Hall.

Melford Hall   This is the ancestral home of Beatrix Potter, who often visited. Jemima PuddleDuck still occupies a chair in one of the bedrooms upstairs, and some of her other figures are on display. The house, built between 1554 and 1578, has paintings, fine furniture, and Chinese porcelain. The gardens alone make a visit here worthwhile.

Long Melford (off A135), Sudbury, Suffolk. (℃ **01787/379228**. Admission £5.50 ($11) adults, £2.75 ($5.50) children, £14 ($28) family ticket. Apr and Oct 1–29 Sat–Sun 1:30–5pm; May–Sept Wed–Sun 1:30–5pm.

7 Dedham

101km (63 miles) NE of London; 13km (8 miles) NE of Colchester

Remember Constable's painting, *The Vale of Dedham?* Dedham Vale lies between the towns of Colchester and Ipswich in a wide valley through which runs the River Stour, the boundary between Essex and Suffolk. It's not only the link with Constable that has made this vale so popular. It is one of the most beautiful, unspoiled areas left in southeast England. In this little Essex village on the Stour River, you're in the heart of Constable Country. One of the most memorable walks in East Anglia is along a public footpath from Dedham to Flatford Mill (see below), which lies 1.5km (1 mile) farther down the river. Set in the midst of water meadows of the Stour, Dedham is filled with Tudor, Georgian, and Regency houses. Constable painted its church and its tower.

GETTING THERE

Trains depart every 20 minutes from London's Liverpool Street Station for the 50-minute ride to Colchester. For schedules and information, call (℃ **0845/748-4950** or visit **www.nationalrail.co.uk**. From Colchester, it's possible to take a taxi from the railway station to the bus station, then board a bus run by Beestons for the 8km (5-mile) trip to Dedham. (Buses leave about once an hour.) Most people take a taxi from Colchester directly to Dedham.

National Express buses depart from London's Victoria Coach Station for Colchester, where you have the choice of taking either another bus or a taxi to Dedham. For schedules and information, call (℃ **0870/580-8080** or visit **www.nationalexpress.com**.

If you're driving from the London Ring Road, travel northeast on the A12 to Colchester, turning off at East Bergholt onto a small secondary road leading east to Dedham.

WHERE TO STAY

If the famous, but pricey, inns of Dedham are too much for your budget, call on **May's Barn Farm,** May's Lane (off Long Rd. W.) in Dedham ((℃ **01206/323191**), which rents large, comfortably, and traditionally furnished bedrooms for £48 to £55 ($96–$110) a night in a double or twin. In-rooms amenities include a TV, beverage maker, and hair dryer.

Dedham Hall/Fountain House Restaurant   A 3-minute walk east of the center of town, this well-managed hotel flourishes under the direction of Jim and Wendy Sarton. Set on 2 hectares (5 acres) of grazing land whose centerpiece is a pond favored by geese and wild swans, it consists of a 400-year-old brick-sided cottage linked to a

200-year-old home of stately proportions. The older section is reserved for the breakfast room, a bar, and a sitting room for residents of the six second-floor bedrooms. A cluster of three converted barns provides accommodations for many artists who congregate here several times throughout the year for painting seminars and art workshops.

Brook St., Dedham CO7 6AD. © **01206/323027.** www.dedhamhall.demon.co.uk. 16 units. £95 ($190) double; £155 ($310) double half-board. MC, V. **Amenities:** Restaurant; bar; room service. *In room:* TV, minibar, beverage maker, hair dryer, iron, safe.

Maison Talbooth *★★★* This small, exclusive hotel is in a handsomely restored Victorian country house on a bluff overlooking the river valley, with views that stretch as far as the medieval Church of Stratford St. Mary. Accommodations consist of spacious suites distinctively furnished by one of England's best-known decorators. High-fashion colors abound, antiques are mixed discreetly with reproductions, and the original architectural beauty has been preserved. Fresh flowers, fruit, and a private bar are standard amenities in the suites. If accommodations are not available here, the staff can book you into neighboring hotels with which they are affiliated.

Stratford Rd., Dedham, Colchester, Essex CO7 6HN. © **01206/322367.** Fax 01206/323689. www.milsom-hotels. co.uk. 14 units. £170–£350 ($340–$700) double. Rates include continental breakfast. AE, DC, MC, V. Take Stratford Rd. 1km (½ mile) west of the town center. **Amenities:** Restaurant; bar; outdoor pool; tennis court; spa; room service; babysitting; laundry service. *In room:* TV, minibar, hair dryer.

WHERE TO DINE
Le Talbooth *★★★* ENGLISH/FRENCH A hand-hewn, half-timbered weaver's house is the setting for this restaurant standing amid beautiful gardens on the banks of the River Stour. Le Talbooth was featured in Constable's *Vale of Dedham.* You descend a sloping driveway leading past flowering terraces. A well-mannered staff will usher you to a low-ceilinged bar for an aperitif.

Owner Gerald Milsom has brought a high standard of cooking to this rustically elegant place, where a well-chosen wine list complements the good food. An à la carte menu changes six times a year, and special dishes are altered daily, reflecting the best produce available at the market. Expect elaborate creations that somehow never destroy the natural flavor. If anything, the well-chosen and prepared sauces enhance dishes such as lobster tail and monkfish cooked in vermouth and rosemary sauce or farm-grown duck breast in a jasmine sauce. Another specialty is veal-and-kidney pudding with bordelaise jus.

Gun Hill. © **01206/323150.** Reservations recommended. Main courses £16–£28 ($32–$56). AE, DC, MC, V. Daily noon–2pm and 7–9:30pm.

VISITING THE PAINTERS' HOMES
Just 1.5km (1 mile) from the village center is the **Sir Alfred Munnings Art Museum,** East Lane (© **01206/322127;** www.siralfredmunnings.co.uk), home of Sir Alfred Munnings, president of the Royal Academy from 1944 to 1949 and painter extraordinaire of racehorses and other animals. The house and studio, which have sketches and other works, are open from Easter Sunday to early October on Sunday, Wednesday, and bank holidays (plus Thurs and Sat during Aug) from 2 to 5pm. Admission is £3 ($6) for adults, £2 ($4) students and seniors, and 50p ($1) for children.

The English landscape painter John Constable (1776–1837) was born at East Bergholt, 3.2km (2 miles) northeast of Dedham. Near the village is **Flatford Mill,** East Bergholt (© **01206/298260**), the subject of one of his most renowned works.

The mill was given to the National Trust in 1943 and has since been leased to the Field Studies Council for use as a residential center. The center offers more than 170 short courses each year in all aspects of art and the environment. Fees are from £140 ($280) for a weekend and from £400 ($800) for a full week. The fee includes accommodations, meals, and tuition. For additional information, visit www.field-studies-council. org/flatfordmill or write to Field Studies Council, Flatford Mill Field Centre, East Bergholt, Colchester CO7 6UL.

8 Woodbridge & Aldeburgh

Woodbridge: 130km (81 miles) NE of London, 76km (47 miles) S of Norwich, 29km (18 miles) NE of Dedham; Aldeburgh: 156km (97 miles) NE of London, 66km (41 miles) SE of Norwich

On the Deben River, the market town of Woodbridge is a yachting center. Its best-known resident was Edward Fitzgerald, Victorian poet and translator of the *Rubaiyat of Omar Khayyam*. You can base in Woodbridge and use it to explore Aldeburgh as well. Woodbridge is also a good base for exploring Framlingham Castle and Sutton Hoo (see below).

Woodbridge is filled with riverside walks along quays, and you can stroll around the town in an hour or two, taking in the wide variety of architecture, including pink-washed Tudor cottages. There is also a vast array of antiques shops for browsing.

On the North Sea, 24km (15 miles) from Woodbridge, Aldeburgh is an exclusive resort, and it attracts many Dutch visitors, who make the sea crossing via Harwich and Felixstowe, both major entry ports for traffic from the Continent. Aldeburgh dates from Roman times and has long been known as a small port for North Sea fisheries. The Aldeburgh Festival, held every June, is the most important arts festival in East Anglia, and one of the best attended in England.

ESSENTIALS

GETTING THERE   Woodbridge is on the rail line to Lowestoft from either Victoria Station or Liverpool Street Station in London. Get off two stops after Ipswich. For schedules and information, call (© **0845/748-4950** or visit **www.nationalrail.co.uk**. The nearest rail station to Aldeburgh is on the same line, at Saxmundham, six stops after Ipswich. From Saxmundham, you can take a taxi or one of six buses that run the 9.5km (6 miles) to Aldeburgh during the day.

One National Express bus a day passes through Aldeburgh and Woodbridge on the way from London's Victoria Coach Station to Great Yarmouth. It stops at every country town and narrow lane along the way, so the trip to Aldeburgh takes a woeful 4½ hours. For information, call (© **0870/580-8080** or visit **www.nationalexpress.com**. Many visitors reach both towns by Eastern County Bus Company's service from Ipswich. That company's no. 80/81 buses run frequently between Woodbridge and Aldeburgh.

If driving from London's Ring Road, take the A12 northeast to Ipswich, then continue northeast on the A12 to Woodbridge. To get to Aldeburgh, stay on the A12 until you reach the junction with the A1094, then head east to the North Sea.

VISITOR INFORMATION   The **Tourist Information Centre** is at the Cinema, 152 High St., Aldeburgh ((© **01728/453637;** www.visit-woodbridge.co.uk), and is open year-round Monday to Friday 9am to 5:30pm, Saturday 9:30am to 5:30pm.

SPECIAL EVENTS   Aldeburgh was the home of Benjamin Britten (1913–76), renowned composer of the operas *Peter Grimes* and *Billy Budd,* as well as many orchestral works. Many of his compositions were first performed at the **Aldeburgh Festival,**

which he founded in 1946. The festival takes place in June, featuring internationally known performers. There are other concerts and events throughout the year. Write or call the tourist office for details, or check out **www.aldeburgh.co.uk**. The Snape Maltings Concert Hall nearby is one of the more successful among the smaller British concert halls; it also houses the Britten-Pears School of Advanced Musical Studies, established in 1973.

WHERE TO STAY
NEAR WOODBRIDGE
Seckford Hall ✹✹✹   This ivy-covered estate's pure Tudor, crow-stepped gables, mullioned windows, and ornate chimneys capture the spirit of the days of Henry VIII and his strong-willed daughter Elizabeth (the latter may have held court here). Today, it provides some of the finest accommodations in Suffolk. You enter through a heavy, studded Tudor door into a flagstone hallway with antiques. The butler will show you to your bedroom. Many rooms have four-poster beds, one of them a monumental 1587 specimen. Bedrooms are statements in luxury and elegance.

If you arrive before sundown, you may want to stroll through the 14-hectare (34-acre) gardens, which include a rose garden, herbaceous borders, and greenhouses.

On A12 (2.5km/1½ miles from the Woodbridge rail station), Woodbridge, Suffolk IP13 6NU. ✆ 01394/385678. Fax 01394/380610. www.seckford.co.uk. 32 units. £140–£150 ($280–$300) double; £180–£215 ($360–$430) suite. Rates include English breakfast. AE, DC, MC, V. Free parking. **Amenities:** 2 restaurants; 2 bars; indoor heated pool; golf course; health club; salon; Jacuzzi; room service; babysitting; laundry service. *In room:* TV, minibar (in some rooms), beverage maker, hair dryer, trouser press, iron.

IN ALDEBURGH
The Brudenell Hotel   Located on the waterfront, this hotel is no match for the Wentworth (see below) but is a good choice. It was built at the beginning of the 20th century and was remodeled and redecorated to achieve a pleasant interior. Many of the bedrooms face the sea, and each has comfortable beds.

The Parade, Aldeburgh, Suffolk IP15 5BU. ✆ 01728/452071. Fax 01728/454082. www.brudenellhotel.co.uk. 42 units. £62–£124 ($124–$248) per person double. Rates include breakfast. AE, MC, V. Free parking. **Amenities:** Restaurant; bar; room service; babysitting; laundry service; dry cleaning. *In room:* TV, beverage maker, hair dryer, iron.

The Wentworth Hotel ✹   A traditional country-house hotel with tall chimneys and gables, the Wentworth overlooks the sea. Built in the early 19th century as a private residence, it was converted into a hotel around 1900. The Pritt family has welcomed the world since 1920, including Sir Benjamin Britten and novelist E. M. Forster. In summer, tables are placed outside so that guests can enjoy the sun; in winter, open fires in the lounges, even the cozy bar, are a welcome sight. Many guest rooms have panoramic views. A 19th-century building across the road from the main house offers a comfortable, seven-room annex. The standards here match those of the main house. *Note:* A minimum stay of 2 nights is required.

Wentworth Rd., Aldeburgh, Suffolk IP15 5BD. ✆ 01728/452312. Fax 01728/454343. www.wentworth-aldeburgh. com. 35 units. £58–£285 ($116–$570) per person double. Rates include English breakfast and dinner. AE, DC, MC, V. Free parking. Closed Dec 27–Jan 9. **Amenities:** Restaurant; bar; room service; laundry service. *In room:* TV, beverage maker, hair dryer.

WHERE TO DINE
ALDEBURGH
The Lighthouse BRITISH/SEAFOOD   This is the showcase of a gastro center that takes in a greengrocer selling exotic products, a wine merchant, a cooking school, and

a cafe-bar that is one of the most popular gathering spots in town. The highlight, though, is this bistro fish restaurant in a sort of Swedish-modern space, featuring a blackboard menu. That menu features seafood specials, including the catch of the day, perhaps succulent Suffolk crab. Meat and poultry dishes are of a high standard, appearing in such dishes as duck confit with fresh spinach or rack of lamb seasoned with mint.

77 High St. ℂ 01728/453377. Reservations recommended. Main courses £9.50–£17 ($19–$34). AE, MC, V. Mon–Fri noon–2pm; Sat–Sun noon–2:30pm; daily 6:30–10pm.

ATTRACTIONS OUTSIDE WOODBRIDGE

Sixteen kilometers (10 miles) to the north of Woodbridge stands **Framlingham Castle** ℛ, in the village of Framlingham along the B1119 (ℂ **01728/724-189;** www. english-heritage.org.uk). This is one of the best examples of a 12th-century castle still standing in East Anglia. Admission is £4.70 ($9.40) for adults, £3.50 ($7) seniors, £2.40 ($4.80) for children 11 and younger, and £12 ($24) family ticket. Hours are daily April to September 10am to 6pm, and October to March Thursday to Sunday 10am to 4pm.

   Sutton Hoo ℛ (ℂ **01394-389714;** www.nationaltrust.org.uk), lying 3.2km (2 miles) east of Woodbridge along B1083, is one of the great Anglo-Saxon royal burial sites of England. On a spur of land rising above the Deben River, several large burial mounds were excavated in 1939, revealing famous treasures, including gold ornaments. Admission is £5.90 ($12) for adults, £3 ($6) for children 11 and younger, and £15 ($30) family ticket. In 2009 it's open March 25 to April 2 Wednesday to Sunday 11am to 5pm; April 3 to April 17 daily 11am to 5pm; April 19 to July 2 Wednesday to Sunday 11am to 5pm; July 3 to September 4 daily 11am to 5pm; September 6 to October 29 Wednesday to Sunday 11am to 5pm; and November 4 to December 17 Saturday and Sunday 11am to 4pm.

ATTRACTIONS IN & AROUND ALDEBURGH

Constructed on a shelf of land at sea level, the High Street runs parallel to the often-turbulent waterfront. A cliff face rises some 89m (55 ft.) above the main street. A major attraction is the 16th-century **Moot Hall Museum,** Market Cross Place, Aldeburgh (ℂ **01728/454666**). The hall dates from the time of Henry VIII, but its tall twin chimneys are later additions. The timber-frame structure displays old maps, prints, and Anglo-Saxon burial urns, as well as other items of historical interest. It is open June to August daily from noon to 5pm. It is also open Easter to April Saturday and Sunday (and bank holidays) 2:30 to 5pm; May, September, and October, daily from 2:30 to 5pm. Admission is £1 ($2) for adults and free for children.

   The seashore and the surrounding areas of Aldeburgh have been designated as an Area of Outstanding Natural Beauty (AONB). The wetlands around Aldeburgh are home to the marsh harrier and booming bittern, both endangered species. If you'd like to see some of these waterfowl, you can visit the nearby bird sanctuary of **Minsmere** ℛ, outside Westleton (ℂ **01728/648281**). Westleton lies 15km (9 miles) northwest of Aldeburgh; take B1122 northwest from Aldeburgh to the junction of B1125 north, following the signs into Westleton and the bird sanctuary.

   For a game of golf in the bracing North Sea air, head for our favorite course, the **Aldeburgh Golf Club** at Saxmundham Road (A1094; ℂ **01728/452890**), a challenging 18-hole heathland course of dense gorse, stretching for 6,366 yards. Greens fees are £60 ($120), rising to £65 ($130) on Saturday and Sunday.

9 Norwich (★(★

175km (109 miles) NE of London; 32km (20 miles) W of the North Sea

Norwich still holds to its claim as the capital of East Anglia. Despite its partial indus-trialization, it's a charming and historic city. In addition to its cathedral, it has more than 30 medieval parish churches built of flint. It's also the most important shopping center in East Anglia and has a lot to offer in the way of entertainment and interest-ing hotels, many of them in its narrow streets and alleyways. A big open-air market is busy every weekday, with fruit, flowers, vegetables, and other goods sold from stalls with colored canvas roofs.

ESSENTIALS

GETTING THERE   Hourly train service from London's Liverpool Street Station takes nearly 2 hours. For information, call (℃ **0845/748-4950** or visit **www.national rail.co.uk**.

National Express buses depart London's Victoria Coach Station once each hour for the 3-hour ride. For schedules and information, call (℃ **0870/580-8080** or visit **www. nationalexpress.com**.

If driving from London's Ring Road, head north toward Cambridge on the M11. Turn northeast at the junction with the A11, which takes you to Norwich.

GETTING AROUND   For information about buses serving the area, go to the **Norfolk Bus Information Centre** at Castle Meadow ((℃ **0870/608-2608**). The office there can answer your transportation questions; it's open Monday to Saturday 8:30am to 5pm.

VISITOR INFORMATION   The **Tourist Information Centre** is located in the Forum Building, Norwich, near the marketplace in the center of town ((℃ **01603/ 727927**). It's open April through October Monday to Saturday 9:30am to 6pm and Sunday 10:30am to 4:30pm; and November to March Monday to Saturday 9:30am to 5:30pm.

WHERE TO STAY
EXPENSIVE
De Vere Dunston Hall (★(★   Surrounded by parkland and its own golf course, this gabled house is imbued with an Elizabethan aura, even though the redbrick mansion dates from 1859. With its soaring chimneys, it has been sensitively converted and extended and is now elegantly furnished and imbued with grand character and com-fort. Many of its original 19th-century features are still intact. A wide range of bed-rooms is available, including some family rooms with double sofa beds for children. You can stay in elegant four-poster comfort or try one of the attic rooms, which still boast their original beamed low ceilings. From a golf course to an indoor heated pool and aerobics studios, Dunston Hall also has the best facilities in the area.

Ipswich Rd., Norfolk NR14 8PQ. (℃ **01508/470444.** Fax 01508/470689. www.devereonline.co.uk. 166 units. £198– £238 ($396–$476) double; £260 ($520) suite. AE, DC, MC, V. Free parking. **Amenities:** 3 restaurants; bar; indoor heated pool; 18-hole golf course; 2 outdoor tennis courts; fitness center; aerobics studio; Jacuzzi; sauna; steam room. *In room:* TV, beverage maker, hair dryer, trouser press.

Sprowston Manor Marriott Hotel and Country Club (★(★(★   Norfolk's premier hotel enjoys a long and illustrious history. It was once a private home before it became a hotel in the 1970s. Built in 1559 by a Protestant family prominent in the civil war of the 1640s, it was eventually sold to the lord mayor of Norwich in the late 1800s. It wasn't until 1991, however, that a comprehensive redevelopment added 87 new bedrooms and leisure and conference facilities.

Now owned by Marriott, the hotel lies in 4 hectares (10 acres) of parkland surrounded by the 18-hole Sprowston Park Golf Course. Elegance and informality are its hallmarks. The bedrooms are spacious, quiet, and filled with stylish furniture; some rooms have four-poster beds and others have fireplaces.

Sprowston Park, Wroxham Rd., Norwich, Norfolk NR7 8RP. © 888/236-2427 in the U.S. and Canada, or 01603/410871. Fax 01603/788922. www.marriotthotels.com. 94 units. £140–£198 ($280–$396) double; £230–£240 ($460–$480) suite. Children 14 and younger stay free in parent's room. Rates include breakfast. AE, DC, MC, V. Free parking. **Amenities:** 2 restaurants; 2 bars; indoor heated pool; golf course; health club; spa; sauna; salon; room service; laundry room. *In room:* TV, Wi-Fi, minibar, beverage maker, hair dryer, iron, trouser press, safe.

MODERATE

Holiday Inn   Situated on a sloping hillside about 3km (2 miles) from the city center, this redbrick building offers comfortable contemporary accommodations for business travelers and visitors. Although uninspired, it's a good and safe haven. Many of the bedrooms feature sitting areas with sofas and armchairs. The superior rooms offer extras such as Neutrogena toiletries and bathrobes.

Ipswich Rd., Norwich, Norfolk NR4 6EP. © 0870/400-9060. Fax 01603/506400. www.holiday-inn.com. 120 units. £89–£130 ($178–$260) double. AE, DC, MC, V. Free parking. Take A140 (Ipswich Rd.) 3km (2 miles) from city center and 1.5km (1 mile) from A11 (London Rd.). **Amenities:** Restaurant; bar; indoor heated pool; health club; spa; Jacuzzi; sauna; steam room; business services; room service; laundry service; dry cleaning. *In room:* TV, Wi-Fi, beverage maker, hair dryer, trouser press, safe (in some rooms).

The Maid's Head Hotel   In business since 1272, the Maid's Head claims to be the oldest continuously operated hotel in the United Kingdom. Located next to Norwich Cathedral in the oldest part of the city, it has Elizabethan and Georgian architectural styles. The Georgian section has a prim white entry and small-paned windows. Many of the bedrooms have oak beams evocative of the hotel's earlier days. Each is supplied with bowls of fresh fruit and a complimentary newspaper. Traditional services such as shoe cleaning, breakfast in bed, and afternoon cream teas are offered. The four-poster Queen Elizabeth I Suite (where the Tudor monarch allegedly once slept) is much sought after.

Palace St., Tombland, Norwich, Norfolk NR3 1LB. © 0870/6096110. Fax 01603/613688. www.foliohotels.com. 84 units. £72–£125 ($144–$250) double. AE, DC, MC, V. Free parking. **Amenities:** Restaurant; bar; business services; room service; babysitting; laundry service; dry cleaning. *In room:* TV, Wi-Fi, beverage maker, hair dryer, iron, trouser press.

The Norwich Nelson Premier Inn *Value*   Set beside the River Wensum, near Thorpe Stadium and Foundry Bridge, this renovated four-story hotel is one of the most affordable in town. It lacks the character and atmosphere of the Maid's Head (see above), but provides well-maintained and comfortably furnished bedrooms, some a bit more spacious than others; a few contain four-posters. Rooms open onto a view of the river or else a courtyard.

121 Prince of Wales Rd., Norwich NR1 1DX. © 01603/760260. Fax 01603/620008. www.premierinn.com 159 units. Mon–Thurs £70 ($140) double; Fri–Sun £67 ($134) double. AE, DC, MC, V. Free parking. **Amenities:** 2 restaurants; 2 bars; laundry service; dry cleaning. *In room:* A/C, TV, beverage maker, hair dryer, iron.

INEXPENSIVE

Pearl Continental Hotel   The 18th-century former home of Norwich's Lord Mayor is now an affordable hotel. The refurbished bedrooms are in the main building and in two semidetached cottages. The cottages have bay windows and wooden beams, as well as a private garden. Most bedrooms are midsize, each with a comfortable bed; some are big enough for families.

116 Thorpe Rd., Norwich, Norfolk NR1 1RU. ℂ **01603/620302.** Fax 01603/761706. www.pc-hotels.co.uk. 40 units. £55–£78 ($110–$156) double. Rates include English breakfast. AE, MC, V. Free parking. Take Thorpe Rd. 1km (½ mile) east of City Centre. **Amenities:** Restaurant; bar; room service; babysitting; laundry service; dry cleaning. *In room:* TV, beverage maker.

WHERE TO DINE

Adlard's 🏵🏵🏵 MODERN BRITISH   Chef/proprietor David Adlard and his head chef, Tom Kerridge, are clearly the culinary stars of Norwich. This stylish dining room has a clean, crisp decor of green and white, with candlelit tables and a collection of paintings. David sees to it that service is correct in every way but also relaxed enough to make diners comfortable. The chef specializes in modern British cookery, bringing his own interpretation to every dish. Balanced sauces, split-second timing, and bold but never outrageous combinations of flavors are the trademarks of the cuisine here. Main courses include calf's kidney with sherry or Galician-style hake with clams. Partridge with savoy cabbage and wild mushrooms is another delectable and well-crafted choice.

79 Upper Giles St. ℂ **01603/633522.** Reservations recommended. Main courses lunch £19–£20 ($38–$40), dinner £21–£24 ($42–$48); 2-course fixed-price lunch £22 ($44), 3 courses £28 ($56). AE, MC, V. Tues–Sat 12:30–2pm; Mon–Sat 7–10pm.

The Belgian Monk BELGIAN   Set in the heart of Norwich, within an antique building very close to the Madderhouse Theatre, this restaurant focuses on the hearty, heady grills, stews, and shellfish of Belgium. Dig into such delights as marinated rump steak with grilled peppers and onions or else breast of pork with cracklings (topped with apple fritters) and served with a Madeira sauce. You can also opt for slow-roasted shank of lamb in a rich minty gravy. There's a wine list here but most of the locals tend to avoid it in favor of beer, which you'll order from a comprehensive list of dark and blond Belgian beers. Most visitors opt for a seat beneath the massive ceiling beams of the street-level dining room, but there's additional seating upstairs if you prefer.

7 Pottergate. ℂ **01603/767222.** Reservations recommended. Main courses £7–£19 ($14–$38). AE, MC, V. Mon–Fri noon–3pm and 5:30–10pm; Sat noon–10pm.

St. Benedict's ENGLISH/FRENCH   This modern brasserie gives patrons a warm greeting in a contemporary and rather simple setting, along with affordable and well-prepared food. The chef, Nigel Raffles, shops for some of the freshest of market produce and fashions it into a series of tasty dishes. We recently took delight in his double-baked vegetable-and-cheese soufflé and found the slow-cooked crispy duck perfection itself. It came with a cinnamon sauce and a side of sweet-and-sour red cabbage. The filet of lemon sole is dusted in bread crumbs and pan seared, and made extra enjoyable by the Café de Paris butter and a timbale of watercress and local brown shrimp. The lip-smacking desserts include a luxurious ice praline parfait.

St. Benedict's St. ℂ **01603/765377.** Reservations recommended. Main courses £12–£14 ($24–$28). AE, DC, MC, V. Tues–Sat noon–2pm and 7–10pm.

SEEING THE SIGHTS

Blickling Hall 🏵🏵   Massive yew hedges bordering a long drive frame your first view of Blickling Hall, a great Jacobean house built in the early 17th century, one of the finest examples of such architecture in the country. The long gallery has an elaborate 17th-century ceiling, and the Peter the Great Room, decorated later, has a fine tapestry on the wall. The house is set in ornamental parkland with a formal garden and an orangery.

Blickling, near Aylsham. © **01263/738030.** www.nationaltrust.org.uk. House and gardens £8 ($16) adults, £4 ($8) children; gardens only £5 ($10) adults, £2.50 ($5) children. Late Mar to Oct Wed–Sun and bank holiday Mon 1–5pm. Blickling Hall lies 23km (14 miles) north of the city of Norwich, 2.5km (1½ miles) west of Aylsham on B1354; take A140 toward Cromer and follow the signs. Phone before visit to confirm hours.

The Mustard Shop Museum   The Victorian-style Mustard Shop displays a wealth of mahogany and shining brass. The standard of service and pace of life reflect the personality and courtesy of a bygone age. The Mustard Shop Museum features exhibits on the history of the Colman Company and the making of mustard, including its properties and origins. There are old advertisements, as well as packages and tins. You can browse in the shop, selecting whichever mustards you prefer, including the really hot English type. The shop also sells aprons, tea towels, pottery mustard pots, and mugs.

15 Royal Arcade. © **01603/627889.** Free admission. Mon–Sat 9:30am–5pm. Closed bank holidays.

Norwich Cathedral ✿✿   Dating from 1096, and principally of Norman design, Norwich Cathedral is noted for its long nave with lofty columns. Built in the late Perpendicular style, the spire rises 95m (315 ft.); together with the keep of the castle, it forms a significant landmark on the Norwich skyline. More than 300 *bosses* (knoblike ornamental projections) on the ceiling depict biblical scenes. The impressive choir stalls with handsome misericords date from the 15th century. Edith Cavell, an English nurse executed by the Germans during World War I, is buried on the cathedral's Life's Green. The quadrangular cloisters, which date from the 13th century, are the largest monastic cloisters in England.

The cathedral visitor center includes a refreshment area and exhibition and film room with tape/slide shows about the cathedral. Guided tours run year-round Monday to Saturday at 10:45am, noon, and 2:15pm. The tours are available in five languages—English, French, German, Italian, and Spanish. A short walk from the cathedral is Tombland, one of the most interesting old squares in Norwich.

62 The Close. © **01603/764385.** Free admission; £4 ($8) donation suggested. Oct–May daily 7:30am–6pm; June–Sept daily 7:30am–7pm.

Sainsbury Centre for Visual Arts   The center was the gift of Sir Robert and Lady Sainsbury, who, in 1973, contributed their private collection to the University of East Anglia, 5km (3 miles) west of Norwich on Earlham Road. Together with their son David, they gave an endowment to house the collection. Designed by Foster Associates, the center was opened in 1978 and has since won many national and international awards. The prominent features of the structure are its flexibility, allowing solid and glass areas to be interchanged, and the superb quality of light, which permits optimum viewing of works of art. Special exhibitions are often presented in the 1991 Crescent Wing extension. The Sainsbury Collection is one of the foremost in the country, including modern, ancient, classical, and ethnographic art. Its most prominent works are those by Francis Bacon, Alberto Giacometti, and Henry Moore.

University of East Anglia, Earlham Rd. © **01603/593199.** www.scva.org.uk. Free admission. Tues–Sun 10am–5pm (until 8pm on Wed). Bus: 25, 26, or 27 from Castle Meadow.

Second Air Division Memorial Library   A memorial room honoring the Second Air Division of the 8th U.S. Army Air Force is part of the central library. The library staff will assist veterans who wish to visit their old air bases in East Anglia. At the library, you can find pertinent books, audiovisual materials, and records of the various bomber groups.

The Forum, Millennium Plain. © **01603/774747.** www.2ndair.org.uk. Free admission. Mon–Sat 9am–5pm.

EXPLORING THE NORFOLK BROADS 🏛🏛

One of the most important wetlands of Europe, the Norfolk "Broads" are part of the lush landscape of the **Broads National Park,** 18 Colegate, Norwich, Norfolk NR3 1BQ (© **01603/610734;** www.broads-authority.gov.uk), lying both in Norfolk and Suffolk. Long thought to be natural lakes, they are actually man-made, resulting from peat being excavated for use as fuel. Flooded by a rising water table in the 13th century, these newly formed waterways were named "Broads."

The water comes from a trio of rivers—the Bure, Waveney, and Yare—that meander across these flatlands to the east of Norwich. The rivers converge at a lake, Breydon Water, before flowing into the North Sea at the port of Great Yarmouth.

The area covers 200km (124 miles) of navigable waterways. The dominant trees are alder, sallow, and birch, but you'll also see lots of oak and ash woodland. The fen, woodland, and grazing marshes of the Broads are home to some of the rarest plants and creatures in Britain.

One of Europe's most popular waterways, the Broads attract a million visitors a year with their blend of wildlife and distinctive landscapes.

On the River Bure, the town of **Wroxham** deservedly calls itself "the capital of the Broads." It lies 11km (7 miles) northeast of Norwich and is the best center for exploring the Broads, which, for the most part, are shallow lagoons linked by streams. These waterways are fun to explore by boat, of course, but some visitors prefer to ride bikes along trails in the Broads.

By public transportation, head to Wroxham from Norwich on bus no. 54, the ride taking 30 minutes and costing £2.50 ($5) round-trip. Once in Wroxham, a lot of information about the Broads is available from the **Tourist Office,** Station Road (© **01603/782281**), open Easter to October daily 9am to 1pm and 2 to 5pm. At this office you can get a list of small-boat outfitters renting vessels for touring the Broads. Day launches generally cost £12 to £15 ($24–$30) per hour. Among the best and most reliable outfitters for boat rentals is **Barnes Brinkcraft,** River Bure, Wroxham, along Riverside Road (© **01603/782625**).

If you don't want to handle your own boat, you can take an organized tour. The best ones are offered by **Broads Tours,** near the Wroxham Bridge (© **01603/782207;** www.broads.co.uk). Their cruises last 1½ to 3½ hours. In summer, most departures are at either 11:30am or 2pm. The cost ranges from £6 to £9 ($12–$18) for adults, and from £4.50 to £6.50 ($9–$13) for children 5 to 15 years; it's free for children ages 4 and younger.

Some areas of the Broads are reached only by bike. At the tourist office (see above), you can purchase a pamphlet, *Broads Bike Hire,* listing the best routes and containing much useful information. There are many outfitters renting bikes for touring the Broads. The tourist office keeps a complete list.

SHOPPING

For antiques, books, and crafts, shoppers can search out the historic lanes and alleys of the town center.

Tombland Antiques Centre, 14 Tombland (© **01603/619129**), is a three-floor house opposite the cathedral where 60-plus dealers set up shop. The selection is wide and varied and includes everything from small collectibles to antique furniture.

NORWICH AFTER DARK

From fine art to pop art, there's quite a lot happening around Norwich at night. Information on almost all of it can be found at the box office of the Theatre Royal, Theatre Street (© **01603/630000;** www.theatreroyalnorwich.co.uk), where you can also pick up tickets to just about any event.

The **Theatre Royal** hosts touring companies performing drama, opera, ballet, and modern dance. The reduced Shakespeare Company troupe is among the regular visitors. Ticket prices run from £4 to £19 ($8–$38), with senior and student discounts usually available for Wednesday, Thursday, and Saturday matinees. The box office is open Monday to Saturday 9:30am to 8pm on performance days, closing at 6pm on nonperformance days.

Hosting productions of classic drama on most evenings, **Norwich Playhouse,** Gun Wharf, 42–58 St. George's St. (© **01603/598598;** www.norwichplayhouse.co.uk), offers tickets ranging from £10 to £18 ($20–$36). The box office is open Monday to Saturday 9:30am until 6pm.

An Elizabethan-style theater, **Maddermarket Theatre,** 1 St. John's Alley (© **01603/ 620917;** www.maddermarket.co.uk), is home to the amateur Norwich Players' productions of classical and contemporary drama. Tickets, ranging from £8 to £10 ($16–$20), and schedules are available at the box office, Monday to Saturday 10am to 9pm and 10am to 5pm on nonperformance days.

Located in a converted medieval church, **Norwich Puppet Theatre,** St. James, Whitefriars (© **01603/629921;** www.puppettheatre.co.uk), offers original puppet shows most afternoons and some mornings in an octagonal studio that holds about 50 people. Tickets are £6.50 ($13) adults, £5 ($10) students and seniors, and £4.50 ($9) for children 16 and younger, and are available at the box office Monday to Friday 10am to 7pm and on Saturday on days of performances 1 hour prior to the show's start.

The most versatile entertainment complex in town, **Norwich Arts Centre,** Reeves Yard, St. Benedict's Street (© **01603/660352;** www.norwichartscentre.co.uk), hosts performances of ballet, comedy, and poetry, with an emphasis on ethnic music. Tickets are £6.50 to £16 ($13–$32), and the box office is open Monday to Friday 10am to 7pm. On days of performances, the box office is open until 9pm.

Pay a call on **Adam and Eve,** 17 Bishopgate (© **01603/667423**), the oldest pub in Norwich, founded in 1249, which serves a well-kept John Smith's or Old Peculiar.

Many beer drinkers prefer **Fat Cat** 🐾🐾, 49 W. End St. (© **01603/624436**). Bartenders serve nearly three dozen real ales as well as their own beer (try Meow Mild or Top Cat). If you don't feel feline, opt for Black Dog Mild. Eight draft beers from Belgium and Germany as well as more than a dozen bottled Belgian beers and a dozen country wines are also featured, even Norfolk farm cider. In summer tables are placed outside, and you can get a good lunch here, often meat pies, on any day except Sunday.

Finally, if you have a hankering for gay Norfolk men, dance the night away (on two floors) at the **Media Night Club,** 80 Rose Lane (© **01603/623559;** www.media nightclub.co.uk). Later you can get better acquainted with your catch of the night on one of the black leather sofas. The website lists special nights such as drag shows and the like.

16

East Midlands:
Princess Di & Robin Hood

This region is a mix of dreary industrial sections and incredible scenery, particularly in the **Peak District National Park,** centered in Derbyshire. Byron said that the landscapes in the Peak District rivaled those of Switzerland and Greece. He might have overstated his case just a bit, but he wasn't too far off target. In the East Midlands, you'll also find the tulip land of **Lincolnshire,** the 18th-century spa of **Buxton** in Derbyshire, and the remains of Robin Hood's **Sherwood Forest** in Nottinghamshire. George Washington looked to **Sulgrave Manor** in Northamptonshire as his ancestral home. If you have Pilgrims in your past, you can trace your roots to the East Midlands. Except for Sulgrave Manor and **Althorp House,** where Princess Di spent her girlhood, Northamptonshire is not on the tourist circuit. If you do decide to stop here, the

best place to spend the night is the industrialized county town of **Leicester,** which is also a base to explore many sights in the countryside, including **Belvoir Castle,** the setting for Steven Spielberg's movie *Young Sherlock Holmes,* and **Bosworth Battlefield,** site of one of England's most important battles.

Derbyshire is noted primarily for the Peak District National Park, but it also has a number of historic homes—notably **Chatsworth,** the home of the 11th duke of Devonshire. The best places to base yourself here are in **Buxton** and **Bakewell.**

In Nottinghamshire, the city of **Nottingham** is a good center for exploring what's left of Sherwood Forest, the legendary stamping grounds of Robin Hood.

If you're headed for Lincolnshire, the highlight is the cathedral city of **Lincoln** itself.

1 Sulgrave Manor: Washington's Ancestral Home

Sulgrave Manor 🏛🏛 American visitors will be especially interested in this small mid-16th-century Tudor manor, the ancestral home of George Washington. As part of a plan to dissolve the monasteries, Henry VIII sold the priory-owned manor in 1539 to Lawrence Washington, who had been mayor of Northampton. The Washington family occupied Sulgrave for more than a century, but in 1656, Colonel John Washington left for the New World. Born in Virginia, George Washington was a direct descendant of Lawrence (seven generations removed).

A group of English people bought the manor in 1914 in honor of the friendship between Britain and the United States. Appropriate furnishings and portraits, including a Gilbert Stuart original of the first president, have been donated from both sides of the Atlantic. The Washington family coat of arms on the main doorway—two bars and a trio of mullets—is believed to have been the inspiration for the Stars and Stripes.

Manor Rd. ℭ **01295/760205.** www.sulgravemanor.org.uk. Admission £6.25 ($13) adults, £3 ($6) children ages 5–16, free for children 4 and younger. May–Oct Tues–Thurs and Sat–Sun 2–4pm; Apr Sat–Sun 2–4pm. From Northampton, drive 29km (18 miles) southwest on A43, then take B4525 to Sulgrave. From Stratford-upon-Avon, take A422 via Banbury (whose famous cross entered nursery-rhyme fame) and continue to Brackley; 9.5km (6 miles) from Brackley, leave A422 and join B4525, which goes to the tiny village of Sulgrave. Signs will lead you to Sulgrave Manor.

2 Althorp: Memories of Princess Di

Althorp ✮   Built in 1508 by Sir John Spencer, Althorp has brought a sometimes unwelcome dose of fame to the surrounding rural area as the girlhood home of Princess Diana. It was glamorously revived by Raine Spencer, Diana's stepmother. At least part of the beauty and historical authenticity of this frequently renovated site is the result of her efforts.

Since the death of Lord Spencer, Diana's father, the house has been under the jurisdiction of Charles Spencer, Diana's older brother. Its collection includes paintings by Van Dyck, Reynolds, Gainsborough, and Rubens; an assortment of rare French and English furniture; and porcelain by Sèvres, Bow, and Chelsea.

Following the tragic death of Princess Diana in August 1997, a ticket to Althorp House became extremely difficult to obtain. More than 200 24-hour telephone lines handle orders for tickets. Althorp is open to the public only from July 1, Diana's birthday, to August 30.

Diana was buried on an island in an artificial lake on the property. Visitors do not have access to the island but have a clear view of it across the lake. A museum celebrates Diana's life, complete with schoolgirl letters, her stunning silk wedding dress, and some of her haute couture clothes.

The museum also shows poignant films of her as a carefree child dancing in the gardens and later as a mother riding with her sons, William and Harry, plus videos that include the moving footage of her funeral. The museum makes no mention of Dodi al-Fayed, who died with her in the Paris car crash, and certainly no mention of her former lover James Hewitt. Her estranged husband is also not featured prominently in the exhibition.

Facilities on-site include a restaurant and a shop selling a range of souvenirs associated with Diana. The estate states that these souvenirs do not "cheapen her memory in any way." You decide.

9.5km (6 miles) northwest of Northampton on A428 in Althorp, near Harlestone. ℭ **1604/770107.** www. althorp.com. Admission £13 ($26) adults, £11 ($22) seniors, £6 ($12) children 5–17, £30 ($60) family ticket, free for children 4 and younger. July 1–Aug 30 daily 10am–5pm (last admission 1 hr. before closing).

3 Leicester

172km (107 miles) NW of London; 69km (43 miles) NE of Birmingham; 39km (24 miles) NE of Coventry; 42km (26 miles) S of Nottingham

Hang on to your hats because this county town is definitely no Sleepy Hollow. Leicester, pronounced *Les*-ter, one of the 10 largest cities in England, is by far the most cosmopolitan city in the East Midlands. Because of the scarcity of hotels in the area, many visitors stop in Leicester for the night on visits to Sulgrave Manor and Althorp.

Historically, Leicester was known as Ratae Coritanorum in Roman days. It was also the capital of Lear's kingdom and the seat of the East Mercian bishops back in the 8th century. Some of that past is still preserved today in Leicester's sightseeing attractions

The East Midlands

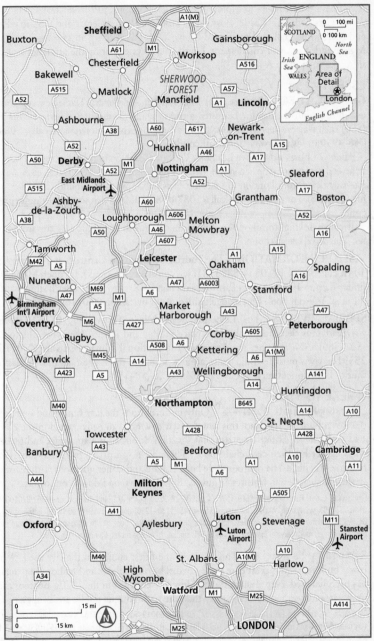

Buxton

Sheffield

A1(M)

M1

A61

Chesterfield

Worksop

Gainsborough

A516

Bakewell

A515

Matlock

SHERWOOD
FOREST

A57

A52

Mansfield

A1

Lincoln

Ashbourne

A38

A60

A617

Newark-
on-Trent

A15

A52

Hucknall

A46

A17

A50

Derby

A52

M1

Nottingham

A1

Sleaford

A515

East Midlands
Airport

A52

A52

Grantham

A17

Boston

Ashby-
de-la-Zouch

A60

Loughborough

A606

Melton
Mowbray

A52

A38

A50

A46

A16

A607

Tamworth

Leicester

A1

A15

M42

A5

Oakham

Spalding

Nuneaton

A47

M69

A6

A47

A6003

Stamford

A16

M1

A5

Birmingham
Int'l Airport

M6

Market
Harborough

A43

A47

Peterborough

Coventry

A427

Corby

A605

Rugby

M45

A508

A6

Kettering

A6

A1(M)

Warwick

A14

A43

Wellingborough

A141

A423

A5

A14

Huntingdon

M40

Northampton

B645

A14

A10

Towcester

A428

St. Neots

Banbury

A43

Bedford

A10

A428

Cambridge

A44

A5

M1

A1

A10

A11

A6

Milton
Keynes

A505

A41

Aylesbury

Luton

Stevenage

M11

Oxford

M40

Luton
Airport

A10

Stansted
Airport

A34

High
Wycombe

St. Albans

A1(M)

Harlow

Watford

M1

M25

A414

0   15 mi

0   15 km

M25

LONDON

569

if you have 3 or 4 hours to explore the city itself and not just its environs, including Ashby Castle, Belvoir Castle, Bosworth Battlefield Visitor Centre and Country Park, and Melbourne Hall—all previewed below. With Di's Althorp and George's Sulgrave Manor added on, you could spent 2 very busy days exploring the attractions of this shire, many of them A-list.

ESSENTIALS

GETTING THERE   Trains depart from London's St. Pancras Station every 25 minutes throughout the day for Leicester, a trip of about 90 minutes. The fare costs £40 ($80) each way on the day of your trip. For schedules and information, call ✆ **0845/748-4950** or visit **www.nationalrail.co.uk**.

About 14 buses a day leave London's Victoria Coach Station for Leicester. They call at several secondary stops en route, thus taking 2 hours and 30 minutes each way. A one-way ticket from London to Leicester costs £15 ($30), and a round-trip ticket goes for £19 ($38). For information, call ✆ **0870/580-8080** or visit **www.nationalexpress. com**.

If you're driving from London, follow the M1 north to Junction 21 toward Leicester. The drive takes 2 hours.

VISITOR INFORMATION   The **Tourist Information Centre** is at 7–9 Every St., Town Hall Square (✆ **0844/8885181;** www.visitleicester.co.uk). It's open Monday to Friday 8am to 10:30pm, and Saturday and Sunday 8am to 8pm. They'll supply a useful map. You can book Blue Badge guided walks by calling ✆ **01162/994444.**

SPECIAL EVENTS   The **Leicester Early Music Festival** (✆ **01162/709984;** www.earlymusicleicester.co.uk) takes place in May and June. Tickets cost £11 to £30 ($22–$60). Also in June, the **Leicester International Music Festival** (✆ **01162/254916;** www.musicfestival.co.uk) attracts some of the biggest names in classical music. Ticket prices vary, but average £4 to £26 ($8–$52).

WHERE TO STAY

Leicester Marriott Hotel ✦✦   Only minutes from the city center and owned by the Royal Bank of Scotland, this was the first new hotel to be launched in the city in 14 years when it swung open its doors in 2006. It has all the amenities and features you'd expect in a first-class chain hotel. There are no surprises, but rarely any disappointments either. The bedrooms are both tasteful and rather luxurious with plenty of space and such design features as duvets, fluffy pillows, and down comforters.

Smith Way, Grove Park, Leicester LE19 15W. ✆ **800/228-9290** in the U.S. and Canada, or 01162/820100. Fax 01162/820101. www.marriott.com. 227 units. £65–£145 ($130–$290) double; £159–£180 ($318–$360) suite. AE, DC, MC, V. Parking £5 ($10). **Amenities:** Restaurant; bar; indoor heated pool; health club; spa; sauna; steam room; business center; room service. *In room:* A/C, TV, Wi-Fi, minibar, beverage maker, hair dryer, iron, safe.

Ramada Jarvis Hotel ✦   This is one of the finest choices in the city itself. When it was built in 1898, no expense was spared. The original oak and mahogany paneling has been retained, even though the building was enlarged in the 1970s. Bedrooms are more streamlined and contemporary than the semi-antique public areas suggest.

73 Granby St., Leicester, Leicestershire LE1 6ES. ✆ **08448/159012.** Fax 01162/554040. www.ramadajarvis.co.uk. 104 units. Mon–Thurs £115 ($230) double; £149 ($298) suite; Fri–Sun £95 ($190) double, £105 ($210) suite. AE, DC, MC, V. Parking £5 ($10). **Amenities:** Restaurant; bar; room service; laundry service; dry cleaning. *In room:* TV, high-speed Internet, beverage maker, hair dryer, trouser press.

Rothley Court Hotel ✺ *Finds*   This hotel stands on the edge of Charnwood Forest, a royal hunting ground for centuries. In 1231, Henry III granted the manor and "soke" (right to hold court under feudal law) to the Knights Templar. The chapel erected next to the existing abbey around 1240 is second only to the Temple in London as the best-preserved Templar chapel in Britain.

On 2.4 hectares (6 acres) of grounds, the hotel is surrounded by open farmland. Stone fireplaces, oak paneling, and stained-glass windows evoke its rich historical associations. Bedrooms have been handsomely restored and are comfortable, with modern conveniences and a number of antique furnishings. The less desirable rooms with standard furnishings are in a modern annex.

Westfield Lane, Rothley, Leicester, Leicestershire LE7 7LG. ✆ 01162/374141. Fax 01162/374483. www.rothleycourt. com. 30 units. £110–£125 ($220–$250) double; £125–£150 ($250–$300) suite. Rates include English breakfast. AE, DC, MC, V. Free parking. Head 9.5km (6 miles) north of Leicester on B5328 Rd., just off A6 between Leicester and Loughborough. **Amenities:** Restaurant (see Berrett's review below); bar; room service; babysitting; laundry service; dry cleaning. *In room:* TV/DVD, beverage maker, hair dryer, iron, trouser press.

WHERE TO DINE

Berrett's Restaurant ENGLISH   Part of the fun of dining at the Rothley Court Hotel (see above) involves a pre- or postmeal visit to one of Britain's best-preserved strongholds of the Knights Templar, a 13th-century semi-fanatical sect that played an important role in the Crusades. Within the venerable walls of a historic manor house surrounded with parks and farmland, you can enjoy a sophisticated blend of modern and traditional English cuisine—say, a medley of monkfish and crayfish with lime juice, coriander, and artichoke hearts; steak Diane with Dijon mustard, shallots, mushrooms, tomatoes, and a cognac sauce; or seared filet of Scottish salmon with nut-brown butter sauce. Not all dishes reach gastronomic heights, but this is as good as it gets in the Leicester area.

In the Rothley Court Hotel, Westfield Lane, Rothley. ✆ 01162/374141. Reservations recommended. Main courses £15–£19 ($30–$38). AE, DC, MC, V. Daily noon–2:30pm; Mon–Thurs 6:30–9:30pm; Fri–Sun 6:30–10pm.

EXPLORING THE TOWN

Leicester is worth a look if you have an afternoon to spare. In addition to Victorian-style **Shires Shopping Centre,** High Street, with its designer and collectible stores, wide walkways, fountains, and sunny skylights, there's **St. Martins Square** in the city center, which has given new life to old restored buildings, with new retailers, cafes, and teashops. A wealth of specialty shops—out .5km (a quarter-mile) on either side of the railway station—and several antiques stores line **Oxford Street** and **Western Boulevard.**

Venture out from the center of town to Belgrave Road, and you'll discover the **Golden Mile,** which takes its name from several jewelry shops found here, each specializing in gold. The store windows along Belgrave Road overflow with fine Indian silks, organza, and cottons. Sari shops also carry a variety of accessories including bags, jewelry, shoes, and shawls.

Jewry Wall and Archeology Museum   Set near the excavation of an ancient Roman bath, this museum has nothing at all to do with Jewish history. Its name derives from a corruption of the Norman French *jurad,* which referred to the governing magistrates of an early medieval town, who used to gather in the shadow of this wall for their municipal decisions. More than 12m (40 ft.) high, the wall is higher

---

Moments   **Launch Yourself into Space**

The most modern attraction in Leicester is the **National Space Centre**, Exploration Drive (© **0870/607-7223;** www.nssc.co.uk), Britain's only attraction dedicated to space science and astronomy. It is crowned by a futuristic Rocket Tower. Allow 3 hours for a journey of discovery where stories, personalities, and technology of the past and present are used to explain space and how it will affect your future. You're taken through eight themed galleries, seeing space rockets, satellites, and capsules, and taking part in hands-on activities. Admission is £12 ($24) for adults, £10 ($20) children ages 4 to 16, £38 to £47 ($76–$94) family ticket, free for children 3 and younger. Hours year-round are Tuesday to Sunday 10am to 5pm (last admission 3:30pm).

---

than any other piece of ancient Roman architecture in Britain. Exhibits within the museum include a pair of ancient Roman mosaics, the Peacock Pavement and the Blackfriars Mosaic, which are the finest of their kind in the British Midlands. Each was laboriously sliced from the masonry of ancient villas within the district and set into new masonry beds here.

St. Nicholas Circle (about .5km/¼ mile from the town center). © **01162/254971.** Free admission. Sat–Sun 11am–4:30pm.

Leicester Abbey   In a verdant public park favored by joggers and picnickers, about 1km (a half-mile) north of Leicester's historic core, these evocative, poetically shattered remains are all that's left of the richest Augustinian monastery in England, built in 1132. In 1530, Cardinal Wolsey came here to die, demoralized and broken after his political and religious conflicts with Henry VIII. The abbey was torn down during the Reformation, and stones were used in the construction of Cavendish House next door.

Abbey Park, Abbey Park Rd. © **01162/221000.** Free admission. Summer daily dawn–dusk; winter daily 7:30am–6pm.

Leicester Guildhall   Built in stages between the 14th and 16th centuries, the city's most prominent public building was Leicester's first town hall and contains one of the oldest libraries in Britain. Plaques commemorate its role as a die-hard last bastion of the Parliamentarians during the civil war. On its ground floor, you'll see a 19th-century police station with a pair of original prison cells, whose mournful graffiti are a powerful testimony to the horrors of the Victorian penal system. Shakespeare's troupe is said to have appeared here.

Guildhall Lane. © **01162/532569.** Free admission. Feb–Nov Sat–Wed 11am–4:30pm; Sun 1–4:30pm.

New Walk Museum and Art Gallery   This multipurpose museum has two distinctly separate features. It contains exhibits of archaeology and natural history: a dinosaur bone found in a field near Leicester; a collection of Egyptian mummies and artifacts brought back to the Midlands by Thomas Cook, the 19th-century travel mogul; and geological exhibits. There is also a collection of paintings by British and European artists (including some by Gainsborough) from the 18th through 20th centuries. The collection of early-20th-century canvasses by German expressionists is one of the largest in Europe. In 2005, the museum added three art galleries: a permanent collection of modern art including such favorites as Degas and Pissarro; a gallery devoted to German expressionism; and a third thematic gallery, highlighting diversity in art, particularly that of south Asia, China, the Caribbean, and Africa.

53 New Walk. © 01162/254900. Free admission; donations accepted. Mon–Sat 10am–5pm; Sun 11am–5pm. Closed Dec–Jan 1.

St. Martin's Cathedral (Leicester Cathedral)   It may not have the soaring grandeur of the cathedrals of York or Lincoln, but this is the most venerated and historic church in Leicester. In 1086, it was one of the region's parish churches, enlarged during the 1300s and 1500s. In 1927, it was designated as the cathedral of Leicester, adding considerably to its pomp and circumstance. The oak vaulting beneath the building's north porch is one of the most unusual treatments of its kind in England. For walking tours, contact the tourist office (see above).

21 St. Martin's Lane. © 01162/625294. Free admission. Daily 8am–6pm.

LEICESTER AFTER DARK

Phoenix Arts Centre, Upper Brown Street (© 01162/554854), hosts dance, music, and theatrical productions from around the world; local dancers, musicians, and actors also perform on its stage, and there's even an occasional film screening.

On weekends, the area around the **Clock Tower** in the center of town is alive with bustling crowds headed out to the clubs and bars on Church Gate, Silver Street, and High Street.

As you may expect of a university town, Leicester has a variety of pubs, but the one favored most by locals is the **Pump and Tap,** Duns Lane (© 01162/540324). Stop by to sample ales by Leicestershire's two home-brewers: Everards and Hoskins.

The biggest after-dark magnet is **Zanzibar,** Gravel Street (© 0116/2511442), drawing hundreds of revelers on Friday or Saturday nights. The cover charge ranges from £2 to £20 ($4–$40), depending on what's being offered. In one room you hear the sounds of pop classics, in the other hip-hop.

HISTORIC SIGHTS NEAR LEICESTER

Ashby Castle   If you've read Sir Walter Scott's *Ivanhoe,* you will remember Ashby-de-la-Zouch, a town that retains a pleasant country atmosphere. The main attraction here is the ruined Norman manor house, Ashby Castle, where Mary, Queen of Scots, was imprisoned. The building was already an antique in 1464 when its thick walls were converted into a fortress.

Ashby-de-la-Zouch (29km/18 miles northwest of Leicester). © 01530/413343. Admission £3.50 ($7) adults, £2.60 ($5.20) seniors and students, £1.80 ($3.60) children 15 and younger, family ticket £8.80 ($18). Apr–June and Sept–Oct Thurs–Mon 10am–5pm; July–Aug daily 10am–6pm; Nov–Mar Thurs–Mon 10am–4pm.

Belvoir Castle   On the northern border of Leicestershire overlooking the Vale of Belvoir (pronounced *Beaver*), Belvoir Castle has been the seat of the dukes of Rutland since the time of Henry VII. Rebuilt by Wyatt in 1816, the castle contains paintings by Holbein, Reynolds, and Gainsborough, as well as tapestries in its magnificent staterooms. The castle was the location of the movies *Little Lord Fauntleroy* and *Young Sherlock Holmes.* In summer, it's the site of medieval jousting tournaments.

11km (7 miles) southwest of Grantham, between A607 to Melton Mowbray and A52 to Nottingham. © 01476/871002. www.belvoircastle.com. Admission castle and grounds £12 ($24) adults, £10 ($20) students and seniors, £6 ($12) children 5–16, £32 ($64) family ticket (2 adults, 3 children). Apr–Sept Tues–Thurs and Sat–Sun 11am–5pm (last entry 4pm).

Bosworth Battlefield Visitor Centre and Country Park This site commemorates the 1485 battle that ended one of England's most important conflicts. The Battle of Bosworth ended the War of the Roses between the houses of York and Lancaster. When the fighting subsided, King Richard III, last of the Yorkists, lay dead, and Henry Tudor, a Welsh nobleman who had been banished to France to thwart his royal ambition, was proclaimed the victor. Henry thus became King Henry VII, and the Tudor dynasty was born.

Today, the appropriate standards fly where the opponents had their positions. You can see the whole scene by taking a 2km (1¼-mile) walk along the marked battle trails. In the center are exhibitions, models, book and gift shops, a cafeteria, and a theater where an audiovisual introduction with an excerpt from the Lord Laurence Olivier film version of Shakespeare's *Richard III* is presented.

29km (18 miles) southwest of Leicester between M1 and M6 (near the town of Nuneaton). ✆ **01455/290429.** Admission £6 ($12) adults, £4 ($8) seniors and children 15 and younger, £15 ($30) family ticket. Visitor center Mar–Oct daily 10am–5pm; Nov–Feb daily 10am–4pm.

Melbourne Hall ✸ Built by the bishops of Carlisle in 1133, Melbourne Hall stands in one of the most famous formal gardens in Britain. The ecclesiastical structure was restored in the 1600s by one of the cabinet ministers of Charles I and enlarged by Queen Anne's vice chamberlain. It was the home of Lord Melbourne, who was prime minister when Victoria ascended to the throne. Lady Palmerston later inherited the house, which contains an important collection of antique furniture and artwork. A special feature is the beautifully restored wrought-iron pergola by Robert Bakewell, a noted 18th-century ironsmith.

24km (15 miles) southwest of Leicester on A50, on Church Sq. ✆ **01332/862502.** www.melbournehall.com. Admission to house and garden £5.50 ($11) adults, £4.50 ($9) seniors and students, £3.50 ($7) children 6–15, free for children 5 and younger; house only £3.50 ($7) adults, £3 ($6) students and seniors, £2 ($4) children 5–15; gardens only £3 ($6) adults, £2 ($4) seniors, students, and children 5–15. House Aug daily 2–4:15pm (closed the 1st 3 Mon of the month). Gardens Apr–Sept Wed, Sat–Sun, and bank holidays 1:30–5:30pm.

4 Derbyshire & Peak District National Park

The most magnificent scenery in the Midlands is found in Derbyshire, between Nottinghamshire and Staffordshire. Some travelers avoid this part of the country because it's ringed by the industrial sprawl of Manchester, Leeds, Sheffield, and Derby. But missing this area is a pity, for Derbyshire has actually been less defaced by industry than its neighbors.

The north of the county, with Peak District National Park, contains waterfalls, hills, moors, green valleys, and dales. In the south, the land is more level, with pastoral meadows. Dovedale, Chee Dale, and Millers Dale are worth a detour. For tips on touring, see below.

EXPLORING PEAK DISTRICT NATIONAL PARK ✸✸

Peak District National Park covers some 1,404 sq. km (542 sq. miles), most of it in Derbyshire, with some spilling over into South Yorkshire and Staffordshire. It stretches from Holmfirth in the north to Ashbourne in the south, and from Sheffield in the east to Macclesfield in the west. The best central place to stay overnight is Buxton (see below).

The peak in the name is a bit misleading, because there is no actual peak—the highest point is just 630m (2,100 ft.). The park has some 4,000 walking trails that cover some of the most beautiful hill country in England.

The southern portion of the park, called **White Peak,** is filled with limestone hills, tiny villages, old stone walls, and hidden valleys. August and September are the best and most beautiful times to hike these rolling hills.

In the north, called **Dark Peak,** the scenery changes to rugged moors and deep gullies. This area is best visited in the spring when the purple heather, so beloved by Emily Brontë, comes into bloom.

If you're planning an extensive visit to the park, write for details to the **Peak District National Park Authority,** Aldern House, Baslow Road, Bakewell, Derbyshire DE45 1AE (© **01629/816200;** www.peakdistrict.org). A list of publications will be sent to you, and you can order whichever you want.

GETTING TO THE PARK   You can reach Buxton (see below) by train from Manchester. It's also possible to travel by bus, the Transpeak, taking 3½ hours from Manchester to Nottingham, with stops at such major centers as Buxton, Bakewell, Matlock, and Matlock Bath. If you're planning to use public transportation, consider the **Derbyshire Wayfarer,** sold at various rail and bus stations; for £8.30 ($17) for adults or £4.15 ($8.30) for students, seniors, and children, you can ride all the bus and rail lines within the peak district for a day.

If you're driving, the main route is the A515 north from Birmingham, with Buxton as the gateway. From Manchester, Route 6 heads southeast to Buxton.

GETTING AROUND THE PARK   Many visitors prefer to walk from one village to another. In our view, the best and most evocative walk in the entire park district is the **Monsal Trail** lying between Buxton and Bakewell (see below). If you're not so hearty, you can take local buses, which connect various villages. Instead of the usual Sunday slowdown in bus service, more buses run on that day than on weekdays because of increased demand, especially in summer.

Another popular way to explore the park is by bicycle. Park authorities operate three **Cycle Hire Centres,** renting bikes for £14 ($28) a day for adults and £10 ($20) for children 15 and younger, with a £20 ($40) deposit, helmet included. Centers are at Mapleton Lane in Ashbourne (© **01335/343156**), near the Fairholmes Information Centre at Derwent (© **01433/651261**), and at the junction of Tissington and High Peak Trails at Parsley Hay (© **01298/84493**).

BUXTON ᴋ: A LOVELY BASE FOR EXPLORING THE PARK
277km (172 miles) NW of London; 61km (38 miles) NW of Derby; 40km (25 miles) SE of Manchester

One of the loveliest towns in Britain, Buxton rivaled the spa at Bath in the 18th century. Its waters were known to the Romans, whose settlement here was called Aquae Arnemetiae. The thermal waters were pretty much forgotten from Roman times until the reign of Queen Elizabeth I, when the baths were reactivated. Mary, Queen of Scots, took the waters here, brought by her caretaker, the earl of Shrewsbury.

Buxton today is mostly the result of 18th-century development directed by the duke of Devonshire. His lordship's grandiose plan to create another Bath or Cheltenham never came to be, but his legacy lives on in many elegant 1700s buildings. The thermal baths closed in 1972, and the town went into decay. But it's slowly being revived, many of its aging properties restored.

Seek out, in particular, the **Crescent,** incorporating the former St. Ann's Hotel. The duke's plan to make this a model of the Royal Crescent in Bath was never realized but it's worth a look anyway. At the eastern end of the Crescent rises the cast-iron and glass canopy sheltering the Cavendish Arcade Shopping Centre in the original 18th-century bathhouses of the spa.

In front of the Crescent is a beautiful park, the **Slopes,** dating from 1818. It leads up to the center of town, the Market Place, which is sleepy all winter but filled with heavy traffic in summer. Buxton's spa days have come and gone, but it's still the best center for exploring the peak district. The climate is amazingly mild, considering that at 300m (1,000 ft.) altitude, Buxton is the second-highest town in England.

ESSENTIALS

GETTING THERE Trains depart from Manchester at least every hour during the day. It's a 50-minute trip.

About half a dozen buses also run between Manchester and Sheffield, stopping in Buxton en route, after a 70-minute ride.

By car, take the A6 from Manchester, heading southeast into Buxton.

VISITOR INFORMATION The **Tourist Office** is at the Crescent (✆ **01298/ 25106;** www.visitbuxton.co.uk) and is open Monday to Friday 8am to 8pm, Saturday and Sunday 10am to 4pm; off-season hours are daily from 10am to 4pm. It provides a free pamphlet, entitled "Buxton Town Trail," that offers a map and detailed instructions for a walking tour, lasting between 75 and 90 minutes, from the town center.

SPECIAL EVENTS The town hosts the **Buxton Festival** (✆ **01298/70395;** www.buxtonfestival.co.uk), a well-known opera festival, during a 2½-week period in July.

WHERE TO STAY

Buxton's Victorian Guest House ★ *Finds* Commissioned by the duke of Devonshire in 1860, this is one of a row of elegant terraced houses lying on a promenade overlooking a lake and the 16-hectare (40-acre) Pavilion Gardens. It is also only a 2-minute walk to the Buxton Opera House. The house is spectacularly decorated and furnished with art, prints, and antiques from both the Victorian and Edwardian eras. All of the bedchambers are individually designed with soft furnishings and bedding. The standard rooms are themed and include the Victorian Craftman's Room and the Egyptian Room. The finest of the accommodations is the premier room decorated in a classical Victorian style and housing a four-poster bed.

3A Broad Walk, Buxton, Derbyshire SK17 6JE. ✆ **01298/78759.** Fax 01298/74732. www.buxtonvictorian.co.uk. 8 units. £68–£92 ($136–$184) double; from £192 ($384) family suite. Rates include full English breakfast. MC, V. Free parking. **Amenities:** Breakfast room; laundry service. *In room:* TV, beverage maker, hair dryer, iron.

Fischer's Baslow Hall ★★★ At the edge of the Chatsworth Estate, at the end of a winding chestnut tree-lined drive, this stately Edwardian country house is the finest choice in the area for either food or lodgings. The six bedrooms in the main house are decorated with lavish fabrics and contain ornate plasterwork ceilings, along with Egyptian cotton bedding and traditionally styled bathrooms with tub and shower. We prefer these accommodations, although you can also rent a large double in the Garden House, built of locally quarried stone with high ceilings and exposed timber joists. In contrast to the main house, the garden rooms are more modern and more minimalist.

Baslow Hall, Calver Rd., Baslow, Derbyshire DE45 1RR. ✆ **01246/583259.** Fax 01246/583818. www.fischers-baslowhall.co.uk. 11 units. £140–£195 ($280–$390) double. Rates include breakfast. AE, DC, MC, V. Free parking. **Amenities:** Restaurant; bar. *In room:* TV, safe (in some).

Old Hall 🖈 This is one of the most historic old inns of Derbyshire. Although other hostelries make the same claim, this is reputed to be the oldest hotel in England, a 16th-century building overlooking the Buxton Opera House. Mary, Queen of Scots, stayed here on several occasions between 1573 and 1582. Daniel Defoe, writing as a guest in 1727, called Old Hall "indeed a very special place," and it remains so in its restored form today. Its mellowed walls and ancient rooms evoke the past, yet it is modernized inside and has kept up-to-date with the times. The bedrooms are generally spacious. Nostalgia buffs seek out Queen Mary's Bower in the oldest part of the hotel, still with its original moldings and a four-poster bed.

The Square, Buxton, Derbyshire SK17 6BD. ℂ 01298/22841. Fax 01298/72437. www.oldhallhotelbuxton.co.uk. 38 units. £120–£130 ($240–$260) double. Rates include English breakfast. AE, DC, MC, V. Free parking. **Amenities:** Restaurant; 3 bars; room service; laundry service. *In room:* TV, beverage maker, hair dryer, iron.

The Palace 🖈🖈 The beautiful restored Victorian architecture of this landmark returns Buxton to its heyday as a spa. For service, cuisine, and comfort, this is the premier choice within the town itself. It maintains tradition but with all the modern facilities, such as a large swimming pool. In fact, the comfort is so grand you may want to make the Palace your base for touring the area. The bedrooms are comfortably well furnished, though often falling short in style. Sometimes they are equipped with half-tester beds, and they are generally spacious. You don't have to leave the premises for good food.

Palace Rd., Buxton, Derbyshire SK17 6AG. ℂ 01298/22001. Fax 01298/72131. www.paramount-hotels.co.uk. 122 units. £83–£123 ($166–$246) double. Rates include breakfast. AE, DC, MC, V. Parking £3.50. **Amenities:** Restaurant; 2 bars; indoor heated pool; fitness center; salon; sauna; steam room; solarium; room service. *In room:* TV, Wi-Fi, beverage maker, hair dryer, trouser press.

WHERE TO DINE

The Columbine 🖈 *Value* CONTINENTAL/MODERN ENGLISH Here is Buxton's most charming restaurant, serving the town's best food. It's reasonably priced but still rivals some of the more formal and expensive country-house hotels outside the center of town. Set behind a facade of gray Derbyshire stone, it was built during the Victorian age as a private home and retains some of its oldest vestiges within an atmospheric cellar. The place is especially popular during the town's annual music festivals; it sometimes prepares pre- and post-theater suppers. Menu items are straightforward and unpretentious, but fresh and flavorful, served in a bistro-style setting. Some of the best items on the menu are likely to include baked saddle of monkfish with a fresh crab risotto, or filet of wild sea bass with stir-fried noodles. A specialty is sautéed filets of red mullet with tiger prawns in a light basil-and-white-wine sauce.

7 Hallbank. ℂ 01298/78752. Reservations recommended. Main courses £11–£13 ($22–$26). MC, V. May–Oct Mon–Sat 7–10pm; Nov–Apr Wed–Mon 7–10pm.

SEEING THE SIGHTS

Water from nine thermal wells is no longer available for spa treatments, but you can visit the 9.3-hectare (23-acre) **Pavilion Gardens** (which are open at all times; admission is free). Originally a concert hall and ballroom under an iron-and-glass roof stood here in the 1870s. They have given way today to a conservatory, restaurant, several bars, and a cafeteria.

Another sight, **Poole's Cavern,** Buxton Country Park, Green Lane (ℂ **01298/ 26978;** www.poolescavern.co.uk), is a cave that was inhabited by Stone Age people, who may have been the first to marvel at the natural vaulted roof bedecked with stalactites.

Visitors can walk through the spacious galleries, viewing the incredible horizontal cave, which is electrically lighted. On a summer day you can take a beautiful walk here by heading south of town for 1.6km (1 mile), following the boardwalk through the Pavilion Gardens and picking up the signposted trail along Temple Road. From Easter to October, the attraction is open daily from 9:30am to 5pm; off-season hours are daily 10am to 4pm. Admission is £6.75 ($14) for adults, £5.50 ($11) for students and seniors, £4 ($8) for children 5 to 16, and free for kids 4 and younger. A family ticket costs £20 ($40).

Set about 2km (1¼ miles) south of Buxton's town center is one of the oddest pieces of public Victorian architecture in the Midlands, **Solomon's Temple,** whose circular design may remind you of a straight castellated Tower of Pisa as interpreted by the neo-Gothic designers of Victorian England. Conceived as a folly in 1895 and donated to the city by a prominent building contractor, Solomon Mycock, it sits atop a tumulus (burial mound) from Neolithic times. Climb a small spiral staircase inside the temple for impressive views over Buxton and the surrounding countryside, especially the hills to the west. It's open all the time, day and night, and admission is free. Our favorite walk in the area is from Poole's Cavern (see above), strolling through Grinlow Woods for 20 minutes until you reach Solomon's Temple.

BAKEWELL

258km (160 miles) NW of London; 42km (26 miles) N of Derby; 60km (37 miles) SE of Manchester; 53km (33 miles) NW of Nottingham

Lying 19km (12 miles) southeast of Buxton, Bakewell is yet another possible base for exploring the southern Peak District, especially the beautiful valleys of Ashwood Dale, Monsal Dale, and Wyedale. Since very few visitors have time to explore this vast territory, we'll let you in on a secret. You can see the park district in a nutshell by taking the **Monsal Trail** ⚑. First, pick up a map at the tourist office (see below). This trail stretches for 4.9km (3 miles) to the north, cutting through some of the county's finest limestone valleys to the bucolic village of Wyedale, which itself lies 1.8km (1 mile) east of Buxton (see above) should you decide to hit the trail from Buxton instead of Bakewell. On the River Wey, Bakewell is just a market town, but its old houses constructed from gray-brown stone and its narrow streets give it a picture-postcard look. Its most spectacular feature is a medieval bridge across the river with five graceful arches.

Still served in local tearooms is the famous Bakewell Pudding, which was supposedly created by accident. One day, a chef didn't put the proper proportions of ingredients into her almond sponge cake batter, and it remained gelatinous and runny. Served apologetically, as a mistake, the pudding was called wonderful, and the tradition has remained ever since. The pudding, made as it is with a rich puff pastry that lies at the bottom of the pudding, and covered with a layer first of jam and then the gelatinous version of the almond sponge cake, is richer than the tarts and relatively difficult to find outside of Bakewell.

The best time to be here is on Monday, **market day,** when local farmers come in to sell their produce. Entrepreneurs from throughout the Midlands also set up flea market stands in the town's main square, the Market Place. Sales are conducted from 8:30am until 5:30pm in winter and until 7:30pm in summer.

ESSENTIALS

GETTING THERE To reach Bakewell from Derby, take the A6 north to Matlock, passing by the town and continuing on the A6 north toward Rowsley. Just past Rowsley, you'll come to a bridge. Follow the signpost across the bridge into Bakewell.

From London, take the M1 motorway north to Junction 28. Then follow the A38 for 5km (3 miles), connecting with the A615 signposted to Matlock. Once you're at Matlock, follow the A6 into Bakewell.

VISITOR INFORMATION The **Bakewell Information Centre,** Old Market Hall, Bridge Street (© **01629/813227**), is open from Easter to October daily 9:30am to 5:30pm; November to February 28, it's open daily 10am to 5pm.

WHERE TO STAY & DINE IN THE AREA

For a look at a working 19th-century flour mill, stop in at **Caudwell's Mill,** Bakewell Road (© **01629/734374**). Here, you can have afternoon tea with freshly baked cakes, breads, and pastries made right here at the mill, and then stroll through a variety of shops, including a handcrafted furniture store, glass-blowing studio, jewelry shop, and art gallery.

The Cavendish Hotel 🏵🏵 Located 6.5km (4 miles) east of Bakewell, the Cavendish is one of the most stately country hotels of England. The stone-sided building was constructed in the 1780s as the Peacock Inn; it is located on the duke of Devonshire's private estate.

The duke and duchess took personal charge of the hotel and its lavish restoration in 1975, furnishing its public areas and more expensive bedrooms with antiques from nearby Chatsworth, a 15-minute walk to the south. The hotel remains aristocratic and charming. Beds are sumptuous with elegant fabrics.

Baslow, Bakewell, Derbyshire DE45 1SP. © **01246/582311.** Fax 01246/582312. www.cavendish-hotel.net. 23 units. £149–£187 ($298–$374) double. AE, DC, MC, V. Free parking. **Amenities:** 2 restaurants; bar; room service; laundry service. *In room:* TV, minibar, beverage maker, hair dryer, trouser press.

Riber Hall 🏵 South of Bakewell on Route 6, this symmetrically gabled structure is built of gray-toned Derbyshire stone. It's from 1450 but was enlarged and discreetly altered by the Jacobeans and then intricately restored to what you'll see today by the present owners. Public areas are as richly historic and atmospheric as anything in the district. Bedrooms occupy the premises of a converted stable and are charmingly furnished, each with a four-poster bed and tasteful chintzes and antiques.

Riber, Matlock, Derbyshire DE4 5JU. © **01629/582795.** Fax 01629/580475. www.riber-hall.co.uk. 14 units. £145–£188 ($290–$376) double. Rates include English breakfast. AE, DC, MC, V. Free parking. **Amenities:** Restaurant; bar; tennis court; room service; laundry service. *In room:* TV, beverage maker, hair dryer, trouser press (in some).

Rutland Arms Hotel A dignified early Georgian building set behind a gray stone facade built in 1804, this town landmark is a good base for visiting nearby Haddon Hall and Chatsworth House. Its original owner operated a prosperous livery stable; some of the bedrooms are in the old stable block in back. The renovated hotel offers cozy, well-maintained bedrooms.

The Square, Bakewell, Derbyshire DE45 1BT. © **01629/812812.** Fax 01629/812309. www.bakewell.demon.co.uk. 35 units. £96–£145 ($192–$290) double. Rates include breakfast. AE, DC, MC, V. Free parking. **Amenities:** Restaurant; bar; room service; laundry service. *In room:* TV, Wi-Fi, beverage maker, hair dryer.

HISTORIC HOMES NEAR BAKEWELL

The tourist office in Bakewell (see above) will provide you with a map outlining the best routes to take to reach each of the attractions below.

Chatsworth ★★★   Here stands one of the great country houses of England, the home of the 11th duke of Devonshire and his duchess, the former Deborah Mitford. With its lavishly decorated interior and a wealth of art treasures, it has 297 rooms, the most spectacular of which are open to the public.

Dating from 1686, the present building stands on a spot where the eccentric Bess of Hardwick built the house in which Mary, Queen of Scots, was held prisoner upon orders of Queen Elizabeth I. Capability Brown (who seems to have been everywhere) worked on the landscaping of the present house. But it was Joseph Paxton, the gardener to the sixth duke, who turned the garden into one of the most celebrated in Europe. Queen Victoria and Prince Albert were lavishly entertained here in 1843. The house contains a great library and such paintings as the *Adoration of the Magi* by Veronese and *King Uzziah* by Rembrandt. On the grounds are spectacular fountains and a playground for children in the farmyard.

The Jane Austen classic, *Pride and Prejudice,* was adapted for the big screen in 1940 starring Laurence Olivier and Greer Garson. Since 1938 it has been made for TV five times. Along comes the latest version directed by Joe Wright, who used Chatsworth as the setting. Chatsworth stars as Pemberley, the family home of Mr. Darcy (played by Matthew Macfayden), whose affair with Elizabeth Bennet (Keira Knightley) is at the heart of the story.

6.5km (4 miles) east of Bakewell, beside the A6 (16km/10 miles north of Matlock). 𝄯 01246/565300. www. chatsworth.org. Admission £12 ($24) adults, £10 ($20) students and seniors, £4.50 ($9) children 4–15, family ticket £28 ($56), free for children 3 and younger. Mar 14–Dec 23 daily 11am–4:30pm.

Hardwick Hall   Built in 1597 for Bess of Hardwick, a woman who acquired an estate from each of her four husbands, it's particularly noted for its "more glass than wall" architecture. The high great chamber and long gallery crown an unparalleled series of late-16th-century interiors, including an important collection of tapestries, needlework, and furniture. The house is surrounded by a 125-hectare (300-acre) country park, featuring walled gardens, orchards, and an herb garden.

Doe Lea, 15km (9½ miles) east of Chesterfield. 𝄯 01246/850430. www.nationaltrust.org.uk. Admission £9 ($18) adults, £4.50 ($9) children. House Mar–Oct Wed–Thurs and Sat–Sun noon–4:30pm; grounds daily 8am–6pm year-round; gardens Mar–Oct Wed–Sun 11am–5:30pm. Take Junction 29 from M1.

5 Nottinghamshire: Robin Hood Country

"Notts," as Nottinghamshire is known, lies in the heart of the East Midlands. Its towns are rich in folklore, and many have bustling markets. Many famous people have come from Nottingham, notably those 13th-century outlaws from Sherwood Forest, Robin Hood and his Merry Men. It also was home to the Romantic poet Lord Byron; you can visit his ancestral home at **Newstead Abbey** (p. 584). D. H. Lawrence, author of *Sons and Lovers* and *Lady Chatterley's Lover,* was born in a tiny miner's cottage in Eastwood, which he later immortalized in his writings.

NOTTINGHAM

195km (121 miles) N of London; 116km (72 miles) SE of Manchester

Though an industrial center, Nottingham is a good base for exploring Sherwood Forest and the rest of the shire. Nottingham is known to literary buffs for its association with author D. H. Lawrence and its medieval sheriff, who played an important role in the Robin Hood story.

It was an important pre-Norman settlement guarding the River Trent, the gateway to the north of England. Followers of William the Conqueror arrived in 1068 to erect a fort here. In a later reincarnation, the fort saw supporters of Prince John surrender to Richard the Lion-Hearted in 1194. Many other exploits occurred here—notably Edward III's capture of Roger Mortimer and Queen Isabella, the assassins of Edward II. From Nottingham, Richard III marched out with his men to face defeat and his own death at Bosworth Field in 1485.

With the arrival of the spinning jenny in 1768, Nottingham was launched into the forefront of the Industrial Revolution. It's still a center of industry and home base to many well-known British firms, turning out such products as John Player cigarettes, Boots pharmaceuticals, and Raleigh cycles.

Nottingham doesn't have many attractions, but it's a young and vital city, and is very student-oriented thanks to its two large universities. Its Hockley neighborhood is as hip as anything this side of Manchester or London. A look at one of the alternative newspapers or magazines freely distributed around town can connect you with the city's constantly changing nightlife scene.

ESSENTIALS

GETTING THERE   The best rail connection is via Lincoln, from which 28 trains arrive Monday to Saturday and about 8 trains on Sunday. The trip takes about 45 minutes. Trains also leave from London's St. Pancras Station; the trip takes about 2½ hours. For information, call © **0845/748-4950** or visit **www.nationalrail.co.uk**.

Buses from London arrive at the rate of about 10 per day. For schedules and information, call © **0870/580-8080** or visit **www.nationalexpress.com**.

If you're driving from London, the M1 motorway runs to a few miles west of Nottingham. Feeder roads, including the A453, are well marked for the short distance into town. The drive takes about 3 to 3½ hours.

VISITOR INFORMATION   Information is available at the **City Information Centre,** 1–4 Smithy Row (© **08444/775678;** www.visitnottingham.com). It's open Monday to Friday 9am to 5:30pm, Saturday 9am to 5pm, and Sunday 10am to 4pm.

SPECIAL EVENTS   Nottingham still gets a lot of reflected glory from its association with Robin Hood and his gang. The **Robin Hood Festival** is a family-friendly, mock-medieval festival scheduled for the first week in August every year. Diversions include food and souvenir stands, jousting and falconry exhibitions, maypole dances, crowd-pleasing jesters juggling their way through crowds, and lots of medieval costume. For information, call © **01623/823202** (www.nottinghamshire.gov.uk/robinhoodfestival).

WHERE TO STAY

Hart's Hotel 𝒜   Nestled high on the ramparts of Nottingham Castle, this is a secluded and tranquil hotel, though located more or less within the city center. No hotel in town offers such panoramic views. Although known for its restaurant (see below), it is also a lovely place at which to spend the night. A privately owned hotel, Hart's offers midsize to spacious bedrooms, each furnished in a modern style with plenty of amenities. The staff is the most helpful in town, arranging admission to a nearby health club or securing tickets to the theater.

Standard Hill, Park Row, Nottingham NG1 6GN. © 0115/9881900. www.hartsnottingham.co.uk. 30 units. £120–£170 ($240–$340) double; £260 ($520) suite. AE, MC, V. Parking £8 ($16). **Amenities:** Restaurant; bar; room service; laundry service; dry cleaning. *In room:* TV, Wi-Fi, minibar, beverage maker, safe.

Lace Market Hotel ⓐ *Finds*   Opposite the Galleries of Justice, this is a boutique hotel—unusual for Nottingham—and an alternative choice for those who shun tired chain hotels for commercial travelers. In the old Lace Market district, it is a restored town house with its original architecture intact. Personal service is provided for the modernized and rather elegant bedrooms furnished with hypoallergenic bedding and deluxe toiletries. Rooms differ in size, including studios which are split-level opening onto views. On-site is one of the town's best restaurants, Merchant's.

High Pavement, Lace Market, Nottingham NG1 1HE. © 0115/8523232. Fax 0115/8523223. www.lacemarket hotel.co.uk. 42 units. £119–£199 ($238–$398) double; £249 ($498) suite. AE, MC, V. Parking £7.70 ($15). **Amenities:** Restaurant; bar; gastro-pub; access to nearby health club; room service; laundry service. *In room:* TV/DVD, Wi-Fi, CD player, beverage maker.

Park Inn Nottingham *Kids*   If you're driving, you'll appreciate this chain hotel's easy access from the A60 highway and its location less than 1.5km (1 mile) north of the city center. It was built in 1968 as a modern alternative to the town's B&Bs. The rooms are standardized but are well maintained; most contain twin beds. Thirty of the bedrooms are suitable for families.

296 Mansfield Rd., Nottingham, Nottinghamshire NG5 2BT. © 01159/359988. Fax 01159/969-1506. www. parkinn.com. 172 units. £79 ($158) double; £120 ($240) suite. Rates include breakfast. AE, DC, MC, V. Free parking. **Amenities:** Restaurant; bar; indoor heated pool; health club; spa; Jacuzzi; sauna; steam room; business center; room service; laundry service; dry cleaning. *In room:* TV, Wi-Fi, beverage maker, hair dryer, trouser press.

Strathdon Hotel   This is a solid and unpretentious member of a nationwide chain. Built in the 1970s of gray-colored brick in the heart of town, it has seven floors, neutral public areas, and two bars. The nondescript bedrooms are equipped to a high standard, evocative of a first-class roadside motel.

44 Derby Rd., Nottingham, Nottinghamshire NG1 5FT. © 01159/418501. Fax 01159/483725. www.strathdon-hotel-nottingham.com. 68 units. £98–£125 ($196–$250) double. AE, DC, MC, V. Free parking. **Amenities:** Restaurant; 2 bars; room service; laundry service. *In room:* TV, Wi-Fi, beverage maker, hair dryer, trouser press.

WHERE TO DINE

Hart's ⓐⓐ MODERN ENGLISH   Hart's lays claim to the best dining in the historic central core of the city, just off the main street. A lovely interior for dining has been created in what was once part of Nottingham's general hospital. Today it invites with its wooden floors, beautifully set tables, and abstract modern paintings on the walls. The location near Nottingham Castle couldn't be more convenient. The cooking technique here is sharp and precise, culminating in a harmonious blend of flavors created from market-fresh ingredients. Excellent appetizers include the likes of leek-and-potato soup with Indian-spiced cod, followed by such well-crafted main courses as loin of venison (served pink) with peppered pineapple and braised endive. Other fine dishes are the pan-fried wild sea bass with poached clams and mussels, or Gressingham duck breast with a red-onion tart.

In the Hart's Hotel, 1 Standard Court, Park Row. © 0115/9110666. Main courses £14–£22 ($28–$44); set lunch Mon–Sat £13–£16 ($26–$32), Sun £22 ($44); set dinner £23 ($46). AE, MC, V. Daily noon–2pm and 7–9:30pm (until 9pm Sun).

Restaurant Sat Bains ⓐⓐⓐ CONTINENTAL   The finest cuisine in the former gastronomic wasteland of Nottingham is served in this dining room installed in a hotel at the end of a small lane, home to a number of low-slung Victorian houses near the River Trent. The setting on this quiet lane is elegant with stone floors, classy black-and-white photographs, and low ceilings. The chef, Sat Bains, continues to polish his classic repertoire by using rigorous, precise cooking techniques and flawless ingredients. He's known for his intriguing "marriages" of flavors such as roast scallops with braised oxtail or Dover sole with Hereford snails. One of our favorite dishes is poached and roasted wild duck accompanied by beans and hazelnuts with a Banyuls sauce.

Old Lenton Lane. © 0115/986-6566. Reservations required. Fixed-price lunch £25–£38 ($50–$76), dinner £47–£120 ($94–$240). AE, DC, MC, V. Tues–Fri noon–1:45pm; Tues–Sat 7–9:30pm. Coming into Nottingham, take the 3rd exit signposted BOOTS INDUSTRIAL ESTATE WEST (Thane Rd.). Then take a very sharp left onto Lenton Lane, which you follow for 450m (1,500 ft.) until you reach the restaurant.

EXPLORING THE AREA

Put on your most comfortable shoes and prepare to tackle the more than 800 shops in and around town—Nottingham boasts some of England's best shopping. Start in the city center, with its maze of pedestrian streets, and work your way out toward the two grand indoor shopping malls, the Victoria and the Broad Marsh, located to the north and to the south of the center of town. Then, head over to Derby Road for your fill of antiques.

Fine Nottingham lace can be found in the **Lace Centre,** Castle Road, across the street from Nottingham Castle (© **01159/413539**), or in the shops around the area known as the **Lace Market** along High Pavement.

Then, to catch up on the hippest and latest in fashion and furnishing trends, explore the many boutiques in the Hockley area, the Exchange Arcade, and the Flying Horse Mall, all in the city center.

Patchings Farm Art Centre, Oxton Road, near Calverton (© **01159/653479;** www.patchingsartcentre.co.uk), is a 24-hectare (60-acre) art haven. Restored farm buildings house three galleries, working art and pottery studios, a gift shop, and art and framing shops.

And long known as Britain's first real crafts center, **Longdale Craft Centre,** Longdale Lane, Ravenshead (© **01623/794858;** www.longdale.co.uk), is a labyrinth of re-created Victorian streets where professional craftspeople work on a range of craft items including jewelry, pottery, and prints.

Nottingham Castle Museum and Art Gallery ⭐   Overlooking the city, Nottingham Castle was built in 1679 by the duke of Newcastle on the site of an old Norman fortress. After restoration in 1878, it opened as a provincial museum surrounded by a charmingly arranged garden. Of particular note is the History of Nottingham Gallery, re-creating the legends associated with the city, plus a rare collection of ceramics and a unique exhibition of medieval alabaster carvings, which were executed between 1350 and 1530. These delicately detailed scenes illustrate the life of Christ, the Virgin Mother, and various saints. Paintings cover several periods but are strong on 16th-century Italian, 17th-century French and Dutch, and the richest English paintings of the past 2 centuries.

The only surviving element of the original Norman castle is a subterranean passage called Mortimer's Hole. The passage leads to **Ye Olde Trip to Jerusalem,** 1 Brewhouse Yard at Castle Road (© **01159/473171;** www.triptojerusalem.com), dating from 1189 and said to be the oldest inn in England (today it's a pub and restaurant). King Edward III is said to have led a band of noblemen through these secret passages, surprising Roger Mortimer and his queen, killing Mortimer and putting his lady in prison. A statue of Robin Hood stands at the base of the castle.

Castle Rd. ⓒ **01159/153700.** Admission Sat–Sun £3.50 ($7) adults, £2 ($4) children and seniors. Mar–Oct daily 10am–5pm (last entrance 4:30pm); Nov–Feb daily 10am–4pm (last entrance 3:30pm).

HISTORIC HOMES NEAR NOTTINGHAM

Newstead Abbey ⓖ   Lord Byron once made his home at Newstead Abbey, one of eight museums administered by the city of Nottingham. Some of the original Augustinian priory, purchased by Sir John Byron in 1540, still survives. In the 19th century, the mansion was given a neo-Gothic restoration. Mementos, including first editions and manuscripts, are displayed inside. You can explore the parkland of some 121 hectares (300 acres), with waterfalls, rose gardens, Monk's Stew Pond, and a Japanese water garden.

On A60 (Mansfield Rd.), 19km (12 miles) north of Nottingham center in Ravenshead. ⓒ **01623/455900.** www. newsteadabbey.org.uk. Admission to house and grounds £6 ($12) adults, £4 ($8) students and seniors, £2.50 ($5) children; gardens only £3 ($6) adults, £2.50 ($5) students and seniors, £1.50 ($3) children. House Apr–Sept daily noon–5pm; gardens year-round daily 9am–dusk.

Wollaton Hall ⓖ   This well-preserved Elizabethan mansion, finished in 1588, is the most ornate in England and a tourist-drawing attraction itself. Today, it houses a natural history museum with lots of insects, invertebrates, British mammals, birds, reptiles, amphibians, and fish. The hall is surrounded by a deer park and garden. See the camellia house with the world's earliest cast-iron front dating from 1823. The bird dioramas here are among the best in Britain.

In Wollaton Park, 5km (3 miles) southwest from Nottingham center. ⓒ **01159/153900.** Free admission. Parking £12 ($24). Mar–Oct daily 11am–5pm; Nov–Feb daily 11am–4pm. Drive southwest along A609 (Ilkeston Rd.), which will become Wollaton Rd.

SHERWOOD FOREST ⓖⓖ

Second only to Germany's Schwarzwald in European lore and legend, **Sherwood Forest** comprises 182 hectares (450 acres) of oak and silver birch trees owned and strictly protected by a local entity, the Thoresby Estate, and maintained by the county of Nottinghamshire. Actually, very little of this area was forest even when it provided cover for Robin Hood, Friar Tuck, and Little John.

Robin Hood, the folk hero of tale and ballad, fired the imagination of a hardworking, impoverished English people, who particularly liked his adopted slogan: "Take from the rich and give to the poor."

Celebrating their freedom in verdant Sherwood Forest, Robin Hood's eternally youthful band rejoiced in "hearing the twang of the bow of yew and in watching the gray goose shaft as it cleaves the glistening willow wand or brings down the king's proud buck." Life was one long picnic beneath the splendid oaks of a primeval forest, with plenty of ale and flavorful venison poached from the forests of an oppressive king. The clever rebellion Robin Hood waged against authority (represented by the haughty, despotic, and overfed sheriff of Nottingham) was full of heroic exploits and a desire to win justice for victims of oppression.

Now, as then, the forest consists of woodland glades, farm fields, villages, and hamlets. But the surroundings are so built up that Robin Hood wouldn't recognize them today.

Sherwood Forest Visitor Centre (ⓒ **01623/823202**) is in Sherwood Forest Country Park at Edwinstowe, 29km (22 miles) north of Nottingham off the A614, or 13km (8 miles) east of Mansfield on the B6034. It stands near the Major Oak, popularly known as Robin Hood's tree, although analysis of its bark reveals that it wasn't around in the 13th century. Many marked walks and footpaths lead from the visitor center through the woodland. There's an exhibition of life-size models of Robin and the other well-known outlaws, as well as a shop with books, gifts, and souvenirs. The center provides as much information as is known about the Merry Men and Maid Marian, whom Robin Hood is believed to have married at Edwinstowe Church near the visitor center. Little John's grave is at Hathersage 58km (36 miles) away, and Will Scarlet's grave is at Blidworth (15km/9½ miles away).

The center also has a visitor information facility and the **Forest Table,** with cafeteria service and meals emphasizing traditional English country recipes.

Open times for the country park are from dawn to dusk, and for the visitor center, April to October daily 10am to 5pm and November to March from 10am to 4:30pm. Entrance to the center is free, and "Robin Hood's Sherwood" exhibition is also free. A year-round program of events is presented, mainly on weekends and during national and school holiday periods. Parking costs £3 ($6) per car per day April to October.

Clumber Park, a 1,537-hectare (3,800-acre) tract of park and woodland maintained by National Trust authorities, is favored by local families for picnics and strolls. It contains a 32-hectare (80-acre) lake at its center, a monumental promenade flanked with venerable lime (linden) trees, and the Gothic Revival **Clumber Chapel.** Built between 1886 and 1889 as a site of worship for the private use of the seventh duke of Newcastle, it's open early March to mid-January, daily 10am to 4pm.

The park itself is open year-round during daylight hours, though its allure and services are at their lowest ebb during November and December. The gift shop and tearoom are open daily in summer 10am to 5pm (closes 4pm off season). Admission to the park, including the chapel, ranges from £5 to £6 ($10–$12), depending on your vehicle.

If you're specifically interested in the botany and plant life, head for the park's **Conservation Centre,** a walled garden with extensive greenhouses, open daily from April to October. For information about the park and its features, contact the **Clumber Park Estate Office,** Worksop, Nottinghamshire S80 3AZ (✆ **01909/476592**).

6 Lincoln ★★

225km (140 miles) N of London; 151km (94 miles) NW of Cambridge; 132km (82 miles) SE of York

The ancient city of Lincoln was the site of a Bronze Age settlement, and later, in the 3rd century, one of four provincial capitals of Roman Britain. In the Middle Ages, it was the center of Lindsey, a famous Anglo-Saxon kingdom. After the Norman Conquest, it grew increasingly important, known for its cathedral and castle. Its merchants grew rich by shipping wool directly to Flanders.

Much of the past remains in Lincoln today to delight visitors who wander past half-timbered Tudor houses, the Norman castle, and the towering Lincoln Cathedral. Medieval streets climbing the hillsides and cobblestones re-create the past. Lincoln, unlike other East Midlands towns such as Nottingham and Leicester, maintains somewhat of a country-town atmosphere. But it also extends welcoming arms to tourists, the mainstay of its economy.

ESSENTIALS

GETTING THERE Trains arrive every hour during the day from London's Kings Cross Station, a 2-hour trip usually requiring a change of train at Newark. Trains also arrive from Cambridge, again requiring a change at Newark. For schedules and information, call ℂ **0845/748-4950** or visit **www.nationalrail.co.uk**.

National Express buses from London's Victoria Coach Station service Lincoln, a 4-hour ride. For schedules and information, call ℂ **0870/580-8080** or visit **www. nationalexpress.com**. Once in Lincoln, local and regional buses service the county from the City Bus Station, off St. Mary's Street opposite the train station.

If you're driving from London, take the M1 north to the junction with the A57, then head east to Lincoln.

VISITOR INFORMATION The **Tourist Information Centre** is at 9 Castle Hill (ℂ **01522/873213;** www.visitnottingham.com) and is open Monday to Friday 9am to 5:30pm, Saturday 9am to 5pm, and Sunday 10am to 4pm.

WHERE TO STAY
MODERATE
Bailhouse & Mews 🌟🌟 Arguably, this is the best little guesthouse in Lincoln, and it's in the very heart of town near the castle and cathedral. It's really like a boutique hotel with a long history (ca. 1350), when it was built as a medieval hall with a beamed roof and low walls that are still preserved in one of the bedrooms. Over the years it has been substantially changed; it was a tavern for much of its life under various names such as the Blue Bell and the Falcon. When new owners took over the building, closed since 1999, they set about restoring it, preserving many of its original features. Bedrooms are spacious and have been decorated tastefully and comfortably, each with a view of the castle. The most dramatic rooms have luxury four-poster beds.

34 Bailgate, Lincoln, Lincolnshire LN1 3AP. ℂ 01522/520883. Fax 01522/521829. www.bailhouse.co.uk. 10 units. £89–£99 ($178–$198) double; £149–£175 ($298–$350) suite. MC, V. Free parking. **Amenities:** Lounge; outdoor pool. *In room:* TV, Wi-Fi.

The Castle Hotel This redbrick, three-story, traditional English hotel is situated in old Lincoln. It has been carefully converted from what was the North District National School, dating from 1858. It boasts splendid views of the castle and cathedral, which are both just a 3-minute walk away. The bedrooms have been individually decorated—one has a four-poster bed—and all are named after British castles. Most bathrooms have a tub/shower combination.

Westgate, Lincoln, Lincolnshire LN1 3AS. ℂ 01522/538801. Fax 01522/575457. www.castlehotel.net. 20 units. £89–£99 ($178–$198) double; £225 ($450) suite. Rates include English breakfast. AE, DC, MC, V. No children 7 or younger. Free parking. **Amenities:** Restaurant; bar; room service; laundry service. *In room:* TV, minibar, beverage maker, hair dryer, trouser press (in some).

Hillcrest Hotel (Value) This is a fine redbrick house built in 1871 as the private home of a local vicar. Though converted into a comfortable, small, licensed hotel, it retains many of its original features. It's on a quiet, tree-lined road overlooking 10 hectares (25 acres) of parkland, in the old high town and within easy walking distance of Lincoln Cathedral and the Roman remains. The bedrooms are well furnished and kept in shape; some rooms have a four-poster bed. Nearly all open onto a view.

15 Lindum Terrace, Lincoln, Lincolnshire LN2 5RT. ℂ 01522/510182. Fax 01522/538009. www.hillcrest-hotel.com. 14 units. £91–£98 ($182–$196) double. Children age 1 and younger stay free with 2 paying adults; children 2–13 £7 ($14) per night; ages 14–18 £17 ($34) per night. Rates include English breakfast. AE, DC, MC, V. From Wragby Rd., connect with Upper Lindum St.; continue to the bottom of this street, make a left onto Lindum Terrace, and the hotel is 180m (600 ft.) along on the right. Free parking. **Amenities:** Restaurant; bar; room service; babysitting; laundry service. *In room:* TV, beverage maker, hair dryer.

Lincoln

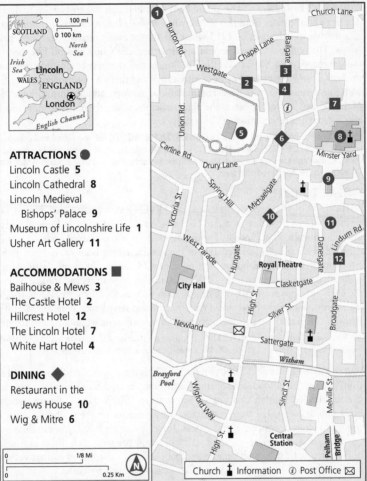

Church ✝ Information ⓘ Post Office ✉

EXPENSIVE

The Lincoln Hotel Lacking the charm of the White Hart (see below), this is still one of the town's leading hotels. When workmen were digging the foundations here in the mid-1960s, they discovered remnants of the north tower of the East Gate of the Roman city wall, a preserved part of which is included in the hotel's rear garden. The hotel faces Lincoln Cathedral and is attached to a Victorian mansion (now the East-gate Bar). The recently refurbished bedrooms are nicely decorated and comfortable.

Eastgate, Lincoln, Lincolnshire LN2 1PN. ⓒ **01522/520348.** Fax 01522/510780. www.thelincolnhotel.com. 72 units. Mon–Thurs £109–£129 ($218–$258) double; Fri–Sun £99–£119 ($198–$238) double. Rates include continental breakfast. AE, DC, MC, V. Free parking. **Amenities:** Restaurant; bar; spa; room service; laundry service. *In room:* TV, beverage maker, hair dryer, trouser press.

White Hart Hotel ⟨★★⟩ The White Hart is named after the emblem of Richard II. The inn's facade dates from the 1700s, when it was a luxurious private home. Its life as a modern hotel began in 1913 when the live-in owners started accepting paying guests. The hotel also hosted several meetings between Churchill and Eisenhower in the darkest days of World War II. The inn is still the best choice in town. Enter through a revolving mahogany door into a large and finely proportioned lounge filled with fine antiques. Each of the accommodations has some antique furniture and views of the old city. Try for a room in the older structure, where the units are more spacious and stylish than those in the lackluster annex.

Bailgate, Lincoln, Lincolnshire LN1 3AR. © **01522/526222.** Fax 01522/531798. www.whitehart-lincoln.co.uk. 48 units. £115–£125 ($230–$250) double; £135–£170 ($270–$340) suite. AE, MC, V. Free parking. .5km (¼ mile) from Lincoln Station. Minimum 2-night stay Sat–Sun. **Amenities:** Restaurant; bar; room service; laundry service. *In room:* TV, beverage maker, hair dryer, trouser press.

WHERE TO DINE

Restaurant in the Jews House ⟨★⟩ CONTINENTAL Constructed around 1150, this stone-fronted building is said to be the oldest occupied house in Europe. Today, it offers the finest food in Lincoln. The dining room has a low-beamed ceiling, a cast-iron fireplace, and medieval features. Two of the massive ceiling beams date from the construction of the original house. Seating about 28 diners, the menu features stylish dishes that change every month according to market ingredients and the inspiration of the chef—perhaps roast rack of Cornish lamb with a stew of chickpeas, chorizo, and sweet peppers, or filet of cod baked with mussels and served with a mousse of basil and Parmesan. The savory dishes are prepared in a modern style without heavy saucing.

The Jews House, 15 The Strait. © **01522/524851.** Reservations recommended. Main courses £8–£17 ($16–$34); fixed-price lunch £18 ($36) for 3 courses. DC, MC, V. Wed–Sat noon–2:30pm; Tues–Sat 7–9pm.

Wig & Mitre ⟨★ Finds⟩ INTERNATIONAL This is not only the best pub in old Lincoln, it serves good food, too. Sitting on the aptly named Steep Hill near the cathedral and loaded with an Old English atmosphere, Wig & Mitre operates somewhat like a pub-brasserie. The main restaurant, behind the bar on the second floor, has oak timbers, Victorian armchairs, and settees. If the restaurant is full, you can dine in the bar downstairs. The eager-to-please staff will tempt you with such dishes as pan-fried pork cutlet; braised beef on caramelized baby onions, roast filet of halibut with wild mushrooms, and an Aberdeen Angus filet steak with anchovy butter.

30–32 Steep Hill. © **01522/535190.** Reservations recommended. Main courses £11–£19 ($22–$38); sandwiches £5.75–£6.75 ($12–$14); fixed-price 3-course menu £17 ($34) served noon–6pm. AE, DC, MC, V. Daily 8am–11pm.

FAVORITE LOCAL PUBS

In addition to the **Wig & Mitre** (see above), drop by **Adam & Eve Tavern,** 25 Lindum Rd. (© **01522/537108**), the oldest pub in Lincoln, dating from 1701, to knock back a Magnet, Old Speckled Hen, or Theakston's Best Bitter in a homey, cottage atmosphere complete with gas fires and a large front garden for warm-weather drinking and browsing.

The **Jolly Brewer,** 27 Broadgate (© **01522/528583**), dates from 1850, and it's a basic wooden-floorboards place where you'll be welcomed into a friendly crowd. If you're hungry, there's pub grub at lunchtime only, and draft ales include Tiger Bitter and Robinson's, as well as rotating guests.

EXPLORING THE CITY

The best lanes for strolling are those tumbling down the appropriately named Steep Hill to the Witham River.

The cathedral is a good starting point for your shopping tour of Lincoln, as the streets leading down the hill (you won't be working against gravity this way) are lined with a mélange of interesting stores. Wander in and out of these historic lanes, down Steep Hill, along Bailgate, around the Stonebow gateway and Guildhall, and then down High Street. Following this route, you'll find all sorts of clothing, books, antiques, arts and crafts, and gift items.

While walking down Steep Hill, stop in the **Harding House Gallery,** 53 Steep Hill (© **01522/523537;** www.hardinghousegallery.co.uk), to see some of the best local crafts: ceramics, teddy bears, textiles, wood, metal sculptures, and jewelry.

Lincoln Castle   A short walk from the cathedral, this 900-year-old fortress was once one of the most powerful strongholds in medieval England. Lincoln Castle dates from the time of William the Conqueror in 1068. Nothing remains of his original fortress. On one of the mounds where the original castle stood is the Lucy Tower, dating from the late 12th century. The East Gate also dates from the 12th century. The castle came under siege in the wars of 1135 to 1154 and again in 1216 to 1217. During the 19th century, it functioned as a prison. You can see the prison chapel with its self-locking cubicles; these cages kept prisoners from seeing each other. Inside its exhibition rooms is displayed one of only four surviving copies of the Magna Carta. Much of the appeal of a visit here involves walking along the top of the wall that surrounds the fortress, overlooking the castle's grassy courtyard, the city of Lincoln, and its cathedral.

© 01522/511068. www.lincolnshire.gov.uk. Admission £3.90 ($7.80) adults, £2.60 ($5.20) students and children 15 and younger. Apr–Nov Mon–Sat 9:30am–5:30pm, Sun 11am–5:30pm; Nov–Mar Mon–Sat 9:30am–4pm.

Lincoln Cathedral 😊😊😊   No other English cathedral dominates its surroundings as does Lincoln's. Visible from up to 48km (30 miles) away, the central tower is 81m (271 ft.) high, which makes it the second tallest in England. The central tower once carried a huge spire, which, before heavy gale damage in 1549, made it the tallest in the world at 158m (525 ft.).

Construction on the original Norman cathedral was begun in 1072, and it was consecrated 20 years later. It sustained a major fire and, in 1185, an earthquake. Only the central portion of the West Front and lower halves of the western towers survive from this period.

The present cathedral is Gothic in style, particularly the Early English and Decorated periods. The nave is 13th century, but the black font of Tournai marble originates from the 12th century. In the Great North Transept is a rose medallion window known as the Dean's Eye. Opposite it, in the Great South Transept, is its cousin, the Bishop's Eye. East of the high altar is the Angel Choir, consecrated in 1280, and so called after the sculpted angels high on the walls. The exquisite woodcarving in St. Hugh's Choir dates from the 14th century. Lincoln's roof bosses, dating from the 13th and 14th centuries, are handsome, and a mirror trolley assists visitors in their appreciation of these features, which are some 21m (70 ft.) above the floor. Oak bosses are in the cloister.

In the Seamen's Chapel (Great North Transept) is a window commemorating Lincolnshire-born Captain John Smith, one of the pioneers of early settlement in America and the first governor of Virginia. The library and north walk of the cloister were built in 1674 to designs by Sir Christopher Wren. In the Treasury is fine silver plate from the churches of the diocese.

C 01522/544544. www.lincolncathedral.com. Admission £4 ($8) adults; £3 ($6) seniors, students, and children. June–Aug Mon–Fri 7:15am–8pm, Sat–Sun 7:15am–6pm; Sept–May Mon–Sat 7:15am–6pm, Sun 7:15am–5pm.

Lincoln Medieval Bishops' Palace   On the south side of the cathedral, this site was the headquarters of the biggest diocese in England during the Middle Ages. Launched in 1150, it held great power until it was sacked during the civil war in the 1640s. Allowed to ruin over the centuries, it has been opened to the public, who can explore its ruins, including an intact entrance tower, a public hall, and a vaulted undercroft. You can also wander its grounds, taking in panoramic views of the city.

Minster Yard. *C* 01522/527468. Admission £3.90 ($7.80) adults, £2.90 ($5.80) students and seniors, £2 ($4) children. Apr–June daily 10am–5pm; July–Aug daily 10am–6pm; Sept–Oct daily 10am–4pm; Nov–Mar Thurs–Mon 10am–4pm.

Museum of Lincolnshire Life   This is the largest museum of social history in the Midlands. Housed in what was originally built as an army barracks in 1857, it's a short walk north of the city center. Displays here range from a Victorian schoolroom to a collection of locally built steam engines.

Burton Rd. *C* 01522/528448. Admission £2.20 ($4.40) adults; £1.50 ($3) students, children, and seniors; £5.90 ($12) family ticket. Apr–Sept daily 10am–5pm; Oct–Mar Mon–Sat 10am–5pm. Closed Dec 24–25, Dec 31, and Jan 1.

Usher Art Gallery   Established in 1927 at the bequest of its founder, James Ward Usher (one of the city's prominent jewelers), the gallery is a repository for paintings and an impressive collection of antique clocks, 20th-century ceramics, and artifacts and literary mementos, plus portraits of Lincolnshire-born Alfred Lord Tennyson. Most impressive is the collection of miniatures from the 16th to 19th centuries, and an exhibition of 17th-century Dutch and Italian paintings. Our favorites are the works of Peter de Wint (1784–1849), including his moving depiction of *Lincoln Cathedral*.

Lindum Rd. *C* 01522/527980. Free admission. Daily 10am–5pm.

17

The Northwest: Manchester, Liverpool & Chester

The great industrial shadow of the 19th century cast such darkness over England's northwest that the area has been relatively neglected by visitors. Most Americans rush through, heading for the Lake District and Scotland. But in spite of its industry and bleak commercial area, the northwest still has a lot to offer, including some beautiful countryside that remains unspoiled.

We will concentrate, however, on only three of its more important cities—**Manchester, Liverpool,** and **Chester**—plus a side trip to **Blackpool,** a huge Coney Island–style resort. You may want to visit it not so much for its beaches as for its kitschy, old-world appeal.

1 Manchester: Gateway to the North ⋆⋆

325km (202 miles) NW of London; 138km (86 miles) N of Birmingham; 56km (35 miles) E of Liverpool

One of the largest cities in England, **Manchester** is becoming increasingly important, as major airlines now fly here from North America, making the city a gateway to northern England. In recent years, Manchester has made great strides to shake its image as an industrial wasteland. Though chimneys still spike the skyline, they no longer make the metropolitan sky an ash-filled canopy. Abandoned warehouses are being renovated to provide sleek new loft apartments. Rustic factory equipment turns up in museums rather than piling up in salvage yards. Even the old Victorian architecture has been given a face-lift. The overall effect is a gritty kind of charm.

Manchester's roots date from A.D. 79, when the Romans settled here. It remained under Roman occupation until A.D. 410 when the empire began its fall. The city's west gate has since been reconstructed upon its original site, and reminders from the city's storied role as a leader during the Industrial Revolution are literally everywhere.

But then in the mid–17th century, the city began to capitalize on the wealth of opportunity that the burgeoning textile industry offered. Manchester eventually became the Dickensian paradigm of the gritty industrial city. The railways were equally responsible for catapulting the city to the forefront of the industrial movement. England found Manchester both a convenient terminus and a refinement center through which raw goods became viable exports. It is apt indeed that the **Museum of Science and Industry** (p. 603) resides here.

Many of the factory laborers were immigrants who flocked to the city for the promise of work. The atrocity of their conditions is well documented. But these immigrants had a profound effect on the city's culture. Today, Manchester's nearly 20,000 descendants of Chinese immigrants constitute England's highest Chinese population outside

London. The Chinese residents have amalgamated their surroundings to fit their heritage. Falkner Street, particularly the monumental Imperial Chinese Archway, is brought to life by the murals, gardens, and vibrant decor that pay homage to the once-displaced working force.

The most recent stars of Manchester have been members of the Manchester United Football (that is, soccer) team, one of the most visible and successful in the world, with ardent legions of fans, and the rock group Oasis. They're best known in America for their album *(What's the Story) Morning Glory.* These rock stars haven't exactly done for Manchester what the Beatles did to put Liverpool on the map, but they certainly have made an impression. Of course, these self-styled "hard-drinking, groupie-shagging, drug-snorting geezers" make the Beatles seem like choirboys. As Manchester is increasingly cited for its hipness, Oasis, whose *Definitely Maybe* was the fastest-selling debut album in British history, helped make it so.

The once-dreary Manchester Docklands, evoking a painting by local son L. S. Lowry, has a spiffy new life following a £200-million ($400-million) restoration. It's called simply "the Lowry," and the complex is filled with theaters, shops, galleries, and restaurants. A plaza provides space for up to 10,000 at outdoor performances.

ESSENTIALS
GETTING THERE

BY PLANE More and more North Americans are flying directly to **Manchester International Airport** (© **0161/489-300;** www.manchesterairport.co.uk), located 24km (15 miles) south of the town center, to begin their explorations of the United Kingdom. **British Airways (BA;** © **800/247-9297** in the U.S. and Canada, or 0870/850-9850; www.british-airways.co.uk) has daily flights departing New York's JFK airport for Manchester at 6pm, arriving after 7 hours in the air. You can also fly from BA's many North American gateways nonstop to London, and from here take the almost shuttlelike service from either Gatwick or Heathrow airport to Manchester, a 50-minute flight.

American Airlines (© **800/433-7300** in the U.S. and Canada; www.aa.com) offers a daily nonstop flight to Manchester from Chicago's O'Hare Airport that departs at 5:35pm, arriving the following morning. American also flies from London's Heathrow back to Chicago.

BMI/British Midland (© **020/8745-7321** in London or 800/788-0555 in the U.S.; www.flybmi.com) flies from London's Heathrow to Manchester, and also flies to Manchester from Washington, D.C.; Chicago; Las Vegas; and some major cities in Canada, including Toronto.

Delta Airlines (© **800/241-4141;** www.delta.com) flies daily from New York's JFK and from Atlanta; **US Airways** (© **800/622-1015;** www.usairways.com) flies once a day from Philadelphia; and **Virgin Atlantic** (© **800/862-8621;** www.virgin-atlantic.com) flies once a day from Orlando.

Manchester is also served by flights from the Continent. For example, **Lufthansa** (© **800/645-3880;** www.lufthansa.com) has frequent nonstop flights each week between Frankfurt and Manchester, depending on the season. Flight time is 1 hour and 45 minutes.

Trains connect the airport terminal to the Piccadilly Railway Station in the center of Manchester. These trains depart from the airport every 5 to 10 minutes for the 15- to 20-minute ride to the center. Direct rail lines link the airport to surrounding northern destinations such as Edinburgh, Liverpool, and Windermere.

The Northwest

Buses nos. 43 and 105 run between the airport and Piccadilly Gardens Bus Station every 15 minutes (hourly, during the evenings and on Sun); the ride takes 55 minutes.

BY TRAIN, BUS & CAR   Trains from London's Euston Station travel directly to Manchester (© **0845/748-4950;** www.nationalrail.co.uk); the trip takes 2½ to 3 hours.

National Express (© **0870/580-8080;** www.nationalexpress.com) buses serve the Manchester region from London's Victoria Coach Station.

If you're driving from London to Manchester, go north on the M1 and the M6. At Junction 21A, go east on the M62, which becomes the M602 as you enter Manchester. The trip from London to Manchester usually takes from 3 to 3½ hours, but it could be longer because of traffic and construction.

GETTING AROUND   It's not a good idea to try to hoof it in Manchester. It's better to take the bus and **Metrolink.** Timetables, routes, fare information, and a copy of a helpful leaflet, the *Passenger's Guide,* are available from **Travelshop,** a general information booth within the Piccadilly Gardens Bus Station, Portland Street, open Monday to Saturday 7am to 6pm, and Sunday 10am to 6pm. For information, call © **0161/2052000** Monday to Friday 7am to 11pm, and Saturday and Sunday 10am to 6pm.

Buses begin running within Manchester at 6am and operate in full force until 11pm, then continue with limited routes until 3am. Tickets are sold at a kiosk at Piccadilly Gardens Bus Station. A day pass, the **Wayfarer** (© **0161/2052000**), costs £8.80 ($18) and is valid for a complete day of public bus travel.

Metrolink (© **0161/2052000;** www.metrolink.co.uk) streetcars connect the bus stations and provide a useful north-south conduit. Self-service ticket machines dispense zone-based fares. The wheelchair-accessible streetcars operate Monday to Thursday from 6am to midnight, Friday and Saturday from 6am to 1am, and Sunday from 7am to 11pm.

VISITOR INFORMATION   The **Manchester Visitor Centre,** Town Hall Extension, Lloyd Street (© **0871/2228223;** www.visitmanchester.com), is open Monday to Saturday 10am to 5:30pm, and Sunday and bank holidays 10:30am to 4:30pm. To get there, take the Metrolink tram to St. Peter's Square. Especially useful is a series of four free pamphlets with information on accommodations, dining, city attractions, and cultural/entertainment options.

WHERE TO STAY
EXPENSIVE
The Lowry Hotel ★★★ *(Finds*   Sexy and sinuous, the Lowry is the best hotel in the region. The hotel rises on the banks of the Irwell River in a gentrified neighborhood of Salford, a sister city whose borders with Manchester grow blurred, and which is most often compared to New York's SoHo. The windows of the bedrooms open onto a distinctively modern footbridge linking this once blighted industrial zone to the heart of town. The steel-and-glass edifice exudes a sense of airy, spacious luxury living. This government-rated five-star hotel (rare in this part of England) is part of the Chapel Wharf development. The Lowry offers bedrooms of maximum comfort with deluxe yet minimalist furnishings and state-of-the-art marble-trimmed bathrooms. Many patrons visit just to sample the international cuisine of the hotel's River Restaurant (p. 598).

Manchester

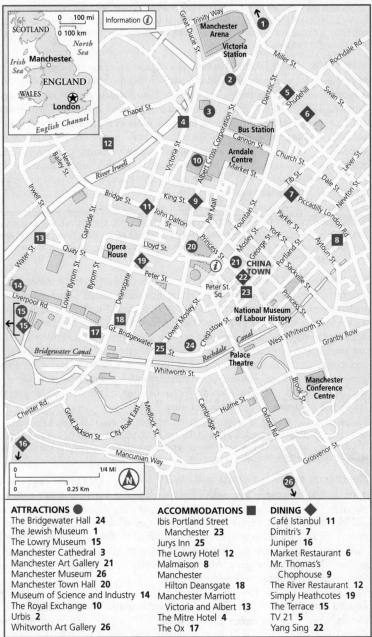

Information ⓘ

Inset map: SCOTLAND, North Sea, Irish Sea, Manchester, ENGLAND, WALES, London, English Channel

Map labels: Trinity Way, Great Ducie St., Manchester Arena, Victoria Station, Miller St., Rochdale Rd., Dantzic St., Shudehill, Swan St., Chapel St., Albert Cross Corporation St., Bus Station, Cannon St., Arndale Centre, Church St., Lever St., Market St., Victoria St., Tib St., Dale St., Newton St., King St., Pall Mall, Piccadilly London Rd., Bridge St., John Dalton St., Fountain St., Parker St., New Bailey St., River Irwell, Gartside St., Quay St., Lloyd St., Princess St., Mosley St., George St., York St., Portland St., Sackville St., Ayroun St., Irwell St., Water St., Lower Byrom St., Byrom St., Opera House, Peter St., Deansgate, China Town, Peter St. Sq., National Museum of Labour History, Liverpool Rd., Gt. Bridgewater St., Lower Mosley St., Chepstow St., Rochdale Canal, West Whitworth St., Granby Row, Bridgewater Canal, Whitworth St., Palace Theatre, Manchester Conference Centre, Chester Rd., Great Jackson St., City Road East, Medlock St., Cambridge St., Hulme St., Oxford Rd., Grosvenor St., Brook St., Mancunian Way

Scale: 0 1/4 Mi, 0 0.25 Km
N

ATTRACTIONS ●
The Bridgewater Hall **24**
The Jewish Museum **1**
The Lowry Museum **15**
Manchester Cathedral **3**
Manchester Art Gallery **21**
Manchester Museum **26**
Manchester Town Hall **20**
Museum of Science and Industry **14**
The Royal Exchange **10**
Urbis **2**
Whitworth Art Gallery **26**

ACCOMMODATIONS ■
Ibis Portland Street
  Manchester **23**
Jurys Inn **25**
The Lowry Hotel **12**
Malmaison **8**
Manchester
  Hilton Deansgate **18**
Manchester Marriott
  Victoria and Albert **13**
The Mitre Hotel **4**
The Ox **17**

DINING ◆
Café Istanbul **11**
Dimitri's **7**
Juniper **16**
Market Restaurant **6**
Mr. Thomas's
  Chophouse **9**
The River Restaurant **12**
Simply Heathcotes **19**
The Terrace **15**
TV 21 **5**
Yang Sing **22**

50 Dearmans Place, Chapel Wharf. © **01618/274000.** Fax 01618/274001. www.thelowryhotel.com. 165 units. £285–£315 ($570–$630) double; from £735 ($1,470) suite. AE, DC, MC, V. Parking £12 ($24). **Amenities:** Restaurant; bar; fitness center; spa; sauna; steam room; business center; room service. *In room:* TV, Wi-Fi, CD player, minibar, hair dryer (in some), trouser press (in some), safe.

Manchester Hilton Deansgate ✦

The city's most visible and most avant-garde competitor to the also-recommended Lowry Hotel, the Hilton is housed within a reflective pencil-thin skyscraper (the Beetham Tower) which, at 47 stories, £150 million, and 171m (561 ft.), is the tallest residential building in Britain. "Why residential?" you might ask. It's because the lower 23 floors of the building are devoted to conventional hotel rooms and the infrastructure, while floors 24 to 47 are private condominiums. The hotel boasts a streamlined, somewhat startling design of public rooms that are spartan, minimalist, almost Zen-like in their artful simplicity. Some find it refreshing, others find it dehumanizing. But in any event, the skinny, soaring building is fast approaching—along with the Lowry Hotel and the Imperial War Museum North—status as an iconic symbol of the city itself.

303 Deansgate, Manchester M3 4LQ. © **0161/870-1600.** Fax 0161/870-1650. www.hilton.co.uk/manchesterdeansgate. 279 units. £152–£220 ($304–$440) double; from $345 ($690) suite. AE, DC, MC, V. Parking £15 ($30). **Amenities:** Restaurant; bar; fitness center; business center; room service; laundry service; dry cleaning. *In room:* A/C, TV, Wi-Fi (in some), minibar, hair dryer, safe.

Malmaison ✦

This is one of the best examples in Manchester of combining old architectural features with the new. Behind an Edwardian facade, a dramatic and strikingly modern design (some locals refer to it as "a kind of tarty, New York–inspired look") reigns, enough of a statement that pop stars visiting from London often make it a point to stay here. In the heart of the city, only a minute's walk from Piccadilly Station, individually designed and "modern-as-tomorrow" bedrooms wait. The accommodations are striking, outfitted as they are in red, black, and ivory. Expect great big beds and very contemporary bathrooms with power showers. Some of the staff define the place by what it's not: "It's not baroque, it's not froufrou, and it's definitely not a Marriott," observed one of them.

Piccadilly, Manchester M1 3AQ. © **01612/781000.** Fax 01612/781002. www.malmaison-manchester.com. 167 units. £150–£180 ($300–$360) double; from £225 ($450) suite. AE, DC, MC, V. Parking £12 ($24). **Amenities:** Restaurant; bar; health club; spa; sauna; steam room; business center; laundry service. *In room:* TV, high-speed Internet, CD player, CD library, minibar, coffeemaker, hair dryer, iron.

Manchester Marriott Victoria and Albert ✦✦ *Finds*

One of the most unusual hotels in Britain occupies a renovated brick-sided pair of warehouses, originally conceived in 1843 to store bales of cotton being barged along the nearby Irwell River and the Manchester Ship Canal to looms and mills throughout the Midlands. Before its present incarnation through Marriott, it was owned by Granada TV as lodgings for their out-of-town media collaborators, but since its takeover by Marriott, it has become a bit more mainstream and a more in keeping with the high-quality and comfortable standards of that well-respected chain.

Bedrooms drip with the authenticity and charm of the Victorian age. Each has exposed brick walls, massive ceiling beams, an individualized shape and themed decor, and, in many cases, the ornate cast-iron columns of its earlier warehouse manifestation.

Water St., Castlefield, Manchester M3 4JQ. © **800/228-9290** in U.S. and Canada, or 01618/321188. Fax 01618/ 342484. www.marriott.com. 148 units. £135–£155 ($270–$310) double; from £235 ($470) suite. Rates include full

English breakfast. AE, DC, MC, V. Parking £12 ($24). **Amenities:** Restaurant; bar; fitness center; room service; laundry service; dry cleaning. *In room:* A/C, TV, high-speed Internet, minibar, coffeemaker, hair dryer, iron, trouser press, safe.

MODERATE

Jurys Inn *(Value)*   Suitable for both commercial travelers and vacationers, this large hotel lies in the center of Manchester. It stands beside the Concert Hall and Exhibition Center, and many of Manchester's major attractions, including museums and galleries, lie within walking distance. All the bedrooms are of the standard peas-in-a-pod variety, but they are well maintained and comfortable. The hotel is good value for the money in that the accommodations are large enough to house three adults or else two adults and two children. Both first-class meals in the main restaurant and delicious bar food in the pub are served here.

56 Great Bridgewater, St. Manchester M1 5LE. © 0161/953-8888. Fax 0161/953-9090. www.jurys-manchester-hotels.com. 265 units. £87–£145 ($174–$290) double. AE, DC, MC, V. Parking £11 ($22). **Amenities:** Restaurant; bar; laundry service; dry cleaning; babysitting. *In room:* A/C, TV, high-speed Internet, beverage maker, hair dryer.

INEXPENSIVE

Ibis Portland Street Manchester   This budget chain doesn't promise more than what it is—a basic, motel-like room suitable for overnighting at an affordable price. In a modern building without soul, Ibis lies in the center of town near the Piccadilly train station. The location is convenient to a wide range of places to eat as well as some of the best pubs in Manchester. The bed is cozy, the bathroom is functional—and that's about it.

96 Portland St., Manchester MI 4GY. © 0161/234-0600. Fax 0161/234-0610. www.accorhotels.com. 127 units. £61–£75 ($122–$150) double. MC, V. Parking £16 ($32). **Amenities:** Restaurant; bar. *In room:* A/C, TV, Wi-Fi.

The Mitre Hotel *(Value)*   The best of the budget hotels, the historic Mitre is the most central hotel in Manchester. Located at the Cathedral Gates and convenient to the big shopping complexes, it was reconstructed, but dates from 1815. It's had a rough history, surviving Hitler's Blitz of 1940 and an IRA bomb in 1996. It lies just a 3-minute walk from Manchester's Victoria Station if you're arriving with luggage. The ground-floor bar is wildly popular during soccer matches. The bedrooms are mostly small to midsize and a bit dowdy, but they're well maintained and comfortable enough.

1–3 Cathedral Gates, Manchester M3 1SW. © 0161/834-4128. Fax 0161/839-1646. www.mitrehotel.com. 32 units, 26 with bathroom. £55 ($110) double without bathroom; £99 ($198) double with bathroom. MC, V. Parking £14 ($28). **Amenities:** Cafe-bar; cocktail bar; laundry service. *In room:* TV, Wi-Fi, beverage maker.

The Ox *(Value)*   This is what the British call a "gastro-pub" with rooms, meaning it offers an excellent cuisine in its restaurant and a guest room above should you tie on a bender—or even if you don't. All the bedrooms have double or twin beds, are small to midsize, and are comfortably if rather simply furnished, each with a private bathroom. In the heart of the city, the Ox offers an atmosphere that is cozy and inviting. We've crashed here a few times and found it to be one of the best bargains in town.

We're also fond of its restaurant, offering both vegetarian and Pacific Rim seafood dishes. There is a daily choice of specials. Locals "pig out" on the mixed grill with pork and leek sausage, rump steak, lamb chop, black pudding, smoked bacon, lamb kidneys and liver, and fried mushroom and grilled tomatoes. An individual meat pie is also a daily special, with main courses costing from £9.95 to £15 ($20–$30). Even if you're not staying here, consider dropping in for a reasonably priced meal made with market-fresh ingredients.

71 Liverpool Rd., Castlefield, Manchester M3 4NQ. © 0161/839-7740. Fax 0161/839-7740. www.theox.co.uk. 9 units. £55–£65 ($110–$130) double; £75–£80 ($150–$160) triple. DC, MC, V. Parking £10 ($20). **Amenities:** Restaurant; bar. *In room:* TV, beverage maker, iron.

WHERE TO DINE

For some of the best value meals in Manchester, patronize the Ox (see above).

EXPENSIVE

Juniper 🌸🌸 ECLECTIC   Hailed as a winning choice, Juniper lies 4.9km (3 miles) outside Manchester. The chef, Paul Kitching, is often credited for "the menu's playful way with ingredients." Signature dishes include roast saddle of Cumbrian hare with foie gras, watercress, yogurt, spices, sugared cashews, and melon syrup juice. The setting isn't glamorous—in a parade of shops—but the food certainly is, especially the seafood, such as Dover sole filets served with preserved lemon and parsley in a creamy broth. For starters, try such divine concoctions as pieces of chicken breast, red pepper, carrots, and mushrooms bound together in a light jelly and topped with intense tomato custard. Ever had chocolate mayonnaise? For dessert, we endorse the locally famed lemon tart with rosemary sorbet. What's the downside here? Several readers complain of rudeness on the part of the staff.

21 The Downs, Altrincham, Greater Manchester. © 01619/294008. Reservations required. Main courses £20–£26 ($40–$52). AE, MC, V. Fri–Sat noon–2pm; Tues–Sat 7–9:30pm.

Market Restaurant ENGLISH   Few other restaurants capitalize as successfully on a sense of old-fashioned English nostalgia as this one. Set in the heart of town, it promotes itself with an allegiance to very fresh ingredients and a slightly dowdy but homelike decor that hasn't changed very much since the beginning of World War II. About a third of the dishes are vegetarian. Main dishes you are likely to savor include Parmesan-crusted turkey breast with red-pepper relish or a smoked haddock pancake with a spicy cream sauce. A filet of beef comes wrapped in bacon and served in port-wine gravy with Stilton butter. A dessert delight is a chocolate pot with whipped Jersey cream and shortbread.

104 High St. © 01618/343743. Reservations recommended. Main courses £10–£19 ($20–$38). AE, DC, MC, V. Wed–Fri noon–2pm and 6–9:30pm; Sat 7–9:30pm.

The River Restaurant 🌸🌸🌸 MODERN BRITISH/CONTINENTAL   This is the most stylish, sophisticated, and sought-after restaurant in Manchester and the region around it, a culinary landmark that's on virtually everybody's list of "important" dining spots. Set one floor above lobby level of the also-recommended hotel, it's decorated in a flawlessly simple kind of postmodern minimalism, wherein a mostly white background acts as a foil for prisms of multicolored light and the superb cuisine of chef Eyck Zimmer. Great efforts are taken within the oft-changing menu to incorporate such local ingredients as Lancaster and Cheshire cheeses, cream, lamb, chicken, berries, vegetables, and fruit. What emerges from the kitchens evokes the best of Britain, as interpreted by some very savvy Continent-trained chefs and staff. Begin a meal here with pressed crabmeat served with mango, cucumber, and coriander oil, or with oyster ravioli with leeks. Main courses might include roast cod in a curry-flavored crust; a fricassee of lobster and scallops with herb-flavored gnocchi; lamb poached in olive oil with a purée of white beans; or a filet of Cheshire beef with garlic, snails, and horseradish-flavored mashed potatoes. Desserts evoke nostalgia for anyone who's ever read Charles Dickens: Apple financier with clotted cream ice cream, or an English custard tart with prunes and pear.

In the Lowry Hotel, 50 Dearmans Place, Chapel Wharf. ✆ **0161/827-4041.** Reservations recommended. Main courses £14–£30 ($28–$60); set-price menus £20–£30 ($40–$60). AE, DC, MC, V. Daily noon–3pm and 6–10:30pm.

Yang Sing ✪ CANTONESE   Manchester's large population of Asian immigrants considers Yang Sing their favorite restaurant as proven by the cacophony of languages spoken within its labyrinth of dining rooms. It's loud and spread out, but efficient with a fast turnover of tables and a large fan base that's partly due to its status as the largest and most visible Chinese restaurant in the region. The decor is inspired by colonial, 1930s-era Shanghai. Delicate dim sum dumplings are served in a blissful array of choices from a pair of oversize carts in the dining room's center. Menu items cover the gamut of the Cantonese repertoire. Flavorful examples include stir-fried scallop with seasonal greens; sizzling filet of chicken in black-currant-and-blackberry sauce; braised duckling with a spicy bean casserole; and finely chopped loin of pork, stir-fried with French beans and preserved Chinese olive leaves.

34 Princess St. ✆ **01612/362200.** Reservations required. Main courses £22–£30 ($44–$60); 4-course fixed-price menu £30 ($60), 5 courses £38 ($76). AE, MC, V. Mon–Thurs noon–11:45pm; Fri–Sat noon–12:15am; Sun 11:45am–10:45pm. Metrolink tram to Piccadilly.

MODERATE

Cafe Istanbul TURKISH   Modern and appealing, with touches of exoticism that sometimes evoke an old Marlene Dietrich flick on the late, late show, this is the most savory spot in Manchester for Turkish cuisine. Decorated in a vague Mediterranean style, it draws a hip, young crowd, many who have traveled abroad and are in search of those exotic flavors discovered in their travels. The selection of *meze* (Turkish appetizers) alone is worth the trek here, and the wine list is extensive but without price gouging. Try any of the lamb kabobs (the house specialty) or the grilled seafood.

79/81 Bridge St. ✆ **01618/339942.** Reservations required. Main courses £10–£14 ($20–$28). MC, V. Mon–Sat noon–11pm; Sun noon–10pm.

Mr. Thomas's Chophouse TRADITIONAL ENGLISH   This mellow Manchester pub is also the city's oldest restaurant, established in 1872. Tall and thin, and bristling with history and a sense of Industrial Revolution nostalgia, it's the restaurant we most highly recommend for insights into the gritty cheerfulness and congenially battered charm of this region of England. The structure itself is a good example of the British Art Nouveau, and one of the first cast-iron buildings in Manchester. Under brown ceilings, within a decor that hasn't changed very much since 1901, guests dine at tables placed on the checkerboard floors. Real ales are very popular here, including Boddingtons and Timothy Taylor's. The most traditional British food served in the city center is offered here at lunch, including dishes such as braised oxtail with cabbage and dumplings, and steak-and-kidney pudding. The pan-fried plaice with mushy peas is a local favorite, as is the French onion soup for a starter. Crabmeat risotto, corned beef hash cakes, fish pie, and venison and claret casserole are other always-reliable staples.

52 Cross St. ✆ **0161/8322245.** Reservations not needed. Main courses £10–£18 ($20–$36). AE, MC, V. Daily 11:30am–3pm and 5:30–9:30pm.

Simply Heathcotes ✪ *Value* LANCASTRIAN/ENGLISH   Installed in old registry offices, this restaurant is spacious and with a contemporary decor. It's reached via a sweeping staircase. The setting is ideal for the modern brasserie cuisine served here. You can "graze" from light modern dishes such as a Caesar salad with chicken breast, or something more rib sticking—notably the best lamb shepherd's pie in town, or breast of Goosnargh duck with braised red cabbage. Other good-tasting mains include grilled filet of trout with braised leeks or pan-fried sage gnocchi with roasted squash. You might also try oxtail-and-kidney pudding. Children's specials are also offered. Sunday classics always feature roast sirloin of local beef with Yorkshire pudding.

Jacksons Row, Deansgate. ⓒ 0161/835-3536. Reservations recommended. Main courses £15–£25 ($30–$50); Sun 2-course lunch £16 ($32), 3 courses £18 ($36). AE, MC, V. Mon–Sat noon–2:30pm; Mon–Fri 5:30–10pm; Sat 5:30–11pm; Sun noon–9pm.

The Terrace ⭐ MODERN BRITISH   This citadel of good food is installed within an avant-garde, ultracontemporary setting in the Lowry Theatre (p. 605) in the Salford district, sometimes known as Manchester's restored dockland area. Ingredients, as prepared by chef Watson-Gumby, are market fresh and served with flair by a well-trained staff. Most dishes are light and completely in step with the tenets of modern Continental cookery. Delights from the ever-changing menu include roasted pork with sage, apples, an onion tartlet, pumpkin purée, and red-wine jus; pan-fried duck breast with chestnut and parsley mash, blackberry, and pink-peppercorn jus; and Cheshire beef filet with roasted onions. The restaurant is open for dinner when there is a theatrical performance.

Pier 8, Salford Quays. ⓒ 01618/762121. Reservations recommended. Main courses £11–£25 ($22–$50); 2-course lunch £14 ($28), 3 courses £17 ($34); 2-course dinner £18 ($36), 3 courses £20 ($40). AE, DC, MC, V. Daily noon–3pm and 5–7pm (last order). Metrolink tram marked ECCLES.

INEXPENSIVE

Dimitri's GREEK   This bistro is a warm and friendly place in the city center. It's so popular, especially with a young crowd, that you should call a day in advance for a table. Greek delicacies are the way to go, though Spanish and Italian dishes, including tapas, are served nightly. Dimitri's also serves up some of the best veggie dishes in Manchester. On weekends, sit at the bar with a savory blend of Greek coffee and listen to a live jazz band.

1 Campfield Arcade. ⓒ 01618/393319. Reservations recommended. Main courses £4.50–£7 ($9–$14). AE, MC, V. Daily 11am–11:30pm.

TV 21 AMERICAN   Don't come here expecting gastronomy, or even behavior that's particularly reverential or polite. It's one of the best examples of the artfully trashy, satirical hangouts where drinks and cocktails are just as important (perhaps more so) than the platters of food that its clientele might eventually get around to ordering after they can't stave off their hunger pangs any longer. Best of all, the food is flavorful and cheap—a boon for 20-somethings looking for sociological insights and perhaps love and romance in Manchester. The decorative theme here is based on what the owners refer to as "Trash TV." Menu items include, among others, sandwiches, quesadillas, spaghetti Bolognese, Thai-style curries with sticky rice, "cheeky chicken pie," sirloin steaks, lasagna, and burgers. Apple crumble or bread and butter pudding are uncharacteristically (for here) traditional desserts.

10 Thomas St. ⓒ 0161/839-5021. Reservations not necessary. Sandwiches, salads, and platters £5–£9 ($10–$18). MC, V. Sun–Tues noon–midnight; Wed–Thurs noon–1am; Fri–Sat noon–2am.

SEEING THE SIGHTS

Imperial War Museum North ⭐⭐   Usually identified as one of the most striking museums in the north of England, it contains thousands of objects associated with 20th-century European wars, including tanks and armored motorized vehicles like your parents or grandparents drove if they were involved in with the conflicts of World War II. These, set as they are into a multimedia hodgepodge of sound, light, and clips from old movies and documentaries, evoke the wrenching emotions of a world at war. Easily as interesting as the exhibits inside is the steel, concrete, and glass shell designed by architect Daniel Libeskind, whose shape evokes a globe wrenched to pieces by global conflict. Inside, floors slope, and walls careen at dizzying angles to evoke a world gone psychotic. Special exhibitions commemorate, among others, the Falklands War and other global conflicts in which Britain played a role. You'll find the place about 2 miles southwest of Manchester's city center, within a grimy industrial landscape crisscrossed with canals, waterways, and weirdly evocative relics of the Industrial Revolution.

The Quays, Trafford Wharf. © 0161/836-4040. http://north.iwm.org.uk. Free admission. Mar–Oct daily 10am–6pm; Nov–Feb daily 10am–5pm. Metrolink: Harbour City or bus 205.

The Jewish Museum   These compact and somewhat claustrophobic premises were originally built in the Moorish Revival style in 1874 as a Sephardic synagogue. Set on the city's northern fringe, it's one of only two such museums in Britain (the other is in London). It traces the culture and history of Manchester's Jewish community, estimated today at around 27,000. Part of the emphasis is on the experiences of immigrants, many from eastern Europe, whose recorded voices describe life in Manchester's Jewish quarter in the years before World War II.

Cheetham Hill Rd. © 01618/349879. www.manchesterjewishmuseum.com. Admission £3.95 ($7.90) adults; £2.95 ($5.90) children, students, and seniors; £9.50 ($19) family ticket. Mon–Thurs 10:30am–4pm; Sun 10:30am–5pm; Fri by appointment. Closed Jewish holidays. Bus: 89, 135, or 167.

The Lowry Museum (aka "the Lowry")   At the restored docklands area, the Lowry, the industrial city landscapes of the artist L. S. Lowry (1887–1976) are showcased as never before, within a hypermodern arts complex that in some ways symbolizes the emergence of Manchester itself as a centerpiece of avant-garde architecture. Lowry (the artist, not to be confused with either the museum, the hotel, or the theater that bears his name) depicted the horror of the England's industrial north, before it disappeared forever. His matchstick people are dwarfed by the smokestacks and viaducts in his paintings. Lowry's paintings, as seen here, imposed a vision of a grim and gloomy urban sprawl. Lowry found a cohesion and lyric beauty in these industrial landscapes. His best-known paintings are from 1905 to 1925. The artist was especially fond of depicting the crudeness of capitalism, forcing workers into boxlike row houses, as railroads nearby rattled across viaducts belching smoke.

The Lowry. Pier 8, the Quays. © 01618/762000. www.thelowry.com. Free admission. Sun–Fri 11am–5pm; Sat 10am–5pm. Bus: 51, 52, 71, 73, or M11.

Manchester Art Gallery   Following an extensive expansion and rejuvenation, this gallery today is the proud owner of one of the best and most prestigious art collections in the north of England. Literally doubled in size, the gallery displays works that are wide-ranging—from the pre-Raphaelites to old Dutch masters, from the land- and seascapes of Turner to Lowry's industrial panoramas.

Designed by Sir Charles Barry, this gallery has been a landmark since 1882. Today's fine collection is also noted for its paintings by Ford Madox Brown and Holman Hunt. The gallery's decorative art collection is one of the finest outside London, especially in its 17th- and 18th-century pieces, its metalwork, and porcelain. The silver, in particular the Assheton Bennett collection, is especially distinguished.

If you're here between Easter and September, consider a visit to **Heaton Hall** (© **01617/731231;** www.manchestergalleries.org), the museum's annex, 6.5km (4 miles) to the east. It's the centerpiece of 263 hectares (650 acres) of rolling parkland and accessible via the Metrolink tram (get off at Heaton Park). Built of York stone in 1772 and filled with furniture and decorative art of the 18th and 19th centuries, it is open only between Easter and September. Opening hours may vary; however, they are generally Thursday to Sunday 11am to 5:30pm. Call the Manchester Visitor Centre (see "Visitor Information," earlier in this chapter) to confirm. Admission is free.

Mosley St. at Princess St. © 01612/358888. www.manchestergalleries.org. Free admission. Tues–Sun 10am–5pm.

Manchester Cathedral   𝕣   Manchester started out as a small medieval parish in

1421, and continued to grow and expand its borders. In 1847, it was a big, bustling city and it had achieved cathedral status with the creation of a new diocese. The cathedral's nave, the widest of its kind in Britain, is formed by six bays, as is the choir. The choir stalls are beautifully carved and date from the early 16th century. The carvings depict a humorous interpretation of life in the Middle Ages. The choir screen is a woodcarving from the same era. Central to the 19th-century grass-roots movement that helped abolish slavery throughout the British Empire, and frequently associated with the kinds of socialist free thinking for which Manchester itself is identified, it's one of the most resilient religious buildings in Britain, having survived vandals during the 17th-century civil wars, a direct hit by a Nazi firebomb in 1941, and damage from an IRA bombing in 1996. Of special note is the "Fire Window," a replacement for a window destroyed during World War II, whose colors evoke the infernos of the Nazi Blitz.

Victoria St. © 01618/332220. www.manchestercathedral.org. Free admission. Mon–Fri 8am–7pm; Sat 8am–5pm; Sun 8:30am–7:30pm.

Manchester Museum   This venerable museum showcases an eclectic and some-

times eccentric collection of the spoils brought back by local industrialists from their adventurous forays outside of England, displaying archaeological finds from all over the world, including England's largest collection of ancient Egyptian mummies outside the British Museum in London.

University of Manchester, Oxford Rd., near Booth St. © 01612/752634. www.museum.man.ac.uk. Free admission. Tues–Sat 10am–5pm; Sun–Mon 11am–4pm. Metrolink tram to St. Peter's Sq., then bus 41, 42, 47, 16, or 11.

Manchester Town Hall   𝕣   Alfred Waterhouse designed this massive neo-Gothic

structure that first opened in 1877, and extensions were added just before World War II. The tower rises nearly 90m (295 ft.) above the town. The Great Hall and its signature hammer-beam roof houses 12 pre-Raphaelite murals by Ford Madox Brown, commissioned between 1852 and 1856. The paintings chronicle the town's storied past, from the 1st-century Roman occupation to the Industrial Revolution of the 19th century.

Albert Sq. © 01612/345000. Free admission. Mon–Fri 9am–5pm. Closed Dec 25–26 and Jan 1.

Urbis   Shimmering, glassy, avant-garde, and massive, and positioned as close to the

commercial core of Manchester as a building can be, Urbis arose like a symbol of the "new Manchester" from the rubble of an IRA bomb that devastated the downtown area in 1996. It was built as an homage to the concept of "the City" as an inevitable byproduct of the human experience. The fantastic structure is clad in 2,200 hand-made plates of glass with a "ski slope" copper roof. Inside, along with changing exhibits, you'll find high-tech interactive displays providing insights into Manchester life along with various explorations of urban culture and art. Other than its core exhibit, noted above, its interior is as changeable and quixotic as its shimmering exterior. Few museums in Europe seem as deliberately undefined, or seem to change exhibits as frequently and as radically.

Cathedral Gardens. © **01612/605-8200**. www.urbis.org.uk. Free admission. Mon–Wed and Sun 10am–6pm; Thurs–Sat 10am–8pm.

Whitworth Art Gallery Whitworth was originally established in 1889 with a bequest to the city from a wealthy industrialist. The gallery was opened to the public in 1908. Behind the magnificent redbrick facade lies a light and spacious interior. The gallery is one of the richest research sources in England for antique patterns of wallpaper and textiles and the weaving techniques that produced them. It also features a superb collection of 18th- and 19th-century watercolors on display, including many by Turner.

South of the University of Manchester, on Oxford Rd., near the corner of Denmark Rd. © **01612/757450**. www.whitworth.man.ac.uk. Free admission. Mon–Sat 10am–5pm; Sun noon–4pm. Metrolink to St. Peter's Sq., then bus 41, 42, or 45.

EXPLORING CASTLEFIELD

Manchester had its origins in **Castlefield,** immediately southwest of the city's historic core, which local authorities have designated an "urban heritage park." Interlaced with canals that helped transport building supplies during the city's late-19th-century heyday, Castlefield's known as a place to escape from more crowded venues downtown. Long ago, it was a densely populated neighborhood that housed as many as 2,000 civilians beginning in A.D. 79, when Manchester was Mamucium, a fortified Roman camp strategically positioned between other Roman outposts, Chester and Carlisle. The roots of modern-day Manchester grew from here, providing the basic goods and services that supplied the soldiers in the nearby fort. After the Romans abandoned their fortress in A.D. 411, the settlement, by then known as Mancestra, stood alone throughout the Dark Ages.

Manchester slumbered for centuries until its heyday came in the 18th and 19th centuries. The development of the **Bridgewater Canal,** which transferred raw materials and coal to Manchester's factories from outlying regions, spurred the city's industrial growth. Warehouses arose around the wharves, their names suggesting their wares (for example, Potato Wharf). Later, Liverpool Road housed the world's first passenger railway station, today home to the Museum of Science and Industry (see below).

Though the city atrophied for decades after its reign as industrial capital of the world, an interest in urban renewal emerged in the 1970s. Many of the city's grand canals and warehouses have been restored, and Castlefield is once again a thriving, vibrant district loaded with a curious mixture of antique and ultramodern buildings randomly positioned next to each other. Such neighboring districts as the Northern Quarter seem to specialize in funky bars and shops selling all manner of used clothing and 1960s-era nostalgia.

The Museum of Science and Industry Set within five separate and antique buildings, the premises were built in 1830 as the first railway station in the world. Its many exhibits celebrate the Industrial Revolution and its myriad inventions and developments, such as printing, the railway industry, electricity, textile manufacturing, and industrial machinery, plus the history of flight and aerospace exploration.

Liverpool Rd. (1.5km/1 mile north of Manchester's center), Castlefield. ⓒ 01618/322244. www.msim.org.uk. Free admission. Daily 10am–5pm. Closed Dec 24–26 and Jan 1. Parking £5 ($10). Bus: 33. Metrolink: G-Mex or Deans Gate.

SHOPPING

Not only does Manchester offer a vast number and variety of boutiques, shops, galleries, and crafts centers, but it's also one of the best hunting grounds for bargains in all of England.

Most of the larger shopping areas in the city are pedestrian only. These include **King Street** and **St. Ann's Square,** full of exclusive boutiques and designer stores; **Market Street,** with its major chain and department stores; **Arndale Centre,** Manchester's largest covered shopping center; and the revitalized **Piccadilly** and **Oldham streets,** for fashion, music, and plenty of bargains. **Deansgate Street** is not pedestrian only but does have a lot of adventure-sports shops.

For the young at heart, interested in everything from World War II RAF bomberpilot gear to outrageous club wear, it's one-stop shopping at **Affleck Palace,** 52 Church St. This complex provides 50 of the most widely varied shops in the city divided among four floors.

ANTIQUES & FINE ART Those who like rooting through dusty stacks of stuff in search of treasures will find Manchester and the greater Manchester area prime hunting grounds. More pricey antiques can be found along **Bury New Road** in Prestwich village, just outside of Manchester.

ARTS & CRAFTS You can rack up a lot of one-of-a-kind items while exploring the many shops devoted to craftspeople and their art. For ceramics, glass, textiles, jewelry, toys, dollhouses, and the like, visit the exquisite Victorian building that houses **Manchester Craft Centre,** 17 Oak St. (ⓒ **01618/324274**).

DEPARTMENT STORES For a northern outpost of London's chic department store, head for **Harvey Nichols,** 21 New Cathedral St. (ⓒ **0161/828-8888**), in the city center. The store often has sales and is always packed with the latest designer goods. For lunch, you can dine in an affordable restaurant and brasserie on the second floor. Far cheaper fashion is found at **Marks & Spencer,** 7 Market St. (ⓒ **0161/831-7341**), the world's largest department store. Among its thousands of offerings, it is also known for its food department.

MARKETS Here in the north, markets are a tradition and offer you a chance to jump in and barter with the locals. Tourists tend to steer clear of them, so this is a great chance for an authentic experience.

Though markets tend to sell everyday items and foodstuff, some stalls are devoted to flea-market goods and "antiques." Market days vary throughout the city, but you're bound to find at least one in full swing each day of the workweek.

The major ones include Arndale Market and Market Hall in Manchester Arndale Centre, Grey Mare Lane Market and Beswick District Shopping Centre in Beswick, and Moss Side Market and Moss Lane East in Moss Side.

MILL SHOPS Manchester is an industrial stronghold with lots of textile mills. Most mills used to have a store, or mill shop, on-site where customers could come to buy mill goods. Today, more and more of the mills are setting up shop in towns across the country.

Bury New Road in Cheetham Hill, near Boddington's Brewery, has a great selection of factory shops, discount stores, warehouses, cash-and-carry outlets, and street stalls on Sunday mornings. Some of the stores along this road do not sell to the general public and others require a minimum purchase.

NOSTALGIA   Thanks partly to its burgeoning gay and lesbian community, Manchester has functioned like a magnet or vacuum cleaner, pulling in the kind of plasticized, airport-lobby kitsch that might have been discarded in horror a dozen or more years ago. The '60s-inspired vinyl of the Carnaby Street era flourishes and thrives at **Oklahoma,** 74–76 High St. (© **0161/834-1136**), one of the most visible purveyors of kitsch in the city's funky Northern Quarter. Its decor is mostly constructed from recycled plastic, and crammed to the rafters with things kitschier—both new and recycled—than most mainstream psyches could possibly imagine. Come here for the kind of tongue-in-cheek gag items that might have been conceived during a psychedelic fog by a dyed-in-the-wool drag queen on mescaline. There's a cafe on the premises.

MANCHESTER AFTER DARK
THE PERFORMING ARTS

The **Lowry Theatre** ★★, Pier 8, Salford Quays (© **0870/787-5780**), has become Manchester's premier center for the performing and visual arts, encompassing two main theaters, studio space, and exhibition galleries. To find out what's happening at the time of your visit, search www.thelowry.com. You can visit the Galleries of Lowry Monday to Friday and Sunday 11am to 5pm, Saturday 10am to 5pm; admission is free. Take Metrolink Harbour City or bus no. 69, 290, or 291.

For drama with an unobstructed view, go to the nation's largest theater-in-the-round. The **Royal Exchange** ★★, St. Ann's Square (© **01618/339833;** www.royalexchange.co.uk), is housed in a futuristic glass-and-steel structure built within the Great Hall of Manchester's former Cotton Exchange and offers 48 weeks of in-house dramaturgy every year.

Home of the renowned **Halle Orchestra,** the **Bridgewater Hall,** Lower Mosley Street (© **01619/079000;** www.bridgewater-hall.co.uk), is a state-of-the-art, 2,400-seat concert hall. In addition to the orchestra's season, it also presents other classical performances as well as some pop and comedy, too.

The **University of Manchester's Department of Music,** Coupland Street (© **01612/754982**), is home to one of the nation's most distinctive classical string quartets, the **Lindsay String Quartet,** which performs a series of eight evening concerts in the department's auditorium during the year. For a real bargain, check out its luncheon recital series, which is free.

The internationally acclaimed **BBC Philharmonic** performs concerts year-round at Bridgewater Hall (© **01619/079000**). The calendar of performances is highly variable, so it's best to call for schedules.

THE CLUB & MUSIC SCENE

Above all else, Manchester is known for its contributions to pop music. From the Smiths and New Order to Oasis and the Stone Roses, the "Manchester sound" has been known throughout the world for more than 2 decades. Yet, surprisingly enough, live music went by the wayside in the early 1990s, and clubs were in short supply until they started making a steady comeback in the last couple of years.

South, 4A King St. (© **01618/317756**), is a small industrial-style club. A 10-minute walk north of Piccadilly Gardens, this club has a sophisticated young aura, with '60s and '70s music on Friday and a hot house DJ on Saturday.

Manchester Gay Life

Loud, proud, and straight-friendly, Manchester's so-called **Gay Village** spreads across Canal Street in a once-seedy factory district that's flanked on one side by a canal with locks. The scene begins northeast of Princess Street and is active day and night. On any given day, gays and lesbians hang out at one of the sidewalk tables that border the canal. The bars are frequented by both young gay men and lesbians. The neighborhood contains as many as 25 different GLBT watering holes, each with their regular clienteles and niche markets, but a trio of bars that's particularly popular includes include **Queer**, 4 Canal St. (© **0161/ 228-1360**), a gay-lifestyle cafe/bar in the heart of the village. Entrance is free and food is served day and night. A cruisy crowd frequents the joint with its large booths. Queer is open Monday to Saturday 11am to 2am, Sunday 11am to 12:30am. On another front, **Churchills**, 37 Chorlton St. (© **0161/236-5529**), arguably has the friendliest atmosphere. The surroundings are safe and comfortable at this pub club that features everything from drag disco to karaoke nights. Both full meals and bar snacks are offered, and there's no cover. It's open Monday to Saturday noon to 2am, Sunday noon to 12:30am. Finally, **Cruz 101**, 101 Princess St. (© **0161/950-0101**), is perhaps the best-attended gay venue, with music ranging from disco to funky house. It's really two clubs in one, with a large main floor and a smaller lower level. It was created from an old abandoned textile mill. Cover ranges from £4 to £5 ($8–$10), depending on the night and entertainment. It's open Monday, Thursday, and Sunday 11pm to 5am, Wednesday 11pm to 3:30am, Friday and Saturday 11pm to 6am.

For cutting-edge music, check the stage at **Star & Garter,** Farefield Street (© **01612/736726**), on Wednesday through Friday, when harder rock and hard-core acts will get in your face.

Peveril of the Peak, Great Bridgewater Street (© **01612/366364**), is easy enough to find—just look for a 380-year-old triangular building covered from top to bottom in antique green-glazed tiles. No one seems to know why it was designed or built that way, but you can step inside its woodsy-looking paneled interior and enjoy a pint of Theakston's Best Bitter, Yorkshire Terrier, or Webster's Best Bitter while you puzzle over it.

Other hot clubs include **Matt and Phred's,** 85 Oldham St. (© **0161/8317002**), which features some of the best jazz in town. It's open Monday to Saturday 5pm to 2am.

BARS & LOUNGES

One of Manchester's most intriguing bars lies one floor above lobby level within the city's best-recommended and most prestigious hotel. It's the **River Bar,** in the Lowry Hotel, 50 Dearmans Place, Chapel Wharf (© **0161/827-4000**) a rambling, contemporary citadel of understated posh whose clientele derives from the young, the beautiful, and the restless from the city that surrounds it. But at least part of the attraction derives from whatever media-hungry clients might be in residence at the time. In other words, don't assume that you'll be surrounded with dour business travelers here: You're more likely to meet troupes of actors, rock musicians, professional athletes (including professional wrestlers and kick boxers), and media folk than not, and as such, the place usually rocks and rolls. Cocktails cost from £7.50 to £10 ($15–$20) each, and platters of food, including salads, sandwiches, tapas, and upscale versions of fish and chips, go from £10 to £18 ($20–$36) each.

Other hot spots for a drink include **Lammar's,** Fourways House, 57 Hilton St. (© **0161/237-9058**), in the Northern Quarter. With its kitschy decor and high camp, it was named after a fabled local drag queen, Foo Foo Lammar. To the sounds of recorded jazz, a young crowd drinks in the bar or retreats to a lounge. Out back tapas are served. **Dukes 92,** Castle Street (© **0161/839-8646**), lies in Castlefield opening onto Lock 92 of the Rochdale Canal. You can sit outside and take in the view, perhaps get inspected yourself. The lounge is installed in a former stable, and it's a huge place, almost like one of the old cotton warehouses of yore. The bar passes out some free snacks, and you can also order pizzas and the like.

2 Liverpool ⚑

353km (219 miles) NW of London; 166km (103 miles) NW of Birmingham; 56km (35 miles) W of Manchester

Liverpool, with its famous waterfront on the River Mersey, is a great shipping port and industrial center and is now a UNESCO World Heritage Site. It's even been called "the next Barcelona." But forget about those palm trees, and carry an umbrella. King John launched Liverpool on its road to glory when he granted it a charter in 1207. Before that, it had been a tiny 12th-century fishing village, but it quickly became a port for shipping men and materials to Ireland. In the 18th century, it grew to prominence because of the sugar, spice, and tobacco trade with the Americans. By the time Victoria came to the throne, Liverpool had become Britain's biggest commercial seaport.

Recent refurbishing of the Albert Dock, the establishment of a maritime museum, and the conversion of warehouses into little stores similar to those in San Francisco's Ghirardelli Square have made this an up-and-coming area once again, with many attractions for visitors. Liverpudlians are proud of their city, with its new hotels, two cathedrals, shopping and entertainment complexes, and parks. And, of course, whether they're fans of the Fab Four or not, most visitors to Liverpool want to see where Beatlemania began.

ESSENTIALS

GETTING THERE Liverpool has its own airport, **John Lennon Airport** (© **0871/5218484;** www.liverpooljohnlennonairport.com), which has frequent daily flights from many parts of the United Kingdom, including London, the Isle of Man, and Ireland.

Frequent express trains depart London's Euston Station for Liverpool, a 3-hour trip. For schedules and information, call © **0845/748-4950** or visit **www.nationalrail. co.uk**. There is also frequent service from Manchester, a 45-minute ride away.

National Express buses depart London's Victoria Coach Station every 3 hours for the 4½-hour trip to Liverpool. Buses also arrive every hour from Manchester, a 1-hour ride away. For schedules and information, call © **0870/580-8080** or visit **www. nationalexpress.com**.

If you're driving from London, head north on the M1, then northwest on the M6 to the junction with the M62, which heads west to Liverpool.

VISITOR INFORMATION The **Tourist Information Centre** is at 8 Place, Whitechapel (© **01512/332008;** www.visitliverpool.com), and is open Monday and Wednesday to Saturday 9am to 6pm, Tuesday 10am to 6pm, and Sunday 11am to 4pm.

SPECIAL EVENTS   At the end of August and running into the first couple of days of September, the annual **International Beatles Week** attracts about 100,000 fans to Liverpool for a 7-day celebration highlighted with concerts performed by bands from Argentina to Sweden (with names such as Lenny Pane, Wings Over Liverpool, and the Beats). You can hear the news today at the Sgt. Pepper concert and take in many other Beatles tributes, auctions, and tours.

WHERE TO STAY
EXPENSIVE

Atlantic Tower 🌟🌟   Showcased in an austere high-rise evoking the bow of a great luxury liner, this first-class hotel is one of the top two big hotels in the city (the other being Britannia Adelphi; see below). It caters largely to business travelers. You check in at a spacious lobby and are shown to one of the well-furnished but fairly standard bedrooms. Many bedrooms, though quite small, provide views of the River Mersey, and you can request a minibar. Average—not grand—comfort can be found here. The best units are the corner bedrooms, which are triangular in shape and face the river. Bedrooms are frequently renovated as need arises.

30 Chapel St., Liverpool, Merseyside L3 9RE. 🏢 **0871/376-9025.** Fax 0871/376-9125. 225 units. £90–£130 ($180–$260) per person double weekdays, £99 ($198) weekends; £119–£149 ($238–$298) per person suite. Rates include breakfast. AE, DC, MC, V. Parking £12 ($24). **Amenities:** 2 restaurants; bar; room service; laundry service; dry cleaning. *In room:* TV, beverage maker, hair dryer, trouser press.

Britannia Adelphi Hotel 🌟   This grand hotel, built in 1914, is known for its fine Edwardian rooms and good cuisine. Past the elegant entrance, you enter an overblown world of marble corridors, molded ceilings, and dark polished wood. These traditional features are complemented by modern luxuries because the hotel has been completely refurbished. Many still view this as the best address in town, but we rank it second behind the Atlantic Tower (see above). Each recently refurbished bedroom is well furnished and comes with double-glazed windows. The mezzanine bedrooms are likely to be noisy.

Ranelagh Place, Liverpool, Merseyside L3 5UL. 🏢 **0871/2220029.** Fax 0871/2227009. www.adelphi-hotel.co.uk. 402 units. £125–£165 ($250–$330) double; £135–£195 ($270–$390) suite. Children 11 and younger stay free in parent's room. AE, DC, MC, V. Parking £10 ($20). **Amenities:** 3 restaurants; 2 bars; heated indoor pool; health club; Jacuzzi; sauna; steam room; salon; room service; laundry service; dry cleaning. *In room:* TV, high-speed Internet (in some), beverage maker, hair dryer, trouser press.

Hope Street Hotel 🌟🌟 *(Finds)*   This converted carriage house, constructed to evoke a palace in Venice, is Liverpool's first boutique hotel—and it's our preferred stopover. Perched on a hill with panoramic views, it stands across from the home of the Liverpool Philharmonic. Exposed brickwork and cast-iron columns from the mid–19th century, along with exposed beam ceilings and waxed oaken floors, create a warm, cozy atmosphere, evocative of Liverpool's shipbuilding past. Each room is beautifully furnished with oversize beds, Egyptian cotton sheets, radiant heat, and natural light, along with custom-made cherrywood furniture. In the private bathroom, we love the "rain dance shower heads" the size of dinner plates. The on-site bar is the town's most sophisticated, often a venue for visiting celebs, and the London Carriage Works restaurant is separately recommended (p. 611).

40 Hope St., Liverpool L1 9DA. 🏢 **0151/709-3000.** Fax 0151/709-2454. www.hopestreethotel.co.uk. 48 units. £140–£200 ($280–$400) double; from £225 ($450) suite. AE, DC, MC, V. Parking £10 ($20). **Amenities:** 2 restaurants; bar; room service; laundry service; dry cleaning. *In room:* TV/DVD, Wi-Fi, CD player, beverage maker, hair dryer, trouser press.

Liverpool

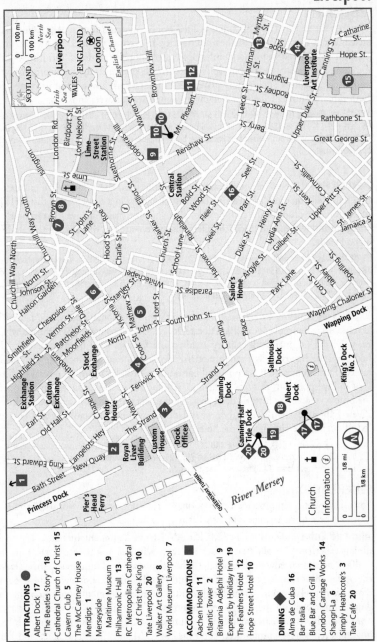

ATTRACTIONS ●
Albert Dock **17**
"The Beatles Story" **18**
Cathedral Church of Christ **15**
Cavern Club **5**
The McCartney House **1**
Mendips **1**
Merseyside
Maritime Museum **9**
Philharmonic Hall **13**
RC Metropolitan Cathedral
of Christ the King **10**
Tate Liverpool **20**
Walker Art Gallery **8**
World Museum Liverpool **7**

ACCOMMODATIONS ■
Aachen Hotel **11**
Atlantic Tower **2**
Britannia Adelphi Hotel **9**
Express by Holiday Inn **19**
The Feathers Hotel **12**
Hope Street Hotel **10**

DINING ◆
Alma de Cuba **16**
Bar Italia **4**
Blue Bar and Grill **17**
London Carriage Works **14**
Shangri-La **6**
Simply Heathcote's **3**
Tate Café **20**

MODERATE

The Feathers Hotel   This brick-fronted hotel comprises four separate Georgian-style town houses. It sits in the heart of the city, adjacent to the modern Metropolitan Cathedral. The bedrooms are comfortable, with simple traditional furniture—there are some four-poster beds—but don't expect much charm. Executive bedrooms offer additional amenities such as CD players and PlayStations. Some 40 units come with both tub and shower. There's a 2-night minimum stay on weekends.

117–125 Mt. Pleasant, Liverpool, Merseyside L3 5TF. ℂ 01517/099655. Fax 01517/093838. www.feathers.uk.com. 66 units. £69–£120 ($138–$240) double; £130 ($260) triple. Rates include buffet breakfast. AE, MC, V. Parking £6.50 ($13). Bus: 80 (the airport bus). **Amenities:** Restaurant; bar; room service; laundry service; dry cleaning. *In room:* TV, beverage maker.

INEXPENSIVE

Aachen Hotel   Five minutes from the city center near the Roman Catholic cathedral, this well-run establishment is a landmark building in a conservation district. The modernized bedrooms are comfortable, though a bit plain; hallway bathrooms are adequate and well maintained. Complete with an on-site bar, this efficient hotel offers a good value.

89–91 Mt. Pleasant, Liverpool, Merseyside L3 5TB. ℂ 0151/7093477. Fax 0151/7091126. www.aachenhotel.co.uk. 18 units, 12 with bathroom. £50 ($100) double without bathroom; £60 ($120) with bathroom; £90 ($180) triple with bathroom. Rates include English breakfast. AE, DC, MC, V. Parking £10 ($20). **Amenities:** Breakfast room; bar. *In room:* TV/DVD, coffeemaker, hair dryer, trouser press, safe.

Express by Holiday Inn 𝒦 (*Value*)   Some of the most reasonable accommodations in Liverpool are centrally located at Albert Dock in this reconverted warehouse where many of the original 19th-century architectural features have been preserved. The bedrooms are handsomely though modestly decorated, each spacious and well maintained. Furnishings are functional and harmonious in style. There are several Holiday Inns in Liverpool, but this one is the best. Ask for one of the accommodations opening onto a view of the historic dock area. A continental breakfast is served daily in the Lively Express Bar with its harbor views, and many quality restaurants and bars are found outside the entrance to the hotel.

Britannia Pavillion, Albert Dock, Liverpool LE 4AD. ℂ 0151/7091133. Fax 0151/7091144. www.ichotelsgroup.com. 135 units. £70 ($140) double. AE, DC, MC, V. Parking £13 ($26) nearby. **Amenities:** Restaurant; bar; business services; laundry service. *In room:* TV, coffeemaker, hair dryer, safe.

WHERE TO DINE

For such a world-famous city, Liverpool has yet to play host to a world-class restaurant, but here is the current crop of what is available.

Alma de Cuba 𝒦 (*Finds*) LATIN AMERICAN   It's fiesta time nightly at this hot new dining experience installed on a back street in a former Catholic church from the 1700s. The church now simmers in the lights of thousands of candles as patrons enjoy the best mojitos this side of Havana, the kind Papa Hemingway sipped in the good ol' days. Stained-glass windows and wall-mounted antlers form the backdrop for the ground-floor bar and the mezzanine restaurant. The tapas-style bar menu is a treat unto itself. Here you can order chorizo sausage and cheese or else blue-fin crab croquettes, even tender cumin-laced lamb meatballs. Main dishes have spice and flair, including the slow-roasted duck with star anise and the roasted free-range chicken breast in a pistachio crust. Vegetarians delight in the roasted fig and peach tart tatin with sun-dried tomatoes and a spinach-and-fennel hummus. Serious carnivores will go for the whole, boned, and rolled roast suckling pig.

St. Peter's Church, Seel St. ℂ **0151/7027394**. Reservations recommended. Tapas £2.50–£4.50 ($5–$9); main courses £13–£28 ($26–$56). AE, DC, MC, V. Restaurant daily noon–2:30pm and 6–10:30pm; tapas Sun–Wed noon–10pm, Thurs–Sat noon–7pm.

Bar Italia ITALIAN/CONTINENTAL   In the center of the business district, this bustling little trattoria serves affordable and tasty dishes with a certain Continental flair. Roman art on the walls evokes a Mediterranean feel, and on wintry nights, the brick fireplace adds a cozy touch. The chefs here select the choicest ingredients to turn out savory dishes, such as pan-fried breast of duck with crushed black peppercorns in a cream-and-brandy sauce, or pan-fried filet steak, also with a brandy sauce. A filet of pork is served with a spicy barbecue sauce, and pasta tubes are stuffed with spicy meat and a béchamel sauce.

48A Castle St. ℂ **01512/363375**. Reservations recommended. Main courses £8–£20 ($16–$40). MC, V. Mon–Fri 11:30am–3pm; Tues–Sat 5:30–11pm.

Blue Bar and Grill ✿ ENGLISH/INTERNATIONAL   This is an elegant and sophisticated contemporary restaurant and bar along the historic Liverpool water-front. Guests come here throughout the day for items such as tasty international tapas, vegetarian specialties, fresh fish dishes, and American fusion cookery. Ingredients are market fresh and can be enjoyed informally on the downstairs level or more grandly at the upstairs gallery, where you can order fish steaks and even roast suckling pig. The cafe makes the best sandwiches in town, including the Thanksgiving, made with oven-roasted turkey and served with brambly-apple stuffing. Plates to share include a Med Platter, with a taste of the Mediterranean, including blue-fin tuna salad and a lamb dish. For lunch, many diners drop in for a soup and sandwich.

Edward Pavilion, Albert Dock. ℂ **0151/702-5831**. Reservations not needed. Cafe platters and sandwiches £14–£21 ($28–$42). MC, V. Mon–Thurs 11am–11pm; Fri–Sat 11am–11:45pm.

London Carriage Works ✿ MODERN EUROPEAN   In a double-fronted Geor-gian house, close to the Philharmonic Hall, this enticing restaurant, among the best in Liverpool, gives you a ground-floor restaurant, a basement cafe, and bar. It's really like a brasserie you'd find on the Continent. For the most part, the food is light in tex-ture and full of flavor. A certain robustness permeates the cuisine. Well-crafted mains include chargrilled portobello mushrooms with a butternut squash purée; pan-seared calves' liver with pancetta and balsamic baby onions, or Colchester oysters on ice fla-vored with shallots and white-wine vinegar.

In the Hope Street Hotel, 60 Hope St. ℂ **01517/052222**. Reservations required. Main courses £14–£24 ($28–$48). MC, V. Mon–Fri noon–2:30pm; Mon–Sat 6–10:30pm.

Shangri-La CANTONESE   One of the biggest and most consistently popular restaurants in the city center serves a wide-ranging choice of mostly Cantonese food, with special emphasis on the cuisine of Shanghai. With room for around 300 guests, it contains two separate dining rooms, each with its own bar, and a red, gold, and green decor reminiscent of a Confucian temple. Many regulars opt to begin a meal with dim sum, the delicate steamed or fried dumplings whose variations are almost infinite. Expect well-flavored treatments of virtually every succulently stir-fried veg-etable that's in season at the moment and myriad preparations of fish, shellfish, duck, pork, chicken, and beef. Specialties include fried scallops and asparagus served in a "bird's nest," or sautéed king prawns and cashew nuts.

In the Ashcroft Building, 37 Victoria St. (℗ **01512/550708.** Reservations not necessary. Main courses £8–£15 ($16–$30); fixed-price lunch £7 ($14). AE, DC, MC, V. Sun–Thurs noon–midnight; Fri–Sat noon–3am.

Simply Heathcote's ENGLISH   An outpost of the "chef of the north," Paul Heathcote brings his Lancashire hot pot to the center of Liverpool. It's been an enduring success since opening in 2001. The stylish decor is designed along clean, modern lines, and the freshest of ingredients are used. Try pan-fried sage gnocchi with roast squash in a blue-cheese cream sauce, or peppered filet steak, or even the chargrilled ham steak with a béarnaise sauce. Of course, those old favorites such as Heathcote's black pudding hash browns also appear on the menu. Other temptations include roast pheasant with caramelized spiced apple, beet, and Savoy cabbage.

25 The Strand, Beetham Plaza. (℗ **01512/363536.** Reservations required. Main courses £15–£25 ($30–$50); 2-course fixed-price Sun lunch £16 ($32), 3 courses £18 ($36). MC, V. Mon–Sat noon–2:30pm and 6–10pm; Sun noon–9pm.

Tate Café ENGLISH   When we're in Liverpool, we like to lunch at this cafe connected with its famous gallery. You can launch your day here with a late breakfast or else indulge in a hearty and delightful lunch, with as many cups of freshly brewed coffee as you wish. On summer days try for one of the dockside seats. Freshly made salads with crisp greens and well-stuffed sandwiches are regularly featured, though you may also want to opt for more substantial fare, such as a tender lamb shank with sweet potatoes or grilled salmon with an assortment of vegetables julienne. The grilled chicken breast is another pleasing favorite. Beer, lager, and wine are also served.

The Colonnades, Albert Dock. (℗ **01517/027581.** Reservations not needed. Main courses £11–£20 ($21–$40); sandwiches £5.50–£8.50 ($11–$17). AE, MC, V. Tues–Sun 10am–6pm.

SEEING THE SIGHTS

If you'd like a Beatles-related bus tour, **Cavern City Tours** (℗ **01512/369091;** www.cavernclub.org) presents a daily 2-hour Magical Mystery Tour. This bus tour covers the most famous attractions associated with the Beatles. Tickets cost £13 ($26) and are sold at the Tourist Information Centre at 8 Place, Whitechapel. Tours depart from the same center daily at 2:30pm, or from the Gower Street bus stop at Albert Dock at 2:10pm.

In the Britannia Pavilion at Albert Dock, you can visit the **Beatles Story** (℗ **01517/091963;** www.beatlesstory.com), a museum housing memorabilia of the famous group, including a yellow submarine with live fish swimming past the portholes. It's open daily from 10am to 6pm. Admission is £10 ($20) for adults, £7 ($14) for students, £5 ($10) for children, and a family ticket is £25 ($50).

Everyone's curious about **Penny Lane** and **Strawberry Field.** Actually, the Beatles' song about Penny Lane didn't refer to the small lane itself but to the area at the top of the lane called Smithdown Place. Today, this is a bustling thoroughfare for taxis and buses—hardly a place for nostalgic memories.

John Lennon lived nearby and attended school in the area. When he studied at Art College, he passed here almost every day. To reach Penny Lane and the area referred to, head north of Sefton Park. From the park, Green Bank Lane leads into Penny Lane itself, and at the junction of Allerton Road and Smithdown Road stands the Penny Lane Tramsheds. This is John Lennon country—or what's left of it.

Only the most die-hard fans will want to make the journey to Strawberry Field along Beaconsfield Road, which is reached by taking Menlove Avenue east of the center. Today, you can stand at the iron gates and look in at a children's home run by the Salvation Army. As a child, John played on the grounds, and in 1970 he donated a large sum of money to the home.

Because these sights are hard to reach by public transport and lie outside the center, you may want to take one of the Cavern City Tours (see above) that feature both Strawberry Field and Penny Lane.

A fun thing to do is to take the famous **Mersey Ferry** that travels from the Pier Head to both Woodside and Seacombe. Service operates daily from early morning to early evening throughout the year. Special cruises run throughout the summer including trips along the Manchester Ship Canal. For more information, contact **Mersey Ferries,** Victoria Place, Seacombe, Wallasey (© **01516/390609;** www.merseyferries. co.uk).

Albert Dock ★ Built of brick, stone, and cast iron, this showpiece development on Liverpool's waterfront opened in 1846, saw a long period of decline, and has now been extensively renovated and refurbished. The dockland warehouses now house shops, restaurants, cafes, an English pub, and a cellar wine bar. One pavilion encompasses the main building of the Merseyside Maritime Museum (see below) and another is the home of the Tate Liverpool (see below). Parking is available.

22 Edward Pavilion, Albert Dock, Liverpool L3 4AF. © **01517/087334.** www.albertdock.com. Free admission. Shops daily 10am–6pm; bars and restaurants daily 11am–11pm. Smart Bus from city center.

Cathedral Church of Christ ★★ The great new Anglican edifice overlooking the River Mersey was begun in 1904 and was largely completed 74 years later; it was the last Gothic-style cathedral to be built worldwide. Dedicated in the presence of Queen Elizabeth II in 1978, it is the largest church in England and the fifth-largest in the world. Its vaulting under the tower is 53m (175 ft.) high, the highest in the world, and its length, 186m (619 ft.), makes it one of the longest cathedrals in the world. The organ has nearly 10,000 pipes, the most found in any church. The tower houses the highest (66m/219 ft.) and the heaviest (31 tons) bells in the world, and the Gothic arches are the highest ever built. From the tower, you can see to North Wales.

A visitor center and refectory feature an aerial sculpture of 12 huge sails, with a ship's bell, clock, and light that changes color on an hourly basis. You can enjoy full meals in the charming refectory.

St. James Mt. © **01517/027255.** www.liverpoolcathedral.org.uk. Admission to cathedral free; £3 ($6) donation suggested; tower and embroidery gallery £4.25 ($8.50) adults, £3 ($6) children. Cathedral daily 8am–6pm. Tower Mar–Oct daily 11am–5pm; winter Mon–Sat 10am–3:30pm, Sun noon–2:30pm.

The McCartney House The house where the McCartneys lived in Liverpool before Paul's meteoric rise to superstardom has been purchased by the National Trust. Working from old photographs taken by Paul's brother Michael, the house has been restored to its original 1950s appearance, complete with patterned brown sofa and armchair with white linen antimacassars, where Paul and John scribbled out their first songs. The Chinese willow print wallpaper doesn't reach the corners because the family was too poor to buy enough. Hardly Graceland, it does give an insight into the humble beginnings of one of the world's most famous and influential entertainers. The house is open to the public only through guided tours organized by the National

A Coming Attraction

The pride of Liverpudlians, the **Museum of Liverpool Life** at Albert Dock has closed down for a massive overhaul, with a reopening date set for 2010. The new complex will be a bigger and better version of the former museum, which has been a popular attraction since 1993. The museum is expected to be in the avant-garde of all city museums around the world, tracing the city's unique contribution to Western civilization.

Trust. Four tours depart Wednesday to Sunday at 10:30 and 11:20am from the Conservation Centre at Whitechapel and at 2:15 and 3:55pm from Speke Hall, the Walk. Groups are limited to 14 people at any one time. Book well in advance.

20 Forthlin Rd., Allerton 16. ℂ **0870/900-0256.** www.nationaltrust.org.uk. Admission £13 ($26) adults, £2 ($4) ages 5–16.

Mendips The stucco house where John Lennon lived as a boy was purchased by his wife, Yoko Ono, and was restored by the National Trust. Curators have re-created the late 1950s look of the house, right down to the posters of Rita Hayworth, Elvis Presley, and Brigitte Bardot in Lennon's bedroom. The future music great lived here with his Aunt Mimi and Uncle George, composing his early songs on the front porch and in his bedroom. Admission is by guided tour only. Tours depart Wednesday to Sunday at 10:30am and 11:20am from the Conservation Centre at Whitechapel and at 2:15pm and 3:55pm from Speke Hall, the Walk.

251 Menlove Ave. ℂ **0870/900-0256.** www.nationaltrust.org.uk. Admission £13 ($26) adults, £2 ($4) children 15 and younger. See above for tour times.

Merseyside Maritime Museum 🅐 Set in the historic heart of Liverpool's waterfront, this museum provides a unique blend of floating exhibits, craft demonstrations, working displays, and special events. In addition to restored waterfront buildings, exhibitions present the story of mass emigration through Liverpool in the last century, shipbuilding on Merseyside, the Battle of the Atlantic Gallery, and Transatlantic Slavery. There is wheelchair access.

Albert Dock. ℂ **01514/784499.** www.liverpoolmuseums.org.uk. Free admission. Daily 10am–5pm. Bus: Albert Dock Shuttle from city center.

Roman Catholic Metropolitan Cathedral of Christ the King 🅐🅐 About 1km (a half-mile) away from the Anglican cathedral stands the Roman Catholic cathedral—the two are joined by a road called Hope Street. The construction of the cathedral, designed by Sir Edwin Lutyens, was started in 1930, but when World War II interrupted in 1939, not even the granite-and-brick vaulting of the crypt was complete. At the end of the war it was estimated that the cost of completing the structure as Lutyens had designed it would be some £27 million ($54 million). Architects throughout the world were invited to compete to design a more realistic project to cost about £1 million ($2 million) and to be completed in 5 years. Sir Frederick Gibberd won the competition and was commissioned to oversee the construction of the circular cathedral. Construction was completed in 1967. Today the cathedral offers seating for more than 2,000. Above the altar rises a multicolored glass lantern weighing 2,000 tons and rising to a height of 87m (290 ft.). Called a space-age cathedral, it has a bookshop, a tearoom, and tour guides.

Mt. Pleasant. ℂ **01517/099222**. www.liverpoolmetrocathedral.org.uk. Free admission. Daily 8am–6pm (until 5pm on winter Sun). Bus: Albert Dock Shuttle from city center.

Tate Liverpool ⊛ This museum displays much of the National Collection of 20th-century art, complemented by changing art exhibitions of international standing such as the prints of Joan Miró or the sculptures of the iconoclastic British sculptress Rachel Whiteread. The tourist office has full details on all special exhibitions, or you can call the museum directly.

Albert Dock. ℂ **01517/027400**. www.tate.org.uk/liverpool. Free admission except special exhibitions. Sept–May Thurs–Sun 10am–5:50pm; June–Aug daily 10am–5:50pm. Bus: Albert Dock Shuttle from city center.

Walker Art Gallery ⊛⊛ One of Europe's finest art galleries offers an outstanding collection of European art from 1300 to the present day. The gallery is especially rich in European Old Masters, Victorian and pre-Raphaelite works, and contemporary British art. It also has an award-winning sculpture gallery, featuring works from the 18th and 19th centuries. Seek out, in particular, Simone Martini's *Jesus Discovered in the Temple* and Salvator Rosa's *Landscape with Hermit*. Rembrandt is on show, as is an enticing *Nymph of the Fountain* by Cranach. The work of British artists is strongest here, ranging from *Horse Frightened by a Lion* by Stubbs to *Snowdon from Llan Nantlle* by Richard Wilson. Among the pre-Raphaelites are Ford Madox Brown and W. R. Yeames. The French Impressionists represented include Monet, Seurat, and Degas, among others. Modern British paintings include works by Lucian Freud and Stanley Spencer.

William Brown St. ℂ **01514/784199**. www.liverpoolmuseums.org.uk. Free admission. Daily 10am–5pm. Closed Dec 23–26 and Jan 1.

World Museum Liverpool ⊛ One of Britain's finest museums features collections from all over the world—from the earliest beginnings with giant dinosaurs through centuries of great art and inventions. Reopening in 2005 after a major overhaul, the galleries doubled in space. At the Natural History Centre, you can use microscopes and video cameras to learn about the natural world. Living displays from the vivarium and aquarium form a large part of the collections, and a planetarium features daily programs covering modern space exploration—an armchair tour toward the beginning of the universe and the far-flung reaches of the cosmos. The latest features added are a World Cultures Gallery, with 1,500 amazing artifacts from across the globe, including Oceania, and the Weston Discovery Centre, a hands-on museum. There is a small charge for the planetarium and temporary exhibitions.

William Brown St. ℂ **01514/784393**. www.liverpoolmuseums.org.uk. Free admission. Daily 10am–5pm.

SHOPPING

Pedestrian shopping areas with boutiques, specialty shops, and department stores include Church Street, Lord Street, Bold Street, Whitechapel, and Paradise Street. On the river, Albert Dock also houses a collection of small shops.

For shopping centers, go to **Cavern Walks** on Mathew Street, the heart of Beatle-land (ℂ **01512/369082**), or **Quiggins Centre,** 12–16 School Lane (ℂ **01517/ 092462**).

If you want to buy that special piece of Beatles memorabilia, wander through the **Beatles Shop,** 31 Mathew St. (ℂ **01512/368066**), or the **Heritage Shop,** 12 The Colonnades, Albert Dock (ℂ **01517/097474**).

Tips **In the Footsteps of the Fab Four**

Wherever you turn in Liverpool today, somebody is hawking a Beatles tour. But if you'd like to see a few of the famous spots on your own, stop in at the **Cavern Club,** 8–10 Mathew St., now touted as "The Most Famous Club in the World," and pick up a Cavern City Tour map to find famous Beatles locations in the city center. The Beatles played 292 gigs here between 1961 and 1963. Manager Brian Epstein first saw them here on November 9, 1961, and by December 10, he had signed a contract with the band. For tour information call © **01512/ 361965.**

For a huge selection of British crafts, visit **Bluecoat Display Centre,** College Lane (© **01517/094014**), with its gallery of metal, ceramics, glass, jewelry, and wood pieces by some 350 British craftspeople.

Frank Green's, 97 Oakfield Rd., Anfield (© **01512/603241**), is where you'll find prints by this famous local artist who has been capturing the Liverpool scene on canvas since the 1960s. His work includes city secular buildings, churches, and street life.

A couple of other specialty shops that warrant a visit include **William Forbes,** Unit 19, Sefton Lane Industrial Estate, Maghull (© **0870/752-2444**), which has been making nautical instruments longer than anyone in the known world; and **Thornton's,** 16 Whitechapel (© **01517/086849**), where you can choose from a dizzying selection of Continental and traditional English chocolates, toffees, and mints.

LIVERPOOL AFTER DARK

Liverpool's nightlife is nothing if not diverse. The evening *Liverpool Echo* is a good source of daily information about larger and fine-arts events; the youth-oriented *L: Scene* magazine will provide you with a thorough calendar of club dates and gigs; and the free *City X Blag,* available in most clubs and pubs, will do the same. Available free in gay clubs and pubs, *Pulse* lists gay activities and events throughout the region.

The **Student Entertainment Office** (© **01517/944143**) at the University of Liverpool can tell you about the range of activities sponsored by the school, or you can stop by the student union on Mount Pleasant and check out the bulletin board. Another good place for finding out about the underground scene is **Quiggins Centre,** School Lane (© **01517/092462**).

Open year-round, the **Empire Theatre,** Lime Street, hosts visiting stage productions ranging from dramas and comedies to ballets and tributes. Book through Ticketmaster at © **0870/606-3536.**

Philharmonic Hall, Hope Street (© **01512/102895;** www.liverpoolphil.com), is home to the **Royal Philharmonic Orchestra,** one of the best orchestras outside of London, which usually performs twice weekly. When the orchestra is not on, there are often concerts by touring musicians, and films are sometimes shown as well.

At the **Zanzibar Club,** 43 Seel St. (© **01517/070633**), DJs spin drum-and-bass and hip-hop Wednesday to Monday nights, with the occasional rock or pop booking thrown in for good measure.

Beatles fans flock to the **Cavern Club,** 8–10 Mathew St. (© **01512/369091;** www.cavernclub.org), thinking that this is where the Fab Four appeared. Demolished years ago, the old Cavern Club has faded into history. However, locals still go to this new version to hear live bands on Thursday to Sunday nights (regrettably, not as good as the dear, departed ones). The cover depends on the event and can range from £1 to £8 ($2–$16). For a more nostalgic evening, head for the **Cavern Pub,** 5 Mathew St. (© **01512/364041**), where many English bands got their start before going on to greater glory. The names of the groups who appeared here from 1957 to 1973 are recorded on a plaque.

Lucy in the Sky with Diamonds, Mathew Street (© **0151/236-0096**), also attracts Beatles fans, with its good, reasonably priced food and music. It is decorated with memorabilia from Liverpool's musical past, including pictures, posters, and artifacts from the '60s. Cynthia Lennon (John's first wife) did the terra-cotta decoration around the entrance. It's open Monday to Saturday 8am to 5pm.

A cafe by day, **Baa Bar,** 43–45 Fleet St. (© **01517/088673**), serves an eclectic menu, and free dancing to a DJ brings in a lot of the evening's business. A pub with a Fab Four spin, **Ye Cracke,** 13 Rice St. (© **01517/094171**), was a favorite watering hole of John Lennon in pre- and early Beatles days (but expect regulars to suggest you quit living in the past if you ask about it). Better just soak up the little-changed atmosphere over a pint of Oak Wobbly Bob, Cains, or Haywood Oak.

GAY BARS IN LIVERPOOL

You won't find as frenetic or as varied a nightlife scene in Liverpool as you will in, say, Manchester or Leeds. But something about the rough-and-tumble streets of this monument to the Industrial Revolution makes for hard-party times at some of the city's gay bars. At **Masquerade,** 10 Cumberland St. (© **01512/367786**), a gay version of a Victorian pub, the scene is the most consistently crowded and animated of the several gay bars in its neighborhood near the Moorfields Railway Station, off Dale Street. Come to the street-level bar to drink, talk, and watch the occasional cabaret artiste, whose acts are presented after 8pm every Friday and Saturday (5pm on Sun). Head for the basement-level dance floor for a bit of boogying with the 'Pudlians. At **G-Bar,** Eberle Street (© **01512/364416**), the street level is a pseudo-Gothic piece of kitsch that only a rave party could fully appreciate. The cellar has a floor where crowds of gay and sexually neutral fans dance, dance, dance. There's even a "love lounge" where you may catch up on a bit of dialogue, or whatever, in circumstances that are highly relaxing. Cover is from £5 to £7 ($10–$14), depending on the night of the week.

The **Lisbon,** 35 Victoria St. (© **01512/316831**), is set close to Moorfield Railway Station. This is the quietest and calmest of the pubs listed in this section, luring a nicer blend of men than at some of the seedier gay dives nearby.

3 The Walled City of Chester ⋆⋆⋆

333km (207 miles) NW of London; 31km (19 miles) S of Liverpool; 147km (91 miles) NW of Birmingham

A Roman legion founded Chester on the Dee River in the 1st century A.D. It reached its pinnacle as a bustling port in the 13th and 14th centuries but declined following the gradual silting up of the river. While other walls of medieval cities of England were either torn down or badly fragmented, Chester still has 3km (2 miles) of fortified city walls intact. The main entrance into Chester is Eastgate, which dates only from the 18th century. Within the walls are half-timbered houses and shops, though not all of them date from Tudor days. Chester is unusual in that some of its builders used black-and-white timbered facades even during the Georgian and Victorian eras.

Chester today has aged gracefully and is a lovely old place to visit, if you don't mind the summer crowds. It has far more charm and intimacy than either Liverpool or Manchester and is one of the most interesting medieval cities in England.

ESSENTIALS

GETTING THERE   About 21 trains depart London's Euston Station every 2 hours daily for the 2¼-hour trip to Chester. Trains also run every hour between Liverpool and Chester, a 45-minute ride. For schedules and information, call © **0845/748-4950** or visit **www.nationalrail.co.uk**.

Four **National Express** buses run between Birmingham and Chester; the trip takes 2½ hours. The same bus line also offers service between Liverpool and Chester. It's also possible to catch a National Express coach from London's Victoria Coach Station to Chester. For schedules and information, call © **0870/580-8080** or visit **www. nationalexpress.com**.

If you're driving from London, head north on the M1, then take the M6 at the junction near Coventry. Continue northwest to the junction with the A54, which leads west to Chester.

VISITOR INFORMATION   The **Tourist Information Centre** is on Vicars Lane (© **01244/351609;** www.visitchester.com). It offers a hotel-reservation service as well as information. Arrangements can also be made for coach or walking tours of Chester (including a ghost-hunter tour). It's open April to October Monday to Saturday 9:30am to 5:30pm; off season, Monday to Saturday 9:30am to 5pm.

SPECIAL EVENTS   July is an active time in Chester, as the **Chester Summer Music Festival** (© **01244/320722;** Mon–Sat 10am–5pm) hosts orchestras and other classical performers from around Britain in lunch concerts, with tickets averaging £6 ($12), and small indoor evening concerts, where tickets cost from £6 to £30 ($12–$60). Exact dates are subject to change but usually take place from around July 7 to July 22.

WHERE TO STAY

VERY EXPENSIVE

The Chester Grosvenor and Grosvenor Spa 𝒢𝒢𝒢   This fine, half-timbered, five-story building in the heart of Chester is considered one of the most luxurious hotels in northern England. Owned and named after the family of the dukes of Westminster, its origin can be traced from the reign of Queen Elizabeth I. It has hosted its share of royalty, including Prince Albert, Princess Diana, and Prince Rainier. The high-ceilinged, marble-floored foyer of the hotel, with its 200-year-old chandelier and carved wooden staircase, sets the tone. Each large, well-furnished bedroom is individually styled, with silks from France and handmade furnishings from Italy. Each comes with a heated towel rack, Floris toiletries, and bathrobes.

Eastgate, Chester, Cheshire CH1 1LT. © **01244/324024.** Fax 01244/313246. www.chestergrosvenor.co.uk. 80 units. £195–£285 ($390–$570) double; £395–£850 ($790–$1,700) suite. 1 child 11 and younger stays free in parent's room. AE, DC, MC, V. **Amenities:** 2 restaurants (including Arkle, p. 621); 2 bars; health club; spa; sauna; steam room; business center; room service; laundry service; dry cleaning. *In room:* A/C, TV/DVD, high-speed Internet, CD player, minibar, hair dryer, iron, trouser press, safe.

EXPENSIVE

Crabwall Manor 𝒢𝒢   Chester's premier country-house hotel, the imposing crenelated Crabwall Manor traces its origins from the 16th century, though most of the present building dates from the early 1800s. It has a more peaceful location than

Chester

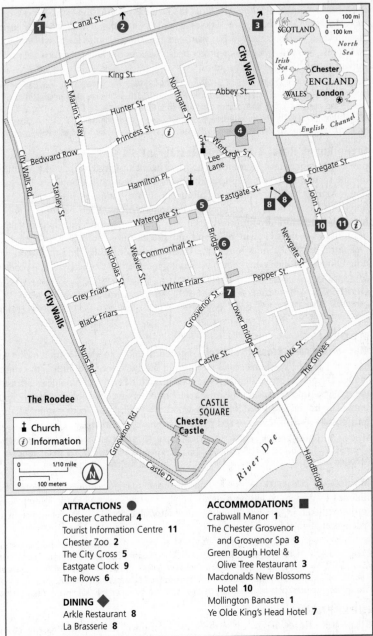

ATTRACTIONS ●
Chester Cathedral **4**
Tourist Information Centre **11**
Chester Zoo **2**
The City Cross **5**
Eastgate Clock **9**
The Rows **6**

DINING ◆
Arkle Restaurant **8**
La Brasserie **8**

ACCOMMODATIONS ■
Crabwall Manor **1**
The Chester Grosvenor
  and Grosvenor Spa **8**
Green Bough Hotel &
  Olive Tree Restaurant **3**
Macdonalds New Blossoms
  Hotel **10**
Mollington Banastre **1**
Ye Olde King's Head Hotel **7**

the Chester Grosvenor, though it lacks the facilities and the top-notch service of its more highly rated competitor. Standing amid 4.4 hectares (11 acres) of private grounds and gardens, the capably managed hotel offers quite large, well-furnished bedrooms. Two rooms have four-poster beds. Relax in the full-service spa after working out in the hotel's aerobics studio.

Parkgate Rd., Mollington, Chester, Cheshire CH1 6NE. ℂ 01244/851666. Fax 01244/851400. www.crabwallmanor hotel.co.uk. 48 units. £110–£170 ($220–$340) double; £160–£270 ($320–$540) suite. Rates include breakfast. Children 15 and younger stay free when sharing room with up to 2 paying adults. AE, DC, MC, V. Take A540 3.5km (2¼ miles) northwest of Chester. **Amenities:** Restaurant; bar; indoor heated pool; health club; Jacuzzi; sauna; steam room; room service; laundry service; dry cleaning. *In room:* A/C, TV, beverage maker, hair dryer, iron, trouser press.

Green Bough Hotel & Olive Tree Restaurant ★★★   *Condé Nast* awarded this property the Johansens Award for "The Most Excellent City Hotel 2004." Maintaining the same inn-keeping standards that won them that honor, hoteliers Janice and Philip Martin have turned this establishment into the most exclusive small luxury hotel in Chester, both for cuisine and accommodations. Each bedroom has been restored and beautifully furnished, each individually designed with elegant fabrics, beautiful wallpapers, Italian tiles, and antique cast-iron or carved wooden beds. Delightful on-site facilities feature the Champagne Lounge Bar and the award-winning Olive Tree Restaurant, known for serving imaginatively conceived local produce.

60 Hoole Rd., Chester, Cheshire CH2 3NL. ℂ 01244/326241. Fax 01244/326265. www.greenbough.co.uk. 15 units. £175–£195 ($350–$390) double; £245–£345 ($490–$690) suite. Rates include English breakfast. AE, DC, MC, V. **Amenities:** Restaurant; bar; room service; laundry service; dry cleaning. *In room:* TV, beverage maker, hair dryer, trouser press, safe (in some).

MODERATE

Macdonald New Blossoms Hotel   This hotel enjoys an ideal location in the very heart of Chester. Blossoms Hotel has been in business since the mid–17th century, though the present structure was rebuilt late in Victoria's day. An old open staircase in the reception room helps set the tone here, but otherwise the public rooms are uninspired. Bedrooms are fitted with dark-wood pieces and firm beds—some of them four-posters (or half-testers)—and many rooms have recently been refurbished.

St. John's St., Chester, Cheshire CH1 1HL. ℂ 01244/323186. Fax 01244/346433. www.macdonaldhotels.com. 67 units. £120 ($240) double; £140 ($280) suite. AE, DC, MC, V. **Amenities:** Restaurant; bar; room service; laundry service; dry cleaning. *In room:* TV, high-speed Internet, beverage maker, hair dryer, iron, trouser press.

Mollington Banastre ★ (Kids)   This Victorian mansion is a gabled house surrounded by gardens. It has been successfully converted into one of the leading country-house hotels in Cheshire. Rooms have comfortable doubles or twin beds; eight are spacious enough for families and two have four-poster beds.

Parkgate Rd., Chester, Cheshire CH1 6NN. ℂ 01244/851471. Fax 01244/851165. www.mollingtonbanastrehotel.com. 63 units. £131–£171 ($262–$342) double. Rates include breakfast. Children 14 and younger stay free in parent's room. AE, DC, MC, V. Take A540 3km (2 miles) northwest of the center of Chester. Or take Junction 16 of M56 and continue for 2.5km (1½ miles). **Amenities:** 2 restaurants; 2 bars; indoor heated pool; squash courts; health club; spa; Jacuzzi; sauna; croquet; salon; room service; laundry service; dry cleaning. *In room:* TV, beverage maker, hair dryer, iron, trouser press.

INEXPENSIVE

Stone Villa Hotel ★ (Value)   On the outskirts of town, just off the A56, this award-winning B&B lies in a tranquil cul-de-sac. In the post-millennium, it has twice won the coveted "Best B&B Award" in Cheshire. In fair weather, the entrance to this old stone-built villa is covered with plants, opening onto a walled floodlit car park in

front. Bedrooms range from standard to executive (the most expensive rooms are larger and contain flatscreen TVs). Their homemade breakfasts are among the best of any B&B in the area, containing everything from porridge drizzled with Drambuie and local honey to vegetarian sausages.

Stone Place, Hoole, Chester CH2 3NR. ℂ **01244/345014.** Fax 01244/345015. www.stonevillahotel.co.uk. 10 units. £75–£85 ($150–$170) double; £90 ($180) triple or family unit. MC, V. **Amenities:** Breakfast room. *In room:* TV, Wi-Fi, fridge, beverage maker, hair dryer, iron, trouser press, safe.

Ye Olde King's Head Hotel ⭐ A 5-minute walk from the bus station, this place is a 16th-century museum piece of black-and-white architecture. From 1598 to 1707, the well-known Randle Holme family, noted heraldic painters and genealogists (some of their manuscripts have made it to the British Museum) occupied it. Since 1717, the King's Head has been a licensed inn. Many of the walls and ceilings are sloped and highly pitched, with exposed beams. The host rents standard-size bedrooms, although they're nowhere near the equal of the public rooms for charm and character.

48–50 Lower Bridge St., Chester, Cheshire CH1 1RS. ℂ **01244/324855.** Fax 01244/315693. 8 units. £60 ($120) double; £80 ($160) family room. Rates include breakfast. AE, DC, MC, V. **Amenities:** Restaurant; bar. *In room:* TV, coffeemaker, hair dryer, trouser press.

WHERE TO DINE

Arkle Restaurant ⭐⭐⭐ *(Finds* ENGLISH/CONTINENTAL   Arkle is the premier restaurant in this part of England. The 45-seat formal, gourmet restaurant has a superb *chef de cuisine* and a talented 40-strong team that uses the freshest ingredients to create modern British and Continental dishes prepared with subtle touches and a certain lightness, complemented by an extensive wine cellar. Tempting main courses include grilled line-caught sea bass with a vegetable compote and shellfish vinaigrette or Lancaise duck with a hot peppercorn crust, served with ravioli and foie gras. Other temptations include breast of grouse with huckleberries. Desserts are equally luscious and tempting. Arkle has an award-winning cheese selection and a choice of at least six unique breads daily. Children 11 and younger aren't permitted in the restaurant, and men are requested to wear a jacket—no jeans allowed.

In the Chester Grosvenor Hotel, Eastgate. ℂ **01244/324024.** Reservations required. 3-course fixed-price menu £55 ($110); fixed-price *menu gourmand* £65 ($130). AE, DC, MC, V. Tues–Sat 7–9:30pm.

La Brasserie ENGLISH/FRENCH   This is the best all-around dining choice in Chester for convenience and quality. Most of the main courses are priced at the lower end of the scale. In a delightful Parisian-style setting, the Brasserie has an extensive à la carte menu to suit most tastes and pocketbooks. You get robust flavors and hearty ingredients. Dishes transcend usual brasserie fare, as evoked by veal kidney with curry, smoked almonds, crispy shallots, and basmati; breast of duck with ravioli, pickled beets and sour cream; and Gloucestershire free-range chicken roasted with seasonal mushrooms.

In the Chester Grosvenor Hotel, Eastgate St. ℂ **01244/324024.** Reservations recommended. Main courses £14–£25 ($28–$50). AE, DC, MC, V. Mon–Fri 7am–10pm; Sat 7:30am–10:30pm; Sun 7:30am–10pm.

SEEING THE SIGHTS

In a big Victorian building opposite the Roman amphitheater, the largest uncovered amphitheater in Britain, the **Tourist Information Centre** (see above), screens a free 20-minute video presentation about Chester and offers guided walking tours of the city; tours depart daily at 10:30am in the winter and at 10:30am and 2pm in the summer.

To the accompaniment of a hand bell, the **town crier** appears at the City Cross—the junction of Watergate, Northgate, and Bridge streets—from May to September noon Tuesday to Saturday to shout news about sales, exhibitions, and attractions in the city.

In the center of town, you'll see the much-photographed **Eastgate clock.** Climb the nearby stairs and walk along the top of the **city wall** for a view down on Chester. Passing through centuries of English history, you'll go by a cricket field, see the River Dee (formerly a major trade artery), and get a look at many 18th-century buildings. The wall also goes past some Roman ruins, and it's possible to leave the walkway to explore them. The walk is charming and free.

The **Rows** are double-decker layers of shops, one tier on the street level, the others stacked on top and connected by a footway. The upper tier is like a continuous galleried balcony—walking in the rain is never a problem here.

Chester Cathedral ✸   The present building, founded in 1092 as a Benedictine abbey, was made an Anglican cathedral church in 1541. Many architectural restorations were carried out in the 19th century, but older parts have been preserved. Notable features include the fine range of monastic buildings, particularly the cloisters and refectory, the chapter house, and the superb medieval woodcarving in the choir (especially the misericords). Also worth seeing are the long south transept with its various chapels, the consistory court, and the medieval roof bosses in the Lady Chapel.

Abbey Sq. Ⓒ 01244/324756. www.chestercathedral.com. Admission £4 ($8) adults, £3 ($6) seniors, £1.50 ($3) children. Mon–Sat 9am–5pm; Sun 12:30–4pm.

Chester Zoo ✸ *Kids*   The Chester Zoo is the largest repository of animals in the north of England. It is also the site of some of the most carefully manicured gardens in the region—44 hectares (110 acres) that feature unusual shrubs, rare trees, and warm-weather displays of carpet bedding with as many as 160,000 plants timed to bloom simultaneously.

Many rare and endangered animal species breed freely here; the zoo is particularly renowned for the most successful colonies of chimpanzees and orangutans in Europe. The water bus, a popular observation aid that operates exclusively in summer, allows you to observe hundreds of water birds that make their home on the park's lake. Also, a monorail stops at the extreme eastern and western ends of the zoo, making visits less tiring. Youngsters love the Monkey's Island exhibit.

Off A41, Upton-by-Chester, 3km (2 miles) north of the town center. Ⓒ 01244/380280. www.chesterzoo.org. Admission £15 ($30) adults, £11 ($22) seniors and children 3–15, £50 ($100) family ticket; free for kids 2 and younger; monorail £2 ($4) adults, £1.50 ($3) children; free for kids 2 and younger. Reduced rates in winter. Daily 10am; closing times vary, call for details. Closed Dec 25–26. From Chester's center, head north along Liverpool Rd.

SHOPPING

Chester has three main shopping areas. The **Grosvenor Precinct** is filled with classy, expensive shops and boutiques that sell a lot of trendy fashion and art items. This area is bordered on three sides by Eastgate, Bridge, and Pepper streets.

For stores with more character and lower prices, explore the **Rows,** a network of double-layered streets and sidewalks with an assortment of shops. The Rows runs along Bridge, Watergate, Eastgate, and Northgate streets. Shopping upstairs is much more adventurous than down on the street. Thriving stores operate in this traffic-free

---

Finds **Following the Antiques Experts**

To find a good deal on antiques, try a quick trip to the town of **Boughton;** every transatlantic dealer seems to go here. Along the A41, a mile from the heart of town, Boughton is filled with antiques shops along Christledon Road. It doesn't have the charm of Chester, but shopping values are often better here than in the more historic city. Some outlets have as many as a dozen showrooms, even though they often are hidden behind rather dreary facades.

---

paradise: tobacco shops, restaurants, department stores, china shops, jewelers, and antiques dealers. For the best look, take a walk on arcaded Watergate Street.

Another shopping area to check out is **Cheshire Oaks,** a huge retail village of 60 shops, mainly clothing, perfume, and shoe outlet stores. Cheshire Oaks is located about 13km (8 miles) north of Chester on the M53.

Chester has a large concentration of antiques and craft shops. Some better ones include **Lowe & Sons,** 11 Bridge St. Row (© **01244/325850**), with antique silver and estate jewelry; the **Antique Shop,** 40 Watergate St. (© **01244/316286**), specializes in brass, copper, and pewter items.

CHESTER AFTER DARK

If you want to relax in a pub, grab a pint of Marston's at the **Olde Custom House,** Watergate Street (© **01244/324435**), a 17th-century customhouse with many original features still intact. The **Pied Bull,** 57 Northgate St. (© **0845/4566399**), is an 18th-century coaching inn where you can still eat, drink, or rent a room. Real ales on tap include Bitter and Traditional. At **Ye Olde King's Head,** Lower Bridge Street (© **01244/324855**), ales are not the only spirits you may encounter. This B&B pub, built in 1622, is said to be haunted by three ghosts; a crying woman and baby in room no. 6 and a ghost whose initials "ST" appear in steam on the bathroom mirror of room no. 4. If you prefer your spirits in a glass, stick to the pub, where you can sip on a Pedigree, or Greenall's Original or Local.

Live Irish music and atmosphere can be sampled at the **Red Lion,** 59 Northgate St. (© **01244/321750**), where you can hear traditional music on Sunday nights for the price of a pint of Guinness. **Alexanders,** Rufus Court off Northgate Street (© **01244/340005**), offers more varied entertainment.

4 Blackpool: Playground of the Midlands

396km (246 miles) NW of London; 142km (88 miles) W of Leeds; 90km (56 miles) N of Liverpool; 82km (51 miles) NW of Manchester

This once-antiquated Midlands resort is struggling to make a comeback by marketing itself to a new generation of vacationers. The result may remind you of Atlantic City or even Las Vegas (with a weird Victorian twist). The city has a winter population of 125,000 that swells to three or four times that in summer.

The country's largest resort makes its living from conferences, tour groups, families, and couples looking for an affordable getaway. Its 11km (7 miles) of beaches, 9.5km (6 miles) of colored lights, and dozens of Disney-like attractions and rides make Blackpool one of the most entertaining (and least apologetic) pieces of razzle-dazzle in England.

Disadvantages include unpredictable weather that brews over the nearby Irish Channel; a sandy, flat-as-a-pancake landscape that's less than inspiring; and a (sometimes undeserved) reputation for dowdiness. But some love the brisk sea air, the architectural remnants of Britain's greatest Imperial Age, the lack of pretentiousness, and the poignant nostalgia that clings to the edges of such places as Coney Island, where people look back fondly on the carefree fun they had in a simpler time.

ESSENTIALS

GETTING THERE   Two trains from Manchester arrive every hour (trip time: 1½ hr.), and one every 2 hours from Liverpool (trip time: 1½ hr.). For information, call ✆ 0845/748-4950 or visit **www.nationalrail.co.uk**.

National Express buses arrive from Chester at the rate of three per day (trip time: 4 hr.); from Liverpool at the rate of six per day (trip time: 3½ hr.); from Manchester, five per day (trip time: 2 hr.); and from London, six per day (trip time: 6½ hr.). For schedules and information, call ✆ **0870/580-8080** or visit **www.nationalexpress.com**.

If you're driving from Manchester, take the M61 north to the M6 then the M55 toward Blackpool. The trip takes about 1 hour.

VISITOR INFORMATION   The helpful **Tourist Office,** located at 1 Clifton St. (✆ **01253/478222;** www.blackpooltourism.com), is open November to March Monday to Friday 9am to 5pm and Saturday 9am to 5pm; April to October, it's Monday to Saturday 9am to 5pm and Sunday 10am to 4pm.

WHERE TO STAY

EXPENSIVE

De Vere Herons' Reach ✮   This hotel symbolizes Blackpool's renewal. It was erected on 96 flat and sandy hectares (236 acres) in 1992, adjacent to the town's zoo and Stanley Park. Designed in a postmodern style that some visitors liken to a mansard-roofed French château, it evokes Las Vegas with a Midlands accent, partly because of the cheerful razzle-dazzle its hardworking staff throws into their jobs and partly because of the many diversions on hand. Bedrooms are traditional but modern, done with light woods; despite their relative youth, they were renovated early in 2003 and offer such extras as PlayStations. Most rooms open onto views of a golf course, and each offers the most comfortable beds in Blackpool hoteldom. Eight rooms are large enough for families.

E. Park Dr., Blackpool, Lancashire FY3 8LL. ✆ **01253/838866.** Fax 01253/798800. www.devereonline.co.uk. 174 units. £128–£233 ($256–$466) double. Rates include breakfast. AE, DC, MC, V. Free parking. **Amenities:** 2 restaurants; 3 bars; indoor heated pool; 18-hole golf course; 3 outdoor tennis courts; 3 squash courts; exercise room; spa; Jacuzzi; sauna; 3 pool tables; salon; room service; babysitting; laundry service; dry cleaning. *In room:* TV, coffeemaker, hair dryer, trouser press.

The Imperial Hotel ✮✮   This is Blackpool's choice address. Noted as a stylish venue for group conferences, this hotel was built by the Victorians—Charles Dickens was a guest—as a massive redbrick pile, and it's still a major landmark in town. Recent renovations added vestiges of 19th-century country-house stateliness to the public areas and some of the bedrooms, and a scattering of artwork related to such genteel pleasures as "the hunt." Accommodations are well appointed and some offer sea views.

N. Promenade, Blackpool, Lancashire FY1 2HB. ✆ **01253/623971.** Fax 01253/751784. www.paramount-hotels. co.uk. 183 units. £149–£195 ($298–$390) double; £223–£254 ($446–$508) suite. Rates include breakfast. AE, DC, MC, V. Parking £2.50 ($5). **Amenities:** 2 restaurants; bar; indoor heated pool; health club; Jacuzzi; sauna; steam room; solarium; room service; babysitting; laundry service. *In room:* TV, Wi-Fi, coffeemaker, hair dryer, trouser press, safe.

The Savoy Hotel *Kids*   The roots of this hotel stretch from the late 19th century, when its redbrick tower and bay windows beckoned vacationers to its seaside location near the North Pier. Since then, ongoing refurbishment has kept the place well carpeted, well painted, and well upholstered. Bedrooms are conservatively up-to-date and restful. Most rooms are quite spacious, many offering sea views, though individual shape and size can vary considerably. Fourteen are large enough to rent to families, and each room has twin or double beds.

Queens Promenade, Blackpool FY2 9SJ. ☎ **01253/352561.** Fax 01253/595549. www.savoyhotelblackpool.com. 131 units. £88–£137 ($176–$274) double; £117–£187 ($234–$374) suite. Rates include breakfast. AE, DC, MC, V. Free parking. **Amenities:** Restaurant; bar; room service; babysitting; laundry service. *In room:* TV, coffeemaker, hair dryer, trouser press.

INEXPENSIVE

The Berwyn Hotel   The plot of land the Berwyn sits on isn't any bigger than those of most of the equivalent guesthouses in Blackpool, but you'll feel that you're in a large estate thanks to its overlooking the city's municipal park, Gynn Gardens. There are many windows set into the ground-floor facade of this house (ca. 1910) that flood the interior with sunlight and views. The hotel was transformed in 1942 into the spacious and much-modernized establishment of today. Bedrooms are simple, even ordinary, but comfortable and restful. Rates decrease for stays of 2 nights or more, and there are senior discounts available. Evening meals, some of the best served within any comparable establishment here, cost a supplement of £10 ($20) per person.

1 Finchley Rd., Gynn Sq., Blackpool FY1 2LP. ☎ **01253/352896.** Fax 01253/594391. www.berwynhotel.co.uk. 20 units. £50–£74 ($100–$148) double. Rates include breakfast. AE, DC, MC, V. Free parking. **Amenities:** Dining room; bar. *In room:* TV, coffeemaker, hair dryer.

Burlees Hotel   There are many dozens of guesthouses similar to the Burlees dotting this urban landscape, but it's a bit better maintained than the norm. Presenting a bow-windowed, stucco-sheathed facade to a neighborhood of equivalent houses, it's run by the Lawrence family. The rooms, if not grand, are comfortably furnished. The garden faces south, a fact prized by those who maintain it.

40 Knowle Ave., North Shore, Blackpool FY2 9TQ. ☎ **01253/354535.** www.burlees-hotel.co.uk. 9 units. £40–£50 ($80–$100) double. Discounts available for stays of 3 nights or more. Rates include breakfast Sat–Sun. AE, DC, MC, V. Free parking. Closed 2 weeks at Christmas. **Amenities:** Dining room; bar; lounge. *In room:* TV, coffeemaker, hair dryer, no phone.

Grosvenor View Guesthouse   Built as halves of a brick-fronted house in the 1930s, these premises were merged by a previous owner into the free-standing guesthouse of today. Public areas are bright thanks to the large bay windows, whose leaded glass breaks sunlight into geometric shapes. Bedrooms are well kept and comfortably furnished. A pair of TV lounges provides places to socialize.

7–9 King Edward Ave., North Shore, Blackpool FY2 9TD. ☎ **01253/352851.** www.grosvenorviewblackpool.com. 15 units, 11 with bathroom. £25 ($50) per person double without bathroom, £30 ($60) with bathroom. Rates include breakfast. AE, MC, V. Free parking. **Amenities:** Dining room; laundry service. *In room:* TV, coffeemaker, no phone.

WHERE TO DINE

Harry Ramsden's SEAFOOD   This is one of the most appealing of a chain of 60 restaurants whose mission is to export British fish and chips to the world at large. The restaurant's allure has resonated deeply in Blackpool, where one of the chain's most opulent restaurants offers a takeout counter selling a portion of haddock and chips suitable for munching during a promenade on the nearby pier. More appealing is the terra-cotta and wood-paneled restaurant, where the nostalgia of yesteryear is preserved with a uniformed staff, big chandeliers, and reminders of the Art Deco age. In addition to fish and chips, there's a steak-and-kidney pudding "filled with savory goodness," plain salmon with tartar sauce or lemon, meat sausages, and vegetarian selections.

60–63 Promenade. © 01253/294386. Reservations recommended. Main courses £7.50–£11 ($15–$22). AE, DC, MC, V Sun–Thurs 11:30am–9pm; Fri–Sat 11:30am–10pm.

Twelve 🕈🕈 ENGLISH/INTERNATIONAL   To eat well in Blackpool, you some-times have to leave town. There is no better choice awaiting you than Twelve, which stands opposite the tallest working windmill in Europe, dating from 1794. Co-own-ers Caroline Upton and Paul Moss converted a former dance studio in this stellar din-ing spot. Although minimalist, the place is stunningly modern in spite of its antique backdrop. The cuisine is perfection itself, even the al dente vegetables in a land of mushy peas, and the specially prepared desserts are divine. High-quality produce is used in the preparation of such dishes as Lakeland red deer or pan-fried breast of wild mallard with a wild mushroom ravioli. Baby Scottish halibut is enticingly served with mussels, and a duo of Bowland forest lamb includes both a pan-fried filet and a braised shoulder, bound together in a rosemary sauce. A winner of a dessert is the banana Betty with crème brûlée, banana ice cream, and a banana milkshake.

Marsh Mill Village, Marsh Mill in Wyre, Fleetwood Rd. S. © 01253/821212. Reservations required. Main courses £15–£25 ($30–$50); fixed-price menu £25 ($50) Fri–Sat only. AE, MC, V. Thurs noon–2pm; Tues–Sun 6:30–10pm. Closed 2 weeks Jan. North of Blackpool on Fleetwood Rd. (from Blackpool head northeast for 8.8km/5½ miles by A584).

WHAT TO SEE & DO

Blackpool is famous for the **Illuminations,** an extravaganza of electric lights affixed to just about any stationary object along the Promenade. It features hundreds of illumi-nated figures, including Diamonds Are Forever, Santa's Workshop, Lamp Lighters, and Kitchen Lites. The tradition began in 1879 with just eight electric lights and has grown with time and technology to include 9.5km (6 miles) of fiber optics, low-volt-age neon tubes, and traditional lamps. The illuminations burn bright into the night from the end of August to the beginning of November. Take a tram ride down the Promenade for a great view of these tacky but festive lights.

Without a doubt, the most famous landmark in this town is the **Tower** along the Central Promenade (© **01253/622242**). In 1891, during the reign of Queen Victo-ria, a madcap idea started floating around to construct a 155m (518-ft.) tower that resembled a half-size version of Paris's Eiffel Tower. The idea was first formally pre-sented to the town leaders of Brighton, who laughed at the idea, thinking it was a joke. But the forward-thinking leaders of Blackpool, when presented the plan, immediately saw the advantages of having such an attraction and quickly approved the tower's con-struction. You be the judge.

Lighted by more than 10,000 bulbs, this landmark has become a tower of fun. This indoor-entertainment complex features the Tower Ballroom (one of the great Victo-rian ballrooms of Britain), the Tower Circus, the Hornpipe Galley, and the Dawn of Time dinosaur ride for kids, as well as the Tower Aquarium. An elevator takes visitors to the top of the Tower for a 97km (60-mile) view. The Tower is open from February to March Wednesday 10am to 5pm, and Saturday and Sunday 10am to 6pm; from April to October, hours are daily from 10am to 11pm. The circus has two to three shows daily (except Fri evening). Tower admission is £8.50 to £13 ($17–$26).

18

The Lake District: Home of the Poets

The Lake District, one of the most beautiful parts of Great Britain, is actually quite small, measuring about 56km (35 miles) wide. Most of the district is in Cumbria, though it begins in the northern part of Lancashire.

Bordering Scotland, the far-northwestern part of the shire is generally divided geographically into three segments: the **Pennines,** dominating the eastern sector (loftiest point at Cross Fell, nearly 900m/3,000 ft. high); the **Valley of Eden;** and the **lakes and secluded valleys of the west,** by far the most interesting.

So beautifully described by the Romantic poets, the area enjoys literary associations with William Wordsworth, Samuel Taylor Coleridge, Charlotte Brontë, Charles Lamb, Percy Bysshe Shelley, John Keats, Alfred Lord Tennyson, and Matthew Arnold. In Queen Victoria's day, the district was one of England's most popular summer retreats.

The largest town is Carlisle, by the Scotland border, which is a possible base for exploring Hadrian's Wall (p. 690)—but for now, we concentrate on the district's lovely lakeside villages. **Windermere** is the best base for exploring the Lake District.

1 Kendal

435km (270 miles) NW of London; 103km (64 miles) NW of Bradford; 116km (72 miles) NW of Leeds; 14km (9 miles) SE of Windermere

The River Kent winds its way through a rich valley of limestone hills and cliffs, known as fells, and down through the "Auld Grey Town" of Kendal, whose moniker refers to the large number of gray stone houses found in and about the town. Many visitors to the Lake District simply pass through Kendal on their way to more attractive destinations—the town is a gateway rather than a true stopping place. It has never depended entirely on tourism. This fact should not deter you, however, from taking a bit of time to discover some of this market town's more intriguing areas.

Kendal contains the ruins of a castle where Catherine Parr, the last wife of Henry VIII, was allegedly born. Recent speculation about her actual birthplace has led to a clouding of the historical record. Even if she wasn't born here, it is still said that she most likely lived at the castle at some time in her life. Among other historic sites, Kendal has a 13th-century parish church that merits a visit.

Today, Kendal is famous for its mint cake and its surrounding limestone fells, which offer excellent vistas of the area and make for great hikes.

ESSENTIALS

GETTING THERE Trains from London's Euston Station do not go directly to Kendal; seven daily trains arrive in Oxenholme, about 2.5km (1½ miles) away. From here, you'll be able to take a cab or board one of the local trains that leave approximately every hour to Kendal proper (trip time from Kendal to London: 3½ hr.). For information, call © **0845/748-4950** or visit **www.nationalrail.co.uk**.

To Kendal from London by bus, take one of the three daily National Express buses (trip time: 7 hr.). For schedules and information, call **National Express** at © **0870/580-8080** or visit **www.nationalexpress.com**.

If driving, take the M1 out of London, and then the M6 to Kendal (trip time: 5 hr.).

VISITOR INFORMATION   The **Tourist Information Centre of Kendal,** Town Hall, Highgate (© **01539/725758**), is open Monday to Saturday 9am to 5pm.

WHERE TO STAY

The Castle Green Hotel in Kendal ✦   Set on 5.6 hectares (14 acres) of woodlands and gardens, this Best Western affiliate is one of the finest hotels in the area. Though it looks like a rambling country estate, it was once a series of offices that have been cleverly converted into comfortable bedrooms. Each room is stylish and well furnished, many opening onto panoramic views. The best, albeit most expensive, accommodations are the executive studio suites with a lot of extra space. Guests enjoy free membership in the hotel's health club. The Castle Green also has one of the best pubs, Alexander's, and one of the best restaurants, Greenhouse, in the area. On the downside, the staff could be more cordial.

Kendal, Cumbria LA9 6BH. © **01539/734000.** Fax 01539/735522. www.castlegreen.co.uk. 100 units. £138 ($276) double; £178 ($356) suite. Rates include English breakfast. AE, DC, MC, V. Signposted from the M6, Junction 37. **Amenities:** Restaurant; pub; indoor heated pool; fitness center; steam room; solarium; salon; room service; laundry service; dry cleaning. *In room:* TV, beverage maker, hair dryer.

Garden House Hotel   Built in 1812, this is an inviting Georgian country house. It was once a convent for local nuns and has been a hotel for the past 30 years or so. It's nestled in .8 hectare (2 acres) of walled garden and green pastureland, and is perfectly serene. Some guest rooms have fireplaces; one has a four-poster bed. The public areas include a somewhat formal sitting room, an informal lounge and bar with lots of seating, an elegant breakfast room with a dark-mahogany fireplace, and a restaurant conservatory.

Fowling Lane, Kendal, Cumbria LA9 6PH. © **01539/731131.** Fax 01539/764216. www.gardenhousehotel.co.uk. 11 units. £89 ($178) double; £110 ($220) double with four-poster bed; £125 ($250) triple. Rates include English breakfast. MC, V. **Amenities:** Restaurant; bar; croquet lawn; car rental; room service. *In room:* TV, beverage maker, hair dryer, trouser press.

WHERE TO DINE

Déjà Vu TRADITIONAL & MODERN FRENCH   The interior of this small and cozy French cabaret is inspired by one of van Gogh's landscape paintings. People come for good food and a fun time. A wide range of appetizers evokes a taste of Paris, featuring fresh scallops *mille-feuille* with a basil cream sauce, or filet of venison with a red-wine-and-raspberry sauce. Follow with such mains as pan-fried sea bass filet with roasted cherry tomatoes or pan-roasted duck breast cooked pink and served with a blueberry sauce. Desserts feature many classic French favorites, including the delicious peach tartlet.

124 Stricklandgate. © **01539/724843.** Reservations recommended. Main courses £9.50–£15 ($19–$30). AE, DC, MC, V. Mon–Sat noon–2pm; daily 5:30–10pm.

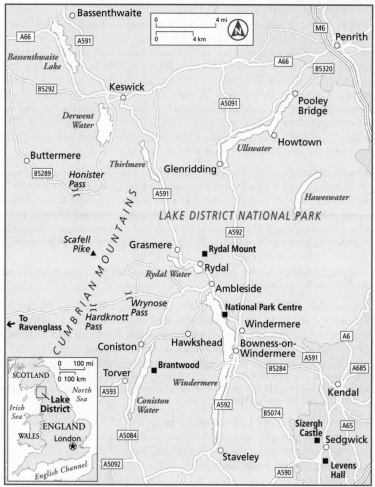

The New Moon ✦ INTERNATIONAL   This bistro cooks up the best food in Kendal. Set in a building that's more than 250 years old and was once a grocery store, the dining room offers patrons a close, friendly, and informal environment. The food is well crafted without being gimmicky. The owners take pride in offering market-fresh ingredients when available. Try such dishes as braised local lamb shank with roasted root vegetables or roast turkey with chestnut stuffing. A special delight is the pan-fried duck breast in a crème de cassis jus. For dessert, try Bailey's crème brûlée with fresh fruits, or else the sticky toffee pudding with toffee sauce.

129 Highgate. ✆ **01539/729254**. Reservations not needed. Main courses £12–£14 ($24–$28); early-bird dinners £10–£13 ($20–$26) before 6:30pm Tues–Fri. MC, V. Tues–Fri 11:30am–2:30pm and 5:30–9pm; Sat 11:30am–2:30pm and 6–9:30pm.

SEEING THE SIGHTS

Abbot Hall Art Gallery   The Georgian elegance of Kendal's Abbot Hall Art Gallery has created an ideal setting for its display of fine art. Paintings by the town's famous son, 18th-century portrait painter George Romney, fill the walls of rooms furnished by Gillows of Lancaster. A major display of work by 20th-century British artists such as Graham Sutherland, John Piper, and Ben Nicholson is on permanent display. Visitors can see the region through the eyes of the many painters who have been inspired by the landscapes in another of the gallery's permanent exhibitions housed in the Peter Scott Gallery.

Kirkland. ✆ **01539/722464**. www.abbothall.org.uk. Admission £5 ($10) adults, £4 ($8) children, £14 ($28) family ticket. Apr–Oct Mon–Sat 10:30am–5pm (until 4pm Nov–Mar). Closed Dec 22–Jan 15.

Kendal Museum   One of England's oldest museums offers a journey of discovery from Roman times to the present. A natural history section includes a nature trail from mountaintop to lakeside, bringing you face to face with many of the inhabitants of the area. The World Wildlife Gallery displays a vast collection of exotic animals. One of the exhibitions introduces visitors to the fell-tops' best-known visitor, Alfred Wainwright, who walked, talked, and wrote with a passion and flair about the region. Wainwright worked diligently until his death in 1991.

Station Rd. ✆ **01539/721374**. www.kendalmuseum.org.uk. Admission £2.80 ($5.60) adults, £2.20 ($4.40) seniors, free for children. Thurs–Sat noon–5pm.

Levens Hall   This Elizabethan mansion was constructed in the 1500s by James Bellingham. Today, the house is filled with Jacobean furniture and a working model steam collection. The estate also has a **topiary garden** 🏵🏵 dating from 1692, with a host of yews and box hedges clipped into a variety of intriguing shapes.

Levens Park, Levens (6.5km/4 miles south of Kendal). ✆ **01539/560321**. www.levenshall.co.uk. Admission house and gardens £10 ($20) adults, £4.50 ($9) children, £25 ($50) family ticket (2 adults, 3 children); gardens only £7 ($14) adults, £3.50 ($7) children, £19 ($38) family ticket (2 adults, 3 children). Apr to mid-Oct Sun–Thurs noon–5pm (gardens open at 10am). Last entry at 4:30pm.

Museum of Lakeland Life   From the re-creation of a Victorian Kendal street, complete with pharmacy and market, visitors can discover the lost crafts and trades of the region and the ways of life that accompanied them.

Kendal, Cumbria. ✆ **01539/722464**. www.lakelandmuseum.org.uk. Admission £3.75 ($7.50) adults, £2.75 ($5.50) children, £11 ($22) family (2 adults, 4 children). Mon–Sat 10:30am–4pm (until 5pm Apr–Oct). Closed mid-Dec to mid-Jan.

Sizergh Castle   The castle has a fortified tower that dates from the 14th century. Inside, visitors can see a collection of Elizabethan carvings and paneling, fine furniture, and portraits. The complete garden, largely from the 18th century, incorporates a rock garden and a famous planting of hardy ferns and dwarf conifers. The castle is surrounded by a show of fiery colors in autumn.

5.5km (3½ miles) south of Kendal (northwest of interchange A590/591). ✆ **01539/560951**. www.nationaltrust. org.uk. Admission £6.70 ($13) adults, £3.30 ($6.60) children, £17 ($34) family ticket (2 adults, 2 children); shop and gardens £4 ($8) adults, £2 ($4) children. Apr–Oct Sun–Thurs 1–5pm; shop and gardens Sun–Thurs 11am–5pm.

KENDAL AFTER DARK

One of the best entertainment centers in the Lake District is the **Brewery Arts Centre,** Highgate (✆ **01539/725133;** www.breweryarts.co.uk), which includes two cinemas, a theater, the Green Room restaurant, two cafe bars, and other venues in a converted brewery. The box office for all attractions is open Monday to Saturday 10am to 8:30pm and Sunday 11am to 8:30pm.

2 Windermere & Bowness ★★

441km (274 miles) NW of London; 16km (10 miles) NW of Kendal; 89km (55 miles) N of Liverpool

The largest lake in England is Windermere, whose eastern shore washes up on the town of Bowness (or Bowness-on-Windermere), with the town of Windermere 2.5km (1½ miles) away. From either town, you can climb **Orrest Head** in less than an hour for a panoramic view of the Lakeland. From that vantage point, you can even view **Scafell Pike,** rising to a height of 963m (3,210 ft.)—it's the tallest peak in all of England.

ESSENTIALS
GETTING THERE   Trains to Windermere meet the main line at Oxenholme for connections to both Scotland and London. You can obtain information about rail services in the area by calling the railway information line at ⓒ **0845/748-4950,** or visit **www.nationalrail.co.uk**. Frequent connections are possible throughout the day. To get to Bowness and its ferry pier from Windermere, turn left from the rail terminal and cross the center of Windermere until you reach New Road, which eventually changes its name to Lake Road before it approaches the outskirts of Bowness. It's about a 20-minute walk downhill. The Lakeland Experience bus also runs from the Windermere Station to Bowness every 20 minutes.

The **National Express** bus link, originating at London's Victoria Coach Station, serves Windermere, with connections also to Preston, Manchester, and Birmingham. For schedules and information, call ⓒ **0870/580-8080** or visit **www.national express.com**. Local buses operated mainly by **Stagecoach** (ⓒ **0870/608-2608;** www. stagecoachbus.com) go to Kendal, Ambleside, Grasmere, and Keswick. Call for information on various routings within the Lake District.

If you're driving from London, head north on the M1 and the M6 past Liverpool until you reach the A685 junction heading west to Kendal. From Kendal, the A591 continues west to Windermere.

VISITOR INFORMATION   The **Tourist Information Centre** at Windermere is on Victoria Street (ⓒ **01539/446499;** www.visitwindermere.co.uk). It's open November to March Monday to Saturday 9am to 5pm and Sunday 10am to 5pm, and April to October Sunday to Thursday 9am to 6pm and Friday to Saturday until 6:30pm.

WHERE TO STAY
EXPENSIVE
Holbeck Ghyll ★★★   This is the most tranquil oasis in the area and offers the most refined cuisine. Overlooking Lake Windermere, this country-house hotel was once a 19th-century hunting lodge owned by Lord Lonsdale, one of the richest men in Britain, and has a high price tag but offers a lot for the money. An inglenook fireplace welcomes visitors. The most elaborate room is a honeymoon and anniversary room that has a four-poster bed and a bathroom with a spa tub for two. But each unit is fitted with a luxury bed, often crowned by a canopy or a padded headboard. Rooms are individually designed, coming in various shapes and sizes, and most of them open onto a view of the lake. Six rooms are in a separate lodge added in 1998, and these are even finer than the rooms in the main building. Lodge rooms are interconnecting with

panoramic lake views, individual balcony or patio areas, and fresh flowers; four units have kitchenettes. Luxurious bathrooms have separate shower cubicles, as well as a tub. Children 7 or younger are not welcome in the restaurant.

Holbeck Lane (on A591 5.5km/3½ miles northwest of town center), Windermere, Cumbria LA23 1LU. ℭ 01539/432375. Fax 01539/434743. www.holbeckghyll.com. 21 units. £115–£140 ($230–$280) per person double; from £145 ($290) per person suite. Rates include English breakfast and dinner. Children 16 and younger stay for half-price when sharing parent's room. AE, DC, MC, V. **Amenities:** Restaurant; bar; putting green; tennis court; gym; spa; croquet lawn; room service; laundry service; dry cleaning. *In room:* TV/DVD, CD player, kitchenette (4 units), beverage maker, hair dryer, trouser press.

Langdale Chase Hotel ⭐⭐   A grand old lakeside house, this hotel resembles a villa on Italy's Lake Como. It has better rooms than Miller Howe (see below), though the food is not as good. The bedrooms contain excellent furniture, and many were recently refurbished. Most of the bedrooms open onto panoramic views of the lake. Five bedrooms are in a converted cottage on the grounds, and these are equal in comfort to those units in the main building. An oft-requested bedroom lies over the boathouse on the lake. Bathrooms are tiled and come with adequate shelf space and combination tub/shower. The interior of the Victorian stone château, with its many gables, balconies, large mullioned windows, and terraces, is a treasure-trove of antiques. The main lounge hall looks like a setting for one of those English drawing-room comedies. On the walls are distinctive paintings, mostly Italian primitives, though one is alleged to be a Van Dyck.

On A591 (3km/2 miles north of town, toward Ambleside), Windermere, Cumbria LA23 1LW. ℭ 01539/432201. Fax 01539/432604. www.langdalechase.co.uk. 27 units. £105–£135 ($210–$270) per person double. Rates include breakfast and dinner. AE, DC, MC, V. **Amenities:** Restaurant; bar; croquet lawn; room service; babysitting; laundry service. *In room:* TV, beverage maker, hair dryer, iron.

Lindeth Fell Hotel ⭐   High above the town is this traditional large Lakeland house, built of stone and brick in 1907. Many of its rooms overlook the handsome gardens and the lake. The owners, the Kennedys, run the place more like a country house than a hotel, achieving an atmosphere of comfort in pleasingly furnished surroundings. Bedrooms open onto beautiful views, especially on the lakeside of the house; many are quite spacious, others are snug, but all have comfortable beds.

Lyth Valley Rd. (on A5074 1.5km/1 mile south of Bowness), Bowness-on-Windermere, Cumbria LA23 3JP. ℭ 01539/443286. Fax 01539/447455. www.lindethfell.co.uk. 14 units. £156–£220 ($312–$440) double. Rates include breakfast and dinner. MC, V. Closed Jan–Feb 14. **Amenities:** Restaurant; bar; putting green; croquet lawn; room service; laundry service; dry cleaning. *In room:* TV, Wi-Fi, beverage maker, hair dryer, trouser press.

The Linthwaite House Hotel ⭐   This hotel, built in 1900, is surrounded by woodlands and gardens, with a panoramic view of Lake Windermere, Bell Isle, and the distant mountains. The bedrooms are beautifully decorated and offer many amenities, including bathrobes and satellite TVs. As befits its former role as an Edwardian gentleman's house, this hotel has individually decorated bedrooms that come in various shapes and sizes. All rooms are fitted with sumptuously comfortable beds and come with a tub/shower combination.

Crook Rd., Bowness-on-Windermere, Cumbria LA23 3JA. ℭ 01539/488600. Fax 01539/488601. www.linthwaite.com. 27 units. £154–£310 ($308–$620) double; £280–£330 ($560–$660) suite. Rates include English breakfast. AE, DC, MC, V. **Amenities:** Restaurant; bar; complimentary use of nearby spa; room service; laundry service; dry cleaning. *In room:* TV, Wi-Fi, beverage maker, hair dryer, trouser press.

Miller Howe Hotel ☆☆   International guests come to this inn, which bears the unique imprint of its creator, former actor John Tovey, who treats his guests as if they had been invited to a house party. His country estate overlooks Lake Windermere (with views of the Langdale Pikes) and offers stylish accommodations and exquisite cuisine. The house was built in 1916 in the Edwardian style, sitting on 2.2 hectares (5½ acres) of statue-dotted garden and parkland. Each of the large, graciously furnished rooms is supplied with binoculars to help guests fully enjoy the view; other amenities include CD players and umbrellas. Beds are sumptuous, often canopy-draped, each with colorful spreads and padded headboards. There are even copies of *Punch* from the 1890s.

The chef nightly prepares a five-course menu gourmand that is one of the best in the area.

Rayrigg Rd. (on A592 between Windermere and Bowness), Windermere, Cumbria LA23 1EY. ℂ **01539/442536**. Fax 01539/445664. www.millerhowe.com. 16 units. Winter £95–£145 ($190–$290) per person per night; high season £105–£180 ($210–$360). Rates include English breakfast and 5-course dinner. AE, MC, V. **Amenities:** Restaurant; 3 lounges; conservatory room; croquet lawn; room service; laundry service; dry cleaning. *In room:* TV, CD player, hair dryer, trouser press.

The Samling ☆☆☆ *(Finds)*   Standing on 27 hectares (67 acres) opening onto panoramic views of Lake Windermere, this hotel was fashioned from a late-18th-century stone-built manse with three gables set off with scalloped fretwork. Wordsworth used to come here to pay his rent on Dove Cottage in neighboring Grasmere. Samling bills itself as an "un-country house" hotel, free of "snooty nostalgic stuff." The tranquil hotel is becoming a secret address for the rich and famous such as soccer star David Beckham. Rooms are more spacious in a converted stable block; you'll think you're at a ski lodge. In the main building bedrooms have more of a traditional British aura. Even if not a guest, consider an elegant £55 ($110) set-price gourmet dinner here.

Ambleside Rd., Windermere, Cumbria LA23 1LR. ℂ **015394/31922**. www.thesamling.com. 11 suites. £200–£430 ($400–$860) double. Rates include breakfast. AE, DC, MC, V. **Amenities:** Restaurant; bar; laundry service. *In room:* TV, hair dryer.

MODERATE

Cedar Manor ☆   One of the most desirable country-house hotels in the area is Cedar Manor. Originally built in 1860, with gables and chimneys, it was the summer getaway home for a wealthy industrialist from Manchester. But since those times, it has been converted into a hotel of exceptional merit with well-furnished and spacious bedrooms. Each room is individually designed and well maintained; some have canopied or four-poster beds. The hotel takes its name from a cedar tree, perhaps from India, which has grown in the garden for some 2 centuries.

Ambleside Rd. (A591), Windermere, Cumbria LA23 1AX. ℂ **01539/443192**. Fax 01539/445970. www.cedarmanor. co.uk. 11 units. £86–£100 ($172–$200) double; £110–£140 ($220–$280) suite. Rates include breakfast. 2-night minimum stay Sat–Sun. AE, MC, V. **Amenities:** Restaurant; lounge; laundry service; dry cleaning. *In room:* TV, Wi-Fi, fridge (in some), beverage maker, hair dryer.

Lindeth Howe   This is a country house in a scenic position above Lake Windermere, with 2.4 hectares (6 acres) of garden. Part stone and part red brick, with a roof of green Westmoreland slate, the house was built for a wealthy mill owner in 1879, but its most famous owner was Beatrix Potter, who installed her mother here while she lived across the lake at Sawrey. The present owner, Norman Stoller, has furnished it in fine style. Nine of the bedrooms have lake views and are comfortably furnished. Three rooms have handsome four-poster beds, and some rooms have spa bathrooms. Three rooms are large enough for families.

Longtail Hill, Storrs Park, Bowness-on-Windermere, Cumbria LA23 3JF. © **01539/445759**. Fax 01539/446368. www. lindeth-howe.co.uk. 36 units. £110–£250 ($220–$500) double. Rates include breakfast. AE, MC, V. Take B5284 south of Bowness. **Amenities:** Restaurant; bar; indoor heated pool; health club; sauna; solarium; room service; laundry service; dry cleaning. *In room:* TV, beverage maker, hair dryer, iron (in some rooms), trouser press.

INEXPENSIVE

Beaumont Hotel   This stone-sided Lakeland villa, originally built in the 1850s, is on a quiet residential street about a minute's walk from Windermere's commercial center. Mr. and Mrs. John Dixon massively upgraded what had been a rather dowdy interior. Each of the bedrooms is named after one of the characters in the Beatrix Potter sagas (our favorite is Jemima PuddleDuck) and contains either some kind of elaborate canopy or a four-poster bed, fitted with a quality mattress. All the accommodations have been refurbished, with showers, carpets, and curtains. No meals are served other than breakfast, so the owners keep local restaurant menus on hand for their guests to consult. Children 9 and younger are not accepted.

Holly Rd., Windermere, Cumbria LA23 2AF. © **01539/447075**. Fax 01539/488311. www.lakesbeaumont.co.uk. 10 units. £80–£115 ($160–$230) double. Rates include English breakfast. MC, V. **Amenities:** Complimentary use of nearby health club. *In room:* TV, beverage maker, hair dryer.

Fir Trees ⚔   One of the finest guesthouses in Windermere, this well-run inn provides hotel-like standards at B&B prices. Opposite St. John's Church, halfway between the villages of Bowness and Windermere, Fir Trees is a Victorian house furnished with antiques. Proprietors Bob and Bea Towers offer a warm welcome and beautifully maintained bedrooms. Some units are large enough for families; a few have four-poster beds. The Towers provide their guests with information on restaurants, country pubs, or where to go and what to see.

Lake Rd., Windermere, Cumbria LA23 2EQ. © **01539/442272**. Fax 01539/442512. www.fir-trees.com. 9 units. £32–£48 ($64–$96) per person double. Rates include English breakfast. MC, V. **Amenities:** Free use of nearby health club. *In room:* TV, beverage maker, hair dryer.

WHERE TO DINE

Lucy 4 at the Porthole BRITISH/FRENCH   In a white-painted Lakeland house near the center of town, this restaurant serves French, English, and Italian cuisine. Amid a decor enhanced by rows of wine and liqueur bottles and nautical accessories, you can enjoy well-flavored specialties that change with the seasons. Try the ballottine of Lakeland lamb (lamb shoulder infused with fresh rosemary, plus a touch of anchovy and garlic, braised in red wine). Also excellent is the filet of beef Rossini chargrilled to your liking and topped with a Madeira-scented chicken liver parfait. Crispy sea bass is coated with a fragrant sauce of homemade Thai red curry and cooked with coconut milk, lemon grass, and ginger, with a touch of chili.

3 Ash St. © **01539/442793**. Reservations recommended. Main courses £12–£17 ($24–$34). AE, DC, MC, V. Mon–Fri 5–10:30pm; Sat–Sun noon–10:30pm.

Queens Head ⚔ MODERN BRITISH   Once voted Cumbria Dining Pub of the year, and still as good, this unusual and popular 17th-century coaching inn uses a huge Elizabethan four-poster bed as its serving counter and has other eclectic antiques among its traditional wooden bar furniture. The menu, which changes every 6 weeks, also combines common items in unusual ways, making traditional dishes more exotic. Some of the best main dishes include slow-roasted breast of Barbary duck and confit of the leg served with a plum sauce, or else a risotto of wild mushrooms and roast salsify with a poached egg and Parmesan crisp. Finish with one of their lovely puddings, perhaps an orange-and-chocolate tart with a Grand Marnier zabaglione (whipped egg dessert). There's a full bar and a good wine selection, or you can quaff a pint of Mitchell's Lancaster Bomber, Tetley's, or Boddington's. Looking for a place to stay? The Queens Head has nine well-furnished rooms with doubles priced at £105 ($210).

A582 north of Windermere, Cumbria LA23 1TW. (℃ 01539/432174. Fax 01539/431938. Reservations recommended. Main courses £8.50–£16 ($17–$32); fixed-price menu £19 ($38). MC, V. Daily noon–2pm and 6:30–9pm.

FAVORITE LOCAL PUBS

Drive a short distance south of Windermere to Cartmel Fell, situated between the A592 and the A5074, and you'll find a pub-lover's dream. The **Mason Arms,** Strawberry Bank (℃ **01539/568486**), is a Jacobean pub with original oak paneling and flagstone floors. Sturdy, comfortable wooden furniture is spread through a series of five rooms in which you can wander or settle. The outside garden, attractive in its own right, offers a dramatic view of the Winster Valley beyond. The pub offers so many beers that they have a 24-page catalog to help you order, plus a creative, reasonable menu that includes several tasty vegetarian options. Beer prices start at £2.50 ($5).

Southeast of the village, off the A5074 in Crosthwaithe, the **Punch Bowl** (℃ **01539/568234**) is a 16th-century pub; the central room features a high-beamed ceiling with upper minstrel galleries on two sides. Outdoors, a stepped terrace on the hillside offers a tranquil retreat. Theakston's Best Bitter, Jennings Cumberland, and Cocker Hoop are available on tap.

Established in 1612, the **Hole in t' Wall,** Lowside (℃ **01539/443488**), is the oldest pub in Bowness, a real treasure for its character and friendliness. The barroom is decorated with a hodgepodge of antiquated farming tools, and there's a large slate fireplace lending warmth on winter days plus a good selection of real ales on tap. The menu, determined daily, illustrates real ingenuity in an eclectic mix of vegetarian, seafood, and local game dishes. A small flagstone terrace in the front encourages lingering on warmer days and evenings.

EXPLORING THE AREA

There is regular **steamer service** around Windermere, the largest of the lakes (about 17km/11 miles long). It's also possible to take a steamer on Coniston Water, a small lake that Wordsworth called "a broken spoke sticking in the rim." Coniston Water is a smaller and less heavily traveled lake than Windermere.

Launch and steamer cruises depart from Bowness daily throughout the year operated by **Windermere Lake Cruises Ltd.** (℃ **01539/443360;** www.windermere-lakecruises. co.uk). Round-trip service is available among Bowness, Ambleside, and Lakeside at rates ranging from £8 to £14 ($16–$28) for adults and £4.50 to £7.50 ($9–$15) for children; it's £22 to £37 ($44–$74) for a family ticket. There is a 45-minute "Island Cruise" for £6 ($12) for adults, £3 ($6) for children, and £16 ($32) for a family ticket.

At Lakeside, you can ride a steam train to Haverthwaite. A combination boat/train ticket is £14 ($28) for adults, £8 ($16) for children, and £35 ($70) for a family ticket.

An attraction at Lakeside, near Newby Bridge, is the **Aquarium of the Lakes** (℃ **01539/530153;** www.aquariumofthelakes.co.uk), with an exhibit of fish and wildlife. The aquarium is open daily from 9am to 4pm November to March, and from 9am to 5pm April to October. Combination boat/admission tickets from Ambleside are £20 ($40) for adults, £11 ($22) for children, and £57 ($114) for a family ticket; from Bowness, tickets are £14 ($28) for adults, £8 ($16) for children, and £43 ($86) for a family ticket. Aquarium-only admission is £7.50 ($15) for adults, £5 ($10) for children, and £22 ($44) for a family ticket (two adults and two children).

Directly south of Windermere, **Bowness** is an attractive old lakeside town with lots of Victorian architecture, much of it dating from Queen Victoria's day. This has been an important center for boating and fishing for a long time, and you can rent boats of all descriptions to explore the lake.

Windermere Steamboat Centre ⍟   This museum houses the finest collection of steamboats in the world. Important examples of these elegant Victorian and Edwardian vessels have been preserved in working order. The steamboats are exhibited in a unique wet dock where they are moored in their natural lakeside setting. The fine display of touring and racing motorboats in the dry dock links the heyday of steam with some of the most famous names of powerboat racing and the record-breaking attempts on Windermere, including Sir Henry Segrave's world water-speed record set in 1930.

Each boat has an intriguing story, including the SL *Dolly*, built around 1850 and probably the oldest mechanically driven boat in the world. The vessel was raised from the lake bed of Ullswater in 1962 and, following restoration, ran for 10 years with its original boiler. The *Dolly* is still steamed on special occasions.

The SL *Swallow* (1911) is steamed most days; a 50-minute trip on the lake costs £5.50 ($11) for adults and £2.50 ($5) for children. The crew serves tea or coffee made using the Windermere steam kettle.

Rayrigg Rd. ✆ 01539/445565. www.steamboat.co.uk. Admission £5 ($10) adults, £2.50 ($5) children, £9.50 ($19) family ticket. Daily 10am–5pm. Closed Nov to mid-Mar.

The World of Beatrix Potter   This exhibit uses the latest technology to tell the story of Beatrix Potter's fascinating life. A video wall and special film describe how her tales came to be written and how she became a pioneering Lakeland farmer and conservationist. There is also a shop with a wealth of top-quality Beatrix Potter merchandise, from Wedgwood ceramics to soft toys. It's mobbed on summer weekends; try to come at any other time.

The Old Laundry, Bowness-on-Windermere. ✆ 01539/488444. www.hop-skip-jump.com. Admission £6 ($12) adults, £5 ($10) children. Easter–Oct daily 10am–5:30pm; rest of year daily 10am–4:30pm. Take A591 to Lake Rd. and follow the signs.

3 Ambleside & Rydal

448km (278 miles) NW of London; 23km (14 miles) NW of Kendal; 6.5km (4 miles) N of Windermere

An idyllic retreat at the north end of Lake Windermere, Ambleside is just a small village, but it's one of the major places to stay in the Lake District, attracting pony trekkers, hikers, and rock climbers. It's wonderful in warm weather and even through late autumn, when it's fashionable to sport a raincoat.

Between Ambleside and Wordsworth's former retreat at Grasmere is Rydal, a small village on one of the smallest lakes, Rydal Water. The village is noted for its sheepdog trials at the end of summer. It's 2.5km (1½ miles) north of Ambleside on the A591.

ESSENTIALS

GETTING THERE   Take a train to Windermere (see "Windermere & Bowness," earlier in this chapter), then continue the rest of the way by bus.

Stagecoach (© 0870/608-2608; www.stagecoachbus.com) has hourly bus service from **Grasmere** and **Keswick** (see "Grasmere" and "Keswick," later in this chapter) and from Windermere. All these buses into Ambleside are labeled either no. 555 or 556.

If you're driving from Windermere, continue northwest on the A591.

VISITOR INFORMATION   The **Tourist Information Centre** is at Market Cross Central Building, in Ambleside (© 01539/432582); it's open daily 9am to 5:30pm.

WHERE TO STAY
EXPENSIVE

Kirkstone Foot ✟   This country house is one of the finest places to stay in the area. There's the main 17th-century manor house, plus several apartments for rent in the surrounding parklike grounds. The original building is encircled by a well-tended lawn, whereas the interior is cozily furnished with overstuffed chairs and English paneling. The comfortable accommodations—11 in the main house and 16 in the less desirable outlying units—are tastefully decorated. The rooms that face the front are the most sought after. One room is spacious enough for families. The hotel requires a minimum stay of 3 nights.

Kirkstone Pass Rd., Ambleside, Cumbria LA22 9EH. © **01539/432232.** Fax 01539/432805. www.kirkstonefoot. co.uk. 27 units. £200–£495 ($400–$990) double. Rates include English breakfast. MC, V. Take Rydal Rd. north, turning right onto Kirkstone Pass Rd. **Amenities:** Restaurant; bar; babysitting. *In room:* TV, beverage maker, hair dryer, kitchens (in apts).

Rothay Manor ✟✟ *Kids*   At this spot, which is reminiscent of a French country inn, the stars are the cuisine, the well-chosen French and American wines, and comfortable, centrally heated bedrooms and suites. It's our top choice in an area where the competition is stiff in the country-house race. Most bedrooms have shuttered French doors opening onto a sunny balcony and a mountain view (two are wheelchair accessible). Throughout the estate you'll find an eclectic combination of antiques (some Georgian blended harmoniously with Victorian), flowers, and enticing armchairs.

The manor is a great place for families, renting both family rooms and family suites (big enough for a brood of six), and also providing cots at no additional fee. "Baby-listening" devices are available, and there's a children's "high tea" served around 6 to 6:30pm, which is really a dinner, with burgers, fish sticks, pizzas, and the like. A children's play park is nearby.

Rothay Bridge, Ambleside, Cumbria LA22 0EH. © **01539/433605.** Fax 01539/433607. www.rothaymanor.co.uk. 19 units. £155–£180 ($310–$360) double; £210 ($420) suite. Rates include English breakfast. AE, DC, MC, V. Take A593 1km (½ mile) south of Ambleside. **Amenities:** Restaurant; bar; free use of nearby health club; room service; babysitting; laundry service. *In room:* TV, beverage maker, hair dryer.

Wateredge Inn ✟   This is a winning little choice with an idyllic lakeside setting. The center of this hotel was formed long ago from two 17th-century fishing cottages. Wateredge was, in fact, listed as a lodging house as early as 1873, and further additions were made in the early 1900s. Situated in a beautiful garden overlooking Lake Windermere, the hotel also serves some of the best food in the area. Public rooms have many little nooks for reading and conversation. However, on sunny days guests prefer to relax in the chairs on the lawn. The rooms vary in size and appointments; some are spacious, others much smaller. Furnishings are continually renewed and upgraded as the need arises. The Windermere room has a two-person tub with a separate walk-in shower.

Borrans Rd. (on A591, 1.5km/1 mile south of Ambleside), Waterhead, Ambleside, Cumbria LA22 0EP. ⓒ 01539/ 432332. Fax 01539/431878. www.wateredgeinn.co.uk. 22 units. £80–£170 ($160–$340) double. Rates include English breakfast. AE, MC, V. **Amenities:** Restaurant; bar; nearby health club. *In room:* TV, beverage maker, hair dryer.

MODERATE TO INEXPENSIVE

Glen Rothay Hotel   Built in the 17th century as a wayfarer's inn, this hotel adjoins Dora's Field, immortalized by Wordsworth. Set back from the highway, it has a stucco-and-flagstone facade. Inside, the place has been modernized, but original details remain, including beamed ceilings and paneling. The comfortable bedrooms upstairs are tastefully furnished. Most rooms have twin or double beds, but a couple offer four-posters. The tiled bathrooms are small and compact, each with a shower.

On A591, Rydal, Ambleside, Cumbria LA22 9LR. ⓒ 01539/434500. Fax 01539/34505. www.theglenrothay.co.uk. 8 units. £70 ($140) double; from £80 ($160) suite. Rates include English breakfast. MC, V. On A591 2.5km (1½ miles) northwest of Ambleside. **Amenities:** Restaurant; bar; room service. *In room:* TV, beverage maker, hair dryer.

Queens Hotel   In the heart of this area is the Queens, an old-fashioned family-run hotel where guests are housed and fed well. It began as a private home in the Victorian era and was later transformed into a hotel. Bedrooms are a bit smallish but reasonably comfortable, and the small bathrooms have shower stalls and tubs.

Market Place, Ambleside, Cumbria LA22 9BU. ⓒ 01539/432206. Fax 01539/432721. www.queenshotelambleside. com. 26 units. Sun–Thurs £58–£76 ($116–$152) double; Fri–Sat £76–£94 ($152–$188) double. AE, MC, V. **Amenities:** 2 restaurants; 2 bars. *In room:* TV, beverage maker, hair dryer.

Riverside Hotel ⋆   Secluded on a quiet lane, this is a small country hotel formed by combining three adjoining riverside houses dating from the 1820s. It has the solid slate-block walls and slate roof common to Cumbria and, despite its peaceful location, lies a few minutes' walk from the center of Ambleside. Each of the painstakingly decorated rooms is comfortably furnished—one features a four-poster bed, and two suites have a Jacuzzi. One room is large enough for families.

Near Rothay Bridge, Under Loughrigg, Ambleside, Cumbria LA22 9LJ. ⓒ 01539/432395. Fax 01539/432440. www. riverside-at-ambleside.co.uk. 6 units. £78–£98 ($156–$196) double. Rates include English breakfast. MC, V. Closed 3 weeks in Dec. From Windermere on A591, take the left fork at Waterhead toward Coniston. Follow Coniston Rd. for about 1.5km (1 mile) until you come to the junction at Rothay Bridge. Turn left across the bridge and then immediately make a sharp right along the small lane signposted UNDER LOUGHRIGG. **Amenities:** Access to nearby health club. *In room:* TV, beverage maker, hair dryer.

WHERE TO DINE

Glass House ⋆ MODERN BRITISH/MEDITERRANEAN   In the early 1990s, the owners of this popular restaurant renovated what had originally been built in the 1400s as a water-driven mill for the crushing of wheat into flour. Today, you'll find a split-level combination of medieval and postmodern architecture, with big sunny windows, interior views of the mill's original cogs and gears, lots of oaken interior trim and, on the buildings outside, a moss-covered, full-scale replica of the original water wheel. Menu items are more sophisticated and elegant than what's served by any of its competitors. Some of the best mains include smoked salmon in a chive-butter sauce or roast free-range Lakeland chicken stuffed with chive and cream cheese.

Rydal Rd. ⓒ 01539/432137. Reservations recommended. Main courses £13–£20 ($26–$40). MC, V. Wed–Mon noon–2pm and 6:30–10pm.

Lucy 4 MODERN BRITISH   Under the same management as Lucy's on a Plate (see below), this is a wine bar lying a few steps from the larger branch. Lucy 4 serves the best tapas in town, everything from feta-stuffed peppers and chili to warm tortilla chips with eggplant dip. These tapas are served both hot and cold. The grilled sardines with lemon butter are succulent, and the figs Italiano are plump and stuffed with cheese and served with a balsamic syrup. The potato cakes are the best in the Lake District, made with feta, fresh herbs, and deep-fried olives with a fruity chutney. For the vegetarian, a platter of Mediterranean style vegetables is chargrilled and offered with a freshly made pesto dressing. For the ultimate dessert, if you didn't go for one of the hot "puds," you can order a chocolate fondue with a selection of fabulous fruit and marshmallows to dip at your leisure.

St. Mary's Lane. © 01539/34666. Reservations not needed. Tapas £5–£9 ($10–$18). AE, DC, MC, V. Mon–Fri 5–10:30pm; Sat–Sun 1–10:30pm.

Lucy's on a Plate ★ *Finds* MODERN BRITISH   The most bustling cafe in town becomes one of the best and most popular restaurants after dark, when it's dinner by candlelight. During the day you can also drop in to the adjoining deli and stock up on enough delights to fill a picnic basket to be enjoyed in some lakeside setting. Local farm produce is used whenever possible to create a series of well-crafted dishes. For mains in the evening, you can sample the likes of a chargrilled rib-eye with matchstick potatoes and onion marmalade, or else a bowl of fresh mussels cooked in a coconut-milk sauce. The restaurant is famous for its hot puds, especially its sublime sticky toffee pudding or its "wicked" hot-chocolate sponge.

Church St. © 01539/431191. Reservations not needed. Main courses £10–£21 ($20–$42). AE, DC, MC, V. Daily 10am–9pm.

WHERE TO SHARE A PINT

The friendliest pub in Ambleside is the **Golden Rule,** Smithy Brow (© **01539/ 432257**), named for the brass yardstick mounted over the bar. Its country-hunt theme features comfortable leather furniture and cast-iron tables. You can step into one side room and throw darts, or go into the other for a quiet, contemplative pint. Behind the bar, a small but colorful garden provides a serene setting in warm weather. There's inexpensive pub grub if you get hungry.

Located 5km (3 miles) west of town, off the A593 in Little Langdale, **Three Shires** (© **01539/437215**), a stone-built pub in the Three Shires Inn with a stripped timber-and-flagstone interior, offers stunning views of the valley and wooded hills. You can get good pub grub here, as well as a pint of Black Sheep Bitter, Ruddles County, or Webster's Yorkshire. Malt whiskies are well represented.

EXPLORING THE AREA

Rydal Mount ★   This was the home of William Wordsworth from 1813 until his death in 1850. Part of the house was built as a farmer's lake cottage around 1575. A descendant of Wordsworth now owns the property, which displays numerous portraits, furniture, and family possessions, as well as mementos and the poet's books. A 1.8-hectare (4½-acre) garden, landscaped by Wordsworth, is filled with rare trees, shrubs, and other features of interest.

Off A591, 2.5km (1½ miles) north of Ambleside. © 01539/433002. www.rydalmount.co.uk. Admission house and garden £5.50 ($11) adults, £4.50 ($9) seniors and students, £2 ($4) children ages 5–15, £13 ($26) family ticket, free for kids 4 and younger. Mar–Oct daily 9:30am–5pm; Nov–Dec and Feb Wed–Mon 10am–4pm.

4 Grasmere ✶✶

454km (282 miles) NW of London; 29km (18 miles) NW of Kendal; 69km (43 miles) S of Carlisle

On a lake of the same name, **Grasmere** was the home of Wordsworth from 1799 to 1808. He called this area "the loveliest spot that man hath ever known."

ESSENTIALS

GETTING THERE   Take a train to Windermere (see "Windermere & Bowness," earlier in this chapter) and continue the rest of the way by bus.

   Stagecoach (✆ **0870/608-2608;** www.stagecoachbus.com) runs hourly bus service to Grasmere from **Keswick** (see "Keswick," later in this chapter) and Windermere. Buses in either direction are marked no. 555 or 556.

   If you're driving from Windermere, continue northwest along the A591.

WHERE TO STAY & DINE
EXPENSIVE

Swan Hotel   Sir Walter Scott used to slip in here for a secret drink early in the morning, and Wordsworth mentioned the place in "The Waggoner." In fact, the poet's wooden chair is in one of the rooms. Many bedrooms are in a modern wing, added in 1975, that fits gracefully onto the building's older core (only the shell of the original 1650 building remains). Bedrooms are comfortably furnished, each with a twin or double bed (one room has a four-poster bed).

On A591 (on the road to Keswick, 1km/½ mile outside Grasmere), Grasmere, Cumbria LA22 9RF. ✆ **0870/4008132.** Fax 01539/435741. www.macdonaldhotels.com. 38 units. £124–£178 ($248–$356) double; £174–£208 ($348–$416) suite. Rates include breakfast. AE, DC, MC, V. **Amenities:** Restaurant; bar; room service; laundry service; dry cleaning. *In room:* TV, beverage maker, hair dryer, iron, trouser press.

Wordsworth Hotel ✶✶   This choice in the heart of the village is situated in a 1.2-hectare (3-acre) garden next to the churchyard where Wordsworth is buried. An old stone Lakeland house that was once the hunting lodge of the earl of Cadogan, the Wordsworth has been completely refurbished to provide luxuriously appointed bedrooms with views of the fells, as well as modern bathrooms. Three rooms have four-poster beds. The original master bedroom contains a Victorian bathroom with a brass towel rail and polished pipes and taps. Bedrooms come with character and comfort, and the canopied beds are rather sumptuous. Three rooms are spacious enough for families.

Grasmere, Cumbria LA22 9SW. ✆ **01539/435592.** Fax 01539/435765. www.grasmere-hotels.co.uk. 35 units. £180–£250 ($360–$500) double; from £260 ($520) suite. Rates include English breakfast and dinner. AE, DC, MC, V. Turn left on A591 at the GRASMERE VILLAGE sign and follow the road over the bridge, past the church, and around an S-bend; the Wordsworth is on the right. **Amenities:** Restaurant; bar; heated indoor pool; exercise room; Jacuzzi; sauna; room service; laundry service. *In room:* TV, Wi-Fi, beverage maker, hair dryer, trouser press.

MODERATE

Gold Rill ✶✶   Paul and Cathy Jewsbury operate the best-located hotel in Grasmere, alongside the lake yet only a 2-minute walk to the center of the village. Surrounded by well-maintained gardens, the hotel stands on .8 hectare (2 acres) of land with its own heated outdoor pool and a private pier. It's really a sprawling country house of grand comfort and taste. Each midsize to spacious bedroom is individually furnished, including a king-size bed in some. Those who consider themselves romantics can arrange in advance for champagne, strawberries, and fresh flowers to be placed in the room. Guests can enjoy pub lunches or else a fine evening dinner, often prepared with local produce.

Red Bank Rd., Grasmere, Cumbria LA22 9PU. ☎ **01539/435486.** www.gold-rill.com. 31 units. £126–£146 ($252–$292) double. Rates include full English breakfast. MC, V. **Amenities:** Restaurant; bar; heated outdoor pool; room service; laundry service. *In room:* TV, beverage maker, hair dryer.

Grasmere Red Lion Hotel ⚜ *Kids*   This 200-year-old coaching inn is only a short stroll from Wordsworth's Dove Cottage, and it's assumed that the poet often stopped here for a meal or drink, or to warm himself by the fire. Refurbished, the hotel offers comfortably furnished bedrooms, half with Jacuzzis in the bathrooms. Your best bet is to ask for one of the eight modern bedrooms, which are better appointed. The older rooms are fine as well, each fitted with firm beds. Four rooms are spacious enough for families and offer bunk beds.

Red Lion Sq., Grasmere, Cumbria LA22 9SS. ☎ **01539/435456.** Fax 01539/435579. www.hotelgrasmere.uk.com. 47 units. Sun–Thurs £102–£155 ($204–$310) double; Fri–Sat £117–£170 ($234–$340) double. Rates include English breakfast. AE, DC, MC, V. **Amenities:** Restaurant; 2 bars; indoor heated pool; exercise room; Jacuzzi; sauna; steam room; room service; laundry service. *In room:* TV, Wi-Fi, beverage maker, hair dryer, trouser press.

White Moss House ⚜   This 1730 Lakeland cottage, once owned by Wordsworth, overlooks the lake and the fells. You'll be welcomed here by Peter and Susan Dixon, who will pamper you with morning tea in bed, turn down your bedcovers at night, and cater to your culinary preferences. The rooms are individually decorated, comfortably furnished, and well heated in nippy weather. Brockstone, a cottage annex that is a 5-minute drive along the road, can accommodate two, three, or four guests comfortably in utter peace.

On A591 (2.5km/1½ miles south of town), Rydal Water, Grasmere, Cumbria LA22 9SE. ☎ **01539/435295.** Fax 01539/435516. www.whitemoss.com. 6 units. £78–£118 ($156–$236) double. Rates include breakfast and dinner. AE, MC, V. Closed Dec–Jan. **Amenities:** Restaurant; bar; access to nearby health club; room service; laundry service; dry cleaning. *In room:* TV, beverage maker, hair dryer, trouser press.

INEXPENSIVE

Riversdale *Value*   This lovely old house, built in 1830 of traditional Lakeland stone, is situated on the outskirts of the village of Grasmere along the banks of the River Rothay. The bedrooms are tastefully decorated and offer every comfort, including hospitality trays, as well as views of the surrounding fells. Bedrooms, most often midsize, have quality furnishings. The staff has a wealth of information on day trips, whether by car or hiking. The delightful breakfasts are served in a dining room overlooking Silver How and the fells beyond Easdale Tarn.

Grasmere, Cumbria LA22 9RQ. ☎ **01539/435619.** www.riversdalegrasmere.co.uk. 3 units. £68–£88 ($136–$176) double. Rates include English breakfast. No credit cards. Drive 16km (10 miles) north of Windermere along A591 (signposted KESWICK), then turn left by the Swan Hotel. In 360m (1,200 ft.), you'll find the inn on the left side of the road facing the river. No children 17 or younger accepted. **Amenities:** Breakfast room. *In room:* Beverage maker, hair dryer, no phone.

A LITERARY LANDMARK

Dove Cottage/The Wordsworth Museum ⚜   Wordsworth lived with his writer-and-diarist sister, Dorothy, at Dove Cottage, which is now part of the Wordsworth Museum and administered by the Wordsworth Trust. Wordsworth, the poet laureate, died in the spring of 1850 and was buried in the graveyard of the village church at Grasmere. Another tenant of Dove Cottage was Thomas De Quincey *(Confessions of* *an English Opium Eater).* The Wordsworth Museum houses manuscripts, paintings, and memorabilia. Various special exhibitions throughout the year explore the art and literature of English Romanticism.

Open to researchers who have made prior arrangements, **Jerwood Center** stands next to the cottage, preserving all the major collections related to the Lake poets. More than 50,000 documents, works of art, and other general memorabilia are housed at the center.

On A591, south of the village of Grasmere on the road to Kendal. © **01539/435544.** www.wordsworth.org.uk. Admission to Dove Cottage and the adjoining museum £6.50 ($13) adults, £4.10 ($8.20) children. Daily 9:30am–5:30pm. Closed Dec 24–26 and mid-Jan to early Feb.

5 Coniston & Hawkshead

423km (263 miles) NW of London; 84km (52 miles) S of Carlisle; 31km (19 miles) NW of Kendal

At Coniston, you can visit the village famously associated with John Ruskin. It's also a good place for hiking and rock climbing. The Coniston "Old Man" towers in the background at 790m (2,633 ft.), giving mountain climbers one of the finest views of the Lake District.

Just 6.5km (4 miles) east of Coniston is the village of Hawkshead, with its 15th-century grammar school where Wordsworth studied for 8 years (he carved his name on a desk that is still there). Nearby, in the vicinity of Esthwaite Water, is the 17th-century Hill Top Farm, former home of author Beatrix Potter.

ESSENTIALS

GETTING THERE   Take a train to Windermere and proceed the rest of the way by bus. From April to September, **Mountain Goat** (© **01539/445161**) operates eight buses per day to Hawkshead.

By car from Windermere, proceed north on the A591 to Ambleside, cutting southwest on the B5285 to Hawkshead.

Windermere Lake Cruises Ltd. (© **01539/443360;** www.windermere-lakecruises. co.uk) operates a ferry service in summer from Bowness, directly south of Windermere, to Hawkshead. It reduces driving time considerably (see "Windermere & Bowness," earlier in this chapter).

WHERE TO STAY

Coniston Lodge Hotel   A third generation of Lakeland hoteliers, Elizabeth and Anthony Robinson, invite you into their well-run lodge, which is almost as much a home as it is a small hotel. All of its bedrooms are individually furnished, one with a four-poster bed. Each room is comfortable and attractive, and carries the name of a local mountain tarn. The hotel has a garden and a communal sitting room where guests gather to watch the "telly." The dining room is country-cottage style, with antique accessories. Home-cooked English and Lakeland dishes are served, using fresh local produce.

Station Rd., Coniston, Cumbria LA21 8HH. © **01539/441201.** Fax 015394/41201. www.coniston-lodge.com. 6 units. £103–£110 ($206–$220) double. Rates include full breakfast. AE, MC, V. **Amenities:** Restaurant. *In room:* TV, beverage maker, hair dryer, trouser press.

Grizedale Lodge   This is one of the better B&Bs in the area. It was built in 1902 as a hunting lodge for the chairman of the Cunard Line. Mr. and Mrs. Aspey offer handsomely furnished bedrooms with compact private bathrooms with showers. Some of the rooms have four-poster beds and offer panoramic views.

Grizedale, Hawkshead LA22 0QL. © **01539/436532.** Fax 01539/436572. www.grizedale-lodge.com. 8 units. £85–£100 ($170–$200) double. Rates include breakfast. AE, MC, V. From Hawkshead take Newby Bridge Rd. for about 450m (1,500 ft.), then turn right (signposted GRIZEDALE & FOREST PARK CENTER) and follow this road for 3km (2 miles). **Amenities:** Bar; room service. *In room:* TV, beverage maker, hair dryer, no phone.

The Sun Hotel   This is the most popular, traditional, and attractive pub, restaurant, and hotel in Coniston. It's a country-house hotel of much character, dating from 1902, though the inn attached to it is from the 16th century. Situated on beautiful grounds above the village, 135m (450 ft.) from the town center, it lies at the foot of the Coniston "Old Man." Each bedroom, ranging in size from small to midsize, is decorated with style and flair; one has a four-poster bed. Three are big enough for families.

Brow Hill (off A593), Coniston, Cumbria LA21 8HQ. © **01539/441248.** Fax 01539/441219. www.thesunconiston. com. 10 units. £90–£110 ($180–$220) double. Rates include English breakfast. MC, V. **Amenities:** Restaurant; bar. *In room:* TV, beverage maker, hair dryer.

WHERE TO DINE

Queen's Head ENGLISH/INTERNATIONAL   This is the most famous pub in town. Behind a mock black-and-white timber facade, it's a 17th-century structure of character. It serves a special brew, Robinson's Stockport, from old-fashioned wooden kegs. Temptations on the menu include a loin of tuna seared with Cajun spice and roast eggplant, or filet of sea bass on a bed of watercress. Another specialty is skate wing cooked in white wine, garlic butter, and cracked peppercorns.

The Queen's Head may be more inn than pub; it rents 14 bedrooms with a private bathroom, TV, and phone. The comfortably old-fashioned bedrooms rent for £75 to £130 ($150–$260) for a double (two with four-poster beds). English breakfast is included.

Main St., Hawkshead. © **01539/436271.** Fax 01539/436722. Reservations recommended. Main courses £14–£19 ($28–$38). AE, MC, V. Daily noon–2:30pm and 6:15–9:30pm.

WHERE TO ENJOY A PINT

A display case of fishing lures is the first tip-off, then there's the pond itself—yes, it's true, you can fish while you drink at the **Drunken Duck,** Barn Gates (© **01539/ 436347**). Or you can just sit on the front porch and gaze at Lake Windermere in the distance. Inside, you can choose from an assortment of cushioned settees, old pews, and tub or ladder-back chairs, then order a beef filet in red-wine sauce or minted lamb casserole to go with a pint of Mitchell's Lancaster Bomber, Yates Bitter, or Yates Drunken Duck Bitter, brewed especially for the pub. If you want stronger spirits, there are more than a dozen malt whiskies to choose from.

Overlooking the central square of the village, the **Kings Arms Pub** in the Kings Arms Hotel (© **01539/436372**) offers a pleasant front terrace and lots of plush leather-covered seating inside the cozy barroom. Traditional pub grub is supplemented with a few pasta dishes, burgers, and steaks. Ales include Greenall's Original, Tetley's, and Theakston's XB. Malt whiskies are also well represented.

EXPLORING THE AREA

Of the many places to go boating in the Lake District, Coniston Water in the Lake District National Park may be the best. Coniston Water lies in a tranquil wooded valley between Grizedale Forest and the high fells of Coniston Old Man and Wetherlam. The **Coniston Boating Centre,** Lake Road, Coniston (℗ **01539/441366**), occupies a sheltered bay at the northern end of the lake. The center provides launching facilities, boat storage, and parking. You can rent rowboats that carry two to six people, sailing dinghies carrying up to six passengers, or Canadian canoes that transport two. There is a picnic area and access to the lakeshore. From the gravel beach, you may be able to spot the varied water birds and plants that make Coniston Water a valuable but fragile habitat for wildlife.

You can also cruise the lake in an original Victorian steam-powered yacht, the *Gondola.* Launched in 1859 and in regular service until 1937, this unique boat was rescued and completely restored by the National Trust. Since 1980 it has become a familiar sight on Coniston Water; sailings to Park-a-Moor and Brantwood run throughout the summer. Service is subject to weather conditions, of course. Trips are possible from April to October, costing £6 ($12) round-trip for adults or £4 ($8) for children.

Coniston Launch (℗ **01539/436216;** www.conistonlaunch.co.uk) is a traditional timber boat that calls at Coniston, Monk Coniston, Torver, and Brantwood. (Discounts are offered in combination with admission to Brantwood house; see below.) This exceptional boating outfitter offers special cruises in summer (the "Swallows and Amazons" tour was inspired by Arthur Ransome's classic story).

Summitreks operates from the lakeside at Coniston Boating Centre, offering qualified instruction in canoeing and windsurfing. You can rent a wide range of equipment from the nearby office at Lake Road (℗ **01539/441212;** www.summitreks.co.uk).

In Hawkshead, the **Beatrix Potter Gallery** (℗ **01539/436355**) has an annually changing exhibition of Beatrix Potter's original illustrations from her children's storybooks. The building was once the office of her husband, solicitor William Heelis, and the interior remains largely unaltered since his day. To get here, take bus no. 505 from Ambleside and Coniston to the square in Hawkshead.

Brantwood ❀   John Ruskin, poet, artist, and critic, was one of the great figures of the Victorian age and a prophet of social reform, inspiring such diverse men as Proust, Frank Lloyd Wright, and Gandhi. He moved to his home, Brantwood, on the east side of Coniston Water, in 1872 and lived here until his death in 1900. The house today is open for visitors to see his memorabilia, including some 200 of his pictures.

Part of the 101-hectare (250-acre) estate is open as a nature trail. The Brantwood stables, designed by Ruskin, have been converted into a tearoom and restaurant, the Jumping Jenny. Also in the stable building is the Coach House Craft Gallery, which follows the Ruskin tradition of encouraging contemporary craftwork of the finest quality. Literary fans may want to pay a pilgrimage to the graveyard of the village church, where Ruskin was buried; his family turned down the invitation to have him interred at Westminster Abbey.

Coniston. ℗ 01539/441396. www.brantwood.org.uk. Admission £5.95 ($12) adults, £4.50 ($9) students, £1.20 ($2.40) children 5–16, £12 ($24) family ticket (2 adults, 3 children); garden walk £4 ($8). Mid-Mar to mid-Nov daily 11am–5:30pm; mid-Nov to mid-Mar Wed–Sun 11am–4:30pm. Closed Dec 25–26.

John Ruskin Museum   At this institute, in the center of the village, you can see Ruskin's personal possessions and mementos, pictures by him and his friends, letters, and his collection of mineral rocks.

Yewdale Rd., Coniston. © **01539/441164**. www.ruskinmuseum.com. Admission £4.25 ($8.50) adults, £2 ($4) children, £11 ($22) family ticket (2 adults, 2 or 3 children). Mid-Mar to mid-Nov daily 10am–5:30pm; mid-Nov to mid-Mar Wed–Sun 10:30am–3:30pm.

6 Keswick

473km (294 miles) NW of London; 50km (31 miles) NW of Kendal; 35km (22 miles) NW of Windermere

Keswick opens onto Derwentwater, one of the loveliest lakes in the region, and the town makes a good base for exploring the northern half of Lake District National Park. Keswick has two landscaped parks, and above the small town is a historic stone circle thought to be some 4,000 years old.

St. Kentigern's Church dates from A.D. 553, and a weekly market held in the center of Keswick can be traced from a charter granted in the 13th century. It's a short walk to Friar's Crag, the classic viewing point on Derwentwater. The walk will also take you past boat landings with launches that operate regular tours around the lake.

Around Derwentwater are many places with literary associations that evoke memories of Wordsworth, Robert Southey, Coleridge, and Hugh Walpole. Several of Beatrix Potter's stories were based at Keswick. The town also has a professional repertory theater that schedules performances in the summer, a swimming pool complex, and an 18-hole golf course at the foot of the mountains 6.5km (4 miles) away.

ESSENTIALS

GETTING THERE   Take a train to Windermere (see "Windermere & Bowness," earlier in this chapter) and proceed the rest of the way by bus.

Stagecoach (© **0870/608-2608**; www.stagecoachbus.com) has a regular bus service from Windermere and Grasmere (bus no. 555).

If you're driving from Windermere, drive northwest on the A591.

VISITOR INFORMATION   The **Tourist Information Centre,** at Moot Hall, Market Square (© **01768/772645**), is open daily April to September 9:30am to 5:30pm, and October to March daily 9:30am to 4:30pm. It's closed Christmas and New Year's Day.

WHERE TO STAY

The Edwardene Hotel   This 1885 house of gray slate stands in a residential area, about a 3-minute walk from the town center. Rising three floors, the gabled house is well maintained with tasteful, comfortable rooms. These accommodations take their names from the Lakeland landscape—Myrtle, Bramble, Heather, Poppy, and so on. Attention is paid to detail by its hospitable owners, and guests assemble on chilly nights in the lounge by the fireplace. Cumberland sausages and free-range eggs are featured at breakfast.

26 Southey St., Keswick, Cumbria, CA12 4EF. © **017687/73586**. Fax 017687/73824. www.edwardenehotel.com. 11 units. £72–£76 ($144–$152) double; £108 ($216) family room. MC, V. **Amenities:** Breakfast room. *In room:* TV, beverage maker, hair dryer.

Grange Country House   A tranquil retreat, this charming hotel and gardens are situated on a hilltop. Dating from the 1840s, it is furnished in part with antiques. Guests enjoy the crackling log fires in chilly weather. Many of the attractively furnished, well-kept rooms have scenic views of the Lakeland hills. There is continual upgrading of the bedrooms, which come in various shapes and sizes; each is individually decorated and most have double or twin beds.

Manor Brow, Ambleside Rd. (on the southeast side of Keswick, overlooking the town, just off A591), Keswick, Cumbria CA12 4BA. ✆ 01768/772500. www.grangekeswick.com. 10 units. £90–£98 ($180–$196) double. Rates include English breakfast. MC, V. Closed Dec–Feb. **Amenities:** Breakfast room; lounge; room service. *In room:* TV, beverage maker, hair dryer.

Highfield Hotel ✪ (Value)

Constructed in the late 1880s, two former private residences have been skillfully converted into this well-run hotel. The houses were built to take full advantage of mountain and lake views. A veranda, balconies, turrets, and bay windows characterize the architecture. A 5-minute walk from the center of town, the house is furnished in a traditional British way. All the bedrooms are good size and handsomely decorated, many with bay windows where you can sit and soak up the view. The most magnificent room is the spacious and elegant Woodford Room, with a four-poster bed and raised seating area. The main dining room is elegant yet informal with daily-changing menus, using, whenever possible, the best of local produce, such as Borrowdale salmon.

The Heads, Keswick, Cumbria CA12 5ER. ✆ **01768/772508.** Fax 01768/780634. www.highfieldkeswick.co.uk. 19 units. £120–£160 ($240–$320) double. Rates include breakfast and dinner. AE, MC, V. Closed mid-Nov to mid-Feb. **Amenities:** Restaurant; bar. *In room:* TV, beverage maker.

Skiddaw Hotel (Kids)

This hotel lies behind an impressive facade and entrance marquee built right onto the sidewalk in the heart of Keswick at the market square. The owners have refurbished the interior, retaining the best features. Bedrooms are compact and eye-catching, and have been refurbished. Seven rooms are large enough for families. The upgraded Summit rooms offer extras such as bathrobes and mineral water. Guests may use the indoor pool and spa at Armathwaite Hall (p. 648; about 9.5km/6 miles from Keswick) and golf at Keswick Golf Club during the week. For weekend bookings, there is a 2-night minimum stay.

Market Sq., Keswick, Cumbria CA12 5BN. ✆ **01768/772071.** Fax 01768/774850. www.skiddawhotel.co.uk. 40 units. £128–£168 ($256–$336) double. Rates include English breakfast. MC, V. **Amenities:** Restaurant; bar; access to nearby pool, golf, and spa; sauna; room service; laundry service; dry cleaning. *In room:* TV, beverage maker, hair dryer.

Swinside Lodge ✪

Isolated on a knoll that overlooks Lake Derwentwater, and solidly built in the 1850s as a home for the manager of the enormous estate that surrounded it at the time, this is a cozy, well-managed bed-and-breakfast hotel where evening meals are better than the norm. The venue is run by Eric and Irene Fell, with cuisine prepared by Andrew Carter. Bedrooms are outfitted with painted, cream-colored furniture, and pastel-colored fabrics that deliberately don't convey a sense of the Edwardian age. Several public rooms and lounges have shelves of books and diversionary games that take the boredom off any rainy day. Children 4 and younger are discouraged.

Grange Rd., Newlands, Cumbria CA12 5UE. ✆ **01768/772948.** Fax 01768/773312. www.swinsidelodge-hotel.co.uk. 7 units. £176–£216 ($352–$432) double. Rates include dinner and breakfast for 2 occupants. MC, V. From Keswick, take A66 southwest for 5km (3 miles), following the signs to Portinscale and to Grange. **Amenities:** Restaurant; 3 lounges. *In room:* TV, beverage maker, hair dryer.

WHERE TO DINE

Underscar Manor ✪ ENGLISH/FRENCH

The area's best cuisine is found at this Italianate manor, also a hotel, set high in the hills with panoramic vistas over Keswick and Derwentwater. Set on 16 hectares (40 acres) in the foothills of Skiddaw, the chintzy conservatory restaurant offers formal service (men are requested to wear jackets). The ambitious menu is just as classic as the setting. Standard recipes are given modern twists, and service is impeccable. Ingredients are top quality and menus are based on the season, with everything perfectly served from sublime breast of local pheasant wrapped in Parma ham, to casserole of local venison with potato dumplings flavored with bacon and chives. Another specialty is chargrilled filets of lemon sole served with an herb-laced risotto. No children 11 or younger are accepted.

Applethwaite, near Keswick. (✆) **017687/75000.** Reservations required. Main courses £22–£26 ($44–$52); 3-course fixed-price lunch £28 ($56); 5-course fixed-price dinner £38 ($76). AE, MC, V. Daily noon–1pm and 7–9:30pm.

SEEING THE SIGHTS

Mirehouse   A tranquil Cumbrian family home that has not been sold since 1688, Mirehouse has unusually wide-ranging literary and artistic connections. The piano is played on afternoons when guests stop by to visit. The park around it stretches to Bassenthwaite Lake and has extensive gardens, plus woodland adventure playgrounds. It is in easy reach of the ancient lakeside church and the Old Sawmill Tearoom, which is known for its generous Cumbrian cooking.

On A591, 5.5km (3½ miles) north of Keswick. (✆) **01768/772287.** www.mirehouse.com. Admission to house and gardens plus a lakeside walk £4.80 ($9.60) adults, £2.40 ($4.80) children and seniors, £14 ($28) family ticket (2 adults, 4 kids ages 5–16); gardens only £2.60 ($5.20) adults, £1.30 ($2.60) children. House Apr–Oct Sun and Wed (also Fri in Aug) 2–4:30pm; tearoom and grounds Apr–Oct daily 10am–5:30pm.

SIDE TRIPS FROM KESWICK
BORROWDALE

One of the most scenic parts of the Lake District, Borrowdale stretches south of Derwentwater to Seathwaite in the heart of the county. The valley is walled in by fell sides, and it's an excellent center for exploring, walking, and climbing. Many use it as a base for exploring **Scafell,** England's highest mountain, at 963m (3,210 ft.).

This resort is in the Borrowdale Valley, the southernmost settlement of which is Seatoller. The village of Seatoller, at 353m (1,176 ft.), is the terminus for buses to and from Keswick.

After leaving Seatoller, the B5289 takes you west through the Honister Pass and Buttermere Fell, one of the most dramatic drives in the Lake District. The road is lined with towering boulders. The lake village of Buttermere also merits a stopover for its lake-country scenery.

Where to Stay & Dine
Borrowdale Gates Hotel ✿   The proprietors of this hotel, Terry and Christine Parkinson, welcome travelers from around the world; even former prime minister John Major has dropped in for afternoon tea. Their 1860 Victorian country house, built of Lakeland stone, received an addition of nine rooms that faithfully matches the Victorian style. All the rooms range in size from medium to large and are decorated with rich Victorian colors and period reproductions. Every year some rooms are upgraded and refurbished. The place is warm, cozy, and inviting. The public areas, with their antiques and open-log stone fireplaces, sprawl along the ground floor and include a bar, a restaurant and dining area, and four sitting lounges. They are all airy and bright, with views of the surrounding gardens.

Grange-in-Borrowdale, Keswick CA12 5UQ. (✆) **01768/777204.** Fax 01768/777254. www.borrowdale-gates.com. 29 units. Sun–Thurs £140–£200 ($280–$400) double; Fri–Sat £160–£210 ($320–$420) double. Rates include English breakfast and dinner. AE, MC, V. Free parking. From Keswick, take B5289 6.5km (4 miles) south to Grange; go over the bridge, and the inn sits on the right, just beyond the curve in the road. **Amenities:** Restaurant; bar. *In room:* TV, beverage maker, hair dryer, trouser press.

Borrowdale Hotel ⭐ When the weather is damp, log fires welcome guests in this Lakeland stone building, which was originally a coaching inn (ca. 1866). The rooms are comfortable and many have fine views. Each of the midsize to spacious bedrooms is well designed and furnished. Four rooms contain four-poster beds; several rooms are suitable for families. Bathrooms are well maintained and most offer a tub/shower combination.

Borrowdale Rd. (B5289), Borrowdale, Keswick, Cumbria CA12 5UY. ℂ **01768/777224.** Fax 01768/777338. www. theborrowdalehotel.co.uk. 36 units. Sun–Thurs £132–£184 ($264–$368) double; Fri–Sat £144–£194 ($288–$388) double. Rates include English breakfast and dinner. MC, V. Free parking. On B5289, 5.5km (3½ miles) south of Keswick. **Amenities:** Restaurant; bar; access to nearby health club; room service; laundry service. *In room:* TV, beverage maker, hair dryer, trouser press (in some).

Lodore Falls Hotel ⭐ This hotel overlooks Derwentwater from fields where cows graze. With its spike-capped mansard tower, symmetrical gables, and balcony-embellished stone facade, it seems straight out of the Swiss Alps. (Ironically, the Swiss owners who built this place in the 19th c. were named England. Their tradition of good rooms, food, and service continues today.) The interior has been completely modernized, and the well-furnished bedrooms vary in size; it's worth opting for one of the larger ones. On weekends there is a 2-night minimum stay.

Borrowdale Rd. (B5289), Borrowdale, Keswick, Cumbria CA12 5UX. ℂ **01768/777285.** Fax 01768/777343. www. lodorefallshotel.co.uk. 71 units. £142–£206 ($284–$412) double; £264–£350 ($528–$700) suite. Rates include breakfast. MC, V. Indoor parking £5 ($10); outdoor parking free. On B5289 5.5km (3½ miles) south of Keswick. **Amenities:** Restaurant; bar; 2 heated pools (1 indoor, 1 outdoor); outdoor tennis court; spa; gym; sauna; children's playground; room service; laundry service; rooms for those w/limited mobility. *In room:* TV, beverage maker, hair dryer, trouser press.

BASSENTHWAITE

In the Lake District National Park, 9.5km (6 miles) north of Keswick, Bassenthwaite is one of the most beautiful of Lakeland villages and makes the best center for exploring the woodlands of Thornthwaite Forest and Bassenthwaite Lake nearby. Bassenthwaite Lake is the northernmost and only true "lake" in the Lake District, and it's visited yearly by many species of migratory birds from the north of Europe.

Where to Stay & Dine

Armathwaite Hall Hotel ⭐⭐ Rich in history, this hotel goes back to the 1300s when it was built as a house for Benedictine nuns. During the Middle Ages, it was plundered frequently, leaving the sisters wretchedly poor. By the 17th century, a series of wealthy landowners had completed the severe Gothic design of its stately facade, and an architecturally compatible series of wings were added in 1844. It was converted into a hotel during the 1930s. Sir Hugh Walpole, who once stayed here, found it "a house of perfect and irresistible charm." Ringed with almost 160 hectares (400 acres) of woodland (some bordering the lake), the place offers a magnificent entrance hall sheathed with expensive paneling. The bedrooms are also handsomely furnished, with padded headboards crowning comfortable beds fitted with fine linen. Four-poster and family rooms are available.

Bassenthwaite Lake (on B5291, 11km/7 miles northwest of Keswick, 2.5km/1½ miles west of Bassenthwaite), Keswick, Cumbria CA12 4RE. ℂ **01768/776551.** Fax 01768/776220. www.armathwaite-hall.com. 43 units. £210–£290 ($420–$580) double; £330–£350 ($660–$700) suite. Rates include English breakfast. AE, DC, MC, V. **Amenities:** Restaurant; bar; indoor heated pool; outdoor tennis court; health club; sauna; steam room; billiards room; salon; room service; babysitting; laundry service. *In room:* TV, Wi-Fi, beverage maker, hair dryer, trouser press.

The Castle Inn Hotel   Don't expect a castle. Though this place plays up its historical importance, you'll find there is an "old" core (no one on the staff is sure of how old), with many newer additions that don't exactly gracefully merge into a unified whole. The result is a hotel that's neither whimsically antique nor strikingly modern—but it is not dowdy. Bedrooms come in various shapes and sizes, including some beautifully appointed and spacious "superior" units. Five are large enough for families. The more modern but equally comfortable rooms are in a new wing. Two of the old-fashioned rooms contain four-poster beds.

Bassenthwaite (9.5km/6 miles north of Keswick on A591), Cumbria CA12 4RG. ℭ **01768/776401.** Fax 01768/776604. www.castleinncumbria.co.uk. 48 units. £100–£120 ($200–$240) double. Rates include half-board. AE, MC, V. From Keswick, take A591 9.5km (6 miles) north of town; the inn is on the left. **Amenities:** Restaurant; bar; indoor heated pool; health club; Jacuzzi; sauna; steam room; bike rental; table tennis; badminton; billiards; room service; laundry. *In room:* TV, Wi-Fi, beverage maker, hair dryer.

Overwater Hall ⭒   Built in the late 18th century, this is a Georgian mansion with battlements added to it by the Victorians. It is reminiscent of a castle and comes complete with a ghost story. All the bedrooms, though standard in size, are extremely ritzy (which may be why Overwater's phantom has chosen to stay), having been furnished with top-quality antiques. One room has an oak-paneled four-poster bed. Guests can enjoy the regal surroundings of the public rooms with their intricate and rich cove molding and formal Victorian antiques. The drawing room is a great place for afternoon tea, and the piano bar actually has a baby grand piano. On weekends there is a 2-night minimum stay.

Overwater, Ireby, near Keswick CA5 1HH. ℭ **01768/776566.** Fax 017687/76921. www.overwaterhall.co.uk. 13 units. £180–£250 ($360–$500) double. Rates include English breakfast and dinner. MC, V. **Amenities:** Restaurant; bar; lounge; putting green; room service. *In room:* TV, beverage maker, hair dryer.

The Pheasant ⭒   This former 17th-century coaching inn sits near the northwestern tip of Bassenthwaite Lake. A series of extensions were later added. Everything about it evokes old-fashioned English coziness. Fireplaces warm a moderately eccentric bar area, a mishmash of antique and merely old-fashioned furniture, and individually decorated bedrooms whose windows overlook 24 hectares (60 acres) of forest and parkland associated with the hotel. Two bedrooms offer sitting areas.

Bassenthwaite Lake near Cockermouth, Cumbria CA13 9YE. ℭ **01768/776234.** Fax 01768/776002. www.the-pheasant.co.uk. 13 units. Winter £130–£150 ($260–$300) double, £170–£180 ($340–$360) suite; summer £160–£170 ($320–$340) double, £190–£200 ($380–$400) suite. Rates include breakfast. MC, V. **Amenities:** Restaurant; bar; room service. *In room:* TV (on request), beverage maker, hair dryer.

7 Ullswater ⭒

477km (296 miles) NW of London; 42km (26 miles) SE of Keswick

Set in a region that is home to contrasting vistas of gently rolling fields and dramatic mountain rises, Ullswater is a favorite with those who enjoy spectacular natural beauty. Ullswater itself is a 14km (9-mile) expanse of water stretching from Pooley Bridge to Patterdale and is the second-largest lake in the district. It is a magnet for outdoor types of all levels of ability, offering activities that range from walks and hikes around the shore to rock climbing, mountain biking, canoeing, sailing, and even windsurfing.

This part of the Lakeland, where the majesty of nature tends to entrance and envelop, has always held a special attraction for artists and writers. The area gained most of its fame from writings by the likes of Wordsworth during the early 19th century. It was on the shores of Ullswater that Wordsworth saw his "host of golden daffodils." Aira Force waterfall, near the National Trust's Gowbarrow, inspired both Wordsworth and Coleridge by its beauty. While using this area as a base for outdoor activities, you can also easily explore the many places of prehistoric and historical significance, from the times of the ancient Celts right through to modern day. Two noteworthy sites include Long Meg and her "daughters," an ancient stone circle near Penrith; and **Hadrian's Wall,** marking the northern extent of the Roman Empire, east of Carlisle (p. 690).

In Ullswater, two 19th-century **steamers** provide the best way to see the area's panoramic mountain scenery around the lake. In season, there are two scheduled services daily between Glenridding, Howtown, and Pooley Bridge as well as five shorter 1-hour cruises. Passengers may choose to walk back along the lakeside path or break for lunch at either end of the lake. The steamers run every day but December 25 and January 1. Round-trip tickets between Glenridding, Howtown, and Pooley Bridge cost £8.40 to £11 ($17–$22) for adults or £4.20 to £5.65 ($8.40–$11) for children, with a family ticket ranging from £23 to £31 ($46–$62). The higher prices are charged in midsummer. For more information, call © **01768/482229** or see **www.ullswater-steamers.co.uk**. Glenridding is on the A592 at the southern end of Ullswater. Pooley Bridge is 8km (5 miles) from the M6 Junction 40 to Penrith.

ESSENTIALS

GETTING THERE   About three trains from London's Euston Station arrive daily in Penrith, this region's main rail junction. Usually, a change of trains isn't necessary. For schedules and information, call © **0845/748-4950** or visit **www.nationalrail. co.uk**. Once in Penrith, passengers usually take a taxi to Ullswater.

Two **Stagecoach** buses (© **0870/608-2608;** www.stagecoachbus.com) stop at the Penrith Bus Station daily on their way between Carlisle and Keswick. Passengers must take a taxi from Penrith to Ullswater.

If you're driving from Penrith, go southeast on the B5320.

WHERE TO STAY & DINE

Brackenrigg Inn ✦ *(Value)*   Since the price tags at Sharrow Bay (see below) are a bit lethal, many discerning travelers book into this traditional inn and restaurant overlooking Ullswater. The lakeside coaching inn has kept up-to-date with the times, serving good food and offering a comfortable bed for the night. Beautiful views unfold from the bar, dining room, lounge, terrace, garden, and bedrooms. Units come in a wide range from smaller, standard doubles to the more spacious superior rooms, or even the premium ground-floor suites. There's a lot of local character here, with a convivial bar, an open fire, and even a dartboard. Chefs specialize in the market-fresh food of Cumbria "but without all the fuss." The succulent lamb dishes are some of the best in the area.

At Watermillock (on A592), Cumbria CA11 0JN. © **017684/86206.** Fax 017684/86945. www.brackenrigginn.co.uk. 17 units. £40 ($80) per person including breakfast; £60 ($120) per person including dinner. MC, V. **Amenities:** Restaurant; bar. *In room:* TV.

Sharrow Bay Country House Hotel ✦✦✦   This was Britain's first country-house hotel, and it's the oldest British member of Relais & Châteaux. Sitting on 4.8 hectares (12 acres), it's an unusual Victorian house with a low angled roof and wide eaves. It was a private home until purchased by Francis Coulson in 1948. Realizing its potential, Coulson restored the structure, sleeping on the floor while work was in progress. Three years later he was joined by Brian Sack, and together they turned Sharrow into one of England's finest places to dine. Today, the hotel offers 26 antiques-filled bedrooms, 17 of them in the gatehouse and cottages. Individually decorated, each is named after one or another of the glamorous (and often famous) women who have swept in and out of the lives of the articulate owners. Some of the rooms offer views of the lakes, trees, or Martindale Fells.

Howtown Rd., Lake Ullswater, near Penrith, Cumbria CA10 2LZ. © 01768/486301. Fax 01768/486349. www. sharrowbay.co.uk. 26 units. £340–£420 ($680–$840) double; £440–£470 ($880–$940) suite for 2. Rates include half-board. 2-night minimum stay Sat–Sun. AE, DC, MC, V. Howtown Rd. 3km (2 miles) south of Pooley Bridge. **Amenities:** Restaurant; bar; 2 lounges; room service; laundry service; dry cleaning. *In room:* TV, minibar, hair dryer, trouser press.

8 Penrith

467km (290 miles) NW of London; 50km (31 miles) NE of Kendal

This one-time capital of Cumbria, in the old Kingdom of Scotland and Strathclyde, takes its name, some say, from the Celts who called it "Ford by the Hill." The namesake hill is marked today by a red-sandstone beacon and tower. Because of Penrith's central location above the northern Lake District and beside the Pennines, this thriving market center was important to Scotland and England from its very beginning, eventually prompting England to take it over in 1070.

The characteristically red-sandstone town has been home to many famous and legendary figures, including Richard, duke of Gloucester; William Cookson, the grandfather of poet William Wordsworth; and Dorothy Wordsworth, William's sister. Today, Penrith remains best known as a lively market town.

ESSENTIALS

GETTING THERE   To bus from London, take one daily **National Express** (© **0870/580-8080;** www.nationalexpress.co.uk) bus leaving from London's Victoria Station at 11pm, arriving in Penrith at 5:30am.

To drive, take the M1 out of London, getting on the M6 to Penrith. The trip should take no more than 6 hours.

VISITOR INFORMATION   The **Tourist Information Centre,** Robinson's School, Middlegate, Penrith (© **01768/867466;** www.visiteden.co.uk), is open in summer Monday to Saturday from 9am to 6pm and Sunday from 10am to 5pm; off-season hours are Monday to Saturday 9am to 5pm and Sunday 10am to 4pm.

WHERE TO STAY & DINE

George   This is a 300-year-old coaching inn, built right in the heart of town. It welcomed Bonnie Prince Charlie in 1745. The front of the George looks out on a street of small specialty shops, and the guest rooms, spread among three floors, are individually decorated with light colors and up-to-date furnishings. The owners have upgraded all the bedrooms. On weekends a minimum stay of 2 nights is required.

Devonshire St., Penrith, Cumbria CA11 7SU. © **01768/862696.** Fax 01768/868223. www.lakedistricthotels.net/ georgehotel. 34 units. £106–£150 ($212–$300) double; £172 ($344) suite. Rates include full Cumbrian breakfast. MC, V. **Amenities:** Restaurant; bar; free use of nearby indoor pool and gym; room service; laundry service. *In room:* TV, beverage maker, hair dryer.

North Lakes Hotel ★ *(Kids)* This is Penrith's finest accommodations and the most family-friendly hotel in the area. The exterior may lack character, but you'll find compensation inside. A member of the Shire Inns chain, this hotel is designed to meet the needs of businesspeople during the week and vacationers on weekends. Rooms are bright and spacious, decorated with classic wood furniture, large couches, and soft pastel accents. Six rooms are large enough for rental to families, and some have bunk beds. Guests enjoy an inviting lobby sitting area with a grand, barn-style, open ceiling with rustic beams, and a huge stone fireplace.

Ullswater Rd., Penrith, Cumbria CA11 8QT. ℂ 01768/868111. Fax 01768/868291. www.shirehotels.co.uk. 84 units. £150–£174 ($300–$348) double; £184–£200 ($368–$400) suite. Children 15 and younger stay free in parent's room. Rates include English breakfast. AE, DC, MC, V. **Amenities:** Restaurant; bar; 2 pools (indoor heated, children's); 2 squash courts; health club; spa; sauna; steam room; room service; babysitting; laundry service; dry cleaning. *In room:* TV, Wi-Fi, beverage maker, hair dryer, trouser press.

Queen's Head Inn ★ Lying 4km (2½ miles) south of Penrith, this is a discovery from 1719, once the property of the Wordsworths. Today it is an inviting country pub and restaurant with overnight accommodations. It is found in the center of the village of Tirril, nestled on the edge of the Lake District National Park. Filled with bric-a-brac and memorabilia, the country inn is full of character. Expect oak beams, wooden settles, and even a roaring fire in the often chilly month of June. It's an atmosphere of hunting prints and horse brasses along with farm tools and hunting horns. Most patrons come here to enjoy the Tirril beers on tap, although you may also enjoy wines from the family-owned vineyards. Good food has always been a tradition of the inn, and you can enjoy traditional British food here, including such noteworthy dishes as braised shoulder of Lakeland lamb in its own red-currant gravy. Local venison and pheasant appear in winter or locally smoked Ullswater trout in summer. The bedrooms are well maintained and most comfortable.

Tirril, near Penrith, Cumbria CA10 2JF. ℂ **01768/863219.** Fax 01768/863243. www.queensheadinn.co.uk. 7 units. £90 ($180) double. Rates include breakfast. MC, V. **Amenities:** Restaurant; pub. *In room:* No phone.

EXPLORING THE AREA

A small town of 12,500 people, Penrith still has lots of shops to explore. Major shopping areas include the covered **Devonshire Arcade** with its name-brand stores and boutiques; the pedestrian-only **Angel Lane** and **Little Dockray,** with an abundance of family-run specialty shops; and **Angel Square** just south of Angel Lane.

The 130-year-old **Briggs & Shoe Mines,** Southend Road (ℂ **01768/899001**), is a shoe-shopping extravaganza. It is the largest independent shoe shop in the Lakelands, carrying famous names and offering great bargains, including sportswear, walking boots, clothing, and accessories.

Acorn Bank Garden & Watermill For a stroll in an English garden, see the Acorn Bank Garden with its varied landscape of blooming bulbs, plants, and walled spaces. Its claim to fame is its extensive herb garden, said to be the best in all of northern England. The Acorn Bank Garden is part of an estate dating from 1228 that includes a partially restored water mill, parts of which also date from the 13th century, and a red-sandstone Tudor house (presently not open to the public).

Temple Sowerby, 9.5km (6 miles) east of Penrith on A6. ℂ 017683/61893. www.nationaltrust.org.uk. Admission £3.40 ($6.80) adults, £1.70 ($3.40) children, £8.50 ($17) family ticket (2 adults, 2 children). Wed–Sun 10am–5pm (last admission at 4:30pm). Closed Nov to mid-Mar.

Penrith Castle   This park contains the massive ruins of the castle, whose construction began in 1399, ordered by William Strickland, the bishop of Canterbury. For the next 70 years, the castle continued to grow in size and strength until it finally became the royal castle and oftentimes residence for Richard, duke of Gloucester.

Just across from the train station along Ullswater Rd. No phone. Free admission. Always accessible.

Penrith Museum   For perspective on Penrith and the surrounding area, a visit here isn't a bad idea. Originally constructed in the 1500s, the museum building was turned into a poor girls' school in 1670. Today, the museum surveys the archaeology and geology of Penrith and the Eden Valley, which was a desert millions of years ago.

Robinson's School, Middlegate. ✆ **01768/212228**. Free admission. Mon–Sat 10am–4pm.

19

Yorkshire & Northumbria: Brontë, Moors & Dales

Yorkshire, known to readers of Emily Brontë's *Wuthering Heights* and James Herriot's *All Creatures Great and Small,* embraces the moors and dales of North Yorkshire.

Across this vast region came Romans, Anglo-Saxons, Vikings, monks of the Middle Ages, kings of England, lords of the manor, craftspeople, hill farmers, and wool growers, all leaving their marks. You can still see Roman roads and pavements, great abbeys and castles, stately homes, open-air museums, and crafts centers, along with parish churches, old villages, and cathedrals.

Some cities and towns still carry the taint of the Industrial Revolution, but you can also find wild and remote beauty—limestone crags, caverns along the Pennines, mountainous uplands, rolling hills, chalk land wolds, heather-covered moorlands, broad vales, and tumbling streams. Yorkshire offers not only beautiful inland scenery but also 161km (100 miles) of shoreline, with rocky headlands, cliffs, sandy bays, rock pools, sheltered coves, fishing villages, bird sanctuaries, former smugglers' dens, and yachting havens. And in the summer, the moors in **North York Moors National Park** bloom with purple heather. You can hike along the 177km (110-mile) **Cleveland Way National Trail,** which encircles the park.

Yorkshire's most visited city is the walled city of **York. York Minster,** part of the cathedral circuit, is noted for its 100 stained-glass windows. In West Yorkshire is the literary shrine of **Haworth,** the home of the Brontës.

Northumbria is made up of the counties of Northumberland, Cleveland, and Durham. The Saxons, who came to northern England centuries ago, carved out this kingdom, which at the time stretched from the Firth of Forth in Scotland to the banks of the Humber in Yorkshire. Vast tracts of that ancient kingdom remain natural and unspoiled. This slice of England has more than its share of industrial towns, but you should explore the wild hills and open spaces and cross the dales of the eastern Pennines.

The whole area evokes ancient battles and bloody border raids. Space constraints don't permit us to cover this area in great detail, and it's often overlooked by the rushed North American visitor, but we suggest at least a venture to **Hadrian's Wall,** a Roman structure that was one of the wonders of the Western world. The finest stretch of the wall lies within **Northumberland National Park,** between the stony North Tyne River and the county boundary at Gilsland. And about 64km (40 miles) of the 242km (150-mile) **Pennine Way** meanders through the park; Pennine Way is one of Britain's most challenging hiking paths.

On the way north to Hadrian's Wall, we suggest you spend the night in the ancient cathedral city of **Durham.** This great medieval city is among the most dramatically sited and most interesting in the north.

1 York *(★(★(★*

327km (203 miles) N of London; 42km (26 miles) NE of Leeds; 142km (88 miles) N of Nottingham

Few cities in England are as rich in history as York. It is still encircled by its 13th- and 14th-century city walls, about 4km (2½ miles) long, with four gates. One of these, Micklegate, once grimly greeted visitors coming from the south with the heads of traitors. To this day, you can walk on the footpath of the medieval walls.

The crowning achievement of York is its minster, or cathedral, which makes the city an ecclesiastical center equaled only by Canterbury. It's easily visible on a drive up to Edinburgh in Scotland. Or, after visiting Cambridge, you can make a swing through the great cathedral cities of Ely, Lincoln, York, and Ripon.

There was a Roman York (Hadrian came this way), then a Saxon York, a Danish York, a Norman York (William the Conqueror slept here), a medieval York, a Georgian York, and a Victorian York (the center of a flourishing rail business). A large amount of 18th-century York remains for visitors to explore today, including Richard Boyle's restored Assembly Rooms.

You may want to visit the Shambles; once the meat-butchering center of York, it dates from before the Norman Conquest. The messy business is gone now, but the ancient street survives, filled today with jewelry stores, cafes, and buildings that huddle so closely together that you can practically stand in the middle of the pavement, arms outstretched, and touch the houses on both sides of the street.

ESSENTIALS

GETTING THERE   British Midland flights arrive at **Leeds Bradford International Airport** (② 01132/509696; www.lbia.co.uk), a 50-minute flight from London's Heathrow Airport. For schedules and fares, call the airline at ② **0870/607-0555** (www.flybmi.com). Connecting buses at the airport take you east and the rest of the distance to York.

From London's Kings Cross Station, York-bound trains leave every 30 minutes. The trip takes 2 hours. For information, call ② **0845/748-4950** or visit **www.nationalrail. co.uk**.

Four **National Express** buses depart daily from London's Victoria Coach Station for the 4½-hour trip to York. For schedules and information, call ② **0870/580-8080** or visit **www.nationalexpress.com**.

If you're driving from London, head north on the M1, cutting northeast below Leeds at the junction with the A64, heading east to York.

VISITOR INFORMATION   The **Tourist Information Centre** at De Grey Rooms, Exhibition Square (② **01904/550099;** www.york-tourism.co.uk), is open in winter Monday to Saturday 9am to 5pm and Sunday 10am to 4pm; summer hours are Monday to Saturday 9am to 6pm and Sunday 10am to 5pm. Another Tourist Information Centre at the railway station has the same hours.

WHERE TO STAY

EXPENSIVE

Dean Court Hotel *★*   This 1850 building, today a Best Western hotel, lies right beneath the towers of the minster. It was originally constructed to provide housing for the clergy of York Minster and then converted to a hotel after World War I. It may not be the most atmospheric choice in York, but refurbishments have vastly improved the accommodations. The rooms are very comfortable, with quality linens on the beds and bathrooms equipped with tub/shower combinations. Two rooms are spacious enough for use by families.

Duncombe Place, York, North Yorkshire YO1 7EF. ✆ 800/780-1234 in the U.S., or 01904/625082. Fax 01904/620305. www.bw-deancourt.co.uk. 39 units. £130–£205 ($260–$410) double; £199–£209 ($398–$418) family room. Rates include English breakfast. AE, DC, MC, V. Parking £10 ($20). **Amenities:** 2 restaurants; bar; room service; babysitting; laundry service; dry cleaning. *In room:* TV, Wi-Fi, beverage maker, hair dryer, trouser press.

Middlethorpe Hall Hotel ✸✸✸ Set on an 11-hectare (26-acre) park, this hotel is on the outskirts of York, near the racecourse and away from the traffic. It's clearly York's leading hotel. Built in 1699, the stately, red-brick William and Mary country house was purchased by Historic House Hotels and beautifully restored, both inside and out. Lots of antiques create the ambience of a classic manor house. The rooms are located in the main house and restored outbuildings. Accommodations in the annex (a converted stable block) have slightly less drama and flair. All the bedrooms have been styled to evoke the aura of a country house, though all the modern comforts have been installed as well.

Bishopthorpe Rd. (on A64, 2.5km/1½ miles south of town), York, North Yorkshire 4023 2GB. ✆ 800/735-2478 in the U.S. and Canada, or 01904/641241. Fax 01904/620176. www.middlethorpe.com. 30 units. £185–£330 ($370–$660) double; £265–£430 ($530–$860) suite. Rates include continental breakfast. AE, MC, V. Free parking. **Amenities:** 2 restaurants; bar; indoor heated pool; Jacuzzi; gym; spa; sauna; steam room; room service; laundry service; dry cleaning. *In room:* TV, Wi-Fi, hair dryer, trouser press.

Park Inn York ✸ Within the ancient city walls, this modern hotel overlooks the River Ouse and is the leading hotel within the center of York. Built in the 1970s, the hotel is the largest in town and is conveniently located for sightseeing. Many of the well-furnished and modern bedrooms have views looking toward the minster. Ten rooms are spacious enough for families. Each comes with a well-maintained private bathroom.

North St., York, North Yorkshire YO1 6JF. ✆ 01904/459988. Fax 01904/641793. www.parkinn.co.uk. 200 units. £99–£119 ($198–$238) double. Rates include English breakfast. AE, DC, MC, V. Parking £10 ($20). **Amenities:** Restaurant; 2 bars; health club; sauna; room service; laundry service; dry cleaning. *In room:* TV, Wi-Fi, beverage maker, hair dryer, trouser press.

MODERATE

Mount Royale Hotel ✸ A short walk west of York's city walls, in a neighborhood known as the Mount, this hotel is the personal statement of two generations of the Oxtaby family. They work hard to create a friendly, homey atmosphere. The main house was built as a private home in 1833, though several years ago the owners merged a neighboring house of the same era into the original core. Accommodations and public rooms are furnished with both modern pieces and antiques. Garden suites have private terraces leading to the garden.

119 The Mount, York, North Yorkshire YO2 2DA. ✆ 01904/628856. Fax 01904/611171. www.mountroyale.co.uk. 24 units. £99–£166 ($198–$332) double; £210 ($420) suite. Rates include English breakfast. AE, DC, MC, V. Free parking. **Amenities:** Restaurant; bar; outdoor heated pool; sauna; steam room; salon; room service; laundry service. *In room:* TV, Wi-Fi, beverage maker, hair dryer, trouser press.

INEXPENSIVE

Alexander House ✸ (Value) Only 7 minutes from the city center, this beautifully restored and elegantly decorated Victorian town house boasts York's most tranquil, delightful sitting room, where porcelain and art works make it even more inviting. Your hosts, David and Gillian, retained many of the original features of the house while

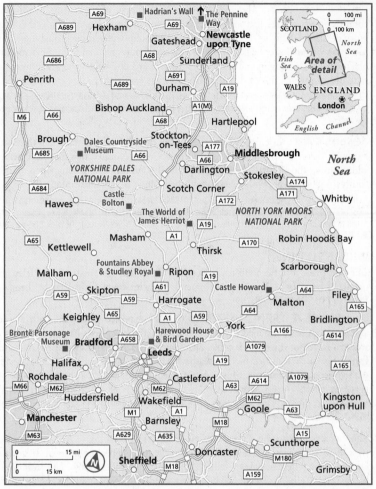

installing modern comforts. The midsize bedrooms are attractively and comfortably furnished, with lovely bathrooms of sparkling white porcelain and elegant toiletries.

54 Bishopthorpe Rd., York YO23 1JS. ⓒ **01904/625016.** www.alexanderhouseyork.co.uk. 4 units. £79–£85 ($158–$170) double. Rates include English breakfast. MC, V. Free parking. *In room:* TV, beverage maker, hair dryer.

Beechwood Close Hotel　Beechwood is a large house that is surrounded by trees, a garden with a putting green, and a parking area. Mr. and Mrs. Blythe run the small hotel, which offers comfortable bedrooms with tasteful furnishings. Each small bathroom is well maintained; most have tub/shower combinations. The hotel is a 15-minute walk to the minster, either by road or along the river.

19 Shipton Rd. (on A19 north of the city), Clifton, York, North Yorkshire YO30 5RE. ⓒ **01904/658378.** Fax 01904/647124. www.beechwood-close.co.uk. 14 units. £80 ($160) double (including breakfast); £95 ($190) double (including breakfast and dinner). AE, DC, MC, V. Free parking. **Amenities:** Restaurant; bar; business services; room service; laundry service. *In room:* TV, beverage maker, hair dryer, iron.

Cottage Hotel *Value*   About a 10-minute walk north of York Minster, this hotel comprises two refurbished and extended Victorian houses overlooking the village green of Clifton. The hotel offers cozy, small bedrooms with simple furnishings. Three rooms have four-poster beds. Some 400-year-old timbers rescued from the demolition of a medieval building in one of the city's historic streets (Micklegate) grace the restaurant and bar, which does a thriving business in its own right.

3 Clifton Green, York, North Yorkshire YO3 6LH. ℂ **0845/4566399.** Fax 01904/611230. 25 units. £60–£80 ($120–$160) double. Rates include English breakfast. MC, V. Free parking. **Amenities:** Restaurant; bar. *In room:* TV, beverage maker.

Heworth Court   Just a 10- to 15-minute walk east of the city center is this three-story red-brick Victorian structure (many of its bedrooms are located in a modern extension added during the 1980s). The rooms are agreeably furnished, and some open onto the courtyard. Each comes with a comfortable bed, plus a compact bathroom.

76 Heworth Green, York, North Yorkshire YO3 7TQ. ℂ **01904/425156.** Fax 01904/415290. www.heworth.co.uk. 28 units. £49–£79 ($98–$158) per person double. Rates include English breakfast. AE, DC, MC, V. Free parking. Take the A1036 to the east side of the city. **Amenities:** Restaurant; bar; laundry service. *In room:* TV, Wi-Fi, beverage maker, hair dryer.

WHERE TO DINE

The best place for afternoon tea is **Betty's Café & Tea Rooms,** 6–8 St. Helen's Sq. (ℂ **01904/659142**). We also recommend **Theatre Royal Café Bar,** St. Leonard's Place (ℂ **01904/623568**).

Blue Bicycle ✦ FRENCH/SEAFOOD   This respected restaurant with a warm ambience has been installed in a former brothel, the brass beds having given way to wooden tables for diners. The cooks earn their good reputation nightly for their fresh fish dishes, such as grilled filets of sea bass. The chefs prepare a Moroccan fish curry with apricots and mint couscous or else roasted monkfish with a chorizo risotto. The eggplant fritters are a delight.

34 Fossgate. ℂ **01904/673990.** Reservations required. Main courses £15–£20 ($30–$40). AE, DC, MC, V. Daily noon–2:30pm and 6–9:30pm.

The Ivy Brasserie/The Cellar Bar ✦ FRENCH/ENGLISH   A 10-minute walk west of York Minster, this dining complex is the most appealing in town. It is within an ivy-covered Regency town house that's also a 30-room hotel. The least formal venue is the Cellar Bar, a crowded, paneled, candlelit hideaway in the basement. The hearty menu items include steaks, fish, and ale. On the ground level, the Ivy Brasserie is more upscale and includes dishes such as a whole grilled Dover sole. Meat eaters gravitate to the rump of lamb with a roast-onion salsa. Skate is stuffed with a crab mousse, and another specialty is braised pork belly with pan-fried monkfish and roast pigs' cheeks.

In the Grange Hotel, 1 Clifton (off Bootham Rd.). ℂ **01904/644744.** Fax 01904/612453. Reservations recommended for Ivy; not necessary for Cellar Bar. Ivy Brasserie main courses £13–£19 ($26–$38); main courses in Cellar Bar £9.75–£11 ($20–$22). AE, DC, MC, V. Ivy Brasserie Mon–Sat 6–10pm; Sun noon–2pm. Cellar Bar daily 11am–11pm.

Melton's Restaurant ✦ *Kids* CONTINENTAL/ENGLISH   Some local food critics claim that Michael and Lucy Hjort serve the finest food in York, though we give that honor to the Ivy. The small and unpretentious restaurant is approximately 1.5km (1 mile) from the heart of the city. Mr. Hjort trained with the famous Roux brothers of Le Gavroche in London, but he doesn't charge their astronomical prices.

In what has always been known as a culinary backwater town, the Hjorts have created some excitement with this family-friendly place. Their menu changes frequently but could include pan-fried halibut with a saffron-and-mussel risotto, or else leg of black-faced lamb with savoy cabbage. A breast of turkey appears rolled in herbs and served with cranberries and bacon noisettes.

7 Scarcroft Rd. ⓒ **01904/634341.** www.meltonsrestaurant.co.uk. Reservations required. Main courses £15–£19 ($30–$38); fixed-price menu (available on limited basis) £26 ($52). MC, V. Tues–Sat noon–2pm; Mon–Sat 5:30–9:30pm. Closed 1 week in early Aug and Dec 24–Jan 14.

1331 Gastro Bar INTERNATIONAL   About a 5-minute walk from the minster, 1331 is in the heart of York, on a small street near Stonegate (walk up a narrow staircase to the second floor). There is a modern lounge area with a comfortable bar. The chefs use fresh ingredients, supplied locally if possible, and turn out high-quality dishes served in an intimate relaxed atmosphere. Vegetarians can sample such menu items as stuffed baked mushrooms topped with melted goat cheese. For meat devotees, try the braised lamb shank cooked slowly in the oven and served with rosemary and red onions. A beef-and-mushroom stroganoff is another winning dish, as are tender strips of filet of beef slow cooked with brandy and served with a Dijon mustard sauce. There's also a modern lounge area with a comfortable bar.

13 Grape Lane. ⓒ **01904/661130.** Reservations required. Main courses £8–£17 ($16–$34). AE, DC, DISC, MC, V. Restaurant Tues–Sat noon–10pm; Sun noon–5pm. Bar Tues–Thurs 11am–midnight; Fri–Sat 11am–2am.

SEEING THE SIGHTS

The best way to see York is to go to **Exhibition Square** (opposite the Tourist Information Centre), where a volunteer guide will take you on a **free 2-hour walking tour** of the city. You'll learn about history and lore through numerous intriguing stories. Tours run April to September daily at 10:15am and 2:15pm, plus 6:45pm from June to August; from November to March, a daily tour starts at 10:15am. Groups can book by prior arrangement by contacting the **Association of Volunteer Guides,** De Grey Rooms, Exhibition Square, York YO1 2HB (ⓒ **01904/640780;** www.york.touristguides. btinternet.co.uk).

Jorvik Viking Centre 🐾   This Viking city, discovered many feet below present ground level, was reconstructed as it stood in 948, and underwent major refurbishment in 2001. In a "time car," you travel back through the ages to 1067, when Normans sacked the city, and then you ride slowly through the street market peopled by faithfully modeled Vikings. You also go through a house where a family lived and down to the river to see the ship chandlers at work and a Norwegian cargo ship unloading. At the end of the ride, you pass through the Finds Hut, where thousands of artifacts are displayed. The time car departs at regular intervals.

Coppergate. ⓒ **01904/543400.** www.jorvik-viking-centre.co.uk. Admission £7.95 ($16) adults, £6.60 ($13) students and seniors, £5.50 ($11) children ages 5–15, £22 ($44) family ticket. Rates may change depending on the event. Apr–Oct and Feb daily 10am–5pm; Nov–Jan and Mar daily 10am–4:30pm.

National Railway Museum 🐾🐾🐾   This was the first national museum to be built outside London, and it has attracted millions of train buffs. Adapted from an original steam-locomotive depot, the museum gives visitors a chance to see how Queen Victoria traveled in luxury and to look under and inside steam locomotives. In addition, there's a collection of railway memorabilia, including a penny machine for purchasing tickets on the railway platform and an early-19th-century clock. More than 40 locomotives are on display. One, the *Agenoria,* dates from 1829 and is a contemporary of Stephenson's well-known *Rocket*. Of several royal coaches, the most interesting is Queen Victoria's Royal Saloon; it's like a small hotel, with polished wood, silk, brocade, and silver accessories.

Leeman York Rd. ⓒ **01904/621261**. www.nrm.org.uk. Free admission. Daily 10am–6pm. Closed Dec 24–26.

Treasurer's House The Treasurer's House lies on a site where a continuous succession of buildings has stood since Roman times. The main part of the house, built in 1620, was refurbished by Yorkshire industrialist Frank Green at the turn of the 20th century; he used this elegant town house to display his collection of 17th- and 18th-century furniture, glass, and china. An audiovisual program and exhibit explain the work of the medieval treasures and the subsequent fascinating history of the house. It has an attractive small garden in the shadow of York Minster.

Minster Yard. ⓒ **01904/624247**. www.nationaltrust.org.uk. Admission £5.50 ($11) adults, £2.80 ($5.60) children, £14 ($28) family ticket. Mar 16–Oct Sat–Thurs 11am–4:30pm; Nov–Mar 15 Sat–Thurs 11am–3pm.

York Castle Museum On the site of York's Castle, this is one of the finest folk museums in the country. Its unique feature is a re-creation of a Victorian cobbled street, Kirkgate, named for the museum's founder, Dr. John Kirk. He acquired his large collection while visiting his patients in rural Yorkshire at the beginning of 20th century. The period rooms range from a neoclassical Georgian dining room to an overstuffed and heavily adorned Victorian parlor to the 1953 sitting room with a "brand-new" television set purchased to watch the coronation of Elizabeth II. In the Debtors' Prison, former prison cells display crafts workshops. There is also a superb collection of arms and armor. In the Costume Gallery, displays are changed regularly to reflect the collection's variety. Half Moon Court is an Edwardian street, with a Gypsy caravan and a pub (sorry, the bar's closed!). During the summer, you can visit a water mill on the bank of the River Foss.

The Eye of York off Tower St. ⓒ **01904/687687**. www.yorkcastlemuseum.org.uk. Admission £6.50 ($13) adults, £5.50 ($11) seniors and students, £4 ($8) children. Daily 9:30am–5pm. Closed Dec 25–26 and Jan 1.

York Minster One of the great cathedrals of the world, York Minster traces its origins from the early 7th century; the present building, however, dates from the 13th century. Like the cathedral at Lincoln, York Minster is characterized by three towers built in the 15th century. The central tower is lantern shaped in the Perpendicular style, and on a clear day, the top of the tower offers panoramic views of York and the Vale of York. The climb up a stone spiral staircase is steep and only recommended for the fit.

The outstanding characteristic of the cathedral is its **stained glass** from the Middle Ages, in glorious vibrant blues, ruby reds, forest greens, and honey-colored ambers. See especially the Great East Window, the work of a 15th-century Coventry-based glass painter. In the north transept is an architectural gem of the mid–13th century: the Five Sisters Window, with its five lancets in grisaille glass. The late-15th-century choir screen in its Octagonal Chapter House has an impressive lineup of historical figures—everybody from William the Conqueror to the overthrown Henry VI. At a reception desk near the entrance to the minster, groups can arrange for a guide, if one is available. Conducted tours are free, but donations toward the upkeep of the cathedral are requested.

At the converging point of Deangate, Duncombe Place, Minster Yard, and Petergate. ⓒ **01904/557216**. www.york minster.org. Chapter House £5.50 ($11) adults, £4.50 ($9) seniors and students, free for children 15 and younger; crypt, foundations, and treasury £4 ($8) adults, £3 ($6) seniors and students, £2 ($4) children. Chapter House, undercroft, and tower Mon–Sat 9am–5:30pm, Sun noon–5:30pm (closing time in winter 5pm). Call ahead to verify times, as they are subject to change.

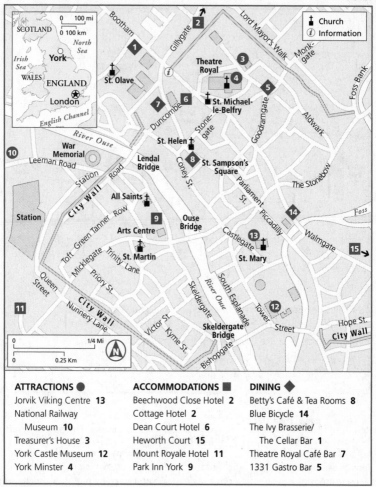

SHOPPING

Several of the main areas to explore include **Gillygate** for antiques dealers, **St. Mary's Square** and its **Coppergate** pedestrian mall for name brands and chain stores. One of the best streets for shopping is **Stonegate** with an array of independent outlets.

Several specialty shops that have ideal gift items include **Maxwell and Kennedy,** 79 Low Petergate (☏ **01904/610034**), a candy store specializing in both Belgian chocolate and Cambridge Wells dark, milk, and white chocolate; and **Mulberry Hall,** 17 Stonegate (☏ **01904/620736;** www.mulberryhall.co.uk), housed in a medieval house from 1436, with 16 showrooms on three floors devoted to the best in British and European porcelain, fine china, crystal, and some antiques. For your furry friends, the **Cat Gallery,** 27 Stonegate (☏ **01904/611053**), is Britain's largest feline-themed store.

York Minster

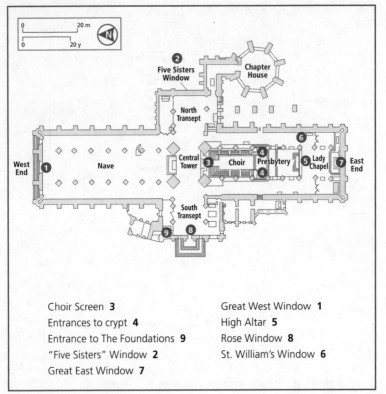

Choir Screen **3**

Entrances to crypt **4**

Entrance to The Foundations **9**

"Five Sisters" Window **2**

Great East Window **7**

Great West Window **1**

High Altar **5**

Rose Window **8**

St. William's Window **6**

A YORK PUB-CRAWL

One of the city's oldest inns, the **Black Swan,** Peaseholme Green (© **01904/679131;** www.blackswanyork.co.uk), is a fine, timber-framed house that was the home of the lord mayor of York in 1417; the mother of General James Wolfe of Quebec also lived here. In front of a log fire in a brick inglenook, you can enjoy pub meals such as fish and chips, burgers, and steaks. This is one of York's "musical pubs," featuring live folk music on Monday and Thursday, jazz on Wednesday and Sunday, and hip-hop every second and fourth Friday, with a small cover charge starting at £4 ($8).

Situated at the base of the Ouse Bridge, a few steps from the edge of the river, the 16th-century **Kings Arms Public House,** King's Staith (© **01904/659435**), is boisterous and fun. A historic monument in its own right, it's filled with charm and character and has the ceiling beams, paneling, and weathered brickwork you'd expect. Because of its location by the river, the pub can flood if rain is heavy enough. Expect a virtually indestructible decor, the kind that can (and often does) sit under water for days at a time. In summer, rows of outdoor tables are placed beside the river. Your hosts serve a full range of draft and bottled beers, the most popular of which (Samuel Smith's) is still brewed in Tadcaster, only 16km (10 miles) away. The ghost walk we recommend leaves here every night at 7:30pm.

On a pedestrian street in Old York, **Ye Olde Starre Inne,** 40 Stonegate (℗ **01904/ 623063**), dates from 1644 and is York's oldest licensed pub. An inn (of one kind or another) has stood on this spot since A.D. 900. The pub (said to be haunted by an old woman, a little girl, and a cat) features cast-iron tables, an open fireplace, oak Victorian settles, and time-blackened beams. The owners added a year-round glassed-in garden so guests can enjoy the view of the minster from their tables.

2 Leeds ⭐

328km (204 miles) NW of London; 121km (75 miles) NE of Liverpool; 69km (43 miles) NE of Manchester; 119km (74 miles) N of Nottingham

The foundations for a permanent community were laid nearly 2,000 years ago when the Romans set up a small camp here called Cambodunum, but the next step toward modern Leeds didn't come until the 7th century when the Northumbrian King Edwin established a residence. Kirkstall Abbey was founded in 1152, and in 1207 Leeds finally obtained its charter.

During the medieval era, Leeds took the golden fleece as its coat of arms, representative of its growth and importance as a wool town. In time, it became the greatest center of cloth trade in the region. Industrial advancements have played a great role in the growth of the city, with the introduction of steam power leading to the development of the coal fields to the south. Other innovations allowed the continued expansion of its textile industry, as well as the rapid development of such upstart industries as printing, tailoring, and engineering. The Victorian era marked the city's glory days.

After languishing for years and being dismissed for its industrial blight, the city is moving progressively forward again today. It's experiencing some economic growth, and many of the great Victorian buildings have been renovated in its bustling central core: the Corn Exchange, the Grand Theatre, and the Victoria Quarter. A "24-hour City Initiative" makes Leeds the only U.K. location that not only allows but also encourages round-the-clock work and entertainment options; it's an up-and-coming city with a lot of new energy.

ESSENTIALS

GETTING THERE   Leeds Bradford International Airport (℗ 01132/509696; www.lbia.co.uk), about 14km (9 miles) north of town, has daily flights to and from London's Heathrow and Gatwick airports and most major regional U.K. airports, with air transport taking less than an hour from London. There is also a 24-hour direct rail link between Manchester airport and Leeds. **Taxi** fare from the airport to the center of Leeds costs £20 ($40).

Trains from London's Kings Cross Station arrive hourly during the day, with the trip taking about 2 hours. For information, call ℗ **0845/748-4950** or visit **www. nationalrail.co.uk**.

Leeds is also serviced daily by **National Express** buses from London. For schedules and information, call ℗ **0870/580-8080** or visit **www.nationalexpress.com**.

Leeds lies at the crossroads of the north-south M1 and the east-west M62 routes, making it easily accessible by car from anywhere in England or Scotland.

VISITOR INFORMATION   The **Gateway Yorkshire Regional Travel & Tourist Information Centre,** the Arcade, City Station (℗ 01132/425242), is open Monday through Saturday 9am to 5:30pm and Sunday 10am to 4pm. The city's own website (www.leeds.gov.uk) offers information on transportation, lodging, dining, shopping, and entertainment in the city.

Information on local bus and train routes and times is available by calling **Metroline** at © **01132/457676.**

SPECIAL EVENTS In July, more than 40,000 opera lovers turn out at **Temple Newsam,** Temple Newsam Road, off Selby Road (© **01132/645535;** www.leeds. gov.uk/templenewsam), for the single performance of **Opera in the Park,** the largest free outdoor opera concert in the United Kingdom. The gargantuan **Party in the Park** (© **01132/478222**), also held at Temple Newsam, is one of the largest free pop and rock concerts in the United Kingdom. It's usually held the day following Opera in the Park and features some of the hottest acts in rock music.

Film buffs turn out in droves for the annual **Leeds International Film Festival** (© **01132/243801;** www.leedsfilm.com). Screened at cinemas throughout Leeds, it's the only theme-based film festival in the United Kingdom. It regularly features British as well as world-premiere films and hosts film-related lectures, seminars, and workshops. In 2009, the festival takes place from November 5 to November 16.

WHERE TO STAY

If you'd like advice on local lodging, or if you'd just like to tell someone your price range and requirements and let them book you a room, contact the **Gateway Yorkshire Accommodation Booking Line** (© **0800/808050** or 01132/425242). For a £4 ($8) handling fee and a refundable deposit of 10% of your first night's stay, they'll find you a bed for the night.

42 The Calls 🌟🌟🌟 Overlooking the River Aire in the heart of Leeds, this small but deluxe hotel is the city's most tranquil and elegant choice, created from an 18th-century grain mill in a once-dilapidated waterfront area that's all high tech and high comfort now. Rooms range from the more traditional to units such as the Black Room, with a huge black bed and black-striped walls, or room no. 303, with an original winch hanging from the ceiling—a nod to the building's origins. Business travelers will appreciate the three phones in every room, full-size work desk, individual fax machine on request, and dictation by arrangement.

42 The Calls, Leeds LS2 7EW. © **01132/440099.** Fax 01132/344100. www.42thecalls.co.uk. 41 units. £130–£210 ($260–$420) double; £260–£375 ($520–$750) suite. AE, DC, MC, V. Parking £12 ($24). **Amenities:** 2 restaurants; bar; access to nearby health club; car-rental desk; courtesy car; room service; babysitting; laundry service; dry cleaning. *In room:* TV, Wi-Fi, beverage maker, hair dryer, iron, trouser press.

Haley's Hotel & Restaurant 🌟 *Value* Located in a quiet, tree-lined cul-de-sac just off the main Otley-Leeds road (A660), this town-house hotel, set up in a Victorian mansion, makes it easy to forget you're near a major metropolitan area. The hotel's rooms are comfortably laid out and opt for tasteful individuality, each with its own period-specific, polished, natural-wood antiques. Features include work desks with telephones and efficiently organized private bathrooms, many with tubs or showers. As for the beds, management accurately quotes Charles Dickens: "It would make anyone go to sleep, that bedstead would, whether they wanted to or not." The staff is diligent, accommodating guests with such options as a late supper or shoe-cleaning service.

Shire Oak Rd. (3km/2 miles from Leeds City Centre and 11km/7 miles from Leeds Bradford International Airport), Headingley, Leeds LS6 2DE. © **01132/784446.** Fax 01132/753342. www.haleys.co.uk. 29 units. £120–£125 ($240–$250) double. Rates include breakfast and dinner. AE, MC, V. Free parking. **Amenities:** Restaurant (see review below); bar; room service; babysitting; laundry service; dry cleaning. *In room:* TV, Wi-Fi, beverage maker, hair dryer, iron, trouser press.

Malmaison ⚑ *(Finds)* This former tram and bus garage is today a hotel of charm and character. The local newspaper hailed its rebirth as "sexy, cool, and slinky," and so it is—a stylish hotel that is intimate and cool. A great range of well-styled and individually designed bedrooms await you, some of them in subtle taupes with contrasting deep tones, such as plum, charcoal, and ocher. The hotel also has a high-tech fitness suite. Downstairs is a super little bar and brasserie under a vaulted ceiling.

Sovereign Quay, Leeds LS1 1DQ. ✆ **01133/981000.** Fax 0113/398-1002. www.malmaison-leeds.com. 100 units. £145–£180 ($290–$360) double; from £399 ($798) suite. AE, DC, MC, V. Parking £10 ($20). **Amenities:** Restaurant; bar; fitness center; room service; laundry service; dry cleaning. *In room:* TV, high-speed Internet, CD player, minibar, beverage maker, hair dryer, trouser press.

Oulton Hall ⚑⚑ A painstakingly restored 1850s Italianate mansion, this hotel offers an atmosphere of pure elegance, from the black-and-white-tiled front entrance and the damask-hung walls of the public rooms with their great crystal chandeliers, to the library with its mahogany wall paneling and window seat. You can enjoy butler service in the drawing room, a drink in the plush red-leather interior of the Calverley Bar, or a stroll through formal gardens re-created from the original 19th-century plans. Most of the well-furnished bedrooms are in the modern wing; the grand suites are in the original house. Bedrooms enjoy views of the well-manicured grounds and championship golf course.

Rothwell Lane (9km/5½ miles east from Leeds by A61 and A639), Oulton, Leeds LS26 8HN. (℃ **01132/821000.** Fax 01132/828066. www.devere.co.uk. 152 units. £95–£155 ($190–$310) double; £245–£295 ($490–$590) suite. Rates include English breakfast. AE, DC, MC, V. Free parking. **Amenities:** 2 restaurants; bar; indoor heated pool; 9- and 18-hole golf courses; driving range; health club; Jacuzzi; sauna; croquet lawn; salon; room service; laundry service; dry cleaning. *In room:* TV, Wi-Fi, minibar, beverage maker, hair dryer, trouser press.

Quebecs ✸✸ *Finds* As a sign of the renaissance of the city of Leeds, this gorgeous 1891 neo-Renaissance pile of red brick has been glamorously restored and converted into a hotel. The Victorian shell has been preserved; otherwise, the hotel is imbued with state-of-the-art amenities. The broad winding oak staircase and the ornate stained-glass windows are still there, along with handcrafted oak panels. A few minutes' walk from City Square and the main train station, the central hotel offers bedrooms that are beautifully and traditionally decorated in chic colors such as camel brown and Wedgwood blue. The best accommodations are two mezzanine suites with spiral staircases leading to the sleeping quarters.

9 Quebec St., Leeds LS1 2HA. (℃ **01132/448989.** Fax 01132/449090. www.summithotels.com. 45 units. £120–£210 ($240–$420) double; from £200 ($400) suite. AE, DC, MC, V. Parking £10 ($20). **Amenities:** Restaurant; bar; room service; laundry service; dry cleaning. *In room:* A/C, TV, Wi-Fi, minibar, beverage maker, hair dryer, iron, safe.

WHERE TO DINE

Anthony's Restaurant ✸✸✸ MODERN BRITISH Anthony James Flinn just may be the greatest chef in Yorkshire. He certainly is number one in Leeds. He's the most innovative, even provocative, chef around, and his creations are cutting edge—or, in his words, "molecular gastronomy," whereby physics and chemistry are applied to the kitchen. Don't you always like your baby squid with mango sherbet or your sliver of pigs' ears with cubes of honey jelly? Shredded crab comes on Jabugo ham with salted peanut foam, and fork-tender pork comes startlingly pink in the new style of preparation. For dessert? Smoked brie ice cream—but, of course.

19 Boar Lane. (℃ **0113/245-5922.** Reservations required. Main courses £20–£26 ($40–$52); set lunch £20 ($40) for 2 courses; set dinner £55 ($110). AE, DC, MC, V. Tues–Sat noon–2pm and 7–9:30pm.

Haley's Restaurant ENGLISH This hotel restaurant, in a beautifully restored Victorian mansion, is so popular among locals that even the guests have to reserve long in advance. Chef John Vennell changes his menu monthly to take advantage of the freshest and best market ingredients. Starters may feature a tantalizing tasting of king prawns marinated and grilled in lemon-grass paste on a lemon risotto flavored with tamarind sauce. A heavenly tartlet is made with roast beets and goat cheese and served with a soft quail egg. Some of the best main courses include filet steak stuffed with blue Stilton and wrapped in Parma ham, or else rack of lamb with a juniper-and-thyme crust, flavored with a Madeira sauce. The wine cellar has offerings from around the world.

In Haley's Hotel, Shire Oak Rd., Headingley (see hotel review above for directions). (℃ **01132/784446.** Reservations required well in advance. Main courses £14–£17 ($28–$34); fixed-price menus £19–£24 ($38–$48). AE, DC, MC, V. Mon–Sat 7:15–9:30pm; Sun 12:15–1:45pm. Closed Dec 26–30.

Heathcotes ✸✸ CONTINENTAL Part of a small, relatively upscale chain, this popular restaurant occupies an early-19th-century granary. Set beside the water in the city's revitalized canal-front district, its theatrical lighting showcases the massive beams and trusses that formed the skeleton of the building's original architecture. Menu items include a pleasing mixture of comfort food and more innovative cuisine. Start with a warm ham hock and potatoes with a soft poached egg and hollandaise tartar, or seared king scallops and black pudding with a mustard dressing. For a main dish, you face such temptations as Bramley roast breast of Goosnargh duck with mulled-red-wine pear and star anise, or else pan-fried filet of haddock with savoy cabbage. Menus change frequently with the seasons.

Canal Wharf, Water Lane. © 01132/446611. Reservations recommended. Main courses £13–£25 ($26–$50); fixed-price 2-course menu Sun noon–6pm £16 ($32), 3 courses £18 ($36). AE, MC, V. Mon–Sat noon–2:30pm and 6–10pm; Sun noon–9:30pm.

EXPLORING LEEDS

Despite its longtime reputation as a grimy northern industrial city, Leeds will surprise you with the beauty and diversity of its **City Centre,** where £400 million ($800 million) has been invested during the past decade in both new construction and renovation of warehouses and landmark Victorian structures into homes, lodgings, shops, and restaurants along the waterfront and in the central shopping district.

The Henry Moore Institute   Located next door to the City Art Gallery, this is one of the largest sculpture galleries in Europe. The institute is named after the greatest British sculptor of the 20th century, Henry Moore (1898–1986), who was a Yorkshireman. Three galleries of changing exhibitions display the various aspects of sculpture. The works of many of Moore's contemporaries are often displayed. Lectures throughout the year supplement the institute's exhibitions.

74 The Headrow. © 01132/467467. www.henry-moore-fdn.co.uk. Free admission. Daily 10am–5:30pm (Wed until 9pm).

Leeds City Art Gallery   Spread over three floors, this gallery, founded in 1888, houses England's best collection of 20th-century art outside of London, including collections of French post-Impressionist paintings, contemporary British sculpture, prints, watercolors, and drawings. Throughout the year it also hosts visiting exhibits, enhanced by workshops, talks, and other related events. The library reopened in May 2007 following a wholesale £1.7-million ($3.4-million) restoration, including a new exhibition gallery for touring art shows and multimedia installations. Located within the gallery, the **Craft Centre and Design Gallery** (© 01132/478241) showcases contemporary ceramics, jewelry, prints, textiles, and applied arts from around the world; it also hosts openings and exhibits by local and regional artists.

74 The Headrow. © 01132/478248. www.leeds.gov.uk/artgallery. Free admission. Mon–Tues and Thurs–Sat 10am–5pm; Wed 10am–8pm; Sun 1–5pm.

Royal Armouries Museum   A notable construction along the waterfront, this £42-million ($84-million) facility is the home of London Tower's Royal Armouries, England's oldest museum, with exhibits that include the working arsenal of the medieval kings. It is designed to exhibit the many pieces that have been in perpetual storage because of inadequate facilities in London. The museum illustrates the development and use of arms and armor for war, sport, hunting, self-defense, and fashion.

Armouries Dr. © 01132/201985. www.armouries.org.uk. Free admission. Daily 10am–5pm. Closed Dec 24–25.

Temple Newsam House   This was the birthplace, in 1545, of the ill-fated Lord Darnley, husband of Mary, Queen of Scots. Construction began on this Tudor-Jacobean mansion in 1521, and substantial remodeling occurred in both the 17th and late 18th centuries. It stands as an odd but beautiful tribute to several eras of architecture. Today, it houses a splendid collection of silver and Chippendale furniture. The surrounding 480 hectares (1,200 acres) of parkland includes Home Farm, a breeding ground for rare farm animals, and the venue for Opera in the Park (p. ###).

Temple Newsam Rd. (off Selby Rd.; 6.5km/4 miles from Leeds City Centre off the A63). © 01132/645535. www. leeds.gov.uk/templenewsam. Admission: House £3.50 ($7) adults, £2.50 ($5) children 5–16; house and farm £5.50 ($11) adults, £3.50 ($7) children 5–16. Apr–Oct Tues–Sun 10:30am–5pm (last admission at 4:15pm); Nov–Mar Tues–Sun 10:30am–4pm (last admission at 3:15pm).

LEEDS AFTER DARK

Thanks to a city initiative aimed at relaxing licensing restrictions and increasing late-night entertainment options, it's safe to say that Leeds now rocks round-the-clock. And it was already humming with classical concerts, opera, jazz, dance, theater, cinema, rock and dance clubs, cafes, and pubs.

THE CLUB & MUSIC SCENE   Leeds has a thriving rock scene, with recent bands such as Sisters of Mercy and the Mission rising out of the music scene. Today's up-and-coming music scene is, not surprisingly, very influenced by the Manchester scene (see chapter 17), but innovative bands such as Black Star Liner, Bedlam A Go Go, and Embrace show that Leeds still has a musical voice all its own.

The **Cockpit,** Bridge House, Swinegate (© 01132/441573; www.thecockpit.co. uk), can host about 600 fans, who turn out to hear the latest indie bands in a converted railway arch setting. It's usually open Tuesday, Wednesday, Friday, and Saturday night with a cover ranging from £3 to £5 ($6–$10).

You'll find the jazz you're looking for at **Arts Café,** 42 Call Lane (© 01132/ 438243), a European-style cafe-bar that offers tapas, bottled beers, and coffees.

Considering its size, there is a substantial gay scene in Leeds. The most popular club at the moment is **Queens Court,** Lower Briggate (© 01132/459449; www.queens-court.co.uk). Downstairs is a restaurant and bar. Queens Court is open Monday to Wednesday noon to 2am, Thursday noon to midnight, Friday and Saturday noon to 3am, and Sunday noon to 11pm. The cover charge ranges from £2 to £4 ($4–$8). Another current hot spot for gay men is the **Bridge Inn,** 1–5 Bridge Inn (© 01132/ 444734), which has a friendly-local-pub atmosphere and becomes increasingly clubby as the night progresses (no cover).

PUBS   Stop by **Whitelocks,** Turks Head Yard (© 01132/453950), in the alley of Briggate, next to Marks & Spencer. There's a copper-topped bar with a handmade ceramic-tile front, a marble sandwich bar, old advertising mirrors, and stained-glass windows. Locals keep the conversation flowing in a thick, northern accent. If you get hungry, there's cheap traditional pub grub. Tap selections are varied and quite good, including McEwan's 80, Younger's IPA, and Theakston's Old Peculier.

Hearkening back to Leeds's glory days, **Victoria,** Great George Street (© 01132/ 451386), is every bit as Victorian as its name suggests, with ornate globe lamps, etched mirrors, and a well-adorned bar. Politicians and lawyers frequent the place. Join in the conversation or sit back and listen while you enjoy a pint of Tetley's Mild and maybe a bar snack or two.

THE PERFORMING ARTS   **Leeds Town Hall,** the Headrow (© 01132/477989), hosts orchestras from around the globe as part of the city's annual **International Concert Season** and is also home to the world-famous **Leeds International Pianoforte Competition,** held every 3 years. Opera North offers three to four productions during its season from October to April at the **Leeds Grand Theatre and Opera House,** 46 New Briggate (© 01132/456014), featuring a well-renovated 1,500-seat auditorium behind its original 1878 Victorian facade.

Side Trip to Holy Island (Lindisfarne)

This island is the cradle of Christianity in northern England, lying 6 miles east of the A1, north of Bamburgh and 8 miles southeast of Berwick-upon-Tweed.

In 635 St. Aidan established a monastery here, which reached the zenith of its power under St. Cuthbert, who turned it into the foremost center of learning in Christendom.

But in 875 Vikings destroyed the community, and only a few monks escaped. However, they did manage to remove Cuthbert's bones in time, reburying them at the cathedral at Durham.

Lindisfarne is a tidal island, and vehicles can only cross when the tide allows. Opening times vary significantly every day, so check locally before going over.

As you cross the causeway you'll see **Lindisfarne Castle,** Lindisfarne (© 01289/389244), which was built about 1550 as a fort to protect the harbor. In 1903 it was converted by Sir Edwin Lutyens into a comfortable home for Edward Huson, the founder of *Country Life.* Many of the original architectural features are intact, and there is also a walled garden, the work of Gertrude Jekyll, which lies nearby. Admission is £5.20 ($10), and visits are possible from late March to October Tuesday to Sunday 10:30am to 3pm (subject to change).

In the village stands **Lindisfarne Priory** (© 01289/389200), which dates from the 11th century when it was partially restored by monks from Durham. A museum displays ancient artifacts, including Anglo-Saxon carvings. Hours are April to September daily 10am to 6pm; February, March, and October daily 10am to 4pm, and November to January Saturday and Sunday 10am to 4pm. Admission is £3.70 ($7.40).

For your base check into the **Manor House Hotel,** Holy Island (© 01289/389207; fax 01289/389310; www.manorhouselindisfarne.co.uk), which sits beside the ruins of Lindisfarne Priory. The manor house stands in the market place in the heart of the village, opening onto panoramic views. Open February to December, the manor rents 10 comfortable and well-furnished bedrooms, opening onto sea views. The rate is £63 ($126) per person, including breakfast and dinner. For sea-view rooms, this half-board rates rises to £75 ($150) per person, going up to £90 ($180) per person for the master bedroom.

Theatergoers are much impressed by the facilities at the £12-million ($24-million) **West Yorkshire Playhouse,** Playhouse Square, Quarry Hill (© 01132/137700; www.wyplayhouse.com), home to the "national theatre of the north." Playhouse artistic director Jude Kelly started out strong in the early inaugural seasons, with 17 productions, including eight British or world premieres. There has been no slowing down since then, and you can find a dramatic offering at most any time in either the Playhouse's Quarry Auditorium, which seats 750, or the Courtyard, which seats 350. The Playhouse, which is the cornerstone of a proposed £70-million ($140-million) Quarry Hill arts complex, also hosts other events throughout the year, including the annual Jazz at the Playhouse series.

The **Yorkshire Dance Centre,** St. Peters Building, York Street (© 01132/438765), houses the internationally renowned **Phoenix Dance Troupe.**

3 Bradford *

341km (212 miles) N of London; 52km (32 miles) NE of Manchester; 14km (9 miles) W of Leeds

This city of nearly half a million souls retains a rich ethnic heritage from the succession of immigrants who came to work the mills beginning in the mid–19th century. High-tech firms, galleries, and museums have displaced many of the textile factories of the past. But generations of Irish, German, Italian, eastern European, Asian, and African-Caribbean immigrants give this West Yorkshire town an international flavor today. Centrally located between the Yorkshire Dales and the Pennines, Bradford provides a nice diversion and is convenient to a historic countryside where the Brontës once dwelled and armor-clad soldiers clashed in the Wars of the Roses.

ESSENTIALS

GETTING THERE **Leeds Bradford International Airport** (© 01132/509696; www.lbia.co.uk) is located about 16km (10 miles) from Bradford, and a number of scheduled flights connect it to London's Heathrow and Gatwick airports and most major regional U.K. airports. A **taxi** from the airport to town costs about £10 ($20), and Bradford is reached by **car** via the M62 and the M606.

Most rail links go through nearby Leeds (see above), but at least one direct **train** each day connects London's Kings Cross Station with Bradford (a 3-hr. trip). Train travel from Manchester takes about 1 hour, and 3 hours from Birmingham.

VISITOR INFORMATION Call the **Bradford Tourist Information Centre,** City Hall, Centenary Square (© 01274/433678). The center assists visitors in selecting accommodations and provides public transit timetables and city guides. Hours are Monday 10am to 5pm, Tuesday to Saturday 9:30am to 5pm. On the Web, there are two websites for Bradford: **www.city-of-bradford.com** and **www.visitbradford.com**.

WHERE TO STAY

Best Western Guide Post Hotel Catering to both business and leisure travelers, this is a winning choice. You get a warm welcome as you're shown to your spacious, well-furnished room equipped with a compact bathroom with shower. The more expensive executive rooms have a spacious lounge area. The reasonable price combined with room size makes this a good choice for families as well.

Common Rd. (5km/3 miles from Junction 26 of M62), Low Moor, Bradford, West Yorkshire BD12 0ST. © 01274/ 607866. Fax 01274/671085. www.guideposthotel.net. 43 units. £67–£97 ($134–$194) double; £77–£115 ($154–$230) suite. Rates include English or continental breakfast. AE, DC, MC, V. **Amenities:** Restaurant; bar; room service; laundry service; dry cleaning. *In room:* TV, Wi-Fi, beverage maker, hair dryer, iron, trouser press.

Great Victoria Hotel Built in 1875, the Victoria in the city center is entirely restored. Once the showpiece of the Lancashire and Yorkshire Railway, the hotel provides stylish accommodations at affordable rates. The well-furnished and recently renovated bedrooms all are comfortable and clean. Bathrooms are equipped with power showers. Four rooms are large enough for families.

Bridge St., Bradford, West Yorkshire BD1 1JX. © 01274/728706. Fax 01274/736358. www.tomahawkhotels.co.uk. 60 units. £119–£139 ($238–$278) double; £159 ($318) suite. Rates include breakfast. AE, DC, MC, V. From M62, take Junction 26 to M606, then to A6177 and A611, and exit at roundabout to Hallings; turn right at traffic light, and hotel is on left. **Amenities:** Restaurant; bar; sauna; children's programs; business services; room service; laundry service; dry cleaning. *In room:* TV, beverage maker, hair dryer, trouser press.

WHERE TO DINE

Bradford is called "the curry capital of the U.K.," boasting a vast array of Asian restaurants featuring dishes from Kashmir, Gujarat, the Punjab, and beyond. Many of the best of these curry houses are found along Morley Street near the National Museum of Photography, Film & Television. Our favorite along this street is **Kashmir,** 27 Morley St. (© **01274/726513**), which, although a very simple place, serves authentic and excellently prepared Indian food.

An even better choice is **Mumtaz,** Great Horton Road (© **01274/571861**), Bradford's leading Kashmiri curry house, drawing large crowds of hungry diners. Meat, fish, and vegetable curries are prepared with great skill and flavor. Expat Indians prefer to accompany their meal with *masala lassi,* a yogurt drink, or perhaps sweet mango juice, as liquor isn't served.

Bradford is not a great restaurant town except for its curry houses, and some travelers prefer to dine at their hotel restaurants.

EXPLORING BRADFORD

Bradford's museums, mill shops, and restaurants provide the main attractions for tourists. The city also boasts Bradford University, one of the better regional universities in the United Kingdom.

The **Industrial Museum and Horse at Work,** Moorside Mills, Moorside Road (© **01274/435900**), depicts mill life for worker and owner in the 1870s and offers Shire horse rides for kids and adults. The museum is open Tuesday to Saturday 10am to 5pm and Sunday noon to 5pm; admission is free. The **Saltaire,** Salt's Mill, is the restored model factory-community developed in the mid–19th century by mill owner and philanthropist Titus Salt. The **1853 Gallery** at Saltaire (© **01274/531163**) exhibits more than 400 works by local artist David Hockney, among others.

Visitors can travel by steam-driven train on the **Keighley & Worth Valley Railway** (© **01535/645214;** www.kwvr.co.uk) for a tour of Brontë Country in Haworth (see below), through Oakworth's Edwardian station and Damen's Station, billed as Britain's smallest rail station. It operates daily in summer and only on Saturday in the winter.

National Museum of Photography, Film & Television, Little Horton Lane (© **0870/7010200;** www.nmpft.org.uk), captures the history of photography, film, and television in audiovisual presentations that span 150 years. The five-story-high IMAX screen, the largest in England, explores a dazzling variety of cinematic images in a series of new and continuing exhibitions. Admission to the museum is free; the IMAX movie costs £7 ($14) for adults, £5 ($10) for children. Advance booking is recommended. The museum is open Tuesday to Sunday 10am to 8pm.

Bradford's textile industry is still represented in dozens of area mill shops where bargain hunters may find a great variety of mohair, pure-wool yarns, fabrics, sportswear, and other clothing and accessories. Some mill shops provide tours of factory spinning, weaving, and textile finishing.

BRADFORD AFTER DARK

Alhambra Theatre, Morley Street (© **01274/432000;** www.bradford-theatres.co. uk), offers a variety of presentations ranging from amateur to professional. At certain times of the year, leading actors of the English stage and screen may appear here. You can also see children's theater, ballet, and musicals. Ticket prices vary depending upon the type of performance. The theater is closed for a few weeks in August.

But perhaps you're just looking for a local pub. In the city center, the **Shoulder of Mutton,** 28 Kirkgate (© **01274/726038**), has a beer garden that comes complete with flower beds and hanging baskets. The oldest brewery in Yorkshire, it was originally Samuel Smith's Old Brewery. Lunch is available, and they also sell real ale here. As many as 200 drinkers can crowd in here on a summer night.

As an alternative, try the **Fighting Cock,** 21–23 Preston St. (© **01274/726907**), an old-fashioned alehouse with bare floors and 12 different bitters. The best ales are Exmoor Gold, Timothy Taylor's, Black Sheep, and Green King Abbott, but they also sell foreign-bottled beers and farm ciders. On nippy nights, coal fires keep the atmosphere mellow. Bar snacks are among the most reasonable in town; the house specialty is chili (the chef guards the recipe).

4 Haworth: Home of the Brontës ★★

72km (45 miles) SW of York; 34km (21 miles) W of Leeds

Haworth, on the moor of the Pennines, is the famed home of the Brontës, the most-visited literary shrine in England after Stratford-upon-Avon.

ESSENTIALS

GETTING THERE To reach Haworth by rail, take the Arriva Train from Leeds City Station to Keighley (it leaves approximately every 30 min.). Change trains at Keighley and take the Keighley and Worth Valley Railway to Haworth and Oxenhope. Train services operate every weekend year-round, with 7 to 12 departures. From late June to September, trains also run four times a day Monday through Friday. For general inquiries, call © **01535/645214** (www.kwvr.co.uk); for a 24-hour timetable, dial the tourist office at © **01535/642329.**

Keighley & District Bus Co. offers bus service between Keighley and Haworth. Bus nos. 663, 664, and 665 will get you there. For information, call © **01535/603284.**

Driving time from York to Haworth is about 1 hour, 15 minutes. Head west toward Leeds on the A64. West toward Leeds on the A64, the route is extremely complicated, with many different turnoffs onto various routes, so plot your way carefully before setting out to avoid getting lost. It's best to set out with a detailed map or else download the complicated directions from MapQuest.

VISITOR INFORMATION The **Tourist Information Centre,** at 2–4 West Lane, Haworth (© **01535/642329**), is open May to August daily 9:30am to 5:30pm, September to April daily 9:30am to 5pm; the center is closed December 24 to December 26.

WHERE TO STAY

Weaver's Restaurant (see "Where to Dine," below) also offers rooms for rent.

Ashmount Country House ★★ *Finds* This is the grandest B&B in this part of England, real government-rated five-star luxury living. Were they to return today, the Brontë sisters might call it decadent. The country house was the ancestral home of Dr. Amos Ingham, family physician to Charlotte and Patrick Brontë. Nestled below the evocative moors of Wuthering Heights, the home has been completely modernized with spacious, luxurious bedrooms, yet its quaint old-fashioned charm has been painstakingly preserved. Bedrooms rest under high ceilings and for the luxury-minded there are exquisite hot-tub suites.

Mytholmes Lane, Haworth, West Yorkshire BD22 8EZ. ℂ **01535/645-726.** Fax 01535/642-550. www.ashmount haworth.co.uk. 9 units. £70–£140 ($140–$280) double; £140 ($280) suite. Rates include English breakfast. AE, MC, V. **Amenities:** Breakfast room; room service; garden. *In room:* TV, Wi-Fi, CD player.

Old White Lion Hotel   At the top of a cobblestone street, this hotel dates from 1700 when it was built with a solid stone roof. It's almost next door to the church where the Reverend Brontë preached, as well as the parsonage where the family lived. Paul and Christopher Bradford welcome visitors to their warm, cheerful, and comfortable hotel. Though full of old-world charm, all rooms are completely up-to-date. Room size varies considerably, but each room is attractively furnished and has a comfortable bed and a small bathroom, most with a tub/shower combination. Two rooms are large enough for families.

6–10 West Lane, Haworth near Keighley, West Yorkshire BD22 8DU. ℂ **01535/642313.** Fax 01535/646222. www. oldwhitelionhotel.com. 14 units. £76 ($152) double. Rates include English breakfast. AE, DC, MC, V. **Amenities:** Restaurant; bar; room service. *In room:* TV, beverage maker, hair dryer.

WHERE TO DINE

Weaver's Restaurant ⍟ *Value* MODERN BRITISH   The best restaurant in the Brontë hometown, this spot is British to the core. In an inviting, informal atmosphere, it serves excellent food made with fresh ingredients. Jane and Colin Rushworth are quite talented in the kitchen. Dinners may include such classic dishes as slow-cooked Yorkshire lamb. If available, try one of the Gressingham ducks, which are widely praised in the United Kingdom. Other highly favored dishes include local farm chicken in a creamy green-peppercorn sauce or steamed filets of sea bass with a shallot-and-white-wine sauce. For dessert, try a British cheese or one of the homemade delicacies. The restaurant is likely to be closed for vacation for a certain period each summer, so call in advance to check. They also rent three bedrooms of high caliber that cost £95 ($190) for a double, including breakfast.

15 West Lane. ℂ **01535/643822.** Reservations recommended. Main courses £12–£18 ($24–$36); 3-course fixed-price menu £17 ($34). AE, DC, MC, V. Wed–Sun noon–2pm; Tues–Sat 6:30–9:30pm.

LITERARY LANDMARKS

Anne Brontë wrote two novels, *The Tenant of Wildfell Hall* and *Agnes Grey;* Charlotte wrote two masterpieces, *Jane Eyre* and *Villette,* which depicted her experiences as a teacher, as well as several other novels; and Emily is the author of *Wuthering Heights,* a novel of passion and haunting melancholy. Charlotte and Emily are buried in the family vault under the **Church of St. Michael** (Anne is buried at the **Church of St. Mary** in Scarborough). Try **www.visitbrontecountry.com** for information.

While in Haworth, you'll want to visit the **Brontë Weaving Shed,** Townend Mill (ℂ **01535/646217**). The shop is not far from the Brontë parsonage and features the famous Brontë tweed, which combines browns, greens, and oranges to evoke the look of the local countryside. The shed is open for visitors Monday to Saturday 10am to 5:30pm and Sunday 11am to 5pm.

Brontë Parsonage Museum ⍟   The parsonage where the Brontë family lived has been preserved as this museum, which houses their furniture, personal treasures, pictures, books, and manuscripts. The stone-sided parsonage, built near the top of the village in 1777, was assigned for the course of his lifetime as the residence of the Brontës' father, Patrick, the perpetual curator of the Church of St. Michael and All Angel's Church. Regrettably, the church tended by the Brontës was demolished in 1870; it was rebuilt in its present form the same year. The parsonage contains a walled garden very similar to the one cultivated by the Brontës, five bedrooms, and a collection of family furniture (some bought with proceeds from Charlotte's literary success), as well as personal effects, pictures and paintings, and original manuscripts. It also contains the largest archive of Brontë family correspondence in the world.

The museum is maintained by a professional staff selected by the Brontë Society, an organization established in 1893 to perpetuate the memory and legacy of Britain's most famous literary family. Contributions to the society are welcomed. The museum tends to be extremely crowded in July and August.

Church St. ✆ 01535/642323. www.bronte.org.uk. Admission £5.50 ($11) adults, £4 ($8) students and seniors, £2 ($4) children 5–16, free for children 4 and younger, £13 ($26) family ticket (2 adults, 3 children). Oct–Mar daily 11am–5pm; Apr–Sept daily 10am–5:30pm. Closed Jan and at Christmas.

5 Yorkshire's Country Houses, Castles & More

Yorkshire's battle-scarred castles, Gothic abbeys, and great country-manor houses are unrivaled anywhere in Britain. Here are some of the highlights.

IN NORTH YORKSHIRE

Castle Howard ✶✶   In its dramatic setting of lakes, fountains, and extensive gardens, Castle Howard, the 18th-century palace designed by Sir John Vanbrugh, is undoubtedly the finest private residence in Yorkshire. This was the first major achievement of the architect who later created the lavish Blenheim Palace near Oxford. The Yorkshire palace was begun in 1699 for the third earl of Carlisle, Charles Howard. The striking facade is topped by a painted and gilded dome, which reaches more than 24m (80 ft.) into the air. The interior boasts a 58m-long (192-ft.) gallery, as well as a chapel with magnificent stained-glass windows by the 19th-century artist Sir Edward Burne-Jones. Besides the collections of antique furniture and sculpture, the castle has many important paintings, including a portrait of Henry VIII by Holbein and works by Rubens, Reynolds, and Gainsborough. The seemingly endless grounds, including two rose gardens, also include the domed Temple of the Four Winds, by Vanbrugh, and the richly designed family mausoleum, by Hawksmoor.

Malton (24km/15 miles northeast of York, 5km/3 miles off A64). ✆ 01653/648444. www.castlehoward.co.uk. Admission £11 ($22) adults, £9.50 ($19) students and seniors, £6.50 ($13) children 4–16. Mar 2–Oct 31 grounds daily 10am–4:30pm; house daily 11am–4pm (during winter, call to verify times).

Fountains Abbey & Studley Royal ✶✶✶   On the banks of the Silver Skell, the abbey was founded by Cistercian monks in 1132 and is the largest monastic ruin in Britain. In 1987, it was awarded World Heritage status. The ruins provide the focal point of the 18th-century landscape garden at Studley Royal, one of the few surviving examples of a Georgian green garden. It's known for its conservation work in the water gardens, ornamental temples, follies, and vistas. The garden is bounded at its northern edge by a lake and 160 hectares (400 acres) of deer park.

At Fountains, 6.5km (4 miles) southwest of Ripon off B6265. ✆ 01765/608888. www.fountainsabbey.org.uk. Admission £7.50 ($15) adults, £4 ($8) children, £20 ($40) family. Nov–Feb daily 10am–4pm; Mar–Oct daily 10am–5pm. Closed Dec 24–25 and Fri in Nov–Jan. It's best to drive, though it can be reached from York by public transportation. From York, take bus no. 142 leaving from the York Hall Station to Ripon, 37km (23 miles) to the northwest (A59, A1, and B6265 lead to Ripon). From Ripon, it will be necessary to take a taxi 6.5km (4 miles) to the southwest, though some prefer to take the scenic walk.

IN WEST YORKSHIRE

Harewood House & Bird Garden ★★ (Kids)   Thirty-five kilometers (22 miles) west of York, the home of the earl and countess of Harewood is one of England's great 18th-century houses. It has always been owned by the Lascelles family. The fine Adam interior has superb ceilings and plasterwork and furniture made especially for Harewood by Thomas Chippendale. There are also important collections of English and Italian paintings and Sèvres and Chinese porcelain.

The gardens, designed by Capability Brown, include terraces, lakeside and woodland walks, and a 1.8-hectare (4½-acre) bird garden with exotic species from all over the world, including penguins, macaws, flamingos, and snowy owls. Other facilities include an art gallery, shops, a restaurant, and a cafeteria. Parking is free, and there is a picnic area, plus an adventure playground for the children. Highest rates are charged June 28 to September 7.

At the junction of A61 and A659, midway between Leeds and Harrogate, at Harewood Village. (C) **01132/281010.** www.harewood.org. House, grounds, bird garden, and the terrace gallery £10–£12 ($20–$24) adults, £6.20–£7.70 ($12–$15) children, £9–£11 ($18–$22) seniors, £36–£42 ($72–$84) family ticket. Mid-Feb to mid-Nov daily house, bird garden, and adventure playground 11am–4:30pm; terrace gallery 11am–5pm; mid-Nov to mid-Dec daily garden and grounds 10am–4pm, bird garden 10am–3pm. From York, head west along B1224 toward Wetherby and follow the signs to Harewood from there.

6 Yorkshire Dales National Park ★

This national park consists of some 1,813 sq. km (700 sq. miles) of water-carved country. In the dales, or valleys, you'll find dramatic white-limestone crags, roads, and fields bordered by dry-stone walls, fast-running rivers, isolated sheep farms, and clusters of sandstone cottages.

Malhamdale receives more visitors annually than any dale in Yorkshire. Two of the most interesting historic attractions are the 12th-century ruins of Bolton Priory and the 14th-century Castle Bolton, to the north in Wensleydale.

Richmond, the most frequently copied town name in the world, stands at the head of the dales and, like Hawes (see below), is a good center for touring the surrounding countryside.

EXPLORING THE DALES

For orientation purposes, head first for **Grassington,** 16km (10 miles) north of Skipton and 40km (25 miles) west of Ripon. Constructed around a cobbled marketplace, this stone-built village is ideal for exploring Upper Wharfedale, one of the most scenic parts of the dales. In fact, the Dales Way footpath passes right through the heart of the village.

Drop in to the **National Park Centre,** Colvend, Hebden Road ((C) **01756/751690;** www.yorkshiredales.org.uk), which is open April through October daily from 10am to 5pm. From November to March, hours are Wednesday, Friday, Saturday, and Sunday 10am to 4pm. Maps, bus schedules through the dales, and a choice of guidebooks are available here to help you navigate your way. If you'd like a more in-depth look than what you can do on your own, you can arrange for a qualified guide who knows the most beautiful places and can point out the most interesting geological and botanical features of the wilderness.

Sixteen kilometers (10 miles) west of Grassington (reached along the B6265), **Malham** is a great place to set out on a hike in summer. Branching out from here, you can set out to explore some of the most remarkable limestone formations in Britain. First, it's best to stop in for maps and information at the **National Park Centre** (© **01969/ 652380**), which is open from Easter to October daily from 10am to 5pm; off season, it is open only Saturday and Sunday from 10am to 4pm. Amazingly, this village of 200 or so souls receives a half-million visitors annually. May or September is the time to come; the hordes descend from June to August.

The scenery in this area has been extolled by no less an authority than Wordsworth, and it has been painted by Turner. You can explore a trio of scenic destinations—**Malham Cove, Malham Tarn,** and **Gordale Scar**—on a circular walk of 13km (8 miles) that takes most hikers 5 hours. If your time (and your stamina) is more limited, you can take a circular walk from the heart of the village to Malham Cove and Gordale Scar in about 2 hours. At least try to walk 1.5km (1 mile) north of the village to Malham Cove, a large natural rock amphitheater. Gordale Scar is a deep natural chasm between overhanging limestone cliffs, and Malham Tarn is a lake in a desolate location.

Kettlewell lies 13km (8 miles) northwest of Malham and 9.5km (6 miles) north of Grassington. This is the main village in the Upper Wharfedale and is a good base for hiking through the local hills and valleys, which look straight out of *Wuthering Heights*. Narrow pack bridges and riverside walks characterize the region, and signs point to the **Dales Way** hiking path.

After Kettlewell, you can drive for 6.5km (4 miles) on B6160 to the hamlet of **Buckden,** the last village in the Upper Wharfedale. Once here, follow the sign to **Kidstone Pass,** still staying on B6160. At **Aysgarth** 𝕬𝕬, the river plummets over a series of waterfalls, one of the dramatic scenic highlights of the Yorkshire Dales.

MASHAM: A ROOM IN A CASTLE

For luxury lovers, the little village of Masham makes the best base—certainly the most luxurious—for an overnight stay to explore the Yorkshire Dales. Swinton Park stands at the gateway to the Dales.

Swinton Park 𝕬𝕬𝕬　If you weren't born in an aristocrat's vine-covered castle, you can stay here and have the experience after all. Mark Cunliffe-Lister, nephew of the earl and countess of Swinton, has converted this historic manor into a luxury hotel. Set in 80 hectares (200 acres) of parkland, lakes, and gardens, this family estate is a good base for exploring the Yorkshire Dales National Park, lying 52km (32 miles) northwest of York. Even with a pedigree going back to the 1500s, the castle is up-to-date with a spa and fitness area in a conservatory. There is also a bar in the family museum, a private cinema, and even a Victorian game room. Each of the spacious and beautifully designed bedrooms is individually designed, taking the theme of a Yorkshire dale, castle, abbey, or town.

Swinton Park, Masham, North Yorkshire HG4 4JH. © **01765/680900.** Fax 01765/680901. www.swintonpark.com. 30 units. £150–£270 ($300–$540) double; £300–£350 ($600–$700) suite. Rates include Yorkshire breakfast. AE, DC, MC, V. **Amenities:** Restaurant; bar; fitness center; spa; sauna; Jacuzzi; room service; babysitting; laundry service; dry cleaning. *In room:* TV, Wi-Fi, beverage maker, iron, trouser press.

HAWES: A BASE FOR EXPLORING YORKSHIRE DALES NATIONAL PARK

About 105km (65 miles) northwest of York, on the A684, Hawes is the natural center of Yorkshire Dales National Park and a good place to stay. On the Pennine Way, it's England's highest market town and the capital of Wensleydale, which is famous for its cheese. Trains from York take you to Garsdale, which is 8km (5 miles) from Hawes. From Garsdale, bus connections will take you into Hawes.

While you're there, you may want to check out the **Dales Countryside Museum,** Station Yard (© **01969/666210;** www.yorkshiredales.org.uk), which traces folk life in the Dales, a story of 10,000 years of human history. The museum is open April to October daily from 10am to 5pm. Winter hours vary; you'll have to check locally. Admission is £4 ($8) for adults, £3 ($6) for students and seniors, and free for ages 11 and younger.

WHERE TO STAY

Cockett's Hotel & Restaurant   This is an atmospheric choice, still sporting many remnants of its construction in 1668. In case you need reminding, the date of its construction is carved into one of its lintels. Set in the center of town, it's a two-story, slate-roofed, stone cottage whose front yard is almost entirely covered with flagstones. Rooms are done in an old-world style with exposed wooden beams; they're snug, cozy, and well maintained.

Market Place, Hawes, North Yorkshire DL8 3RD. © **01969/667312.** Fax 01969/667162. www.cocketts.co.uk. 8 units. £64–£79 ($128–$158) double. Rates include English breakfast. MC, V. **Amenities:** Restaurant; bar. *In room:* TV, beverage maker, hair dryer, trouser press.

Simonstone Hall   Just north of Hawes, you can stay and dine at Simonstone Hall. Constructed in 1733, this building has been converted into a comfortable, family run, country-house hotel with a helpful young staff. It's the former home of the earls of Wharncliffe. The public rooms and the bedrooms are equally ideal for relaxation and comfort. Most bedrooms are spacious, and all are furnished tastefully with antiques. Each comes with a quality bed and an efficiently organized shower bathroom.

2.5km (1½ miles) north of Hawes on the road signposted to Muker, Hawes, North Yorkshire DL8 3RD. © **01969/667255.** Fax 01969/667741. www.simonstonehall.co.uk. 18 units. £110–£190 ($220–$380) double. Rates include breakfast. AE, MC, V. **Amenities:** Restaurant; bar; room service. *In room:* TV, beverage maker, hair dryer.

7 North York Moors National Park ⊛

The moors, on the other side of the Vale of York, have a wild beauty all their own, quite different from that of the dales. This rather barren moorland blossoms in summer with purple heather. Bounded on the east by the North Sea, it embraces a 1,440-sq.-km (554-sq.-mile) area, which has been preserved as a national park.

If you're looking for a hot, sunny beach vacation, the North Yorkshire coast isn't for you—the climate is cool because of the brisk waters of the North Sea. Even summer months don't get very hot. Many Britons do visit North Yorkshire for beach vacations, however, so you will find a beach-town atmosphere along the coast, with brightly colored stalls lining the seafront.

The national park is perfect for solitary strolls and peaceful drives. For remnants of the area's exciting days of smugglers and brave explorers, visitors can follow the Captain Cook Heritage Trail along the coast. The fishing industry is still alive in the area, though the whaling ships of yesteryear have been anchored.

ESSENTIALS

GETTING THERE   Because the park sprawls over such a large area, you can access it from five or six different gateways. Most visitors enter it from the side closest to York, by following either the A19 north via the hamlet of **Thirsk,** or by detouring to the northeast along the A64 and entering via **Scarborough.** You can also get in through **Helmsley,** where the park's administrative headquarters are located; just follow the roads from York that are signposted HELMSLEY. Gateways along the park's northern edges, which are less convenient to York, include the villages of **Whitby** (accessible via A171) and **Stokesley** (accessible via A19).

VISITOR INFORMATION   For information on accommodations and transportation before you go, contact **North York Moors National Park,** the Old Vicarage, Bondgate, Helmsley, York YO62 5BP (© **01439/770657;** www.moors.uk.net). You can get advice, specialized guidebooks, maps, and information at the **Sutton Bank Visitor Centre,** Sutton Bank, near Thirsk, North Yorkshire YO7 2EK (© **01845/597426**). Another well-inventoried information source, which, unlike the others, is open year-round, is the **Moors Centre,** Danby Lodge, Lodge Lane, Danby, near Whitby, YO21 2JE (© **01439/772737**).

EXPLORING THE MOORS

Bounded by the Cleveland and Hambleton hills, the moors are dotted with early burial grounds and ancient stone crosses. **Pickering** and **Northallerton,** both market towns, serve as gateways to the moors.

The North York Moors will always be associated with doomed trysts between unlucky lovers and ghosts who wander vengefully across the rugged plateaus of their lonely and windswept surfaces. Though the earth is relatively fertile in the river valleys, the thin, rocky soil of the heather-clad uplands has been scorned by local farmers as wasteland, suitable only for sheep grazing and healthy (but melancholy) rambles. During the 19th century, a handful of manor houses were built on their lonely promontories by moguls of the Industrial Revolution, but not until 1953 was the 1,440-sq.-km (554-sq.-mile) district designated the North York Moors National Park.

Encompassing England's largest expanse of moorland, the park is famous for the diversity of heathers, which thrive between the sandstone outcroppings of the uplands. If you visit between October and February, you'll see smoldering fires across the landscape—deliberately controlled attempts by shepherds and farmers to burn the omnipresent heather back to stubs. Repeated in age-old cycles every 15 years, the blazes encourage the heather's renewal with new growth for the uncounted thousands of sheep that thrive in the district.

Though public bridle and footpaths take you to all corners of the moors, two noteworthy and clearly demarcated trails make up the most comprehensive moor walks in Europe. The shorter of the two is the **Lyle Wake Walk,** a 64km (40-mile) east-to-west trek that connects the hamlets of Osmotherly and Ravenscar. It traces the rugged path established by 18th-century coffin bearers. The longer trek (the **Cleveland Walk**) is a 177km (110-mile) circumnavigation of the national park's perimeter. A good section skirts the edge of the Yorkshire coastline; other stretches take climbers up and down a series of steep fells in the park's interior.

Don't even consider an ambitious moor trek without good shoes, a compass, an ordinance survey map, and a detailed park guidebook. With descriptions of geologically interesting sites, safety warnings, and listings of inns and farmhouses (haunted or otherwise) offering overnight stays, the guidebooks sell for less than £4 ($8) each at any local tourist office.

The isolation and the beauty of the landscape attracted the founders of **three great abbeys:** Rievaulx near Helmsley, Byland Abbey near the village of Wass, and Ampleforth Abbey. Nearby is **Coxwold,** one of the most beautiful villages in the moors. The Cistercian Rievaulx and Byland abbeys are in ruins, but the Benedictine Ampleforth still functions as a monastery and well-known Roman Catholic boys' school. Though many of its buildings date from the 19th and 20th centuries, they do contain earlier artifacts.

The old market town of Thirsk, in the Vale of Mowbray, 39km (24 miles) north of York on the A19, is near the western fringe of the park. It has a fine parish church, but what makes it such a popular stopover is its association with the late James Herriot (1916–95), author of *All Creatures Great and Small*. Mr. Herriot used to practice veterinary medicine in Thirsk. You can drop in at a visitor center, the **World of James Herriot,** 23 Kirkgate (© **01845/524234**), which is dedicated to his life and to veterinary science. The Kirkgate surgery where he practiced from 1930 until his death in 1995 and the house next door have been transformed into *The Herriot Experience*. You can view the surgery and see various exhibitions and displays on veterinary science. It's open daily from Easter to September from 10am to 5pm and from October to Easter from 11am to 4pm (last admission is always 1 hr. before closing). Admission is £5.20 ($10) adults, £3.80 ($7.60) children 5 to 15, £4.20 ($8.40) seniors, family ticket £15 ($30).

EXPLORING THE NORTH YORKSHIRE COAST

Along the eastern boundary of the park, North Yorkshire's 72km (45-mile) coastline shelters such traditional seaside resorts as Filey, Whitby, and Scarborough, the latter claiming to be the oldest seaside spa in Britain, located supposedly on the site of a Roman signaling station. The spa was founded in 1622, when mineral springs with medicinal properties were discovered. In the 19th century, its Grand Hotel, a Victorian structure, was acclaimed the best in Europe. The Norman castle on the big cliffs overlooks the twin bays.

It's easy to follow the main road from Bridlington north to Scarborough and on to Robin Hood's Bay and Whitby. As you drive up the coast, you'll see small fishing ports and wide expanses of moorland.

BRIDLINGTON
29km (18 miles) SE of Scarborough

Bridlington is a good starting point for a trip up the North Yorkshire coast. A fishing port with an ancient harbor, the wide beach and busy seafront markets draw crowds who enjoy relaxing on the sand or browsing through the gift shops and stalls that line the streets. Flamborough Head is one of the most distinguishable features on England's east coast. Jutting out into the North Sea, it features a 26m-tall (85-ft.) lighthouse that stands atop a chalk cliff towering 51m (170 ft.) above the sea. A path that winds up the cliffs ends at Bempton, site of a bird sanctuary that is one of the finest reserves on the coast. You can enjoy watching the seabirds or simply take in the view of the sea off Flamborough, the final resting place of more than a few ships. Bridlington also has many country houses that are open for tours, in addition to Pickering and Helmsley castles and the deserted village of Wharram Percy.

Where to Stay
Flamborough Manor   The current manor house of Flamborough dates from 1800. It was fully restored by local craftspeople and now boasts comfortable accommodations and a friendly atmosphere. Bedrooms are tastefully appointed and have small bathrooms equipped with showers and adequate shelf space. Many visitors come to the house to browse through the variety of antiques sold in the converted stable block or to purchase a Gansey sweater. (These intricate fishermen's sweaters are hand-made in the traditional way, an almost-lost process that has been revived by Lesley Berry, the house's proprietor.) Children 7 and younger are not allowed.

Flamborough, Bridlington, East Yorkshire YO15 1PD. ℂ/fax **01262/850943**. www.flamboroughmanor.co.uk. 2 units. £78–£88 ($156–$176) double. Rates include English breakfast. AE, MC, V. *In room:* TV, beverage maker, hair dryer, no phone.

SCARBOROUGH
29km (18 miles) NW of Bridlington; 55km (34 miles) NE of York; 407km (253 miles) N of London

Scarborough, one of the first seaside resorts in Britain, has been attracting visitors for more than 3 centuries. A mineral spring discovered in the early 17th century led to the establishment of a spa that lured clients with promises of its water's healing benefits. In the 18th century, swimmers were attracted to the waters off the coast—sea bathing had come into vogue, and the beaches of England swarmed with tourists taking part in the craze.

The city of Scarborough is divided into two unique districts separated by a green headland that holds the remains of Scarborough Castle, which dates from Norman times. South of the headland, the town conforms to its historical molds. High cliffs and garden walks interspersed with early Victorian residences dominate the landscape. The north side is more touristy; souvenir shops and fast-food stands line the promenade. Rock candy (brightly colored hard candy that can be etched with the saying of your choice) and candy floss (cotton candy) satisfy even the most die-hard sweet tooth.

For more information about what to see and do while you're in Scarborough, visit the **Tourist Information Centre,** Pavilion House, Valley Bridge Road (ℂ **01723/373333**), open May to September daily 9:30am to 6pm; the rest of the year it's open Monday to Saturday 10am to 4:30pm.

Trains leave London approximately every 30 minutes headed for York, where you'll have to transfer to another train. The entire trip takes just 2 hours and 10 minutes. For more information on schedules and prices, call ℂ **0845/748-4950** or visit **www. nationalrail.co.uk**. Three buses a day leave London heading for York; another will take you from York to Scarborough. If you're taking the bus, plan on spending most of a day riding. For **National Express** bus service, call ℂ **0870/580-8080** or visit **www.nationalexpress.com**.

Where to Stay
The Crown Spa Hotel *Kids*   Maintained in a style that's in keeping with its "Grand Hotel" origins in 1844, this hotel overlooks South Bay and Scarborough Castle from its setting above a cliff top, just above the quieter side of the town's beachfront. In recent years, extensive renovations have brought everything up-to-date. The accommodations are comfortable, with many rooms offering pleasant views over the sea. Most of the rooms, ranging from midsize to spacious, have been rejuvenated. Seven rooms are large enough for families.

Esplanade, Scarborough, North Yorkshire YO11 2AG. ℂ **01723/357400**. Fax 01723/357404. www.scarborough hotel.com. 87 units. £118–£152 ($236–$304) double; £196–£276 ($392–$552) suite. Rates include breakfast. AE, MC, V. Free parking. **Amenities:** 2 restaurants; bar; indoor heated pool; gym; spa; Jacuzzi; sauna; steam room; room service; laundry service; dry cleaning. *In room:* TV, Wi-Fi, beverage maker, hair dryer, trouser press.

The Palm Court Hotel   This inn provides guests with modern amenities in an elegant, old-world atmosphere. Inviting common areas, such as the lounge and cocktail bar, provide ideal settings for sharing a drink with friends. Rooms are tastefully furnished and among the most comfortable in Scarborough. Most accommodations are generally spacious, and six are rented to families.

St. Nicholas Cliff, Scarborough, North Yorkshire YO11 2ES. (C) **01723/368161.** Fax 01723/371547. www.palm courtscarborough.co.uk. 44 units. £82–£92 ($164–$184) double. Rates include English breakfast. AE, DC, MC, V. Parking £1.10 ($2.20) per hour. **Amenities:** Restaurant; bar; indoor heated pool; room service; babysitting; laundry service; dry cleaning. *In room:* TV, Wi-Fi, beverage maker, hair dryer, trouser press.

Wrea Head Country House Hotel ⋇ This Victorian country house is situated just north of Scarborough on 5.6 hectares (14 acres) of beautifully kept grounds. Several very compelling common rooms, such as a library and comfortable bar, entice guests to sit and relax. The rooms vary in size and are individually styled with tasteful furnishings, including first-rate beds and well-maintained bathrooms with tub/shower combinations. Two rooms are ideal for families.

Barmoor Lane, Scalby, Scarborough, North Yorkshire YO13 0PB. (C) **01723/378211.** Fax 01723/355936. www.english rosehotels.co.uk. 20 units. £119–£180 ($238–$360) double; £200 ($400) suite. Rates include breakfast. AE, MC, V. Free parking. **Amenities:** Restaurant; bar; room service; babysitting; laundry service. *In room:* TV, beverage maker, hair dryer, trouser press.

Where to Dine

Lanterna ⋇ ITALIAN Small, straightforward, and charming, this is a high-quality Italian restaurant whose owners, the Alessio family, maintain a strict allegiance to the recipes and ingredients (especially truffles) of their original home in northern Italy. Set in the center of old town, without any view of the sea, it offers places for 30 diners at a time in a room that's ringed with art photographs of Italian wine, food products, and, of course, truffles. Menu items include lots of fresh fish (the owners make a trip to the fish market every morning at 7:30am), including whole sea bass roasted "on its bone" with olive oil and herbs. Pastas are made fresh almost every day and may include a succulent version of venison ravioli. A particularly unctuous starter is *tajarin* (strips of flat pasta), served with a relatively bland sauce of mushrooms and cream. The intent of this mild dish involves allowing the nutty, woodsy flavor of the truffles—added table-side at the last minute—to emerge, unencumbered by other, more strident flavors.

33 Queen St. (C) **01723/363616.** Reservations recommended. Main courses £13–£38 ($26–$76). MC, V. Mon–Sat 7–9:30pm. Closed 2 weeks in Oct (dates vary).

Exploring the Town

The ruins of **Scarborough Castle,** Castle Road ((C) **01723/372451;** www.english-heritage.org.uk), stand on the promontory near a former Viking settlement. From the castle, you can look out over the North Bay, the beaches, and the gardens along the shore. Throughout the summer, fairs and festivals celebrate days of yore with mock battles, pageantry, and falconry displays. The castle is open daily as follows: July and August 9:30am to 6pm; October and February 10am to 5pm; November to January 10am to 4pm; March to June and September 10am to 6pm. Admission is £4 ($8) for adults, £3 ($6) for seniors and persons with disabilities, £2 ($4) for children, £10 ($20) family ticket. Children 4 years old and younger enter free.

Nearby is the medieval **Church of St. Mary,** Castle Road (no phone), where Anne Brontë, the youngest of the three sisters of literary fame, was buried in 1849. She died in Scarborough after being brought from her home in Haworth in hopes that the sea air would revive her health.

Also located at the Crescent is the **Art Gallery** ((C) **01723/374753**). The gallery's permanent collection features pieces ranging from 17th-century portraits to 20th-century masterworks. Many of the works relate to the Scarborough area. Changing exhibitions by young artists and local craftspeople are also displayed. If you're interested in learning how to create your own works of art, you may want to spend a while at the **Crescent Arts Workshop,** located in the basement of the gallery. Local artists offer courses and demonstrations in their respective mediums. The Art Gallery is open from June to September, Tuesday to Sunday 10am to 5pm. The rest of the year it is open Tuesday to Sunday 11am to 4pm. Admission is £2 ($4) for adults, £1.50 ($3) for seniors and children. Children 4 and younger are admitted free. For information about workshop offerings, call © **01723/351461** or visit their website at **www.crescentarts. co.uk**.

Local history collections and displays of important archaeological finds can be found at the **Rotunda Museum,** Vernon Road (© **01723/374839;** www.rotunda museum.org.uk). The museum is housed in a circular building, constructed in 1829 for William Smith, the "Father of English Geology," to display his collection; it was one of the first public buildings in England built specifically for use as a museum. The Rotunda is open June to September Tuesday to Sunday 10am to 5pm; from October to May, hours are Tuesday, Saturday, and Sunday from 11am to 4pm. Admission is £2.50 ($5) for adults, £1.50 ($3) for seniors and children 5 to 16, and £6 ($12) for a family ticket. Children 4 and younger are admitted free.

Of course, Scarborough still has the springs that established its popularity. The **Spa,** South Bay (© **01723/376774**), no longer offers guests the opportunity to partake of the waters; it is now an entertainment and conference center in the midst of elegant gardens and buildings dating from several eras. In summer, there is a concert of some kind every day (usually classical and often held outdoors). Unless you just want to wander through the grounds, entertaining in itself, you may want to call ahead for concert times and prices.

Scarborough After Dark

Alan Ayckbourn, a popular contemporary playwright, calls Scarborough home. The **Stephen Joseph Theatre,** Westborough, performs many of his plays as well as other favorites. Call the box office at © **01723/370541** for information about shows and prices, or check out **www.sjt.uk.com**.

Most action takes place at **zero,** in Westborough (© **01723/503170**), where DJs rule the night when live bands aren't appearing. Its chief rival is **Vivaz** on Huntriss Row (© **01723/368222**). The club with its dance floor was designed to host live music. Otherwise, hot DJs dictate the music. The club sometimes sponsors "Dirty Nights."

ROBIN HOOD'S BAY

21km (13 miles) NW of Scarborough

Though Robin Hood's Bay was once a notorious port for smugglers, it has no connection with the well-known outlaw who shares the village's name. The tiny fishing port is tucked into a deep ravine; in fact, space is so limited that cars can't enter the village center. The villagers live in cottages precariously balanced on the steep cliffs, where narrow roads curve between the dwellings.

Where to Stay

Raven Hall Hotel *Kids*   Many guests never leave the grounds of the hotel for entertainment, though Raven Hall makes a good base from which to venture out into Scarborough and nearby Robin Hood's Bay. The rooms have pleasant views of the water, the moors, or the garden. Each of the traditionally furnished bedrooms is renovated and comes with a comfortable bed. Nearly half of the rooms here are large enough for families. Two rooms have four-poster beds.

Ravenscar, North Scarborough YO13 0ET. © 01723/870353. Fax 01723/870072. www.ravenhall.co.uk. 53 units. £98–£168 ($196–$336) double. Rates include English breakfast. 2-night minimum stay Fri–Sat. AE, DC, MC, V. **Amenities:** Restaurant; bar; indoor heated pool; 9-hole golf course; putting green; 2 outdoor tennis courts; gym; sauna; lawn bowling; game room; room service; laundry service. *In room:* TV, beverage maker, hair dryer, trouser press.

WHITBY
11km (7 miles) NW of Robin Hood's Bay; 564km (350 miles) NE of London

The resort town of Whitby, at the mouth of the River Esk, has a rich and interesting history. It began as a religious center in the 7th century when Whitby Abbey was first founded. Later, Whitby became a prominent whaling port and eventually, like most coastal towns, an active participant in the smuggling trade.

Several famous explorers have pushed off from the beaches of Whitby, including Captain James Cook. Captain Cook, as the king's surveyor, circumnavigated the globe twice in ships constructed by local carpenters and craftsmen. He also claimed Australia and New Zealand for Great Britain.

Literary references to Whitby add intrigue to the town. Herman Melville paid tribute to William Scoresby, captain of some of the first ships that sailed to Greenland and inventor of the crow's nest, in his novel *Moby-Dick,* and Bram Stoker found his inspiration for *Dracula* in the quaint streets of Whitby.

Whitby Tourist Information Centre, Langbourne Road (© **01947/602674**), is open daily May to September from 9:30am to 6pm. The rest of the year it opens daily 10am to 4:30pm.

One bus a day travels between London and Whitby. The trip takes approximately 7 hours and is a direct route. Call the **National Express** bus service at © **0870/580-8080** or visit **www.nationalexpress.com** for more details. To get to Whitby from London by train, you'll have to ride to Middlesbrough or Scarborough, then transfer to the train or bus to Whitby. The number of trains to Whitby varies, so call ahead. The number for rail information is © **0845/748-4950** (www.nationalrail.co.uk).

Where to Stay
Dunsley Hall *Kids*   Five kilometers (3 miles) north of Whitby in the small hamlet of Dunsley, Dunsley Hall is from the turn of the 20th century, when it was built by a Hartlepool shipping magnate who lived here with his family until 1940. Some of the original carpets and furnishings remain, and they now add historical charm to the well-appointed hotel. Guests can enjoy a stroll through the carefully tended gardens. Two of the spacious bedrooms are set aside for families, and bathrooms are small but well maintained; each has a shower unit (some have bathtubs). In 2007 a new wing opened with eight stylish bedrooms, more desirable than those in the main building.

Dunsley, Whitby, North Yorkshire YO21 3TL. © 01947/893437. Fax 01947/893505. www.dunsleyhall.com. 26 units. £125–£190 ($250–$380) double; £200 ($400) family suite. Rates include breakfast. AE, MC, V. **Amenities:** Restaurant; bar; indoor heated pool; exercise room; sauna; breakfast-only room service; laundry service; dry cleaning. *In room:* TV, beverage maker, hair dryer, trouser press.

Where to Dine
Many hotels in the area offer half-board plans (with dinner) in addition to bed-and-breakfast rates; it may save you time and money if you take advantage of these. If you don't, or if you're looking for lunch, try **Trencher's,** New Quay Road (© **01947/ 603212**), for terrific fish and chips. Fresh filets of haddock or cod are fried in a crispy

batter and served with thick-cut fries. For good food in an even better atmosphere, stop by **White Horse and Griffin,** Church Street (© **01947/604857;** http://white horseandgriffin.co.uk). While surrounded by the character of the 18th-century structure, you may enjoy pot-roasted pheasant with cider or crispy pork belly with a mustard sauce. Whitby cod is baked under a crust of crab and served on a bed of fresh spinach. The White Horse and Griffin also rents out 10 comfortable bedrooms, each with a private bathroom, TV, and beverage maker, costing £65 ($130) a night in a double, including breakfast.

Seeing the Sights

The ruins of **Whitby Abbey,** Abbey Lane (© **01947/603568**), lie high on the East Cliff, where they are visible from almost anywhere in town. The abbey dates from the 12th century and adjoins the site of a Saxon Monastery that was established in A.D. 657. Caedmon, the first identifiable English-language poet, was a monk here. On this site in A.D. 664, the date for Easter was decided. The abbey is open from Easter to September daily from 10am to 6pm; October daily from 10am to 5pm; and the rest of the year, Thursday to Monday, closing at 4pm. Admission is £4.20 ($8.40) for adults, £3.20 ($6.40) for seniors, £2.10 ($4.20) for children 5 to 16, and £11 ($22) for a family ticket.

Another religious site is the uniquely designed **Church of St. Mary** (© **01947/603421**). Stairs (199 of them) leading to the church begin at the end of Church Street. If you have the stamina to climb them, you can walk through the rather spooky churchyard; it was here that Lucy was taken as Dracula's victim in Bram Stoker's novel. The church itself is an eclectic mix of architectural styles.

Whitby Museum, Pannett Park (© **01947/602908;** www.whitbymuseum.org.uk), features exhibits that center on the city's history. Of course, ship models and details of Captain Cook's adventures are essential to the museum, but there are also displays about the archaeology and natural history of the area. The Pannett Art Gallery has a permanent collection featuring paintings by George Weatherill. There are also constantly changing special exhibits. The museum and gallery are open Tuesday to Sunday 9:40am to 4:30pm (last admission at 4pm). Admission to the museum is £3 ($6) for adults, £1 ($2) for children, and £7 ($14) for a family ticket; there is no charge for the gallery.

Captain Cook Memorial Museum, Grape Lane (© **01947/601900;** www.cook museumwhitby.co.uk), deals more specifically with the life and achievements of the famous explorer James Cook. It is open daily April to October 9:45am to 5pm, daily March 11am to 3pm, and the last two weekends of February 11am to 3pm. Last entry is 30 minutes before closing. Admission is £4 ($8) for adults, £3 ($6) for students and seniors, £3 ($6) for children, and £11 ($22) for a family ticket.

The **Whitby Tourist Information Centre** (© **01947/602674**) can give anglers information about fishing along the town's coastline. Fishing is free all along the Whitby shore. If you'd rather go out to sea to reel in a big one, there are boats for hire at points throughout the city. The cost usually includes tackle and bait.

Golfers should visit the **Whitby Golf Club,** Low Straggleton (© **01947/600660**). The 6,134-yard course is open to visiting golfers daily. **Raven Hall Hotel Golf Course,** Ravenscar (© **01723/870353**), is open to nonguests all day, every day. The 9-hole course is well tended and offers panoramic views of the moors and the sea. This is also the best place in the area for **tennis.**

8 Durham (★(★(★

403km (250 miles) N of London; 24km (15 miles) S of Newcastle upon Tyne

This medieval city took root in 1090 after the Normans, under William the Conqueror, took over and began construction of Durham's world-renowned cathedral and castle on a peninsula surrounded by the River Wear. The cathedral, "Half Church of God, half Castle 'gainst the Scots," was built as a shrine to protect the remains of St. Cuthbert, while also providing a sturdy fortress against the warring Scots to the north.

The cathedral castle thrust Durham into its role as a protective border post for England. For centuries, Durham Castle was the seat of the prince bishops—kings of the wild northern territories in all but name—and a pilgrimage site for Christians coming to pay tribute to St. Cuthbert, a monk on Lindisfarne. His life of contemplation and prayer led to his consecration as a bishop in 685 and his sainthood after death.

Today, Durham boasts a university (built on the cornerstone of the castle) and is a good base for exploring this stretch of the North Sea coast, as well as the unspoiled rolling hills and waterfalls of the Durham Dales in the North Pennines.

ESSENTIALS

GETTING THERE   Trains from London's Kings Cross Station arrive hourly during the day, with the trip taking about 3 hours, and trains from York leave every 15 minutes, arriving approximately an hour later. Durham lies on the main London-Edinburgh rail line. For information, call (♪ **0845/748-4950** or visit **www.nationalrail. co.uk**.

National Express buses from London arrive twice daily, with the trip taking about 5 hours. For information, call **National Express** at (♪ **0870/580-8080** or visit **www. nationalexpress.com**.

If you're driving from London, follow the A1(M) north to Durham.

VISITOR INFORMATION   The **Durham Tourist Office** is at Millennium Place (♪ **01913/843720;** www.durhamtourism.co.uk) and is open year-round Monday to Saturday from 9:30am to 5:30pm and Sunday from 11am to 4pm.

SPECIAL EVENTS   At the **Durham Folk Festival,** held the last weekend in July, you can sing, clog, or just cavort to music; almost every event is free. The weekend also includes free camping along the River Wear, though you'd better arrive early on Friday if you want to get a choice spot. In early June, crowds swarm along the riverbank to cheer the crew racing the **Durham Regatta.**

WHERE TO STAY

Durham Marriott Hotel Royal County (★   This is where we prefer to stay in Durham. Though some critics consider this an anonymous chain hotel (it's part of the Marriott chain), it has many winning features in its three Georgian buildings, plus a convenient location right in the heart of Durham. Skillfully converted from a row of riverside houses, it was once the family home of the Queen Mother before being turned into one of the region's premier hotels. Many of its original details have been retained, including an oak staircase that was transported here from Loch Leven, the Scottish castle where Mary, Queen of Scots, was held prisoner. The bedrooms all maintain a high standard of comfort and furnishings, though they vary in size. Most rooms are large enough to rent to families.

Old Elvet, Durham DH1 3JN. (♪ **800/228-9290** in U.S. and Canada, or 01913/866821. Fax 01913/860704. www. marriott.com. 150 units. £155–£180 ($310–$360) double; from £225 ($450) suite. AE, DC, MC, V. **Amenities:** 2

restaurants; bar; heated indoor pool; health club; Jacuzzi; sauna; room service; babysitting; laundry service; dry cleaning. *In room:* TV, high-speed Internet, minibar, beverage maker, hair dryer, iron, trouser press.

Georgian Town House *Value* This is the most desirable B&B in Durham, an unusually decorated place lying on a steep, cobbled Georgian terrace street, close to everything, including the cathedral. It is a wonder of decoration, especially the reception hallway with its stenciled pillars and leaf patterns. It's almost like entering an arbor in sunny Sicily. In the lounge, papier-mâché "stars" and "moons" twinkle on the walls. Sofas are placed around the fireplace where guests can mingle. Rooms, except for a cramped single, are tastefully decorated and are light and airy. The house has a panoramic view of the cathedral and castle. Children 4 and younger are not accepted at this establishment.

10 Crossgate, Durham DH1 4PS. ℂ/fax **01913/868070**. www.durham.bedbreakfastaccommodation.co.uk. 7 units. £75–£100 ($150–$200) double. Rates include breakfast. No credit cards. *In room:* TV, beverage maker.

Three Tuns Hotel Still going strong after all these years, this hotel is the reincarnation of a 16th-century coaching inn that once housed travelers heading north into Scotland. Almost all traces of its former role are gone. Bedrooms have been completely modernized and furnished to a high, if not exciting, standard. The best and most spacious rooms are the executive units, but each room has a good comfort level. Two rooms are large enough for families. The public rooms have more character and are roomy and inviting.

New Elvet, Durham DH1 3AQ. ℂ **01913/864326**. Fax 01913/861406. www.swallow-hotels.com. 50 units. £115 ($230) double; £175 ($350) suite. Rates include breakfast. AE, DC, MC, V. **Amenities:** Restaurant; bar; room service; babysitting; laundry service; dry cleaning. *In room:* TV, beverage maker, hair dryer, iron, trouser press.

WHERE TO DINE

Bistro 21 *✧* CONTINENTAL A big hit locally, this is a bright, farm-themed bistro. Chef Paul O'Hara's cuisine is precise and carefully prepared, with market-fresh ingredients that are allowed to keep their natural essence without being overly sauced or disguised. We especially recommend the blackboard specials, such as fish cakes with buttery spinach or pork chops with creamed cabbage and potatoes. The food is full of flavor, borrowing from all over Europe—certainly the Mediterranean—but also offering traditional British fare at times, such as deep-fried plaice and chips. You can finish with one of the rich desserts, including double chocolate truffle cake. But if you want to be terribly old-fashioned and very English, you'll ask for the toffee pudding with butterscotch sauce. It's prepared to perfection.

Aykley Heads House, Aykley Heads. ℂ **01913/844354**. Reservations recommended. Main courses £14–£23 ($28–$46); fixed-price lunch £14–£17 ($28–$34). AE, DC, MC, V. Mon–Fri noon–2pm and 7–10:30pm; Sat noon–2pm and 6–10:30pm.

SEEING THE SIGHTS

Durham Castle *✧* Facing the Durham Cathedral from the opposite side of the "Palace Green," this was the seat of the prince bishops of Durham for more than 800 years. In 1832, it became the first building of the fledgling local college, now Durham University; it still houses University College. During university breaks, it offers unique bed-and-breakfast accommodations to the public.

Palace Green. ℂ **01913/343800**. www.durhamcastle.com. Admission £5 ($10) adults, £3.50 ($7) children, £12 ($24) family ticket. Guided tours June–Sept daily 10am–12:30pm and 2–4:30pm; other times of the year Mon, Wed, Sat–Sun 2–4:30pm. Closed during university Christmas breaks.

Durham Cathedral ✸✸✸   Under construction for more than 40 years, the cathedral was completed in 1133, and today is Britain's largest, best-preserved Norman stronghold and one of its surviving Romanesque palaces. The structure is not only breathtaking to view, it is also architecturally innovative, the first English building with ribbed vault construction. It is also the first stone-roofed cathedral in Europe, an architectural necessity because of its role as a border fortress.

The treasury houses such relics as the original 12th-century door knocker, St. Cuthbert's coffin, ancient illuminated manuscripts, and more. You can still attend daily services in the sanctuary.

Palace Green. 𝒸 **01913/864266.** www.durhamcathedral.co.uk. Free admission to cathedral (donation required); tower £3 ($6) adults, £1.50 ($3) children, £8 ($16) family ticket; treasury £2.50 ($5) adults, 70p ($1.40) children, £6 ($12) family ticket; monks' dormitory £1 ($2) adults, 30p (60¢) children, £2 ($4) family ticket; audiovisual visitors' exhibition £1 ($2) adults, 30p (60¢) children, £2 ($4) family ticket. Guided tours £4 ($8) adults, free for children 15 and under. Cathedral mid-June to Aug daily 9:30am–8pm; Sept–Apr Mon–Sat 9:30am–6:15pm, Sun 12:30–6:15pm. Treasury Mon–Sat 10am–4:30pm; Sun 2–4:30pm. Monks' dormitory Apr–Sept Mon–Sat 10am–3:30pm; Sun 12:30–3:15pm. Audiovisual visitors' exhibition Mar–Oct Mon–Sat 10am–3pm. Guided tours July to mid-Sept Mon–Sat at 10:30am and 2pm (also 11:30am during Aug).

Oriental Museum   This is the nation's only museum devoted entirely to Eastern culture and art. The display covers all major periods of art from ancient Egypt through India, as well as relics from Tibet, China, and Japan.

Elvet Hill off South Rd. 𝒸 **01913/345694.** www.dur.ac.uk/oriental.museum. Admission £1.50 ($3) adults, 75p ($1.50) seniors and children 5–16, £3.50 ($7) family ticket. Mon–Fri 10am–5pm; Sat–Sun noon–5pm.

OUTDOOR PURSUITS

Fishing is a good sport all along the rivers Tees and Wear, and in the several reservoirs and ponds throughout the county. Boating is also available, and **Brown's Boat House,** Elvet Bridge (𝒸 **01913/863779**), rents rowboats for pulls up or down the Wear, as well as offering short cruises April to October, at the price of £6.50 ($13) for adults and £4 ($8) for children.

Hikers can take the challenge provided by the 435km (270 miles) of trails (64km/40 miles of which are in the country) along the **Pennine Way,** the **Weardale Way's** 126km (78-mile) course along the River Wear from Monkwearmouth in Sunderland to Cowshill in County Durham, or the **Teesdale Way,** running 145km (90 miles) from Middleton in Teesdale to Teesmouth in Cleveland. Rambles along the public footpaths in town are supplemented by more than 80km (50 miles) of hiking trails, which follow the tracks of a former railroad outside of town. Seven such trails make use of interlinked routes and range from the 7.5km (4.5-mile) **Auckland Walk** to the 17km (11-mile) **Derwent Walk.** If you don't feel like going it alone, there are also more than 200 guided walks throughout the county, providing background on the history, culture, and plant and animal life of the surrounding area; contact the tourist office (see "Visitor Information," above).

Cyclists can opt for road biking along quiet country lanes and converted railway routes, or mountain biking in **Hamsterley Forest.** The acclaimed **C2C national cycle route** passes through the Durham Dales and North Durham, on a 225km (140-mile) signposted route. Both road and mountain-bike rentals are available at several locations, including **Cycle Force 2000 Ltd.,** 87 Claypath St. (𝒸 **01913/840319**), open Monday to Friday 9am to 5:30pm, Saturday 9am to 5pm, and Sunday from 11am to 3pm. A bike rental costs £14 ($28) per day, with a £36 ($72) deposit.

DURHAM AFTER DARK

Much of Durham's nightlife revolves around its university students. When school is in session, the **Hogs Head,** 58 Saddler St. (© **01913/869550**), is a popular traditional English-style pub. It's open Thursday to Saturday 11am to 1am and Sunday to Wednesday 11am until midnight. **Coach and Eight,** Bridge House, North Road (© **01913/860056**), has disco Thursday to Sunday nights and is open Monday to Thursday 11am to 11pm, Friday and Saturday 11am to 1:30pm, and Sunday 11am to 10:30pm.

SIDE TRIPS TO THE DURHAM DALES, BARNARD CASTLE & BEAMISH

This densely populated county of northeast England was once pictured as a dismal place, with coal fields, ironworks, mining towns, and shipyards. Yet the **Durham Dales,** occupying the western third of the county, is a popular panorama of rolling hills, valleys of quiet charm, and wild moors. **Teesdale** is particularly notable for its several waterfalls, including **High Force,** the largest waterfall in England, which drops a thundering 21m (70 ft.) to join the River Tees. It is equally known for the rare wildflowers that grow in the sugar limestone–based soil of the region; they have helped it earn protection as a National Nature Reserve.

Also notable is **Weardale,** once the hunting ground of Durham's prince bishops, with its idyllic brown sandstone villages. For more information on the wide range of options the area has to offer, contact the **Durham Dales Centre,** Castle Garden, Stanhope, Bishop Auckland, County Durham DL13 2FJ (© **01388/527650;** fax 01388/527461; www.durhamdalescentre.co.uk). Hours are April to October daily 10am to 5pm; November to March daily 10am to 4pm.

The 12th-century **Barnard Castle** ★ (© **01833/690909**) is an extensive Norman ruin overlooking the River Tees. It's open April to September daily 10am to 6pm, October to March Thursday to Monday 10am to 4pm. Admission is £3.50 ($7) for adults, and £2 ($4) for students and children 15 and younger.

Barnard Castle is also home to the **Bowes Museum** ★ (© **01833/690606;** www. bowesmuseum.org.uk), a sprawling French-style château housing one of Britain's most important collections of European art, including paintings from Goya to El Greco, plus tapestries, ceramics, costumes, musical instruments, and French and English furniture. There is also a children's gallery. The museum is open daily from 11am to 5pm. Admission is £7 ($14) for adults, and £6 ($12) for students, seniors, and children 16 and older. Children 15 and younger enter free. Buses run from Durham several times daily.

North of England Open Air Museum   West of Chester-le-Street, 13km (8 miles) southwest of Newcastle upon Tyne, and 19km (12 miles) northwest of Durham City, this is a vivid re-creation of an early-19th-century village. A costumed staff goes through the motions of daily life in shops, houses, pubs, a newspaper office, and garage, as well as a Methodist chapel, village school, home farm, and railway station. An average summer visit takes around 4 hours, and a winter visit, including the town and railway only, takes about 2 hours.

Just off A693 in Beamish. © **0191/370-4000.** www.beamish.org.uk. Admission spring and summer £16 ($32) adults, £10 ($20) children, free for children 4 and younger; winter £6 ($12) for all, free for children 4 and younger. Spring and summer daily 10am–5pm; off season Sat–Sun and Tues–Thurs 10am–4pm. Closed Dec 13–Jan 3.

9 Hexham, Hadrian's Wall *★*/*★* & the Pennine Way

489km (304 miles) N of London; 60km (37 miles) E of Carlisle; 34km (21 miles) W of Newcastle upon Tyne

Above the Tyne River, the historic old market town of Hexham has narrow streets, an old market square, a fine abbey church, and a hall. It makes a good base for exploring Hadrian's Wall and the Roman supply base of Corstopitum at Corbridge-on-Tyne, the ancient capital of Northumberland.

ESSENTIALS

GETTING THERE   Take one of the many daily trains from London's Kings Cross Station to Newcastle upon Tyne. At Newcastle, change trains and take one in the direction of Carlisle. The fifth stop after Newcastle will be Hexham. For schedules and information, call *©* **0845/748-4950** or visit **www.nationalrail.co.uk**.

Hexham lies 23km (14 miles) southeast of Hadrian's Wall. If you are primarily interested in the wall (rather than in Hexham), get off the Carlisle-bound train at the third stop (Haltwhistle), which is 4km (2½ miles) from the wall. At either of these hamlets, you can take a taxi to whichever part of the wall you care to visit. Taxis line up readily at the railway station in Hexham but less often at the other villages. If you get off at one of the above-mentioned villages and don't see a taxi, call *©* **01434/321064** and a local taxi will come to get you. Many visitors ask their taxi drivers to return at a pre-arranged time (which they gladly do) to pick them up after their excursion on the windy ridges near the wall.

National Express coaches to Newcastle and Carlisle connect with Northumbria bus no. 685. Trip time to Hexham from Carlisle is about 1½ hours and from Newcastle about 1 hour. For information, call *©* **0870/580-8080** or visit **www.national express.com**. Local bus services connect Hexham with North Tynedale and the North Pennines.

If you're driving from Newcastle upon Tyne, head west on the A69 until you see the cutoff south to Hexham.

VISITOR INFORMATION   The **Tourist Information Centre** at Hexham is at the Wentworth Car Park (*©* **01434/652220**). It's open from Easter to October Monday to Saturday 9am to 6pm (until 5pm in Oct) and Sunday 10am to 5pm; November to March, hours are limited to Monday to Saturday 9am to 5pm.

NEARBY PLACES TO STAY & DINE

Anchor Hotel   This is the social center of the village. Ideally situated for visitors to the wall and its surroundings, between Haltwhistle (14km/9 miles away) and Hexham (11km/7 miles), this riverside village pub was once a coaching inn on the route from Newcastle to Carlisle. The building, which was constructed in 1700 near the edge of the North Tyne River (which still flows within a few feet of its foundations), sits in the heart of the tiny village of Haydon Bridge. The cozy bar is a local hangout. In the country dining room, wholesome evening meals are served. The bedrooms, albeit a bit small, are comfortably furnished with cozy beds.

John Martin St. (on A69, 11km/7 miles west of Hexham), Haydon Bridge, Northumberland NE47 6AB. *©* 01434/ 684227. Fax 01434/688413. www.anchorhotel-haydonbridge.co.uk. 10 units. £60 ($120) double. Rates include English breakfast. AE, MC, V. **Amenities:** Restaurant; bar. *In room:* TV, beverage maker, hair dryer, iron.

George Hotel   Standing on the banks of the Tyne, this country hotel opens onto gardens leading to the riverbank. It's a convenient base for visiting Hadrian's Wall. The hotel dates from the 18th century, when the original structure was built of Roman stone. It has been extensively refurbished to a high standard, and all bedrooms are comfortably furnished and well equipped.

Chollerford, Humshaugh, near Hexham, Northumberland NE46 4EW. ℂ 0845/4566399. Fax 01434/681727. 47 units. £80–£140 ($160–$280) double. Rates include English breakfast. AE, DC, MC, V. Take A6079 8km (5 miles) north of Hexham. **Amenities:** Restaurant; bar; indoor heated pool; health club; sauna; steam room; spa; room service; laundry service; dry cleaning. In room: TV, beverage maker, hair dryer, iron, trouser press.

Hadrian Hotel   Ideal for a stopover along Hadrian's Wall, the Hadrian lies on the only street of the hamlet of Wall, 5.5km (3½ miles) north of Hexham. It's an ivy-covered 18th-century building erected of stones gathered long ago from the site of the ancient wall. The owners have carefully refurbished the place. Each renovated bedroom is attractive, and all the rooms have been modernized and offer comfortable double or twin beds. Three rooms have a tub only. One room has a shower only, and two rooms have neither tub nor shower. The hotel has a private garden and a beer garden that serves as a warm-weather extension of its pub.

Wall, near Hexham, Northumberland NE46 4EE. ℂ 01434/681232. Fax 01434/681512. www.hadrianhotel.com. 6 units. £65 ($130) double. Rates include English breakfast. MC, V. **Amenities:** Restaurant; 2 bars. In room: TV, beverage maker, hair dryer.

Langley Castle Hotel ✸ *(Finds)*   This stately home is located on 4 hectares (10 acres) of woodlands at the edge of Northumberland National Park, southwest of Haydon Bridge and about 11km (7 miles) west of Hexham. It's the only medieval fortified castle home in England that receives paying guests. The castle, built in 1350, was largely uninhabited after being damaged in 1400 during an English-and-Scottish war, until it was purchased in the late 19th century by Cadwallader Bates, a historian, who spent the rest of his life carefully restoring the property. Medieval features include the 14th-century spiral staircase, stained-glass windows, huge open fireplaces, and many turrets. The luxuriously appointed bedrooms vary in size; some have whirlpools or saunas in the well-maintained bathrooms. An adjacent building has extra rooms.

Langley-on-Tyne, Hexham, Northumberland NE47 5LU. ℂ 01434/688888. Fax 01434/684019. www.langleycastle. com. 18 units. £129–£169 ($258–$338) double; from £229 ($458) suite. Rates include English breakfast. AE, MC, V. From Hexham, go west on A69 to Haydon Bridge, then head south on A686 for 3km (2 miles). **Amenities:** Restaurant; bar; gift shop; room service; babysitting; laundry service; dry cleaning. In room: TV, minibar, beverage maker, hair dryer, iron, trouser press.

HADRIAN'S WALL & ITS FORTRESSES

Hadrian's Wall ✸✸, which extends for 118km (73 miles) across the north of England, from the North Sea to the Irish Sea, is particularly scenic for a stretch of 16km (10 miles) west of Housesteads, which lies 4km (2¾ miles) northeast of Bardon Mill on the B6318. Only the lower courses of the wall have been preserved intact; the rest were reconstructed in the 19th century using original stones. From the wall, there are incomparable views north to the Cheviot Hills along the Scottish border and south to the Durham moors.

The wall was built in A.D. 122 after the visit of the emperor Hadrian, who was inspecting far frontiers of the Roman Empire and wanted to construct a dramatic line between the empire and the barbarians. Legionnaires were ordered to build a wall across the width of the island of Britain, stretching 118km (73 miles), beginning at the North Sea and ending at the Irish Sea.

The wall is one of Europe's top Roman ruins. The western end is accessible from Carlisle, which also has an interesting museum of Roman artifacts; the eastern end can be reached from Newcastle upon Tyne (where you can see some remains on the city outskirts, as well as a nice museum at the university).

You can find more information about Hadrian's Wall at the website **www.hadrian swallcountry.org**.

From early May to late September, the Tynedale Council and the Northumberland National Park run a **bus service** that visits every important site along the wall, then turns around in the village of Haltwhistle and returns to Hexham. Buses depart from a point near the railway station in Hexham six times a day. Call © **01434/652220** for more information. The cost is £7 ($14) for adults, £5 ($10) for children, and £14 ($28) for a family ticket. Many visitors take one bus out, then return on a subsequent bus 2, 4, or 6 hours later. Every Sunday, a national park warden leads a 2½-hour walking tour of the wall, in connection with the bus service. The Hexham tourist office (see "Visitor Information," above) provides further details.

Housesteads Roman Fort and Museum 🔎🔎   Along the wall are several Roman forts, the largest and most well-preserved of which was called Vercovicium by the Romans. This substantially excavated fort, on a dramatic site, contains the only visible example of a Roman hospital in Britain.

5km (3 miles) northeast of Bardon Mill on B6318. © 01434/344363. Admission £4.10 ($8.20) adults, £3.10 ($6.20) students and seniors, £2.10 ($4.20) children 5–16. Apr–Sept daily 10am–6pm; Oct–Mar daily 10am–4pm. Closed Dec 25–26 and Jan 1.

Roman Army Museum 🔎   Close to the village of Greenhead, the Roman Army Museum traces the influence of Rome from its early beginnings to the expansion of the empire, with emphasis on the role of the Roman army and the garrisons of Hadrian's Wall. A barracks room depicts army living conditions. Realistic life-size figures make this a strikingly visual museum experience.

Within easy walking distance of the Roman Army Museum is one of the most imposing and high-standing sections of Hadrian's Wall, **Walltown Crags;** the height of the wall and magnificent views to the north and south are impressive.

At the junction of A69 and B6318, 29km (18 miles) west of Hexham. © 01697/747485. www.vindolanda.com. Admission £4.20 ($8.40) adults, £3.70 ($7.40) students and seniors, £2.50 ($5) children, £12 ($24) family ticket. Feb–Mar and Oct to mid-Nov daily 10am–5pm; Apr–Sept daily 10am–6pm. Closed late Nov to early Feb.

Vindolanda   This is another well-preserved fort south of the wall, the last of eight successive forts to be built on this site. An excavated civilian settlement outside the fort has an interesting museum of artifacts of everyday Roman life.

Just west of Housesteads, on a minor road 2km (1¼ miles) southeast of Twice Brewed off B6318. © 01434/344277. www.vindolanda.com. Admission £5.20 ($10) adults, £4.30 ($8.60) students and seniors, £3 ($6) children. Feb 11–Mar and Oct–Nov daily 10am–5pm; Apr–Sept daily 10am–6pm; Dec–Feb 10 daily 10am–4pm.

HIKING THE PENNINE WAY IN NORTHUMBERLAND NATIONAL PARK

Northumberland National Park, established in 1956, encompasses the borderlands that were a buffer zone between the warring English and Scots during the 13th and 14th centuries. Today, the park comprises almost 1,035 sq. km (400 sq. miles) of the least populated area in England and is noted for its rugged landscape and associations with the northern frontier of the ancient Roman Empire.

Touching the border with Scotland, the park covers some of the most tortuous geology in England, the Cheviot Hills, whose surfaces have been wrinkled by volcanic pressures, inundated with seawater, scoured by glaciers, silted over by rivers, and thrust upward in a complicated series of geological events. Much of the heather-sheathed terrain here is used for sheep grazing; woolly balls of fluff adorn hillsides ravaged by high winds and frequent rain.

Northumberland Park includes the remains of Hadrian's Wall, one of the most impressive classical ruins of northern Europe. Footpaths run alongside it, and there are a variety of walks in the country to the north and south of the monument. One of the most challenging hiking paths in Britain, the **Pennine Way** ★★, snakes up the backbone of the park. The 129km (80 miles) of the 403km (250-mile) path that are in the park are clearly marked; one of the most worthwhile (and safest) hikes is between Bellingham and the Hamlet of Riding Wood.

You can purchase a map of the trails, priced at 50p ($1), at almost any local tourist office in the district. There are **National Park Centres** at Once Brewed (© 01434/344396), Rothbury (© 01669/620887), and Ingram (© 01665/578890). The Head Office is at Eastburn, South Park, Hexham, Northumberland NE46 1BS (© 01434/605555; www.nnpa.org.uk).

20

Cardiff & South Wales: Dylan Thomas Country

No longer the dreary coal-exporting port it was so often depicted as in the 20th century, **Cardiff,** the capital of Wales, is hot and happening—one of the most attractive cities of Britain to visit. Cardiff (*Caerdydd* in Welsh) is a large seaport built on the tidal estuary of the Taff River.

Enriched by the Industrial Revolution, Cardiff declined after World War II with the closing of coal mines, railroads, and factories. The old industrial city is now a progressive, inviting modern port, as exemplified by the waterfront along Cardiff Bay. Here you'll find renewal at its best, with restaurants, hotels, and a hands-on exhibit, Techniquest.

Cardiff can be your launching pad for the treasures of South Wales, which has turned a bright, new face to the world and is no longer known for its depressing stories of slag heaps, dreary cottages, and denuded hillsides that were once proudly forested.

In fact, South Wales is imbued with some of the great beauty spots of Britain: **Brecon Beacons National Park,** 835 sq. km (519 sq. miles) of beauty and pleasure grounds with nature reserves; **Gower Peninsula,** an area of outstanding natural beauty stretching for 23km (14 miles) from the Mumbles to Worms Head in the West; and, finally, **Pembrokeshire Coast National Park,** one of the smallest national parks of Britain (only 362 sq. km/225 sq. miles) but an area acclaimed for its coastal scenery.

On the western side of Cardiff, the city of **Swansea** on Swansea Bay of the Bristol Channel, seems a natural starting place for a visit to southwest Wales. After a sojourn in the vicinity of the port city, the beautiful **Gower Peninsula,** Swansea's neighbor, draws you westward. You can explore where Dylan Thomas, the country's outstanding 20th-century poet, was born, and then move on to the west to Laugharne, where the poet lived, wrote, and is buried.

Swansea is on the western edge of West Glamorgan County. When the counties of Wales were realigned and consolidated in 1973, Pembrokeshire and Carmarthenshire, familiar names in Welsh history, became part of Dyfed County, an even older designation for the area they occupy. In this southwestern corner of the country, you'll be introduced to the land of St. David and Celtic crosses, of craggy coastlines and the cromlechs marking the burial places of prehistoric humans.

In addition to Swansea, you'll find two more excellent bases outside Cardiff— **Tenby,** one of the most famous coastal resorts of Wales, its charm and character dating from the Middle Ages, plus **St. Davids,** a tiny cathedral city, birthplace of the patron saint of Wales.

Two major attractions that you may want to seek out even on a rushed visit are **Pembroke Castle,** oldest castle in west Wales and seat of the earls of Pembroke; and **Tintern Abbey,** in the Wye Valley, founded in 1131, once one of the richest and most important monastic houses of Wales.

1 Cardiff ⓐ

249km (155 miles) W of London; 177km (110 miles) SW of Birmingham; 64km (40 miles) SE of Swansea

If you remember Cardiff's dull, industrial reputation from yesteryear, you may not want to fit the capital of Wales into your already busy schedule. But to omit it would be a shame because it has blossomed into one of the most inviting cities of Britain and is an ideal base for exploring its own attractions, plus the major scenic beauty spots of South Wales.

ESSENTIALS

GETTING THERE   In recent years, Cardiff has greatly expanded its air facilities, and flights now wing in from across Europe, although there are still no direct flights between London and Cardiff. Airlines that service **Cardiff International Airport** (ⓒ **01446/711111;** www.cial.co.uk) include **KLM** (ⓒ **0870/507-4074;** www.klm. com), which offers transfers, through Amsterdam, to points around the world. **BMI Baby** (ⓒ **0871/224-0224;** www.bmibaby.com) flies from Cardiff to Belfast, Edinburgh, and Glasgow. **Aer Arann** (ⓒ **0870/8767676;** www.aerarann.com) flies between Cardiff and Cork, Dublin, and Galway.

The **Cardiff Bus Service** (ⓒ **0871/2002233**) operates bus no. X91, which travels between the airport and the bus station at hourly intervals from 7:15am to 8:25pm, Monday to Friday. On Saturdays, the X91 operates from 7:25am to 8:25pm, and on Sundays services X5 and X91 operate between 9:05am and 8:25pm. The cost of a one-way trip is £3.70 ($7.40).

Trains arrive in Cardiff at the Central Station on Wood Street, in back of the bus station. Trains from London pull in at the rate of one every half-hour during the day; the trip takes 2 hours. Trains also arrive every hour from Glasgow and Edinburgh; trip time is 7 hours. Trains from Glasgow often stop at Bristol; trains from Edinburgh often stop at Bristol or Birmingham. For rail information and schedules, call ⓒ **0845/ 748-4950** or visit **www.nationalrail.co.uk.** For bus and motor routes into Cardiff, call ⓒ **0870/580-8080** or visit **www.nationalexpress.com.** The trip is about 3½ hours from London.

GETTING AROUND   If you don't have a car, you must depend on taxis, buses, or your trusty feet to get around in Cardiff.

There's fairly good bus service, even to the sights in the environs. Your hotel staff will usually be able to help you plan a day's outing. Note that prices of bus routes vary according to the number of zones you want to travel in. One-way travel within zone 1 (the commercial heart of the city) costs £1 ($2) for adults, and 70p ($1.40) for children. One-way travel across all four zones of the city (a very large metropolitan area, taking in far-flung suburbs) costs £1.80 ($3.60) for adults, and £1.20 ($2.40) for children.

For bus routes, go to **BWS Caerdydd,** Wood Street (ⓒ **0870/608-2608**), which is the office of Cardiff City Transport. Across from the bus station, it is open Monday to Friday 8:30am to 5:30pm, Saturday 9am to 4:30pm. Bus service on Sunday morning tends to be infrequent, and service stops completely every night at 11pm.

Taxis are usually easy to find, especially in the busy shopping areas, and most cab fares within Cardiff range from £5 to £11 ($10–$22) each. The most prominent taxi stands are at the rail and bus station and at St. David's Hall. Or you can have your hotel or the place where you've dined call you a taxi. Wonder of wonders, the meter starts ticking only when you get into the vehicle, not when it leaves the station, as is the case in most U.K. cities. For service, call **Capital Cabs** at ⓒ **02920/777777.**

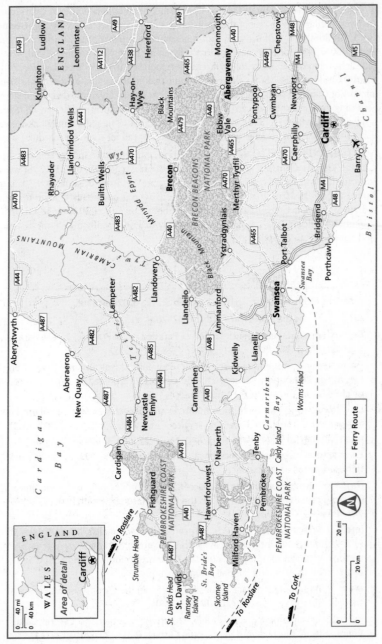

South Wales

One of the most efficient ways to see Cardiff and the attractions within its central core involves joining up with one of the open-top bus tours conducted by **City Sightseeing** (© **1708/866000** for information about its services throughout the United Kingdom, or 029/20473432 for information specifically about its services within Cardiff; www. city-sightseeing.com). Tours follow a clearly signposted itinerary that begins outside Cardiff Castle (at Castle St.). Tours cover a route that incorporates the most visible monuments of Cardiff. Participants can get on or off the bus at any of the designated stops, returning for the next bus to carry them on to the next monument. Adults pay £8 ($16), students and seniors £6 ($12), children ages 5 to 15 £4 ($8), and a family ticket costs £20 ($40). Tour times change from month to month; call for a current schedule.

VISITOR INFORMATION   For information about Cardiff and its environs, the **Cardiff Visitors Centre** is at the Old Library, the Hayes (© **0870/121-1258;** www. visitcardiff.com), in the heart of the city. Hours are Monday to Saturday 9:30am to 6pm and Sunday 10am to 4pm. In July and August it is open daily 9:30am to 7pm. A branch office at Cardiff Bay, the Tube, Harbour Drive (© **02920-463833**), lying 2.5km (1½ miles) to the south, is open Monday to Friday 9:30am to 5pm, Saturday and Sunday 10am to 5pm.

FAST FACTS: Cardiff

American Express An office is at 3 Queen St. (© **02920/649305**).

Area Code The area code for Cardiff is **02920**.

Dentist For dental emergencies, contact Parade Dental Practice, 23 The Parade (© **029/2048-1486**).

Doctor For medical emergencies, dial © **999** and ask for an ambulance. Doctors are on 24-hour-call service. A full list of doctors is posted at all post offices, or else visitors can ask at their hotel desk.

Drugstores To get a prescription filled, go to Boots the Chemist, with outlets all over town. The main dispensing service is at 5 Wood St. (© **029/2037-7043**), open Monday to Friday 8am to 6:30pm, Saturday 9am to 6pm.

Emergencies To summon police or call firefighters, dial © **999**, the same number used to call an ambulance.

Hospitals The most visible and best-accessorized hospital in Cardiff is the University Hospital of Wales (also known as the Heath Hospital), Heath Park (© **02920/747747**).

Internet Access To stay in touch, you can go to McDonald's, 12–14 Queen St. (© **02920/222604**). Internet access is free but customers must carry their own laptops. It's open Monday to Thursday 7:30am to midnight, Friday and Saturday 7:30am to 3am, and Sunday 7:30am to 11pm.

Maps You can obtain detailed maps for free from the Cardiff Visitors Centre at the Old Library, the Hayes (© **0870/121-1258**).

Police In an emergency, dial © **999**. Otherwise, contact the Central Cardiff Police Station, King Edward VII Avenue, Cathays Parks (© **02920/222111**).

Post Office The main post office is at 45–46 Queens Arcade, Queen Street (© **0845-722-3344;** www.postoffice.co.uk), open Monday to Saturday from 9am to 5:30pm.

Cardiff

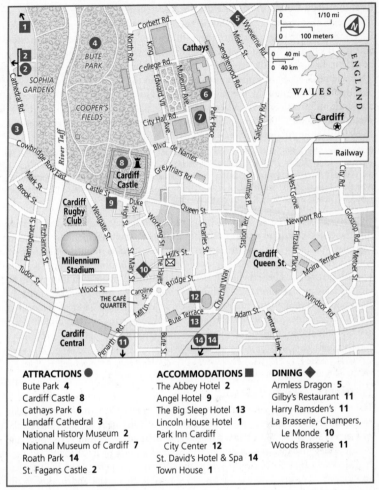

ATTRACTIONS ●
Bute Park **4**
Cardiff Castle **8**
Cathays Park **6**
Llandaff Cathedral **3**
National History Museum **2**
National Museum of Cardiff **7**
Roath Park **14**
St. Fagans Castle **2**

ACCOMMODATIONS ■
The Abbey Hotel **2**
Angel Hotel **9**
The Big Sleep Hotel **13**
Lincoln House Hotel **1**
Park Inn Cardiff
City Center **12**
St. David's Hotel & Spa **14**
Town House **1**

DINING ◆
Armless Dragon **5**
Gilby's Restaurant **11**
Harry Ramsden's **11**
La Brasserie, Champers,
Le Monde **10**
Woods Brasserie **11**

WHERE TO STAY
EXPENSIVE

Angel Hotel ⚐   This elegant Victorian hotel across from Cardiff Castle was *the* place to stay in South Wales when it was first built. Over the years it has attracted everybody from Greta Garbo to the Beatles to every prime minister of Britain. It will never regain its old supremacy, as greater hotels such as Cardiff Bay and St. David's Hotel & Spa have long surpassed it, but the Angel is still there and still good—and it has regained some of its old prestige following a restoration—a world of neo-Doric decor, *trompe l'oeil* ceilings, Waterford crystal chandeliers, and hand-stippled faux-marble columns. As befits a hotel of this age, rooms come in a wide variety of styles and sizes.

Castle St., Cardiff CF10 1SZ. ℭ **02920/649200.** Fax 029/2039-6212. www.paramount-hotels.co.uk. 102 units. £65–£200 ($130–$400) double; £125–£300 ($250–$600) suite. AE, DC, MC, V. Parking £5 ($10). **Amenities:** Restaurant; bar and lounge; room service; babysitting. *In room:* A/C, TV, Wi-Fi, beverage maker, hair dryer, iron, trouser press.

Egerton Grey Country House Hotel ⊛ (Kids)   Sixteen kilometers (10 miles) west of the city, this elegant country-house hotel lies in a bucolic setting in the Vale of Glamorgan. The house dates from the 17th century and has been carefully restored, and it's filled with antiques and well-chosen accessories, including paintings and porcelain. In nippy weather you can warm yourself by the open fires. Standing amid 2.8 hectares (7 acres) of gardens, it faces the sea in the hamlet of Porthkerry, within easy driving distance of the Brecon Beacons and Gower Peninsula. It was once a rectory and private residence but was opened as a small luxurious house in 1988. All the rooms are spacious and exceedingly comfortable; some have four-poster beds. The suites offer beautiful coastal views.

Porthkerry, near Barry and Cardiff, Vale of Glamorgan CF62 3BZ. ⓒ **01446/711666.** Fax 01446/711690. www. egertongrey.co.uk. 10 units. £140–£150 ($280–$300) double; £170 ($340) suite. AE, MC, V. Free parking. From Junction 33 of M4 follow signs to the airport, bypassing Barry and turning left at the small roundabout, signposted PORTHKERRY. After about 457m (1,500 ft.), turn left again at the signpost to the hotel. **Amenities:** Restaurant; bar; room service; babysitting; laundry service. *In room:* TV, beverage maker, hair dryer, trouser press.

New House Country ⊛   On the fringe of Cardiff this elegant Georgian mansion is our choice for a tranquil retreat from the city. Opening onto panoramic views—on a clear day you can see the North Devon coast—the hotel is imbued with an inviting country-house flavor, as evoked by open fires, exquisite furnishings, and beautifully restored bedrooms. The individually designed bedrooms, many with four-poster beds, are spacious and comfortable. Although traditional, there is modern luxury here. Bathrooms are roomy and sumptuous, with deluxe toiletries. Most of the bedrooms are in a large annex, and rooms here are as good as those in the main building. Three are large enough for families.

Thornhill, Cardiff CF14 9UA. ⓒ **02920-520280.** Fax 029/2052-0324. www.newhousehotel.com. 36 units. £140–£170 ($280–$340) double; £190–£195 ($380–$390) suite. AE, DC, MC, V. Free parking. **Amenities:** Restaurant; bar; lounge; exercise room; room service. *In room:* A/C (in some), TV, beverage maker, hair dryer, iron.

St. David's Hotel & Spa ⊛⊛⊛ (Finds)   A strikingly contemporary structure, St. David's dwarfs the competition, rising above the modern waterfront development. A seven-story atrium towers above the lobby, an unusual sight for a Welsh hotel. An immediate hit, it is the first five-star hotel to arrive in Wales and is the only one in South Wales that qualifies as one of the Leading Hotels of the World. You get the highest level of service in South Wales, the ultimate in comfort, and the best leisure facilities. St. David's is especially known for its extensive spa and beauty facilities. Roomy and beautifully furnished bedrooms offer floor-to-ceiling windows and open onto private balconies with panoramic sweeps of the bay.

Havannah St., Cardiff Bay, Cardiff CF10 5SD. ⓒ **02920/454045.** Fax 029/2048-7056. www.thestdavidshotel.com. 132 units. £260 ($520) double; £290–£550 ($580–$1,100) suite. AE, DC, MC, V. Parking £8 ($16). **Amenities:** 2 restaurants; bar; indoor heated pool; health club; spa; Jacuzzi; sauna; business center; room service; babysitting; laundry service; dry cleaning. *In room:* A/C, TV, fax, high-speed Internet, minibar, beverage maker, hair dryer, trouser press, safe.

MODERATE

Park Inn Cardiff City Centre ⊛ (Kids)   Adjacent to the Cardiff International Arena, this refurbished hotel is stylish and classic, ideal for both business travelers and vacationers. There's a vibrant spirit about the place that attracts us. Spacious and well-furnished bedrooms are grouped around a central atrium, which gives access to the hotel's fashionable public rooms. The accommodations are among the city's finest, with some of the best amenities. A few family rooms are available, and children are given a very hospitable welcome.

Mary Ann St., Cardiff CF10 2JH. © **02920/341441.** Fax 029/2022-3742. www.parkinn.com. 146 units. £90–£180 ($180–$360) double. Rates include breakfast. AE, DC, MC, V. Parking £5 ($10). **Amenities:** Restaurant; Irish-themed bar; room service; babysitting; laundry service; dry cleaning. *In room:* TV, beverage maker, hair dryer, iron, trouser press, safe.

INEXPENSIVE

The Abbey Hotel   Built in 1898 as a home for a wealthy sea captain and his family, this house retains many of its original features and is one of the better and more reasonably priced B&Bs. Richard Burton once attended elocution lessons in the public lounge back when the hotel was a private school. Bedrooms are small but comfortably and tastefully furnished and have shower-only bathrooms. A few have four-posters. The on-site restaurant only occasionally serves lunch and dinner.

149–51 Cathedral Rd., Cardiff CF11 9PJ. © **02920/390896.** Fax 029/2023-8311. www.bandb4u.co.uk. 26 units (shower only). £60–£70 ($120–$140) double; £75–£95 ($150–$190) triple. Rates include continental breakfast. MC, V. Free parking. **Amenities:** Restaurant; bar. *In room:* TV, Wi-Fi, beverage maker, hair dryer (in some).

The Big Sleep Hotel ⭐ *Value*   What are pictures of the actor John Malkovich doing scattered throughout this hotel? The actor, who made a career out of playing "evil bastards," is one of the major shareholders. And his hotel has been named one of *Condé Nast Traveller's* "coolest places to stay." A rather dull office tower built in the 1960s has been successfully transformed into a hotel with a certain chic minimalism but with most affordable prices. Each of the midsize bedrooms is individually decorated with contemporary pieces, a rather smart styling. The best rooms are the "New on Ninth," though they cost more. If there's a downside, it's that some of the bedrooms overlook the rail tracks nearby, a rather noisy location.

Bute Terrace, Cardiff CF10 2FE. © **02920/636363.** Fax 029/2063-6364. www.thebigsleephotel.com. 81 units. Mon–Thurs £58–£89 ($116–$178) double, Fri–Sat £55–£65 ($110–$130) double, Sun £45–£50 ($90–$100) double; daily £99–£135 ($198–$270) suite. Rates include breakfast. AE, MC, V. Free parking. **Amenities:** Breakfast room; bar; laundry service; dry cleaning. *In room:* TV, beverage maker, hair dryer, iron.

Lincoln House Hotel *Kids*   This Victorian house provides a cozy and reasonably priced nest along popular Cathedral Road. The majestic home was created in 1900 by joining together two older residences, resulting in a superb and completely restored hotel. Surprisingly, the hotel is named for Abraham Lincoln, not the English cathedral city of Lincoln. The four-poster units exude romance, but there are also modern facilities. Rooms are spacious, and furnishings offer both style and comfort. Several family rooms are available.

118 Cathedral Rd., Cardiff CF11 9LQ. © **02920/395558.** Fax 029/2023-0537. www.lincolnhotel.co.uk. 18 units. £90–£110 ($180–$220) double; £150 ($300) suite. Rates include buffet breakfast. AE, MC, V. Free parking. **Amenities:** Bar; room service; laundry service; dry cleaning. *In room:* TV, Wi-Fi, beverage maker, hair dryer, iron, trouser press.

Town House ⭐ *Value*   This is the best B&B in Cardiff, preferable even to the neighboring Lincoln (see above). A classic Victorian town house, it lies in the shadow of the great Norman castle and has been completely restored and tastefully decorated. Its original architectural details are still here, including the mosaic-tiled floors in the elegantly decorated hallway, the stained-glass windows so beloved of Victorians, and even the original fireplaces in the public lounge and dining area. A cosmopolitan guesthouse, it attracts guests from San Francisco to Sydney. The roomy bedrooms are immaculately furnished and have excellent bathrooms. The location is a 10-minute walk from the City Centre.

70 Cathedral Rd., Cardiff CF11 9LL. ℂ **02920/239399.** Fax 029/2022-3214. www.thetownhousecardiff.co.uk. 8 units. £65–£80 ($130–$160) double. Rates include breakfast. AE, MC, V. Free parking. **Amenities:** Breakfast room. *In room:* TV, beverage maker, hair dryer.

WHERE TO DINE
EXPENSIVE

Armless Dragon WELSH   About 1.6km (1 mile) north of the center in a busy suburb, this popular restaurant occupies a 19th-century stone core and is known for its unpretentious and nutritious food. The kitchen hires skilled chefs whose suppliers offer the best in Welsh produce and meats. The cooks are strong on their "taste of Wales" dishes, as exemplified by such delights as deep-fried *laverballs* (seaweed balls) coated in sunflower and sesame seeds. Starters are divvied up among "Land," "Sea," and "Earth" platters, each comprising five miniature appetizers. One Land appetizer, for example, features smoked Monmouthshire chicken with avocado and ham crisps. Among the best-prepared mains are skate wing with a cockle-and-leek sauce, or else loin of pork chop with wild mushrooms. Brecon lamb appears with a rosemary cake and spring greens.

97 Wyeverne Rd. ℂ 02920/382357. Reservations recommended. Main courses £12–£22 ($24–$44); fixed-price lunch £10 ($20). MC, V. Tues–Fri noon–2pm; Tues–Thurs 7–9pm; Fri–Sat 7–9:30pm. Closed Dec 25–26.

Le Gallois—Y Cymro ✦ CONTINENTAL   For the flavors of the Mediterranean, this restaurant is without peer in Cardiff. The chef and patron, Padrig Jones, served under the *enfant terrible* of English chefs, the famous Marco Pierre White, and Jones learned his lessons well, scoring some knockout dishes from his own culinary imagination as well. In a stylish, contemporary atmosphere, this family-run favorite is two-tiered with clean, bold lines. Fashion and technique are evident in the specialties. The pot-roasted pigs' cheeks with truffle mash is better than dear old Mom made. You might also opt for the pan-fried filet of salmon with a beet vinaigrette and cauliflower purée. Also praiseworthy is the shank of lamb with a tomato couscous. A dessert specialty is Black Forest parfait with a warm blackberry compote.

6–10 Romilly Crescent, Canton. ℂ 02920/341264. Reservations required. Main courses £17–£25 ($34–$50); fixed-price lunch £10–£22 ($20–$44). AE, MC, V. Mon–Sat noon–2:30pm; Mon–Thurs 6–10:30pm; Fri–Sat 7–10:30pm.

MODERATE

Gilby's Restaurant SEAFOOD/WELSH   Near the Culverhouse Cross roundabout, two old converted farm buildings are now the venue for some of the finest viands in and around Cardiff. It's a lively place, popular with punters who come here mainly for seafood, such as fresh lobster and oysters caught on nearby shores, along with crab from Pembroke. A young team in the kitchen turns out one tempting dish after another. Our preferred selection is the grilled whole fish, although you can also delight in other main courses, such as baked whole sea bass stuffed with citrus and served with tomato croquettes. Filet of salmon appears with red-onion lyonnaise potatoes. Other delights are the honey-glazed Gressingham duck breast with poached chestnuts, or a medley of rack and rump of lamb. For dessert, the chef is justly proud of his hot chocolate fondant with a soft, gooey center and pistachio ice cream.

Old Port Rd., Culverhouse Cross. ℂ 02920/670800. Reservations recommended. Main courses £16–£20 ($32–$40); fixed-price lunch Tues–Sat £14 ($28), Sun £20 ($40); fixed-price early dinner Tues–Fri £19 ($38). AE, MC, V. Tues–Sat noon–2:30pm and 5:45–10pm; Sun noon–3:30pm. From M4 133 follow signs for Airport/Cardiff W.; take A4050 Barry/Bairport Rd., turning right at the 1st roundabout.

Woods Brasserie MODERN BRITISH/CONTINENTAL   In the old Pilotage Building down by the dock, this is a haven of modernity, serving not only the best of

Britain, but also dishes inspired by the cuisines of the Pacific Rim and the Mediterranean. Sean McCarthy roams the world for inspiration and finds it in his spicy and savory combinations. He is addicted to Asian flavorings, such as a sweet chili sauce used to perk up pork tenderloin (ginger and garlic help, too). Well-crafted starters include pressed terrine of pheasant with mulled-wine jelly, or a ravioli of salmon with lobster with artichoke purée. Mains include pan-roasted corn-fed chicken breast or chargrilled rib-eye of Aberdeen Angus with Jerusalem artichokes.

Pilotage Building, Stuart St., Cardiff Bay. © 02920/492400. Reservations required. Main courses £11–£17 ($21–$33); fixed-price lunch £15–£18 ($30–$36); fixed-price pre-theater dinner £17–£20 ($34–$40). AE, DC, MC, V. Mon–Sat noon–2pm and 7–10pm; Sun noon–3pm.

INEXPENSIVE
Harry Ramsden's SEAFOOD   This member of a chain serves the best fish and chips in Wales, at least according to its devotees. Until we finish sampling hundreds of others, we'll have to let the claim remain. Under crystal chandeliers, with nostalgic pictures displayed, this is both a place for traditional British cuisine, mainly seafood, as well as entertainment. Begin perhaps with a prawn cocktail or a smoked salmon salad. You can opt for fish platters, such as a 14-ounce batter-fried haddock with chips. If you finish the entire thing, you can have any dessert you want for free. You can also order such mains as New Zealand red cod or chargrilled swordfish steak, even a fish pie. Meat and poultry dishes are also served, including chicken breasts or chargrilled sirloin steaks.

Landsey House, Stuart Place. © 02920/463334. Reservations recommended. Main courses £6–£10 ($12–$20). AE, DC, MC, V. Summer Mon–Thurs 11:30am–9pm; Fri–Sat 11:30am–10pm; Sun noon–8pm. Closes 1 hr. earlier off season.

La Brasserie, Champers, Le Monde *Kids* CONTINENTAL   Benigno Martinez enjoys one of the best dining formulas in the city—a three-in-one winner—a wine bar, a brasserie, and a Spanish bodega. A bustling, informal atmosphere prevails, and much of young Cardiff turns up here nightly, beginning with the bar food in Champers, which in this case means the tastiest tapas in town. La Brasserie was originally built as a warehouse in the 19th century. You order your drinks from a wood-topped bar and food from an attendant, who waits behind a well-stocked display case. The establishment serves 50 kinds of wine. Opt for the spit-roasted suckling pig or a platter of fresh oysters. Game including grouse, woodcock, and partridge is featured in season. Le Monde concentrates on fresh fish, including a delectable Marseilles-style fish soup and sea bass baked in rock salt. At Champers you get a lively Spanish atmosphere with a cuisine to match.

60 St. Mary St. © 02920/387376. Reservations not needed. Main courses £11–£20 ($22–$40). MC, V. Mon–Sat noon–2:30pm and 7pm–midnight; Sun noon–4pm. Closed Dec 15–26.

EXPLORING THE TOWN
The Welsh capital has many interesting things to see, from antiquities to such modern pieces as Epstein's controversial carving, *Christ in Majesty,* at Llandaff Cathedral. If you're in Cardiff for only a short time, try to see the major sights described below.

CARDIFF BAY'S INNER HARBOR ☆
Allow 2 hours to visit this redeveloped area of the old dockland of Tiger Bay, lying about 2.5km (1½ miles) south of the town center. The salty old sea dogs of yesteryear who used to hang out here between sails wouldn't recognize the place today. No longer tawdry, it bustles with shops, restaurants, pubs, and attractions.

In the 19th century, when the area was called Tiger Bay, it became notorious among sailors around the world. The setting for many a novel, Tiger Bay meant poverty, crime, and violence. Today, the panoramic view of the harbor is worth the visit alone, as are the scenic promenades along the bay and even a science center.

Drop in at the **Cardiff Bay Visitor Centre,** the Tube, Harbour Drive (© **02920/ 463833**), next to the Welsh Industrial and Maritime Museum, to pick up any information about the area. Information is free at the center, which is open Monday to Friday 9:30am to 5pm, and Saturday and Sunday 10am to 5pm.

Techniquest ✰, Stuart Street (© **02920/475475;** www.techniquest.org), Britain's leading science discovery center, is the chief attraction here. Here you can enjoy 160 hands-on exhibits, and visit both a Science Theatre and Planetarium. Some 100,000 people—both young and old—visit it annually. Admission is £6.90 ($14) for adults, £4.80 ($9.60) for children ages 4 to 16 (free for children ages 3 and younger), or £20 ($40) for a family ticket. Techniquest is open Monday to Friday 9:30am to 4:30pm, Saturday and Sunday 10:30am to 5pm. Last admission is 45 minutes before closing.

THE TOP ATTRACTIONS

Caerphilly Castle ✰✰   About 13km (8 miles) north of Cardiff is this imposing moated fortress built partly on the site of a Roman fort. It was constructed by Earl Gilbert de Clare, Lord of Glamorgan, as protection against invasion by the Welsh prince Llywelyn ap Gwynedd in the 13th century. The massive water defenses of the castle form the second-largest castle area in Britain. You will note the leaning tower as you approach the castle, a result of efforts by Cromwell to blow up the towers. Perhaps you'll see the castle ghost, the Green Lady. She is supposed to be the spirit of a French princess who loved a handsome Welsh prince. When her husband, the Norman lord of Caerphilly, learned of the matter, he sent her into exile, but her ghost is still supposed to be here, lamenting her lost love. You should come here mainly to see the impressive layout of the castle, with its defenses and great gatehouse, along with a fortified dam separating the outer moat from the inner moat. Wander also into the Great Hall. What you don't get is a luxurious interior filled with fascinating paintings or antiques.

On the A469 at Caerphilly. © 02920/883143. Admission £3.50 ($7) adults, £3 ($6) children ages 15 and younger. Apr–May and Oct daily 9:30am–5pm; June–Sept daily 9:30am–6pm; Nov–Mar Mon–Sat 9:30am–4pm. Bus: 26 from Cardiff leaves for Caerphilly every hour during the day (also bus 71 or 72). Caerphilly train with several departures daily from Central Station in Cardiff.

Cardiff Castle ✰   Some 1,900 years of history are embodied in this castle located in the heart of the city. The Romans first built a forum on this site, and you can see the remains of massive 3m-thick (10-ft.) stone walls. The Normans constructed a castle on what was left of the Roman fort, and much of the Norman work still exists, added to by medieval lords. It came under assault in the Anglo-Welsh wars and was besieged during the English Civil War. The third marquis of Bute, by then the owner, had it restored in the 19th century by Victorian architect William Burges, who transformed the interior into the extravaganza of whimsy, color, and rich architectural detail you see today. The Welsh Regimental Museum and the First Queen's Dragoon Guards Regimental Museum are also here. Admission includes the full conducted tour.

Castle St. © 02920/878100. www.cardiffcastle.com. Admission £7.50 ($15) adults, £5.95 ($12) students, £5.95 ($12) seniors, £4.50 ($9) children. Mar–Oct daily 9:30am–6pm; Nov–Feb daily 9:30am–5pm. Last admission 1 hr. before closing. Closed Dec 25–26 and Jan 1. Bus: 32 or 62.

Llandaff Cathedral ⚐★   This cathedral is in the tiny city of Llandaff, which stood just outside the western boundary of Cardiff until 1922, when it was made a part of the capital. It retains its village atmosphere, with modern shops in old half-timbered buildings. The cathedral stands in a green hollow at a place where religious history goes back 1,400 years. It began as a religious community founded by St. Teilo in the 6th century, with many churches under its aegis scattered throughout South Wales. A 10th-century Celtic cross is all that's left of the pre-Norman church. Among relics of the Norman church erected on-site is a fine arch behind the high altar. The west front, built in the 13th century, is one of the best medieval works of art in Wales. Cromwell's army used the cathedral as a beer house and post office; then in 1941 a German bomb severely damaged the building. Postwar reconstruction gave the cathedral two fine new features: the Welsh Regiment Chapel and Sir Jacob Epstein's soaring sculpture *Christ in Majesty*. Epstein's striking work, which dominates the interior of the structure, has elicited mixed reactions from viewers. The ruin of the 800-year-old Bishop's Palace has been made into a peaceful public garden. Call for times of services.

Cathedral Rd. ⓒ **02920/564554.** www.llandaffcathedral.org.uk. Free admission (donations requested). Daily 7am–7pm. Bus: 25, 33, 33A, or 62.

National History Museum ⚐★★   One of the best places to visit in all of Wales is this museum, which provides a glimpse of Welsh life in centuries past. In the wooded parkland of an Elizabethan mansion, you can visit a treasury of ancient buildings that have been brought from their original sites all over the country and re-erected, in some cases even restored, to their former use. In this superb collection of traditional buildings, widely distributed over the 40 hectares (100 acres) of parkland, you can see a 15th-century Tudor farmhouse furnished in the fashion of its day, cottages, a tollhouse, a schoolhouse, a chapel, and a cockpit. You'll also see a woolen mill and a flour mill from long ago put back into use so that people of the present can see how such work was done back in the days before electricity, steam power, or other modern conveniences. A wood-turner and a cooper (barrel maker) are also at work, using the tools and materials of another age.

Besides the open-air museum, you can also visit the handsome headquarters building of the **Welsh Folk Museum** with its wealth including costumes, agricultural farm equipment used to till Welsh fields centuries ago, and articles of material culture, from Welsh dressers and cooking utensils to love spoons and early-day toys.

Also on the grounds is **St. Fagans Castle,** the 16th-century mansion that was given to the National Museum of Wales by the earl of Plymouth as a center for the folk museum. The mansion house, built inside the curtain wall of a Norman castle, with its formal gardens, has been refurbished and restored to the way it was at the end of the 18th century.

St. Fagans. ⓒ **02920/573500.** www.museumwales.ac.uk. Free admission. Daily 10am–5pm. Bus: 32 or 320 leaving from the bus station in Cardiff every hour during the day.

National Museum Wales ⚐★   This imposing white, classic building with a columned entrance and a large cupola houses eclectic art and science collections. Along with City Hall, it stands at the Civic Centre. The diverse exhibits here focus on natural science, industry, archaeology, and geology, plus there are extensive collections of silver, china, and glass (some dating from 1250). The emphasis is on the story of Wales from earliest times. There are also modern and classic sculptures and works from Old Masters and modern artists from van Gogh to Kokoschka.

Much of the museum's ambience comes from the openness and light that fills the main entrance and hall below the high ceiling. From the floor of the rotunda, you can look up to the mezzanine gallery that girdles the main hall. The exhibits are at the head of the impressive staircase from the main hall. Also on this level is the French Impressionist collection—our favorite part of the museum—which includes Monet's *Waterlilies,* Renoir's *Parisian Girl,* and Manet's haunting *The Rabbit.* Here you can also see Rodin's bronze couple *The Kiss* and paintings by Rubens, Cézanne, Augustus John, and Brangwyn. A well-stocked bookstore is situated off the main hall.

Cathays Park in the Civic Centre. ℂ 02920/397951. www.nmgw.ac.uk. Free admission except for special exhibitions (prices vary). Tues–Sun 10am–5pm. Closed some public holidays. Bus: 32 or 62.

PARKS & GARDENS

Cardiff has been called a city of parks, with some 1,092 hectares (2,700 acres) of well-designed parklands. **Bute Park,** in the heart of the city, spreads its green swath along the River Taff for the pleasure of residents and visitors.

Of special interest, **Roath Park,** Lake Road West (ℂ 02920/445900), is east of the city center, offering facilities for boating and fishing on its 13-hectare (32-acre) lake, as well as tennis courts and bowling greens. Rose and dahlia gardens, a subtropical greenhouse, a children's play area, and an island bird sanctuary add to the pleasures found here. The lighthouse clock tower in the lake is a memorial to Captain Scott. Admission is free, and it's open daily from 10:30am to 1pm and 2 to 4:30pm (bus: 32 or 62).

Close to 5km (3 miles) from Cardiff, **Dyffryn Gardens,** St. Nicholas (ℂ 02920/593328; www.dyffryngardens.org.uk), stands in a secluded valley in the Vale of Glamorgan. This park of 20 hectares (50 acres) contains a landscaped botanical garden. Herbaceous borders, a rose garden, a rock garden, and the largest heather garden in Wales are found here, along with an extensive arboretum. Grass walks invite you for long, leisurely strolls through the grounds. A palm house, orchid house, cactus and succulent house, along with seasonal display houses of potted plants, are also on view. The gardens were restored to their original design as conceived by Thomas Mawson in 1906. From November to February admission is £3 ($6) for adults, £2 ($4) for seniors and students, and £1 ($2) for children. A family ticket costs £17 ($34). From March to October admission is £6 ($12) for adults, £4 ($8) for seniors and students, £2 ($4) for children, with a family ticket going for £15 ($30). The gardens are open daily April to September 10am to 6pm, October 10am to 5pm, and November to April 10am to 4pm.

SHOPPING

Whether you're looking for gifts to take home, hunting for souvenirs, or just browsing, you'll like the shops of Cardiff. They are many and varied, ranging from a multiplicity of offerings in a modern shopping precinct, St. David's Centre—a stone's throw from the castle—to the stalls of a covered market.

The **main shopping streets** are St. Mary, High, Castle, Duke, and Queen streets, plus the Hayes. Most of this area has been made into a pedestrian mall, with trees, shrubs, and gracious Edwardian arcades. These arcades, a dozen in all, are the most famous shopping precincts in all of Wales. The best known is the **Castle Arcade,** constructed in 1887. The interior has a fascinating first-floor wooden gallery with a wooden second floor overhanging it. Dating from 1858, the **Royal Arcade** is the oldest of the city's shopping arcades. Look for the original Victorian storefronts at nos.

29, 30, and 32. The **Morgan Arcade** from 1896 is the best preserved. Note the first-floor Venetian windows and the original slender wooden storefronts such as nos. 23 and 24. All in all, the arcades stretch to a length of 797m (2,655 ft.) in the city.

In **St. David's Shopping Centre** is a branch of **Marks & Spencer,** 72 Queen St. (© **02920/378211**), one of the country's oldest branches of a major chain store, offering clothing with emphasis on British-made goods. A food section contains a range of high-quality specialty items. This is the anchor store in the enclosed center, which has shops opening off wide walkways. You can get to St. David's by bus no. 2, 3, 7, 8, or 9. Shops are usually open Monday to Saturday 8:30am to 6:30pm (Thurs until 9pm).

The best Welsh craft shop in the center is **Castle Welsh Crafts,** 1 Castle St. (© **02920/ 343038**), opposite the castle entrance. Shipping service is available, and VAT-refund forms are available for overseas visitors.

Markets are held at several sites. The **Central Indoor Market** on St. Mary Street is open Monday to Saturday. The **Outdoor Fruit and Vegetable Market,** St. David Street and Mary Ann Street, is open Monday to Saturday. On Bessemer Road, an **open-air market** is held on Sunday morning.

For a novel shopping jaunt, visit **Jacob Antique Centre,** West Canal Wharf (© **02920/390939**), to see what's for sale from Grandmother Welsh's attic. Perhaps a Victorian fireplace, 19th-century jewelry, antique brass or hardware, pocket watches, and certainly furnishings mainly from Victoria's heyday. You can get there on bus no. 2 or 3.

Close to St. David's Centre, **Capitol Shopping Centre** along Queen Street is another place to shop for bargains or special gifts. In the complex is one of Britain's best men's stores, **Austin Reed,** Unit 4, Capitol Shopping Centre (© **02920/ 228357**). You can get there on bus no. 70, 78, 80, or 82.

At the **Martin Tinney Gallery,** 18 St. Andrews Crescent (© **02920/641411**), a short distance from the Cardiff rail station, you'll find the region's best commercial galleries. Finally, **Craft in the Bay,** the Flourish, Lloyd George Avenue (© **02920/ 484611**), features the largest selection of handmade quality crafts in Wales—baskets, pottery, jewelry, handcrafted furniture, ceramics, and the like.

CARDIFF AFTER DARK

There's no Soho in Cardiff, but you can find many interesting places to go after dark.

St. David's Hall (see below) is one of Britain's leading centers of music, offering an extensive program, including visits by international conductors, soloists, and orchestras. Top rock and pop artists also appear there. The most outstanding local troupe is the **Welsh National Opera,** which *Punch* magazine acclaimed as "the world's best opera company."

For information about after-dark diversions, pick up a brochure from the Cardiff tourist office, "Cardiff 2009," which is revised annually. In it you'll find a selective rundown of the city's most worthwhile entertainment.

THE PERFORMING ARTS

Built at the cost of £106 million ($212 million), the **Wales Millennium Centre** ✸✸✸ has made its debut at Cardiff Bay (© **02920/636400;** www.wmc.org.uk), the home base for seven leading cultural organizations, including the Welsh National Opera and the Dance Company of Wales. Set against a backdrop of Welsh slate walls and a golden roof, the 1,900-seat auditorium overlooks the waterfront. Right from the beginning, it has established itself as one of the world's leading venues for the performing arts, attracting companies from all over the world, including the Australian Ballet. The center houses the Donald Gordon Theatre and the Weston Studio, plus an array of places to dine, drink, and watch free entertainment. Tickets prices vary depending on the attraction. On our last visit, for example, prices began at £10 ($20) for the cheapest seat in the house, going up to £38 ($76).

St. David's Hall (or *Neuadd Dewi Sant* in Welsh), the Hayes (© **02920/878889;** www.newtheatrecardiff.co.uk), was designed in an octagonal format of shimmering glass and roughly textured concrete; it is the most comprehensive forum for the arts in Wales. A number of world-class orchestras appear regularly, along with popular music stars—everybody from Tina Turner to Welsh-born Tom Jones. Dance, films, and classical ballet, among other events, are also presented.

The hall maintains an information desk for the sale of tickets throughout the day. It also has dining facilities, plus a changing exhibition of art. Prince Charles laid the hall's cornerstone, and the Queen Mother officially opened the arts center in 1983. The top-notch acoustics are attributed to its interior arrangements of a series of interlinked sloping terraces, any of which can be opened or closed for seating depending on the size of the audience.

Instant confirmed bookings for events are available by phone with a Visa or MasterCard daily 10am to 6 or 8pm, depending on the concert schedule. The box office is open Monday to Saturday 9:30am to 8pm (but only until 5:30pm on days when there's no performance). On Sunday, the box office opens 1 hour before the start of a scheduled performance. Ticket prices depend on the event. Take bus no. 1 or 2.

Cardiff's main repertory theater, **Sherman Theatre,** Senghennydd Road (© **02920/ 646900;** www.shermantheatre.co.uk), is on the campus of the University of Wales. It has two auditoriums—the Main Theatre and the more intimate Arena Theatre. More than 600 performances a year are staged here, including drama, dance, and Welsh folkloric performances. The box office is open Monday to Saturday from 10am to 8pm (until 5:30pm if no performance is scheduled). The cost for most tickets is £12 to £15 ($24–$30) for adults or £10 to £11 ($20–$22) for students and children. Take bus no. 70, 78, 80, or 82.

Finally, **Chapter,** Market Road, in Canton (© **02920/304400;** www.chapter.org), is an arts center complete with a theater; two movie facilities; three galleries and artists' studios; video, photography, and silk-screen workshops; a dance studio; a bookshop; two bars; and a cafe. Its box office is open Monday to Friday 11am to 8:30pm, Saturday 2 to 8:30pm, and Sunday 3 to 8:30pm. Take bus no. 17, 18, or 31.

MUSIC CLUBS

The hottest action is likely to be found at **Clwb ifor Bach** (the **Welsh Club**) at 11 Womanby St. (© **029/2023-2199**), whose activities spread across three levels, including the top floor, which rocks to live bands, including some of the best in Wales. There's something different happening every night the club is open, perhaps a live band session called "Bullet for My Valentine." Cover ranges from £3.50 to £8 ($7–$16), and the club rocks Wednesday to Monday, usually from 7:30pm to either 2 or 3am.

Liquid, St. Mary's St. (© **029/645-464**), has the best sound and lighting systems, with striking visuals. Management plays all the best funk, house, electro, R&B, whatever, with the town's best DJs. Charging from £5 to £12 ($10–$24) entrance fee, Liquid pours over Friday and Saturday 9:30pm to 5am.

Another hot venue, attracting massive crowds to its three floors of action, is **Risa,** Millennium Plaza (© **029/377-184**). Live entertainment is on the top floor, which presents comedy. On the main level are a bar and lounges, with a dance floor underneath. Risa is open Thursday 7pm to 1am, and Wednesday, Friday, and Saturday noon to 2am. The cover charge ranges from £2 to £3 ($4–$6).

PUBS & BARS

A traditional favorite is the **Park Vaults,** in the Thistle Hotel, Park Place (© **0871/ 3769011**), a cozy pub and bistro format. Stained-glass windows evoke Victorian nostalgia. You can also come here for a pub dinner. Take bus no. 8 or 9.

More modern and attracting a younger crowd, **Salt,** Stuart Street, Mermaid Quay (© **02920/494375**), is a two-story bar that serves some of the best cocktails in town. Take bus no. 8.

A hangout for rugby fans, **City Arms,** 10 Quay St. (corner of Quay and Womanby sts.; © **02920/225258**), attracts sports enthusiasts and is the most likely venue for any pop star or celebrity visiting Wales. Take bus no. 50, 51, 52, 70, 71, or 72.

GAY CLUBS

Exit Club, 48 Charles St. (© **02920/640102;** www.matgocreative.co.uk/exit), is a hot spot that is usually crowded and cruisy. Its precincts accommodate the Richard Burton or Dylan Thomas wannabes of the 21st century. Surveying the dance floor of heavy-drinking hot guys, one patron claimed, "You want to get 'em before they're too pissed." There's no cover before 9:30pm; after that hour, you pay from £2 to £3 ($4–$6). The club is open Sunday to Thursday 8pm to 2am, Friday and Saturday 8pm to 3am. Sunday is cabaret night.

2 Abergavenny

262km (163 miles) W of London; 78km (48 miles) NE of Swansea; 49km (31 miles) NE of Cardiff

This flourishing market town of nearly 10,000 people is called "the Gateway to Wales," and it's certainly the gateway to the Brecon Beacons, which lie to the west. The Welsh word *aber* means the mouth of a river, and Abergavenny lies at the mouth of the River Gavenny, where it joins the River Usk. The town is in a valley with mountains and hills spread around it. Humankind has found this a good, sometimes safe place to live for some 5,000 years, as revealed by archaeological finds from the late Neolithic Age. The Romans established one of their forts here; centuries later a Norman castle was built nearby.

The best time to visit Abergavenny is for its Wednesday **flea market** (© **01873/ 735811;** www.abergavennymarket.co.uk), from 6am to 5pm. An **antiques market** is staged every third Sunday of the month.

Abergavenny is renowned as a center for outdoor holiday activities, including pony trekking, hill walking and climbing, golfing, hang gliding, and fishing. A Leisure Centre provides for indoor sports. The tourist office (see below) keeps an up-to-date list of activities available at any season.

ESSENTIALS

GETTING THERE   The town is linked by rail to both Shrewsbury and Hereford (in England) and to Newport, a distance of 31km (19 miles) to the southwest, in Wales. From Newport, rail connections are made to Cardiff, Bristol, and London. The Abergavenny Rail Station is on Station Road, off Monmouth Road. It usually takes

2½ hours if you're arriving from London. For rail information and schedules, call
℃ 0845/748-4950 or visit www.nationalrail.co.uk.

The no. X3 or X4 Stagecoach Bus from Hereford arrives 10 times per day. Bus no.
X43 arrives 7 times per day from Brecon, and bus no. X20 arrives at the rate of 12 per
day from Newport (from which connections are made to Cardiff). For information,
call ℃ 0870/608-2608 or visit www.stagecoachbus.com.

If driving, from Hereford, take the A465 southwest; from Cardiff take the M4
motorway east toward London but cut north along the A4042 toward Abergavenny.

VISITOR INFORMATION   Abergavenny's Civic Society has laid out a **Town
Trail,** marking buildings and other points of interest with brass plaques. For more info
about the town and its environs, get in touch with the **Tourist Information Centre,**
Swan Meadow, Monmouth Road (℃ **01873/857588;** www.abergavenny.co.uk); it's
open Easter to October daily 10am to 1pm and 2 to 5:30pm, and November to Easter
daily 10am to 4pm.

WHERE TO STAY NEARBY

Bear 🐾 *(Value*   This 15th-century coaching inn is hailed for its evocative atmosphere,
bedrooms, and cuisine—a winning combination. About 8km (5 miles) northwest of
Abergavenny in a charming little town, the hotel grew in fame back in the days when
stagecoaches from London would pull in here. The place has been upgraded to keep
up with modern times, but the old character has been respected—for example, some
units with four-posters also have Jacuzzi tubs. In summer, a secluded outdoor garden
is the place to sit and ponder a Welsh twilight. A modern addition is a range of superior bedrooms bordering a courtyard; this annex was designed in the style of an old
Tudor manse. Or you can opt for the individually furnished bedrooms in the main
building, which come in a variety of styles.

High St., Crickhowell, Powys NP8 1BW. ℃ **01873/810408.** Fax 01873/811696. www.bearhotel.co.uk. 34 units.
£80–£130 ($160–$260) double; £150 ($300) suite. Rates include breakfast. AE, MC, V. On A40 between Abergavenny
and Brecon. **Amenities:** Restaurant; bar. *In room:* TV, beverage maker, hair dryer.

Llansantffraed Court 🐾🐾   You'll have to drive 16km (10 miles) from Abergavenny to reach it, but this hotel is worth the journey. As you head up the drive, an
impressive redbrick country house in William and Mary style comes into view. It's set
on extensive and well-kept grounds with a small lake, everything opening onto distant
views of the Brecon Beacons. The midsize bedrooms are comfortably furnished, each
with en-suite bathrooms, and some offer panoramic views of the surrounding mountains. Some of the accommodations contain four-posters. The dining room, serving
Welsh and French cuisine, is decorated with oak beams and oil paintings and has an
outdoor terrace.

Llanvihangel Gobion, Abergavenny NP7 9BA. ℃ **01873/840678.** Fax 01873/840674. www.llch.co.uk. 21 units.
£115–£135 ($230–$270) double; £175 ($350) suite. Rates include breakfast. AE, DC, MC, V. At A465/A40 Aber-
gavenny intersection, take B4598 signposted to USK. Continue toward Raglan until you see the hotel. **Amenities:**
Restaurant; bar; croquet lawn; archery; fishing; clay pigeon shooting; room service; laundry service; dry cleaning. *In
room:* TV, Wi-Fi, minibar, beverage maker.

WHERE TO DINE

Walnut Tree Inn 🐾 WELSH   This popular restaurant wins praise all over the
British Isles—and rightly so. Energetic and enthusiastic, the chefs cultivate an inventive and fresh cuisine. Come here for full-flavored dishes that may include roast partridge with chestnut stuffing or wild duck with morel mushrooms and game gravy.

You might also try the local favorite of saddle of hare with celeriac and a red-wine sauce.

Llandewi Skirrid. ℂ 01873/852797. Reservations recommended. Main courses £11–£20 ($22–$40). MC, V. Tues–Sat noon–2:30pm and 7–10pm. Closed 2 weeks at Christmas. Take B4521 4.8km (3 miles) northeast of Abergavenny.

SEEING THE SIGHTS

Only fragments of the 12th-century **Abergavenny Castle,** on Castle Street, remain, but a gruesome segment of its history is remembered. An early owner of the fortress, the Norman knight William de Braose, angered at the slaying of his brother-in-law by Welsh lords of Gwent, invited a group of them to dinner and had them murdered as they sat unarmed at his table. Visitors today fare much better. Admission is free, and it's open daily from dawn to dusk.

The **Abergavenny Museum,** Castle Street (ℂ **01873/854282;** www.abergavenny museum.co.uk), is in a house attached to the 19th-century hunting lodge on the castle grounds. The museum contains archaeological artifacts, farming tools, and a fascinating collection of old prints and pictures. A Welsh farmhouse kitchen and the contents of an old saddler's shop are on display. Admission is free. The museum is open March to October Monday to Saturday 11am to 1pm and 2 to 5pm, Sunday 2 to 5pm; and November to February, Monday to Saturday 11am to 1pm and 2 to 4pm.

St. Mary's Parish Church, Monk Street, is all that's left of a 12th-century Benedictine priory church. Little remains of the original Norman structure, as the building was redone from the 13th to the 15th century. It is believed that Cromwell's troops, which were billeted in Abergavenny for a while during the siege of Raglan Castle, did some damage to the church and its tombs. In the Herbert Chapel are a number of sarcophagi of lords of Abergavenny and family members, with requisite effigies on top. The oldest brass memorial in the church records a death in 1587. The 15th-century Jesse Tree in the Lewis Chapel is an unusual, 3.4m-long (10-ft.) woodcarving portraying Christ's family tree growing out of the body of Jesse, father of David. There is also a Norman font, as well as some 14th-century oak choir stalls. In spite of vandalism that has been committed in the church throughout the centuries, the building is kept open most days for worship and inspection; official hours are daily 9am to 7pm. For information, call the vicarage (ℂ **01873/853168;** www.stmarys-priory.org).

SIDE TRIPS FROM ABERGAVENNY
TINTERN ABBEY

The famous Wye Valley winds north from Chepstow, passing by the Lancaut Peninsula at the foot of the Windcliffe, a 243m (800-ft.) hill with striking views over the Severn estuary and the English border as far as the south part of the Cotswolds. About 1.6km (1 mile) or so farther north, you come to the little village of Tintern.

Now in magnificent ruins, **Tintern Abbey** ✦✦ (ℂ **01291/689251**) is in the exact center of this riverside village and is the focal point of the town. The Cistercian abbey is one of the greatest monastic ruins of Wales, and it was only the second Cistercian foundation in Britain and the first in Wales. The abbey was founded in 1131 and was active until the Dissolution of the Monasteries by King Henry VIII. Most of the standing structure dates from the 13th century, when the abbey was almost entirely rebuilt. It became one of the richest and most important monastic houses in Wales. Wordsworth was one of the first to appreciate the serene beauty of the abbey remains, as his poetry attests. There is ample parking quite near the entrance, and refreshments are available nearby.

Admission is £3.70 ($7.40) for adults and £3.30 ($6.60) for students, seniors, and children; it's £11 ($22) for a family ticket. The abbey is open April to May and October daily 9:30am to 5pm; June to September daily 9:30am to 6pm; and November to March 18 Monday to Saturday 9:30am to 4pm, and Sunday 11am to 4pm.

To get here from Abergavenny, take the A40 east to Monmouth, from which you can connect with the A466 south along the trail of Offa's Dyke to Tintern.

3 Brecon & Brecon Beacons National Park

275km (171 miles) W of London; 64km (40 miles) N of Cardiff

This busy little market town is the main base for touring Brecon Beacons National Park. Brecon, situated where the Usk and Honddu rivers meet, is the center of a farming section.

The Romans thought the area was a good place for a military encampment to discourage the Celts, and in A.D. 75 they built a fort, **Y Gaer,** about 4km (2½ miles) west of the present town. To get to Y Gaer, you walk across private farm fields. You can look around free.

Brecon Castle, built in 1093, is practically nonexistent, but it was militarily important when Llywelyn the Great and later Owain Glyndwr were battling against outsiders who wanted sovereignty in Wales. However, at the close of the civil war after Cromwell's visitations, the people of Brecon, tired of centuries of strife, pulled the castle down. All that's left is a section of wall joined to the Castle of Brecon Hotel and the Ely Tower, named for the bishop of Ely imprisoned there by Richard III. Access to the ruins is free, and there's no time limit on when it can be viewed. Oddly, it lies on the grounds of the Castle of Brecon Hotel and requires a transit through the hotel lobby to view it.

Of special interest is the fortified red-sandstone priory church of St. John the Evangelist, with its massive tower, now the **Cathedral of Swansea and Brecon,** Priory Hill (© **01874/623857;** www.breconcathedral.org.uk). It stands high above the River Honddu. The oldest parts of the cathedral date from the 12th century. It's open daily 8am to 6:30pm and admission is free.

ESSENTIALS

GETTING THERE   Sixty Sixty Buses (© **01443/692060;** www.sixtysixty.co.uk) runs buses from Cardiff, taking 90 minutes. Connections are also made from Merthry Tydfil, taking 40 minutes.

From Cardiff, motorists can head north along A470.

VISITOR INFORMATION   The Brecon Tourist Information Office, in the Cattle Market Car Park (© **01874/622485**), is open daily 9:30am to 5:30pm in summer, and Monday to Friday 9:30am to 5pm and Saturday and Sunday 9:30am to 4pm in winter.

WHERE TO STAY & DINE

All of the following establishments, with the exception of Cantre Selyf, serve lunch and dinner and are open to nonguests.

EXPENSIVE

Llangoed Hall 🐷🐷🐷   Sir Bernard Ashley, widower of Laura Ashley, presides over one of the great country houses of Wales. In the Wye Valley, 18km (11 miles) northeast of Brecon, the house opens onto panoramic views of the Black Mountains. A former

Jacobean manor house, it was redesigned in 1912 by the celebrated architect Cloug Williams-Ellis, who had wanted to create the aura of a great Edwardian country house party. Sir Bernard has gone even beyond the Edwardians in this fantasy, creating grand luxury—with the help of floor-to-ceiling Laura Ashley fabrics, of course—that and his own personal art collection. The individually decorated bedrooms and suites are spacious and elegant, with Laura Ashley fabrics at every turn.

From Welsh lamb to freshly caught salmon, Llangoed Hall serves the most refined cuisine in the area. You can make a reservation to enjoy a superb dinner for £40 ($80) per person.

Llyswen, Brecons, Powys LD3 0YP. ℂ **01874/754525.** Fax 01874/754545. www.llangoedhall.com. 23 units. £210–£350 ($420–$700) double; £385–£400 ($770–$800) suite. Rates include Welsh breakfast. AE, DC, MC, V. On A470, 3.2km (2 miles) northwest of Llyswen. **Amenities:** Restaurant; 2 outdoor tennis courts; clay shooting; fishing; rafting; rock climbing; room service; laundry service; dry cleaning. *In room:* TV, beverage maker, hair dryer.

MODERATE

Felin Fach Griffin ✨ *(Finds)*   This is an exceptional discovery for Wales, much of it looking as if you'd wandered back through a time portal. Old-fashioned though it may look, it is absolutely comfortable and up-to-date. Crisp white linen and soft goosedown pillows top ornate beds placed on stripped floorboards and will make you want to linger in bed long into the morning. Bedrooms are beautifully maintained and quietly elegant, and three have four-poster beds.

Felin Fach (A470, directly east of Brecon), Powys LD3 0UB. ℂ **01874/620111.** Fax 01874/620120. www.eatdrink sleep.ltd.uk. 7 units. £98–£125 ($196–$250) double. Rates include full breakfast. MC, V. **Amenities:** Restaurant; bar; room service. *In room:* Beverage maker, hair dryer, iron.

Nant Ddu Lodge ✨ *(Kids)*   This is your best bet for staying in the heart of the Brecon Beacons National Park. Originally built as a shooting lodge during the 19th century for Lord Tredegar, its name translates as "Black Stream," but that is hardly meant to suggest pollution, as its situation is idyllic for walking, climbing, fishing, and escaping from urban pressures. Though unified with a common hunter's theme, each of the small to midsize bedrooms is different from its neighbor. There are panoramic views of the mountains from all the bedrooms. Family rooms with sofa beds are available.

Diners can choose between the busy Bistro, the hotel's restaurant, or else eat in the intimate bar.

Cwm Taf, Brecon, CF Powys CF48 2HY. ℂ **01685/379111.** Fax 01685/377088. www.nant-ddu-lodge.co.uk. 31 units. £90–£100 ($180–$200) double; £125 ($250) suite. Rates include buffet breakfast. AE, MC, V. Beside the A470, 8km (5 miles) north of Merthyr Tydfil and 19km (12 miles) south of Brecon. **Amenities:** Bistro; bar; indoor heated pool; health club; spa; sauna; solarium; room service. *In room:* TV, beverage maker, hair dryer, trouser press.

Three Cocks Hotel ✨ *(Value)*   This 15th-century inn, surrounded by the countryside of the Brecon Beacons, is one of the best-known little inns of Wales. It deserves its fame. As you pass through the tiny hamlet of Three Cocks, don't blink, or you might miss the inn. The place is really small but has a certain charm. It's a stone building, which over the years has incorporated the trunk of a live tree into one of its walls. The inn and its elegant restaurant are operated by Mr. and Mrs. Michael Winstone, who extend very cordial hospitality to their guests. Downstairs is an elegant paneled drawing room, and upstairs are midsize bedrooms that have modern furnishings. Throughout the inn are rich furnishings with antiques, Oriental rugs, and oil paintings; log fires burn on chilly nights.

The Three Cocks is known throughout the area for the high-quality fare served in both its restaurant and pub.

Three Cocks, Brecon, Powys LD3 0SL. © **01497/847215.** Fax 01497/847339. www.threecockshotel.com. 7 units. £75–£110 ($150–$220) double. Rates include Welsh breakfast. MC, V. On A438, 18km (11 miles) northeast of Brecon and 6.4km (4 miles) southwest of Hay-on-Wye. **Amenities:** Restaurant; lounge. *In room:* No phone.

INEXPENSIVE

Cantre Selyf ✸ *Finds* One of the historic properties of Brecon, this town house dates from the 17th century. Close to St. Mary's Church, this Georgian house is one of the most convenient locations in town. When viewed only from the front, the property looks rather small, but it's a nice spread, complete with a large walled garden enclosed by a Norman wall. Much of the 17th-century architecture remains inside, although subsequent additions were made in the following century. The bedrooms still have their former beamed ceilings, cast-iron beds, and Georgian fireplaces. Guests meet fellow guests in the formal sitting room.

5 Lion St., Brecon, Powys LD3 7AU. © **01874/622904.** Fax 01874/622315. www.cantreselyf.co.uk. 3 units. £60–£72 ($120–$144) double. Rates include full breakfast. No credit cards. Closed Dec. **Amenities:** Breakfast room; lounge; bar; room service; laundry service. *In room:* TV, beverage maker, hair dryer, iron.

Griffin Inn ✸ *Value* Though hardly in the league of Llangoed (see above), this little oasis is infinitely more affordable. Outside Brecon, it was originally constructed in the 15th century as a cider house. Today it's an inn popular with fishermen who come hoping to get lucky while casting into the River Wye. Behind its ivy-covered facade, four generations of the Stockton family have received guests into their tidy bedrooms, offering them good pub grub as well. The inn itself is one of the oldest in the Upper Wye Valley, and lake fishing, pony trekking, and hiking are part of the summer fun in the Brecon Beacons. A few years ago, the Griffin was voted "Britain's Pub of the Year," so drinking is big here and the food is popular with locals. But we gravitate to the small to midsize bedrooms and their somewhat cramped bathrooms, soaking up the atmosphere of old beams and exposed stonework.

Good, unfussy food is served in both the restaurant and the Fisherman's Bar.

Llyswen, near Brecon, Powys LD3 0UR. © **01874/754241.** Fax 01874/754592. www.griffininn-llyswen.co.uk. 7 units. £60–£70 ($120–$140) double. MC, V. Lies 16km (10 miles) northeast of Brecon at the junction of A4079 and A470. **Amenities:** Restaurant; bar. *In room:* TV, beverage maker.

SEEING THE SIGHTS
BRECON BEACONS NATIONAL PARK ✸✸✸

Brecon Beacons National Park comprises 835 sq. km (519 sq. miles) of land from the Black Mountains in the west. National parks in the British Isles are maintained differently from those in the United States. Here people own land, live, and work within the park boundaries, though the landscape is safeguarded, and access to the park area is provided.

The park takes its name from the mountain range in the center of the park area. Pen y Fan, the highest peak in the range, rises to nearly 914m (3,000 ft.). The park contains sandstone moors covered with bracken and limestone crags with wooded gorges. Vast stretches of open common land lie in pastoral country. Farming is the main industry of the park. You can enjoy drives over the mountains, but walking and pony trekking are the best ways to explore the park.

There are nature reserves, a mountain center, and 51km (32 miles) of canal. The limestone area contains Britain's deepest cave system. A number of ancient monuments and historic buildings lie within the park boundaries.

For information regarding the park and its facilities, call one of the **National Park Information Centres,** the main one being at Wharton Mount, Glamorgan Street, in

Brecon (© **01874/624437**). Other information numbers include © **01873/853254** in Abergavenny and © **01550/720693** in Llandovery.

The park's southern boundary is only 40km (25 miles) from Cardiff, 23km (14 miles) from Swansea, and 16km (10 miles) from Newport. Abergavenny lies on the eastern boundary.

Run by the Brecon Beacons National Park Committee, the **National Park Centre,** near Libanus (© **01874/623366;** www.brecon-beacons.com), 8km (5 miles) south-west of Brecon, offers a good point from which to begin your tour of the park. The center, a spacious lounge, has displays explaining the major points of interest, talks and films, an informative staff, a picnic area, a refreshments buffet, and toilets. The entire building is wheelchair accessible.

The center is open daily, except Christmas Day, from 9:30am; the buffet is open 10:30am (10am July–Aug). Closing times vary according to the time of year. The center shuts its doors at 5pm in March to June, September, and October; at 6pm in July and August; and at 4:30pm from November to February. Closing is a half-hour later on Saturday, Sunday, and bank holidays from April to June and in September. The buffet closing time varies, so check when you go to the center.

Over the millennia, the force of flowing water has carved underground caverns through the extensive limestone regions in the southwestern portions of the Brecon Beacons National Park. Experienced cavers can explore many of these by making arrangements with one of the caving clubs, through the National Park Information Centres. However, only the **Dan-yr-Ogof Showcaves,** Abercraf (© **01639/730801;** www.dan-yr-ogof-showcaves.co.uk), are open to the general public, including children. Midway between Brecon and Swansea on the A4067, this is the largest show cave complex in western Europe. Visitors are able to follow dry, firm walkways to see stalagmite and stalactite formations under floodlights.

The Brecon Beacon's **Dinosaur Park** is filled with life-size models of creatures that disappeared 65 million years ago. Children are especially awed by the massive reptiles, particularly by one of the oldest—and the most terrifying—dinosaurs, tyrannosaurus rex.

Tours through Dan-yr-Ogof, Cathedral Cave, Bone Cave, and the Dinosaur Park last about 2½ hours. The complex is open from Easter to the end of October daily from 10am to 3pm (it closes at 5pm in high season). The charge is £11 ($22) for adults and £6.50 ($13) for children; children 3 and younger are admitted free. Admission also includes Mr. Morgan's Farmyard (an open farm where people can mingle with the animals), a re-created Iron Age village, a replica of an ancient stone circle, and a horse center. There are a restaurant, craft shop, museum, dry-ski slope, and information center at the caves.

4 Swansea & Gower Peninsula ⨁

307km (190 miles) W of London; 64km (40 miles) W of Cardiff; 131km (82 miles) W of Bristol

Vikings, Normans, English, Welsh, industry, seaport activity, holiday magic, and cultural prominence—all have combined to make the Swansea of today. It's tough, bold, and fun. Parks abound, and the tender loving care bestowed on them has caused Swansea to be a winner of the "Wales in Bloom" award year after year.

Swansea entered recorded history some 800 years ago, bearing a Viking name believed derived from "Sweyn's ey," or Sweyn's island. The Sweyn in question may well have been Sweyn Forkbeard, king of Denmark (987–1014), known to have been active in the Bristol Channel. Normans founded the marcher lordship of Gower, with its capital at Swansea, and a small trading community grew up here, as seagoing business, including coal exportation, became important through the Middle Ages. In the early 18th century at the town at the mouth of the River Tawe (Swansea's Welsh name is Abertawe), copperworks began to be built, and soon it was the copper capital of the world, as well as a leading European center for zinc refining, tin plating, steel making, and many chemical activities.

This "ugly, lovely city," as native son Dylan Thomas described it, has today pretty well obliterated the ugliness. Devastation of the town center by German air raids during World War II led to complete rebuilding. Traditional industries in the lower Swansea Valley have vanished, leaving economic woes and an industrial wasteland. Reclamation and redevelopment, however, have long been underway. The leveling of old mine tips and slag heaps and the planting of trees in their stead points to a more attractive Swansea for both today and tomorrow. Clean industries are coming in, but they are being placed out in wooded areas and suitable industrial parks, and they do not cast a pall over the city. Nonetheless, if your time clock allows for only one of the major cities of South Wales, make it Cardiff.

ESSENTIALS

GETTING THERE Trains arrive from both Cardiff and from London every hour throughout the day. The trip takes about an hour from Cardiff, about 3 hours from London. The Swansea Railway Station is on High Street. For reservations and information, call © **0845/748-4950** or visit **www.nationalrail.co.uk**.

National Express Coaches (© **0870/580-8080;** www.nationalexpress.com) arrive in Swansea from London, Manchester, Birmingham, and Cardiff. Many of these connections include stops with about an hour's wait.

From Cardiff, motorists can continue west along the M4.

GETTING AROUND Swansea is serviced by a good bus network, with buses leaving from the Quadrant Bus Station, at the Quadrant Shopping Centre. Bus nos. 4, X12, X13, 25, and 404 link the train station at 35 High St. and the bus station. For bus schedules and information, call © **0870/608-2608** or visit **www.firstgroup.com**. Because distances are usually short, consider calling a taxi—either **Data Cabs** (© **01792/474747**) or **Swallow Cabs** (© **01792/895533**).

VISITOR INFORMATION The **City of Swansea Information Centre,** Plymouth Street (© **01792/468321;** www.visitswanseabay.com), is open year-round, Monday to Saturday 9:30am to 5:30pm; Easter to September, it's also open Sunday 10am to 4pm.

WHERE TO STAY

Fairyhill ✪ If you want to escape from the world, head to this stone-built 18th-century manor set on 10 hectares (25 acres) of wooded grounds that also hold a lake and a fishing stream. It's an ideal base for exploring not only Swansea but also the little-populated Gower Peninsula that juts out into the British Channel west of Swansea and offers a good deal of natural beauty. After passing through a sumptuously appointed lounge, you are directed to one of the individually styled bedrooms—most often medium-size. Crackling log fires and deep-cushioned sofas create the aura of a cozy, snug country house. A real "taste of Wales" emerges from the menu. *Note:* Children 7 and younger are not accepted as guests.

Reynoldston SA3 1BS. © **01792/390139.** Fax 01792/391358. www.fairyhill.net. 8 units. £165–£275 ($330–$550) double. Rates include Welsh breakfast. MC, V. Outside Reynoldston off the A4118 from Swansea (18km/11 miles) away. **Amenities:** Restaurant; brasserie; bar; croquet lawn; room service; massage. *In room:* TV, beverage maker, iron.

Swansea

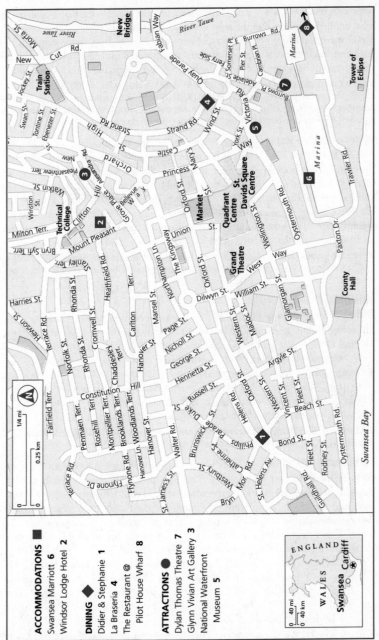

ACCOMMODATIONS ■
Swansea Marriott **6**
Windsor Lodge Hotel **2**

DINING ◆
Didier & Stephanie **1**
La Braseria **4**
The Restaurant @
Pilot House Wharf **8**

ATTRACTIONS ●
Dylan Thomas Theatre **7**
Glynn Vivian Art Gallery **3**
National Waterfront
Museum **5**

ENGLAND
WALES
Swansea Cardiff ✶

0 — 40 mi
0 — 40 km

New
Bridge

River Tawe

River Tawe

Morfa St.

Cut Rd.

New
Jockey St.

Train
Station

Swan St.
Tontine St.
Ebenezer St.

High St.
Strand Rd
Orchard St.

Alexandra Rd
New
Pleasantview Terr.

Watkin St.
Winston St.

Technical
College

Milton Terr.
Bryn Syfi Terr.
Stanley Terr.

Clifton
Grove Place
Bellevue Way

Mount Pleasant

Harries St.
Hewson St.

Rhonda St.
Cromwell St.
Norfolk St.
Rhonda St.

Heathfield Rd.
Chaddesley Terr.

Carlton Terr.

Fairfield Terr.
Penmaen Terr.
Rosehill Terr.
Montpellier Terr.
Brooklands Terr.
Woodlands Terr.

Constitution Hill

Terrace Rd

Ffynone Dr.
Hanover Ln.
Hanover St.

St. James's St.
Walter Rd.

Carlton Terr.
Hanover St.
Mansel St.
Northampton Ln.
The Kingsway

Page St.
Nicholl St.
George St.
Henrietta St.
Russell St.

Duke St.
Brunswick St.
Catherine St.

Westbury St.
Bryn

Mor Rd.

Dilwyn St.
Union St.

Oxford St.
Princess Way
Castle St.

Mary's
Market

Grand
Theatre

William St.
Western St.
Madoc St.

West Way

Phillips Parade

St. Helens Av.
Bond St.

Fleet St.
Rodney St.
Guildhall Rd

Helens Rd
Oxford St.
Western St.
Vincent St.
Argyle St.
Beach St.
Fleet St.

Oystermouth Rd.

Strand Rd
Wind St.

Quay Parade
Fabian Way

Ferry Side
Adelaide St.
Somerset Pl.
E. Burrows Rd

Pier St.
Cambrian Pl.

Burrows Pl.

Victoria Rd
York St.
Way

St.
Davids
Centre

Quadrant
Centre

Square
Centre

Wellington St.

Oystermouth Rd.

Glamorgan St.

County
Hall

Paxton Dr.

Marina

Marina

Trawler Rd.

Tower of
Eclipse

Swansea Bay

4
3
2
1
5
6
7
8

N

0 — 1/4 mi
0 — 0.25 km

Swansea Marriott ✫✫   This is the town's premier choice—the best amenities, the most dramatic location, and the most luxurious bedrooms. The four-story structure lies on the marina, opening onto panoramic views over the bay. By Swansea standards, it is large and bustling, attracting an equal mix of business clients and visitors. The hotel offers spacious bedrooms and roomy bathrooms, each immaculate and comfortable.

Maritime Quarter, Swansea SA1 3SS. ✆ 800/228-9290 in the U.S. and Canada, or 01792/642020. Fax 01792/650345. www.marriott.com. 119 units. £95–£139 ($190–$278) double. Rates include breakfast. AE, DC, MC, V. **Amenities:** Restaurant; bar; indoor heated pool; health club; whirlpool; sauna; business center; room service; laundry service; dry cleaning. *In room:* A/C, TV, minibar, beverage maker, hair dryer, iron, trouser press.

Windsor Lodge Hotel   Architecturally undistinguished, this is a nonetheless welcoming family-run hotel, close to the town center and about a 5-minute walk from the train station. It offers good value and cozy bedrooms with decent furnishings and modern decor, and tidy bathrooms for the night. The building itself is 2 centuries old and has been sheltering wayfarers to Swansea for decades. You never know who is likely to turn up. We once encountered former U.S. president Jimmy Carter and Rosalynn Carter leaving the inn after having enjoyed a lunch here. Your hosts maintain midsize bedrooms that are well cared for and provide a good night's sleep.

Mt. Pleasant, Swansea SA1 6EG. ✆ 01792/642158. Fax 01792/648996. www.windsor-lodge.co.uk. 19 units. £70 ($140) double. Rates include breakfast. AE, DC, MC, V. **Amenities:** Restaurant; bar; room service. *In room:* TV, beverage maker.

WHERE TO DINE

Didier & Stephanie ✫ FRENCH   Swansea, believe it or not, is becoming known for its fine dining, as exemplified by this sophisticated restaurant where you might see Michael Douglas and his wife, Catherine Zeta-Jones, popping in for a visit on one of their frequent visits to her hometown. Inside this little Swansea house, you'll encounter a cozy, welcoming decor and a tempting menu of Gallic-inspired recipes often using Welsh-grown fresh produce. Start with the smoked duck breast or the terrine of rabbit in a Cumberland sauce, and perhaps follow with such specialties as a rosemary-flavored rack of Welsh lamb or something from the local sea.

56 St. Helens Rd. ✆ 01792/655603. Reservations required. Main courses £14–£17 ($28–$34); set lunch £11–£16 ($22–$32). AE, DC, MC, V. Tues–Sat noon–1:30pm and 7–9pm.

La Braseria SPANISH   No, this is not Madrid, although this Spanish bodega (in Swansea, of all places) lying only a 5-minute walk from the train station evokes thoughts of sunny Spain. It's a marvelous change of pace when you've had too many leeks and too much Welsh lamb. The food, prepared daily from fresh ingredients, complements the list of Spanish wines and champagne; this is not the place for "lager louts." Come here for the town's best chargrilled meats. Tossed on that grill is everything from tender suckling pig to great chunks of beef to ostrich. Flavors are straightforward here, as the cooks don't like to mess up their grills with a lot of sauces. Likewise, they prepare the catch of the day in the same way, be it shark, bass, or snapper. Specific choices change according to the seasons, the availability of ingredients, and the inspirations of the chefs. In addition to items from the grill, you may opt for a savory kettle of mussels.

28 Wind St. ✆ 01792/469683. Reservations not accepted except for large parties. Main courses £7–£20 ($14–$40); fixed-price 2-course lunch £8.50 ($17). AE, DC, MC, V. Mon–Sat noon–2:30pm and 7–11:30pm.

The Restaurant @ Pilot House Wharf ⭐ MODERN BRITISH/SEAFOOD   In the former pilot house at the Swansea Marina, this seafood restaurant lies above a fishing tackle shop. It couldn't be more maritime, and you are served some of the freshest and best seafood in Wales, each dish based on the catch of the day. The owner said that the fishermen "land their catch within a salmon's leap of my back door." That's how fresh it is. Most of the dishes are solidly British, but there are a few Mediterranean touches as well. Full-flavor dishes include pot-roasted free-range chicken with smoked bacon, or braised half shoulder of Welsh lamb. Roast breast of pheasant is accompanied by black pudding and a Calvados sauce, and a haunch of venison that would have pleased Henry VIII also appears on the menu with a sauce made of plums and Jack Daniel's.

Trawler's Rd., Swansea. © **01792/466200.** Reservations recommended. Fixed-price lunch menu £11–£15 ($22–$30); main courses £15–£20 ($30–$40). DC, MC, V. Daily noon–2pm; Mon–Sat 6:30–9:30pm.

SEEING THE SIGHTS

In a once-dirty waterfront area, a **Maritime Quarter** has emerged. Lying between the city center and the seafront, it is centered on the historic South Dock and its Half Tide Basin and is complete with urban villages and a modern marina on the Swansea Yacht Haven. Open spaces, a promenade, and a seawall round out the scene.

The chief attraction here is the **National Waterfront Museum** ⭐⭐, Oystermouth Road, Maritime Quarter (© **01792/638950;** www.waterfrontmuseum.co.uk), open daily 10am to 5pm, charging no admission. Bus no. 118 runs here from the center of town. It's altogether fitting that Swansea has a maritime museum. After all, the copper plates that sheathed the hulls of the British fleet, making Nelson's ships faster than their enemies, were cast in Swansea. The exhibits are vast, including a display of the steel rails produced in Dowlaid that opened up the American Midwest in the mid-1800s.

The museum explores the history of industrial Wales through a series of exhibits— Wales, incidentally, was the world's first industrial nation. Transportation is strong here, including a Cardiff-built monoplane and a full-size replica of the famous Pen-y-darren locomotive. The story of immigration and emigration in Wales is told, focusing on how the metal and coal industries created wealth attracting workers to Wales, but also making Welsh expertise an exportable commodity to other countries.

A statue of Dylan Thomas stands in the Maritime Quarter, and the **Dylan Thomas Theatre** is nearby at 7 Gloucester Place (© **01792/473238;** www.dylanthomastheatre. org.uk). Many different types of plays are presented here (check the local newspapers for listings), not just works by Dylan Thomas. The poet was born in the Uplands, a residential area of Swansea, at 5 Cwmdonkin Dr., a steep street off Walter Road. You can walk in **Cwmdonkin Park** (pronounced *Quam*-don-kin) close by, which the poet made famous in his writings.

Swansea is one of the few Welsh cities to have a beach within walking distance of the center. A **promenade** leads all the way to Oystermouth, 6.4km (4 miles) away, although you can drive the route on the A4067. Along the way you pass rugby and cricket grounds and the entrance to the city's largest park, Singleton. About halfway down the bay is a 9-hole golf course and a well-equipped resort beach, in an area known as Blackpill. It includes the entrances to the city's country park, Clyne Valley, and the Clyne Gardens. Before long you come to the villages of Westcross and Norton, and then comes Oystermouth, which has a Norman castle renowned for its imposing position on a headland commanding a view of the bay and Swansea.

Eight kilometers (5 miles) south of Swansea, across Swansea Bay, lies the **Mumbles** 𝕲. It has been compared to the Bay of Naples because of its shape and beauty, especially after dark. This former fishing village has two faces (both pleasing): By day it has a tranquil atmosphere, but when the sun goes down Mumbles bursts into action and becomes a nightlife center, with crowded pubs, clubs, and restaurants. Mumbles has been attracting tourists since Victorian times, when the handsome pier was built, as in most British sea towns. It protrudes 274m (900 ft.) from Mumbles Head into the bay and affords sweeping views. Away from the seafront, you can see tiny fishermen's cottages built into the limestone rock. Souvenirs and examples of local crafts are in shops that cling to the hillside. Yachting, swimming, fishing, beach games, and bowling are enjoyed here.

Glynn Vivian Art Gallery 𝕲 (Finds)   Founded in 1911, although little known, this gallery is one of the treasure-troves of art in Wales. It was created by Richard Glynn Vivian, scion of a copper industrialist family. An inveterate traveler and art collector, he wanted to pass on his treasures to the world. The special reason to visit is to see the 20th-century collection of Welsh artists, including Ceri Richards, Josef Herman, and Evan Walters. We are especially fond of Alfred Janes's penetrating portrait of Dylan Thomas, painted in 1964. There are also displays of elegant porcelain and pottery, both European and Asian. On-site is an unusual gift shop with a selection of original works by Welsh artists, including ceramics, glass, and jewelry.

Alexandra Rd. ℂ **01792/516900.** www.glynnviviangallery.org. Free admission. Tues–Sun 10am–5pm.

SWANSEA AFTER DARK

Long gone are the days when Swansea's nocturnal entertainment consisted of a handful of battered pubs with a jukebox blaring out pre-Beatles tunes. Since the 1990s gentrification of many areas of Swansea's central core, there has been an explosion of nightlife options, many of them focusing on the city's nightlife-related pride and joy—**Wind** (it rhymes with "wined and dined") **Street.** The best way to explore the place involves popping in and out of any of the pubs, bars, and shops that appeal to you along this cobble-covered thoroughfare, especially on evenings when the city council has blocked off traffic, transforming it into a pedestrian-only walkway that on weekend evenings becomes very crowded.

Some of our favorites include the **Bank Statement,** 57–58 Wind St. (ℂ **01792/455477**), a pub and restaurant contained within the grandly ornate premises of what was built as a bank during the Victorian age. Nearby is the **Bar SA1,** 2 Wind St. (ℂ **01792/630941**), where a 19th-century storefront serves up copious portions of pub grub, platters, and foaming mugs full of local ale. More self-consciously trendy, evoking a hip bar in faraway London, is the **No Sign Wine Bar,** 56 Wind St. (ℂ **01792/465300**), where you're likely to see members of the local TV news team, off-duty, sampling whatever French, Chilean, or California vintage happens to be uncorked at the moment.

Other streets, each nearby, but none as densely packed as Wind Street with bars and restaurants, also have goodly numbers of nightlife offerings. **Exchange Bar,** 10 Strand (ℂ **01792/462896**), offers glimpses of Ireland, with live music and generous amounts of Celtic *joie de vivre.* The **Potters Wheel,** 85 The Kings Way (ℂ **01792/465113**), a member of the same chain as the above-mentioned Bank Statement, offers food and drink in a setting that's nostalgically evocative of turn-of-the-20th-century Wales.

In addition to the **Dylan Thomas Theatre** (see above), Swansea has a cultural side as well. The **Grand Theatre,** Singleton Street (ℂ **01792/475715**), adjacent to the

Quadrant Shopping Centre, is a Victorian theater that has been refurbished and redeveloped into a multimillion-dollar theater complex. The venue hosts international opera, ballet, and theater companies, plus 1-night stands that often feature internationally known entertainers. It also has its own schools of song and dance.

SIDE TRIPS FROM SWANSEA
GOWER PENINSULA ✸

The first area in Britain designated "an area of outstanding natural beauty," Gower is a broad peninsula stretching about 22km (14 miles) from the Mumbles to Worms Head in the west. This attraction begins 6.4km (4 miles) west of Swansea on A4067. The coastline of Gower starts at Bracelet Bay, just around the corner from the Mumbles. You can drive—at least to some parts of the peninsula—but the best way to see its sometimes-rugged, sometimes-flat coast is to walk, even for short distances if you don't have time to make the complete circuit.

There are many and varied beaches on Gower: **Caswell Bay,** with its acres of smooth, golden sand and safe swimming; **Langland,** a family attraction with facilities for golf, swimming, tennis, and surfing; and **Rotherslade,** which at high tide features some of the largest waves around the peninsula crashing onto the shore. Secluded **Pwil-du** is a place to sunbathe in solitude, despite the crowds elsewhere along the coast, and there are numerous other small coves tucked away beneath the cliffs. **Oxwich Bay** is one of the largest on the peninsula, with 4.8km (3 miles) of uninterrupted sand, where you can enjoy beach games, picnics, water-skiing, and sailing. Windsurfing is popular at Oxwich, too. Oxwich village, at one end of the bay, is a typical Gower hamlet of cottages and tree-lined lanes. There is a nature reserve here that is home to some rare orchid species.

After the commercial and often-crowded Oxwich beach, you may be happy to see **Slade,** which has to be approached on foot down a steep set of steps. The spotless beach is usually wind-free. Around the next corner, you'll find the villages of **Horton** and **Port Eynon,** with a long, curving beach backed by sand dunes. Refreshments are available on the beach, and the two villages offer nighttime entertainment.

From Port Eynon, a spectacular 7.2km (4.5-mile) cliff walk leads past Culver Hole, Paviland Cave, Mewslade, and Fall Bay to Worms Head and Rhossilli. The **Paviland Caves** can be explored. It is here that 100,000-year-old human remains have been found. **Worms Head** is a twisted outcrop of rock shaped into the form that sometimes, depending on the tides, looks like a prehistoric worm sticking its head up out of the water. **Rhossilli** is a long, sweeping bay and a beach reached from the treeless village of Rhossilli, with a church and houses perched 61m (200 ft.) up on the cliff tops. This is an international center for hang gliding. Halfway along the beach at Llangennith is the most popular surfing site on the peninsula. Rolling dunes connect it with Broughton Bay and Whitford Sands, and eventually you come to **Penclawdd,** a little village where a centuries-old cockle industry still thrives. If the tide is right, you can see the pickers with their rakes and buckets gleaning the crustaceans from the flats.

Although the coastal attractions are Gower's biggest lure, there are pleasant farms, attractive country roads, and places of interest inland. **Parc le Breos (Giant's Grave)** burial chamber, almost in the center of the peninsula, close to Parkmill on the A4118, is an ancient legacy from Stone Age people. The remains of at least four people were found there. A central passage and four chambers are in a cairn about 21m (70 ft.) long. **Pennard Castle** has suffered under ravages of weather and time, but from the north you can see the curtain wall almost intact. Admission is free.

Weobley Castle, Llanrhidian (© **01792/390012**), on North Gower, is actually a fortified house rather than a castle. There was no space for a garrison, and the rooms were for domestic purposes. On the northern edge of bare upland country, it overlooks the Llanrhidian marshes and the Loughor estuary. There are substantial remains of this 13th- and 14th-century stronghold, and the view is panoramic. Weobley is off the Llanrhidian-Cheriton road, 11km (7 miles) west of Gowerton. It is open daily 9:30am to 6pm (closes at 5pm in winter). Entrance costs £13 ($26) for adults or £2.50 ($5) for students and children ages 16 and younger.

Even though it is protected from development, Gower has been invaded by caravans (mobile homes), recreational vehicles, beach huts, retirement homes, and bungalows. Nevertheless, you can still find solitude in secluded bays and especially in the center of the peninsula, along the Cefn Bryn ridge or on Rhossili Down. From the top of **Cefn Bryn,** 185m (609 ft.) above sea level, you can see the entire peninsula and far beyond on clear days. By taking the Green Road, which runs the length of the ridge from Penmaen, you'll find a path about 1km (a half-mile) east of Reynoldston that leads to **Arthur's Stone,** a circular burial chamber. The mound of earth that once covered it has been weathered away, but you can see the huge capstone that protected the burial place. From Rhossili Down, at 192m (632 ft.), the English coast comes into view. Here also are megalithic tombs, cairns, and barrows.

LAUGHARNE: MEMORIES OF DYLAN THOMAS

Laugharne (pronounced *Larne*), 24km (15 miles) east of Tenby, is a hamlet overlooking broad waters. This ancient township on the estuary fed by the River Taf (not be confused with the River Taff in Cardiff) and the River Cywyn, was for centuries a bone of contention between Welsh, English, Cromwellians, and royal supporters. However, it did not come into the limelight of public attention until after the death of its adopted son, Swansea-born Dylan Thomas, and his acclaim as one of the great poets of the 20th century.

Head west from Swansea along the A4070, which becomes the A484 signposted north to Carmarthen. Once in Carmarthen, continue west along the A40 to St. Clears, where you cut southeast along the A4066 to Laugharne.

Where to Dine

Stable Door Restaurant ✿ TAPAS/SPANISH   A stable block in days gone by, this is the finest dining choice in the area, serving Mediterranean-style meals with taste and flair. It operates behind walls that were originally built in the 14th century to house horses Edward I brought from England during the construction of a nearby castle. Later, Oliver Cromwell's forces shot cannon into it when the masters of the castle switched their loyalties back to the Royalist side. Today, it's the most likable and enjoyable restaurant in the area, serving a menu of fresh ingredients that is varied and artfully prepared. Chefs prepare the best tapas in the south of Wales, and other starters include a platter of bell peppers with ricotta, feta cheese, sun-dried tomatoes, and olives. One of our favorites is fried potatoes with a chili-and-garlic sauce, given extra flavor by a homemade tomato sauce. Filet of beef skewers are marinated with cumin and served with red-onion marmalade. Marinated Spanish sardines appear on toast with arugula and cherry tomatoes.

Market Lane. © **01994/427777.** www.laugharne-restaurant.co.uk. Reservations recommended. Main courses £5–£18 ($10–$36). MC, V. Thurs–Sun noon–2pm and 6–9pm. Closed Jan–Feb 14.

Seeing the Sights

Dylan Thomas Boathouse ⊛, along a little path named Dylan's Walk, is the waterside house where the author lived with his wife, Caitlin, and their children until his death in 1953 during a visit to America. In the boathouse, a white-painted little three-story structure wedged between the hill and the estuary, you can see the family's rooms, photographs, interpretive panels on his life and works, an audio and audiovisual presentation that portrays him reading some of his work, a small art gallery, a book and record shop, and a little tearoom where you can have tea and Welsh cakes while you listen to the poet's voice and look out over the tranquil waters of the wide estuary.

On the way along the path, before you come to the boathouse, there's a little shack where this untidy wretch of a man wrote many of his minor masterpieces. You can't enter it, but you can look through an opening and see his built-in plank desk. Wadded-up scraps of paper on the floor give the feeling that he may have just stepped out to visit a favorite pub. Admission is £3.50 ($7) for adults, £2.95 ($5.90) seniors, £1.75 ($3.50) for children. Hours are May to October daily 10am to 5:30pm, and November to April daily 10:30am to 3:30pm. For more information, call ⓒ **01994/427420** or visit **www.dylanthomasboathouse.com**.

The poet is buried in the churchyard near the **Parish Church of St. Martin,** which you pass as you drive into town. A simple wooden cross marks his grave. A visit to the church is worthwhile. It dates from the 14th century and is entered through a lych-gate (iron gate), with the entrance to the church guarded by ancient yew trees. Memorial stones and carvings are among the interesting things to see.

Laugharne Castle, a handsome ruin called the home of the "Last Prince of Wales," sits on the estuary at the edge of the town. A castle here, Aber Corran, was first mentioned in 1113, believed to have been built by the great Welsh leader Rhys ap Gruffydd. The present romantic ruins date from Tudor times. Dylan Thomas described the then ivy-mantled structure as a "castle brown as owls."

National Botanic Museum ⊛ Lying 32km (20 miles) northwest of Swansea, this mammoth project is the first modern botanic garden in Britain dedicated to science, education, and leisure. A project costing £45 million ($90 million), this 229-hectare (568-acre) Regency estate was developed by financier William Paxton in the late 18th century, with walled gardens, lakes, and cascades. Its centerpiece is a magnificent Great Glasshouse, the largest single-span greenhouse in the world, blending in naturally with the rolling and bucolic Tywi Valley. The greenhouse is dedicated to threatened Mediterranean climates of the world, and its interior includes a ravine, rock faces, bridges, and waterfalls.

Middleton Hall, Llanarthne. ⓒ **01558/668768.** www.gardenofwales.org.uk. Mar–Oct admission £8 ($16) adults, £6 ($12) seniors, £3 ($6) children 5–16, £17 ($34) family ticket; Nov–Feb £5 ($10) adults, £3 ($6) seniors, free for children 16 and younger. Mar–Oct daily 10am–6pm (last admission at 5pm); Nov–Feb daily 10am–4:30pm (last admission at 3:30pm).

5 Pembrokeshire

This county boasts Britain's smallest national park, Pembrokeshire Coast National Park. It's unique in that it extends over cliff and beaches, whereas most parks encompass mountains or hill country. The coastline takes in 290km (180 miles) of sheer rugged beauty, with towering cliffs and turbulent waters. **Tenby** is the chief resort for exploring the park, but **Pembroke** and **St. Davids** also make worthy stopovers.

TENBY ⭐

The leading resort in Pembrokeshire, Tenby is packed with vacationers during the summer months, but it has a charm and character dating from medieval times, which makes it an interesting place to visit at any time of year. The location is 85km (53 miles) west of Swansea and 148km (92 miles) west of Cardiff.

The main southern rail line through Tenby is run by Arriva Trains Wales (© **0870/ 900-0773;** www.arrivatrainswales.co.uk). Trains run from Swansea seven times a day Monday to Friday and six times a day on Saturday and Sunday. For more detailed information, call **National Rail** at © **0845/748-4950.** For visitor information, go to the **Tourist Information Office** at the Croft (© **01834/842402**). It is open November to March Monday to Saturday 10am to 4pm, April and May daily 10am to 5pm, and June to October daily 10am to 5:30pm (until 6pm July–Aug).

WHERE TO STAY & DINE

Fourcroft Hotel *Kids*   This is our favorite hotel within the town itself, though we prefer the greater elegance and secluded location of Penally Abbey (see below). On the cliffs above Tenby's sheltered North Beach, the hotel lies a 5-minute walk from the medieval walled town center. Fourcroft forms part of a landmarked Georgian terrace, built more than 150 years ago as summer homes for Londoners. The front bedrooms are generally more spacious and open onto a view of the sea. All the rooms, however, have modern comfort, ranging from midsize to spacious, with roomy, well-kept bathrooms. Guests can use a private garden walk leading to the beach.

North Beach, Tenby, Pembrokeshire SA70 8AP. © 01834/842886. Fax 01834/842888. www.fourcroft-hotel.co.uk. 40 units. £100–£150 ($200–$300) double. Rates include Welsh breakfast. AE, DC, MC, V. Limited free parking (6 spaces). **Amenities:** Restaurant; bar; outdoor heated pool; whirlpool; sauna; game room; kids' playground; room service. *In room:* TV, beverage maker, hair dryer.

Penally Abbey ⭐   This country-house hotel—the finest lodging in the area— opens onto a gracious, timeless world. The house is 2 centuries old, but parts of its foundation date from the 6th century, when a monastery was established here. Today the flowering garden partially conceals the ruins of St. Deniol's Chapel and a Flemish chimney of a long-ago homestead. The wide-open sea and the still-functioning Cistercian monastery on Caldy Island contribute to the panoramic sweep from the terraces. The house is built of Pembrokeshire stone, containing ogee-headed doors, large square windows, and Gothic-inspired architectural details. The spacious bedrooms are full of character, often enhanced by a four-poster bed. We prefer the rooms in the family house to the newer ones in the two annexes.

Penally, Tenby, Pembrokeshire SA70 7PY. © 01834/843033. Fax 01834/844714. www.penally-abbey.com. 17 units. £140–£180 ($280–$360) double; £220 ($440) suite. Rates include breakfast. Discounts for children sharing parent's room. AE, MC, V. 3.2km (2 miles) southwest of town by A4139. **Amenities:** Restaurant; bar; heated indoor pool. *In room:* TV, minibar, beverage maker, hair dryer.

SEEING THE SIGHTS

There was already a Welsh village here when the Normans built **Tenby Castle,** now in ruins. Today the castle attracts interest because of its location on the headland overlooking the town and harbor. The town walls had four gates, one of which, the West Gate, known as Five Arches, remains. The west wall is in good condition. Tenby was also a target during the civil war.

Tenby Museum and Art Gallery, Castle Hill (© **01834/842809;** www.tenby museum.org.uk), is housed near the ruins of Tenby Castle. Exhibits cover the geology, archaeology, and natural history of the district, as well as the history of Tenby from the 12th century. In the art gallery you'll see works by Augustus and Gwen John, and Charles Norris, a local artist of the early 19th century. The museum and gallery are open April to October daily 10am to 5pm and November to March Monday to Friday 10am to 5pm. Admission costs £4 ($8) for adults, £3 ($6) for seniors and students, and £2 ($4) for children. A family ticket costs £9 ($18).

Tudor Merchant's House, Quay Hill (© **01834/842279;** www.nationaltrust.org. uk), is a beautifully furnished medieval dwelling of the 15th century with a fine Flemish chimney. On three interior walls, paintings with designs similar to Flemish weaving patterns were discovered under years of whitewash. It's open April to October Sunday to Friday 11am to 4:30pm. Admission costs £2.50 ($5) for adults or £1.20 ($2.40) for children 15 and younger.

Tenby's parish church, **St. Mary's,** dates from the 13th century and is the largest parish church in Wales. Giraldus Cambrensis (Gerald the Welshman), a great religious leader of the 13th century, was the first rector. Charging no admission, it is open daily from 8am to 6pm.

In the bay just 3.2km (2 miles) south of Tenby, little **Caldy Island** ⊛ has long been a Roman Catholic venue. A Celtic monastic cell is believed to have been here, and today it is farmed by Cistercian monks, whose abbey is the island's outstanding attraction. From the 12th century until the Dissolution of the Monasteries by Henry VIII, a Benedictine priory was here. For the next few centuries, lay people living on the island farmed and quarried limestone until, in 1906, English Benedictines established a community here.

The Benedictines left solid evidence of their occupation: the refectory, gatehouse, and priory's lodging, which is now used as a guesthouse. In 1929, the Cistercian order took over the island, and today they produce perfume, chocolate, and dairy products, all sold locally. Only male visitors are allowed to enter the monastery, but anyone can visit St. David's Church, the Old Priory, and St. Illtud's Church, with its leaning stone spire. Inside St. Illtud's is a 6th-century Ogham stone, a relic of the time when monks from Ireland came here to establish their religious house. The writing on the Ogham stones was Celtic, which was then translated into Latin by the monks.

Allow about 2 hours for a visit. Access to the island is via a boat that runs only between Easter and late October Monday to Friday 10am to 3pm. The vessels depart every 20 minutes; the crossing also takes 20 minutes. A round-trip passage costs £11 ($22) for adults, and £6 ($12) for children 14 and younger. For information about all aspects of the island, including boat access, call © **01834/844453** or go to **www.caldey-island.co.uk**.

PEMBROKE

At a point 92km (57 miles) west of Swansea and 156km (97 miles) west of Cardiff, the ancient borough of Pembroke is the most English town in South Wales. It was never really a typical Welsh town because the Normans and the English had such a strong hold on it. It was settled by English and Flemish people, and its first language was always English. It is visited for two reasons today—to see Pembroke Castle, one of the most impressive in South Wales, and to use it as a base for exploring the national park.

Pembroke received its charter about 1090 from King Henry I and was built around Pembroke Castle, a great fortress set on a rocky spur above the town. The town walls formed the castle's outer ward, and the entire complex, a 22km-wide (14-mile) medieval defense system, can still be viewed as a fortified town, with the castle as its hub.

Most trains coming to Pembroke require transfers in Swansea, an hour's travel away. From Swansea, there are six trains per day, and from Swansea, trains fan out to many other points within Britain. For railway information, call © **0870/900-0773** or visit **www.arrivatrainswales.co.uk** (also © **0845/748-4950**; www.nationalrail.co.uk).

Bus connections into Pembroke from Tenby run about every hour throughout the day Monday through Saturday, with limited service on Sunday. For bus information about service from Wales into Pembroke, call © **0870/608-2608** or visit www.first group.com. For information about long-distance bus transit from London or big cities of the English Midlands, call **National Express** at © **0870/580-8080** or visit **www. nationalexpress.com**.

Pembroke maintains a tourist information office—**Pembroke Visitor Centre,** Commons Road (© **01646/622388**)—that's open between Easter and October daily from 10am to 5pm (until 5:30pm July–Aug). The rest of the year, people should contact the year-round **Tourist Information Centre,** 19 Old Bridge, Haverfordwest (© **01437/763110**). Between November and Easter, it's open Monday to Saturday 10am to 4pm. From Easter to October, it's open Monday to Saturday 10am to 5pm (June–Sept until 5:30pm). Mid-July to August, it's also open on Sunday, 10am to 4pm.

WHERE TO STAY

Coach House Hotel   Built along traditional lines after World War II (though the facade dates from medieval times), the Coach House is the best place for lodgings within the town itself, although the Court (see below) at Lamphey is far more elegant. Bedrooms are small to midsize, each comfortably furnished with a private bathroom with tub or shower. Set on the main thoroughfare of Pembroke, the hotel has a classic facade of black and white. View it mainly as an overnight stopover and don't expect a lot of style.

116 Main St., Pembroke, Pembrokeshire SA71 4HN. © **01646/684602.** Fax 01646/687456. 14 units. £75 ($150) double. Rates include breakfast. AE, MC, V. **Amenities:** Restaurant; bar; laundry service. *In room:* TV, Wi-Fi, beverage maker.

Lamphey Court Hotel ⓐ   This impressive Georgian mansion set on several acres of landscaped gardens adds a touch of class to the area. This Best Western affiliate is by far the finest place for lodging and dining in the area. Both the public rooms and the bedrooms have a certain luxurious grandeur. Many units are spacious enough for family suites. Stay in the house where the units are more traditional or in an 11-room annex. Local produce is cooked to perfection in the formal restaurant. Bar food is also available.

Lamphey, Pembrokeshire SA71 5NT. © **800/528-1234** in the U.S., or 01646/672273. Fax 01646/672480. www. lampheycourt.co.uk. 37 units. £105–£165 ($210–$330) double. Rates include breakfast. AE, DC, MC, V. Take A477 to Pembroke, turning left at Village Milton; Lamphey is signposted from there. **Amenities:** Restaurant; bar; heated indoor pool; lighted tennis court; health club; spa; Jacuzzi; sauna; solarium; room service; babysitting. *In room:* TV, beverage maker, hair dryer, trouser press.

WHERE TO DINE

Ferry Inn ⓐ *Finds* WELSH/SEAFOOD   This is a creeper-clad riverside inn found under the landmark Cleddau Bridge. From its nautically themed bar and its water-bordering terrace, you'll have a view of the estuary. There is also a garden and limited parking. The food is well prepared and based on market-fresh ingredients. As befits its setting, seafood specials are featured. We've enjoyed the fresh local trout, grilled to perfection—but you can order it baked. Broiled sea bass is another winner, as is the baked monkfish, properly seasoned and cooked without being dried out. You can also order tender and flavorful Welsh sirloin steaks or else savory lamb kabobs.

Pembroke Ferry. © **01646/682947.** Reservations recommended. Main courses £7–£20 ($14–$40). MC, V. Mon–Sat 11:30am–2pm and 7–10:30pm; Sun noon–1:30pm and 7–9:30pm. Take A477 3.2km (2 miles) from the center of Pembroke, following the signs pointing to Pembroke Ferry. Go right at a garage where there are signs posted for Cleddau Bridge, making a left turn at the roundabout.

VISITING THE CASTLE

Pembroke Castle 🎯🎯   With its massive keep and walls, the castle still looks formidable, although little inside it remains. It is the oldest castle in west Wales, and for more than 300 years it was the seat of the earls of Pembroke. It was founded by the Montgomerys in 1093, and work began on the fine masonry a century later with the circular great tower, or keep. Dominating the castle, the tower stands 22m (75 ft.) high and is the finest of its type in Britain. Home to such great leaders as Earl William Marshal, regent to Henry III, and to the early Tudors, the castle was also the birthplace of Henry VII ("Harri Tewdwr"). During the civil war, the castle was held in turn for both Parliament and the king. Cromwell arrived in person to start the siege that led to its final surrender. A vast cavern underneath the castle, called the Wogan, is where food and water were stored. The water defenses of the fortress can still be traced in a millpond on the north and in marshes on the south, outside the walls, as well as in the River Pembroke over which it looms.

Main St. © **01646/681510.** www.pembrokecastle.co.uk. Admission £3.50 ($7) for adults; £2.50 ($5) seniors, students, and children 5–15; £10 ($20) family ticket. Apr–Sept daily 9:30am–6pm; Mar and Oct daily 10am–5pm; Nov–Feb daily 10am–4pm.

ST. DAVIDS 🎯🎯

St. Davids and its environs are in a part of the Pembrokeshire Coast National Park that had inhabitants far back in Paleolithic and Mesolithic times. About 5,000 years ago, New Stone Age (Neolithic) farmers arrived and made their homes here. They didn't leave many traces, but their tombs, or cromlechs, have survived. Many lie on or near St. Davids Head, on Newport Bay, and in the Preseli foothills. Many people believe that the massive blue or foreign stones at Stonehenge came from the Preseli hills more 4,000 years ago. Bronze Age cairns have also been found in the Preseli region.

Iron Age Celts came here, bringing with them from Gaul the beginnings of the Welsh and Gaelic languages. Near St. Davids, walls built during that era are still in use around fields. The Romans ignored this part of Wales, and contacts with Ireland, where fellow Celts lived, were strong. Irish tribes settled in Dyfed in the 3rd and 4th centuries, and then the monastic movement in the early Christian church was brought by Irish and spread by Welsh missionaries, when a vigorous Christian community was established on the St. Davids Peninsula.

The coming of the Normans did not really affect this section of Wales, and Welsh is still widely spoken here. In Tudor times and later, village seafaring came in, taking the mining output of coal, silver, and lead out of small village ports. All this has changed, of course, and today the coastal area is a popular holiday territory, with beaches, boating, fishing, and other leisure pursuits taking over.

There's a tremendous allure to one of Britain's most visited surf beaches, **Whitesands** 🎯, which is located 3.2km (2 miles) northwest of St. Davids. From June to early September, lifeguards are on duty. Access to this windswept beach is free, but there's a

A Word About Welsh

"Let me not understand you, then; speak it in Welsh"

—Shakespeare's *Henry IV*

Of all the Celtic languages still in use, Welsh is still spoken by the greatest number of people, although most Welsh men or women also speak English. It is not a dialect of English, as commonly believed, but a distinct language with its own pedigree that is older than English.

An Indo-European language, Welsh is more allied to French, German, and the Scandinavian languages than English. The Welsh people and their language originated with the Celts who came from Britain from across central Europe, a mixture of the Germanic peoples in the north, the Slavs in the East, and the Hellenic people in the South. These tribes belonged to the Roman Empire and spoke Celtic languages most closely related to present-day Welsh.

The Welsh language, called *Cymraeg,* borrows heavily from English today, although it's based on a completely different grammatical system. Only one-eighth of Welsh people speak Welsh as a first language. The language is one of the most difficult in the world to learn. If you want to tell a Welsh girl (or boy) that you love her or him, it's said "dw I'n dy garu di" (doo een duh *gar*-ee dee). It sounds better in French.

£2 ($4) charge for parking. Whitesands is noted for some of the consistently best surf waves in Britain. As such, it's the site of surfing exhibitions, where participants arrive from as far away as Huntington Beach, California.

The tiny cathedral city of St. Davids is the birthplace of the patron saint of Wales. The countryside around it is centuries away from the hurry of modern times. The cathedral lies in a grassy hollow of the River Alun, chosen by St. David for its small monastic community because the site was hidden from approach by attackers, yet it was conveniently only a mile from the waters of St. Bride's Bay.

Dewi Sant (later St. David), son of a Welsh chieftain and a Welsh woman named Non, was a Celtic religious leader in the 6th century. The little church he and his monks built where the present cathedral stands was burned down in 645, rebuilt, sacked and burned by the Danes in 1078, and then burned again in 1088. After that, a Norman cathedral was built, its organization changing from the Celtic monastic to diocesan type. The stone village of St. Davids grew up on the hill around the church.

St. Davids lies 117km (73 miles) west of Swansea and 180km (112 miles) west of Cardiff. Motorists take the A487 to reach St. Davids from Haverfordwest, 24km (15 miles) away. **Richard Brothers** (✆ **01239/613756;** www.richardbros.co.uk) runs buses from Haverfordwest to St. Davids every hour; a one-way ticket costs only £5 ($10) round-trip for adults, and £3 ($6). Haverfordwest is the nearest rail station.

For information, the tourist office is at the **Grove** (✆ **01437/720392**), open from Easter to October daily 9:30am to 5:30pm. From November to Easter, it's open Monday to Saturday 10am to 4pm.

WHERE TO STAY

Ramsey House *(Value)*   The town's best bargain lies 1km (a half-mile) from the cathedral on the road to Porthclais, standing amid manicured gardens and looking very much like the private house it is. Just 1km (a half-mile) from the house, you can reach the Pembrokeshire Coast Path that takes you along some of the most panoramic coastal scenery in Wales. The owners show you one of their immaculately kept mid-size bedrooms, each with a cozy and efficient private bathroom. We prefer the second-floor rooms because of their views, either of the sea, cathedral, or open country. For those who don't like stairs, there are ground-floor rooms.

Lower Moor, St. Davids, Pembrokeshire SA62 6RP. (C) 01437/720321. Fax 01437/720025. www.ramseyhouse.co.uk. 5 units. £80 ($160) double. Rates include breakfast and dinner. No credit cards. No children allowed. **Amenities:** Restaurant; bar; laundry service. *In room:* TV, Wi-Fi, beverage maker, hair dryer.

Warpool Court Hotel ✿   This hotel, a 5-minute walk from the heart of the city, is the town's premier address, far outstancing all competitors. A country house overlooking the sea, it is privately owned and set amid secluded gardens of great natural beauty. The vine-covered structure overlooks one of the most beautiful coastal stretches in Wales. Originally the cathedral choir school, it has been successfully transformed into a hotel with a courteous staff. Most of the rooms are midsize to spacious, and some are large enough for families. The more expensive rooms offer sea views. Asa Williams, who lived here early in the 20th century, decorated some 3,000 tiles, which are positioned throughout the house.

St. Davids, Pembrokeshire SA62 6BN. (C) 01437/720300. Fax 01437/720676. www.warpoolcourthotel.com. 25 units. £80–£145 ($160–$290) per person. Rates include breakfast. AE, DC, MC, V. **Amenities:** Restaurant; bar; covered heated pool (Easter–Oct only); tennis court; croquet lawn; game room; babysitting. *In room:* TV, beverage maker, hair dryer.

WHERE TO DINE
Morgan's Brasserie ✿ WELSH/CONTINENTAL   Unless you dine at one of the inns, this is by far the best independent restaurant in town and has been since it opened in 1993. Peruse the menu while admiring the art collection on the walls. The chef is known for making use of local produce and market-fresh ingredients. The fresh fish is rushed here from the Pembrokeshire coast after it lands at the nearby port of Milford Haven. Blackboard menus display the catch of the day. Meat eaters will also find the most reliable Welsh spring lamb or "black steaks" from the countryside, even game in season. Well-prepared mains include roast breast of Gressingham duck with a Grand Marnier–laced orange sauce, a leek and parsnip steamed pudding with an herb-and-truffle sauce, or filet of hake in a cider-and-black-peppercorn sauce.

20 Nun St. (C) 01437/720508. Reservations recommended. Main courses £13–£20 ($26–$40). MC, V. Mon–Sat noon–1:45pm and 6:30–10:30pm. Closed Jan.

SEEING THE SIGHTS
With its ornately carved roof and a Norman nave, **St. Davids Cathedral** ✿✿, Cathedral Close ((C) 01437/721885; www.stdavidscathedral.org.uk), is a magnificent example of medieval religious architecture. Its reliquary contains what are supposed to be the bones of St. David. The nave, a product of 3 centuries of craftsmanship, is a place of medieval beauty. The choir stalls, from the late 15th century, have witty, even light-hearted misericord carvings. Visitors are welcome at the cathedral, open daily from 8:30am to 6:30pm. During the months of July and August, there are regular tours on Monday, Tuesday, Thursday, and Friday starting at 2:30pm. Tours last about 90 minutes. Tour costs are £4 ($8) for adults, £2.50 ($5) seniors, and £1.20 ($2.40) for children 6 to 16. Tickets should be purchased in the Cathedral bookshop in the nave before joining the tour. Donations are accepted to help with the upkeep of the building.

Associated with the cathedral, the ruins of **Bishop's Palace,** Cathedral Close (© **01437/720517**), stand across the meadow and river, with the gatehouse, battlements, and curtain walls showing how even such a place needed fortification in medieval days. An outstanding sight is the elegant arcaded parapet that runs along both main walls. You can visit the palace ruins; note especially the fine piscina at the east end of the chapel's south wall. The site is open April to May daily 9:30am to 5pm, June to September daily 9:30am to 6pm, October daily 9:30am to 5pm, and November to March Monday to Saturday 9:30am to 4pm and Sunday 11am to 4pm. Admission is £3.10 ($6.20) for adults and £2.70 ($5.40) for seniors, students, and children.

The cathedral is no longer Roman Catholic, nor is it Church of England. It is a member of the Church of Wales. When St. David was canonized in the 12th century, the pope declared that two pilgrimages to St. Davids were worth one to Rome, and three pilgrimages equaled one to Jerusalem. You can make such a pilgrimage today; although the pope's promise may not have been honored since the days of Henry VIII, we can promise you an interesting and educational tour of St. Davids peninsula.

Porth Clais, at the mouth of the River Alun about 1.6km (1 mile) south from St. Davids, was the seaport used by travelers to Ireland and elsewhere for centuries before and after the birth of Christ and then by pilgrims making their way to St. Davids. In medieval days it became a coal port, and limekilns were used to reduce limestone to slaked lime for use on fields, in building, and for household purposes. The restored limekilns can be seen.

A little eastward around the bay on a headland is **St. Non's Chapel,** now in ruins, supposedly built on the spot where St. David was born. It is dedicated to his mother. St. Non's Well is there also, reportedly in full flow. Its waters were said to have healing properties in the past. The site can be viewed 24 hours a day without charge.

21

North Wales: The Peaks of Snowdonia

North Wales is a rewarding target for those willing to seek it out. Distinctly different from England, it is linguistically and culturally different from most of Britain and is known for its beauty spots, a land of mountains and lakes interspersed with castles. The most powerful of the Welsh princes held sway here, and the residents remain staunchly nationalistic. British families flock to the coastal resorts on holidays, especially in July and August, whereas others prefer to seek out the footpaths of Snowdonia National Park.

Mountain peaks and steep wooded slopes, spectacular estuaries and rugged cliffs brooding over secluded coves, lakes, little rivers, and valleys with tiny towns looking as if they were carved out of granite—all these join to make up **Snowdonia National Park.** The park, with slate mines, moors, heavy forests, mountain lakes, grain fields, pastures, swift-moving rivers, and sandy beaches, takes its name from Snowdon, at 1,085m (3,560 ft.) the highest peak in Wales and England. Most of the Snowdonia area is in the County of Gwynedd, once the ancient Welsh kingdom of that name. Its prince, Owen ap Gwynedd, never agreed to let himself be reduced to the status of baron under the English kings. Because his terrain was mountainous and

wild, it helped him stave off an invasion by forces accustomed to fighting on flat land.

The rocky, majestic crags of Snowdonia National Park are rivaled by the mighty walls and soaring towers of **Caernarfon Castle,** the best example of castle building in medieval Wales. Caernarfon (formerly spelled Caernarvon) and its neighbors, Anglesey and the Lleyn Peninsula, reaching out from its northwest and west, are all part of the County of Gwynedd. Legends of holy islands and druidic mysteries flourished among the Celtic peoples who lived in this area in long-ago centuries.

Many of the native-born people of this region are of blood stock little changed over the centuries. Most are bilingual, with English as their second tongue, and signs are usually in both languages.

The County of Clwyd, in northeastern Wales, has miles of sandy beaches along its north coast; highland ranges, peat bogs, and deep valleys lush with greenery in the center; coal country to the southeast; and industry, agriculture, and sheep farming in the section nearest the estuary of the River Dee and the English border. What is now Clwyd (by order of Parliament since 1973) was before that time Denbighshire and Flintshire.

1 Llanberis

376km (233 miles) W of London; 11km (7 miles) SE of Caernarfon

The starting point for going up Snowdon by mountain railway, Llanberis nestles between Lake Padarn and Lake Peris. Views of outstanding beauty greet your eyes, both man-made sights and natural wonders.

The **Snowdon Mountain Railway** runs from Llanberis to within a few yards of the top of the Snowdon peak at about 1,085m (3,560 ft.). The only rack-and-pinion train in Britain, it is also the steepest train ride, and the view from the top platform, where the train stops, is one of the most panoramic in the country. It's possible to see some 160km (100 miles) away into Ireland, especially the peaks of the Wicklow Mountain chain, on the clearest and brightest of days. Another "great little train" in the region is the Llanberis Lake Railway, which takes you along Lake Padarn. The purpose of the trains in this area and in the Vale of Ffestiniog to the south was to bring the "gray gold" from slate caverns for shipping all over the world. For information and schedules, call © **0871/7200033** or visit **www.snowdonrailway.co.uk**. *Note:* If you book by phone at least a day in advance for a 9am departure, ticket prices are cut in half. Trains run to the summit between May and October, costing £22 ($44) for adults round-trip and £15 ($30) for children 14 and younger.

Padarn Country Park (© **01286/870892**), open daily until dusk, has marked footpaths that will take you past the Vivian Quarry, with its dramatic slate cliffs and deep pools, through galleries where slate was worked, and to lookouts from which the Snowdon range and the lakes can be viewed. The entrance to these 283 hectares (700 acres) of countryside is signposted from High Street and begins .8km (a half-mile) north of the town center.

Craft workshops and a woodcraft center are open at the park, where you can watch artisans work in clay, copper, slate, and wood. One workman specializes in Celtic folk harps, including miniature models and do-it-yourself kits.

Dolbadarn Castle ruins overlook Lake (Llyn) Padarn in the Llanberis pass, .8km (a half-mile) east of Llanberis, a relic of the time when the pass was used by the conquering armies. It is notable for its location and a mortared masonry tower that still stands. You can take a look around the meager ruins for free.

ESSENTIALS

GETTING THERE   The nearest rail station is at Bangor, 14km (9 miles) north of Llanberis. Buses run frequently throughout the day (Mon–Sat) from Bangor to Llanberis. Contact the **Arriva Bus Company** (© **0871/200-2233;** www.arriva.co.uk). Because of the many stops en route, buses take about 25 minutes each way.

Buses between Llanberis and Caermarfon run Monday to Saturday every half-hour, every 1 to 2 hours on Sunday. Bus timetables are available from the Llanberis Tourist Information Office (see below) and the Caernarfon Tourist Information Centre (see "Caernarfon," later in this chapter).

Motorists from Caernarfon head southeast along the A4086.

VISITOR INFORMATION   The **Llanberis Tourist Information Office,** 41B High St. (© **01286/870765**), is open from Easter to the end of October daily from 9:30am to 5:30pm. The rest of the year, it's open Monday, Friday, Saturday, and Sunday from 10:30am to 4pm.

North Wales

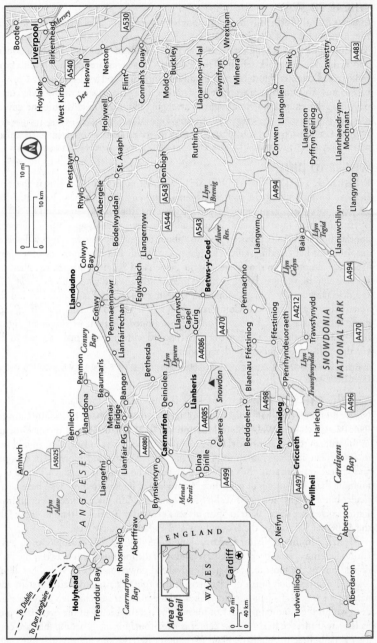

Map labels:

Bootle, Liverpool, Birkenhead, *Mersey*, A530, Hoylake, A540, Heswall, Neston, West Kirby, *Dee*, Holywell, Flint, Connah's Quay, Mold, Buckley, Llanarmon-yn-Ial, Gwynfryn, Minera, Wrexham, Oswestry, A483, Chirk, Corwen, Llangollen, Llanarmon Dyffryn Ceiriog, Llanrhaeadr-ym-Mochnant, Prestatyn, Rhyl, Abergele, St. Asaph, Denbigh, Ruthin, A543, *Llyn Brenig*, A544, A543, *Alwen Res.*, Llangwm, Langynog, Llanuwchllyn, *Llyn Tegid*, Bala, A494, Bodelwyddan, Llangernyw, Eglwsbach, Betws-y-Coed, Penmachno, *Llyn Celyn*, A494, Colwyn Bay, Llandudno, Conwy, *Conwy Bay*, Penmaenmawr, Llanfairfechan, Llanrwst, Capel Curig, A470, Ffestiniog, A212, Penrhyndeudraeth, Trawsfynydd, SNOWDONIA NATIONAL PARK, A470, Penmon, Beaumaris, Bangor, Bethesda, Deiniolen, *Llyn Ogwen*, Llanberis, A4086, Snowdon, Blaenau Ffestiniog, *Llyn Trawsfynydd*, A496, Benllech, Llanddona, Menai Bridge, Caernarfon, A4085, Cesarea, Beddgelert, A498, Porthmadog, Harlech, Amlwch, A5025, Llangefni, Llanfair PG, A4080, Brynsiencyn, Dina Dinlle, A499, Criccieth, A497, Pwllheli, *Cardigan Bay*, *Llyn Alaw*, ANGLESEY, *Menai Strait*, Nefyn, Abersoch, Rhosneigr, Aberffraw, Treardur Bay, Holyhead, *Caernarfon Bay*, *To Dublin*, *To Dún Laoghaire*, Tudweiliog, Aberdaron

Inset: ENGLAND, WALES, Cardiff, Area of detail, 40 mi, 40 km

Scale: 10 mi, 10 km

WHERE TO STAY

Legacy Royal Victoria Hotel   Although it's a venue for local weddings and social functions and is a bit stuffy, this is nonetheless the most prestigious address in town. The Royal Victoria is long established at the foothills of Snowdon, between Padarn and Peris lakes, a bucolic setting. The bedrooms in general are spacious and recently modernized, with comfortable and endurable furniture and well-maintained private bathrooms. Four rooms are set aside for families. The place bustles with activity, often providing live entertainment at night or arranging mountain treks during the day.

Llanberis, Gwynedd LL55 4TY. ℂ **0870/8329903.** Fax 0870/8329904. www.royal-victoria-hotel.co.uk. 106 units. £48–£115 ($96–$230) double. Rates include breakfast. AE, DC, MC, V. Free parking. **Amenities:** Restaurant (large dining room w/conservatory opening onto the lakes); bar; room service. *In room:* TV, beverage maker, hair dryer, trouser press.

WHERE TO DINE

Y Bistro ☝ TRADITIONAL WELSH   When it comes to food, this is the only ticket in town. Nothing else matters—there's not even a good inn here. For more than 25 years, we've been popping in here to see what the Robertses (Nerys and Danny) are offering on their "taste of Wales" menu, and we've never been disappointed. Nerys has appeared on numerous British TV shows about cuisine and has won many deserved accolades for her cooking skills. The place is so Welsh that it even offers wines from Wales . . . although you should stick to the French and Spanish vintages. Excellent use is made of local produce. Here's a chance to learn some Welsh when ordering. *Eog peris* is a delectable locally smoked salmon in a creamy sauce; *ffryth* is a chilled melon flavored with orange zest and Cointreau, a delightful way to launch yourself in such game dishes as a perfectly roasted and herb-seasoned pheasant or succulent pigeon breasts. The Welsh wine tastes better when cooked with grapes to make a sauce to flavor the melt-in-your-mouth pork tenderloins.

45 High St. ℂ **01286/871278.** Reservations required. Main courses £13–£17 ($26–$34). MC, V. Tues–Sat 7:30–9:30pm. Closed Tues in winter.

SEEING THE SIGHTS

Nearly a kilometer (a half-mile) north of the center of Llanberis in Padarn Country Park (see above), the **Welsh Slate Museum** (ℂ **01286/870630**) is a minor museum in the workshops of Dinorwic slate quarry, one of the largest in Britain until it closed in 1969. Slate-mining communities were intensely Welsh, nonconformist in religion, and radical in politics, as films shown here reveal. The exhibitions, which should take no more than 30 minutes of your time, are mainly of interest to those who have a particular interest in this aspect of Welsh life of long ago. Admission is free. It's open from Easter to October daily 10am to 5pm; off season Sunday to Friday 10am to 4pm. Take the A4086 at the start of the lake railway and Padarn Country Park.

   Electric Mountain Visitor Centre, along the A4086 (ℂ **01286/870636**), is a sci-entific-looking observation center, functioning as the meeting point between the public and one of the most technologically advanced power stations in Wales. Set about .4km (a quarter-mile) north of Llanberis, it incorporates a hydroelectric system harnessing the waters of a pair of nearby lakes, whose turbines and channels are concealed deep within the mountains so as not to spoil the natural beauty of the nationally protected site. Entrance to the visitor center is free. Tours for the general public are conducted daily June to August 9:30am to 5:30pm. Reservations are advised. Once you get here, if a staff member isn't busy with other tasks, you can take a tour of the turbines for a fee of £7 ($14) for adults, £5.50 ($11) seniors, £3.50 ($7) for children 14 and younger, and £17 ($34) for a family ticket.

2 Betws-y-Coed ★

363km (226 miles) W of London; 70km (44 miles) SE of Holyhead

This idyllic Snowdonia village, with tumbling rivers, waterfalls, and mountains, is nestled in the tree-lined valley of the River Conwy. It has an antique church with a Norman font; old bridges, stone houses, and hotels on rocky outcrops; and woodland paths.

Although crowded in summer, this town is one of the best centers for exploring North Wales. It's mainly a one-street town, but you get the feel that you're in the great outdoors far removed from England's polluted cities of the Midlands. There's an alpine feeling about the place.

The town is known for its eight bridges, of which our favorite is the Waterloo Bridge at the village's southern end, the construction of Telford in 1815 in cast iron. There's also a suspension bridge near St. Michael's Church. If you walk upon it, it sways in the wind but seems perfectly safe. The most regal bridge is Pont-y-Pair, "the bridge of the cauldron," bounding the Llugwy River to the north. In fact, walking across the bridges of Betws-y-Coed and taking in the views is one of the main reasons to come here.

ESSENTIALS

GETTING THERE   The **Conwy Valley** line between Llandudno and Blaenau Ffestiniog passes through Betws-y-Coed with three trains daily. For rail information and schedules, call ℂ **0845/748-4950** or visit **www.nationalrail.co.uk**.

The **Express** bus company services Betws-y-Coed from both Llandudno and Porthmadog. For schedules, call ℂ **0871/200-2233** or visit **www.arriva.co.uk**.

Motorists from Llandudno can take A470 south.

VISITOR INFORMATION   For information about the town and Snowdonia National Park, head for the **local tourist office** at Holyhead Road in the town center (ℂ **01690/710426**). It's open from Easter to October daily 10am to 1pm and 1:30 to 6pm; off-season hours are daily 9:30am to 1pm and 1:30 to 4:30pm.

WHERE TO STAY & DINE
EXPENSIVE

Tan-y-Foel Country House Hotel ★★★ (Finds   A 16th-century manor house, this gem is the best hotel in the area, opening onto a panoramic sweep of Conwy Valley, with Snowdonia looming in the background. Stay here if you can, forsaking all other places. Vibrant fabrics and modern paintings bring you into the 21st century, but the atmosphere is still yesterday. It is set on 3.2 hectares (8 acres) of woodlands and pastures 3.2km (2 miles) north of town. Charm and grace prevail in the public and private rooms. The latter are moderate to spacious, each individually furnished with immaculate little bathrooms. Two rooms are in an annex and have less charm. We prefer one of the four bedrooms opening onto the front of the hotel, as they offer the best views. Children 11 and under are not accepted.

In an intimate setting, the chef and owner, Janet Pitman, one of the best chefs in this part of Wales, takes care with her three-course dinner, which she changes daily. Dinner costs £42 ($84) per person, and is an elegant meal featuring such specialties as Welsh black beef and such catches of the day as fresh turbot or sea bass.

Capel Garmon, near Betws-y-Coed, Llanrwst, Conwy LL26 0RE. ℂ 01690/710507. Fax 01690/710681. www.tyfhotel. co.uk. 6 units. £144–£195 ($288–$390) double. Rates include breakfast. MC, V. From Betws-y-Coed, take A5 onto A470, heading north to Llanrwst, turning at the signpost for Capel Garmon. Children 11 and younger not accepted. **Amenities:** Restaurant; laundry service; dry cleaning. In room: TV/DVD, hair dryer, iron.

MODERATE

The Park Hill Hotel ✿

About a 5-minute walk west of town, this small Victorian hotel is surrounded by secluded gardens and opens onto panoramic views of the Conwy and Llugwy valleys. For such a small hotel, it offers some exceptional recreational facilities and is also known for its justly praised cuisine. Your hosts, Jaap and Ghislaine Buis, run a good little inn, with moderately sized bedrooms and small but well-kept bathrooms. Three rooms have shower-only bathrooms and six have tub/shower combos. Front rooms are preferable to those on the side. Furnishings are traditional, and one room is graced with a four-poster.

Traditional meals are based on longtime Welsh favorites and served along with modern dishes using local produce. Expect Welsh lamb and fresh fish from the Conwy estuary and local rivers.

Llanwvst Rd., Betws-y-Coed, Gwynedd LL24 0HD. ⓒ/fax **01690/710540.** www.park-hill-hotel.co.uk. 9 units. £60–£78 ($120–$156) double. Rates include breakfast. MC, V. Children 5 and younger not accepted. **Amenities:** Restaurant, bar; indoor pool; whirlpool; sauna. *In room:* TV, beverage maker, no phone.

Ty Gwyn ✿

This is one of the most charming hotels and pubs in town. You could ask Theodore Roosevelt, if he were still around. Much has changed since the American president stayed here in the late 1800s, but much is still the same as well. Laden with carved beams and local artifacts, Ty Gwyn is low slung, sitting on the opposite side of Waterloo Bridge from the rest of town. Inside it's a world of old prints and chintz, time-darkened beams, and copper pans. Originally it was a coaching inn from the 16th century, drawing horsemen traveling between London and the ferryboats to Ireland. The rooms, often small, are still comfortably furnished, often with a four-poster or a half-tester bed (ca. 1800). The best unit has a "health spa" tub, small lounge, and private balcony. There are four rooms without private bathrooms.

The restaurant's menu features local Welsh dishes as well as more exotic fare from Thailand and elsewhere. There is always a homemade soup of the day and a wide selection of vegetarian dishes.

Along the A5, Betws-y-Coed, Gwynedd LL24 6SG. ⓒ **01690/710383.** www.tygwynhotel.co.uk. 13 units, 9 with bathroom. £48 ($96) double without bathroom; £68 ($136) with bathroom; £92–£120 ($184–$240) four-poster room. Rates include breakfast. Children 11 and younger stay free in same room with up to 2 paying adults. MC, V. **Amenities:** Restaurant; pub. *In room:* TV, beverage maker, no phone.

SEEING THE SIGHTS

If time is short, we'd skip the minor sights of town—that is, after you've walked over those bridges—and head instead for one of the beauty spots of Wales, the **Swallow Falls** ✿ and **Miners Bridge.** Take the A5 for 3.2km (2 miles) to the west of Betws-y-Coed. The Swallow Falls is one of the most mystical and evocative—also one of the most powerful—of its kind in Wales. It's composed of a series of waterfalls strung together, creating a mist. Miners Bridge is a wooden footbridge impregnated with pitch for preservation and dating from the late 18th century. It's not a conventional flat bridge, but a steeply inclined staircase-style bridge, with elevation much higher on one end than on the other. The Miners Bridge doesn't charge anything to visit—and, as such, many walkers opt for a brisk half-hour riverfront walk from the center of Betws-y-Coed, with the bridge as their final destination. You'll pay £1 ($2) to see the falls, however. There's no attendant—just drop a coin into a tollbooth, and visit anytime you want, night or day.

Again, and only if you have time, there are two more evocative places to visit in the area. One is **Dolwyddelan Castle** at the hamlet of Dolwyddelan (ⓒ **01690/750366**).

Standing lonely on a ridge, this castle was the birthplace of Llywelyn the Great, according to tradition. It was certainly his royal residence. Restored to its present condition in the 19th century, the castle's remains look out on the rugged grandeur of Moel Siabod peak. A medieval road from the Vale of Conwy ran just below the west tower, which made this a strategic site for a castle to control passage. About 1.6km (1 mile) from Dolwyddelan, the castle is accessible by a rough track off the A470 to the southwest of Betws-y-Coed, on the road to Blaenau Ffestiniog. To enter, adults pay £2.50 ($5), children ages 4 to 16 pay £2 ($4), and children 3 and younger enter free; a family ticket costs £7 ($14). It's open April to September Monday to Saturday 10am to 6pm, Sunday from 11am to 4pm; off-season hours are Monday to Saturday 10am to 4pm, Sunday from 11am to 4pm.

One of the premier literary sights of Wales, **Ty Mawr,** Wybrnant, Penmachno (© **01690/760213;** www.nationaltrust.org.uk), lies 11km (7 miles) southeast of Betws-y-Coed. From the town, head southwest for 5.6km (3½ miles), going west of Penmachno along B4406 the rest of the way. At the head of the little valley of Gwybernant, this cottage is where Bishop William Morgan was born in the 16th century. He was the first person to translate the Bible into Welsh, and his translation is viewed even today as a masterpiece and the foundation of modern Welsh literature. It's an isolated stone-walled cottage with a slate roof that you might pass by unless you knew its pedigree. Between April and September, it's open Thursday to Sunday noon to 5pm. In October, it is open Thursday to Sunday noon to 4pm. Admission is £3 ($6) for adults, £1.50 ($3) for children, and £7.50 ($15) for a family ticket.

3 The Lleyn Peninsula ★★

Separating Cardigan Bay and its northern arm, Tremadog Bay, from Caernarfon Bay, the gentle western Lleyn Peninsula thrusts out alone into the Irish Sea. It's bounded by the mountains of Snowdonia on the east and by the sea. Having little communication with the outside world before the coming of railroads and highways, the peninsula has a large Welsh-speaking population, although most people also have English as a second language, made necessary by the influx of people coming here to retire, to do business, or just to take holidays.

The peninsula takes its name from an Irish tribe, the Celtic Legine or Laigin, who didn't have very far to go from home to invade the country of fellow Celts. They were followed by missionaries and pilgrims in the Christian era. The distance from Ireland is so short that when you stand on National Trust property high on a cliff above St. Mary's Well you can often see the Wicklow Mountains of Ireland with the naked eye.

The Lleyn Peninsula has beaches, hills, farmland, moorland, villages nestled in the hollows, trees, heather, gorse, and country lanes. There are traces of hill forts here, and you can find standing stones, monastery ruins, pilgrim trails, holy wells (four of them), and nonconformist chapels. Sporting enthusiasts find fishing, golf, watersports, and rough shooting.

For information on the peninsula, get in touch with the **Tourist Information Centre,** Min Y Don, Station Square, Pwllheli (© **01758/613000).** The two best towns on the peninsula are Porthmadog and Criccieth (see below).

Pwllheli, lying 13km (8 miles) to the west of Criccieth, is the principal transportation hub of the peninsula, with daily buses arriving from London. Buses also pull in here every hour from Bangor. You may not want to linger in Pwllheli, but take a connecting bus to either Porthmadog or Criccieth, which make better centers.

Arriva Trains Wales line, which begins at Aberystwyth, with a change of trains at Dovey Junction, takes you to both Porthmadog and Criccieth. Call © **0845/748-4950** or visit **www.nationalrail.co.uk** for more information.

PORTHMADOG

The estuary of the River Glaslyn has long been the scene of shipping and fishing activity, emptying as it does into Tremadog Bay and thence into Cardigan Bay.

This is the main town east of the Lleyn Peninsula. It grew up as a slate-shipping port on the coast near the mouth of the River Glaslyn. T. E. Lawrence (Lawrence of Arabia) was born in Tremadog, close by.

The town was named after a "Celtification" of the English name of its builder, William Madocks, a mining mogul who built the town from scratch between 1808 and 1811. The harbor that later figured so prominently in the town's history was custom-built between 1821 and 1825. In the 1870s, as many as 1,000 vessels a year pulled into harbor here to haul away slate. At its peak in 1873, 116,000 tons of Blaenau slate were shipped from this harbor to points throughout the empire and the world.

The location is 428km (266 miles) west of London and 32km (20 miles) south of Caernarfon. The **Wales Information Centre,** High Street (© **01766/512981**), is open daily from Easter to October 10am to 6pm. Off-season hours are Thursday to Tuesday 9:30am to 5pm.

WHERE TO STAY & DINE

Hotel Portmeirion 🌟🌟🌟 *(Finds)*   Sir Clough Williams-Ellis set out to build an idyllic village on a romantic coast. Standing amid one of the finest scenic settings in Wales, this hotel existed as an early Victorian villa before it was converted into an evocative hotel in 1926. Writers such as H. G. Wells and George Bernard Shaw became habitués, Noel Coward wrote *Blithe Spirit* here in 1941, and the cult TV classic *The Prisoner* was filmed here in the late '60s. The hotel overlooks Cardigan Bay from its own private peninsula. The decor inside is exotic: fabrics from Kashmir, paintings from Rajasthan, tiles from Delft, and wallpaper from New York. Many of the rooms have half-tester or four-poster beds. About a dozen units are in the main house, the rest in a cluster of "village houses." Four accommodations are designated for families. The best sea views are from the rooms in the main house, however.

The main restaurant here, **Castell Deudraeth Bar & Grill,** offers brasserie-style menus featuring a virtual showcase of fresh local produce—crab and scallops from the Lleyn Peninsula, lamb from the farms around Bala, rock oysters from the island of Anglesey, and much more. Much cheaper is the self-service restaurant, which serves freshly cooked hot and cold meals daily but only from 10am to 5pm.

Portmeirion, Gwynedd LL48 6ET (off A487, signposted from Minffordd, 3.2km/2 miles west of Portmeirion). © 01766/770000. Fax 01766/770300. www.portmeirion-village.com. 53 units. £167 ($334) double; from £188 ($376) suite. Rates include breakfast. AE, DC, MC, V. Free parking. **Amenities:** 2 restaurants; bar; outdoor pool; outdoor tennis court; room service; babysitting. *In room:* TV, beverage maker, hair dryer.

SEEING THE SIGHTS

The view of the mountains of Snowdonia from Porthmadog Cob, the embankment, is panoramic. Porthmadog is the coastal terminal of the Ffestiniog Railway, and a small museum may be visited at the station. The town has access to beaches at Borth-y-Gest and Black Rock Sands, where cars may be driven onto the beach. Other than the scenery, attractions are not exceptional.

The production of traditional tapestries and tweeds can be observed at the small **Brynkir Woollen Mill,** Golan, Garndolbenmaen (© **01766/530236**), in a beautiful rural setting. The products are available for sale at the mill shop. Admission is free; it is open Monday through Friday from 10am to 4pm. Head out the A487 for 5.6km (3½ miles) from Porthmadog.

CRICCIETH

Now in ruins, **Criccieth Castle** (© **01766/522227**), built as a native Welsh stronghold, is on a grassy headland and offers a commanding view of Tremadog Bay. During its years as an active fortress, it changed hands—Welsh to English and back and forth—until it was finally sacked and burned in 1404 by Owain Glyndwr, never to rise again as a fortification. The castle houses an interesting exhibition on the theme of the native castles of Welsh princes. On a fine day, from its heights you can see westward to the tip of the peninsula, north and east to Snowdonia, and far down the bay to the south. Admission costs £3 ($6) for adults and £2.50 ($5) for students and children ages 5 to 16, free for children ages 4 and younger. A family ticket goes for £8.30 ($17). It's open April and May daily from 10am to 5pm, June to September daily 10am to 6pm, October daily 10am to 5pm, and November to March Friday and Saturday 9:30am to 4pm, and Sunday 11am to 4pm. The castle's exhibition center is closed the rest of the year, but you can still enjoy the panoramic view.

About 3km (2 miles) west of Criccieth in Llanystumdwy, you can visit **Highgate,** the boyhood home of David Lloyd George, prime minister of Britain in the war years of 1914 to 1918 , and also the **Lloyd George Museum** (© **01766/522071**), designed by Sir Clough Williams-Ellis of Portmeirion resort village fame (see above). The museum outlines the statesman's life, and the main displays illustrate his political career and include a collection of "freedom" caskets, a "talking head" portrayed by Philip Madoc, the actor, with excerpts of three of Lloyd George's famous speeches, and an audiovisual display. Admission is £3 ($6) for adults, £2 ($4) for children, and £7 ($14) for a family ticket. From April to June, it is open Monday to Saturday from 10:30am to 5pm (open Mon–Fri in May); July to September daily from 10:30am to 5pm; and October Monday to Friday from 11am to 4pm. Lloyd George's grave is nearby on the banks of the swift-running River Dwyfor, shaded by large oak trees. The name of the hamlet, Llanystumdwy, means "the church at the bend of the River Dwyfor."

St. Cybi's Well, Llangybi, is 6.4km (4 miles) northwest of Criccieth on a minor road. Of 6th-century origin, only two chambers remain of the holy well, although in the mid–18th century a bathhouse was built to surround the font. You can visit it free.

North of the well is the site of a small Iron Age hill fort. **Tourist information** about the Criccieth area is available from Porthmadog (see above).

WHERE TO STAY & DINE

Bron Eifion Country House Hotel 🏚🏚   On 2 hectares (5 acres) of well-manicured gardens, this baronial mansion is the finest and most elegant place to stay in the area. This tranquil Welsh country estate lies close to the Snowdonia National Park and makes a good base for exploring the area. The interior looks like it would make a good place to stage an Agatha Christie murder mystery. You'll surely be impressed by the grand stairway and the minstrels' gallery, with its lofty timbered roof. Rooms are spacious and traditionally furnished; some have four-poster beds. You can wander the tended gardens evoking the South of France.

Popular with locals and visitors alike, the **Orangery Restaurant** offers one of the most beautiful settings for dining in the area, its chef featuring freshly prepared local ingredients deftly handled and delicately flavored. A set menu costs £30 ($60) per person, and it's an elegant, tasty presentation, beginning perhaps with smoked salmon, featuring lamb or other meats as a main course, and ending with a fresh dessert or else (our favorite) Welsh artisan cheese with a fig-and-beet chutney and a slice of fresh walnut and raisin bread.

Criccieth, Gwynedd LL52 05A. ℭ **800/780-7234** in the U.S., or 01766/522385. Fax 01766/523796. www.broneifion. co.uk. 19 units. £65–£98 ($130–$196) per person double. Rates include full Welsh breakfast. AE, MC, V. Lies .8km (½ mile) outside Criccieth on A497 signposted PWLLHELI. **Amenities:** Restaurant; lounge; room service; babysitting; laundry service. *In room:* TV, beverage maker, hair dryer, trouser press.

The Lion Hotel *(Kids)*   This former private home from the 18th century lies in the town's most enviable spot: beside the village green behind a painted stone facade. The lager-drinking pubbers of town head here at sundown, and it's a lively, cozy nest for an overnight stop and some good Welsh cookery. Rooms are homelike and often small but comfortably furnished with tidy housekeeping and somewhat cramped bathrooms. Families are especially welcome here, as the hotel sets aside separate bedrooms for them and offers early dinners for children. The inn also has such devices as "baby-listening" facilities along with cots and highchairs that are provided. In addition to staying in the main building, you can also find lodgings in the Castle Cottage, offering a dozen well-furnished bedrooms.

Y Maes, Criccieth, Gwynedd LA52 0AA. ℭ **01766/522460.** Fax 01766/523075. www.lionhotelcriccieth.co.uk. 46 units. £70–£80 ($140–$160) double. Rates include breakfast. AE, MC, V. **Amenities:** Restaurant; bar; room service; babysitting. *In room:* TV, beverage maker, hair dryer, trouser press (in some).

4 Caernarfon *(★(★)*

400km (249 miles) W of London; 100km (68 miles) W of Chester; 48km (30 miles) SE of Holyhead; 14km (9 miles) SW of Bangor

In the 13th century, when King Edward I of England had defeated the Welsh after long and bitter fighting, he felt the need for a castle in this area as part of his network of fortresses in the still-rebellious country. He ordered the construction of one on the site of an old Norman castle at the western end of the Menai Strait, where the River Seiont flows into the sea, a place from which his sentinels could command a view of the land around all the way to the mountains and far out across the bay to the Irish Sea. Based either on his firsthand observations (historians believed he might have visited Constantinople during his involvement in the Crusades) or on ancient drawings of Constantinople procured by his architect, the Savoy-born James St. George, the walls were patterned after the fortifications surrounding ancient Byzantium. Most of the walls of the 13th-century town still stand, although growth outside the walls has been inevitable.

The main reason to come here today is to see the castle. After that, you will have seen the best of Caernarfon and can press on to another town for the night or else stay at one of the local inns. The downside? Tourist buses overrun the place in summer. Other than the castle, there is nothing in the town that needs to take up too much of your time.

ESSENTIALS

GETTING THERE   There's no railway station in Caernarfon; the nearest connection is through Bangor, to which Caernarfon is linked by bus.

Buses run between Caernarfon and Bangor, a 25-minute ride, every 20 minutes throughout the day. Bus timetables are available by either calling the tourist office (see below), dialing © **0871/200-2233,** or visiting **www.arriva.co.uk**.

If you're driving from Bangor, head southwest along the A487; from Porthmadog (see above) head north along the A487.

VISITOR INFORMATION   The **Caernarfon Tourist Information Centre** is at Oriel Pendeitsh, 1 Castle St. (© **01286/672232;** www.visitcaernarfon.com). From May through October it's open daily 9:30am to 5:30pm; November to April, it's open Monday to Saturday 10am to 4:30pm.

WHERE TO STAY & DINE

Celtic Royal Hotel ⊛   Carved out of a 19th-century grand hotel shell and massively enlarged, this is the blockbuster and leading choice in town. Its uniformed, well-trained staff grew accustomed long ago to groups of visitors pulling in by motorcoach to see the famous castle, just a 3-minute walk away. The hotel's current look derives from a 1996 face-lift and radical enlargement of what had become a dowdy and outmoded "grand hotel" built in 1843. Today, most of the antique original vestiges lie within the hotel's lobby, with bedrooms and dining facilities placed within modern, three-story wings that contain all of the conveniences you'd expect from a first-class property. The midsize bedrooms are blandly uncontroversial, outfitted in pastels with comfortable furnishings.

The main restaurant, **Brasserie Draco,** is a chic setting for a Mediterranean-inspired cuisine. In addition, you can head for the on-site Havana Bistro/Bar, which is much more informal and less expensive, offering an array of freshly cooked local food and a well-stocked bar.

Bangor St., Caernarfon, Gwynedd LL55 1AY. © **01286/674477.** Fax 01286/674139. www.celtic-royal.co.uk. 110 units. £115 ($230) double. Rates include breakfast. AE, MC, V. Free parking. **Amenities:** 2 restaurants; bar; indoor heated pool; gym; sauna; steam room; Jacuzzi; vertical tanning bed; room service; laundry service; dry cleaning. *In room:* TV, beverage maker, hair dryer.

Seiont Manor ⊛⊛ (Kids)   In the tranquil Welsh countryside, this is one of the best bases for exploring Snowdonia National Park. It can also be an excellent base for visiting the Isle of Anglesey. With a slight exaggeration, the owners proclaim, "We're a Pandora's box of wondrous treasures." Constructed from the original farmstead of a Georgian manor house, the hotel has been tastefully converted into a honeycomb of spacious rooms, each with good-size bathrooms and all with views over 60 hectares (150 acres) of parkland. Come here for seclusion, a sense of style, and some of the best leisure facilities in the area. It's also a great family favorite. Several bedrooms are reserved for families. Each of the rooms has a small balcony or a terrace.

One of the town's best three-course dinners is served here nightly, for £28 ($56), featuring such dishes as seared scallops enlivened with an orange-and-horseradish cream sauce. The chef prepares a simple but high-quality cuisine for contemporary tastes. In addition to the good food, you get to enjoy views of the lake through the conservatory windows.

Llanrug, Caernarfon, Gwynedd LL55 2AQ. © **01286/673366.** Fax 01286/672840. www.handpicked.co.uk. 28 units. £190–£220 ($380–$440) double; from £250 ($500) suite. Rates include breakfast. AE, DC, MC, V. From Caernarfon, head east on A4086 for 3.2km (2 miles). **Amenities:** Restaurant; bar; indoor pool; gym; sauna; solarium; fishing; room service; babysitting; laundry service; dry cleaning. *In room:* TV, beverage maker, hair dryer.

Stables ⊛ (Kids)   Those who don't like living in a stable should rethink their prejudice. This unusual hotel was constructed around stone stables that were famous locally many years ago for horse breeding. Some of the trained horses here eventually ended up helping fight South Africa's Boer War. Today those stables have been considerably enlarged with modern wings and slate roofs whose materials and angles match those of the original core. Most of the good-size and comfortably furnished accommodations with commodious private bathrooms are in an L-shaped annex whose innermost corner shelters a swimming pool. Several of the bedrooms have four-poster beds.

The on-site bar and bistro offers an extensive menu daily with specials posted on a blackboard. There is also a fine range of cask ales to wash down the Welsh specialties. You receive good value for the quality food served here.

Llanwnda, near Caernarfon. Gwynedd LL54 5SD. ✆ **01286/830711**. Fax 01286/830413. www.stableshotel.co.uk. 23 units. £64–£89 ($128–$178) double. Rates include breakfast. MC, V. From Caernarfon, drive the A499 9.6km (6 miles) east and follow signs to Pwllheli. **Amenities:** Restaurant; pub; outdoor pool; room service; babysitting. *In room:* TV, beverage maker, hair dryer (in some).

SEEING THE SIGHTS

Every Saturday (plus Mon May–Sept), a market is held in **Castle Square,** where there's a statue of David Lloyd George, prime minister of Great Britain between 1916 and 1922, who is generally credited, along with King George V, for leading the United Kingdom through the rigors of World War I. He's also credited with introducing what's defined today as Britain's national healthcare system. Born in Manchester, he was reared on the nearby Lleyn Peninsula, and was later instrumental in preserving the remnants of the town's famous castle (see below).

The nearest thing Wales ever had to a royal palace is **Caernarfon Castle** 𝒦𝒦𝒦, described by Dr. Samuel Johnson after a visit in 1774 as "an edifice of stupendous majesty and strength." Legend has it that after the birth, in 1301, of the son of Edward I in this castle, he showed the infant boy to the Welsh, calling him "the native-born prince who can speak no English." Since that time the title "Prince of Wales" has belonged to every male heir-apparent to the English throne. The eyes of the world were on Caernarfon in 1969 when it was the scene of the investiture of Charles as prince of Wales.

The castle is open to visitors. Although in some places only the shell of the wall remains, some rooms and stone and wooden steps remain so that you can climb up into it. Eagle Tower has an exhibition on the ground floor showing the history of the fortress and of the town around it. In the northeast are exhibits on the princes of Wales. You can also visit the **Regimental Museum of the Royal Welch Fusiliers** (the regiment retains the Old English spelling of the word *Welsh*), which occupies all three floors of Queen's Tower and contains many items of interest relating to the regiment and its military history. In 2000, millions of pounds were spent on the renovation and enlargement of this historic castle, with additional exhibition space for the museum set up within the Chamberlain Tower. It is the castle as a whole that's of interest—not one special exhibition or hall. Allow 1½ hours.

Between June and the September, the castle is open daily from 9:30am to 6pm. From April to May, and during all of October, it's open daily from 9:30am to 5pm. From November to April, it's open Monday to Saturday 9:30am to 4pm and Sunday 11am to 4pm. Admission costs £4.90 ($9.80) for adults and £4.50 ($9) for students and children 15 and younger. For more information, call ✆ **01286/677617.**

Today the town's quays are less animated than they were during the heyday of the region's slate mining, when boats lined up to haul roofing tiles off to points as far away as London, the United States, the mainland of Europe, and India. In the mid-1990s, a full-service marina, with about 60 slips, was built to accommodate the increasing numbers of yachts and pleasure craft that moor here when not in use.

The Romans recognized the strategic importance of northwest Wales and maintained a fort at **Segontium** for some 3 centuries. Excavations on the outskirts of Caernarfon on the A4085 have disclosed foundations of barracks, bathhouses, and other structural remains. Finds from the excavations are displayed in the **museum** (© **01286/675625;** www.segontium.org.uk) on the site, open year-round Tuesday to Sunday 12:30 to 4:30pm. Admission is free. Some archaeologists and historians think that native Britons may have been displaced from the site, which was one of their strongholds at the time of the Roman invasion. There are no outstanding relics here; allow about 30 minutes to walk about.

5 The Isle of Anglesey ★★

The Welsh name of this island is Mon (the Romans called it Mona), and it is called Mon, Mam Cymru, or Anglesey, Mother of Wales. If this is true, we must say that the child doesn't much resemble the mother. The scenery differs totally from that of the mainland, with low-lying farmland interrupted here and there by rocky outcrops. The landscape is dotted with single-story whitewashed cottages, and the rolling green fields stretch down to the sea—all against a backdrop of the mountains of Snowdonia across the Menai Strait, which divides this island from the rest of Wales.

Visitors cross the strait by one of the two bridges built by celebrated engineers of the 19th century: the **Menai Suspension Bridge,** designed by Thomas Telford and completed in 1826, and the **Britannia Bridge,** originally a railroad bridge, which was the work of Robert Stephenson. The Britannia, a neighbor of the suspension bridge, had to be rebuilt after a devastating fire that destroyed its pitch and timberwork; it now carries both trains and cars on two different levels. The bridges are about 1.6km (1 mile) west of Bangor on the mainland.

Many people have passed through Anglesey on the train that operates between London and Holyhead, for a ferry journey to Ireland. A stopover for a day in Anglesey is recommended. Neolithic tombs of Stone Age settlers have been found on the island, as have Iron Age artifacts. The Romans left artifacts behind, as did the early Christians who settled here.

The coming of steamers and then of the railroad brought Victorian-era visitors. However, if you're not really sold on antiquity, there's a lot to do on Anglesey that is totally in tune with today. Yachting, sea fishing, and leisure centers that offer swimming, squash, and other activities are within easy reach wherever you stay. Golf, tennis, nature walks, pony trekking, canoeing—whatever—are offered in the daytime, and in the evening you can wine, dine, and even dance to the latest music.

ESSENTIALS

GETTING THERE   The island has good bus service. For information about bus service on the island, call **Arriva Cymru** at © **0871/200-2233** or visit **www.arriva. co.uk.** The major route (bus no. 4) runs between Bangor and Holyhead via Llangefni. Buses operate at the rate of two per hour during the day Monday to Saturday, but on Sunday service is curtailed. Bus no. 57 goes from Bangor to Beaumaris every 30 minutes during the day Monday to Saturday. Service is about once every 2 hours on a Sunday. All buses cross the Menai Bridge at the town of Menai Bridge (see below).

VISITOR INFORMATION   To find out about activities on the island, call or write for a brochure from the **Wales Tourist Board Information Centre,** Railway Station Site, Llanfairpwllgwyngyllgogerychwyrndrobwllllantysiliogogogoch (yes, this is the real name; see below), Isle of Anglesey (✆ **01248/713177**). It's open November to March daily 10am to 5pm, April to November daily 9:30am to 5:30pm.

MENAI BRIDGE

The small town of Menai Bridge, 4km (2½ miles) west of Bangor, has several points of interest. Take a stroll westward along the Belgian Promenade, a walk constructed along the strait during World War II by Belgian refugees. You can go under the bridge, past some standing stones, which were recently erected, and Coed Cyrnol, a pinewood, to **Church Island.** The island's 14th-century **Church of St. Tysilio** was originally founded in the 7th century by St. Tysilio, son of the royal house of Powys and grandson of St. Pabo. St. Pabo is believed to have been a northern British chief who sought asylum on Anglesey. Call the tourist office (✆ **01248/713177**) for information (see above).

Menai Bridge is the site every October 24 of the **Ffair-y-Borth fair,** which has been held here since the 16th century. Today, it's really a flea market, not worth a trip unless you're in the area. This is an excellent place from which to view the Menai Strait sailing regatta in August each year.

WHERE TO STAY & DINE

Gazelle   This former posting inn beside the Menai Straits is your top choice for a combined hotel, restaurant, and pub in the area. If you're arriving late in the day, it can be your overnight stopover and gateway to Anglesey, which you can explore the next day. Nearly 5km (3 miles) from the center of Menai Bridge, beside the road signposted to Beaumaris, the hotel's quay-side pub has panoramic views of both the waterfront and the mountains. It's the best place to meet locals and visitors, the latter of whom often have yachts moored nearby. The inn is attractively decorated; old Welsh dressers and time-blackened settles give the place character. Bedrooms are small to moderate in size, each simply decorated but comfortable. Bathrooms are just adequate for the function—nothing more—and contain showers only.

The Gazelle has the best food in the area, so try to dine here even if you're not staying as a guest.

Glyngarth, Menai Bridge, Isle of Anglesey LL59 5PD. ✆ **01248/713364.** Fax 01248/713167. www.thegazellehotel. com. 9 units. £75–£100 ($150–$200) double. Rates include breakfast. MC, V. 3.2km (2 miles) northeast of Menai Bridge along A545. **Amenities:** Restaurant; bar; babysitting. *In room:* TV, beverage maker, hair dryer, iron.

LLANFAIR PG (LLANFAIRPWLLGWYNGYLLGOGERYCHWYRN-DROBWLLLLANTYSILIOGOGOGOCH)

Practically a suburb of Menai Bridge is a village to the west that has been heard of all over the world. Its fame is its name: Llanfairpwllgwyngyllgogerychwyrndrobwllllan-tysiliogogogoch, or something like that. It means "St. Mary's Church in the Hollow of the White Hazel near a Rapid Whirlpool and the Church of St. Tysilio near the Red Cave." It has been suggested that perhaps the name was invented as a tourist attraction. You can get the longest train platform ticket in the world from the station here, giving the full name. On maps and most references it is usually called "Llanfair PG" to differentiate it from several other Llanfairs in Wales. The first Women's Institute in Britain was founded here in 1915.

You're sure to see the **Marquess of Anglesey Column,** standing 27m (90 ft.) high on a mount 76m (250 ft.) above sea level. It has a statue of the marquess on top, to which visitors can climb (115 steps up a spiral staircase). The marquess lost a leg while he was second in command to the duke of Wellington at Waterloo and was thereafter called "One Leg" ("Ty Coch" in Welsh). The column is open year-round daily 9am to 5pm, charging £1.50 ($3) for adults, 75p ($1.50) for seniors and children.

WHERE TO STAY & DINE

Carreg Môn Country Hotel   Set at the edge of the village, within a 10-minute walk from the center, this hotel dates from the late 1800s, when it was a privately owned manor house. Today, much altered and enlarged from its original design, it sports a white-painted brick facade and a modern wing that contains the simple but efficient and well-scrubbed small-to-midsize bedrooms, with little bathrooms containing shower stalls. This is the only conventional hotel in town, providing more rooms than any of its smaller and less accessorized competitors. Since the building's transformation into a hotel occurred during the mid-1970s, some of the infrastructure might seem a bit dated, but overall, it provides comfortable and safe lodgings.

Traditional Welsh cookery is always a feature at this reliable country restaurant, with local lamb, black beef, and freshly caught seafood a nightly feature. The home-cooked dishes are backed up with a fully stocked bar and a decent wine list.

Church Lane, Llanfair PG, Anglesey LL61 5YH. Ⓒ 01248/714224. Fax 01248/715983. www.carregmonhotel.co.uk. 29 units. £65–£85 ($130–$170) double; £85–£110 ($170–$220) family room. Rates include breakfast. AE, DC, MC, V. Free parking. **Amenities:** Restaurant; bar; cocktail lounge; room service. *In room:* TV, beverage maker, hair dryer, trouser press, iron.

Penrhos Arms ENGLISH/WELSH   In the town with the long name, this is your best bet for pub grub for the night. It's especially inviting after you've climbed the Anglesey monument and are ready for a cold beer. You can't miss it, as it lies in the center of the village opposite the famous rail station of the village with the impossible name. The food is typical and standard, but it's made from fresh ingredients. If you like steak with mushrooms, fried seafood, or sausage and mashed potatoes, this is for you.

The pub also lets four bedrooms, each comfortable and costing £55 ($110) for a double, with breakfast included. Expect a TV and a small cubicle with a shower and toilet. Rooms have a chintz-filled decor inspired by Laura Ashley but no phones.

Holyhead Rd., Llanfair PG, Anglesey LL61 5YQ. Ⓒ 01248/714892. Reservations not needed. Main courses £6–£15 ($12–$30). DC, MC, V. Mon–Sat 11am–11pm; Sun noon–10:30pm.

SEEING THE SIGHTS

About 1.6km (1 mile) southwest of the village with the long name, on the A4080, from a turn off the A5 almost opposite the Marquess of Anglesey Column, is **Plas Newydd, Llanfair PG** ⟅⟅ (Ⓒ **01248/714795**; www.nationaltrust.org.uk), standing on the shores of the Menai Straits. It was the home of the seventh marquess of Anglesey but is now owned by the National Trust. An ancient manor house, it was converted between 1783 and 1809 into a splendid mansion in the Gothic and neoclassical styles. Its Gothic Hall features a gallery and elaborate fan vaulting. In the long dining room, see the magnificent *trompe l'oeil* mural by Rex Whistler. A military museum houses relics and uniforms of the Battle of Waterloo where the first marquess of Anglesey lost his leg. The beautiful woodland garden and lawns are worth visiting. The mansion is open to visitors. The gardens are open Saturday to Wednesday noon to 5pm from March to October, whereas the home can be visited only Saturday to Wednesday from noon to 5pm from Easter to November 2. A combined ticket for both the house and garden costs £6.60 ($13) for adults and £3.30 ($6.60) for children 15 and younger; it's £17 ($34) for a family ticket.

6 Holyhead & Holy Island

550km (342 miles) NW of London; 346km (215 miles) NW of Cardiff; 305km (190 miles) N of Swansea

The largest town on Anglesey, Holyhead (it's pronounced *Holly*-head—don't ask us why) is not actually on Anglesey at all but on Holy Island. However, the two islands have long been linked. Packet boats between Holyhead and Ireland were recorded as far back at 1573.

The harbor of Holyhead was reconstructed in 1880 and now serves as a terminal for container-bearing ships.

People have come to this far point of northern Wales for a long, long time by water. Celtic invaders, early Christian missionaries, Romans, Vikings—whoever—have made their way here, and in many cases stayed on for centuries.

ESSENTIALS

GETTING THERE   Holyhead is the terminus of the **North Wales Coast** rail line. Trains arrive hourly during the day from Cardiff, Bangor, Llandudno, Chester, Birmingham, and London. For information and schedules, call © **0845/748-4950** or visit www.nationalrail.co.uk. **Arriva** no. 4 buses pull into Holyhead from Bangor every 30 minutes during the day. There is no station here; buses arrive along both London Road and Market Street. For information and schedules, call © **0871/200-2233** or visit **www.arriva.co.uk**.

A causeway carries motorists across on the A5, which comes all the way from London, and the Four Mile Bridge on B4545 also links Holy Island to Anglesey.

Two unrelated ferryboat companies operate service between Holyhead and the Irish port of Dun Laoghaire, a railway and highway junction close to Dublin. (Some of them continue on even into Dublin harbor.) Both companies run swift and conventional ferryboat service (transit time 1½ hr. swift; 3½ hr. conventional each way, with three to five departures daily). On the Stena Line, foot passengers are allowed on the swift ferry, but passengers with car can travel on the conventional ferries. The Irish ferries carry both passengers and cars. Transit costs £42 ($84) round-trip on the conventional ferryboats, £46 ($92) round-trip on the catamarans for passengers traveling and returning on the same day. For more information, contact either the **Stena Line** (© **0870/570-7070;** www.stenaline.co.uk) or **Irish Ferries** (© **0870/5171717;** www.irishferries.com). Irish Ferries operates only between Holyhead and Dublin; it does not operate between Holyhead and Dun Laoghaire.

VISITOR INFORMATION   Information is available at the **Holyhead Information Centre,** Stena Line, Terminal 1 (© **01407/762622**), open year-round Monday to Saturday 8:30am to 6pm.

WHERE TO STAY & DINE

Boathouse Hotel   If you decide to overnight before taking a ferry in the morning, this hotel is just a few minutes' walk from the terminal. The town's finest inn, it lies in a stellar position looking out over the water and the Holyhead Mountains, which can be seen from your bedroom. The midsize rooms are pleasantly and comfortably furnished, and the bathrooms, though small, are spick-and-span, with shower units. One unit is large enough for families.

A widely varied selection of freshly made bar snacks is available in the hotel's bistro, along with daily specialties as noted on the blackboard. The chef specializes in freshly caught fish and lobster.

Newry Promenade, Newry Beach, Holyhead LL65 1YF. ℂ **01407/762094.** Fax 01407/764898. www.boathouse-hotel.co.uk. 19 units. £80 ($160) double; £90 ($180) family room. Rates include breakfast. AE, MC, V. Free parking. **Amenities:** Restaurant; bar; lounge; room service. *In room:* TV, beverage maker, hair dryer.

Bull Hotel *Kids*   A bustling hotel, the long-popular Bull stands right at the approach to Holyhead. We'd give its competitor, the Boathouse (see above), a slight edge, but the Bull is almost as good. We prefer the more comfortable midsize rooms in the main building, as opposed to the newer and more sterile ones in the annex, but both are comfortable, containing tidy bathrooms with showers. Four rooms are large enough for families. Both locals and visitors meet in the restaurant to savor an array of both Welsh specialties and international dishes, including black beef, lamb, and freshly caught seafood.

London Rd. Valley, Holyhead LL65 3DP. ℂ **01407/740351.** Fax 01407/742328. 14 units. £60 ($120) double. Rates include breakfast. DC, MC, V. **Amenities:** Restaurant; 2 bars. *In room:* TV, beverage maker.

SEEING THE SIGHTS

Holyhead Mountain *🎿* is the highest point in Anglesey, at 216m (710 ft.). From the rocky height, you can see the Isle of Man, the Mourne Mountains in Ireland, Snowdonia, and Cumbria on a clear day. The summit is the site of an ancient hill fort and the ruins of an Irish settlement from the 2nd to the 4th century A.D. The towering cliffs of North and South Stack are home to thousands of seabirds, and gray seals breed in the caves below. At the southern point of the mountain, **South Stack** is an automatic lighthouse built in 1808. It's 27m (91 ft.) high (60m/197 ft. above mean high water) and can be seen for 32km (20 miles). It's noted for its antique walls, its strategic position, and a state-of-the-art light beam. The lighthouse is open Easter to September daily from 10:30am to 5pm, charging £4 ($8) for adults, £3 ($6) for seniors and students, and £2 ($4) for children 15 and younger. For information, call ℂ **01407/763207.**

On Friday and Saturday, **general markets** are held in Holyhead.

St. Cybi's Church, Market Street (no phone), near the town center, is on the site of a 6th-century church; a Roman fort from the 3rd century also stood here. The site is open daily from 10am to 4pm; admission is free. Services are at 9:15am and 6pm. For information, contact the tourist office (see above).

7 Conwy *🎿*

387km (241 miles) NW of London; 59km (37 miles) E of Holyhead; 35km (22 miles) NE of Caernarfon

Unlike Llandudno, its 19th-century neighbor, Conwy is an ancient town. With its mighty medieval castle and complete town walls, this is a richly historic place.

The Conwy estuary is crossed by three bridges that lead to Conwy. The handsome suspension bridge was built in 1826 by Thomas Telford, bridge-builder extraordinaire. It looks as if it runs right into the castle, but it doesn't. It's closed to vehicular traffic now, but you can walk across it for free and marvel at how it served as the main entrance to the town for so long, with its narrow lanes and the sure bottleneck at the castle end. It replaced the ferry that was previously the only means of crossing the river. An exhibit of Telford's work is in the tollhouse. You can also see Robert Stephenson's tubular railroad bridge built in 1848, and the modern arched road bridge, completed in 1958.

St. Mary's, the parish church, stands inside the town walls on the site of a 12th-century Cistercian abbey. In it are a Byzantine processional cross, a beautiful Tudor cross, and a 15th-century screen of fine workmanship. The churchyard contains a grave associated with William Wordsworth's poem *We Are Seven*.

ESSENTIALS

GETTING THERE   Trains run between Conwy and Llandudno, Bangor, and Holyhead, with easy connections to the rest of Wales. Llandudno is only a 3-minute ride from Conwy. For schedules and information, call ℂ **0845/7484950.**

   Arriva buses from Bangor heading for Llandudno pass through Conwy every 15 minutes during the day Monday to Saturday, and hourly on Sunday. Call ℂ **0871/200-2233** or visit **www.arrivabus.co.uk** for schedules and more information.

   Motorists from England head west along the North Wales coastline on A548.

VISITOR INFORMATION   **Conwy Castle Visitor Centre,** Castle Street (ℂ **01492/592248**), dispenses information from Easter to May daily 9:30am to 5pm, June to September daily 9:30am to 6pm, October daily 9:30am to 5pm, and November to Easter Monday to Saturday 9:30am to 4pm and Sunday 11am to 4pm.

WHERE TO STAY & DINE

Groes Inn 🏨🏨   Oozing with 4 centuries of atmosphere and old-fashioned charm, this inn dates from 1573 and was the first licensed house in Wales. Although it has expanded over the years, the original core is still here, evoked by log fires, antiques, and open-beamed, time-blackened ceilings. For history buffs, it's the finest choice in the area. The accommodations are in a separate house away from the pub noise, and each midsize unit is comfortably furnished. Rooms open onto bucolic views of sheep grazing in the fields and of rolling hills. The best units have balconies or private terraces. One room has a four-poster bed. Stop in for a lager or a hearty, home-cooked pub dinner.

Tyn-y-Groes, Conwy LL32 8TN. ℂ **01492/650545.** Fax 01492/650855. www.groesinn.com. 14 units. £103–£189 ($206–$378) double. Rates include breakfast. AE, DC, MC, V. Lies 4.8km (3 miles) south of Conwy on B5106. **Amenities:** Restaurant; pub; room service. *In room:* TV, beverage maker, hair dryer.

The Old Rectory 🏨   The Welsh motto for the house, *Hardd Hafan Hedd*, means "a beautiful haven of peace"—and so it is. From its hillside perch, with terraced gardens, the inn sweeps across the Conwy Estuary for a view of Conwy Castle and the Snowdonia mountain range. Once the Tudor home of the rectors of the parish for centuries, it is furnished with paintings and antiques. A night here is like entering a bygone era. Each good-size bedroom has its own charm and style; a few have four-poster or half-tester beds. Comfort is foremost, from the sleep-inducing bed to the well-maintained private bathroom.

   Wendy Vaughan is a grand chef, producing high-quality and creative dishes that have a light touch and artistic presentation.

Llansanffraid, Glan Conwy, Conwy LL28 5LF. ℂ **01492/580611.** Fax 01492/584555. www.oldrectorycountryhouse.co.uk. 6 units. £99–£159 ($198–$318) double. Rates include Welsh breakfast. MC, V. Take the A470 4.8km (3 miles) from Conwy; Old Rectory is .8km (½ mile) south from A55/A470 junction on the left. No children 4 or younger. **Amenities:** Restaurant; bar. *In room:* TV, hair dryer, beverage maker, iron.

SEEING THE SIGHTS

Aberconwy House   This is the only remaining medieval merchant's house in Conwy, a town that used to have hundreds of them. Dating from the 14th century, this structure is owned by the National Trust and houses an exhibition depicting the life of Conwy from Roman times. It includes a re-created 18th-century kitchen and a mussel-fishing corner, with the traditional instruments still used by the industry.

Castle St. and High St. ℂ **01492/592246**. www.nationaltrust.org.uk. Admission £3 ($6) adults, £1.50 ($3) children 15 and younger, £7.50 ($15) family ticket. Apr–Oct Wed–Mon 11am–5pm (last admission at 4:30pm).

Conwy Castle 🖈🖈   The town centers on Conwy Castle. Edward I had this master-piece of medieval architecture built after he conquered the last native prince of Wales, Llywelyn. The English king put up massive castles to convince the Welsh that he was the supreme authority. The castle follows the contours of a narrow strip of rock, the eight towers commanding the estuary of the River Conwy. The town wall that pro-tected the borough, chartered by Edward in 1284, is almost intact, with 21 flanking towers and three twin-towered gateways. Visitors to the town can walk the walls. This is one castle you can't possibly miss seeing, as the road runs almost close enough for you to touch the walls in place. Allow an hour to visit.

Castle St. ℂ **01492/592358**. Admission £4.50 ($9) adults, £4 ($8) seniors and students, £3.50 ($7) children 15 and younger, £14 ($28) family ticket. Apr–May and Oct daily 9:30am–5pm; June–Sept daily 9:30am–6pm; Nov–Mar Mon–Sat 9:30am–4pm, Sun 11am–4pm. Closed Dec 24–26 and Jan 1.

8 Llandudno 🖈

391km (243 miles) NW of London; 69km (43 miles) E of Holyhead

This Victorian seaside resort—the largest in Wales—nestles in a crescent between the giant headlands of the **Great Orme** and the **Little Orme,** which received their names from early Vikings who thought they resembled sea serpents when their bases were shrouded in mist. This premier resort of Wales has two beaches, one on the northern edge of town, flanking a boardwalk and the Irish Sea, and the other on the west side of town, opening onto the mountains of Snowdonia and the Conwy Estuary.

Llandudno was built beginning around 1850 by the Mostyn family, after whom many local roads, avenues, and sites are named. It was conceived as a means to cash in on the already-proven proclivity of the British of Queen Victoria's day—particu-larly the great middle classes—to go to the seashore in summer. It is built in a typi-cally Victorian way with a promenade along the beach. The Victorian elegance and tradition of Llandudno have been maintained in the architecture of its buildings, but there the days-gone-by atmosphere stops.

ESSENTIALS

GETTING THERE   Virgin Trains operate from London's Euston Station, many of which require changes of equipment in either Crewe, Birmingham, or Chester, and in some cases, all of them. Overall, with waiting time included, it takes about 4½ hours to reach Llandudno from London by train. However, one Virgin train per day goes direct with no changes, taking 3¼ hours. For information about this or any other rail-way schedule in Wales, call ℂ **0845/748-4950**, or go to **www.nationalrail.co.uk**.

During the day, the **Arriva Bus Company** (ℂ **0871/200-2233;** www.arriva.co.uk) maintains buses to and from neighboring Bangor. Buses depart every 15 to 60 minutes.

If driving from England, take the M6 to the M56, then head across North Wales along the A55.

VISITOR INFORMATION   The **Llandudno Tourist Information Centre,** Mostyn Street (ℂ **01492/876413**), is open between April and October daily from

9:30am to 5:30pm. From November to March, it's open Monday to Friday 9:30am to 4:30pm.

WHERE TO STAY
VERY EXPENSIVE

Bodysgallen Hall ★★★ *Finds*   This is the finest address in the north of Wales, a dramatic 17th-century country house set in 80 hectares (200 acres) of parkland and manicured gardens. It would be the only suitable address for the novelist Henry James, were he alive today. Skillfully restored, it offers architectural merit combined with 21st-century comfort. The hall has a 13th-century tower that was a lookout post for Conwy Castle, 2.5km (1½ miles) away. You can still climb the tower for a panoramic view. Each of the spacious and elegant bedrooms evokes a certain period in their styles and colors; some have four-poster beds. Some of the units, as good as those in the main house, are in converted cottages.

3.2km (2 miles) southeast along A470 from Llandudno, Llandudno LL30 IRS. ✆ 01492/584466. Fax 01492/582519. www.bodysgallen.com. 33 units. £175–£315 ($350–$630) double; £385–£395 ($770–$790) suite. Rates include breakfast. MC, V. Free parking. No children 7 or younger. **Amenities:** Restaurant; bar; indoor pool; outdoor tennis court; health club; whirlpool; spa; sauna; steam room; laundry service; dry cleaning. *In room:* TV, Wi-Fi, fridge, hair dryer.

EXPENSIVE

Empire Hotel ★★★   In an ocean of tacky hotels, this one is a winner, the best within the town itself. Off the Promenade, near the Great Orme cable car, it looks down on the pier and Happy Valley, about 274m (900 ft.) away. Family managed, it is furnished with antiques and fine paintings in the Victorian tradition. Bedrooms are medium-size to spacious—luxuriously furnished. A Victorian annex, "No. 72," contains eight of the establishment's finest rooms, filled with Victorian antiques, touches of silk, and a bathtub-cum-Jacuzzi. We prefer these to the accommodations in the main building. You get luxury and style throughout.

Church Walks, Llandudno, Conwy LL30 2HE. ✆ 01492/860555. Fax 01492/860791. www.empirehotel.co.uk. 58 units. £90–£100 ($180–$200) double; £120 ($240) suite. AE, DC, MC, V. Free parking. **Amenities:** 2 restaurants; bar; 2 pools (1 indoor, 1 outdoor); spa; whirlpool; sauna; room service; laundry service; dry cleaning. *In room:* TV, Wi-Fi, fridge, beverage maker, hair dryer, safe.

St. Tudno Hotel ★★   For fans of *Alice in Wonderland,* this is the only place to stay in town. Alice Liddell, immortalized by Lewis Carroll in *Alice in Wonderland,* checked in here at the age of 8 on her first visit to Llandudno in 1861. It's a Victorian terraced seafront hotel that escapes the tacky curse of many of its neighbors. The hotel has kept abreast of the times—you won't fall down the rabbit hole if checking in here—and is one of the top seafront hotels in North Wales. Richly decorated inside, it is opulent and luxurious, with first-class service. Martin and Janette Bland offer a beautiful product with individually designed bedrooms that come in a variety of sizes. Rooms in the rear have slightly less glamour but are more tranquil and a lot cheaper. Traditionalists prefer to check into the Alice Suite. Public rooms evoke the Victorian era.

North Parade, Promenade, Llandudno, Gwynedd LL30 2LP. ✆ 01492/874411. Fax 01492/860407. www.st-tudno. co.uk. 18 units. £57–£115 ($114–$230) per person double; £145–£155 ($290–$310) per person suite. Rates include breakfast. AE, DC, MC, V. Free parking. Closed Oct 29–Apr 22. **Amenities:** Restaurant; bar; lounge/cafe; heated indoor pool; room service. *In room:* A/C (in some), TV, minibar, beverage maker, hair dryer.

INEXPENSIVE

Tan Lan Hotel ★ *Value*   This is your best bet for the night if you're seeking good-value accommodations on the tranquil west shore of Llandudno. It lies under the

Llandudno

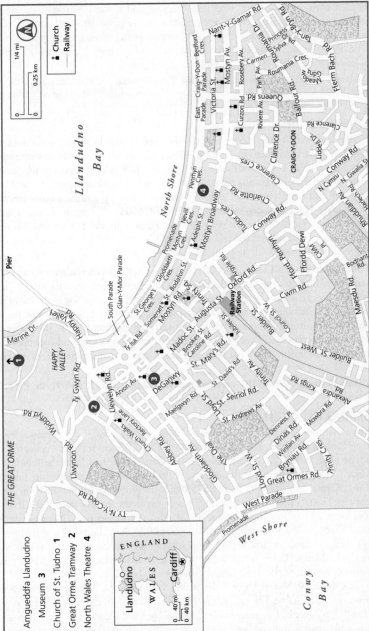

Amgueddfa Llandudno
Museum **3**
Church of St. Tudno **1**
Great Orme Tramway **2**
North Wales Theatre **4**

Church
Railway

1/4 mi
0.25 km

Llandudno
Bay

North Shore

THE GREAT ORME

Pier

HAPPY
VALLEY

CRAIG-Y-DON

Railway
Station

West Shore

Conway
Bay

ENGLAND
WALES
Llandudno
Cardiff
40 mi
40 km

Marine Dr.
Wyddfyd Rd.
Ty Gwyn Rd.
Happy Valley Rd.
Llwynon Rd.
Llewelyn Rd.
Anvon Av.
Church Walks
Rectory Lane
Abbey Rd.
Gloddaeth Av.
TY N-y-Coed Rd.
South Parade
Glan-Y-Mor Parade
Promenade
Gloddaeth Cres.
St. George's Cres.
Isa Rd.
Somerset St.
Mostyn Rd.
Bodafon St.
Trinity Sq.
Madoc St.
Brookes St.
Caroline Rd.
St. Mary's Rd.
Maelgwyn Rd.
Lloyd St.
The Oval
Lloyd St. W.
St. David's Rd.
St. Andrews Av.
Seiriol Rd.
Denness Pl.
Dinas Rd.
Winllan Av.
Bryniau Rd.
Great Ormes Rd.
Mowbra Rd.
Trinity Cres.
Trinity Av.
Kings Rd.
Alexandra Rd.
Builder St. West
Maesdu Rd.
Bodnant Rd.
Cwm Rd.
Cwm Pl.
Ffordd Dewi
Ffordd Penrhyn
Council St. W.
Builder St.
Oxford Rd.
Jubilee St.
Argyle Rd.
Augusta St.
DeGanwy
Mostyn St.
Nevill Cres.
Adelphi St.
Mostyn Cres.
Promenade Cres.
Tudor Cres.
Mostyn Broadway
Charlotte Rd.
Conway Rd.
Perrhyn Cres.
Clarence Cres.
Clarence Rd.
Clarence Dr.
CRAIG-Y-DON
Balfour Rd.
Clarence Rd.
Liddell Dr.
Conway Rd.
N Cymru
Hafren Rd.
Gwalia St.
Rhuddlan Av.
East Parade
Craig-Y-Don Parade
Victoria St.
Curzon Rd.
Queens Rd.
Riviere Av.
Carmen
Princess Dr.
Park Av.
Rosebery Av.
Mostyn Av.
Bedford Cres.
Nant-Y-Gamar Rd.
Roumania Dr.
Roumania Cres.
Meadow Gdns.
Tan-Y-Bryn Rd.
Ffern Bach Rd.

West Parade
Promenade

1
2
3
4

Great Orme, and its owners offer cozy lodgings and a warm welcome. The rooms upstairs are a bit quieter, but all are medium-size, brightly decorated, and well furnished. A trio of units is big enough for families, and children get a warm welcome. The dining room, decorated in the best tradition of the English play *Separate Tables,* is known for a varied menu—nothing too experimental.

Great Ormes Rd., West Shore, Llandudno, Conwy LL30 2AR. © **01492/860221.** Fax 01492/870219. www.tanlanhotel. co.uk. 17 units. £70 ($140) double. Rates include breakfast. MC, V. Free parking. Closed Oct 23–Mar 16. **Amenities:** Restaurant; bar; lounge; garden for drinks. *In room:* TV, beverage maker, hair dryer.

WHERE TO DINE

If you don't want a long, drawn-out, sit-down meal (see below), drop in at the **Cottage Loaf,** Market Square (© **01492/870762**), which is the village tavern with a summer beer garden. It serves the best pub grub in town, with generous main courses (each a meal in itself) costing from £6.50 ($13); it's open Monday to Saturday 11am to 11pm and Sunday noon to 10:30pm. One of the best places for a quick lunch is the **Cocoa House,** George Street (© **01492/876601**). The establishment got its name during the heyday of the temperance movement in Wales. That time has now passed, and the cafe has a full liquor license. Daily 10am to 4:30pm, it offers good-tasting lunches made with fresh ingredients, from £6 ($12).

The Seahorse ❧ WELSH/CONTINENTAL   Don and Gill Hadwin run a restaurant both upstairs and in the basement. Their cuisine and friendly service have brought them a faithful list of habitués. The cooks turn out satisfying meals full of flavor. Crispy duck breast is served with a tangy plum sauce, or else you can sample chicken breast stuffed with smoked cheddar and wild mushrooms. The fish dishes are especially recommended, notably the grilled tuna steak with a lime-and-coriander butter or else swordfish which has been marinated in lemon and garlic before reaching the grill.

7 Church Walks. © **01492/875315.** Reservations required. Fixed-price menu £27 ($54). AE, MC, V. Tues–Sat 5:30–11pm.

SEEING THE SIGHTS

From the summit of the **Great Orme** ❧ (206m/679 ft.), you get a panoramic view of the North Wales coast. You can walk up to the top if you're really energetic, but we advise other means. At Happy Valley, exotic sheltered gardens lie at the foot of the Great Orme, near the pier at the west end of the Llandudno Bay promenade. Take the **Great Orme Tramway** (© **01492/879306;** www.greatormetramway.com) to reach the top. The tramway has been carrying passengers to the summit since 1902. It operates every 20 minutes only between late March and October daily 10am to 6pm. It costs £5.20 ($10) round-trip for adults, £3.60 ($7.20) for children 13 and younger. It is closed in winter, during which period you can drive along a spectacular cliff-edge road, the Marine Drive, which winds uphill in a circular route that reaches a point near the summit of the Great Orme. Cars pay a toll of £2.50 ($5) each.

Just above the Marine Drive is the ancient **Church of St. Tudno,** from which the town derives its name. The present stone building dates from the 12th century, but the church was founded 600 years earlier. Between April and October, it's open 24 hours a day, and between June and September, there are open-air worship services every Sunday at 11am. For more information about the church and its services, or to gain entrance during other times of the year, contact the rector, John Nice, at © **01492/876624.**

At the end of the north-shore promenade, one of Britain's finest Victorian piers was built jutting 699m (2,295 ft.) into the bay at the base of the Great Orme, with an ornate covered pavilion at the end. You can find entertainment, food, fishing, or just relaxation on the pier. The north-shore beach is busy in summer, with traditional British seaside activities, including donkey rides, Punch-and-Judy shows, boat trips, and a children's fun land across the promenade.

The seafront's most visible public monument is the **North Wales Theatre,** the Promenade (© **01492/872000;** www.nwtheatre.co.uk). Built in the early 1990s, it had what amounted to the longest stage in Britain, until the more recent construction of a theater in Bournemouth surpassed it by a mere 15 centimeters (6 in.). Throughout the year, it's the venue for a changing roster of entertainment that includes everything from opera to rock-'n'-roll concerts. Most shows begin at 8pm and tickets cost £9 to £35 ($18–$70).

Amgueddfa Llandudno Museum, 17–19 Gloddaeth St. (© **01492/876517**), displays the development of Llandudno as a seaside resort. Period rooms are open to viewers. It is open Easter through October Tuesday to Saturday 10:30am to 1pm and 2 to 5pm, Sunday 2:15 to 5pm; and Tuesday to Saturday 1:30 to 4:30pm the rest of the year. Admission is £3 ($6) for adults, £2 ($4) for children, and £5 ($10) family ticket.

Appendix:
Fast Facts, Toll-Free
Numbers & Websites

1 Fast Facts: England & Wales

AMERICAN EXPRESS There are outlets at Heathrow Airport including at Terminal 4 (© **020/8897-0134**) and at Terminal T3 (© **020/8759-6845**). There is also an American Service Express Travel Service in London at 78 Brompton Rd., Knightsbridge, SW3 (© **020/761-7905**). In Wales, the Amex office is at 3 Queen St. in Cardiff (© **02920/649305**).

AREA CODES The country code for England and Wales is **44**. The area code for London is **020**; Cardiff's area code is **029**.

ATM NETWORKS & CASHPOINTS See "Money & Costs," in chapter 3.

BUSINESS HOURS With many, many exceptions, business hours are Monday to Friday 9am to 5pm. In general, stores are open Monday to Saturday 9am to 5:30pm. In country towns, there is usually an early closing day (often Wed or Thurs), when the shops close at 1pm.

CAR RENTALS See "Toll-Free Numbers & Websites," p. 756.

DRINKING LAWS The legal drinking age is 18. Children 15 and younger aren't allowed in pubs, except in certain rooms, and then only when accompanied by a parent or guardian. Don't drink and drive. Penalties are stiff.

Breaking decades of tradition, England in 2005 abandoned its strict, often draconian, liquor laws, allowing 24-hour alcohol sales in England and Wales. Many pubs no longer close at 11pm, which used to be "last call." Of course, it's up to the publican, but many, if they elect to do so, could stay open day and night. It's not total nirvana for the pub owners, however. Some counties are stationing undercover officers in pubs to fine staff members who serve liquor to visibly drunk customers, and the problems of drunk drivers on the highway, policemen fear, will only increase.

DRIVING RULES See "Getting There & Getting Around," in chapter 3.

DRUGSTORES In Britain, they're called "chemists." Every police station in the country has a list of emergency chemists. Dial "0" (zero) and ask the operator for the local police, who will give you the name of one nearest you.

ELECTRICITY British electricity is 240 volts AC (50 cycles), roughly twice the voltage in North America, which is 115 to 120 volts AC (60 cycles). American plugs don't fit British wall outlets. Always bring suitable transformers and/or adapters—if you plug an American appliance directly a European electrical outlet without a transformer, you'll destroy your appliance and possibly start a fire. Electronic equipment with motors intended to revolve at a fixed number of revolutions per minute probably won't work properly even with transformers.

EMBASSIES & CONSULATES The **U.S. Embassy** is at 24 Grosvenor Sq., London, W1 (✆ **020/7499-9000;** www. usembassy.org.uk; Tube: Bond St.). Hours are Monday to Friday 8am to 5:30pm, Saturday 10am to 4pm. However, for passport and visa information, go to the **U.S. Passport and Citizenship Unit**, 55–56 Upper Grosvenor St., London, W1 (✆ **020/7894-0563;** Tube: Marble Arch or Bond St.). Passport and Citizenship Unit hours are Monday to Friday 8:30am to 12:30pm.

The **Canadian High Commission,** Macdonald House, 38 Grosvenor St., London, W1 (✆ **020/7258-6600;** www. international.gc.ca/Canada-europa/united_kingdom; Tube: Bond St.), handles visas for Canada. Hours are Monday to Friday 8 to 11am for immigration services, and 9:30am to 1:30pm for passports.

The **Australian High Commission** is at Australia House, the Strand, London, WC2 (✆ **020/7379-4334;** www.australia.org.uk; Tube: Charing Cross or Aldwych). Hours are Monday to Friday 9am to 5pm; for immigration services, hours are 9 to 11am, and for passports, 9:30am to 3:30pm.

The **New Zealand High Commission** is at New Zealand House, 80 Haymarket at Pall Mall, London, SW1 (✆ **020/7930-8422;** www.nzembassy.com; Tube: Charing Cross or Piccadilly Circus). Hours are Monday to Friday 10am to 4pm.

The **Irish Embassy** is at 17 Grosvenor Place, London, SW1 (✆ **020/7235-2171;** http://ireland.embassyhomepage.com; Tube: Hyde Park Corner). Hours are Monday to Friday 9:30am to 1pm and 2 to 5pm.

EMERGENCIES Dial **999** for police, fire, or ambulance. Give your name, address, and telephone number and state the nature of the emergency.

GASOLINE (PETROL) See "Gasoline," p. 64.

HOLIDAYS Britain observes New Year's Day, Good Friday, Easter Monday, May Day (first Mon in May), spring and summer bank holidays (the last Mon in May and Aug, respectively), Christmas Day, and Boxing Day (Dec 26).

HOT LINES These emergency numbers exist in London. If you're in some sort of substance abuse or legal emergency, call **Release** (✆ **020/7729-9904**), open Monday to Friday 11am to 1pm. The **Rape and Sexual Abuse Hotline** (✆ **0845/122-1331**) is open daily, Monday to Friday noon to 2:30pm and 7 to 9:30pm, and on weekends and bank holidays 2:30 to 5pm. **Alcoholics Anonymous** (✆ **020/7833-0022**) answers its help line daily 10am to 10pm. For issues related to sexual health and sexually transmitted diseases, call the **Sexual Health Information Line** at ✆ **0800/567-123.**

INSURANCE **Medical Insurance** For travel overseas, most U.S. health plans (including Medicare and Medicaid) do not provide coverage, and the ones that do often require you to pay for services upfront and reimburse you only after you return home.

As a safety net, you may want to buy travel medical insurance, particularly if you're traveling to a remote or high-risk area where emergency evacuation might be necessary. If you require additional medical insurance, try **MEDEX Assistance** (✆ 410/453-6300; www.medexassist.com) or **Travel Assistance International** (✆ 800/821-2828; www.travelassistance.com; for general information on services, call the company's **Worldwide Assistance Services, Inc.** at ✆ 800/777-8710).

Canadians should check with their provincial health plan offices or call **Health Canada** (✆ 866/225-0709; www.hc-sc.gc.ca) to find out the extent of their coverage and what documentation and receipts they must take home in case they are treated overseas.

Travel Insurance The cost of travel insurance varies widely, depending on the destination, the cost and length of your trip, your age and health, and the type of trip you're taking, but expect to pay between 5% and 8% of the vacation itself. You can get estimates from various providers through **InsureMyTrip.com** (© 800/487-4722). Enter your trip cost and dates, your age, and other information, for prices from more than a dozen companies.

Most big travel agents offer their own insurance and will probably try to sell you their package when you book a holiday. Think before you sign. **Britain's Consumers' Association** recommends that you insist on seeing the policy and reading the fine print before buying travel insurance. The **Association of British Insurers** (© 020/7600-3333; www.abi. org.uk) gives advice by phone and publishes *Holiday Insurance,* a free guide to policy provisions and prices. You might also shop around for better deals. Try **Columbus Direct** (© 0870/033-9988; www.columbusdirect.net).

Trip Cancellation Insurance Trip-cancellation insurance will help retrieve your money if you have to back out of a trip or depart early, or if your travel supplier goes bankrupt. Trip cancellation traditionally covers such events as sickness, natural disasters, and State Department advisories. The latest news in trip-cancellation insurance is the availability of **expanded hurricane coverage** and the **"any-reason"** cancellation coverage—which costs more but covers cancellations made for any reason. You won't get back 100% of your prepaid trip cost, but you'll be refunded a substantial portion. **TravelSafe** (© 888/885-7233; www.travelsafe.com) offers both types of coverage. Expedia also offers any-reason cancellation coverage for its air-hotel packages. For details, contact one of the following recommended insurers: **Access America** (© 800/284-8300; www. accessamerica.com), **Travel Guard International** (© 800/826-4919; www.travel guard.com), **Travel Insured International** (© 800/243-3174; www.travelinsured. com), and **Travelex Insurance Services** (© 800/228-9792; www.travelex-insurance.com).

INTERNET ACCESS It's hard nowadays to find a city that *doesn't* have a few cybercafes. Although there's no definitive directory for cybercafes—these are independent businesses, after all—two places to start looking are at **www.cybercaptive. com** and **www.cybercafe.com**.

LEGAL AID The American Services section of the U.S. Embassy (see above) will give you advice if you run into trouble abroad. They can advise you of your rights and will even provide a list of attorneys (for which you'll have to pay if services are used). But they cannot interfere on your behalf in the legal process of Great Britain. For questions about American citizens who are arrested abroad, including ways of getting money to them, telephone the **Citizens Emergency Center** of the Office of Special Consulate Services in Washington, D.C. (© 202/647-5225). Citizens of other nations should go to their London-based consulate for advice.

LOST & FOUND Be sure to tell all of your credit card companies the minute you discover your wallet has been lost or stolen, and file a report at the nearest police precinct. Your credit card company or insurer may require a police report number or record of the loss. Most credit card companies have an emergency toll-free number to call if your card is lost or stolen; they may be able to wire you a cash advance immediately or deliver an emergency credit card in a day or two. American cardholders can call the toll-free numbers below in case of an emergency—**Visa** at © **0800/891-725, American Express** at © **0800/587-6023,** and **MasterCard** at © **020/7557-5000** (the latter is not a toll-free number).

If you need emergency cash over the weekend when all banks and American Express offices are closed, you can have money wired to you via **Western Union** (_©_ **800/325-6000;** www.westernunion. com).

MAIL   An airmail letter to North America costs 56p ($1.12) for 10 grams; postcards also require a 56p ($1.12) stamp; letters generally take 7 to 10 days to arrive in the United States. The British postal system is among the most reliable in the world so you don't need to depend on Federal Express or some other carrier unless you're in a great hurry.

MAPS   See "Maps," in chapter 3.

MEASUREMENTS   See the chart on the inside front cover of this book for details on converting metric measurements to nonmetric equivalents.

NEWSPAPERS & MAGAZINES   In London the _Times, Daily Telegraph, Daily Mail,_ and _Guardian_ are dailies carrying the latest news. The _International Herald Tribune,_ published in Paris, and an international edition of _USA Today,_ beamed via satellite, are available daily (_USA Today_ is printed as a newsletter). Copies of _Time_ and _Newsweek_ are sold at most newsstands. Magazines such as _Time Out_ and _Where_ contain useful information about the latest happenings in London.

PASSPORTS   For Residents of the United States: Whether you're applying in person or by mail, you can download passport applications from the U.S. Department of State website at http://travel.state. gov. To find your regional passport office, either check the U.S. Department of State website or call the toll-free number of the **National Passport Information Center** (_©_ **877/487-2778**) for automated information.

For Residents of Canada: Passport applications are available at travel agencies throughout Canada or from the central **Passport Office,** Department of Foreign Affairs and International Trade, Ottawa, ON K1A 0G3 (_©_ **800/567-6868;** www.ppt.gc.ca). **Note:** Canadian children who travel must have their own passport. However, if you hold a valid Canadian passport issued before December 11, 2001, that bears the name of your child, the passport remains valid for you and your child until it expires.

For Residents of Ireland: You can apply for a 10-year passport at the **Passport Office,** Setanta Centre, Molesworth Street, Dublin 2 (_©_ **01/671-1633;** www.irlgov.ie/iveagh). Those under age 18 and over 65 must apply for a 3-year passport. You can also apply at 1A South Mall, Cork (_©_ **021/494-4700**) or at most main post offices.

For Residents of Australia: You can pick up an application from your local post office or any branch of Passports Australia, but you must schedule an interview at the passport office to present your application materials. Call the **Australian Passport Information Service** at _©_ **131-232** or visit the government website at **www.smart traveler.gov.au**.

For Residents of New Zealand: You can pick up a passport application at any New Zealand Passports Office or download it from their website. Contact the **Passports Office** at _©_ **0800/225-050** in New Zealand or 04/474-8100, or log on to www.passports.govt.nz.

POLICE   Dial _©_ **999** if the matter is serious. Losses, thefts, and other criminal matters should be reported to the police immediately.

SMOKING   As of July 1, 2007, a smoking ban went into effect in England. Smoking is now banned in all indoor public places such as pubs, restaurants, clubs, and hotels, although hotels can set aside some rooms for smokers.

TAXES   To encourage energy conservation, the British government levies a 25%

tax on gasoline (petrol). There is also a 19.5% national value-added tax (VAT) that is added to all hotel and restaurant bills and is included in the price of many items you purchase. This can be refunded if you shop at stores that participate in the Retail Export Scheme (signs are posted in the window).

TELEPHONES See "Staying Connected," in chapter 3.

TIME Britain follows **Greenwich Mean Time** (5 hr. ahead of Eastern Standard Time). For most of the year, including summer, Britain is 5 hours ahead of the time observed in the Eastern United States. Because of different daylight saving time practices in the two nations, there's a brief period (about a week) in autumn when Britain is only 4 hours ahead of New York and a brief period in spring when it's 6 hours ahead of New York.

TIPPING For cabdrivers, add about 10% to 15% to the fare on the meter. However, if the driver loads or unloads your luggage, add something extra.

In hotels, porters receive 75p ($1.50) per bag, even if you have only one small suitcase. Hall porters are tipped only for special services. Maids receive £1 ($2) per day. In top-ranking hotels, the concierge will often submit a separate bill showing charges for newspapers and other items; if he or she has been particularly helpful, tip extra.

Hotels often add a service charge of 10% to 15% to most bills. In smaller bed-and-breakfasts, the tip is not likely to be included. Therefore, tip people for special services, such as the waiter who serves you breakfast. If several people have served you in a bed-and-breakfast, you may ask that 10% to 15% be added to the bill and divided among the staff.

In both restaurants and nightclubs, a 15% service charge is added to the bill, which is distributed among all the help. To that, add another 3% to 5%, depending on the service. Waiters in deluxe restaurants and nightclubs are accustomed to the extra 5%. Sommeliers (wine stewards) get about £1 ($2) per bottle of wine served. Tipping in pubs isn't common, but in wine bars, the server usually gets about 75p ($1.50) per round of drinks.

Barbers and hairdressers expect 10% to 15%. Tour guides expect £2 ($4), though it's not mandatory. Gas station attendants are rarely tipped, and theater ushers don't expect tips.

TOILETS They're marked by PUBLIC TOILETS signs in streets, parks, and Tube stations; many are automatically sterilized after each use. The English often call toilets "loos." You'll also find well-maintained lavatories in all larger public buildings, such as museums and art galleries, large department stores, and railway stations. It's not really acceptable to use the lavatories in hotels, restaurants, and pubs if you're not a customer, but we can't say that we always stick to this rule. Public lavatories are usually free, but you may need a small coin to get in or to use a proper washroom.

2 Toll-Free Numbers & Websites

MAJOR U.S. AIRLINES
(*flies internationally as well)

American Airlines*
✆ 800/433-7300 (in the U.S. and Canada)

✆ 020/7365-0777 (in the U.K.)
www.aa.com

Continental Airlines*
✆ 800/231-0856 (in the U.S. and Canada)

℗ 084/5607-6760 (in the U.K.)
www.continental.com

Delta Air Lines*

℗ 800/221-1212 (in the U.S. and
   Canada)
℗ 084/5600-0950 (in the U.K.)
www.delta.com

Northwest Airlines

℗ 800/225-2525 (in the U.S.)
℗ 870/0507-4074 (in the U.K.)
www.flynaa.com

United Airlines*

℗ 800/864-8331 (in the U.S. and
   Canada)
℗ 084/5844-4777 in the U.K.
www.united.com

US Airways*

℗ 800/428-4322 (in the U.S. and
   Canada)
℗ 084/5600-3300 (in the U.K.)
www.usairways.com

MAJOR INTERNATIONAL AIRLINES

Aeroméxico

℗ 800/237-6639 (in the U.S.)
℗ 020/7801-6234 (in the U.K.,
   information only)
www.aeromexico.com

Air Canada

℗ 888/247-2262 (in the U.S. and
   Canada)
℗ 0871/220-1111 (in the U.K.)

Air France

℗ 800/237-2747 (in the U.S.)
℗ 800/375-8723 (in the U.S. and
   Canada)
℗ 087/0142-4343 (in the U.K.)
www.airfrance.com

Air India

℗ 212/407-1371 (in the U.S.)
℗ 91 22 2279 6666 (in India)
℗ 020/8745-1000 (in the U.K.)
www.airindia.com

Air New Zealand

℗ 800/262-1234 (in the U.S.)
℗ 800/663-5494 (in Canada)
℗ 0800/028-4149 (in the U.K.)
www.airnewzealand.com

Alitalia

℗ 800/223-5730 (in the U.S.)
℗ 800/361-8336 (in Canada)
℗ 087/0608-6003 (in the U.K.)
www.alitalia.com

BMI

℗ 800/788-0555 (in the U.S. and
   Canada)
℗ 0870/607-0555 (in the U.K.)
www.flybmi.com

British Airways

℗ 800/247-9297 (in the U.S. and
   Canada)
℗ 087/0850-9850 (in the U.K.)
www.british-airways.com

Caribbean Airlines (formerly BWIA)

℗ 800/920-4225 (in the U.S. and
   Canada)
℗ 084/5362 4225 (in the U.K.)
www.caribbean-airlines.com

Cubana

℗ 888/667-1222 (in Canada)
℗ 020/7538-5933 (in the U.K.)
www.cubana.cu

EgyptAir

℗ 212/581-5600 (in the U.S.)
℗ 020/7734-2343 (in the U.K.)
℗ 09/007-0000 (in Egypt)
www.egyptair.com

Emirates Airlines

℗ 800/777-3999 (in the U.S.)
℗ 087/0243-2222 (in the U.K.)
www.emirates.com

Finnair

℗ 800/950-5000 (in the U.S. and
   Canada)
℗ 087/0241-4411 (in the U.K.)
www.finnair.com

Iberia Airlines
© 800/722-4642 (in the U.S. and Canada)
© 087/0609-0500 (in the U.K.)
www.iberia.com

Icelandair
© 800/223-5500, ext. 2 prompt 1 (in the U.S. and Canada)
© 084/5758-1111 (in the U.K.)
www.icelandair.com
www.icelandair.co.uk (in the U.K.)

Korean Air
© 800/438-5000 (in the U.S. and Canada)
© 0800/413-000 (in the U.K.)
www.koreanair.com

Lufthansa
© 800/399-5838 (in the U.S.)
© 800/563-5954 (in Canada)
© 087/0837-7747 (in the U.K.)
www.lufthansa.com

Olympic Airlines
© 800/223-1226 (in the U.S.)
© 514/878-9691 (in Canada)
© 087/0606-0460 (in the U.K.)
www.olympicairlines.com

Qantas Airways
© 800/227-4500 (in the U.S.)
© 084/5774-7767 (in the U.K. or Canada)
© 13 13 13 (in Australia)
www.qantas.com

Swiss Air
© 877/359-7947 (in the U.S. and Canada)
© 084/5601-0956 (in the U.K.)
www.swiss.com

TACA
© 800/535-8780 (in the U.S.)
© 800/722-TACA (8222; in Canada)
© 087/0241-0340 (in the U.K.)
© 503/2267-8222 (in El Salvador)
www.taca.com

Thai Airways International
© 212/949-8424 (in the U.S.)
© 020/7491-7953 (in the U.K.)
www.thaiair.com

Virgin Atlantic Airways
© 800/821-5438 (in the U.S. and Canada)
© 087/0574-7747 (in the U.K.)
www.virgin-atlantic.com

BUDGET AIRLINES

Aegean Airlines
© 210/626-1000 (in the U.S., Canada, and the U.K.)
www.aegeanair.com

Aer Lingus
© 800/474-7424 (in the U.S. and Canada)
© 087/0876-5000 (in the U.K.)
www.aerlingus.com

Air Berlin
© 087/1500-0737 (in the U.K.)
© 018/0573-7800 (in Germany)
© 180/573-7800 (all others)
www.airberlin.com

Avolar
© 888/3-AVOLAR (888/326-8527; in the U.S.)
© 800/21-AVOLAR (800/326-8527; in Mexico)
© 086/6370-4065 (in the U.K.)
www.avolar.com.mx

BMI Baby
© 087/1224-0224 (in the U.K.)
© 870/126-6726 (in the U.S.)
www.bmibaby.com

easyJet
© 870/600-0000 (in the U.S.)
© 090/5560-7777 (in the U.K.)
www.easyjet.com

JetBlue Airways
℃ 800/538-2583 (in the U.S.)
℃ 801/365-2525 (in the U.K. or Canada)
www.jetblue.com

Ryanair
℃ 1 353 1 249 7700 (in the U.S.)
℃ 081/830-3030 (in Ireland)
℃ 087/1246-0000 (in the U.K.)
www.ryanair.com

Southwest Airlines
℃ 800/435-9792 (in the U.S., the U.K., and Canada)
www.southwest.com

CAR-RENTAL AGENCIES

Auto Europe
℃ 888/223-5555 (in the U.S. and Canada)
℃ 0800/2235-5555 (in the U.K.)
www.autoeurope.com

Avis
℃ 800/331-1212 (in the U.S. and Canada)
℃ 084/4581-8181 (in the U.K.)
www.avis.com

Budget
℃ 800/527-0700 (in the U.S.)
℃ 087/0156-5656 (in the U.K.)
℃ 800/268-8900 (in Canada)
www.budget.com

Dollar
℃ 800/800-4000 (in the U.S.)
℃ 800/848-8268 (in Canada)
℃ 080/8234-7524 (in the U.K.)
www.dollar.com

Enterprise
℃ 800/261-7331 (in the U.S.)
℃ 514/355-4028 (in Canada)
℃ 012/9360-9090 (in the U.K.)
www.enterprise.com

Hertz
℃ 800/645-3131
℃ 800/654-3001 (for international reservations)
www.hertz.com

Kemwel (KHA)
℃ 877/820-0668
www.kemwel.com

National
℃ 800/CAR-RENT (800/227-7368)
www.nationalcar.com

Thrifty
℃ 800/367-2277
℃ 918/669-2168 (international)
www.thrifty.com

MAJOR HOTEL & MOTEL CHAINS

Best Western International
℃ 800/780-7234 (in the U.S. and Canada)
℃ 0800/393-130 (in the U.K.)
www.bestwestern.com

Clarion Hotels
℃ 800/CLARION or 877/424-6423 (in the U.S. and Canada)
℃ 0800/444-444 (in the U.K.)
www.choicehotels.com

Comfort Inns
℃ 800/228-5150
℃ 0800/444-444 (in the U.K.)
www.comfortinn.com

Courtyard by Marriott
℃ 888/236-2427 (in the U.S.)
℃ 0800/221-222 (in the U.K.)
www.marriott.com/courtyard

Days Inn
℃ 800/329-7466 (in the U.S.)
℃ 0800/280-400 (in the U.K.)
www.daysinn.com

Doubletree Hotels
℃ 800/222-TREE (800/222-8733; in the U.S. and Canada)
℃ 087/0590-9090 (in the U.K.)
www.doubletree.com

Fairfield Inn by Marriott
ⓒ 800/228-2800 (in the U.S. and Canada)
ⓒ 0800/221-222 (in the U.K.)
www.marriott.com/fairfieldinn

Four Seasons
ⓒ 800/819-5053 (in the U.S. and Canada)
ⓒ 0800/6488-6488 (in the U.K.)
www.fourseasons.com

Hilton Hotels
ⓒ 800/HILTONS (800/445-8667; in the U.S. and Canada)
ⓒ 087/0590-9090 (in the U.K.)
www.hilton.com

Holiday Inn
ⓒ 800/315-2621 (in the U.S. and Canada)
ⓒ 0800/405-060 (in the U.K.)
www.holidayinn.com

Hyatt
ⓒ 888/591-1234 (in the U.S. and Canada)
ⓒ 084/5888-1234 (in the U.K.)
www.hyatt.com

InterContinental Hotels & Resorts
ⓒ 800/424-6835 (in the U.S. and Canada)
ⓒ 0800/1800-1800 (in the U.K.)
www.ichotelsgroup.com

Marriott
ⓒ 877/236-2427 (in the U.S. and Canada)
ⓒ 0800/221-222 (in the U.K.)
www.marriott.com

Quality
ⓒ 877/424-6423 (in the U.S. and Canada)
ⓒ 0800/444-444 (in the U.K.)
www.qualityinn.com

Radisson Hotels & Resorts
ⓒ 888/201-1718 (in the U.S. and Canada)
ⓒ 0800/374-411 (in the U.K.)
www.radisson.com

Ramada Worldwide
ⓒ 888/2-RAMADA (888/272-6232; in the U.S. and Canada)
ⓒ 080/8100-0783 (in the U.K.)
www.ramada.com

Residence Inn by Marriott
ⓒ 800/331-3131
ⓒ 800/221-222 (in the U.K.)
www.marriott.com/residenceinn

Sheraton Hotels & Resorts
ⓒ 800/325-3535 (in the U.S.)
ⓒ 800/543-4300 (in Canada)
ⓒ 0800/3253-5353 (in the U.K.)
www.starwoodhotels.com/sheraton

Westin Hotels & Resorts
ⓒ 800/937-8461 (in the U.S. and Canada)
ⓒ 0800/3259-5959 (in the U.K.)
www.starwoodhotels.com/westin

Wyndham Hotels & Resorts
ⓒ 877/999-3223 (in the U.S. and Canada)
ⓒ 050/6638-4899 (in the U.K.)
www.wyndham.com

Index

Also see Accommodations and Restaurant indexes, below.

ACCOMMODATIONS IN LONDON

RESTAURANTS IN LONDON

The new way to
get AROUND town.

Make the most of your stay. Go Day by Day!

The all-new Day by Day series shows you the best places to visit and the best way to see them.

- Full-color throughout, with hundreds of photos and maps
- Packed with 1–to–3–day itineraries, neighborhood walks, and thematic tours
- Museums, literary haunts, offbeat places, and more
- Star-rated hotel and restaurant listings
- Sturdy foldout map in reclosable plastic wallet
- Foldout front covers with at-a-glance maps and info

The best trips start here. **Frommer's®**

A Branded Imprint of ⊛WILEY
Now you know.

A Guide for Every Type of Traveler

Frommer's Complete Guides

For those who value complete coverage, candid advice, and lots of choices in all price ranges.

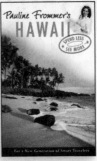

Pauline Frommer's Guides

For those who want to experience a culture, meet locals, and save money along the way.

MTV Guides

For hip, youthful travelers who want a fresh perspective on today's hottest cities and destinations.

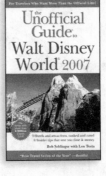

Day by Day Guides

For leisure or business travelers who want to organize their time to get the most out of a trip.

Frommer's With Kids Guides

For families traveling with children ages 2 to 14 seeking kid-friendly hotels, restaurants, and activities.

Unofficial Guides

For honeymooners, families, business travelers, and others who value no-nonsense, *Consumer Reports*–style advice.

For Dummies Travel Guides

For curious, independent travelers looking for a fun and easy way to plan a trip.

Visit Frommers.com

 WILEY
Now you know.

Explore over 3,500 destinations.

Frommers.com makes it easy.

Find a destination. ✓ Book a trip. ✓ Get hot travel deals.
Buy a guidebook. ✓ Enter to win vacations. ✓ Listen to podcasts. ✓ Check out
the latest travel news. ✓ Share trip photos and memories. ✓ And much more.

Frommers.com

FROMMER'S® COMPLETE TRAVEL GUIDES

FROMMER'S® DAY BY DAY GUIDES

PAULINE FROMMER'S GUIDES: SEE MORE. SPEND LESS.

FROMMER'S® PORTABLE GUIDES

Acapulco, Ixtapa & Zihuatanejo
Amsterdam
Aruba, Bonaire & Curacao
Australia's Great Barrier Reef
Bahamas
Big Island of Hawaii
Boston
California Wine Country
Cancún
Cayman Islands
Charleston
Chicago
Dominican Republic

Florence
Las Vegas
Las Vegas for Non-Gamblers
London
Maui
Nantucket & Martha's Vineyard
New Orleans
New York City
Paris
Portland
Puerto Rico
Puerto Vallarta, Manzanillo &
    Guadalajara

Rio de Janeiro
San Diego
San Francisco
Savannah
St. Martin, Sint Maarten, Anguila &
    St. Bart's
Turks & Caicos
Vancouver
Venice
Virgin Islands
Washington, D.C.
Whistler

FROMMER'S® CRUISE GUIDES

Alaska Cruises & Ports of Call

Cruises & Ports of Call

European Cruises & Ports of Call

FROMMER'S® NATIONAL PARK GUIDES

Algonquin Provincial Park
Banff & Jasper
Grand Canyon

National Parks of the American West
Rocky Mountain
Yellowstone & Grand Teton

Yosemite and Sequoia & Kings
    Canyon
Zion & Bryce Canyon

FROMMER'S® WITH KIDS GUIDES

Chicago
Hawaii
Las Vegas
London

National Parks
New York City
San Francisco

Toronto
Walt Disney World® & Orlando
Washington, D.C.

FROMMER'S® PHRASEFINDER DICTIONARY GUIDES

Chinese
French

German
Italian

Japanese
Spanish

SUZY GERSHMAN'S BORN TO SHOP GUIDES

France
Hong Kong, Shanghai & Beijing
Italy

London
New York
Paris

San Francisco
Where to Buy the Best of Everything.

FROMMER'S® BEST-LOVED DRIVING TOURS

Britain
California
France
Germany

Ireland
Italy
New England
Northern Italy

Scotland
Spain
Tuscany & Umbria

THE UNOFFICIAL GUIDES®

Adventure Travel in Alaska
Beyond Disney
California with Kids
Central Italy
Chicago
Cruises
Disneyland®
England
Hawaii

Ireland
Las Vegas
London
Maui
Mexico's Best Beach Resorts
Mini Mickey
New Orleans
New York City
Paris

San Francisco
South Florida including Miami &
    the Keys
Walt Disney World®
Walt Disney World® for
    Grown-ups
Walt Disney World® with Kids
Washington, D.C.

SPECIAL-INTEREST TITLES

Athens Past & Present
Best Places to Raise Your Family
Cities Ranked & Rated
500 Places to Take Your Kids Before They Grow Up
Frommer's Best Day Trips from London
Frommer's Best RV & Tent Campgrounds in the U.S.A.

Frommer's Exploring America by RV
Frommer's NYC Free & Dirt Cheap
Frommer's Road Atlas Europe
Frommer's Road Atlas Ireland
Retirement Places Rated